Critical values of the *t* Distribution

MW00522910

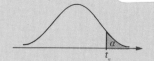

Degrees of Freedom	$t_{.100}$	$t_{.050}$	$t_{.025}$	$t_{.010}$	$t_{.005}$
1	3.078	6.314	12.706	31.821	63.657
2	1.886	2.920	4.303	6.965	9.925
3	1.638	2.353	3.182	4.541	5.841
4	1.533	2.132	2.776	3.747	4.604
5	1.476	2.015	2.571	3.365	4.032
6	1.440	1.943	2.447	3.143	3.707
7	1.415	1.895	2.365	2.998	3.499
8	1.397	1.860	2.306	2.896	3.355
9	1.383	1.833	2.262	2.821	3.250
10	1.372	1.812	2.228	2.764	3.169
11	1.363	1.796	2.201	2.718	3.106
12	1.356	1.782	2.179	2.681	3.055
13	1.350	1.771	2.160	2.650	3.012
14	1.345	1.761	2.145	2.624	2.977
15	1.341	1.753	2.131	2.602	2.947
16	1.337	1.746	2.120	2.583	2.921
17	1.333	1.740	2.110	2.567	2.898
18	1.330	1.734	2.101	2.552	2.878
19	1.328	1.729	2.093	2.539	2.861
20	1.325	1.725	2.086	2.528	2.845
21	1.323	1.721	2.080	2.518	2.831
22	1.321	1.717	2.074	2.508	2.819
23	1.319	1.714	2.069	2.500	2.807
24	1.318	1.711	2.064	2.492	2.797
25	1.316	1.708	2.060	2.485	2.787
26	1.315	1.706	2.056	2.479	2.779
27	1.314	1.703	2.052	2.473	2.771
28	1.313	1.701	2.048	2.467	2.763
29	1.311	1.699	2.045	2.462	2.756
30	1.310	1.697	2.042	2.457	2.750
40	1.303	1.684	2.021	2.423	2.704
60	1.296	1.671	2.000	2.390	2.660
120	1.289	1.658	1.980	2.358	2.617
∞	1.282	1.645	1.960	2.326	2.576
C.I.	80%	90%	95%	98%	99%

Critical Points of Z for Selected Levels of Significance

	Level of Significance α:	
	0.05	0.01
One-Tailed Test	+ or 1.645 −	+ or 2.326 −
Two-Tailed Test	+ and 1.96 −	+ and 2.576 −

Note: + or − means we use the positive value in the table for a right-hand-tailed test and the negative value for a left-hand-tailed test. In a two-tailed test, we use both the positive and the negative values.

Source: Tabular data from M. Merrington, "Table of Percentage Points of the *t*-Distribution," *Biometrika* 32 (1941) p. 300. Reproduced by permission of the *Biometrika* trustees.

Instructor's Edition

SECOND EDITION

COMPLETE BUSINESS
STATISTICS

AMIR D. ACZEL
Bentley College

IRWIN

Homewood, IL 60430
Boston, MA 02116

PREFACE TO THE ANNOTATED INSTRUCTOR'S EDITION

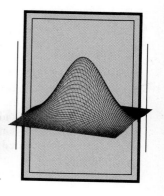

The first edition of *Complete Business Statistics* was widely acclaimed by business statistics professors at the best universities and colleges in the United States and abroad. Revising the book for second edition was, therefore, a big challenge for me. I wanted to keep all the features that have made the book successful, and yet improve it. This Preface will highlight the features that made the first edition successful, as well as the additions and improvements in the second edition. I will also outline some suggestions on how to teach statistics effectively using my textbook, and how to get the most out of the book in a course of any level.

Margin Notes

Throughout the text, answers to many of the even-numbered problems are provided in the margins. These answers appear only in the instructor's edition. Answers to many of the odd-numbered problems appear in Appendix B in both the instructor and student versions.

ADDITIONAL PROBLEMS

Answers

15–51. A quality-control engineer believes that the proportion of defective items in a production process is a random variable with a probability distribution that is approximated by the following probability mass function.

x	P(x)
0.1	0.1
0.2	0.3
0.3	0.2
.0.4	0.2
0.5	0.1
0.6	0.1

The engineer collects a random sample of items and finds that 5 out the 16 items in the sample are defective. Find the engineer's posterior probability distribution of the proportion of defective items.

15–52.

92.11%:
[0.2, 0.4]

15–52. Continuing problem 15–51, determine a credible set for the proportion of defective items with probability close to 0.95. Interpret the meaning of the credible set.

15–53. For problem 15–51, suppose that the engineer collects a second sample of 20 items and finds that 5 items are defective. Update the probability distribution of the population proportion you computed in problem 15–51 to incorporate the new information.

15–54. What are the main differences between the Bayesian approach to statistics and the classical approach? Discuss these differences.

15–55. What is the added advantage of the normal probability distribution in the context of Bayesian statistics?

15–56.

$M'' = 99.81$
$\sigma'' = 0.9806$

[98.89, 101.96]

15–56. The average life of a battery is believed to be normally distributed with an unknown mean, μ. The mean is viewed as a random variable with expected value of 45 hours and standard deviation of 5 hours. The population standard deviation is believed to be 10 hours. A random sample of 100 batteries gives a sample mean of 102 hours. Find the posterior probability distribution of the population mean, μ.

15–57. For problem 15–56, give a highest-posterior-density credible set of probability 0.95 for the population mean.

15–58. For problem 15–56, a second sample of 60 batteries gives a sample mean of 101.5 hours. Update the distribution of the population mean, and give a new HPD credible set of probability 0.95 for μ.

15–59. What is a payoff table? What is a decision tree? Can a payoff table be used in decision making without a decision tree?

15–60. What is a subjective probability, and what are its limitations?

15–61. Discuss the advantages and the limitations of the de Finetti game. What is the main principle behind the game?

15–62. Why is Bayesian statistics controversial? Try to argue for, and then against, the Bayesian methodology.

15–63. Suppose that I am different in terms of the following two choices: a sure $3,000 payoff, and a payoff of $5,000 with probability 0.2 and $500 with probability 0.8. Am I a risk taker or a risk-averse individual (within the range $500 to $5,000)? Explain.

15–64.

Alternative
$E = \$4,000$
is optimal.

15–64. An investment is believed to earn $2,000 with probability 0.2, $2,500 with probability 0.3, and $3,000 with probability 0.5. An alternative investment may earn zero with probability 0.1, $3,000 with probability 0.2, $4,000 with probability 0.5, and $7,000 with probability 0.2. Construct a decision tree for this problem, and determine the investment with the highest expected monetary outcome. What are the limitations of the analysis?

15–65. Assess your own utility in the range of values of problem 15–64, and redo that problem using utilities instead of dollars. Has the optimal decision changed? Explain.

15–66.

Merge;
$E = \$2.45$ million.

15–66. A company is considering merging with a smaller firm in a related industry. The company's chief executive officer believes that the merger has a 0.55 probability of success. If the merger is successful, the company stands to gain in the next two years $5 million with probability 0.2; $6 million with probability 0.3; $7 million with probability 0.3; and $8 million with probability 0.2. If the attempted merger should fail, the company stands to lose $2 million (due to loss of public goodwill) over the next two years with probability 0.5 and to lose $3 million over this period with probability 0.5. Should the merger be attempted? Explain.

15–67. For problem 15–66, suppose that the chief executive may hire a consulting firm for a fee of $725,000. The consulting firm will advise the CEO about the possibility of success of the merger. This consulting firm is known to have correctly predicted the outcomes of 89% of all successful mergers and the outcomes of 97% of all unsuccessful ones. What is the optimal decision?

PEDAGOGY

Chapter Introductions

The introductions to all the chapters are related historical stories or interesting applications of the subject matter discussed in the chapter. These stories are designed to whet the student's appetite to learn statistics and to provide a glimpse of the richness of the field, and not necessarily to relate to business applications. The intensive, comprehensive applications of statistics in business come later and are found everywhere in the book except the chapter introductions. My intent is to stimulate and captivate the interest of the student.

I N T R O D U C T I O N

 n June 18, 1964, a woman was robbed while walking home along an alley in San Pedro, California. Some time later, police arrested Janet Collins and charged her with the robbery. The interesting thing about this case of petty crime is that the prosecution had *no* direct evidence against the defendant. Janet Collins was convicted of robbery on purely statistical grounds.

The case, *People* v. *Collins*, drew much attention because of its use of probability—or, rather, what was perceived as a probability—in determining guilt. An instructor of mathematics at a local college was brought in by the prosecution and testified as an expert witness in the trial. The instructor "calculated the probability" that the defendant was a person *other* than the one who committed the crime as 1 in 12,000,000. This led the jury to convict the defendant.

The Supreme Court of California later reversed the "guilty" verdict against Janet Collins when it was shown that the method of calculating the probability was incorrect. The mathematics instructor had made some very serious errors.[1]

Despite the erroneous procedure used in deriving the probability, and the justified reversal of the conviction by the Supreme Court of California, the *Collins* case serves as an excellent analogy for statistical hypothesis testing. Under the American legal system, the accused is assumed innocent until proven guilty "beyond a reasonable doubt." We will call this the *null hypothesis*—the hypothesis that the accused is *innocent*. We will hold the null hypothesis as true until a time when we can prove, beyond a reasonable doubt, that it is false and that the *alternative hypothesis*—the hypothesis that the accused is guilty—is true. We want to have a small probability (preferably *zero*) of convicting an innocent person, that is, of rejecting a null hypothesis when the null hypothesis is actually true.

In the *Collins* case, the prosecution claimed that the accused was guilty since, otherwise, an event with a very small probability had just been observed. The argument was that if Collins were *not* guilty, then another woman fitting her exact characteristics had committed the crime. According to the prosecution, the probability of this event was 1/12,000,000, and since the probability was so small, Collins was very likely the person who committed the robbery.

In statistical hypothesis testing, our null hypothesis will state something about one or more population parameters. For example, the null hypothesis may be that the population mean is equal to some number. The alternative hypothesis will be that the population mean is different from the number stated in the null hypothesis. We will assume that the null hypothesis is true and that the population mean is as stated. Then we will look at some evidence derived from a random sample. If our obtained sample mean should happen to fall so far away from the population mean as to constitute an event with a small presampling probability, then we will reject the null hypothesis in favor of the alternative hypothesis. ∎

[1] The instructor *multiplied* the probabilities of the separate events comprising the reported description of the robber: the event that a woman has blond hair, the event that she drives a yellow car, the event that she is seen with a black man, the event that the man has a beard. Recall that the probability of the intersection of several events is equal to the product of the probabilities of the separate events *only if* the events are independent. In this case, there was no reason to believe that the events were independent. There were also some questions about how the separate "probabilities" were actually derived since they were presented by the instructor with no apparent justification. See W. Fairley and F. Mosteller, "A Conversation About Collins," *University of Chicago Law Review* 41, no. 2 (Winter 1974) pp. 242–53.

Boxed Equations, Formulas, Definitions

The pedagogy makes use of boxes and color in setting out important equations and definitions. In some cases, several different definitions or alternative formulas are presented in a way that helps the student find them and use them appropriately.

The standard error of the sample mean:[5]
$$\text{SE}(\bar{X}) = \sigma_{\bar{x}} = \sigma/\sqrt{n} \qquad (5\text{-}3)$$

When sampling from a *normal* distribution with mean μ and standard deviation σ, the sample mean $\bar{X}$ has a normal **sampling distribution:**
$$\bar{X} \sim N(\mu, \sigma^2/n) \qquad (5\text{-}4)$$

Figures and Graphs

This book is unique in the use it makes of figures and graphs. Each concept is illustrated by supportive graphs. There are also a number of composite figures that illustrate several different concepts and their interaction.

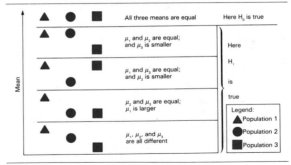

FIGURE 9–5 The Deviations of the Triangles, Squares, and Circles from Their Sample Means and the Deviations of the Sample Means from the Grand Mean

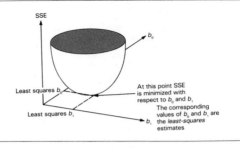

FIGURE 10–10 The Particular Values b_0 and b_1 that Minimize SSE

Notation

I have tried throughout to use the easiest, most common statistical notation. This helps make a difficult subject easier for the student. I have tried to reduce the use of Greek letters and other symbols and to rely on English words as much as possible. I also chose notation that is unambiguous. In the case of the normal curve, for example, I use the notation Normal (mean, variance) with the variance written as a squared number to avoid confusion with the standard deviation.

Notation

We now introduce some general notation for random variables and distributions that will prove to be especially useful in work with the normal probability model; however, it has uses also in the case of other random variables.

We will denote the distribution, mean, and variance of a random variable by a simple notational statement:

$$X \sim D(\mu, \sigma^2) \qquad (4\text{–}2)$$

This statement says in words: "The random variable X is distributed according to a probability distribution D, with mean equal to μ, and standard deviation equal to σ (equivalently, variance equal to σ^2)." This is the general notation for a random variable, with the distribution denoted by D. If we were talking about the binomial distribution, we would use the letter B to denote it. For a normally distributed random variable, we use the letter N. If we deal with a random variable with a normal distribution with mean $\mu = 5.7$ and standard deviation $\sigma = 2$, we say:

$$X \sim N(5.7, 2^2)$$

Note that we wrote the variance σ^2 as 2^2, rather than its value, 4. We will always follow the convention of writing the variance as a squared quantity. This will prevent us from confusing the value of the variance with the value of the standard deviation. Here it is perfectly clear that the variance is $2^2 = 4$ and the standard deviation is 2.

CASE

1

HIGHEST U.S. BANK YIELDS FOR IRAS

*T*he following data are reproduced from *Money* magazine (February 1991, p. 23).

Bank Rating	Institution (state)	Yield on Jan. 4	Minimum Deposit	Additional Deposits	Annual Fee
	Six-Month IRA				
★★★	Loyola Federal Savings (Md.)	7.84%	$500	No	None
★★★	Citibank/S.D.	7.72	250	No	None
★★★	La Jolla (Calif.)	7.68	1,000	No	$10
★★★	Beach Savings (Calif.)	7.60	2,500	No	15
★★★	Key Bank USA (N.Y.)	7.60	1,000	No	None
★★★	Atlantic Bank of N.Y.	7.30	500	No	None
	One-Year IRA				
★★★	First Deposit National (N.H.)	8.00	10,000	No	None
★★★	First Trade Union Savings (Mass.)	7.90	500	No	None
★★★	Loyola Federal Savings (Md.)	7.90	500	No	None
★★★	Beach Savings (Calif.)	7.88	500	No	15
★★★	Colonial National (Del.)	7.85	250	No	None
★★★	Citibank/S.D.	7.82	250	No	None
	18-Month IRA				
★★★	La Jolla (Calif.)	8.17	100	Yes	10
★★★	Loyola Federal Savings (Md.)	8.07	100	Yes	None
★★★	First Deposit National (N.H.)	8.00	10,000	No	None
★★★	Colonial National (Del.)	7.94	250	No	None
★★★	Key Bank USA (N.Y.)	7.82	1,000	No	None
★★★	Beach Savings (Calif.)	7.74	100	Yes	None
	Five-Year IRA				
★★★	Colonial National (Del.)	8.25	250	No	None
★★★	Washington Savings (Md.)	8.24	500	No	None
★★★	Loyola Federal Savings (Md.)	8.22	500	No	None
★★★	First Trade Union Savings (Mass.)	8.14	500	No	None
★★★	Atlantic Bank of N.Y.	8.10	500	No	None
★★★	Metropolitan Bank for Savings (Va.)	8.08	1,000	No	None

For each maturity (six months, one year, etc.), find the mean, median, range, and standard deviation of both the percent yield and the minimum deposit. Draw a histogram or a box plot, and identify outlying observations. Discuss your results.

Cases

Another improvement you will notice in this edition is the inclusion of more cases. While the first edition of the book had 8 cases, there are now 17—one per chapter. When we initially interviewed business statistics professors about their use of cases, the typical response was: "We don't use cases," or "Cases are not relevant in an introductory course." Yet, 8 cases that appeared in the first edition of the book were so well received that we decided to expand. The cases were perceived as realistic, challenging exercises in the actual application of business statistics methods in the real world. Reviewers quickly noted the difference between my cases and what other business statistics authors call "cases"—many of them designed for "illustrative" rather than assignment purposes and actually having little to do with statistics. Many first edition reviewers indicated that these cases have become an integral and important part of their course, and I hope that the 9 new ones will be found to be equally effective.

5–5 Degrees of Freedom

The concept of *degrees of freedom* is crucial for the understanding of many important statistical distributions. The concept also underlies the reason why our sample variance S^2 is the unbiased estimator of σ^2. Here lies the answer to our big question: Why divide by $n - 1$ and not by n?

Suppose we consider four data points, X_1, X_2, X_3, and X_4. The values of the data points are:

$$x_1 = 10 \qquad x_2 = 12 \qquad x_3 = 16 \qquad x_4 = 18$$

Let us compute the sample mean of these data.

$$\bar{x} = \frac{\sum_{i=1}^{4} x_i}{n} = \frac{(x_1 + x_2 + x_3 + x_4)}{4}$$

$$= \frac{(10 + 12 + 16 + 18)}{4} = \frac{56}{4} = 14$$

FIGURE 5–12 The Four Deviations of the Data Points from Their Mean

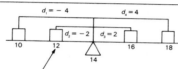

If any data point is assumed unknown, we can solve for its deviation from the mean because the sum of all four deviations is equal to zero.

Explanation of Statistical Concepts and Ideas

Among the most highly praised features of the book were the thorough, easy-to-understand explanations of statistical concepts and ideas. Based on specific suggestions from reviewers and adopters, many of these explanations have been expanded and improved. They reflect the teaching philosophy that statistics can be understood by anyone if explained the right way. In the explanations, I have made every effort to be intuitive and to stress concepts rather than formulas. Each of these concepts is illustrated by one or more examples.

Real-World Examples and Problems

The problems and exercises have been greatly expanded in the new edition. As in the figrst edition, my problems have been drawn from practical work with statistics, and relevant articles in the business literature and professional research journals in business and economics. I have listened carefully to reviewers' suggestions about the level and the type of problems to include in the new edition. In each chapter, I have added challenging statistical problems (usually at the very end of the Additional Problems sets). Other new problem types are the memo problems—suggestion from reviewers who like to incorporate writing practice into their course. Here the student is expected to explain the statistical findings of a problem solution in the form of a memorandum to a manager or client. Also included in the second edition is a new type of problem which asks students to interpret the output. This is an important addition since statistical analysis is increasingly done on computer. We hope this will help to make sure that besides understanding statistics, the student also will be able to interpret numbers, graphs, and tables provided by the computer.

EXAMPLE (b)

Club Med has over 30 major resorts worldwide, from Tahiti to Switzerland. Many of the beach resorts are in the Caribbean, and at one point the club wanted to test whether or not the resorts on Guadeloupe, Martinique, Haiti, Paradise Island, and St. Lucia were all equally well liked by vacationing club members. The analysis was to be based on a survey questionnaire filled out by a random sample of 40 respondents in each of the resorts. From every returned questionnaire, a general satisfaction score, on a scale of 0 to 100, was computed. Analysis of the survey results yielded the statistics given in Table 9–4.

TABLE 9–4 Club Med Survey Results

Resort (i)	Mean Response ($\bar{x}_i$)
1. Guadeloupe	89
2. Martinique	75
3. Haiti	73
4. Paradise Island	91
5. St. Lucia	85

SST = 112,564   SSE = 98,356

The results were computed from the responses using a computer program that calculated the sums of squared deviations from the sample means and from the grand mean. Given the values of SST and SSE, construct an ANOVA table and conduct the hypothesis test. (Note: the reported sample means in Table 9–4 will be used in the next section.)

SOLUTION

Let us first construct an ANOVA table and fill in the information we have: SST = 112,564; SSE = 98,356; $n = 200$; and $r = 5$. This has been done in Table 9–5. We now compute SSTR as the difference between SST and SSE and enter it in the appropriate place in the table. We then divide SSTR and SSE by their respective degrees of freedom to give us MSTR and MSE. Finally, we divide MSTR by MSE to give us the F ratio. All these quantities are entered in the ANOVA table. The result is the complete ANOVA table for the study, Table 9–6.

Table 9–6 contains all the pertinent information for this study. We are now ready to conduct the hypothesis test.

H_0: $\mu_1 = \mu_2 = \mu_3 = \mu_4 = \mu_5$ (average vacationer satisfaction for each of the five resorts is equal)

H_1: Not all μ_i ($i = 1, \ldots, 5$) are equal (on the average, vacationer satisfaction is not equal among the five resorts)

TABLE 9–5 Preliminary ANOVA Table for Club Med Example

Source of Variation	Sum of Squares	Degrees of Freedom	Mean Square	F Ratio
Treatment	SSTR =	$r - 1 = $ 4	MSTR =	$F = $
Error	SSE = 98,356	$n - r = $ 195	MSE =	
Total	SST = 112,564	$n - 1 = $ 199		

TABLE 9–6 ANOVA Table for Club Med Example

Source of Variation	Sum of Squares	Degrees of Freedom	Mean Square	F Ratio
Treatment	SSTR = 14,208	$r - 1 = 4$	MSTR = 3,552	$F = 7.04$
Error	SSE = 98,356	$n - r = 195$	MSE = 504.4	
Total	SST = 112,564	$n - 1 = 199$		

As shown in Table 9–6, the test statistic value is $F_{(4, 195)} = 7.04$. As often happens, the exact number of degrees of freedom we need does not appear in Appendix C, Table 5. We use the nearest entry, which is the critical point for F with 4 degrees of freedom for the numerator and 200 degrees of freedom for the denominator. The critical point for $\alpha = 0.01$ is $C = 3.41$. The test is illustrated in Figure 9–11.

Since the computed test statistic value falls in the rejection region for $\alpha = 0.01$, we reject the null hypothesis and note that the p-value is smaller than 0.01. We may conclude that, based on the survey results and our assumptions, it is likely that the five resorts studied are not equal in terms of average vacationer satisfaction. Which resorts are more satisfying than others? This question will be answered when we return to this example in the next section.

2–30. One of the greatest problems in marketing research and other survey fields is the problem of nonresponse to surveys. In home interviews the problem arises from absence from home at the time of the visit or, sometimes, plain refusal to answer questions. A market researcher believes that a respondent will answer all questions with probability 0.94 if found at home. He further believes that the probability that a given person will be found at home is 0.65. Given this information, what percentage of the interviews will be successfully completed?

2–32. An investment analyst collects data on stocks and notes whether or not dividends were paid and whether or not the stocks increased in price over a given period. Data are presented in the following table.

	Price Increase	No Price Increase	Total
Dividends paid	34	78	112
No dividends paid	85	49	134
Total	119	127	246

a. If a stock is selected at random out of the analyst's list of 246 stocks, what is the probability that it increased in price?

b. If a stock is selected at random, what is the probability that it paid dividends?

c. If a stock is randomly selected, what is the probability that it both increased in price and paid dividends?

d. What is the probability that a randomly selected stock neither paid dividends nor increased in price?

e. Given that a stock increased in price, what is the probability that it also paid dividends?

f. If a stock is known not to have paid dividends, what is the probability that it increased in price?

g. What is the probability that a randomly selected stock was worth holding during the period in question; that is, what is the probability that it either increased in price, or paid dividends, or both?

Use of the Computer

Every chapter contains a section, "Using the Computer." These sections, taken together, constitute a complete guide for using the computer in a business statistics course. All the necessary commands and subcommands and options for doing statistics using MINITAB are listed and explained. These are demonstrated with many examples. In addition, there explanations of how to use other computer packages: SAS, SPSS, and SYSTAT, and a variety of examples. The book is also available with a shrink-wrapped version of BUSINESS MYSTAT, by Systat Inc.

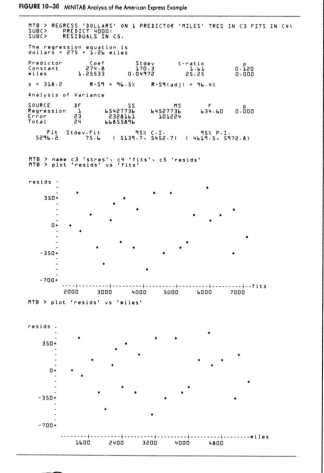

FIGURE 10–30 MINITAB Analysis of the American Express Example

Chapter Summaries and Review of Terminology

When we began this revision, we considered revising the summaries to fit into a more traditional list-of-terms and summary paragraph format. However, my experience has been that students find the current format more useful because it better describes and reinforces the logic and order of the chapter and the relationships between key terms and concepts.

4–9 Summary and Review of Terms

In this chapter, we discussed the **normal probability distribution**, the most important probability distribution in statistics. We defined the **standard normal random variable** as the normal random variable with mean 0 and standard deviation 1. We saw how to use a table of probabilities for the standard normal random variable and how to transform a normal random variable with any mean and any standard deviation to the standard normal random variable using the **normal transformation.**

We also saw how the standard normal random variable may, in turn, be transformed into any other normal random variable with a specified mean and standard deviation, and how this allows us to find values of a normal random variable that conform with some probability statement. We discussed a method of determining the mean and/or the standard deviation of a normal random variable from probability statements about the random variable. We saw how the normal distribution is used as a model in many real-world situations, both as the true distribution (a continuous one) and as an approximation to discrete distributions. In particular, we illustrated the use of the normal distribution as an approximation to the binomial distribution.

In the following chapters, we will make much use of the material presented here. Most of statistical theory relies on the normal distribution and on distributions that are derived from it.

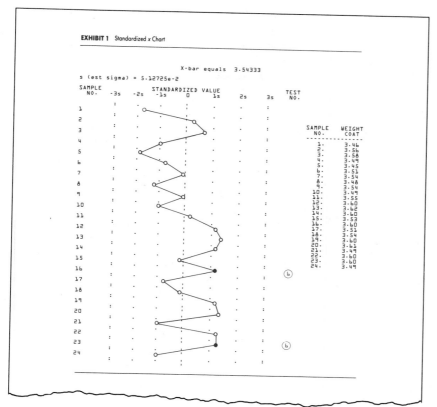

EXHIBIT 1   *Standardized x Chart*

CONTENT

Quality Control

Quality control is undoubtedly one of the fastest growing areas of interest to business statisticians. Clearly, this is an area where statistical planning, experimentation, and analysis can lead to tremendous improvements in our society, going beyond the realm of industrial production processes. To reflect the importance of this application of statistics, a new Chapter 13, "Quality Control and Improvement," was added. Dr. Lloyd Nelson of the Nashua Corporation, one of the nation's experts on quality control, has kindly provided a most interesting case for inclusion in this chapter (Case 13). Many other people contributed ideas and suggestions for the presentation of the ideas of quality control, including an introductory story on the first known use of quality control—the Royal Mint in London, starting around AD 1100 and continuing with minor changes to this very day. (The story is based on Professor Stephen Stigler's fascinating research of the Trial of the Pyx. See the introduction to Chapter 13.) The chapter includes thorough discussions of all commonly used control charts, as well as other quality-control tools. In addition to the new chapter, the topic of quality control is *integrated* throughout the text. Every chapter in the second edition has problems, and many chapters have examples, dealing with quality control and production issues. In Chapter 7 (Hypothesis Testing), for example, the introduction to section 7-6, Example (n), problems 7-28, 7-48, all deal with quality improvement and control. A table of quality-control constants for use in setting limits for control charts has also been added.

More Probability Distributions

In Chapter 3, "Random Variables," a brief discussion of other probability distributions has been included. The first edition of the book was generally oriented toward the normal-theory approach. My purpose has been (and still is) to get the student, as quickly as possible, to be comfortable with the normal distribution and its uses. This approach is effective in a *statistics* course, but may be somewhat limited when the purpose of the course is also to provide some familiarity with probability distributions used in other areas such as operations research, operations management, decision theory, and related fields. So, the chapter now includes discussions of the binomial, Poisson, geometric, hypergeometric, multinomial, exponential, uniform, and other probability distributions. The *binomial* table has been improved. You no longer need to use a formula for finding probabilities when p is greater than 0.5.

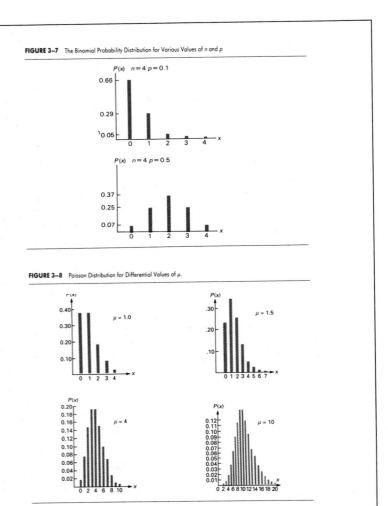

FIGURE 3-7 The Binomial Probability Distribution for Various Values of n and p

FIGURE 3-8 Poisson Distribution for Differential Values of μ.

4–41. Pierre operates a currency exchange office at Orly Airport in Paris. His office is open at night when the airport bank is closed, and he makes most of his business on returning American tourists who need to change their remaining French francs back to U.S. dollars. From experience, Pierre knows that the demand for dollars on any given night during high season is approximately normally distributed with mean $25,000 and standard deviation $5,000. If Pierre carries too much cash in dollars overnight, he pays a penalty: interest on the cash. On the other hand, if he runs short of cash during the night, he needs to send a person downtown to an all-night financial agency to get the required cash. This, too, is costly to him. Therefore, Pierre would like to carry overnight an amount of money such that the demand on 85% of the nights will not exceed this amount. Can you help Pierre find the required amount of dollars to carry?

An International Orientation

One of the book's strengths is its global orientation. As the world becomes smaller and domestic firms are affected by international competition, it becomes ever more important to understand how business is done abroad, how international markets operate, and how other cultures affect business. This book is one of the few that has a strong international flavor. Many of the examples, problems, and cases deal with global issues and multinational corporations. Besides promoting the understanding of business statistics in a global setting, the international applications are more exciting.

EXAMPLE (f)   Twenty-one percent of the executives in a large advertising firm are at the top salary level. It is further known that 40% of all the executives at the firm are women. Also, 6.4% of all executives are women *and* are at the top salary level. Recently, a question arose among executives at the firm as to whether there is any evidence of salary inequity. Assuming that some statistical considerations (explained in later chapters) are met, do the percentages reported above provide any evidence of salary inequity?

SOLUTION   To solve this problem, we pose it in terms of probabilities and ask whether the probability that a randomly chosen executive will be at the top salary level is approximately equal to the probability that the executive will be at the top salary level *given* the executive is a woman. To answer, we need to compute the probability that the executive will be at the top level given the executive is a woman. Defining T as the event of a top salary and W as the event that an executive is a woman, we get:

$$P(T|W) = \frac{P(T \cap W)}{P(W)} = \frac{0.064}{0.40} = 0.16$$

Since 0.16 is smaller than 0.21, we may conclude (subject to statistical considerations) that salary inequity does exist at the firm, as an executive is less likely to make a top salary if she is a woman.

The preceding example may incline us to think about the relations among different events. Are different events related, or are they *independent* of each other? In this example, we concluded that the two events, being a woman and being at the top salary level, are related in the sense that the event W made the event T less likely. The next section quantifies the relations among events and defines the concept of independence.

Gender Issues and Ethics

The book has been written with great sensitivity to ethics and morality. I have made every effort to exclude from examples and problems companies or countries that I believe did not behave "nicely." Companies that use animal testing, the fur industry, and companies that discriminate against women or minorities were all excluded to the best of my ability and awareness. I use a nonsexist language throughout, preferring the use of "he or she" to any other, or using he and she alternately in problems. I also give several examples of the use of statistics in proving discrimination cases.

COMPREHENSIVENESS

Everyone who has seen the first edition agreed that the book lived up to its name: *Complete Business Statistics*. I felt that it was important that the book be comprehensive and cover all statistical tools that find at least some application in business and related fields. The idea was to present the basic topics usually covered in an introductory course, and to include additional topics to allow the instructor (or the interested, independent student) the option to explore other areas. For example, Chapter 6 is devoted to confidence intervals, which are usually two-sided. There are, however, situations where we want to estimate an upper bound or a lower bound only for a given parameter. This is why an optional section on one-sided confidence intervals is included. Even if an instructor has absolutely no interest in covering the topic, it is still nice to know that a question from a student "What if we only care about an upper bound?" can be answered by referring the student to the optional section. The same holds true for discussions of the power of a test, transformations in regression, and many other topics. In the second edition, the areas that are usually considered optional are clearly marked by a footnote.

In order to allow space for the inclusion of the new chapter on quality control, some reductions had to be made elsewhere. One subject that was found to be used by few instructors was the Box-Jenkins forecasting methodology. This topic was greatly reduced, and now appears as a short summary.

THE EDUCATIONAL PACKAGE

The textbook comes with:

- An *Instructor's Manual* containing the solutions of all the problems and cases.
- A *Student Problem-Solving Guide* authored by Dr. Michael Sklar of Emory University.
- A *Test Bank* and a *Computerized Test Bank* written by Richard Duffy of M.I.T.
- An *Instructor's Lecture Guide* containing transparency masters, useful graphs and figures, ways of presenting various topics, and other useful instructor's aids.
- A *Data Disk* containing all large data sets from the text.
- An optional shrink-wrapped disk and guide for the *Business Mystat* package.

SOME SUGGESTIONS ON HOW TO USE THE BOOK

The book is designed so that it can be used in a variety of courses and course sequences. A typical first course in business statistics could cover Chapters:

1. Introduction and Descriptive Statistics
2. Probability
3. Random Variables
4. The Normal Distribution
5. Sampling and Sampling Distributions
6. Confidence Intervals
7. Hypothesis Testing
10. Simple Linear Regression

In each chapter, you may choose to cover the basic sections, adding any optional topics you desire as time permits. While many variations are possible, for a one-term course we recommend you consider one of two alternatives. The first is to include Chapter 8 on the comparison of two populations and Chapter 9 on the analysis of variance. The other would be to include Chapters 1–7 followed by Chapter 13 on quality and then Chapter 10 on simple regression.

In a two-semester course, the second course could include the chapters:

7., 10. (Review)
11. Multiple Regression
12. Forecasting
13. Quality Control and Improvement
14. Nonparametric Statistics
15. Bayesian Statistics and Decision Analysis

Alternatively, you may choose to cover Chapter 16 on multivariate methods and/or Chapter 17 on sampling methods instead of any of the chapters above. Again, optional sections may be covered at your discretion and depending on student interest. The nonparametrics chapter is very comprehensive and you will likely have to choose your favorite topics from among the many presented here.

In a three-semester course I would cover all of the topics in the book, in any of a variety of sequential orders. The book is designed for flexibility and variety. Enjoy it!

Throughout the revision process on the text and teaching package we have worked hard to maintain the cleanliness of the first edition. I would like to thank Edwin Sexton at Virginia Military Institute as well as colleagues and adopters, especially Richard Duffy at M.I.T., for finding and reporting errors. Still, for those errors that remain I take full responsibility and request that you forward any you find to me or to Irwin. A postage-paid form appears in the instructor's manual for this purpose. We will correct any errors as quickly as possible.

SECOND EDITION

COMPLETE BUSINESS
STATISTICS

AMIR D. ACZEL
Bentley College

IRWIN

Homewood, IL 60430
Boston, MA 02116

SECOND EDITION

COMPLETE BUSINESS
STATISTICS

AMIR D. ACZEL
Bentley College

IRWIN
Homewood, IL 60430
Boston, MA 02116

This symbol indicates that the paper in this book is made from recycled paper. Its fiber content exceeds the recommended minimum of 50% waste paper fibers as specified by the EPA.

© RICHARD D. IRWIN, INC., 1989 and 1993

All rights reserved. No part of this publication may be reproduced, stored in a retrieval system, or transmitted, in any form or by any means, electronic, mechanical, photocopying, recording, or otherwise, without the prior written permission of the publisher.

Senior sponsoring editor	Richard T. Hercher, Jr.
Developmental editor	Karen E. Perry
Marketing manager	Kurt Messersmith
Project editor	Margaret Haywood
Production manager	Diane Palmer
Designer	Terri Ellerbach
Art coordinator	Mark Malloy
Compositor	Interactive Composition Corporation
Typeface	10/12 Times Roman
Printer	Von Hoffmann Press, Inc.

Library of Congress Cataloging-in-Publication Data

Aczel, Amir D.
  Complete business statistics / Amir D. Aczel. — 2nd ed.
    p.   cm.
  Includes index.
  ISBN 0-256-08613-3

  ISBN 0-256-12651-8 (Instructor's Edition)
  1. Commercial statistics. 2. Statistics. I. Title.
HF1017.A26 1992
519.5—dc20   92–8933

Printed in the United States of America
1 2 3 4 5 6 7 8 9 0 VH 9 8 7 6 5 4 3 2

To my father, Captain E. L. Aczel, and to the memory of my mother, Miriam Aczel

PREFACE

As with the first edition of this book, I have tried to achieve several important goals. First, I wanted a book that *really* explained statistical thinking and the ideas of statistical inference rather than just giving formulas and examples as do many business statistics books. I also wanted to stress an *intuitive* understanding of statistical procedures and an understanding of what statistics is all about. For example, this book explains the logical principle behind the analysis of variance rather than just the computations. Once the student understands this principle, the complicated sums of squares suddenly make sense and the final result is not just a number—it is a complete picture of what the data are trying to tell us about an actual problem. As another example, this is one of very few statistics books at this level that actually explain the meaning of *degrees of freedom*.

My second goal was to write a book that is firmly rooted in the real world. I carefully chose exceptional problems and examples that I came across in actual business situations; in doing so, I drew on my experience in the field of marketing research. I also chose a wide selection of real problems and examples from the fields of finance, management, transportation, tourism, accounting, public administration, economics, production, the fashion industry, advertising, and other areas. Many of the examples and problems originate in the professional business literature; other problems are company-specific and originate in statistical consulting projects. Among these, I have also made an effort to mix international settings and situations.

My third goal was to present a wide range of statistical topics. I sought to write a *complete* book of business statistics, and I included several important topics that are avoided by other authors. This is the only book I know of at this level that includes a chapter on multivariate statistical methods.

After an introduction to descriptive statistics (Chapter 1), the book moves on to a thorough treatment of probabilistic reasoning and the concepts of probability theory—the basis for all of statistical inference. The book then provides the student with a detailed explanation of random variables, expected values, the variance, and the standard deviation. There is an entire chapter devoted to the normal distribution—including some optional advanced topics not commonly covered as well as a wide range of problems demonstrating the usefulness of the normal probability model. Once the student is comfortable with probability and random variables, the ideas of sampling are carefully explained. Estimation and confidence intervals are next, followed by a very thorough discussion of statistical hypothesis testing. Hypothesis tests are explained at several different levels, including the philosophy behind a statistical hypothesis test, when and how tests should be conducted, and how to carefully interpret their results. This is one book that truly explains the meaning of statistical *significance*.

Every chapter in this book introduces the basics of the theory and then expands the discussion to include more advanced material. Chapter 11 on multiple regression, for example, contains many advanced topics. At the beginning undergraduate level, however, an instructor may choose the earlier sections, leaving out more complicated topics such as transformations. He or she is left with a thorough, clear, and easy-to-understand discussion of multiple regression models. The presentation is complete and includes a discussion of the *pitfalls* to avoid when conducting a regression analysis.

Books written specifically for an introductory course, however, often fail to discuss the perceived "difficult" topics in regression and other areas. This is one reason why statisticians so often encounter misuse of statistical methods and the consequent distortion of results and implications. This is especially true nowadays that computers and software packages for statistical analysis are so prevalent that everyone has access to "statistics." It is now more important than ever before to teach business practitioners and others the *correct* use of statistics. Computing power should go hand in hand with—not replace—statistical reasoning, correct selection of a statistical model, careful evaluation of the underlying assumptions, and cautious interpretation of results. It is my hope that this book stresses these aspects of any analysis more completely and understandably than other statistics texts. It is, in fact, the development and implementation of new statistical software that made me realize just how important it is that we teach the advanced topics. When a microcomputer can be used to perform complicated multivariate analysis, statistical instruction that does not cover such topics is behind the times.

The book integrates theory and examples with use of the computer. The main computer package demonstrated is MINITAB. This package was chosen because it is very easy to use. Each chapter where data analysis is conducted contains a section on the use of the computer. MINITAB is explained in some detail to allow the student to use it with little or no prior preparation. Three other packages are explained and used in the book: SPSS, SYSTAT, and SAS.

Many people were helpful to me in preparing this book. I would like to thank Professor Robert Fetter of Yale University for his many helpful comments and suggestions. I gratefully acknowledge the help of the following reviewers who contributed to the first edition: Professor Michael Sklar, Emory University; Professor John Sennetti, Texas Tech University; Professor Jamie Eng, San Francisco State University; Professor Chaim M. Ehrman, Loyola University of Chicago; Professor Samuel Kotz, University of Maryland; Professor Andrew Seila, University of Georgia; Professor Paul Rubin, Michigan State University; Professor Amitava Mitra, Auburn University; Professor Randall Anderson, California State University; Professor Charles Feinstein, University of Santa Clara; Professor Peter Seagle, State University of New York—Albany; Professor Michael Broida, Miami University of Ohio; Professor Gary Franko, Siena College; Professor Mary Sue Younger, University of Tennessee; Professor Robert Des Jardines, University of North Carolina at Chapel Hill; Professor Marvin Puterman, University of British Columbia; Professor Ralph St. John, Bowling Green State University; Professor Charles Warnock, Hong Kong University; Professor Thomas Knowles, Illinois Institute of Technology; Professor Donald Robinson, Illinois State University; and Professor Peg Young, George Mason University.

I also thank the following reviewers who contributed to the second edition. Their insightful comments helped to fine tune the text and supplement package.

Sung K. Ahr—Washington State University

James Behel—Harding University

Sherman Chottiner—Syracuse University

Chaim M. Ehrman—Loyola University

Nicholas Farnum—California State University, Fullerton

Stuart Kellog—University of Miami, Coral Gables

Brenda Masters—Oklahoma State University

G. Steven Rhiel—Old Dominion University

Don Robinson—Illinois State University

Marjorie Rubash—Bradley University

Amy Schmidt—Bentley College

Vincent Showers—Bradley University

Jay Sounderpandian—University of Wisconsin, Parkside

Ron Suich—California State University, Fullerton

Peter Westfall—Texas Tech University

Othmar Winkler—Georgetown University

John Wong—Wichita State University

I would like to thank the following colleagues, friends, and students, who also helped with the project. I am most grateful to Professor Erl Sorensen for countless suggestions, encouragement, and advice. James Zeitler of Bentley College has also been very helpful. I am grateful to my colleagues Dominique Haughton, Norm Josephy, Nick Teebagy, Andrew Stollar, Richard Fristensky, John Leeth, Scott Callan, Amy Schmid, and Joseph Kane for many suggestions. I acknowledge help from students Harpreet Singh, Joseph Lessard, Jay Goldberg, Garrett Tight, and Karl Haase. I would also like to thank Professor Frederick Mosteller, Harvard University; Professor Arnold Zellner, University of Chicago; and Professor Johannes Ledolter, University of Iowa, for helpful comments.

I would like to thank Bruce Powell of Richard D. Irwin, Inc., who first suggested that I write this book. Furthermore, I am indebted to my editor, Richard T. Hercher Jr., for all his help, encouragement, enthusiasm, and support throughout this project. I would also like to thank Karen Perry, developmental editor; Margaret Haywood, project editor; David Mason, copy editor; Terri Ellerbach, designer; and many others of the highly professional staff at Irwin for all their help and hard work.

Among others, I am indebted to the *Biometrika* trustees for permission to reprint various statistical tables from *Biometrika* publications, and to the American Marketing Association for permission to reprint many tables and other information from the *Journal of Marketing* and the *Journal of Marketing Research*. I would also like to acknowledge the New York Times Company for its kind permission to reprint several articles. Finally, I thank my wife, Debra, for all her help in editing the manuscript and for her many suggestions and ideas.

Amir D. Aczel

CONTENTS IN BRIEF

CONTENTS

3 Random Variables   90

4 The Normal Distribution   134

5 | Sampling and Sampling Distributions   164

6 | Confidence Intervals   196

7 | Hypothesis Testing   234

8 The Comparison of Two Populations 306

9 Analysis of Variance 348

Simple Linear Regression and Correlation   410

Multiple Regression   462

12 Time Series, Forecasting, and Index Numbers   556

13 Quality Control and Improvement 602

14 Nonparametric Methods and Chi-Square Tests 624

15 Bayesian Statistics and Decision Analysis 704

16 Multivariate Analysis 760

Sampling Methods   820

COMPLETE BUSINESS
STATISTICS

1

INTRODUCTION AND DESCRIPTIVE STATISTICS

INTRODUCTION

It is better to be roughly right than precisely wrong

—*Maynard Keynes*

You all have probably heard the story about Malcolm Forbes, who once got lost floating for miles in one of his famous balloons and finally landed in the middle of a cornfield. He spotted a man coming toward him and asked, "Sir, can you tell me where I am?" The man said, "Certainly, you are in a basket in a field of corn." Forbes said, "You must be a statistician." The man said, "That's amazing, how did you know that?" "Easy," said Forbes, "your information is concise, precise, and absolutely useless!"[1]

T he purpose of this book is to convince you that information resulting from a good statistical analysis is always concise, often precise, and never useless! The spirit of statistics is, in fact, very well captured by the quotation above from Keynes. This book should teach you how to be at least roughly right a high percentage of the time.

The word *statistics* is derived from the Italian word *stato*, which means "state." Similarly, *statista* refers to a person involved with the affairs of state, and *statistics* originally meant the collection of facts useful to the *statista*. Statistics in this sense was used in 16th-century Italy and then spread to France, Holland, and Germany. We note, however, that surveys of people and property actually began in ancient times.[2]

Today, statistics is not restricted to information about the state but extends to almost every realm of human endeavor. Neither do we restrict ourselves to merely collecting numerical information, called *data*. Our data are summarized, displayed in meaningful ways, and analyzed. Statistical analysis often involves an attempt to generalize from the data. In that sense, statistics is a science—the science of *inference*. Data, summarized or otherwise, are used in the inference along with the tools of probability theory and inductive reasoning. The result is an inference from the *sample* (the data) to a general *population* from which the sample is assumed to have been randomly selected.

The **population** consists of the set of all measurements in which the investigator is interested. The population is also called the **universe**.

---

[1] From an address by R. Gnanadesikan to the American Statistical Association, reprinted in *American Statistician* 44, no. 2 (May 1990), p. 122.

[2] See Anders Hald, *A History of Probability and Statistics and Their Applications before 1750* (New York: Wiley, 1990), pp. 81–82.

Continued on next page

> A **sample** is a subset of measurements selected from the population. Sampling from the population is often done **randomly,** such that every possible sample of *n* elements will have an equal chance of being selected. A sample selected in this way is called a **simple random sample,** or just a **random sample.**

In this chapter, we will concentrate on the processing, summarization, and display of data—the first step in statistical analysis. In the next chapter, we will explore the theory of probability, the connection between the random sample and the population. Later chapters build on the concepts of probability and develop a system that allows us to draw a logical, consistent inference from our sample to the underlying population.

Why worry about inference and about a population? Why not just look at our data and interpret them? Mere inspection of the data will suffice when interest centers on the particular observations you have. If, however, you want to draw meaningful conclusions with implications extending beyond your limited data, statistical inference is the way to do it.

In marketing research, we are often interested in the relationship between advertising and sales. A data set of randomly chosen sales and advertising figures for a given firm may be of some interest in itself, but the information in it is much more useful if it leads to implications about the underlying process—the relationship between the firm's level of advertising and the resulting level of sales. An understanding of the true relationship between advertising and sales—the relationship in the population of advertising and sales possibilities for the frm—would allow us to predict sales for any level of advertising and thus to set advertising at a level that maximizes profits.

A pharmaceutical manufacturer interested in marketing a new drug may be required by the Food and Drug Administration to prove that the drug does not cause serious side effects. The results of tests of the drug on a random sample of people may then be used in a statistical inference about the entire population of people who may use the drug if it is introduced.

A bank may be interested in assessing the popularity of automatic teller machines. The machines may be tried on a randomly chosen group of bank customers. The conclusions of the study could then be generalized by statistical inference to the entire population of the bank's customers.

A quality control engineer at a plant making disk drives for computers needs to make sure that no more than 3% of the drives produced are defective. The engineer may routinely collect random samples of drives and check their quality. Based on the random samples, the engineer may then draw a conclusion about the proportion of defective items in the entire population of drives.

These are just a few examples illustrating the use of statistical inference in business situations. In the rest of this chapter, we will introduce the descriptive statistics needed to carry out basic statistical analyses. The next chapters will develop the elements of the inference from samples to populations. ∎

1–2 Percentiles and Quartiles

Given a set of numerical observations, we may order them according to magnitude. Once we have done this, it is possible to define the boundaries of the set. Any student who has taken a nationally administered test, such as the Scholastic Aptitude Test (SAT), is familiar with *percentiles*. Your score on such a test is compared with the scores of all people who took the test at the same time, and your position within this group is defined in terms of a percentile. If you are in the 90th percentile, 90% of the people who took the test received a score lower than yours. We define a percentile as follows.[3]

> The *P*th **percentile** of a group of numbers is that value below which lie *P*% (*P* percent) of the numbers in the group. The position of the *P*th percentile is given by $(n + 1)P/100$, where n is the number of data points.

Let us look at an example.

A large department store collects data on sales made by each of its salespeople. The data, number of sales made on a given day by each of 20 salespeople, are given below.

6, 9, 10, 12, 13, 14, 14, 15, 16, 16, 16, 17, 17, 18, 18, 19, 20, 21, 22, 24

The data have already been arranged in ascending order. Find the 50th, 80th, and 90th percentiles of this data set.

To find the 50th percentile, we need to determine the data point in position $(n + 1)P/100 = (20 + 1)(50/100) = (21)(0.5) = 10.5$. Thus, we need the data point in position 10.5. Counting the observations from smallest to largest, we find that the 10th observation is 16, and so is the 11th. Therefore, the observation that would lie in position 10.5 (halfway between the 10th and 11th observations) is 16. Thus, the 50th percentile is 16.

Similarly, we find the 80th percentile of the data set as the observation lying in position $(n + 1)P/100 = (21)(80/100) = 16.8$. The 16th observation is 19, and the 17th is 20; therefore, the 80th percentile is a point lying 0.8 of the way from 19 to 20, that is, 19.8.

The 90th percentile is found as the observation in position $(n + 1)P\,100 = (20 + 1)(90/100) = (21)(0.9) = 18.9$, which is 21.9.

Certain percentiles have greater importance than others because they break down the **distribution** of the data (the way the data points are *distributed* along the number line) into four groups. These are the quartiles. **Quartiles** are the percentage points that break down the data set into quarters—first quarter, second quarter, third quarter, and fourth quarter.

> The **first quartile** is the 25th percentile. It is that point below which lie 1/4 of the data.

Similarly, the second quartile is the 50th percentile, as we computed in Example (a). This is the most important point and has a special name: the *median*.

> The **median** is the point below which lie half the data. It is the 50th percentile.

---

[3] Note that this definition may not work for small data sets and extreme percentiles.

We define the third quartile correspondingly:

> The **third quartile** is the 75th percentile point. It is that point below which lie 75 percent of the data.

The 25th percentile is often called the **lower quartile;** the 50th percentile point, the median, is called the **middle quartile;** and the 75th percentile is called the **upper quartile.**

Find the lower, middle, and upper quartiles of the data set in Example (a).

SOLUTION

Based on the procedure we used in computing the 80th and 90th percentiles, we find that the lower quartile is the observation in position $(21)(0.25) = 5.25$, which is 13.25. The middle quartile was already computed (it is the 50th percentile, the median, which is 16). The upper quartile is the observation in position $(21)(75/100) = 15.75$, which is 18.75.

> We define the **interquartile range** as the difference between the first and third quartiles.

The interquartile range is a measure of the spread of the data. In Example (a), the interquartile range is equal to: Third quartile − First quartile = $18.75 - 13.25 = 5.5$.

PROBLEMS

Answers

1–1.   The following data are numbers of passengers on flights of Delta Air Lines between San Francisco and Seattle over 33 days in April and early May.

> 128, 121, 134, 136, 136, 118, 123, 109, 120, 116, 125, 128, 121, 129, 130, 131, 127, 119, 114, 134, 110, 136, 134, 125, 128, 123, 128, 133, 132, 136, 134, 129, 132

Find the lower, middle, and upper quartiles of this data set. Also find the 10th, 15th, and 65th percentiles. What is the interquartile range?

1–2.

Median = 8
1st quartile = 9
3rd quartile = 15.5

1–2.   The following data are annualized returns on a group of 15 stocks.

> 12.5, 13, 14.8, 11, 16.7, 9, 8.3, −1.2, 3.9, 15.5, 16.2, 18, 11.6, 10, 9.5

Find the median, the first and third quartiles, and the 55th and 85th percentiles for these data.

1–3.   The following data are scores on a management examination taken by a group of 22 people.

> 88, 56, 64, 45, 52, 76, 54, 79, 38, 98, 69, 77, 71, 45, 60, 78, 90, 81, 87, 44, 80, 41

1–4.

Median = 3
1st quartile = 2
3rd quartile = 5

Find the median and the 20th, 30th, 60th, and 90th percentiles.

1–4.   Following are the numbers of daily bids received by the government of a developing country from firms interested in winning a contract for the construction of a new port facility.

2, 3, 2, 4, 3, 5, 1, 1, 6, 4, 7, 2, 5, 1, 6

Find the quartiles and the interquartile range. Also find the 60th percentile.

1–5. Find the median, the interquartile range, and the 45th percentile of the following data.

23, 26, 29, 30, 32, 34, 37, 45, 57, 80, 102, 147, 210, 355, 782, 1,209

1–3 Measures of Central Tendency

Percentiles, and in particular quartiles, are measures of the relative positions of points within a data set or a population (when our data set constitutes the entire population). The median is a special point, since it lies in the center of the data in the sense that half the data lie below it and half above it. The median is thus a measure of the *location* or *centrality* of the observations.

In addition to the median, there are two other commonly used measures of central tendency. One is the *mode* (or modes—there may be several of them), and the other is the *arithmetic mean,* or just the *mean.* We define the mode as follows.

The **mode** of the data set is the value that occurs most frequently.

Let us look at the frequencies of occurrence of the data values in Example (a), shown in Table 1–1. We see that the value 16 occurs most frequently. There are three data points with this value—more points than for any other value in the data set. Therefore, the mode is equal to 16.

The most commonly used measure of central tendency of a set of observations is the mean of the observations.

The **mean** of a set of observations is their **average**. It is equal to the sum of all observations divided by the number of observations in the set.

Let us denote the observations by $x_1, x_2, \ldots, x_n$. That is, the first observation is denoted by x_1, the second by x_2, and so on to the nth observation, x_n. (In Example (a) $x_1 = 6$, $x_2 = 9$, $\ldots$, and $x_n = x_{20} = 24$.) The sample mean is denoted by $\bar{x}$.

TABLE 1–1 Frequencies of Occurrence of Data Values in Example (a)

Value	Frequency
6	1
9	1
10	1
12	1
13	1
14	2
15	1
16	3
17	2
18	2
19	1
20	1
21	1
22	1
24	1

> **Mean of a sample:**
> $$\bar{x} = \frac{\sum\limits_{i=1}^{n} x_i}{n} = (x_1 + x_2 + \cdots + x_n)/n \qquad (1\text{--}1)$$

where Σ is summation notation. The summation extends over all data points.

When our observation set constitutes an entire population, instead of denoting the mean by $\bar{x}$ we use the symbol μ (the Greek letter mu). For a population, we use N as the number of elements instead of n. The population mean is defined as follows.

> **Mean of a population:**
> $$\mu = \frac{\sum\limits_{i=1}^{N} x_i}{N} \qquad (1\text{--}2)$$

The mean of the observations in Example (a) is found as:

$$\bar{x} = (x_1 + x_2 + \cdots + x_{20})/20 = (6 + 9 + 10 + 12 + 13 + 14 + 14 + 15$$
$$+ 16 + 16 + 16 + 17 + 17 + 18 + 18 + 19 + 20 + 21 + 22 + 24)/20$$
$$= 317/20$$
$$= 15.85$$

The mean of the observations of Example (a), their average, is 15.85.

Figure 1–1 shows the data of Example (a) drawn on the number line along with the mean, median, and mode of the observations. If you think of the data points as little balls of equal weight located at the appropriate places on the number line, the mean is that point where all the weights would balance. It is the *fulcrum* of the point-weights, as shown in Figure 1–1.

What characterizes the three measures of centrality, and what are the relative merits of each? The mean summarizes all of the information in the data. It is the average of all observations. The mean is a single point that can be viewed as the point where all the mass—the weight—of the observations is concentrated. It is the center of mass of the data. If all the observations in our data set were the same size, then (assuming the total is the same) each would be equal to the mean.

The median, on the other hand, is an observation (or a point between two observations) in the center of the data set. One-half of the data lie above this observation, and one-half of the data lie below it. When we compute the median, we do not consider the exact location of each data point on the number line; we only consider

FIGURE 1–1   *Mean, Median, and Mode for Example (a)*

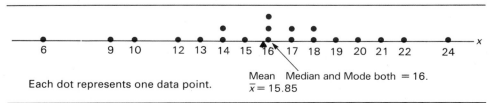

Each dot represents one data point.

Mean   Median and Mode both = 16.
$\bar{x} = 15.85$

FIGURE 1-2   A Symmetrically Distributed Data Set

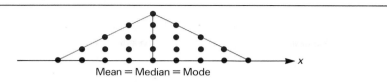

Mean = Median = Mode

whether or not it falls in the half lying above the median or the half lying below the median.

What does this mean? If you look at the picture of the data set of Example (a), Figure 1-1, you will note that the observation $x_{20} = 24$ lies to the far right. If we shift this particular observation (or any other observation to the right of 16) to the right, say, move it from 24 to 100, what would happen to the median? The answer is: absolutely *nothing* (prove this to yourself by calculating the new median). The exact location of any data point is not considered in the computation of the median, only its relative standing with respect to the central observation. *The median is resistant to extreme observations.*

The mean, on the other hand, is sensitive to extreme observations. Let us see what happens to the mean if we change x_{20} from 24 to 100. The new mean is

$$\bar{x} = (6 + 9 + 10 + 12 + 13 + 14 + 14 + 15 + 16 + 16 + 16 + 17 + 17 \\ + 18 + 18 + 19 + 20 + 21 + 22 + 100)/20 = 19.65$$

We see that the mean has shifted almost four units to the right to accommodate the change in the single data point x_{20}.

The mean, however, does have strong advantages as a measure of central tendency. *The mean is based on information contained in all the observations in the data set,* rather than being an observation lying "in the middle" of the set. The mean also has some desirable mathematical properties that make it useful in many contexts of statistical inference. In cases where we want to guard against the influence of a few outlying observations (called *outliers*), however, we may prefer to use the median.

The mode is less useful than either the mean or the median. The mode tells us our data set's most frequently occurring value. There may be several modes. In Example (a), our data would possess two modes if we had another data point equal to 18, for example. Of the three measures of central tendency, we are most interested in the mean.

If a data set or population is *symmetric* (that is, if one side of the distribution of the observations is a mirror image of the other) and if the distribution of the observations has only one mode, then the mode, the median, and the mean are all equal. Such a situation is demonstrated in Figure 1-2. Generally, when the data distribution is not symmetric, then the mean, median, and mode will not all be equal. The relative positions of the three measures of centrality in such situations will be discussed in Section 1-6.

In the next section, we discuss measures of variability of a data set or population.

PROBLEMS

1-6.   Discuss the differences among the three measures of centrality.

1-7.   Find the mean, median, and mode(s) of the observations in problem 1-1.

Answers

1–8.

1–8. Do the same as problem 1–7 using the data of problem 1–2.

1–9. Do the same as problem 1–7 using the data of problem 1–3.

1–10. Do the same as problem 1–7 using the data of problem 1–4.

1–11. Do the same as problem 1–7 using the observation set in problem 1–5.

1–8.
─────

Mean = 11.2533
Median = 11.6
no Mode

1–10.
─────

Mean = 3.466
Median = 3
Modes = 1 and 2

1–4 Measures of Variability

Consider the following two data sets.

> Set I: 1, 2, 3, 4, 5, 6, 6, 7, 8, 9, 10 ,11
> Set II: 4, 5, 5, 5, 6, 6, 6, 6, 7, 7, 7, 8

Compute the mean, median, and mode of each of the two data sets. As you see from your results, the two data sets have the same mean, the same median, and the same mode, all equal to 6. The two data sets also happen to have the same number of observations, $n = 12$. But the two data sets are different. What is the main difference between them?

Figure 1–3 shows data sets I and II. The two data sets have the same central tendency (as measured by any of the three measures of centrality), but they have a different *variability*. In particular, we see that data set I is more variable than data set II. The values in set I are more spread out: they lie further away from their mean than do those of set II.

There are several measures of **variability,** or **dispersion.** We have already discussed one such measure—the interquartile range. (Recall that the interquartile range is defined as the difference between the upper quartile and the lower quartile.) The interquartile range for data set I is 5.5, and the interquartile range of data set II is 2 (show this). The interquartile range is one measure of the dispersion or variability of a set of observations. Another such measure is the *range*.

> The **range** of a set of observations is the difference between the largest observation and the smallest observation.

FIGURE 1–3 Comparison of Data Sets I and II

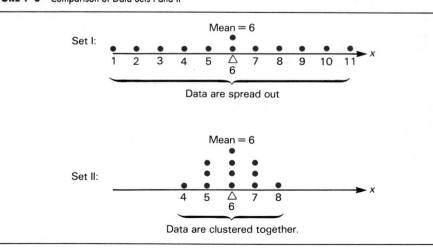

The range of the observations in Example (a) is: Largest number − Smallest number = 24 − 6 = 18. The range of the data in set I is 11 − 1 = 10, and the range of the data in set II is 8 − 4 = 4. We see that, conforming with what we expect from looking at the two data sets, the range of set I is greater than the range of set II. Set I is more variable.

The range and the interquartile range are measures of the dispersion of a set of observations, the interquartile range being more resistant to extreme observations. There are also two other, more commonly used measures of dispersion. These are the *variance* and the square root of the variance—the *standard deviation*.

The variance and the standard deviation are more useful than the range and the interquartile range because, like the mean, they use the information contained in all the observations in the data set or population. (The range contains information only on the distance between the largest and smallest observations, and the interquartile range contains information only about the difference between upper and lower quartiles.) We define the variance as follows.

> The **variance** of a set of observations is the average squared deviation of the data points from their mean.

When our data constitute a sample, the variance is denoted by s^2, and the averaging is done by dividing the sum of the squared deviations from the mean by $n − 1$. (The reason for this will become clear in Chapter 5.) When our observations constitute an entire population, the variance is denoted by σ^2, and the averaging is done by dividing by N. (σ is the Greek letter sigma; we call the variance *sigma-squared*. The capital sigma is known to you as the symbol we use for summation, Σ.)

Sample variance:

$$s^2 = \frac{\sum_{i=1}^{n} (x_i - \bar{x})^2}{n - 1} \qquad (1\text{--}3)$$

Recall that $\bar{x}$ is the sample mean, the average of all the observations in the sample. Thus, the numerator in equation 1–3 is equal to the sum of the squared differences of the data points x_i (where $i = 1, 2, \ldots, n$) from their mean, $\bar{x}$. When we divide the numerator by the denominator $n − 1$, we get a kind of average of the items summed in the numerator. This average is based on the assumption that there are only $n − 1$ data points. (Note, however, that the summation in the numerator extends over all n data points, not just $n − 1$ of them.) This will be explained in section 5–5.

When we have an entire population at hand, we denote the total number of observations in the population by N. We define the population variance as follows.

Population variance:

$$\sigma^2 = \frac{\sum_{i=1}^{N} (x_i - \mu)^2}{N} \qquad (1\text{--}4)$$

where μ is the population mean.

Unless noted otherwise, we will assume that all our data sets are samples and do not constitute entire populations; thus, we will use equation 1–3 for the variance, and not equation 1–4. We now define the standard deviation.

The **standard deviation** of a set of observations is the (positive) square root of the variance of the set.

The standard deviation of a sample is the square root of the sample variance, and the standard deviation of a population is the square root of the variance of the population.[4]

Sample standard deviation:

$$s = \sqrt{s^2} = \sqrt{\frac{\sum\limits_{i=1}^{n} (x_i - \overline{x})^2}{n-1}} \qquad (1\text{–}5)$$

Population standard deviation:

$$\sigma = \sqrt{\sigma^2} = \sqrt{\frac{\sum\limits_{i=1}^{n} (x_i - \mu)^2}{N}} \qquad (1\text{–}6)$$

Why would we use the standard deviation when we already have its square, the variance? The standard deviation is a more meaningful measure. The variance is the average squared deviation from the mean. It is squared because if we just compute the deviations from the mean and then average them, we get zero (prove this with any of the data sets). Therefore, when seeking a measure of the variation in a set of observations, we square the deviations from the mean; this removes the negative signs, and thus the measure is not equal to zero. The measure we obtain—the variance—is still a *squared* quantity; it is an average of squared numbers. By taking its square root, we "unsquare" the units and get a quantity denoted in the original units of the problem (e.g., dollars instead of dollars squared, which would have little meaning in most applications). The variance tends to be large because it is in squared units. Statisticians like to work with the variance because its mathematical properties simplify computations. People applying statistics prefer to work with the standard deviation because it is more easily interpreted.

Let us find the variance and the standard deviation of the data in Example (a). It is convenient to carry out hand computations of the variance by use of a table. After doing the computation using equation 1–3, we will show a shortcut that will help in the calculation. Table 1–2 shows how the mean, $\overline{x}$, is subtracted from each of the values and the results are squared and added together. At the bottom of the last column we find the sum of all squared deviations from the mean. Finally, the sum is

---

[4] A note about calculators: If your calculator is designed to compute means and standard deviations, find the key for the standard deviation. Typically, there will be two such keys. Consult your owner's handbook to be sure you are using the key that will produce the correct computation for a sample (division by $n-1$) versus a population (division by N).

TABLE 1-2 Calculations Leading to the Sample Variance in Example (a)

x	$(x - \bar{x})$	$(x - \bar{x})^2$
6	$6 - 15.85 = -9.85$	97.0225
9	$9 - 15.85 = -6.85$	46.9225
10	$10 - 15.85 = -5.85$	34.2225
12	$12 - 15.85 = -3.85$	14.8225
13	$13 - 15.85 = -2.85$	8.1225
14	$14 - 15.85 = -1.85$	3.4225
14	$14 - 15.85 = -1.85$	3.4225
15	$15 - 15.85 = -0.85$	0.7225
16	$16 - 15.85 = 0.15$	0.0225
16	$16 - 15.85 = 0.15$	0.0225
16	$16 - 15.85 = 0.15$	0.0225
17	$17 - 15.85 = 1.15$	1.3225
17	$17 - 15.85 = 1.15$	1.3225
18	$18 - 15.85 = 2.15$	4.6225
18	$18 - 15.85 = 2.15$	4.6225
19	$19 - 15.85 = 3.15$	9.9225
20	$20 - 15.85 = 4.15$	17.2225
21	$21 - 15.85 = 5.15$	26.5225
22	$22 - 15.85 = 6.15$	37.8225
24	$24 - 15.85 = 8.15$	66.4225
	0	378.5500

divided by $n - 1$, giving s^2, the sample variance. Taking the square root gives us s, the sample standard deviation.

By equation 1-3, the variance of the sample is equal to the sum of the third column in the table, 378.55, divided by $n - 1$: $s^2 = 378.55/19 = 19.923684$. The standard deviation is the square root of the variance: $s = \sqrt{19.923684} = 4.4635954$, or, using two-decimal accuracy,[5] $s = 4.46$.

If you have a calculator with statistical capabilities, you may avoid having to use a table such as Table 1-2. If you need to compute by hand, there is a shortcut formula for computing the variance and the standard deviation.

Shortcut formula for the sample variance:

$$s^2 = \frac{\sum\limits_{i=1}^{n} x_i^2 - \left(\sum\limits_{i=1}^{n} x_i\right)^2/n}{n - 1} \qquad (1\text{-}7)$$

Again, the standard deviation is just the square root of the quantity in equation 1-7. We will now demonstrate the use of this computationally simpler formula with the data of Example (a). We will then use this simpler formula and compute the variance and the standard deviation of the two data sets we are comparing: set I and set II.

As before, a table will be useful in carrying out the computations. The table for finding the variance using equation 1-7 will have a column for the data points, x,

---

[5] In quantitative fields such as statistics, there is always the problem of decimal accuracy. How many digits after the decimal point should we carry? This question has no easy answer; everything depends on the required level of accuracy. As a rule, we will use only two decimals, since this suffices in most applications. In some procedures, such as regression analysis, it is recommended that more digits be used in computations (these computations, however, are usually done by computer).

TABLE 1–3 Shortcut Computations for the Variance in Example (a)

x	x²
6	36
9	81
10	100
12	144
13	169
14	196
14	196
15	225
16	256
16	256
16	256
17	289
17	289
18	324
18	324
19	361
20	400
21	441
22	484
24	576
317	5,403

and a column for the squared data points, x^2. Table 1–3 shows the computations for the variance of the data in Example (a).

Using equation 1–7, we find:

$$s^2 = \frac{\sum_{i=1}^{n} x_i^2 - \left(\sum_{i=1}^{n} x_i\right)^2/n}{n-1} = \frac{5{,}403 - (317)^2/20}{19} = \frac{5{,}403 - 100{,}489/20}{19}$$
$$= 19.923684$$

The standard deviation is obtained as before: $s = \sqrt{19.923684} = 4.46$. Using the same procedure demonstrated with Table 1–3, we find the following quantities leading to the variance and the standard deviation of set I and of set II. Both are assumed to be samples, not populations.

Set I: $\Sigma x = 72$, $\Sigma x^2 = 542$, $s^2 = 10$, and $s = \sqrt{10} = 3.16$
Set II: $\Sigma x = 72$, $\Sigma x^2 = 446$, $s^2 = 1.27$, and $s = \sqrt{1.27} = 1.13$

As expected, we see that the variance and the standard deviation of set II are smaller than those of set I. While each has a mean of 6, set I is more variable. That is, the values in set I vary more about their mean than do those of set II, which are clustered more closely together.

The sample standard deviation and the sample mean are very important statistics used in inference about populations. In the next section we discuss the analysis of grouped data.

PROBLEMS

1–12. Explain why we need measures of variability and what information these measures convey.

1–13. What is the most important measure of variability and why?

1–14. What is the computational difference between the variance of a sample and the variance of a population?

1–15. Find the range, the variance, and the standard deviation of the data set in problem 1–1 (assumed to be a sample).

1–16. Do the same as problem 1–15 using the data in problem 1–2.

1–17. Do the same as problem 1–15 using the data in problem 1–3.

1–18. Do the same as problem 1–15 using the data in problem 1–4.

1–19. Do the same as problem 1–15 using the data in problem 1–5.

Answers

1–16.

Range = 19.2
Variance = 25.9

1–18.

Range = 6
Variance = 3.98

1–5 Grouped Data and the Histogram

It often happens that data are grouped. This happened naturally in Example (a), where we had a group of three points with a value of 16 and three groups of two points (14s, 17s, and 18s). In other cases, especially when we have a large data set, the collector of the data may break the data into groups even if the points in each group are not equal in value. The data collector may set some (often arbitrary) group boundaries for ease of recording the data. When considering the salaries of 5,000 executives, for example, the data may be reported in the form: 1,548 executives in the salary range $30,000 to $35,000; 2,365 executives in the salary range $35,001 to $40,000; and so on. In this case, the data collector or analyst has processed all the salaries and put them into groups with defined boundaries. In such cases, there is a loss of information. We are unable to find the mean, variance, and other measures because we do not know the actual values. There are, however, formulas that allow us to find the approximate mean, variance, and standard deviation. The formulas assume that all data points in a group are placed in the *midpoint* of the interval. In this example, we would assume that all 1,548 executives in the $30,001–$35,000 *class* make exactly ($30,000 + $35,000)/2 = $32,500; we estimate similarly for executives in the other groups.

> We define a group of data values within specified group boundaries as a **class.**

When data are grouped into classes, we may also plot a frequency distribution of the data. Such a frequency plot is called a *histogram*.

> A **histogram** is a chart made of bars of different heights. The height of each bar represents the **frequency** of values in the class represented by the bar. Adjacent bars share sides.

We demonstrate the use of histograms and the computation of statistics for grouped data in the following example. Note that a histogram is used only for measured, or ordinal, data.

Management of an appliance store recorded the amounts spent at the store by the 184 customers who came in during the last day of the big sale. The data, amounts spent, were grouped into categories as follows: $0 to less than $100, $100 to less than $200, and so on up to $600, a bound higher than the amount spent by any single buyer. The classes and the frequency of each class are shown in Table 1–4. The frequencies, denoted by $f(x)$, are shown in a histogram in Figure 1–4.

EXAMPLE (b)

TABLE 1–4 Classes and Frequencies, Example (b)

x Spending Class ($)	f(x) Frequency (number of customers)
0 to less than 100	30
100 to less than 200	38
200 to less than 300	50
300 to less than 400	31
400 to less than 500	22
500 to less than 600	13
	184

FIGURE 1–4 A Histogram of the Data in Example (b)

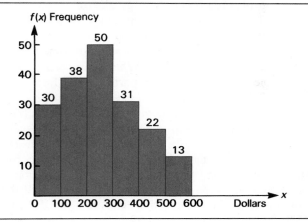

As you can see from Figure 1–4, a histogram is just a convenient way of plotting the frequencies of grouped data. Here the frequencies are *absolute frequencies*, or **counts** of data points. It is also possible to plot *relative frequencies*.

> The **relative frequency** of a class is the count of data points in the class divided by the total number of data points.

The relative frequency in the first class, $0 to less than $100, is equal to count/total = $30/184 = 0.163$. We can similarly compute the relative frequencies for the other classes. The advantage of relative frequencies is that they are standardized: they add to 1.00. The relative frequency in each class represents the proportion of the total sample in the class. Table 1–5 gives the relative frequencies of the classes.

TABLE 1–5 Relative Frequencies, Example (b)

x Class ($)	f(x) Relative Frequency
0 to less than 100	0.163
100 to less than 200	0.207
200 to less than 300	0.272
300 to less than 400	0.168
400 to less than 500	0.120
500 to less than 600	0.070
	1.000

FIGURE 1–5 A Histogram of the Relative Frequencies in Example (b)

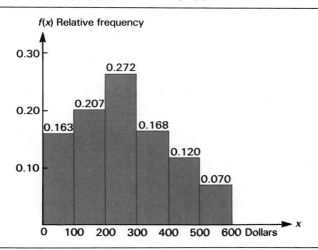

Figure 1–5 is a histogram of the relative frequencies of the data in this example. Note that the shape of the histogram of the relative frequencies is the same as that of the absolute frequencies, the counts. The shape of the histogram does not change; only the labeling of the $f(x)$ axis is different.

Relative frequencies—proportions that add to 1.00—may be viewed as probabilities, as we will see in the next chapter. Hence, such frequencies are very useful in statistics, and so are their histograms.

Let us now see how we can compute statistics for grouped data. We will start with the mode. The mode of a grouped data set is called a **modal class:** it is the class, or group of values, with the highest frequency of occurrence. From either histogram, Figure 1–4 or Figure 1–5, we see that the most frequent class of values in the data of Example (b) is the class "$200 to less than $300." We determine this from the fact that the highest rectangle in the histogram corresponds to this class.

The median of a grouped data set is that point on the horizontal scale of the histogram that divides the area of the histogram into two equal parts. We define the **median class** as the class containing the median. The median class is thus the class containing the observation with rank $(n + 1)(0.5)$. In Example (b) the median class is the one containing the observation lying in position 92.5, the class "$200 to less than $300" (see Table 1–4). If we assume that the values in each class are evenly distributed over the class interval, it is possible to estimate the median itself.

The median for grouped data is estimated as $L + (j/f)W$, where L is the lower limit of the median class interval, f is the frequency of the median class, W is the width of the median class interval, and j is the number of values needed to reach the median after L is reached.

In Example (b), $L = 200$, $j = 92.5 - 68 = 24.5$, $f = 50$, and $W = 100$. The median is therefore estimated as: $200 + (24.5/50)100 = 249$.

Let k be the number of groups or classes. Let us define the count, or absolute frequency of occurrence, in class i as f_i. Let us also define the midpoint of class i as m_i. Using these definitions, the mean and the variance of a grouped data set (considered a sample, not a population) are given in equations 1–8 and 1–9, respectively.

Mean of grouped data:

$$\bar{x} = \frac{\sum\limits_{i=1}^{k} f_i m_i}{n}$$

(1–8)

Variance of grouped data:

$$s^2 = \frac{\sum\limits_{i=1}^{k} f_i(m_i)^2 - \frac{\left(\sum\limits_{i=1}^{k} f_i m_i\right)^2}{n}}{n-1}$$

(1–9)

The standard deviation, s, is (as always) the square root of the variance, s^2.

We will now demonstrate the use of equations 1–8 and 1–9 with the data of Example (b). We have

$$\bar{x} = [(50)(30) + (150)(38) + (250)(50) + (350)(31) + (450)(22) + (550)(13)]/184 = \$258.70$$

and

$$s^2 = \{[(30)(50)^2 + (38)(150)^2 + (50)(250)^2 + (31)(350)^2 + (22)(450)^2 + (13)(550)^2] - [(30)(50) + (38)(150) + (50)(250) + (31)(350) + (22)(450) + (13)(550)]^2/184\}/183 = 21,454.03$$

The standard deviation is

$$s = \sqrt{21,454.03} = 146.47$$

(All these numbers are accurate to the second decimal place only.)

You may construct a table of values with columns f_i, m_i, $f_i m_i$, and $f_i(m_i)^2$ for ease of calculation of the above quantities. On the other hand, if your calculator computes statistics, you may use the statistics function in computing means and standard deviations of grouped data sets. You should consult your owner's manual for instructions on how to do this.

PROBLEMS

1–20. The October 12, 1987, issue of *Fortune* magazine lists the world's richest people and their wealth, in U.S. dollars, according to the magazine's estimates. The data are as follows (in billions of dollars).

25.0, 20.0, 8.7, 7.5, 7.4, 6.0, 5.7, 5.5, 5.0, 5.0, 4.4, 4.0, 4.0, 3.6, 3.4, 3.1, 3.0, 3.0, 2.9, 2.8, 2.8, 2.5, 2.5, 2.5, 2.4, 2.4, 2.4, 2.2, 2.0, 2.0, 2.0, 1.9, 1.8, 1.7, 1.6, 1.5, 1.5, 1.5, 1.5, 1.4, 1.3, 1.3, 1.3, 1.3, 1.2, 1.2, 1.2, 1.2, 1.1, 1.1, 1.1, 1.0, 1.0, 1.0, 1.0, 1.0, 1.0, 1.0, 1.0, 1.0.

Draw a histogram of the frequencies of the above data and a histogram of the relative frequencies of these data.

1–21.   More and more employers are using psychological testing as an aid in determining whether or not there is a good fit between the company and a prospective employee. The following data are counts of scores of a group of people who took the psychological examination administered by a company. Scores are grouped into categories with a class width of 10.

Score Class	Count
41– 50	5
51– 60	7
61– 70	10
71– 80	16
81– 90	11
91–100	9

Draw a histogram of the score counts. Find the mean score and the standard deviation. What is the modal class? What is the median class? Also compute the relative frequencies.

1–22.   The following data are a sample of the equivalent numbers of pages of information that can be stored on Kodak's optical disk for computers. Data are in million-page equivalents.

2.01, 2.32, 2.45, 2.00, 2.22, 2.67, 2.03, 2.08, 2.09, 2.55, 2.33, 2.31, 2.22, 2.10,
2.15, 2.17, 2.43, 2.22, 2.18, 2.19, 2.30, 2.42, 2.00, 2.03, 2.04, 2.05, 2.11, 2.16,
2.19, 2.00, 2.06, 2.07, 2.05, 2.00, 2.27, 2.40, 2.05, 2.03, 2.02, 2.35, 2.39, 2.07,
2.08, 2.11, 2.34, 2.37, 2.09, 2.15, 2.33, 2.25, 2.16, 2.13, 2.20, 2.11, 2.06, 2.41, 2.03.

Group the data into classes of equal width, and draw a histogram of the counts. Also compute the relative frequency in each group. Use the grouped data in computing the mean and the variance. Also compute the mean and variance of the ungrouped data, and compare your results with the values you get for the grouped data. Is the difference great? Explain.

1–23.   An analyst kept track of the daily price of a certain commodity over 35 days and grouped the data as follows: \$2.10–\$2.50, 4 days; \$2.60–\$3.00, 6 days; \$3.11–\$3.50, 8 days; \$3.60–\$4.00, 7 days; \$4.10–\$4.50, 6 days; and \$4.60–\$5.00, 4 days. (The commodity price moves in \$0.10 increments.) Draw a histogram of these data. Find the modal class. Find the mean and the standard deviation.

1–6   Skewness and Kurtosis

In addition to measures of location such as the mean or median, and measures of variation such as the variance or standard deviation, there are two attributes of a frequency distribution of a data set that may be of interest to us. These are *skewness* and *kurtosis*.

> **Skewness** is a measure of the degree of asymmetry of a frequency distribution.

When the distribution stretches to the right more than it does to the left, we say that the distribution is *right-skewed*. Similarly, a *left-skewed* distribution is one that stretches asymmetrically to the left. Three examples are shown in Figure 1–6: a symmetric distribution, a right-skewed distribution, and a left-skewed distribution.

Recall that a symmetric distribution with a single mode has mode = mean = median. Generally, for a right-skewed distribution, the mean is to the right of the median, which in turn lies to the right of the mode (assuming a single mode). The opposite is true for left-skewed distributions.

FIGURE 1–6   Skewness of Distributions

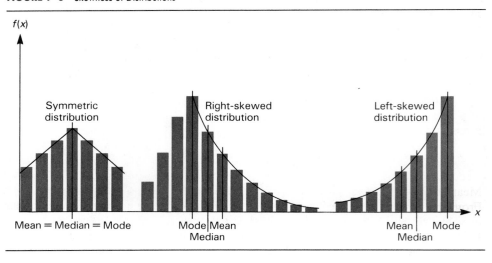

FIGURE 1–7   Kurtosis of Distributions

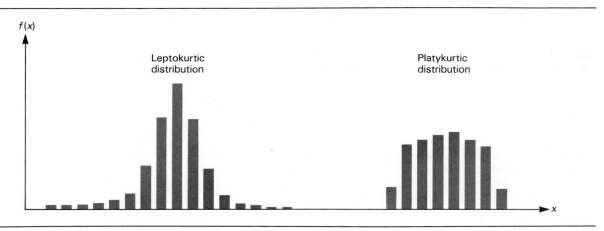

Kurtosis is a measure of the flatness (versus peakedness) of a frequency distribution.

Flat distributions are called *platykurtic*, and peaked distributions are called *leptokurtic*. Neutral distributions—not too flat and not too peaked—are called *mesokurtic*. Figure 1–7 shows two examples of kurtosis.

1–7   Relations between the Mean and the Standard Deviation

The mean is a measure of the centrality of a set of observations, and the standard deviation is a measure of their spread. There are two general rules that establish a relation between these measures and the set of observations. The first is called Chebyshev's theorem, and the second is the empirical rule.

Chebyshev's Theorem

A mathematical theorem attributed to Chebyshev establishes the following rules:

1. At least 3/4 of the observations in a set will lie within 2 standard deviations of the mean.
2. At least 8/9 of the observations in a set will lie within 3 standard deviations of the mean.

In general, the rule states that at least $1 - 1/k^2$ of the observations will lie within k standard deviations of the mean. (We note that k does not have to be an integer.) In Example (a) we found that the mean was 15.85 and the standard deviation was 4.46. According to rule 1 above, at least 3/4 of the observations should fall in the interval Mean $\pm 2s = 15.85 \pm 2(4.46)$, which is defined by the points 6.93 and 24.77. From the data set itself, we see that only one observation, 6, lies outside this range of values. Since there are 20 observations in the set, 19/20 are within the specified range, so the rule that at least 3/4 will be within the range is satisfied.

The Empirical Rule

If the distribution of the data is mound-shaped—that is, if the histogram of the data is more or less symmetric with a single mode or high point—then tighter rules will apply.

1. Approximately 68% of the observations will be within 1 standard deviation of the mean.
2. Approximately 95% of the observations will be within 2 standard deviations of the mean.
3. A vast majority of the observations (all of them, or almost all of them) will be within 3 standard deviations of the mean.

Verify that the empirical rule holds rather well for the data set in Example (a), even though the distribution of the data set is not perfectly symmetric.

PROBLEMS

1–24. Check the applicability of Chebyshev's theorem and the empirical rule for the data set in problem 1–1.

1–25. Check the applicability of Chebyshev's theorem and the empirical rule for the data set in problem 1–2.

1–26. Check the applicability of Chebyshev's theorem and the empirical rule for the data set in problem 1–3.

1–27. Check the applicability of Chebyshev's theorem and the empirical rule for the data set in problem 1–4.

1–28. Check the applicability of Chebyshev's theorem and the empirical rule for the data set in problem 1–5.

1–8   Scales of Measurement

In statistics we deal with data, and data are measurements. It is therefore important to define the kinds of measurement scales we will be using. There is a hierarchy of scales of measurement, going from weakest to strongest. The weaker the scale of measurement, the less we are able to assume about the relations among elements on the scale. There are four generally used scales, listed here from weakest to strongest.

Nominal Scale

In the **nominal scale** of measurement, numbers are used simply as labels for groups or classes. If our data set consists of blue, green, and red items, we may designate blue as 1, green as 2, and red as 3. In this case, the numbers 1, 2, and 3 stand only for the category to which a data point belongs. Thus, "nominal" stands for "name" of category. The nominal scale of measurement is used for *qualitative* rather than quantitative data: blue, green, red; male, female; professional classification; geographic classification; and so on.

Ordinal Scale

In the **ordinal scale** of measurement, data elements may be ordered according to their relative size. Four products ranked by a consumer may be ranked as 1, 2, 3, and 4, where 4 is the best and 1 is the worst. In this scale of measurement we do not know how much better one product is than others, only that it is better.

Interval Scale

In the **interval scale** of measurement, we can assign a meaning to distances between any two observations. The data are on an *interval* of numbers, and distances between elements can be measured in units. In January 1992, the Dow Jones average was 3108; in December 1991, it was 2914. These numbers are on an interval scale.

Ratio Scale

The **ratio scale** is the strongest scale of measurement. Here not only distances between pairs of observations have a meaning, but there is a meaning also to ratios of distances. Salaries, for example, are measured on a ratio scale: a salary of $50,000 is twice as large as a salary of $25,000. Such a comparison, however, is not possible with temperatures, which are on an interval scale but not on a ratio scale (we cannot say that 50° is twice as warm as 25°). The ratio scale contains a *meaningful zero* (0° in temperature is not meaningful in this respect). The distinction between the interval and ratio scales, however, is not always immediately clear.

1–9 Methods of Displaying Data

In section 1–5, we saw how a histogram is used to display frequencies of occurrence of values in a data set. In this section, we will see a few other ways of displaying data, some of which are descriptive only. We will introduce frequency polygons, cumulative frequency plots (called *ogives*), pie charts, and bar charts. We will also see examples of how descriptive graphs can sometimes be misleading. We will start with pie charts.

Pie Charts

A **pie chart** is a simple descriptive display of data that sum to a given total. The chart is a display of percentages of the total. This type of chart is very popular in budget reports, economic analysis studies, and newspapers and magazines.

TABLE 1–6 Australian Export Income (Six Months Ended December 1985)

Exports	Income ($m)
Coal	2,664
Wheat	1,177
Wool	1,049
Iron ore	1,017
Petroleum crude oil	812
Petroleum products	620

FIGURE 1–8 Pie Chart of Australian Export Income

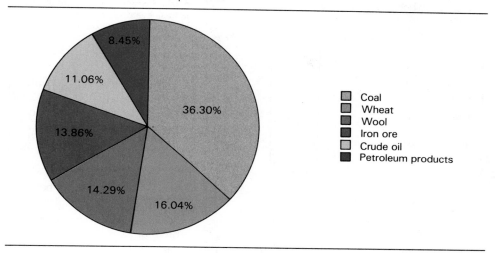

FIGURE 1–9
Bar Graph of 1983 Income of U.S. Regions

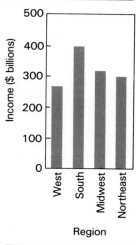

Table 1–6 shows the main export categories of Australia with export income amounts for 1985.[6] Figure 1–8 is a pie chart display of these data. A pie chart is probably the most illustrative way of displaying quantities as percentages of a given total. The total area of the "pie" represents 100% of the quantity of interest (the sum of the variable values in all categories), and the size of each "slice" is the percentage of the total represented by the category the slice denotes.

Bar and Column Graphs

Bars (horizontal rectangles) and columns (vertical rectangles) are often used to display categorical data where there is no emphasis on the percentage of a total represented by each category. Table 1–7 shows total per capita income, in billions of dollars, in the different regions of the United States in 1983.[7] Figure 1–9 is a bar graph of these data. Figure 1–10 is a column graph of these data.

The two types of graphs are essentially the same. In some cases, it may be more convenient for the purpose at hand to use one versus the other. For example, if we want to write the name of the category inside the rectangle to which the category corresponds, then a bar graph may be more convenient. If we want to stress the height of the different columns as measures of the quantity of interest, a column graph should be used.

FIGURE 1–10
Column Graph of 1983 Income of U.S. Regions

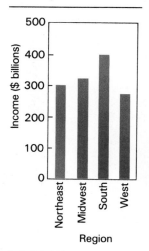

[6] *Barron's* (June 10, 1986).

[7] Data are from the 1986 edition of the *Statistical Abstract of the United States* (Washington, D.C.: U.S. Bureau of the Census).

TABLE 1–7 Total per Capita Income in the United States, 1983

Region	Income ($billions)
Northeast	296.6
Midwest	316.4
South	400.4
West	266.8

FIGURE 1–11 Examples of Pie Charts, Bar Graphs, and Column Graphs

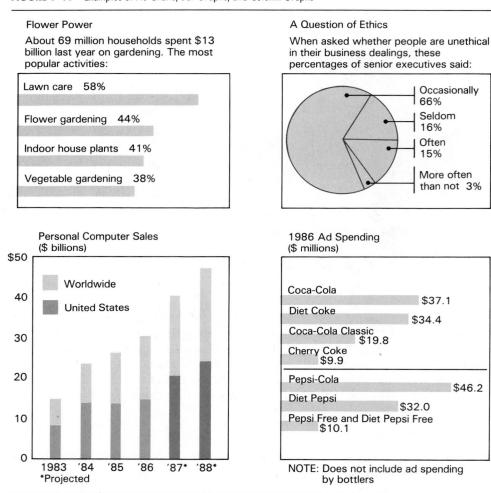

Sources: National Gardening Association; McFeely Wackerie Jett; InfoCorp; and Furman Selz Mager Dietz and Birney.

Figure 1–11 shows examples of pie charts, bar graphs, and column graphs. These charts are reprinted, by permission, from *The Wall Street Journal* (June 3, September 14, September 18, and November 2, 1987, issues).

Frequency Polygons and Ogives

A **frequency polygon** is similar to a histogram except that there are no rectangles, only a point in the midpoint of each interval at a height proportional to the frequency or relative frequency (in a relative-frequency polygon) of the category of the inter-

TABLE 1–8 Pizza Sales

Sales ($000)	Relative Frequency
6–14	0.20
15–22	0.30
23–30	0.25
31–38	0.15
39–46	0.07
47–54	0.03

FIGURE 1–12 Relative-Frequency Polygon for Pizza Sales

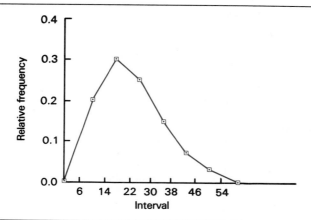

val. The rightmost and leftmost points are zero. Table 1–8 gives the relative frequency of sales volume, in thousands of dollars per week, for pizza at a local establishment.

A relative-frequency polygon for these data is shown in Figure 1–12. Note that the frequency is located in the middle of the interval as a point with height equal to the relative frequency of the interval. Note also that the point zero is added at the left boundary and the right boundary of the data set: the polygon starts at zero and ends at zero even if zero is not part of the data.

An **ogive** is a cumulative-frequency (or cumulative relative-frequency) graph. An ogive starts at 0 and goes to 1.00 (for a relative-frequency ogive) or to the maximum cumulative frequency. The point with height corresponding to the cumulative frequency is located at the right end point of each interval. An ogive for the data in Table 1–8 is shown in Figure 1–13. While the ogive shown is for the cumulative *relative* frequency, an ogive can also be used for the cumulative absolute frequency.

A Caution about Graphs

A picture is indeed worth a thousand words, but pictures can sometimes be deceiving. Often, this is where "lying with statistics" comes in: presenting data graphically on a stretched or compressed scale of numbers with the aim of making the data show whatever you want them to show. This is one important argument against a merely descriptive approach to data analysis and an argument for statistical *inference*. Statistical tests tend to be more objective than our eyes and are less prone to deception as long as our assumptions (random sampling and other assumptions)

FIGURE 1–13   Ogive of Pizza Sales

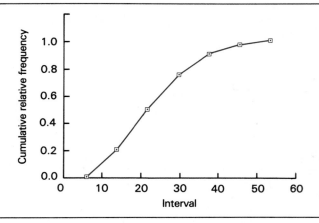

FIGURE 1–14   Two Graphic Displays of the Crash of '87

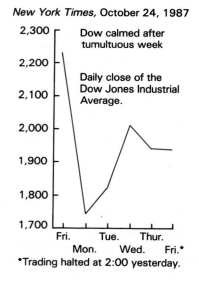

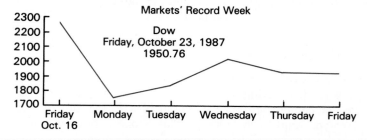

Sources: © 1987 *The New York Times*. Reprinted by permission. © 1987 *Investor's Daily*. Reprinted by permission.

hold. As we will see, statistical inference gives us tools that allow us to objectively evaluate what we see in the data.

Pictures are sometimes deceptive even though there is no intention to deceive. When someone shows you a graph of a set of numbers, there may really be no particular scale of numbers that is "right" for the data.

We will demonstrate how deceptive graphs can be—even with no intention to deceive—with the Crash of '87. On "Bloody Monday," October 19, 1987, the Dow fell 508 points. This much is certain. The question is: How can we best present this decline on a graph? What is the correct distance to use for each day on the horizontal scale (the *x*-axis) of the graph? By the end of that eventful week, almost every newspaper and magazine in the nation had a graph of the Crash of '87 in its pages. Figure 1–14 shows the fluctuations in the Dow over the period October 16 to October 23 as portrayed by *The New York Times* and as portrayed by *Investor's Daily*. The data are the same, yet note the difference in the two graphs. There certainly was no intention to deceive anyone: both publications aimed at conveying the same information to their readers. Yet the graphs are very different because the scales are different. Which scale is correct?

If you think the graphs in Figure 1–14 seem illusive (or at least inconsistent), consider the graph in Figure 1–15. This display is reprinted by permission from *Time* magazine (November 4, 1987). The superposition of the graph of the Dow's movements with plots of the prime rate, dollar index, trade deficit, and budget deficit—not to mention Uncle Sam lying on the spikes formed by these plots— might lead the viewer to conclude that there is a relationship between the Dow's

FIGURE 1–15   A Third Graphic Portrayal of the Crash of '87

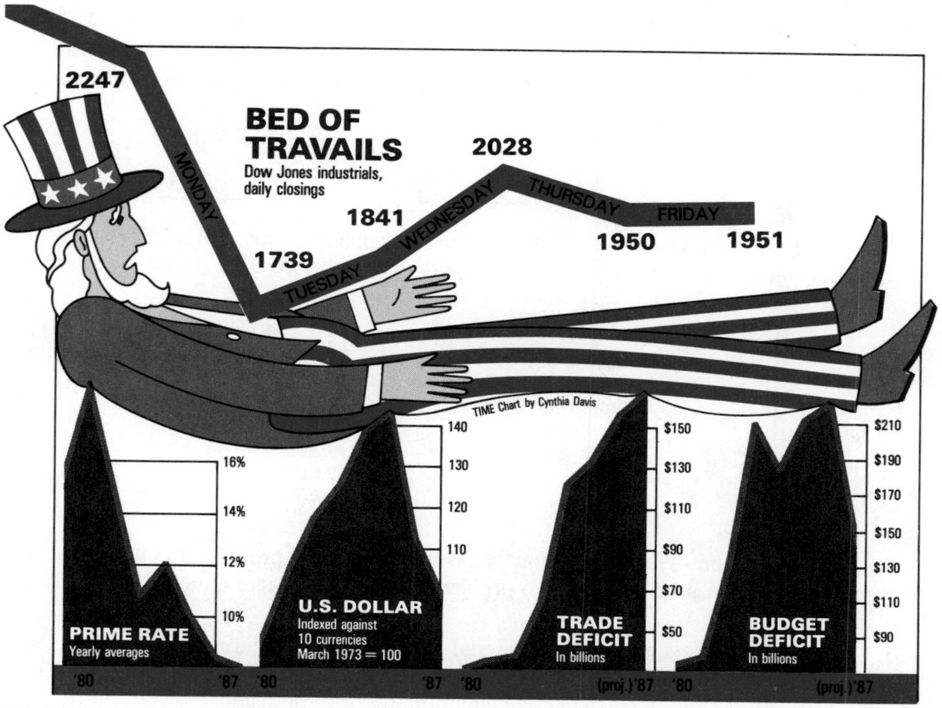

Source: © 1987 TIME Inc. All rights reserved. Reprinted by permission from TIME.

FIGURE 1–16   A Picture Graph that Is Both Imaginative and Correct

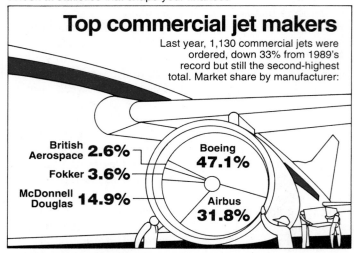

Source: ESG Aviation Services.

movements and the other four variables. While such relationships *may* exist, they are neither proved nor even effectively demonstrated by this rather casual superposition. What is the significance of the "spikes," anyway?

Do not get the impression that all fancy-looking graphs are deceptive, and that accurate graphing must be uninventive and boring. As an example of a creative graph that is perfectly accurate in its description of the provided data, consider the pie chart shown in Figure 1–16. The display is reproduced by permission from *USA Today* (February 11, 1991).

PROBLEMS

1–29.   The following data are estimated worldwide appliance sales (in millions of dollars). Use the data to construct a pie chart for the worldwide appliance sales of the listed manufacturers.

Electrolux	$5,100
General Electric	4,350
Matsushita Electric	4,180
Whirlpool	3,950
Bosch-Siemens	2,200
Philips	2,000
Maytag	1,580

1–30.   Draw a column graph and a bar graph for the data in problem 1–29. Is any one of the three kinds of plot used in these two problems more appropriate than the others for these data? If so, why?

1–31.   The following data are gross national product (GNP) figures for the years 1980 to 1985. Data are from the 1987 edition of the *Survey of Current Business*, published by the U.S. Department of Commerce. Draw a column graph of these data.

Year	GNP ($billions)
1980	11,995
1981	13,262
1982	13,614
1983	14,504
1984	15,913
1985	16,757

1–32. The following data, from *The Wall Street Journal,* are U.S. liquid consumption figures, in gallons per capita, for 1976 and 1986. Draw a single bar graph, with the figures for each category for each of the two years drawn side by side. Interpret the findings.

	1986	1976
Soft drinks	42.1	28.6
Coffee*	25.4	29.4
Beer	23.9	21.8
Milk	20.3	21.9
Tea*	7.4	7.4
Juices	6.3	6.8
Powdered drinks	6.1	5.5
Bottled water	5.7	1.5
Wine	2.5	1.7
Distilled spirits	1.6	2.0

*Based on three-year moving average

Source: Furman Selz Mager Dietz & Birney

1–33. The following data are Dow Jones industry-group closing prices for January 11, 1991.[8] Draw a bar graph for these data.

Groups Leading (and strongest stocks in group)

Group	Close	CHG	%CHG
Semiconductor	221.19 +	5.57 +	2.58
Natl Semicndtr	4 7/8 +	1/2 +	11.43
Intel Corp	39 3/4 +	1 +	2.58
Adv Micro Dvc	5 +	1/8 +	2.56
Transportation equip	182.23 +	3.01 +	1.68
Paccar Inc	33 1/2 +	1 1/2 +	4.69
Navistar Intl	3 +	1/8 +	4.35
Trinity Indus	20 +	5/8 +	3.23
Diversified tech	233.32 +	3.53 +	1.54
Rockwell Intl	24 1/8 +	3/4 +	3.21
TRW Inc	36 +	1 +	2.86
Minn Mining	81 5/8 +	2 +	2.51
Coal	226.16 +	3.32 +	1.49
Addington Res	10 1/2 +	1/2 +	5.00
Pittston Co	17 7/8 +	3/8 +	2.14
Ashland Coal	21 1/8 +	1/8 +	0.60
Containers/pkging	434.34 +	6.29 +	1.47
Temple-Inland	30 +	1 1/4 +	4.35
Stone Cont	9 3/4 +	1/8 +	1.30
Crown Cork	55 7/8 +	3/8 +	0.68

Groups Lagging (and weakest stocks in group)

Group	Close	CHG	%CHG
Commu-wo / AT&T	176.53 −	8.41 −	4.55
Motorola Inc	47 3/4 −	2 3/4 −	5.45
Harris Corp	19 1/8 −	1/4 −	1.29
Scientific-Atl	11 7/8	unch	unch
Oil drilling	94.52 −	2.69 −	2.77
Parker Drilling	6 1/8 −	1/2 −	7.55
Rowans Cos	9 1/8 −	3/8 −	3.95
Helmerich	24 −	3/8 −	1.54
Banks-East	140.12 −	2.80 −	1.96
MNC Fcnl	2 1/8 −	5/8 −	22.73
Midlantic Corp	3 3/8 −	5/8 −	15.63
1st Fidelity	14 1/8 −	5/8 −	4.24
Trucking	200.62 −	3.17 −	1.56
Roadway Svcs	38 1/2 −	1 1/4 −	3.14
Yellow Freight	28 1/8 −	1/2 −	1.75
Consol Freight	11 7/8	unch	unch
Home furnishings	154.62 −	2.19 −	1.40
Whirlpool Corp	21 5/8 −	1 1/8 −	4.95
Black & Decker	9 −	1/8 −	1.37
Shaw Industries	19 7/8 −	1/8 −	0.63

[8] *The Wall Street Journal* (January 14, 1991).

1–34. Using the following data, draw a pie chart of 1986 production of the different drinks made by the Coca-Cola Company.

Coca-Cola Classic	1,294.3 (million units)
Diet Coke	490.8
New Coke	185.1
Cherry Coke	115.6
Caffeine-free Diet Coke	85.6
Caffeine-free Coke	19.0
Diet Cherry Coke	15.0

1–35. Draw a pie chart for the data in problem 1–34.

1–36. Draw a column chart for the endowments (stated in billions of dollars) of each of the universities specified in the following list.

Harvard	$3.4
Texas	2.5
Princeton	1.9
Yale	1.7
Stanford	1.4
Columbia	1.3
Texas A&M	1.1

1–37. The following are the amounts from the sales slips of a department store (in dollars): 3.45, 4.52, 5.41, 6.00, 5.97, 7.18, 1.12, 5.39, 7.03, 10.25, 11.45, 13.21, 12.00, 14.05, 2.99, 3.28, 17.10, 19.28, 21.09, 12.11, 5.88, 4.65, 3.99, 10.10, 23.00, 15.16, 20.16. Draw a frequency polygon for these data (start by defining intervals of the data and counting the data points in each interval).

1–38. Draw a relative-frequency polygon for the data in problem 1–37.

1–39. Draw an ogive for the data in problem 1–37.

1–40. A stockbroker kept a record of the number of times a stock that she was following was within given price ranges. The data follow.

Price Range	Number of Days
$10–11.99	2
12–13.99	5
14–15.99	12
16–17.99	4
18–20	1

Compute the relative frequencies of occurrence of each price range, and draw a frequency polygon for these frequencies. Also draw a histogram and an ogive.

1–10 Exploratory Data Analysis

Exploratory data analysis (EDA) is the name given to a large body of statistical and graphical techniques. These techniques provide ways of looking at data to determine relationships and trends, identify outliers and influential observations, and quickly describe or summarize data sets. Pioneering methods in this field, as well as the name *exploratory data analysis,* derive from the work of John W. Tukey.[9]

---

[9] John W. Tukey, *Exploratory Data Analysis* (Reading, Mass.: Addison-Wesley, 1977).

Stem-and-Leaf Displays

A **stem-and-leaf display** is a quick way of looking at a data set. It contains some of the features of a histogram but avoids the loss of information in a histogram that results from aggregating the data into intervals. The stem-and-leaf display is based on the tallying principle, | || ||| |||| ||||, but also uses the decimal base of our number system. In a stem-and-leaf display, the *stem* is the number without its rightmost digit (the leaf). The stem is written to the left of a vertical line separating the stem from the leaf. For example, suppose we have the numbers 105, 106, 107, 107, 109. We would display them as:

$$10 \mid 56779$$

With a more complete data set with different stem values, the last digit of each number is displayed at the appropriate place to the right of its stem digit(s). Stem-and-leaf displays help us identify, at a glance, numbers in our data set that have high frequency. Let us look at an example.

EXAMPLE (c)

Artificial reality is the name given to a new system of simulating real situations on a computer in a way that gives people the feeling that what they see on the computer screen is a real situation. Flight simulators were the forerunners of artificial reality programs. A particular artificial reality program has been designed to give production engineers experience in real processes. Engineers are supposed to complete certain tasks as responses to what they see on the screen. The following data are the time, in seconds, it took a group of 42 engineers to perform a given task.

11, 12, 12, 13, 15, 15, 15, 16, 17, 20, 21, 21, 21, 22, 22, 22, 23, 24, 26, 27, 27, 27, 28, 29, 29, 30, 31, 32, 34, 35, 37, 41, 41, 42, 45, 47, 50, 52, 53, 56, 60, 62

SOLUTION

The data are already arranged in increasing order. We see that the data are in the 10s, 20s, 30s, 40s, 50s, and 60s. We will use the first digit as the stem and the second digit of each number as the leaf. The stem-and-leaf display of our data is shown in Figure 1–17.

As you can see, the stem-and-leaf display is a very quick way of arranging the data in a kind of a histogram (turned sideways) that allows us to see what the data look like. Here, we note that the data do not seem to be symmetrically distributed; rather, they are skewed to the right.

FIGURE 1–17   Stem-and-Leaf Display of the Task Performance Times of Example (c)

Stem	Leaf
1	122355567
2	0111222346777899
3	012457
4	11257
5	0236
6	02

We may feel that this display does not convey very much information because there are too many values with first digit 2. To solve this problem, we may split the groups into two subgroups. We will denote the stem part as 1* for the possible numbers 10, 11, 12, 13, 14 and as 1. for the possible numbers 15, 16, 17, 18, 19. Similarly, the stem 2* will be used for the possible numbers 20, 21, 22, 23, and 24; stem 2. will be used for the numbers 25, 26, 27, 28, and 29; and so on for the other numbers. Our stem-and-leaf diagram for the data of Example (c) using this convention is shown in Figure 1–18. As you can see from the figure, we now have a more spread out histogram of the data. The data still seem skewed to the right; the low 20s are the modal class.

If desired, a further refinement of the display is possible by using the symbol * for a stem followed by the leaf values 0 and 1; the symbol t for leaf values 2 and 3; the symbol f for leaf values 4 and 5; s for 6 and 7; and . for 8 and 9. Also, the class containing the median observation is often denoted with its stem value in parentheses. We demonstrate this version of the display for the data of Example (c) in Figure 1–19. Note that the median is 27 (why?).

Note that for the data set of this example, the refinement offered in Figure 1–19 may be too much: we may have lost the general picture of the data. In cases where there are many observations with the same value (e.g., 22, 22, 22, 22, 22, 22, 22, . . .), it may be necessary to use a more stretched out display in order to get a good picture of the way our data are clustered.

Box Plots

A *box plot* (also called a *box-and-whisker plot*) is another way of looking at a data set in an effort to determine its central tendency, spread, skewness, and the existence of outliers.

A **box plot** is a set of five summary measures of the distribution of the data:

1. The median of the data
2. The lower quartile
3. The upper quartile
4. The smallest observation
5. The largest observation

FIGURE 1–18   Refined Stem-and-Leaf Display for Data of Example (c)

1*	1223
1.	55567
2*	011122234
2.	6777899
3*	0124
3.	57
4*	112
4.	57
5*	023
5.	6
6*	02

FIGURE 1-19 Further Refined Stem-and-Leaf Display of Data of Example (c)

```
                          1*  | 1
                           t  | 223
                           f  | 555
                           s  | 67
                           .
                          2*  | 0111
                           t  | 2223
                           f  | 4
     (Median in this class) (s) | 6777
                              | 899
                          3*  | 01
                           t  | 2
                           f  | 45
                           s  | 7
                           .
                          4*  | 11
                           t  | 2
                           f  | 5
                           s  | 7
                           .
                          5*  | 0
                           t  | 23
                           f  |
                           s  | 6
                           .
                          6*  | 0
                           t  | 2
```

There are two qualifications to the preceding statements. First, recall that there are several different ways of defining the quartiles. Since all of the definitions are quite similar, however, we may safely assume that the *hinges* of the box plot are essentially the quartiles of the data set. (We will define hinges shortly.) The median is a line inside the box.

Second, the *whiskers* of the box plot are made by extending a line from the upper quartile to the largest observation and from the lower quartile to the smallest observation, only if the largest and smallest observations are within a distance of 1.5 times the interquartile range from the appropriate hinge (quartile). If one or more observations are farther away than that distance, they are marked as suspected outliers. If these observations are at a distance of over three times the interquartile range from the appropriate hinge, they are marked as outliers. The whisker then extends to the largest or smallest observation that is at a distance less than or equal to 1.5 times the interquartile range from the hinge.

Let us make these definitions clearer by using a picture. Figure 1–20 shows the parts of a box plot and how they are defined. The median is marked as a vertical line across the box. The **hinges** of the box are the upper and lower quartiles (the rightmost and leftmost sides of the box). The interquartile range (IQR) is the distance from the upper quartile to the lower quartile (the length of the box from hinge to hinge): $IQR = Q_U - Q_L$. We define the **inner fence** as a point at a distance of

FIGURE 1–20   The Box Plot

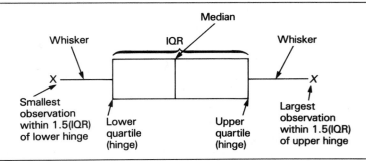

1.5(IQR) above the upper quartile; similarly, the lower inner fence is $Q_L -$ 1.5(IQR). The **outer fences** are defined similarly but are at a distance of 3(IQR) above or below the appropriate hinge. Figure 1–21 shows the fences (these are not shown on the actual box plot; they are only guidelines for defining the whiskers, suspected outliers, and outliers) and demonstrates how we mark outliers.

Box plots are very useful for the following purposes.

1. To identify the location of a data set based on the median.
2. To identify the spread of the data based on the length of the box, hinge to hinge (the interquartile range), and the length of the whiskers (the range of the data without extreme observations: outliers or suspected outliers).
3. To identify possible skewness of the distribution of the data set. If the portion of the box to the right of the median is longer than the portion to the left of the median, and/or the right whisker is longer than the left whisker, the data are right-skewed. Similarly, a longer left side of the box and/or left whisker implies a left-skewed data set. If the box and whiskers are symmetric, the data are symmetrically distributed with no skewness.
4. To identify suspected outliers (observations beyond the inner fences but within the outer fences) and outliers (points beyond the outer fences).
5. To compare two or more data sets. By drawing a box plot for each data set and displaying the box plots on the same scale, we can compare several data sets.

FIGURE 1–21   The Elements of a Box Plot

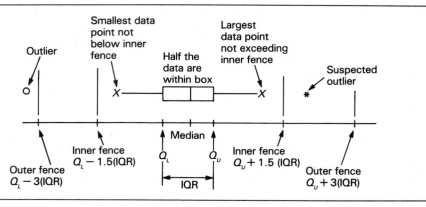

FIGURE 1–22   Box Plots and Their Uses

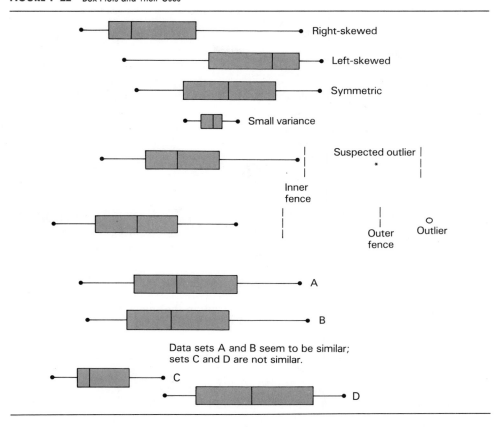

It has even been suggested that a special form of a box plot may be used for conducting a test of the equality of two population medians.[10] The various uses of a box plot are demonstrated in Figure 1–22.

Let us now construct a box plot for the data of Example (c). For this data set, the median is 27, and we find that the lower quartile is 20.75 and the upper quartile is 41. The interquartile range is IQR = 41 − 20.75 = 20.25. One and one-half times this distance is 30.38; hence, the inner fences are −9.63 and 71.38. Since no observation lies beyond either point, there are no suspected outliers and no outliers, so the whiskers extend to the extreme values in the data: 11 on the left side and 62 on the right side. The box plot for the data of Example (c) is shown in Figure 1–23, along with the MINITAB program that produced it.

As you can see from the figure, there are no outliers or suspected outliers in this data set. The data set is skewed to the right. This confirms our observation of the skewness from consideration of the stem-and-leaf diagrams of the same data set, in Figures 1–17 to 1–19.

---

[10] See J. Chambers, W. Cleveland, B. Kleiner, and P. Tukey, *Graphical Methods for Data Analysis* (Boston: Duxbury Press, 1983).

FIGURE 1–23   MINITAB-Produced Box Plot for the Data of Example (c)

```
MTB > read 'ccc.dat' into c1
    42 ROWS READ

C1
    11      12      12      13

MTB > PRINT C1
C1
    11      12      12      13      15      15      15      16      17      20      21      21      21
    22      22      22      23      24      26      27      27      27      28      29      29      30
    31      32      34      35      37      41      41      42      45      47      50      52      53
    56      60      62

MTB > BOXPLOT FOR DATA IN C1
```

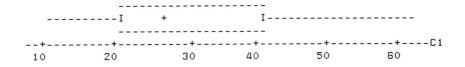

```
MTB >

MTB > stop
```

PROBLEMS

1–41.   The following data are monthly steel production figures, in millions of tons.

7.0, 6.9, 8.2, 7.8, 7.7, 7.3, 6.8, 6.7, 8.2, 8.4, 7.0, 6.7, 7.5, 7.2, 7.9, 7.6, 6.7, 6.6, 6.3, 5.6, 7.8, 5.5, 6.2, 5.8, 5.8, 6.1, 6.0, 7.3, 7.3, 7.5, 7.2, 7.2, 7.4, 7.6.

Draw a stem-and-leaf display of these data.

1–42.   Draw a box plot for the data in problem 1–41. Are there any outliers? Is the distribution of the data symmetric or skewed? If it is skewed, to what side?

1–43.   What are the uses of a stem-and-leaf display? What are the uses of a box plot?

1–44.   Worker participation in management is a new concept that involves employees in corporate decision making. The following data are the percentages of employees involved in worker participation programs in a sample of firms. Draw a stem-and-leaf display of the data.

5, 32, 33, 35, 42, 43, 42, 45, 46, 44, 47, 48, 48, 48, 49, 49, 50, 37, 38, 34, 51, 52, 52, 47, 53, 55, 56, 57, 58, 63, 78

1–45.   Draw a box plot of the data in problem 1–44, and draw conclusions about the data set based on the box plot.

1–46.   Consider the four box plots in the following output, and draw your conclusions about the data sets.

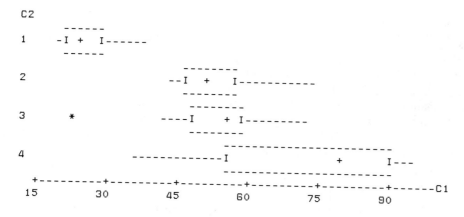

1–47. Presented in the following list are data on government expenditures by Western Hemisphere countries, expressed as a percentage of a nation's gross domestic product. (Data are for 1979–1981.)[11]

Argentina: 12.7; Bahamas: 13.2; Belize: 14.0; Bolivia: 13.6; Brazil: 8.9; Canada: 19.4; Chile: 12.4; Colombia: 8.0; Costa Rica: 18.3; Cuba: 2.1; Dominican Republic: 7.8; Ecuador: 15.0; El Salvador: 15.1; Guadeloupe: 32.3; Guatemala: 7.7; Guyana: 28.9; Haiti: 87.4; Honduras: 14.6; Jamaica: 21.5; Martinique: 26.0; Mexico: 10.8; Netherlands Antilles: 21.3; Nicaragua: 11.6; Panama: 15.3; Paraguay: 7.3; Peru: 12.5; Puerto Rico: 17.1; Surinam: 16.4; Trinidad and Tobago: 16.8; Uruguay: 13.5; USA: 20.7; Venezuela: 13.1

Construct a box plot for the data on the listed countries. Are there any outliers (or suspected outliers)? Can you identify possible reasons for outliers in this case?

1–48. The following data are the daily price quotations for a certain stock over a period of 45 days. Construct a stem-and-leaf display for these data. What can you conclude about the distribution of daily stock prices over the period under study?

10, 11, 10, 11, 11, 12, 12, 13, 14, 16, 15, 11, 18, 19, 20, 15, 14, 14, 22, 25, 27, 23, 22, 26, 27, 29, 28, 31, 32, 30, 32, 34, 33, 38, 41, 40, 42, 53, 52, 47, 37, 23, 11, 32, 23

1–49. Discuss ways of dealing with outliers: their detection and what to do about them once they are detected. Can you always discard an outlier? Why or why not?

1–50. Define the inner fences and the outer fences of a box plot; also define the whiskers and the hinges. What portion of the data is represented by the box? By the whiskers?

1–51. The following data are the number of ounces of silver per ton of ore for two mines.

Mine A: 34, 32, 35, 37, 41, 42, 43, 45, 46, 45, 48, 49, 51, 52, 53, 60, 73, 76, 85
Mine B: 23, 24, 28, 29, 32, 34, 35, 37, 38, 40, 43, 44, 47, 48, 49, 50, 51, 52, 59

Construct a stem-and-leaf display for each data set, and a box plot for each data set. Compare the two displays and the two box plots. Draw conclusions about the data.

1–52. Can you compare two *populations* by looking at box plots or stem-and-leaf displays of random samples from the two populations? Explain.

---

[11] From *International Marketing Data and Statistics* (London: Euromonitor Publications, 1983).

1–11 Other Statistics

In this section, we present two statistics often omitted in basic statistics books but that are very useful in some areas, especially finance. You are likely to encounter these statistics in courses in other areas, and it will therefore be worthwhile to introduce them here. The first statistic is the *coefficient of variation,* or CV for short. The second statistic is the *geometric mean,* an average that uses multiplication rather than addition as the basic operation. The geometric mean is very useful for dealing with interest rates, for example, because this mean accounts for compounding of interest. We will start with the coefficient of variation.

The Coefficient of Variation

Recall that the standard deviation is a measure of the dispersion of a population or a sample. The standard deviation is an absolute measure of dispersion; it does not take into consideration the magnitude of the values in the population or sample. Sometimes, however, we need a *relative* measure of the dispersion of a set of numbers, that is, a measure of dispersion that accounts for the magnitudes of the observations. The **coefficient of variation** is such a measure.

Suppose that the standard deviation of a sample is 20. If you assume normality of the observations set, then roughly 95% of the observations will lie within 40 units of the mean. How meaningful is the information conveyed by this measure? If the data are dollars in some accounts, there would be a big difference in the interpretation of $s = \$20$ between the case where the data are amounts such as \$50 or \$60 and the case where the amounts are, say, \$1 million or so. In the first case, a standard deviation of 20 means that the amounts vary a lot (relative to their size of \$50 or \$60). However, for amounts in the order of \$1 million, what is the meaning of a variation of plus or minus \$40? Obviously, such variation is a drop in the bucket. In the comparison of such cases, you can see that an absolute measure of dispersion, such as the standard deviation, does not convey much information. The coefficient of variation is designed especially to be a relative measure of dispersion. The CV allows us to *consider the dispersion as a proportion of the mean*, that is, the dispersion in proportion to the average magnitude of the data. The formula for the CV is thus the standard deviation divided by the mean. For a *sample,* we have:

$$CV = \frac{s}{\bar{x}} \qquad\qquad (1\text{–}10)$$

If a sample of accounts has mean $\bar{x} = 60$ and standard deviation $s = 20$, then the CV is: $s/\bar{x} = 20/60 = 0.33$. On the other hand, if the average account in the sample is $\bar{x} = 1{,}000{,}000$ and $s = 20$, then the CV is equal to: $s/\bar{x} = 20/1{,}000{,}000 = 0.00002$, which is much smaller and conveys the information that, relative to their size, the data in the second sample do not vary much.

The Geometric Mean

Until now, every time we computed the mean of a sample we did so by adding the data and then dividing by the sample size, n. When computed this way, the mean is called the *arithmetic* mean. There is another kind of mean, called the *geometric mean,* which is useful in some situations.

Consider interest rates. Let us assume that you have some amount of money invested that pays you a certain percentage of interest each year and that the percentage varies from year to year. Suppose that over $n = 5$ years, you are paid a rate i_1 at year 1, i_2 at year 2, i_3 at year 3, i_4 at year 4, and i_5 at year 5. The interest is *compounded* once a year. That is, after year 1, an amount equal to your principal times i_1 is added to your account. If you want to find the average interest rate paid to you over the five years, you could add $i_1, i_2, \ldots, i_5$ and divide by 5. Then you would be computing the arithmetic mean of the five interest rates.

On the other hand, note the following. If your principal is P, then after year 1 you will have $P(1 + i_1)$ in your account. In the account at the end of year 2, you will have $P(1 + i_1)(1 + i_2)$, and so on. After the five years have passed, you will have: $F = P(1 + i_1)(1 + i_2)(1 + i_3)(1 + i_4)(1 + i_5)$. If you think of the average interest rate, i, that would give you the same amount F after five years if it were constantly applied each year, this would be the *geometric* average of the interest rates you are paid. The rate i is the average of $i_1, i_2, \ldots, i_5$ in a multiplicative sense. It is the rate that solves the equation: $(1 + i)^n = (1 + i_1)(1 + i_2) \times (1 + i_3)(1 + i_4)(1 + i_5)$. It is the mean in a sense that preserves the idea of *compounding*. The solution of the equation is:

$$(1 + i) = \sqrt[n]{(1 + i_1)(1 + i_2)(1 + i_3)(1 + i_4)(1 + i_5)}$$

$(1 + i)$ is, then, the geometric mean of $(1 + i_1), \ldots, (1 + i_5)$.

For example, suppose that $n = 2$ years, $i_1 = 0.10$, and $i_2 = 0.05$. The geometric mean of $(1 + i_1)$ and $(1 + i_2)$ is: $(1 + i) = \sqrt{(1.10)(1.05)} = 1.0747$, giving an interest rate of 0.0747 or 7.47%. If we compute an arithmetic average of i_1 and i_2, we get $(0.05 + 0.10)/2 = 0.075$, which is slightly different. In situations such as these, a geometric mean is more meaningful.

The formula for the geometric mean of n items $x_1, x_2, \ldots, x_n$ is:

Geometric mean:

$$\overline{x}_G = \sqrt[n]{x_1 x_2 \cdots x_n}$$

(1–11)

In this book, we will confine our analysis to the arithmetic mean, $\overline{x}$.

PROBLEMS

1–53. What are the advantages of the coefficient of variation? What is the difference between the standard deviation and the coefficient of variaton?

1–54. The standard deviation of returns on an investment is a measure of the risk of the investment. Under what conditions is the coefficient of variation a more useful measure of risk than the standard deviation in comparing several investment opportunities? Explain.

1–55. The following are data on the number of business travelers per week staying at two hotels. For each hotel, find the mean weekly number of business travelers, the standard deviation, and the coefficient of variation. Compare the two hotels based on the statistics you computed.

Hotel A: 987, 988, 990, 967, 973, 945, 993, 965, 944, 930, 948, 958
Hotel B: 124, 138, 110, 147, 198, 136, 140, 162, 187, 119, 155, 149

Answer

1–56.

Geometric: 12.3146%
Arithmetic: 12.3333%

1–56. An investment pays you 12% interest the first year, 10% the next year, and 15% the third year. What is the average interest rate computed using a goemetric mean? What is the arithmetic mean of the three interest rates? Which of the two averages is more meaningful and why?

1–57. What are the uses of the geometric mean, and how does it differ from the arithmetic mean?

1–12 Using the Computer

Since statistics involves the processing of numerical data—often large sets of data—computers play a major role. The connection between statistics and computers is so strong, in fact, that most computer software packages with capabilities for handling numerical data have statistical analysis routines.

Among the best-known computer packages designed primarily for conducting statistical analysis are SAS (Statistical Analysis System, SAS Institute, Cary, N.C.), SPSS (Statistical Package for the Social Sciences, SPSS Inc., Chicago, Ill.), SYSTAT (SYSTAT, Inc., Evanston, Ill.), and MINITAB (a registered trademark of MINITAB, Inc., 3081 Enterprise Drive, State College, PA 16801); there are several others.

In this book we will use primarily the MINITAB package. MINITAB is not the most commonly used package in business and industry; there you are much more likely to use SPSS, SAS, or one of the other fine statistical packages. MINITAB, however, is possibly the easiest to use of all commonly available statistical packages. The data do not have to be specified in a rigid way. As long as blanks separate data, the data column format does not have to be strictly adhered to. This and other features make MINITAB a more "forgiving" package than most. It can be used with little preparation and, as a result, you will have more time to concentrate on learning the statistical concepts.

As always, a price is paid for simplicity: the MINITAB package is not quite as powerful as some of the others. Results are often rounded to few decimal places, and MINITAB does not have capabilities in one or two areas covered in this book. In such cases, we will use another package. However, familiarity with MINITAB will enable you to use any statistical package that you may later have access to or own.

MINITAB works with columns of data. When you enter a single data set into the computer, the data go into column 1, or C1. If you have two data sets, where one set represents one variable (say, personal income) and the other set a second variable (say, experience of the same person), one data set is entered into C1 and the second set into C2. This is basically the only "logic" of MINITAB you need to understand. It tells you how to enter and define your data.

We will demonstrate the use of MINITAB in producing descriptive statistics with the data of Example (a). The MINITAB command to enter the data into the first column, when done within the program, is

```
SET   into   C1
```

Later we will work with files of data that are defined separately. In such cases, we will tell the program to call the appropriate data set and analyze it. In this example, however, we will enter the data within the program itself, using the SET command. (The necessary commands will always be capitalized in our explanations; lower-case letters will be used for words needed only for our own documentation, which will be ignored by the computer.) When we finish entering the data, we give the command:

```
END
```

Then we tell the computer what we want it to do with our data. The command

```
MEAN  of  C1
```

for example, will produce the mean of our data set. Similarly, the command

```
STDEV  of  C1
```

will give us the standard deviation of our data set. In our example, we will use a general command:

```
DESCRIBE  C1
```

This command will give us the mean and standard deviation of our data set, along with other statistics. We will also use the command

```
HISTOGRAM  of  C1
```

to produce a histogram of our data set. To get out of MINITAB, just type:

```
STOP
```

Figures 1–24 and 1–25 show the commands, the data, and the output for the two operations DESCRIBE and HISTOGRAM, respectively. Compare the results with the ones we obtained without use of a computer.

The results include mean, median, and standard deviation, as well as the lower and upper quartiles, Q1 and Q3, respectively. In addition, the results provide the minimum and maximum values, which allow us to compute the range (their difference). Note that the computer chose the group boundaries for the histogram and gave us the midpoint of each interval.

Computer graphics is a fast-growing field. There are computer packages that allow you to plot any data set in two or three dimensions, and the graphs are continually improving. The computer language S is one example of a powerful graphical

FIGURE 1–24 MINITAB-Produced Descriptive Statistics, Example (a)

```
MTB > SET INTO C1
DATA> 6 9 10 12 13 14 14 15 16 16 16 17 17 18 18 19 20 21 22 24
DATA> END
MTB > DESCRIBE C1

              N      MEAN    MEDIAN    TRMEAN    STDEV    SEMEAN
C1           20    15.850    16.000    15.944    4.464     0.998

             MIN       MAX        Q1        Q3
C1         6.000    24.000    13.250    18.750
```

FIGURE 1–25 MINITAB-Produced Histogram, Example (a)

```
MTB > HISTOGRAM C1

Histogram of C1    N = 20

Midpoint   Count
       6       1   *
       8       0
      10       2   **
      12       1   *
      14       3   ***
      16       4   ****
      18       4   ****
      20       2   **
      22       2   **
      24       1   *
MTB > STOP
```

data analysis tool. Other packages for microcomputers include MacSpin for the Apple® Macintosh®. This program allows you to look at data in several dimensions (three at a time) and to rotate the data in space to detect relationships and outliers.

The MINITAB package has EDA capabilities. The command for a box plot is:

```
BOXPLOT (name of data column)
```

and the command for a stem-and-leaf display is:

```
STEM-AND-LEAF (name of data column)
```

The construction of a box plot was demonstrated in Figure 1–23. Now we will show how to use MINITAB to produce a stem-and-leaf display using the data of Example (c). The commands and the output are shown in Figure 1–26. Compare the stem-and-leaf display in the figure with the one we constructed by hand, in Figure 1–17.

FIGURE 1–26 MINITAB Commands and Output for Stem-and-Leaf Display of Example (c)

```
MTB > read 'ccc.dat' into c1
     42 ROWS READ
MTB > STEM-AND-LEAF C1

Stem-and-leaf of C1       N = 42
Leaf Unit = 1.0

      4    1 1223
      9    1 55567
     18    2 011122234
    (7)    2 6777899
     17    3 0124
     13    3 57
     11    4 112
      8    4 57
      6    5 023
      3    5 6
      2    6 02
```

1–13   Summary and Review of Terms

In this chapter we introduced many terms and concepts. We defined a **population** as the set of all measurements in which we are interested. We defined a **sample** as a smaller group of measurements chosen from the larger population (the concept of random sampling will be discussed in detail in Chapter 4). We defined the process of using the sample for drawing conclusions about the population as **statistical inference.**

We discussed **descriptive statistics** as quantities computed from our data. We also defined the following statistics: **percentile,** a point below which lie a specified percentage of the data, and **quartile,** a percentile point in multiples of 25. The first quartile, the 25th percentile point, is also called the lower quartile. The 50th percentile point is the second quartile, also called the middle quartile, or the **median.** The 75th percentile is the third quartile, or the upper quartile. We defined the **interquartile range** as the difference between the upper and lower quartiles. We said that the median is a measure of central tendency, and we defined two other measures of central tendency: the **mode,** which is a *most frequent* value, and the **mean.** We called the mean the most important measure of central tendency, or location, of the data set. We said that the mean is the average of all the data points and is the point where the entire distribution of data points balances.

We defined measures of variability: the **range,** the **variance,** and the **standard deviation.** We defined the range as the difference between the largest and smallest data points. The variance was defined as the average squared deviation of the data points from their mean. For a sample (rather than a population), we saw that this averaging is done by dividing the sum of the squared deviations from the mean by $n - 1$ instead of by n. We defined the standard deviation as the square root of the variance.

We discussed grouped data and **frequencies** of occurrence of data points in **classes** defined by intervals of numbers. We defined **relative frequencies** as the absolute frequencies, or counts, divided by the total number of data points. We saw how to construct a **histogram** of a data set: a graph of the frequencies of the data. We mentioned **skewness,** a measure of the asymmetry of the histogram of the data set. We also mentioned **kurtosis,** a measure of the flatness of the distribution. We introduced **Chebyshev's theorem** and the **empirical rule** as ways of determining the proportions of data lying within several standard deviations of the mean.

We defined four scales of measurement of data: **nominal**—*name* only; **ordinal**—data that can be *ordered* as greater than or less than; **interval**—with meaningful distances as *intervals* of numbers; and **ratio**—a scale where *ratios* of distances are also meaningful.

The next topic we discussed was graphical techniques. These extended the idea of a histogram. We saw how a **frequency polygon** may be used instead of a histogram. We also saw how to construct an **ogive:** a cumulative frequency graph of a data set. We also talked about **bar graphs, column graphs,** and **pie charts:** three types of charts for displaying data, both categorical and numerical.

Then we discussed **exploratory data analysis,** a statistical area devoted to analyzing data using graphical techniques and other techniques that do not make restrictive assumptions about the structure of the data. Here we encountered two useful techniques for plotting data in a way that sheds light on their structure: **stem-and-leaf displays** and **box plots.** We saw that a stem-and-leaf display, which can be drawn quickly, is a type of histogram that makes use of the decimal structure of our number system. We saw how a box plot is made out of five quantities: the median, the two **hinges,** and the two **whiskers.** And we saw how the whiskers, as well as outliers and suspected outliers, are determined by the **inner fences** and **outer fences;** the first lies at a distance of 1.5 times the interquartile range from the hinges, and the second is found at 3 times the interquartile range from the hinges.

Finally, we mentioned two statistics not commonly associated with statistical inference but that have uses in other areas, such as finance: the **geometric mean** of n numbers, computed as the nth root of the product of the numbers; and the **coefficient of variation,** defined as the standard deviation divided by the mean.

ADDITIONAL PROBLEMS

Answers

1–58. The following data, obtained from *Business Week* (March 3, 1986), are the annual percentages of Japanese cars in the United States for the years 1974 through 1986.

1–58.
___
Mean = 16.48
Median = 18.3
Std. deviation = 5.76

6.7, 9.5, 9.3, 12.3, 12.0, 16.6, 21.3, 21.8, 22.6, 20.9, 18.3, 20.1, 22.8

Find the mean, median, and standard deviation of these data. (Assume the data constitute a sample.)

1–59. Choose a stock from among the ones listed in *The Wall Street Journal*, and follow its price for two weeks. Find the mean price and the variance. (Assume the data are a sample.)

1–60. Twenty randomly chosen people are shown a television commercial and asked to rank it as to overall appeal on a scale of 0 to 100. The results are given below.

1–60.
___
Mean = 74.7
Variance = 194.43

89, 75, 59, 96, 88, 71, 43, 62, 80, 92, 76, 72, 67, 60, 79, 85, 77, 83, 87, 53

Find the mean, variance, and standard deviation of the sample of ratings.

1–61. The following data are the number of tons shipped weekly across the Pacific by a shipping company.

398, 412, 560, 476, 544, 690, 587, 600, 613, 457, 504, 477, 530, 641, 359, 566, 452, 633, 474, 499, 580, 606, 344, 455, 505, 396, 347, 441, 390, 632, 400, 582

Assume these data represent an entire population. Find the population mean and the population standard deviation.

1–62. The following data are grouped daily sales volume figures for an electronics store.

1–62.
___
Mean = 418.6
Variance = 20359.91
Modal class: $400
and less than $500.
Also Median class.
Est. Median = 435.71

Volume Category	Count
$0 to less than $200	3
$200 to less than $300	5
$300 to less than $400	9
$400 to less than $500	14
$500 to less than $600	8
$600 to less than $700	4

a. Find the mean, the variance, and the standard deviation. (Assume the data are a sample.)
b. What is the modal class?
c. What is the median class? Estimate the median of the data.
d. Find the relative frequencies.
e. Draw a histogram of the relative frequencies of the data.

1–63. Group the data in problem 1–61 into classes, and draw a histogram of the frequency distribution.

1–64. In 1987 the FCC was considering charging database companies a fee. Protests from computer user groups prompted a study of these service companies. A random sample of 30 users was selected, and their monthly charges for using a database service were recorded. Data (in dollars, rounded to the nearest dollar) are as follows.

12, 3, 5, 17, 4, 9, 15, 21, 18, 6, 8, 19, 9, 25, 2, 10,
16, 18, 24, 1, 11, 6, 19, 23, 14, 7, 10, 26, 30, 7

Group the data into classes, and draw histograms of the frequency distribution and the relative-frequency distribution. Also find the mean and the standard deviation of the raw data, assumed to be a sample.

1–65. Find the 80th percentile and the interquartile range of the data in problem 1–64.

1–66. Find the 90th percentile, the quartiles, and the range of the data in problem 1–61.

1–67. The following data are grouped annual salary figures, in dollars, for a random sample of executives in a particular industry.

Salary Range	Count
25,000 to 29,999	12
30,000 to 34,999	23
35,000 to 39,999	37
40,000 to 44,999	19
45,000 to 49,999	15
50,000 to 54,999	9

Draw a histogram of the frequency distribution of the executive salaries. Find the mean salary and the standard deviation of the salaries. What is the modal class?

1–68. The following data are numbers of color television sets manufactured per day at a given plant: 15, 16, 18, 19, 14, 12, 22, 23, 25, 20, 32, 17, 34, 25, 40, 41. Draw a frequency polygon and an ogive for these data.

1–69. Construct a stem-and-leaf display for the data in problem 1–68.

1–70. Construct a box plot for the data in problem 1–68. What can you say about the data?

1–71. The following data are the number of cars passing a point on a highway per minute: 10, 12, 11, 19, 22, 21, 23, 22, 24, 25, 23, 21, 28, 26, 27, 27, 29, 26, 22, 28, 30, 32, 25, 37, 34, 35, 62. Construct a stem-and-leaf display of these data. What does the display tell you about the data?

1–72. For the data in problem 1–71, construct a box plot. What does the box plot tell you about these data?

1–73. Following are data on U.S. market share for Japanese car makers:[12]

Who's Hot and Who's Not

	1990 U.S. Market Share*	Percent Change from Previous Year
Toyota	7.64%	17.5
Honda	6.12	14.3
Nissan	4.49	−1.5
Mazda	2.52	7.2
Mitsubishi	1.38	34.0
Subaru	0.80	−14.9
Isuzu	0.80	−2.4
Suzuki	0.15	−28.6
Daihatsu	0.11	—

*Vehicles sold under Japanese nameplates, including cars and light trucks.

Answers

1–64.

Mean = 13.166
Std. deviation = 7.874

1–66.

90th percentile = 632.7
Range = 346

[12] From *Business Week* (January 21, 1991), p. 37.

Draw a bar graph of these data and a pie chart showing the total percentage of Japanese cars in the U.S. market for the period of this study.

Problems 1–74 through 1–77 refer to the following data on corporate profitability (five-year average return on equity). They are reproduced by permission from the Annual Report on American Industry, *Forbes*, January 7, 1991.

Company	Percent
Apparel & shoes	
LA Gear	83.2
Reebok International	45.1
Gitano Group	41.5
Liz Claiborne	40.2
Philips-Van Heusen	36.0
NIKE	26.8
Stride Rite	24.7
Fruit of the Loom	22.5
VF	19.9
Kellwood	19.2
Russell	18.5
Leslie Fay Cos.	16.0
Crystal Brands	7.4
Oxford Industries	4.2
Salant	3.6
Median	22.5
Photography & toys	
Fuqua Industries	16.3
Mattel	14.8
Eastman Kodak	13.6
Hasbro	13.4
Brunswick	12.8
Tonka	8.5
Polaroid	7.4
Median	13.4
Home furnishings	
LADD Furniture	24.8
Rubbermaid	22.9
Newell Co.	19.3
Leggett & Platt	18.8
Kimball International	16.8
La-Z-Boy Chair	16.4
Thomas Industries	14.7
Premark Intl.	13.0
Oneida	12.6

Company	Percent
Springs Industries	10.3
Bassett Furniture Inds.	7.9
Interco	5.3
Median	15.6
Gas distributors	
MCN	18.9
Nicor	16.8
Peoples Energy	15.6
UtiliCorp United	14.5
Laclede Gas	14.5
Piedmont Natural Gas	14.5
Washington Gas Light	13.9
Kansas Power & Light	13.7
Southwest Gas	13.6
Brooklyn Union Gas	13.2
Wicor	13.1
UGI	12.0
Atlanta Gas Light	11.4
Eastern Enterprises	9.2
Diversified Energies	8.4
Median	13.7
Major oils	
Exxon	14.2
Amoco	12.9
Mobil	12.1
Chevron	8.1
Texaco	7.6
Median	12.1
Software	
Oracle Systems	50.6
Microsoft	50.4
Novell	46.6
Lotus Development	36.1
Computer Associates	30.4
Automatic Data	19.4

Company	Percent
General Motors EDS	17.3
First Financial Mgmt.	16.8
Computer Sciences	15.2
Median	30.4
Beverages	
Coca-Cola	39.1
PepsiCo	28.5
Anheuser-Busch Cos.	23.6
Brown-Forman	22.8
Seagram	13.2
Coca-Cola Enterprises	5.9
Adolph Coors	3.8
Median	22.8
Automobiles & trucks	
Ford Motor	25.5
Oshkosh Truck	23.1
Paccar	19.8
Chrysler	18.6
Fleetwood Enterprises	17.3
General Motors	13.3
Navistar Intl.	1.6
Median	18.6
Business services	
Rollins	50.4
Kelly Services	31.6
Olsten	24.7
Pinkerton	21.2
Adia Services	18.2
Wackenhut	15.4
PHH	13.4
American Building	10.3
National Education	10.3
Volt Info Sciences	1.6
Median	16.8

1–74. For each of the nine industry groups in the preceding data set, find the mean and the median. Compare your results with the medians reported in the table. Which of the two measures is more meaningful and why? Discuss.

1–75. For each of the industry groups in the data set, find the range, the variance, and the standard deviation.

1–76. Construct a box plot and a stem-and-leaf display for each industry group in the *Forbes* data set. Also construct a box plot for the entire data set, ignoring industry classification. Write a summary about outliers.

1–77. In the *Forbes* data set, ignore the industry groups and combine all the return data. Find the mean, median, mode, range, standard deviation, quartiles, and 10th and 90th percentiles. How do firms in the various industry groups compare in performance level with an average firm in the combined group?

Answers

The following table lists the leading fixed 30-year mortgage rates in the 24 largest metro areas, based on mortgages of $75,000.[13]

Region	Institution	Rate as of Jan. 4	Percent Down	Points	Monthly payment
Atlanta	Citizens & Southern	9.00%	5	3.25	$603.47
Baltimore	Paine Webber Mortgage Finance	9.25	5	2.50	617.01
Boston	First New England Mortgage	9.13	5	2.00	610.23
Chicago	Sears Mortgage	9.25	5	3.00	617.01
Cleveland	Third Federal S&L	9.00	20	3.00	603.47
Dallas	Texas Commerce	9.13	10	3.00	610.23
Denver	WestAmerica Mortgage	8.75	20	4.00	590.03
Detroit	Detroit Savings	9.25	5	2.88	617.01
Houston	Liberty Savings	9.00	5	3.38	603.47
Los Angeles	Estate Mortgage	9.38	10	2.00	623.81
Miami	First Financial of Boston	9.00	5	3.50	603.47
Minneapolis	Metropolitan Financial Mortgage	9.13	5	3.25	610.23
New York City	Executive Mortgage	9.25	10	2.50	617.01
N. New Jersey	Maryland National Mortgage	9.13	5	2.75	610.23
Philadelphia	Huntington Mortgage	9.13	5	3.00	610.23
Phoenix	GMAC Mortgage	9.13	10	2.50	610.23
Pittsburgh	NVR Mortgage	9.00	5	2.75	603.47
San Diego	Weyerhaeuser Mortgage	9.25	5	2.75	617.01
San Francisco	Fleet Mortgage	9.50	10	2.00	630.64
Seattle	Olympic Savings	9.25	5	2.00	617.01
St. Louis	Magnum Mortgage	9.25	5	2.50	617.01
S.W. Connecticut	Shelter Mortgage	9.00	10	2.75	603.47
Tampa	American Home Funding	9.50	5	1.50	630.64
Washington, D.C.	TransCoastal Mortgage	9.00	5	3.00	603.47

National average: 9.66%, 9.96% a month ago, 9.92% a year ago.

1–78. In the table above, find the mean and the median rate (as of January 4). Compare the mean with the median. Also compare the mean with the national average reported at the bottom of the table. Discuss the reasons for the differences you may find.

1–78.
———
Mean = 9.1525
Median = 9.13

1–79. Find the variance and the standard deviation of mortgage rates. Does Chebyshev's theorem apply to this data set? Does the empirical rule seem to apply?

1–80. Find the mode(s) of the distribution of rates and of the distribution of points from the leading mortgage rates table.

1–80.
———
Rate modes: 9.00, 9.25

1–81. Again referring to the table above, draw a box plot of monthly payments. Do you identify any outliers? Which cities, if any, are unusual with respect to any of the variables in the table?

1–82. Draw a stem-and-leaf display of monthly payments and of points using the data in the table above. Also draw histograms of these variables. What do you learn about the distributions of these variables?

---

[13] Reproduced by permission from *Money* (February 1991), p. 26.

1–83.   Interpret the following MINITAB computer output.

```
MTB > describe c1

                N      MEAN   MEDIAN   TRMEAN   STDEV   SEMEAN
CI             12     39.08    34.00    33.90   19.31     5.57

               MIN      MAX       Q1       Q3
C1           30.00   100.00    32.00    35.75
MTB > histo c1

Histogram of C1   N = 12

Midpoint  Count
      30      8 ********
      40      3 ***
      50      0
      60      0
      70      0
      80      0
      90      0
     100      1 *
```

HIGHEST U.S. BANK YIELDS FOR IRAs

*T*he following data are reproduced from *Money* magazine (February 1991, p. 23).

Bank Rating	Institution (state)	Yield on Jan. 4	Minimum Deposit	Additional Deposits	Annual Fee
	Six-Month IRA				
★★★	Loyola Federal Savings (Md.)	7.84%	$500	No	None
★★★	Citibank/S.D.	7.72	250	No	None
★★★	La Jolla (Calif.)	7.68	1,000	No	$10
★★★	Beach Savings (Calif.)	7.60	2,500	No	15
★★★	Key Bank USA (N.Y.)	7.60	1,000	No	None
★★★	Atlantic Bank of N.Y.	7.30	500	No	None
	One-Year IRA				
★★★	First Deposit National (N.H.)	8.00	10,000	No	None
★★★	First Trade Union Savings (Mass.)	7.90	500	No	None
★★★	Loyola Federal Savings (Md.)	7.90	500	No	None
★★★	Beach Savings (Calif.)	7.88	500	No	15
★★★	Colonial National (Del.)	7.85	250	No	None
★★★	Citibank/S.D.	7.82	250	No	None
	18-Month IRA				
★★★	La Jolla (Calif.)	8.17	100	Yes	10
★★★	Loyola Federal Savings (Md.)	8.07	100	Yes	None
★★★	First Deposit National (N.H.)	8.00	10,000	No	None
★★★	Colonial National (Del.)	7.94	250	No	None
★★★	Key Bank USA (N.Y.)	7.82	1,000	No	None
★★★	Beach Savings (Calif.)	7.74	100	Yes	None
	Five-Year IRA				
★★★	Colonial National (Del.)	8.25	250	No	None
★★★	Washington Savings (Md.)	8.24	500	No	None
★★★	Loyola Federal Savings (Md.)	8.22	500	No	None
★★★	First Trade Union Savings (Mass.)	8.14	500	No	None
★★★	Atlantic Bank of N.Y.	8.10	500	No	None
★★★	Metropolitan Bank for Savings (Va.)	8.08	1,000	No	None

For each maturity (six months, one year, etc.), find the mean, median, range, and standard deviation of both the percent yield and the minimum deposit. Draw a histogram or a box plot, and identify outlying observations. Discuss your results.

2

PROBABILITY

INTRODUCTION

The development of the theory of probability is usually attributed to European gamblers and mathematicians of the 17th century. Many books on probability and statistics tell the story of the Chevalier de Mére, a French gambler who enlisted the help of the well-known mathematician Blaise Pascal in an effort to obtain the probabilities of winning at certain games of chance. The resulting work on probability by Pascal (1623–1662) as well as work by Pierre de Fermat (1601–1665), Galileo (1564–1642), Abraham De Moivre (1667–1754), and others is believed by many to form the earliest known basis of probability theory. Thus the mid-1600s are usually accepted as the time of the development of the theory of probability.

A **probability** is a quantitative measure of uncertainty—a number that conveys the strength of our belief in the occurrence of an uncertain event. Since life is full of uncertainty, people have always been interested in evaluating probabilities, and it seems very surprising that the theory of probability should have emerged as late as the 1600s. Since the assessment of uncertainty incorporates the idea of learning from experience as well as the idea of inductive reasoning, the statistician I. J. Good suggests that "the theory of probability is much older than the human species."[1] Recent historical discoveries have shown that Good may be correct in this assessment. At least, these discoveries cast some doubt on the commonly held view that the theory of probability was developed in Europe in the 1600s.

The great Indian epic *Mahábarata* was written before A.D. 400. In the third book is the story of Rtuparna, a king who demonstrates a knowledge of statistics to Nala, a man possessed by the demigod of dicing. Rtuparna is described as able to estimate the number of leaves on a tree based on the number of leaves on a randomly chosen branch. This form of estimation is the essence of statistical inference. The story seems to prove that the early Indians knew something about statistics. Rtuparna further says:

I of dice possess the science
and in numbers thus am skilled

---

which seems to suggest a familiarity with the laws of probability.[2]

Not much is known about works such as the *Mahábarata,* and further investigations will have to be concluded before we are able to determine to what extent probability and its relationship to statistical inference were known to the Indians of the fourth century. They certainly had some familiarity with the subject.

---

[1] I. J. Good, "Kinds of Probability," *Science,* no. 129 (February 20, 1959), pp. 443–47.
[2] See Ian Hacking, *The Emergence of Probability* (New York: Cambridge University Press, 1975), p. 7.

Continued on next page

The Rabbis of the early centuries following the destruction of the second Temple in Jerusalem also had some familiarity with the laws of probability. As evidenced in the Talmud (written about the same time as the *Mahábarata*), probability arguments were widely used for determining issues related to dietary laws, paternity, taxes, adultery, and other matters. There are some indications that these early scholars were familiar with the rules of addition and multiplication of probabilities and were able to compare probabilities and make judgments based on their relative magnitudes.[3]

Today, the theory of probability is an indispensable tool in the analysis of situations involving uncertainty. It forms the basis for inferential statistics as well as for other fields that require quantitative assessments of chance occurrences, such as quality control, management decision analysis, and areas in physics, biology, engineering, and economics.

While most analyses using the theory of probability have nothing to do with games of chance, gambling models provide the clearest examples of probability and its assessment. The reason is that games of chance usually involve dice, cards, or roulette wheels—mechanical devices. If we assume there is no cheating, these mechanical devices tend to produce sets of outcomes that are *equally likely,* and this allows us to compute probabilities of winning at these games.

Suppose that a single die is rolled and that you win a dollar if the number 1 or 2 appears. What are your chances of winning a dollar? Since there are six *equally likely* numbers (assuming the die is fair) and you win as a result of either of two numbers appearing, the probability that you win is 2/6, or 1/3.

As another example, consider the following situation. An analyst follows the price movements of IBM stock for a period of time and wants to assess the probability that the stock will go up in price in the next week. This is a different type of situation. The analyst does not have the luxury of a known set of equally likely outcomes, where "IBM stock goes up next week" is one of a given number of these equally likely possibilities. Therefore, the analyst's assessment of the probability of the event will be a *subjective* one. The analyst will base his or her assessment of this probability on knowledge of the situation, guesses, or gut feelings. Different people may assign different probabilities to this event depending on their experience and knowledge; hence the name *subjective* probability.

Objective probability is probability based on symmetry of games of chance or similar situations. It is also called *classical probability*. This probability is based on the idea that certain occurrences are equally likely (the term *equally likely* is intuitively clear and will be used as a starting point for our definitions): the numbers 1, 2, 3, 4, 5, and 6 on a fair die are each equally likely to occur. Another type of objective probability is long-term *relative-frequency* probability. If, in the long run, 20 out of 1,000 consumers given a taste test for a new soup like the taste, then we say that the probability that a given consumer will like the soup is 20/1,000 = 0.02. Like the probability in games of chance and other symmetrical situations, relative-frequency probability is objective in the sense that no personal judgment is involved.

Subjective probability, on the other hand, involves personal judgment, information, intuition, and other subjective evaluation criteria. The area of subjective

---

[3] See Nachum L. Rabinovitch, "Probability in the Talmud," *Biometrika* 56, no. 2 (1969), pp. 437–41.

probability is relatively new, having been first developed in the 1930s.[4] The area is somewhat controversial; it is closely associated with Bayesian statistics and decision analysis, which we discuss in Chapter 15. An expert assessing the probability of success of a merger offer is making a personal judgment based on what he or she knows and feels about the situation. Subjective probability is also called *personal probability:* one person's subjective probability may very well be different from another person's subjective probability of the same event.

Whatever the kind of probability involved, the same set of mathematical rules holds for manipulating and analyzing probability. We now give the general rules for probability as well as formal definitions. Some of our definitions will involve counting the number of ways in which some event may occur. The counting idea is implementable only in the case of objective probability, although *conceptually* this idea may apply to subjective probability as well, if we can imagine a kind of lottery with a known probability of occurrence for the event of interest. ∎

2–2 Basic Definitions: Events, Sample Space, and Probabilities

In order to understand probability, it is useful to have some familiarity with sets and with operations involving sets. We define a set as follows.

> A **set** is a collection of elements.

The elements may be people, sheep, desks, cars, files in a cabinet, or even numbers. We may define our set as the collection of all sheep in a given pasture, all people in a room, all cars in a given parking lot at a given time, all the numbers between 0 and 1, or all integers. The number of elements in a set may be infinite, as in the last two examples (the number of integers is called *countably infinite,* while the numbers between any two numbers on the line, such as 0 and 1, are *uncountably infinite;* all other sets we mentioned are finite).

We now define a universal set:

> The **universal set** is the set containing *everything* in a given context. We denote the universal set by X.

We next define the empty set:

> The **empty set** is the set containing *no elements*. It is denoted by Ø.

Given a set A, we may define its complement:

> The **complement** of set A is the set containing all the elements in the universal set X that are *not* members of set A. We denote the complement of A by $\overline{A}$. The set $\overline{A}$ is often called "not A."

---

[4] The earliest published works on subjective probability are Frank Ramsey's *The Foundation of Mathematics and Other Logical Essays* (London: Kegan Paul, 1931) and the Italian statistician Bruno de Finetti's "La Prévision: Ses Lois Logiques, ses Sources Subjectives," *Annales de L'Institut Henri Poincaré* 7, no. 1 (1937). Following these came other papers by de Finetti, L. J. Savage, I. J. Good, B. O. Koopman, and others.

FIGURE 2-1
A Set, A, and Its Complement, $\overline{A}$

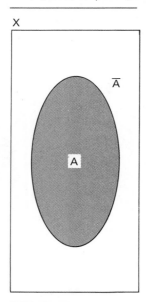

X

$\overline{A}$

A

A **Venn diagram** is a schematic drawing of sets that demonstrates the relationships between different sets. In a Venn diagram, sets are shown as circles, or other closed figures, within a rectangle corresponding to the universal set, X. Figure 2–1 is a Venn diagram demonstrating the relationship between a set, A, and its complement, $\overline{A}$.

As an example of a set and its complement, consider the following. Let the universal set, X, be the set of all students at a given university. Define A as the set of all students who own a car (at least one car). The complement of A, $\overline{A}$, is thus the set of all students at the university who do *not* own a car.

Consider two sets, A and B, within the context of the same universal set, X (we say that A and B are *subsets* of the universal set, X). We now define the intersection of A and B:

The **intersection** of A and B, denoted A ∩ B, is the set containing all elements that are members of *both* A and B.

The union of two sets A and B is defined as follows.

The **union** of A and B, denoted A ∪ B, is the set containing all elements that are members of *either* A *or* B, *or both*.

As you can see from these definitions, the union of two sets contains the intersection of the two sets. Figure 2–2 is a Venn diagram showing two sets, A and B, and their intersection, A ∩ B. Figure 2–3 is a Venn diagram showing the union of the same sets.

FIGURE 2-2
Sets A and B and Their
Intersection

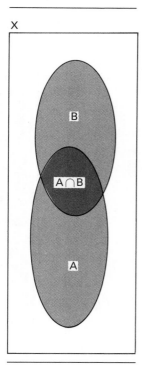

X

B

A∩B

A

As an example of the union and intersection of sets, consider again the set of all students at a university who own a car. This is set A. Now define set B as the set of all students at the university who own a bicycle. The universal set, X, is, as before, the set of all students at the university. A ∩ B is the intersection of A and B—it is the set of all students at the university who own *both* a car and a bicycle. A ∪ B is the union of A and B—it is the set of all students at the university who own either a car or a bicycle, or both.

Two sets may have no intersection: they may be **disjoint.** In such a case, we say that the intersection of the two sets is the empty set, ∅. In symbols, when A and B are disjoint, A ∩ B = ∅. As an example of two disjoint sets, consider the set of all students enrolled in a business program at a particular university and all the students at the university who are enrolled in an art program (assume no student is enrolled in both programs). A Venn diagram of two disjoint sets is shown in Figure 2–4.

In probability theory we make use of the idea of a set and of operations involving sets. We will now provide some basic definitions of entities relevant to the computation of probability. These are an *experiment,* an *event,* and a *sample space.*

We define an **experiment** as a process that leads to one of several possible **outcomes.** An outcome of an experiment is some observation or measurement.

Drawing a card out of a deck of 52 cards is an experiment. One outcome of the experiment is that the queen of diamonds is drawn. Measuring the temperature at a given moment is also an experiment, and the temperature measured is an outcome of the experiment.

A single outcome of an experiment is called a *basic outcome* or an *elementary event*. Any particular card drawn from a deck is a basic outcome. The set of all possible outcomes of an experiment, the set of all elementary events, is the *sample space*.

> The **sample space** is the universal set, X, pertinent to a given experiment. The sample space is the set of all possible outcomes of an experiment.

The sample space for the experiment of drawing a card out of a deck is the set of all cards in the deck. The sample space for the experiment of reading the temperature is the set of all numbers in the range of temperatures.

We now define an event:

> An **event** is a subset of a sample space. It is a set of basic outcomes. We say that the event occurs if the experiment gives rise to a basic outcome belonging to the event.

For example, the event "an ace is drawn out of a deck of cards" is the set of the 4 aces within the sample space consisting of all 52 cards. This event occurs whenever one of the 4 aces (the basic outcomes) is drawn.

The sample space for the experiment of drawing a card out of a deck of 52 cards is shown in Figure 2–5. The figure also shows event A, the event that an ace is drawn.

In this context, for a given experiment we have a sample space with equally likely basic outcomes: when a card is drawn out of a well-shuffled deck, every one of the cards (the basic outcomes) is as likely to occur as any other. In such situations, it seems reasonable to define the probability of an event as the *relative size* of the event with respect to the size of the sample space. Since there are 4 aces and there are 52 cards, the size of A is 4 and the size of the sample space is 52. Therefore, the probability of A is equal to 4/52.

As we have seen, sample spaces need not be finite, as in the case of a deck of cards: they can even be uncountably infinite, as in the experiment of measuring the temperature. A temperature is a single point on the number line, and there is an uncountably infinite number of such points. Still, if we make the assumption that every

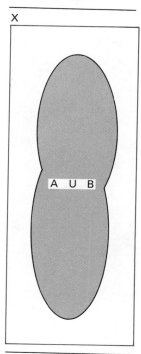

FIGURE 2–3
The Union of A and B

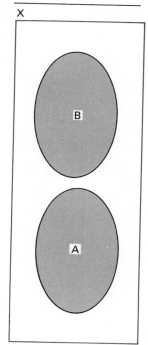

FIGURE 2–4
Two Disjoint Sets

FIGURE 2–5 Sample Space for Drawing a Card

	H	D	C	S	
The event A, "an ace is drawn" →	A	A	A	A ←	The outcome "ace of spades" means that event A has occurred
	K	K	K	K	
	Q	Q	Q	Q	
	J	J	J	J	
	10	10	10	10	
	9	9	9	9	
	8	8	8	8	
	7	7	7	7	
	6	6	6	6	
	5	5	5	5	
	4	4	4	4	
	3	3	3	3	
	2	2	2	2	

FIGURE 2–6

Probability as a Relative
Measure of Size

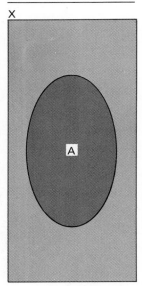

X

$$P(A) = \frac{|A|}{|X|} = \frac{\blacksquare}{\square + \blacksquare}$$

interval of a given length is as likely to occur as any other interval *of the same length,* then we will have extended the *equal-likelihood* principle. We may now define the probability of an event:

> Assuming equal likelihood, the probability of event A is the relative size of A with respect to the size of the sample space, X.

This definition makes use of our extended equal-likelihood assumption and so may not be appropriate in cases where this assumption is not reasonable.

Denoting the size of set A by $|A|$ and the size of sample space X by $|X|$, the definition of probability may be written as a formula.[5]

> Probability of event A:
>
> $$P(A) = \frac{|A|}{|X|} \qquad (2\text{–}1)$$

In cases where the number of elements in the sample space is finite, the size of a set is just the number of elements in the set. In cases where there are infinitely many elements, we may define size as the length of an interval, area, or volume, depending on the situation. For finite sample spaces, the definition of probability, equation 2–1, may be simplified. Let $n(A)$ be the number of elements in set A, and let $n(X)$ be the number of elements in sample space X. Then we have

$$P(A) = \frac{n(A)}{n(X)} \qquad (2\text{–}2)$$

The probability of drawing an ace is $P(A) = n(A)/n(X) = 4/52$.

Figure 2–6 demonstrates the idea of probability as a relative measure of the size of the set corresponding to an event with respect to the size of the entire sample space.

We will now demonstrate the use of equations 2–1 and 2–2 with a few examples. Example (a) is an extension of the card drawing experiment we have been discussing.

EXAMPLE (a)

Let us consider two possible events that may occur when a single card is drawn out of a well-shuffled deck of 52 cards. Let A denote the event that an ace is drawn, and let S denote the event that a spade is drawn. We now consider the sample space for this experiment and note the sets A and S, as well as their intersection, A ∩ S, and their union, A ∪ S. Let us use equation 2–2 and directly evaluate the probability of event A, the probability of event S, the probability of A ∩ S, and the probability of A ∪ S. Note that the event A ∩ S is the event that the card drawn is both an ace and a spade, that is, the ace of spades. The event A ∪ S is the event that the card drawn is either an ace or a spade, or both. Figure 2–7 shows the sample space for this experiment and the events A and S, their union, and their intersection. By direct counting and equation

[5] More on the idea of probability as the relative size of a set may be found in the very readable book: K. L. Chung, *Probability Theory with Stochastic Processes* (New York: Springer-Verlag, 1979).

FIGURE 2–7   The Events A and S and Their Union and Intersection

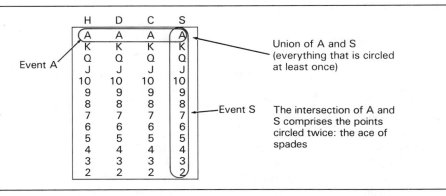

2–2, we get: $P(A) = 4/52$, $P(S) = 13/52$, $P(A \cup S) = 16/52$, and $P(A \cap S) = 1/52$.

In this example we obtained probabilities by direct counting. Later, we will see how probabilities of unions, and in some cases intersections, may be obtained from the probabilities of the original events and other information.

The following two examples demonstrate the use of probability in situations more complicated than the drawing of cards out of a deck. In Example (b) a subjective probability needs to be assessed. Since only limited information is available, an equal-likelihood assumption is made (this may not necessarily be a valid assumption in the presence of other information). The problem is solved based on this assumption and the resulting sample space.

In Example (c) we have an uncountably infinite sample space: an interval of numbers. Here a solution is obtained using the equal-likelihood assumption for all intervals of the same length and equation 2–1, with the size of a set being the length of the interval.

EXAMPLE (b)

As a result of litigation following Texaco's takeover of Getty Oil, a Texas jury decided in November 1985 that Texaco owed Pennzoil an amount that in time increased to $11 billion—the largest award in history. A quick settlement would have been a sensible way to end the battle between the two oil giants, but, apparently, an agreement between the two sides could not be reached. Months later—as a protective move—Texaco filed for bankruptcy. While preparing for the bankruptcy hearings, Texaco's top counsel, David Boies, went through records of all previous hearings presided over by Bankruptcy Judge Schwartzberg. Suppose that Boies found that out of 45 similar bankruptcy cases, Judge Schwartzberg made a favorable decision 13 times. Based on this information *only*, what should be Boies' assessment of the probability of a favorable outcome for Texaco as it goes before the judge?

SOLUTION

In such cases, typically, a subjective probability assessment is made. Here we assume that the probability assessment depends only on information about the judge's previous rulings. We thus consider a sample space with 45 equally likely points, 13 of which lead to the event in question. Using equation 2–2, the desired probability is: $P(A) = 13/45 = 0.289$.

EXAMPLE (c)

As international fishing pressures mount and the populations of such desirable food fish as salmon and halibut decrease, research is being done on shifting fishing efforts to other species. Recent years saw the development of a North Pacific fishery for pollock, a bottom fish used mainly in the production of imitation crab. Researchers at West Coast universities are looking for ways to protect this species from future overexploitation and are using sonar to detect schools of the bottom fish and track their migratory routes. Understanding the migratory behavior of these fish would lead to the setting of international fishing restrictions in certain areas and, it is hoped, protect the fish.

Pollock schools swim at random depths: they are as likely to be at any depth from the bottom of the ocean up to 120 meters above the ocean floor. If the sonar can only detect the fish when they are at least 10 meters above the ocean floor, what is the probability that a given school located in the region (off the Aleutian Islands) will be detected if one sonar reading is taken?

SOLUTION

In this example, the sample space is uncountably infinite: therefore, we will not measure the size of an event by the number of points. Instead, we will measure size by length: the distance above the bottom of the ocean. The total sample space has length 120 because the fish are assumed to be found at a random depth anywhere from 0 to 120 meters above the ocean floor. We define event D as the event that the school will be discovered. The size of D is 110 because the event will occur only if the fish are at least 10 meters above the ocean floor ($120 - 10 = 110$ meters). Using equation 2–1, we find the probability that the fish will be found (assuming they are in the area) as:

$$P(D) = \frac{|D|}{|X|} = \frac{110}{120} = 0.9167$$

We have made several assumptions in this example. First, we assumed that any length of, say, 1 meter along the total distance of 0 to 120 meters is equally likely to contain the fish. We also assumed that the school is like a point: it has no size; its location is randomly obtained, like throwing a pointlike dart at a board. These two assumptions lead to what is called the *continuous uniform distribution*. We will discuss probability distributions in the next chapter as well as give a formal definition of a distribution. Here the notion is intuitively clear. Incidentally, because of our assumption that the school is like a point and has no size, we are assuming that the probability that the school will be found at any exact, prespecified depth is zero. Nonzero probabilities are only given to intervals, such as 1 meter, 5 meters, and 10 meters in the range 0 to 120. This assumption is made in all *continuous* probability models. Figure 2–8 shows the sample space and event D.

PROBLEMS

2–1. What are the two main types of probability?

2–2. What is an event? What is the union of two events? What is the intersection of two events?

2–3. Define a sample space.

2–4. Define the probability of an event.

FIGURE 2–8 Sample Space and Event for Example (c)

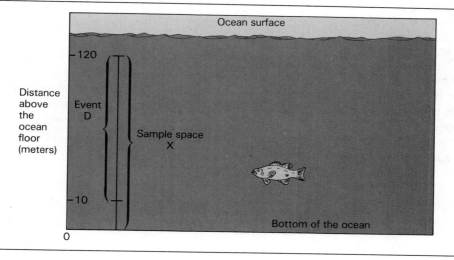

2–5. The Ford Motor Company advertises its cars on radio and on television. The company is interested in assessing the probability that a randomly chosen person is exposed to at least one of these two modes of advertising Ford cars. If we define event R as the event that a randomly chosen person was exposed to a radio advertisement and event T as the event that the person was exposed to a television commercial, define R ∪ T and R ∩ T in this context.

2–6. A brokerage firm deals in stocks and bonds. An analyst for the firm is interested in assessing the probability that a person who inquires about the firm will eventually purchase stock (event S) or bonds (event B). Define the union and the intersection of these two events.

2–7. A 1986 article in *Newsweek* by the mathematician John Paulos makes the point that most people have no grasp of the probabilities of events that may affect them: they tend to have great fear of publicized events with small probability, while not worrying at all about events with much higher probability. As an example, Paulos gives the following data: In 1985, 28 million Americans traveled abroad, and 39 of them were killed by terrorists. Based on this information, what is the probability of being killed by terrorists while traveling abroad? Compare this with another statistic reported by Paulos: 1 in 5,300 Americans was killed in an automobile accident in 1985.

2–8. An airline passenger lost her luggage. When it finally arrived a few days later, she casually asked the ticket agent how often things like this happen. The ticket agent said that, in his experience, a piece of luggage in that particular airport was reported lost about once every two days. He also said that two flights arrive every day, each flight carrying approximately 200 passengers. The average passenger was reported to check in an average of two pieces of luggage. Given this information, what is the probability that you will not find your suitcase (or one of your suitcases, if you check more than one) upon arrival at this airport?

2–9. A certain operation on a time-shared computer takes anywhere from 1/100 to 4/100 of a second, and the operation time is no more likely to be in any subinterval in this range than in any other subinterval of the same length. What is the probability that the operation will take over 2/100 of a second?

2–10. *The unfair subway.*[6] Marvin gets off work at random times between 3 and 5 P.M. His mother lives uptown, his girlfriend downtown. He takes the first subway that comes in either direction and eats dinner with the person he is first delivered to. His mother complains that he

---

[6] This problem is reprinted, by permission, from Frederick Mosteller, *Fifty Challenging Problems in Probability* (New York: Dover, 1987).

never comes to see her, but he says she has a 50–50 chance. He has had dinner with her twice in the last 20 working days. Explain.

2–3   Basic Rules for Probability

We have explored probability on a somewhat intuitive level and have seen rules that help us evaluate probabilities in special cases: when we have a known sample space with equally likely basic outcomes (and the extension of this case to infinite sample spaces). We will now look at some general probability rules that hold regardless of the particular situation or kind of probability (objective or subjective). First, let us give a general definition of probability.

> *Probability is a measure of uncertainty.* The probability of event A is a numerical measure of our belief in the occurrence of the event.

Probability obeys certain rules. The first rule sets the range of values that the probability measure may take.

For any event, the probability $P(A)$ satisfies:

$$0 \le P(A) \le 1 \qquad\qquad (2\text{–}3)$$

When an event cannot occur, its probability is zero. The probability of the empty set is zero: $P(\varnothing) = 0$. In a deck where half the cards are red and half are black, the probability of drawing a green card is zero because the set corresponding to that event is the empty set: there are no green cards.

In infinite sample spaces, there are events with zero probability. The probability that the temperature at noon tomorrow will be *exactly* 72° is zero because temperature is measured on a continuous scale of numbers, and there are uncountably infinitely many values the temperature may take. The relative *size* of the set containing only one point, 72, with respect to the size of any interval of numbers is zero. In continuous sample spaces, events with zero probability do occur, but the fact that their probability is zero means that we are unable to predict them in advance. Suppose that you guess that the temperature tomorrow at noon will be exactly 72°. If the temperature should be 72.000001°, your guess is incorrect. Since there are infinitely many possibilities, the probability of any particular one is zero. We will return to this point at the end of the next chapter.

Events that are certain to occur have probability 1.00. The probability of the entire sample space, X, is equal to 1.00: $P(X) = 1.00$. If we draw a card out of a deck, one of the 52 cards in the deck will *certainly* be drawn, and so the probability of the sample space, the set of all 52 cards, is equal to 1.00.

In infinite spaces there are, again, qualifications to this rule: you may delete any finite number of points from an interval of numbers and still have a remaining set of probability 1.00. This is so because the probability of any particular point in an infinite space is zero, and so is the probability of any finite collection of points. The probability that the temperature tomorrow will be any number except exactly 72.00 is still equal to 1.00. Now that we have noted these technicalities, let us not worry about them until the next chapter.

FIGURE 2–9 Interpretation of a Probability

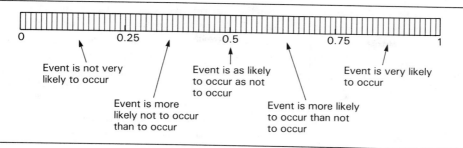

Within the range of values 0 to 1, the greater the probability, the more confidence we have in the occurrence of the event in question. A probability of 0.95 implies a very high confidence in the occurrence of the event. A probability of 0.80 implies a high confidence. When the probability is 0.5, the event is as likely to occur as it is not to occur. When the probability is 0.2, the event is not very likely to occur. When we assign a probability of 0.05, we believe the event is unlikely to occur, and so on. Figure 2–9 is an informal aid in interpreting probability.

Note that probability is a measure that goes from 0 to 1. In everyday conversation, we often describe probability in less formal terms. For example, people sometimes talk about odds. If the odds are 1 to 1, the probability is 1/2; if the odds are 1 to 2, the probability is 1/3; and so on. Also, people sometimes say, "The probability is 30%." We will avoid such quantifications and will always deal with probability as a number between 0 and 1.00. Its interpretation should be clear.

Our second rule for probability defines the probability of the complement of an event in terms of the probability of the original event. Recall that the complement of set A is denoted by $\overline{A}$.

$$P(\overline{A}) = 1 - P(A) \qquad (2\text{–}4)$$

As a simple example, if the probability of rain tomorrow is 0.3, then the probability of no rain tomorrow must be $1 - 0.3 = 0.7$. If the probability of drawing an ace is 4/52, then the probability of the drawn card not being an ace is $1 - 4/52 = 48/52$.

We now state a very important rule, the **rule of unions.** The rule of unions allows us to write the probability of the union of two events in terms of the probabilities of the two events and the probability of their intersection:[7]

$$P(A \cup B) = P(A) + P(B) - P(A \cap B) \qquad (2\text{–}5)$$

(The probability of the intersection of two events, $P(A \cap B)$, is called their **joint probability.**) The meaning of this rule is very simple and intuitive: When we add the

---

[7] The rule can be extended to more than two events. In the case of three events, we have: $P(A \cup B \cup C) = P(A) + P(B) + P(C) - P(A \cap B) - P(A \cap C) - P(B \cap C) + P(A \cap B \cap C)$. With more events, this becomes even more complex. Rule 2–10 in the next section is better for solving such probabilities.

probabilities of A and B, we are measuring, or counting, the probability of their intersection *twice*—once when measuring the relative size of A within the sample space, and once when doing this with B. Since the relative size, or probability, of the intersection of the two sets is counted twice, we subtract it once so that we are left with the true probability of the union of the two events (refer to Figure 2–7). Note that instead of finding the probability of A ∪ B by direct counting, as we did in Example (a), we can use the rule of unions: We know that the probability of an ace is 4/52, the probability of a spade is 13/52, and the probability of their intersection—the drawn card being the ace of spades—is 1/52. By rule 2–5, $P(A \cup S) = 4/52 + 13/52 - 1/52 = 16/52$, which is exactly what we found from direct counting.

The law of unions is especially useful when we do not have the sample space for the union of events but do have the separate probabilities. For example, suppose your chance of being offered a certain job is 0.4, your probability of getting another job is 0.5, and your probability of being offered both jobs (i.e., the intersection) is 0.3. Using the rule of unions, your probability of being offered at least one of the two jobs (their union) is $0.4 + 0.5 - 0.3 = 0.6$.

Mutually Exclusive Events

When the sets corresponding to two events are disjoint, that is, have no intersection, the two events are called **mutually exclusive** (see Figure 2–4). For mutually exclusive events, the probability of the intersection of the events is zero. This is so because the intersection of the events is the empty set, and we know that the probability of the empty set, ∅, is zero.

For mutually exclusive events A and B:

$$P(A \cap B) = 0. \tag{2–6}$$

This fact gives us a special rule for unions of mutually exclusive events. Since the probability of the intersection of the two events is zero, there is no need to subtract $P(A \cap B)$ when computing the probability of the union of the two events. Therefore,

---

For mutually exclusive events A and B:

$$P(A \cup B) = P(A) + P(B) \tag{2–7}$$

This is not really a new rule since we can always use equation 2-5 for the union of two events: if the events happen to be mutually exclusive, we subtract zero as the probability of the intersection.

Continuing our cards example, what is the probability of drawing either a heart or a spade? We have: $P(H \cup S) = P(H) + P(S) = 13/52 + 13/52 = 26/52 = 1/2$. We need not subtract the probability of an intersection, since no card is a spade *and* a heart.

2–11. ShopperTrak is a hidden electric eye designed to count the number of shoppers entering a store.[8] When two shoppers enter a store together, one walking in front of the other, the following probabilities apply: There is a 0.98 probability that the first shopper will be detected, a 0.94 probability that the second shopper will be detected, and a 0.93 probability that both of them will be detected by the device. What is the probability that the device will detect at least one of two shoppers entering together?

2–12. A machine produces components for use in cellular phones. At any given time, the machine may be in one, and only one, of three states: operational, out of control, or down. From experience with this machine, a quality-control engineer knows that the probability that the machine is out of control at any moment is 0.02, and the probability that it is down is 0.015.

a. What is the relationship between the two events "machine is out of control" and "machine is down"?

b. When the machine is either out of control or down, a repairperson must be called. What is the probability that a repairperson must be called right now?

c. Unless the machine is down, it can be used to produce a single item. What is the probability that the machine can be used to produce a single component right now? What is the relationship between this event and the event "machine is down"?

2–13. Following are age and sex data for 20 midlevel managers at a service company: 34 F, 49 M, 27 M, 63 F, 33 F, 29 F, 45 M, 46 M, 30 F, 39 M, 42 M, 30 F, 48 M, 35 F, 32 F, 37 F, 48 F, 50 M, 48 F, 61 F. A manager must be chosen at random to serve on a company-wide committee that deals with personnel problems. What is the probability that the chosen manager will be either a woman or over 50 years old, or both? Solve both directly from the data, and by using the law of unions. What is the probability that the chosen manager will be under 30?

2–14. In a marketing research survey, people are interviewed about product usage. One of the questions is about the brand of toothpaste used. If it is known that 14% of the population use brand A and 9% use another brand, B, what is the probability that a randomly chosen person will be a user of one of the two brands? (We assume that only one brand is used at a given time.)

2–15. Suppose that 25% of the population in a given area is exposed to a television commercial for Ford automobiles, and 34% is exposed to Ford's radio advertisements. Also, it is known that 10% of the population is exposed to both means of advertising. If a person is randomly chosen out of the entire population in this area, what is the probability that he or she was exposed to at least one of the two modes of advertising?

2–16. Suppose it is known that 85% of the people who inquire about investment opportunities at a brokerage house end up purchasing stock, and 33% end up purchasing bonds. It is also known that 28% of the inquirers end up getting a portfolio with both stocks and bonds. If a person is just making an inquiry, what is the probability that he or she will get either stock or bonds, or both (that is, open any portfolio)?

2–17. In problem 2–9, what is the probability that the operation will take less than 2/100 of a second?

2–18. In problem 2–14, suppose that the question is what toothpaste was used during the last month, allowing for the possibility that more than one toothpaste was used during the month. Suppose it is known that 1% of the people used both toothpastes during the month. What is the probability that the randomly chosen person used at least one of the two brands during the month?

Answers

2–12.

a. Mutually exclusive
b. 0.035
c. 0.985

2–14.

0.23

2–16.

0.90

2–18.

0.22

[8] *Business Week* (February 4, 1991), p. 85.

2–20.

a. 4/7
b. 5/7
c. 6/7

2–19.   A firm has 550 employees; 380 of them have had at least some college education, and 412 of the employees underwent a vocational training program. Furthermore, 357 employees are both college-educated and have had the vocational training. If an employee is chosen at random, what is the probability that he or she is either college-educated or has had the training, or both?

2–20.   The following table of the performance of financial indexes is reproduced, by permission, from *Money* magazine (February 1991).

	Percent Gain (or loss) to Jan. 1, 1991				
	1 Year	**3 Years**	**5 Years**	**10 Years**	**Percent Yield**
S&P 500 stock index	(3.1)	48.7	85.7	268.6	3.8
Dow Jones industrial average	(5.6)	38.3	65.8	216.5	3.9
Russell 2000 small-company stock index	(19.5)	16.9	12.7	125.3	2.3
Average equity fund	(5.3)	35.7	58.9	222.2	3.3
Salomon Bros. investment-grade bond index	9.1	34.8	59.6	240.8	8.5
Shearson Lehman Bros. long-term Treasury index	6.3	38.4	66.7	265.0	8.3
Shearson Lehman Bros. municipal bond index*	7.7	32.3	59.3	180.4	6.8

* All figures to Dec. 1, 1990.

An investor chooses a financial index for her personal use in evaluating investments. Let us assume that the choice is made at random, with equal probability for each of the indexes in the table above, and without the investor knowing the information in this table.

a. What is the probability that the index the investor has chosen lost money in the year ending January 1, 1991?

b. What is the probability that the chosen index gained at least 200% in the 10 years preceding this date?

c. What is the probability that the index either had a yield of at least 5% in the last year or gained at least 35% in the preceding three years, or both?

d. Are the event "index lost money in the preceding year" and the event "index had a yield of at least 4%" mutually exclusive? Explain.

2–4 De Morgan's Rules

The English mathematician Augustus De Morgan (1806–1871) discovered an important relationship between unions and intersections of sets. His rules involve the operation of taking complements of sets. The first rule says that the complement of a union of a collection of sets is equal to the intersection of the complements of the sets in the collection. The second rule says that the complement of an intersection of a collection of sets is equal to the union of the complements of the sets in the collection. We will consider only the first rule because it is the one useful in probability calculations. In the case of two sets only, the rule is:

De Morgan's rule:

$$\overline{(A \cup B)} = \overline{A} \cap \overline{B} \qquad (2\text{--}8)$$

The rule is demonstrated in Figure 2–10. Points in the complement of the set $A \cup B$ are the points that are not in A *and* not in B. Therefore, these points are in the intersection of $\overline{A}$ and $\overline{B}$. Thus, $\overline{(A \cup B)} = \overline{A} \cap \overline{B}$.

FIGURE 2–10 A Venn Diagram Demonstration of De Morgan's Rule

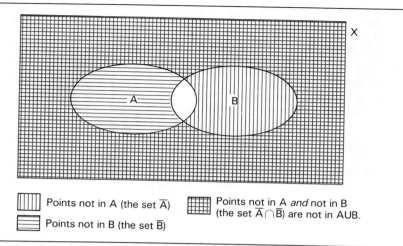

| | Points not in A (the set $\overline{A}$) |
| | Points not in B (the set $\overline{B}$) |

Points not in A *and* not in B (the set $\overline{A} \cap \overline{B}$) are not in A∪B.

Since the probability of the complement of an event is equal to 1 minus the probability of the event, De Morgan's rule (equation 2–8) becomes the following when stated in terms of probabilities of events.

$$P(A \cup B) = 1 - P(\overline{A} \cap \overline{B}) \qquad (2-9)$$

This rule may be extended to any collection of events $A_1, A_2, \ldots, A_n$:

$$P(A_1 \cup A_2 \cup \cdots \cup A_n) = 1 - P(\overline{A}_1 \cap \overline{A}_2 \cap \cdots \cap \overline{A}_n) \qquad (2-10)$$

The rule says that the probability of at least one of the events A_i occurring is equal to 1 minus the probability that all *n* events will *not* occur. The logic behind this rule is that *if at least one of several events occurs, then it is not the case that all the events do not occur*. Let us look at an example.

A salesperson is trying to conclude five deals and feels that the probability that all five deals will not go through is 0.40. What is the probability that at least one deal will be concluded? Using equation 2–10, we find the probability $P(A_1 \cup A_2 \cup \cdots \cup A_5) = 1 - 0.40 = 0.60$.

The usefulness of De Morgan's rule derives from its applicability in the case of independent events, as will be seen in section 2–6. The probability of an intersection of independent events may be obtained from the probabilities of the separate events, leading to the probability of the union of the complements.

PROBLEMS

2–21. Draw a picture similar to Figure 2–10 with three interesecting sets, and derive a rule that will be an extension of equation 2–8 for three sets A, B, and C.

2–22. For the situation with three events, derive a probability rule using the picture you drew for the previous problem.

2–23. Pier 1 Imports is a national chain of stores that sells imported oriental furniture and other home items. The company maintains a mailing list of customers based on their zip

Answer

0.96

codes. On March 10, 1991, a catalog was sent to customers in three zip code areas. A local store manager believes that there is a 0.25 probability that there will be no response from customers in the three areas. What is the probability of a response from at least one of the three areas?

2–24. A machine has four different components. It is known that there is a 0.04 probability that all four components will fail. What is the probability that at least one of the four components will work?

2–25. In the situation of the previous problem, can you determine the probability that *exactly* one of the four components will work? Explain.

2–5 Conditional Probability

As a measure of uncertainty, probability depends on information. Thus, the probability you would give the event "IBM stock price will go up tomorrow" depends on what you know about the company and its performance; the probability is *conditional* upon your information set. If you know much about the company, you may assign a different probability to the event than you would in the case you know little about the company. We may define the probability of event A *conditional upon* the occurrence of event B. In this example, event A may be the event that the stock will go up tomorrow, and event B may be a favorable quarterly report. The definition of **conditional probability** is as follows.

Conditional probability of event A given the occurrence of event B:

$$P(A|B) = \frac{P(A \cap B)}{P(B)} \qquad (2–11)$$

assuming $P(B) \neq 0$

The vertical line in $P(A|B)$ is read *given*, or *conditional upon*. The probability of event A given the occurrence of event B is defined as the probability of the intersection of A and B, divided by the probability of event B.

Suppose a single die is rolled, and let 6 denote the event that the number 6 shows. We know that $P(6) = 1/6$. Suppose that we do not know what number came up, but we are told that it is an even number (event E). The information about the occurrence of event E *reduces our sample space*, thus changing the probability of event 6.

The sample space for the original event of rolling a die is shown in Figure 2–11 as the six points 1 through 6. Also shown is the reduced sample space corresponding to event E. Once you are given the fact that the number that came up is even, the sample space is immediately reduced to the three even numbers circled in Figure 2–11. The new sample space has three equally likely points, so the probability of 6 *conditional* on the number being even is increased from 1/6 to 1/3. This example is

FIGURE 2–11 Sample Space for Rolling a Die, and the Reduced Sample Space Given an Even Number

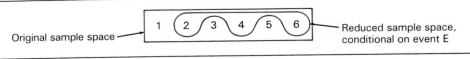

Original sample space

Reduced sample space, conditional on event E

useful for showing the validity of the definition of conditional probability: from equation 2–11 we have

$$P(6|E) = \frac{P(6 \cap E)}{P(E)} = \frac{1/6}{1/2} = \frac{1}{3}$$

which agrees with what we know from observing the reduced sample space and from counting one point out of three. The probability of the intersection of 6 and E is 1/6 because the intersection of the two events is just the event 6. The probability of E is, of course, 1/2.

There are two other useful forms of the definition of conditional probability, which are algebraically equivalent to equation 2–11:

and

$$P(A \cap B) = P(A|B)P(B) \qquad\qquad (2\text{–}12)$$

$$P(A \cap B) = P(B|A)P(A) \qquad\qquad (2\text{–}13)$$

Equation 2–12, or its equivalent, equation 2–13, which has A and B interchanged, is very useful in many applications. Following are a few examples.

EXAMPLE (d)

A consulting firm is bidding for two jobs, one with each of two large multinational corporations. The company executives estimate that the probability of obtaining the consulting job with firm A, event A, is 0.45. The executives also feel that *if* the company should get the job with firm A, then there is a 0.90 probability that firm B will also give the company the consulting job. What are the company's chances of getting *both* jobs?

SOLUTION

We are given $P(A) = 0.45$. We also know that $P(B|A) = 0.90$, and we are looking for $P(A \cap B)$, which is the probability that both A and B will occur. From equation 2–13, we have $P(A \cap B) = P(B|A)P(A) = 0.90 \times 0.45 = 0.405$.

EXAMPLE (e)

A certain MBA program requires its applicants to achieve a score of at least 500 on the Graduate Management Test (GMAT) and at least 600 on the GRE mathematics test. A student feels that her chances of obtaining at least the minimum required score on the GRE are 0.75 and that her chances of achieving the required level on *both* tests are 0.50. If the student passes the GRE at a score higher than required, what are her chances of passing the GMAT at the required level?

SOLUTION

$$P(A|B) = \frac{P(A \cap B)}{P(B)} = \frac{0.50}{0.75} = 0.6666$$

EXAMPLE (f)

Twenty-one percent of the executives in a large advertising firm are at the top salary level. It is further known that 40% of all the executives at the firm are women. Also, 6.4% of all executives are women *and* are at the top salary level. Recently, a question arose among executives at the firm as to whether there is any evidence of salary inequity. Assuming that some statistical considerations (explained in later chapters) are met, do the percentages reported above provide any evidence of salary inequity?

SOLUTION

To solve this problem, we pose it in terms of probabilities and ask whether the probability that a randomly chosen executive will be at the top salary level is approximately equal to the probability that the executive will be at the top salary level *given* the executive is a woman. To answer, we need to compute the probability that the executive will be at the top level given the executive is a woman. Defining T as the event of a top salary and W as the event that an executive is a woman, we get:

$$P(T|W) = \frac{P(T \cap W)}{P(W)} = \frac{0.064}{0.40} = 0.16$$

Since 0.16 is smaller than 0.21, we may conclude (subject to statistical considerations) that salary inequity does exist at the firm, as an executive is less likely to make a top salary if she is a woman.

The preceding example may incline us to think about the relations among different events. Are different events related, or are they *independent* of each other? In this example, we concluded that the two events, being a woman and being at the top salary level, are related in the sense that the event W made the event T less likely. The next section quantifies the relations among events and defines the concept of independence.

PROBLEMS

Answers

2-26.

0.32

2-28.
_____
2.5%

2-26. A financial analyst believes that if interest rates decrease in a given period, then the probability that the stock market will go up is 0.80. The analyst further believes that interest rates have a 0.40 chance of decreasing during the period in question. Given the above information, what is the probability that the market will go up and interest rates will go down during the period in question?

2-27. A bank loan officer knows that 12% of the bank's mortgage holders lose their jobs and default on the loan in the course of five years. She also knows that 20% of the bank's mortgage holders lose their jobs during this period. Given that one of her mortgage holders just lost his job, what is the probability that he will now default on the loan?

2-28. An express delivery service promises overnight delivery of all packages checked in before 5 P.M. The delivery service is not perfect, however, and sometimes delays do occur. Management knows that if delays occur in the evening flight to a major city from which distribution is made, then a package will not arrive on time with probability 0.25. It is also known that 10% of the evening flights to the major city are delayed. What percentage of the packages arrive late? (Assume that all packages are sent out on the evening flight to the major city and that all packages arrive on time if the evening flight is *not* delayed.)

2-29. The following table gives numbers of claims at a large insurance company by kind and by geographical region.

	East	South	Midwest	West
Hospitalization	75	128	29	52
Physician's visit	233	514	104	251
Outpatient treatment	100	326	65	99

Compute column totals and row totals. What do they mean?

a. If a bill is chosen at random, what is the probability that it is from the Midwest?

b. What is the probability that a randomly chosen bill is from the East?

c. What is the probability that a randomly chosen bill is either from the Midwest or from the South? What is the relation between these two events?

d. What is the probability that a randomly chosen bill is for hospitalization?

e. Given that a bill is for hospitalization, what is the probability that it is from the South?

f. Given that a bill is from the East, what is the probability that it is for physician's visit?

g. Given that a bill is for outpatient treatment, what is the probability that it is from the West?

h. What is the probability that a randomly chosen bill is either from the East or for outpatient treatment (or both)?

i. What is the probability that a randomly selected bill is either for hospitalization or from the South (or both)?

2–30.   One of the greatest problems in marketing research and other survey fields is the problem of nonresponse to surveys. In home interviews the problem arises from absence from home at the time of the visit or, sometimes, plain refusal to answer questions. A market researcher believes that a respondent will answer all questions with probability 0.94 if found at home. He further believes that the probability that a given person will be found at home is 0.65. Given this information, what percentage of the interviews will be successfully completed?

2–31.   The secret to increasing market share is winning over new customers and maintaining them. Maintaining customers is called *brand loyalty* and is one of the most thoroughly researched areas in marketing. The manufacturers of a certain perfume know there is a 0.02 probability that a given consumer will adopt their product and maintain brand loyalty for at least six months. They also know that there is a 0.05 probability that a randomly chosen consumer will adopt the brand. Suppose a consumer just switched to their brand. What is the probability of continued use over the next six months?

2–32.   An investment analyst collects data on stocks and notes whether or not dividends were paid and whether or not the stocks increased in price over a given period. Data are presented in the following table.

2–32.

0.484
0.455
0.138
0.199
0.285
0.634
0.801

	Price Increase	No Price Increase	Total
Dividends paid	34	78	112
No dividends paid	85	49	134
Total	119	127	246

a. If a stock is selected at random out of the analyst's list of 246 stocks, what is the probability that it increased in price?

b. If a stock is selected at random, what is the probability that it paid dividends?

c. If a stock is randomly selected, what is the probability that it both increased in price and paid dividends?

d. What is the probability that a randomly selected stock neither paid dividends nor increased in price?

e. Given that a stock increased in price, what is the probability that it also paid dividends?

f. If a stock is known not to have paid dividends, what is the probability that it increased in price?

g. What is the probability that a randomly selected stock was worth holding during the period in question; that is, what is the probability that it either increased in price, or paid dividends, or both?

2–33.   A cover article in *Business Week* deals with the salaries of top executives at large corporations.[9] The following table is compiled from data given in four tables in the article

[9] "Executive Pay: Who Got What in '86," *Business Week* (May 4, 1987).

Answer

and lists the number of firms in the study where the top executive officer made over $1 million a year. The table also lists firms according to whether or not shareholder return was positive during the period in question.

	Top Executive Made More than $1 Million	Top Executive Made Less than $1 Million	Total
Shareholders made money	1	6	7
Shareholders lost money	2	1	3
Total	3	7	10

a. If a firm is randomly chosen from the list of 10 firms studied, what is the probability that its top executive made over $1 million a year?

b. If a firm is randomly chosen from the list, what is the probability that its shareholders lost money during the period studied?

c. Given that one of the firms in this group had negative shareholder return, what is the probability that its top executive made over $1 million?

d. Given that a firm's top executive made over $1 million, what is the probability that the firm's shareholder return was positive?

2–34.

——

0.45

2–34. At the end of 1990, some airline industry analysts felt that if Continental Airlines could sell one of its main assets, the Seattle–Tokyo route, then there would be a 0.75 probability that the company would survive. It was further believed that there was a 0.60 probability that the airline would be allowed to sell this route. What was Continental's survival probability based on these estimates?

2–6 Independence of Events

In Example (f) we concluded that the probability that an executive made a top salary was lower when the executive was a woman, and we concluded that the two events T and W were *not independent*. We now give a formal definition of statistical independence of events.

Two events, A and B, are said to be **independent** of each other if and only if the following three conditions hold:

Conditions for the independence of two events A and B:

$$P(A|B) = P(A) \qquad\qquad (2\text{–}14)$$

$$P(B|A) = P(B) \qquad\qquad (2\text{–}15)$$

and, most useful:

$$P(A \cap B) = P(A)P(B) \qquad\qquad (2\text{–}16)$$

Equations 2–14 and 2–15 are intuitively clear: Equation 2–14 says that the probability of A *given* the occurrence of B is equal to the probability of A without the condition that B occurs. It tells us that event B has no effect on event A in the sense that its occurrence or nonoccurrence does not affect the chances of occurrence of event A. Event B has no information content that helps us to predict event A. Equation 2–15 says the same thing about the probability of event B, with A as the conditioning event.

Equation 2–16 is the most useful of the three definitions of independence. It is easily derivable from either equation 2–14 or 2–15 using equation 2–12 or 2–13;

the proof is left as an exercise. Equation 2–16 is useful because it tells us that in the special case that the two events are *independent*, the probability of their intersection—their *joint* probability—is equal to the product of the two separate probabilities. When two events are *not* known to be independent, we do not have this luxury—the ability to obtain their joint probability just by multiplying the unconditional (also called *marginal*) probabilities. In general, we need to know the conditional probability of one event given the other one, and from it determine the joint probability by using equation 2–12 or 2–13. This is one reason we often make the assumption of statistical independence. Caution must be exercised, however, in making the assumption of independence, because if the assumption is not valid, our results will not be correct. We demonstrate the concept of independence with the following examples.

The probability that a consumer will be exposed to an advertisement for a certain product by seeing a commercial on television is 0.04. The probability that the consumer will be exposed to the product by seeing an advertisement on a billboard is 0.06. The two events, being exposed to the commercial and being exposed to the billboard ad, are assumed to be independent. (*a*) What is the probability that the consumer will be exposed to both advertisements? (*b*) What is the probability that he or she will be exposed to at least one of the ads?

EXAMPLE (g)

(*a*) Since the two events are independent, the probability of the intersection of the two (i.e., being exposed to *both* ads) is: $P(A \cap B) = P(A)P(B) = 0.04 \times 0.06 = 0.0024$. (*b*) We note that being exposed to at least one of the advertisements is, by definition, the union of the two events, and so the rule for union applies. The probability of the intersection was computed above, and we have $P(A \cup B) = P(A) + P(B) - P(A \cap B) = 0.04 + 0.06 - 0.0024 = 0.0976$. The computation of such probabilities is important in advertising research. Probabilities are meaningful also as proportions of the population exposed to different modes of advertising, and are thus important in the evaluation of advertising efforts.

SOLUTION

As noted earlier, De Morgan's rule is especially useful in conjunction with the assumption of independence of events (when this assumption can be made). We now state De Morgan's rule (equation 2–10) for the special case where the n events A_1, A_2, . . . , A_n are independent.

De Morgan's rule in the case of independent events:

$$P(A_1 \cup A_2 \cup \cdots \cup A_n) = 1 - P(\overline{A}_1 \cap \overline{A}_2 \cap \cdots \cap \overline{A}_n)$$
$$= 1 - P(\overline{A}_1)P(\overline{A}_2) \cdots P(\overline{A}_n) \qquad (2–17)$$

Given a collection of events that are independent of each other, De Morgan's rule tells us that the probability of their union (that is, the probability of occurrence of *at least one* of the events) is 1 minus the product of the probabilities of the complements of the events. Suppose that the probability of getting one job offer is 0.4 and the probability of getting another job offer is 0.3; the two applications are independent of each other. Then, by equation 2–17, the probability of getting at least one job offer is $1 - (0.6)(0.7) = 1 - 0.42 = 0.58$. Example (h) will demonstrate the use of the rule in a more complicated situation.

Random Sampling

Much of statistics involves random sampling from some population. When we sample randomly from a large population, or when we sample randomly with replacement from a population of any size, the elements are independent of one another. For example, suppose that we have an urn containing 10 balls, 3 of them red and the rest blue. We randomly sample one ball, note that it is red, and return it to the urn. What is the probability that a second ball we choose at random will be red? The answer is still 3/10 because the second drawing does not "remember" that the first ball was red. Sampling with replacement in this way ensures independence of the elements from one another. The same holds for random sampling without replacement (i.e., without returning each element to the population before the next draw) if the population is relatively large in comparison with the size of the sample. Unless otherwise specfied, we will assume random sampling from a large population.

Random sampling from a large population implies independence.

EXAMPLE (h)

A marketing research firm is interested in interviewing a consumer who fits certain qualifications, for example, use of a certain product. It is known that 10% of the public in a certain area use the product and would thus qualify to be interviewed. The company selects a random sample of 10 people from the population as a whole. What is the probability that at least 1 of these 10 people qualifies to be interviewed?

SOLUTION

First, we note that if a sample is drawn at random, then the event that any one of the items in the sample fits the qualifications is independent of the other items in the sample. This is an important property in statistics. Let Q_i, where $i = 1, 2, \ldots, 10$, be the event that person i qualifies. Then the probability that at least 1 of the 10 people will qualify is the probability of the union of the 10 events Q_i ($i = 1, \ldots, 10$). We are thus looking for $P(Q_1 \cup Q_2 \cup \cdots \cup Q_{10})$, which, by De Morgan's rule, is equal to $1 - P(\overline{Q}_1 \cap \overline{Q}_2 \cap \cdots \cap \overline{Q}_{10})$. But since the events Q_i are independent, so are their complements $\overline{Q}_i$, and the probability of the intersection of the complements is therefore equal to the *product* of the probabilities of the separate events. Now, since 10% of the people qualify, the probability that person i does not qualify, $P(\overline{Q}_i)$, is equal to 0.90 for each $i = 1, \ldots, 10$. Therefore, the required probability is equal to $1 - (0.9)(0.9)\cdots(0.9)$ (10 times), or $1 - (0.9)^{10}$. This is equal to 0.6513.

Be sure that you understand the difference between *independent* events and *mutually exclusive* events. These two concepts are very different, although they usually cause some confusion when introduced. When two events are mutually exclusive, they are *not* independent. In fact, they are dependent events in the sense that if one happens, the other one cannot happen. The probability of the intersection of two mutually exclusive events is equal to zero. The probability of the intersection of two independent events is *not* zero; it is equal to the product of the probabilities of the separate events.

Equations 2–14 through 2–16 may also be used for checking whether or not two events are independent. If events A and B are independent, the rules hold; if they are not, the rules do not hold.

Suppose we know that the probability that the width of a machine-made part will be within specified bounds is 0.90, and the probability that its length will be within the bounds is 0.85. Suppose further that 80% of the parts are within specified bounds for length *and* width. Are the two events "width within bounds" and "length within bounds" independent?

From equation 2–16 we know that for independent events the joint probability is equal to the product of the marginal probabilities. We need to check whether $P(A \cap B) = P(A)P(B)$ in this case. Here $(0.90)(0.85) = 0.765 \neq 0.80$. Therefore, the two events are not independent.

PROBLEMS

2–35. In problem 2–32, are the events "dividends paid" and "price increase" independent?

2–36. In problem 2–33, are positive shareholder returns independent of the top executive's salary being over $1 million?

2–37. The probability that the price of a commodity will go up tomorrow is 0.3, and the probability that the price of silver will go up tomorrow is 0.2. It is further known that 6% of the time the prices of both the commodity and of silver go up. Are the prices of the commodity and of silver independent of each other?

2–38. The Holly Sugar Company makes sugar cubes. Quality checks revealed that about one in one hundred cubes is broken. If you reach for the sugar and randomly choose two cubes, what is the probability that at least one of them will be broken? (Assume independence—this assumption is inherent in random sampling.)

2–39. The chancellor of a state university is applying for a new position. At a certain point in his application process, he is being considered by seven universities. At three of the seven he is a finalist, which means that he is in the final group of three applicants, one of which will be chosen for the position. At two of the seven universities he is a semifinalist, that is, one of six candidates (in each of the two universities). In two universities he is at an early stage of his application and believes there is a pool of about 20 candidates for each of the two positions. Assuming that there is no exchange of information, or influence, across universities as to their hiring decisions, and that the chancellor is as likely to be chosen as any other applicant, what is the chancellor's probability of getting at least one job offer?

2–40. Saflok® is an electronic door lock system made in Troy, Michigan, and used in modern hotels and other establishments. To open a door you must insert the electronic card into the lock slip. Then a green light indicates that you can turn the handle and enter; or a yellow light indicates that the door is locked from inside, and you cannot enter. Personal experience at one hotel shows the following: When the door *should* open (when not locked from inside), one in every 30 entry attempts results in a yellow light, and the door does not open. Assuming that every attempt to enter the room is independent of any previous attempt, what is the probability of getting a yellow light every time in three consecutive attempts to enter your room (when the door is not locked from inside)?

2–41. Refer to the lost baggage problem, problem 2–8. When the passenger got off the plane, she went to pick up her suitcase, which she "found" and took home. She soon discovered, however, that she had picked up a suitcase identical to hers that was owned by another passenger. When she took the suitcase back to the airport, she was told that the other passenger had filed for lost baggage and been informed that his bag (actually hers!) was lost in transit. The airline agent told the passenger that in the last year there was only one case where two identical suitcases were mistakenly switched. Use the data given for flight frequency and number of passengers in problem 2–8 along with the new information in computing the probability that when you fly, your suitcase will be *both* switched and lost (delayed in transit) as happened here. Assume independence of the two events (this is a reasonable assumption if we leave out the possibility that if your bag *does* arrive, you will be less likely to pick up an identical suitcase).

2–42. A package of documents needs to be sent to a given destination, and it is important

Answers

2–36.
___
No

2–38.
___
0.0199

2–40.
___
0.000037

2–42.
___
0.9989

that it arrive within one day. To maximize the chances of on-time delivery, three copies of the documents are sent via three different delivery services. Service A is known to have a 90% on-time delivery record, service B has an 88% on-time delivery record, and the record for service C is 91% on-time delivery. What is the probability that at least one copy of the documents will arrive at its destination on time?

2–43. An electronic device has four independent components with a reliability of 0.85 each. The device works only if all four components are functional. What is the probability that the device will work when needed?

2–44.

0.9993

2–44. A device similar to the one in problem 2–43 has three components, but the device works as long as at least one of the components is functional. The reliabilities of the components are 0.96, 0.91, and 0.80. What is the probability that the device will work when needed?

2–45. A company sells picture books by telephone. From experience, it is known that 1 out of 65 calls produces a sale. If a salesperson makes 20 calls during an afternoon, what is the probability that at least one book will be sold? Comment on an assumption you must use.

2–46.

0.9844

2–46. A market researcher needs to interview people who drive to work. In the area where the study is undertaken, 75% of the people drive to work. If three people agree to be interviewed, what is the probability that at least one satisfies the requirement? What is the necessary assumption, and how does it apply?

2–47. Prove equation 2–16 using equations 2–14 and 2–12.

2–48.

0.831

2–48. An article on managing quality reports that at the end of the 1980s the market share for General Motors of Canada Ltd. was 35.9%.[10] If four cars were randomly chosen in Canada at that time, what is the probability that at least one was made by GM of Canada?

2–49. (*The Von Neumann device.*) Suppose that one of two top executives is to be randomly chosen, with equal probability, to attend an important meeting. One executive claims that using a coin to make the choice is not fair because the probability that is will land on a "head" or "tail" is not exactly 0.50. How can the coin still be used for making the choice? (*Hint:* Toss the coin *twice,* basing your decision on two possible outcomes.) Explain your answer.

2–50.

0.0039, 0.6836

2–50. When randomly sampling four items from a population, what is the probability that all four elements will come from the top quartile of the population distribution? What is the probability that at least one of the four elements will come from the bottom quartile of the distribution?

2–7 Combinatorial Concepts

In this section we briefly discuss a few combinatorial concepts and give some formulas useful in the analysis. The interested reader may find more on combinatorial rules and their applications in the classic book by W. Feller or in other books on probability.[11]

> If there are *n* events and event *i* can occur in N_i possible ways, then the number of ways in which the sequence of *n* events may occur is $N_1 N_2 \cdots N_n$.

Suppose that a bank has two branches, each branch has two departments, and each department has three employees. Then there are (2)(2)(3) choices of employees, and the probability that a particular one will be randomly selected is 1/(2)(2)(3) = 1/12.

---

[10] "Total Quality: Wave of the Future," *Canadian Business Review* (Spring 1990), p. 17.

[11] William Feller, *An Introduction to Probability Theory and Its Applications,* vol. I, 3d ed. (New York: John Wiley & Sons, 1968).

FIGURE 2–12   Tree Diagram for Computing the Total Number of Employees by Multiplication

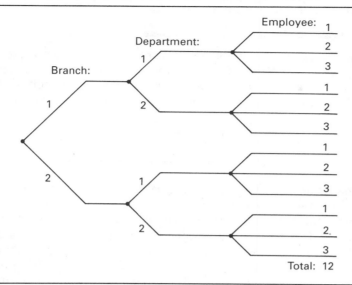

We may view the choice as done sequentially: first a branch is randomly chosen, then a department within the branch, and then the employee within the department. This is demonstrated in the tree diagram in Figure 2–12.

> For any positive integer n, we define n **factorial** as:
> $n(n - 1)(n - 2) \cdots (1)$. We denote n factorial by $n!$. The number $n!$ is the number of ways in which n objects can be ordered. By definition, $0! = 1$.

For example, 6! is the number of possible arrangements of six objects. We have: $6! = (6)(5)(4)(3)(2)(1) = 720$. Suppose that six applications arrive at a center on the same day, all written at different times. What is the probability that they will be read in the order they were written? Since there are 720 ways to order six applications, the probability of a particular order (the order in which the applications were written) is 1/720.

> **Permutations** are the possible ordered selections of r objects out of a total of n objects. The number of permutations of n objects taken r at a time is denoted $n\mathbf{P}r$.
>
> $$n\mathbf{P}r = \frac{n!}{(n - r)!} \qquad (2\text{–}18)$$

Suppose that 4 people are to be randomly chosen out of 10 people who agreed to be interviewed in a market survey. The 4 people are to be assigned to 4 interviewers. How many possibilities are there? The first interviewer has 10 choices, the second 9 choices, the third 8, and the fourth 7. Thus, there are $(10)(9)(8)(7) = 5{,}040$ selections. You can see that this is equal to $n(n - 1)(n - 2) \cdots (n - r + 1)$, which is equal to $n!/(n - r)!$. If choices are made randomly, the probability of any predetermined assignment of 4 people out of a group of 10 is 1/5,040.

Combinations are the possible selections of r items from a group of n items regardless of the order of selection. The number of combinations is denoted by $\binom{n}{r}$ and is read *n choose r*. An alternative notation is $n\,\mathbf{C}r$. We define the number of combinations of r out of n elements as:

$$\binom{n}{r} = \frac{n!}{r!(n - r)!} \qquad (2-19)$$

This is the most important of the combinatorial rules given in this chapter and is the only one we will use extensively. This rule is basic to the formula of the binomial distribution presented in the next chapter and will find use also in other chapters.

Suppose that 3 out of the 10 members of the board of directors of a large corporation are to be randomly selected to serve on a particular task committee. How many possible selections are there? Using equation 2–19, we find that the number of combinations is $\binom{10}{3} = 10!/3!7! = 120$. If the committee is chosen in a truly random fashion, what is the probability that the 3 committee members chosen will be the 3 senior board members? This is 1 combination out of a total of 120, so the answer is $1/120 = 0.00833$.

EXAMPLE (i)

A certain university held a meeting of administrators and faculty members to discuss some important issues of concern to both groups. Out of eight members, two were faculty, and both were missing from the meeting. If two members are absent, what is the probability that they should be the two faculty members?

SOLUTION

By definition, there are $\binom{8}{2}$ ways of selecting two people out of a total of eight people, disregarding the order of selection. Only one of these ways corresponds to the pair being the two faculty members. Therefore, the probability is $1/\binom{8}{2} = 1/(8!/2!6!) = 1/28 = 0.0357$. This assumes randomness.

PROBLEMS

Answers

2–52.

9!

2–54.

120

2–51. A company has four departments: manufacturing, distribution, marketing, and management. The number of people in each department is 55, 30, 21, and 13, respectively. Each department is expected to send one representative to a meeting with the company president. How many possible sets of representatives are there?

2–52. Nine sealed bids for oil drilling leases arrive at a regulatory agency in the morning mail. In how many different orders can the nine bids be opened?

2–53. Fifteen locations in a given area are believed likely to have oil. An oil company can only afford to drill at eight sites, sequentially chosen. How many possibilities are there, in order of selection?

2–54. A committee is evaluating six equally qualified candidates for a job. Only three of the six will be invited for an interview; among the chosen three, the order of invitation is of importance because the first candidate will have the best chance of being accepted, the second will be made an offer only if the committee rejects the first, and the third will be made an offer only if the committee should reject both the first and the second. How many possible ordered choices of three out of six candidates are there?

2–55. In the analysis of variance (discussed in Chapter 9) we compare several population means to see which is largest. After the primary analysis, pairwise comparisons are made. If we want to compare seven populations, each with all the others, how many pairs are there? (We are looking for the number of choices of seven items taken two at a time, regardless of order.)

2–56. In a shipment of 14 computer parts, 3 are faulty and the remaining 11 are in working order. Three elements are randomly chosen out of the shipment. What is the probability that all three faulty elements will be the ones chosen?

2–56.
———
1/364

2–57. *Megabucks* is a lottery game played in Massachusetts with the following rules. A random drawing of 6 numbers out of all 36 numbers from 1 to 36 is made every Wednesday and every Saturday. The game costs $1 to play, and to win a person must have the correct six numbers drawn, regardless of their order. (The numbers are sequentially drawn from a bin and are arranged from smallest to largest. When a player buys a ticket prior to the drawing, the player must also arrange his or her chosen numbers in ascending order.) The jackpot depends on the number of players and is usually worth several million dollars.[12] What is the probability of winning the jackpot?

2–58. In *Megabucks*, a player who correctly chooses five out of the six winning numbers gets $400. What is the probability of winning $400?

2–58.
———
180/1947792

2–59. *Mass Millions* is a similar lottery game. In this game, however, 6 numbers must be chosen out of a total of the 48 numbers from 1 to 48. What is the probability of winning the jackpot (also worth several million dollars) of this game?

2–60. In *Mass Millions*, if you are fortunate enough to have guessed five out of the six numbers on the balls drawn from the bin, you get to play an extra ball that is drawn. If your missing correct number is on the bonus ball, you win $50,000. What is the probability of winning at least $50,000 in this game?

2–60.
———
7/12271512

2–8   The Law of Total Probability and Bayes' Theorem

In this section we present two useful results of probability theory. The first one, **the law of total probability,** allows us at times to evaluate probabilities of events that are difficult to obtain alone, but become easy to calculate once we *condition* on the occurrence of a related event. We first assume that the related event occurs, and then we assume it does not occur. The resulting conditional probabilities help us compute the total probability of occurrence of the event of interest.

The second rule, the famous **Bayes' theorem,** is easily derived from the law of total probability and the definition of conditional probability. The rule, discovered in 1761 by the English clergyman Rev. Thomas Bayes, has had a profound impact on the development of statistics and is responsible for the emergence of a new philosophy of science. Bayes himself is said to have been unsure of his extraordinary result, which was presented to the Royal Society by a friend in 1763—after Bayes' death.

The Law of Total Probability

Consider two events A and B. Whatever may be the relation between the two events, we can *always* say that the probability of A is equal to the probability of the intersection of A and B, plus the probability of the intersection of A and the complement of B (event $\overline{B}$).

---

[12] On February 16, 1991, for example, the jackpot was $6,864,468 and was shared by three winners.

FIGURE 2–13
Partition of Set A into Its
Intersections with the Two Sets
B and B̄, and the Implied Law
of Total Probability

$P(A) = P(A \cap B) + P(A \cap \bar{B})$

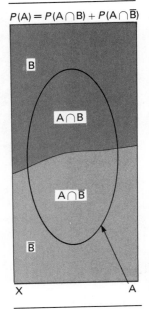

The law of total probability:

$$P(A) = P(A \cap B) + P(A \cap \bar{B}) \qquad (2\text{–}20)$$

The sets B and B̄ form a **partition** of the sample space. A partition of a space is the division of the space into a set of events that are mutually exclusive (disjoint sets) *and* cover the whole space. Whatever event B may be, either B or B̄ *must* occur, but not both. Figure 2–13 demonstrates this situation and the law of total probability.

The law of total probability may be extended to more complex situations, where the sample space X is partitioned into more than two events. Say we partition the space into a collection of n sets $B_1, B_2, \ldots, B_n$. The law of total probability in this situation is given as equation 2–21.

$$P(A) = \sum_{i=1}^{n} P(A \cap B_i) \qquad (2\text{–}21)$$

Figure 2–14 shows the partition of a sample space into the four events B_1, B_2, B_3, and B_4 and shows their intersections with set A.

We demonstrate the rule with a more specific example. Define A as the event that a picture card is drawn out of a deck of 52 cards (the picture cards are the aces, kings, queens, and jacks). Letting H, C, D, and S denote the events that the card drawn is a heart, club, diamond, or spade, respectively, we find that the probability of a picture card is $P(A) = P(A \cap H) + P(A \cap C) + P(A \cap D) + P(A \cap S) = 4/52 + 4/52 + 4/52 + 4/52 = 16/52$, which is what we know the probability of a picture card to be just by counting 16 picture cards out of a total of 52 cards in the deck. This demonstrates equation 2–21. The situation is shown in Figure 2–15. As can be seen from the figure, the event A is the set-addition of the intersections of A with each of the four sets H, D, C, and S.

The law of total probability can be extended by using the definition of conditional probability. Recall that $P(A \cap B) = P(A|B)P(B)$ (equation 2–12) and, similarly, $P(A \cap \bar{B}) = P(A|\bar{B})P(\bar{B})$. Substituting these relationships into equation 2–20 gives us another form of the law of total probability. This law and its extension to a partition consisting of more than two sets are given in equations 2–22 and 2–23.

FIGURE 2–14   The Partition of Set A into Its Intersection with Four Partition Sets

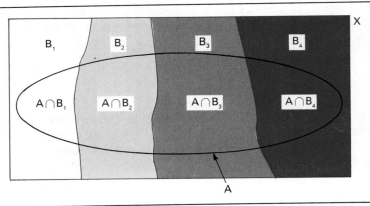

FIGURE 2–15   The Total Probabilty of Drawing a Picture Card as the Sum of the Probabilities of Drawing a Card in the Intersections of Picture and Suit

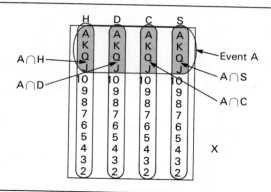

The law of total probability using conditional probabilities:

Two-set case

$$P(A) = P(A|B)P(B) + P(A|\bar{B})P(\bar{B}) \qquad (2\text{--}22)$$

More than two sets in the partition

$$P(A) = \sum_{i=1}^{n} P(A|B_i)P(B_i) \qquad (2\text{--}23)$$

where there are *n* sets in the partition: B_i, $i = 1, \ldots , n$.

An analyst believes the stock market has a 0.75 probability of going up in the next year if the economy should do well, and a 0.30 probability of going up if the economy should not do well during the year. The analyst further believes there is a 0.80 probability that the economy will do well in the coming year. What is the probability that the stock market will go up next year (using the analyst's assessments)?

EXAMPLE (j)

We define U as the event that the market will go up and W as the event the economy will do well. Using equation 2–22, we find: $P(U) = P(U|W)P(W) + P(U|\bar{W})P(\bar{W}) = (0.75)(0.80) + (0.30)(0.20) = 0.66$.

SOLUTION

Bayes' Theorem

We now develop the well-known Bayes' theorem. The theorem allows us to *reverse* the conditionality of events: we can obtain the probability of *B* given *A* from the probability of *A given B* (and other information).

By the definition of conditional probability, equation 2–11,

$$P(B|A) = \frac{P(A \cap B)}{P(A)} \qquad (2\text{--}24)$$

By another form of the same definition, equation 2–12,

$$P(A \cap B) = P(A|B)P(B) \qquad (2\text{–}25)$$

Substituting equation 2–25 into equation 2–24 gives us

$$P(B|A) = \frac{P(A|B)P(B)}{P(A)} \qquad (2\text{–}26)$$

From the law of total probability using conditional probabilities, equation 2–22, we have

$$P(A) = P(A|B)P(B) + P(A|\overline{B})P(\overline{B})$$

Substituting this expression for $P(A)$ in the denominator of equation 2–26 gives us Bayes' theorem.

Bayes' theorem:

$$P(B|A) = \frac{P(A|B)P(B)}{P(A|B)P(B) + P(A|\overline{B})P(\overline{B})} \qquad (2\text{–}27)$$

As we see from the theorem, the probability of B given A is obtained from the probabilities of B and $\overline{B}$ and from the conditional probabilities of A given B and A given $\overline{B}$.

The probabilities $P(B)$ and $P(\overline{B})$ are called **prior probabilities** of the events B and $\overline{B}$; the probability $P(B|A)$ is called the **posterior probability** of B. It is possible to write Bayes' theorem in terms of $\overline{B}$ and A, thus giving the posterior probability of $\overline{B}$, $P(\overline{B}|A)$.) Bayes' theorem may be viewed as a means of transforming our *prior* probability of an event, B, into a *posterior* probability of the event B—posterior to the known occurrence of event A.

The use of prior probabilities in conjunction with other information—often obtained from experimentation—has been questioned. The controversy arises in more involved statistical situations where Bayes' theorem is used in *mixing* the objective information obtained from sampling with prior information that *could* be subjective. We will explore this topic in more detail in Chapter 15. We now give some examples of the use of the theorem.

EXAMPLE (k)

Consider a test for an illness. The test has a known reliability:

1. When administered to an ill person, the test will indicate so with probability 0.92.
2. When administered to a person who is not ill, the test will erroneously give a positive result with probability 0.04.

Suppose the illness is rare and is known to affect only 0.1% of the entire population. If a person is randomly selected from the entire population and is given the test and the result is positive, what is the posterior probability (posterior to the test result) that the person is ill?

Let Z denote the event that the test result is positive and I the event that the person tested is ill. The preceding information gives us the following probabilities of events:

$$P(I) = 0.001, \qquad P(\bar{I}) = 0.999, \qquad P(Z|I) = 0.92, \qquad P(Z|\bar{I}) = 0.04$$

We are looking for the probability that the person is ill *given* a positive test result; that is, we need $P(I|Z)$. Since we have the probability with the *reversed* conditionality, $P(Z|I)$, we know that Bayes' theorem is the rule to be used here. Applying the rule, equation 2–27, to the events Z, I, and $\bar{I}$, we get:

$$P(I|Z) = \frac{P(Z|I)P(I)}{P(Z|I)P(I) + P(Z|\bar{I})P(\bar{I})} = \frac{(0.92)(0.001)}{(0.92)(0.001) + (0.04)(0.999)}$$
$$= 0.0225$$

This result may surprise you. A test with a relatively high reliability (92% correct diagnosis when a person is ill and 96% correct identification of people who are not ill) is administered to a person, the result is *positive,* and yet the probability that the person is actually ill is only 0.0225!

The reason for the low probability is that we have used *two* sources of information here: the reliability of the test *and* the very small probability (0.001) that a randomly selected person is ill. The two pieces of information were *mixed* by Bayes' theorem, and the posterior probability reflects the mixing of the high reliability of the test with the fact that the illness is rare. The result is perfectly correct as long as the information we have used is accurate. Indeed, subject to the accuracy of our information, if the test should be administered to a large number of people selected randomly from the *entire* population, it would be found that about 2.25% of the people in the sample who test positive are indeed ill.

Problems with Bayes' theorem arise when we are not careful with the use of prior information. In this example, suppose the test is administered to people in a hospital. Since people in a hospital are more likely to be ill than people in the population as a whole, the overall-population probability that a person is ill, 0.001, no longer applies. If we should apply this low probability in the hospital, our results would not be correct. This caution extends to all situations where prior probabilities are used: we must always examine the appropriateness of the prior probabilities.

Bayes' theorem may be extended to a partition of more than two sets. This is done using equation 2–23, the law of total probability involving a partition of sets: $B_1, B_2, \ldots, B_n$. The resulting extended form of Bayes' theorem is given in equation 2–28. The theorem gives the probability of one of the sets in the partition, B_1, given the occurrence of event A. A similar expression holds for any of the events B_i.

Extended Bayes' theorem:

$$P(B_1|A) = \frac{P(A|B_1)P(B_1)}{\displaystyle\sum_{i=1}^{n} P(A|B_i)P(B_i)} \qquad (2\text{--}28)$$

We demonstrate the use of equation 2–28 with the following example. In the solution, we use a table format to facilitate computations. We also demonstrate the computations using a tree diagram.

EXAMPLE (I)   An economist believes that during periods of high economic growth, the U.S. dollar appreciates with probability 0.70; in periods of moderate economic growth, the dollar appreciates with probability 0.40; and during periods of low economic growth, the dollar appreciates with probability 0.20. During any period of time, the probability of high economic growth is 0.30, the probability of moderate growth is 0.50, and the probability of low economic growth is 0.20. Suppose the dollar has been appreciating during the present period. What is the probability we are experiencing a period of high economic growth?

SOLUTION   Our partition consists of three events: high economic growth (event H), moderate economic growth (event M), and low economic growth (event L). The prior probabilities of the three states are: $P(H) = 0.30$, $P(M) = 0.50$, and $P(L) = 0.20$. Let A denote the event that the dollar appreciates. We have the following conditional probabilities: $P(A|H) = 0.70$, $P(A|M) = 0.40$, and $P(A|L) = 0.20$. Applying equation 2–28 using three sets ($n = 3$), we get:

$$P(H|A) = \frac{P(A|H)P(H)}{P(A|H)P(H) + P(A|M)P(M) + P(A|L)P(L)}$$

$$= \frac{(0.70)(0.30)}{(0.70)(0.30) + (0.40)(0.50) + (0.20)(0.20)} = 0.467$$

We can obtain this answer, along with the posterior probabilities of the other two states, M and L, by using a table. In the first column of the table we write the prior probabilities of the three states H, M, and L. In the second column we write the three conditional probabilities $P(A|H)$, $P(A|M)$, and $P(A|L)$. In the third column we write the joint probabilities $P(A \cap H)$, $P(A \cap M)$, and $P(A \cap L)$. The joint probabilities are obtained by multiplying across in each of the three rows (these operations make use of equation 2–12). The sum of the entries in the third column is the total probability of event A (by equation 2–21). Finally, the posterior probabilities $P(H|A)$, $P(M|A)$, and $P(L|A)$ are obtained by dividing the appropriate joint probability by the total probability of A at the bottom of the third column. For example, $P(H|A)$ is obtained by dividing $P(H \cap A)$ by the probability $P(A)$. The operations and the results are given in Table 2–1, and demonstrated in Figure 2–16.

Note that both the prior probabilities and the posterior probabilities of the three states add to 1.00, as required for probabilities of all the possibilities in a given situation. We conclude that, given that the dollar has been appreciating, the probability that our period is one of high economic growth is 0.467, the probability that it is one of moderate growth is 0.444, and the probability that our period is one of low economic growth is 0.089. The advantage of using a table is that we can obtain all posterior probabilities at

TABLE 2–1   Bayesian Revision of Probabilities, Example (I)

Event	Prior Probability	Conditional Probability	Joint Probability	Posterior Probability
H	$P(H) = 0.30$	$P(A\|H) = 0.70$	$P(A \cap H) = 0.21$	$P(H\|A) = \frac{0.21}{0.45} = 0.467$
M	$P(M) = 0.50$	$P(A\|M) = 0.40$	$P(A \cap M) = 0.20$	$P(M\|A) = \frac{0.20}{0.45} = 0.444$
L	$P(L) = 0.20$	$P(A\|L) = 0.20$	$P(A \cap L) = \underline{0.04}$	$P(L\|A) = \frac{0.04}{0.45} = \underline{0.089}$
	Sum = $\overline{1.00}$		$P(A) = 0.45$	Sum = 1.000

FIGURE 2–16   Tree Diagram for Example (I)

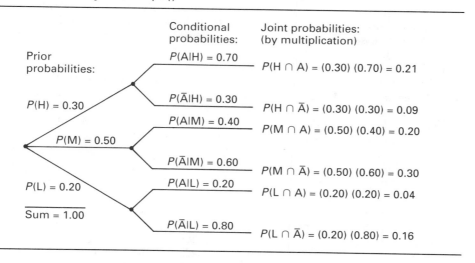

Conditional probabilities:

Joint probabilities: (by multiplication)

Prior probabilities:

$P(A|H) = 0.70$

$P(H \cap A) = (0.30)(0.70) = 0.21$

$P(H) = 0.30$

$P(\bar{A}|H) = 0.30$

$P(H \cap \bar{A}) = (0.30)(0.30) = 0.09$

$P(A|M) = 0.40$

$P(M \cap A) = (0.50)(0.40) = 0.20$

$P(M) = 0.50$

$P(\bar{A}|M) = 0.60$

$P(M \cap \bar{A}) = (0.50)(0.60) = 0.30$

$P(L) = 0.20$

$P(A|L) = 0.20$

$P(L \cap A) = (0.20)(0.20) = 0.04$

$\overline{\text{Sum} = 1.00}$

$P(\bar{A}|L) = 0.80$

$P(L \cap \bar{A}) = (0.20)(0.80) = 0.16$

once. If we use the formula directly, we need to apply it once for the posterior probability of each state.

2–61. In a takeover bid for a certain company, management of the raiding firm believes that the takeover has a 0.65 probability of success if a member of the board of the raided firm resigns, and a 0.30 chance of success if she does not resign. Management of the raiding firm further believes that the chances for a resignation of the member in question are 0.70. What is the probability of a successful takeover?

2–62. A drug manufacturer believes there is a 0.95 chance that the FDA will approve a new drug the company plans to distribute if the results of current testing show that the drug causes no side effects. The manufacturer further believes there is a 0.50 probability that the FDA will approve the drug if the test shows that the drug does cause side effects. A physician working for the drug manufacturer believes there is a 0.20 probability that tests will show that the drug causes side effects. What is the probability that the drug will be approved by the FDA?

2–63. An import-export firm has a 0.45 chance of concluding a deal to export agricultural equipment to a developing nation if a major competitor does not bid for the contract, and a 0.25 probability of concluding the deal if the competitor does bid for it. It is estimated that the competitor will submit a bid for the contract with probability 0.40. What is the probability of getting the deal?

2–64. A realtor is trying to sell a large piece of property. He believes there is a 0.90 probability that the property will be sold in the next six months if the local economy continues to improve throughout the period, and a 0.50 probability the property will be sold if the local economy does not continue its improvement during the period. A state economist consulted by the realtor believes there is a 0.70 chance the economy will continue its improvement during the next six months. What is the probability that the piece of property will be sold during the period?

2–65. Holland America Cruise Lines has three luxury cruise ships that sail to Alaska during the summer months. Since the business is very competitive, it is important that the ships run full during the summer if the company is to turn a profit on this line. A tourism expert hired by Holland America believes there is a 0.92 chance the ships will sail full during the

Answers

2–62.
_____
0.86

2–64.
_____
0.78

coming summer if the dollar does not appreciate against European currencies, and a 0.75 chance they will sail full if the dollar does appreciate in Europe (appreciation of the dollar in Europe draws American tourists there, away from American destinations). Economists believe the dollar has a 0.23 chance of appreciating against European currencies soon. What is the probability the ships will sail full?

2–66. In the Saflok® problem, problem 2–40, suppose that 90% of the time when the card is inserted, the door should open because it is not locked from inside. When the door should open, a green light will appear with probability 0.98. When the door should not open, a green light may still appear (an electronic error) 5% of the time. Suppose that you just inserted the card and the light is green. What is the probability that the door will actually open?

2–67. A chemical plant has an emergency alarm system. When an emergency situation exists, the alarm sounds with probability 0.95. When an emergency situation does not exist, the alarm system sounds with probability 0.02. A real emergency situation is a rare event, with probability 0.004. Given that the alarm has just sounded, what is the probability that a real emergency situation exists?

2–68. When the economic situation is "high," a certain economic indicator rises with probability 0.6. When the economic situation is "medium," the economic indicator rises with probability 0.3. When the economic situation is "low," the indicator rises with probability 0.1. The economy is high 15% of the time, it is medium 70% of the time, and it is low 15% of the time. Given that the indicator has just gone up, what is the probability that the economic situation is high?

2–69. An oil explorer orders seismic tests to determine whether oil is likely to be found in a certain drilling area. The seismic tests have a known reliability: when oil does exist in the testing area, the test will indicate so 85% of the time; when oil does not exist in the test area, 10% of the time the test will erroneously indicate that it does exist. The explorer believes that the probability of existence of an oil deposit in the test area is 0.4. If a test is conducted and indicates the presence of oil, what is the probability that an oil deposit really exists?

2–70. Before marketing new products nationally, companies often test them on samples of potential customers. Such tests have a known reliability. For a particular product type, it is known that a test will indicate success of the product 75% of the time if the product is indeed successful and 15% of the time when the product is not successful. From past experience with similar products, a company knows that a new product has a 0.60 chance of success on the national market. If the test indicates that the product will be successful, what is the probability that it really will be successful?

2–71. A market research field worker needs to interview married couples about use of a certain product. The researcher arrives at a residential building with three apartments. From the names on the mailboxes downstairs, the interviewer infers that a married couple lives in one apartment, two men live in another, and two women live in the third apartment. The researcher goes upstairs and finds that there are no names or numbers on the three doors, so that it is impossible to tell in which of the three apartments the married couple lives. The researcher chooses a door at random and knocks. A woman answers the door. Having seen a woman at the door, what *now* is the probability of having reached the married couple? Make the (possibly unrealistic) assumptions that if the two men's apartment was reached, a woman cannot answer the door; if the two women's apartment was reached, then only a woman can answer; and that if the married couple was reached, then the probability of a woman at the door is 1/2. Also assume a 1/3 prior probability of reaching the married couple. Are you surprised by the numerical answer you obtained?

2–9 Summary and Review of Terms

In this chapter, we discussed the basic ideas of probability. We defined **probability** as a relative measure of our belief in the occurrence of an **event**. We defined a **sample space** as the set of all possible outcomes in a given situation and saw that an event is a set within the sample space. We set some rules for handling probabilities:

the **rule of unions,** the definition of **conditional probability,** the **law of total probability, De Morgan's rule,** and **Bayes' theorem.** We also defined **mutually exclusive events** and **independence of events.** We saw how certain computations are possible in the case of independent events, and we saw how we may test whether events are independent.

In the next chapter, we will extend the ideas of probability and discuss random variables and probability distributions. These will bring us closer to statistical inference, the main subject of this book.

ADDITIONAL PROBLEMS

2–72. WLDN (AM 1120) is Walden Pond Radio, an offbeat radio station located near Walden Pond in eastern Massachusetts. On January 29, 1991, the following conversation was heard on this radio station.

Weatherman: And the temperature now is 37 degrees.
DJ: But our thermometer outside the studio is not very accurate, is it?
Weatherman: You are right, Joe. As soon as the sun hits it, the mercury just bounces all over the place. I would say that there is only a 3% chance that the temperature we report at any given time is correct.

Assume that "correct" means correct to within a degree, and that temperature readings are independent of each other. Use the information above to answer the following two questions.

a. If I listen to the temperature report on this radio station at three different times, what is the probability that I will hear at least one correct temperature?

b. In three times, what is the probability that all three reported temperatures are correct?

2–73. AT&T was running commercials in 1990 aimed at luring back customers who may have switched to one of the other long-distance phone service providers. One such commercial shows a businessman trying to reach Phoenix and mistakenly getting Fiji, where a half-naked native on a beach responds incomprehensibly in Polynesian. When asked about this advertisement, AT&T admitted that the portrayed incident did not actually take place but added that this was an enactment of something that "could happen".[13] Suppose that one in 200 long-distance telephone calls is misdirected. What is the probability that at least one in five attempted telephone calls reaches the wrong number? (Assume independence of attempts.)

2–74. Refer to the information in the previous problem. Given that your long-distance telephone call is misdirected, there is a 2% chance that you will reach a foreign country (such as Fiji). Suppose that I am now going to dial a single long-distance number, what is the probability that I will erroneously reach a foreign country?

2–75. The probability that a builder of airport terminals will win a contract for construction of terminals in country A is 0.40, and the probability that it will win a contract in country B is 0.30. The company has a 0.10 chance of winning the contracts in both countries. What is the probability that the company will win at least one of these two prospective contracts?

2–76. The probability that a consumer entering a retail outlet for microcomputers and software packages will buy a computer of a certain type is 0.15. The probability that the consumer will buy a particular software package is 0.10. There is a 0.05 probability that the consumer will buy both the computer and the software package. What is the probability that the consumer will buy either the computer, or the software package, or both?

2–77. The probability that a graduating senior will pass the CPA examination is 0.60. The probability that the graduating senior will both pass the CPA examination and get a job offer

Answers

2–72.
———
0.0873,
0.000027

2–74.
———
0.0001

2–76.
———
0.2

---

[13] While this may seem virtually impossible due to the different dialing procedure for foreign countries, AT&T argues that erroneously dialing the prefix 679 instead of 617, for example, would get you Fiji instead of Massachusetts.

Answers

2–78.

0.60

2–80.

No

2–82.

0.388

2–84.

0.5905,
0.4095

2–86.

0.132

is 0.40. Suppose that the student just found out that she passed the CPA examination. What is the probability that she will be offered a job?

2–78. Two stocks, A and B, are known to be related in that both are in the same industry. The probability that stock A will go up in price tomorrow is 0.20, and the probability that both stocks A and B will go up tomorrow is 0.12. Suppose that tomorrow you find that stock A did go up in price. What is the probability that stock B went up as well?

2–79. The probability that production will increase if interest rates decline more than one-half of a percentage point for a given period is 0.72. The probability that interest rates will decline by more than one-half of a percentage point in the period in question is 0.25. What is the probability that, for the period in question, both the interest rate will decline and production will increase?

2–80. A large foreign automaker is interested in identifying its target market in the United States. The automaker conducts a survey of potential buyers of its high-performance sports car and finds that 35% of the potential buyers consider engineering quality among the car's most desirable features and that 50% of the people surveyed consider sporty design to be among the car's most desirable features. Out of the people surveyed, 25% consider *both* engineering quality and sporty design to be among the car's most desirable features. Based on this information, do you believe that potential buyers' perceptions of the two features are independent? Explain.

2–81. Consider the situation in problem 2–80. Three consumers are chosen randomly from among a group of potential buyers of the high-performance automobile. What is the probability that all three of them consider engineering quality to be among the most important features of the car? What is the probability that at least one of them considers this quality to be among the most important ones? How do you justify your computations?

2–82. A financial service company advertises its services in magazines, runs billboard ads on major highways, and advertises its services on the radio. The company estimates that there is a 0.10 probability that a given individual will see the billboard ad during the week, a 0.15 chance that he or she will see the ad in a magazine, and a 0.20 chance that he or she will hear the advertisement on the radio during the week. What is the probability that a randomly chosen member of the population in the area will be exposed to at least one method of advertising during a given week? (Assume independence.)

2–83. An accounting firm carries an advertisement in *The Wall Street Journal*. The firm estimates that 60% of the people in the potential market read *The Wall Street Journal*; research further shows that 85% of the people who read the *Journal* remember seeing the advertisement when questioned about it afterward. What percentage of the people in the firm's potential market see and remember the advertisement?

2–84. A quality control engineer knows that 10% of the microprocessor chips produced by a machine are defective. Out of a large shipment, five chips are chosen at random. What is the probability that none of them is defective? What is the probability that at least one is defective? Explain.

2–85. A fashion designer has been working with the colors green, black, and red in preparing for the coming season's fashions. The designer estimates that there is a 0.3 chance that the color green will be "in" during the coming season, a 0.2 chance that black will be among the season's colors, and a 0.15 chance that red will be popular. Assuming that colors are chosen independently of each other for inclusion in new fashions, what is the probability that the designer will be successful with at least one of her colors?

2–86. A company president always invites one of her three vice presidents to attend business meetings and claims that her choice of the accompanying V.P. is random. One of the three has not been invited even once in five meetings. What is the probability of such an occurrence if the choice is indeed random? What conclusion would you reach based on your answer?

2–87. A multinational corporation is considering starting a subsidiary in an Asian country. Management realizes that the success of the new subsidiary depends, in part, on the ensuing political climate in the target country. Management estimates that the probability of success (in terms of resulting revenues of the subsidiary during its first year of operation) is 0.55 if the prevailing political situation is favorable, 0.30 if the political situation is neutral, and 0.10 if the political situation during the year is unfavorable. Management further believes that the probabilities of favorable, neutral, and unfavorable political situations are 0.6, 0.2, and 0.2, respectively. What is the success probability of the new subsidiary?

2–88.   The probability that a shipping company will obtain authorization to include a certain port of call in its shipping route is dependent on whether or not certain legislation is passed. The company believes there is a 0.5 chance that *both* the relevant legislation will pass *and* it will get the required authorization to visit the port. The company further estimates that the probability that the legislation will pass is 0.75. If the company should find that the relevant legislation just passed, what is the probability that authorization to visit the port will be granted?

2–89.   The probability that a bank customer will default on a loan is 0.04 if the economy is high and 0.13 if the economy is not high. Suppose the probability that the economy will be high is 0.65. What is the probability that the person will default on the loan?

2–90.   Housing starts (the number of residential construction projects per month) are considered a leading indicator of economic activity. Housing starts have turned upward prior to the emergence of economic recovery in six of the eight postwar recessions.[14] If housing starts are currently increasing, what is the probability that an economic recovery will follow? Comment on your method of estimating this probability.

2–91.   SwissAir maintains a mailing list of people who have taken trips to Europe in the last three years. The airline knows that 8% of the people on the mailing list will make arrangements to fly SwissAir during the period following their being mailed a brochure. In an experimental mailing, 20 people are mailed a brochure. What is the probability that at least one of them will book a flight with SwissAir during the coming season?

2–92.   A company's internal accounting standards are set so as to ensure that no more than 5% of the accounts are in error. From time to time, the company collects a random sample of accounts and checks to see how many are in error. If the error rate is indeed 5%, and 10 accounts are chosen at random, what is the probability that none will be in error?

2–93.   At a certain university, 30% of the students who take basic statistics are freshmen, 35% are sophomores, 20% are juniors, and 15% are seniors. From records of the statistics department it is found that out of the freshmen who take the basic statistics course 20% get As; out of the sophomores who take the course 30% get As; out of the juniors 35% get As; and out of the seniors who take the course 40% get As. Given that a student got an A in basic statistics, what is the probability that he or she is a senior?

2–94.   The probability that a new product will be successful if a competitor does not come up with a similar product is 0.67. The probability that the new product will be successful in the presence of a competitor's new product is 0.42. The probability that the competing firm will come out with a new product during the period in question is 0.35. What is the probability that the product will be a success?

2–95.   In an effort to increase productivity, the Motorola Corporation has instituted new book-balancing procedures. These procedures are reported to ensure that credit or debit entries in the general ledger are correct 99.92% of the time.[15] If a random sample of 1,000 book entries are selected (out of the company's more than 1.3 million monthly entries), what is the probability that at least one error will be found?

2–96.   Blackjack is a popular casino game where the objective is to reach a card count greater than the dealer's without exceeding 21. One version of the game is referred to as the "hole card" version. Here, the dealer starts by drawing a card for himself/herself and putting it aside, face down, without the players seeing what it is. This is the dealer's *hole card* (and the origin of the expression "an ace in the hole"). At the end of the game, the dealer has the option of turning this additional card face up if it may help him or her win the game. The no-

Answers

2–88.
——
0.6666

2–90.
——
0.75

2–92.
——
0.599

2–94.
——
0.583

---

[14] "As Housing Starts Go, So Goes the Economy," *Business Week,* (February 4, 1991), p. 20.
[15] "Make Your Office More Productive," *Fortune* (February 25, 1991), pp. 72–76.

Answers

hole-card version of the game is exactly the same, except that at the end of the game the dealer has the option of *drawing* the additional card from the deck for the same purpose (assume that the deck is shuffled prior to this draw). *Conceptually,* what is the difference between the two versions of the game? Is there any *practical* difference between the two versions as far as a player is concerned?

2–97. Diamonds may soon become useful in making semiconductors for use in communication satellites. Theory predicts that chips from diamond films would run faster than the currently used silicon chips, tolerate higher temperatures than silicon chips, and would be immune to radiation damage (encountered in space).[16] Suppose that the probabilities of these three events are 0.9, 0.9, and 0.95, respectively. The three events are believed to be independent. Cost considerations suggest that diamond semiconductors should be developed only if we can be at least 70% sure that all three properties described above hold. Should the project be considered?

2–98. Recall from Chapter 1 that the median is that number such that 1/2 the observations lie above it and 1/2 the observations lie below it. If a random sample of two items is to be drawn from some population, what is the probability that the population median will lie between these two data points?

2–99. Extend your result from the previous problem to a general case as follows. A random sample of n elements is to be drawn from some population and arranged according to their value, from smallest to largest. What is the probability that the population median will lie somewhere between the smallest and the largest values of the drawn data?

2–100. (This problem is a little harder than the rest. Once you have solved it, experiment with different starting probabilities and different discounting factors.) A research journal states: "Rejection rate for submitted manuscripts: 86%." A prospective author believes that the editor's statement reflects the probability of acceptance of any author's *first* submission to the journal. The author further believes that for any subsequent submission, an author's acceptance probability is 10% lower than the probability he or she had for acceptance of the preceding submission. Thus, the author believes that the probability of acceptance of a first submission to the journal is $1 - 0.86 = 0.14$, the probability of acceptance of the second submission is 10% lower, that is $(0.14)(0.90) = 0.126$, and so on for the third submission, fourth submission, etc. Suppose the author plans to continue submitting papers to the journal indefinitely until one is accepted. What is the probability that at least one paper will eventually be accepted by the journal?[17]

---

[16] "Will Diamond Transistors Leave Silicon in the Dust?" *Business Week* (February 11, 1991), p. 80.

[17] Since its appearance in the first edition of the book, this interesting problem has been generalized. See N. H. Josephy and A. D. Aczel, "A Note on a Journal Selection Problem," *ZOR-Methods and Models of Operations Research* 34 (1990), pp. 469–76.

THE PATRIOT ANTIMISSILE SYSTEM

*P*art of the great success of the war against Iraq was due to the incredibly high performance of Raytheon Corporation's Patriot Missile System. The Patriot missile was designed to intercept enemy missiles and destroy them in the air. The missile's rate of successful intercepts of Iraqi Scud missiles aimed at Israel and Saudi Arabia surprised even its makers. At a speech made at Raytheon's headquarters in Andover, Massachusetts, on February 15, 1991, President Bush praised the company and stated that (in a part of the campaign against Iraq) 41 out of 42 incoming Scud missiles were intercepted by the Patriot system. Exhibit 1, reproduced by permission from *Time* (February 14, 1991, p. 47) demonstrates how the missile system works.

From publicly available sources, we may infer the following about the Patriot system. There is a 99% chance that the system's radar will detect an incoming enemy missile such as the Scud. Once the missile is detected, a Patriot missile is immediately fired and has a 98.5% chance of exploding close enough to the incoming missile so that its fragments will damage the incoming missile. If this happens, there is a 65% chance that the enemy warhead will explode in the air and thus cause no damage. What is the probability that an incoming missile will be totally destroyed in the air? Interpret the president's statement. Based on the numbers, what event was President Bush likely referring to in his address?[18]

---

[18] Some news reports in March 1992 have questioned the early assessments of the Patriot's successes, and at this writing only 10% of missile firings during the war are confirmed as hits.

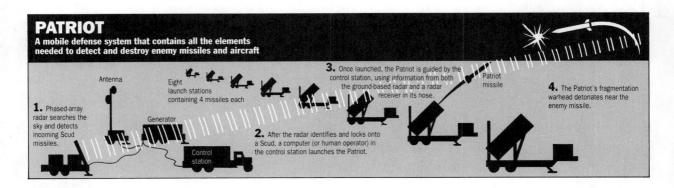

PATRIOT
A mobile defense system that contains all the elements needed to detect and destroy enemy missiles and aircraft

Antenna

Eight launch stations containing 4 missiles each

3. Once launched, the Patriot is guided by the control station, using information from both the ground-based radar and a radar receiver in its nose.

Patriot missile

4. The Patriot's fragmentation warhead detonates near the enemy missile.

1. Phased-array radar searches the sky and detects incoming Scud missiles.

Generator

Control station

2. After the radar identifies and locks onto a Scud, a computer (or human operator) in the control station launches the Patriot.

RANDOM VARIABLES

INTRODUCTION

n 1725, two well-known Swiss mathematicians, the brothers Daniel and Nicholas Bernoulli, went to St. Petersburg, Russia. While there, the two developed the idea of what has become known as the Petersburg paradox.

Consider the following game of chance. A coin is tossed, and if a head appears, you win two dollars. If a head does not appear, the coin is tossed again. If a head appears now, you win four dollars. If a head does not appear, the coin is tossed again; if a head appears this time, you win eight dollars; and so on. How much should you be willing to pay for the privilege of playing this game?

Unlike other games, this game is worth an *infinite* amount of money. The probabilities of obtaining greater and greater rewards at this game become very small very quickly, but at the same time the possible rewards become fantastically high. It turns out that no finite sum of money is a fair price for playing the game. After reading this chapter, you will understand the reason for this. The game, however, is a mathematical oddity and has no practical implications.

The amount of money you may win at a particular game of chance is an example of a *random variable*. The maximum amount of money you should be willing to pay for playing the game (assuming you are not a risk taker, a concept discussed in Chapter 15) is the *mean,* or *expected value,* of the random variable. In this chapter, we will define random variables and probability distributions. We will distinguish two kinds of random variables: discrete and continuous. We will define the mean and the standard deviation of a random variable and see how they are computed. We will also discuss special random variables that occur in practice, particularly the binomial random variable.

3–2 Discrete Random Variables

In Chapter 2, we discussed events and their probabilities. Here we extend these notions to more involved situations. We will be interested in the *numerical values* associated with the outcomes of an experiment (such as rolling a die). Since the outcome of an experiment may vary from trial to trial, the associated numerical value (the number appearing on the die) is a *variable*. Since the outcomes are determined by chance, the variable is *random*. We define a random variable as follows.

> A **random variable** is a variable that takes on different numerical values, determined by chance.

A random variable may also be viewed as a function of the sample space of the experiment, but we will not make use of this definition. The probability law governing the random variable—the assignment of probabilities to the different possible values of the random variable—is called the *probability distribution* of the random variable.

Random variables may be either *discrete* or *continuous*. A discrete random variable is one that takes on values that may be counted, such as 0, 1, 2, 3, . . . , although the values need not be integers and need not be positive.

A random variable is **discrete** if it can assume at most a countable number of values.

A **continuous** random variable, on the other hand, is one that may take on any value in an interval of numbers (its possible values are uncountably infinite).

For a discrete random variable, we may list the probabilities of the different values the variable may take. This is done by a table of values, a formula, or a graph. Each value of the random variable is assigned a probability, called a *probability mass*.

The **probability distribution** of a discrete random variable, also called the **probability mass function** of the random variable, is a list, a formula, or a graph that assigns a probability to each value of the random variable.

Let us now establish some notation. We will denote a random variable by a capital letter, usually X, although any capital letter will do. When two variables are involved (as in later chapters), we will call one of them X and the other Y, and so on if more variables are considered.

We will use lower-case letters to denote particular values of a random variable. Thus, the notation $P(X = x)$ stands for the probability that the random variable X will take on the *particular value x*. For example, $P(X = 5) = 0.2$ means that the probability that the random variable X will take on the value $x = 5$ is 0.2. We will sometimes use the shortened notation $P(x)$ for $P(X = x)$; here we say $P(5) = 0.2$. The following rules must be satisfied by the probability distribution of any discrete random variable.

The probability distribution of a discrete random variable X must satisfy the following two conditions.

$$1. \quad P(x) \geq 0 \text{ for all values } x \qquad\qquad (3\text{--}1)$$

$$2. \quad \sum_{\text{all } x} P(x) = 1 \qquad\qquad (3\text{--}2)$$

These conditions must hold because the $P(x)$ values are probabilities. Equation 3–1 states that all probabilities must be greater than or equal to zero, as we know from Chapter 2. For the second rule, equation 3–2, note the following. For each value x, $P(x) = P(X = x)$ is the probability of the event that the random variable equals x. Since by definition *all x* means all the values the random variable X may take, and since X may take on only one value at a time, the occurrences of these values are mutually exclusive events, and one of them must take place. Therefore, the sum of all the probabilities $P(x)$ must be 1.00.

EXAMPLE (a)

Each day a local newspaper receives orders for advertisements to appear in the following morning's issue. The number of ads to be placed depends on many factors, such as the day of the week, the season, the economy in general, and the state of local business. The number of ads placed daily in the paper is random. Let X denote the number of ads placed in the paper daily. Thus, X is a random variable; it is an uncertain quantity governed by some probability law. Since the number of ads to be placed daily may only

TABLE 3–1 Probability Distribution of the Daily Number of Ads Placed in the Newspaper

x	P(x)
0	0.1
1	0.2
2	0.3
3	0.2
4	0.1
5	0.1
	1.00

have integer values such as 0, 1, 2, 3, . . . , X is a discrete random variable. Table 3–1 is a list of the possible number of ads placed daily and their corresponding probabilities. This list is the probability distribution of the random variable X.

Note that the probabilities of the different values of the random variable are all non-negative, and they sum to 1.00 as required (otherwise, there would be missing values with a probability greater than zero that should have been included). Note that the random variable does not take on any value greater than five. We are assuming that the newspaper cannot print more than five ads on any day.

The probability distribution tells us many things about the random variable in question. For example, we know that the probability that three ads will be placed on a given day is 0.2, and the probability that two ads will be placed is 0.3. Since occurrences of different values of the random variable are mutually exclusive events, the probability that either two or three ads will be placed on a given day (the union of the two events $X = 2$ and $X = 3$) is just the sum of the two probabilities: $P(2) + P(3) = 0.3 + 0.2 = 0.5$. The probability that anywhere from one to four ads will be placed on a given day is 0.8 (the sum of the probabilities of the values 1 to 4). Other probabilities are obtained similarly by finding in the table the probabilities of the required values of the random variable.

We may want to visualize the probability distribution of a random variable. We do this by way of a graph of the probabilities against the values x. Figure 3–1 is a graph showing the probability distribution of the number of ads placed daily. The probability of each value is the height of the line above the particular value of the random variable. For example, the height of the line over the value $x = 0$ is 0.1 because $P(X = 0) = 0.1$.

FIGURE 3–1
A Graph of the Probability Distribution of the Number of Ads Placed Daily with the Newspaper [Example (a)]

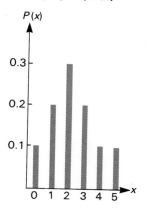

In practice, where do probabilities such as the ones given in Table 3–1 come from? The paper keeps records of information on the number of ads appearing every day. The long-term frequencies of occurrence of the different values are computed from these records, and we consider these frequencies of occurrence as probabilities of the number of advertisements.

In other cases, probabilities may be derived from theoretical considerations. These lead to probability distributions of special random variables useful in statistics. Such distributions are tabulated and may be found in statistics books. Such tables are included in Appendix C of this book. We will encounter a few of these distributions in this chapter and in the following ones.

Cumulative Distribution Function

The probability distribution of a discrete random variable lists the probabilities of occurrence of different values of the random variable. We may be interested in *cumulative* probabilities of the random variable. That is, we may be interested in the probability that the value of the random variable is *at most* some value x. This is the sum of all the probabilities of the values i of X that are less than or equal to x. We define the *cumulative distribution function* (also called *cumulative probability function*) as follows.

The **cumulative distribution function,** $F(x)$, of a discrete random variable X is

$$F(x) = P(X \leq x) = \sum_{\text{all } i \leq x} P(i) \qquad\qquad (3\text{–}3)$$

Table 3–2 gives the cumulative distribution function of the random variable of Example (a). Note that each entry of $F(x)$ is equal to the sum of the corresponding values of $P(i)$ for all values i less than or equal to x. For example, $F(3) = P(X \leq 3) = P(0) + P(1) + P(2) + P(3) = 0.1 + 0.2 + 0.3 + 0.2 = 0.8$. Of course, $F(5) = 1.00$ because $F(5)$ is the sum of the probabilities of all values that are less than or equal to 5, and 5 is the largest value of the random variable.

Figure 3–2 shows $F(x)$ for the number of ads placed with the paper on a given day. All cumulative distribution functions are nondecreasing and equal 1.00 at the largest possible value of the random variable.

Let us consider a few probabilities. The probability that the number of ads

TABLE 3–2   The Cumulative Distribution Function of the Number of Ads [Example (a)]

x	P(x)	F(x)
0	0.1	0.1
1	0.2	0.3
2	0.3	0.6
3	0.2	0.8
4	0.1	0.9
5	0.1	1.00
	1.00	

FIGURE 3–2   Cumulative Distribution Function of Number of Ads

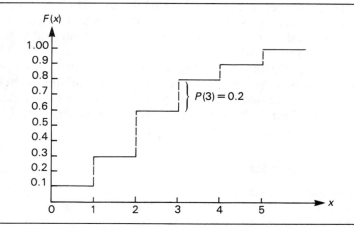

placed in tomorrow's paper will be less than or equal to three is given by $F(3) = 0.8$. This is illustrated, using the probability distribution, in Figure 3–3.

The probability that *more than* one ad will be placed, $P(X > 1)$, is equal to $1 - F(1) = 1 - 0.3 = 0.7$. This is so because $F(1) = P(X \le 1)$, and $P(X \le 1) + P(X > 1) = 1$ (the two events are complements of each other). This is demonstrated in Figure 3–4.

The probability that anywhere from one to three ads will be placed is $P(1 \le X \le 3)$. From Figure 3–5 we see that this is equal to $F(3) - F(0) = 0.8 - 0.1 = 0.7$. (This is the probability that the number of ads placed will be less than or equal to three and greater than zero.) This, and other probability questions, could certainly be answered directly, without use of $F(x)$. We could just add the probabilities: $P(1) + P(2) + P(3) = 0.2 + 0.3 + 0.2 = 0.7$. The advantage of

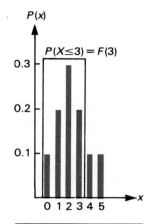

FIGURE 3–3
The Probability that at Most Three Ads Will Be Placed

FIGURE 3–4 The Probability that More than One Ad Will Be Placed

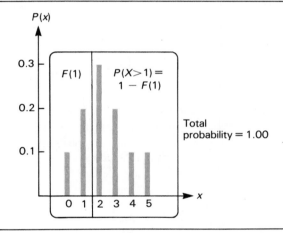

FIGURE 3–5 The Probability that Anywhere from One to Three Ads Will Be Placed

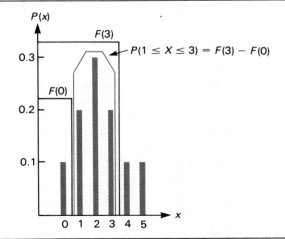

$F(x)$ is that probabilities may be computed by few operations (usually subtraction of two values of $F(x)$, as in this example), whereas use of $P(x)$ often requires lengthier computations.

If the probability distribution is available, use it directly. If, on the other hand, you have a cumulative distribution function for the random variable in question, you may use it as we have demonstrated. In either case, it is always helpful to draw a picture of the probability distribution. Then look at the signs in the probability statement, such as $P(X \leq x)$ versus $P(X < x)$, to see which values to include and which ones to leave out of the probability computation.

PROBLEMS

Answers

3–1. The number of telephone calls arriving at an exchange during any given minute between noon and 1:00 P.M. on a weekday is a random variable with the following probability distribution.

x	P(x)
0	0.3
1	0.2
2	0.2
3	0.1
4	0.1
5	0.1

a. Verify that $P(x)$ is a probability distribution.
b. Find the cumulative distribution function of the random variable.
c. Use the cumulative distribution function to find the probability that between 12:34 and 12:35 P.M. more than two calls will arrive at the exchange.

3–2.

c. 0.80

d. 0.90

3–2. Typing errors per page for a certain typing pool are known to follow the probability distribution:

x	P(x)
0	0.01
1	0.09
2	0.30
3	0.20
4	0.20
5	0.10
6	0.10

a. Verify that $P(x)$ is a probability distribution.
b. Find the cumulative distribution function.
c. Find the probability that at most four errors will be made on a page.
d. Find the probability that at least two errors will be made on a page.

3–3. The percentage of people (to the nearest ten) responding to an advertisement is a random variable with the following probability distribution.

x(%)	P(x)
0	0.10
10	0.20
20	0.35
30	0.20
40	0.10
50	0.05

a. Show that $P(x)$ is a probability distribution.

b. Find the cumulative distribution function.

c. Find the probability that more than 20% will respond to the ad.

3–4.   An automobile dealership records the number of cars sold each day. The data are used in calculating the following probability distribution of daily sales.

x	P(x)
0	0.1
1	0.1
2	0.2
3	0.2
4	0.3
5	0.1

a. Find the probability that the number of cars sold tomorrow will be between two and four (both inclusive).

b. Find the cumulative distribution function of the number of cars sold per day.

c. Show that $P(x)$ is a probability distribution.

3–5.   Consider the roll of a pair of dice, and let X denote the sum of the two numbers appearing on the dice. Find the probability distribution of X, and find the cumulative distribution function. What is the most likely sum?

3–6.   The number of intercity shipment orders arriving daily at a transportation company is a random variable X with the following probability mass function.

x	P(x)
0	0.1
1	0.2
2	0.4
3	0.1
4	0.1
5	0.1

a. Verify that $P(x)$ is a proper probability mass function.

b. Find the cumulative probability function of X.

c. Use the cumulative probability function computed in b to find the probability that anywhere from one to four shipment orders will arrive on a given day.

d. When more than three orders arrive on a given day, the company incurs additional costs due to the need to hire extra drivers and loaders. What is the probability that extra costs will be incurred on a given day?

e. Assuming that the number of orders arriving on different days are independent of each other, what is the probability that no orders will be received over a period of five working days?

f. Again assuming independence of orders on different days, what is the probability that extra costs will be incurred two days in a row?

3–7.   The number of wooden sailboats constructed per month in a small shipyard is a random variable with the following probability distribution.

x	P(x)
2	0.2
3	0.2
4	0.3
5	0.1
6	0.1
7	0.05
8	0.05

Answers

3–4.

a. 0.7

3–6.

c. 0.8

d. 0.2

e. 0.00001

f. 0.04

Answers

3–8.
_____

b. 0.6
c. 0.9

a. Find the probability that the number of boats constructed next month will be between four and seven (both inclusive).

b. Find the cumulative distribution function of X.

c. Use $F(x)$ computed in b to evaluate the probability that the number of boats constructed in a month will be less than or equal to six.

d. Find the probability that the number of boats made will be greater than three and less than or equal to six.

3–8. The number of defects in a machine-made product is a random variable, X, with the following probability distribution:

x	P(x)
0	0.1
1	0.2
2	0.3
3	0.3
4	0.1

a. Show that $P(x)$ is a probability distribution.

b. Find the probability $P(1 < X \leq 3)$.

c. Find the probability $P(1 \leq X \leq 4)$.

d. Find $F(x)$.

3–9. Returns on investments overseas, especially in Europe and the Pacific Rim, are expected to be higher than those of American markets in the 1990s, and analysts are now recommending investments in international portfolios.[1] An investment consultant believes that the probability distribution of returns (in percent per year) on one such portfolio is as given below.

x (%)	P(x)
9	0.05
10	0.15
11	0.30
12	0.20
13	0.15
14	0.10
15	0.05

a. Verify that $P(x)$ is a proper probability distribution.

b. What is the probability that returns will be at least 12%?

c. Find the cumulative distribution of returns.

3–3 Expected Values of Discrete Random Variables

In Chapter 1, we discussed summary measures of data sets. The most important summary measures discussed were the mean and the variance (and also the square root of the variance, the standard deviation). We saw that the mean is a measure of *centrality*, or *location*, of the data or population, and that the variance and the standard deviation measure the *variability*, or *spread*, of our observations.

Recall in particular how we computed the mean and the variance of a set of grouped data (equations 1–8 and 1–9). For the mean, we multiplied the data (the midpoints) by their frequencies and summed, and then we divided by the sum of the

_____

[1] "Your Money," *Working Woman* (March 1991), p. 58.

frequencies (n). Since a probability distribution may be viewed as a distribution of long-term frequencies, we may define the mean of a probability distribution in a similar way. The mean of a probability distribution of a random variable is a measure of the centrality of the probability distribution. It is a measure that considers both the values of the random variable and their probabilities. The mean is a *weighted average* of the possible values of the random variable—the weights being the probabilities.

The mean of the probability distribution of a random variable is called the *expected value* of the random variable (sometimes called the *expectation* of the random variable). The reason for this name is that the mean is the average value of the random variable, and therefore it is the value we "expect" to occur. We denote the mean by two notations: μ for *mean* (as in Chapter 1 for a population) and $E(X)$ for *expected value of X*. In situations where no ambiguity is possible, we will often use μ. In cases where we want to stress the fact that we are talking about the expected value of a particular random variable (here, X), we will use the notation $E(X)$. The expected value of a discrete random variable is defined as follows.

The **expected value** of a discrete random variable X is equal to the sum of all values of the random variable, each value multiplied by its probability.

$$\mu = E(X) = \sum_{\text{all } x} xP(x) \qquad (3\text{--}4)$$

Suppose a coin is tossed. If it lands heads you win a dollar, but if it lands tails you lose a dollar. What is the expected value of this game? Intuitively, you know you have an even chance of winning or losing the same amount, and so the average or expected value is zero. Your payoff from this game is a random variable, and we find its expected value from equation 3–4: $E(X) = (1)(1/2) + (-1)(1/2) = 0$. The definition of an expected value, or mean, of a random variable thus conforms with our intuition. Incidentally, games of chance with an expected value of zero are called *fair games*.

Let us now return to Example (a) and find the expected value of the random variable involved—the expected number of ads placed with the newspaper on a given day. It is convenient to compute the mean of a discrete random variable using a table. In the first column of the table we write the values of the random variable. In the second column we write the probabilities of the different values, and in the third column we write the products $xP(x)$ for each value x. We then add the entries in the third column, giving us $E(X) = \sum xP(x)$, as required by equation 3–4. This is shown for Example (a) in Table 3–3.

TABLE 3–3 Computing the Expected Number of Ads [Example (a)]

x	P(x)	xP(x)
0	0.1	0
1	0.2	0.2
2	0.3	0.6
3	0.2	0.6
4	0.1	0.4
5	0.1	0.5
	1.00	2.3 ⟵ Mean, $E(X)$

FIGURE 3–6
The Mean of a Discrete
Random Variable as a Center
of Mass [Example (a)]

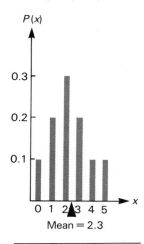

As indicated in the table, $\mu = E(X) = 2.3$. We can say that, on the average, 2.3 ads are placed daily. As this example shows, the mean does not have to be one of the values of the random variable. There are no days with 2.3 ads, but 2.3 is the average number of ads. It is the *expected* number of ads on a given day, although here the exact expectation will not be realized on any day.

As the weighted average of the values of the random variable, with probabilities as weights, the mean is the *center of mass* of the probability distribution. This is demonstrated for Example (a) in Figure 3–6.

Let us now return to the example with which we opened this chapter and compute the expected value of the Petersburg game. The probability of winning two dollars is $1/2$ (the probability that the coin lands heads the first time). Similarly, the probability of winning four dollars is the probability that the coin lands tails the first time and heads the second time. The probability of this event is (by independence): $(1/2)(1/2) = 1/4$. By the same argument, the probability of winning eight dollars is $1/8$, and so on. Let us now use equation 3–4 to compute the expected value of the game:

$$E(X) = \Sigma x P(x) = 2(1/2) + 4(1/4) + 8(1/8) + \cdots = 1 + 1 + 1 + \cdots = \infty$$

Since the game continues until the first time heads appears, we must allow for the event occurring at *any* toss, and therefore the sum has infinitely many terms. Since every term is equal to 1.00, the sum of all the terms is infinite. Thus, theoretically, no finite amount of money is a fair price for playing this game, which has an infinite expected payoff. The game has no practical implications. Since the probabilities of winning greater and greater amounts decrease very quickly, you will probably not gain a very large amount of money at any play of this game.

The Expected Value of a Function of a Random Variable

It is possible to compute the expected value of a *function* of a random variable. Let $h(X)$ be a function of the discrete random variable X.

> The expected value of $h(X)$, a function of the discrete random variable X, is:
>
> $$E[h(X)] = \sum_{\text{all } x} h(x)P(x) \qquad (3\text{–}5)$$

The function $h(X)$ could be X^2, $3X^4$, log X, or any function. As we will see shortly, equation 3–5 is most useful for computing the expected value of the special function $h(X) = X^2$. But let us first look at a simpler example, where $h(X)$ is a *linear* function of X. A linear function of X is a straight-line relation: $h(X) = a + bX$, where a and b are numbers.

EXAMPLE (b)

Monthly sales of a certain product, recorded to the nearest thousand, are believed to follow the probability distribution given in Table 3–4. Suppose that the company has a fixed monthly production cost of $8,000 and that each item brings $2. Find the expected monthly profit from product sales.

The company's profit function from sales of the product is $h(X) = 2X - 8,000$. Equation 3–5 tells us that the expected value of $h(X)$ is the sum of the values of $h(X)$, each value multiplied by the probability of the particular value of X. We thus add two columns to Table 3–4: a column of values of $h(x)$ for all x and a column of the products $h(x)P(x)$. At the bottom of this column we find the required sum $E[h(X)] = \sum_{\text{all } x} h(x)P(x)$. This is done in Table 3–5. As shown in the table, expected monthly profit from sales of the product is $5,400.

TABLE 3–4 Probability Distribution of Monthly Product Sales [Example (b)]

Number of Items, x	P(x)
5,000	0.2
6,000	0.3
7,000	0.2
8,000	0.2
9,000	0.1
	1.00

TABLE 3–5 Computing Expected Profit for Example (b)

x	h(x)	P(x)	h(x)P(x)
5,000	2,000	0.2	400
6,000	4,000	0.3	1,200
7,000	6,000	0.2	1,200
8,000	8,000	0.2	1,600
9,000	10,000	0.1	1,000
		$E[h(X)] =$	5,400

In the case of a linear function of a random variable, as in Example (b), there is a possible simplification of our calculation of the mean of $h(X)$. The simplified formula of the expected value of a linear function of a random variable is as follows.

The expected value of a linear function of a random variable:

$$E(aX + b) = aE(X) + b \qquad (3\text{–}6)$$

where a and b are fixed numbers

Equation 3–6 holds for *any* random variable, discrete or continuous. Once you know the expected value of X, the expected value of $aX + b$ is just $aE(X) + b$. In Example (b) we could have obtained the expected profit by finding the mean of X first, and then multiplying the mean of X by 2 and subtracting from this the fixed cost of $8,000. The mean of X is 6,700 (prove this), and the expected profit is therefore: $E[h(X)] = E(2X - 8,000) = 2E(X) - 8,000 = 2(6,700) - 8,000 = 5,400$, as we obtained using Table 3–5.

As mentioned earlier, the most important expected value of a function of X is the expected value of $h(X) = X^2$. This is because this expected value helps us compute the *variance* of the random variable X and, through the variance, the standard deviation.

The Variance and the Standard Deviation of a Random Variable

The variance of a random variable is the expected squared deviation of the random variable from its mean. The idea is similar to that of the variance of a data set or a population, defined in Chapter 1. Probabilities of the values of the random variable are used as weights in the computation of the expected squared deviation from the mean of a discrete random variable. The definition of the variance follows. As with a population, we denote the variance of a random variable by σ^2. Another notation for the variance of X is $V(X)$.

The **variance** of a discrete random variable X is given by:

$$\sigma^2 = V(X) = E[(X - \mu)^2] = \sum_{\text{all } x} (x - \mu)^2 P(x) \qquad (3-7)$$

Using equation 3–7, it is possible to compute the variance of a discrete random variable by subtracting the mean μ from each value x of the random variable, squaring the result, multiplying it by the probability $P(x)$, and finally adding the results for all x. Let us apply equation 3–7 and find the variance of the number of daily ads in Example (a):

$$\sigma^2 = \sum (x - \mu)^2 P(x)$$

$$= (0 - 2.3)^2(0.1) + (1 - 2.3)^2(0.2) + (2 - 2.3)^2(0.3)$$
$$+ (3 - 2.3)^2(0.2) + (4 - 2.3)^2(0.1) + (5 - 2.3)^2(0.1)$$

$$= 2.01$$

There is, however, an easier way of computing the variance of a discrete random variable. It can be shown mathematically that equation 3–7 is equivalent to the following computational form of the variance.

Computational formula for the variance of a random variable:

$$\sigma^2 = V(X) = E(X^2) - [E(X)]^2 \qquad (3-8)$$

Equation 3–8 has the same relation to equation 3–7 as equation 1–7 has to equation 1–3 for the variance of a set of points.

Equation 3–8 states that the variance of X is equal to the expected value of X^2 minus the squared mean of X. In computing the variance using this equation, we use the definition of the expected value of a function of a discrete random variable, equation 3–5, in the special case $h(X) = X^2$. We compute x^2 for each x, multiply it by $P(x)$, and add for all x. This gives us $E(X^2)$. To get the variance, we subtract from $E(X^2)$ the mean of X, squared.

We now compute the variance of the random variable in Example (a) using this method. This is done in Table 3–6. The first column in the table gives the values of X, the second column gives the probabilities of these values, the third column gives the products of the values and their probabilities, and the fourth column is the product of the third column and the first (because we get $x^2 P(x)$ by just multiplying each entry $xP(x)$ by x from column one). At the bottom of the third column we find

TABLE 3–6 Computations Leading to the Variance of the Number of Ads in Example (a) Using the Short-Cut Formula (equation 3–8)

x	P(x)	xP(x)	x²P(x)
0	0.1	0	0
1	0.2	0.2	0.2
2	0.3	0.6	1.2
3	0.2	0.6	1.8
4	0.1	0.4	1.6
5	0.1	0.5	2.5
	1.00	2.3 ← Mean of X	7.3 ← Mean of X²

the mean of X, and at the bottom of the fourth column we find the mean of X^2. Finally, we perform the subtraction $E(X^2) - [E(X)]^2$ to get the variance of X:

$$V(X) = E(X^2) - [E(X)]^2 = 7.3 - (2.3)^2 = 2.01$$

This is the same value we found using the other formula for the variance, equation 3–7. Note that equation 3–8 holds true for *all* random variables, discrete or otherwise. Once we obtain the expected value of X^2 and the expected value of X, we can compute the variance of the random variable using this equation.

For random variables, as for data sets or populations, the standard deviation is equal to the (positive) square root of the variance. We denote the standard deviation of a random variable X by σ or by SD(X).

The **standard deviation** of a random variable:

$$\sigma = \text{SD}(X) = \sqrt{V(X)} \qquad (3–9)$$

In Example (a), the standard deviation is: $\sigma = \sqrt{2.01} = 1.418$.

What are the variance and the standard deviation, and how do we interpret their meaning? By definition, the variance is the average squared deviation of the values of the random variable from their mean. Thus, it is a measure of the *dispersion* of the possible values of the random variable about the mean. The variance gives us an idea of the variation or uncertainty associated with the random variable: the larger the variance, the further away from the mean are possible values of the random variable. Since the variance is a squared quantity, it is often more useful to consider its square root—the standard deviation of the random variable. When comparing two random variables, the one with the larger variance (standard deviation) is the more variable one. The risk associated with an investment is often measured by the standard deviation of investment returns. When comparing two investments with the same average (*expected*) return, the investment with the higher standard deviation is considered riskier (although a higher standard deviation implies that returns are expected to be more variable—both below *and above* the mean).

Variance of a Linear Function of a Random Variable

There is a formula, analogous to equation 3–6, that gives the variance of a linear function of a random variable. For a linear function of X given by $aX + b$, we have the following:

Variance of a linear function of a random variable:

$$V(aX + b) = a^2 V(X) = a^2\sigma^2 \qquad (3\text{--}10)$$

where a and b are fixed numbers

Using equation 3–10, we will find the variance of the profit in Example (b). The profit is given by $2X - 8,000$. We need to find the variance of X in this example. We find $E(X^2) = (5,000)^2(0.2) + (6,000)^2(0.3) + (7,000)^2(0.2) + (8,000)^2(0.2) + (9,000)^2(0.1) = 46,500,000$. The expected value of X is $E(X) = 6,700$. The variance of X is thus: $V(X) = E(X^2) - [E(X)]^2 = 46,500,000 - (6,700)^2 = 1,610,000$. Finally, we find the variance of the profit, using equation 3–10, as: $2^2(1,610,000) = 6,440,000$. The standard deviation of the profit is $\sqrt{6,440,000} = 2,537.72$.

Chebyshev's Theorem

The standard deviation is useful in obtaining bounds on the possible values of the random variable with certain probability. The bounds are obtainable from a well-known theorem, *Chebyshev's theorem* (the name is sometimes spelled Tchebychev, Tchebysheff, or any of a number of variations). The theorem says that for any number k greater than 1.00, the probability that the value of a given random variable will be *within k standard deviations* of the mean is at least $1 - 1/k^2$. In Chapter 1, we listed some results for data sets that are derived from this theorem.

Chebyshev's theorem

For a random variable X with mean μ and standard deviation σ, and for any number $k > 1$,

$$P(|X - \mu| < k\sigma) \geq 1 - 1/k^2 \qquad (3\text{--}11)$$

Let us see how the theorem is applied by selecting values of k. While k does not have to be an integer, we will use integers. When $k = 2$, we have: $1 - 1/k^2 = 0.75$: the theorem says that there is at least a 0.75 probability that the value of the random variable will be within a distance of two standard deviations away from the mean. Letting $k = 3$, we find that there is at least a 0.89 probability that X will be within three standard deviations of its mean. We can similarly apply the rule for other values of k. The rule holds for data sets and populations in a similar way. When applied to a sample of observations, the rule says that at least 75% of the observations lie within two standard deviations of the sample mean, $\bar{x}$. It says that at least 89% of the observations lie within three standard deviations of the mean, and so on. Applying the theorem to the random variable of Example (a), which has mean 2.3 and standard deviation 1.418, we find that there is at least a 0.75 probability that X will be anywhere from $2.3 - 2(1.418)$ to $2.3 + 2(1.418) = -0.536$ to 5.136. From the actual probability distribution in this example, Table 3–1, we know that the probability that X will be between 0 and 5 is 1.00.

Often, we will know the distribution of the random variable in question, in which case we will be able to use the distribution for obtaining actual probabilities rather than the bounds offered by Chebyshev's theorem. If the exact distribution of the random variable is not known, but we may assume an approximate distribution, the approximate probabilities may still be better than the general bounds offered by Chebyshev's theorem.

PROBLEMS

3–10. Find the expected value of the random variable in problem 3–1. Also find the variance of the random variable and its standard deviation.

3–11. Find the mean, variance, and standard deviation of the random variable in problem 3–2.

3–12. What is the expected percentage of people responding to an advertisement when the probability distribution is the one given in problem 3–3? What is the variance of the percentage of people who respond to the advertisement?

3–13. Find the mean, variance, and standard deviation of the number of cars sold per day using the probability distribution in problem 3–4.

3–14. What is the expected number of dots appearing on two dice? (Use the probability distribution you computed in your answer to problem 3–5.)

3–15. Use the probability distribution in problem 3–6 to find the expected number of shipment orders per day. What is the probability that on a given day there will be more orders than the average?

3–16. Find the mean, variance, and standard deviation of the number of wooden sailboats constructed in a month using the probability distribution in problem 3–7.

3–17. According to Chebyshev's theorem, what is the minimum probability that a random variable will be within four standard deviations of its mean?

3–18. At least 8/9 of a population lie within how many standard deviations of the population mean? Why?

3–19. The average annual return on a certain stock is 8.3%, and the variance of the returns on the stock is 2.3. Another stock has average return of 8.4% per year and variance of 6.4. Which stock is riskier? Why?

3–20. Returns on a certain business venture, to the nearest $1,000, are known to follow the probability distribution:

x	P(x)
−2,000	0.1
−1,000	0.1
0	0.2
1,000	0.2
2,000	0.3
3,000	0.1

a. What is the most likely monetary outcome of the business venture?

b. Is the venture likely to be successful? Explain.

c. What is the long-term average earning of business ventures of this kind? Explain.

d. What is a good measure of the risk involved in a venture of this kind? Why? Compute this measure.

3–21. Management of an airline knows that 0.5% of the airline's passengers lose their luggage on domestic flights. Management also knows that the average value claimed for a lost piece of luggage on domestic flights is $600. The company is considering increasing fares by an appropriate amount to cover expected compensation to passengers who lose their luggage. By how much should the airline increase fares? Why? Explain using the ideas of a random variable and its expectation.

Answers

3–10.

1.8, 2.76, 1.66

3–12.

21.5, 162.75

3–14.

7

3–16.

4.05, 2.75, 1.66

3–18.

3

3–20.

a. 2000
b. yes
c. 800
d. s.d. = 1469.69

Answers

3-22.
___
45250

3-24.
___
12.39

3-28.
___
68687500

3-22. Refer to problem 3-7. Suppose that the sailboat builders have fixed monthly costs of $25,000 and an additional construction cost of $5,000 per boat. Find the expected monthly cost of the operation. What property of expected values are you using?

3-23. Refer to problem 3-4. Suppose the car dealership's operation costs are well approximated by the square root of the number of cars sold, multiplied by $300. What is the expected daily cost of the operation? Explain.

3-24. In problem 3-2, suppose that a penalty is imposed on the typing pool of an amount equal to the square of the number of errors per page. What is the expected penalty per page? Explain.

3-25. What is the meaning of the expected value of a random variable, and what are its uses?

3-26. Explain the meaning of the variance of a random variable. What are possible uses of the variance?

3-27. Why is the standard deviation of a random variable more meaningful than its variance for interpretation purposes?

3-28. Refer to problem 3-22. Find the variance and the standard deviation of the monthly production cost.

3-4 The Binomial Distribution

Consider the following examples.

1. A coin is tossed four times. Let H denote the number of heads that appear.
2. It is known that 30% of the people in a given city prefer to use public transportation. A random sample of 20 people is selected. Let T be the number of people in the sample found to prefer public transportation.
3. It is known that 15% of the items produced by a machine are defective. A random sample of 12 items is chosen. Let D be the number of defective items found in the sample.

What characterizes the random variables H, T, and D? They are just a few of the many examples of discrete random variables following a special probability distribution known as the *binomial distribution*. The binomial distribution is based on an experiment consisting of a sequence of *Bernoulli trials*. The trials are named after a third member of the Bernoulli family, James Bernoulli (1654–1705), who was the first to propose them.

Bernoulli trials are a sequence of *n* identical trials satisfying the following assumptions.

1. Each trial has two possible outcomes, called *success* and *failure*. The two outcomes are mutually exclusive and exhaustive.
2. The probability of success, denoted by *p*, remains constant from trial to trial. The probability of failure is denoted by *q*, where $q = 1 - p$.
3. The *n* trials are independent. That is, the outcome of any trial does not affect the outcomes of other trials.

The terms *success* and *failure* are statistical terms and do not necessarily have the everyday meaning attached to the two words. In fact, when dealing with defective items in a production process, we may define the outcome "item is defective" as a success. Success refers to the occurrence of a particular event (e.g., "item is defective"), and failure refers to the nonoccurrence of the event. We define the *binomial random variable* as a random variable that counts the number of successes in a sequence of n Bernoulli trials.

> A random variable, X, that counts the number of successes in n Bernoulli trials, where p is the probability of success in any given trial, is said to follow the binomial distribution with parameters n and p. We call X a **binomial random variable.**

Note that the random variables in all three examples are binomial. The first, H, follows a binomial distribution with $n = 4$ and $p = 0.5$ (we assume a fair coin). Successive tosses of a coin are independent, the only outcomes are heads or tails (success versus failure), and the probability of either remains constant from toss to toss.

In the second example, our random variable T is binomial with $n = 20$ and $p = 0.3$. Recall from Chapter 2 that the assumption of random sampling implies the independence of outcomes. Note an important point: We are implicitly assuming that the number of people in the city is large so that the outcome of any trial does not affect the proportion of the remaining people in the city who prefer to use public transportation (i.e., the probability of the event "prefer public transportation" for any person in the sample is not seriously affected by the outcome for any other sampled person). If there were only 10 people in our population, 3 of whom preferred public transportation, the situation would be different. The probability that our first person (assume people are sampled in some order) prefers public transportation would indeed be 0.3. The probability that the next sampled person prefers public transportation, however, is either $2/9 = 0.22$ or $3/9 = 0.33$, *depending* on whether the first person prefers public transportation or does not. In this case, assumptions 2 and 3 of the Bernoulli process would be violated, and T would *not* be binomial. The assumptions are not seriously violated as long as the size of the population, N, is large compared with the sample size n (a generally accepted rule of thumb is $N/n \geq 10$).

Finally, we see that D follows a binomial distribution with parameters $n = 12$ and $p = 0.15$. We assume that the machine produces a large number of items and that the sampling is done randomly from this large population. This reduces the chance that the sample is drawn from a batch of adjacent items that could be similar to each other (either more likely to be defective than the entire population, or less so).

Binomial Probabilities

Now that we have set the assumptions required for a binomial probability distribution, let us see how the probabilities are computed. In the coin tossing example, the coin is tossed four times, and the random variable H is defined as the number of heads that appear. We want to find the probability distribution of H. The possible values of H are 0, 1, 2, 3, and 4. Let us look, in particular, at the event $H = 2$. This is the event that the four tosses of the coin produce exactly two heads. We want to evaluate the probability of this event, $P(H = 2)$.

First, let us find the number of ways in which this event may occur. The sequences of four tosses of the coin that result in exactly two heads are HHTT, HTHT, HTTH, THHT, THTH, and TTHH: there are six such sequences. Now we need to find the probability of each particular sequence. Owing to the independence of the four trials, the probability of a particular sequence, say, the sequence HHTT, is the product of the probabilities of the events heads, heads, tails, and tails, which is *ppqq*. Since the order of appearance of heads or tails does not affect the probabilities, we see that this probability, p^2q^2, is the probability of any one of the six sequences. Since there are six possible sequences leading to the value H = 2, we multiply p^2q^2 by 6, giving us $P(H = 2) = 6p^2q^2$. Finally, for a fair coin $p = q = 0.5$; therefore, $P(H = 2) = 6(0.5)^4 = 0.375$.

It is possible to compute the probabilities of the other events, $P(H = 0)$, $P(H = 1)$, $P(H = 3)$, and $P(H = 4)$ in a similar way. It would be more useful, however, if we could generalize the procedure by which we obtained the preceding probability and develop a formula for the binomial probabilities. We note the following:

1. The probability of any *given sequence* of *x* successes out of *n* trials with probability of success *p* and probability of failure *q* is equal to:

$$p^x q^{n-x}$$

Note that in our coin tossing example, $p = q = 0.5$, $n = 4$, and $x = 2$, giving $(0.5)^2(0.5)^2 = (0.5)^4$.

2. The number of different sequences of *n* trials that result in exactly *x* successes is equal to the number of choices of *x* elements out of a total of *n* elements. This number is denoted $n\,Cx$, or $\binom{n}{x}$, and from equation 2–19 we know that it is equal to:

$$\frac{n!}{x!(n-x)!}$$

In our coin tossing example,

$$\binom{n}{x} = \binom{4}{2} = \frac{4!}{2!(4-2)!} = \frac{(4)(3)(2)(1)}{(2)(1)(2)(1)} = 6$$

as we obtained earlier by direct counting.

Since there are $\binom{n}{x}$ sequences and each sequence has probability $p^x q^{n-x}$, the probability of *x* successes in *n* trials is the product of the two expressions. The resulting binomial probability law follows. We will use the simplified notation $P(x)$ for the probability: $P(X = x$ successes in *n* trials, where the probability of success is *p*).

The binomial probability distribution:

$$P(x) = \binom{n}{x}p^x q^{n-x} = \frac{n!}{x!(n-x)!}p^x q^{n-x} \qquad (3\text{–}12)$$

where:
p is the probability of success in a single trial,
$q = 1 - p$,
n is the number of trials,
and *x* is the number of successes

By substituting values of *x*, *n*, *p*, and *q* into equation 3–12, we are able to determine all the probabilities, that is, the probability *distribution*, of our binomial random

TABLE 3–7 The Binomial Distribution

Number of Successes, x	Probability P(x)
0	$\binom{n}{0}p^0q^n$
1	$\binom{n}{1}p^1q^{n-1}$
2	$\binom{n}{2}p^2q^{n-2}$
3	$\binom{n}{3}p^3q^{n-3}$
$\vdots$	$\vdots$
n	$\binom{n}{n}p^nq^0$
	1.00

variable of interest. Table 3–7 shows how the binomial probabilities for all values of a random variable are obtained using equation 3–12.

Table 3–8 gives the binomial probability distribution of the random variable H in our example. Use equation 3–12, or the equivalent, Table 3–7, to verify the probabilities in the table. Recall that 0! is defined as 1.00; and $p^0 = 1$ (for $p \neq 0$).

As the number of trials, n, increases, the computation of the probability distribution using equation 3–12 becomes more tedious. To facilitate use of the binomial probability model, the distribution has been tabulated for various values of n and p. Such a table of probabilities is Table 1 in Appendix C. The table lists the cumulative binomial probabilities, $F(x)$. Recall from equation 3–3 that the cumulative function $F(x)$ is the sum of the probabilities of all values i less than or equal to x:

$$F(x) = P(X \leq x) = \sum_{\text{all } i \leq x} P(i)$$

Table 3–9 is a reproduction of the part of Table 1 corresponding to $n = 5$. In the column $p = 0.50$, we find the cumulative probabilities corresponding to the probability distribution given in Table 3–8. (Note: The cumulative probabilities for $x = 5$ are omitted because they are all equal to 1.00. Accuracy is to the third decimal only; the 1.000 in the last row of the column corresponding to $p = 0.05$ should be interpreted accordingly.) For $p = 0.50$, note, for example, that $P(X = 3) = \sum_{i=0}^{3} P(i) - \sum_{i=0}^{2} P(i) = F(3) - F(2) = 0.813 - 0.500 = 0.313$, which corresponds to what we find in Table 3–8. In general, $P(x) = F(x) - F(x - 1)$ as can be deduced from equation 3–3.

TABLE 3–8 The Binomial Probability Distribution of H, the Number of Heads Appearing in Four Tosses of a Fair Coin

h	P(h)
0	$(5!/0!5!)(0.5)^0(0.5)^5 = 0.031$
1	$(5!/1!4!)(0.5)^1(0.5)^4 = 0.156$
2	$(5!/2!3!)(0.5)^2(0.5)^3 = 0.313$
3	$(5!/3!2!)(0.5)^3(0.5)^2 = 0.313$
4	$(5!/4!1!)(0.5)^4(0.5)^1 = 0.156$
5	$(5!/5!0!)(0.5)^5(0.5)^0 = 0.031$
	1.000

TABLE 3–9   Reproduction of Part of the Table of the Cumulative Binomial Distribution (Table 1 in Appendix C)

n = 5

x	0.01	0.05	0.10	0.20	0.30	0.40	0.50	0.60	0.70	0.80	0.90	0.95	0.99
0	.951	.774	.590	.328	.168	.078	.031	.010	.002	.000	.000	.000	.000
1	.999	.977	.919	.737	.528	.337	.187	.087	.031	.007	.000	.000	.000
2	1.000	.999	.991	.942	.837	.683	.500	.317	.163	.058	.009	.001	.000
3	1.000	1.000	1.000	.993	.969	.913	.813	.663	.472	.263	.081	.023	.001
4	1.000	1.000	1.000	1.000	.998	.990	.969	.922	.832	.672	.410	.226	.049

For random variable T, the number of people in a random sample of 20 who prefer to use public transportation, we find from Table 1 (using $p = 0.3$) that the probability that at most 5 in the sample will be found to prefer public transportation is $F(5) = 0.416$. Let us look at an example.

EXAMPLE (c)

In his article "Stock Market Signals to Managers" (*Harvard Business Review* November–December 1987), Alfred Rappaport reports results of a study indicating that 60% of all top executives of American firms believe that their company's stock is undervalued by the market. Suppose that a random sample of 15 top executives is selected. What is the probability that *at most three* of them will be found to believe their company's stock is undervalued?

SOLUTION

We need $P(X \leq 3)$ for a binomial random variable with $n = 15$ and $p = 0.60$. Looking at Table 1, we find $F(3) = 0.002$.

As a prelude to the topic of Chapter 7, hypothesis testing, let us interpret our findings in the following way. Suppose a claim is made that 60% of the top executives think their company's stock is undervalued. To *test* this *hypothesis,* you gather a random sample of 15 top executives and find that only 3 of them feel this way. If indeed 60% of all top executives (60% of the *population* of top executives) are in this category, what is the probability that a random sample of 15 will lead to 3 or fewer successes? The answer is the number we have just computed: 0.002. Since this probability is rather small, *either* we have just observed an event with a very small probability *or* the proportion of all executives who feel their company stock is undervalued is not as high as claimed. In hypothesis testing, when the probability of the observed event is small given that the hypothesis presented to us is true, we usually conclude that the hypothesis is false. We will discuss this topic in detail in Chapter 7 and in following chapters.

Mean, Variance, and Shape of the Binomial Distribution

The mean of a binomial distribution is equal to the number of trials, n, times the probability of success in a single trial, p. The variance is equal to the number of trials times p, times q. These formulas and the standard deviation are as follows.

Mean of a binomial distribution:

$$\mu = E(X) = np \qquad\qquad (3\text{-}13)$$

Variance of a binomial distribution:

$$\sigma^2 = V(X) = npq \qquad\qquad (3\text{-}14)$$

Standard deviation of a binomial distribution:

$$\sigma = SD(X) = \sqrt{npq} \qquad\qquad (3\text{-}15)$$

Recall that the mean of the distribution is the expected value of the random variable. Using equations 3–13 and 3–14, we find that the expected value of H, the number of heads appearing in four tosses of a fair coin, is $E(X) = np = 4(0.5) = 2.00$. This conforms with our intuition: as a long-run average, we expect that two out of four tosses of a fair coin will result in heads. The variance of H is $npq = 4(0.5)(0.5) = 1.00$. In this particular case, the standard deviation is also 1.00.

Find the mean and the standard deviation of the random variables T and D. In Example (c), assuming p is indeed 0.60, the expected number of executives who believe their company's stock is undervalued is $E(X) = np = 15(0.60) = 9$. The variance of this random variable is $V(X) = npq = 15(0.60)(0.40) = 3.6$. The standard deviation is $SD(X) = \sqrt{3.6} = 1.897$.

It is possible to use Chebyshev's theorem to obtain probability bounds on the value of a random variable using its mean and standard deviation. In cases where the probability distribution is known, we may find probabilities of values directly. Suppose, however, that we are interested in probabilities for a binomial random variable that is not tabulated. For example, let $n = 100$ and $p = 0.25$. Using Chebyshev's theorem with $k = 2$, we know that there is at least a 0.75 probability $(1 - 1/k^2 = 1 - 1/4 = 0.75)$ that the number of successes will be within $\mu \pm 2\sigma$, that is, within the bounds: $np \pm 2(\sqrt{npq}) = 100(0.25) \pm 2\sqrt{(100)(0.25)(0.75)} = 25 \pm 2(4.33) = 16.34$ and 33.66. We used Chebyshev's theorem to demonstrate the significance of knowing the standard deviation of a distribution. In the next chapter we will see a much better approximation for probabilities associated with a binomial random variable with a large number of trials: an approximation based on the normal distribution.

The shape of the probability distribution of a binomial random variable is symmetrical when $p = 0.50$. The distribution is skewed to the right when $p < 0.5$ and skewed to the left when $p > 0.5$, both if the number of trials is small. As n increases, the distribution becomes more and more symmetric. Figure 3–7 shows the binomial distribution for various values of n and p.

Sampling with or without Replacement

We noted earlier that the binomial distribution is appropriate when we are sampling from a population that is much larger than the sample. As a rule of thumb, we said that N/n should be at least 10. This is true for a sampling scheme *without replacement:* the sample is drawn and not returned into the population. If, on the other hand, we sample an item, note whether it is a success or a failure and *return* it to the population before the next item is selected for the sample, we are *sampling with re-*

FIGURE 3–7   The Binomial Probability Distribution for Various Values of *n* and *p*

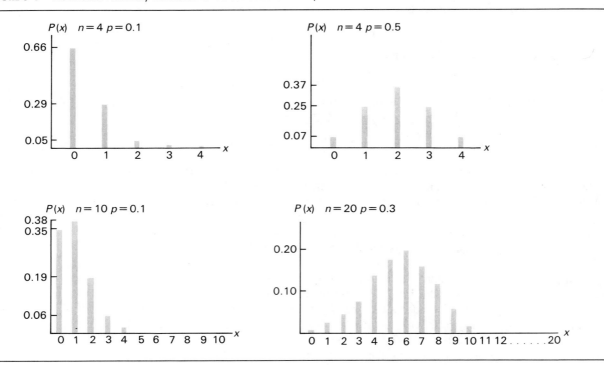

placement. When sampling with replacement, the population need not be much larger than the sample for the binomial assumption to hold. The reason for this can be seen if we consider a simple case where the population consists of 10 items, 4 of which are successes and 6 are failures. For the item first selected, $p = 0.4$. Once the item is returned to the population and has an equal chance of being selected again, the probability of success for the second item is also $p = 0.4$, and the two drawings are independent. Sampling with replacement is not a frequently used procedure and will not be discussed further in this book.

PROBLEMS

3–29.   A study of the videocassette recorder (VCR) industry reveals that 75% of all VCRs sold in the United States are of the VHS type; the remaining 25% are of the Beta type.[2] Of the many orders received by a movie rental agency on a Friday night, five separate orders fail to mention the type of VCR owned. The rental agent has all five requested movies available on either kind of cassette but needs to know the type of machine each customer has (a Beta cassette is unsuitable for a VHS machine and vice versa). Unable to contact the five customers and hoping to minimize the resulting disappointments, the agent decides to send all of them VHS-type movies.

a. Let S be the total number of suitable cassettes out of the five sent to the customers. What assumptions must be satisfied for a binomial distribution of S?

b. What is the probability that all five customers will receive the correct type of movie? Can

[2] R. Rosenbloom and M. Cusumano, "The Birth of the VCR Industry," *California Management Review* (Summer 1987).

you solve this part of the problem without knowledge of any of the material in this chapter? Explain.

c. Write the probability distribution of S in a table format.

d. What is the probability that at least one customer will be satisfied? (Again, can you solve this part without the information in this chapter?)

e. What is the probability that exactly three customers will receive movies of the correct type?

f. What is the probability that at most two customers will be satisfied?

g. What is the expected number of satisfied customers?

h. Find the variance of S.

3–30. Three of the 10 airplane tires at a hangar are faulty. Four tires are selected at random for a plane; let F be the number of faulty tires found. Is F a binomial random variable? Explain.

3–30.
———
No

3–31. A salesperson finds that, in the long run, two out of three sales calls are successful. Twelve sales calls are to be made; let X be the number of concluded sales. Is X a binomial random variable? Explain.

3–32. A large shipment of computer chips is known to contain 10% defective chips. If 100 chips are randomly selected, what is the expected number of defective ones? What is the standard deviation of the number of defective chips? Use Chebyshev's theorem to give bounds such that there is at least a 0.75 chance that the number of defective chips will be within the two bounds.

3–32.
———
[7.86, 22.14]

3–33. A new treatment for baldness is known to be effective in 70% of the cases treated. Four bald members of the same family are treated; let X be the number of successfully treated members of the family. Is X a binomial random variable? Explain.

3–34. What are Bernoulli trials? What is the relationship between Bernoulli trials and the binomial random variable?

3–35. In a given area, the probability that a person is exposed to an advertisement of a paper company is 0.20. If 10 people are randomly chosen from among the population in the area, what is the probability that at least 5 of them were exposed to the advertisement? What is the probability that at most 2 were exposed to the advertisement?

3–36. Records of a health insurance company show that 30% of its policyholders over 50 years of age submit a claim during the year. Fifteen policyholders over 50 years of age are selected at random. What is the probability that at least 10 will submit a claim during the coming year? What are the mean and standard deviation of the distribution?

3–36.
———
0.0037, 4.5, 1.77

3–37. In *acceptance sampling* in quality control, a lot is accepted only if the number of items that do not conform to production specifications out of a given total is no greater than some preset value. Suppose that out of a large collection of produced items, 20% are nonconforming. A random sample of 20 items is selected in an acceptance sampling scheme that requires that no more than 2 items out of 20 be nonconforming. What is the probability that the lot will be rejected?

3–38. Samuel Adams beer made by one of the nation's smallest breweries, Boston Brewing Co., is the only American beer exported to Germany. About 3,000 barrels are shipped to Germany each year.[3] Suppose that the beer is served on draft and randomly sent to establishments in an area of Germany where 27,000 barrels of German beer are also served annually. If 5 Americans arrive in this area and order draft beer, what is the probability that at least 2 of them will actually be served American beer? What assumptions are you making? If 10 Americans arrive, what is the expected number of drinkers to be served the Boston beer?

3–38.
———
0.0815, 1

3–39. Every week the Barbados Tourist Board interviews six randomly chosen vacationers on the island about their experience. In general, each vacationer's comments can be classified as mainly positive or mainly negative. The responses are then published in the *Visitor* news-

---

[3] "Wooing Jacques and Fritz Six-Pack," *Business Week* (February 4, 1991), p. 93.

Answer

3–40.

0.4845

paper. Suppose that only 5% of all visitors to Barbados are dissatisfied with their visit. What is the probability that at least two visitors out of the six interviewed will express negative comments?

3–40.   A study found that 70% of all employees believed that employee involvement in a firm was important for improving quality.[4] If 15 employees are randomly chosen, what is the probability that at most 10 of them will be found to believe that employee involvement can improve quality?

3–5   Other Discrete Probability Distributions[5]

The binomial probability distribution is among the most commonly used discrete distributions in statistics. There are several other useful discrete distributions. In this section, we will give brief descriptions of some of these distributions. These are the *Poisson,* the *hypergeometric,* the *multinomial,* and the *geometric* probability distributions. These distributions are not in the main direction of statistical inference followed in this book but find use in areas of probability modeling, operations research, and other areas. All of these distributions are discussed in detail in advanced books on probability.

The Poisson Distribution

The Poisson distribution is useful in describing a random variable that counts the number of occurrences in a particular interval of time: the number of equipment failures per week, the number of traffic accidents per month, and so on. The Poisson distribution is a good approximation for the binomial when the number of trials, n, is large ($n \geq 20$) and the probability of success (the probability of an *occurrence* in this context) is small ($p \leq 0.05$).

Poisson distribution:

$$P(x) = \frac{\mu^x e^{-\mu}}{x!} \qquad \text{for } x = 0, 1, 2, 3, \ldots \qquad (3\text{–}16)$$

where μ is the mean of the distribution (and also happens to be the variance) and e is the base of the natural logarithms ($e = 2.71828 \ldots$)

When using the Poisson as an approximation to a binomial random variable, we set $\mu = np$ and use equation 3–16. We demonstrate the use of the Poisson distribution as an approximation for the binomial with the following example.

EXAMPLE (d)

Today, people have more and more opportunities to get customized products rather than the usual uniform products of the past. Telephone manufacturers now offer 1,000 different choices for a telephone (as combinations of color, type, options, portability, etc.).[6]

---

[4] "Is Industry Ready for Adult Relationships?" *Industry Week* (January 21, 1991), p. 18.

[5] This is an optional section, which may be skipped without loss of continuity.

[6] R. McKenna, "Marketing Is Everything," *Harvard Business Review* (January–February 1991), p. 72.

A company is opening a large regional office, and each of its 200 managers is allowed to order his or her own choice of a telephone. Assuming independence of choices, and that each of the 1,000 different combinations of telephone are equally likely, what is the probability that a particular choice will be made by none, one, two, or three of the managers?

Here we have a binomial random variable with large n (200) and small p ($1/1{,}000 = 0.001$), so the Poisson approximation should work well. The parameter value is $\mu = np = 200(0.001) = 0.2$. Using equation 3–16, we get:

$$P(X = 0) = (0.2)^0 e^{-0.2}/0! = 0.8187$$
$$P(X = 1) = (0.2)^1 e^{-0.2}/1! = 0.1637$$
$$P(X = 2) = (0.2)^2 e^{-0.2}/2! = 0.0164$$
$$P(X = 3) = (0.2)^3 e^{-0.2}/3! = 0.0011$$

To avoid having to compute every probability using equation 3–16, a table is provided. This is Appendix C, Table 12. Use the table to verify the probabilities calculated directly in the solution of this example.

The Poisson distribution has other important applications in addition to its use as an approximation to the binomial. This distribution is useful in describing the number of occurrences over a fixed interval of time or space. The Poisson distribution requires the following assumptions.

Poisson assumptions:

1. The probability that an event will occur in a short interval of time (or space) is proportional to the size of the interval.
2. In a very small interval, the probability that two events will occur is close to zero.
3. The probability that any number of events will occur in a given interval is independent of where the interval begins.
4. The probability of any number of events occurring over a given interval is independent of the number of events that occurred prior to the interval.

In this general context, the parameter μ stands for the average number of occurrences in the period of time or space in question (e.g., 12 accidents per week, 2 typing errors per page, etc.). Figure 3–8 shows the Poisson distribution for various values of μ.

The Hypergeometric Distribution

In cases where we sample without replacement from a population that is relatively small compared with the sample size, we know that the binomial distribution is not appropriate. In such cases the random variable counting the number of successes in n trials follows the hypergeometric distribution. Denoting our random variable by X, the number of elements in the entire population by N, the number of successes in the entire population by S, and (as with the binomial) the number of trials by n, the probability distribution of X is given below.

FIGURE 3–8 Poisson Distribution for Different Values of μ.

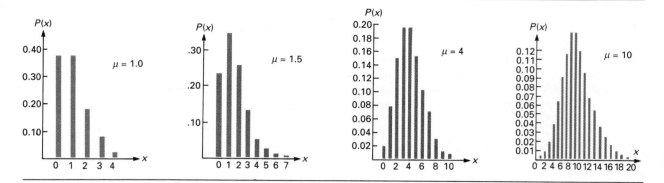

Hypergeometric distribution:

$$P(x) = \binom{S}{x}\binom{N-S}{n-x} \Big/ \binom{N}{n} \qquad (3-17)$$

The mean of the hypergeometric distribution is $\mu = np$ where $p = S/N$. The variance is $\sigma^2 = (N - n/N - 1)npq$.

Since we usually sample from a large population, the hypergeometric distribution is somewhat less useful than the binomial. It is important to understand, however, that this is the correct distribution when sampling without replacement. We illustrate the use of this distribution in the following example.

EXAMPLE (e)

Suppose that automobiles arrive at a dealership in lots of 10 and that for time and resource considerations, only 5 out of each 10 are inspected for safety. The 5 cars are randomly chosen from the 10 in the lot. If 2 out of the 10 cars in a lot are below standards for safety, what is the probability that at least 1 out of the 5 cars to be inspected will be found not meeting the safety standards?

SOLUTION

Here we have a hypergeometric random variable with $N = 10$, $S = 2$, $n = 5$, and $x = 1$ or 2. Using equation 3–17, we get:

$$P(1) = \binom{2}{1}\binom{8}{4} \Big/ \binom{10}{5} = \frac{2!}{1!1!}\frac{8!}{4!4!} \Big/ \frac{10!}{5!5!} = 0.556$$

$$P(2) = \binom{2}{2}\binom{8}{3} \Big/ \binom{10}{5} = \frac{2!}{2!0!}\frac{8!}{3!5!} \Big/ \frac{10!}{5!5!} = 0.222$$

and the answer is $P(1) + P(2) = 0.556 + 0.222 = 0.778$.

The Multinomial Distribution

Recall that in the binomial experiment we classify outcomes as successes or failures, for example, user versus nonuser of a product. It is possible to generalize the experiment to situations where outcomes may be classified into more than two categories. Suppose there are k categories of outcomes. Instead of user versus nonuser of a product, suppose a member of the population may be classified as "user of product A," "user of product B," . . . , "user of product K." The probability distribution of (X_1 = number of users of product A, X_2 = number of users of product B, . . . , X_k = number of users of product K) in a sample of size n is the *multinomial distribution* with parameters n and $p_1, p_2, \ldots, p_k$ (where p_i is the probability of occurrence of category i). The p_i terms must add to 1.00, they are constant from trial to trial, and trials are independent. A formula for the multinomial distribution follows.

> **Multinomial distribution:**
>
> $$P(x_1, x_2, \ldots, x_k) = \frac{n!}{x_1! \, x_2! \cdots x_k!} p_1^{x_1} p_2^{x_2} \cdots p_k^{x_k} \qquad (3\text{--}18)$$

The Geometric Distribution

Consider the binomial experiment with its usual assumptions. Instead of counting the number of successes in n trials, let our random variable X count the *number of trials until the first success*. Our random variable has a *geometric probability distribution*:

> **Geometric distribution:**
>
> $$P(x) = pq^{x-1} \qquad (3\text{--}19)$$
>
> where $x = 1, 2, 3, \ldots$ and p and q are the binomial parameters. The mean and variance of the geometric distribution are: $\mu = 1/p$ and $\sigma^2 = q/p^2$.

The number of items we need to sample until the first defective item is found is a geometric random variable. The expected value $\mu = 1/p$ conforms with our intuition: if the proportion of defective items is $p = 0.1$, then it seems logical that, *on the average*, we would have to sample 10 items until the first defective item is found. The geometric distribution is illustrated in the next example.

A recent study indicates that Pepsi-Cola has a market share of 33.2%, versus 40.9% for Coca-Cola.[7] A marketing research firm wants to conduct a new taste test for which it needs Pepsi drinkers. Potential participants for the test are selected by random screening of soft drink users to find Pepsi drinkers. What is the probability that the first ran-

EXAMPLE (f)

---

[7] "Pepsi Keeps on Going After No. 1," *Fortune* (March 11, 1991), pp. 62–70.

domly selected drinker qualifies? What is the probability that two soft drink users will have to be interviewed to find the first Pepsi drinker? Three? Four?

SOLUTION

The first person qualifies if there is "success" in a single trial when the probability of success is 0.332. Using the geometric distribution with $x = 1$, we find from equation 3–19: $P(1) = (0.332)(0.668)^0 = 0.332$. Similarly, the first person will be a non-Pepsi drinker and the second will qualify with probability $P(2) = (0.332)(0.668)^1 = 0.2218$. Two non-Pepsi drinkers will be interviewed before the first Pepsi user with probability $P(3) = (0.332)(0.668)^2 = 0.1481$. And finally, $P(4) = (0.332)(0.668)^3 = 0.099$.

PROBLEMS

Answers

3–42.
———
0.7492

3–44.
———
0.2642

3–46.
———
0.994

3–48.
———
10

3–41. In an effort to reach "zero defects" in its production process, a manufacturing firm managed to achieve 0.1% defective items produced. To check this rate, random samples are selected from time to time. Assuming this rate of defectives, what is the probability that out of a random sample of 100 items none will be found defective? One? Two? Three? (Use the Poisson approximation.)

3–42. The 3i company is the United Kingdom's largest venture capital provider, with a 35% share of the UK market.[8] Seven out of a total of exactly 20 firms under investigation are 3i-financed. If a random sample of 8 out of the 20 firms is to be selected for further scrutiny, what is the probability that at most 3 of them are 3i-financed?

3–43. As stated in the previous problem, 35% of all UK ventures are 3i-financed. If venture-capitalized firms are to be selected randomly until the first 3i-financed firm is found, what is the probability that three firms will be selected, with only the third being 3i-financed?

3–44. The arrival of cars at a service station follows a Poisson distribution with parameter value of one car per minute. What is the probability that at least two cars will arrive in a given minute?

3–45. Foreign banks now face extensive IRS reporting requirements.[9] Out of 15 banks with branches in Manhattan's Upper East Side, 6 are foreign-owned. The IRS plans to select a random sample of 10 out of the 15 banks for investigation. What is the probability that at least 3 of the selected banks will be foreign-owned?

3–46. One in 5,000 salmon caught in Alaska's Bristol Bay has parasites that make it unfit for human consumption. Use the Poisson approximation to find the probability that out of a shipment of 1,800 fish, two at most will have to be destroyed due to parasites.

3–47. An academic department has 11 faculty members, 4 of whom are tenured. Five faculty members are to be randomly selected from the entire department to serve on a committee. What is the probability that the tenured members in this committee will constitute a majority?

3–48. I am stranded on a highway with a dead battery and no jumper cables. Every once in a while a car stops and the driver offers to help me. However, I have to let these drivers go if they have no jumper cables. If 10% of the cars carry jumper cables, then—on the average—how many cars will stop without being able to help before I find someone who can help me?

3–6 Continuous Random Variables

Instead of depicting probability distributions by simple graphs, where the height of the line above each value represents the probability of that value of the random variable, let us use a histogram. We will associate the *area* of each rectangle of the his-

---

[8] "The Cautious Venture Capitalist," *Euromoney* (January 1991), pp. 41–46.

[9] "Foreign Banks Face IRS Scrutiny," *Bankers Monthly* (February 1991), p. 33.

FIGURE 3–9 A Histogram of the Probability Distribution of the Time to Complete a Task, with Time Measured to the Nearest Minute

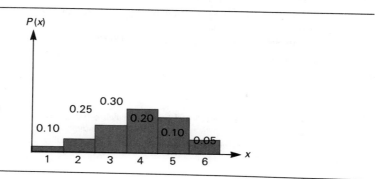

togram with the probability of the particular value represented. Let us look at a simple example. Let X be the time, measured in minutes, it takes to complete a given task. A histogram of the probability distribution of X is shown in Figure 3–9.

The probability of each value is the area of the rectangle over the value and is written on top of the rectangle. Since the rectangles all have the same base, the height of each rectangle is proportional to the probability. Note that the probabilities add to 1.00, as required. Now suppose that X can be measured more accurately. The distribution of X, with time now measured to the nearest half minute, is shown in Figure 3–10.

Let us continue the process. Time is a *continuous* random variable; it can take on any value measured on an *interval* of numbers. We may, therefore, refine our measurement to the nearest quarter minute, the nearest five seconds, or the nearest second, or we can use even more finely divided units. As we refine the measurement scale, the number of rectangles in the histogram increases and the width of each rectangle decreases. The probability of each value is still measured by the area of the rectangle above it, and the total area of all rectangles remains 1.00, as required of all probability distributions. As we keep refining our measurement scale, the discrete distribution of X *tends* to a continuous probability distribution. The steplike surface formed by the tops of the rectangles in the histogram tends to a smooth function. This function is denoted by $f(x)$ and is called the *probability density function* of the continuous random variable X. Probabilities are still measured as areas under

FIGURE 3–10 A Histogram of the Probability Distribution of Time to Complete a Task, with Time Measured to the Nearest Half Minute

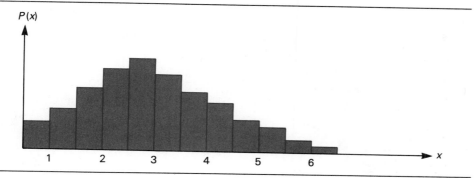

the function. The probability that the task will be completed in two to three minutes is the area under $f(x)$ between the points $x = 2$ and $x = 3$. Histograms of the probability distribution of X with our measurement scale refined further and further are shown in Figure 3–11. Also shown is the density function, $f(x)$, of the limiting *continuous* random variable X. The density function is the limit of the histograms as the number of rectangles approaches infinity and the width of each rectangle approaches zero.

FIGURE 3–11 Histograms of the Distribution of Time to Complete a Task as Measurement Is Refined to Smaller and Smaller Intervals of Time, and the Limiting Density Function, $f(x)$.

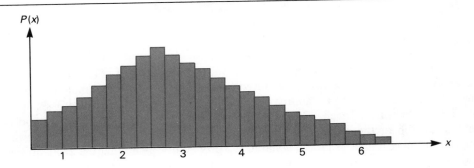

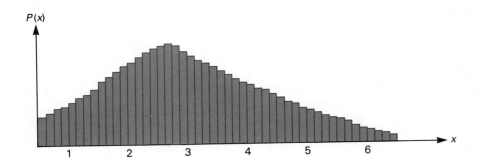

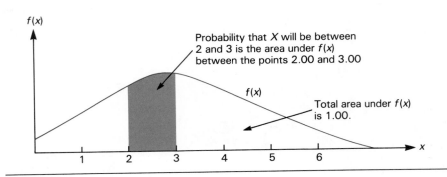

Now that we have developed an intuitive feel for continuous random variables, and for probabilities of intervals of values as areas under a density function, let us make some formal definitions.

A **continuous random variable** is a random variable that can take on any value in an interval of numbers.

The probabilities associated with a continuous random variable X are determined by the **probability density function** of the random variable. The function, denoted $f(x)$, has the following properties.

1. $f(x) \geq 0$ for all x.
2. The probability that X will be between two numbers a and b is equal to the area under $f(x)$ between a and b.
3. The total area under the entire curve of $f(x)$ is equal to 1.00.

Recall from Chapter 2 that when the sample space is continuous, the probability of any single given value is zero. For a continuous random variable, therefore, the probability of occurrence of any *given* value is *zero*. We see this from property 2, noting that the *area* under a curve between a point and itself is the area of a line, which is zero. *For a continuous random variable, nonzero probabilities are associated only with intervals of numbers.*

We define the cumulative distribution function, $F(x)$, for a continuous random variable similarly to the way we defined it for a discrete random variable: $F(x)$ is the probability that X is less than (or equal to) x.

The **cumulative distribution function** of a continuous random variable:[10]

$F(x) = P(X \leq x) =$ Area under $f(x)$ between the *smallest* possible value of X (often $-\infty$) and the point x.

The cumulative distribution function, $F(x)$, is a smooth, nondecreasing function that increases from 0 to 1.00. The connection between $f(x)$ and $F(x)$ is demonstrated in Figure 3–12.

We now give an example of a continuous random variable. The simplest continuous distribution is the *uniform* distribution over an interval. A continuous random variable has the uniform distribution over an interval I if it is equally likely to be in any subinterval of I as in any other subinterval of the same length. The density of a uniform random variable over the interval $I = [0,5]$ is as follows.

Uniform [0,5] density:

$$f(x) = \begin{cases} 1/5 & \text{for } 0 \leq x \leq 5 \\ 0 & \text{otherwise} \end{cases} \qquad (3\text{--}20)$$

---

[10] If you are familiar with calculus, you know that the area under a curve of a function is given by the *integral* of the function. The probability that X will be between a and b is the *definite integral* of $f(x)$ between these two points: $P(a < X < b) = \int_a^b f(x)dx$. In calculus notation, we define the cumulative distribution function as: $F(x) = \int_{-\infty}^{x} f(y)dy$.

FIGURE 3–12   The Probability Density Function and the Cumulative Distribution Function of a Continuous Random
Variable

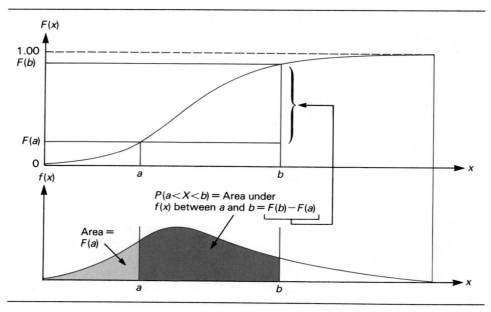

This density is shown in Figure 3–13. Note that the entire area under the curve is equal to the area of the rectangle with base 5 and height 1/5 and is therefore equal to 1.00, as required. Also, $f(x) \geq 0$ for all x. To find the probability that X will be between 1 and 3, $P(1 \leq X \leq 3)$, we need to compute the area under $f(x)$ between 1 and 3. This is the area of the rectangle with base $3 - 1 = 2$ and height 1/5. The probability is thus 2/5. This is also shown in the figure.

The expected value of a continuous random variable is the average value that would result from repeated drawing of values of the random variable. It is the center of the "mass" associated with the area under the graph of the density function if we assume this area were covered by some material, such as cardboard, of uniform

FIGURE 3–13   The Uniform [0,5] Density

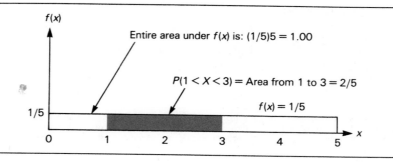

FIGURE 3–14   The Mean of a Continuous Distribution as the Center of the Mass under the Density Function

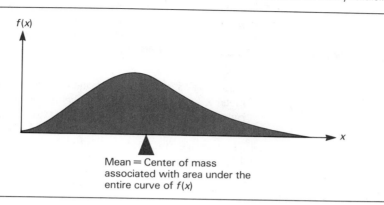

Mean = Center of mass
associated with area under the
entire curve of $f(x)$

thickness.[11] This is demonstrated in Figure 3–14. Using this intuitive principle, we find the mean of the uniform [0,5] distribution to be $E(X) = 2.5$.

Most continuous random variables with which we will work have density functions more complicated than the uniform density. Areas under the densities of these random variables, needed for probability calculations, are obtainable from tables such as the ones in Appendix C. The next chapter is devoted to the most important continuous distribution we will use: the normal distribution.

The Exponential Distribution [12]

We now present another example of a continuous random variable in common use in areas of applied probability. The random variable that measures the time between two occurrences that have a Poisson distribution is an *exponential* random variable. For example, if the number of cars that arrive at a service station per minute has a Poisson distribution, then the time between the arrivals of two consecutive cars (time being measured on a continuous scale) has an exponential distribution. The exponential distribution is the continuous limit of the discrete geometric distribution.

The exponential distribution:

The density function is

$$f(x) = \lambda e^{-\lambda x} \quad \text{for} \quad x \geq 0, \lambda > 0 \qquad (3\text{–}21)$$

The mean of the exponential distribution is $\mu = 1/\lambda$, and the variance is also $1/\lambda$. The cumulative distribution is

$$F(x) = 1 - e^{-\lambda x} \quad \text{for} \quad x \geq 0 \qquad (3\text{–}22)$$

We demonstrate the use of the exponential distribution with the following example.

---

[11] Using calculus, we define the expected value of a continuous random variable X as: $E(X) = \int_{-\infty}^{\infty} x f(x) dx$. A similar relation, $E(X^2) = \int_{-\infty}^{\infty} x^2 f(x) dx$, allows us to compute the variance of X with the aid of equation 3–8. Calculus is not required for understanding the material in this book.

[12] Optional subsection.

EXAMPLE (g)   The time a particular machine operates before breaking down (time between break-downs) is known to have an exponential distribution with parameter $\lambda = 2$. Time is measured in hours. What is the probability that the machine will work continuously for at least one hour? What is the average time between breakdowns?

SOLUTION   **FIGURE 3–15**

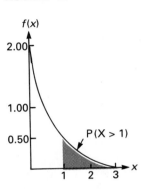

Figure 3–15 shows the exponential density with parameter $\lambda = 2$. We require the area under the curve to the right of the point $x = 1$. Using equation 3–22, we get $P(X \geq 1) = 1 - F(1) = 1 - (1 - e^{-2(1)}) = 0.1353$. The average time between breakdowns is $\mu = 1/\lambda = 1/2$ hour.

PROBLEMS

Answers

3–49.   What is the main difference between a continuous random variable and a discrete one?

3–50.   How do we obtain probabilities of intervals of numbers for a continuous random variable?

3–51.   Let X be a continuous random variable. Explain why $P(X = a) = 0$ for any given number a.

3–52.   How is the cumulative probability function $F(x)$ defined for a continuous random variable?

3–53.   Let X have the probability density function:

$$f(x) = \begin{cases} (1/2)x & \text{for } 0 \leq x \leq 2 \\ 0 & \text{otherwise} \end{cases}$$

a.   Sketch the probability density function.
b.   Show that $f(x)$ is a probability density function.
c.   Find the probability that X will be between 0 and 1.

3–54.   Write the density of a uniform [0,7] random variable. (Hint: the total area under $f(x)$ must equal 1.00.)

3–55.   Use the density of problem 3–54 to find the probability that X will be between 0 and 2.

3–56.   What is the expected value of the uniform [0,7] random variable of problem 3–54?

3–57.   For the random variable of problem 3–53, find the probability that X will be greater than 1.5.

3–58.   The time between customer arrivals at a bank has an exponential distribution with a

3–54.
———
1/7 between 0 and 7

3–56.
———
3.5

3–58.
———
0.5134

mean time between arrivals of 3 minutes. If a customer just arrived, what is the probability that another customer will not arrive for at least 2 minutes?

3–59. Light bulbs have an exponentially distributed life with mean 100 hours. What is the probability that the light bulb I am now putting in will last at least 65 hours?

3–60. What is the standard deviation of the lifetime of a light bulb in the previous problem?

Answer

3–60.

10

3–7 Using the Computer

Computers are often used for determining probabilities associated with random variables such as the binomial, Poisson, exponential, and others. We will now demonstrate how such probabilities are obtained for these random variables using the MINITAB package. Use the command PDF (probability distribution function) for the probability mass function of a discrete random variable or values of the density of a continuous random variable. The comand CDF is used for obtaining values of the cumulative distribution function. The particular distribution of interest is specified in a *subcommand*. Putting a semicolon at the end of the command PDF or CDF makes the computer ask for a subcommand. Then type BINOMIAL, POISSON, or EXPONENTIAL, followed by the parameter value(s). For the exponential, we also need to specify after the CDF command, the value x for which we require the cumulative probability. Note also that the parameter value for the exponential distribution in MINITAB is the mean rather than λ. Three examples are demonstrated in Figure 3–16.

FIGURE 3–16 Examples of the Use of MINITAB in Obtaining Probabilities for the Binomial, Poisson, and Exponential Distributions

```
MTB > PDF;
SUBC> BINOMIAL N=4 P=0.5.

     BINOMIAL WITH N =    4   P = 0.500000
       K          P( X = K )
       0            0.0625
       1            0.2500
       2            0.3750
       3            0.2500
       4            0.0625

MTB > PDF;
SUBC> POISSON M=0.01.

     POISSON WITH MEAN =    0.010
       K          P( X = K )
       0            0.9900
       1            0.0099
       2            0.0000

MTB > CDF 1;
SUBC> EXPONENTIAL M=2.
       1.0000      0.3935
MTB > STOP
```

3–8   Summary and Review of Terms

In this chapter we extended the ideas of probability presented in Chapter 2. We defined a **random variable** as a variable that takes on different numerical values determined by chance. We made a distinction between a **discrete** random variable—one that takes on discrete values—and a **continuous** random variable—one that may take on any value in an interval of numbers. We defined the **probability distribution** of a random variable as the rule that assigns probabilities to the different values of the random variable. In the discrete case, we saw that the probability distribution, $P(x)$, assigns probabilities to the numerical values the random variable may take. In the continuous case, we defined a **probability density function**, $f(x)$, and saw that probabilities are assigned only to intervals of numbers and are determined by areas under the density function. We defined the **cumulative distribution function** of a random variable, $F(x)$, as the function giving the probability that X is less than or equal to x. We also defined the **expected value** of a random variable as the mean of the probability distribution, and we defined the **variance** and the **standard deviation** for a discrete random variable. We saw how to compute the mean and variance of a function of a random variable; we also saw how to obtain probability bounds using **Chebyshev's theorem.** We discussed the **binomial distribution** as the discrete probability distribution of the number of successes in n independent trials with a fixed probability of success in all trials. We also discussed a few other probability distributions: the **Poisson, hypergeometric, geometric,** and **multinomial** discrete distributions, and the continuous **uniform** and **exponential** distributions.

ADDITIONAL PROBLEMS

3–61.   The Bombay Company offers reproductions of classic 18th- and 19th-century English furniture pieces, which have become popular in recent years.[13] The following table gives the probability distribution of the number of Raffles tables sold per day at a particular Bombay store.

Number of Tables	Probability
0	0.05
1	0.05
2	0.10
3	0.15
4	0.20
5	0.15
6	0.15
7	0.10
8	0.05

a. Show that the probabilities above form a proper probability distribution.

b. Find the cumulative distribution function of the number of Raffles tables sold daily.

c. Using the cumulative distribution function, find the probability that the number of tables sold in a given day will be at least three and less than seven.

d. Find the probability that at most five tables will be sold tomorrow.

e. What is the expected number of tables sold per day?

f. Find the variance and the standard deviation of the number of tables sold per day.

---

[13] E. F. Cone, "The Big Money in Raffles Tables," *Forbes* (December 28, 1987).

g. Use Chebyshev's theorem to determine bounds of at least 0.75 probability on the number of tables sold daily. Compare with the actual probability for these bounds using the distribution itself.

3–62. The number of orders for installation of a computer information system arriving at an agency per week is a random variable, X, with the following probability distribution.

x	P(x)
0	0.10
1	0.20
2	0.30
3	0.15
4	0.15
5	0.05
6	0.05

a. Prove that $P(x)$ is a probability distribution.
b. Find the cumulative distribution function of X.
c. Use the cumulative distribution function to find the probabilities: $P(2 < X \leq 5)$, $P(3 \leq X \leq 6)$, and $P(X > 4)$.
d. What is the probability that either four or five orders will arrive in a given week?
e. Assuming independence of weekly orders, what is the probability that three orders will arrive next week and the same number of orders the following week?
f. Find the mean and the standard deviation of the number of weekly orders.

3–63. Consider the situation in the previous problem, and assume that the distribution holds for all weeks throughout the year and that weekly orders are independent from week to week. Let Y denote the number of weeks in the year in which no orders are received (assume a year of 52 weeks).

a. What kind of random variable is Y? Explain.
b. What is the expected number of weeks with no orders?

3–64. An analyst kept track of the daily price quotation for a given stock. The frequency data led to the following probability distribution of daily stock price.

Price in Dollars, x	P(x)
17	0.05
17 1/8	0.05
17 1/4	0.10
17 3/8	0.15
17 1/2	0.20
17 5/8	0.15
17 3/4	0.10
17 7/8	0.05
18	0.05
18 1/8	0.05
18 1/4	0.05

Assume that the stock price is independent from day to day.

a. If 100 shares are bought today at 17 1/4 and must be sold tomorrow, by prearranged order, what is the expected profit, disregarding transaction costs?
b. What is the standard deviation of the stock price? How useful is this information?
c. What are the limitations of the analysis in part a? Explain.

3–65. In problem 3–62, suppose that the company makes $1,200 on each order but has to pay a fixed weekly cost of $1,750. Find the expected weekly profit and the standard deviation of weekly profits.

Answers

3–62.

c. 0.35, 0.40
d. 0.20
e. 0.225
f. 2.4, 1.562

3–64.

a. 31.875
b. 0.3149

Answers

3–66. An advertisement claims that two out of five doctors recommend a certain pharmaceutical product. A random sample of 20 doctors is selected, and it is found that only 2 of them recommend the product.

   a. Assuming the advertising claim is true, what is the probability of the observed event?

   b. Assuming the claim is true, what is the probability of observing two *or fewer* successes?

   c. Given the sampling results, do you believe the advertisement? Explain.

   d. What is the expected number of successes in a sample of 20?

3–67. Five percent of the many cars produced at a plant are defective. Ten cars made at the plant are sent to a dealership. Let X be the number of defective cars in the shipment.

   a. Under what conditions can we assume that X is a binomial random variable?

   b. Making the required assumptions, write the probability distribution of X.

   c. What is the probability that two or more cars are defective?

   d. What is the expected number of defective cars?

3–68. Refer to the situation in the previous problem. Suppose that the cars at the plant are checked one by one, and let X be the number of cars checked until the first defective car is found. What type of probability distribution does X have?

3–69. Suppose that 5 of a total of 20 company accounts are in error. An auditor selects a random sample of 5 out of the 20 accounts. Let X be the number of accounts in the sample that are in error. Is X binomial? If not, what distribution does it have? Explain.

3–70. The time, in minutes, necessary to perform a certain task has the uniform [5,9] distribution.

   a. Write the probability density of this random variable.

   b. What is the probability that the task will be performed in less than eight minutes? Explain.

   c. What is the expected time required to perform the task?

3–71. Suppose X has the following probability density function.

$$f(x) = \begin{cases} (1/8)(x-3) & \text{for } 3 \le x \le 7 \\ 0 & \text{otherwise} \end{cases}$$

   a. Graph the density function.

   b. Show that $f(x)$ is a density function.

   c. What is the probability that X is greater than 5.00?

3–72. In a nationally televised interview in 1988, the head of the Federal Deposit Insurance Corporation (FDIC) revealed that the agency maintains a secret list of banks suspected of being in financial trouble. The FDIC chief further stated that of the nation's 14,000 banks, 1,600 were on the list at the time. Suppose that, in an effort to diversify your savings, you randomly choose six banks and split your savings among them. What is the probability that no more than three of your banks are on the FDIC's suspect list?

3–73. Corporate raider Asher Adelman, teaching a course at Columbia University's School of Business in 1987, made the following proposal to his students. He would pay $100,000 to any student who would give him the name of an undervalued company, which Adelman would then buy.[14] Suppose that Adelman has 15 students in his class and that 5% of all companies in this country are undervalued. Suppose also that due to liquidity problems, Adelman can give the award to at most three students. Finally, suppose each student chooses a single company at random and without consulting others. What is the probability that Adelman would be able to make good on his promise?

3–74. An applicant for a faculty position at a certain university is told by the department chair that she has a 0.95 probability of being invited for an interview. Once invited for an interview, the applicant must make a presentation and win the votes of a majority (at least 8) of the department's 14 current members. From previous meetings with 4 of these members, the

---

[14] Columbia has since questioned this offer on ethical grounds, and the offer has been retracted.

candidate believes that 3 of them would certainly vote for her while 1 would not. She also feels that any member she has not yet met has a 0.50 probability of voting for her. Department members are expected to vote independently and with no prior consultation. What are the candidate's chances of getting the position?

3–75. (This is a hard problem.) Consider the situation in problem 3–29. Prove that the agent's strategy is best. First, consider the following alternative strategy. Instead of sending all five customers a VHS cassette, the agent tosses a coin each time and sends the customer a VHS movie if heads comes up and a Beta movie if tails appears. Prove that this strategy is not as good as sending all customers VHS movies if the agent wants to minimize the probability of sending a movie of the wrong type. (Hint: Use the law of total probability, Chapter 2.) Second, redo the analysis with a coin that has a 0.75 probability (or any other probability) of landing heads. Finally, generalize your result and prove that the VHS-only strategy is best.

3–76. The Nielsen Company rates television programs. The ratings for the three networks during prime time on Friday, February 1, 1991, were as follows. Also shown is the proportion of viewers watching each program.

Program	Network	Rating	Proportion
20/20	ABC	13.8	0.44
George Burns 95th Birthday	CBS	10.4	0.33
Midnight Caller	NBC	7.5	0.23

a. What is the mean rating given a program that evening?

b. How many standard deviations above or below the mean is the rating for each one of the programs?

3–77. A major ski resort in the eastern United States closes in late May. Closing day varies from year to year depending on when the weather becomes too warm for making and preserving snow.[15] The day in May and the number of years in which closing occurred that day are reported in the table below.

Day	Number of Years
21	2
22	5
23	1
24	3
25	3
26	1
27	2
28	1

a. Based only on this information, estimate the probability that you could ski at this resort after May 25 next year.

b. What is the average closing day based on past history?

3–78. Ten percent of the items produced at a plant are defective. A random sample of 20 items is selected. What is the probability that more than 3 items in the sample are defective? If items are selected randomly until the first defective item is encountered, how many items, on the average, will have to be sampled before the first defective item is found?

3–79. Lee Iacocca has volunteered to drive one of his Chryslers into a brick wall to demonstrate the effectiveness of airbags used in these cars.[16] Airbags are known to activate at

[15] "Warm Weather Bargains," *Skiing* (March 1991), p. 72.

[16] "Surviving the Crash," *The Economist* (March 2, 1991), pp. 65–66.

Answers

3–76.
―――
a. 11.229
b. +1.02, −0.33, −1.48

3–78.
―――
0.133, 10

Answer

random when the car decelerates anywhere from 9 to 14 miles per hour per second. The probability mass function for the deceleration speed at which bags activate is given below.

MPH/Second	Probability
9	0.12
10	0.23
11	0.34
12	0.21
13	0.06
14	0.04

a. If the airbag activates at a deceleration of 12 MPH/second or more, Iacocca would get hurt. What is the probability of his being hurt in this demonstration?

b. What is the mean deceleration at airbag activation moment?

c. What is the standard deviation of deceleration at airbag activation time?

3–80.

0.3935

3–80. In the previous problem, the time that it takes the airbag to completely fill up from the moment of activation has an exponential distribution with mean 1 second. What is the probability that the airbag will fill up in less than $1/2$ second?

DIRECT SHARE MARKETING AT WORK: "THE MILLIONAIRES' BANK"[17]

Pacific Bank raised its start-up capital in 1983 by subscriptions to units of $1 million each. As a result, a local San Francisco newspaper coined the name, "The Millionaires' Bank." There actually are only four investors who contributed a full million dollars. Most of the units are owned by groups of several individuals with a $20,000 minimum investment.

The unit arrangement is designed to ensure "management sufficient time and stability to achieve the bank's goals," according to the shareowners' Agreement and Proxy. During the bank's first five years, voting power was limited to the twenty-two "unit holders," who were all preapproved by the bank's board of directors. Any shareholder wishing to sell shares had to offer them first to others within the units before they could be sold to "outsiders."

When raising capital, organizers of the bank decided not to use a securities firm, either as an underwriter or as a commissioned agent. They also decided that they would pay no compensation—not even stock warrants or options—to the bank's officers or directors for their efforts in marketing shares.

Putting together an impressive and well-known team of managers and directors was the most important step for share marketing. Not only were the top executives experienced in running profitable and fast-growing banks, but they also had a history of ultimately merging those institutions into larger banks, returning a multiple of the shareowners' investment.

About 150 original shareowners were largely "locked in" to their investment during the five-year life of the units with no trading market for their shares. However, rapid growth required more equity, and existing shareholders invested another $5.7 million in a 1987 "rights offering" of one share for each share owned. The price was about 120 percent of book value, and the bank got a "fairness opinion" from a securities firm, declaring that the price was fair to shareowners whether or not they exercised their rights.

When the units expired in 1988, shares had been spread among over 300 holders. When these holders were offered another one-for-five subscription right the next year, the offering was 150 percent subscribed at a price very close to book value. Later in 1989, Pacific Bank made a direct offering to the general public at a price per share of about 130 percent of book value that was also oversubscribed.

Little marketing effort went into that public offering. The bank cleared the offering circular with the OCC and sent it to prospective investors along with a rather low-key letter from the bank's chairman. The key to success was the prospects who received that package—it included the bank's employees, a third of whom became shareowners.

---

[17] Adapted by permission from *The Bankers Magazine* (March/April 1991), p. 41.

Most of the new shareowners came from a file that bank management had been compiling in a computer for several years. It consisted of any customer who ever mentioned a desire to own shares in the bank. This list had gradually grown into the hundreds and was all the bank needed to find investors for another $24 million of equity capital.

Since January 1990, the shares of Pacific Bank have been quoted on the NASDAQ system. There are now 700 shareowners, and several securities firms act as market makers, providing continuous bid and asked prices.

1. If bank employees are randomly approached, what is the probability that in a random sample of 10, at least 3 shareholders will be found?
2. In a random sample of 100 shareholders, what is the probability of finding at most three millionaires?
3. If shareholders attend meetings at random, what is the probability that of 15 attending shareholders, exactly 5 will be original shareholders locked in for 5 years?

4

THE NORMAL DISTRIBUTION

INTRODUCTION

F igure 4–1 shows the binomial probability distribution with $p = 0.5$ and an increasing number of trials: $n = 6$, $n = 10$, and $n = 14$. Note the emerging pattern (the overlaid curve) as the number of trials increases. This smooth, bell-shaped curve is the **normal probability density function.** The normal random variable is a continuous random variable that appears here as the *limit* of the discrete binomial random variable as the number of trials, n, increases. The normal distribution appears not only as a limit of the binomial distribution, but also in a very wide variety of other situations. It is the distribution of many random variables in situations where a large number of random effects from different sources come into play. The normal distribution was originally called the *law of errors,* the random effects of different magnitude and source considered "errors." The normal distribution is so prevalent, in fact, that Sir Francis Galton called it "the supreme law of unreason."

On November 12, 1733, a French-born mathematician who emigrated to England, Abraham De Moivre (1667–1754), privately published a small pamphlet and distributed it to his personal friends. The pamphlet was soon forgotten, and almost a century later the Marquis de Laplace (1749–1827) and Carl Friedrich Gauss (1777–1855) were jointly credited with the discovery of the normal distribution. To this day, the distribution is often called the *Gaussian* distribution. In 1924 the English statistician Karl Pearson happened upon a surviving copy of the forgotten pamphlet of 1733. Reading it, Pearson discovered to his great surprise that De Moivre had developed the formula for what we see in Figure 4–1—the tendency of the binomial distribution toward the normal distribution as n increases. The pamphlet contained the mathematical formula of the normal density. This formula, for a normal random variable with mean μ and standard deviation σ, is given as equation 4–1.

The probability density function of a normal random variable with mean μ and standard deviation σ:

$$f(x) = (1/\sqrt{2\pi}\sigma)e^{-(x-\mu)^2/2\sigma^2} \qquad \text{for } -\infty < x < \infty \qquad (4\text{–}1)$$

where e and π are the numbers 2.718 . . . and 3.141 . . . , respectively

---

Fortunately, Pearson had his own journal, *Biometrika,* and he was able to set the record straight. In an article published that year, Pearson recorded that De Moivre was actually the first to discover the normal distribution.[1]

---

[1] Karl Pearson, "Historical Note on the Origin of the Normal Curve of Errors," *Biometrika,* XVI (1924), pp. 402–4.

Continued on next page

FIGURE 4–1
Binomial Distributions with
p = 0.5 and Increasing Number
of Trials n

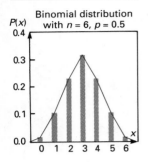

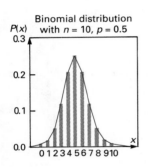

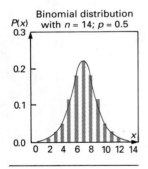

As for De Moivre, what else do we know about him? Unfortunately, not much. We know that he was a member of the Royal Society and that he made his living as a mathematics tutor and coffeehouse advisor to gamblers. De Moivre died at the age of 87, and some believe he was able to predict the exact day of his death by noting that every day he required a few more minutes of sleep. He is said to have died the day his sleep requirement reached 24 hours.

Why is the normal distribution important in statistics? Statistics is based on sampling, and by an important theorem called the *central limit theorem,* the distributions of many sampling results tend to the normal distribution as the sample size, *n,* increases. The normal distribution is thus quite useful in evaluating the accuracy of sampling outcomes, as we will see in the following chapters. ■

4–2 The Normal Probability Distribution

The normal random variable is continuous and has a density function given by equation 4–1. As with all continuous random variables, the probability that a normal random variable X will equal any particular value is zero. This holds for random variables that are *truly* continuous, such as time or size, measured on a continuous scale. The normal distribution is also used, however, as an excellent approximation for distributions of discrete random variables in a variety of situations. For example, profits of business ventures of a certain kind are approximately normally distributed. In this context, it does not necessarily mean that the probability of earning exactly $1,200 is equal to zero (although the probability may be small). Use of the normal distribution does mean that the probability that earnings will be in a given interval of numbers, say, $1,100 to $1,300, is approximated by the probability of this interval computed for a normal random variable with a given mean and standard deviation.

FIGURE 4–2   Normal Distributions with Different Means and Standard Deviations

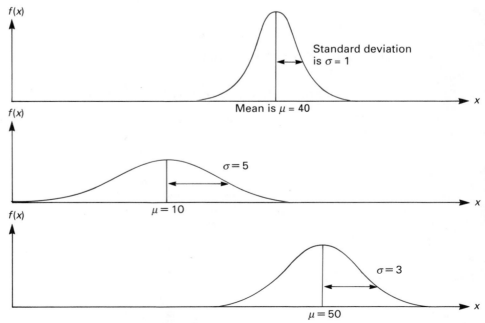

Equation 4–1 contains two parameters: the mean of the normal random variable, μ, and its standard deviation, σ. There are, therefore, infinitely many possible normal random variables, depending on the value of the mean and the value of the standard deviation. The shape of all normal densities is the same: a symmetric bell shape. Knowing the mean of the normal random variable and its standard deviation (or equivalently, its variance) fixes a *particular* normal random variable out of the infinite collection of such variables. This gives us the exact density function and allows us to compute probabilities associated with intervals of values.

Figure 4–2 shows several normal distributions with different means and standard deviations. *The mean of the distribution is a measure of its location:* It tells us where on the numbers line the distribution is centered. (Since the normal density is symmetrical with one peak in the center, the *mean*, μ, is also the *mode* and the *median* of the probability distribution; thus, μ is also the point where the density function is highest and the point that splits the area under the curve in half. The area to each side of μ is equal to 0.5.) *The standard deviation of the distribution is a measure of the spread, or variability, of the distribution.* When the standard deviation is large, the density function is *wide* and, hence, also *low* (because the total area under the curve must equal 1.00). When the standard deviation is small, the curve is narrow and high. The normal distribution has an additional interesting property. The distance on the curve from the mean (the center line) to the inflection point of the density function (that point where the slope of the function starts to decrease) is equal to *one standard deviation.*

Notation

We now introduce some general notation for random variables and distributions that will prove to be especially useful in work with the normal probability model; however, it has uses also in the case of other random variables.

We will denote the distribution, mean, and variance of a random variable by a simple notational statement:

$$X \sim D(\mu, \sigma^2) \qquad (4-2)$$

This statement says in words: "The random variable X is distributed according to a probability distribution D, with mean equal to μ, and standard deviation equal to σ (equivalently, variance equal to σ^2)." This is the general notation for a random variable, with the distribution denoted by D. If we were talking about the binomial distribution, we would use the letter B to denote it. For a normally distributed random variable, we use the letter N. If we deal with a random variable with a normal distribution with mean $\mu = 5.7$ and standard deviation $\sigma = 2$, we say:

$$X \sim N(5.7, 2^2)$$

Note that we wrote the variance σ^2 as 2^2, rather than its value, 4. We will always follow the convention of writing the variance as a squared quantity. This will prevent us from confusing the value of the variance with the value of the standard deviation. Here it is perfectly clear that the variance is $2^2 = 4$ and the standard deviation is 2.

4–3 The Standard Normal Distribution

Since, as noted earlier, there are infinitely many possible normal random variables, one of them is selected to serve as our *standard*. Probabilities associated with values of this standard normal random variable are tabulated. A special transformation then

FIGURE 4–3   The Standard Normal Density Function

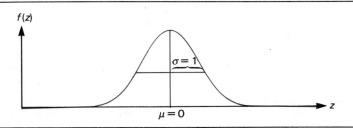

allows us to apply the tabulated probabilities to *any* normal random variable. The standard normal random variable has a special name, Z (rather than the general name X we use for other random variables).

> We define the **standard normal random variable,** Z, as the normal random variable with mean $\mu = 0$ and standard deviation $\sigma = 1$.

In the notation established in the previous section, we say:

$$Z \sim N(0, 1^2) \tag{4-3}$$

Since $1^2 = 1$, we may in this particular case drop the square sign, as no confusion of the standard deviation and the variance is possible. A graph of the standard normal density function is given in Figure 4–3.

Finding Probabilities of the Standard Normal Distribution

Probabilities of intervals are areas under the density $f(z)$ over the intervals in question. From the range of values in equation 4–1, $-\infty < x < \infty$, we see that any normal random variable is defined over the entire real line. Thus, the intervals in which we will be interested are sometimes *semi-infinite* intervals, such as a to ∞ or b to $-\infty$ (where a and b are numbers). While such intervals have infinite length, the probabilities associated with them are finite; they are, in fact, no greater than 1.00, as required of all probabilities. The reason for this is that the area in either of the "tails" of the distribution (the two narrow ends of the distribution, extending toward $-\infty$ and $+\infty$) becomes very small very quickly as we move away from the center of the distribution.

Tabulated areas under the standard normal density are probabilities of intervals extending from the mean, $\mu = 0$, to points z to its right. Table 2 in Appendix C gives areas under the standard normal curve between 0 and points $z > 0$. The total area under the normal curve is equal to 1.00, and since the curve is symmetric, the area from 0 to $-\infty$ is equal to 0.5. The *table area* associated with a point z is thus equal to the value of the cumulative distribution function, $F(z)$, minus 0.5.

> We define the **table area** as:
> $$TA = F(z) - 0.5 \tag{4-4}$$

The table area, TA, is shown in Figure 4–4. Part of Table 2 is reproduced here as

FIGURE 4–4   The Table Area, TA, for a Point z of the Standard Normal Distribution

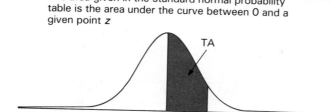

The area given in the standard normal probability
table is the area under the curve between 0 and a
given point z

TA

0   z

Table 4–1. Let us see how the table is used in obtaining probabilities for the standard normal random variable. In the following examples, refer to Figure 4–4 and Table 4–1.

1. Let us find the probability that the value of the standard normal random variable will be between 0 and 1.56. That is, we want $P(0 < Z < 1.56)$. In Figure 4–4, substitute 1.56 for the point z on the graph. We are looking

TABLE 4–1   Standard Normal Probabilities

z	.00	.01	.02	.03	.04	.05	.06	.07	.08	.09
0.0	.0000	.0040	.0080	.0120	.0160	.0199	.0239	.0279	.0319	.0359
0.1	.0398	.0438	.0478	.0517	.0557	.0596	.0636	.0675	.0714	.0753
0.2	.0793	.0832	.0871	.0910	.0948	.0987	.1026	.1064	.1103	.1141
0.3	.1179	.1217	.1255	.1293	.1331	.1368	.1406	.1443	.1480	.1517
0.4	.1554	.1591	.1628	.1664	.1700	.1736	.1772	.1808	.1844	.1879
0.5	.1915	.1950	.1985	.2019	.2054	.2088	.2123	.2157	.2190	.2224
0.6	.2257	.2291	.2324	.2357	.2389	.2422	.2454	.2486	.2517	.2549
0.7	.2580	.2611	.2642	.2673	.2704	.2734	.2764	.2794	.2823	.2852
0.8	.2881	.2910	.2939	.2967	.2995	.3023	.3051	.3078	.3106	.3133
0.9	.3159	.3186	.3212	.3238	.3264	.3289	.3315	.3340	.3365	.3389
1.0	.3413	.3438	.3461	.3485	.3508	.3531	.3554	.3577	.3599	.3621
1.1	.3643	.3665	.3686	.3708	.3729	.3749	.3770	.3790	.3810	.3830
1.2	.3849	.3869	.3888	.3907	.3925	.3944	.3962	.3980	.3997	.4015
1.3	.4032	.4049	.4066	.4082	.4099	.4115	.4131	.4147	.4162	.4177
1.4	.4192	.4207	.4222	.4236	.4251	.4265	.4279	.4292	.4306	.4319
1.5	.4332	.4345	.4357	.4370	.4382	.4394	.4406	.4418	.4429	.4441
1.6	.4452	.4463	.4474	.4484	.4495	.4505	.4515	.4525	.4535	.4545
1.7	.4554	.4564	.4573	.4582	.4591	.4599	.4608	.4616	.4625	.4633
1.8	.4641	.4649	.4656	.4664	.4671	.4678	.4686	.4693	.4699	.4706
1.9	.4713	.4719	.4726	.4732	.4738	.4744	.4750	.4756	.4761	.4767
2.0	.4772	.4778	.4783	.4788	.4793	.4798	.4803	.4808	.4812	.4817
2.1	.4821	.4826	.4830	.4834	.4838	.4842	.4846	.4850	.4854	.4857
2.2	.4861	.4864	.4868	.4871	.4875	.4878	.4881	.4884	.4887	.4890
2.3	.4893	.4896	.4898	.4901	.4904	.4906	.4909	.4911	.4913	.4916
2.4	.4918	.4920	.4922	.4925	.4927	.4929	.4931	.4932	.4934	.4936
2.5	.4938	.4940	.4941	.4943	.4945	.4946	.4948	.4949	.4951	.4952
2.6	.4953	.4955	.4956	.4957	.4959	.4960	.4961	.4962	.4963	.4964
2.7	.4965	.4966	.4967	.4968	.4969	.4970	.4971	.4972	.4973	.4974
2.8	.4974	.4975	.4976	.4977	.4977	.4978	.4979	.4979	.4980	.4981
2.9	.4981	.4982	.4982	.4983	.4984	.4984	.4985	.4985	.4986	.4986
3.0	.4987	.4987	.4987	.4988	.4988	.4989	.4989	.4989	.4990	.4990

FIGURE 4–5   Finding the Probability that Z Is Less than −2.47

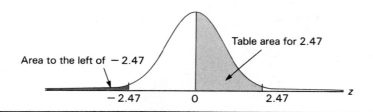

for the table area in the row labeled 1.5 and the column labeled .06. In the table, we find the probability 0.4406.

2. Let us find the probability that Z will be less than −2.47. Figure 4–5 shows the required area for the probability $P(Z < -2.47)$. By the symmetry of the normal curve, the area to the left of −2.47 is exactly equal to the area to the right of 2.47. We find:

$$P(Z < -2.47) = P(Z > 2.47) = 0.5000 - 0.4932 = 0.0068$$

3. Find $P(1 < Z < 2)$. The required probability is the area under the curve between the two points 1 and 2. This area is shown in Figure 4–6. The table gives us the area under the curve between 0 and 1, and the area under the curve between 0 and 2. Areas are additive; therefore, $P(1 < Z < 2) = $ TA(for 2.00) − TA(for 1.00) = 0.4772 − 0.3413 = 0.1359.

In cases where we need probabilities based on values with greater than second-decimal accuracy, we may use a linear interpolation between two probabilities obtained from the table. For example, $P(0 \leq Z \leq 1.645)$ is found as the midpoint between the two probabilities $P(0 \leq Z \leq 1.64)$ and $P(0 \leq Z \leq 1.65)$. This is found, using the table, as the midpoint of 0.4495 and 0.4505, which is 0.45. If even more accuracy is required, we may use computer programs designed to produce standard normal probabilities.

Finding Values of Z Given a Probability

In many situations, instead of finding the probability that a standard normal random variable will be within a given interval, we may be interested in the reverse: finding an interval with a given probability. Consider the following examples.

1. Find a value z of the standard normal random variable such that the proba-

FIGURE 4–6   Finding the Probability that Z Is between 1 and 2

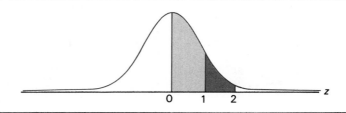

FIGURE 4–7 Using the Normal Table to Find a Value, Given a Probability

z	.00	.01	.02	.03	.04	.05	.06	.07	.08	.09
0.0	.0000	.0040	.0080	.0120	.0160	.0199	.0239	.0279	.0319	.0359
0.1	.0398	.0438	.0478	.0517	.0557	.0596	.0636	.0675	.0714	.0753
0.2	.0793	.0832	.0871	.0910	.0948	.0987	.1026	.1064	.1103	.1141
0.3	.1179	.1217	.1255	.1293	.1331	.1368	.1406	.1443	.1480	.1517
0.4	.1554	.1591	.1628	.1664	.1700	.1736	.1772	.1808	.1844	.1879
0.5	.1915	.1950	.1985	.2019	.2054	.2088	.2123	.2157	.2190	.2224
0.6	.2257	.2291	.2324	.2357	.2389	.2422	.2454	.2486	.2517	.2549
0.7	.2580	.2611	.2642	.2673	.2704	.2734	.2764	.2794	.2823	.2852
0.8	.2881	.2910	.2939	.2967	.2995	.3023	.3051	.3078	.3106	.3133
0.9	.3159	.3186	.3212	.3238	.3264	.3289	.3315	.3340	.3365	.3389
1.0	.3413	.3438	.3461	.3485	.3508	.3531	.3554	.3577	.3599	.3621
1.1	.3643	.3665	.3686	.3708	.3729	.3749	.3770	.3790	.3810	.3830
1.2	.3849	.3869	.3888	.3907	.3925	.3944	.3962	.3980	.3997	.4015
1.3	.4032	.4049	.4066	.4082	.4099	.4115	.4131	.4147	.4162	.4177
1.4	.4192	.4207	.4222	.4236	.4251	.4265	.4279	.4292	.4306	.4319
1.5	.4332	.4345	.4357	.4370	.4382	.4394	.4406	.4418	.4429	.4441

bility that the random variable will have a value between 0 and z is 0.40. We look *inside* the table for the value closest to 0.40; we do this by searching through the values inside the table, noting that they increase from 0 to numbers close to 0.5000 as we go down the columns and across rows. The closest value we find to 0.40 is the table area .3997. This value corresponds to 1.28 (row 1.2 and column .08). This is illustrated in Figure 4–7.

2. Find the value of the standard normal random variable that cuts off an area of 0.90 to its left. Here, we reason as follows. Since the area to the left of the given point, z, is greater than 0.50, z *must be on the right side of 0.* Furthermore, the area to the left of 0 all the way to $-\infty$ is equal to 0.5. Therefore, TA $= 0.9 - 0.5 = 0.4$. We need to find the point z such that TA $= 0.4$. We know the answer from the preceding example: $z = 1.28$. This is shown in Figure 4–8.

3. Find a 0.99 probability interval, symmetric about 0, for the standard normal random variable. The required area between the two z values that are equidistant from 0 on either side is 0.99. Therefore, the area under the curve between 0 and the positive z value is TA $= 0.99/2 = 0.495$. We now look in our normal probability table for the area closest to 0.495. The area 0.495 lies exactly between the two areas 0.4949 and 0.4951, corresponding to $z = 2.57$ and $z = 2.58$. Therefore, a simple linear interpo-

FIGURE 4–8 Finding z Such that $P(Z \le z) = 0.9$

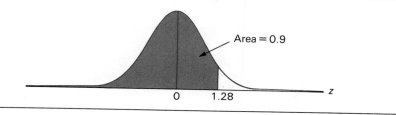

FIGURE 4–9 A Symmetric 0.99 Probability Interval about 0 for a Standard Normal Random Variable

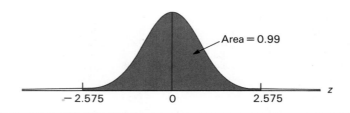

lation between the two values gives us $z = 2.575$. This is correct to within the accuracy of the linear interpolation. The answer, therefore, is $z = \pm 2.575$. This is shown in Figure 4–9.

PROBLEMS

Answers

4–2.
——
0.8185

4–4.
——
0.0013

4–6.
——
0.0062

4–8.
——
0.9772

4–10.
——
0.0239

4–12.
——
±1.645

4–14.
——
−1.04

4–16.
——
0

4–1. Find the following probabilities: $P(-1 < Z < 1)$, $P(-1.96 < Z < 1.96)$, $P(-2.33 < Z < 2.33)$, $P(Z < 2.58)$, $P(-3 < Z < 3)$.

4–2. What is the probability that a standard normal random variable will be between the values -2 and 1?

4–3. Find the probability that a standard normal random variable will have a value between -0.89 and -2.66.

4–4. Find the probability that a standard normal random variable will have a value greater than 3.02.

4–5. Find the probability that a standard normal random variable will be between 2 and 3.

4–6. Find the probability that a standard normal random variable will have a value less than or equal to -2.5.

4–7. Find the probability that a standard normal random variable will be greater in value than -2.33.

4–8. Find the probability that a standard normal random variable will have a value between -2 and 15.

4–9. Find the probability that a standard normal variable will have a value less than -45.

4–10. Find the probability that a standard normal random variable will be between -0.01 and 0.05.

4–11. A sensitive measuring device is calibrated so that errors in the measurements it provides are normally distributed with mean 0 and variance 1.00. Find the probability that a given error will be between -2 and 2.

4–12. Find two values defining tails of the normal distribution with an area of 0.05 each.

4–13. Is it likely that a standard normal random variable will have value less than -4? Explain.

4–14. Find a value such that the probability that the standard normal random variable will be above it is 0.85.

4–15. Find a value of the standard normal random variable cutting off an area of 0.575 to its left.

4–16. Find a value of the standard normal random variable cutting off an area of 0.50 to its right. (Do you need the table for this probability? Explain.)

4–17. Find z such that $P(Z > z) = 0.28$.

4–18. Find two values, equidistant from 0 on either side, such that the probability that a standard normal random variable will be between them is 0.40.

4–19. Find two values of the standard normal random variable, z and $-z$, such that $P(-z < Z < z) = 0.95$.

4–20. Find two values of the standard normal random variable, z and $-z$, such that the two corresponding "tail areas" of the distribution (the area to the right of z and the area to the left of $-z$) add up to 0.01.

4–21. The deviation of a magnetic needle away from the magnetic pole in a certain area in northern Canada is a normally distributed random variable with mean 0 and standard deviation 1.00. What is the probability that the absolute value of the deviation from the north pole at a given moment will be more than 2.4?

Answers

4–18.

±0.524

4–20.

±2.576

4–4 The Transformation of Normal Random Variables

The importance of the standard normal distribution derives from the fact that any normal random variable may be transformed to the standard normal random variable. We want to transform X, where $X \sim N(\mu, \sigma^2)$, into the standard normal random variable $Z \sim N(0, 1^2)$. Look at Figure 4–10. Here we have a normal random variable, X, with mean $\mu = 50$ and standard deviation $\sigma = 10$. We want to transform this random variable to a normal random variable with $\mu = 0$ and $\sigma = 1$. How can we do this?

We move the distribution from its center of 50 to a center of 0. This is done by *subtracting* 50 from all the values of X. Thus, we shift the distribution 50 units back so that its new center is 0. The second thing we need to do is to make the width of the distribution, its standard deviation, equal to 1. This is done squeezing the width down from 10 to 1. Because the total probability under the curve must remain 1.00, the distribution must grow upward to maintain the same area. This is shown in Figure 4–10. Mathematically, squeezing the curve to make the width 1 is equivalent to dividing the random variable by its standard deviation. Under the assumption of flexibility, the area under the curve adjusts so that the total remains the same. *All probabilities* (areas under the curve) *adjust accordingly*. The mathematical transformation from X to Z is thus achieved by first subtracting μ from X and then dividing the result by σ.

FIGURE 4–10 Transforming a Normal Random Variable with Mean 50 and Standard Deviation 10 into the Standard Normal Random Variable

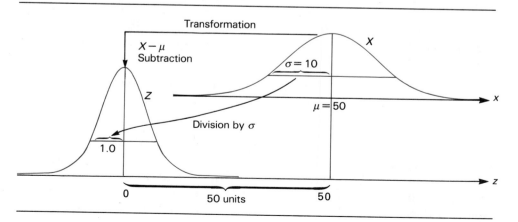

> The transformation of X to Z:
>
> $$Z = \frac{X - \mu}{\sigma}$$
>
> (4–5)

The transformation of equation 4–5 takes us from a random variable X with mean μ and standard deviation σ to the standard normal random variable. We also have an opposite, or *inverse*, transformation, which takes us from the standard normal random variable Z to the random variable X with mean μ and standard deviation σ. The inverse transformation is given by equation 4–6.

> The inverse transformation of Z to X:
>
> $$X = \mu + Z\sigma$$
>
> (4–6)

You can verify mathematically that equation 4–6 does the opposite of equation 4–5. Note that multiplying the random variable Z by the number σ increases the width of the curve from 1 to σ, thus making σ the new standard deviation. Adding μ makes μ the new mean of the random variable. The actions of multiplying and then adding are the opposite of subtracting and then dividing. We note that the two transformations, one an inverse of the other, transform a *normal* random variable into a *normal* random variable. If a transformation is carried out on a random variable that is not normal, the result will not be a normal random variable.

Using the Normal Transformation

Let us consider our random variable X with mean 50 and standard deviation 10, $X \sim N(50, 10^2)$. Suppose we want the probability that X is greater than 60. That is, we want to find $P(X > 60)$. We cannot evaluate this probability directly, but if we can transform X to Z, we will be able to find the probability in the Z table, Table 2. Using equation 4–5, the required transformation is $Z = (X - \mu)/\sigma$. Let us carry out the transformation. In the probability statement, $P(X > 60)$, we will substitute Z for X. If, however, we carry out the transformation on one side of the probability inequality, we must also do it on the other side. In other words, transforming X into Z requires us also to transform the value 60 into the appropriate value of the standard normal distribution. We transform the value 60 into the value $(60 - \mu)/\sigma$. The new probability statement is:

$$P(X > 60) = P\left(\frac{X - \mu}{\sigma} > \frac{60 - \mu}{\sigma}\right) = P\left(Z > \frac{60 - \mu}{\sigma}\right)$$

$$= P\left(Z > \frac{60 - 50}{10}\right) = P(Z > 1)$$

Why does the inequality still hold? We subtracted a number from each side of an inequality; this does not change the inequality. In the next step we divide both sides of the inequality by the standard deviation, σ. The inequality does not change because we can divide both sides of an inequality by a positive number, and a standard deviation is always a positive number. (Recall that dividing by 0 is not permissible; and dividing, or multiplying, by a negative value would reverse the direction of the inequality.) From the transformation, we find that the probability that a normal random variable with mean 50 and standard deviation 10 will have a value greater than 60 is exactly the probability that the standard normal random variable Z will be greater than 1. The latter probability can be found using Table 2. We find: $P(X > 60) = P(Z > 1) = 0.5000 - 0.3413 = 0.1587$. Let us now look at a few examples of the use of equation 4–5.

An Italian automaker believes that the number of kilometers driven on one of its engine models is normally distributed with mean 160,000 kilometers and standard deviation 30,000 kilometers. What is the probability that a given engine of this type will last anywhere from 100,000 to 180,000 kilometers before it needs to be replaced?

EXAMPLE (a)

Figure 4–11 shows the normal distribution for $X \sim N(160{,}000, 30{,}000^2)$ and the required area on the scale of the original problem and on the transformed z scale. We have the following (where the probability statement inequality has three sides and we carry out the transformation of equation 4–5 on all three sides).

SOLUTION

$$P(100{,}000 < X < 180{,}000) = P\left(\frac{100{,}000 - \mu}{\sigma} < \frac{X - \mu}{\sigma} < \frac{180{,}000 - \mu}{\sigma}\right)$$

$$= P\left(\frac{100{,}000 - 160{,}000}{30{,}000} < Z < \frac{180{,}000 - 160{,}000}{30{,}000}\right)$$

$$= P(-2 < Z < 0.6666) = 0.4772 + 0.2475 = 0.7247$$

(Table area values were obtained by linear interpolation.) Thus, there is a 0.7247 chance that a given engine of this kind will last anywhere from 100,000 to 180,000 kilometers before it needs to be replaced.

FIGURE 4–11   Probability Computation for Example (a)

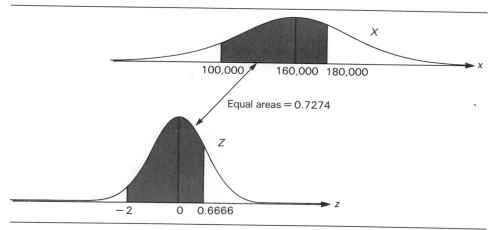

EXAMPLE (b)

The concentration of impurities in a semiconductor used in the production of micropro-cessors for computers is a normally distributed random variable with mean 127 parts per million and standard deviation 22. A semiconductor is acceptable only if its concentra-tion of impurities is below 150 parts per million. What proportion of the semiconductors are acceptable for use?

SOLUTION

$X \sim N(127, 22^2)$, and we need $P(X < 150)$. Using equation 4–5, we have:

$$P(X < 150) = P\left(\frac{X - \mu}{\sigma} < \frac{150 - \mu}{\sigma}\right) = P\left(Z < \frac{150 - 127}{22}\right)$$
$$= P(Z < 1.045) = 0.5 + 0.3520 = 0.8520$$

(The TA of 0.3520 was obtained by interpolation.) Thus, 85.2% of the semiconductors are acceptable for use. This also means that the probability that a randomly chosen semiconductor will be acceptable for use is 0.8520. The solution of this example is illus-trated in Figure 4–12.

FIGURE 4–12   Probability Computation for Example (b)

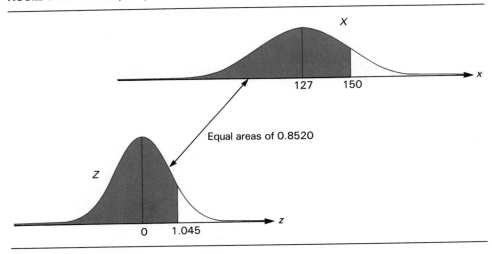

EXAMPLE (c)

Fluctuations in the prices of precious metals such as gold have been empirically shown to be well approximated by a normal distribution when observed over short intervals of time. In mid-September 1986, the daily price of gold (1 troy oz.) was believed to have a mean of $409 and a standard deviation of $12. A broker, working under these assump-tions, wanted to find the probability that the price of gold the next day will be between $420 and $425 per troy ounce. In this eventuality, the broker had an order from a client to sell the gold in the client's portfolio. What is the probability that the client's gold will be sold the next day?

SOLUTION

Figure 4–13 shows the setup for this problem and the transformation of X, where $X \sim N(409, 12^2)$, into the standard normal random variable Z. Also shown are the re-

FIGURE 4–13   Probability Computation for Example (c)

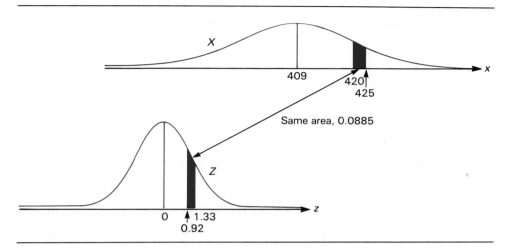

quired areas under the X curve and the transformed Z curve. We have:

$$P(420 < X < 425) = P\left(\frac{420 - \mu}{\sigma} < \frac{X - \mu}{\sigma} < \frac{425 - \mu}{\sigma}\right)$$

$$= P\left(\frac{420 - 409}{12} < Z < \frac{425 - 409}{12}\right)$$

$$= P(0.9166 < Z < 1.3333) = 0.4088 - 0.3203 = 0.0885$$

(Both TA values were obtained by a linear interpolation, although this is not necessary if less accuracy is acceptable).

Let us summarize the transformation procedure used in computing probabilities of events associated with a normal random variable $X \sim N(\mu, \sigma^2)$.

Transformation formulas of X to Z, where a and b are numbers:

$$P(X < a) = P\left(Z < \frac{a - \mu}{\sigma}\right)$$

$$P(X > b) = P\left(Z > \frac{b - \mu}{\sigma}\right)$$

$$P(a < X < b) = P\left(\frac{a - \mu}{\sigma} < Z < \frac{b - \mu}{\sigma}\right)$$

PROBLEMS

4–22.   For a normal random variable with mean 674 and standard deviation 55, find the probability that its value will be below 600.

4–23.   Let X be a normally distributed random variable with mean 410 and standard deviation 2. Find the probability that X will be between 407 and 415.

Answer

4–22.

0.0893

Answers

4–24.

0.003

4–26.
———
0.266

4–28.

0.9332, 0.3085, 0.0062

4–30.
———
0.3085, 0.0228, 0.7333

4–32.
———
0.00003

4–24.   If X is normally distributed with mean 500 and standard deviation 20, find the probability that X will be above 555.

4–25.   For a normally distributed random variable with mean -44 and standard deviation 16, find the probability that the value of the random variable will be above 0.

4–26.   A normal random variable has mean 0 and standard deviation 4. Find the probability that the random variable will be above 2.5.

4–27.   Let X be a normally distributed random variable with mean $\mu = 16$ and standard deviation $\sigma = 3$. Find $P(11 < X < 20)$. Also find $P(17 < X < 19)$ and $P(X > 15)$.

4–28.   The time it takes an international telephone operator to place an overseas phone call is normally distributed with mean 45 seconds and standard deviation 10 seconds.

a. What is the probability that my call will go through in less than one minute?

b. What is the probability that I will get through in less than 40 seconds?

c. What is the probability that I will have to wait more than 70 seconds for my call to go through?

4–29.   The number of votes cast in favor of a controversial proposition is believed to be approximately normally distributed with mean 8,000 and standard deviation 1,000. The proposition needs at least 9,322 votes in order to pass. What is the probability that the proposition will pass? (Assume numbers are on a continuous scale.)

4–30.   Under the system of floating exchange rates, the rate of foreign money to U.S. dollar is affected by many random factors, and this leads to the assumption of a normal distribution of small daily fluctuations. The rate of German marks per U.S. dollar is believed in a certain period to have a mean of 2.06 and a standard deviation of 0.08. Find the following.

a. The probability that tomorrow's rate will be above 2.10.

b. The probability that tomorrow's rate will be below 1.90.

c. The probability that tomorrow's exchange rate will be between 2.00 and 2.20.

4–31.   The production level at a plant is believed to be approximately normally distributed with mean 134,786 items per week and standard deviation 13,000. Find the probability that weekly production will exceed 150,000 items. Also find the probability that production will drop below 100,000 units in a given week. Suppose that labor disputes arise and production during the week drops below 80,000. Management blames the union for deliberately slowing down production, while the union claims that production is within acceptable level variations. Given the assumptions of normality and the stated mean and variance, do you believe the union? Explain.

4–32.   Certain diet drinks are stated to have, on the average, only 5 calories per serving. If the caloric content of servings are normally distributed with the stated 5 calories as the mean and with standard deviation of 0.5 calorie, what is the probability that a given serving will contain more than 7 calories?

Let us look more closely at the relationship between X, a normal random variable with mean μ and standard deviation σ, and the standard normal random variable. The fact that the standard normal random variable has mean 0 and standard deviation 1 has some important implications. When we say that Z is greater than 2, we are also saying that Z is more than 2 *standard deviations above its mean*. This is so because the mean of Z is 0 and the standard deviation is 1; hence, $Z > 2$ is the same event as $Z > [0 + 2(1)]$.

Now consider a normal random variable X with mean 50 and standard deviation 10. Saying that X is greater than 70 is exactly the same as saying that X is 2 standard deviations above its mean. This is so because 70 is 20 units above the mean, 50, and

20 units $= 2(10)$ units, or two standard deviations of X. Thus, the event $X > 70$ is the same as the event $X >$ (two standard deviations above the mean). This event is identical to the event $Z > 2$. Indeed, this is what results when we carry out the transformation of equation 4–5:

$$P(X > 70) = P\left(\frac{X - \mu}{\sigma} > \frac{70 - \mu}{\sigma}\right) = P\left(Z > \frac{70 - 50}{10}\right) = P(Z > 2)$$

Normal random variables are related to each other by the fact that the probability that a normal random variable will be above (or below) its mean a certain number of standard deviations is exactly equal to the probability that any other normal random variable will be above (or below) its mean the same number of (its) standard deviations. In particular, this property holds for the standard normal random variable. The probability that a normal random variable will be greater than (or less than) z units above its mean is the same as the probability that the standard normal random variable will be greater than (less than) z. The change from a z *value* of the random variable Z to z *standard deviations* above the mean for a given normal random variable X should suggest to us the inverse transformation, equation 4–6:

$$x = \mu + z\sigma$$

That is, the value of the random variable X may be written in terms of the number (z) of standard deviations (σ) it is above or below the mean (μ). Three examples are useful here. We know from the standard normal probability table that the probability that Z is greater than -1 and less than 1 is 0.6826 (show this). Similarly, we know that the probability that Z is greater than -2 and less than 2 is 0.9544. Also, the probability that Z is greater than -3 and less than 3 is 0.9974. These probabilities may be applied to *any* normal random variable as follows.[2]

1. The probability that a normal random variable will be within a distance of *1 standard deviation* from its mean (on either side) is 0.6826, or *approximately 0.68*.
2. The probability that a normal random variable will be within *2 standard deviations* of its mean is 0.9544, or *approximately 0.95*.
3. The probability that a normal random variable will be within *3 standard deviations* of its mean is 0.9974.

We use the inverse transformation, equation 4–6, when we want to get from a given probability to the value or values of a normal random variable X. We illustrate the procedure with a few examples.

PALCO Industries, Inc. is a leading manufacturer of cutting and welding products. One of the company's products is an acetylene gas cylinder used in welding. The amount of nitrogen gas in a cylinder is a normally distributed random variable with mean 124 units

EXAMPLE (d)

---

[2] This is the origin of the *empirical rule* (in Chapter 1) for mound-shaped data distributions. Mound-shaped data sets approximate the distribution of a normal random variable, and hence the proportions of observations within given number of standard deviations away from the mean roughly equal those predicted by the normal distribution. Compare the empirical rule (section 1–7) with the numbers given here.

FIGURE 4–14 The Solution of Example (d)

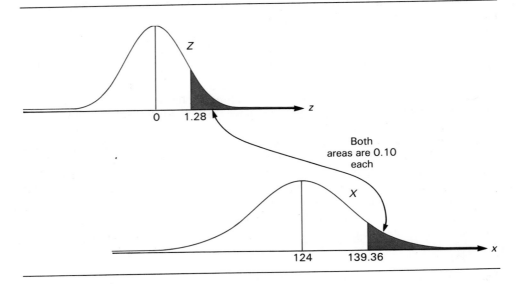

of volume and standard deviation 12. We want to find the amount of nitrogen, x, such that 10% of the cylinders contain more nitrogen than this amount.

SOLUTION   We have $X \sim N(124,12^2)$. We are looking for the value of the random variable X such that $P(X > x) = 0.10$. In order to find it, we look for the value of the standard normal random variable Z such that $P(Z > z) = 0.10$. Figure 4–14 illustrates how we find the value z and transform it to x. If the area to the right of z is equal to 0.10, the area between 0 and z (the table area) is equal to $0.5 - 0.10 = 0.40$. We look inside the table for the z value corresponding to TA = 0.40 and find $z = 1.28$ (actually, TA = 0.3997, which is close enough to 0.4). We need to find the appropriate x value. Here we use equation 4–6:

$$x = \mu + z\sigma = 124 + (1.28)(12) = 139.36$$

Thus, 10% of the acetylene cylinders contain more than 139.36 units of nitrogen.

EXAMPLE (e)   The amount of fuel consumed by the engines of a jetliner on a flight between two cities is a normally distributed random variable, X, with mean $\mu = 5.7$ tons and standard deviation $\sigma = 0.5$. Carrying too much fuel is inefficient as it slows the plane. If, however, too little fuel is loaded on the plane, an emergency landing may be necessary. The airline would like to determine the amount of fuel to load so that there will be a 0.99 probability that the plane will arrive at its destination.

SOLUTION   We have: $X \sim N(5.7,0.5^2)$. First, we must find the value z such that $P(Z < z) = 0.99$. Following our methodology, we find that the required table area is TA = $0.99 - 0.5 = 0.49$, and the corresponding z value is 2.33. Transforming the z value to an x value, we get: $x = \mu + z\sigma = 5.7 + (2.33)(0.5) = 6.865$. Thus, the plane should be loaded with 6.865 tons of fuel to give a 0.99 probability that the fuel will last throughout the flight. The transformation is shown in Figure 4–15.

FIGURE 4–15 The Solution of Example (e)

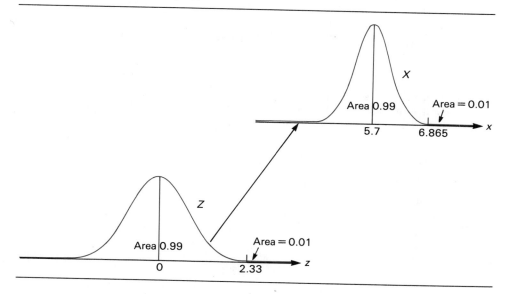

Weekly sales of Campbell's soup cans at a grocery store are believed to be normally distributed with mean 2,450 and standard deviation 400. The store management wants to find two values, symmetrically on either side of the mean, such that there will be a 0.95 probability that sales of soup cans during the week will be between the two values. Such information is useful in determining levels of orders and stock.

EXAMPLE (f)

Here $X \sim N(2,450,400^2)$. From the section on the standard normal random variable, we know how to find two values of Z such that the area under the curve between them is 0.95 (or any other area). We find that $z = 1.96$ and $z = -1.96$ are the required values. We now need to use equation 4–6. Since there are *two* values, one the negative of the other, we may combine them in a single transformation:

SOLUTION

$$x = \mu \pm z\sigma \qquad\qquad (4-7)$$

Applying this special formula we get: $x = 2,450 \pm (1.96)(400) = 1,666$ and $3,234$. Thus, management may be 95% sure that sales on any given week will be between 1,666 and 3,234 units.

Summary of the procedure of obtaining values of a normal random variable, given a probability:

1. Draw a picture of the normal distribution in question and the standard normal distribution.
2. In the picture, shade in the area corresponding to the probability.
3. Use the table to find the z value (or values) that give the required probability.
4. Use the transformation from Z to X to get the appropriate value (or values) of the original normal random variable.

PROBLEMS

4–33. If X is a normally distributed random variable with mean 120 and standard deviation 44, find a value x such that the probability that X will be less than x is 0.56.

4–34. For a normal random variable with mean 16.5 and standard deviation 0.8, find a point of the distribution such that there is a 0.85 probability that the value of the random variable will be above it.

4–35. For a normal random variable with mean 19,500 and standard deviation 400, find a point of the distribution such that the probability that the random variable will exceed this value is 0.02.

4–36. Find two values of the normal random variable with mean 88 and standard deviation 5 lying symmetrically on either side of the mean and covering an area of 0.98 between them.

4–37. For $X \sim N(32, 7^2)$, find two values, x_1 and x_2, symmetrically lying on each side of the mean, with $P(x_1 < X < x_2) = 0.99$.

4–38. If X is a normally distributed random variable with mean -61 and standard deviation 22, find the value such that the probability that the random variable will be above it is 0.25.

4–39. Let X be a normally distributed random variable with mean 97 and standard deviation 10. Find x such that $P(102 < X < x) = 0.05$.

4–40. Let X be a normally distributed random variable with mean 600 and variance 10,000. Find two values x_1 and x_2 such that $P(X > x_1) = 0.01$ and $P(X < x_2) = 0.05$.

4–41. Pierre operates a currency exchange office at Orly Airport in Paris. His office is open at night when the airport bank is closed, and he makes most of his business on returning American tourists who need to change their remaining French francs back to U.S. dollars. From experience, Pierre knows that the demand for dollars on any given night during high season is approximately normally distributed with mean $25,000 and standard deviation $5,000. If Pierre carries too much cash in dollars overnight, he pays a penalty: interest on the cash. On the other hand, if he runs short of cash during the night, he needs to send a person downtown to an all-night financial agency to get the required cash. This, too, is costly to him. Therefore, Pierre would like to carry overnight an amount of money such that the demand on 85% of the nights will not exceed this amount. Can you help Pierre find the required amount of dollars to carry?

4–42. The demand for unleaded gasoline at a service station is normally distributed with mean 27,009 gallons per day and standard deviation 4,530. Find two values that will give a symmetric 0.95 probability interval for the amount of unleaded gasoline demanded daily.

4–43. The percentage of protein in a certain brand of dog food is a normally distributed random variable with mean 11.2% and standard deviation 0.6%. The manufacturer would like to state on the package that the product has a protein content of at least $x_1\%$ and no more than $x_2\%$. They want their statement to be true for 99% of the packages sold. Determine the values x_1 and x_2.

4–44. Japanese travel agencies have recently discovered the beauty of Jamaica and are sending large groups of Japanese, many of them honeymooners, to vacation on this Caribbean island. On the average, a Japanese tourist pays $2,700 for a seven-day trip including airfare.[3] Assume that a tourist's total cost per trip is normally distributed with mean being the stated average and with standard deviation of $150. Only 5% of the Japanese tourists to Jamaica pay more than what amount for their vacation? Also give 95% bounds on the amount of money paid by a Japanese tourist for the vacation.

4–45. The CAC Index of the Paris stock market fluctuates widely but can be inferred to have a normal distribution with mean of 400 francs and standard deviation of 75 francs.[4] Give

---

[3] Japan's Newlyweds Fall for Jamaica," *Fortune* (January 14, 1991), p. 13.

[4] "World Stock Markets," *The Wall Street Journal* (March 7, 1991).

two bounds, symmetric about the mean, such that (knowing nothing else about the CAC Index value in recent days) you are 80% sure that the value of the index is anywhere between the two bounds.

4–6   More Complex Problems[5]

In this section, we show how more complicated problems related to normal random variables may be solved. The problems we solve are: finding the mean, finding the standard deviation, and finding both the mean and standard deviation of a normal random variable, using information about probabilities of the random variable. The problems require the solution of one or two linear equations.

Suppose we know that the mean of a normal random variable is 120, and we know that the probability that the random variable will be above 125 is 0.05. We do not know the standard deviation of the random variable. How can we find the value of the standard deviation, σ? Let us set up the problem in probability statement notation and see what we get. We have:

$$P(X > 125) = 0.05$$

We now transform to Z, so we can work with the probability. We know that $Z = (X - \mu)/\sigma$, and so:

$$P\left(Z > \frac{125 - \mu}{\sigma}\right) = 0.05$$

Since $\mu = 120$, we have:

$$P\left(Z > \frac{5}{\sigma}\right) = 0.05$$

Now we need to find z such that $P(Z > z) = 0.05$. From the table, we find $z = 1.645$. Finally, equating $z = 1.645$ with $z = 5/\sigma$, we get $\sigma = 5/1.645 = 3.04$. We illustrate the procedure of solving for an unknown mean with Example (g).

The net weight of a single cereal box is a normally distributed random variable. The variance of the net weights is known to be $\sigma^2 = 0.25$. Since the production process has changed, the mean is unknown (although the variance is believed not to have changed). A check of the weight of some boxes indicates that 20% of the boxes have net weight greater than 16.5 oz. Based on this information, find the mean net weight, μ, of the cereal boxes.

EXAMPLE (g)

We have:

SOLUTION

$$P(X > 16.5) = 0.20$$

Transforming X to Z we get:

$$P\left(\frac{X - \mu}{\sigma} > \frac{16.5 - \mu}{\sigma}\right) = 0.20$$

---

[5] Optional section.

Since $\sigma^2 = 0.25$, $\sigma = 0.5$ and:

$$P\left(Z > \frac{16.5 - \mu}{0.5}\right) = 0.20$$

We now need to find that particular point of the standard normal distribution, $z = (16.5 - \mu)/0.5$, such that the area under the curve to its right is equal to 0.20. From the table, using TA = $0.5 - 0.2 = 0.3$, we get $z = 0.84$. We now need to solve the equation for μ:

$$\frac{16.5 - \mu}{0.5} = 0.84$$

We get: $\mu = 16.5 - (0.84)(0.5) = 16.08$. Thus, the mean net weight of a box of cereal is $\mu = 16.08$ oz.

We may also solve for both an unknown mean and an unknown variance (or standard deviation) of a normal distribution. From algebra, we know that to solve for two unknowns, we need two equations. Therefore, we will need to have two probability statements about the normal random variable in question. The two statements will lead to two equations with the unknowns μ and σ. Let us look at an example.

EXAMPLE (h) For a certain new automobile, gasoline consumption on the highway is normally distributed with an unknown mean and unknown standard deviation. The manufacturer does know, however, that 80% of the time the automobile gets more than 28 miles per gallon (mpg) on the highway, and 40% of the time it gets more than 32 mpg on the highway. Find the mean and the standard deviation of highway gasoline consumption.

SOLUTION We have two probability statements:

$$P(X > 28) = 0.80 \qquad \text{and} \qquad P(X > 32) = 0.40$$

Let us transform these statements into statements about the random variable Z.

$$P\left(Z > \frac{28 - \mu}{\sigma}\right) = 0.80 \qquad \text{and} \qquad P\left(Z > \frac{32 - \mu}{\sigma}\right) = 0.40$$

We now look for the two z values, the first having an area to its right equal to 0.80 and the second having an area to its right equal to 0.40. From the table, we find that the first value is $z_1 = -0.84$, and the second value is $z_2 = 0.25$. Substituting these values into the expressions for μ and σ in the probability statements, we get two equations:

$$\frac{28 - \mu}{\sigma} = -0.84 \qquad \text{and} \qquad \frac{32 - \mu}{\sigma} = 0.25$$

Multiplying each equation by σ to get rid of denominators gives us the two equations:

$$28 - \mu = -0.84\sigma$$
$$32 - \mu = 0.25\sigma$$

We now solve the equations by substitution:

$$\mu = 28 + 0.84\sigma$$
$$\mu = 32 - 0.25\sigma$$

Equating the two expressions for μ gives: $28 + 0.84\sigma = 32 - 0.25\sigma$. Solving the resulting equation for σ gives us: $\sigma = 4/1.09 = 3.67$. Finally, substituting this value for σ into any of the equations gives us: $\mu = 31.08$.

PROBLEMS

4-46. The time it takes a train to go from one station to another is a normally distributed random variable with mean 129 minutes and an unknown variance. Thirty percent of the time, the train makes the trip in more than 142 minutes. Find the variance of the length of a single trip.

4-47. The weight of a tropical fruit experimentally grown in the United States is normally distributed with known variance of 0.04 and an unknown mean. The growers do know that 65% of the fruits have weights less than 0.5 lb. Find the expected weight of a randomly chosen fruit.

4-48. Weekly earnings on a certain import venture are approximately normally distributed with a known mean of $3,250, and an unknown standard deviation. Ten percent of the time, earnings are over $4,000. Find the standard deviation of weekly earnings.

4-49. The number of orders received monthly by a mail order firm is approximately normally distributed with standard deviation 560 and an unknown mean. Ninety percent of the time, monthly orders exceed 12,439. Find the mean number of orders per month.

4-50. The construction time for certain buildings is a normally distributed random variable with an unknown mean and variance. We do know, however, that 75% of the time, construction takes less than 12 months, and 45% of the time, construction takes less than 10 months. Find the mean and the standard deviation of construction time.

4-51. The weight of goods shipped in containers of a certain size is a normally distributed random variable. It is known that 65% of the containers have net weight above 4.9 tons, and 25% of the containers have net weight less than 4.2 tons. Find the mean and the standard deviation of the net weight of a container.

Data for the next three problems come from E. I. Ronn and A. K. Verma, "Pricing Risk Adjusted Deposit Insurance: An Option Based Model," *Journal of Finance* (September 1986), pp. 871-95.

4-52. Rates of return on bank assets are approximately normally distributed. For Bankers Trust NY Corp, the standard deviation is 1.75 (data are in annualized percentages). If the probability that the return will be above 7.4% is 0.55, find the mean annualized percentage return.

4-53. The average face value of total debt (in millions of dollars) for First Interstate Bancorp. is reported to be 36,405. If the face value of total debt is believed to be normally distributed and we know that 5% of the time it is over 45,000, what is the standard deviation of the face value of total debt for First Interstate Bancorp.?

4-54. The standard deviation of the annual value of assets for First Pennsylvania Corp. is reported as 46.2. Assuming a normal distribution of the annual value of assets, and that the probability is 0.90 that assets value will be under $4,048 million, find the mean annual assets value.

4-55. Cover Story is a monthly ranking of celebrities' popularity as reflected in the number of appearances by the celebrities on the pages of hundreds of national publications. A celebrity's rating, computed in some way based on the number of such appearances, is a random variable. For Cher, the rating has an average of 5.2 points.[6] If ratings are normally dis-

Answers

4-46.
615.49

4-48.
585.94

4-50.
10.315, 2.5

4-52.
7.6205

4-54.
3,988.86 millions

---

[6]Cover Story, *Advertising Age* (February 4, 1991).

Answer

1.5990 million,
0.3909 million

tributed and 80% of the time Cher's rating is below 7.0, what is Cher's standard deviation of ratings?

4–56.   The number of viewers of Cablevision systems is random and varies from day to day.[7] It may be assumed that 60% of the time there are more than 1.5 million viewers, and 90% of the time the number of viewers is below 2.1 million. Assuming a normal distribution, find the mean and the standard deviation of the daily number of Cablevision viewers.

4–7   The Normal Distribution as an Approximation to Other Probability Distributions

The normal distribution is, by its very nature, the limiting probability distribution in many situations. In fact, the majority of the probability distributions discussed in this book tend to the normal distribution as some quantity relevant to the distribution, such as sample size, increases indefinitely. For example, the t distribution and the chi-square distribution—two important probability distributions used in statistics and introduced in the next chapters—tend to the normal distribution as the sample size from which they arise increases. As was noted in the beginning of this chapter, the normal distribution was originally discovered as the limit of the binomial distribution as n increases. We now return to this situation and show how the normal distribution serves as an approximation to the binomial.

As n, the number of trials in the binomial experiment, increases, the discrete binomial probability distribution tends to the continuous normal probability distribution. This means that, for large n, we may approximate a binomial probability with the probability obtained for a normal random variable with the same mean and the same standard deviation as the binomial. Let us look at an example.

EXAMPLE (i)

Suppose that the proportion of people who use a certain product is $p = 0.50$. A random sample of seven people is chosen, and we want to evaluate the probability that at most four of them will be product users. We want to do this both directly and by way of a normal approximation. The situation is demonstrated in Figure 4–16, where the sum of the weights to the left of and including 4, that is, $F(4)$, is shown. Also shown is the normal approximation to the required probability: the area under the normal curve to the left of the point 4.5. (We use 4.5 because we want to include 4 but not 5, and the best way to do this—using a continuous approximation to a discrete distribution[8]—is to draw the line centered between the two points 4 and 5.)

The normal distribution we use is one with mean and standard deviation identical to those of the given binomial. We have: $\mu = np = (0.5)(7) = 3.5$ and $\sigma = \sqrt{np(1 - p)} = \sqrt{(7)(0.5)(0.5)} = 1.323$. The normal approximation to the binomial probability $F(4)$ is:

$$P(X < 4.5) = P\left(Z < \frac{4.5 - \mu}{\sigma}\right)$$
$$= P\left(Z < \frac{4.5 - 3.5}{1.323}\right) = P(Z < 0.756)$$

for which the value from the normal table, added to 0.5 as required, gives us 0.7749. The true probability, obtained from the binomial table (Table 1), is $F(4) = 0.7734$. Thus, the approximation, even with a small number of trials ($n = 7$), is quite good. Let

---

[7] F. Meeks, "Bell TV?" *Forbes* (March 4, 1991), p. 42.

[8] This is sometimes called a *continuity correction*.

FIGURE 4–16   Approximating a Binomial Distribution with $n = 7$ and $p = 0.5$ by a Normal Distribution [Example (i)]

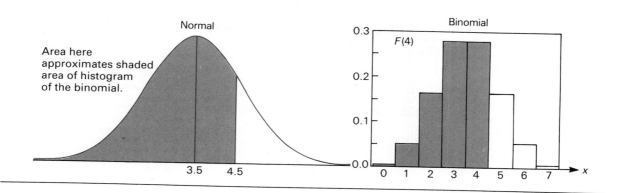

us now see what happens when the number of trials increases. Suppose that we now take a sample of 11 people, and we want to find the probability that at most 4 of them are users of the product of interest. Again, we evaluate the probability two ways. First, we refer directly to the binomial table: $F(4) = 0.2744$ (see Table 1 with $p = 0.5$ and $n = 11$). Then we use the approximating normal random variable with mean $\mu = np = 11(0.5) = 5.5$ and standard deviation $\sigma = \sqrt{np(1 - p)} = 1.6583$. We find:

$$P(X < 4.5) = P\left(Z < \frac{4.5 - 5.5}{1.6583}\right) = P(Z < -0.603) = 0.2732$$

(from Table 2, with interpolation). Again, the approximation is excellent. The situation is shown in Figure 4–17.

As the number of trials, n, increased from 7 to 11, the normal approximation to the binomial improved by three units in the fourth decimal place. We showed how the normal distribution is used in approximating a binomial with $p = 0.5$. In this case, the approximation is best and works well with relatively small n because the binomial distribution is *symmetric*. When $p \neq 0.5$, the binomial distribution is not symmetric, and the convergence to a normal distribution is slower. Approximations to the binomial with

FIGURE 4–17   Approximating a Binomial Distribution with $n = 11$ and $p = 0.5$ by a Normal Distribution [Example (i)]

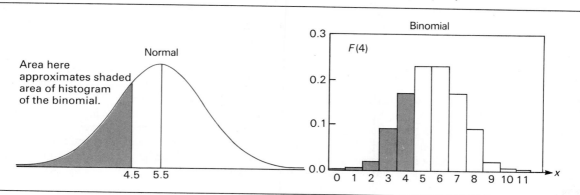

$p \neq 0.5$ improve more dramatically as n increases than was the case in our example. When can we safely use the normal distribution as an approximation to the binomial? A rule of thumb says that the normal approximation works well when both np and $n(1 - p)$ are greater than 5. Of course, the larger n is, the better the approximation. Also, the closer p is to 0.5, the better the approximation and the lower the minimum n required for good approximation accuracy.

Approximating a binomial probability using the normal distribution:

$$P(a \leq X \leq b) \doteq P\left(\frac{a - np}{\sqrt{np(1 - p)}} \leq Z \leq \frac{b - np}{\sqrt{np(1 - p)}}\right)$$

for n large ($n \geq 50$) and p not too close to 0 or 1.00.
Or:

$$P(a \leq X \leq b) \doteq P\left(\frac{a - 0.5 - np}{\sqrt{np(1 - p)}} \leq Z \leq \frac{b + 0.5 - np}{\sqrt{np(1 - p)}}\right)$$

for n only moderately large ($20 \leq n < 50$). This is the continuity correction.

If p is either small (close to 0) or large (close to 1.00), use the Poisson approximation instead. The normal approximation is usually considered adequate if $np(1 - p) > 9$.

PROBLEMS

Answers

In the following problems, use a normal distribution to compute the required probabilities. Whenever you can, compare your answers with the true binomial probabilities obtained from the binomial table, Table 1 in Appendix C. In each problem, also state the assumptions necessary for a binomial distribution, and indicate whether the assumptions are reasonable.

4–57. The manager of a restaurant knows from experience that 70% of the people who make reservations for the evening show up for dinner. The manager decides one evening to overbook and accept 20 reservations when only 15 tables are available. What is the probability that more than 15 parties will show up?

4–58.
_____
0.99997

4–58. An advertising research study indicates that 40% of the viewers exposed to an advertisement try the product during the following four months. If 100 people are exposed to the ad, what is the probability that at least 20 of them will try the product in the following four months?

4–59. A computer system contains 45 identical microchips. The probability that any microchip will be in working order at a given time is 0.80. A certain operation requires that at least 30 of the chips be in working order. What is the probability that the operation will be carried out successfully?

4–60.
_____
0.8985

4–60. Sixty percent of the managers who enroll in a special training program will successfully complete the program. If a large company sends 28 of its managers to enroll in the program, what is the probability that at least half of them will pass?

4–61. A large state university sends recruiters throughout the state in order to recruit graduating high school seniors to enroll in the university. From the university's records, it is known that 25% of the students who are interviewed by the recruiters actually enroll. If last spring the university recruiters interviewed 1,889 graduating seniors, what is the probability that at least 500 of them will enroll this fall?

4–62.
_____
Less than 0.00003

4–62. Several automobile manufacturers are currently experimenting with adapting car engines to run on hydrogen.[9] A particular 3.8-liter engine is believed to have a 0.6 probability of developing 170 horsepower in the hydrogen version (rather than its 208 horsepower in the usual gasoline version). If 200 cars are randomly tested, what is the probability that at least 150 of them will develop 170 horsepower?

4–63. In the situation of the previous problem, only 30% of the cars fitted with the hydrogen engine can last 50,000 miles before a major breakdown. If 500 cars are sold, what is the probability that at least 80% of them will last 50,000 miles without a breakdown? (Assume independence.)

4–8 Using the Computer

Computer packages, including MINITAB, can be used to evaluate probabilities for normal random variables. Again, we can use the command CDF followed by the value for which we need the cumulative normal probability. We end the command with a semicolon, after which the computer looks for a subcommand. Then we type: NORMAL. If we put a period right after NORMAL, the computer assumes we need the standard normal. Otherwise, we specify two numbers, one for the mean and one for the standard deviation before typing the final period and pressing "return." Two examples are demonstrated in Figure 4–18. Verify the simple answers using the normal table.

4–9 Summary and Review of Terms

In this chapter, we discussed the **normal probability distribution,** the most important probability distribution in statistics. We defined the **standard normal random variable** as the normal random variable with mean 0 and standard deviation 1. We saw how to use a table of probabilities for the standard normal random variable and how to transform a normal random variable with any mean and any standard deviation to the standard normal random variable using the **normal transformation.**

We also saw how the standard normal random variable may, in turn, be transformed into any other normal random variable with a specified mean and standard deviation, and how this allows us to find values of a normal random variable that conform with some probability statement. We discussed a method of determining the mean and/or the standard deviation of a normal random variable from probability statements about the random variable. We saw how the normal distribution is used as a model in many real-world situations, both as the true distribution (a continuous one) and as an approximation to discrete distributions. In particular, we il-

FIGURE 4–18   Examples of Using MINITAB to Find Normal Probabilities

```
MTB > cdf 1.00;
SUBC> normal mean=o stddev=1.
      1.0000     0.8413

MTB > cdf 20;
SUBC> normal mean=10, stddev=5.
     20.0000     0.9772
MTB > stop
```

---

[9] "Fill 'er up—with Hydrogen, Please," *Business Week* (March 4, 1991), p. 59.

lustrated the use of the normal distribution as an approximation to the binomial distribution.

In the following chapters, we will make much use of the material presented here. Most of statistical theory relies on the normal distribution and on distributions that are derived from it.

ADDITIONAL PROBLEMS

Answers

4-64.

0.7642

4-66.

0.1587, 0.9772

4-68.

791,580.00

4-70.

[7.02, 8.98]

4-72.

1,556,
[1,373, 3,323]

4-64. The time, in hours, a copying machine may work without breaking down is a normally distributed random variable with mean 549 and standard deviation 68. Find the probability that the machine will work for at least 500 hours without breaking down.

4-65. The yield, in tons of ore per day, at a given coal mine is approximately normally distributed with mean 785 tons and standard deviation 60. Find the probability that at least 800 tons of ore will be mined on a given day. Find the proportion of working days in which anywhere from 750 to 850 tons are mined. Find the probability that on a given day, the yield will be below 665 tons.

4-66. Scores on a management aptitude examination are believed to be normally distributed with mean 650 (out of a total of 800 possible points) and standard deviation 50. What is the probability that a randomly chosen manager will achieve a score above 700? What is the probability that the score will be below 750?

4-67. Assume that the price of a share of TWA stock is normally distributed with mean 48 and standard deviation 6. What is the probability that on a randomly chosen day in the period for which our assumptions are made (the first part of 1986), the price of the stock will be over $60 per share? Below $60 per share? Above $40 per share? Between $40 and $50 per share? (Some data for this problem were obtained from *The Wall Street Journal*, September 11, 1986.) What are the limitations of your analysis?

4-68. The amount of oil pumped daily at Standard Oil's facilities in Prudhoe Bay is normally distributed with mean 800,000 barrels and standard deviation 10,000 (from the *Standard Oil Scene*, Summer 1986). In determining the amount of oil the company must report as its lower limit of daily production, the company wants to choose an amount such that for 80% of the days, at least the reported amount, x, is produced. Determine the value of the lower limit x.

4-69. Models of the pricing of stock options make the assumption of a normal distribution. An analyst believes that the price of an IBM stock option with expiration date December 12, 1988, is a normally distributed random variable with mean $8.95 and variance 4. The analyst would like to determine a value such that there is a 0.90 probability that the price of the option will be above that value. Find the required value.

4-70. Weekly rates of return (on an annualized basis) for certain securities over a given period of time are believed to be normally distributed with mean 8.00% and variance 0.25. Give two values, x_1 and x_2, such that you are 95% sure that annualized weekly returns will be between the two values.

4-71. The impact of a television commercial, measured in terms of excess sales volume over a given time period, is believed to be approximately normally distributed with a mean 50,000 and variance 9,000,000. Find 0.99 probability bounds on the volume of excess sales that would result from a given airing of the commercial.

4-72. A travel agency believes that the number of people who sign up for tours to Hawaii during the Christmas–New Year holiday season is an approximately normally distributed random variable with mean 2,348 and standard deviation 762. For reservation purposes, the agency's management wants to find the number of people such that the probability is 0.85 that at least that many people will sign up. They also need 0.80 probability bounds on the number of people who will sign up for the trip.

4-73. A loans manager at a large bank believes that the percentage of her customers who default on their loans during each quarter is an approximately normally distributed random variable with mean 12.1% and standard deviation 2.5%. Give a lower bound, x, with 0.75

probability that the percentage of people defaulting on their loans is at least x. Also give an upper bound, x', with 0.75 probability that the percentage of loan defaulters is below x'.

4–74.   The power generated by a solar electric generator is normally distributed with mean of 15.6 kilowatts and standard deviation of 4.1 kilowatts. We may be 95% sure that the generator will deliver at least how many kilowatts?

4–75.   Short-term interest rates fluctuate daily. It may be assumed that the rate in Switzerland in 1990 was approximately normally distributed with mean 8.9% and standard deviation of 0.8%.[10] Find a value such that 95% of the time during that year the short-term rate in Switzerland was below this value.

4–76.   In quality-control projects, engineers use charts where item values are plotted and compared with 3-standard deviation bounds above and below the mean for the process. When items are found to fall outside the bounds, they are considered nonconforming, and the process is stopped when "too many" items are out of bounds. Assuming a normal distribution of item values, what percentage of values would you *expect* to be out of bounds when the process is in control? Accordingly, how would you define "too many"? What do you think is the rationale for this practice?

4–77.   Total annual textbook sales in a certain discipline are normally distributed. Forty-five percent of the time, sales are above 671,000 copies, and 10% of the time, sales are above 712,000 copies. Find the mean and the variance of annual sales.

4–78.   Typing speed on a new kind of keyboard for people at a certain stage in their training program is approximately normally distributed. The probability that the speed of a given trainee will be above 65 words per minute is 0.45. The probability that the speed will be better than 70 words per minute is 0.15. Find the mean and the standard deviation of typing speed.

4–79.   The number of people responding to a mailed information brochure on cruises of the Royal Viking Line through an agency in San Francisco is approximately normally distributed. The agency found that 10% of the time, over 1,000 people respond immediately after a mailing, and 50% of the time, at least 650 people respond right after the mailing. Find the mean and the standard deviation of the number of people who respond following a mailing.

4–80.   The Tourist Delivery Program was developed by several European automakers. In this program, a tourist from outside Europe—most are from the United States—may purchase an automobile in Europe and drive it in Europe for as long as six months, after which the manufacturer will ship the car to the tourist's home destination at no additional cost. In addition to the time limitations imposed, some countries impose mileage restrictions so that tourists will not misuse the privileges of the program. In setting the limitation, some countries use a normal distribution assumption. It is believed that the average number of miles driven by a tourist in the program is normally distributed with mean 4,500 and standard deviation 1,800. If a country wants to set the mileage limit at a point such that 80% of the tourists in the program will want to drive fewer miles, what should the limit be?

4–81.   The number of newspapers demanded daily at a large metropolitan area is believed to be an approximately normally distributed random variable. If more newspapers are demanded than are printed, the paper suffers an opportunity loss, in that it could have sold more papers, and also a loss of public goodwill. On the other hand, if more papers are printed than will be demanded, the unsold papers are returned to the newspaper office at a loss. Suppose that management believes it is most important to guard against the first type of error, unmet demand, and would like to set the number of papers printed at a level such that 75% of the time, demand for newspapers will be below that point. How many papers should be printed daily if the average demand is 34,750 papers and the standard deviation of demand is 3,560?

4–82.   Arrival times of airplanes at their destination airports are normally distributed. Air traffic controllers must deal with these random arrivals in arranging for a free runway for a landing. The arrival time depends on many factors, such as weather conditions, flight duration, and flight altitude. Suppose that for a certain type of flight, arrival time is a normally

---

[10] "International Financial Markets," *Financial Market Trends* (October 1990), p. 11.

Answers

4–84.

120.3, 0.5

4–86.

0.006

4–88.

0.5

4–90.

Greater than 0.99997

distributed random variable with mean 42.0 minutes after the hour and standard deviation 2.4 minutes. If an air traffic controller wants to hold a runway for the plane until a time such that she can be 98% sure that the plane will not arrive any later, until what time should the controller wait?

4–83. Pollution has caused the death of large numbers of trees in German forests. The proportion of dying trees in a certain region is as high as 0.30. Sometimes it happens that so many trees die, there are not enough trees to prevent erosion of the soil, and this causes the destruction of the entire forest. In a particular location, there are 238 trees. Scientists believe that if pollution should kill as many as 50 trees, all 238 trees in the location will eventually die. Assuming that the probability that any single tree will die from pollution is indeed 0.30, and that trees are affected independently of each other, what is the probability that out of 238 trees at least 50 will die, thus endangering the forest?

4–84. The amount of electricity demanded in a midsized town is normally distributed. The utility serving the area needs estimates of electricity consumption in order to arrange for the purchase of electricity in excess of what they produce when demand exceeds production. They also want to be able to reduce their production when consumption is at lower levels and thus keep down the cost of electric power. Management knows that the standard deviation of demand in January is 5.1 megawatts. Management also knows that there is a 0.20 probability that electric demand in January will exceed 124.6 megawatts. What is the mean electric demand during the month of January? If the utility should decide to produce exactly the average electric demand for the month, what is the probability that demand will be less than production?

4–85. In setting warranties on appliances, manufacturers want to set the time limit in such a way that few appliances will have to be repaired at the manufacturer's expense, yet they want the buyer to have some degree of protection against malfunctions over a period of time after the purchase. A manufacturer of a certain appliance would like to set the expiration time of the warranty at such a level that 90% of the appliances made will remain in working order throughout the period. What should the time period be if the life of the appliance is normally distributed with mean 38 months and standard deviation 11 months?

4–86. Redo problem 3–66 of Chapter 3 using a normal approximation to the binomial distribution. Compare the two results.

4–87. Emery Worldwide now specializes in transporting animals by air and making them feel comfortable while on board the aircraft. Recently, Emery flew six gorillas from Cincinnati to San Diego and treated them royally with large amounts of fresh fruit.[11] Such flights are very costly and average $40,000. The fare depends on the kind of animals and their particular requirements and is negotiated individually. Assuming the cost is normally distributed with standard deviation of $10,000, what is the probability that the next animal flight will cost between $25,000 and $35,000?

4–88. Project costs are normally distributed with mean $1.5 million. What is the probability that the next project will cost at least $1.5 million?

4–89. In the situation of the previous problem, 75% of the projects cost over $1 million. What is the standard deviation of project costs?

4–90. Twenty-four percent of Wells-Fargo Bank's loans are in real estate.[12] If a random sample of 2,000 of the bank's loans is selected for examination, what is the probability that at least 20% of the loans in the sample are in real estate?

4–91. *The round-numbers trap.* Supposedly, the IRS looks for "nice" numbers in taxpayers' returns for further investigation, which may lead to an audit. Thus for example, a return form reporting an expense item of $3,000 would lead to initial scrutiny while numbers such as $3,137.12 would not.[13] A random sample of 10,000 returns is selected by the IRS out of a population of returns where 10% contain round numbers. What is the probability that at least 800 returns in the sample will contain round numbers?

---

[11] "Of Course, Sir, Sit Wherever You Like," *Business Week* (March 11, 1991), p. 41.

[12] "Bank Bulls," *Forbes* (March 4, 1991), p. 115.

[13] *Tax Guide for College Teachers* (College Park, MD: Academic Information Service, 1991).

OVERALL PERFORMANCE OF CASH EQUIVALENTS FOR STOCKS

A study was conducted on cash equivalents for stock. Annualized rates of return for these stocks were computed, and then the mean and the standard deviation were calculated for these percentages of return. The average for all stocks in the study was found to be 3.76%, and the standard deviation was found to be 3.48%.[14] A random sample of 105 of the returns is presented below.

4.2929	2.5078	0.0497	4.8775	4.7823	1.9127	5.6990
8.2220	5.1947	−0.0513	0.1797	7.7884	−0.3332	3.4602
−2.1203	2.1744	4.7451	4.2653	0.9926	7.5047	11.4342
1.4832	9.2090	4.5709	3.0776	0.5469	6.3069	−2.5981
3.6459	5.6322	4.0596	−1.8470	5.6297	5.5510	0.4241
2.3822	0.2255	0.5892	10.5601	3.4567	2.2958	9.1093
3.1829	7.6588	−2.1161	8.0557	5.9172	8.5991	3.4134
8.6449	3.8811	18.9001	2.9253	3.3914	4.8913	1.3166
10.9781	3.0342	1.5353	8.7480	3.1827	5.3145	4.8544
2.7868	5.6929	6.0649	0.4156	6.3927	2.6705	0.9061
0.4027	8.2145	7.3652	6.5483	−0.1128	−2.1665	6.5056
4.4936	0.0100	2.5397	3.3327	8.3862	2.2782	7.3212
1.9865	4.8451	1.7055	7.4952	0.0577	4.4249	8.6370
6.0416	3.9232	1.2513	4.0367	3.3105	5.8972	9.4582
5.6092	6.2703	5.4551	7.0799	−1.6761	1.2563	1.8623

a. Plot a histogram of the data. Compute the mean and the standard deviation of the data, and compare them with the numbers in the study. Now compute specific percentage points of the data distribution that may be compared with percentage points of a normal distribution with the same mean and standard deviation. Based on your results, can you conclude that the data distribution is approximately normal?

b. Assuming a normal distribution is appropriate, consider the following. The original investment in each case is $1,000. Once you sell the stock and realize your return, the brokerage house deducts an amount equal to 5% of your earnings as their commission. What can you say about the distribution of the net returns (after commissions are paid)? Explain.

---

[14] G. Kester, "Market Timing," *Financial Analysts Journal* (September–October 1990), p. 64.

SAMPLING AND SAMPLING DISTRIBUTIONS

INTRODUCTION

S tatistics is a science of *inference*. It is the science of generalization from a *part* (the randomly chosen sample) to the *whole* (the population).[1] Recall from Chapter 1 that the population is the entire collection of measurements in which we are interested, and the sample is a smaller set of measurements selected from the population. A random sample of n elements is a sample selected from the population in such a way that every set of n elements is as likely to be selected as any other set of n elements.[2] It is important that the sample be drawn randomly from the entire population under study. This makes it likely that our sample will be truly representative of the population of interest and minimizes the chance of errors. As we will see in this chapter, random sampling also allows us to compute the probabilities of sampling errors, thus providing us with knowledge of the degree of accuracy of our sampling results. The need to sample correctly is best illustrated by the well-known story of the *Literary Digest*.

DIGEST POLL GIVES LANDON 32 STATES

LANDON LEADS 4–3 IN LAST DIGEST POLL

Final Tabulation Gives Him 370 Electoral Votes to 161 for President Roosevelt

Governor Landon will win the election by an electoral vote of 370 to 161, will carry thirty-two of the forty-eight States, and will lead President Roosevelt about four to three in their share of the popular vote, if the final figures in The Literary Digest poll, made public yesterday, are verified by the count of the ballots next Tuesday.

The New York Times, Friday, October 30, 1936.
Copyright © 1936 by The New York Times Company. Reprinted by permission.

---

[1] Not all of statistics concerns inferences about populations. One branch of statistics, called *descriptive statistics,* deals with describing data sets—possibly with no interest in an underlying population. The descriptive statistics of Chapter 1, when *not* used for inference, fall in this category.

[2] This is the definition of *simple random sampling,* and we will assume throughout that all our samples are simple random samples. Other methods of sampling are discussed in Chapter 17.

Continued on next page

ROOSEVELT'S PLURALITY IS 11,000,000

HISTORY'S LARGEST POLL

46 STATES WON BY PRESIDENT,
MAINE AND VERMONT BY LANDON

MANY PHASES TO VICTORY

Democratic Landslide Looked Upon as Striking
Personal Triumph for Roosevelt

By Arthur Krock

As the the count of ballots cast Tuesday in the 1936 Presidential election moved toward completion yesterday, these facts appeared: Franklin Delano Roosevelt was re-elected President, and John N. Garner Vice President, by the largest popular and electoral majority since the United States became a continental nation—a margin of approximately 11,000,000 plurality of all votes cast, and 523 votes in the electoral college to 8 won by the Republican Presidential candidate, Governor Alfred M. Landon of Kansas. The latter carried only Maine and Vermont of the forty-eight States of the Union . . . .

The New York Times, Thursday, November 5, 1936.
Copyright © 1936 by The New York Times Company. Reprinted by permission.

In 1936, the widely quoted *Literary Digest* embarked on the project of predicting the results of the presidential election to be held that year. The magazine boasted it would predict, to within a fraction of the percentage of the votes, the winner of the election—incumbent President Franklin Delano Roosevelt or the Republican governor of Kansas, Alfred M. Landon. The *Digest* tried to gather a sample of staggering proportion—10 million voters! One problem with the survey was that only a fraction of the people sampled, 2.3 million, actually provided the requested information. Should a link have existed between a person's inclination to answer the survey and his or her voting preference, the results of the survey would have been *biased*: slanted toward the voting preference of those who did answer. It is unknown whether such a link did exist in the case of the *Digest*. (This problem is known as *nonresponse bias* and is discussed in Chapter 17.) A very serious problem with the *Digest*'s poll, and one known to have affected the results, is the following.

The sample of voters chosen by the *Literary Digest* was obtained from lists of telephone numbers, automobile registrations, and names of *Digest* readers. Remember that this was 1936—not as many people owned phones or cars as today, and the ones who did tended to be wealthier and more likely to vote Republican (and the same goes for readers of the *Digest*). The selection procedure for the sample of voters was thus biased (slanted toward one kind of voter) because the sample was not randomly chosen from the entire population of voters. Figure 5–1 demonstrates

FIGURE 5–1   A Good Sampling Procedure and the One Used by the *Literary Digest*

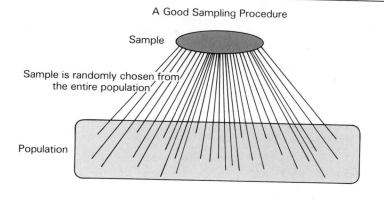

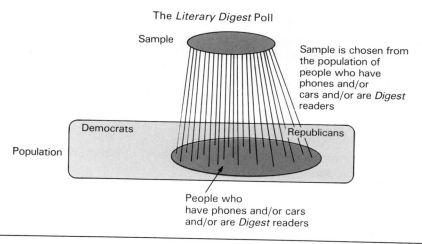

a correct sampling procedure versus the sampling procedure used by the *Literary Digest*.

As a result of the *Digest* error, the magazine does not exist today; it went bankrupt soon after the 1936 election. Some say that hindsight is useful and that today we know more statistics, making it easy for us to deride mistakes made more than 50 years ago. Interestingly enough, however, the ideas of sampling bias were understood in 1936. A few weeks *before* the election, there appeared a small article in *The New York Times* criticizing the methodology of the *Digest* poll. Few paid it any attention.

Sampling is very useful in many situations besides political polling, including business and other areas where we need to obtain information about some population. Our information often leads to a *decision*. There are also situations, as demonstrated by the examples in the introduction to this book, where we are interested in a *process* rather than a single population. One such process is the relationship between advertising and sales. In these more involved situations, we still make the assumption of an underlying population—here, the population of *pairs* of possible advertising and sales values. Conclusions about the process are reached based on information in our data, which are assumed to constitute a random sample from the entire population. The ideas of a population and of a random sample drawn from the population are thus essential to all of inferential statistics.

In statistical inference we are concerned with populations; the samples are of no interest to us in their own right. We wish to use our *known* random sample in the extraction of information about the *unknown* population from which it is drawn. The information we extract is in the form of summary statistics: a sample mean, a sample standard deviation, or other measures computed from the sample. A statistic such as the sample mean is considered an *estimator* of a population *parameter*—the population mean. In the next section, we discuss and define sample estimators and population parameters. Then we explore the relationship between statistics and parameters via the *sampling distribution*. Finally, we discuss desirable properties of statistical estimators. ■

5–2 Sample Statistics as Estimators of Population Parameters

A population may be a large, sometimes infinite, collection of elements. The population has a *frequency distribution*—the distribution of the frequencies of occurrence of its elements. The population distribution, when stated in relative frequencies, is also the probability distribution of the population. This is so because the relative frequency of a value in the population is also the probability of obtaining the particular value when an element is randomly drawn from the entire population. As with random variables, we may associate with a population its mean and its standard deviation. In the case of populations, the mean and the standard deviation are called *parameters*. They are denoted by μ and σ, respectively.

> A numerical measure of a population is called a **population parameter,** or simply a **parameter.**

Recall that in Chapter 4 we referred to the mean and the standard deviation of a normal probability distribution as the distribution parameters. Here we view parameters as descriptive measures of populations. Inference drawn about a population parameter is based on sample statistics.

> A numerical measure of the sample is called a **sample statistic,** or simply a **statistic.**

Population parameters are estimated by sample statistics. When a sample statistic is used to estimate a population parameter, the statistic is called an *estimator* of the parameter.

> An **estimator** of a population parameter is a sample statistic used to estimate the parameter. An **estimate** of the parameter is a *particular* numerical value of the estimator obtained by sampling. When a single value is used as an estimate, the estimate is called a **point estimate** of the population parameter.

The sample mean, $\overline{X}$, is the sample statistic used as an estimator of the population mean, μ. Once we sample from the population and obtain a value of $\overline{X}$ (using equation 1–1), we will have obtained a *particular* sample mean; we will denote this particular value by $\overline{x}$. We may have, for example, $\overline{x} = 12.53$. This value is our estimate of μ. The estimate is a point estimate because it constitutes a single number. In this chapter, every estimate will be a point estimate—a single number that, we hope, lies close to the population parameter it estimates. Chapter 6 is entirely devoted to the concept of an *interval estimate*—an estimate constituting an interval of numbers rather than a single number. An interval estimate is an interval believed likely to contain the unknown population parameter. It conveys more information than just the point estimate on which it is based.

In addition to the sample mean, which estimates the population mean, other statistics are useful. The sample standard deviation, S, is used as an estimator of the population standard deviation σ. A particular estimate obtained will be denoted by s. (This estimate is computed from the data using equation 1–4 or an equivalent formula.)

As demonstrated by the political polling example with which we opened this chapter, interest often centers not on a mean or standard deviation of a population, but rather on a population *proportion*. The population proportion parameter is also called a binomial proportion parameter.

> The **population proportion,** p, is equal to the number of elements in the population belonging to the category of interest, divided by the total number of elements in the population.

The population proportion of voters for Governor Landon in 1936, for example, was the number of people who intended to vote for the candidate, divided by the total number of voters. The estimator of the population proportion p is the *sample proportion* $\hat{P}$, defined as the number of *binomial successes* in the sample (i.e., the number of elements in the sample that belong to the category of interest) divided by the sample size, n. A particular estimate of the population proportion p is the sample proportion $\hat{p}$.

The **sample proportion:**

$$\hat{p} = \frac{x}{n} \tag{5–1}$$

where x is the number of elements in the sample found to belong to the category of interest, and n is the sample size

Suppose that we want to estimate the proportion of consumers in a certain area that are users of a certain product. The (unknown) population proportion is p. We estimate p by the statistic $\hat{P}$, the sample proportion. Suppose a random sample of 100 consumers in the area reveals that 26 of them are users of the product. Our point estimate of p is then $\hat{p} = x/n = 26/100 = 0.26$.

In summary, we have the following estimation relationships.

Estimator (Sample statistic)		Population parameter
$\overline{X}$	estimates →	μ
S	estimates →	σ
$\hat{P}$	estimates →	p

Let us consider sampling to estimate the population mean, and let us try to visualize how this is done. Consider a population with a certain frequency distribution.

FIGURE 5–2   A Population Distribution, a Random Sample from the Population, and Their Respective Means

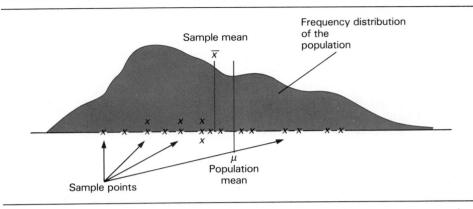

The frequency distribution of the values of the population is the probability distribution of the value of an element in the population, drawn at random. Figure 5–2 shows a frequency distribution of some population, and the population mean, μ. If we knew the exact frequency distribution of the population, we would be able to determine μ directly in the same way we determine the mean of a random variable when we know its probability distribution. In reality, the frequency distribution of a population is not known; neither is the mean of the population. We try to estimate the population mean by the sample mean, computed from a random sample. Figure 5–2 shows the values of a random sample obtained from the population and the resulting sample mean, $\bar{x}$, computed from the data.

In this example, $\bar{x}$ happens to lie close to μ, the population parameter it estimates, although this does not always happen. The sample statistic $\bar{X}$ is a *random variable* whose actual value depends on the particular random sample obtained. The random variable $\bar{X}$ has a relatively high probability of being close to the population mean it estimates, and it has decreasing probabilities of falling further and further away from the population mean. Similarly, the sample statistic S is a random variable with a relatively high probability of being close to σ, the population parameter it estimates. Also, when sampling for a population proportion, p, the estimator $\hat{P}$ has a relatively high probability of being close to p. How high a probability, and how close to the parameter? The answer to this question is the main topic of this chapter, presented in the next section. Before discussing this important topic, we will say a few things about the mechanics of obtaining random samples.

Obtaining a Random Sample

All along we have been referring to random samples. We have stressed the importance of the fact that our sample should always be drawn randomly from the entire population about which we wish to draw an inference. How do we draw a random sample?

To obtain a random sample from the entire population, we need a list of all the elements in the population of interest. Such a list is called a *frame*. The frame allows us to draw elements from the population by randomly generating the numbers of the elements to be included in the sample. Suppose we need a simple random sample of 100 people from a population of 7,000. We make a list of all 7,000 people and assign each person an identification number. This gives us a list of 7,000 numbers—our frame for the experiment. Then we generate by computer or by other means a

TABLE 5–1   Random Numbers

10480	15011	01536	02011	81647	91646	69179	14194
22368	46573	25595	85393	30995	89198	27982	53402
24130	48360	22527	97265	76393	64809	15179	24830
42167	93093	06243	61680	07856	16376	93440	53537
37570	39975	81837	16656	06121	91782	60468	81305
77921	06907	11008	42751	27756	53498	18602	70659

set of 100 random numbers in the range of values from 1 to 7,000. This procedure gives every set of 100 people in the population an equal chance of being included in the sample.

As mentioned, a computer (or an advanced calculator) may be used for generating random numbers. We will demonstrate an alternative method of choosing random numbers—a random numbers table. Table 5–1 is a part of such a table. A random number table is given in Appendix C as Table 14. To use the table, we start at any point, pick a number from the table, and continue in the same row or the same column (it does not matter which), systematically picking out numbers with the number of digits appropriate for our needs. If a number is outside our range of required numbers, we ignore it. We also ignore any number already obtained.

For example, suppose that we need a random sample of 10 data points from a population with a total of 600 elements. This means that we need 10 random drawings of elements from our frame of 1 through 600. To do this, we note that the number 600 has three digits; therefore, we draw random numbers with three digits. Since our population has only 600 units, however, we ignore any number greater than 600 and take the next number, assuming it falls in our range. Let us decide arbitrarily to choose the first three digits in each set of five digits in Table 5–1, and proceed by row, starting in the first row and moving to the second row, continuing until we have obtained our 10 required random numbers. We get the following random numbers: 104, 150, 15, 20, 816 (discard), 916 (discard), 691 (discard), 141, 223, 465, 255, 853 (discard), 309, 891 (discard), 279. Our random sample will, therefore, consist of the elements with serial numbers 104, 150, 15, 20, 141, 223, 465, 255, 309, and 279. A similar procedure would be used for obtaining the random sample of 100 people from the population of 7,000 mentioned earlier. Random number tables are included in books of statistical tables. Random numbers can also be generated by computer. The output below demonstrates the generation of 12 random integers, uniformly distributed from 0 to 9, using MINITAB.

```
MTB > RANDOM 12 C1;
SUBC> INTEGER 0 9.
MTB > PRINT C1

C1
    3    6    9    7    2    5    4    1    5    7    6    6
```

In many situations it is not possible to obtain a frame of the elements in the population. In such situations we may still randomize some aspect of the experiment and thus obtain a random sample. For example, we may randomize the location and the time and date of the collection of our observations, as well as other factors involved. In estimating the average mpg rating of an automobile, for example, we may randomly choose the dates and times of our trial runs as well as the particular automobiles used, the drivers, the roads used, and so on. More will be said about sampling techniques in Chapter 17.

PROBLEMS

Answers

5–2.
———
97.923, 2,686.38

5–4.
———
15.333, 2.555

5–6.
———
0.6111

5–1.   Discuss the concepts of a parameter, a sample statistic, an estimator, and an estimate. What are the relations among these entities?

5–2.   An auditor selected a random sample of 12 accounts from all accounts receivable of a given firm. The amounts of the accounts, in dollars, are as follows: 87.50, 123.10, 45.30, 52.22, 213.00, 155.00, 39.00, 76.05, 49.80, 99.99, 132.00, 102.11. Compute an estimate of the mean amount of all accounts receivable. Give an estimate of the variance of all the amounts.

5–3.   In problem 5–2, suppose the auditor wants to estimate the proportion of all the firm's accounts receivable with amounts over $100. Give a point estimate of this parameter.

5–4.   Following is a random sample of personal incomes of industry workers in the state of New York, in thousands of dollars per year: 14.5, 13.2, 15.4, 12.8, 19.3, 13.4, 16.5, 17.2, 17.8, 11.5, 13.6, 18.8. Compute point estimates of the mean and the standard deviation of the population of incomes of industry workers in the state.

5–5.   The following is a random sample of the total compensation, in millions of dollars per year, received by executives in a category labeled "the nation's highest paid executives":[3] 0.79, 1.59, 0.99, 1.12, 3.42, 5.21, 7.86, 13.23. Compute a point estimate of the proportion of all executives in the nation's "highest paid" category with salaries over $1 million per year. Also compute a point estimate of the average salary of an executive in this category.

5–6.   A market research worker interviewed a random sample of 18 people about their use of a certain product. The results, in terms of Y or N (for Yes, a user of the product, or No, not a user of the product), are as follows: Y N N Y Y Y N Y N Y Y Y N Y N Y Y N. Estimate the population proportion of users of the product.

5–7.   Use a random numbers table (you may use Table 5–1) to find identification numbers of elements to be used in a random sample of size $n = 25$ from a population of 950 elements.

5–8.   Find five random numbers from 0 to 5,600.

5–9.   Assume that you have a frame of 40 million voters (something the *Literary Digest* should have had for an unbiased polling). Randomly generate the numbers of five sampled voters.

5–10.   Suppose you need to sample the concentration of a chemical in a production process that goes on continuously 24 hours a day, seven days a week. You need to generate a random sample of six observations of the process over a period of one week. Use a computer, a calculator, or a random numbers table to generate the six observation times (to the nearest minute).

5–3   Sampling Distributions

> The **sampling distribution** of a statistic is the probability distribution of all possible values the statistic may take when computed from random samples of the same size, drawn from a specified population.

Let us first look at the sample mean, $\overline{X}$. The sample mean is a random variable. The possible values of this random variable depend on the possible values of the elements in the random sample from which $\overline{X}$ is to be computed. The random sample, in turn, depends on the distribution of the population from which it is drawn. As a random variable, $\overline{X}$ has a *probability distribution*. This probability distribution is the sampling distribution of $\overline{X}$.

---

[3]Kevin J. Murphy, "Top Executives Are Worth Every Nickel They Get," *Harvard Business Review* (March–April 1986).

TABLE 5–2   Possible Values of Two Sample Points from a Uniform Population of the Integers 1 through 8

		First sample point:							
		1	2	3	4	5	6	7	8
Second	1	1,1	2,1	3,1	4,1	5,1	6,1	7,1	8,1
sample	2	1,2	2,2	3,2	4,2	5,2	6,2	7,2	8,2
point:	3	1,3	2,3	3,3	4,3	5,3	6,3	7,3	8,3
	4	1,4	2,4	3,4	4,4	5,4	6,4	7,4	8,4
	5	1,5	2,5	3,5	4,5	5,5	6,5	7,5	8,5
	6	1,6	2,6	3,6	4,6	5,6	6,6	7,6	8,6
	7	1,7	2,7	3,7	4,7	5,7	6,7	7,7	8,7
	8	1,8	2,8	3,8	4,8	5,8	6,8	7,8	8,8

The **sampling distribution of** $\overline{X}$ is the probability distribution of all possible values the random variable $\overline{X}$ may take when a sample of size n is taken from a specified population.

Let us derive the sampling distribution of $\overline{X}$ in the simple case of drawing a sample of size $n = 2$ items from a population uniformly distributed over the integers 1 through 8. That is, we have a large population consisting of equal proportions of the values 1 to 8. At each draw, there is a 1/8 probability of obtaining any of the values 1 through 8 (alternatively, we may assume there are only eight elements, 1 through 8, and that the sampling is done with replacement). The sample space of the values of the two sample points drawn from this population is given in Table 5–2.

Using the sample space from the table, we will now find all possible values of the sample mean $\overline{X}$ and their probabilities. We compute these probabilities using the fact that all 64 sample pairs shown are equally likely. This is so because the population is uniformly distributed and because in random sampling each drawing is independent of the other; therefore, the probability of a given pair of sample points is the product $(1/8)(1/8) = 1/64$. From Table 5–2, we compute the sample mean associated with each of the 64 pairs of numbers and find the probability of occurrence of each value of the sample mean. The values and their probabilities are given in Table 5–3. The table thus gives us the sampling distribution of $\overline{X}$ in this particular

TABLE 5–3   The Sampling Distribution of $\overline{X}$ for a Sample of Size 2 from a Uniformly Distributed Population of the Integers 1 through 8

Particular Value $\overline{x}$	Probability of $\overline{x}$
1	1/64
1.5	2/64
2	3/64
2.5	4/64
3	5/64
3.5	6/64
4	7/64
4.5	8/64
5	7/64
5.5	6/64
6	5/64
6.5	4/64
7	3/64
7.5	2/64
8	1/64
	1.00

FIGURE 5–3   The Population Distribution and the Sampling Distribution of the Sample Mean

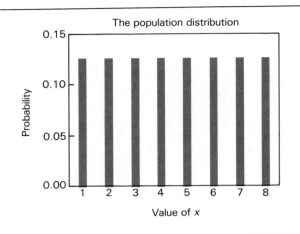
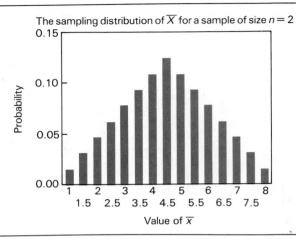

sampling situation. Verify the values in Table 5–3 using the sample space given in Table 5–2. Figure 5–3 shows the uniform distribution of the population and the sampling distribution of $\overline{X}$, as listed in Table 5–3.

Let us find the mean and the standard deviation of the *population*. We can do this by treating the population as a random variable (the random variable being the value of a single item randomly drawn from the population; each of the values 1 through 8 has a 1/8 probability of being drawn). Using the appropriate equations from Chapter 3, we find: $\mu = 4.5$ and $\sigma = 2.29$ (verify these results).

Now let us find the expected value and the standard deviation of the random variable $\overline{X}$. Using the sampling distribution listed in Table 5–3, we find $E(\overline{X}) = 4.5$ and $\sigma_{\overline{X}} = 1.62$ (verify these values by computation). Note that the expected value of $\overline{X}$ is equal to the mean of the population: each is equal to 4.5. The standard deviation of $\overline{X}$, denoted $\sigma_{\overline{X}}$, is equal to 1.62, and the population standard deviation, σ, is 2.29. But observe an interesting fact: $2.29/\sqrt{2} = 1.62$. The facts we have discovered in this example are not an accident—they hold in all cases. The expected value of the sample mean, $\overline{X}$, is equal to the population mean, μ, and the standard deviation of $\overline{X}$ is equal to the population standard deviation divided by the square root of the sample size. The standard deviation of the sample mean, $\sigma_{\overline{X}}$, is also called the *standard error* of $\overline{X}$.

The expected value of the sample mean:[4]

$$E(\overline{X}) = \mu \tag{5–2}$$

---

[4] The proof of equation 5–2 relies on the fact that the expected value of the sum of several random variables is equal to the sum of their expected values. Also, from equation 3–6 we know that the expected value of aX, where a is a number, is equal to a times the expected value of X. We also know that the expected value of each element X drawn from the population is equal to μ, the population mean. Using these facts, we find the following: $E(\overline{X}) = E(\Sigma X/n) = (1/n)E(\Sigma X) = (1/n)n\mu = \mu$.

> The standard error of the sample mean:[5]
>
> $$SE(\overline{X}) = \sigma_{\overline{x}} = \sigma/\sqrt{n} \qquad (5\text{–}3)$$

We know the two parameters of the sampling distribution of $\overline{X}$: we know the mean of the distribution (the expected value of $\overline{X}$) and we know its standard deviation (the standard error of $\overline{X}$). What about the shape of the sampling distribution? If the population itself is *normally distributed*, the sampling distribution of $\overline{X}$ is also normal.

> When sampling from a *normal* distribution with mean μ and standard deviation σ, the sample mean $\overline{X}$ has a **normal sampling distribution:**
>
> $$\overline{X} \sim N(\mu, \sigma^2/n) \qquad (5\text{–}4)$$

Thus, when we sample from a normally distributed population with mean μ and standard deviation σ, the sample mean has a normal distribution with the same *center*, μ, as the population but with *width* (standard deviation) that is $1/\sqrt{n}$ the size of the width of the population distribution. This is demonstrated in Figure 5–4, which shows a normal population distribution and the sampling distribution of $\overline{X}$ for different sample sizes.

FIGURE 5–4   A Normally Distributed Population and the Sampling Distribution of the Sample Mean for Different Sample Sizes

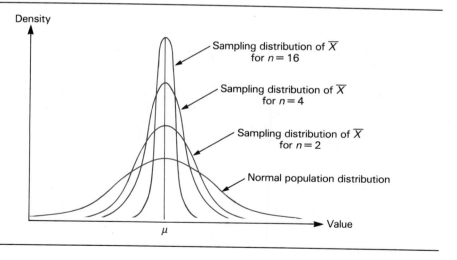

---

[5] The proof of equation 5–3 relies on the fact that, when several random variables are *independent* (as happens in random sampling), the variance of the sum of the random variables is equal to the sum of their variances. Also, from equation 3–11, we know that the variance of aX is equal to $a^2V(X)$. The variance of each X drawn from the population is equal to σ^2. Using these facts, we find: $V(\overline{X}) = V(\Sigma X/n) = (1/n)^2(\Sigma\sigma^2) = (1/n)^2(n\sigma^2) = \sigma^2/n$. Hence, $SD(\overline{X}) = \sigma/\sqrt{n}$.

The fact that the sampling distribution of $\bar{X}$ has mean μ is very important. It means that, *on the average*, the sample mean is equal to the population mean. The distribution of the statistic is *centered* over the parameter to be estimated, and this makes the statistic $\bar{X}$ a good estimator of μ. This fact will become clearer in the next section, where we discuss estimators and their properties. The fact that the standard deviation of $\bar{X}$ is $\sigma/\sqrt{n}$ means that as the sample size *increases*, the standard deviation of $\bar{X}$ *decreases*, making $\bar{X}$ more likely to be close to μ. This is another desirable property of a good estimator, to be discussed later. Finally, when the sampling distribution of $\bar{X}$ is normal, this allows us to compute probabilities that $\bar{X}$ will be within specified distances of μ. What happens in cases where the population itself is *not* normally distributed?

In Figure 5–3, we saw the sampling distribution of $\bar{X}$ when sampling is done

FIGURE 5–5   The Sampling Distribution of $\bar{X}$ as the Sample Size Increases

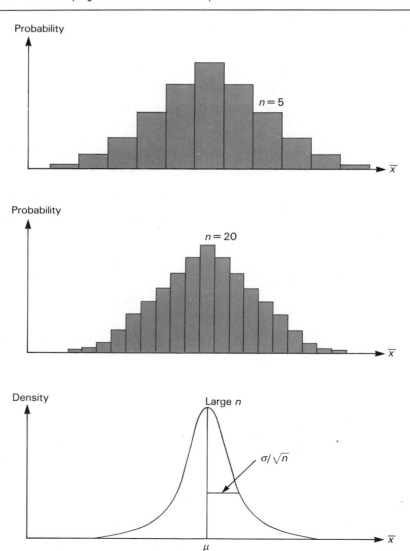

from a uniformly distributed population and with a sample of size $n = 2$. Let us now see what happens as we increase the sample size. Figure 5–5 shows results of a simulation giving the sampling distribution of $\overline{X}$ when the sample size is $n = 5$, when the sample size is $n = 20$, and the *limiting* distribution of $\overline{X}$—the distribution of $\overline{X}$ as the sample size increases indefinitely. As can be seen from the figure, the limiting distribution of $\overline{X}$ is, again, the *normal distribution*.

The Central Limit Theorem

The result we have just stated, that the distribution of the sample mean $\overline{X}$ tends to the normal distribution as the sample size increases, is one of the most important results in statistics. It is known as the *central limit theorem*.

The Central Limit Theorem

When sampling from a population with mean μ and finite standard deviation σ, the sampling distribution of the sample mean, $\overline{X}$, will tend to a normal distribution with mean μ and standard deviation $\sigma/\sqrt{n}$ as the sample size n becomes large.

$$\text{For "large enough" } n, \quad \overline{X} \sim N(\mu, \sigma^2/n) \quad\quad (5\text{–}5)$$

The central limit theorem is remarkable because it states that the distribution of the sample mean $\overline{X}$ tends to a normal distribution *regardless* of the distribution of the population from which the random sample is drawn. The theorem allows us to make probability statements about the possible range of values the sample mean may take. It allows us to compute probabilities of how far away $\overline{X}$ may be from the population mean it estimates. For example, using our rule of thumb for the normal distribution, we know that the probability that the distance between $\overline{X}$ and μ will be less than $\sigma/\sqrt{n}$ is approximately 0.68. This is so because, as you remember, the probability that the value of a normal random variable will be within one standard deviation of its mean is 0.6826; here our normal random variable has mean μ and standard deviation $\sigma/\sqrt{n}$. Other probability statements can be made as well; we will see their use shortly. When is a sample size, n, "large enough" so that we may apply the theorem?

The central limit theorem says that, *in the limit*, as n goes to infinity $(n \to \infty)$, the distribution of $\overline{X}$ becomes a normal distribution (regardless of the distribution of the population). The *rate* at which the distribution approaches a normal distribution does depend, however, on the shape of the distribution of the parent population. If the population itself is normally distributed, the distribution of $\overline{X}$ is normal for *any* sample size n, as stated earlier. On the other hand, for population distributions that are very different from a normal distribution, a relatively large sample size is required to achieve a good normal approximation for the distribution of $\overline{X}$. Figure 5–6 shows several parent population distributions and the resulting sampling distributions of $\overline{X}$ for different sample sizes.

Since we often do not know the shape of the population distribution, it would be useful to have some general rule of thumb telling us when a sample is large enough so that we may apply the central limit theorem.

In general, a sample of 30 or more elements is considered large enough for the central limit theorem to take effect.

We emphasize that this is a *general*, and somewhat arbitrary, rule. A larger

FIGURE 5–6   The Effects of the Central Limit Theorem: The Distribution of $\overline{X}$ for Different Populations and Different Sample Sizes

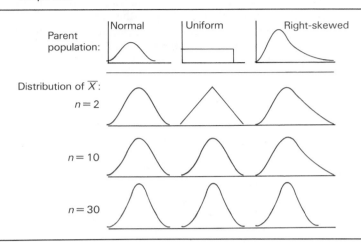

minimum sample size may be required for a good normal approximation when the population distribution is very different from a normal distribution. By the same token, a smaller minimum sample size may suffice for a good normal approximation when the population distribution is close to a normal distribution.

Throughout this book, we will make reference to *small* samples versus *large* samples. By a small sample, we generally mean a sample of fewer than 30 elements. A large sample will generally mean a sample of 30 or more elements. The results we will discuss as applicable for large samples will be more meaningful, however, the larger the sample size. (By the central limit theorem, the larger the sample size, the better the approximation offered by the normal distribution.) The "30 rule" should, therefore, be applied with caution. Let us now look at an example of the use of the central limit theorem.

EXAMPLE (a)   Mercury makes a 2.4 liter V-6 engine, the Laser XRi, used in speedboats. The company's engineers believe that the engine delivers an average power of 220 horsepower (HP) and that the standard deviation of power delivered is 15 HP. A potential buyer intends to sample 100 engines (each engine to be run a single time). What is the probability that the sample mean, $\overline{X}$, will be less than 217 HP?

SOLUTION   In solving problems such as this one, we use the techniques of Chapter 4. There we used μ as the mean of the normal random variable and σ as its standard deviation. Here our random variable $\overline{X}$ is normal (at least approximately so, by the central limit theorem because our sample size is large) and has mean μ. Note, however, that the standard deviation of our random variable $\overline{X}$ is $\sigma/\sqrt{n}$ and not just σ. We proceed as follows:

$$P(\overline{X} < 217) = P\left(Z < \frac{217 - \mu}{\sigma/\sqrt{n}}\right)$$

$$= P\left(Z < \frac{217 - 220}{15/\sqrt{100}}\right) = P(Z < -2) = 0.0228$$

Thus, if the population mean is indeed $\mu = 220$ HP and the standard deviation is $\sigma = 15$ HP, there is a rather small probability that the potential buyer's tests will result in a sample mean lower than 217 HP.

Figure 5–7 should help clarify the distinction between the population distribution and the sampling distribution of $\overline{X}$. The figure emphasizes the three aspects of the central limit theorem:

1. When the sample size is large enough, the sampling distribution of $\overline{X}$ is normal.
2. The expected value of $\overline{X}$ is μ.
3. The standard deviation of $\overline{X}$ is $\sigma/\sqrt{n}$.

The last statement is the key to the important fact that as the sample size increases, the variation of $\overline{X}$ about its mean μ decreases. Stated another way, as we buy *more information* (take a larger sample), our *uncertainty* (measured by the standard deviation) about the parameter being estimated *decreases*.

The History of the Central Limit Theorem

What we call the central limit theorem actually comprises several theorems developed over the years. The first such theorem was discussed at the beginning of Chapter 4 as the discovery of the normal curve by Abraham De Moivre in 1733. Recall that De Moivre discovered the normal distribution as the *limit* of the binomial distribution. The fact that the normal distribution appears as a limit of the binomial distribution as *n* increases is a form of the central limit theorem. Around the turn of this century, Liapunov gave a more general form of the central limit theorem, and in 1922 the final form we use in applied statistics was given by Lindeberg. The proof of the necessary condition of the theorem was given in 1935 by W. Feller [see W. Feller, *An Introduction to Probability Theory and Its Applications* (New York: Wiley, 1971), vol. 2]. A proof of the central limit theorem is beyond the scope of this book, but the interested reader is encouraged to read more about it in the given reference or in other books.

FIGURE 5–7 A (Nonnormal) Population Distribution and the Normal Sampling Distribution of the Sample Mean When a Large Sample Is Used

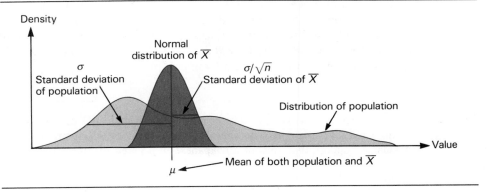

The Standardized Sampling Distribution
of the Sample Mean When σ Is Not Known

In order to use the central limit theorem, we need to know the population standard deviation, σ. When σ is not known, we use its estimator, the sample standard deviation, S, in its place. In such cases, the distribution of the standardized statistic

$$\frac{\bar{X} - \mu}{S/\sqrt{n}} \tag{5-6}$$

(where S is used in place of the unknown σ) is no longer the standard normal distribution. *If the population itself is normally distributed, the statistic in equation 5–6 has a t distribution with n − 1 degrees of freedom.* The t distribution is flatter in the middle and has wider tails than the standard normal distribution. Values and probabilities of t distributions with different degrees of freedom are given in Table 3 in Appendix C. The t distribution and its uses will be discussed in detail in Chapter 6. The idea of degrees of freedom is explained in the last section of this chapter.

The Sampling Distribution of the Sample Proportion, $\hat{P}$

The sampling distribution of the sample proportion, $\hat{P}$, is the binomial distribution with parameters n and p, where n is the sample size and p is the population proportion. Recall that the binomial random variable, X, counts the number of successes in n trials. Since $\hat{P} = X/n$ and n is fixed (determined before the sampling), the distribution of the number of successes, X, is also the distribution of $\hat{P}$.

As the sample size, n, increases, the central limit theorem applies here as well. In the beginning of Chapter 4, we saw how the binomial distribution approaches the normal distribution when $p = 0.5$—the case of a symmetric distribution for all n. The symmetry of the distribution makes the convergence to a normal distribution relatively fast. Figure 5–8 shows the effects of the central limit theorem in the case where the binomial distribution is *not* symmetric. We use a distribution with $p = 0.3$ (a distribution skewed to the right, when n is small).

We now state the central limit theorem when sampling for the population proportion, p.

> As the sample size, n, increases, the sampling distribution of $\hat{P}$ approaches a *normal distribution* with mean p and standard deviation $\sqrt{p(1 - p)/n}$

(The standard deviation of $\hat{P}$ is also called its *standard error*.) In order for us to use the normal approximation for the sampling distribution of $\hat{P}$, the sample size needs to be large. A commonly used rule of thumb says that the normal approximation to the distribution of $\hat{P}$ may be used only if *both np and n(1 − p) are greater than 5.* We demonstrate the use of the theorem with Example (b).

EXAMPLE (b)

In recent years, convertible sport coupes have become very popular in Japan. Toyota is currently shipping Celicas to Los Angeles, where a customizer does a roof lift and ships them back to Japan.[6] Suppose that 25% of all Japanese in a given income and lifestyle

---

[6] "Tokyo Flips Its Lid for Convertibles," *Business Week* (November 2, 1987).

FIGURE 5–8   The Sampling Distribution of $\hat{P}$ When $p = 0.3$, as n Increases

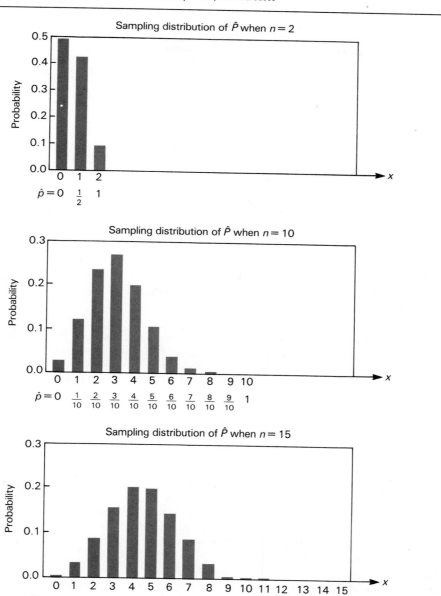

category are interested in buying Celica convertibles. A random sample of 100 Japanese consumers in the category of interest is to be selected. What is the probability that at least 20% of those in the sample will express an interest in a Celica convertible?

We need $P(\hat{P} \geq 0.20)$. Since $np = 100(0.25) = 25$ and $n(1 - p) = 100(0.75) = 75$, both numbers greater than 5, we may use the normal approximation to the distribution of $\hat{P}$. The mean of $\hat{P}$ is $p = 0.25$, and the standard deviation of $\hat{P}$ is $\sqrt{p(1 - p)/n} =$

SOLUTION

0.0433. We have:

$$P(\hat{P} \geq 0.20) = P\left(Z \geq \frac{0.20 - 0.25}{0.0433}\right) = P(Z \geq -1.15) = 0.8749$$

Sampling distributions are essential to statistics. In the following chapters, we will make much use of the distributions discussed in this section, as well as others that will be introduced as we go along. In the next section, we discuss properties of good estimators.

PROBLEMS

Answers

5–12.
___

Normal population.

5–18.
___

0.0446

5–20.
___

0.0912

5–22.
___

0.9923

5–11. What is a sampling distribution, and what are the uses of sampling distributions?

5–12. A sample of size $n = 5$ is selected from a population. Under what conditions is the sampling distribution of $\overline{X}$ normal?

5–13. In problem 5–12, suppose the population mean is $\mu = 125$ and the population standard deviation is 20. What are the expected value and the standard error of $\overline{X}$?

5–14. What is the most significant aspect of the central limit theorem?

5–15. Under what conditions is the central limit theorem most useful in sampling to estimate the population mean?

5–16. What are the limitations of small samples?

5–17. When sampling from a population with population proportion $p = 0.1$, using a sample size $n = 12$, what is the sampling distribution of $\hat{P}$? Is it reasonable to use a normal approximation for this sampling distribution? Explain.

5–18. If the population mean is 1,247, the population variance is 10,000, and the sample size is 100, what is the probability that $\overline{X}$ will be less than 1,230?

5–19. When sampling from a population with standard deviation $\sigma = 55$, using a sample of size $n = 150$, what is the probability that $\overline{X}$ will be at least eight units away from the population mean μ?

5–20. The Colosseum, once the most popular monument in Rome, dates from about A.D. 70. Since then earthquakes have caused considerable damage to the huge structure, and engineers are currently trying to make sure the building will survive future shocks.[7] The Colosseum can be divided into several thousand small sections. Suppose that the average section can withstand a quake measuring 3.4 on the Richter scale with a standard deviation of 1.5. A random sample of 100 sections is selected and tested for the maximum earthquake force they can withstand. What is the probability that the average section in the sample can withstand an earthquake measuring at least 3.6 on the Richter scale?

5–21. Seventy percent of the art auctioned by Sotheby's in Japan is Japanese art since the demand for Western art in that country is declining.[8] If a random sample of 200 art pieces is selected from among the ones auctioned by Sotheby's, what is the probability that at least 80% of the art pieces in the sample will be Japanese?

5–22. An economist wishes to estimate the average family income in a certain population. The population standard deviation is known to be $4,500, and the economist uses a random sample of size $n = 225$. What is the probability that the sample mean will fall within $800 of the population mean?

5–23. When sampling for the proportion of defective items in a large shipment, where the population proportion is 0.18 and the sample size is 200, what is the probability that the sample proportion will be at least 0.20?

---

[7] "Colosseum Faces Further Ruin," *International Management* (February 1991), p. 17.

[8] "Japan Becomes the Land of the Falling Gavel," *Business Week* (February 25, 1991), p. 68.

5–24. A study of the investment industry claims that 58% of all mutual funds outperformed the stock market as a whole last year. An analyst wants to test this claim and obtains a random sample of 250 mutual funds. The analyst finds that only 123 of the funds outperformed the market during the year. Determine the probability that another random sample would lead to a sample proportion as low or lower than the one obtained by the analyst, assuming the proportion of all mutual funds that outperformed the market is indeed 0.58.

5–25. The average amount in all checking accounts at a bank is known to be $657, and the standard deviation of the amounts is $232. A random sample of 144 accounts is to be selected for some purpose. What is the probability that the sample mean will be below $600?

5–26. It has been suggested that an investment portfolio selected randomly by throwing darts at the stock market page of *The Wall Street Journal* may be a sound (and certainly well-diversified) investment.[9] Suppose that you own such a portfolio of 16 stocks randomly selected from all stocks listed on the New York Stock Exchange (NYSE). On a certain day, you hear on the news that the average stock on the NYSE rose 1.5 points. Assuming that the standard deviation of stock price movements that day was 2 points and assuming stock price movements were normally distributed around their mean of 1.5, what is the probability that the average stock in your portfolio increased in price?

5–27. An advertisement for Citicorp Insurance Services, Inc., claims "one person in seven will be hospitalized this year." Suppose you keep track of a random sample of 180 people over an entire year. Assuming Citicorp's advertisement is correct, what is the probability that fewer than 10% of the people in your sample will be found to have been hospitalized (at least once) during the year? Explain.

5–28. Shimano mountain bikes are displayed in chic clothing boutiques in Milan, Italy, and the average price for the bike in the city is $700.[10] Suppose that the standard deviation of the bike prices is $100. If a random sample of 60 boutiques is selected, what is the probability that the average price for a Shimano mountain bike in this sample will be between $680 and $720?

5–29. A quality-control analyst wants to estimate the proportion of imperfect jeans in a large warehouse. The analyst plans to select a random sample of 500 pairs of jeans and note the proportion of imperfect pairs. If the actual proportion in the entire warehouse is 0.35, what is the probability that the sample proportion will deviate from the population proportion by more than 0.05?

Answers

5–24.
———
0.0024

5–26.
———
0.9987

5–28.
———
0.8786

5–4 Estimators and Their Properties[11]

The sample statistics we discussed, $\bar{X}$, S, and $\hat{P}$, as well as other sample statistics to be introduced later, are used as estimators of population parameters. In this section, we discuss some important properties of good statistical estimators. These properties are *unbiasedness, efficiency, consistency,* and *sufficiency*.

> An estimator is said to be **unbiased** if its expected value is equal to the population parameter it estimates.

Consider the sample mean $\bar{X}$. From equation 5–2, we know $E(\bar{X}) = \mu$. *The sample mean, $\bar{X}$, is, therefore, an unbiased estimator of the population mean μ.* This means that if we were to sample repeatedly from the population and compute $\bar{X}$ for each of our samples, *in the long run*, the average value of $\bar{X}$ will be the parameter of inter-

---

[9] See the very readable book by Burton G. Malkiel, *A Random Walk Down Wall Street*, 4th ed. (New York: W. W. Norton, 1985).

[10] "Three Men and a Derailleur," *Forbes* (January 21, 1991), p. 46.

[11] An optional, but recommended, section.

FIGURE 5–9   The Sample Mean, $\overline{X}$, as an Unbiased Estimator of the Population Mean, μ

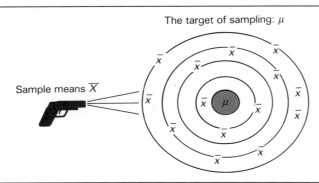

est, μ. This is an important property of the estimator because it means that there is no systematic *bias* away from the parameter of interest.

If we view the gathering of a random sample and the calculating of its mean as *shooting at a target*—the target being the population parameter, say, μ—then the fact that $\overline{X}$ is an unbiased estimator of μ means that the device producing the estimates is aiming at the *center* of the target (the parameter of interest), with no systematic deviation away from it.

> Any *systematic* deviation of the estimator away from the parameter of interest is called a **bias.**

The concept of unbiasedness is demonstrated for the sample mean $\overline{X}$ in Figure 5–9.

Figure 5–10 demonstrates the idea of a biased estimator of μ. The hypothetical estimator we denote by Y is centered on some point, M, that lies away from the parameter μ. The distance between the expected value of Y (the point M) and μ is the *bias*.

It should be noted that, in reality, we usually sample *once* and obtain our estimate. The multiple estimates shown in Figures 5–9 and 5–10 serve only as an illus-

FIGURE 5–10   An Example of a Biased Estimator of the Population Mean, μ

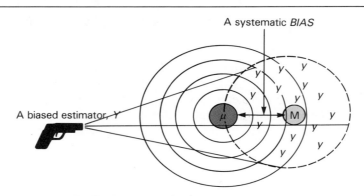

tration of the expected value of an estimator as the center of a large collection of the actual estimates that would be obtained in repeated sampling. (Note also that, in reality, the "target" at which we are "shooting" is one-dimensional—on a straight line rather than on a plane.)

The next property of good estimators we discuss is *efficiency*.

An estimator is **efficient** if it has a relatively small variance (and standard error).

Efficiency is a relative property. We say that one estimator is efficient *relative* to another. This means that the estimator has a smaller variance (also a smaller standard error) than the other. Figure 5–11 shows two hypothetical unbiased estimators of the population mean, μ. The two estimators, which we denote by X and Z, are unbiased: their distributions are centered at μ. The estimator X, however, is more efficient than the estimator Z because it has a smaller variance than that of Z. This is seen from the fact that repeated estimates produced by Z have a larger spread about their mean, μ, than repeated estimates produced by X.

Another desirable property of estimators is *consistency*.

An estimator is said to be **consistent** if its probability of being close to the parameter it estimates increases as the sample size increases.

The sample mean $\overline{X}$ is a consistent estimator of μ. This is so because the standard error of $\overline{X}$ is $\sigma_{\overline{X}} = \sigma/\sqrt{n}$. As the sample size, n, increases, the standard error of $\overline{X}$ decreases and, hence, the probability that $\overline{X}$ will be close to its expected value μ increases.

We now define a fourth property of good estimators, *sufficiency*.

An estimator is said to be **sufficient** if it contains all the information in the data about the parameter it estimates.

FIGURE 5–11 Two Unbiased Estimators of μ, Where the Estimator X Is Efficient Relative to the Estimator Z

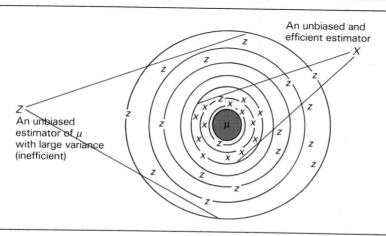

Applying the Concepts of Unbiasedness, Efficiency, Consistency, and Sufficiency

We may evaluate possible estimators of population parameters as to whether or not they possess important properties of estimators and thus choose the best estimator to be used.

For a *normally distributed population,* for example, both the sample mean and the sample median are *unbiased* estimators of the population mean, μ. The sample mean, however, is more *efficient* than the sample median. This is so because the variance of the sample median happens to be 1.57 times as large as the variance of the sample mean. In addition, the sample mean is a *sufficient* estimator because in computing it we use the *entire* data set. The sample median is not sufficient; it is found as the point in the middle of the data set, regardless of the exact magnitudes of all other data elements. The sample mean, $\overline{X}$, is the *best* estimator of the population mean, μ, because it is unbiased and has the smallest variance of all unbiased estimators of μ. The sample mean is also *consistent.* (It should be noted that, while the sample mean is best, the sample median is sometimes used because it is more resistant to extreme observations.)

The sample proportion, $\hat{P}$, is the best estimator of the population proportion, p. Since $E(\hat{P}) = p$, the estimator $\hat{P}$ is unbiased. It also has the smallest variance of all unbiased estimators of p.

What about the sample variance, S^2? The sample variance, as defined in equation 1–3 is an unbiased estimator of the population variance, σ^2. Recall equation 1–3:

$$S^2 = \frac{\Sigma(X - \overline{X})^2}{n - 1}$$

It seems logical to divide the sum of squared deviations in the equation by n rather than by $n - 1$ because we are seeking the *average* squared deviation from the sample mean. There are n deviations from the mean, so why not divide by n? It turns out that if we were to divide by n rather than by $n - 1$, our estimator of σ^2 would be biased. Although the bias becomes small as n increases, we will always use the statistic given in equation 1–3 as an estimator of σ^2. The reason for dividing by $n - 1$ rather than n will become clearer in the next section, where we discuss the concept of degrees of freedom.

It should be noted that, while S^2 is an unbiased estimator of the population variance σ^2, the sample standard deviation S (the square root of S^2) is *not* an unbiased estimator of the population standard deviation σ. Still, we will use S as our estimator of the population standard deviation, ignoring the small bias that results and relying on the fact that S^2 is the unbiased estimator of σ^2.

PROBLEMS

Answers

5–30.

B

5–32.

1,300

5–30. Suppose that you have two statistics, A and B, as possible estimators of the same population parameter. Estimator A is unbiased, but has a large variance. Estimator B has a small bias, but has only one-tenth the variance of estimator A. Which estimator is better? Explain.

5–31. Suppose that you have an estimator with a relatively large bias. The estimator is consistent and efficient, however. If you have a generous budget for your sampling survey, would you use this estimator? Explain.

5–32. Suppose that in a sampling survey to estimate the population variance, the biased estimator (with n instead of $n - 1$ in the denominator of equation 1–3) was used instead of the unbiased one. The sample size used was $n = 100$, and the estimate obtained was 1,287. Can you find the value of the unbiased estimate of the population variance?

5–33. What are the advantages of a sufficient statistic? Can you think of a possible disadvantage of sufficiency?

5–34. Suppose that you have two biased estimators of the same population parameter. Estimator A has a bias equal to $1/n$ (that is, the mean of the estimator is $1/n$ units away from the parameter it estimates), where n is the sample size used. Estimator B has a bias equal to 0.01 (the mean of the estimator is 0.01 units away from the parameter of interest). Under what conditions is estimator A better than B?

5–35. Why is consistency an important property?

Answer

5–34.

When $n > 100$.

5–5   Degrees of Freedom

The concept of *degrees of freedom* is crucial for the understanding of many important statistical distributions. The concept also underlies the reason why our sample variance S^2 is the unbiased estimator of σ^2. Here lies the answer to our big question: Why divide by $n - 1$ and not by n?

Suppose we consider four data points, $X_1, X_2, X_3,$ and X_4. The values of the data points are:

$$x_1 = 10 \qquad x_2 = 12 \qquad x_3 = 16 \qquad x_4 = 18$$

Let us compute the sample mean of these data.

$$\bar{x} = \frac{\sum\limits_{i=1}^{4} x_i}{n} = \frac{(x_1 + x_2 + x_3 + x_4)}{4}$$

$$= \frac{(10 + 12 + 16 + 18)}{4} = \frac{56}{4} = 14$$

Now, let us ask the question: Given that we know that the mean of our set of four data points is $\bar{x} = 14$, how many of our data points $X_1, X_2, X_3,$ and X_4 are "free to move"? In other words, of four data points with a known mean, how many points do not have predetermined values? Let us experiment with our data. First, assume that the value of our fourth data point, X_4, is not known to us. Would this data point be free to move, that is, free to take on any value? In this case, our data are:

$$10, 12, 16, \text{ and } X_4 \text{ (the unknown fourth point)}$$

However, note the following. We know the mean of the four data points. The mean is 14, and so we have, by definition of the mean:

$$\frac{(10 + 12 + 16 + X_4)}{4} = 14$$

From this equation, we can solve for the unknown value of the fourth data point, X_4.

$$10 + 12 + 16 + X_4 = 56$$

or

$$X_4 = 56 - 10 - 12 - 16 = 18$$

So, if in a set of n data points we do not know *one* of the points but we do know the mean of all n data points, then the "unknown" point is actually known: it is predetermined. The point is fixed—not free to move. We can solve for the exact value the data point must have, using the known values of the remaining $n - 1$ data points and the sample mean.

What happens if we have *two* missing values? Suppose we do not know two of the data points, X_3 and X_4. Are these two missing values fixed or free to move? Again, using the definition of the mean, we have the following.

$$\frac{(10 + 12 + X_3 + X_4)}{4} = 14$$

or

$$10 + 12 + X_3 + X_4 = 56$$

We have one equation with two unknowns; thus, the equation cannot be solved for the two missing values. When two data points are unknown to us, there is a degree of freedom for these values; the values are free to move. Assign any value to one of the two missing points (this is the degree of freedom—the data point can be anything), and the last missing value will be *determined*, as we can solve for it using the now-known three points and the mean of all four. A similar thing happens if three points are unknown (now we have *two* degrees of freedom because you may freely choose any value for any two of the missing three points), and so on.

We may conclude that when we have n data points *and* we know their mean, the mean acts as a *restriction* on the data, leaving us with only $n - 1$ *degrees of freedom*. Let us now view the situation in terms of deviations from the mean. Figure 5–12 shows the four data points of our example, their mean, and the deviations from the mean. The mean is a restriction in the sense that deviations from the mean must sum to zero. In our particular example, the deviations from the mean are:

$$d_1 = x_1 - \bar{x} = 10 - 14 = -4 \qquad d_2 = x_2 - \bar{x} = 12 - 14 = -2$$
$$d_3 = x_3 - \bar{x} = 16 - 14 = 2 \qquad d_4 = x_4 - \bar{x} = 18 - 14 = 4$$

We see that the sum of the four deviations of the data points from their mean is:

$$d_1 + d_2 + d_3 + d_4 = (-4) + (-2) + 2 + 4 = 0$$

Any three of the four deviations from the known mean are free to move and will not violate the restriction $\bar{x} = 14$ as long as the fourth deviation is constrained to be the number required to make the sum of all four deviations from the mean zero. Again,

FIGURE 5–12   The Four Deviations of the Data Points from Their Mean

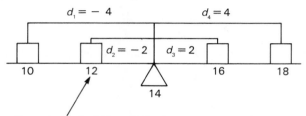

If any data point is assumed unknown, we can solve
for its deviation from the mean because the sum of all
four deviations is equal to zero.

we see that once the mean is known, $n - 1$ out of our n points are free to move. There are $n - 1$ degrees of freedom.

Now consider the sample variance, S^2. Equation 1–3 tells us that the sample variance is the sum of the squared deviations of the data points from their mean, $\Sigma(x_i - \bar{x})^2$, divided by $n - 1$. Since the computation involves the known quantity $\bar{x}$ and n data points (n deviations of data points from their mean in the sum of squares in the numerator of the equation), we know from the preceding discussion that only $n - 1$ of the data points (or, equivalently, $n - 1$ of the n deviations from the mean) are actually free to move. Therefore, if we want an average squared deviation from the mean as our measure of variation within the sample, *this average should be based on only $n - 1$ free points*. This is why we divide by $n - 1$ when we compute S^2, the unbiased estimator of the population variance, σ^2.

The concept of degrees of freedom will prove very important for us in other applications as well: in Chapter 8, on two-sample analysis, in Chapter 9, on analysis of variance, and in the chapters on regression analysis and forecasting. In these applications, we will see degrees of freedom that are different from $n - 1$. It is important to develop an intuitive understanding of the concept of degrees of freedom.

> The number of **degrees of freedom** is equal to the total number of measurements (these are not always raw data points), less the total number of restrictions on the measurements. A *restriction* is a quantity computed from the measurements.

For example, suppose we have two independent samples that are combined together, and we know the mean of each sample. If the first sample has n_1 data points and the second sample has n_2 data points, then the degrees of freedom (df) associated with the combined deviations from the two sample means are the total number of data points minus the total number of restrictions: df $= n_1 + n_2 - 2$.

This demonstrates that the degrees of freedom associated with independent samples are additive. The degrees of freedom associated with the first sample are $n_1 - 1$ and the degrees of freedom associated with the second sample are $n_2 - 1$. The degrees of freedom associated with the combined sample are: df $= n_1 + n_2 - 2 = (n_1 - 1) + (n_2 - 1)$. As a final example illustrating the concept of degrees of freedom, we consider a business situation.

A company manager has a total budget of $150,000 to be completely allocated to four different projects. How many "degrees of freedom" does the manager have?

EXAMPLE (c)

Fixing the total of several items is the same as fixing the mean of the items, because the total is just the mean multiplied by the number of items. In this case, saying that the total budget for the four projects is $150,000 is the same as fixing the mean allocation to $150,000/4 = $37,500. Now the manager is free to choose (within the total budget) whatever amount she desires for allocation to any three of the four projects. Once the first three allocations are made, however, the manager has no choice as to the fourth allocation: it is constrained to be exactly equal to the difference between the total budget of $150,000 and the sum of the allocations for the first three projects. The manager thus has three degrees of freedom.

SOLUTION

PROBLEMS

5–36.
———
107

5–38.
———
No.

5–36. Three random samples of sizes, 30, 48, and 32, respectively, are collected, and the three sample means are computed. What is the total number of degrees of freedom for deviations from the means?

5–37. In simple linear regression analysis, which will be introduced in Chapter 10, we will use a data set with n observations, from which we will compute two estimates—a slope and an intercept. The data vary around the line with the computed slope and intercept. What are the degrees of freedom for the deviations of the data points about the line?

5–38. Your bank sends you a summary statement, giving the average amount of all checks you wrote during the month. You have a record of the amounts of 17 out of the 19 checks you wrote during the month. Using this and the information provided by the bank, can you figure out the amounts of the two missing checks? Explain.

5–39. In problem 5–38, suppose you know the amounts of 18 of the 19 checks you wrote and the average of all the checks. Can you figure out the amount of the missing check? Explain.

5–40. Explain the relation between S^2 and the concept of degrees of freedom.

5–6 Using the Computer

In MINITAB, the command "SAMPLE k rows from C1 C2 . . . , put into C7 C8 . . ." takes a random sample of numbers (rows) from one or more columns and puts them into specified columns. This allows us to select random samples from given data. The command RANDOM will select a random sample from a known distribution generated by the computer. We specify the command RANDOM, followed by the number of observations we want (we may also list the columns into which these data are to be put) and a semicolon. Then comes the subcommand specifying the distribution (UNIFORM, BINOMIAL, POISSON, EXPONENTIAL, or any other distribution in the MINITAB library). Then we type the parameter value(s) of the distribution and end with a period.

We will now demonstrate the generation of the sampling distribution of the sample mean, $\overline{X}$, using MINITAB. This is done in Figure 5–13. Look carefully at the commands; in order to achieve efficiency in the command usage, we have to take means of samples across *rows* with the command RMEAN, rather than MEAN. The sample size, n, is the number of columns used (here 10), and the number following RANDOM is the number of times the procedure is to be done (the number of resulting sample means, here 200). Notice how the sampling distribution of $\overline{X}$ from a uniform $(0,1)$ distribution approaches normality with a sample of size 10.

5–7 Summary and Review of Terms

In this chapter, we saw how samples are randomly selected from populations for the purpose of drawing inferences about **population parameters**. We saw how **sample statistics** computed from the data—the sample mean, the sample standard deviation, and the sample proportion—are used as **estimators** of population parameters. We presented the important idea of a **sampling distribution** of a statistic, the probability distribution of the values the statistic may take. We saw how the **central limit theorem** implies that the sampling distributions of the sample mean and the sample proportion approach normal distributions as the sample size increases. Sampling distributions of estimators will prove to be the key to the construction of confidence intervals in the following chapter, as well as the key to the ideas presented in later

FIGURE 5–13

```
MTB > random 200 c1-c10;
SUBC> uniform 0 1.
MTB > rmean c1-c10 c11
MTB > histo c11

Histogram of c11
  Midpoint   Count
     0.20       1   *
     0.25       3   *
     0.30      16   ****
     0.35      68   **************
     0.40     124   ************************
     0.45     175   ***********************************
     0.50     230   **********************************************
     0.55     176   ************************************
     0.60     125   *************************
     0.65      61   ************
     0.70      18   ****
     0.75       3   *
```

chapters. We also presented important properties we would like our estimators to possess: **unbiasedness, efficiency, consistency,** and **sufficiency.** Finally, we discussed the idea of **degrees of freedom.**

ADDITIONAL PROBLEMS

5–41. Suppose you are sampling from a population with mean $\mu = 1,065$ and standard deviation $\sigma = 500$. The sample size is $n = 100$. What are the expected value and the variance of the sample mean, $\bar{X}$?

5–42. Suppose you are sampling from a population with population variance $\sigma^2 = 1,000,000$. You want the standard deviation of the sample mean to be at most 25. What is the minimum sample size you should use?

5–43. When sampling from a population with mean 53 and standard deviation 10, using a sample of size 400, what are the expected value and the standard error of the sample mean?

5–44. When sampling for a population proportion from a population with actual proportion $p = 0.5$, using a sample of size $n = 120$, what is the standard error of our estimator $\hat{P}$?

5–45. What are the expected value and the standard error of the sample proportion, $\hat{P}$, if the true population proportion is 0.2 and the sample size is $n = 90$?

5–46. For a fixed sample size, what is the value of the true population proportion, p, that maximizes the variance of the sample proportion, $\hat{P}$? (Hint: Try several values of p on a grid between 0 and 1.)

5–47. An article by J. C. Anderson and J. M. Kraushaar in the *Accounting Review* (July 1986) states: "The only commonly acknowledged attribute of these accounting populations is that of high positive skewness." Discuss the problems involved in sampling from the population in question. How would you solve these problems?

5–48. In problem 5–41, what is the probability that the sample mean will be at least 1,000? Do you need to use the central limit theorem to answer this question? Explain.

5–49. In problem 5–43, what is the probability that the sample mean will be between 52 and 54?

Answers

5–42.
___
1,600

5–44.
0.0456

5–46.
___
0.5

5–48.
___

0.9032

Answers

5–50.
___

0.8632

5–52.
___

100

5–58.
___

[18.46, 20.54]
and [18.63, 20.37]

5–60.
___

3,297.99 to 3,350.01

5–64.
___

All but S.

5–66.
___

121

5–50. In problem 5–44, what is the probability that the sample proportion will be least 0.45?

5–51. An article by B. Dietrich-Campbell and E. Schwartz on valuing debt options, in the *Journal of Financial Economics* (July 1986), reports that for a sample of 486 bonds, the average price was $424 and the sample standard deviation was $130. Assume that the *population* standard deviation was $130. Based on the reported sample mean, would you believe a claim that the population mean is $500? Explain.

5–52. The proportion of defective microcomputer disks of a certain kind is believed to be anywhere from 0.06 to 0.10. The manufacturer wants to draw a random sample and estimate the proportion of all defective disks. How large should the sample be to ensure that the standard error of the estimator is *at most* 0.03?

5–53. Explain why we need to draw random samples and how such samples are drawn. What are the properties of a (simple) random sample?

5–54. Explain the idea of a bias and its ramifications.

5–55. Is the sample median a biased estimator of the population mean? Why do we usually prefer the sample mean to the sample median as an estimator for the population mean? If we use the sample median, what must we assume about the population? Compare the two estimators.

5–56. Explain why the sample variance is defined as the sum of squared deviations from the sample mean divided by $n - 1$ and not by n.

5–57. Average weekly family expenditure on entertainment for a population in a given region is $19.50, and the population standard deviation is $5.30. What is the probability that a random sample of size 100 will yield a sample mean of over $20.00?

5–58. In problem 5–57, give 0.95 probability bounds on the value of the sample mean that would be obtained. Also give 0.90 probability bounds on the value of the sample mean.

5–59. The average premium for family medical insurance in the United States is $3,324 per year.[12] If a random sample of 1,000 families from around the country is selected, what is the probability that the sample mean will deviate from this stated figure by more than 0.062 standard deviations of the population?

5–60. In the situation presented in the previous problem, assume that the population standard deviation is $500. The sample mean has a 90% chance of falling within what two bounds?

5–61. Thirty-eight percent of all shoppers at a large department store are holders of the store's charge card. If a random sample of 100 shoppers is taken, what is the probability that at least 30 of them will be found to be holders of the card?

5–62. When sampling from a normal population with an unknown variance, is the sampling distribution of the sample mean normal? Explain.

5–63. When sampling from a normal population with a known variance, what is the smallest sample size required for applying a normal distribution for the sample mean?

5–64. Which of the following estimators are unbiased estimators of the appropriate population parameters: $\bar{X}$, $\hat{P}$, S^2, S? Explain.

5–65. Suppose a new estimator for the population mean is discovered. The new estimator is unbiased and has variance equal to σ^2/n^2. Discuss the merits of the new estimator as compared with the sample mean.

5–66. Three independent random samples are collected, and three samples means are computed. The total size of the combined sample is 124. How many degrees of freedom are associated with the deviations from the sample means in the combined data set? Explain.

5–67. Discuss, in relative terms, the sample size needed for an application of a normal distribution for the sample mean when sampling from each of the following populations. (Assume the population standard deviation is known in each case.)

___
[12] "Power Shift," *Forbes* (February 18, 1991), p. 80.

a. A normal population

b. A mound-shaped population, close to normal

c. A discrete population consisting of the values 1006, 47, and 0, with equal frequencies

d. A slightly skewed population

e. A highly skewed population

5–68. When sampling from a normally distributed population, is there an advantage to taking a large sample? Explain.

5–69. Suppose that you are given a new sample statistic to serve as estimator of some population parameter. You are unable to assume any theoretical results such as the central limit theorem. Discuss how you would empirically determine the sampling distribution of the new statistic.

5–70. In 1983, the federal government claimed that the state of Alaska had overpaid 20% of the Medicare recipients in the state. The director of the Alaska Department of Health and Social Services planned to check this claim by selecting a random sample of 250 recipients of Medicare checks in the state and determining the number of overpaid cases in the sample. Assuming the federal government's claim is correct, what is the probability that less than 15% of the people in the sample will be found to have been overpaid?

5–71. A new kind of alkaline battery is believed to last an average of 25 hours of continuous use (in a given kind of flashlight). Assume that the population standard deviation is 2 hours. If a random sample of 100 batteries is selected and tested, is it likely that the average battery in the sample will last less than 24 hours of continuous use? Explain.

5–72. Häagen-Dazs ice cream has recently introduced a frozen yogurt aimed at health-conscious ice cream lovers. Before marketing the product, the company wanted to estimate the proportion of grocery stores currently selling Häagen-Dazs ice cream that would sell the new product.[13] If 80% of the grocery stores would sell the product and a random sample of 200 stores is selected, what is the probability that the percentage in the sample will deviate from the population percentage by no more than 7 percentage points?

5–73. Japan's birthrate is believed to be 1.57 per woman.[14] Assume that the population standard deviation is 0.4. If a random sample of 200 women is selected, what is the probability that the sample mean will fall between 1.52 and 1.62?

5–68.

Yes

5–70.

0.0241

5–72.

0.9866

[13] "Häagen-Dazs Frozen Yogurt," *Fortune* (February 11, 1991), p. 124.

[14] "The Mommy Track, Japanese-Style," *Business Week* (March 11, 1991), p. 46.

FORTUNE'S 50 BEST STOCKS OF 1990

The following table (Exhibit 1), reprinted by permission from *Fortune*[15], reports stock prices for December 31, 1990, for 50 stocks listed on the New York Stock Exchange that *Fortune* anlaysts consider "best."

Consider the 50 stocks a *population,* and directly compute the population mean and the population standard deviation of the stock prices. Then generate random samples of varying sample size (*n* = 5, 10, 15, etc.), and form the sampling distribution of the sample mean for stock prices. Do the same for total return to investors. Use a computer for convenience. What do you observe?

EXHIBIT 1 The 50 Best

		Stock Price	Dividends per Share	Total Return to Investors
1	**Cabletron Systems** (telecommunications)	$28.50	—	204%
2	**United States Surgical** (medical supplies)	$71.38	$0.48	163%
3	**L.E. Myers Co. Group** (power line construction)	$15.12	$0.12	126%
4	**Oregon Steel Mills**	$24.00	$0.42	103%
5	**Clayton Homes** (manufactured homes)	$13.75	—	96%
6	**International Rectifier** (power semiconductors)	$11.00	—	91%
7	**Fabri-Centers of America** (fabric retailer)	$25.75	—	87%
8	**Jacobs Engineering** (engineering and const.)	$25.50	—	87%
9	**Chiquita Brands Int'l** (produce marketing)	$32.00	$0.35	87%
10	**Christiana** (owns drilling equipment company)	$17.50	—	87%
11	**Storage Technology** (information processing)	$21.50	—	83%
12	**Conner Peripherals** (disk drives)	$23.62	—	80%
13	**Suave Shoe** (footwear)	$9.50	$0.10	79%
14	**Fansteel** (diversified manufacturing)	$12.38	$0.85	78%
15	**RLI** (property and casualty insurance)	$14.50	$0.41	77%
16	**House of Fabrics** (fabric retailer)	$30.38	$0.24	77%
17	**Merry-Go-Round Enterprises** (clothing retailer)	$25.25	$0.08	72%
18	**Oakwood Homes** (manufactured homes)	$11.13	$0.08	69%
19	**Freeport-McMoRan Copper** (mining)	$16.00	$1.38	64%
20	**Milton Roy** (precision instruments)	$28.00	$0.54	59%
21	**Home Depot** (home improvement retailer)	$38.63	$0.10	59%
22	**NCR** (computers)	$90.75	$1.38	57%
23	**CUC Int'l** (mktg. programs for credit card holders)	$22.25	—	53%
24	**Nike** (athletic footwear and apparel)	$40.25	$0.40	53%
25	**Gottschalks** (retailer)	$13.38	—	53%
26	**Blockbuster Entertainment** (videocassette stores)	$25.88	—	52%
27	**Fund American Cos.** (insurance holding company)	$51.87	$0.68	52%

28	Rhône-Poulenc Rorer Group (drugs)	$70.00	$0.84	51%
29	Alberto-Culver (health and beauty aids)	$33.25	$0.20	50%
30	Donaldson (diversified manufacturing)	$32.75	$0.43	49%
31	Service Corp. Int'l (funeral services)	$22.50	$0.56	49%
32	Federal Signal (diversified manufacturing)	$30.63	$0.64	47%
33	Imcera Group (med. prods., specialty chemicals)	$75.00	$1.00	46%
34	Vista Chemical (commodity and specialty chems.)	$53.75	$1.90	45%
35	Healthsouth Rehabilitation (medical rehab)	$25.00	—	45%
36	Kent Electronics (electronic components)	$12.13	—	45%
37	General Motors E (information processing)	$38.63	$0.56	44%
38	Beverly Enterprises (nursing homes)	$8.63	—	44%
39	Vivra (kidney dialysis, home nursing care)	$25.50	—	44%
40	Whittaker (aerospace, biotech)	$11.12	—	43%
41	Varian Associates (defense electronics)	$30.50	$0.26	42%
42	Compaq Computer (personal computers)	$56.38	—	42%
43	IBP (meat processing)	$20.88	$0.60	41%
44	A.L. Laboratories (drugs)	$25.38	$0.16	40%
45	General Mills (food, restaurants)	$49.00	$1.19	39%
46	American Barrick Resources (gold)	$21.75	$0.09	38%
47	Universal Foods (frozen potatoes, yeast)	$32.13	$0.70	38%
48	Millipore (scientific equipment and supplies)	$36.13	$0.42	38%
49	Ashland Coal	$23.13	$0.36	37%
50	Marion Merrell Dow (drugs)	$36.25	$0.59	37%

[15] "The Best and Worst Stocks of 1990," *Fortune* (January 28, 1991), p. 58.

CONFIDENCE INTERVALS

I N T R O D U C T I O N

A nthropologists, armed with knowledge of molecular biology and statistics, announced in 1988 that they had discovered Eve. A long and involved research study resulted in the implication that all human beings are genetically descended from *one* woman.[1] The scientists did not claim to have found the *first* woman, but rather a common ancestor of all of humanity. The scientists' Eve was the most genetically successful woman living in our distant past, a woman whose progeny are all people living in the world today, regardless of race, ethnic origin, or native continent. This finding brings with it far-reaching implications, which have already stirred up heated debates at scientific conferences. The most controversial implication is that humans did not slowly evolve in different parts of the world, as many anthropologists believed. The evolution to modern *Homo sapiens,* according to the new theory, occurred only in *one* place (scientists are still uncertain where, although it is believed to have been somewhere in Asia or Africa). Sometime between 90,000 and 180,000 years ago, Eve's descendants left their homeland and began their slow migration to all parts of the world, replacing local populations as they went along and eventually settling the entire planet. What we call racial characteristics or external differences of appearance all developed *after* these migrations. How did the scientists develop and demonstrate these incredible assertions?

Scientists asked a random sample of 147 pregnant women of all races, ethnic origins, and continents of birth to donate their babies' placentas. The genetic matter in the placentas, strings of the protein DNA, was then carefully scrutinized with interest centered on a particular type of mitochondrial DNA inherited only from one's mother. The scientists found that the genetic matter in the placentas of all the sampled babies contained segments of DNA traceable to a single source—a woman they called Eve. Statistical estimation was then used in analyzing the number of mutations inherent in the genetic material. Based on their random sample, the scientists estimated the average percentage of mutated mitochondrial DNA in the entire population of living people at 2–4%. This is an **interval estimate** of a population parameter. Such an interval has associated with it a measure of **confidence** (usually stated as a percentage, often 95% or 99%). Since the scientists also knew the approximate rate of mutation over time, they were able to use the interval estimate of the average percentage of mutated mitochondrial DNA in the present-day population and extrapolate back in time toward the beginning of these mutations. This led them to conclude, with a high degree of confidence, that Eve lived anywhere between 140,000 and 290,000 years ago. In this chapter, we discuss the computation and interpretation of interval estimates of population parameters. An interval estimate with its associated measure of confidence is usually called a *confidence interval.*

In the last chapter, we saw how sample statistics are used as estimators of population parameters. We defined a point estimate of a parameter as a single value obtained from the estimator. We saw that an estimator, a sample statistic, is a random

---

[1] See, for example, the cover article in *Newsweek* (January 11, 1988).

Continued on next page

variable with a certain probability distribution—its sampling distribution. A given point estimate is a single realization of the random variable. The actual estimate may or may not be close to the parameter of interest. Therefore, if we only provide a point estimate of the parameter of interest, we are not giving any information about the *accuracy* of the estimation procedure. For example, saying that the sample mean is 550 is giving a point estimate of the population mean. This estimate does not tell us how close μ may be to its estimate, 550. Suppose, on the other hand, that we also said: "We are *99% confident* that μ is in the interval [449, 551]." This conveys much more information about the possible value of μ. Now compare this interval with another one: "We are *90% confident* that μ is in the interval [400, 700]." This interval conveys less information about the possible value of μ, both because it is wider and because the level of confidence is lower. (When based on the same information, however, an interval of lower confidence level is narrower.)

> A **confidence interval** is a *range of numbers* believed to include an unknown population parameter. Associated with the interval is a measure of the *confidence* we have that the interval does indeed contain the parameter of interest.

The sampling distribution of the statistic gives a *probability* associated with a range of values the statistic may take. After the sampling has taken place and a *particular estimate* has been obtained, this probability is transformed into a *level of confidence* for a range of values that may contain the unknown parameter.

In the next section, we will see how to construct confidence intervals for the population mean, μ, when the population standard deviation, σ, is known. Then we will alter this unrealistic situation and see how a confidence interval for μ may be constructed without knowledge of σ. Other sections present confidence intervals in other situations. ■

6–2 Confidence Interval for the Population Mean When the Population Standard Deviation Is Known

The central limit theorem tells us that when we select a large random sample from any population with mean μ and standard deviation σ, the sample mean, $\overline{X}$, is (at least approximately) normally distributed with mean μ and standard deviation $\sigma/\sqrt{n}$. If the population itself is normal, $\overline{X}$ is normally distributed for any sample size. Recall that the standard normal random variable Z has a 0.95 probability of being within the range of values -1.96 and 1.96 (you may check this using Table 2 in Appendix C). Transforming Z to the random variable $\overline{X}$ with mean μ and standard deviation $\sigma/\sqrt{n}$, we find that—*before the sampling*—there is a 0.95 probability that $\overline{X}$ will fall within the interval:

$$\mu \pm 1.96 \frac{\sigma}{\sqrt{n}} \qquad (6-1)$$

Once we have obtained our random sample, we have a particular value, $\overline{x}$. This particular $\overline{x}$ either lies within the range of values specified by equation 6–1 or does not lie within this range. Since we do not know the (fixed) value of the population parameter μ, we have no way of knowing whether $\overline{x}$ is indeed within the range given in equation 6–1. Since the random sampling has already taken place and a particular $\overline{x}$ has been computed, we no longer have a random variable and may no longer talk about probabilities. We do know, however, that since the presampling probability

FIGURE 6-1   The Probability Distribution of $\overline{X}$ and Some Resulting Values of the Statistic in Repeated Samplings

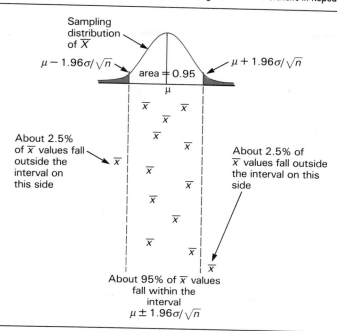

that $\overline{X}$ will fall in the interval in equation 6–1 is 0.95, about 95% of the values of $\overline{X}$ obtained in a large number of repeated samplings will fall within the interval. Since we have a single value $\overline{x}$ that was obtained by this process, we may say that we are *95% confident that $\overline{x}$ lies within the interval.* This idea is demonstrated in Figure 6–1.

Consider a particular $\overline{x}$ and note that the distance between $\overline{x}$ and μ is the same as the distance between μ and $\overline{x}$. Thus, $\overline{x}$ falls inside the interval $\mu \pm 1.96\sigma/\sqrt{n}$ *if and only if μ happens to be inside the interval* $\overline{x} \pm 1.96\sigma/\sqrt{n}$. In a large number of repeated trials, this would happen about 95% of the time. We therefore call the interval $\overline{x} \pm 1.96\sigma/\sqrt{n}$ *a 95% confidence interval for the unknown population mean* μ. This is demonstrated in Figure 6–2.

Instead of measuring a distance of $1.96\sigma/\sqrt{n}$ on either side of μ (an impossible task since μ is unknown), we measure the same distance of $1.96\sigma/\sqrt{n}$ on either side of our *known* sample mean, $\overline{x}$. Since, *before the sampling,* the random interval $\overline{X} \pm 1.96\sigma/\sqrt{n}$ had a 0.95 probability of capturing μ, *after the sampling* we may be 95% confident that our particular interval $\overline{x} \pm 1.96\sigma/\sqrt{n}$ indeed contains the population mean μ. We cannot say that there is a 0.95 *probability* that μ is inside the interval, because the interval $\overline{x} \pm 1.96\sigma/\sqrt{n}$ is not random, and neither is μ. The population mean μ is unknown to us but is a fixed quantity—not a random variable.[2] Either μ lies inside the confidence interval (in which case the probability of this event is 1.00), or it does not (in which case the probability of the event is 0). We do know, however, that 95% of all possible intervals constructed in this manner will

---

[2] We are using what is called the *classical* interpretation of confidence intervals. An alternative view, the Bayesian approach, will be discussed in Chapter 15. The Bayesian approach allows us to treat an unknown population parameter as a random variable. As such, the unknown population mean μ may be stated to have a 0.95 *probability* of being within an interval.

FIGURE 6-2   The Construction of a 95% Confidence Interval for the Population Mean μ

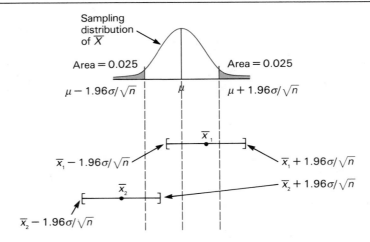

The sample mean $\overline{x}_1$ falls inside the interval $\mu \pm 1.96\sigma/\sqrt{n}$. Therefore, the confidence interval based on $\overline{x}_1$, which is $\overline{x}_1 \pm 1.96\sigma/\sqrt{n}$, contains μ. Another sample mean, $\overline{x}_2$, falls outside the interval $\mu \pm 1.96\sigma/\sqrt{n}$. Therefore, the confidence interval based on $\overline{x}_2$, which is $\overline{x}_2 \pm 1.96\sigma/\sqrt{n}$, does not contain μ.

contain μ. Therefore, we may say that we are *95% confident* that μ lies in the particular interval we have obtained.

> A 95% confidence interval for μ when σ is known and sampling is done from a normal population, or a large sample is used:
>
> $$\overline{x} \pm 1.96 \frac{\sigma}{\sqrt{n}} \qquad (6\text{-}2)$$

To compute a 95% confidence interval for μ, all we need to do is substitute the values of the required entities in equation 6-2. Suppose, for example, that we are sampling from a normal population, in which case the random variable $\overline{X}$ is normally distributed for any sample size. We use a sample of size $n = 25$, and we get a sample mean $\overline{x} = 122$. Suppose we also know that the population standard deviation is $\sigma = 20$. Let us compute a 95% confidence interval for the unknown population mean, μ. Using equation 6-2, we get:

$$\overline{x} \pm 1.96 \frac{\sigma}{\sqrt{n}} = 122 \pm 1.96 \frac{20}{\sqrt{25}} = 122 \pm 7.84 = [114.16, 129.84]$$

Thus, we may be 95% confident that the unknown population mean μ lies anywhere between the values 114.16 and 129.84.

In business and other applications, the 95% confidence interval is commonly used. There are, however, many other possible levels of confidence. You may choose any level of confidence you wish, find the appropriate z value from the standard normal table, and use it instead of 1.96 in equation 6-2 to get an interval of the chosen level of confidence. Using the standard normal table, we find, for example, that for a 90% confidence interval we use the z value 1.645, and for a 99% confidence interval we use $z = 2.58$ (or, using an accurate interpolation, 2.576). Let us formalize the procedure and make some definitions.

> We define $z_{\alpha/2}$ as the z value that cuts off a right-tail area of $\alpha/2$ under the standard normal curve.

For example, 1.96 is $z_{\alpha/2}$ for $\alpha/2 = 0.025$ because $z = 1.96$ cuts off an area of 0.025 to its right. (We find from Table 2 that, for $z = 1.96$, TA = 0.475; therefore, the right-tail area is $\alpha/2 = 0.025$.) Now consider the two points 1.96 and −1.96. Each of them cuts off a tail area of $\alpha/2 = 0.025$ in the respective direction of its tail. The area between the two values is therefore equal to $1 - \alpha = 1 - 2(0.025) = 0.95$. The area under the curve excluding the tails, $1 - \alpha$, is called the **confidence coefficient.** (And the combined area in both tails, α, is called the **error probability.** This probability will be important to us in the next chapter.) The confidence coefficient multiplied by 100, expressed as a percentage, is the **confidence level.**

A $(1 - \alpha)$ 100% confidence interval for μ when σ is known and sampling is done from a normal population, or with a large sample:

$$\bar{x} \pm z_{\alpha/2}\frac{\sigma}{\sqrt{n}} \tag{6–3}$$

Thus, for a 95% confidence interval for μ we have:

$$(1 - \alpha)100\% = 95\%$$
$$1 - \alpha = 0.95$$
$$\alpha = 0.05$$
$$\frac{\alpha}{2} = 0.025$$

From the normal table, we find $z_{\alpha/2} = 1.96$. This is the value we substitute for $z_{\alpha/2}$ in equation 6–3.

For example, suppose we want an 80% confidence interval for μ. We have $1 - \alpha = 0.80$ and $\alpha = 0.20$; therefore, $\alpha/2 = 0.10$. We now look in the standard normal table for the value of $z_{0.10}$, that is, the z value that cuts off an area of 0.10 to its right. We have: TA = $0.5 - 0.1 = 0.4$, and from the table we find $z_{0.10} = 1.28$. The confidence interval is therefore: $\bar{x} \pm 1.28\sigma/\sqrt{n}$. This is demonstrated in Figure 6–3.

Let us compute an 80% confidence interval for μ using the information presented earlier. We have: $n = 25$, and $\bar{x} = 122$. We also assume $\sigma = 20$. To compute an 80% confidence interval for the unknown population mean, μ, we use equation 6–3 and get:

$$\bar{x} \pm z_{\alpha/2}\frac{\sigma}{\sqrt{n}} = 122 \pm 1.28\frac{20}{\sqrt{25}} = 122 \pm 5.12 = [116.88, 127.12]$$

Comparing this interval with the 95% confidence interval for μ we computed ear-

FIGURE 6–3   The Construction of an 80% Confidence Interval for μ

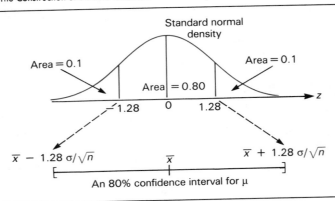

lier, we note that the present interval is *narrower*. This is an important property of confidence intervals.

> When sampling from the same population, using a fixed sample size, *the higher the confidence level, the wider the interval.*

Intuitively, a wider interval has more of a presampling chance of "capturing" the unknown population parameter. If we want a 100% confidence interval for a parameter, the interval must be $[-\infty, \infty]$. The reason for this is that 100% confidence is derived from a presampling probability of 1.00 of capturing the parameter, and the only way to get such a probability using the standard normal distribution is by allowing Z to be anywhere from $-\infty$ to ∞. If we are willing to be more realistic (nothing is *certain*) and accept, say, a 99% confidence interval, our interval would be finite and based on $z = 2.58$. The width of our interval would then be $2(2.58\sigma/\sqrt{n})$. If we further reduce our confidence requirement to 95%, the width of our interval would be $2(1.96\sigma/\sqrt{n})$. Since both σ and n are fixed, the 95% interval must be narrower. The more confidence you require, the more you need to sacrifice in terms of a wider interval.

If you want both a narrow interval *and* a high degree of confidence, you need to buy a large amount of information—take a large sample. This is so because the larger the sample size, n, the narrower the interval. This makes sense in that if you buy more information, you will have less uncertainty.

> When sampling from the same population, using a fixed confidence level, *the larger the sample size, n, the narrower the confidence interval.*

Suppose that the 80% confidence interval developed earlier was based on a sample size $n = 2,500$ instead of $n = 25$. Assuming that $\bar{x}$ and σ are the same, the new confidence interval should be 10 times as narrow as the previous one (because $\sqrt{2,500} = 50$, which is 10 times as large as $\sqrt{25}$). Indeed, the new interval is:

$$\bar{x} \pm z_{\alpha/2}\frac{\sigma}{\sqrt{n}} = 122 \pm 1.28\frac{20}{\sqrt{2,500}} = 122 \pm 0.512 = [121.49, 122.51]$$

This interval has width $2(0.512) = 1.024$, while the width of the interval based on a sample of size $n = 25$ is $2(5.12) = 10.24$. This demonstrates the value of information. The two confidence intervals are shown in Figure 6–4.

FIGURE 6–4 Width of a Confidence Interval as a Function of Sample Size

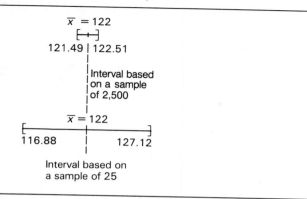

6–1. What is a confidence interval, and why is it useful? What is a confidence level?

6–2. Explain why in classical statistics it makes no sense to describe a confidence interval in terms of probability.

Answers

6–3. Explain how the postsampling confidence level is derived from a presampling probability.

6–4. Suppose that you computed a 95% confidence interval for a population mean. The user of the statistics claims your interval is too wide to have any meaning in the specific use for which it is intended. Discuss and compare two methods of solving this problem.

6–5. A realtor needs to estimate the average value of a residential property of a given size in a certain area. The realtor believes that the standard deviation of the property values is $\sigma = \$5,500.00$ and that property values are approximately normally distributed. A random sample of 16 units gives a sample mean of \$89,673.12. Give a 95% confidence interval for the average value of all properties of this kind.

6–6. In problem 6–5, suppose that a 99% confidence interval is required. Compute the new interval, and compare it with the 95% confidence interval you computed in problem 6–5.

6–6.
———
[86,131.12, 93,215.12]

6–7. A car manufacturer wants to estimate the average mpg highway rating for a new model. From experience with similar models, the manufacturer believes the mpg standard deviation is 4.6. A random sample of 100 highway runs of the new model yields a sample mean of 32 mpg. Give a 95% confidence interval for the population average mpg highway rating.

6–8. In problem 6–7, do we need to assume that the population of mpg values is normally distributed? Explain.

6–8.
———
No.

6–9. A wine importer needs to report the average percentage of alcohol in bottles of French wine. From experience with previous kinds of wine, the importer believes the population standard deviation is 1.2%. The importer randomly samples 60 bottles of the new wine and obtains a sample mean $\bar{x} = 9.3\%$. Give a 90% confidence interval for the average percentage of alcohol in all bottles of the new wine.

6–10. A company is considering installing a facsimile machine at one of its offices. As part of the decision process as to whether or not to install the machine, the company's manager wants to estimate the average number of documents that would be transmitted daily if the machine were installed. From experience at other offices, the company manager believes the standard deviation of the number of documents sent daily is 32. The manager also believes the number of documents transmitted daily is a normally distributed random variable. The machine is tested over a random sample of 15 days, and the resulting sample mean is 267. Give a 99% confidence interval for the average number of documents that would be transmitted daily if the machine were installed.

6–10.
———
[245.72, 288.28]

Answers

6–12.
_____

[21.608, 22.392]

6–14.
_____

[8,483.11, 8,640.89]

6-16.
_____

4 times as large

6–11. In problem 6–10, suppose that the manager would be interested in installing the machine if she could be fairly confident that the average number of documents transmitted daily would be above 245. Do the findings in problem 6–10 justify installing the machine? Explain.

6–12. Beechcraft, Inc., wants to estimate the average time it takes their Beechjet corporate jet to climb from sea level to 41,000 feet. From previous experience, company engineers believe that the standard deviation of climbing times is 2 minutes. The model is tested in 100 random trials, and it is found that the sample mean is 22 minutes. Give a 95% confidence interval for the average climbing time from sea level to 41,000 feet.

6–13. A mining company needs to estimate the average amount of copper ore per ton mined. A random sample of 50 tons gives a sample mean of 146.75 pounds. The population standard deviation is assumed to be 35.2 pounds. Give a 95% confidence interval for the average amount of copper in the "population" of tons mined. Also give a 90% confidence interval and a 99% confidence interval for the average amount of copper per ton.

6–14. A survey reports that people with family incomes in the $75,000 to $100,000 range report an average of $8,562 in interest paid per year when filing their tax returns with the IRS.[3] Assuming that this result is based on a random sample of 2,000 taxpayers from all over the country and that the population standard deviation is $1,800, give a 95% confidence interval for the population average interest paid per year.

6–15. The average household saving in Japan is reported to be 9.3% of income per year.[4] Assuming that the finding is based on a random sample of 5,000 households and that the population standard deviation is 1.6%, give a 90% confidence interval for Japan's population average of household percentage of savings per year.

6-16. Suppose you have a confidence interval based on a sample of size n. Using the same level of confidence, how large a sample is required to produce an interval of half the width?

6-17. The width of a 95% confidence interval for μ is 10 units. If everything else stays the same, how wide would a 90% confidence interval be for μ?

6–3　Confidence Invervals for μ When σ Is Unknown— The t Distribution

In constructing confidence intervals for μ, we assume a normal population distribution or a large sample size (for normality via the central limit theorem). Until now, we have also assumed a known population standard deviation. This assumption was necessary for theoretical reasons so that we could use standard normal probabilities in constructing our intervals.

In real sampling situations, however, the population standard deviation, σ, is rarely known. The reason for this is that both μ and σ are population parameters. When we sample from a population with the aim of estimating its unknown mean, it is quite unlikely that the other parameter of the same population, the standard deviation, will be known.

The t Distribution

As we mentioned in Chapter 5, when the population standard deviation is not known, we may use the sample standard deviation, S, in its place. *If the population is normally distributed*, the standardized statistic

$$t = \frac{\overline{X} - \mu}{S/\sqrt{n}} \qquad (6\text{–}4)$$

_____

[3] "Take a Peek at Your Peers' Deductions," *Business Week* (March 11, 1991), p. 110

[4] T. Ohta, "International Perspective: Japan's Financial Role in the 1990s," *Business Economics* (January 1991), p. 22.

has a **t distribution** with $n - 1$ degrees of freedom. The degrees of freedom of the distribution are the degrees of freedom associated with the sample standard deviation, S (as explained in the last chapter). The t distribution is also called *Student's distribution,* or *Student's t distribution.* What is the origin of the name *Student*?

W. S. Gossett was a scientist at the Guinness brewery in Dublin, Ireland. In 1908, Gossett discovered the distribution of the quantity in equation 6–4. He called the new distribution the t distribution. The Guinness brewery, however, did not allow its workers to publish findings under their own names. Therefore, Gossett published his findings under the pen name Student. As a result, the distribution became known also as Student's distribution.

The t distribution is characterized by its degrees-of-freedom parameter, df. For any integer value, df = 1, 2, 3, . . . , there is a corresponding t distribution. The t distribution resembles the standard normal distribution, Z: it is symmetric and bell-shaped. The t distribution, however, is flatter than Z in the middle part and has wider tails.

> The mean of a t distribution is zero. For df > 2, the variance of the t distribution is equal to df/(df − 2).

We see that the mean of t is the same as the mean of Z, but the variance of t is larger than the variance of Z. As df increases, the variance of t approaches 1.00, which is the variance of Z. Having wider tails and a larger variance than Z is a reflection of the fact that the t distribution has a greater inherent *uncertainty*. The uncertainty comes from the fact that σ is unknown and is estimated by the *random variable S*. The t distribution thus reflects the uncertainty in *two* random variables, $\overline{X}$ and S, while Z reflects only an uncertainty due to $\overline{X}$. The greater uncertainty in t (which makes confidence intervals based on t wider than those based on Z) is the price we pay for not knowing σ and having to estimate it from our data. As df increases, the t distribution approaches the Z distribution. Figure 6–5 shows several t distributions, with different numbers of degrees of freedom, along with the standard normal distribution, which is their limit as df goes to infinity.

Values of t distributions for selected tail probabilities are given in Table 3 in Appendix C (reproduced here as Table 6–1). Since there are infinitely many t distributions—one for every value of the degrees-of-freedom parameter—the table contains probabilities for only some of these distributions. For each distribution, the table gives values that cut off given areas under the curve to the *right*. The t table is thus a table of values corresponding to right-tail probabilities.

Let us consider an example. A random variable with a t distribution with 10 degrees of freedom has a 0.10 probability of exceeding the value 1.372. It has a 0.025 probability of exceeding the value 2.228, and so on for the other values listed in the table. Since the t distributions are symmetric about zero, we also know, for example, that the probability that a random variable with a t distribution with 10 degrees of freedom will be less than −1.372 is 0.10. These facts are demonstrated in Figure 6–6.

As we noted earlier, the t distribution approaches the standard normal distribution as the df parameter approaches infinity. The t distribution with "infinite" degrees of freedom is defined as the standard normal distribution. The last row in Appendix C, Table 3 (Table 6–1) corresponds to df = ∞, the standard normal distribution. Note that the value corresponding to a right-tail area of 0.025 in that row is 1.96, which we recognize as the appropriate z value. Similarly, the value corresponding to a right-tail area of 0.005 is 2.576, and the value corresponding to a right-tail area of 0.05 is 1.645. These, too, are values we recognize for the standard normal distribution. Look upward from the last row of the table to find cutoff values

FIGURE 6–5

Several t Distributions Showing the Convergence to the Standard Normal Distribution as the Degrees of Freedom Increase

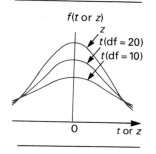

TABLE 6–1   Values and Probabilities of t Distributions

Degrees of Freedom	$t_{.100}$	$t_{.050}$	$t_{.025}$	$t_{.010}$	$t_{.005}$
1	3.078	6.314	12.706	31.821	63.657
2	1.886	2.920	4.303	6.965	9.925
3	1.638	2.353	3.182	4.541	5.841
4	1.533	2.132	2.776	3.747	4.604
5	1.476	2.015	2.571	3.365	4.032
6	1.440	1.943	2.447	3.143	3.707
7	1.415	1.895	2.365	2.998	3.499
8	1.397	1.860	2.306	2.896	3.355
9	1.383	1.833	2.262	2.821	3.250
10	1.372	1.812	2.228	2.764	3.169
11	1.363	1.796	2.201	2.718	3.106
12	1.356	1.782	2.179	2.681	3.055
13	1.350	1.771	2.160	2.650	3.012
14	1.345	1.761	2.145	2.624	2.977
15	1.341	1.753	2.131	2.602	2.947
16	1.337	1.746	2.120	2.583	2.921
17	1.333	1.740	2.110	2.567	2.898
18	1.330	1.734	2.101	2.552	2.878
19	1.328	1.729	2.093	2.539	2.861
20	1.325	1.725	2.086	2.528	2.845
21	1.323	1.721	2.080	2.518	2.831
22	1.321	1.717	2.074	2.508	2.819
23	1.319	1.714	2.069	2.500	2.807
24	1.318	1.711	2.064	2.492	2.797
25	1.316	1.708	2.060	2.485	2.787
26	1.315	1.706	2.056	2.479	2.779
27	1.314	1.703	2.052	2.473	2.771
28	1.313	1.701	2.048	2.467	2.763
29	1.311	1.699	2.045	2.462	2.756
30	1.310	1.697	2.042	2.457	2.750
40	1.303	1.684	2.021	2.423	2.704
60	1.296	1.671	2.000	2.390	2.660
120	1.289	1.658	1.980	2.358	2.617
∞	1.282	1.645	1.960	2.326	2.576

FIGURE 6–6   Table Probabilities for a Selected t Distribution (df = 10)

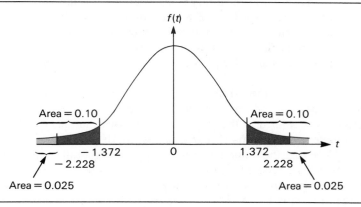

of the same right-tail probabilities for t distributions with different degrees of freedom. Suppose, for example, that we want to construct a 95% confidence interval for μ using the t distribution with 20 degrees of freedom. We may identify the value 1.96 in the last row (the appropriate z value for 95%) and then move up in the same column until we reach the row corresponding to df = 20. Here we find the required value $t_{\alpha/2} = t_{0.025} = 2.086$.

A $(1 - \alpha)$ 100% confidence interval for μ when σ is not known (assuming a normally distributed population):

$$\bar{x} \pm t_{\alpha/2} \frac{s}{\sqrt{n}} \qquad (6\text{–}5)$$

where $t_{\alpha/2}$ is the value of the t distribution with $n - 1$ degrees of freedom that cuts off a tail area of $\alpha/2$ to its right

---

EXAMPLE (a)

A stock market analyst wants to estimate the average return on a certain stock. A random sample of 15 days yields an average (annualized) return of $\bar{x} = 10.37\%$ and a standard deviation of $s = 3.5\%$. Assuming a normal population of returns, give a 95% confidence interval for the average return on this stock.

SOLUTION

Since the sample size is $n = 15$, we need to use the t distribution with $n - 1 = 14$ degrees of freedom. In Table 3, in the row corresponding to 14 degrees of freedom and the column corresponding to a right-tail area of 0.025 (this is $\alpha/2$), we find: $t_{0.025} = 2.145$. (We could also have found this value by moving upward from 1.96 in the last row.) Using this value, we construct the 95% confidence interval as follows:

$$\bar{x} \pm t_{\alpha/2} \frac{s}{\sqrt{n}} = 10.37 \pm 2.145 \frac{3.5}{\sqrt{15}} = [8.43, 12.31]$$

Thus, the analyst may be 95% sure that the average annualized return on the stock is anywhere from 8.43% to 12.31%.

Looking at the t table, we note the *convergence* of the t distributions to the Z distribution—the values in the rows preceding the last get closer and closer to the corresponding z values in the last row. Although the t distribution is the correct distribution to use whenever σ is not known (assuming the population is normal), when df is *large* we may use the standard normal distribution as an adequate approximation to the t distribution. Thus, instead of using 1.98 in a confidence interval based on a sample of size 121 (df = 120), we will just use the z value 1.96.

We divide estimation problems into two kinds: small-sample problems and large-sample problems. Example (a) demonstrated the solution of a small-sample problem. In general, *large sample* will mean a sample of 30 items or more, and *small sample* will mean a sample of size less than 30. For small samples, we will use the t distribution as demonstrated above. For large samples, we will use the Z distribution as an adequate approximation. We note that the larger the sample size, the better the normal approximation. Remember, however, that this division of large versus small samples is arbitrary.

Whenever σ is not known (and the population is assumed normal), the correct distribution to use is the t distribution with $n - 1$ degrees of freedom. Note, however, that for large degrees of freedom, the t distribution is approximated well by the Z distribution.

If you wish, you may always use the more accurate values obtained from the t table (when such values can be found in the table) rather than the standard normal approximation. In this chapter and elsewhere (with the exception of some examples in Chapter 14), we will assume that the population satisfies, at least approximately, a normal distribution assumption. For large samples, this assumption is less crucial.

A large-sample $(1 - \alpha)100\%$ confidence interval for μ:

$$\bar{x} \pm z_{\alpha/2}\frac{s}{\sqrt{n}} \qquad\qquad (6\text{--}6)$$

We demonstrate the use of equation 6–6 in Example (b).

EXAMPLE (b)

An economist wants to estimate the average amount in checking accounts at banks in a given region. A random sample of 100 accounts gives $\bar{x} = \$357.60$ and $s = \$140.00$. Give a 95% confidence interval for μ, the average amount in any checking account at a bank in the given region.

SOLUTION

We find the 95% confidence interval for μ as follows.

$$\bar{x} \pm z_{\alpha/2}\frac{s}{\sqrt{n}} = 357.60 \pm 1.96\frac{140}{\sqrt{100}} = [330.16, 385.04]$$

Thus, based on the data and the assumption of random sampling, the economist may be 95% confident that the average amount in checking accounts in the area is anywhere from $330.16 to $385.04.

PROBLEMS

Answers

6–18.

[12.95, 16.05],
[13.20, 15.80].

6–20.
─────
[30.45, 37.95]

6–18. A telephone company wants to estimate the average length of long-distance calls during weekends. A random sample of 50 calls gives a mean $\bar{x} = 14.5$ minutes and standard deviation $s = 5.6$ minutes. Give a 95% confidence interval and a 90% confidence interval for the average length of a long-distance phone call during weekends.

6–19. An insurance company handling malpractice cases is interested in estimating the average amount of claims against physicians of a certain specialty. The company obtains a random sample of 165 claims and finds $\bar{x} = \$16,530$ and $s = \$5,542$. Give a 95% confidence interval and a 99% confidence interval for the average amount of a claim.

6–20. The manufacturer of batteries used in small electrical appliances wants to estimate the average life of a battery. A random sample of 12 batteries yields $\bar{x} = 34.2$ hours and $s = 5.9$ hours. Give a 95% confidence interval for the average life of a battery.

6–21. A tire manufacturer wants to estimate the average number of miles that may be driven on a tire of a certain type before the tire wears out. A random sample of 32 tires is chosen; the tires are driven on until they wear out, and the number of miles driven on each tire is recorded. The data, in thousands of miles, are as follows:

32, 33, 28, 37, 29, 30, 25, 27, 39, 40, 26, 26, 27, 30, 25, 30, 31, 29, 24, 36, 25, 37, 37, 20, 22, 35, 23, 28, 30, 36, 40, 41

Give a 99% confidence interval for the average number of miles that may be driven on a tire of this kind.

6–22. It is estimated that the average household charitable contribution to cultural institutions is $193.[5] Assume that this sample mean is based on a sample of size 500 and that the sample standard deviation is $78. Give a 95% confidence interval for the population mean contribution for all households.

6–22.

[186.163, 199.837]

6–23. Pier 1 Imports is a nationwide retail outlet selling imported furniture and other home items. From time to time, the company surveys its regular customers by obtaining random samples based on customer zip codes. In one mailing, customers were asked to rate a new table from Thailand on a scale of 0 to 100. The ratings of 25 randomly selected customers are as follows: 78, 85, 80, 89, 77, 50, 75, 90, 88, 100, 70, 99, 98, 55, 80, 45, 80, 76, 96, 100, 95, 90, 60, 85, 90. Give a 99% confidence interval for the rating of the table that would be given by an average member of the population of regular customers. Assume normality.

6–24. An executive placement service needs to estimate the average salary of executives placed in a given industry. A random sample of 40 executives gives $\bar{x} = \$42,539$ and $s = \$11,690$. Give a 90% confidence interval for the average salary of an executive placed in this industry.

6–24.

[39498.46, 45579.54]

6–25. A bank is interested in extending its automated teller machine service to a new community. As part of the research prepared as an aid in making the decision, the bank's management undertakes an experiment to determine the average amount of a transaction, in dollars per person per day. A random sample of 10 experimental transactions on a trial run of the machine is collected. The following data (in dollars) are the result: 53, 40, 39, 10, 12, 60, 72, 65, 50, 45. Give a 95% confidence interval for the average amount of a transaction.

6–26. For advertising purposes, the Beef Industry Council needs to estimate the average caloric content of 3 oz. top loin steak cuts. A random sample of 400 pieces gives a sample mean of 212 calories and a sample standard deviation of 38 calories. Give a 95% confidence interval for the average caloric content of a 3 oz. cut of top loin steak. Also give a 98% confidence interval for the average caloric content of a cut.

6–26.

[208.28, 215.72]
[207.58, 216.42]

6–27. A transportation company wants to estimate the average length of time goods are in transit across the country. A random sample of 20 shipments gives $\bar{x} = 2.6$ days and $s = 0.4$ days. Give a 99% confidence interval for the average transit time.

6–28. To aid in planning the development of a tourist shopping area, a state agency wants to estimate the average dollar amount spent by a tourist in an existing shopping area. A random sample of 56 tourists gives $\bar{x} = \$258$ and $s = \$85$. Give a 95% confidence interval for the average amount spent by a tourist at the shopping area.

6–28.

[235.74, 280.26]

6–29. A large drugstore wants to estimate average weekly sales for a brand of soap. A random sample of 13 weeks gives the following numbers: 123, 110, 95, 120, 87, 89, 100, 105, 98, 88, 75, 125, 101. Give a 90% confidence interval for average weekly sales.

6–30. Citibank Visa gives its cardholders "bonus dollars," which may be spent in partial payment for gifts purchased with the Visa card. The company wants to estimate the average amount of bonus dollars that will be spent by a cardholder enrolled in the program during a year. A trial run of the program with a random sample of 225 cardholders is carried out. The results are $\bar{x} = \$259.60$ and $s = \$52.00$. Give a 95% confidence interval for the average amount of bonus dollars that will be spent by a cardholder during the year.

6–30.

[252.81, 266.39]

6–31. An accountant wants to estimate the average amount of an account of a service company. A random sample of 46 accounts yields $\bar{x} = \$16.50$ and $s = \$2.20$. Give a 95% confidence interval for the average amount of an account.

6–32. An art dealer wants to estimate the average value of works of art of a certain period and type. A random sample of 20 works of art is appraised. The sample mean is found to be

6–32.

[4839.47, 5438.52]

[5] *Working Woman* (March 1991), p. 58.

$5,139 and the sample standard deviation $640. Give a 95% confidence interval for the average value of all works of art of this kind.

6-33. A management consulting agency needs to estimate the average number of years of experience of executives in a given branch of management. A random sample of 28 executives gives $\bar{x} = 6.7$ years and $s = 2.4$ years. Give a 99% confidence interval for the average number of years of experience for all executives in this branch.

6-34.

[8.79, 9.01]

6-34. The Food and Drug Administration (FDA) needs to estimate the average content of an additive in a given food product. A random sample of 75 portions of the product gives $\bar{x} = 8.9$ units and $s = 0.5$ units. Give a 95% confidence interval for the average number of units of additive in any portion of this food product.

6-35. The management of a supermarket needs to make estimates of the average daily demand for milk. The following data are available (number of half-gallon containers sold per day): 48, 59, 45, 62, 50, 68, 57, 80, 65, 58, 79, 69. Assuming that this is a random sample of daily demand, give a 90% confidence interval for average daily demand for milk.

6-36. The following table, reprinted by permission from *Entertainment Weekly,* shows ratings of 10 movies by seven independent movie critics and the average rating for each film.[6]

6-36.

[3.113, 4.030]
[1.102, 2.355]
[0.955, 2.279]
[2.114, 3.486]
[2.666, 3.362]
[0.333, 3.227]
[0.797, 1.974]
[2.753, 4.076]
[1.170, 2.315]
[1.157, 2.976]

	Peter Travers, Rolling Stone	Gene Siskel, Siskel & Ebert	Roger Ebert, Siskel & Ebert	Mike Clark, USA Today	Jay Carr, Boston Globe	Kathy Huffhines, Detroit Free Press	Owen Gleiberman, Entertainment Weekly	Average
The Grifters	A	B+	A	B−	A−	B+	A	A−
He Said, She Said	D	D	C	C−	C−	B	C−	C−
King Ralph	C−	C	—	C+	D−	D	C	C−
L.A. Story	C	C	A	C+	B	B+	B	B−
Once Around	B	A−	B+	B−	B−	B−	B	B
Popcorn	F	—	—	D+	C+	C+	B	C
Scenes from a Mall	D	D	D	C−	D+	D	B−	D+
The Silence of the Lambs	A	C	B+	A	B+	B+	A	B+
Sleeping with the Enemy	D	C	D+	D	C+	C+	C+	C−
White Fang	C	B	B	D−	C	—	C−	C

Assign the usual numerical values to the letter grades (A=4, B=3, C=2, D=1, F=0; a "+" adds a 0.3 to the score, and a "−" reduces the score by 0.3). Assume that the seven movie critics constitute a random sample from a *population* of well-educated, informed, and opinionated regular moviegoers. Give a 95% confidence interval for the mean grade that would be given each of the 10 movies by members of this population.

6-37. Contact lenses can cause sore eyes due to protein buildup on the surface of the lens. A new technology promises a cure for this problem. A layer of polymer is deposited on the lens and prevents the tear proteins from building up on the lens. The polymer must have an average thickness of 10 atoms.[7] A random sample of 15 locations on a particular lens gives the following thickness readings (number of atoms): 9, 9, 8, 11, 12, 10, 9, 8, 13, 12, 10, 11, 10, 9, 7. Give a 90% confidence interval for the average polymer thickness on the entire lens. Does the population average value of 10 atoms lie inside the confidence interval? Explain the meaning of your answer.

6-38.

[11.937, 13.886]

6-38. The following table, reproduced by permission from *American Banker,* shows total assets in millions of dollars for a random sample of 20 large regional banking companies in

[6] *Entertainment Weekly* (March 8, 1991), p. 41.

[7] "A Nonstick Lens to Cure Red-eye," *Business Week* (January 28, 1991), p. 95.

the United States (where "large" is defined as having total assets of at least $10 billion).[8] Use the information in the table to construct a 95% confidence interval for the average total assets of all large regional banking companies in the United States.

		Assets 12/31/89 ($ million)
1	U.S. Bancorp., Portland, Ore.	16,975
2	CoreStates Financial Corp., Philadelphia	16,849
3	Southeast Banking Corp., Miami	16,525
4	KeyCorp, Albany, N.Y.	15,461
5	Boatmen's Bancshares, Inc., St. Louis	14,542
6	First City Bancorp of Texas, Inc., Houston	14,081
7	First of America Bank Corp., Kalamazoo, Mich.	12,793
8	Signet Banking Corp., Richmond, Va.	12,476
9	Harris Bankcorp, Inc., Chicago	12,374
10	UJB Financial Corp., Princeton, N.J.	12,172
11	Comerica, Inc., Detroit	12,149
12	Meridian Bancorp, Inc., Reading, Pa.	11,925
13	Huntington Bancshares, Inc., Columbus, Ohio	11,680
14	First American Bankshares, Inc., Washington, D.C.	11,490
15	Michigan National Corp., Farmington Hills	11,480
16	Crestar Financial Corp., Richmond, Va.	11,361
17	Ameritrust Corp., Cleveland	11,233
18	Northern Trust Corp., Chicago	10,938
19	Society Corp., Cleveland	10,903
20	Valley National Corp., Phoenix	10,549

6–4 Large-Sample Confidence Intervals for the Population Proportion, *p*

Sometimes interest centers on a qualitative, rather than a quantitative, variable. We may be interested in the relative frequency of occurrence of some characteristic in a population. For example, we may be interested in the proportion of people in a population who are users of some product or the proportion of defective items produced by a machine. In such cases, we want to estimate the population proportion, p.

The estimator of the population proportion, p, is the sample proportion, $\hat{P}$. In Chapter 5, we saw that when the sample size is large, $\hat{P}$ has an approximately normal sampling distribution. The mean of the sampling distribution of $\hat{P}$ is the population proportion, p, and the standard deviation of the distribution of $\hat{P}$ is $\sqrt{pq/n}$, where $q = 1 - p$. Since the standard deviation of the estimator depends on the unknown population parameter, its value is also unknown to us. It turns out, however, that for large samples we may use our actual estimate $\hat{p}$ instead of the unknown parameter p in the formula for the standard deviation. We will, therefore, use $\sqrt{\hat{p}\hat{q}/n}$ as our estimate of the standard error of $\hat{P}$. Recall our large-sample rule of thumb: For estimating p, a sample is considered large enough when both $n \cdot p$ and $n \cdot q$ are greater than 5. (We guess the value of p when determining whether the sample is large enough. As a check, we may also compute $n\hat{p}$ and $n\hat{q}$ once the sample is obtained.)

---

[8] *American Banker Top Numbers 1990* (New York: American Banker, 1990), p. 56.

A large-sample $(1 - \alpha)100\%$ confidence interval for the population proportion, p:

$$\hat{p} \pm z_{\alpha/2}\sqrt{\frac{\hat{p}\hat{q}}{n}} \qquad (6\text{--}7)$$

where the sample proportion, $\hat{p}$, is equal to the number of successes in the sample, x, divided by the number of trials (the sample size), n, and $\hat{q} = 1 - \hat{p}$

We demonstrate the use of equation 6–7 in Example (c).

EXAMPLE (c)

A marketing research firm wants to estimate the share that foreign companies have in the American market for certain products. A random sample of 100 consumers is obtained, and it is found that 34 people in the sample are users of foreign-made products; the rest are users of domestic products. Give a 95% confidence interval for the share of foreign products in this market.

SOLUTION

We have $x = 34$ and $n = 100$, so our sample estimate of the proportion is $\hat{p} = x/n = 34/100 = 0.34$. We now use equation 6–7 to obtain the confidence interval for the population proportion, p. A 95% confidence interval for p is:

$$\hat{p} \pm z_{\alpha/2}\sqrt{\frac{\hat{p}\hat{q}}{n}} = 0.34 \pm 1.96\sqrt{\frac{(0.34)(0.66)}{100}}$$

$$= 0.34 \pm 1.96(0.04737) = 0.34 \pm 0.0928$$

$$= [0.2472, 0.4328]$$

Thus, the firm may be 95% confident that foreign manufacturers control anywhere from 24.72% to 43.28% of the market.

Suppose the firm is not happy with such a wide confidence interval. What can be done about it? This is a problem of *value of information*, and it applies to all estimation situations. As we stated earlier, for a fixed sample size, the higher the confidence you require, the wider will be the confidence interval. The sample size is in the denominator of the standard error term, as we saw in the case of estimating μ. If we should increase n, the standard error of $\hat{P}$ will decrease, and there will be less uncertainty about the parameter being estimated. If the sample size cannot be increased but you still want a narrower confidence interval, you must reduce your confidence level. Thus, for example, if the firm agrees to reduce the confidence level to 90%, z will be reduced from 1.96 to 1.645, and the confidence interval will shrink to:

$$0.34 \pm 1.645(0.04737) = 0.34 \pm 0.07792 = [0.2621, 0.4179]$$

The firm may be 90% confident that the market share of foreign products is anywhere from 26.21% to 41.79%. If the firm wanted a high confidence (say 95%) *and* a narrow confidence interval, it would have to take a larger sample. Suppose that a random sample of $n = 200$ customers gave us the same result, that is: $x = 68$, $n = 200$ and $\hat{p} = x/n = 0.34$. What would be a 95% confidence interval in this case? Using equation 6–7, we get:

$$\hat{p} \pm z_{\alpha/2}\sqrt{\frac{\hat{p}\hat{q}}{n}} = 0.34 \pm 1.96\sqrt{\frac{(0.34)(0.66)}{200}} = [0.2743, 0.4057]$$

This interval is considerably narrower than our first 95% confidence interval, which was based on a sample of 100.

When estimating proportions using small samples, the binomial distribution may be used in forming confidence intervals. Since the distribution is discrete, it may not be possible to construct an interval with an exact, prespecified confidence level such as 95% or 99%. We will not demonstrate the method here.

PROBLEMS

6–39. The maker of portable exercise equipment, designed for health-conscious people who travel too frequently to use a regular athletic club, wants to estimate the proportion of traveling businesspeople who may be interested in the product. A random sample of 120 traveling businesspeople indicates that 28 of them may be interested in purchasing the portable fitness equipment. Give a 95% confidence interval for the proportion of all traveling businesspeople who may be interested in the product.

6–40. The makers of a medicated facial skin cream are interested in determining the percentage of people in a given age group who may benefit from the ointment. A random sample of 68 people results in 42 successful treatments. Give a 99% confidence interval for the proportion of people in the given age group who may be successfully treated with the facial cream.

6–41. An article on secretaries' salaries in the *The Wall Street Journal* (July 8, 1986) reports: "Three-fourths of surveyed secretaries said they make less than $25,000 a year." Suppose that the *Journal* based its results on a random sample of 460 secretaries drawn from every category of business. Give a 95% confidence interval for the proportion of secretaries earning less than $25,000 per year.

6–42. A Pitney Bowes advertisement appearing in business magazines shows an irate manager kneeling on his desktop in a room full of playful seals, with his disgraced assistant looking at the floor. The caption reads: "SEALS? I said, bring in more DEALS!" Suppose the company wanted to test the comic effect of the ad and gathered a random sample of 80 viewers, 58 of whom thought the advertisement was funny. Give a 90% confidence interval for the proportion of people who consider this ad funny.

6–43. A study was undertaken to investigate the relative success of IBM "clones" in the microcomputer market. A random sample of 590 companies revealed that 88 were using computers made by either of two main competitors of IBM. Give a 95% confidence interval for the combined market share of the two "clone" companies.

6–44. A recent article describes the success of business schools in Europe and the demand on that continent for the MBA degree. The article reports that a survey of 280 European business positions resulted in the conclusion that only one-seventh of the positions for MBAs at European businesses are currently filled. Assuming that these numbers are exact and that the sample was randomly chosen from the entire population of interest, give a 90% confidence interval for the proportion of filled MBA positions in Europe.

6–45. A recent article about accounting systems describes how Solutions Inc., a consulting firm in Richmond, Virginia, is able to compare a client's needs with 70 different accounting systems and find the best system for each business. According to the company's president, 50% of all companies made the wrong choice of an accounting system.[9] If this assertion is based on a random sample of 200 firms, give a 95% confidence interval for the proportion of all firms that use the wrong accounting system.

Answers

6–40.
[0.4658, 0.7695]

6–42.
[0.6429, 0.8071]

6–44.
[0.1085, 0.1773]

---

[9] "Accounting: Finding the System that Fits Your Firm," *Nation's Business* (March 1991), p. 9.

Answers

6–46.

[0.5297, 0.6103]

6–48.

[0.4026, 0.5654]

6–50.

[0.7857, 0.8143]

6–46. The United States now controls 57% of the world's market for software.[10] Suppose that this conclusion is based on a random sample of 1,000 software products worldwide, 570 of which are made in America. Construct a 99% confidence interval for the worldwide proportion of software packages made by American firms.

6–47. A machine produces safety devices for use in helicopters. A quality-control engineer regularly checks samples of the devices produced by the machine, and if too many of the devices are defective, the production process is stopped and the machine is readjusted. If a random sample of 52 devices yields 8 defectives, give a 98% confidence interval for the proportion of defective devices made by this machine.

6–48. Before launching its Buyers' Assurance Program, American Express wanted to estimate the proportion of cardholders who would be interested in this automatic insurance coverage plan. A random sample of 250 American Express cardholders was selected and sent questionnaires. The results were that 121 people in the sample expressed interest in the plan. Give a 99% confidence interval for the proportion of all interested American Express cardholders.

6–49. An airline wants to estimate the proportion of business passengers on a new route from New York to San Francisco. A random sample of 347 passengers on this route is selected, and 201 of them are found to be business travelers. Give a 90% confidence interval for the proportion of business travelers on the airline's new route.

6–50. In 1990, 3,000 volunteers assisted scientists in projects in 50 countries, and 80% of all these volunteers were single.[11] Assuming that the 3,000 volunteers constitute a random sample of people who would assist in research abroad, give a 95% confidence interval for the proportion of single people who would volunteer.

6–51. A recent survey of 200 randomly selected products shows that the success rate of new industrial products is 59%.[12] Give a 99% confidence interval for the proportion of all new industrial products that are successful.

6–5 The Finite-Population Correction Factor[13]

Until now, we have implicitly assumed an "infinite" population. That is, we have assumed that the population was much larger than the sample. This is often the case in practice. Still, there are cases where we sample (without replacement) a sizable fraction of a finite population. In such cases, the standard error of our estimator needs to be corrected to reflect the fact that the sample constitutes a nonnegligible fraction of the entire population.

When the size of the sample, n, constitutes at least 5% of the size of the population, N, we have to use a finite-population correction factor and modify the standard error of our estimator. In Chapter 5, we gave the standard error of our estimator, $\bar{X}$, in equation 5–3: $\sigma_{\bar{x}} = \sigma/\sqrt{n}$. Note that the standard error, as stated, does *not* account for the relative size of the sample with respect to the size of the sampled population. The standard error in equation 5–3 depends only on the absolute size of the sample, n (and on the magnitude of the population standard deviation). When the sample constitutes a considerable fraction of the population, equation 5–3 does not correctly reflect the standard deviation of the sample mean. The reason is the following. If the sample size is *equal* to the population size, that is, $n = N$, the standard error of $\bar{X}$ is equal to *zero*. This is so because when we sample the *entire* popu-

---

[10] "Can the U.S. Stay Ahead in Software?" *Business Week* (March 11, 1991), p. 98.

[11] "How to Survive with One Paddle in a Two-Paddle Boat," *Condé Nast Traveler* (March 1991), p. 132.

[12] U. Yucelt, "New Product Forecasting: Survey Results," *The Journal of Business Forecasting* (Winter 1990–91), p. 20.

[13] This is an optional section.

lation, we know the exact population mean, and there is no uncertainty—the standard error is zero. As the sample size, n, approaches the population size, N, the standard error of $\overline{X}$ should approach zero. This is not reflected in equation 5–3 because—according to that equation—the standard error of $\overline{X}$ is equal to zero only when the sample size is infinite. In cases where we sample a sizable fraction of the population, we thus need to account for the reduction in the *actual* standard error of $\overline{X}$ as n becomes close to N. This reduction in the standard error of the statistic is achieved by multiplying the standard error by a finite-population correction factor.

Finite-population correction factor:

$$\sqrt{\frac{N - n}{N - 1}} \qquad (6\text{–}8)$$

Note that the expression in equation 6–8 is close to 1.00 when the sample size is small relative to the population size. The expression approaches zero as the sample size approaches the population size, as required. When sampling for the population mean, we multiply the standard error of $\overline{X}$ by the correction factor. We thus have the following large-sample confidence interval for μ when the sample size is a sizable fraction of the population size.

A large-sample $(1 - \alpha)100\%$ confidence interval for μ using a finite-population correction:

$$\overline{X} \pm z_{\alpha/2} \frac{s}{\sqrt{n}} \sqrt{\frac{N - n}{N - 1}} \qquad (6\text{–}9)$$

The finite-population correction factor (equation 6–8) may also be used to modify the standard error of the sample proportion in estimating a population proportion, p.

A large-sample $(1 - \alpha)100\%$ confidence interval for p using a finite-population correction:

$$\hat{p} \pm z_{\alpha/2} \sqrt{\frac{\hat{p}\hat{q}}{n}} \sqrt{\frac{N - n}{N - 1}} \qquad (6\text{–}10)$$

EXAMPLE (d)

A company has 1,000 accounts receivable. To estimate the average amount of these accounts, a random sample of 100 accounts is chosen. In the sample, the average amount is $\overline{x} = \$532.35$, and the standard deviation is $s = \$61.22$. Give a 95% confidence interval for the average of all 1,000 accounts.

SOLUTION

Here we have $N = 1,000$ and $n = 100$, so the sampling fraction is $n/N = 100/1,000 = 0.10$. Since the fraction is greater than 0.05, we need to use a confidence interval with a finite-population correction factor. Using equation 6–9, we get:

$$\bar{x} \pm z_{\alpha/2}\frac{s}{\sqrt{n}}\sqrt{\frac{N-n}{N-1}} = 532.35 \pm 1.96\left(\frac{61.22}{10}\right)\left(\sqrt{\frac{900}{999}}\right)$$
$$= 532.35 \pm 1.96(6.122)(\sqrt{0.9009})$$
$$= 532.35 \pm 11.39 = [520.96, 543.74]$$

PROBLEMS

Answers

6-52.
___
[613.24, 683.40]

6-54.
___
[48.73, 51.27]

6-56.
___
[1,138.29, 1,301.71]

6-58.
___
[1.85, 2.15]

6-60.
___
[0.1111, 0.2623]

6-52. A community branch of a large bank has 1,253 checking accounts. A random sample of 200 of these accounts was selected, and the average balance in the sample was found to be $648.32. The sample standard deviation was found to be $210.00. Give a 99% confidence interval for the average balance in a checking account at the branch.

6-53. In problem 6-52, give a 90% confidence interval for the average amount in checking accounts at the branch.

6-54. An article about nonalcoholic beer indicates that brands of the new beer contain an average of 50 calories per bottle, and the standard deviation is 5 calories.[14] If these results are obtained from a random sample of 50 bottles drawn from a single shipment of 300 bottles, give a 95% confidence interval for the average caloric content of a bottle in this shipment of 300 bottles.

6-55. A company wants to estimate the proportion of its employees who are satisfied with a new management decision. Out of a total of 1,242 employees, 160 were randomly selected and interviewed. Of the ones interviewed, 85 indicated that they were satisfied with the new decision. Give a 95% confidence interval for the proportion of all employees who are satisfied with the new decision.

6-56. A marketer of candy products wants to estimate the average number of candy bars sold in a given month in all 538 candy stores in a given area. A random sample of 100 stores gives $\bar{x} = 1,220$ and $s = 550$. Give a 90% confidence interval for the average number of candy bars sold in all 538 stores.

6-57. A large supermarket receives weekly shipments of 1,520 cartons of eggs. To estimate reimbursements for shipment damages, the supermarket opens a random sample of 100 cartons to determine whether eggs are damaged. If, in a regular weekly sampling, 12 cartons are found to contain damaged eggs, give a 95% confidence interval for the proportion of cartons that are damaged in the entire shipment of 1,520.

6-58. A random sample of 65 stocks selected from among the stocks listed in the Standard & Poor's 500 Index are found to have gone up by an average of 2 points with a standard deviation of 0.5 points. Give a 99% confidence interval for the average price change of all 500 stocks in the index.

6-59. The five-year average return-on-equity figures for 50 computer hardware manufacturers are shown on page 217.[15] Draw a random sample of 15 data points, and use it in constructing a 95% confidence interval for the population mean return. Try with and without adjusting, using the finite-population correction. Is the population mean inside the interval? Experiment with other sample sizes.

6-60. A shipment of 1,000 items is sampled to determine the proportion of defective items. A random sample of 150 items reveals that 28 are defective. Give a 99% confidence interval for the proportion of defectives.

---

[14] *Business Week* (October 6, 1986).

[15] Reproduced by permission from "Annual Report on American Industry," *Forbes* (January 7, 1991), p. 122.

Company	5-Year Average (%)	Company	5-Year Average (%)
Conner Peripherals	46.4	Marshall Industries	16.1
Everex Systems	44.3	Maxtor	16.1
Compaq Computer	42.7	Applied Materials	15.6
Mark IV Industries	40.9	Dynatech	15.4
Apple Computer	37.2	Texas Instruments	15.4
Merisel	29.8	Intergraph	15.3
Micron Technology	27.4	SCI Systems	14.1
Cray Research	24.8	Northern Telecom	13.8
EG&G	23.5	IBM	13.8
Premier Industrial	23.1	Tandem Computers	13.7
Sun Microsystems	22.5	Motorola	12.3
Seagate Technology	21.0	Scientific-Atlanta	11.7
Western Digital	20.0	Carlisle Cos	11.5
AMP	19.9	Silicon Graphics	10.8
3Com	19.7	Analog Devices	10.0
Amdahl	18.9	MAI Systems	9.0
Quantum	18.8	Penn Central	6.9
Vishay Intertech	18.8	Wyle Laboratories	6.9
NCR	18.4	Avnet	6.4
Thomas & Betts	18.1	Bell Industries	6.0
AST Research	17.6	Harris Corp	6.0
Molex	17.0	Varian Associates	5.1
Intel	16.7	Perkin-Elmer	3.6
Digital Equipment	16.2	Tektronix	3.2
Hewlett-Packard	16.2	M/A-Com	1.1

6–6 Confidence Intervals for the Population Variance[16]

In some situations, our interest centers on the population variance (or, equivalently, the population standard deviation). This happens in production processes, queuing (waiting line) processes, and other situations. As we know, the sample variance, S^2, is the (unbiased) estimator of the population variance, σ^2.

To compute confidence intervals for the population variance, we must learn to use a new probability distribution: the *chi-square distribution*. Chi (pronounced $k\bar{i}$) is one of two X letters in the Greek alphabet and is denoted by χ. Hence, we denote the chi-square distribution by χ^2.

The chi-square distribution, like the t distribution, has associated with it a degrees-of-freedom parameter, df. In the application of the chi-square distribution to estimation of the population variance, $df = n - 1$ (as with the t distribution in its application to sampling for the population mean). Unlike the t and the normal distributions, however, the chi-square distribution is *not* symmetric.

> The **chi-square distribution** is the probability distribution of the sum of several independent, squared standard normal random variables.

As a sum of squares, the chi-square random variable cannot be negative and is therefore bounded on the left by zero. The resulting distribution is skewed to the right. Figure 6–7 shows several chi-square distributions with different numbers of degrees of freedom.

---

[16] This is an optional section, but the chi-square distribution presented in this section should be introduced before Chapter 14.

FIGURE 6–7 Several Chi-Square Distributions with Different Values of the df Parameter

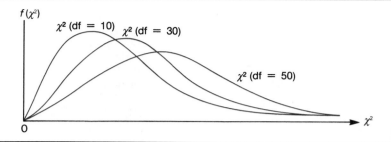

The mean of a chi-square distribution is equal to the degrees of freedom parameter, df. The variance of a chi-square distribution is equal to twice the number of degress of freedom.

Note in Figure 6–7 that as df increases, the chi-square distribution looks more and more like a normal distribution. In fact, as df increases, the chi-square distribution approaches a normal distribution with mean df and variance 2(df).

Table 4 in Appendix C gives values of the chi-square distribution with different degrees of freedom, for given tail probabilities. An abbreviated version of part of the table is given on the next page as Table 6–2. We apply the chi-square distribution to problems of estimation of the population variance using the following property.

In sampling from a normal population, the random variable

$$\chi^2 = \frac{(n-1)S^2}{\sigma^2} \qquad (6\text{–}11)$$

has a chi-square distribution with $n-1$ degrees of freedom

The distribution of the quantity in equation 6–11 leads to a confidence interval for σ^2. Since the χ^2 distribution is not symmetric, we cannot use equal values with opposite signs (such as ± 1.96 as we did with Z) and must construct the confidence interval using the two distinct tails of the distribution.

A $(1-\alpha)100\%$ confidence interval for the population variance, σ^2 (where the population is assumed normal):

$$\left[\frac{(n-1)s^2}{\chi^2_{\alpha/2}}, \frac{(n-1)s^2}{\chi^2_{1-\alpha/2}}\right] \qquad (6\text{–}12)$$

where $\chi^2_{\alpha/2}$ is the value of the chi-square distribution with $n-1$ degrees of freedom that cuts off an area of $\alpha/2$ to its right and $\chi^2_{1-\alpha/2}$ is the value of the distribution that cuts off an area of $\alpha/2$ to its left (equivalently, an area of $1-\alpha/2$ to its right)

We now demonstrate the use of equation 6–12 with an example.

TABLE 6-2 Values and Probabilities of Chi-Square Distributions

				Area in Right Tail						
df	.995	.990	.975	.950	.900	.100	.050	.025	.010	.005
1	.0⁴393	.0³157	.0³982	.0²393	0.158	2.71	3.84	5.02	6.63	7.88
2	.0100	.0201	.0506	.103	.211	4.61	5.99	7.38	9.21	10.6
3	.0717	.115	.216	.352	.584	6.25	7.81	9.35	11.3	12.8
4	.207	.297	.484	.711	1.06	7.78	9.49	11.1	13.3	14.9
5	.412	.554	.831	1.15	1.61	9.24	11.1	12.8	15.1	16.7
6	.676	.872	1.24	1.64	2.20	10.6	12.6	14.4	16.8	18.5
7	.989	1.24	1.69	2.17	2.83	12.0	14.1	16.0	18.5	20.3
8	1.34	1.65	2.18	2.73	3.49	13.4	15.5	17.5	20.1	22.0
9	1.73	2.09	2.70	3.33	4.17	14.7	16.9	19.0	21.7	23.6
10	2.16	2.56	3.25	3.94	4.87	16.0	18.3	20.5	23.2	25.2
11	2.60	3.05	3.82	4.57	5.58	17.3	19.7	21.9	24.7	26.8
12	3.07	3.57	4.40	5.23	6.30	18.5	21.0	23.3	26.2	28.3
13	3.57	4.11	5.01	5.89	7.04	19.8	22.4	24.7	27.7	29.8
14	4.07	4.66	5.63	6.57	7.79	21.1	23.7	26.1	29.1	31.3
15	4.60	5.23	6.26	7.26	8.55	22.3	25.0	27.5	30.6	32.8
16	5.14	5.81	6.91	7.96	9.31	23.5	26.3	28.8	32.0	34.3
17	5.70	6.41	7.56	8.67	10.1	24.8	27.6	30.2	33.4	35.7
18	6.26	7.01	8.23	9.39	10.9	26.0	28.9	31.5	34.8	37.2
19	6.84	7.63	8.91	10.1	11.7	27.2	30.1	32.9	36.2	38.6
20	7.43	8.26	9.59	10.9	12.4	28.4	31.4	34.2	37.6	40.0
21	8.03	8.90	10.3	11.6	13.2	29.6	32.7	35.5	38.9	41.4
22	8.64	9.54	11.0	12.3	14.0	30.8	33.9	36.8	40.3	42.8
23	9.26	10.2	11.7	13.1	14.8	32.0	35.2	38.1	41.6	44.2
24	9.89	10.9	12.4	13.8	15.7	33.2	36.4	39.4	43.0	45.6
25	10.5	11.5	13.1	14.6	16.5	34.4	37.7	40.6	44.3	46.9
26	11.2	12.2	13.8	15.4	17.3	35.6	38.9	41.9	45.6	48.3
27	11.8	12.9	14.6	16.2	18.1	36.7	40.1	43.2	47.0	49.6
28	12.5	13.6	15.3	16.9	18.9	37.9	41.3	44.5	48.3	51.0
29	13.1	14.3	16.0	17.7	19.8	39.1	42.6	45.7	49.6	52.3
30	13.8	15.0	16.8	18.5	20.6	40.3	43.8	47.0	50.9	53.7
30	10.0⁴393	10.0³157	10.0³982	10.0²393	10.158	10.71	10.84	10.02	10.63	10.88

EXAMPLE (e)

In an automated process, a machine fills cans of coffee. If the average amount filled is different from what it should be, the machine may be adjusted to correct the mean. If the *variance* of the filling process is too high, however, the machine is out of control and needs to be repaired. Therefore, from time to time regular checks of the variance of the filling process are made. This is done by randomly sampling filled cans, measuring their amounts, and computing the sample variance. A random sample of 30 cans gives an estimate $s^2 = 18,540$. Give a 95% confidence interval for the population variance σ^2.

SOLUTION

Figure 6-8 shows the appropriate chi-square distribution with $n - 1 = 29$ degrees of freedom. From Table 6-2 we get, for df = 29, $\chi^2_{0.025} = 45.7$ and $\chi^2_{0.975} = 16.0$. Using these values, we compute the confidence interval as follows:

$$\left[\frac{29(18,540)}{45.7}, \frac{29(18,540)}{16.0} \right] = [11,765, 33,604]$$

We can be 95% sure that the population variance is between 11,765 and 33,604.

FIGURE 6-8 Values and Tail Areas of a Chi-Square Distribution with 29 Degrees of Freedom

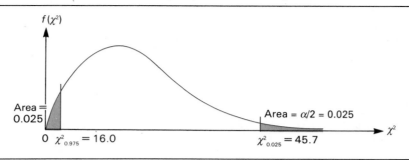

PROBLEMS

In the following problems, assume normal populations.

6-61. The service time in queues should not have a large variance; otherwise, the queue tends to build up. A bank regularly checks service time by its tellers to determine its variance. A random sample of 22 service times (in minutes) gives $s^2 = 8$. Give a 95% confidence interval for the variance of service time at the bank.

6-62. A sensitive measuring device should not have a large variance in the errors of measurements it makes. A random sample of 41 measurement errors gives $s^2 = 102$. Give a 99% confidence interval for the variance of measurement errors.

6-63. A random sample of 60 accounts gives a sample variance of 1,228. Give a 95% confidence interval for the variance of all accounts.

6-64. In problem 6-21, give a 99% confidence interval for the variance of the number of miles that may be driven on a tire.

6-65. In problem 6-25, give a 95% confidence interval for the variance of the population of transaction amounts.

6-66. In problem 6-26, give a 95% confidence interval for the variance of the caloric content of all 3 oz. cuts of top loin steak. (Hint: Use a normal approximation to the chi-square distribution.)

6-67. In problem 6-27, give a 95% confidence interval for the variance of the transit time for all goods.

Answers

6-62.
―――
[61.11, 197.04]

6-64.
―――
[19.25, 74.92]

6-66.
―――
[1,268.03, 1,676.68]

FIGURE 6-9
The Standard Error of a
Statistic as a Function of
Sample Size

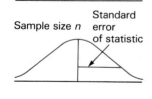

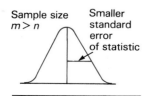

6-7 Sample-Size Determination

One of the most common questions a statistician is asked before any actual sampling takes place is: "How large should my sample be?" From a *statistical* point of view, the best answer to this question is: "Get as large a sample as you can afford. If possible, 'sample' the entire population." If you need to know the mean or proportion of a population, and you can sample the entire population (i.e., carry out a census), you will have all the information and will know the parameter exactly. Clearly, this is better than any estimate. This, however, is unrealistic in most situations due to economic constraints, time constraints, and other limitations. "Get as large a sample as you can afford" is the best answer if we ignore all costs, because the larger the sample, the smaller the standard error of our statistic. The smaller the standard error, the less uncertainty with which we have to contend. This is demonstrated in Figure 6-9.

When the sampling budget is limited, the question often is how to find the *minimum* sample size that will satisfy some precision requirements. In such cases, you should explain to the designer of the study that he or she must first give you answers to the following three questions.

1. How close do you want your sample estimate to be to the unknown parameter? The answer to this question is denoted by B (for "bound").
2. What do you want the confidence level to be so that the distance between the estimate and the parameter is less than or equal to B?
3. The last, and often misunderstood, question that must be answered is: What is your estimate of the variance (or standard deviation) of the population in question?

Only after you have answers to all three questions can you give an answer as to the minimum required sample size. Often the statistician is told: "How can I give you an estimate of the variance? I don't know. You are the statistician." In such cases, try to get from your client some idea about the variation in the population. If the population is approximately normal and you can get 95% bounds on the values in the *population, divide the difference between the upper and lower bounds by 4*; this will give you a rough guess of σ. Or you may take a small, inexpensive *pilot* survey and estimate σ by the sample standard deviation. Once you have obtained the three required pieces of information, all you need to do is substitute the answers into the appropriate formula that follows.

Minimum required sample size in estimating the population mean, μ:

$$n = \frac{z_{\alpha/2}^2 \sigma^2}{B^2} \qquad\qquad (6\text{–}13)$$

Minimum required sample size in estimating the population proportion, p:

$$n = \frac{z_{\alpha/2}^2 pq}{B^2} \qquad\qquad (6\text{–}14)$$

Equations 6–13 and 6–14 are derived from the formulas for the corresponding confidence intervals for these population parameters based on the normal distribution. In the case of the population mean, B is the half-width of a $(1 - \alpha)100\%$ confidence interval for μ, and therefore

$$B = z_{\alpha/2}\frac{\sigma}{\sqrt{n}} \qquad\qquad (6\text{–}15)$$

Equation 6–13 is the solution of equation 6–15 for the value of n.

Equation 6–14, for the minimum required sample size in estimating the population proportion, is derived in a similar way. Note that the term pq in equation 6–14 acts as the population variance in equation 6–13. In order to use equation 6–14, we need a guess of p, the unknown population proportion. Any prior estimate of the parameter will do. When none is available, we may take a pilot sample, or—in the absence of any information—we use the value $p = 0.5$. This value maximizes pq and thus assures us a minimum required sample size that will work for any value of p.

EXAMPLE (f)

A marketing research firm wants to conduct a survey to estimate the average amount spent on entertainment by each person visiting a popular resort. The people who plan the survey would like to be able to determine the average amount spent by all people visiting the resort to within $120, with 95% confidence. From past operation of the resort, an estimate of the population standard deviation is $\sigma = \$400$. What is the minimum required sample size?

SOLUTION

Using equation 6–13, the minimum required sample size is

$$n = \frac{z_{\alpha/2}^2 \sigma^2}{B^2}$$

We know that $B = 120$, and σ^2 is estimated at $400^2 = 160,000$. Since we want a 95% confidence, $z_{\alpha/2} = 1.96$. Using the equation, we get:

$$n = \frac{(1.96)^2 160,000}{120^2} = 42.684$$

Therefore, the minimum required sample size is 43 people (we cannot sample 42.684 people, so we go to the next higher integer).

EXAMPLE (g)

The manufacturers of a sports car want to estimate the proportion of people in a given income bracket who are interested in the model. The company wants to know the population proportion, p, to within 0.10 with 99% confidence. Current company records indicate that the proportion p may be around 0.25. What is the minimum required sample size for this survey?

SOLUTION

Using equation 6–14, we get:

$$n = \frac{z_{\alpha/2}^2 pq}{B^2} = \frac{(2.576)^2(0.25)(0.75)}{0.10^2} = 124.42$$

The company should, therefore, obtain a random sample of at least 125 people. Note that a different guess of p would have resulted in a different sample size.

PROBLEMS

Answers

6–68.

114

6–70.

97

6–68. "A new kind of company is evolving in the United States—manufacturing companies that do little manufacturing. Instead, they import components or products from low-wage countries, slap their own names on them, and sell them in America."[17] An agency wants to estimate the percentage of American manufacturing firms in this category to within 5% with 95% confidence. A guess is that the percentage of such firms is about 8%. What is the minimum size of a random sample of firms to investigate?

6–69. What is the required sample size for determining the proportion of defective items in a production process if the proportion is to be known to within 0.05 with 90% confidence? No guess as to the value of the population proportion is available.

6–70. How many test runs of an automobile are required for determining its average mpg

---

[17] *Business Week* (March 3, 1986).

rating on the highway to within 2 mpg with 95% confidence, if a guess is that the variance of the population of mpg is about 100?

6–71.   A company that conducts surveys of current jobs for executives wants to estimate the average salary of an executive at a given level to within $2,000 with 95% confidence. From previous surveys it is known that the variance of executive salaries is about 40,000,000. What is the minimum required sample size?

6–72.   Find the minimum required sample size for estimating the average return on investments of a certain kind to within 0.5% per year with 95% confidence. The standard deviation of returns is believed to be 2% per year.

6–72.
——
62

6–73.   A company believes its market share is about 14%. Find the minimum required sample size for estimating the actual market share to within 5% with 90% confidence.

6–74.   Find the minimum required sample size for estimating the average number of designer shirts sold per day to within 10 units with 90% confidence if the standard deviation of the number of shirts sold per day is about 50.

6–74.
——
68

6–75.   Find the minimum required sample size of accounts if the proportion of accounts in error is to be estimated to within 0.02 with 95% confidence. A rough guess of the proportion of accounts in error is 0.10.

6–8   One-Sided Confidence Intervals[18]

In closing this chapter, we want to note that it is also possible to construct confidence intervals with only one side. When are such confidence intervals useful? We may be interested in finding an *upper bound* only, or a *lower bound* only, for a population parameter with a given level of confidence. For example, suppose we are interested in finding a bound such that we are 95% confident that the population mean is no greater than that bound. In such a case, we construct a right-hand confidence interval for the population mean. The left-hand bound is, then, defined as $-\infty$. Similarly, we may be interested in finding a bound such that we are 95% sure that the population mean is no smaller than the given bound. This is a left-hand confidence interval, and the right-hand bound of the interval is, then, defined as $+\infty$. Equations 6–16 and 6–17 give a right-hand and a left-hand confidence interval for μ, respectively.

A right-hand $(1 - \alpha)100\%$ confidence interval for μ:

$$\left[-\infty, \overline{X} + z_\alpha \frac{s}{\sqrt{n}} \right]$$ (6–16)

A left-hand $(1 - \alpha)100\%$ confidence interval for μ:

$$\left[\overline{X} - z_\alpha \frac{s}{\sqrt{n}}, +\infty \right]$$ (6–17)

Note that α replaces $\alpha/2$ because we have only *one* side where an error of probability α may take place in the estimation. This is illustrated in Figure 6–10.

---

[18] This is an optional section.

FIGURE 6–10   Using One Tail of a Distribution Leads to a One-Sided Confidence Interval

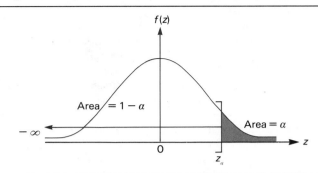

We now demonstrate the use of one-sided confidence intervals for the population mean with a right-hand interval. Formulas similar to equations 6–16 and 6–17 for the population proportion also apply.

EXAMPLE (h)

A company wants to estimate a 95% upper bound for average daily production. A random sample of 36 days gives $\bar{x} = 1{,}150$ units and $s = 312$ units.

SOLUTION

Using equation 6–16, we get the following right-hand confidence interval.

$$\left[-\infty, \bar{x} + z_\alpha \frac{s}{\sqrt{n}}\right] = \left[-\infty, 1{,}150 + 1.645 \frac{312}{\sqrt{36}}\right]$$

$$= [-\infty, 1235.54]$$

Note that we used the z value 1.645 rather than 1.96. This is because 1.645 cuts off an area of 0.05 to its *right*, which is what we need here (1.96 and -1.96 would cut off a *combined* area of 0.05 on both sides).

PROBLEMS

Answers

6–76.
———
246.42

6–78.
———
39674

6–80.
———
15.8

6–82.
———
251.54

6–76.   Give a 90% left-hand confidence interval for the population mean if $\bar{x} = 250$, $s = 28$, and $n = 100$.

6–77.   Give a 95% upper bound for the proportion of defective items produced by a machine if 15 items are found to be defective in a random sample of 100 items.

6–78.   Give a 99% lower bound for the average number of miles that can be driven on a tire of a given make if a random sample of 100 tires gives $\bar{x} = 42{,}000$ miles and $s = 10{,}000$ miles.

6–79.   Give a 99% lower bound for the proportion of salespeople in a given industry who make commissions of over \$10,000 a year if a random sample of 200 of these salespeople shows that 32 earn commissions of over \$10,000 a year.

6–80.   In problem 6–18, give a 95% upper bound for the average length of a long-distance phone call during weekends.

6–81.   In problem 6–19, give a 90% lower bound for the average amount of a claim.

6–82.   In problem 6–30, give a 99% lower bound for the average amount of bonus dollars spent per cardholder.

6–83.   In problem 6–39, give a 90% upper bound for the proportion of traveling businesspeople who may be interested in the product.

6–9 Using the Computer

In this chapter, we will again use the computer package MINITAB. The command for the construction of confidence intervals for the population mean is ZINTERVAL (followed by 90, for 90% confidence, for example, and then the column number) or TINTERVAL (confidence, column), depending on whether the interval is to be based on the normal or the *t* distribution, respectively. ZINTERVAL assumes a known population standard deviation. You may specify the confidence level either as a percent or as a decimal value. In the case of ZINTERVAL, you may specify the population standard deviation after the confidence level. The default confidence level is 95%. Figure 6–11 shows a data set entered into the computer, the file of necessary commands for a 95% confidence interval for μ, and the resulting output. The data are a random sample of 15 daily price quotations of a certain stock.

MINITAB can also be used to find cumulative probabilities to given values (CDF command) and to find values for a given cumulative probability (INVCDF command), for the *t* distribution and for the chi-square distribution. The distribution is specified in the subcommand along with the number of degrees of freedom. This is demonstrated in Figure 6–12. Compare the probabilities and values computed with table values of the *t* and chi-square distributions.

6–10 Summary and Review of Terms

In this chapter, we learned how to construct **confidence intervals** for population parameters. We saw how confidence intervals depend on the sampling distributions of the statistics used as estimators. We also encountered two new sampling distributions: the **t distribution**, used in estimating the population mean when the population standard deviation is unknown, and the **chi-square distribution**, used in estimating the population variance. The use of either distribution assumes a normal population. We saw how the new distributions, as well as the normal distribution, allow us to construct confidence intervals for population parameters. We saw how to determine

FIGURE 6–11 MINITAB-Produced Confidence Interval for Average Stock Price

```
MTB> SET C1
DATA> 17.125
DATA> 17
DATA> 17.375
DATA> 17.25
DATA> 16.625
DATA> 16.875
DATA> 17
DATA> 17
DATA> 17.25
DATA> 18
DATA> 18.125
DATA> 17.5
DATA> 17.375
DATA> 17.5
DATA> 17.25
DATA> END
MTB> TINTERVAL C1
```

	N	MEAN	STDEV	SE MEAN	95.0 PERCENT C.I.
C1	15	17.283	0.397	0.102	(17.064, 17.503)

FIGURE 6-12   Using MINITAB for *t* Distribution and Chi-Square Distribution Probabilities

```
MTB > CDF 2.00;
SUBC> T df=24.
      2.0000     0.9715

MTB > INVCDF 0.95;
SUBC> T df=24.
      0.9500     1.7109

MTB > CDF 35;
SUBC> CHISQUARE 25.
      35.0000    0.9118

MTB > INVCDF 0.99;
SUBC> CHISQUARE 20.
      0.9900    37.5662
```

the minimum required sample size for estimation. Finally, we saw how one may construct one-sided confidence intervals for population parameters.

ADDITIONAL PROBLEMS

Answers

6-84.

125

6-86.

[713.51, 766.45]

6-88.

[0.3087, 0.3673]

6-84.   An industry that has been growing steadily in recent years is that of firms that create names for new businesses [*Time* (November 3, 1986)]. These firms constantly test the appeal of names being considered for use by their clients. One such firm wants to gather a random sample to test the appeal of a potential name for a high-tech company. The name maker wants to estimate the proportion of people who will respond favorably to the name to within 0.10 of the true population proportion with 99% confidence. The company has a rough idea that the population proportion may be around 0.75. What is the minimum required sample size?

6-85.   An investment analyst needs to estimate the average investment amount in mutual fund portfolios by institutional investors. A random sample of 15 institutional investors gives a sample mean of $11.32 million and a sample standard deviation of $4.4 million. Give a 95% confidence interval for the mean investment by all institutional investors in this type of portfolio.

6-86.   An insurance company needs to estimate the average amount claimed by 1,455 policyholders over one year. A random sample of 300 policyholders reveals that the sample mean claim is $739.98 and the sample standard deviation is $312.70. Give a 90% confidence interval for the average amount claimed by the 1,455 policyholders.

6-87.   Radio Shack® markets many of its products by direct-mail advertising of reduced-price items. Before a large mailing, the company wants to estimate the proportion of people who will respond positively to an advertisement for a certain stereo component. The company needs to know the minimum sample size required for estimating the population proportion to within 0.10 with 95% confidence. From previous mailings, Radio Shack knows that the population proportion is around 0.45. Find the minimum required sample size.

6-88.   In problem 6-87, suppose that a test mailing of 1,000 brochures resulted in 338 sales of the stereo component. Give a 95% confidence interval for the population proportion of sales that would result from a marketwide mailing.

6-89.   Boeing, Inc., needs to estimate the variance of the number of possible failure-free landings on a brand of airplane tires being considered for use on the 767 jet made by Boeing. A random testing of 100 tires gives $s^2 = 870,432.76$. Give a 99% confidence interval for the variance of the number of landings before failure for all tires of this brand.

6–90. A new computer software package by Nestor, Inc., allows users to simulate pattern recognition on desktop computers. Fifteen trial runs of the new package are carried out. The time, in seconds, required to recognize a pattern in each run is: 12, 13, 10, 17, 14, 16, 9, 15, 12, 18, 11, 14, 10, 9, 19. Give a 95% confidence interval for the average time required for performing this task.

6–91. An ice cream manufacturer wants to estimate the proportion of people who like the taste of emulsified protein in ice cream. A random sample of 200 people shows that 54 of them like the taste. Give a 99% confidence interval for the proportion of people who like the taste of emulsified protein in ice cream.

6–92. A battery manufacturer knows that the standard deviation of the life, in hours, of a certain type of battery is around 4.5. The manufacturer wants to estimate the average life of all batteries of this kind to within one hour with 95% confidence. What is the minimum required sample size?

6–93. In problem 6–90, give a 95% confidence interval for the variance of the simulation time.

6–94. In problem 6–91, give a 95% lower bound on the proportion of people who like the taste of emulsified protein.

6–95. A ski resort operator wants to estimate the average length of stay of skiers at the resort. A random sample of 67 skiers gives a sample mean stay of 2.5 days and a sample standard deviation of 1.1 days. Give a 90% confidence interval for the average length of stay of all skiers at this resort.

6–96. In problem 6–95, give a 90% confidence interval for the variance of length of stay.

6–97. In a random sample of 2,000 switches used in video display apparatus, 5 switches are found to be defective. Give a 99% confidence interval for the proportion of defective switches in the entire (large) population. How do you interpret this particular confidence interval?

6–98. In problem 6–97, suppose the entire population of switches consists of a shipment of 4,520. Redo the problem to account for this information.

6–99. A random sample of 128 condominiums in Minneapolis reveals a sample mean price of $356,080 and a sample standard deviation of $79,100. Give a 98% confidence interval for the average price of a condominium in Minneapolis.

6–100. An express delivery service needs to estimate the average weight of a package sent overnight. A random sample of 20 packages is selected. The weights, in pounds, are as follows: 0.4, 1.2, 3.7, 1.1, 2.3, 5.0, 0.2, 4.1, 0.8, 6.8, 9.8, 7.5, 3.5, 4.7, 3.3, 2.8, 1.0, 5.9, 4.6, 0.1. Give a 95% confidence interval for the average weight of all packages sent overnight.

6–101. In problem 6–100, give a 95% confidence interval for the variance of the weights of all packages sent overnight.

6–102. In problem 6–99, assume that the 128 condominiums were selected from a population of 500 condominiums in a certain area of the city. How would you correct your confidence interval in that problem to account for this fact?

6–103. What assumption must be made about the population if we are to use either the *t* distribution or the chi-square distribution? Make this assumption in all problems involving either distribution.

6–104. A recent study reveals that the average after-tax income of an entry-level American executive is $24,500.[19] Assuming that the result is based on a random sample of 100 executives and that the sample standard deviation is $2,500, give a 99% confidence interval for the average after-tax income of all American entry-level executives. Write your answer in the form of a memo.

6–105. Use the Federal Reserve data set (Appendix D). Select a random sample, and construct a 95% confidence interval for the federal funds rate. Experiment with various sample sizes.

---

[19] "Executive Life," *Fortune* (March 11, 1991), p. 53.

Answers

6–90.

[11.47, 15.06]

6–92.

78

6–94.

0.2184

6–96.

[0.9286, 1.6638]

6–98.

[0.000352, 0.004648]

6–100.

[2.187, 4.693]

6–102.

[342,038.86, 370,121.14]

6–104.

[23,856, 25,144]

6–106. Interpret the following computer output.

```
MTB > TINTERVAL 90 C1

            N      MEAN    STDEV   SE MEAN    90.0 PERCENT C.I.
   C1      48     53.604   3.120    0.450    ( 52.848,  54.360)
```

Compare the results with the ones you would get if you used the normal distribution instead of the t distribution.

6–107. Recall that the median of a population is the point such that half the population values lie below it and half the population values lie above it.[20] Suppose that a random sample of two elements is selected from a population. We want to construct a confidence interval for the population *median* (if we assume the population distribution is symmetric, however, this is also a confidence interval for the population mean). We define the confidence interval as [the smaller of the two sample values, the larger of the two sample values]. What is the confidence level of such a confidence interval?

6–108. Generalize the procedure of problem 6–107 as follows. We select a random sample of size n and define the confidence interval for the population median as [lowest sample value, highest sample value]. What is the confidence level of such an interval? What is one big limitation of this procedure?

6–108.

$1 - 1/2^{n-1}$

---

[20] This problem and the next one are harder than the rest but instructive.

THE WORLD'S TOP 200 BANKS

E xhibit 1 is a list of the top 200 banks in the world, reprinted by permission from *American Banker Top Numbers 1990**. Consider the list as a population. Draw random samples of various sizes, and estimate the average total deposits for a bank on this list. (You may scan the data to approximate their range. Divide this number by 4 to estimate the standard deviation, and from it find a reasonable sample size to be used.) Give 95% and 99% confidence intervals. Also use random sampling to estimate the proportion of banks of certain nations (American banks, Japanese banks, European banks, etc.). Give 90% and 95% confidence intervals for these proportions. Also estimate the population total, knowing that $N = 200$.

*Data Source: The primary source of data is *American Banker's* questionnaire to the 1,200 largest banks in the world. Data were checked against annual reports whenever possible. Consolidated data, if available, are used for all banks that own over 50% of other banks. The consolidation includes only those affiliates in which ownership exceeds 50%. *Total deposits* are funds due depositors, banks (including central banks), and national, state, and local governments. *Note:* Banks that did not provide current data are excluded from the listing. *Date of figures:* Data for most banks are for Dec. 31, 1989 and Dec. 31, 1988. *Exceptions:* Data for Australian and New Zealand banks are for June 30, 1989, Sept. 30, 1989, and March 31, 1990; Canadian bank data are for fiscal yearend Oct. 31, 1989; and all Japanese bank data are for fiscal yearend March 31, 1990. *Exchange rates:* Whenever possible, the New York cable rate is used, and this rate is for same date as bank's figures. See "Foreign Currency Exchange Guide and Exchange Rate Comparisons" for key to currency abbreviations. **(h)**— A subsidiary of Compagnie Financiere de Credit Industriel et Commercial. **(q)**— A subsidiary Compagnie Financiere de Paribas, Paris, a financial holding company. **(a)**— Consolidated data. **(t)**— Figures are included in the consolidated figures of parent bank. For that reason, the data for the bank are not included in the aggregate data totals for the Top 500 Banks. **(u)**— Data are not consolidated for affiliates more than 50% owned. **(v)**— Bank is owned by another bank, which does not consolidate subsidiary banks in its data. **(†)**— Rank based on revised asset total for 1988. **(‡)**— Restated to reflect changes in consolidation in 1989. **(¹)**— On Dec. 31, 1989, Banca Catolica Veneto merged with Nuevo Banco Ambrosiano, Milan to form Banca Ambrosiano Veneto, Milan. The data for Dec. 31, 1988, are for the former Nuevo Banco Ambrosiano. **(Compiled by American Banker, Copyright 1990.)**

EXHIBIT 1   The Top 200 Banks in the World

Rank 12/89	Bank	Country	Deposits 12/31/89 (U.S. dollars)	Exchange Rate (U.S. dollars)	Deposits 12/31/89 (nation's currency)	Deposits 12/31/88 (U.S. dollars)	Rank 1988	Gain in Rank
1	Dai-ichi Kangyo Bank Ltd., Tokyo	Japan	314,780,128,477s	0.006289	Y50,052,493,000,000	312,465,781,696s	1	
2	Sumitomo Bank Ltd., Osaka	Japan	288,242,189,906s	0.006289	Y45,832,754,000,000	296,000,827,792s	2	
3	Mitsubishi Bank Ltd., Tokyo	Japan	278,806,752,894s	0.006289	Y44,332,446,000,000	272,510,345,476s	4	+1
4	Fuji Bank, Ltd., Tokyo	Japan	278,642,534,526s	0.006289	Y44,306,334,000,000	283,585,351,228s	3	
5	Sanwa Bank Ltd., Osaka	Japan	275,972,495,553s	0.006289	Y43,881,777,000,000	269,032,279,492s	5	
6	Industrial Bank of Japan, Ltd., Tokyo	Japan	213,287,598,710s	0.006289	Y33,914,390,000,000	215,397,605,132u	6	
7	Banque Nationale de Paris	France	192,525,991,000s	0.173000	FF1,112,867,000,000	158,549,122,000s	13	+6
8	Mitsubishi Trust & Banking Corp., Tokyo	Japan	192,294,268,943u	0.006289	Y30,576,287,000,000	185,955,516,200u	8	
9	Deutsche Bank, Frankfurt	Germany	184,378,642,070s	0.590000	DM312,506,173,000	175,600,895,540s	15	+6
10	Tokai Bank Ltd., Nagoya	Japan	179,030,994,347s	0.006289	Y28,467,323,000,000	210,759,455,544	10	
11	Norinchukin Bank, Tokyo	Japan	176,329,604,709	0.006289	Y28,037,781,000,000		7	
12	Credit Lyonnais, Paris	France	176,099,987,000s	0.173000	FF1,017,919,000,000	148,842,971,595s	17	+5
13	Sumitomo Trust & Banking Co., Ltd., Osaka	Japan	171,664,091,192u	0.006289	Y27,295,928,000,000	177,932,182,096u	9	
14	Credit Agricole Mutuel, Paris	France	169,711,546,800s	0.173000	FF980,991,600,000	141,973,000,000u	19	+5
15	Barclays Bank Plc, London	United Kingdom	167,127,660,000s	1.610000	P103,806,000,000	157,357,472,000s	14	
16	National Westminster Bank Plc, London	United Kingdom	163,014,110,000s	1.610000	P103,251,000,000	153,645,648,000s	16	
17	Mitsui Trust & Banking Co., Ltd., Tokyo	Japan	159,219,084,675u	0.006289	Y25,317,075,000,000	161,228,496,316	11	
18	Mitsui Bank, Ltd., Tokyo	Japan	157,894,948,303s	0.006289	Y25,106,527,000,000	159,039,606,488s	12	
19	Bank of Tokyo, Ltd.	Japan	152,933,845,497s	0.006289	Y24,317,673,000,000	132,147,474,612u	22	+3
20	Long-Term Credit Bank of Japan Ltd., Tokyo	Japan	148,398,357,055u	0.006289	Y23,596,495,000,000	147,426,607,488u	18	
21	Societe Generale, Paris	France	141,977,467,000s	0.173000	FF820,679,000,000	123,187,087,000s	24	+3
22	Taiyo Kobe Bank, Ltd., Kobe	Japan	136,538,177,226u	0.006289	Y21,710,634,000,000	138,986,023,792u	20	
23	Dresdner Bank, Frankfurt	Germany	135,670,067,545s	0.590000	DM229,949,267,026	120,317,120,000s	25	+2
24	Yasuda Trust & Banking Co. Ltd., Tokyo	Japan	135,105,775,719s	0.006289	Y21,482,871,000,000	131,788,381,988	23	
25	Daiwa Bank, Ltd., Osaka	Japan	131,680,308,355u	0.006289	Y20,938,195,000,000	134,466,778,400u	21	
26	Hongkong and Shanghai Banking Corp., Hong Kong	Hong Kong	118,504,960,000s	0.128000	H$925,820,000,000	101,841,280,000s	28	+2
27	Citibank NA, New York	United States	111,487,000,000			104,996,000,000	27	
28	Commerzbank, Frankfurt	Germany	106,668,460,000s	0.590000	DM180,794,000,000	94,904,206,676s	30	+2
29	Swiss Bank Corp., Basle	Switzerland	100,865,736,000s	0.648000	SF155,657,000,000	89,572,067,935u	32	+3
30	Toyo Trust & Banking Co., Ltd., Tokyo	Japan	100,172,770,539u	0.006289	Y15,928,251,000,000	105,384,007,332	26	
31	Union Bank of Switzerland, Zurich	Switzerland	96,977,909,016u	0.648000	SF149,657,267,000	93,750,145,230u	31	
32	Westdeutsche Landesbank Girozentrale, Duesseldorf	Germany	96,532,850,000s	0.590000	DM163,615,000,000	86,730,534,166s	34	+2
33	Bayerische Vereinsbank, Munich	Germany	95,993,000,000s	0.590000	DM162,700,000,000	85,089,724,160s	35	+2
34	Nippon Credit Bank, Ltd., Tokyo	Japan	88,179,792,186s	0.006289	Y14,021,274,000,000	96,733,830,308	29	
35	Midland Bank Plc, London	United Kingdom	88,034,800,000s	1.610000	P54,680,000,000	86,753,264,000s	33	
36	Banca Nazionale del Lavoro, Rome	Italy	84,811,188,000s	0.000789	L107,492,000,000,000	76,309,515,000s	40	+4
37	Lloyds Bank Plc, London	United Kingdom	84,355,950,000s	1.610000	P52,395,000,000	82,911,264,000s	36	
38	Bayerische Hypotheken-und Wechsel-Bank, Munich	Germany	83,191,003,340s	0.590000	DM141,001,700,577	70,527,672,594s	43	+5
39	Istituto Bancario San Paolo di Torino, Turin	Italy	79,614,718,017s	0.000789	L100,905,853,000,000	61,899,778,395s	52	+13
40	Kyowa Bank, Ltd., Tokyo	Japan	78,919,006,993s	0.006289	Y12,548,737,000,000	81,096,761,040u	38	
41	Banca Commerciale Italiana, Milan	Italy	77,865,384,300s	0.000789	L98,688,700,000,000	54,179,824,500s	60	+19
42	Saitama Bank Ltd., Urawa	Japan	77,003,434,194s	0.006289	Y12,244,146,000,000	76,037,495,240u	41	
43	Bayerische Landesbank Girozentrale, Munich	Germany	76,595,775,910s	0.590000	DM129,823,349,000	68,858,720,000s	45	+2
44	Royal Bank of Canada, Montreal	Canada	75,986,706,300s	0.852000	C$89,186,275,000	72,146,963,596s	42	
45	Amsterdam-Rotterdam Bank, Amsterdam	Netherlands	75,751,012,000s	0.524000	G144,563,000,000	64,270,884,000s	48	+3
46	Banque Paribas, Paris (q)	France	74,909,000,000s	0.173000	FF433,067,000,000	62,029,650,000s	51	+5
47	Shoko Chukin Bank, Tokyo	Japan	74,764,053,363	0.006289	Y11,888,067,000,000	81,968,920,352	37	
48	NMB Postbank Group, N.V., Amsterdam	Netherlands	74,656,900,000s	0.524000	G142,475,000,000	....	...	

No.	Bank, City	Country	Assets (US$)	Rate	Assets (local currency)	Deposits (US$)	Prev. rank	Change
49	Deutsche Genossenschaftsbank, Frankfurt	Germany	73,936,791,706s	0.590000	DM125,316,596,112	45,252,491,087s	71	+22
50	Bank of America NT&SA, San Francisco	United States	73,295,000,000			69,640,000,000	44	
51	Algemene Bank Nederland, Amsterdam	Netherlands	72,897,832,000s	0.524000	G139,118,000,000	55,980,180,000s	58	+7
52	Canadian Imperial Bank of Commerce, Toronto	Canada	67,199,362,332s	0.852000	C$78,872,491,000	59,376,031,848s	53	+1
53	Credito Italiano, Milan	Italy	65,740,584,600s	0.000789	L83,321,400,000,000	50,645,830,500s	63†	+10
54	Zenshinren Bank, Tokyo	Japan	65,193,396,562	0.006289	Y10,366,258,000,000	77,741,067,948	39	
55	Norddeutsche Landesbank Girozentrale, Hannover	Germany	63,657,289,761s	0.590000	DM107,893,711,459	56,780,612,993s	57	+2
56	Rabobank Nederland, Utrecht	Netherlands	63,651,328,000s	0.524000	G121,472,000,000	62,616,528,000s	50	
57	Generale Bank, Brussels	Belgium	63,112,712,400s	0.028100	BF2,246,004,000,000	57,829,442,000s	56	
58	Bank of Yokohama, Ltd.	Japan	62,453,845,272u	0.006289	Y9,930,648,000,000	62,917,505,496u	49	
59	Chuo Trust & Banking Co., Ltd., Tokyo	Japan	62,310,267,402u	0.006289	Y9,907,818,000,000	66,142,311,624u	47	
60	Chase Manhattan Bank NA, New York	United States	61,720,245,000			58,241,477,000	55	
61	Monte dei Pasachi di Siena	Italy	61,004,240,481s	0.000789	L77,318,429,000,000	52,400,211,120s	61	
62	Credit Suisse, Zurich	Switzerland	60,704,640,000s	0.648000	SF93,680,000,000	66,549,571,095u	46	
63	Hokkaido Takushoku Bank, Ltd., Sapporo	Japan	56,212,352,378u	0.006289	Y8,938,202,000,000	58,792,542,724u	54	
64	Bank of Montreal	Canada	56,166,594,516s	0.852000	C$65,923,233,000	54,290,812,966	59	
65	Banco di Napoli, Naples	Italy	54,904,186,632	0.000789	L69,587,055,300,000	47,904,300,000u	65	
66	Bank Melli Iran, Tehran	Iran	54,327,924,000	0.014000	Ri3,880,566,000,000	46,008,886,000	67	+1
67	Westpac Banking Corp., Sydney	Australia	51,993,784,800s	0.776000	A$67,002,300,000	41,711,271,300s	76	+9
68	Bank of Nova Scotia, Toronto	Canada	51,907,625,436s	0.852000	C$60,924,443,000	47,920,670,686s	64	
69	Groupe Des Banques Populaires, Paris	France	48,729,746,628	0.173000	FF281,674,836,000	40,632,253,527	77	+8
70	Chiba Bank, Ltd.	Japan	48,686,243,188	0.006289	Y7,741,492,000,000	47,266,598,984	66	
71	Banco di Roma, Rome	Italy	48,523,421,100s	0.000789	L61,499,900,000,000	45,775,458,000s	69	
72	Danske Bank, Copenhagen	Denmark	47,297,269,601s	0.151000	DK313,226,951,000	20,275,393,500s	144	+72
73	Joyo Bank, Ltd., Mito	Japan	46,402,895,958	0.006289	Y7,187,359,199,000	43,788,563,032	72	
74	Hokuriku Bank Ltd., Toyama	Japan	45,201,302,003s	0.006289	Y7,378,422,000,000	45,887,972,516	68	
75	Banco Bilbao Vizcaya, Bilbao	Spain	44,927,287,460u	0.009130	SP4,920,842,000,000	43,784,076,420s	73	
76	Banque Bruxelles Lambert, Brussels	Belgium	44,432,377,108s	0.025400	BF1,749,306,185,349	39,273,150,808s	79	+3
77	Sudwestdeutsche Landesbank, Stuttgart	Germany	44,002,790,000s	0.590000	DM74,581,000,000	38,584,000,000u	80	+3
78	Shizuoka Bank Ltd.	Japan	42,779,614,388u	0.006289	Y6,802,292,000,000	40,125,349,768u	78	
79	Manufacturers Hanover Trust Co., New York	United States	42,736,000,000			42,876,000,000	75	
80	Kredietbank N.V., Brussels	Belgium	42,471,897,000s	0.028500	BF1,490,242,000,000	34,590,057,143s	90	+10
81	Toronto Dominion Bank	Canada	41,903,784,792	0.852000	C$49,182,846,000	37,954,165,230	81	
82	Morgan Guaranty Trust Co., New York	United States	40,953,451,000			45,471,746,000	70	
83	Bank of Seoul	Korea	40,784,107,770s	0.001470	KW27,744,291,000,000	32,023,788,845	98	+15
84	Security Pacific National Bank, Los Angeles	United States	40,597,338,000			36,095,333,000	84	
85	Rafidain Bank, Baghdad	Iraq	39,842,170,300	3.100000	ID12,852,313,000	43,416,230,400	74	
86	Hessische Landesbank-Girozentrale, Frankfurt	Germany	39,789,975,988s	0.590000	DM67,440,637,267	37,080,200,467s	83	
87	Banque Indosuez, Paris	France	38,692,661,000s	0.173000	FF223,657,000,000	31,350,378,593s	99	+12
88	ASLK-CGER Bank, Brussels	Belgium	38,493,341,324s	0.028100	BF1,369,869,798,005	35,322,372,171u	87	
89	Cassa di Risparmio delle Provincie Lombarde, Milan	Italy	38,432,190,000u	0.000789	L48,710,000,000,000	52,103,385,000s	62	
90	Royal Bank of Scotland Plc., Edinburgh	United Kingdom	37,592,208,600s	1.619000	£23,219,400,000	31,162,417,000s	100	+10
91	Australia & New Zealand Banking Group, Ltd., Melbourne	Australia	37,569,186,400s	0.776000	A$48,413,900,000	34,063,240,500s	92	+1
92	Banco Central, Madrid	Spain	37,298,259,460s	0.009130	SP4,085,242,000,000	35,091,551,880s	89	
93	Ashikaga Bank, Ltd., Utsunomiya	Japan	37,292,254,351	0.006289	Y5,929,759,000,000	37,831,490,592	82	
94	National Australia Bank, Ltd, Melbourne	Australia	36,829,115,200s	0.776000	A$47,460,200,000	30,662,984,700s	103	+9
95	Banco do Brasil, Brasilia	Brazil	36,516,887,456u	0.112000	BC326,043,638,000	26,151,264,701s	111	+16
96	Wells Fargo Bank NA, San Francisco	United States	36,462,605,000			35,109,059,000	88	
97	PKbanken, Stockholm	Sweden	35,893,501,000s	0.161000	SK222,941,000,000	29,000,471,000s	106	+9
98	Unibank, Copenhagen	Denmark	35,806,026,000	0.151000	DK237,126,000,000	33,783,505,786s	—	
99	Bank fuer Gemeinwirtschaft, Frankfurt	Germany	35,644,584,536s	0.590000	DM60,414,550,061	34,387,798,406s	93	
100	Standard Chartered Bank, London	United Kingdom	35,554,596,000s	1.610000	£22,083,600,000	20,316,120,300s	91	
101	Banco Santander	Spain	34,789,855,870s	0.009130	SP3,810,499,000,000		143	+42

EXHIBIT 1 *(concluded)*   The Top 200 Banks in the World

Rank 12/89	Bank	Country	Deposits 12/31/89 (U.S. dollars)	Exchange Rate (U.S. dollars)	Deposits 12/31/89 (nation's currency)	Deposits 12/31/88 (U.S. dollars)	Rank 1988	Gain in Rank
102	Credit Commercial de France, Paris	France	34,559,789,783s	0.173000	FF199,767,571,000	25,660,112,978s	113	+11
103	Bank of Hiroshima, Ltd.	Japan	34,524,748,456	0.006289	Y5,489,704,000,000	35,479,481,956	85	
104	TSB Bank, Plc., London	United Kingdom	34,505,296,000s	1.613000	P21,392,000,000	23,719,696,000	121†	+17
105	Bank of New York	United States	34,411,451,000	......		16,665,898,000	167	+62
106	Bank Saderat Iran, Tehran	Iran	33,929,214,345	0.014000	Ri2,423,515,310,377	33,719,901,508	94	
107	Home Savings of America, FA, Irwindale, Calif.	United States	33,100,655,000			29,568,816,000	104	
108	Skandinaviska Enskilda Banken, Stockholm	Sweden	32,626,489,000s	0.161000	SK202,649,000,000	31,162,177,000s	101	
109	Chemical Bank, New York	United States	32,312,000,000			33,298,000,000	95	
110	Bank of Fukuoka, Ltd.	Japan	32,254,432,034	0.006289	Y5,128,706,000,000	32,388,573,500	97	
111	Hachijuni Bank, Ltd., Nagano	Japan	30,872,908,537	0.006289	Y4,909,033,000,000	29,357,376,168	105	+2
112	Banco di Sicilia, Palermo	Italy	29,887,222,164s	0.000789	L37,879,876,000,000	25,506,624,645s	114	+2
113	Svenska Handelsbanken, Stockholm	Sweden	29,802,227,000s	0.161000	SK185,107,000,000	26,797,037,000s	110	
114	Banco Espanol de Credito, Madrid	Spain	29,181,497,730u	0.009130	SP3,196,221,000,000	23,316,596,100u	124	+10
115	Creditanstalt-Bankverein, Vienna	Austria	28,979,815,200	0.084000	AS344,997,800,000	26,095,072,000	112	
116	Caja de Pensiones para la Vejez, Barcelona	Spain	28,974,456,720s	0.009130	SP3,173,544,000,000	24,520,852,440s	118	+2
117	Taiwan Cooperative Bank, Taipei	Taiwan	28,162,762,650	0.038380	T$733,787,458,320	21,013,145,505	137	+20
118	Commonwealth Banking Corp., Sydney	Australia	28,088,650,800s	0.756000	A$37,154,300,000	24,611,126,000s	117	
119	Bankers Trust Co., New York	United States	27,879,571,000	......		33,261,373,000	96	
120	Bank of Scotland, Edinburgh	United Kingdom	27,496,143,500s	1.679000	P16,376,500,000	21,645,774,000s	133	+13
121	Hamburgische Landesbank-Girozentrale, Hamburg	Germany	26,730,535,870	0.590000	DM45,305,993,000	23,856,073,920	120	
122	Gunma Bank, Ltd., Maebashi	Japan	26,663,894,663	0.006289	Y4,239,767,000,000	26,969,742,072	109	
123	First National Bank, Chicago	United States	26,403,340,000			27,372,439,000	108	
124	Commonwealth Bank of Australia, Sydney	Australia	25,883,172,000s	0.756000	A$34,237,000,000	23,413,464,400s	122	
125	NCNB Texas National Bank, Dallas	United States	25,623,428,000			20,474,765,000	140	+15
126	Bank Hapoalim, Tel-Aviv	Israel	24,939,824,160s	0.530000	IS47,056,272,000	25,357,400,154s	115	
127	Bank Leumi le-Israel, Tel-Aviv	Israel	24,847,600,980s	0.530000	IS46,882,266,000	24,979,771,914s	116	
128	Deutsche Girozentrale-Deutsche Kommunalbank, Frankfurt	Germany	24,711,416,475u	0.590000	DM41,883,756,738	22,160,688,803u	128	
129	Bank of Taiwan, Taipei	Taiwan	24,301,422,033	0.038380	T$633,179,313,000	20,388,750,785	142	+13
130	Banco Hispano-Americano, Madrid	Spain	24,001,993,950u	0.009130	SP2,628,915,000,000	20,922,795,180s	138	+8
131	Landesbank Rheinland-Pfalz Girozentrale, Mainz	Germany	23,777,000,000s	0.590000	DM40,300,000,000	22,211,433,440s	127	
132	Union Bank of Finland, Ltd., Helsinki	Finland	23,446,604,400s	0.246000	FM95,311,400,000	21,113,496,000s	135	+3
133	National Bank of Greece, Athens	Greece	23,385,165,300u	0.006300	GD3,711,931,000,000	23,262,172,200s	125	
134	Banque Cantonale de Zurich	Switzerland	23,168,946,456	0.648000	SF35,754,547,000	21,026,894,618	136	+2
135	Great Western Bank, FSB, Beverly Hills	United States	23,117,689,000			21,664,188,000	132	
136	Chugoku Bank, Ltd., Okayama	Japan	23,102,088,068	0.006289	Y3,673,412,000,000	23,385,077,504	123	
137	Hyogo Bank, Ltd., Kobe	Japan	23,051,052,833	0.006289	Y3,665,297,000,000	24,101,903,804	119	
138	Swiss Volksbank, Berne	Switzerland	22,894,635,889	0.648000	SF35,331,228,224	21,207,227,320	134	
139	National Bank of Canada, Montreal	Canada	22,702,279,536s	0.852000	C$26,645,868,000	19,892,847,112s	146	+7
140	Allied Irish Banks Plc., Dublin	Ireland	22,530,800,000s	1.580000	IP14,260,000,000	19,122,633,306s	151	+11
141	Yamaguchi Bank, Ltd., Shimonoseki	Japan	22,498,167,976	0.006289	Y3,577,384,000,000	22,803,372,680	126	
142	Banca Popolare di Novara	Italy	22,490,620,947s	0.000789	L28,505,223,000,000	14,958,266,570u	189	+47
143	First National Bank, Boston	United States	22,061,157,000			17,687,897,000	164	+21
144	Juroku Bank, Ltd., Gifu	Japan	21,998,733,330	0.006289	Y3,497,970,000,000	19,035,798,216	153	+9
145	Kansallis-Osake Pankki, Helsinki	Finland	21,362,886,000s	0.246000	FM86,841,000,000	22,015,824,000s	130	
146	National Commercial Bank, Jeddah	Saudi Arabia	21,359,214,082	0.266000	SAR80,297,797,299	19,096,171,265	152	+6
147	First Commercial Bank, Taipei	Taiwan	21,353,446,595	0.038380	T$556,369,114,000	15,076,761,977	187	+40
148	77 Bank, Ltd., Sendai	Japan	21,244,801,721	0.006289	Y3,378,089,000,000	21,986,644,932	131	

149	Hang Seng Bank Ltd., Hong Kong	Hong Kong	20,692,838,400st	H$161,662,800,000	0.128000	15,622,617,600st	175	+26
150	Girozentrale und Bank der Oesterreichischen Sparkassen, Vienna	Austria	20,567,943,643u	AS244,856,471,944	0.084000	11,571,347,266s	241	+91
151	Nippon Trust Bank, Ltd., Tokyo	Japan	20,504,517,242	Y3,260,378,000,000	0.006289	22,088,002,932	129	
152	Nishi-Nippon Bank, Ltd., Fukuoka	Japan	20,355,650,323	Y3,236,707,000,000	0.006289	20,904,133,984	139	
153	Hua Nan Commercial Bank, Ltd., Taipei	Taiwan	19,924,483,878	T$510,884,202,000	0.039000	12,835,260,530	217	+64
154	Banco Exterior de Espana, Madrid	Spain	19,812,465,220s	SP2,170,040,000,000	0.009130	19,491,582,600s	147	
155	Berliner Bank, Berlin	Germany	19,734,328,333s	DM33,448,014,124	0.590000	17,778,753,870s	161	+6
156	Banque Francaise du Commerce Exterieur, Paris	France	19,648,594,024s	FF113,575,688,000	0.173000	18,481,132,503s	156	+35
157	Oesterreichische Laenderbank, Vienna	Austria	19,386,925,488s	AS230,796,732,000	0.084000	14,592,160,880s	192	
158	Berliner Handels und-Frankfurter Bank, Frankfurt	Germany	19,158,957,838s	DM32,472,809,895	0.590000	17,072,169,835s	166	+8
159	Banca Nazionale dell'Agricoltura, Rome	Italy	19,122,232,832u	L24,236,036,543,030	0.000789	17,866,240,997	159	+25
160	Banca Popolare di Milano, Milan	Italy	19,097,625,072s	L24,204,848,000,000	0.000789	15,128,218,485s	185	
161	Bank of Kyoto, Ltd.	Japan	18,824,788,232	Y2,993,288,000,000	0.006289	19,946,098,168	145	+9
162	Arab Banking Corp, Manama	Bahrain	18,695,000,000s			16,305,000,000s	171	
163	Hokkaido Bank, Ltd., Sapporo	Japan	18,685,413,780	Y2,971,126,376,173	0.006289	19,280,559,016	149	
164	Chang Hwa Commercial Bank, Ltd., Taichung	Taiwan	18,655,561,686s	T$486,075,083,000	0.038380	11,586,509,820s	238	+74
165	Bank of Ireland, Dublin	Ireland	18,508,594,000s	IP11,714,300,000	1.580000	13,874,689,800s	199	+34
166	Tokyo Sowa Bank, Ltd.	Japan	18,385,759,324	Y2,923,478,983,000	0.006289	19,401,948,360u	148	
167	Nanto Bank, Ltd., Nara	Japan	18,352,628,979	Y2,918,211,000,000	0.006289	18,870,644,657	154	
168	Continental Bank NA, Chicago	United States	18,178,226,000			17,763,339,000	162	+11
169	Marine Midland Bank NA, Buffalo, N.Y.	United States	18,021,665,000t			16,659,085,000t	168	+1
170	Banco Popular Espanol, Madrid	Spain	18,003,456,130s	SP1,971,901,000,000	0.009130	15,386,384,160s	181	+7
171	Zentralsparkasse und Kommerzialbank, Vienna	Austria	17,924,760,000u	AS213,390,000,000	0.084000	16,133,200,000u	172	
172	Deutsche Bank Luxembourg	Luxembourg	17,879,646,275t	LF638,558,795,520	0.028000	15,404,708,124t	179	
173	First Interstate Bank of California, Los Angeles	United States	17,849,795,000			16,613,623,000	170	+10
174	Bremer Landesbank, Bremen	Germany	17,688,259,000t	DM29,980,100,000	0.590000	15,811,171,600t	174	
175	Iyo Bank, Ltd., Matsuyama	Japan	17,268,348,778	Y2,745,802,000,000	0.006289	17,805,109,380	160	
176	Caisse Centrale des Banques Populaires, Paris	France	17,180,471,467	FF99,309,083,624	0.173000	15,125,735,545t	186	+42
177	Hyakujushi Bank, Ltd., Takamatsu	Japan	17,110,850,640	Y2,720,760,000,000	0.006289	17,903,794,532	158	
178	Shiga Bank, Ltd., Otsu	Japan	17,067,691,944	Y2,713,896,000,000	0.006289	17,921,963,892	157	
179	Land Bank of Taiwan, Taipei	Taiwan	17,057,846,303	T$444,446,229,881	0.038380	12,661,978,200	221	+27
180	Banco di Santo Spirito, Rome	Italy	17,050,155,912sv	L21,609,830,052,840	0.000789	15,966,302,420st	173	
181	Daishi Bank, Ltd., Niigata	Japan	17,004,575,540	Y2,703,860,000,000	0.006289	17,750,668,872	163	+24
182	Suruga Bank, Ltd., Numazu	Japan	16,359,468,787	Y2,601,283,000,000	0.006289	16,624,746,668	169	+18
183	Cassa di Risparmio di Roma, Rome	Italy	16,287,764,106u	L20,643,554,000,000	0.000789	13,121,760,420u	210	+36
184	Glendale Federal Bank, FSB, Calif.	United States	15,869,180,000			15,300,883,000	183	+12
185	Banco Ambrosiano Veneto, Milan[1]	Italy	15,511,214,526s	L19,659,334,000,000	0.000789	13,167,514,305s	209	
186	Westfalenbank, Bochum	Germany	15,362,304,231st	DM26,037,803,781	0.590000	13,548,562,864st	204	+20
187	Credit Lyonnais Bank Nederland, Rotterdam	Netherlands	15,223,538,296st	G29,052,554,000	0.524000	12,458,256,840st	223	+34
188	Hamburger Sparkasse, Hamburg	Germany	15,199,265,385	DM25,761,466,754	0.590000	13,848,038,765	200	
189	California Federal Bank, FSB, Los Angeles	United States	15,194,340,000			18,787,200,000	155	+18
190	Mellon Bank NA, Pittsburgh	United States	15,022,808,000			15,603,197,000	176	
191	Bank fuer Arbeit und Wirtschaft, Vienna	Austria	15,017,998,048u	AS178,785,691,049	0.084000	13,081,493,706u	211	
192	Caja de Madrid	Spain	14,941,701,500s	SP1,636,550,000,000	0.009130	12,188,728,440s	226	
193	Kiyo Bank, Ltd., Wakayama	Japan	14,922,954,274	Y2,372,866,000,000	0.006289	15,447,649,733	178	
194	Christiania Bank og Kreditkasse, Oslo	Norway	14,909,921,000	NK98,741,200,000	0.151000	14,932,936,000s	190	+23
195	American Express Bank Ltd., New York	United States	14,778,000,000s			13,035,000,000s	213	+38
196	Westdeutsche Genossenschafts-Zentralbank, Duesseldorf	Germany	14,689,820,000u	DM24,898,000,000	0.590000	13,927,935,280	196	
197	Sparbankernas Bank, Stockholm	Sweden	14,502,880,000s	SK90,080,000,000	0.161000	12,776,266,000s	220	+36
198	Bancomer, Mexico City	Mexico	14,496,027,180u	MP38,967,815,000	0.000372	11,718,458,246u	236	
199	Centrale Raiffeisenkas van Belgische Boerenbond, Leuven	Belgium	14,339,977,551	BF510,319,485,796	0.028100	11,761,706,739u	235	
200	Republic National Bank, New York	United States	14,250,340,000			13,897,318,000	198	

7

HYPOTHESIS TESTING

INTRODUCTION

O n June 18, 1964, a woman was robbed while walking home along an alley in San Pedro, California. Some time later, police arrested Janet Collins and charged her with the robbery. The interesting thing about this case of petty crime is that the prosecution had *no* direct evidence against the defendant. Janet Collins was convicted of robbery on purely statistical grounds.

The case, *People* v. *Collins,* drew much attention because of its use of probability—or, rather, what was perceived as a probability—in determining guilt. An instructor of mathematics at a local college was brought in by the prosecution and testified as an expert witness in the trial. The instructor "calculated the probability" that the defendant was a person *other* than the one who committed the crime as 1 in 12,000,000. This led the jury to convict the defendant.

The Supreme Court of California later reversed the "guilty" verdict against Janet Collins when it was shown that the method of calculating the probability was incorrect. The mathematics instructor had made some very serious errors.[1]

Despite the erroneous procedure used in deriving the probability, and the justified reversal of the conviction by the Supreme Court of California, the *Collins* case serves as an excellent analogy for statistical hypothesis testing. Under the American legal system, the accused is assumed innocent until proven guilty "beyond a reasonable doubt." We will call this the *null hypothesis*—the hypothesis that the accused is *innocent*. We will hold the null hypothesis as true until a time when we can prove, beyond a reasonable doubt, that it is false and that the *alternative hypothesis*—the hypothesis that the accused is guilty—is true. We want to have a small probability (preferably *zero*) of convicting an innocent person, that is, of rejecting a null hypothesis when the null hypothesis is actually true.

In the *Collins* case, the prosecution claimed that the accused was guilty since, otherwise, an event with a very small probability had just been observed. The argument was that if Collins were *not* guilty, then another woman fitting her exact characteristics had committed the crime. According to the prosecution, the probability of this event was 1/12,000,000, and since the probability was so small, Collins was very likely the person who committed the robbery.

In statistical hypothesis testing, our null hypothesis will state something about one or more population parameters. For example, the null hypothesis may be that the population mean is equal to some number. The alternative hypothesis will be that the population mean is different from the number stated in the null hypothesis. We will assume that the null hypothesis is true and that the population mean is as stated. Then we will look at some evidence derived from a random sample. If our obtained

---

[1]The instructor *multiplied* the probabilities of the separate events comprising the reported description of the robber: the event that a woman has blond hair, the event that she drives a yellow car, the event that she is seen with a black man, the event that the man has a beard. Recall that the probability of the intersection of several events is equal to the product of the probabilities of the separate events *only* if the events are independent. In this case, there was no reason to believe that the events were independent. There were also some questions about how the separate "probabilities" were actually derived since they were presented by the instructor with no apparent justification. See W. Fairley and F. Mosteller, "A Conversation About Collins," *University of Chicago Law Review* 41, no. 2 (Winter 1974) pp. 242–53.

Continued on next page

sample mean should happen to fall so far away from the population mean as to constitute an event with a small presampling probability, then we will reject the null hypothesis in favor of the alternative hypothesis. ∎

7–2 Statistical Hypothesis Testing

We will now define the concepts and sketch the framework of statistical tests of hypotheses. First, we define the null and alternative hypotheses.

> A **null hypothesis,** denoted by H_0, is an assertion about one or more population parameters. This is the assertion we hold as true until we have sufficient statistical evidence to conclude otherwise.

> The **alternative hypothesis,** denoted by H_1, is the assertion of all situations *not* covered by the null hypothesis.[2]

Together, the null and the alternative hypotheses constitute a set of hypotheses that covers all possible values of the parameter or parameters in question. An example of such a pair of hypotheses is the following.

$$H_0: \mu = 100 \qquad\qquad (7\text{–}1)$$
$$H_1: \mu \neq 100$$

The null hypothesis in equation 7–1 is the assertion that the population mean is equal to 100. The alternative hypothesis is the assertion that the population mean is not equal to 100. Only one of the two competing hypotheses may be true, and one of them must be true: either the population mean is equal to 100, or it is equal to any of the infinitely many numbers other than 100.

Often, the null hypothesis represents a status quo situation or an existing belief. We wish to *test* the null hypothesis and see whether we can reject it in favor of the alternative hypothesis. The hypothesis test is carried out using information obtained by random sampling. In a test of the value of the population mean, such as the test in equation 7–1, the *test statistic* we employ is the sample mean, $\overline{X}$.

> A **test statistic** is a sample statistic computed from the data. The value of the test statistic is used in determining whether or not we may reject the null hypothesis.

We decide whether or not to reject the null hypothesis by following a rule called the *decision rule*.

> The **decision rule** of a statistical hypothesis test is a rule that specifies the conditions under which the null hypothesis may be rejected.

An example of a decision rule for the hypothesis test in equation 7–1 is: "Reject the null hypothesis if and only if $\overline{x}$ happens to be either greater than or equal to 105 or less than or equal to 95." We will now see how to determine a decision rule for a statistical hypothesis test.

---

[2] Some authors use the notation H_a or H_A for the alternative hypothesis.

Let us return to our courtroom analogy. The accused is either innocent (H_0 is true) or guilty (H_1 is true). The jury does not know the real *state of nature* (the actual innocence or guilt of the defendant). The jury must, however, make a *decision* as to whether or not they believe she is guilty (*reject* H_0) or innocent (*not reject* H_0).

Let us consider the consequences of the jury's decision. If the jury rejects the null hypothesis and declares the defendant guilty when in reality she is guilty (the state of nature is H_1), then the jury has made a correct decision. If, on the other hand, the defendant is actually innocent (the state of nature is H_0), then the jury has made an *error* and convicted an innocent person. We will call this error a **type I error**. Now consider the other possibility. Suppose the jury decides not to reject the null hypothesis. If the defendant is innocent, a correct decision has been made. If, on the other hand, she is guilty, then the jury has failed to convict a guilty person. We will call the error of failing to reject a false null hypothesis a **type II error**. This is shown in Table 7–1.

A moment's reflection will reveal that—within the American legal system—a type I error is considered more serious. "Innocent until proven guilty" means that we want to guard against the possibility of convicting an innocent person—*more so* than guarding against the other type of error, that of letting a guilty person go free. What are the probabilities of committing the two types of errors?

The probability of committing a type I error is denoted by α.

The probability of committing a type II error is denoted by β.

While we would like both error probabilities, α and β, to be *small*, the preceding discussion implies that it is more important for us to control the level of α. The probability of committing a type I error should be set to a predetermined small number. In criminal court cases, we would like α to be a very small number indeed—again, preferably zero. Let us now look at the statistical analogy.

We do not know the value of the population mean. If we decide to reject the null hypothesis in equation 7–1 when in actuality the population mean is 100, then we are committing a type I error. If we fail to reject the null hypothesis when in reality the population mean is different from 100, then we are committing a type II error. In either of the remaining two possibilities (rejecting the null hypothesis when the population mean is not 100, or *not* rejecting the null hypothesis when the population mean is equal to 100), we are making a correct decision. Since, as stated earlier, the null hypothesis is usually a statement of an existing belief, we would like to control α, the probability of committing a type I error. Of course, we also hope not to commit a type II error, that is, we hope to reject H_0 when H_0 is false. But if we can con-

TABLE 7–1　The State of Nature, the Decision, and the Two Possible Errors

		State of Nature	
		H_0	H_1
Decision	H_0	Correct decision	Type II error
	H_1	Type I error	Correct decision

trol only one of the two error probabilities, then it is α, the probability of a type I error, that should be controlled.[3] In common statistical applications, α is usually set to less stringent standards than one would expect in the legal analogy ("beyond a reasonable doubt"). For us, type I error probabilities will often be $\alpha = 0.05$ or $\alpha = 0.01$.

Let us write α and β using the probability notation of Chapter 2. Both are *conditional probabilities:* α is the probability that, when we sample and obtain a value of the test statistic, we will end up rejecting the null hypothesis when the null hypothesis is actually true; similarly, β is the probability that we will end up not rejecting the null hypothesis when the null hypothesis is actually false. We thus have the following:

$$\alpha = P(\text{Reject } H_0 \mid H_0 \text{ is true}) \qquad (7\text{-}2)$$
$$\beta = P(\text{Not reject } H_0 \mid H_0 \text{ is false}) \qquad (7\text{-}3)$$

A word of explanation is in order here. Usually, we will be presented with a null hypothesis, a statistical assertion, which we will try to *reject.* Before carrying out the actual test, we know the probability that we will make a type I error. This probability, α, is preset to a small number, say 0.05. Knowing that we have a small probability of committing a type I error, that is, of rejecting a null hypothesis when it should not be rejected, makes our rejection of a null hypothesis a *strong conclusion.* Usually, the same cannot be said about accepting (*not rejecting*) the null hypothesis. This is so because, unlike α, the probability β of failing to reject a null hypothesis when the null hypothesis *should* be rejected is usually not preset to a known small number. Thus, failing to reject the null hypothesis is usually a *weak conclusion* because we do not know the probability that we will fail to reject a null hypothesis when the null hypothesis should be rejected. When we reject the null hypothesis, we feel fairly confident that the hypothesis should indeed be rejected. When we fail to reject (i.e., we accept) the null hypothesis, we feel that *we did not have enough evidence to reject the hypothesis.* Either the null hypothesis is indeed true, or more evidence is needed for it to be rejected. For this reason, we prefer to use the terms:

$$\text{reject} \qquad \text{versus} \qquad \textit{fail to reject (or do not reject)}$$

If the word *accept* is used when referring to the null hypothesis, we emphasize that it will mean that *there is not enough evidence to reject the null hypothesis* and will not carry its positive, everyday meaning. Returning to the legal analogy, the fact that many defendants are acquitted for lack of conclusive evidence illustrates our point.

In statistical hypothesis testing, how do we decide whether or not to reject the null hypothesis? It turns out that our understanding of confidence intervals, developed in the last chapter, will allow us to conduct hypothesis tests. This is demonstrated in Example (a).

EXAMPLE (a)

A company that delivers packages within a large metropolitan area claims that it takes an average of 28 minutes for a package to be delivered from your door to the destination. Suppose that you want to carry out a hypothesis test of this claim.

---

[3] As we will see, α is exactly the same error probability we used in Chapter 6 in the construction of confidence intervals.

Consistent with our desire to assume "innocent until proven guilty," we set the null and alternative hypotheses as follows:

$$H_0: \mu = 28$$
$$H_1: \mu \neq 28$$

To conduct the test, we select a random sample of $n = 100$ deliveries. We record the delivery times and compute the sample mean $\bar{x} = 31.5$ minutes and sample standard deviation $s = 5$. We will construct a 95% confidence interval for the mean of *all* delivery times of packages in the area (the population mean, μ). Since the sample is large, we can use the normal distribution. We compute the following confidence interval for μ.

$$\bar{x} \pm z_{\alpha/2} \frac{s}{\sqrt{n}} = 31.5 \pm 1.96 \frac{5}{\sqrt{100}} = 31.5 \pm 0.98 = [30.52, 32.48]$$

Consistent with our interpretation of the meaning of confidence intervals, we can be 95% sure that the average time it takes a package to be delivered across town is anywhere from 30.52 to 32.48 minutes.

Let us take this one step further. If we are 95% confident that it takes, on average, anywhere from 30.52 to 32.48 minutes for a package to be delivered, then we are 95% confident that μ does not lie outside this range of values. Since μ under the null hypothesis is 28, a value outside the confidence interval, we may *reject* the null hypothesis. If the null hypothesis is actually true, then—before the sampling takes place—there is only a 0.05 probability that the constructed interval would not include the population mean. If we reject the null hypothesis whenever the population mean stated in the null hypothesis lies outside the 95% confidence interval for μ, then we have at most a 0.05 probability of committing a type I error. We are thus carrying out our test at the $\alpha = 0.05$ *level of significance*. Here we reject the null hypothesis in favor of the alternative hypothesis and conclude that we believe the average delivery time is *not* 28 minutes. Furthermore, since our confidence interval lies entirely *above* the hypothesized value of the population mean (*hypothesized* will mean "stated in the null hypothesis"), we may further conclude that, based on the information in our random sample, we believe that the average time it takes a package to be delivered in the metropolitan area is more than 28 minutes.

What have we learned from this example? We learned that we may use a confidence interval for a population parameter as our decision rule for a statistical hypothesis test. If we use a confidence interval based on a $(1 - \alpha)$ probability (obtained through the sampling distribution of our statistic), then our probability of a type I error—rejecting a true null hypothesis—is at most α. This is demonstrated in Figure 7–1.

FIGURE 7–1 Confidence Interval for μ and the Null-Hypothesized Population Mean, μ_0, in Example (a)

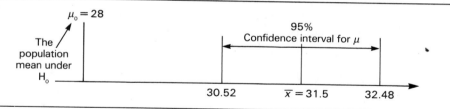

A confidence interval is useful when we are interested in giving a *range* of possible values that we believe the unknown parameter is likely to have. However, if we are only interested in testing a particular hypothesis about the value of a population parameter, we can carry out the test in an easier way by using a test statistic calculated from our data.

Recall that in Chapter 6 we centered the sampling distribution of our statistic $\overline{X}$ over its obtained value because the value of the parameter μ was unknown to us. We used the sampling distribution to establish bounds on either side of the obtained $\overline{x}$ such that we may be, say, 95% sure that the unknown parameter μ lies within these bounds.

Let us now use the same idea in testing hypotheses about the population mean, μ. If someone asserts that the population mean is equal to 28, then let us *center* our sampling distribution of $\overline{X}$ over this hypothesized value of μ. We denote the null-hypothesized value of μ by μ_0. If the null hypothesis is correct, then $\mu_0 = 28$ *is* the mean of the sampling distribution of $\overline{X}$, and the distribution should be centered over that value. If μ_0 is indeed the population mean, then—when we sample from the population and obtain a value of the sample mean—this value, $\overline{x}$, should not fall too far away from μ_0. In fact, when H_0 is true, $\overline{X}$ will have a 0.95 probability (assuming a large sample) of falling within the bounds:

$$\mu_0 \pm 1.96 \frac{s}{\sqrt{n}} \tag{7-4}$$

Thus, if we want to take only a 0.05 chance of making a type I error when we reject the null hypothesis, then we should only reject the null hypothesis if the sample mean $\overline{X}$ should fall outside the bounds given in equation 7–4. The range of values in equation 7–4 is called the *nonrejection* (or acceptance) *region* of the test, and the values outside this range are the *rejection region* of the test.

Our test statistic is $\overline{X}$. The obtained value of the test statistic, $\overline{x}$, is compared with the range of values in equation 7–4. If the test statistic falls outside the bounds, that is, in the rejection region, then we reject the null hypothesis at the $\alpha = 0.05$ level of significance. If $\overline{x}$ falls within the bounds, that is, in the nonrejection range, we do not reject the null hypothesis. In Example (a), the rejection region consists of all values outside the bounds: $\mu_0 \pm 1.96 s/\sqrt{n} = 28 \pm 1.96(5/\sqrt{100}) = [27.02, 28.98]$. Since $\overline{x} = 31.5$, a value *outside* this range, we reject the null hypothesis at the $\alpha = 0.05$ level of significance.

It should be clear from these arguments that when the level of significance is α, *rejection* of the null hypothesis occurs if and only if a confidence interval with confidence coefficient $(1 - \alpha)$ based on the same sample results does *not* include the hypothesized value of the parameter. Similarly, acceptance of the null hypothesis at the significance level α occurs if and only if a confidence interval with confidence coefficient $(1 - \alpha)$ does contain the hypothesized value. This equivalence of hypothesis tests and confidence intervals is demonstrated in Figure 7–2.

Figure 7–3 shows the rejection and nonrejection regions for the test H_0: $\mu = 28$ versus H_1: $\mu \neq 28$. The figure shows the resulting rejection of the null hypothesis due to the fact that the value of the test statistic $\overline{x}$ falls in the rejection region. Let us now formalize our definitions.

The **level of significance** of a statistical hypothesis test is α, the probability of committing a type I error.

FIGURE 7–2   The Equivalence of a 95% Confidence Interval for μ and a Hypothesis Test about μ at the 0.05 Level of Significance

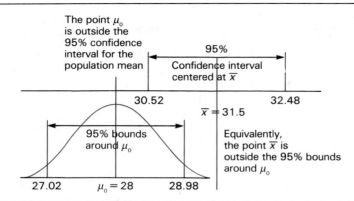

FIGURE 7–3   The Rejection and Nonrejection Regions and the Actual Value of the Test Statistic, Falling in the Rejection Region [Example (a)]

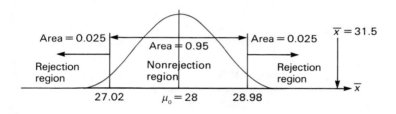

The *decision rule* of a statistical hypothesis test consists of a comparison of the computed value of the test statistic with the values defining the rejection and nonrejection regions. We reject the null hypothesis at the level of significance α if and only if the test statistic falls in the rejection region.

The **rejection region** of a statistical hypothesis test is the range of numbers that will lead us to reject the null hypothesis in case the test statistic falls within this range. The rejection region, also called the **critical region,** is defined by the **critical points.** The rejection region is designed so that, before the sampling takes place, our test statistic will have a probability α of falling within the rejection region if the null hypothesis is true.

The **nonrejection region** is the range of values (also determined by the critical points) that will lead us *not* to reject the null hypothesis if the test statistic should fall within this region. The nonrejection region is designed so that, before the sampling takes place, our test statistic will have a probability $1 - \alpha$ of falling in the nonrejection region if the null hypothesis is true.

The *critical points* define the separation between the rejection and the nonrejection regions. In Example (a), these points were found to be 27.02 and 28.98, with the test statistic $\bar{x}$ in the rejection region (see Figure 7–3).

What about a type II error? What is the probability that such an error will be made? This depends on what value (covered by the *alternative* hypothesis) the parameter actually has. Consider our hypothesis test:

$$H_0: \mu = 28$$

$$H_1: \mu \neq 28$$

We commit a type I error if we reject the null hypothesis when the null hypothesis is actually true—in our example, when the population mean is really 28. On the other hand, we commit a type II error if we accept the null hypothesis when the null hypothesis is false. As you can see, the null hypothesis can be false in many (infinitely many) ways. For example, if the population mean is 29.5, and we conclude that the null hypothesis $\mu = 28$ is true, then we are committing a type II error. The same happens if we accept the null hypothesis when the population mean is 30.7, or 35.9, or 26.432, and so on. In all such situations, if we fail to reject the null hypothesis, we are committing a type II error: accepting a null hypothesis that is false. Thus, the probability of committing a type II error *depends* on the actual value of the parameter in question. The probability of a type II error should, therefore, be denoted by $\beta(\mu)$—a whole collection of values that depend on μ. The concept of β is more complicated than that of α, and we will return to it in a later section.

For now, we will concern ourselves only with α, the probability of a type I error. Recall that, within our framework, a type I error is considered to be more serious than a type II error. We set the value of α before the test takes place (similar to the way we set the confidence level of a confidence interval), and this defines our critical points, which define our rejection and nonrejection regions for the statistical hypothesis test. For the population mean, the critical points were defined in equation 7–4. [In Example (a), these critical points were found to be 27.02 and 28.98.]

The test we have seen in this section is called a *two-tailed test*. A test as stated in equation 7–1 is a two-tailed test because rejection of the null hypothesis is allowed either when we believe the parameter is *greater than* the value stated in the null hypothesis or when we believe it is *less than* the value stated in the null hypothesis. Rejection is allowed when the test statistic falls in either of the *two tails* of the sampling distribution.

A **two-tailed test** is a test with a rejection region consisting of the values in *both* tails of the sampling distribution (under the null hypothesis) of the test statistic.

In the next section, we will see how to conduct a *standardized* two-tailed hypothesis test about a population mean. That is, instead of conducting the test using the actual values of μ_0 and $\bar{x}$, we will convert the test statistic, $\bar{x}$, to a standard normal value—a *z value*. This will be done the way we converted $\bar{X}$ to Z in Chapter 5. Using the new procedure, we will not have to compute the critical points from equation 7–4 as we have done here. The critical points will be values on the *z scale* of numbers (for example, ± 1.96 for a test using $\alpha = 0.05$). The standardized test procedure will be found to be simpler than the method we used in this section, and we will follow it throughout the book.

7-3 A Two-Tailed, Large-Sample Test for the Population Mean

In a two-tailed test, the null hypothesis is stated in terms of an equality. The format is $H_0: \mu = \mu_0$, where μ_0 is some stated number. The alternative hypothesis includes *all* other possible values of the population parameter μ. Logically, if the population parameter is not equal to μ_0, then the alternative hypothesis, $H_1: \mu \neq \mu_0$, is true. This is demonstrated in Figure 7–4.

FIGURE 7–4
The Value of μ under H_0 and the Values of μ under H_1

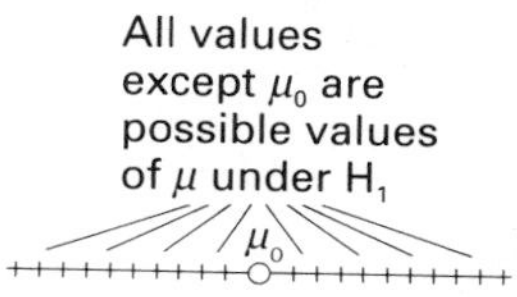

All values except μ_0 are possible values of μ under H_1

You may raise some practical objections at this point. For example, if our null hypothesis is $H_0: \mu = 5.0$, you may ask what we should do if the true population mean is not exactly 5.0, but is equal to 4.99999. In such a case, strictly speaking, we should reject the null hypothesis, as it is not true that $\mu = 5.0$. This, however, is preposterous because 4.99999 is not very different from 5.0. Do we really want to detect such an infinitesimal deviation from the hypothesized value, 5.0? The answer is, of course, no. Usually, we will end up rejecting null hypotheses only when the deviation from the hypothesized value is more *real* than in this hypothetical example. You should know, however, that as the sample size increases, we are better able to detect smaller and smaller deviations from any hypothesized value of the parameter.

In all statistical hypothesis tests, *not only in the two-tailed test*, the equal sign (=) must be stated in the null hypothesis. In the one-tailed tests, which will follow, we will have an *inequality* in the null hypothesis. This inequality, however, will always be a nonstrict inequality and will include the equal sign. This is so because, as we will see, when we carry out a hypothesis test, we center the sampling distribution of the test statistic over the value stated in the null hypothesis. This is the assumption of "innocent until proven guilty"—we *assume* that the mean is as stated in the null hypothesis by centering the distribution of $\bar{X}$ over the hypothesized value, μ_0. The requirement of always having the equal sign in the null hypothesis is thus essential in all hypothesis tests. We now present a standardized form of the two-tailed test.

Standardized Form of the Statistical Hypothesis Test

Recall that if we subtract from a normally distributed random variable its mean and then divide the result by the standard deviation, we get the standard normal random variable, Z. Therefore, assuming that the null hypothesis is true ("innocent until proven guilty"), the mean of $\bar{X}$ is μ_0. We subtract this mean from the obtained $\bar{x}$ and then divide the result by the standard error of $\bar{X}$, which is $\sigma/\sqrt{n}$ (since σ is rarely known, we usually divide by $s/\sqrt{n}$). If the null hypothesis is true, the result (when the sample size is large) should be close to a value drawn from the standard normal distribution. If the null hypothesis is *not* true, the population mean, μ, is either larger than or smaller than μ_0. Hence, when H_0 is not true, the standardized test statistic will tend to be either too large or too small. The terms *too large* and *too small* will mean to us: above, or below, the $\alpha = 0.05$ probability bounds for the standard normal random variable (which are ± 1.96), or the $\alpha = 0.01$ probability bounds for the standard normal random variable (which are ± 2.576), or other bounds for some given significance level. Let us now define our terms in the context of a standardized, large-sample, two-tailed test for the population mean, μ.

The elements of a large-sample, two-tailed (standarized) test for the population mean, μ.

The null hypothesis:	$H_0: \mu = \mu_0$
The alternative hypothesis:	$H_1: \mu \neq \mu_0$

(7–5)

The significance level of the test:

α (often, $\alpha = 0.05$ or 0.01)

The test statistic:

$$z = \frac{\bar{x} - \mu_0}{s/\sqrt{n}}$$ (assuming σ is unknown; otherwise, use $\sigma/\sqrt{n}$ in the denominator) (7–6)

The critical points:

These depend on α. They are the bounds $\pm z_{\alpha/2}$ that capture between them an area of $1 - \alpha$. (When $\alpha = 0.05$, the critical points are ± 1.96; when $\alpha = 0.01$, the critical points are ± 2.576. For other values of α, the critical points may be obtained from the standard normal table.)

The decision rule:

Reject the null hypothesis if either $z > z_{\alpha/2}$ or $z < -z_{\alpha/2}$, where $z_{\alpha/2}$ and $-z_{\alpha/2}$ are the two critical points.

Figure 7–5 demonstrates the standardized test in the context of Example (a). The standardized test shown in the figure is equivalent to the test carried out in the preceding section. In that section, we compared the computed $\bar{x}$ with critical points corresponding to $\alpha = 0.05$ in the scale of the problem itself. Here, instead, we compare $\bar{x}$ converted to a z value with critical points of the Z distribution for $\alpha = 0.05$. These critical points are ± 1.96. The computed z value is (using equation 7–6):

$$z = \frac{\bar{x} - \mu_0}{s/\sqrt{n}} = \frac{31.5 - 28}{5/\sqrt{100}} = 7.0$$

FIGURE 7–5 The Test of Example (a) Carried Out on the z Scale, Where the Test Statistic Is Standardized

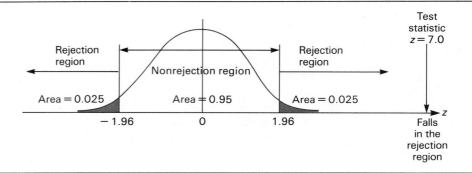

As seen in the figure, the standardized test statistic $z = 7.0$ falls in the right-hand rejection region of the test, and the null hypothesis is rejected at the $\alpha = 0.05$ level of significance.

Recently the airlines and their regulating agencies have been locked in a battle over baggage. The Air Transport Association, the airlines' trade group, believes that most passengers try to carry on board with them as much of their baggage as they possibly can, to avoid long delays at the baggage-claim carousels upon arrival. Consequently, airlines have been spending millions of dollars redesigning storage space in aircraft cabins. Federal regulators, on the other hand, worry about safety when too much baggage is stored in aircraft cabins. As part of a survey to determine the extent of required in-cabin storage capacity, a researcher needs to test the null hypothesis that the average weight of carry-on baggage per person is $\mu_0 = 12$ pounds (traditionally considered the average weight), versus the alternative hypothesis that the average weight is not 12 pounds. The study is undertaken to determine whether the average weight of carry-on baggage is indeed still 12 pounds or whether trends have changed carry-on baggage weight in either direction—either increased it to more than the traditional average of 12 pounds or decreased it to below that average. In other words, the researcher does not take sides as to the direction of possible change in passenger behavior, allowing for the possibility that *less* baggage may now be carried on board, to avoid delays at X-ray checking machines, for example. The analyst wants to test the null hypothesis at $\alpha = 0.05$.

Suppose that the analyst collects a random sample of 144 passengers traveling on different airlines and different routes (both of which are randomly selected) and finds that the average weight of carry-on baggage per passenger is $\bar{x} = 14.6$ pounds and the sample standard deviation is $s = 7.8$. Carry out the statistical hypothesis test, and state your conclusion.

EXAMPLE (b)

The null and alternative hypotheses are:

SOLUTION

$$H_0: \mu = 12$$
$$H_1: \mu \neq 12$$

Using the standardized form of the test (which, certainly leads to the same results as does the other form of the test, which we discussed in the last section) makes things easier. For example, the fact that we want to carry out the test at the $\alpha = 0.05$ level of significance means that we already know the critical points before computing the test statistic. The critical points for Z are ± 1.96. These are shown in Figure 7–6.

We now have an objective decision rule, known even before the sample is collected. We will reject the null hypothesis that the mean weight is 12 pounds if and only if our test statistic, z, falls in the rejection region shown in Figure 7–6. Thus, if we should end

FIGURE 7–6 Determining the Rejection and Nonrejection Regions of the Test of Example (b)

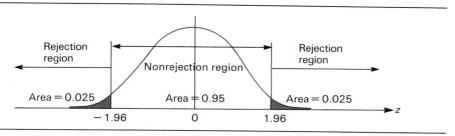

FIGURE 7–7   Conducting the Test of Example (b)

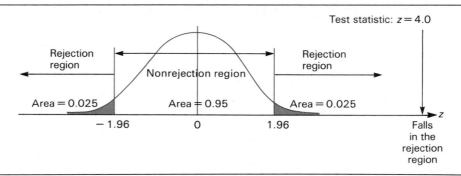

up rejecting the null hypothesis, we will only be taking a 0.05 chance of committing a type I error. We now compute our test statistic using equation 7–6:

$$z = \frac{\bar{x} - \mu_0}{s/\sqrt{n}} = \frac{14.6 - 12}{7.8/\sqrt{144}} = 4.0$$

Since the computed value of the test statistic falls in the rejection region, our decision is to reject the null hypothesis. This is shown in Figure 7–7.

We reject the null hypothesis that the average weight of carry-on baggage per person is equal to 12 pounds in favor of the alternative that it is not equal to 12 pounds. Furthermore, since the rejection occurred in the right tail of the distribution, we may conclude that the average weight is probably higher than 12 pounds. (This conclusion should be made with some care. As we will see later, there is a very small probability that rejection on the right tail may occur when the value of the parameter is actually smaller than the value stated in the null hypothesis—in this example, if the mean is less than 12.)

EXAMPLE (c)

An insurance company executive believes that, over the last few years, the average liability insurance per board seat in companies defined as "small companies" has been $2,000. A recent survey of small business by Growth Resources, Inc., reports that the average liability tab per board seat in their sample is $2,700.[4] Assume that the sample used by Growth Resources contained 100 randomly chosen small firms (as defined by their total annual gross billing) and that the sample standard deviation was $947. Do these sampling results provide evidence to reject the executive's claim that the average liability per board seat is $2,000, using the $\alpha = 0.01$ level of significance?

SOLUTION

We are testing H_0: $\mu = 2,000$ versus the alternative H_1: $\mu \neq 2,000$. Since $\alpha = 0.01$ and our sample size is large, our test statistic is Z and has two critical points: 2.576 and -2.576. The rejection and nonrejection regions defined by these two points are shown in Figure 7–8. Now let us compute the test statistic.

$$z = \frac{\bar{x} - \mu_0}{s/\sqrt{n}} = \frac{2,700 - 2,000}{947/10} = \frac{700}{94.7} = 7.39$$

As seen from Figure 7–8, our test statistic falls in the rejection region, as 7.39 is much larger than the right-hand critical point 2.576. We therefore reject the null hypothesis

---

[4] "Small Business, Big Headache," *Forbes* (October 20, 1986).

FIGURE 7–8   Carrying Out the Hypothesis Test of Example (c)

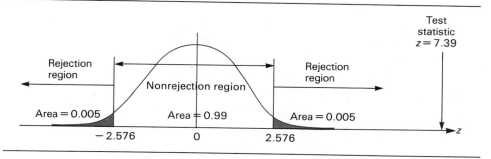

that mean liability insurance per board member in small firms is $2,000 in favor of the alternative that it is not equal to $2,000.

In this example, the computed value of our test statistic turned out to be rather high. The value $z = 7.39$ lies far in the rejection region. In the previous example, the test statistic value was $z = 4$, which is smaller. Is there any information to be obtained from *where* in the rejection region the test statistic falls? The answer to this is yes, and we will discuss this topic in detail in a following section. You should already be intuitively aware that the further in the rejection region the test statistic falls, the *stronger* we feel about rejecting the null hypothesis.

This point is made clearer if we consider the following example. Suppose that you choose a level of significance $\alpha = 0.05$ and your test statistic value is $z = 2.1$. Can you reject the null hypothesis? Clearly you can, because 2.1 is greater than 1.96, which is the right-hand critical point for $\alpha = 0.05$. If you had chosen a significance level $\alpha = 0.01$, however, you would not be able to reject the null hypothesis because the right-hand critical point for $\alpha = 0.01$ is 2.576, and the test statistic value $z = 2.1$ is less than 2.576 and, hence, inside the nonrejection region. This demonstrates that *the further out in the rejection region the test statistic falls, the smaller is the minimum significance level, α, we may use and still be able to reject the null hypothesis.*

EXAMPLE (d)

The average time it takes a computer to perform a certain task is believed to be 3.24 seconds. In 1984, scientists at Bell Laboratories in New Jersey were testing several new algorithms, which they believed might change the speed of computation of the particular task. Scientists did not know whether a particular algorithm they developed would speed up, slow down, or bring no change at all to the average performance time. Therefore, it was decided to test the statistical hypothesis that the average performance time of the task using the new algorithm was the same as it was without the new procedure, versus the alternative hypothesis that the average performance time was no longer 3.24 seconds. A random test of 200 trial computations was carried out, and the result was $\bar{x} = 3.48$ seconds and $s = 2.8$ seconds. At the 0.05 level of significance, can we conclude that average time using the new algorithm is different?

SOLUTION

Here we test the null hypothesis H_0: $\mu = 3.24$ versus the alternative H_1: $\mu \neq 3.24$. Using $\alpha = 0.05$ means that our rejection region is marked by the critical points ± 1.96. We now compute our test statistic using equation 7–6 and get the following.

FIGURE 7–9 Carrying Out the Hypothesis Test of Example (d)

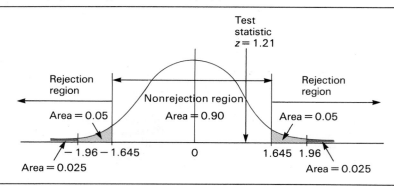

$$z = \frac{\bar{x} - \mu_0}{s/\sqrt{n}} = \frac{3.48 - 3.24}{2.8/\sqrt{200}} = 1.21$$

Our test statistic value is clearly inside the nonrejection region, and we therefore cannot reject the null hypothesis that the average performance time using the new algorithm is still 3.24 seconds. This is shown in Figure 7–9.

Recall that failing to reject a null hypothesis is not a strong or a definitive conclusion. It means that, using the level of significance we have chosen, we do not have enough evidence to reject the claim stated in the null hypothesis. In this particular example, even if we had chosen to use $\alpha = 0.10$, we still would not have been able to reject the null hypothesis because the critical points for this level of significance are ± 1.645, and our test statistic would still be in the nonrejection region. This is also shown in Figure 7–9. The smallest probability of a type I error (the smallest level of significance, α) that will allow us to reject the null hypothesis in this example is greater than 0.10—a value of α considered risky and not often used. The null hypothesis cannot be rejected.

PROBLEMS

Answer

7–2.

Do not reject at both levels.

p-value = 0.053

7–1. An automobile manufacturer substitutes a different engine in cars that were known to have an average mpg rating of 31.5 on the highway. The manufacturer wants to test whether the new engine changes the mpg rating of the automobile model. A random sample of 100 trial runs gives $\bar{x} = 29.8$ mpg and $s = 6.6$ mpg. Using the 0.05 level of significance, is the average mpg rating on the highway for cars using the new engine different from the rating for cars using the old engine?

7–2. A certain prescription medicine is supposed to contain an average of 247 parts per million (ppm) of a certain chemical. If the concentration is higher than 247 ppm, the drug may cause some side effects, and if the concentration is below 247 ppm, the drug may be ineffective. The manufacturer wants to check whether the average concentration in a large shipment is the required 247 ppm or not. A random sample of 60 portions is tested, and it is found that the sample mean is 250 ppm and the sample standard deviation is 12 ppm. Test the null hypothesis that the average concentration in the entire, large shipment is 247 ppm versus the alternative hypothesis that it is not 247 ppm using a level of significance $\alpha = 0.05$. Do the same using $\alpha = 0.01$. What is your conclusion? What is your decision about the shipment? If the shipment were guaranteed to contain an average concentration of 247 ppm, what would your decision be, based on the statistical hypothesis test? Explain.

7–3. A metropolitan transit authority wants to determine whether there is any need for changes in the frequency of service over certain bus routes. The transit authority needs to know whether the frequency of service should increase, decrease, or remain the same. It is determined that if the average number of miles traveled by bus over the routes in question by all residents of a given area is about 5 per day, then no change will be necessary. If the average number of miles traveled per person per day is either above 5 or below 5, then changes in service may be necessary. The authority wants, therefore, to test the null hypothesis that the average number of miles traveled per person per day is 5.0 versus the alternative hypothesis that the average is not 5.0 miles. The required level of significance for this test is $\alpha = 0.05$. A random sample of 120 residents of the area is taken, and it is found that the sample mean is 2.3 miles per resident per day and the sample standard deviation is 1.5 miles. Advise the authority on what should be done. Explain your recommendation. Could you state the same result at different levels of significance? Explain.

7–4. A study was undertaken to determine customer satisfaction in Canadian automobile markets following certain changes in customer service. Suppose that before the changes, average customer satisfaction rating, on a scale of 0 to 100, was 77. A survey questionnaire was sent to a random sample of 350 residents who bought new cars after the changes in customer service were instituted, and the average satisfaction rating for this sample was found to be $\bar{x} = 84$; the sample standard deviation was found to be $s = 28$. Use an α of your choice, and determine whether there is statistical evidence of a change in customer satisfaction. If you determine that a change did occur, state whether you believe customer satisfaction has improved or deteriorated.

7–5. An investment services company claims that the average annual return on stocks within a certain industry is 11.5%. An investor wants to test whether this claim is true and collects a random sample of 50 stocks in the industry of interest. He finds that the sample average annual return is 10.8% and the sample standard deviation is 3.4%. Does the investor have enough evidence to reject the investment company's claim? (Use $\alpha = 0.05$.)

7–6. Tara Pearl founded a multimillion-dollar furniture business that specializes in making futons. Retail prices for the futons vary from outlet to outlet, and it is believed that the average price is $210 for a double futon.[5] To test this hypothesis, Tara's marketing director selects a random sample of 120 outlets and finds a mean price of $225 and a standard deviation of $82. Carry out the test using $\alpha = 0.05$ and also using $\alpha = 0.01$.

7–4 A Two-Tailed, Small-Sample Test for the Population Mean

Until now, we have assumed that the sample size, n, was large (or that the sampling was from a normally distributed population with a known standard deviation). In this section, we will extend our methodology to statistical hypothesis tests for the population mean when the sample size is small. This involves the t distribution. Recall that when we use the t distribution, we must assume that the population itself is normally distributed. Our standardized test statistic for testing hypotheses about the population mean using a small sample is given in equation 7–7.

Small-sample test statistic for the population mean, μ:

$$t = \frac{\bar{x} - \mu_0}{s/\sqrt{n}} \qquad (7–7)$$

When the population is normally distributed and the null hypothesis is true, the test statistic has a t distribution with $n - 1$ degrees of freedom.

Answers

7–4.
p-value less than 0.001.

7–6.
Significant at 0.05, not 0.01.

[5] "Sweet Dreams," *Entrepreneurial Woman* (March 1991), p. 54.

As you can see, the test statistic is identical to the one used earlier for large samples, equation 7–6. The difference is that the distribution of our test statistic is now the *t* distribution with $n - 1$ degrees of freedom instead of the standard normal distribution. Note, however, that *as long as the population standard deviation, σ, is unknown* (and the population is normal), the test statistic in equation 7–7 has a *t* distribution with $n - 1$ degrees of freedom. We use the *z* statistic, equation 7–6, only as a good approximation when the sample size is large. We now demonstrate the use of the *t* statistic with Example (e).

EXAMPLE (e)

According to the Japanese National Land Agency, average land prices in central Tokyo soared 49% in the first six months of 1986.[6] Suppose that an international real estate investment company wants to test this claim versus the alternative that the average land price did not increase by 49% (that is, the null hypothesis is $H_0: \mu = 49$, and it is to be tested against the two-sided alternative $H_1: \mu \neq 49$). The company manages to find a random sample of 18 properties in central Tokyo for which the prices in the second half of 1986 as well as the prices in the first half of that year, are known. For each piece of property, the percentage of price increase is computed. Then the average percentage increase in price for the 18 pieces of property in the sample is computed, along with the standard deviation of the percentage price increases. The calculated sample statistics are $\bar{x} = 38\%$ and $s = 14\%$. Given this information, conduct the statistical hypothesis test using a level of significance $\alpha = 0.01$.

SOLUTION

Since the sample size is small ($n = 18$) and the population standard deviation is not known, we will use the *t* distribution with $n - 1 = 17$ degrees of freedom. We will implicitly assume that percentage increases in all property values in central Tokyo are at least roughly approximated by a normal distribution. (This is a reasonable assumption in this case, as some properties may have increased very much, others very little, and most may have had an increase of around the average percentage.) Since we have chosen to use the $\alpha = 0.01$ level of significance, we need to find the two critical points of the *t* distribution with 17 degrees of freedom that cut off an area of $\alpha/2 = 0.005$ in each tail. From Table 3 in Appendix C we find that the two values are ± 2.898. Our objective decision rule is therefore to reject the null hypothesis if and only if our test statistic *t* given by equation 7–7 is either greater than 2.898 or less than -2.898. Computing the value of the *t* statistic, we find:

$$t = \frac{\bar{x} - \mu_0}{s/\sqrt{n}} = \frac{38 - 49}{14/4.24} = -3.33$$

Since the test statistic falls in the rejection region, we reject the null hypothesis that the average percentage increase in price is 49% in favor of the alternative that the average price increase is not 49%. Furthermore, since the rejection took place on the left-hand tail of the *t* distribution, we are led to believe that the average percentage increase in property values in central Tokyo during the first half of 1986 was less than the 49% claimed by the Japanese National Land Agency. In rejecting their claim, we are taking less than a 0.01 chance of committing a type I error. Figure 7–10 shows the *t* distribution, the rejection and nonrejection regions, and the computed value of the test statistic—located in the left-hand rejection region.

FIGURE 7–10

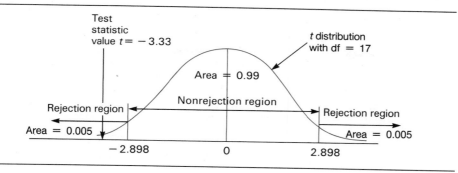

FIGURE 7–11   Rejection of the Null Hypothesis in Example (e) Using Levels $\alpha = 0.01$ and $\alpha = 0.05$

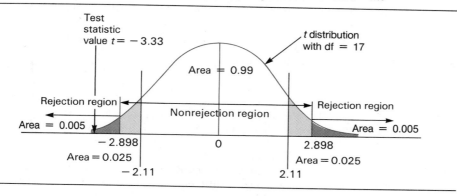

At this point, we will introduce a definition that is useful in all statistical hypothesis tests, whether small- or large-sample, two-tailed or one-tailed.

> We say that a statistical result is **significant** at the level of significance α if the result causes us to *reject our null hypothesis* when we carry out the test using level of significance α.

Thus, in the last example, the result $\bar{x} = 38\%$ was found to be significant at the 0.01 level. Of course, when a result is significant at a given level α, it is also significant at all levels higher than α. This can be seen from the fact that if we had used $\alpha = 0.05$ in the last example, we would have also rejected the null hypothesis; if our test statistic is in the rejection region for $\alpha = 0.01$, it must also be in the rejection region for $\alpha = 0.05$—a larger rejection region. This is demonstrated in the context of Example (e) in Figure 7–11.

Canon, Inc., introduced a copying machine that features two-color copying capability in a compact system copier. The average speed of the standard compact system copier is 27 copies per minute (as advertised in national business magazines and elsewhere). Suppose that the company wants to test whether the new two-color copier has the same average speed as its standard compact copier and it conducts a test of 24 runs of the new machines, giving a sample mean $\bar{x} = 24.6$ and sample standard deviation $s = 7.4$ (copies

EXAMPLE (f)

FIGURE 7-12 Carrying Out the Test of Example (f)

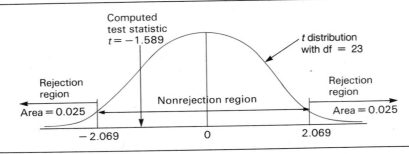

per minute). Using the significance level $\alpha = 0.05$, is there evidence to conclude that the average speed of the new machine is different from that of the standard model?

SOLUTION

We want to test H_0: $\mu = 27$ versus H_1: $\mu \neq 27$. Since the sample size is $n = 24$, we use the t distribution, making the usual implicit assumption about the shape of the population. The critical points for $\alpha = 0.05$, found from Table 3 using df $= 23$, are ± 2.069. We now compute the value of our test statistic.

$$t = \frac{\bar{x} - \mu_0}{s/\sqrt{n}} = \frac{24.6 - 27}{7.4/4.899} = -1.589$$

Is this result significant? No. Since the test statistic falls inside the nonrejection region for $\alpha = 0.05$, we cannot reject the null hypothesis. There is no evidence to conclude that the average speed of the new copier is different from the average speed of the standard compact copier. Our statistical hypothesis test is shown in Figure 7–12.

Usually, when we carry out statistical hypothesis tests, we want to disprove the null hypothesis in favor of the alternative hypothesis. This is so not because there is something intrinsically special about the alternative hypothesis, but rather because of our decision to give the type I error more importance by controlling its probability of occurrence (we set the level of this probability, α, to a given small number: 0.05, 0.01, or another preset value). Thus, as noted earlier, if we accept a null hypothesis, we have not made a strong conclusion; the null hypothesis may be true or may be false, but we cannot reject it without taking a chance greater than α of being wrong when we reject it. In cases where we are able to reject the null hypothesis, we have some degree of confidence in our conclusion—we know that our chance of being wrong is small. This is why a result that leads to the rejection of a null hypothesis is called *significant*. Such a result implies a substantial finding—one with a small, known probability of being false.

PROBLEMS

7-7. A new British newspaper, *The Independent*, was introduced to fill a gap in a changing British society. The newspaper is aimed at affluent, well-educated young professionals. The paper's editors believe that the new paper will appeal to a readership with an average age of 33. If a test of this hypothesis is carried out at the 0.05 level of significance, and a random sample of 20 readers shows that the average age in the sample of readers is 41 and the standard deviation of the sample is 4 years, do you believe the editors' claim? Explain.

7–8. A certain commodity is known to have a price that is stable through time and does not change according to any known trend. Price, however, does change from day to day in a random fashion. If the price is at a certain level one day, it is as likely to be at any level the next day within some probability bounds approximately given by a normal distribution. The mean daily price is believed to be $14.25. To test the hypothesis that the average price is $14.25 versus the alternative hypothesis that it is not $14.25, a random sample of 16 daily prices is collected. The results are $\bar{x} = \$16.50$ and $s = \$5.8$. Using $\alpha = 0.05$, can you reject the null hypothesis?

7–9. Average total daily sales at a small foodstore are known to be $452.80. The store's management recently implemented some changes in displays of goods, order within aisles, and other changes, and it now wants to know whether average sales volume has changed. A random sample of 12 days shows $\bar{x} = \$501.90$ and $s = \$65.00$. Using $\alpha = 0.05$, is the sampling result significant? Explain.

7–10. A study was undertaken to evaluate how stocks are affected by being listed in the Standard & Poor's 500 Index. The aim of the study was to assess average excess returns for these stocks, above returns on the market as a whole. The average excess return on *any* stock is zero because the "average" stock moves with the market as a whole. As part of the study, a random sample of 13 stocks newly included in the S&P 500 Index was selected. Before the sampling takes place, we allow that average "excess return" for stocks newly listed in the Standard & Poor's 500 Index may be either positive or negative; therefore, we want to test the null hypothesis that average excess return is equal to zero versus the alternative that it is not zero. If the excess return on the sample of 13 stocks averaged 3.1% and had a standard deviation of 1%, do you believe that inclusion in the Standard & Poor's 500 Index changes a stock's excess return on investment, and if so, in which direction? Explain.

7–11. A new chemical process is introduced in the production of nickel-cadmium batteries. For batteries produced by the old process, it is known that the average life of a battery is 102.5 hours. To determine whether the new process affects the average life of the batteries, the manufacturer collects a random sample of 25 batteries produced by the new process and uses them until they run out. The sample mean life is found to be 107 hours, and the sample standard deviation is found to be 10 hours. Are these results significant at the $\alpha = 0.05$ level? Are they significant at the $\alpha = 0.01$ level? Explain. Draw your conclusion.

7–12. Average soap consumption in a certain country is believed to be 2.5 bars per person per month. *The standard deviation of the population is known to be $\sigma = 0.8$.* While the standard deviation is not believed to have changed (and this may be substantiated by several studies), it is believed that the mean consumption may have changed either upward or downward. A survey is therefore undertaken to test the null hypothesis that average soap consumption is still 2.5 bars per person per month versus the alternative that it is not. A sample of size $n = 20$ is collected and gives $\bar{x} = 2.3$. The population is assumed to be normally distributed. What is the appropriate test statistic in this case? Conduct the test and state your conclusion. Use an α of your choice. Does the choice of level of significance change your conclusion? Explain.

7–13. What are the assumptions underlying the use of the *t* distribution in testing hypotheses about the population mean?

7–14. Average sales commissions in a certain industry are claimed to be $5,600 per salesperson per year. A researcher wants to test whether or not this claim is true. The researcher collects a random sample of 38 salespeople and finds $\bar{x} = \$6,480$ and $s = \$1,209$. Use $\alpha = 0.01$ to test the claim. State your conclusion.

7–15. It is known that the average stay of tourists in Hong Kong hotels has been 3.4 nights.[7] A tourism industry analyst wanted to test whether recent changes in the nature of tourism to Hong Kong have changed this average. The analyst obtained the following random sample of the number of nights spent by tourists in Hong Kong hotels: 5, 4, 3, 2, 1, 1, 5, 7, 8, 4, 3, 3, 2, 5, 7, 1, 3, 1, 1, 5, 3, 4, 2, 2, 2, 6, 1, 7. Conduct the test using the 0.05 level of significance.

Answers

7–8.

p-value > 0.1
t = 1.55

7–10.

p-value very small
t = 11.18

7–12.

p-value = 0.26

7–14.

small p-value
z = 4.49

---

[7] "Hong Kong's Tourism: Stay a While, Spend a Little," *The Economist* (March 16, 1991), p. 72.

7–5 A Two-Tailed, Large-Sample Test for the Population Proportion

As we know, when the sample size is large, the distribution of the sample proportion, $\hat{P}$, may be approximated by a normal distribution with mean p and standard deviation $\sqrt{pq/n}$. Therefore, for large samples (recall our rule of thumb: both $np > 5$ and $nq > 5$), we can test hypotheses about the population proportion p in a similar manner to the way we constructed confidence intervals for p in the last chapter. The test statistic we use is z, defined in equation 7–8. In computing the test statistic, we use p_0—the hypothesized value of p under the null hypothesis.

Large-sample test statistic for the population proportion, p:

$$z = \frac{\hat{p} - p_0}{\sqrt{p_0 q_0 / n}}$$

(7–8)

where $q_0 = 1 - p_0$.

We will demonstrate the use of this statistic in a two-tailed test for the population proportion in Example (g).

EXAMPLE (g)

Recent changes, referred to as the "Big Bang," in regulation of the investment industry in Britain brought far-reaching consequences. For the first time, the London stock market was opened to foreign investors, and this gave many foreign investors direct access to British securities. The U.S. dollar, which had been declining during the period preceding and following the deregulation, was expected to bring massive American investments to the British Exchange. An investment analyst for Goldman Sachs and Company wanted to test the hypothesis made by British securities experts that 70% of all foreign investors in the British market were American. The analyst gathered a random sample of 210 accounts of foreign investors in London and found that 130 were owned by U.S. citizens. At the $\alpha = 0.05$ level of significance, is there evidence to reject the claim of the British securities experts?

SOLUTION

We want to test the null hypothesis H_0: $p = 0.70$ versus the alternative hypothesis H_1: $p \neq 0.70$. Our test statistic is z, and therefore, using $\alpha = 0.05$, our rejection region is defined by the two critical points ± 1.96. This is shown in Figure 7–13. We now compute the value of the test statistic using equation 7–8 and the calculated sample proportion $\hat{p} = x/n = 130/210 = 0.619$.

$$z = \frac{\hat{p} - p_0}{\sqrt{p_0 q_0 / n}} = \frac{0.619 - 0.70}{\sqrt{(0.7)(0.3)/210}} = -2.5614$$

As can be seen from Figure 7–13, the computed value of the test statistic falls in the left-hand rejection region; hence, at $\alpha = 0.05$ our result is significant. We therefore may state that, based on our random sample of accounts, we believe that the percentage of American accounts in the London Exchange at the time of the study was lower than 70%.

Let us consider our rejection of the null hypothesis in this example a little more carefully. Since we decided, before the sampling took place, that we were willing to take a 0.05 probability of committing a type I error and rejecting a true null hypoth-

FIGURE 7–13   Conducting the Hypothesis Test of Example (g)

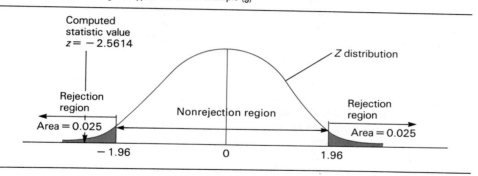

esis, we were able to reject the null hypothesis. If, however, we had decided to take only a 0.01 probability of rejecting a true null hypothesis, we would not have been able to reject it because our test statistic value—although very close to the 0.01 critical point, −2.576—is still inside the nonrejection region for this level of significance (−2.5614 is to the *right* of −2.576).

What can we say about the "real" level of significance of this test? What is the smallest probability of committing a type I error we could have chosen and *still* rejected the null hypothesis? Since our test statistic value falls close to the critical point for $\alpha = 0.01$, the "smallest possible α" we seek is very close to 0.01. To find the exact "smallest possible α" (the actual, or "real" level of significance of our finding), we look in the normal probability table and find the combined area in the two tails cut off by the two values ±2.5614. We find that this value is around 0.0104. We use the combined area in both tails because our test is a two-tailed test; therefore, *if the null hypothesis is true*, then an error could occur either by rejecting on the left tail of the sampling distribution of the statistic Z or by rejecting on the right tail of the distribution. The value we found, 0.0104, is the smallest level of significance at which we may reject the null hypothesis. Such a value, called a *p-value*, will be discussed in detail in Section 7–7.

PROBLEMS

7–16.   A recent survey of schools of business indicates that 16% of the faculty positions in schools of business are currently vacant. A placement service working for a renowned university wants to test whether or not the claim is true and collects information on a random sample of 300 business faculty positions chosen from universities around the country. The results indicate that 51 out of the 300 positions surveyed are vacant. Use $\alpha = 0.05$ to conduct the test.

7–17.   Suppose that the Goodyear Tire Company has historically held 42% of the market for automobile tires in the United States. Recent changes in company operations, especially its diversification to other areas of business, as well as changes in competing firms' operations, prompt the firm to test the validity of the assumption that it still controls 42% of the market. A random sample of 550 automobiles on the road shows that 219 of them have Goodyear tires. Conduct the test at $\alpha = 0.01$.

7–18.   The manufacturer of electronic components needs to inform its buyers of the proportion of defective components in its shipments. The company has been stating that the percentage of defectives is 12%. The company wants to test whether or not the proportion of all components that are defective is as claimed. A random sample of 100 items indicates 17 defectives. Use $\alpha = 0.05$ to test the hypothesis that the percentage of defective components is 12%.

Answers

7–16.

$p = 0.64$

7–18.

$p = 0.12$

Answer
_____

7–19. The percentage of farmers using fertilizers in an African country was known to be 35%. The drought and other events of the last few years are believed to have had a potential impact on the proportion of farmers using fertilizers. An international aid program wants to test whether or not the percentage is still around 35% and gathers a random sample of 150 farmers. The findings reveal that 68 of the farmers use fertilizers. Conduct the test at $\alpha = 0.05$ and at $\alpha = 0.01$. State your conclusion.

7–20. A company's market share is very sensitive to both its level of advertising and the levels of its competitors' advertising. A firm known to have a 56% market share wants to test whether or not this value is still valid in view of recent advertising campaigns of its competitors and its own increased level of advertising. A random sample of 500 consumers reveals that 298 of them use the company's product. Is there evidence to conclude that the company's market share is no longer 56%, using the 0.01 level of significance?

7–21. *Variety* magazine reports ratings of movie videocassettes based on a national survey of stores. *Variety* assigns a volume indicator to each video based on the store popularity ratings. The highest possible score for a video is 130, but anything higher than 100 reflects a particularly strong rental.[8] It is currently believed that 10% of all videos have volume indicator scores over 100. Use the randomly selected group of videos listed below (reprinted by permission from *Variety*) to test this claim. Use your choice of significance level for this test.

Title and Distributor	Volume Indicator	Title and Distributor	Volume Indicator
Die Hard 2 (CBS/Fox)	120.90	*Q&A* (HBO Video)	67.10
Flatliners (RCA/Columbia)	111.73	*Moon 44* (Live)	65.34
Navy Seals (Orion)	108.75	*Back to the Future, Part III*	
Days of Thunder (Paramount)	104.18	(MCA/Universal)	65.20
Young Guns II (CBS/Fox)	103.30	*Henry V* (CBS/Fox)	63.30
Darkman (MCA/Universal)	102.11	*Total Recall* (Live)	63.20
Problem Child (MCA/Universal)	102.04	*Repossessed* (Live)	62.00
The Freshman (RCA/Columbia)	96.70	*Last Exit to Brooklyn*	
Mo' Better Blues (MCA/Universal)	90.00	(RCA/Columbia)	61.40
My Blue Heaven (Warner)	88.60	*The Adventures of Milo & Otis*	
Delta Force 2 (Media)	87.60	(RCA/Columbia)	61.30
The Witches (Warner)	86.20	*Miami Blues* (Orion)	60.40
Robocop 2 (Orion)	85.65	*Glory* (RCA/Columbia)	60.20
Taking Care of Business		*Ernest Goes to Jail* (Touchstone)	59.50
(Hollywood Home)	84.06	*The Lemmon Sisters* (HBO Video)	58.90
The Adventures of Ford Fairlane		*I Love You to Death* (RCA/Columbia)	58.50
(CBS/Fox)	82.90	*The Adventures of Rocky &*	
I Come in Peace (Media)	82.69	*Bullwinkle* (Buena Vista)	55.37
Bird on a Wire (MCA/Universal)	80.40	*Loose Cannons* (RCA/Columbia)	54.70
Dick Tracy (Touchstone)	79.60	*The First Power* (Nelson)	53.00
Another 48 HRS. (Paramount)	78.30	*Fire Birds* (Touchstone)	52.40
Hardware (HBO Video)	77.50	*A Shock to the System* (HBO	
Men at Work (RCA/Columbia)	77.30	Video)	52.00
Betsy's Wedding (Touchstone)	73.40	*Grim Prairie Tales* (Academy)	51.50
The Hunt for Red October		*Lisa* (CBS/Fox)	51.20
(Paramount)	73.10	*The Guardian* (MCA/Universal)	50.70
Ghost Dad (MCA/Universal)	72.90	*The Godfather: The Complete Epic*	
Wild Orchid (RCA/Columbia)	72.10	(Paramount)	50.70
Short Time (Live)	71.70	*Cinema Paradiso* (HBO Video)	50.56
The Godfather II (Paramount)	71.10	*Daddy's Dyin' . . . Who's Got the*	
Cadillac Man (Orion)	70.90	*Will?* (MGM/UA)	49.60
Gremlins 2 (Warner)	70.30	*Deceptions* (Republic)	47.10
The Godfather (Paramount)	69.70	*Longtime Companion* (Vidmark)	46.10
Blind Fury (RCA/Columbia)	68.70	*Revenge* (RCA/Columbia)	45.75
Pretty Woman (Touchstone)	67.40	*The Last of the Finest* (Orion)	45.50

_____
[8] "Top Video Titles," *Variety* (February 18, 1991), p. 30.

7–6 One-Tailed Tests

While reading the examples and problems of the previous sections, you may have wondered about situations where, instead of testing whether or not a population parameter is *equal* to some specified number, we may be interested in testing whether the parameter is greater than (or smaller than) some specified value. Such situations are indeed more realistic and occur very often in practice. When we want to test whether a parameter is greater than or less than some value, our test is not a two-tailed test, but rather a **one-tailed test.** For example, in quality control, it is much more meaningful to test the null hypothesis that the proportion of defective items produced is equal to 0.10 versus the alternative hypothesis that the proportion of defective items is strictly *greater than* 0.10. In this case we would be conducting the right-hand-tailed test given by:

$$H_0: p \leq 0.10$$
$$H_1: p > 0.10 \tag{7-9}$$

Here the assumption of "innocence" is the assumption that the proportion of defective items in a shipment is *at most* 0.10. We will conclude "guilty"—and reject the null hypothesis in favor of the alternative hypothesis—if we find statistical evidence indicating that the proportion of defective items is greater than 0.10. Note that, here too, the equal sign is included in the null hypothesis. This conforms with our requirement that the null hypothesis always include the equal sign. Our test is a right-hand-tailed test because, as we will see, the rejection region is strictly in the right tail of the distribution.

In a given situation, how do we decide whether a test should be carried out as a one-tailed or a two-tailed test? This is an important question, and to answer it we must consider the decision-making framework of hypothesis tests. Recall that our philosophy of hypothesis tests tells us that we will take action (decide "guilty") if we have enough evidence to believe that the situation presented to us in the null hypothesis is not true. *The action is, therefore, always associated with the alternative hypothesis.* Thus, we ask ourselves: In what *situation* do we want to take action? The answer to this question determines the alternative hypothesis. If the test is carried out by the manufacturer, and the manufacturer is interested in determining whether there is a deviation from the value $p = 0.10$ in *either direction,* that is, either up or down from 0.10, then the test is a two-tailed test. This is so because an action is to be taken if the proportion of defectives is below 0.10 (say, notify buyers that their shipment contains fewer defective items than stated by the manufacturer) as well as when the proportion of defective items is above 0.10 (again, the action is to notify buyers). On the other hand, suppose a supplier guarantees that its shipments contain at most 10% defectives, and there is no interest in taking action if fewer than 10% are defective. The buyer may now be the one conducting a hypothesis test to check whether the supplier's claim of no more than 10% defective items is correct. The buyer will only take action if it may be concluded that *more than* 10% are defective. Since the action is to be taken only in such a case, this means that the alternative hypothesis (the one that entails action) is $p > 0.10$, and the test is a right-hand-tailed test. We summarize the distinction between one- and two-tailed tests as follows.

> The tails of a statistical hypothesis test are determined by the need for an action. If action is to be taken if a parameter is greater than some value *a*, then the alternative hypothesis is that the parameter is greater than *a*, and the test is a **right-hand-tailed test.**

For example, if a population mean is claimed to be 50 and we are concerned about the possibility that the mean may be greater than 50 (but do not care if the mean is below 50), then the hypotheses are:

$$H_0: \mu \leq 50$$
$$H_1: \mu > 50$$

which is a right-hand-tailed test.

> If action is to be taken only if the value of a parameter is believed to be less than a stated value *a*, then the alternative hypothesis is that the parameter is less than *a*, and the test is a **left-hand-tailed test.**

For example, if the population mean is claimed to be 50 but action should only be taken if it is below 50, then the null and alternative hypotheses are:

$$H_0: \mu \geq 50$$
$$H_1: \mu < 50$$

> If action is to be taken if the value of a parameter is either greater than or less than *a*, then the test is a two-tailed test.

In our example, the test is:

$$H_0: \mu = 50$$
$$H_1: \mu \neq 50$$

In a one-tailed test, the rejection region is either completely on the left (a left-hand-tailed test) or completely on the right (a right-hand-tailed test). Therefore, we have the following important property.

> In a one-tailed test, the entire probability of a type I error, α, is placed in the tail of rejection.

This changes the critical points of the tests. For example, in a right-hand-tailed test for the population mean, using a large sample size and $\alpha = 0.05$, there is only one critical point: $z = +1.645$. Why? The answer is shown in Figure 7–14.

The distribution of the statistic is normal, and the probability of a type I error is 0.05. We place this probability *entirely* on the right-hand side of the distribution. We have to find that point *a* such that the area to its right is 0.05 (not 0.025, as in the case of a two-tailed test, where the sum of the areas in *both* tails is 0.05). From the

FIGURE 7–14   Critical Point and Rejection and Nonrejection Regions for a Right-Hand-Tailed Test at $\alpha = 0.05$

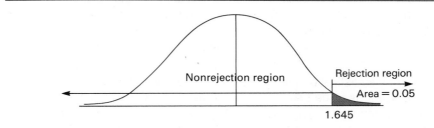

standard normal table, we find that the point z_α that cuts off an area of 0.05 to its right is 1.645. (This is the same point we use together with its negative, -1.645, in a two-tailed test at $\alpha = 0.10$. Here it is used alone.)

The elements of a large-sample, right-hand-tailed (standardized) test for the population mean, μ.

The null hypothesis:	$H_0: \mu \leq \mu_0$
The alternative hypothesis:	$H_1: \mu > \mu_0$ $\quad$ (7–10)

The significance level of the test:

α (often, $\alpha = 0.05$ or 0.01)

The test statistic:

$$z = \frac{\bar{x} - \mu_0}{s/\sqrt{n}} \quad \text{(assuming } \sigma \text{ (7–6)}$$

(assuming σ is unknown; otherwise, use $\sigma/\sqrt{n}$ in the denominator)

The critical point: This depends on α. It is the bound z_α that captures an area of α to its right. (When $\alpha = 0.05$, the critical point is 1.645; when $\alpha = 0.01$, the critical point is 2.326. For other values of α, the critical point may be obtained from the standard normal table.)

The decision rule: Reject the null hypothesis if $z > z_\alpha$ where z_α is the critical point.

Table 7–2 gives the critical points for a test using the normal distribution in the cases of a one-tailed and a two-tailed test with commonly used values of α. When the distribution to be used is the t distribution, the critical point(s) may be determined by finding the value for appropriate degrees of freedom, where the infinite df value (the z value) is the value given in Table 7–2. Critical values for other levels of α are found in the standard normal table. Table 7–2 is only a quick-reference summary table provided for convenience. We demonstrate the use of one-tailed tests using the following examples.

TABLE 7–2 Critical Points of Z for Selected Levels of Significance

	Level of Significance α:		
	0.10	**0.05**	**0.01**
One-Tailed Test	+ or 1.28 −	+ or 1.645 −	+ or 2.326 −
Two-Tailed Test	+ and 1.645 −	+ and 1.96 −	+ and 2.576 −

Note: + or − means we use the positive value in the table for a right-hand-tailed test and the negative value for a left-hand-tailed test. In a two-tailed test, we use both the positive and the negative values.

EXAMPLE (h)

The Environmental Protection Agency (EPA) sets limits on the concentrations of pollutants emitted by various industries. Suppose that the upper allowable limit on the emission of vinyl chloride is set at an average of 55 parts per million (ppm) within a range of two miles around the plant emitting this chemical. To check compliance with this rule, the EPA collects a random sample of 100 readings at different times and dates within the two-mile range around the plant. The findings are that the sample average concentration is 60 ppm and the sample standard deviation is 20 ppm. Is there evidence to conclude that the plant in question is violating the law?

SOLUTION

The EPA is interested in determining whether or not the plant operators are violating the law. The EPA will be taking action against the plant operators only if there is enough evidence to conclude that the average concentration of vinyl chloride within the given range of two miles from the plant is *above* the allowed average of 55 ppm. Therefore, the test is a right-hand-tailed test. Since the sample size is 100, we use the normal distribution. If a level of significance $\alpha = 0.01$ is desired, the critical point to be used is $+2.326$. The test statistic is the same as that used in the two-tailed test and is given by equation 7–6:

$$z = \frac{\bar{x} - \mu_0}{s/\sqrt{n}} = \frac{60 - 55}{20/10} = 2.5$$

As can be seen from Figure 7–15, the value of the test statistic falls in the rejection region for $\alpha = 0.01$, and the EPA may therefore reject the null hypothesis of "innocence" (nonviolation of the emission control rule) in favor of the alternative hypothesis that the plant operators are indeed violating the law. By using $\alpha = 0.01$, the EPA is willing to take at most a 0.01 chance of concluding that the plant operators are guilty when in reality they are innocent.

What are the advantages of a one-tailed test? From this example, we see that when we are interested in rejecting a null hypothesis only in one direction, setting up the test as a one-tailed test in the direction of interest (here a right-hand-tailed test) is advantageous. Suppose the EPA had set up the test as a two-tailed test, with the understanding that action would only be taken if the rejection happened on the

FIGURE 7–15 The One-Tailed Test in Example (h), Compared with a Two-Tailed Test

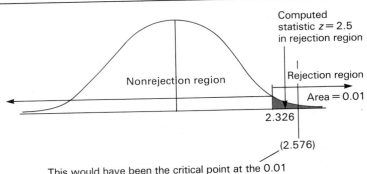

right-hand side. In such a case, the test would have had two critical points at the 0.01 level of significance, ± 2.576, and the obtained test statistic value, $z = 2.5$, would be found inside the nonrejection region for the test (although the null hypothesis would still be rejected if the EPA were willing to use an α of 0.05). Thus, we see that setting up the hypothesis test as a one-tailed test increases the *power* of the test (we will formally define power in a later section) in the sense that this allows us to reject null hypotheses in more cases than would be possible if we use two tails. It is very important, therefore, to first determine whether a test should be one-tailed or two-tailed.

A certain kind of packaged food bears the following statement on the package: "Average net weight 12 oz." Suppose that a consumer group has been receiving complaints from users of the product who believe that they are getting smaller quantities than the manufacturer states on the package. The consumer group wants, therefore, to test the hypothesis that the average net weight of the product in question is 12 oz. versus the alternative hypothesis that the packages are, on average, underfilled. A random sample of 144 packages of the food product is collected, and it is found that the average net weight in the sample is 11.8 oz. and the sample standard deviation is 6 oz. Given these findings, is there evidence that the manufacturer is underfilling the packages?

EXAMPLE (i)

As in every problem, we first need to determine whether the situation entails a one-tailed or a two-tailed test. In this particular example, the required test clearly is one-tailed and the tail of rejection is the left-hand tail. This is seen by answering the question: Under what conditions do we want to take an action? The action always determines the alternative hypothesis, and the null hypothesis then covers all other possibilities (always including the equal sign). Here it is easy to see that since the consumer group is the one carrying out the test, they would be interested in taking action against the manufacturer (complaint, lawsuit, etc.) only if they end up believing, to within a small probability of being wrong, that the manufacturer is underfilling the packages it sells. If the packages are believed to be overfilled or filled with exactly 12 oz. of food, then no action whatsoever will be taken. Since action is to be taken only in the underfilled case, the test is a left-hand-tailed test. As a mnemonic device, you may want to think of "less than" implying a left-hand and "greater than" implying a right-hand test.

SOLUTION

Now that we know what kind of test to perform, we can set up the distribution of the test statistic under the null hypothesis, noting that our sample size, $n = 144$, allows us to use the standard normal distribution. In the statement of the problem, we left out the required probability of a type I error, α. This was done purposely, because, in reality, the choice of α will often be left to the statistician performing the test. You may start, if you wish, by choosing a commonly used value, such as $\alpha = 0.05$. Figure 7–16 shows the distribution and the critical point $z_\alpha = -1.645$, which corresponds to $\alpha = 0.05$ and a left-hand-tailed test using the normal distribution. The figure also shows the value of the test statistic, computed as:

$$z = \frac{\bar{x} - \mu_0}{s/\sqrt{n}} = \frac{11.8 - 12}{6/12} = -0.4$$

As we see, the value of the test statistic falls in the nonrejection region. We cannot reject the null hypothesis $H_0: \mu \geq 12$. There is insufficient evidence to conclude that the manufacturer is underfilling the packages. The fact that we accepted the null hypothesis does not mean that the manufacturer is *not* underfilling the packages; it merely means that, given our data, we cannot reject the null hypothesis without taking a large probability of being wrong. The probability of committing a type I error is large because the

FIGURE 7–16   Nonrejection of the Null Hypothesis in Example (i)

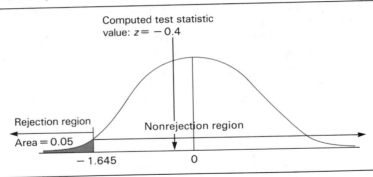

value of our test statistic falls far inside the nonrejection region, and we would have to accept the null hypothesis even if we were to choose a much larger value of α than 0.05.

Recall that a two-tailed test at a given level α is equivalent to constructing a confidence interval for the parameter in question with confidence coefficient $1 - \alpha$ (a confidence interval of level 95%, for example, is equivalent to carrying out a two-tailed hypothesis test for the parameter at the 0.05 level of significance). What about a one-tailed test? *One-tailed tests are equivalent to one-sided confidence intervals.* This means that a one-sided confidence interval would contain the hypothesized value of a parameter if and only if a one-tailed test (in direction opposite to the confidence interval, using the corresponding level of significance, α) would lead to acceptance of the null hypothesis. In the case of Example (i), we could have constructed a right-hand confidence interval for μ. If we do so, $\alpha = 0.05$ implies we need a 95% right-handed confidence interval. The interval is: $[-\infty, \bar{x} + 1.645s/\sqrt{n}] = [-\infty, 12.6225]$. This confidence interval contains the hypothesized value $\mu_0 = 12$, as we would expect from the fact that the one-tailed test led us to accept the null hypothesis that μ is greater than or equal to 12.

As we saw in Chapter 6, the distance from $\bar{x}$ to μ is the same as the distance from μ to $\bar{x}$. Hence, we can measure this distance from our hypothesized value of the parameter to the test statistic as we do in the case of a hypothesis test, or we may measure the distance from our test statistic to the hypothesized value of the parameter, which is what we do in the case of a confidence interval. In either case the results are the same: A null hypothesis will be accepted if and only if the confidence interval contains the hypothesized value of the parameter. The distance between the value of the test statistic and the hypothesized value of the parameter is measured in number of standard deviations of the test statistic. A distance greater than a few standard deviations (1.96 of them, 2.576 of them, etc.) leads to the rejection of the null hypothesis (or, equivalently, noninclusion of the hypothesized value of the parameter in the confidence interval).

The following two examples demonstrate one-tailed hypothesis tests for the mean when the sample size is small, and large-sample one-tailed tests for the population proportion, respectively.

EXAMPLE (i)

A floodlight is stated to last an average of 65 hours. A competitor believes that the average life of the floodlight is less than that stated by the manufacturer and sets out to prove that the manufacturer's claim is false. A random sample of 21 floodlight elements

FIGURE 7–17   Carrying Out the Test of Example (j)

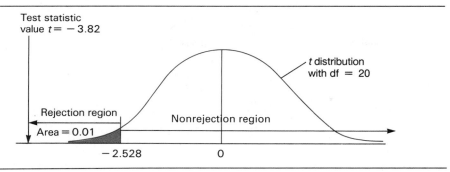

is chosen and shows that the sample average is 62.5 hours and the sample standard deviation is 3. Using $\alpha = 0.01$, determine whether there is evidence to conclude that the manufacturer's claim is false.

SOLUTION

We have the following hypotheses: $H_0: \mu \geq 65$ and $H_1: \mu < 65$. Since this is a left-hand-tailed test at the 0.01 level of significance, we know that if the sample size were large enough for the normal distribution to be used, the critical point would be -2.326. Here the appropriate distribution is the t distribution with $n - 1 = 20$ degrees of freedom. Looking at the t table, Appendix C, Table 3, we find that the appropriate critical value (using the same column in which we have in the bottom row the value 2.326) is $t = -2.528$. This is shown in Figure 7–17, along with the computed value of the test statistic:

$$ t = \frac{\bar{x} - \mu_0}{s/\sqrt{n}} = \frac{62.5 - 65}{3/4.583} = -3.82 $$

Since the test statistic falls in the rejection region, we reject the null hypothesis and conclude that there is statistical evidence that the manufacturer's claim is false. Our probability of a type I error in rejecting the claim is less than 0.01.

EXAMPLE (k)

"After looking at 1,349 hotels nationwide, we've found 13 that meet our standards." This statement by the Small Luxury Hotels Association, which appeared in advertisements of the association in national magazines, implies that the proportion of all hotels in the United States that meet the association's standards is $13/1,349 = 0.0096$. The management of a hotel that was denied acceptance to the association on the grounds that it did not meet the association's standards wanted to prove that the standards set by the association are not quite as stringent as claimed and that, in fact, the proportion of hotels in the United States that would qualify under present standards is higher than 0.0096. The management hired an independent research agency, which visited a random sample of 600 hotels nationwide and found that 7 of them satisfied the exact standards set by the association. Is there evidence to conclude that the population proportion of all hotels in the country satisfying the standards set by the Small Luxury Hotels Association is greater than 0.0096?

SOLUTION

Note that in order to use the normal approximation for the sampling distribution of the sample proportion, $\hat{P}$, we must satisfy the rule that both np and nq be at least equal to 5. In this particular example, it is especially important to check this because under the null hypothesis, the population proportion, p, is very small ($p_0 = 0.0096$). This means that a relatively large sample size is needed. The condition is satisfied because $np_0 = 600(0.0096) = 5.76$. The other condition clearly holds.

FIGURE 7–18   Carrying Out the Test, Using $\alpha = 0.10$, in Example (k)

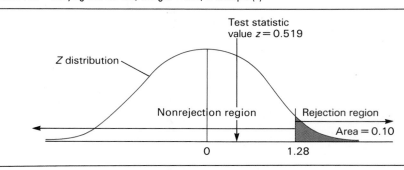

Our test is a right-hand-tailed test, as we are trying to prove that the proportion of hotels that satisfy the standards is greater than $p_0 = 0.0096$. The null and alternative hypotheses are: H_0: $p \le 0.0096$ and H_1: $p > 0.0096$. Again, no particular level of significance, α, is given, so let us first compute the value of the test statistic in this case. From equation 7–8, we find the required value of the test statistic as

$$z = \frac{\hat{p} - p_0}{\sqrt{p_0 q_0/n}} = \frac{(7/600) - 0.0096}{\sqrt{(0.0096)(0.9904)/600}} = 0.519$$

As can be seen, this result is not significant at any conventional level of significance because even if we were to take a 0.10 chance of a type I error, our right-hand critical point would be equal to $+1.28$, and the value of the test statistic would still lie in the nonrejection region. Clearly, for all smaller levels of α, we would also have to accept the null hypothesis. We conclude that there is no statistical evidence to indicate that the association's claims are exaggerated. The test, carried out at the large level of significance $\alpha = 0.10$, is shown in Figure 7–18.

At this point, you may ask why we used a significance level of $\alpha = 0.10$ as the largest value for the probability of a type I error. Couldn't we have used larger values and shown that there really is no sufficient evidence that the null hypothesis is false? The computed test statistic value 0.519 lies inside the acceptance region for values of α even much larger than 0.10. How large would α have to be for us to *reject* the null hypothesis? That is, what is the "true" level of significance of this test—the *smallest* value of α for which we may reject the null hypothesis? This is the *p-value*, the topic of the next section.

PROBLEMS

Answer

In the following problems, first determine whether the required test is one-tailed or two-tailed, and then solve the problem. You will have to make your own decisions: what kind of test to use, whether it is one- or two-tailed, which is the appropriate distribution, and—in many cases—you will have to choose your own level of significance, α. As an aid in deciding whether a test is one-tailed or two-tailed, always ask yourself: Under what conditions do I want to take an action? The answer to this question will indicate to you the alternative hypothesis. (But remember that the equal sign must be in the null hypothesis.)

7–22.
——
$p = 0.0011$

7–22.   An advertisement claims that three out of five doctors recommend a certain pharmaceutical product. The manufacturer of a competing brand of the medicine believes that this claim is exaggerated and sets out to prove so. A random sample of 100 doctors reveals that only 45 of them recommend the brand in question. Can you reject the manufacturer's claim?

7–23. An advertisement for the Princess Hotel of Bermuda lists the price per person for weekend business meetings of more than 15 people as $194 (including airfare). The advertisement, which appeared in leading business journals, claims that $250 per person is the average price charged by hotels on the East Coast for business meetings of comparable length and attendance. The point of the advertisement was that it was cheaper to have a business meeting at the Princess in Bermuda than to have the meeting "at home" on the East Coast. A company planning a business meeting wanted to check whether the reported average price of $250 was correct or whether the Princess had exaggerated the East Coast average to make its own rate look good. A random sample of 19 hotels offering business meeting facilities gave a sample mean of $143 and a sample standard deviation of $52. Is there evidence to conclude that the advertisement for the Princess is false?

7–24. The theory of finance allows for the computation of "excess" returns, either above or below the current stock market average. An analyst wants to determine whether stocks in a certain industry group earn either above or below the market average at a certain time period. The null hypothesis is that there are no excess returns, on the average, in the industry in question. "No average excess returns" means that the population excess return for the industry is zero. A random sample of 24 stocks in the industry reveals a sample average excess return of 0.12 and sample standard deviation of 0.2. State the null and alternative hypotheses, and carry out the test at the $\alpha = 0.05$ level of significance.

7–25. The average weekly earnings for all full-time-equivalent employees are reported to be $344. Suppose that you want to check this claim since you believe it is too low. You want to prove that average weekly earnings of all employees are higher than the amount stated. You collect a random sample of 1,200 employees in all areas and find that the sample mean is $361 and the sample standard deviation is $110. Can you disprove the claim?

7–26. A recent article claims that 25% of Hong Kong's total imports are in the form of capital goods.[9] An international trade company hires a consultant to check this claim. The trade company feels that if there is evidence that more than 25% of Hong Kong's imports are in the form of capital goods, the company may find it profitable to trade with Hong Kong. If, however, the consultant should conclude that only 25% or less of Hong Kong's trade is in the form of capital goods, the trading potential for the company may not be high enough, and no action should be taken. The consultant looks at a random sample of 180 imports to Hong Kong and finds that 52 of these import items are capital goods. Advise the trading company.

7–27. The U.S. Department of Commerce estimates that 17% of all automobiles on the road in the United States at a certain time are made in Japan. An organization that wants to limit imports believes that the proportion of Japanese cars on the road during the period in question is higher than 17% and wants to prove this. A random sample of 2,000 cars is observed, 381 of which are made in Japan. Conduct the hypothesis test at $\alpha = 0.01$ and state whether you believe the reported figure.

7–28. Airplane tires are sensitive to the heat produced when the plane taxis along runways. A certain type of airplane tire used by Boeing is guaranteed to perform well at temperatures as high as 125°F. From time to time, Boeing performs quality control checks to determine whether the average maximum temperature for adequate performance is as stated, or whether the average maximum temperature is lower than 125°, in which case the company must replace all tires. Suppose that a random sample of 100 tires is checked. It is found that the average maximum temperature for adequate performance in the sample is 121° and the sample standard deviation is 2°. Conduct the hypothesis test, and conclude whether the company should take action to replace its tires.

7–29. A marine radar unit for use in small pleasure boats is guaranteed to detect objects as small as a 12-foot boat at an average maximum range of 8 nautical miles. A potential buyer

Answers

7–24.

$t = 2.94$; reject

7–26.

$p = 0.11$

7–28.

$z- = 20$; very small p

[9] J. S. Henley and M. K. Nyaw, "A Reappraisal of the Capital Goods Sector in Hong Kong," *World Development* (June 1985).

Answers

conducts a test of 10 random trials of the radar unit. The results of the trials are that the average maximum distance at which a 12-foot boat was detected was 7.8 nautical miles and the sample standard deviation was 0.4 nautical miles. Use $\alpha = 0.05$ to determine whether the potential buyer should reject the radar manufacturer's claim.

7–30.

$p = 0.089$

7–30.   A study of top executives' midlife crises indicates that 45% of all top executives suffer from some form of mental crisis in the years following corporate success. An executive who had undergone a midlife crisis opened a clinic providing counseling for top executives in the hope of reducing the number of executives who might suffer from this problem. A random sample of 125 executives who went through the program indicated that only 39% of them eventually showed signs of a midlife crisis. Do you believe that the program is beneficial and indeed reduces the proportion of executives who show signs of the crisis?

7–31.   The unemployment rate in Britain during a certain period was believed to have been 11%. At the end of the period in question, the government embarked on a series of projects to reduce unemployment. It was of interest to determine whether the average unemployment rate in the country had decreased as a result of these projects, or whether *previously employed* people were the ones hired for the project jobs, while the unemployed remained unemployed. A random sample of 3,500 people was chosen, and 421 of them were found to be unemployed. Do you believe that the government projects reduced the unemployment rate?

7–32.

$z = 9.6$; very small p

7–32.   Certain eggs are stated to have reduced cholesterol content, with an average of only 2.5% cholesterol. A concerned health group wants to test whether the claim is true. The group believes that more cholesterol may be found, on the average, in the eggs. A random sample of 100 eggs reveals a sample average content of 5.2% cholesterol, and a sample standard deviation of 2.8%. Does the health group have cause for action?

7–33.   The recent move toward internationalization in the financial markets has created an index called the World Market. Movements of stocks in this index reflect the average change in price, in U.S. dollars, of the "average" stock of all issues traded worldwide. For the week of November 24, 1986, the average percentage change in price in the World Market was reported to be -1.1%. An international investment firm regularly checks such reported price changes by collecting a random sample of 180 stocks, proportionally selected from all stock markets included in the World Market. Then a statistical hypothesis test is carried out to determine whether the average percentage change is as reported. The firm has no reason to believe that the actual average world price change is either above or below the reported value; it simply wants to check whether any deviation exists. For the week of November 24, the sample indicated $\bar{x} = -0.9\%$ and $s = 0.4\%$. Should the firm reject the stated average price change in the World Market as incorrect?

7–34.

$t = -8.78$; $t = -27.2$;
both very significant

7–34.   The following advertisement appeared in early 1991 in *Boston* magazine.

INCREASE YOUR BRUNCH BUSINESS WITH BOSTON MAGAZINE'S BRUNCH NOTES.

Whet our readers' appetites for brunch with your ad in Brunch Notes. It's an ideal way to showcase your branch offerings to our 350,000+ monthly readers who are always hungry for new dining experiences.

BOSTON's readers are your best customers. Your ad in Brunch Notes will reach our affluent readers whose average household income is $89,000. And our readers dine out an average of 15.3 times a month.

An agency suspecting that *Boston* magazine was upwardly exaggerating its readers' average household income and frequency of dining out obtained the following data from a random sample of the magazine's readership:

Household income ($1000/year): 45, 52, 30, 67, 90, 58, 35, 60, 44, 28, 50, 37, 69, 108, 46, 33, 48, 40, 65, 72, 39, 61, 56

Dining out (number of times/month): 3, 5, 1, 6, 5, 1, 2, 7, 4, 2, 4, 3, 5, 8, 0, 2, 5, 1, 5, 5, 2, 4, 3

Conduct the appropriate tests, and state your conclusions.

7-35. The following data are three-year gains (percentages) to January 1991 for a random sample of mutual funds. [10]

28.6, 32.9, 35.0, 44.8, 36.5, 42.8, 30.7, 27.4, 39.1, 35.8, 25.9, 30.9, 23.0, 39.1, 27.9, 42.1, 31.6, 33.5, 44.1, 38.2, 41.0, 37.8, 36.5, 28.3, 8.8, 40.8, 37.1, 27.5, 16.3, 29.3, 37.4, 57.3, 9.4, 26.9, 34.8, 61.6, 19.4, 45.2.

Use these data to test the following statement made by salespeople for one mutual fund: "Our three-year return is higher than that of the average mutual fund, which made only 35%."

7-36. An article about transatlantic business claims that British Airways carried 11% of the 27 million people who fly across the Atlantic every year. [11] Suppose that you want to check this claim without any prior suspicion in mind. You get a random sample of passenger files from a random sample of travel agents, and you find that out of 2,000 people in your sample, 341 flew across the Atlantic with British Airways. Conduct the test, and state your conclusions.

7-7 The p-Value

From all our examples, you already have an idea as to the nature of the p-value. Let us return to Example (k) of section 7-6, where we tested the null hypothesis H_0: $p \le 0.0096$ versus the alternative hypothesis H_1: $p > 0.0096$. Our sample size was large, and we used the approximate normal distribution of the sample proportion estimator. We computed the statistic $z = (\hat{p} - p_0)/\sqrt{p_0 q_0/n}$, and we found its value to be 0.519. We stated that this value of the test statistic leads us to accept the null hypothesis even at a significance level $\alpha = 0.10$ because the value 0.519 falls in the acceptance region for $\alpha = 0.10$, defined by the critical point $z = +1.28$. We also noted that we used $\alpha = 0.10$ because it is the largest conventional level of significance employed, and if we have to accept the null hypothesis at this level, surely we have to accept it at smaller values of α, which lead to greater values for the critical point (since 0.519 is smaller than 1.28, it is also smaller than 1.645, which corresponds to $\alpha = 0.05$). However, we know that 0.519 is *much* smaller than 1.28. Is it not true then, that the null hypothesis could also be accepted at values of α larger than 0.10? The answer is yes, and we can—in the case of the normal distribution—actually compute the smallest possible α at which we may reject the null hypothesis. [12]

Let us ask ourselves: At what level, α, can we reject the null hypothesis, given that the value of our test statistic is $z = 0.519$, if we should insist on rejecting the null hypothesis? We know that the area to the right of 1.645 is 0.05, which is why

---

[10] "Guide to Mutual Funds," *Money* (February 1991), pp. 129–68.

[11] "Passing Through Paris," *Forbes* (April 1, 1991), p. 90.

[12] This can be done also with the *t* distribution, as well as other distributions, although it is more difficult (due to the limitations of our tables) and usually requires a computer.

we may reject the null hypothesis at the 0.05 level of significance if our test statistic value is as small as 1.645. Similarly, the area to the right of 1.28 is 0.10, which is why we could reject the null hypothesis at the 0.10 level if our test statistic is as small as 1.28. By this reasoning, let us find the area to the right of the actual computed value of our test statistic. That is, we seek the area to the right of $z = 0.519$. This area represents the smallest probability of a type I error, the smallest possible level α at which we may reject the null hypothesis. From Appendix C, Table 2, the table of probabilities of the standard normal distribution, we find that the area to the right of $z = 0.519$ is $0.5 - 0.1982$ (using an interpolation) $= 0.3018$. This number is called the *p-value*. The number 0.3018 means that, assuming that the null hypothesis is true, there is a 0.3018 probability of obtaining a test statistic value as extreme as we have (0.519) or more extreme (i.e., further to the *right* of $z = 0.519$ since this is a right-hand-tailed test). Since this probability is rather high (much higher than the usually acceptable probability of a type I error: 0.01, 0.05, or even 0.10), we should accept the null hypothesis.

Let us look at another example and then formally define the *p*-value and explore its ramifications. Returning to Example (h), section 7–6, we see that the value of the test statistic in this example is $z = (\bar{x} - \mu_0)/(s/\sqrt{n}) = 2.5$. Clearly, this value of the test statistic leads us to reject the null hypothesis at values of α as small as 0.01 because the critical point for $\alpha = 0.01$ is 2.326, and $z = 2.5$ falls farther to the right—in the rejection region. However, 0.01 is not the *smallest* value of α at which we may reject the null hypothesis. To find the smallest level of significance at which H_0 may be rejected, that is, the *p*-value, we need to find the area to the right of our computed value of the test statistic, $z = 2.5$. Looking in Table 2, we find the required probability as: $0.5 - 0.4938 = 0.0062$. Thus, assuming that the null hypothesis is true, there is only a 0.0062 probability of observing a value of the test statistic as extreme as 2.5 or more extreme (larger than 2.5). If we were willing to take a 0.01 probability of committing a type I error, we could reject the null hypothesis. Even if we were willing to accept a probability of only 0.0062 of committing a type I error, we could still reject the null hypothesis. The *p*-value 0.0062 is the smallest value of α at which we may reject the null hypothesis. Suppose someone wants to take only a 0.001 probability of committing a type I error. Here that person could not reject the null hypothesis because the smallest probability of a type I error at which we may reject this particular hypothesis, given our value of z, is 0.0062.

In Example (i), section 7–6, the obtained value of the test statistic is $z = -0.4$, and the test is a left-hand-tailed test. Here the *p*-value is given as the area to the *left* of $z = -0.4$. Again, using the normal probability table, we find:

FIGURE 7–19   Computing the *p*-Value in Example (k)

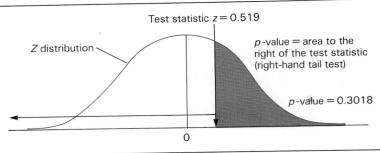

Test statistic $z = 0.519$

Z distribution

p-value = area to the right of the test statistic (right-hand tail test)

p-value = 0.3018

0

p-value $= 0.5 - 0.1554 = 0.3446$. Here we may reject the null hypothesis only if we are willing to take a 0.3446 chance of committing a type I error. We therefore must accept the null hypothesis if we use any conventional level of significance, α. Figures 7–19, 7–20, and 7–21 demonstrate the evaluation of the p-value in Examples (k), (h), and (i), respectively.

We now define the p-value:

> The **p-value** is the smallest level of significance, α, at which a null hypothesis may be rejected using the obtained value of the test statistic.

Another way of looking at the p-value is as follows.

> The p-value is the probability of obtaining a value of the test statistic as extreme as, or more extreme than, the actual value obtained, when the null hypothesis is true.

Logically, if our obtained value of the test statistic is not very likely (i.e., has a small p-value) assuming that the null hypothesis is true, then we should reject the null hypothesis. Similarly, if the obtained value of the test statistic is relatively likely (i.e., has a high p-value, say, above 0.05 or 0.10), then we should accept the null hypothesis because there is no convincing evidence to reject it.

The p-value acts as a "personalized" level of significance that goes with our value of the test statistic. It is the *exact α*, or *attained α*, attached to the test statistic value we have and at which we may reject the null hypothesis. If this "exact α" is

FIGURE 7–20 Computing the p-Value in Example (h)

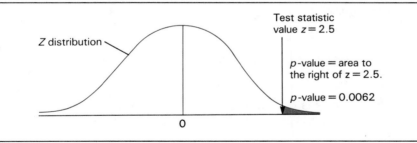

FIGURE 7–21 Computing the p-Value in Example (i)

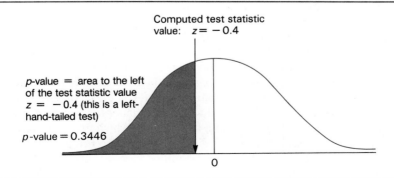

greater than, say, 0.05, then we must accept the null hypothesis at $\alpha = 0.05$. If, on the other hand, the p-value is smaller than 0.05, we may reject the null hypothesis at $\alpha = 0.05$.

Reporting the p-value of a test is therefore a more general (less restrictive) way of reporting results of statistical hypothesis tests: it leaves the choice of α to the person using the results rather than the statistician performing the test. For example, suppose a test is carried out and we report that its p-value is 0.0002. This conveys much information to the reader. It tells him or her that the null hypothesis can be rejected at $\alpha = 0.01$ and that it can be rejected even at smaller values of α, such as 0.001. In fact, this p-value says that the null hypothesis can be rejected at values of α as small as $\alpha = 0.0002$. It also tells the receiver of the information that—assuming the null hypothesis is true—the probability of obtaining a test statistic value as extreme as the value obtained in the experiment, or more extreme than the obtained value, is 0.0002. Here, if one chooses to reject the null hypothesis given the obtained value of the test statistic, one is willing to take a chance of 2 in 10,000 of committing a type I error and thus "convicting an innocent person." Contrast the information content in the statement "p-value $= 0.0002$" with the very limited amount of information in the statement "we reject the null hypothesis at $\alpha = 0.05$," which could have been the reported result of the same test.

Suppose we have another case, where the p-value is 0.06. Reporting this value allows the reader to reject the null hypothesis if he or she is willing to use $\alpha = 0.06$. If the reader wants to use the $\alpha = 0.05$ level of significance, or anything smaller, then he or she will have to accept the null hypothesis. Reporting the p-value allows the reader to choose his or her own α and still know how to interpret the reported results of the experiment. The following are some rules of thumb developed by statisticians as aids in interpreting p-values.

When the p-value is *smaller than 0.01*, the result is called *very significant*.

When the p-value is *between 0.01 and 0.05*, the result is called *significant*.

When the p-value is *between 0.05 and 0.10*, the result is considered by some as *marginally significant* (and by others as not significant).

When the p-value is *greater than 0.10*, the result is considered by most as *not significant*.

Reporting and using the p-value eliminates the necessity of making standard conclusions that may be too restrictive. Reporting a p-value of 0.000003 implies that the result is very unlikely if the null hypothesis is true; therefore, we feel *strongly* about rejecting the null hypothesis. The p-value gets smaller as the test statistic falls further away in the tail of the distribution. Therefore, even if we are unable to compute the p-value exactly, we may have an idea about its size. For example, suppose that we compute the value of a test statistic as $z = 120.97$. In a right-hand-tailed test, this means that the p-value is equal to the area under the standard normal curve to the right of the point 120.97. Without a computer (which may not even give accurate results for a value as large as 120.97), we are unable to compute the exact p-value. We do know, however, that this probability is very, very small. We may then say that the p-value, although unknown, is an extremely small number; hence, we reject the null hypothesis with much conviction.

The further away in the tail of the distribution our test statistic falls, the smaller is the *p*-value and, hence, the more convinced we are that the null hypothesis is false and should be rejected.

Conversely, the closer our test statistic is to the center of the sampling distribution, the larger is the *p*-value; hence, we may be more convinced that we do not have enough evidence to reject the null hypothesis and should therefore accept it.

If you understand the idea of a *p*-value, and use it, your statistical conclusions will be more meaningful and more convincing. Try to report the *p*-value when you can compute it, or at least make a statement about its relative magnitude ("small *p*-value," "very small *p*-value," etc.) when you cannot compute it.

The t Distribution, the Chi-Square Distribution, and Others

In the case of statistical tests where the sampling distribution of the test statistic is the *t* distribution, we see from the *t* table (Appendix C, Table 3), that the exact *p*-values are not obtainable because the table contains values for only a few selected, "standard" values of α, such as 0.01 or 0.05. What do we do in such situations? As mentioned earlier, it is always possible to make some relative statements about the *p*-value. For example, suppose that in a left-hand-tailed test we get a value of the test statistic $t = -2.4$, with df $= 15$. What is the *p*-value? From Appendix C, Table 3, we find that the value 2.4 for a *t* random variable with 15 degrees of freedom falls between the two values 2.131 and 2.602, corresponding to one-tail areas of 0.025 and 0.01, respectively. We may, therefore, conclude that the *p*-value is between 0.01 and 0.025. The use of a computer may allow us to give a more exact *p*-value. We know that the further in the tail the test statistic falls, the smaller the *p*-value. If we get a *t* statistic with 23 degrees of freedom equaling, say, 45.33, then we know that the *p*-value is very, very small (the area to the right of 2.807 is 0.005, from Table 3). The same holds for the chi-square distribution, as well as other distributions we will encounter that have few tabulated tail areas.

Two-Tailed Tests

In a two-tailed test, we find the *p*-value by *doubling* the area in the tail of the distribution beyond the value of the test statistic.

In Example (d), we found that the value of the test statistic was $z = (\overline{x} - \mu_0)/(s/\sqrt{n}) = 1.21$. What is the *p*-value? We must first find the area to the right of 1.21 (since 1.21 is a positive number, the area to its left would be over 0.5; if doubled, this would give the meaningless result of a number over 1.00). We find that the area to the right of $z = 1.21$ is equal to $0.5 - 0.3869$ (from Appendix C, Table 2) $= 0.1131$. Now, since the test is two-tailed, we must double the probability. The *p*-value is therefore equal to $2(0.1131) = 0.2262$. You may gain a feeling for the reason that the *p*-value must be twice the value it is for a one-tailed test from noting the following. The *z* value 1.645 corresponds to $\alpha = 0.05$ in a right-hand-tailed test, but corresponds to $\alpha = 0.10$ in a two-tailed test. In a two-tailed test, there is another tail where possible rejection of the null hypothesis may occur. That tail contains an equal area beyond the negative of the obtained *z* value, on the other side of the distribution. The *p*-value for a one-tailed test and the *p*-value for a two-tailed test are shown in Figure 7–22.

When we calculate the *p*-value, we are calculating the probability of obtaining a value of the test statistic as extreme as, or more extreme than, the value we have. If

FIGURE 7–22   The *p*-Value in a One-Tailed Test versus the *p*-Value in a Two-Tailed Test [Using the Statistic Value in Example (i)]

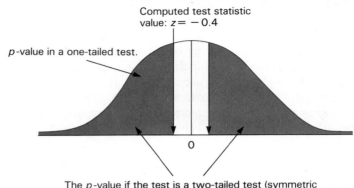

Computed test statistic value: $z = -0.4$

p-value in a one-tailed test.

0

The *p*-value if the test is a two-tailed test (symmetric area on both sides of 0. The area to the left of $z = -0.4$ *and* the area to the right of 0.4).

the null hypothesis in a two-tailed test is true, then we may obtain our value or more extreme values on *both* sides of the distribution, possibly leading us to commit a type I error in either of the two tails of the distribution. We must account for these possibilities and double the area in a single tail when calculating the *p*-value. In Example (d), we must account for values as extreme as, and more extreme than, 1.21 under the null hypothesis. We must account for values greater than or equal to 1.21, but we must also account for the possibility, under the null hypothesis, of obtaining the value -1.21 and all values to its left, which are *as likely* under the null hypothesis as the positive values 1.21 and beyond.

Since in a two-tailed test we may reject both on the left and on the right, and since under H_0 the positive and the negative values of the same absolute magnitude are equally likely, we must allow for this and include in the *p*-value both the area in the tail on which the test statistic falls and an equal area in the other tail of the distribution. This is demonstrated in Figure 7–23.

FIGURE 7–23   The *p*-Value in a Two-Tailed Test

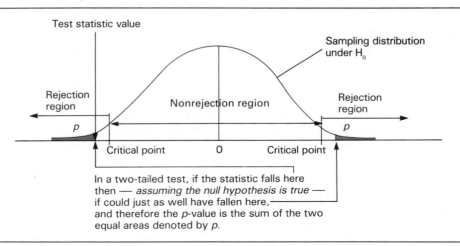

Test statistic value

Sampling distribution under H_o

Rejection region

Nonrejection region

Rejection region

p

p

Critical point   0   Critical point

In a two-tailed test, if the statistic falls here then — *assuming the null hypothesis is true* — if could just as well have fallen here, and therefore the *p*-value is the sum of the two equal areas denoted by *p*.

To summarize:

In a right-hand-tailed test, the *p*-value is the area to the right of the test statistic if the test statistic is positive.

In a left-hand-tailed test, the *p*-value is the area to the left of the test statistic if the test statistic is negative.

In a two-tailed test, the *p*-value is twice the area to the right of a positive test statistic or to the left of a negative test statistic.

For a quick interpretation of reported *p*-values you may want to use the following rule.

For a given level of significance, α:

Reject the null hypothesis if and only if $\alpha \geq p$-value.

In other words, a result is *significant* at level α if the associated *p*-value is less than or equal to α. This rule is useful when looking at tables of reported results, such as computer-generated test results. It is easy to scan the results, comparing *p*-values (often reported as "significance") with, say, the value 0.05. Any result with a *p*-value less than or equal to 0.05 will then be noted as significant at the $\alpha = 0.05$ level. Remember, however, that a *p*-value contains much more information than just whether or not to reject the null hypothesis at a *given* level of significance, α. The *p*-value tells us how unusual our particular sample result is if we assume that the null hypothesis is true. This, in turn, gives us an indication as to how strongly we should feel about rejecting (or not rejecting) the null hypothesis in light of our evidence.

PROBLEMS

In the following problems, report the *p*-value if you can compute it exactly. If you cannot compute the *p*-value, give some bounds on its value or describe it as small, very small, large, etc., and state whether or not you reject the null hypothesis.

Answer

7–37. Several U.S. airlines carry passengers from the United States to countries in the Pacific region, and the competition in these flight routes is keen. One of the leverage factors for United Airlines in Pacific routes is that, whereas most other airlines fly to Pacific destinations two or three times weekly, United offers daily flights to Tokyo, Hong Kong, and Osaka. Before instituting daily flights, the airline needed to get an idea as to the proportion of frequent fliers in these routes who consider daily service an important aspect of business flights to the Pacific. From previous information, the management of United estimated that 60% of the frequent business travelers to the three destinations believed that daily service was an important aspect of airline service. Following changes in the airline industry, marked by reduced fares and other factors, the airline management wanted to check whether or not the proportion of frequent business travelers who believe that daily service is an important feature was still about 60%. A random sample of 250 frequent business fliers revealed that 130 of them thought daily service was important. Compute the *p*-value for this test (is this a one-tailed or a two-tailed test?) and state your conclusion.

7–38. An advertisement for the Toyota Supra model lists the following performance specifications: standing start, 0–50 mph in an average of 5.27 seconds; braking, 60 mph to 0 in 3.15 seconds on the average. An independent testing service hired by a competing manufacturer of high-performance automobiles wants to prove that Toyota's claims are exagger-

7–38.

$p = 0.0026$

Answer

ated. A random sample of 100 trial runs gives the following results: standing start, 0–50 mph in an average of $\bar{x} = 5.8$ seconds and $s = 1.9$ seconds; braking, 60 mph to 0 in an average of $\bar{x} = 3.21$ seconds and $s = 0.6$ seconds. Carry out the two hypothesis tests, state the p-value of each test, and state your conclusions.

7–39.   Borg-Warner manufactures hydroelectric miniturbines that generate low-cost, clean electric power from the energy in small rivers and streams. One of the models was known to produce an average of 25.2 kilowatts of electricity. Recently the model's design was improved, and the company wanted to test whether the model's average electric output had changed. There was no reason to suspect, a priori, a change in either direction. A random sample of 115 trial runs produced an average of 26.1 kilowatts and a standard deviation of 3.2 kilowatts. Carry out a statistical hypothesis test, give the p-value, and state your conclusion. Do you believe that the improved model has a different average output?

7–40.   In early 1986, PepsiCo, Inc., tested a new orange-flavored soft drink, Mandarin Orange Slice. The company's research department determined that if more than 60% of the people who taste the drink like its taste, then the drink will be successful in terms of annual sales volume. Thus, they decided to test the null hypothesis that the proportion of people who respond positively to the new taste is at most 0.60 versus the alternative that the proportion is over 0.60. A random sample of 1,000 people turned out 845 positive responses. What can you say about the p-value of this test? How strongly do you feel about the potential success of Mandarin Orange Slice? Explain.

7–41.   It is claimed that a two-bedroom apartment in Taiwan costs an average of $200,000.[13] This high price supposedly keeps many young Taiwanese couples from owning a home, and a government official in charge of the problem wanted to check whether the stated average is correct or is upwardly inflated. A random sample of 1,000 two-bedroom apartments throughout Taiwan gave a sample mean of $195,200 and a sample standard deviation of $49,750. Conduct the test, and find the p-value. Carefully explain what is happening here, both in statistical terms and in practical terms. Write your conclusions in the form of a memo.

7–42.   The following results on abnormal trading volume of stocks before ex-dividend days are taken from an article in the *Journal of Financial Economics*.[14]

7–40.

$z = 15.8$

7–42.

Yield Group	Trading Size Group	Abnormal Volume ($)	t-Value
very small	1	1	−6,524	−5.16
very small	1	2	−11,433	−5.43
0.003	1	3	−14,957	−2.97
0.012	1	4	60,856	2.51
very small	2	1	−3,023	−5.90
very small	2	2	−7,947	−5.41
0.056	2	3	−9,220	−1.91
0.0016	2	4	116,189	3.17
0.012	3	1	−1,114	−2.50
0.73	3	2	−455	−0.35
0.44	3	3	3,677	0.78
very small	3	4	265,023	7.95
0.13	4	1	811	1.52
very small	4	2	6,560	3.77
very small	4	3	32,288	4.28
very small	4	4	397,997	4.34

The sample size in every case was well over 500; therefore, you may consider the reported t values as z values and use the normal distribution. The test implied in each yield group and

[13] "Rebuilding a Tiger: Who'll Get the Lion's Share?" *Business Week* (March 25, 1991), p. 46.

[14] J. Jakonishok and T. Vermaelen, "Tax-Induced Trading Around Ex-Dividend Days," *Journal of Financial Economics* (July 1986).

trading size group is a test for the existence of average abnormal returns. Without getting into the technical details of these special tests, use the reported z values to determine the p-values. For each yield and trading size combination, state whether or not you believe that average abnormal returns are present in the entire population of stocks in the group. All tests are two-tailed.

7-43. Select a random sample of the problems in the preceding sections of this chapter, and determine the p-values of the hypothesis tests.

7-8 Tests Involving Finite Populations[15]

When we deal with a finite population containing N elements, and when the sample size, n, represents 5% or more of the population, we need to use a finite-population correction factor. Recall from our discussion in Chapter 6 that the finite-population correction factor is given by equation 6-8 as

$$\sqrt{\frac{N - n}{N - 1}}$$

The finite-population correction factor multiplies the standard error of our estimator in hypothesis tests in the same way as in the construction of confidence intervals.

In the case of hypothesis tests of the population mean, μ, we incorporate a finite-population correction factor, by using the standard error given by equation 7-11. (When the population standard deviation, σ, is unknown, we substitute the sample standard deviation, s, for it.)

Standard error of $\overline{X}$ using a finite-population correction factor:

$$\sigma_{\overline{x}} = \frac{\sigma}{\sqrt{n}} \sqrt{\frac{N - n}{N - 1}} \qquad (7\text{--}11)$$

For testing hypotheses about the population proportion, p, the standard error of the sample proportion, $\hat{P}$, that incorporates a finite-population correction factor is given by equation 7-12.

Standard error of $\hat{P}$ using a finite-population correction factor:

$$\sigma_{\hat{P}} = \sqrt{\frac{pq}{n}} \sqrt{\frac{N - n}{N - 1}} \qquad (7\text{--}12)$$

We demonstrate the use of equations 7-11 and 7-12 in hypothesis tests with the following examples.

An accountant wants to test the hypothesis that the average balance of the 1,240 accounts at a sporting goods store is at most $35.00 versus the alternative that the average

EXAMPLE (l)

---

[15] This is an optional section.

account is over $35.00. The sample size used is $n = 100$, and the sampling results are $\bar{x} = \$38.90$ and $s = \$15.00$.

SOLUTION

Since the sample size is $n = 100$, the sampling fraction n/N is $100/1,240 = 0.0806$, which is over 5%. This makes it necessary to use the finite-population correction factor. The hypotheses are H_0: $\mu \leq 35$ and H_1: $\mu > 35$. We now compute the test statistic, using equation 7–11 for the standard error of $\bar{X}$. We get:

$$z = \frac{\bar{x} - \mu_0}{(s/\sqrt{n})\sqrt{(N-n)/(N-1)}} = \frac{38.9 - 35}{(15/10)\sqrt{(1,140/1,239)}} = 2.71$$

Since this is a right-hand-tailed test, we find that the p-value here is equal to 0.0034, and the null hypothesis can be rejected.

EXAMPLE (m)

A company has 2,000 employees. Management wants to test the null hypothesis that no more than half the employees feel positively about the prospect of a takeover bid by a large multinational corporation, against the alternate hypothesis that more than half the employees feel positively about the impending takeover bid. A random sample of 200 employees is chosen, 180 of whom confess to having a positive feeling about the possible takeover bid. Carry out the hypothesis test.

SOLUTION

We want to test the hypotheses H_0: $p \leq 0.5$ and H_1: $p > 0.5$. The test statistic, using equation 7–12 for the standard error of $\hat{P}$, is:

$$z = \frac{\hat{p} - p_0}{\sqrt{p_0 q_0 (N-n)/n(N-1)}} = \frac{(180/200) - 0.5}{\sqrt{(0.5)(0.5)/200}\sqrt{(1800/1999)}} = 11.92$$

The value of the test statistic is very large with a very small p-value (far outside the range of the normal table). We can therefore conclude that there is strong evidence to reject the null hypothesis and believe that over 50% of all employees feel positively about the takeover bid for their company.

PROBLEMS

Answer

7-44.

p = 0.19

7-44. The Australian firm Elders IXL Ltd. became the first foreign concern to own a major British beermaker, Courage Brewing, Ltd., whose beers are sold in Britain's 5,000-odd pubs. Assume that before the takeover, Elders wanted to test the hypothesis that the percentage of pubs in England selling Courage beers is 90% versus the alternative hypothesis that it is over 90%. Elders gathered a random sample of 250 pubs, 229 of which were found to carry Courage beers. What conclusion can be made? (Assume there are exactly 5,000 pubs in England.)

7-45. The Star Company recently signed a contract with Southland Corporation to supply videocassettes for rental in 1,400 7-Eleven stores throughout the country. Before signing the agreement, a test was carried out to determine whether average weekly revenues per store for the rental of videocassettes would be over $300, which was considered the break-even value. Thus, it was desired to test the null hypothesis H_0: $\mu \leq 300$ versus the alternative H_1: $\mu > 300$, and to go ahead with the deal only if the null hypothesis can be rejected at $\alpha = 0.01$. A random sample of 400 of the 1,400 7-Eleven stores was chosen. It was found that the sample mean was $521.05 and the sample standard deviation was $102.50. Conduct the test and state your conclusion. What effect did the finite-population correction have in this case?

7–46. An analyst wants to test the null hypothesis that the average price change for all stocks listed in the Fortune 500 for a given week is zero, versus the alternative hypothesis that the average price change for the Fortune 500 stocks is not zero. A random sample of 45 stocks listed in the Fortune 500 gives $\bar{x} = +\$0.125$ and $s = \$0.275$. What is the p-value? What should the analyst conclude?

7–47. There are 155 banks involved in certain international transactions. A federal agency claims that at least 35% of these banks have total assets of over $10 billion (in U.S. dollars). An independent agency wants to test this claim. It gets a random sample of 50 out of the 155 banks and finds that 15 of them have total assets of over $10 billion. Can the claim be rejected?

7–48. An importer of jewelry from Italy has just received a shipment of 1,500 pieces of jewelry of the same kind. Usually, the shipment is acceptable if no more than 8% of the pieces are damaged. The importer gathers a random sample of 100 pieces and finds that 11 of them are damaged. Should the shipment be rejected on the grounds that over 8% of the total shipment is damaged?

Answers

7–46.

p = 0.0014

7–48.

p = 0.13

7–9 Tests of Hypotheses about the Population Variance[16]

In section 6–6 (Chapter 6), we noted that in some cases it is of interest to draw inferences about the population variance, σ^2. Examples of such situations involve production processes where the variance of the number of items produced by a machine must be controlled to within some upper bound, or the time spent in waiting lines, the variance of which must also be relatively small to prevent the queue from building up. While two-tailed tests *may* be carried out, it is usually of interest to test whether the population variance *exceeds* some level—in which case an action should be taken. Thus, a right-hand-tailed test is most useful. The distribution used is the chi-square distribution with $n - 1$ degrees of freedom, and the test statistic is given by:

Test statistic for the population variance:

$$\chi^2 = \frac{(n - 1)s^2}{\sigma_0^2} \qquad (7\text{–}13)$$

where σ_0^2 is the value of the variance stated in the null hypothesis

---

Tests using the chi-square distribution require the assumption of a *normally distributed population*. The rationale of a hypothesis test for the variance is the following: If the null hypothesis is true and the population variance is indeed σ_0^2, then the quantity in equation 7–13 possesses a chi-square distribution with $n - 1$ degrees of freedom. Hence, the probability that the statistic χ^2 will exceed any value is given by the area to the right of that value under the chi-square curve with $n - 1$ degrees of freedom. For example, suppose that some variable χ^2 has the chi-square distribution with 21 degrees of freedom. Then the probability that the variable will exceed 41.4 is 0.005. This is seen by consulting Appendix C, Table 4, and noting that the critical point for a right-hand tail area of 0.005 for a chi-square variable with 21 degrees of freedom is 41.4. This is shown in Figure 7–24.

Suppose that a null hypothesis about the variance is false and that the population

---

[16] This is an optional section.

FIGURE 7–24   A Critical Point of the Chi-Square Distribution with df = 21

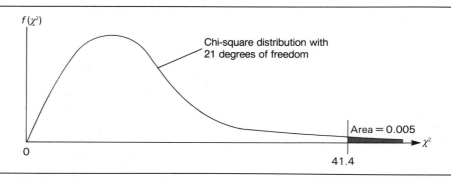

variance is greater than the hypothesized value σ_0^2. Then the quantity in equation 7–13 will be greater than some critical point of the chi-square distribution, leading to the rejection of the null hypothesis. So, if we observe a value of the test statistic, χ^2, larger than, say, the critical point for $\alpha = 0.05$, we may reject the null hypothesis, taking a 0.05 chance of committing a type I error (if the null hypothesis is true, then only 5% of the time we would observe χ^2 values above that critical point). Let us look at an example.

EXAMPLE (n)

A machine makes small metal plates that are used in batteries for electronic games. The diameter of a plate is a random variable with mean 5 mm. As long as the variance of the diameter of the plates is at most 1.00 (mm²), the production process is under control and the plates are acceptable. If, however, the variance exceeds 1.00, the machine must be repaired. A quality-control engineer wants, therefore, to test the following hypotheses: H_0: $\sigma^2 \leq 1.00$ and H_1: $\sigma^2 > 1.00$. The engineer collects a random sample of 31 plates and finds that the sample variance is $s^2 = 1.62$. Is there evidence that the variance of the production process is above 1.00?

SOLUTION

We compute the test statistic χ^2 of equation 7–13:

$$\chi^2 = \frac{(n-1)s^2}{\sigma_0^2} = \frac{(30)(1.62)}{(1.00)} = 48.6$$

From Appendix C, Table 4, we find that, for a chi-square random variable with 30 degrees of freedom, the critical point for $\alpha = 0.05$ in a right-hand-tailed test is 43.77. Therefore, the null hypothesis may be rejected at the 0.05 level of significance. For $\alpha = 0.025$, we find that the critical point is 46.98, so we may still reject the null hypothesis at this level. On the other hand, for $\alpha = 0.01$, the critical point is 50.89, and the null hypothesis must be accepted at this level of significance. These values allow us to establish bounds on the p-value for this test: the p-value is between 0.025 and 0.01. Reject the null hypothesis if you are willing to take a 0.025 chance of a type I error; accept the null hypothesis if you want to take no more than a 0.01 chance of a type I error. Since this is a production process, the engineer should probably decide to stop production and service the machine. The test is shown in Figure 7–25.

When we need to use a chi-square distribution that is not listed in Table 4, approximate values may be used. Also, recall that as the degrees of freedom increase,

FIGURE 7–25   Carrying Out the Test of Example (n)

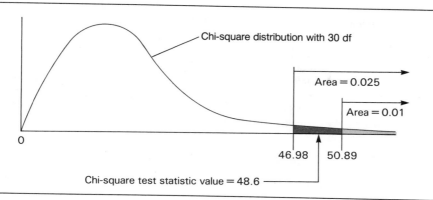

χ^2 approaches a normal distribution with mean df and variance 2 df (this is due to a form of the central limit theorem). This can be used in finding the critical points for a test. For example, if we have a chi-square random variable with 150 degrees of freedom, we may use as an approximation a normal random variable with $\mu = 150$ and standard deviation $\sigma = \sqrt{300}$ (because the variance is twice 150). Find the right-hand critical point for this distribution using $\alpha = 0.05$. The solution is as follows. For the standard normal random variable Z, we know that the critical point would be 1.645. Here we need to find the point for a normal random variable with mean $\mu = 150$ and standard deviation $\sigma = \sqrt{300} = 17.32$. The critical point is $\mu + 1.645\sigma = 150 + (1.645)(17.32) = 178.49$. Let us find the two critical points for a two-tailed test at $\alpha = 0.05$ for a chi-square random variable with 100 degrees of freedom, using the normal approximation. They are: $\mu \pm 1.96\sigma = 100 \pm 1.96(\sqrt{200}) = 100 \pm 1.96(14.1421) = 72.28$ and 127.72. These values are close to the corresponding table values for df = 100.[17]

PROBLEMS

7–49.   An economist wants to test the null hypothesis that the variance of family incomes in the population in a certain region is less than or equal to 25,000,000 (dollars squared) versus the alternative that it is over 25,000,000. A random sample of 25 families gives a sample standard deviation of 7,000. Conduct the test at $\alpha = 0.01$, and state your conclusion.

7–50.   An accountant wants to test the null hypothesis that the variance of the amounts in company accounts is equal to 10,000 (dollars squared) versus the alternative that the variance is not equal to 10,000. A random sample of 30 accounts gives a sample variance of 13,896. Conduct the two-tailed test at the $\alpha = 0.05$ level of significance.

7–51.   Computer integrated manufacturing (CIM) is a method of integrating all manufacturing activities and controlling them by a central computer. The biggest problem faced by companies using CIM is system failure. The problem is that when the computer goes down, the entire manufacturing system shuts down. Stratus is one company that installs CIM systems for its clients. Once Stratus installs a system, it checks not only for the mean time until system failure occurs, but also for the variance of times until failure. If the variance of failure times is believed to be above 530 (days squared), the system is reworked. System testing is carried

Answer

7–50.

not significant

---

[17] A better approximation is possible with the formula: $\chi^2 = \frac{1}{2}(z + \sqrt{2\ df - 1})^2$. In this example, we get $\chi_1^2 = 73.77$ and $\chi_2^2 = 129.07.7$

Answer

out by computer, which allows running the system many times until failure without requiring the use of "real time." One such simulation was equivalent to a random sample of 300 time-until-failure trials and revealed a sample variance of 544. Is there evidence that the system needs reworking?

7–52.

7–52. If the variance of waiting times at a certain bank is believed to be over 1.5 (minutes squared), the system needs adjustment. Such adjustments may include replacing tellers, adding tellers, or enrolling tellers in a training program. The bank regularly checks to see whether or not there is evidence that the variance of waiting times is above the allowed level. A random sample of 60 waiting times gives a sample variance of 1.8 minutes squared. Conduct the test, give an approximate p-value, and state your conclusion.

$p > 0.1$

7–10 The Probability of a Type II Error and the Power of the Test[18]

You may have wondered why, until now, we have only concerned ourselves with the probability of a type I error, α—completely ignoring β, the probability of committing a type II error. Part of the reason for this is that we have determined—consistent with our analogy of the legal system—that a type I error is more serious than a type II error, and, therefore, we should try to control the type I error by setting its probability to a small level, α. From that point, we have carried out our tests at given levels of significance without knowing our probabilities of committing errors of type II.

Another reason we have ignored the type II error probability for so long is that it is complicated to compute, due to the fact that this probability depends on the particular value of the parameter, out of all values covered by the alternative hypothesis. Recall that, in the case of tests for μ, we said that β should actually be written $\beta(\mu)$ to indicate this dependence. We will now see why β depends on the value of the parameter. We will compute the probability β in certain situations, as well as the value $1 - \beta$, called the *power* of the test. As a simple example, let us consider the following hypothesis test:

$$H_0: \mu = 60$$
$$H_1: \mu = 65 \tag{7-14}$$

These hypotheses are of a kind we have not seen before. The set consists of two *simple hypotheses*: either the mean is equal to 60, or it is equal to 65. Usually, our hypotheses are not simple but rather *composite* ones—covering a range of values.

Let us investigate the probability of a type II error in this simple case. Suppose that the sample size is $n = 100$ and that the population standard deviation is known and given as $\sigma = 20$. In our investigation of the probability of a type II error, we will find it convenient to consider the test in the scale of the problem itself, rather than in the standardized z scale. The particular simple test in equation 7–14 is a right-hand-tailed test. We have only two choices: either we conclude that the population mean is equal to 60 (accept the null hypothesis), or we conclude that the population mean is equal to 65 (reject the null hypothesis). Clearly, such a situation rarely arises in a real application because it is too restrictive. This type of hypothesis testing is useful, however, in helping us understand the type II error and its probability.

Let us now determine the rejection region and the critical point for a given level of significance $\alpha = 0.05$. We know that the value of Z for a right-hand-tailed test at $\alpha = 0.05$ is $z = 1.645$. Transforming this value to the scale of the problem in order to determine the critical point, C, we have: $C = \mu_0 + 1.645\sigma/\sqrt{n} = 60 +$

---

[18] In a short course, this section may be optional. However, some discussion of power should be provided from this section.

FIGURE 7-26   Determining the Rejection Region and the Probability of a Type II Error for the Test in Equation 7-14

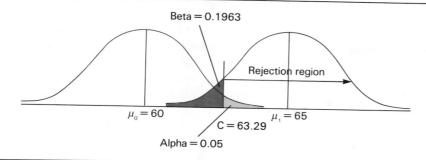

1.645(20/10) = 63.29. The critical point and the rejection region are shown in Figure 7-26.

The figure shows two curves. One is the curve corresponding to the sampling distribution of $\bar{X}$ if the null hypothesis is true; this is the curve centered over the mean $\mu = 60$. The area under this curve to the right of the critical point $C = 63.29$ is equal to 0.05. This is the probability that the sample mean $\bar{X}$ will fall above the critical point when the population mean is indeed equal to 60; it is the probability of a type I error. Now, however, we are also interested in the probability of a type II error. The true state of nature could be only one of two possibilities: either the population mean is 60 (null hypothesis) or it is 65 (alternative hypothesis). Therefore, a type II error occurs if and only if we should decide that the true mean is 60 (i.e., accept the null hypothesis) when in reality the alternative hypothesis is true and the population mean is 65. The question here is: When is a type II error committed? A type II error is committed if the test statistic $\bar{X}$ falls to the left of the critical point C when the population mean is equal to 65. This is so because if the mean is 65 and the test statistic falls to the left of C, then the test statistic is in the acceptance region of the null hypothesis. We then accept a false null hypothesis.

What is the probability, β, of committing such an error? *The probability that $\bar{X}$ will fall to the left of point C when the population mean is $\mu = 65$ is given by the area to the left of C under the normal curve centered over the mean 65.* We have the following conditional probabilities.

Probability of type I error:
$$\alpha = P(\bar{X} > C | \mu = \mu_0) \qquad (7-15)$$

Probability of type II error:
$$\beta = P(\bar{X} < C | \mu = \mu_1) \qquad (7-16)$$

The probability α was preset to 0.05 by construction. The probability of the type II error, β, is not determined by us; it is whatever the area to the left of C under the curve centered at 65 may be. Let us solve equation 7-16 to find the value of β.

$$\beta = P(\bar{X} < C | \mu = \mu_1) = P\left(\frac{\bar{X} - \mu_1}{\sigma/\sqrt{n}} < \frac{C - \mu_1}{\sigma/\sqrt{n}}\right)$$

$$= P\left(Z < \frac{63.29 - 65}{20/10}\right)$$

$$= P(Z < -0.855) = 0.1963$$

Thus, our probability of erroneously deciding to accept the null hypothesis that the population mean is 60, when in reality the population mean is equal to 65, is $\beta = 0.1963$.

We solved equation 7–16 for β by noting the following: If the alternative hypothesis is true, then the population mean is equal to μ_1, which is 65. Under this assumption, $\overline{X}$ is a normally distributed random variable (by the central limit theorem) with mean 65 and with the same standard error as in the case where H_0 is true: $\sigma/\sqrt{n}$. Therefore, in order to evaluate the probability β, we transform $\overline{X}$ into Z using the value μ_1 as the mean of $\overline{X}$.

The situation is shown in Figure 7–26 with both curves and both areas. We conclude that carrying out this hypothesis test allows us a 0.05 chance of rejecting the null hypothesis when the null hypothesis is true, and a 0.1963 chance of accepting the null hypothesis when the null hypothesis is false and the actual population mean is 65. We now define the *power* of a statistical hypothesis test.

> The **power** of a statistical hypothesis test is the probability of rejecting the null hypothesis when the null hypothesis is false.

Thus, the power of a test is the probability of rejecting a null hypothesis that should indeed be rejected. Clearly, the probability of rejecting H_0 when H_0 is false is equal to 1 minus the probability of accepting H_0 when H_0 is false. Thus, we have:

$$\text{Power} = 1 - \beta \qquad (7\text{–}17)$$

The term *power* is quite appropriate. Considering the fact that we want to reject null hypotheses that are false, a test is *powerful* if it gives us a high probability of rejecting a false null hypothesis. Power is a measure of our ability to demonstrate that H_1, rather than H_0, is the correct hypothesis. In the preceding example, the power of the test is equal to $1 - \beta = 1 - 0.1963 = 0.8037$. We have a 0.8037 chance of rejecting the null hypothesis when the true mean is 65 rather than 60 as stated in the null hypothesis.

In most situations, the hypotheses to be tested are not simple hypotheses like the ones we have just considered. Most hypothesis tests are of the composite type; that is, they include a range of values to be tested. Whatever the form of our test, the null hypothesis always contains a single number to be used in carrying out the test (this is the value obtained from the equal sign in the null hypothesis). For example, the null hypothesis $H_0: \mu \leq 60$ is tested as if it were $H_0: \mu = 60$ because 60 is the maximum of all values of μ under the null hypothesis. The assumption of "innocence" means we allow the mean to be as large as 60, and test to see if it is greater than this maximum value. In two-tailed tests, the null hypothesis contains a single value only. However, the alternative hypothesis (except in simple cases such as the one just considered) always contains many—in fact, infinitely many—possible values. If the null hypothesis is $H_0: \mu \leq 60$, then the alternative hypothesis is $H_1: \mu > 60$. How can we define the power of the test in such situations?

Power is the probability of rejecting the null hypothesis when the null hypothesis is false. But in the example above, the null hypothesis can be false in an infinite

TABLE 7-3   The Power of the Test at Selected Values of μ under H_1

Value of μ	β	Power = $1 - \beta$
61	0.8739	0.1261
62	0.7405	0.2595
63	0.5577	0.4423
64	0.3613	0.6387
65	0.1963	0.8037
66	0.0877	0.9123
67	0.0318	0.9682
68	0.0092	0.9908
69	0.0021	0.9979

FIGURE 7-27
Power at Different Values of μ

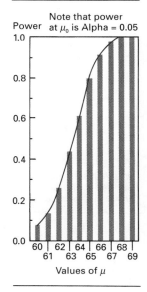

number of ways: the population mean could be 61, or 67, or 72.8653, or 999.87, or *any* value above 60. What, then, is the probability of correctly rejecting the null hypothesis when the population mean is any number above 60? It should be easy to see that this probability depends on the actual value of the population mean. The larger the population mean, μ, the greater the probability that the sample mean, $\overline{X}$, will fall away from 60 and away from the critical point, C, determined by our level of significance, α. The power is demonstrated for the hypothesis test $H_0: \mu \leq 60$ versus $H_1: \mu > 60$ for various values of μ covered by the alternative hypothesis. We assume that the sample size is $n = 100$, the population standard deviation is $\sigma = 20$, and $\alpha = 0.05$. This is shown in Figure 7-27. The actual power, evaluated at each of several selected values of μ, is given in Table 7-3. Note that the figure also shows the power at $\mu = \mu_0 = 60$. This is the probability of rejecting the null hypothesis when $\mu = \mu_0$—the probability of a type I error, $\alpha = 0.05$.

Table 7-3 contains the value of β for each selected value of μ_1 and the corresponding power, $1 - \beta$. (The values selected for the table are integers, although the power is defined for any value μ_1, integer or otherwise.) We see that the power of a test depends on the possible values of the population parameter under the alternative hypothesis. Thus, both the probability of a type II error, β, and its complement, the power, depend on the value of the mean. The dependence of the power on the value of the parameter is called the **power function.** The power function, also called the *power curve*, is shown for our particular test in Figure 7-28.

Note that the values in Table 7-3, which were used in the construction of the function in Figure 7-28, were calculated in exactly the same way we computed the power in the simple hypothesis test described earlier, where the alternative value of the mean was $\mu_1 = 65$. Since our present, composite, one-tailed test has the same critical point, sample size, and assumed standard deviation, the same formula, equation 7-16, applies, and we obtain the values of β by substituting in the equation each appropriate value for the population mean for which we want to compute β and the power. Note that the power as shown for $\mu_1 = 65$ in Table 7-3 conforms with the value we computed earlier in the simple hypothesis test.

The power of a statistical hypothesis test depends on the following factors.

1. The power depends on the distance between the value of the parameter under the null hypothesis and the *true value* of the parameter in question. *The greater this distance, the greater the power.*

FIGURE 7-28
The Power Function (for a One-Tailed Test)

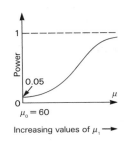

2. The power depends on the population standard deviation. *The smaller the population standard deviation, the greater the power.*

3. The power depends on the sample size used. *The larger the sample, the greater the power.*

4. The power depends on the level of significance of the test. *The smaller the level of significance, α, the smaller the power.*

FIGURE 7–29
The Power Curve for a Two-Tailed Test and the Power Curve for a One-Tailed Test

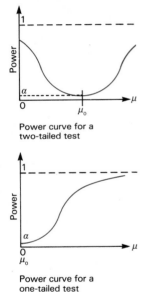

Power curve for a two-tailed test

Power curve for a one-tailed test

Suppose that you look at the values of the power function shown in Table 7–3, and you decide that it is important to be able to reject the null hypothesis if the true population mean is $\mu = 62$. The value $\mu = 62$ falls under the alternative hypothesis; however, for this particular value, the test is rather weak—the power is only 0.2595. That is, if the true population mean is 62, we only have a 0.2595 chance of rejecting the null hypothesis. As we see from the table and from Figure 7–28, the power increases quickly, and if the true mean is equal to 69, we have a 0.9979 chance of rejecting the null hypothesis. That still doesn't solve the problem of what to do if we want to have a high power—a high probability of rejecting the null hypothesis—if the true mean is $\mu = 62$. Looking at the four statements about power, we realize that we cannot control the first two factors. We can, however, use the next two properties. We can either reduce our demands on the level of significance, that is, increase α, or—the better solution—we can increase the sample size. Increasing the sample size is a way of increasing the power of a test without sacrificing the level of significance, α (our protection against a type I error).

Let us now use equation 7–16 to compute the power of the test at $\mu = 62$ if the sample size is increased to $n = 400$ (and the level of significance stays the same, $\alpha = 0.05$). Note that increasing the sample size changes the critical point as well. A larger sample size brings the critical point closer to the center of the distribution (the null-hypothesized value). First we solve for the new critical point. We have: $C = \mu_0 + 1.645\sigma/\sqrt{n} = 60 + 1.645(20/20) = 61.645$. Now we compute the new power for $\mu = 62$. We have, using equation 7–16:

$$\beta = P\left(Z < \frac{C - \mu_1}{\sigma/\sqrt{n}}\right) = P\left(Z < \frac{61.645 - 62}{20/20}\right)$$
$$= P(Z < -0.355) = 0.3613$$

The power is $1 - \beta = 0.6387$. This is much higher than the power we had when the sample size was only 100.

What about two-tailed tests? The power curve for our test of the null hypothesis $H_0: \mu = \mu_0$ versus the two-tailed alternative $H_1: \mu \neq \mu_0$ is shown in Figure 7–29. Also shown, for comparison, is the power curve for a one-tailed test.

EXAMPLE (o)

An advertisement for Saab states that *Car and Driver* magazine recently determined that the new Saab 9000 goes from 0 to 60 mph in 7.7 seconds, while *Road & Track* magazine tested this car at 7.6 seconds in going from 0 to 60 mph. Makers of a competing automobile feel that if the true average number of seconds it takes the Saab 9000 to reach 60 mph from zero is *above* the 7.6 figure claimed by *Road & Track*, and in particular, if it takes an average of 7.7 seconds, as determined by *Car and Driver*, the competitor could advertise its own car as a better model with respect to this performance aspect. Thus, the makers of the competing automobile want to test the Saab 9000 and carry out the following hypothesis test: $H_0: \mu \leq 7.6$ and $H_1: \mu > 7.6$. Since the competitor wants to have a high probability of rejecting the null hypothesis if μ is equal to the value 7.7, covered under the alternative hypothesis, the firm is interested in finding the power of the test evaluated at $\mu_1 = 7.7$.

Suppose that the sample size available for this test is $n = 150$ trials and that the population standard deviation (from previous driving tests) is believed to be $\sigma = 0.4$ seconds. The required level of significance is $\alpha = 0.05$. What is the power? That is, if the true average time is 7.7 seconds, what is the probability of rejecting the null hypothesis that the average time is at most 7.6 seconds?

SOLUTION

First we find the critical point: $C = \mu_0 + 1.654\sigma/\sqrt{n} = 7.6 + 1.645(0.4/12.25) = 7.6537$. Now we find the power at $\mu = 7.7$.

$$\text{Power} = P(\overline{X} > C | \mu = 7.7) = P\left(Z > \frac{7.6537 - 7.7}{0.4/12.25}\right) = P(Z > -1.42) = 0.9222$$

The competitor thus has a 0.9222 chance of rejecting the null hypothesis when the true average time it takes the Saab 9000 to go from 0 to 60 mph is 7.7 seconds. Note that in our calculation we used the probability definition of power directly, without first computing β.

PROBLEMS

7–53. Recent near misses in the air, as well as several fatal accidents, have brought air traffic controllers under close scrutiny. As a result of a high-level inquiry into the accuracy of speed and distance determinations through radar sightings of airplanes, a statistical test was proposed to check the air traffic controllers' claim that a commercial jet's position can be determined, on the average, to within 110 feet in the usual range around airports in the United States. The proposed test was given as: H_0: $\mu \leq 110$ versus the alternative H_1: $\mu > 110$. The test was to be carried out at the 0.05 level of significance using a random sample of 80 airplane sightings. The statistician designing the test wanted to determine the power of this test if the actual average distance at detection is 120 feet. An estimate of the standard deviation is 30 feet. Compute the power at $\mu_1 = 120$ feet.

Answer

7–54. McDonald's Corporation has been steadily moving into more countries around the world. Recent reports show that McDonald's has been interested in opening franchises in Poland. As part of its efforts to sell fast foods in Poland, McDonald's Corporation has been evaluating the potential of using Polish-grown potatoes not only in Poland, but also for distribution in other European countries. The feasibility of such an option depends on the demand for french-fried potatoes in all of McDonald's European franchises. Company analysts believe that if the average weekly demand for fries per franchise per week is above 500 package units, it may be feasible to use Polish-grown potatoes. Thus, the analysts want to test the null hypothesis H_0: $\mu \leq 500$ versus the alternative hypothesis H_1: $\mu > 500$. The company has data on 100 weekly sales randomly obtained from franchises throughout the continent. The test is to be carried out at the 0.05 level of significance, and an estimate of the population variance is 2,500 (units squared). What is the power of the test if the true mean is 520 units per franchise per week?

7–54.

power = 0.99

7–55. The Polaroid Spectra® camera has an electronic device that makes complex focusing and exposure decisions in 50 thousandths of a second. Before each device is installed in a camera, it is tested by quality control inspectors. The device is linked to a simulator that runs a random sample of 80 situations and measures the sample average reaction time of the device. The statistical test is H_0: $\mu \leq 50$ (thousandths of a second) versus the alternative H_1: $\mu > 50$ (thousandths of a second). If the null hypothesis is accepted, the device is considered to have good quality and is installed in a camera; otherwise it is replaced. The test is carried out at the 0.01 level of significance, and the population standard deviation is $\sigma = 20$

Answer

(thousandths of a second). For quality control considerations, inspectors need to have a high power for this test, that is, a high probability of rejecting a faulty device, when the average speed of the device is 60 thousandths of a second. Find the power at this level of μ. Also compute the power at other levels, and sketch the power curve.

7–56. The management of a large manufacturing firm believes that the firm's market share is 45%. From time to time, a statistical hypothesis test is carried out to check whether the assertion is true. The test consists of gathering a random sample of 500 products sold nationally and finding what percentage of the sample constitutes brands made by the firm. Whenever the test is carried out, there is no suspicion as to the direction of a possible change in market share, i.e., increase or decrease; the company wants to detect any change at all. The tests are carried out at the $\alpha = 0.01$ level of significance. What is the probability of being able to statistically determine a true change in the market share of magnitude 5% in either direction? (That is, find the power at $p = 0.50$ or $p = 0.40$. Hint: Use the methods of this section in the case of sampling for proportions. You will have to derive the formulas needed for computing the power.)

7-56.

power = 0.377, 0.375

7–11 Sample Size Determination for Hypothesis Tests[19]

In Chapter 6, we saw how sample size may be determined for a specified width of a confidence interval at a given confidence *coefficient* $(1 - \alpha)$. We can also determine the required sample size in the context of hypothesis tests. In this context, the specifications are those of a statistical test: the level of significance, α, and the power, $1 - \beta$, that we require at some given point covered in the alternative hypothesis. The procedure is illustrated in Figure 7–30.

The situation here is as follows: We wish to test the null hypothesis H_0: $\mu \leq 60$ versus the alternative hypothesis H_1: $\mu > 60$ (the same situation as in section 7–10). This time, we want to determine how large our sample size, n, should be so that when the test is carried out at $\alpha = 0.05$, it will have a 0.90 power if the population mean is $\mu = 65$. That is, $\alpha = 0.05$, β (at $\mu = 65$) $= 0.10$, and we want to find the sample size that will ensure these requirements. To solve, we note the following. The area to the right of the critical point under the left curve (corresponding to $\mu = 60$) is 0.05; the area to the left of the critical point under the right curve (the one corresponding to $\mu = 65$) is equal to 0.10. To find the sample size, n, we have to solve two equations for n. Each equation is obtained from one of the two requirements.

We assume again that the population standard deviation is $\sigma = 20$. We know that the z value corresponding to a right-tail area of 0.05 is 1.645 and that the z value for a left-tail area of 0.10 is -1.28. The two resulting equations are:

$$C = \mu_0 + 1.645\sigma/\sqrt{n} = 60 + 1.645(20/\sqrt{n})$$

and

$$C = \mu_1 - 1.28\sigma/\sqrt{n} = 65 - 1.28(20/\sqrt{n})$$

(7–18)

(Inspecting Figure 7–30 will make this clearer.) We now solve the two equations for n by equating the two expressions for C:

$$60 + 1.645(20/\sqrt{n}) = 65 - 1.28(20/\sqrt{n})$$
$$5 = 2.925(20/\sqrt{n})$$
$$\sqrt{n} = (20)(2.925)/5$$
$$n = (11.7)^2 = 136.89$$

---

[19] This is an optional section.

FIGURE 7–30   Determining the Required Sample Size in Hypothesis Tests

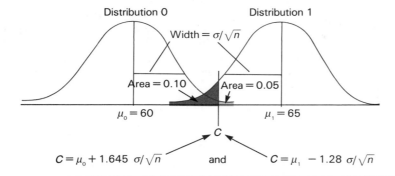

The sample size that makes the width of the two curves such that the area under Distribution O to the right of C is 0.05 and the area under Distribution 1 to the left of C is 0.10, is $n = 137$.

The required sample size is therefore given by the next higher integer: $n = 137$.

In this case, we solved for the required sample size by directly substituting given values into the two expressions for the critical point, C, and then solving the equations. There is, however, a single formula that gives the solution of the two equations. We can find the required sample size by just substituting our information into equation 7–19.

> The minimum required sample size in hypothesis tests of μ to satisfy a given significance level and a given power:
>
> $$n = \left[\frac{(z_0 + z_1)\sigma}{\mu_0 - \mu_1} \right]^2 \qquad (7\text{–}19)$$
>
> where z_0 and z_1 are the required z values determined by the probabilities α and β, respectively, and are used in their *absolute value* form (that is, in our present example we use 1.28 rather than -1.28). The values μ_0 and μ_1 are the population mean under the null hypothesis, and a value of the population mean under the alternative hypothesis at which the specified power is needed, respectively.

Let us compute the required sample size in our example using equation 7–19:

$$n = \left[\frac{(1.645 + 1.28)20}{60 - 65} \right]^2 = 136.89$$

as was obtained earlier. The required sample size is 137.

Note that the procedure we are using assumes normality (we use z values). Our result is a large sample, so the assumption is justified regardless of the shape of the population. If the population is not normally distributed and the obtained sample size is small, the result may not be accurate. Let us now consider an example.

EXAMPLE (p)

The Hawaiian Economic Development Association is interested in promoting sales of Kona coffee. As part of the promotion campaign, the association is interested in determining current consumption levels of Kona coffee at establishments on the U.S. mainland. The association wants to select a random sample of establishments that sell Kona coffee and use the results to test the null hypothesis that average daily consumption of Kona coffee per customer in all establishments serving this kind of coffee is at most 0.4 oz. The test is to be carried out at the 0.01 level of significance, and the association wants to have at least a 0.95 probability of rejecting the null hypothesis if the average consumption is actually 0.5 oz. An estimate of the standard deviation of consumption per customer is 0.2 oz. What is the minimum sample size needed to assure satisfaction of the requirements?

SOLUTION

We use equation 7–19 for the sample size:

$$n = \left[\frac{(z_0 + z_1)\sigma}{\mu_0 - \mu_1} \right]^2 = \left[\frac{(2.326 + 1.645)(0.2)}{0.4 - 0.5} \right]^2$$

$$= 63.07$$

The association, therefore, needs to sample at least 64 establishments.

A formula similar to equation 7–19 is useful in finding the minimum sample size required to achieve a given level of μ and β in the case of hypothesis tests for the population proportion.

The minimum required sample size in hypothesis tests of p to satisfy a given significance level and a given power:

$$n = \left(\frac{z_0\sqrt{p_0 q_0} + z_1\sqrt{p_1 q_1}}{p_0 - p_1} \right)^2 \qquad (7\text{–}20)$$

where z_0 and z_1 are the required z values determined by the probabilities α and β, respectively, and are used in their *absolute value* form. The values p_0 and p_1 are the null-hypothesized population proportion and the value of p under the alternative hypothesis at which the stated power is needed, respectively.

We demonstrate the use of equation 7–20 by the following example.

EXAMPLE (q)

An important factor for Japanese farmers is the amount of rice consumed in Japan. Recent findings indicate that urban Japanese are eating less rice every year, while they are eating more meat and dairy products.[20] A Japanese farmers' organization wants to test the null hypothesis that 80% of Japanese families eat rice at least five times a week against the alternative hypothesis that less than 80% of Japanese families eat rice at least five times a week. Designers of the survey want to have a 0.95 probability of rejecting the null hypothesis if 75% of the

---

[20] "Japanese Farmers Win Protection and Subsidies," *The Wall Street Journal* (December 4, 1986).

FIGURE 7–31   Determining the Required Sample Size in Example (q)

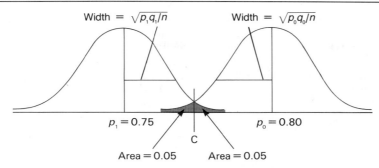

The sample size that makes the two areas equal to
0.05 each is slightly over $n = 751$.

Japanese families eat rice at least five times a week. The test is carried out at $\alpha = 0.05$. How large should the sample be?

SOLUTION

We use equation 7–20. The z values, in absolute value, corresponding to a power of 0.95 and level of significance 0.05, are both $z = 1.645$ (this is a one-tailed test). We get:

$$n = \left(\frac{z_0\sqrt{p_0 q_0} + z_1\sqrt{p_1 q_1}}{p_0 - p_1}\right)^2 = \left(\frac{1.645\sqrt{(0.8)(0.2)} + 1.645\sqrt{(0.75)(0.25)}}{0.80 - 0.75}\right)^2 = 751.095$$

The Japanese farmers' organization should obtain a random sample of 752 families. The situation is shown in Figure 7–31.

PROBLEMS

7–57. A 1984 study by the National Assessment of Educational Progress claims that at most 25% of 11th graders in this country write well enough to succeed in business or academia. An independent agency wants to test whether this claim is true. The agency plans 'o use an α of 0.01 and wants to have a power of 0.95 in this right-hand-tailed test if the true percentage of 11th graders who can write well enough to succeed is 30%. How large should the sample be?

Answer

7–58. The average selling price for an American Eagle gold coin during a certain period in 1986 was $418. The standard deviation of prices of the coin at different dealerships around the country was known to be $4. At the end of the period in question, there was a slight increase in the price of bullion gold. A precious metals investment consultant wanted to test the null hypothesis that the average retail price of the coin remained $418, or was lower, versus the alternative hypothesis that the average price had increased. The test was to be carried out at $\alpha = 0.05$, and the consultant wanted to have a 0.90 power of detecting a shift from the $418 level by as much as $3 upward. Find the required sample size. Assume that the population of prices is normally distributed.

7–58.

16

7–59. A company is considering an offer to exchange preferred stock for common stock and wants to estimate the proportion of its stockholders who favor the exchange. In particular, the company's management feels that certain gains may be achieved if more than 60% of the stockholders favor the swap. The management wants to gather a random sample of shareholders to test the null hypothesis that 60% or fewer of the shareholders favor the exchange, versus the alternative hypothesis that more than 60% favor it. The test is to be carried out at

$\alpha = 0.05$, and they want a 0.99 power if the true percentage of all stockholders in favor of the exchange is as high as 67%. What is the required sample size?

7–60. A study is undertaken to evaluate the public's recall of radio advertisements.[21] We want to test the null hypothesis that the average recall score for the entire population of people who hear the advertisement is 6.5 on a scale of 1 to 10, versus the alternative hypothesis that the average recall score is higher than 6.5. From previous studies, it is estimated that the population standard deviation of recall scores is 2.5. The test is to be conducted at the 0.01 level of significance, and we want to have a power of 0.95 if the true average recall score is equal to 7.0. What is the required sample size?

7–61. A two-tailed test is to be carried out of the null hypothesis that the average transaction time at a bank is 3.8 minutes versus the alternative hypothesis that it is not 3.8 minutes. The test is to be carried out at the 0.05 level of significance. The standard deviation of transaction times is known to be 1.5 minutes. What is the required sample size if the power at $\mu_1 = 4$ minutes is to be 0.90?

7–12 Further Discussion—How Hypothesis Testing Works

In this section, we will look at the mechanics of hypothesis testing and gain an insight into what makes the procedure work. We will also give some general comments about hypothesis tests—aspects to consider when conducting a test, and some caveats.

Let us consider a hypothesis test for the mean of a population. Assume that the sample size n is large and the normal distribution applies. Assume also that the population standard deviation σ is known (when it is not, use s in its place). We have a hypothesized value for the mean, μ_0, and we compute from our sample the sample mean, $\bar{x}$. Now suppose that the test is two-tailed, or, if it is one-tailed, then assume that $\bar{x}$ is away from μ_0 in the direction of the rejection region ($\bar{x}$ larger than μ_0 in the right-hand-tailed test and smaller than μ_0 in a left-hand-tailed test). The first thing taken into consideration is the distance between $\bar{x}$ and μ_0. This is the numerator of our test statistic:

$$z = \frac{\bar{x} - \mu_0}{\sigma/\sqrt{n}} \tag{7–21}$$

Suppose we test H_0: $\mu \leq 60$ versus H_1: $\mu > 60$, and $\bar{x}$ is equal to 70. The distance between $\bar{x}$ and μ_0 is $70 - 60 = 10$ units. This is the numerator in equation 7–21. Now suppose that you report your findings to a person who does not know any statistics. You say: "The claim was that the population mean is no greater than 60; I sampled n items and found that the sample mean was 70." The person to whom you are reporting may say: "Clearly, the population mean cannot be 60, because your sample result is 10 units over the claimed mean!" When we do statistics, however, we make conclusions much more carefully and in a scientific manner. We first must ask ourselves: What is the *significance* of the distance of 10 units from $\bar{x}$ to μ_0? This is a question of *scale*. Do 10 units represent a large distance in the scale of the problem or a small one? The scale depends on two quantities: the population standard deviation and the sample size. Let us see why. Suppose the values of the population are the following: 0, -30, 400, 68, -298, 1,095, and so on. The variance in these values is large, and, therefore, a difference of 10 units between what you find from a sample and the true population mean may be relatively minor (again, the statistical

[21] M. Sewall and D. Sarel, "Characteristics of Radio Commericals and Their Recall Effectiveness," *Journal of Marketing* (January 1986).

FIGURE 7–32   A Distance of 10 Units in Two Different Settings

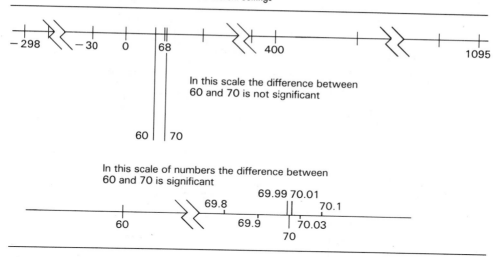

significance depends also on the sample size). On the other hand, a difference of 10 units is *enormous* if the population values are 69.9, 70.01, 69.8, 70.1, 69.99, 70.03, and so on. Here the population is very closely clustered around a mean of about 70, and the distance of 10 units is very significant: the claimed mean of 60 is indeed far away, in this scale, from the sample mean, 70. This is shown in Figure 7–32.

The dependence of the scale of measurement on the population standard deviation (a measure of the variation in the population) is taken into account in equation 7–21 by the fact that we divide the distance $\bar{x} - \mu_0$ by the standard deviation, σ. The second factor that affects the scale of the problem is the sample size. This has to do with the fact that our sample mean, $\bar{x}$, should carry more weight (carry more importance) if it is based on a larger sample. If you invert the fraction in the denominator of equation 7–21 and multiply the numerator of the equation by $\sqrt{n}$, you see how the "importance" factor $\sqrt{n}$ acts as a weight that multiplies the difference between $\bar{x}$ and μ_0. The larger the sample size, the larger the importance given to the difference between our observed $\bar{x}$ and the hypothesized mean, μ_0.

Another way to see how our test statistic in equation 7–21 is a scaled distance is to note something we have known all along. The sample mean is a normally distributed random variable with mean μ and standard deviation (standard error) equal to $\sigma/\sqrt{n}$. As σ decreases, or as n increases, the width of the normal curve centered at the true mean, μ, becomes smaller, and the sample mean $\bar{X}$ becomes "constrained" to fall within smaller distances from μ for any probability level. The sample mean should not be too far away from μ, when measured in standard deviations of the random variable $\bar{X}$. This is exactly what the test statistic z measures: *the distance from $\bar{x}$ to μ in standard deviations of the random variable $\bar{X}$.* This is done by dividing the actual distance between $\bar{x}$ and μ_0 by $\sigma/\sqrt{n}$. This gives us the standardized distance, z. Equation 7–21 assumes that the true population mean is μ_0 (the assumption of "innocence"). If the distance between the sample result $\bar{x}$ and the hypothesized mean μ_0, measured in standard deviations of $\bar{X}$ (and, hence, scaled to the specifications of the problem), is a large distance, then we reject the null hypothesis. Otherwise we accept it. We know, for example, that if the population mean is indeed μ_0, then the standardized distance measured by Z has only a 0.05 chance of

FIGURE 7–33   The Standardized Distance between $\bar{x}$ and μ_0 as Measured by the Test Statistic z

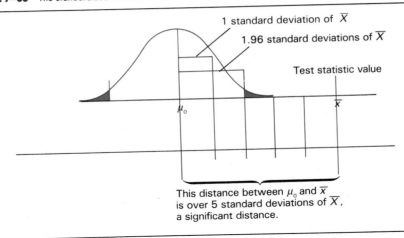

being greater than 1.96 or less than -1.96. Similar facts about the probability of the standardized distance Z are obtained by consulting the normal probability table. This is demonstrated in Figure 7–33.

We see that the standardized test statistic allows us to measure the distance between the value of the statistic and the hypothesized value of the parameter in terms of standard errors of the statistic. A general formula (except for cases involving the population variance, where the mechanism is somewhat different) for a standardized test statistic is:

$$\text{Test statistic} = \frac{\text{Estimate} - \text{Hypothesized parameter}}{\text{Standard error of estimator}} \quad (7\text{–}22)$$

Equation 7–22 is a general form of equation 7–21, a test statistic for the mean. The test statistic has a known probability distribution. The test statistic measures the distance between what is claimed under H_0 and the estimate obtained from the data, in terms of standard errors of the estimator. Such a distance, in standard units (hence, the statistical term *standard deviation*), may or may not be *significant*. When the standardized distance between estimate and hypothesized parameter value has a small (presampling) probability of occurrence, the result is significant and the null hypothesis should be rejected. On the other hand, when the standardized distance between estimate and hypothesized parameter value has a relatively high (presampling) probability, the result is common (not significant) and the null hypothesis must be accepted.

Some Comments and Caveats

1. When you are conducting a right-hand-tailed test and the estimate $\bar{x}$ is smaller than the hypothesized value of the parameter, μ_0, you do not need to compute the value of the test statistic at all. You may immediately accept H_0. This is so because if $\bar{x}$ is less than μ_0, then the value of the test statistic

will be negative, and in a right-hand-tailed test we reject only for some (extreme) *positive* values of the test statistic.

2. If you are conducting a two-tailed test and you end up rejecting the null hypothesis in the right-hand rejection region, one of three things may be true. First, it is possible that, as you concluded, the parameter is greater than the value stated in the null hypothesis. Second, it is possible that the null hypothesis is true (in which case you just observed an event that had a probability of occurrence equal to your p-value) and you committed a type I error. The third possibility is that the null hypothesis is indeed false, as you concluded, but the true value of the parameter is actually *smaller* than the value stated in the null hypothesis. This is an event with an extremely small probability in most situations, but conceivably it can happen. This is so because curves centered to the right of the null-hypothesized value still have tails extending to the left of the left-hand critical point. This is demonstrated in Figure 7–34. This possibility is of little practical importance, but you should understand it. Here you correctly reject the null hypothesis, but for the wrong reason.

3. A two-tailed test has the form H_0: $\mu = 10$ versus H_1: $\mu \neq 10$. Let us think about this logically. The mean could be equal to 10 exactly, or it could equal some other number. If the mean is not 10 but, say, 12, then we probably want to know about it and hope to reject the null hypothesis. Suppose, however, that the population mean is not 10, but 10.001. The fact that the mean differs so slightly from 10 (again, this must be considered within the scale of the problem, but suppose that for practical considerations 10 and 10.001 are no different to us) means that we probably do not want to know about it. In this case, we do not want to reject the null hypothesis.

   A statistical hypothesis test will cause us to reject the null hypothesis if the sample size is large enough. As the sample size increases, the power of the test increases, and this allows us to reject almost any null hypothesis in a two-tailed test. What is the meaning of this rejection? We must be very careful with our interpretations and be aware of the fact that, while we may not want to reject H_0 if the true mean is 10.001 instead of 10.000, a huge sample (say, 10,000) may make us reject this null hypothesis anyway. Therefore, you should understand the following: If we reject H_0 and the p-value is very small, this means that we feel strongly about rejecting H_0. It

FIGURE 7–34   The Possibility of Correctly Rejecting the Null Hypothesis, for the Wrong Reason

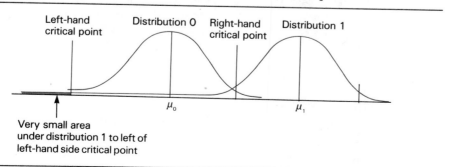

does *not* always mean that the population mean is very far away from the value stated in the null hypothesis; it merely means that there is strong evidence to reject the claim that the mean is exactly 10. The true mean may be very different from 10, or it may be close to 10. In general, beware of inferences made on the basis of very large samples. While rejection of the null hypothesis may be very significant in the statistical sense, it may not be significant in a *practical* sense.

4. The formulation of the null and alternative hypotheses should never be done *after* you have seen the data. This is called *data snooping*, and it is a bad thing. Why? We will demonstrate the answer with an example. Suppose that you are interested in estimating the proportion of consumers who use a certain product. You do not have any idea as to what the proportion may be, but you want to carry out a "hypothesis test." You collect a random sample of 100 consumers and, after looking at the data and noticing that 34 of the consumers indicated that they use the product, you decide to test the null hypothesis that the population proportion is $p = 0.34$. If you use the sample results just obtained, your "hypothesis test" will be meaningless and will never lead to rejection. Here is why:

$$H_0: p = 0.34$$
$$H_1: p \neq 0.34$$
$$z = \frac{\hat{p} - p_0}{\sqrt{p_0 q_0 / n}} = \frac{0.34 - 0.34}{\sqrt{p_0 q_0 / n}} = 0$$

The value we obtain for the test statistic, zero, lies right in the middle of the acceptance region and, thus, cannot lead to rejection of the null hypothesis at any level, α.

In this example, we used all the information in the sample in formulating the "hypotheses," but the same holds true, to a lesser degree, if we just "snoop around" and look at some of our data. Doing this, we lower our power of rejecting any null hypothesis, and we are also cheating. Data snooping is an example of lying with statistics.

5. The null hypothesis plays a special role. It is the hypothesis that enjoys the assumption of "innocence" and requires strong evidence to reject. When we accept the null hypothesis, it does not mean that the null hypothesis is true; it merely means that the data we have do not provide strong evidence for rejecting it. In cases where we want to evaluate hypotheses in a more symmetric way, we may test the two hypotheses $H_0: \mu = 10$ versus $H_1: \mu = 15$, for example, and set α and β to the same level, say, 0.05. Using the method of section 7–11, we can find the sample size, n, that will allow us to carry out our test. Now the two hypotheses are perfectly symmetric; there is no special null hypothesis. We choose to accept a hypothesis if the test statistic falls on its side of the critical point, and we reject the other hypothesis. This is demonstrated in Figure 7–35.

7–13   Using the Computer

Computers are useful in carrying out hypothesis tests. Usually, the user specifies the kind of test to be carried out, one- or two-tailed, and the distribution to be used. Data are entered and read by the program, and the analysis is done. Results are

FIGURE 7–35   A Symmetric Way of Testing Two Statistical Hypotheses

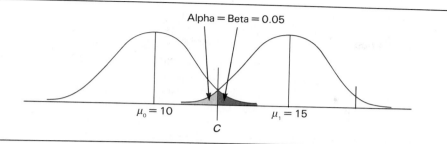

usually reported in a table that gives the value of the estimate, the standard deviation, the standard error of the estimator, the computed test statistic value, and the p-value.

In this chapter, we will again use the package MINITAB. The commands used for a test of the population mean are ZTEST, for a test using the normal distribution, or TTEST, for a test using the t distribution. We demonstrate the use of MINITAB in hypothesis tests for the population mean with Example (r).

EXAMPLE (r)

Federal Express claims in an advertisement that customers can get a report on the exact status of their package within 30 minutes. A competitor wants to test this claim, trying to prove that the average time for an exact status report by Federal Express is over 30 minutes. The null hypothesis is therefore H_0: $\mu \leq 30$, and the alternative hypothesis is H_1: $\mu > 30$. A random sample of 20 status reports is collected. The time required for obtaining the report in each case, in minutes, is as follows: 39, 35, 37, 28, 40, 25, 27, 24, 42, 45, 20, 38, 39, 25, 42, 26, 48, 51, 48, 41. These data are entered into column C1 of MINITAB. (Since we plan to use the t distribution, we must assume that the population is normally distributed.)

SOLUTION

Figure 7–36 shows the MINITAB command needed for executing the analysis. The subcommand ALTERNATIVE=1 specifies that the test is a right-hand-tailed test. (ALTERNATIVE=−1 would specify a left-hand-tailed test, and leaving out the ALTERNATIVE statement would indicate a two-tailed test.) This comes in the row specifying the command: TTEST of MU=30. The output is also shown in the figure. Since the p-value is 0.0045, as reported in the computer output, we may reject the null hypothesis.

FIGURE 7–36   MINITAB Program and Output for Example (r)

```
MTB > TTEST OF MU = 30 ALTERNATIVE = 1 ON DATA IN C1

TEST OF MU = 30.00 VS MU G.T.  30.00

            N       MEAN    STDEV    SE MEAN       T     P VALUE
C1         20      36.00     9.23       2.06     2.91     0.0045
```

7-14 Summary and Review of Terms

In this chapter, we introduced the important ideas of statistical hypothesis testing. We discussed the philosophy behind hypothesis tests, which is similar to the philosophy of a trial in a court of law under the American legal system. This system assumes innocence until guilt is proven beyond a reasonable doubt. We showed how this way of thinking gives a special status to the **null hypothesis.** We defined a statistical test as a test of two competing hypotheses: the null hypothesis and the **alternative hypothesis.** We defined both a **two-tailed test** and a **one-tailed test,** and we saw how the kind of test used depends on the need for action, which determines the alternative hypothesis. We defined **test statistics** for use in tests about population parameters. We saw how we can use the value of the test statistic to determine the rejection or nonrejection of the null hypothesis by comparing it with one or two **critical points.** We defined the **type I error** and the **type II error** and their respective probabilities, α and β. We saw how—due to our agreed-upon philosophy—the **level of significance** (α) is usually predetermined and controlled, whereas β is not. We then explored situations where β can be evaluated, and we saw the importance of the **power** of the test, defined as $1 - \beta$. We learned about the **p-value** and saw how interpreting its meaning facilitates our statistical conclusions. Finally, we saw a way of determining the sample size required for a given level of significance and a given power at some value in the set of values covered under the alternative hypothesis. In the next chapter, we will extend our results to the case of analysis of two samples. There we will study tests that allow us to statistically compare the means of two populations, as well as to compare two population proportions and two population variances. Following chapters will extend the results further, to more involved situations.

ADDITIONAL PROBLEMS

In each of the following problems, state any necessary assumptions.

Answer

7-62.

p = 0.039

7-62.   One of the most ingenious advertising schemes in recent years is Gallo Winery's invention of Bartles and Jaymes, the two down-home entrepreneurs selling a wine cooler. Bartles & Jaymes wine coolers have been rapidly increasing in sales since their introduction, largely due to the believability of television commercials featuring the two elderly gentlemen in their suspenders sitting on the porch with bottles of the wine cooler. As part of marketing research efforts to design new commercials, it was of interest to find out what proportion of the general public knew that Bartles and Jaymes were not real people and that the wine cooler was actually made by Gallo.[22] An assertion by advertising industry experts was that no more than 10% of the public knew the truth. If it could be shown that more than 10% of the public knew that the wine cooler was made by Gallo, then the company would change the television commercials in some way; otherwise nothing would be changed. Thus, it was necessary to test the null hypothesis that the percentage of the public that was aware of the true maker of the wine cooler was less than or equal to 10%, versus the alternative that the population percentage was above 10%. A random sample of 800 people was selected, and 95 of them admitted they knew that the wine cooler was made by Gallo and that Bartles and Jaymes were fictional characters. Should Gallo change its commercials? What is the p-value?

7-63.   Explain the difference between a one-tailed test and a two-tailed test. What are the conditions required for a one-tailed test? What are the necessary conditions for a test to be two-tailed?

---

[22] "Bartles & Jaymes Aren't Real Guys, but You Knew That," *The Wall Street Journal* (July 8, 1986).

7–64. Explain the relationship between a two-tailed test and a confidence interval.

7–65. An advertisement for AT&T encourages people to make overseas phone calls. The advertisement highlights the average cost per minute of calling time to the United Kingdom during "economy" time (6 P.M. to 7 A.M.) as 64 cents. A note explains that the average cost per minute varies depending on the length of the call. An agency wants to test this claim, believing that the average cost per minute is higher than that stated in the ad. A random sample of 100 calls to the United Kingdom during economy time reveals that the average in the sample is 72 cents per minute and the sample standard deviation is 10 cents. Carry out the hypothesis test. Do you believe the advertisement? Explain.

7–66. Which random variable is appropriate for finding probabilities associated with a test for the population variance when the sample size is very large?

7–67. Look at the power curve for either a one-tailed test or a two-tailed test, and explain the meaning of the "power" at the point corresponding to the value of the parameter under the null hypothesis.

7–68. A two-tailed test for the population mean was carried out with sample size $n = 12,785$. The p-value obtained was 0.0002. Can you say that the true value of the parameter is very far from the value stated in the null hypothesis?

7–69. Give an interpretation of the results stated in problem 7–68.

7–70. A large department store is considering launching a campaign to promote use of its charge card. The store's management believes that the average amount charged per month on the store's charge card is $55.00. The management wants to test whether a marketing campaign would increase the amount of charges on the card. A random sample of cardholders is selected, and the campaign is tested on this sample. The sample size is 120 cardholders, and it is found that average charges for the sample are $65.50 and the standard deviation is $22.00. Do you believe the campaign would increase the average charge per cardholder? Explain.

7–71. Explain the difference between α and β.

7–72. Explain the relationship between β and the power of the test.

7–73. Suppose a statistical test results in a p-value of 0.0006. Explain the rationale for rejecting the null hypothesis. How confident are you that the null hypothesis is false?

7–74. What is wrong with data snooping?

7–75. What factors determine the power of a test?

7–76. What factors determine the p-value?

7–77. An advertisement for a Toshiba humidifier states: "Your bedroom may be 67% drier than the Sahara desert." The advertisement then states that the Sahara averages over 30% humidity. A competitor wants to prove that Toshiba's advertisement is incorrect and that the Sahara averages below 30% humidity. The competitor carries out a random set of 100 measurements of humidity in the Sahara desert and finds an average of 27% humidity and a standard deviation of 6% humidity. Are these findings significant? Explain.

7–78. Consider the following computer output for some hypothesis test. Do you accept or reject the null hypothesis? Explain.

MEAN	STDEV	SE MEAN	Z	P VALUE
7.262	5.310	0.819	-3.34	0.0009

7–79. The following results of a hypothesis test are produced by the computer.

N	MEAN	STDEV	SE MEAN	T	P. VALUE
15	17.283	0.397	0.102	7.65	0.0000

a. What are the degrees of freedom involved in this test?
b. Do you accept or reject the null hypothesis?
c. Why did the computer report the p-value as 0.0000? Explain.

Answers

7–66.
Normal

7–68.
No

7–70.
$z = 5.23$

7–78.
Reject

Answers

7–82.

$p = 0.25$

7–86.

power = 0.997
$n = 1284$

7–88.

p slightly over 0.025

7–80. How can we increase the power of a test without increasing the sample size?

7–81. The sales of home appliances have increased greatly in recent years. A study sponsored by the home appliance industry is aimed at testing the hypothesis that 6% of all consumers purchased new appliances during the June–September period. Industry analysts have no prior suspicion as to whether the proportion of consumers who bought new appliances during the period in question is higher or lower than stated and merely want to check the claim. A random sample of 2,000 consumers nationwide shows that 142 of them bought new appliances during the period. Is this a one-tailed or a two-tailed test? What is the p-value? State your conclusion.

7–82. A recent marketing and promotion campaign by Charles of the Ritz more than doubled the sales of the suntan lotion Bain de Soleil, which has become the nation's number 2 suntan product. At the end of the promotional campaign, the company wanted to test the hypothesis that the market share of its product was 0.35 versus the alternative hypothesis that the market share was higher than 0.35. The company polled a random sample of bathers on beaches from Maine to California and Hawaii, and found that out of the sample of 3,850 users of suntan lotions, 1,367 were users of Bain de Soleil. Do you accept or reject the null hypothesis? What is the p-value? Explain your conclusion.

7–83. Efforts are underway to make the American automobile industry more efficient and competitive so that it will be able to survive intense competition from foreign automakers. An industry analyst is quoted as recently saying, "GM is sized for 60% of the market, and they only have 43%." General Motors needs to know its actual market share because such knowledge would help the company make better decisions about trimming down or expanding so that it could become more efficient. A company executive, pushing for expansion rather than for cutting down, is interested in proving that the analyst's claim that GM's share of the market is 43% is false and that, in fact, GM's true market share is higher. The executive hires a marketing research firm to study the problem and carry out the hypothesis test she proposed. The marketing research agency looks at a random sample of 5,500 cars throughout the country and finds that 2,521 of them are GM cars. What should be the executive's conclusion? How should she present her results to GM's vice president for operations?

7–84. Why is it useful to know the power of a test?

7–85. Explain the difference between the p-value and the significance level, α.

7–86. Refer to problem 7–83. Suppose that the executive wanted to have a 0.90 power against the null hypothesis if the true market share of General Motors was 48%, and suppose that the test were to be carried out at $\alpha = 0.01$. What would be the required minimum sample size? Also, with the sample size you obtained, what is the power against the null hypothesis if the true market share is as high as 50%?

7–87. "Corporate women are still struggling to break into senior management ranks, according to a study of senior corporate executives by Korn/Ferry International, New York recruiter. In 1985, of 1,362 top executives surveyed by the firm, only 2%, or 29, were women." Assuming that the sample reported is a random sample, use the results to test the null hypothesis that the percentage of women in top management is 5% or more, versus the alternative hypothesis that the true percentage is less than 5%. If the test is to be carried out at $\alpha = 0.05$, what would be the power of the test if the true percentage of female top executives is 4%?

7–88. The Mellon Bank Corporation recently hired a team to analyze computer CRT systems. This proved to the management that the right choice of a CRT system would increase productivity. Suppose that the average production level at the bank, measured on a scale of 0 to 100, was known to be 78. The team tested a random sample of 24 employees using a proposed new CRT and found that the average productivity level in the sample was 83 and the sample standard deviation was 12. Using $\alpha = 0.05$, conduct the appropriate hypothesis test and state your conclusion. What is the approximate p-value?

7–89. At Armco's steel plant in Middletown, Ohio, statistical quality-control methods have been used very successfully in controlling slab width on continuous casting units. The company claims that a large reduction in the steel slab width variance resulted from the use of these methods. Suppose that the variance of steel slab widths is expected to be 156 (squared units). A test is carried out to determine whether the variance is above the required level, with the intention to take corrective action if it is concluded that the variance is above 156. A random sample of 25 slabs gives a sample variance of 175. Using $\alpha = 0.05$, should corrective action be taken?

7–90. Refer to problem 7–89. Suppose that a random sample of 250 slabs is chosen and that the sample variance is 182. What distribution should be used in this hypothesis test? Carry out the test at $\alpha = 0.05$, and state your conclusion.

7–91. According to the mortgage banking firm Lomas & Nettleton, 95% of all household formations in the second half of 1985 were in the form of rental accommodations. The company believes that lower interest rates for mortgages during the following period reduced the percentage of household formations in the form of rental units. The company therefore wants to test $H_0: p \geq 0.95$ versus the alternative $H_1: p < 0.95$ for the proportion during the new period. A random sample of 1,500 households shows that 1,380 are rental units. Carry out the test, and state your conclusion. Use an α of your choice.

7–92. A recent study was aimed at determining whether people with increased workers' compensation stayed off the job longer than people without the increased benefits.[23] Suppose that the average time off per employee per year is known to be 3.1 days. A random sample of 21 employees with increased benefits yielded the following number of days spent off the job in one year: 5, 17, 1, 0, 2, 3, 1, 1, 5, 2, 7, 5, 0, 3, 3, 4, 22, 2, 8, 0, 1. Conduct the appropriate test, and state your conclusions.

7–93. Environmental changes have recently been shown to improve firms' competitive advantages. The approach is called the Multiple Scenario Approach. A study was designed to find the percentage of the *Fortune* top 1,000 firms that use the Multiple Scenario Approach. The null hypothesis was that 30% or fewer of the firms use the approach. A random sample of 166 firms in the *Fortune* top 1,000 was chosen, and 59 of the firms replied that they used the Multiple Scenario Approach. Conduct the hypothesis test at $\alpha = 0.05$. What is the p-value? (Do you need to use the finite-population correction factor?)

7–94. Junk bonds are high-risk securities issued by entities with questionable ability to repay their debts. These risky securities pay, on the average, high returns to compensate investors for the risk they bear. Drexel Burnham Lambert and other investment banks have recently come up with the latest junk bond: the debt of Third World banks. The investment bankers are trying to sell this debt to investors, promising very high yields. One firm claims that the average return on the risky debt of Peruvian banks is as high as 40% a year. A potential investor wants to check this claim against the alternative that average return on an investment of this kind is less than 40% per year. The potential investor gets a random sample of 14 securities and finds that the average return in the sample is 28% with a standard deviation of 12%. Can the potential investor take action against the investment firm? Give a rough estimate of the p-value.

7–95. Suppose that there are a total of 110 securities of the kind described in problem 7–94. Redo the problem using the finite-population correction factor.

7–96. Executives at Gammon & Ninowski Media Investments, a top television station brokerage, believe that the current average price for an independent television station in the United States is $125 million. An analyst at the firm wants to check whether the executives' claim is true. The analyst has no prior suspicion that the claim is incorrect in any particular direction and collects a random sample of 25 independent TV stations around the country. The results are (in millions of dollars): 233, 128, 305, 57, 89, 45, 33, 190, 21, 322, 97, 103, 132, 200, 50, 48, 312, 252, 82, 212, 165, 134, 178, 212, 199. Test the hypothesis that the average station price nationwide is $125 million versus the alternative that it is not $125 million. Use a significance level of your choice.

7–97. Microsoft Corporation makes software packages for use in microcomputers. The

Answers

7–90.
_____

Chi-square = 286.5

7–92.
_____

$p = 0.15$
(using computer)

7–94.
_____

$p < 0.005$

7–96.
_____

$t = 1.49$
not significant

[23] "Does Better Workers' Comp Mean Longer Absences?" *Business Week* (January 28, 1991), p. 22.

company believes that if at least 25% of present owners of microcomputers of certain types would be interested in a particular new software package, then the company will make a profit if it markets the new package. A company analyst therefore wants to test the null hypothesis that the proportion of owners of microcomputers of the given kinds who will be interested in the new package is at most 0.25, versus the alternative that the proportion is above 0.25. A random sample of 300 microcomputer owners shows that 94 of them are interested in the new Microsoft package. Should the company market its new product? Report the p-value.

7–98.

$p < 0.00003$

7–98. A recent National Science Foundation (NSF) survey indicates that more than 20% of the staff in American research and development laboratories is foreign. Results of the study have been used for pushing legislation aimed at limiting the number of foreign workers in the United States. An organization of foreign-born scientists wants to prove that the NSF survey results do not reflect the true proportion of foreign workers in U.S. labs. The organization collects a random sample of 5,000 laboratory workers in all major labs in the country and finds that 876 are foreign. Can these results be used to prove that the NSF study overestimated the proportion of foreigners in American laboratories?

7–99. Three airlines recently brought suit against a broker selling airline tickets that were earned by travelers through "frequent flyer" bonus programs. Prices for these bonus tickets, which are sold to the broker by people who earn them, are variable. The airlines claim that the average price for such tickets on the New York to Hawaii route is $1,250. The broker wants to prove that the average price is higher than claimed and, hence, that his profit margin upon resale is smaller than claimed by the airlines. An independent investigator is hired, and the investigator gathers a random sample of 18 tickets bought by the broker. The average price paid for tickets in the sample is $1,330 and the sample standard deviation is $120. Is there evidence to support the broker's claim? Use $\alpha = 0.01$.

7–100.

p values:
0.009, 0.0038, 0.114,
0.303, 0.897

7–100. An article on stock-for-debt swaps investigated the existence of excess returns on portfolios including stocks about to be swapped. Two-tailed statistical tests (with samples above the minimum required for the normal assumption to hold) were carried out to determine whether excess returns may occur during the day of the event, five days before or after the event, and at other time spans around the event date. The results are given in the following table.[24] Determine which of the results are significant, and find their p-values using the normal probability table.

Date Relative to Event Date	Portfolio Excess Return	t-Statistic
0	−0.48%	−2.61
−5 to +5	−1.84%	−2.90
+6 to +20	1.12%	1.58
−5 to +20	−0.72%	−1.03
−1 to +20	−0.04%	−0.13

7–101. An article on generic prescription drugs claims that 15% of the prescription drugs sold in the United States are generic.[25] A market analyst for Hoffman-La Roche, the manufacturer of such brand-name drugs as Valium, is interested in testing this claim. If the claim is true, then the company is losing money through the surge in sales of cheaper, non-brand-name medicines of identical chemical composition. The analyst wants to prove that less than 15% of the prescription drugs sold are generic. A random sample of 2,078 prescriptions filled at randomly selected pharmacies throughout the country reveals that 232 of these prescriptions are for generic drugs. What should the analyst conclude?

7–102.

$p < .005$

7–102. Dunhill Tailors of New York City claim that their average custom-tailored suit costs $1,925. A competitor, suspecting that Dunhill is trying to advertise their suits as more ex-

---

[24] J. Peavy and J. Scott, "A Closer Look at Stock-for-Debt Swaps," *Financial Analysts Journal* (May–June 1985).

[25] "Pop Cheaper Pills," *The Economist* (October 18, 1986).

pensive than they really are in an attempt to build a high-class image, gets a random sample of 12 sales slips for Dunhill and finds $\bar{x} = \$1,645$ and $s = \$250$. Carry out the test at $\alpha = 0.05$.

Answer

7–103.   A study of marketing mix and brand switching involved certain statistical tests of the significance of marketing variables. The results are given in the following table.[26] All sample sizes are over 50, and all tests are two-tailed. Which variables are significant? Find the p-value in each case.

Variable	z value
Advertising	0.74
Price	−0.04
Brand	0.25
Form	3.75
Type	−1.74

7–104.   An article about women in business claims that 30% of all small businesses in the United States are owned by women.[27] An analyst wanted to test this claim without any prior intent to prove anything. The analyst looked at a random sample of 2,000 small businesses and found that 852 of them were owned by women. Conduct the test, and state your conclusion.

7–104.

$z = 12.3$; very significant

7–105.   SES, a relatively small satellite communications company based in Luxembourg, has been winning the competition for cable television customers in Europe.[28] A large German competitor of SES believes that the company's claim that its European market share is 25% is exaggerated upward. The German competitor gathers a random sample of 1,000 European cable television viewers and finds that 248 of them are SES subscribers. Conduct the test, and state your conclusions in the form of a memo to the company's president.

---

[26] "A Model of Marketing Mix, Brand Switching, and Competition," *Journal of Marketing Research* (August 1985).

[27] "Selling to Uncle Sam," *Nation's Business* (March 1991), p. 29.

[28] "This Satellite Company Runs Rings Around Rivals," *Business Week* (February 11, 1991), p. 74.

THE ALASKA MARINE HIGHWAY

*T*he Alaska Marine Highway is the ferry system that serves southeast Alaska from the lower 48 states. Since much of southeast Alaska is inaccessible by land due to icefields that separate it from Canada, the Marine Highway is a very important means of transportation to and from the southeast Alaska region. Ferries leave from pier 48 in downtown Seattle every week and travel up the Inside Passage, a protected waterway between groups of forested islands and the mainland. This waterway remains calm even in winter. The ferries stop in the towns of Ketchikan, Wrangell, Petersburg, and Juneau and then continue on to Haines and Skagway. From there travelers may continue by land into interior Alaska. The map in Exhibit 1 shows the route of the Alaska Marine Highway from Seattle to the ports of southeast Alaska. The map also shows the port of Bellingham, Washington.

As early as 1977, rumors have surfaced from time to time about the intention of directors of the Marine Highway to move the base port of the system from Seattle to the town of Bellingham. Despite the lack of official confirmation of such intentions, newspaper articles about a proposed move prompted a group of Bellingham business leaders to form an association to lobby for the move. The association hired a professional legislative lobbyist, Mr. Howard Scaman of Juneau, Alaska. The group wanted Scaman to lobby the Alaska state legislature on their behalf. Since the state of Alaska owns the ferry system, the association believed it should concentrate its efforts on the state legislature. An important factor that favored the association's efforts was the prevailing economic conditions in the state of Alaska.

Until 1984, the Alaska economy boomed as high oil prices brought hefty revenues from royalties from the sale of oil found on state-owned land. With the decline in oil prices after 1984, the state's economy was uncertain. This situation had a profound contradictory effect on operating conditions of the Alaska Marine Highway: While oil had become cheaper—and with it marine fuel—the state of Alaska had less money for support of the Marine Highway and was therefore looking for ways to reduce fuel consumption. One way to reduce fuel consumption by Marine Highway vessels would be to place the base port closer to Alaska. Moving the base from Seattle to Bellingham would achieve that result. Since Bellingham is the Washington port town closest to the Canadian border, it would have been the perfect choice. Alaska state economists quickly calculated that fuel consumption would be reduced by more than $3 million a year if the ferry terminal was to move to Bellingham. Aware of these facts, Mr. Scaman approached the concerned bodies in Juneau. The lobbyist found strong opposition to his plan from a surprising source—Mr. Joe Kemp, director of the Alaska Marine Highway. Kemp agreed with the economists that fuel consumption would be reduced by more than $3 million. He claimed, however, that moving the port to Bellingham would sharply reduce the number of passengers sailing on the ferries.

As negotiations continued, it was agreed that if less than 10% of the passengers would be lost, the move would be a viable solution. Scaman was thus left with the

EXHIBIT 7-1

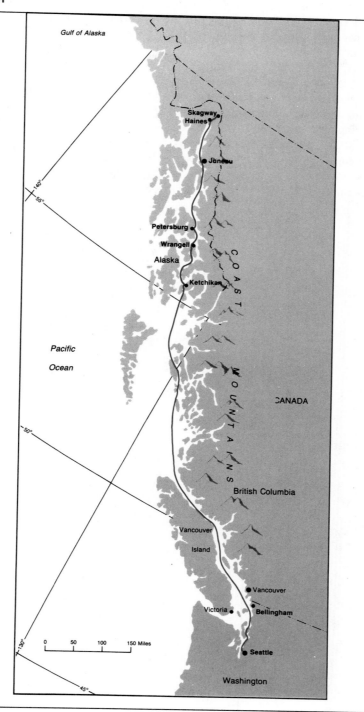

task of proving to the Alaska state legislature, the governor, and the director of the ferry system that moving the base port of the Marine Highway north to Bellingham would *not* result in a loss of passenger traffic of 10% or more. To prove this assertion, Scaman hired a statistician.

You are the statistician. You were hired to design a survey aboard Alaska Marine Highway ferries to determine what percentage of the passengers would not make the trip if the departure port was Bellingham instead of Seattle. Design the survey. Find the minimum required sample size, and give Scaman all the information he needs to start preparing the study. You have a $6,000 budget. A round-trip voyage aboard the ferry costs $400, and you may hire as many people as you need to make the trip and interview people. Other costs, for computing time, printing the questionnaire, and incidentals, are $420. The ferries make one trip every week from May through the end of September. The type of passengers throughout this period varies.

8

THE COMPARISON OF TWO POPULATIONS

INTRODUCTION

T he findings of the study had such potentially far-reaching implications that the Reuters agency, with advance knowledge of the findings, reported the information to its subscribing newspapers more than 24 hours before the article describing the study appeared in the January 28, 1988, issue of the *New England Journal of Medicine*.[1] The large-scale study was begun in 1982. Its subjects were a group of 22,071 male physicians 40 to 84 years of age living in the United States. Each physician was randomly assigned to take one of two kinds of pills: aspirin or beta carotene (as a placebo). Thus, 11,037 physicians were randomly assigned to take aspirin and 11,034 physicians were assigned to take the placebo. No physician knew which of the two kinds of pills he was taking. Each physician was to take his assigned pill every other day until the scheduled conclusion of the study in 1990. However, at a special meeting on December 18, 1987, the Data Monitoring Board of the Physicians' Health Study took the unusual step of recommending the early termination of the randomized aspirin experiment. At this point, the statistical results of the study had already exceeded everyone's expectations. It was shown, with a p-value of less than 0.00001, that a population (of male physicians, at least) taking a single aspirin pill once every two days would have a significantly lower proportion of heart attacks than a similar population not taking aspirin. The study confirmed what doctors have suspected for years—that the wonder drug aspirin can actually help prevent heart attacks.[2]

The comparison of two populations with respect to some population parameter—the population mean, the population proportion, or the population variance—is the topic of this chapter. Testing hypotheses about population parameters in the single-population case, as was done in Chapter 7, is an important statistical undertaking. However, the true usefulness of statistics manifests itself in allowing us to make *comparisons*. Almost daily we compare products, services, investment opportunities, management styles, etc. In this chapter, we will learn how to conduct such comparisons in an objective and meaningful way. We will learn how to find statistically significant differences between two populations. If you understood the methodology of hypothesis testing presented in the last chapter and the idea of a confidence interval from Chapter 6, you will find the extension to two populations straightforward and easy to understand. The first method we will learn is a test for the existence of a difference between the means of two populations. In the next section, we will see how such a comparison may be made in the special case where the observations may be paired in some way. Later we will learn how to conduct a test for the equality of the means of two populations using independent random samples. Then we will see how to compare two population proportions. Finally, we will encounter a test for the equality of the variances of two populations. In addition to statistical hypothesis tests, we will also learn how to construct confidence intervals for the difference between two population parameters. ■

---

[1] The editors of the *New England Journal of Medicine* reacted by barring the London-based Reuters from all new information from the *Journal* for a period of six months.

[2] For details of this interesting study, see "Preliminary Report: Findings from the Aspirin Component of the Ongoing Physicians' Health Study," *New England Journal of Medicine* (January 28, 1988).

8-2 Paired-Observations Comparisons

In this section, we describe a method for conducting a hypothesis test and constructing a confidence interval when our observations come from two populations and are *paired* in some way. What is the advantage of pairing our observations? Suppose that a taste test of two flavors is carried out. It seems intuitively plausible that if we let every person in our sample rate each one of the two flavors (with random choice of which flavor is tasted first), the resulting *paired* responses will convey more information about the taste difference than if we had used two different sets of people, each group rating only one flavor. Statistically, when we use the same people for rating the two products, we tend to remove much of the *extraneous variation* in taste ratings—the variation in people, experimental conditions, and other extraneous factors—and concentrate on the difference between the two flavors. When possible, it is often advisable to pair the observations, as this makes the experiment more precise. We will demonstrate the paired-observations test with an example.

EXAMPLE (a)

Home Shopping Network, Inc., pioneered the idea of merchandising directly to customers through cable television. By watching what amounts to 24 hours of commercials, viewers can call a number to buy products. Before expanding their services, network managers wanted to test whether or not this method of direct marketing increased sales on the average. A random sample of 16 viewers was selected for an experiment. All viewers in the sample had recorded the amount of money they spent shopping during the holiday season of the previous year. The next year, these people were given access to the cable network and were asked to keep a record of their total purchases during the holiday season. The paired observations for each shopper are given in Table 8-1. Faced with these data, Home Shopping Network managers want to test the null hypothesis that their service does not increase shopping volume, versus the alternative hypothesis that it does. The following solution of this problem introduces the *paired-observations t test*.

SOLUTION

The test involves two populations: the population of shoppers who have access to the Home Shopping Network and the population of shoppers who do not. We want to test the null hypothesis that the mean shopping expenditure in both populations is equal ver-

TABLE 8-1 Total Purchases of 16 Viewers with and without Home Shopping

Shopper	Previous Year's Shopping ($)	Current Year's Shopping ($)	Difference ($)
1	334	405	71
2	150	125	−25
3	520	540	20
4	95	100	5
5	212	200	−12
6	30	30	0
7	1,055	1,200	145
8	300	265	−35
9	85	90	5
10	129	206	77
11	40	18	−22
12	440	489	49
13	610	590	−20
14	208	310	102
15	880	995	115
16	25	75	50

sus the alternative hypothesis that the mean for the home shoppers is greater. Using the same people for the test and pairing their observations in a before-and-after way makes the test more precise than it would be without pairing. The pairing removes the influence of factors other than home shopping. The shoppers are the same people; thus, we can concentrate on the effect of the new shopping opportunity, leaving out of the analysis other factors that may affect shopping volume. Of course, we must consider the fact that the first observations were taken a year before. Let us assume, however, that relative inflation between the two years has been accounted for and that people in the sample have not had significant changes in income or other variables since the previous year that might affect their buying behavior.

Under these circumstances, it is easy to see that the variable in which we are interested is the difference between the present year's per-person shopping expenditure and that of the previous year. The population parameter about which we want to draw an inference is the mean difference between the two populations. We denote this parameter by μ_D, the mean difference. This parameter is defined as: $\mu_D = \mu_1 - \mu_2$, where μ_1 is the average holiday season shopping expenditure of people who use home shopping and μ_2 is the average holiday season shopping expenditure of people who do not. Our null and alternative hypotheses are, then,

$$H_0: \mu_D \leq 0$$
$$H_1: \mu_D > 0$$

(8–1)

Looking at the null and alternative hypotheses and the data in the last column of Table 8–1, we note that the test is a simple t test with $n - 1$ degrees of freedom, where our variable is the *difference* between the two observations for each shopper. In a sense, our two-population comparison test has been reduced to a hypothesis test about one parameter—the difference between the means of two populations. The test, as given by equation 8–1, is a right-hand-tailed test, but it need not be. In general, the paired-observations t test can be done as one-tailed or two-tailed. In addition, the hypothesized difference need not be zero. We can state any other value as the difference in the null hypothesis (although zero is most commonly used). The only assumption we make when we use this test is that *the population of differences is normally distributed*. Recall that this assumption was used whenever we carried out a test or constructed a confidence interval using the t distribution. Also note that, for large samples, the standard normal distribution may be used instead. This is also true for a normal population if you happen to know the population standard deviation of the differences, σ_D. The test statistic (assuming σ_D is not known and is estimated by s_D, the sample standard deviation of the differences) is given in equation 8–2.

Test statistic for the paired-observations t test:

$$t = \frac{\overline{D} - \mu_{D_0}}{s_D/\sqrt{n}}$$

(8–2)

where $\overline{D}$ is the sample average difference between each pair of observations, s_D is the sample standard deviation of these differences, and the sample size, n, is the number of pairs of observations (here, the number of people in the experiment). The symbol μ_{D_0} is the population mean difference under the null hypothesis. When the null hypothesis is true and the population mean difference is μ_{D_0}, the statistic has a t distribution with $n - 1$ degrees of freedom.

FIGURE 8–1   Carrying Out the Test of Example (a)

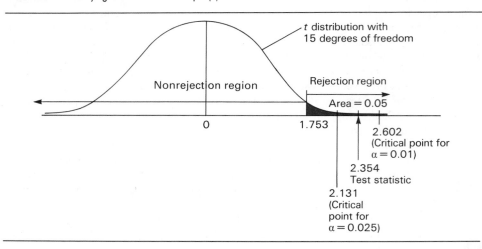

Let us now conduct the hypothesis test. From the differences reported in Table 8–1, we find that their mean is $\overline{D}$ = \$32.81 and their standard deviation is s_D = \$55.75. Since the sample size is small, n = 16, we use the t distribution with $n - 1$ = 15 degrees of freedom. The null-hypothesized value of the population mean is μ_{D_o} = 0. The value of our test statistic is obtained as:

$$t = \frac{32.81 - 0}{55.75/\sqrt{16}} = 2.354$$

This computed value of the test statistic is greater than 1.753, which is the critical point for a right-hand-tailed test at α = 0.05 using a t distribution with 15 degrees of freedom (see Appendix C, Table 3). The test statistic value is smaller than 2.602, which is the critical point for a one-tailed test using α = 0.01, but greater than 2.131, which is the critical point for a right-hand-tail area of 0.025. We may conclude that the p-value is between 0.025 and 0.01. This is shown in Figure 8–1. Home Shopping Network managers may conclude that the test gave moderate evidence for increased shopping volume by network viewers.

EXAMPLE (b)

It has recently been asserted that returns on stocks may change once a story about a company appears in *The Wall Street Journal* column "Heard on the Street." An investment portfolio analyst wants to check the statistical significance of this claim. The analyst collects a random sample of 50 stocks that were recommended as winners by the editor of "Heard on the Street." The analyst proceeds to conduct a two-tailed test of whether or not the annualized return on stocks recommended in the column differs between the month before the recommendation and the month after the recommendation. The analyst decides to conduct a two-tailed rather than a one-tailed test because she wants to allow for the possibility that stocks may be recommended in the column after their price has appreciated (and thus returns may actually decrease in the following month), as well as allowing for an increased return. For each stock in the sample of 50, the analyst computes the return before and after the *event* (the appearance of the story in the column) and the difference in the two return figures. Then the sample average difference of returns is computed, as well as the sample standard deviation of return differences. The results are: $\overline{D}$ = 0.1%, s_D = 0.05%. What should the analyst conclude?

The null and alternative hypotheses are $H_0: \mu_D = 0$ and $H_1: \mu_D \neq 0$. We now use the test statistic given in equation 8–2, noting that the distribution may be well approximated by the normal distribution because the sample size, $n = 50$, is large. We have:

$$z = \frac{\bar{D} - \mu_{D_0}}{s_D/\sqrt{n}} = \frac{0.1 - 0}{0.05/7.07} = 14.14$$

The value of the test statistic falls very far in the right-hand rejection region, and the p-value, therefore, is very small. The analyst should conclude that there is strong evidence that the average returns on stocks increase (because the rejection occurred in the right-hand rejection region) for stocks recommended in "Heard on the Street," as asserted by financial experts. Incidentally, the assumption of normality of the population of return differences—while not crucial in this case because the sample size is large—is supported by research findings on stock returns.

Confidence Intervals

In addition to tests of hypotheses, it is also possible to construct confidence intervals for the average population difference, μ_D. Analogous to the case of a single-population parameter, we define a $(1 - \alpha)100\%$ confidence interval for the parameter μ_D as follows.

A $(1 - \alpha)$ 100% confidence interval for the mean difference μ_D:

$$\bar{D} \pm t_{\alpha/2}\frac{s_D}{\sqrt{n}} \tag{8–3}$$

where $t_{\alpha/2}$ is the value of the t distribution with $n - 1$ degrees of freedom that cuts off an area of $\alpha/2$ to its right. When the sample size, n, is large, we may use $z_{\alpha/2}$ instead.

In Example (b), we may construct a 95% confidence interval for the average difference in annualized return on a stock before and after its being recommended in "Heard on the Street." The confidence interval is:

$$\bar{D} \pm z_{\alpha/2}\frac{s_D}{\sqrt{n}} = 0.1 \pm 1.96\frac{0.05}{7.07} = [0.086\%, 0.114\%]$$

Based on the data, the analyst may be 95% confident that the average difference in annualized return rate on a stock, measured the month before and the month following a positive recommendation in the column, is anywhere from 0.086% to 0.114%.

In this section, we compared population means for paired data. The following sections compare means of two populations where samples are drawn randomly and *independently* of each other from the two populations. When pairing can be done, our results tend to be more precise because the *experimental units* (for example, the people, each trying two different products) are different from each other, but each acts as an independent measuring device for the two products. This pairing of similar items is called *blocking*, and we will discuss it in detail in Chapter 9.

PROBLEMS

Answers

8–1.   A market research study is undertaken to test which of two popular electric shavers, a model made by Norelco or a model make by Remington, is preferred by consumers. A random sample of 25 men who regularly use an electric shaver, but not one of the two models to be tested, is chosen. Each man is then asked to shave one morning with the Norelco and the next morning with the Remington, or vice versa. The order, which model is used on which day, is randomly chosen for each man. After every shave, each man is asked to complete a questionnaire rating his satisfaction with the shaver. From the questionnaire, a total satisfaction score on a scale of 0 to 100 is computed. Then, for each man, the difference between the satisfaction score for Norelco and that for Remington is computed. The score differences (Norelco score − Remington score) are: 15, −8, 32, 57, 20, 10, −18, −12, 60, 72, 38, −5, 16, 22, 34, 41, 12, −38, 16, −40, 75, 11, 2, 55, 10. Which model, if any, is statistically preferred over the other? How confident are you of your finding? Explain.

8–2.

$z = 13.75$

Strong rejection

8–2.   The performance ratings of two sports cars, the Mazda RX7 and the Nissan 300ZX, are to be compared. A random sample of 40 drivers is selected to drive the two models. Each driver tries one car of each model, and the 40 cars of each model are chosen randomly. The time of each test drive is recorded for each driver and model. The difference in time (Mazda time − Nissan time) is computed, and from these differences a sample mean and a sample standard deviation are obtained. The results are $\overline{D} = 5.0$ seconds and $s_D = 2.3$ seconds. Based on these data, which model has higher performance? Explain. Also give a 95% confidence interval for the average time difference, in seconds, for the two models over the course driven.

8–3.   Recent studies indicate that in order to be globally competitive, firms must form global strategic partnerships.[3] An investment banker wants to test whether the return on investment for international ventures is different from return on investment for similar domestic ventures. A sample of 12 firms that recently entered into ventures with foreign companies is available. For each firm, the return on investment for both the international venture (I), and a similar domestic venture (D) is given:

D(%): 10 12 14 12 12   17 9 15 8.5 11 7 15
I(%): 11 14 15 11 12.5 16 10 13 10.5 17 9 19

Assuming that these firms represent a random sample from the population of all firms involved in global strategic partnerships, can the investment banker conclude that there are differences between average returns on domestic ventures and average returns on international ventures? Explain.

8–4.

$z = 1.549$

Cannot reject

8–4.   A study is undertaken to determine how consumers react to energy conservation efforts. A random group of 60 families is chosen. Their consumption of electricity is monitored in a period before and a period after the families are offered certain discounts to reduce their energy consumption. Both periods are the same length. The difference in electric consumption between the period before and the period after the offer is recorded for each family. Then the average difference in consumption and the standard deviation of the difference are computed. The results are $\overline{D} = 0.2$ kW (kilowatts) and $s_D = 1.0$ kW. At $\alpha = 0.01$, is there evidence to conclude that conservation efforts reduce consumption?

8–5.   A nationwide retailer wants to test whether new product shelf facings are effective in increasing sales volume. New shelf facings for the soft drink Country Time are tested at a random sample of 15 stores throughout the country. Data on total sales of Country Time for

---

[3] H. Perlmutter and D. Heenan, "Cooperate to Compete Globally," *Harvard Business Review* (March–April 1986).

each store, for the week before and the week after the new facings are installed, are given below:

```
Store:   1  2  3  4  5  6   7  8  9 10 11 12 13 14 15
Before: 57 61 12 38 12 69   5 39 88  9 92 26 14 70 22
After:  60 54 20 35 21 70   1 65 79 10 90 32 19 77 29
```

Using the 0.05 level of significance, do you believe that the new shelf facings increase sales of Country Time?

8–6. Most international investors managing Asian portfolios invest in both Japan and Hong Kong. Favorable conditions are believed to have brought more of these investments to Hong Kong. A test is carried out during the month of October to determine whether investors have shifted the proportions of their portfolios in favor of Hong Kong investments versus the Japanese investments. A random sample of 25 international investors is collected. These investors voluntarily reveal the proportion of their Hong Kong investments before and after October 15. The difference in proportion (after − before) is computed for each of these investors, and from these differences an average and a standard deviation are obtained. The average difference is +4%, and the standard deviation of differences is 2%. Do you believe that the average international investor has shifted investments to Hong Kong during the period in question? Explain.

8–6.
———
$t_{(24)} = 10$
Strong rejection

8–7. In problem 8–4, suppose that the *population* standard deviation is 1.0 and that the true average reduction in consumption for the entire population in the area is $\mu_D = 0.1$. For a sample size of 60, and $\alpha = 0.01$, what is the power of the test?

8–8. Consider the information in the following table.[4]

8–8.
———
$\overline{D} = 1.25$
$s = 42.89$
$t_{(19)} = 0.13$
No evidence of a
difference

Network	Program	Program Rating (scale: 0 to 100)	
		Men	**Women**
CBS	60 Minutes	99	96
ABC	ABC Monday Night Football	93	25
NBC	Cheers	88	97
ABC	America's Funniest Home Videos	90	35
ABC	America's Funniest People	81	33
NBC	Unsolved Mysteries	61	10
NBC	Matlock	54	50
CBS	Murder, She Wrote	60	48
ABC	Roseanne	73	73
NBC	The Heat of the Night	44	33
ABC	Davis Rules	30	11
CBS	Murphy Brown	25	58
CBS	Rescue 911	38	18
NBC	L.A. Law	52	12
ABC	ABC Sunday Night Movies	32	61
NBC	Empty Nest	16	96
CBS	Designing Women	8	94
NBC	The Cosby Show	18	80
NBC	A Different World	9	20
NBC	NBC Sunday Night Movies	10	6

Assume that the television programs were randomly selected from the population of all prime time TV programs. Also assume that ratings are normally distributed. Conduct a statistical test to determine whether there is a significant difference between average men's and women's ratings of prime time television programs.

---

[4] Adapted from *Variety* (February 25, 1991), p. 63.

8–3 A Test for the Difference between Two Population Means Using Independent Random Samples

It may not always be possible to pair our observations from two populations and carry out a test on the differences. In cases where the paired-observations test of the previous section does not apply, we may still compare the means of two populations by drawing two *independent* random samples from the two populations of interest. The samples drawn from the populations do not have to be the same size. We denote the size of the sample from population 1 by n_1 and the size of the sample from population 2 by n_2.

We will first consider a large-sample test for the difference between two population means. *Large sample* will mean that both sample sizes are large enough to assure us of a good normal approximation for the distributions of the sample means $\overline{X}_1$ and $\overline{X}_2$ via the central limit theorem. Following our rule of thumb from Chapter 5, we will consider the sample sizes large if both $n_1 \geq 30$ and $n_2 \geq 30$ (the large-sample test may also apply to smaller samples if we can assume that both populations are normally distributed with known population variances σ_1^2 and σ_2^2). We assume that the random samples, the sample from population 1 and the sample from population 2, are drawn *independently* of each other.

There are several different hypotheses that may be tested. We may want to test whether the mean of one particular population, say, population 1, is greater than the mean of the other population (a one-tailed test), or we may want to test whether or not the two population means are equal (with no prior intention to prove that one mean is greater than the other—a two-tailed test). Or we may wish to test whether or not the difference between the two population means is greater than (or less than) some particular number, D. Let us look at some particular sets of hypotheses. We will show three hypothesis-testing situations, which we will call situation I, situation II, and situation III. These possible hypothesis tests are not exhaustive. There are other possible tests that may be carried out; these are simple extensions of the three situations discussed here. The test we show, for example, may be a right-hand-tailed test; the analogous left-hand-tailed test is also possible, and you should have no problem carrying it out as well.

Hypothesis-testing situation I:

$$H_0: \mu_1 - \mu_2 = 0$$
$$H_1: \mu_1 - \mu_2 \neq 0$$

This is the most common test for the difference between two population means, μ_1 and μ_2. The null hypothesis states that the two means are equal (their difference is 0), while the two-tailed alternative states that the two population means are not equal.

Hypothesis-testing situation II:

$$H_0: \mu_1 - \mu_2 \leq 0$$
$$H_1: \mu_1 - \mu_2 > 0$$

This is another common set of hypotheses. The null hypothesis says that the mean of population 1 is equal to that of population 2 or is smaller than the mean of population 2. The alternative hypothesis states that the mean of population 1 is greater than the mean of population 2. The alternative hypothesis is the one we try to prove. We want to prove that the mean of population 1 is greater; we choose the label 1 for the population we believe to have the higher mean. The test is a right-hand-tailed test.

Hypothesis-testing situation III:
$$H_0: \mu_1 - \mu_2 \le D$$
$$H_1: \mu_1 - \mu_2 > D$$

This situation is not very common. Here we have some special-purpose test that we want to carry out; namely, we want to prove that the mean of one population is greater than the mean of the other population by at least D units. (A two-tailed test of the hypothesis that the difference between μ_1 and μ_2 is equal to D is also possible.)

The test statistic in all three hypothesis-testing situations is the same. Due to our assumptions about sample size or normal populations with known population variances, the statistic is a z statistic.

Large-sample test statistic for the difference between two population means:

$$z = \frac{(\overline{x}_1 - \overline{x}_2) - (\mu_1 - \mu_2)_0}{\sqrt{\dfrac{s_1^2}{n_1} + \dfrac{s_2^2}{n_2}}} \qquad (8-4)$$

The term $(\mu_1 - \mu_2)_0$ is the difference between μ_1 and μ_2 under the null hypothesis. It is equal to zero in situations I and II and it is equal to the prespecified value D in situation III. The term in the denominator is the standard error of the difference between the two sample means (it relies on the assumption that the two samples are independent).

We demonstrate the test, in situation I, with the following example.

EXAMPLE (c)

Until a few years ago, the market for consumer credit was considered to be segmented. Higher-income, higher-spending people tended to be American Express cardholders, and lower-income, lower-spending people were usually Visa cardholders. In the last few years, Visa has intensified its efforts to break into the higher-income segments of the market by using magazine and television advertising to create a high-class image. Recently, a consulting firm was hired by Visa to determine whether or not average monthly charges on the American Express Gold Card are approximately equal to the average monthly charges on Preferred Visa. A random sample of 1,200 Preferred Visa

FIGURE 8–2   Carrying Out the Test of Example (c)

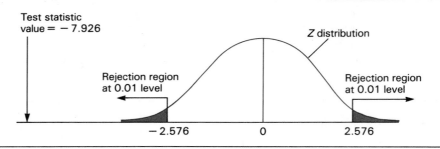

cardholders was selected, and it was found that the sample average monthly charge was $\bar{x}_1 = \$452$ and the sample standard deviation was $s_1 = \$212$. An independent random sample of 800 Gold Card members revealed a sample mean $\bar{x}_2 = \$523$ and $s_2 = \$185$. (Holders of both the Gold Card and Preferred Visa were excluded from the study.) Is there evidence to conclude that the average monthly charge in the entire population of American Express Gold Card members is different from the average monthly charge in the entire population of Preferred Visa cardholders?

SOLUTION

Since we have no prior suspicion (before looking at the two sample means—remember our caution in Chapter 7 about data snooping!) that either of the two populations may have a higher mean, the test is two-tailed. The null and alternative hypotheses are therefore as stated in situation I:

$$H_0: \mu_1 - \mu_2 = 0$$
$$H_1: \mu_1 - \mu_2 \neq 0$$

The value of our test statistic (equation 8–4) is:

$$z = \frac{(452 - 523) - 0}{\sqrt{\dfrac{212^2}{1,200} + \dfrac{185^2}{800}}} = -7.926$$

The computed value of the z statistic falls in the left-hand rejection region for any commonly used α, and the p-value is very small. We conclude that there is a statistically significant difference in average monthly charges between Gold Card and Preferred Visa cardholders. Note that this does not imply any *practical significance*. That is, while a difference in average spending in the two populations may exist, we cannot necessarily conclude that this difference is large. The test is shown in Figure 8–2.

The following example demonstrates the test in situation III.

EXAMPLE (d)

Suppose that the makers of Duracell batteries want to prove that their size AA battery lasts an average of at least 45 minutes longer than Duracell's main competitor, the Energizer. Two independent random samples of 100 batteries of each kind are selected, and the batteries are run continuously until they are no longer operational. The sample average life for Duracell is found to be $\bar{x}_1 = 308$ minutes, and the sample standard deviation is $s_1 = 84$ minutes. The results for the Energizer batteries are $\bar{x}_2 = 254$ minutes and $s_2 = 67$ minutes. Is there evidence to substantiate Duracell's claim that their batteries last, on average, at least 45 minutes longer than Energizer batteries of the same size?

Our null and alternative hypotheses are:

SOLUTION

$$H_0: \mu_1 - \mu_2 \leq 45$$
$$H_1: \mu_1 - \mu_2 > 45$$

The makers of Duracell hope to prove their claim by rejecting the null hypothesis. Recall that accepting a null hypothesis is not a strong conclusion. This is why—in order to prove that Duracell batteries last an average of at least 45 minutes longer—the claim to be proved is stated as the *alternative* hypothesis.

The value of the test statistic in this case is computed as follows:

$$z = \frac{(308 - 254) - 45}{\sqrt{\dfrac{84^2}{100} + \dfrac{67^2}{100}}} = 0.838$$

This value falls in the nonrejection region of our right-hand-tailed test at any conventional level of significance, α. The p-value is equal to 0.2011. We must conclude that there is insufficient evidence to support Duracell's claim.

Confidence Intervals

Recall from Chapter 7 that there is a strong connection between hypothesis tests and confidence intervals. In the case of the difference between two population means, we have:

A large sample $(1 - \alpha)100\%$ confidence interval for the difference between two population means, $\mu_1 - \mu_2$, using independent random samples:

$$(\bar{X}_1 - \bar{X}_2) \pm z_{\alpha/2} \sqrt{\frac{s_1^2}{n_1} + \frac{s_2^2}{n_2}} \qquad (8\text{–}5)$$

Equation 8–5 should be intuitively clear. The bounds on the difference between the two population means are equal to the difference between the two sample means, plus or minus the z coefficient for $(1 - \alpha)100\%$ confidence times the standard error of the difference between the two sample means (which is the expression with the square root sign).

In the context of Example (c), a 95% confidence interval for the difference between the average monthly charge on the American Express Gold Card and the average monthly charge on the Preferred Visa Card is, by equation 8–5:

$$(523 - 452) \pm 1.96 \sqrt{\frac{212^2}{1{,}200} + \frac{185^2}{800}} = [53.44, 88.56]$$

The consulting firm may report to Visa that they are 95% confident that the average

American Express Gold Card monthly bill is anywhere from \$53.44 to \$88.56 higher than the average Preferred Visa bill.

With one-tailed tests, the analogous interval is a one-sided confidence interval. We will not give examples of such intervals in this chapter. In general, we construct confidence intervals for population parameters when we have no *particular* values of the parameters we want to test and are interested in estimation only.

A Small-Sample Test for the Difference between Two Population Means

When the sample sizes are small ($n_1 < 30$, or $n_2 < 30$, or both) and we assume both populations are normally distributed, the test statistic in equation 8–4 has *approximately* a t distribution with degrees of freedom given by:

$$df = \frac{(s_1^2/n_1 + s_2^2/n_2)^2}{\dfrac{(s_1^2/n_1)^2}{n_1 - 1} + \dfrac{(s_2^2/n_2)^2}{n_2 - 1}} \tag{8–6}$$

When df as computed in equation 8–6 is not an integer, we round *downward* to the nearest integer for a conservative estimate of the degrees of freedom. We can also construct a confidence interval similar to equation 8–5 with $z_{\alpha/2}$ replaced by $t_{\alpha/2}$, with df given by equation 8–6. We will demonstrate the analysis with a short, hypothetical example.

Suppose that we want to test the null hypothesis that two population means are equal versus the alternative hypothesis that they are not equal. The two populations are assumed to be normally distributed. A random sample of size 15 from population 1 gives a sample mean of 100 and a sample standard deviation of 5. An independent random sample of size 10 from population 2 gives a sample mean of 110 and a sample standard deviation of 3. The test statistic value is:

$$t = \frac{(100 - 110) - 0}{\sqrt{\dfrac{5^2}{15} + \dfrac{3^2}{10}}} = -6.242$$

This value is a realization of a random variable approximately following a t distribution with degrees of freedom given by:

$$df = \frac{(s_1^2/n_1 + s_2^2/n_2)^2}{\dfrac{(s_1^2/n_1)^2}{n_1 - 1} + \dfrac{(s_2^2/n_2)^2}{n_2 - 1}}$$

$$= \frac{(25/15 + 9/10)^2}{\dfrac{(25/15)^2}{14} + \dfrac{(9/10)^2}{9}} = 22.84$$

We round downward from 22.84 and use the approximation df = 22. The critical points in a two-tailed test with $\alpha = 0.05$ for a t distribution with df = 22 are ± 2.074. Since the computed value of the test statistic, -6.242, is smaller than -2.074, we reject the null hypothesis. A confidence interval for $\mu_1 - \mu_2$ can be similarly constructed. In the next section, we will see an easier small-sample test.

8–9. LINC is a software tool developed by Burroughs Corporation. The program automatically writes some of the coding that programmers have to do manually. LINC supposedly saves programming time and allows programmers to operate more efficiently. In a test of the software package, 45 programmers (group 1) were asked to write a program without LINC and then run the program until it performed with no bugs. The times from start to finish for this group were recorded. Group 2 consisted of 32 programmers who were asked to prepare the same program with the aid of LINC. Before getting the data, it was decided to run the test as a one-tailed test to prove that the package reduces the average programming time. The results were: $\bar{x}_1 = 26$ minutes, $\bar{x}_2 = 21$ minutes, $s_1 = 8$ minutes, and $s_2 = 6$ minutes. Conduct the test, and state your conclusion. Is LINC effective in reducing average programming time?

8–10. The photography department of a glamour magazine needs to choose a camera. Of the two models the department is considering, one is made by Nikon and one by Minolta. The department contracts with an agency to determine if one of the two models gets a higher average performance rating by professional photographers, or whether the average performance ratings of these two cameras are not statistically different. The agency asks 60 different professional photographers to rate one of the cameras (30 photographers rate each model). The ratings are on a scale of 1 to 10. The average sample rating for Nikon is 8.5, and the sample standard deviation is 2.1. For the Minolta sample, the mean is 7.8, and the standard deviation is 1.8. Is there a difference between the average population ratings of the two cameras? If so, which one is rated higher?

8–11. The Marcus Robert Real Estate Company wants to test whether the average sale price of residential properties in a certain size range in Bel Air, California, is approximately equal to the average sale price of residential properties of the same size range in Marin County, California. The company gathers data on a random sample of 32 properties in Bel Air and finds $\bar{x} = \$345{,}650$ and $s = \$48{,}500$. A random sample of 35 properties in Marin County gives $\bar{x} = \$289{,}440$ and $s = \$87{,}090$. Is the average sale price of all properties in both locations approximately equal or not? Explain.

8–12. General Motors Corporation hopes to reduce anticipated production costs of its Saturn model by instituting an assembly schedule that will reduce average production time to about 40 hours per car.[5] In a test run of the new assembly line, 40 cars are built at a sample average time per car of 46.5 hours and a sample standard deviation of 8.0 hours. A test run of 38 cars using the old assembly schedule results in a sample mean of 51.2 hours and a sample standard deviation of 9.5 hours. Is there proof that the new assembly schedule reduces the average production time per car? What is the p-value? Explain.

8–13. Many companies that cater to teenagers have learned that young people respond to commercials that provide dance-beat music, adventure, and a fast pace, rather than words. In one test, a group of 128 teenagers were shown commercials featuring rock music, and their purchasing frequency of the advertised products over the following month was recorded as a single score for each person in the group. Then a group of 212 teenagers were shown commercials for the same products, but with the music replaced by verbal persuasion. The purchase frequency scores of this group were computed as well. The results for the music group were $\bar{x} = 23.5$ and $s = 12.2$; and the results for the verbal group were $\bar{x} = 18.0$ and $s = 10.5$. Assume that the two groups were randomly selected from the entire teenage consumer population. Using the $\alpha = 0.01$ level of significance, test the null hypothesis that both methods of advertising are equally effective versus the alternative hypothesis that they are not equally effective. If you conclude that one method is better, state which one it is, and explain how you reached your conclusion.

Answers

8–10.

$z = 1.386$
No evidence of a
difference

8–12.

$z = 2.357$
Reject H_0

---

[5] "Behind the Hype at GM's Saturn," *Fortune* (November 11, 1985).

Answers

z = 1.208
No evidence

8-14. In 1985, the chief proprietor of Michael's Restaurant in Santa Monica decided to add an 18% service charge to customers' bills in an effort to reduce the dependence of the service staff on variable tipping. Before the change, the proprietor managed to convince the staff to reveal the exact amount of tips they received over a period of 40 days. The average tipping percentage over 40 days was found to be 16.8%. Then for 30 days after the change— after the 18% service charge was added to customers' bills—additional tips given to the service staff averaged 10.5%. The sample standard deviation for the prechange period was 5%, and the sample standard deviation for the postchange period was 4%. Suppose that the proprietor had originally decided to test the null hypothesis that adding the extra charge would reduce the average tip by, at most, 5% versus the alternative hypothesis that the average tip would be reduced by over 5%; and suppose that the period of 40 days before the change and the period of 30 days after the change were independent random samples of 40 and 30 data points, respectively. Carry out the hypothesis test at $\alpha = 0.05$, and state your conclusion.

8-15. A fashion industry analyst wants to prove that models featuring Liz Claiborne clothing earn on average more than models featuring clothes designed by Calvin Klein. For a given period of time, a random sample of 32 Liz Claiborne models reveals average earnings of $4,238.00 and a standard deviation of $1,002.50. For the same period, an independent random sample of 37 Calvin Klein models has mean earnings of $3,888.72 and a sample standard deviation of $876.05.

a. Is this a one-tailed or a two-tailed test? Explain.

b. Carry out the hypothesis test at the 0.05 level of significance.

c. State your conclusion.

d. What is the *p*-value? Explain its relevance.

e. Redo the problem assuming the results are based on a random sample of 10 Liz Claiborne models and 11 Calvin Klein models.

z = 10.14
Strong evidence

8-16. An article on the growing trade gap in high-tech ideas between the United States and Japan claims that more royalties and licensing fees are paid to the United States by Japanese users of American ideas than the other way around.[6] A random sample of 100 American patents used in Japan reveals an average royalty of $1,838.69 and a standard deviation of $461. A random sample of 80 Japanese patents used in the United States has an average royalty payment of $1,050.22 and a standard deviation of $560. Is there evidence to conclude that the Japanese pay, on the average, more to American patent holders than the other way around?

8-17. A brokerage firm is said to provide both brokerage services and "research" if, in addition to buying and selling securities for its clients, the firm also furnishes clients with advice about the value of securities, information on economic factors and trends, and portfolio strategy. The Securities and Exchange Commission (SEC) has been studying brokerage commissions charged by both "research" and "nonresearch" brokerage houses.[7] A random sample of 255 transactions at nonresearch firms is collected, as well as a random sample of 300 transactions at research firms. These samples reveal that the difference between the average sample percentage commission at research firms and the average percentage commission in the nonresearch sample is 2.54%. The standard deviation of the research firms' sample is 0.85%, and that of the nonresearch firms is 0.64%. Give a 95% confidence interval for the difference in the average percentage of commissions in research versus nonresearch brokerage houses.

[6]"Picking Japan's Research Brains," *Fortune* (March 25, 1991), p. 84.

[7]J. Gillis, "Soft Dollars and Investment Research," *Financial Analysts Journal* (July–August 1985).

8–4 A Test for the Difference between Two Population Means, Assuming Equal Population Variances

When the population variances σ_1^2 and σ_2^2 are assumed to be equal, there is another test that can be done for the difference between two population means. This test is especially useful in the case of small samples, as it allows us to conduct a test for the difference between two population means without having to use the complicated expression for the degrees of freedom of the approximate t statistic (equation 8–6). In addition to assuming equal (but usually unknown) population variances, we assume that the two populations of interest are *approximately normally distributed*.

As before, there are many possible hypothesis tests. We will concentrate on the three situations we considered in the previous section:

Situation I: $H_0: \mu_1 - \mu_2 = 0$
              $H_1: \mu_1 - \mu_2 \neq 0$

Situation II: $H_0: \mu_1 - \mu_2 \leq 0$
              $H_1: \mu_1 - \mu_2 > 0$

Situation III: $H_0: \mu_1 - \mu_2 \leq D$
              $H_1: \mu_1 - \mu_2 > D$

We note again that other tests are possible as well. While the tests in situations II and III are right-hand-tailed tests, it is possible in each of these situations to conduct a similar left-hand-tailed test. It is also possible to conduct a two-tailed test, in situation I, using a specified value D as the null-hypothesized difference between μ_1 and μ_2, where D is not necessarily zero. Before we describe the test statistic and its distribution, let us analyze the situation giving rise to our statistic.

We select two independent random samples: a random sample from population 1 and a random sample from population 2. We denote the sample sizes by n_1 and n_2,

FIGURE 8–3 The Degrees of Freedom Associated with Deviations from the Sample Means of Two Independent Samples

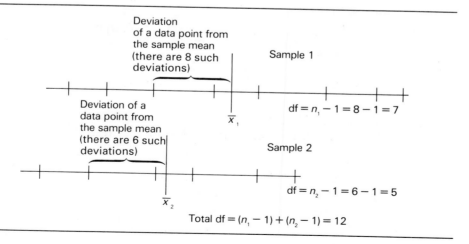

respectively. Once we compute the mean for each sample, $\bar{x}_1$ and $\bar{x}_2$, we lose one degree of freedom in each sample with respect to the computation of the sample standard deviations, s_1 and s_2. (Refer to the explanation in Chapter 5 as to why this happens.) Figure 8–3 shows why, with two independent samples for which the two sample means are computed, the total number of degrees of freedom associated with deviations from the sample means is: df $= (n_1 - 1) + (n_2 - 1) = n_1 + n_2 - 2$. This parameter, df, is associated with the *pooled estimate* of the common population variance, defined as follows.

We assume that the two population variances, σ_1^2 and σ_2^2, are equal. We denote this common variance of the two populations by σ_2. The two sample variances, s_1^2 and s_2^2, are then estimates of the same quantity, σ^2. What we are looking for is a *pooled* variance estimate, s_p^2. The variance estimator from sample 1 has $n_1 - 1$ degrees of freedom, and the variance estimator from sample 2 has $n_2 - 1$ degrees of freedom. We want to pool the two variance estimators S_1^2 and S_2^2 in such a way that the relative weights given to the two estimates produced will be proportional to the degrees of freedom of the estimators. (Obviously, an estimate based on a larger sample—larger df—should be given proportionally more weight in computing the pooled variance than an estimate based on smaller df.)

A **pooled estimate** of the common population variance, based on a sample variance s_1^2 from a sample of size n_1 and a sample variance s_2^2 from a sample of size n_2, is given by:

$$s_p^2 = \frac{(n_1 - 1)s_1^2 + (n_2 - 1)s_2^2}{n_1 + n_2 - 2} \tag{8–7}$$

Equation 8–7 should make sense to you. The equation gives a weighted average of two sample variances, where the weights are the degrees of freedom upon which each estimate is based, and the total weight—the denominator in the formula—is the sum of the degrees of freedom associated with the two estimates: df $= (n_1 - 1) + (n_2 - 1) = n_1 + n_2 - 2$.

The estimate of the standard error of $(\bar{X}_1 - \bar{X}_2)$ is given by:[8]

$$\sqrt{s_p^2\left(\frac{1}{n_1} + \frac{1}{n_2}\right)} \tag{8–8}$$

The expression in equation 8–8 has the same function as $s/\sqrt{n}$ in the case of a single-sample inference about a population mean. We are now ready to define our test statistic.

---

[8] Our assumption of independent random sampling from the two populations implies that $\bar{X}_1$ and $\bar{X}_2$ are *independent* random variables. Thus, the variance of $(\bar{X}_1 - \bar{X}_2)$ is equal to $V(\bar{X}_1 - \bar{X}_2) = V(\bar{X}_1) + V(\bar{X}_2) = (\sigma^2/n_1) + (\sigma^2/n_2) = \sigma^2[(1/n_1) + (1/n_2)]$, where σ^2 is the common population variance. This common variance is estimated by S_p^2.

Test statistic for the difference between two population means, assuming equal population variances:

$$t = \frac{(\bar{x}_1 - \bar{x}_2) - (\mu_1 - \mu_2)_0}{\sqrt{s_p^2\left(\dfrac{1}{n_1} + \dfrac{1}{n_2}\right)}} \qquad (8\text{–}9)$$

where $(\mu_1 - \mu_2)_0$ is the difference between the two population means under the null hypothesis (zero or some number, D). The degrees of freedom of the test statistic t are $n_1 + n_2 - 2$ (the degrees of freedom associated with s_p^2, the pooled estimate of the population variance).

For large samples, we may use the standard normal distribution instead of the t distribution with $n_1 + n_2 - 2$ degrees of freedom. Note that the test statistic in equation 8–9 follows the general form of a standardized test statistic given in Chapter 7: Test statistic = (Estimate − Hypothesized value of parameter)/(Standard error of estimator).

EXAMPLE (e)

Changes in the price of oil have long been known to affect the economy of the United States. An economist wants to check whether the price of a barrel of crude oil affects the U.S. Consumer Price Index (CPI), a measure of price levels and inflation. The economist collects two sets of data: one set comprises 14 monthly observations on increases in the CPI, in percentage per month, when the price of oil is $27.50 per barrel; the other set consists of 9 monthly observations on percentage increase in the CPI when the price of crude oil is $20.00 per barrel. The economist assumes that her data are a random set of observations from a population of monthly CPI percentage increases when oil sells for $27.50 per barrel, and an independent set of random observations from a population of monthly CPI percentage increases when oil sells for $20.00 per barrel. She also assumes that the two populations of CPI percentage increases are normally distributed and that the variances of the two populations are equal. Considering the nature of the economic variables in question, these are reasonable assumptions. If we call the population of monthly CPI percentage increases when oil sells for $27.50 population 1, and that of oil at $20.00 per barrel population 2, then the economist's data are as follows:[9] $\bar{x}_1 = 0.317\%$, $s_1 = 0.12\%$, $n_1 = 14$; $\bar{x}_2 = 0.21\%$, $s_2 = 0.11\%$, $n_2 = 9$. Our economist is faced with the question: Do these data provide evidence to conclude that average percentage increase in the CPI differs when oil sells at these two different prices?

SOLUTION

Although the economist may have a suspicion about the possible direction of change in the CPI as oil prices decrease, she decides to approach the situation with an open mind and let the data speak for themselves. That is, she wants to carry out the two-tailed test, situation I. Her test is: H_0: $\mu_1 - \mu_2 = 0$ versus H_1: $\mu_1 - \mu_2 \neq 0$. Using equation 8–9, the economist computes the value of the test statistic, which has a t distribution with $n_1 + n_2 - 2 = 21$ degrees of freedom:

[9] The data are based on estimates reported by Data Resources, Inc.

$$t = \frac{(0.317 - 0.210) - 0}{\sqrt{\frac{(13)(0.12)^2 + (8)(0.11)^2}{21}\left(\frac{1}{14} + \frac{1}{9}\right)}} = 2.15$$

The computed value of the test statistic, $t = 2.15$, falls in the right-hand rejection region at $\alpha = 0.05$, but not very far from the critical point, 2.080. The p-value is therefore just under 0.05. The economist may thus conclude that, based on her data and the validity of the assumptions made, there is some evidence that the average monthly increase in the CPI is greater when oil sells for $27.50 per barrel than it is when oil sells for $20.00 per barrel.

EXAMPLE (f)

The manufacturers of compact disc players want to test whether a small price reduction is enough to increase sales of their product. Randomly chosen data on 15 weekly sales totals at outlets in a given area before the price reduction show a sample mean of $6,598 and a sample standard deviation of $844. A random sample of 12 weekly sales totals after the small price reduction gives a sample mean of $6,870 and a sample standard deviation of $669. Is there evidence that the small price reduction is enough to increase sales of compact disc players?

SOLUTION

Our null and alternative hypotheses are those of situation II, a one-tailed test, except that we will reverse the notation 1 and 2 so we can conduct a right-hand-tailed test to determine whether reducing the price increases sales (if sales increase, then μ_2 will be greater than μ_1, which is what we want the alternative hypothesis to be). We have: $H_0: \mu_2 - \mu_1 \leq 0$ and $H_1: \mu_2 - \mu_1 > 0$. We assume an equal variance of the populations of sales at the two price levels. Our test statistic has a t distribution with $n_1 + n_2 - 2 = 15 + 12 - 2 = 25$ degrees of freedom. The computed value of the statistic, by equation 8–9, is:

$$t = \frac{(6,870 - 6,598) - 0}{\sqrt{\frac{(14)(844)^2 + (11)(669)^2}{25}\left(\frac{1}{15} + \frac{1}{12}\right)}} = 0.91$$

This value of the statistic falls inside the nonrejection region for any usual level of significance, as shown in Figure 8–4. The manufacturer may conclude that the data

FIGURE 8–4 Conducting the Test of Example (f)

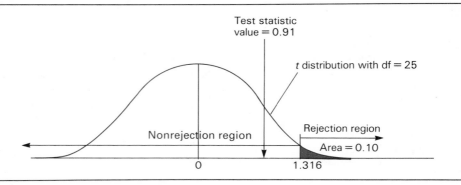

present no evidence that reducing the price by the small amount used in the experiment brings about increases in average sales.

Confidence Intervals

As usual, it is possible to construct confidence intervals for the parameter in question—here, the difference between the two population means. The confidence interval for this parameter is based on the t distribution with $n_1 + n_2 - 2$ degrees of freedom (or z when df is large).

A $(1 - \alpha)100\%$ confidence interval for $(\mu_1 - \mu_2)$, assuming equal population variance:

$$(\bar{x}_1 - \bar{x}_2) \pm t_{\alpha/2} \sqrt{s_p^2 \left(\frac{1}{n_1} + \frac{1}{n_2} \right)} \qquad (8\text{--}10)$$

The confidence interval in equation 8–10 has the usual form: Estimate $\pm$ Distribution coefficient $\times$ Standard error of estimator.

In Example (f), forgetting that the test was carried out as a one-tailed test, let us compute a 95% confidence interval for the difference between the two means. Since the test resulted in acceptance of the null hypothesis (and would have also resulted in acceptance had it been carried out as two-tailed), our confidence interval should contain the null-hypothesized difference between the two population means: zero. This is due to the connection between hypothesis tests and confidence intervals. Let us see if this really happens. The 95% confidence interval for $(\mu_1 - \mu_2)$ is:

$$(\bar{x}_1 - \bar{x}_2) \pm t_{0.025} \sqrt{s_p^2 \left(\frac{1}{n_1} + \frac{1}{n_2} \right)} = (6{,}870 - 6{,}598) \pm 2.06 \sqrt{(595{,}835)(0.15)}$$

$$= [-343.85, \ 887.85]$$

We see that the confidence interval indeed contains the null-hypothesized difference of zero, as expected from the fact that a two-tailed test would have resulted in acceptance of the null hypothesis.

PROBLEMS

In each of the following problems assume that the two populations of interest are normally distributed with equal variance. Assume independent random sampling from the two populations.

8–18. The recent boom in sales of travel books has led to the marketing of other travel-related guides, such as video travel guides and audio walking-tour tapes. Waldenbooks has been studying the market for these travel guides.[10] In one market test, a random sample of 25 potential travelers was asked to rate audiotapes of a certain destination, and another random sample of 20 potential travelers was asked to rate videotapes of the same destination. Both ratings were on a scale of 0 to 100 and measured the potential travelers' satisfaction with the

Answer

8–18.

$z = 4.326$

Reject H_0

---

[10] "Travel Guides Boom," *The Wall Street Journal* (December 11, 1986).

travel guide they tested and the degree of possible purchase intent (with 100 the highest). The mean score for the audio group was 87, and their standard deviation was 12. The mean score for the video group was 64, and their standard deviation was 23. Do these data present evidence that one form of travel guide is better than the other? Advise Waldenbooks on a possible marketing decision to be made.

8–19. Business schools at certain prestigious universities offer nondegree management training programs for high-level executives. These programs supposedly develop executives' leadership abilities and help them advance to higher management positions within two years after program completion. A management consulting firm wants to test the effectiveness of these programs and sets out to conduct a one-tailed test, where the alternative hypothesis is that graduates of the programs under study do receive, on the average, salaries at least $4,000 per year higher than salaries of comparable executives without the special university training. To test the hypotheses, the firm traces a random sample of 28 top executives who earn, at the time the sample is selected, about the same salaries. Out of this group, 13 executives—randomly selected from the group of 28 executives—are enrolled in one of the university programs under study. Two years later, average salaries for the two groups and standard deviations of salaries are computed. The results are: $\bar{x} = 48$ and $s = 6$ for the nonprogram executives, and $\bar{x} = 55$ and $s = 8$ for the program executives. All numbers are in thousands of dollars per year. Conduct the test at $\alpha = 0.05$, and evaluate the effectiveness of the programs in terms of increased average salary levels.

8–20.

$z = 3.256$
Hiring probably increased

8–20. A survey of the National Federation of Independent Business (NFIB) indicates that small businesses intended to increase their hiring as well as their capital expenditures during 1986 as compared with 1985. Suppose that, as part of a follow-up survey by NFIB, 20 small businesses, randomly chosen from the NFIB's list of 2,100 companies, show an average hiring for 1985 equal to 3.2 new employees per firm and a standard deviation of 1.5 hires. A random sample of 30 small businesses taken at the end of 1986 shows an average of 5.1 new hires and a standard deviation of 2.3 hires. At the $\alpha = 0.01$ level of significance, can you conclude that average hiring by all small businesses in 1986 increased as compared with 1985?

8–21. Refer to the survey described in problem 8–20. Suppose that the same two samples of small businesses were used to test the null hypothesis that capital expenditure by small firms in 1985 averaged about the same as in 1986, versus the alternative hypothesis that average capital expenditure in 1986 was higher than in 1985. Use the following results to conduct the test at $\alpha = 0.01$. For the 1985 sample of 20 firms: $\bar{x} = \$21,670$, $s = \$8,300$. For the 1986 sample of 30 firms: $\bar{x} = \$42,889$, $s = \$9,302$.

8–22.

$\bar{x}_O = 8.263$
$s_O = 1.428$
$\bar{x}_N = 9.06$
$s_N = 1.563$
$t_{(40)} = 1.71$
Some evidence

8–22. Ikarus, the Hungarian bus maker, has lost its important Soviet market and is reported on the verge of collapse.[11] The company is now trying a new engine in its buses and has gathered the following random samples of miles-per-gallon figures for the old engine versus the new:

Old engine: 8, 9, 7.5, 8.5, 6, 9, 9, 10, 7, 8.5, 6, 10, 9, 8, 9, 5, 9.5, 10, 8
New engine: 10, 9, 9, 6, 9, 11, 11, 8, 9, 6.5, 7, 9, 10, 8, 9, 10, 9, 12, 11.5, 10, 7, 10, 8.5

Is there evidence that the new engine is more economical than the old one?

8–23. *Air Transport World* recently named the Dutch airline KLM "Airline of the Year." One measure of the airline's excellent management is its research effort in developing new routes and improving service on existing routes. The airline wanted to test the profitability of a certain transatlantic flight route and offered daily flights from Europe to the United States over a period of six weeks on the new proposed route. Then, over a period of nine weeks, daily flights were offered from Europe to an alternative airport in the United States. Weekly profitability data for the two samples were collected, under the assumption that these may be viewed as independent random samples of weekly profits from the two populations (one pop-

---

[11] "Hungary: Economy Shackled by Chain of Debt," *International Management* (March, 1991), p. 20.

ulation is flights to the proposed airport, and the other population is flights to an alternative airport). Data are as follows. For the proposed route, $\bar{x}$ = $96,540 per week and s = $12,522. For the alternative route, $\bar{x}$ = $85,991 and s = $19,548. Test the hypothesis that the proposed route is more profitable than the alternative route. Use a significance level of your choice.

8-24. Authors T. Peters and R. Waterman state in their book *In Search of Excellence* that the giant advertising firm of Ogilvy and Mather is more concerned with customer satisfaction than it is with company profits.[12] Suppose a test is carried out to determine whether or not new management decisions at Ogilvy and Mather increase average customer satisfaction. To test this claim, a random sample of company clients is polled before an important management decision, and customer satisfaction is measured for this sample on a scale of 1 to 10. Then, some time after the management decision has been made and a new company policy implemented, another sample of clients is polled, and their satisfaction scores are computed (on the same scale). Letting the subscript b denoted "before the new decision" and the subscript a denoted "after the new decision," the results of the surveys are: n_b = 18, $\bar{x}_b$ = 7.4, s_b = 1.3; n_a = 23, $\bar{x}_a$ = 8.2, s_a = 2.4. Using these data, do you believe that customer satisfaction is increased, on the average, after the new management decision and the resulting new company policy?

8-25. Mark Pollard, financial consultant for Merrill Lynch, Pierce, Fenner & Smith, Inc., is quoted in national advertisements for Merrill Lynch as saying: "I've made more money for clients by saying no than by saying yes." Suppose that Mr. Pollard allowed you access to his files so that you could conduct a statistical test of the correctness of his statement. Suppose further that you gathered a random sample of 25 clients to whom Mr. Pollard said yes when presented with their investment proposals, and you found that the clients' average gain on investments was 12% and the standard deviation was 2.5%. Suppose you gathered another sample of 25 clients to whom Mr. Pollard said no when asked about possible investments; the clients were then offered other investments, which they consequently made. For this sample, you found that the average return was 13.5% and the standard deviation was 1%. Test Mr. Pollard's claim at α = 0.05. What assumptions are you making in this problem?

8-26. A recent article by A. Chen and L. Merville reports the results of an analysis of stock market returns before and after antitrust trials that resulted in the breakup of AT&T.[13] The study concentrated on two periods: the preantitrust period of 1966 to 1973, denoted period 1, and the antitrust trial period of 1974 to 1981, called period 2. An equation similar to equation 8-9 was used to test for the existence of a difference in mean stock return during the two periods. Conduct a two-tailed test of equality of mean stock return in the population of all stocks before and during the antitrust trials using the following data: n_1 = 21, $\bar{x}_1$ = 0.105, s_1 = 0.09; n_2 = 28, $\bar{x}_2$ = 0.1331, s_2 = 0.122. Use α = 0.05.

8-27. A banker with Continental Illinois National Bank and Trust Company wants to test which method of raising cash for companies—borrowing from public sources or borrowing from private sources—results in higher average amounts raised by a company. The banker collects a random sample of 12 firms that borrowed only from public sources and finds that the average amount borrowed by a company per source is $12,500 and the standard deviation is $3,400. Another sample of 18 firms that borrowed only from private sources gives a sample average per source of $21,000 and a sample standard deviation of $5,000. Do you believe that either private or public sources lend, on the average, more than the other? Explain.

8-28. In problem 8-25, construct a 95% confidence interval for the difference between the average return to investors following a no recommendation and the average return to investors following a yes recommendation. Interpret your results.

Answers

8-24.
___

z = 1.273
No evidence

8-26.
___

z = 0.89
Not significant

8-28.
___

[0.44, 2.56]

[12] T. Peters and R. Waterman, *In Search of Excellence* (New York: Harper & Row, 1982).

[13] A. Chen and L. Merville, "An Analysis of Divestiture Effects Resulting from Deregulation," *Journal of Finance* (December 1986).

8–5 A Large-Sample Test for the Difference between Two Population Proportions

When sample sizes are large enough that the distributions of the sample proportions $\hat{P}_1$ and $\hat{P}_2$ are both approximated well by a normal distribution, the difference between the two sample proportions is also approximately normally distributed, and this gives rise to a test for equality of two population proportions based on the standard normal distribution. It is also possible to construct confidence intervals for the difference between the two population proportions. Assuming the sample sizes are large and assuming independent random sampling from the two populations, the following are possible hypotheses (we consider situations similar to the ones discussed in the previous two sections; other tests are also possible).

Situation I: H_0: $p_1 - p_2 = 0$
                H_1: $p_1 - p_2 \neq 0$

Situation II: H_0: $p_1 - p_2 \leq 0$
                H_1: $p_1 - p_2 > 0$

Situation III: H_0: $p_1 - p_2 \leq D$
                H_1: $p_1 - p_2 > D$

where D is some number other than 0.

In the case of tests about the difference between two population proportions, there are two test statistics. One statistic is appropriate when the null hypothesis is that the difference between the two population proportions is equal to (or greater than or equal to, or less than or equal to) zero. This is the case, for example, in situations I and II. The other test statistic is appropriate when the null-hypothesized difference is some number, D, different from zero. This is the case, for example, in situation III (or in a two-tailed test, situation I, with D replacing 0).

Test statistic for the difference between two population proportions where the null-hypothesized difference is zero:

$$z = \frac{(\hat{p}_1 - \hat{p}_2) - 0}{\sqrt{\hat{p}(1 - \hat{p})\left(\dfrac{1}{n_1} + \dfrac{1}{n_2}\right)}} \qquad (8\text{–}11)$$

where $\hat{p}_1 = x_1/n_1$ is the sample proportion in sample 1 and $\hat{p}_2 = x_2/n_2$ is the sample proportion in sample 2. The symbol $\hat{p}$ stands for the *combined sample proportion in both samples,* considered as a single sample. That is,

$$\hat{p} = \frac{x_1 + x_2}{n_1 + n_2} \qquad (8\text{–}12)$$

Note that 0 in the numerator of equation 8–11 is the null-hypothesized difference between the two population proportions; we retain it only for conceptual reasons—to maintain the form of our test statistic: (Estimate − Hypothesized value of the parameter)/(Standard error of the estimator). When we carry out computations using equation 8–11, we will, of course, ignore subtracting zero. Under the null hypothesis that the difference between the two population proportions is zero, both sample proportions $\hat{p}_1$ and $\hat{p}_2$ are estimates of the same quantity, and therefore—assuming, as always, that the null hypothesis is true—we pool the two estimates when computing the estimated standard error of the difference between the two sample proportions: the denominator of equation 8–11.

When the null hypothesis is that the difference between the two population proportions is a number other than zero, we cannot assume that $\hat{p}_1$ and $\hat{p}_2$ are estimates of the same population proportion (because the null-hypothesized difference between the two population proportions is $D \neq 0$); in such cases we cannot pool the two estimates when computing the estimated standard error of the difference between the two sample proportions. In such cases, we use the following test statistic.

Test statistic for the difference between two population proportions when the null-hypothesized difference between the two proportions is some number, D, other than zero:

$$z = \frac{(\hat{p}_1 - \hat{p}_2) - D}{\sqrt{\dfrac{\hat{p}_1(1 - \hat{p}_1)}{n_1} + \dfrac{\hat{p}_2(1 - \hat{p}_2)}{n_2}}} \qquad (8\text{–}13)$$

We will now demonstrate the use of the test statistics presented in this section with the following examples.

EXAMPLE (g)

A recent article describes how finance incentives by the major automakers are reducing banks' share of the market for automobile loans.[14] The article reports that in 1980, banks wrote about 53% of all car loans, and in 1986, the banks' share was only 43%. Suppose that these data are based on a random sample of 100 car loans in 1980, where 53 of the loans were found to be bank loans; and the 1986 data are also based on a random sample of 100 loans, 43 of which were found to be bank loans. Carry out a two-tailed test of the equality of banks' share of the car loan market in 1980 and in 1986.

SOLUTION

Our hypotheses are those described as situation I, a two-tailed test of the equality of two population proportions. We have: H_0: $p_1 - p_2 = 0$ and H_1: $p_1 - p_2 \neq 0$. Since the null-hypothesized difference between the two population proportions is zero, we can use the test statistic of equation 8–11. First we calculate $\hat{p}$, the combined sample proportion, using equation 8–12:

$$\hat{p} = \frac{x_1 + x_2}{n_1 + n_2} = \frac{53 + 43}{100 + 100} = 0.48$$

We also have: $1 - \hat{p} = 0.52$.

We now compute the value of the test statistic, equation 8–11:

$$z = \frac{\hat{p}_1 - \hat{p}_2}{\sqrt{\hat{p}(1 - \hat{p})\left(\dfrac{1}{n_1} + \dfrac{1}{n_2}\right)}} = \frac{0.53 - 0.43}{\sqrt{(0.48)(0.52)(0.01 + 0.01)}} = 1.415$$

---

[14] "The Market Share Fight over Auto Loans," *Fortune* (October 27, 1986).

FIGURE 8–5 Carrying Out the Test of Example (g)

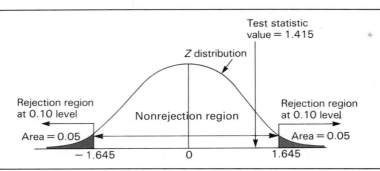

This value of the test statistic falls in the nonrejection region even if we use $\alpha = 0.10$. In fact, the p-value, found using the standard normal table, is equal to 0.157. We conclude that the data present insufficient evidence that the share of banks in the car loan market has changed from 1980 to 1986. The test is shown in Figure 8–5.

EXAMPLE (h)

From time to time, BankAmerica Corporation comes out with its Free and Easy Travelers Cheques Sweepstakes, designed to increase the amounts of BankAmerica traveler's checks sold. Since the amount bought per customer determines the customer's chances of winning a prize, a manager hypothesizes that, during sweepstakes time, the proportion of BankAmerica traveler's checks buyers who buy more than $2,500 worth of checks will be at least 10% higher than the proportion of traveler's checks buyers who buy more than $2,500 worth of checks when there are no sweepstakes. A random sample of 300 traveler's checks buyers, taken when the sweepstakes are on, reveals that 120 of these people bought checks for more than $2,500. A random sample of 700 traveler's checks buyers, taken when no sweepstakes prizes are offered, reveals that 140 of these people bought checks for more than $2,500. Conduct the hypothesis test.

SOLUTION

The manager wants to prove that the population proportion of traveler's checks buyers who buy at least $2,500 in checks when sweepstakes prizes are offered is at least 10% higher than the proportion of such buyers when no sweepstakes are on. Therefore, this should be the manager's alternative hypothesis. We have: H_0: $p_1 - p_2 \leq 0.10$ and H_1: $p_1 - p_2 > 0.10$. The appropriate test statistic is the statistic given in equation 8–13:

$$z = \frac{(\hat{p}_1 - \hat{p}_2) - D}{\sqrt{\dfrac{\hat{p}_1(1 - \hat{p}_1)}{n_1} + \dfrac{\hat{p}_2(1 - \hat{p}_2)}{n_2}}} = \frac{(120/300) - (140/700) - 0.10}{\sqrt{\dfrac{(120/300)(180/300)}{300} + \dfrac{(140/700)(560/700)}{700}}}$$

$$= \frac{(0.4 - 0.2) - 0.1}{\sqrt{[(0.4)(0.6)/300] + [(0.2)(0.8)/700]}} = 3.118$$

This value of the test statistic falls in the rejection region for $\alpha = 0.001$ (corresponding to the critical point 3.09 from the normal table). The p-value is therefore smaller than 0.001, and the null hypothesis is rejected. The manager is probably right. Figure 8–6 shows the result of the test.

FIGURE 8–6 Carrying Out the Test of Example (h)

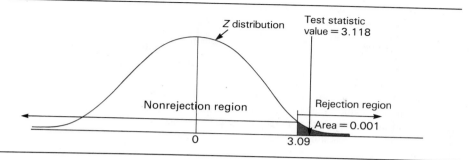

Confidence Intervals

When constructing confidence intervals for the difference between two population proportions, we do not use the pooled estimate because we do not assume that the two proportions are equal. The estimated standard error of the difference between the two sample proportions, to be used in the confidence interval, is the denominator in equation 8–13.

A large-sample $(1 - \alpha)100\%$ confidence interval for the difference between two population proportions:

$$(\hat{p}_1 - \hat{p}_2) \pm z_{\alpha/2} \sqrt{\frac{\hat{p}_1(1 - \hat{p}_1)}{n_1} + \frac{\hat{p}_2(1 - \hat{p}_2)}{n_2}} \qquad (8\text{–}14)$$

In the context of Example (h), let us now construct a 95% confidence interval for the difference between the proportion of BankAmerica traveler's checks buyers who buy more than $2,500 worth of checks during sweepstakes and the proportion of buyers of checks above this amount when no sweepstakes prizes are offered. Using equation 8–14, we get:

$$(0.4 - 0.2) \pm 1.96 \sqrt{\frac{(0.4)(0.6)}{300} + \frac{(0.2)(0.8)}{700}}$$

$$= 0.2 \pm 1.96(0.032) = [0.137, 0.263]$$

The manager may be 95% confident that the difference between the two proportions of interest is anywhere from 0.137 to 0.263.

PROBLEMS

8–29. Airline mergers cause many problems for the airline industry. One variable often quoted as a measure of an airline's efficiency is the percentage of on-time departures. Following the merger of Republic Airlines with Northwest Airlines, the percentage of on-time departures for Northwest planes declined from approximately 85% to about 68%.[15] Suppose that

---

[15] *Business Week* (November 24, 1986).

Answers

the percentages reported above are based on two random samples of flights: a sample of 100 flights over a period of two months before the merger, of which 85 are found to have departed on time; and a sample of 100 flights over a period of two months after the merger, 68 of which are found to have departed on time. Based on these data, do you believe that Northwest's on-time percentage has declined during the period following its merger with Republic?

8–30.

$z = 4.677$

Reject H_0

8–30.   A physicians' group is interested in testing to determine whether more people in small towns choose a physician by word of mouth in comparison with people in large metropolitan areas. A random sample of 1,000 people in small towns reveals that 850 have chosen their physicians by word of mouth; a random sample of 2,500 people living in large metropolitan areas reveals that 1,950 of them have chosen a physician by word of mouth. Conduct a one-tailed test aimed at proving that the percentage of popular recommendation of physicians is larger in small towns than in large metropolitan areas. Use $\alpha = 0.01$.

8–31.   A corporate raider has been successful in 11 of 31 takeover attempts. Another corporate raider has been successful in 19 of 50 takeover bids. Assuming that the success rate of each raider at each trial is independent of all other attempts, and that the information presented can be regarded as based on two independent random samples of the two raiders' overall performance, can you say whether one of the raiders is more successful than the other? Explain.

8–32.

$z = 1.08$

No evidence

8–32.   A random sample of 2,060 consumers shows that 13% of them prefer California wines. Over the next three months, an advertising campaign is undertaken to show that California wines receive awards and win taste tests. The organizers of the campaign want to prove that the three-month campaign raised the proportion of people who prefer California wines by at least 5%. At the end of the campaign, a random sample of 5,000 consumers shows that 19% of them now prefer California wines. Conduct the test at $\alpha = 0.05$.

8–33.   In problem 8–32, give a 95% confidence interval for the increase in the population proportion of consumers preferring California wines following the campaign.

8–34.

$z = 2.248$

p-value = 0.012

8–34.   Recent Federal Reserve Board regulations permit banks to offer their clients commercial paper. A random sample of 650 customers of Chase Manhattan Bank reveals that 48 of them own commercial paper as part of their investment portfolios with the bank. A random sample of customers of Manufacturers Hanover Bank reveals that out of 480 customers, only 20 own commercial paper as part of their investments with the bank. Can you conclude that Chase Manhattan has a greater share of the new market for commercial paper? Explain.

8–35.   Airbus Industrie, the European maker of the A320 medium-range jet capable of carrying 150 passengers, is currently trying to expand its market worldwide. At one point, Airbus managers wanted to test whether or not their potential market in the United States, measured by the proportion of airline industry executives who would prefer the A320, is greater than the company's potential market for the A320 in Europe (measured by the same indicator). A random sample of 120 top executives of U.S. airlines looking for new aircraft were given a demonstration of the plane, and 34 indicated that they would prefer the model to other new planes on the market. A random sample of 200 European airline executives were also given a demonstration of the plane, and 41 of them indicated that they would be interested in the A320. Test the hypothesis that more American airline executives prefer the A320 than their European counterparts.

8–36.

$z = 0.257$

Not significant

8–36.   Data from the Bureau of Labor Statistics indicate that the 1986 unemployment rate in Cleveland was 7.5% and the unemployment rate in Chicago was 7.2%. Suppose that both figures are based on random samples of 1,000 people in each city. Test the null hypothesis that the unemployment rates in both cities are equal versus the alternative hypothesis that they are not equal. What is the p-value? State your conclusion.

8–37.   In problem 8–36, give a 99% confidence interval for the difference in unemployment rates between Cleveland and Chicago in 1986. Explain your results.

8–38.

$z = 0.877$

Not significant

8–38.   Sales of laptop computers have been increasing rapidly and are expected to account for 35% of all personal computer sales in the United States.[16] The marketing manager for

---

[16] "Laptops Take Off," *Business Week* (March 18, 1991), p. 118.

Toshiba wanted to test whether the company's laptop computer accounted for about the same share of the market in California as it did in New York. A random sample of 1,000 laptops sold in California revealed that 285 were made by Toshiba, while a random sample of 1,500 laptops sold in New York revealed that 452 were Toshiba's. Conduct the test, and state your conclusion in the form of a memo to the marketing director.

8–39.   Several companies have been developing electronic guidance systems for cars. Motorola and Germany's Blaupunkt are two firms in the forefront of such research.[17] Out of 120 trials of the Motorola model, 101 were successful; and out of 200 tests of the Blaupunkt model, 110 were successful. Is there evidence to conclude that the Motorola electronic guidance system is superior to the German competitor?

8–6   The *F* Distribution and a Test for Equality of Two Population Variances

In this section, we encounter the last of the major probability distributions useful in statistics, the *F distribution*. The *F* distribution is named after the English statistician Sir Ronald A. Fisher, who discovered it in 1924.

> The **F distribution** is the distribution of the ratio of two chi-square random variables that are independent of each other, each of which is divided by its own degrees of freedom.

If we let χ_1^2 be a chi-square random variable with k_1 degrees of freedom, and χ_2^2 another chi-square random variable independent of χ_1^2 and having k_2 degrees of freedom, the ratio in equation 8–15 has the *F* distribution with k_1 and k_2 degrees of freedom.

An *F* random variable with k_1 and k_2 degrees of freedom:

$$F_{(k_1, k_2)} = \frac{\chi_1^2/k_1}{\chi_2^2/k_2} \qquad (8\text{–}15)$$

The *F* distribution thus has two kinds of degrees of freedom: k_1 is called the *degrees of freedom of the numerator* and is always listed as the first item in the parentheses; k_2 is called the *degrees of freedom of the denominator* and is always listed second inside the parentheses. The degrees of freedom of the numerator, k_1, are "inherited" from the chi-square random variable in the numerator; similarly, k_2 is "inherited" from the other, independent chi-square random variable in the denominator of equation 8–15.

Since there are so many possible degrees of freedom for the *F* random variable, tables of values of this variable for given probabilities are even more concise than the chi-square tables. Table 5 in Appendix C gives the critical points for *F* distributions with different degrees of freedom of the numerator and the denominator corresponding to right-hand-tail areas of 0.10, 0.05, 0.025 and 0.01. The second part of Table 5 gives critical points for $\alpha = 0.05$ and $\alpha = 0.01$ for a wider range of *F* random variables. For example, use Table 5 to verify that the point 3.01 cuts off an area of 0.05 to its right for an *F* random variable with 7 degrees of freedom for the numerator and 11 degrees of freedom for the denominator. This is demonstrated in

---

[17] "Solutions without Problems," *Forbes* (April 1, 1991), p. 120.

FIGURE 8–7 An *F* Distribution with 7 and 11 Degrees of Freedom

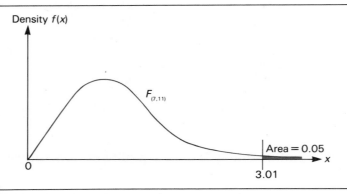

FIGURE 8–8 Several *F* Distributions

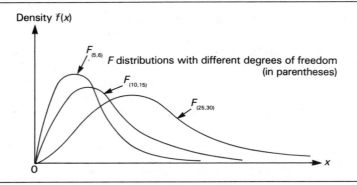

Figure 8–7. Figure 8–8 shows various *F* distributions with different degrees of freedom. The *F* distributions are asymmetric (a quality inherited from their chi-square parents), and their shape resembles that of the chi-square distributions. Note that $F_{(7,11)} \neq F_{(11,7)}$. It is important to keep track of which degrees of freedom are for the numerator and which are for the denominator.

Table 8–2 is a reproduction of a part of Table 5, showing values of *F* distributions with different degrees of freedom cutting off a right-hand-tail area of 0.05.

The *F* distribution is useful in testing the equality of two population variances. Recall that in Chapter 7 we defined a chi-square random variable as:

$$\chi^2 = \frac{(n-1)S^2}{\sigma^2} \tag{8–16}$$

where S^2 is the sample variance from a *normally distributed population*. This was the definition in the single-sample case, where $(n-1)$ was the appropriate number of degrees of freedom. Now suppose that we have two *independent* random samples from two *normally distributed populations*. The two samples will give rise to two sample variances, the random variables S_1^2 and S_2^2 with $n_1 - 1$ and $n_2 - 1$ degrees of freedom, respectively. The ratio of these two random variables is the random variable:

$$\frac{S_1^2}{S_2^2} = \frac{\chi_1^2 \sigma_1^2/(n_1 - 1)}{\chi_2^2 \sigma_2^2/(n_2 - 1)} \tag{8–17}$$

TABLE 8–2   Critical Points Cutting Off a Right-Tail Area of 0.05 for Selected *F* Distributions

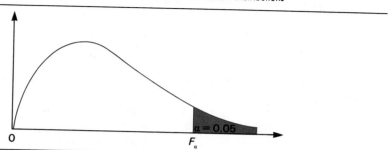

k_2 \ k_1		1	2	3	4	5	6	7	8	9
				Degrees of Freedom of the Numerator						
Degrees	1	161.4	199.5	215.7	224.6	230.2	234.0	236.8	238.9	240.5
of	2	18.51	19.00	19.16	19.25	19.30	19.33	19.35	19.37	19.38
Freedom	3	10.13	9.55	9.28	9.12	9.01	8.94	8.89	8.85	8.81
of the	4	7.71	6.94	6.59	6.39	6.26	6.16	6.09	6.04	6.00
Denomi-	5	6.61	5.79	5.41	5.19	5.05	4.95	4.88	4.82	4.77
nator	6	5.99	5.14	4.76	4.53	4.39	4.28	4.21	4.15	4.10
	7	5.59	4.74	4.35	4.12	3.97	3.87	3.79	3.73	3.68
	8	5.32	4.46	4.07	3.84	3.69	3.58	3.50	3.44	3.39
	9	5.12	4.26	3.86	3.63	3.48	3.37	3.29	3.23	3.18
	10	4.96	4.10	3.71	3.48	3.33	3.22	3.14	3.07	3.02
	11	4.84	3.98	3.59	3.36	3.20	3.09	3.01	2.95	2.90
	12	4.75	3.89	3.49	3.26	3.11	3.00	2.91	2.85	2.80
	13	4.67	3.81	3.41	3.18	3.03	2.92	2.83	2.77	2.71
	14	4.60	3.74	3.34	3.11	2.96	2.85	2.76	2.70	2.65
	15	4.54	3.68	3.29	3.06	2.90	2.79	2.71	2.64	2.59

When the two population variances, σ_1^2 and σ_2^2, are *equal,* the two terms σ_1^2 and σ_2^2 cancel out, and equation 8–17 is equal to equation 8–15, which is the ratio of two independent chi-square random variables, each divided by its own degrees of freedom (k_1 is $n_1 - 1$, and k_2 is $n_2 - 1$). This, therefore, is an *F* random variable with $n_1 - 1$ and $n_2 - 1$ degrees of freedom.

Test statistic for the equality of the variances of two normally distributed populations:

$$F_{(n_1-1,\,n_2-1)} = \frac{s_1^2}{s_2^2}$$

(8–18)

Now that we have encountered the important *F* distribution, we are ready to define the test for the equality of two population variances. Incidentally, the *F* distribution has many more uses than just testing for equality of two population variances. In chapters that follow, we will find this distribution extremely useful in a variety of involved statistical contexts.

A Statistical Test for Equality of Two Population Variances

We assume independent random sampling from the two populations in question. We also assume that the two populations are normally distributed. Let the two populations be labeled 1 and 2. The possible hypotheses to be tested are the following:

A two-tailed test: H_0: $\sigma_1^2 = \sigma_2^2$

$\qquad\qquad\qquad\qquad$ H_1: $\sigma_1^2 \neq \sigma_2^2$

A one-tailed test: H_0: $\sigma_1^2 \leq \sigma_2^2$

$\qquad\qquad\qquad\qquad$ H_1: $\sigma_1^2 > \sigma_2^2$

We will consider the one-tailed test first, because it is easier to handle. Suppose that we want to test whether σ_1^2 is greater than σ_2^2. We collect the two independent random samples from populations 1 and 2, and we compute the statistic in equation 8–18. We must be sure to put s_1^2 in the numerator, because in a one-tailed test, rejection may occur only on the right. If s_1^2 is actually smaller than s_2^2, we can immediately accept the null hypothesis because the statistic value will be less than 1.00 and, hence, certainly within the acceptance region for any level, α.

In a two-tailed test, we may do one of two things:

1. We may use the convention of always placing the *larger* sample variance in the *numerator*. That is, we label the population with the larger sample variance population 1. Then, if the test statistic value is greater than a critical point cutting off an area of, say, 0.05 to its right, we reject the null hypothesis that the two variances are equal at $\alpha = 0.10$ (that is, at *double* the level of significance from the table). This is so because, under the null hypothesis, either of the two sample variances could have been larger than the other, and we are carrying out a two-tailed test on one tail of the distribution. Similarly, if we can get a *p*-value on the one tail of rejection, we need to *double* it to get the actual *p*-value. Alternatively, we can conduct a two-tailed test as described next.

2. We may choose not to relabel the populations such that the larger sample variance is on top. Instead, we find the right-hand critical point for $\alpha = 0.01$ or 0.05 (or another level) from Appendix C, Table 5. We compute the left-hand critical point for the test (not given in the table) as follows.

The left-hand critical point to go along with $F_{(k_1, k_2)}$ is given by:

$$\frac{1}{F_{(k_2, k_1)}} \qquad\qquad (8\text{–}19)$$

where $F_{(k_1, k_2)}$ is the right-hand critical point from the table and $F_{(k_2, k_1)}$ is the right-hand critical point from the table for an *F* random variable with the *reverse order of degrees of freedom*.

Thus, the left-hand critical point is the reciprocal of the right-hand critical point obtained from the table using the reverse order of degrees of freedom for numerator and denominator. Again, the level of significance, α, must be doubled. For example, from Table 8–2, we find that the right-hand critical point for $\alpha = 0.05$ with degrees of freedom for the numerator equal to 6 and degrees of freedom for the denominator equal to 9 is $C = 3.37$. So, for a two-tailed test at $\alpha = 0.10$ (double the significance level from the table), the critical points are 3.37 and the point obtained using equation 8–19, $1/F_{(9,6)}$, which, using the table, is found to be $1/4.10 = 0.2439$. This is shown in Figure 8–9.

We will now demonstrate the use of the test for equality of two population variances with examples.

FIGURE 8–9   The Critical Points for a Two-Tailed Test Using $F_{(6,9)}$ and $\alpha = 0.10$

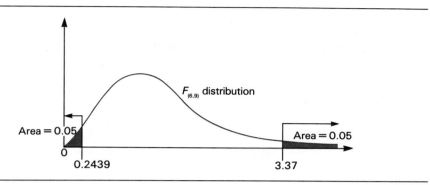

EXAMPLE (i)

One of the problems that insider trading supposedly causes is unnaturally high stock price volatility. When insiders rush to buy a stock they believe will increase in price, the buying pressure causes the stock price to rise faster than under usual conditions. Then, when insiders dump their holdings to realize quick gains, the stock price dips fast. Price volatility can be measured as the variance of prices.

An economist wants to study the effect of the insider trading scandal and ensuing legislation on the volatility of the price of a certain stock. The economist collects price data for the stock during the period before the event (interception and prosecution of insider traders) and after the event. The economist makes the assumptions that prices are approximately normally distributed and that the two price data sets may be considered independent random samples from the populations of prices before and after the event. As we mentioned earlier, the theory of finance supports the normality assumption. (The assumption of random sampling may be somewhat problematic in this case, but later we will deal with time-dependent observations more effectively.) Suppose that the economist wants to test whether or not the event has decreased the variance of prices of the stock. The 25 daily stock prices before the event give $s_1^2 = 9.3$ (dollars squared) and the 24 stock prices after the event give $s_2^2 = 3.0$ (dollars squared). Conduct the test at $\alpha = 0.05$.

Our test is a right-hand-tailed test. We have H_0: $\sigma_1^2 \le \sigma_2^2$ and H_1: $\sigma_1^2 > \sigma_2^2$. We compute the test statistic of equation 8–18:

$$F_{(n_1-1,\, n_2-1)} = F_{(24,\, 23)} = \frac{s_1^2}{s_2^2} = \frac{9.3}{3.0} = 3.1$$

As can be seen from Figure 8–10, this value of the test statistic falls in the rejection region for $\alpha = 0.05$ and for $\alpha = 0.01$. The critical point for $\alpha = 0.05$, from Table 5, is equal to 2.01 (see 24 degrees of freedom for the numerator and 23 degrees of freedom for the denominator). Referring to the F table for $\alpha = 0.01$ with 24 degrees of freedom for the numerator and 23 degrees of freedom for the denominator gives a critical point of 2.70. The computed value of the test statistic, 3.1, is greater than either of these values. The p-value is smaller than 0.01, and the economist may conclude that (subject to the validity of the assumptions) the data present significant evidence that the event in question has reduced the variance of the stock's price.

FIGURE 8–10 Carrying Out the Test of Example (i)

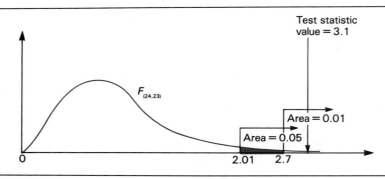

EXAMPLE (i)

Recall that in section 8–4 we made the special assumption that the variances of the two populations were equal. We can use the F test to determine whether or not our assumption of equal variance indeed holds. The test for equality for two population variances is, of course, a two-tailed test: H_0: $\sigma_1^2 = \sigma_2^2$ and H_1: $\sigma_1^2 \neq \sigma_2^2$. Let us use the data of Example (e), $n_1 = 14$, $s_1 = 0.12$; $n_2 = 9$, $s_2 = 0.11$, to test the assumption of equal population variances.

The test statistic is the same as in the previous example, given by equation 8–18:

$$F_{(13,8)} = \frac{s_1^2}{s_2^2} = \frac{0.12^2}{0.11^2} = 1.19$$

Here we placed the larger variance in the numerator because it was already labeled 1 (we did not purposely label the larger variance as 1). We can carry this out as a one-tailed test, even though it is really two-tailed, remembering that we must double the level of significance. Choosing $\alpha = 0.05$ from the table makes this a test at true level of significance equal to $2(0.05) = 0.10$. The critical point, using 12 and 8 degrees of freedom for numerator and denominator, respectively, is 3.28. (This is the closest value, since our table does not list critical points for 13 and 8 degrees of freedom.) As can be seen, our test statistic falls inside the nonrejection region, and we may conclude that at the 0.10 level of significance, there is no evidence that the two population variances are different from each other.

Let us now see how this test may be carried out using the alternative method of solution: finding a left-hand critical point to go with the right-hand one. The right-hand critical point remains 3.28 (Let us assume that this is the exact value for 13 and 8 de-

FIGURE 8–11 Carrying Out the Two-Tailed Test of Example (i)

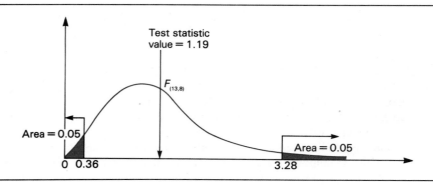

grees of freedom). The left-hand critical point is found by equation 8–19 as: $1/F_{(8,13)} = 1/2.77 = 0.36$ (recall that the left-hand critical point is the inverse of the critical point corresponding to reversed-order degrees of freedom). The two tails are shown in Figure 8–11. Again, the value of the test statistic falls inside the nonrejection region for this test at $\alpha = 2(0.05) = 0.10$.

Confidence Intervals

Using the right-hand-tail value of an F distribution obtained from the table and the left-hand-tail value obtained using equation 8–19, we may construct a confidence interval for the ratio of two population variances. The confidence interval will have level $(1 - 2\alpha)100\%$, where α is the right-hand area from the table.

A $(1 - 2\alpha)100\%$ confidence interval for σ_1^2/σ_2^2:

$$\left[\frac{s_1^2/s_2^2}{F_\alpha}, \frac{s_1^2/s_2^2}{F_{1-\alpha}} \right] \tag{8–20}$$

where F_α is the value obtained from the table and $F_{1-\alpha}$ is the left-hand-tail value of the distribution obtained through equation 8–19 as the reciprocal of the F value with reversed-order degrees of freedom.

Let us see how this confidence interval is constructed for the case of Example (j). Let us construct a 90% confidence interval for the ratio of the two population variances. Since we accepted the null hypothesis that the two population variances are equal, a confidence interval (using the same level: $\alpha = 0.05$, $2\alpha = 0.10$) for the *ratio* of the two variances should contain the point 1.00. This is so because if two quantities are approximately equal, their ratio should be approximately equal to 1.00. A 90% confidence interval for σ_1^2/σ_2^2 is given by:

$$\left[\frac{(0.12)^2/(0.11)^2}{3.28}, \frac{(0.12)^2/(0.11)^2}{0.36} \right] = [0.363, 3.306]$$

The confidence interval does indeed contain the point 1.00 as a possible ratio of the two population variances.

In this section we encountered the F distribution. Like the t distribution and the chi-square distribution, the F distribution relies on the assumption that the population is normally distributed. The reason for this is that all these distributions are derived from the standard normal random variable: The chi-square distribution is defined as the distribution of the sum of k independent squared standard normal random variables, Z (k is the number of degrees of freedom). The t distribution is defined as the ratio of Z to the square root of a chi-square random variable divided by its degrees of freedom (the t distribution has the same number of degrees of freedom, k, as its chi-square parent). The F distribution is the distribution of the ratio of two independent chi-square random variables, each divided by its degrees of freedom. Finally, the F distribution with degrees of freedom 1 and k (the special case with only *one* degree of freedom for the numerator) is also the distribution of the random variable obtained by squaring a t random variable with k degrees of freedom. The relationships among the distributions are shown in Figure 8–12.

FIGURE 8–12   The Relationships among Probability Distributions Useful in Statistics

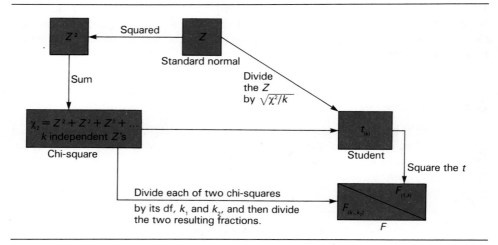

PROBLEMS

In the following problems, assume that all populations are normally distributed.

8–40.   Compaq Computer Corporation has an assembly plant in Houston, where the company's Deskpro 386 computer is being built. Engineers at the plant are considering a new production facility and are interested in going on line with the new facility if and only if they can be fairly sure that the variance of the number of computers assembled per day using the new facility is lower than the production variance of the old system. A random sample of 40 production days using the old production method gives a sample variance of 1,288, and a random sample of 15 production days using the proposed new method gives a sample variance of 1,112. Conduct the appropriate test at $\alpha = 0.05$.

8–41.   Test the validity of the equal-variance assumption in problem 8–27.

8–42.   Test the validity of the equal-variance assumption for the data presented in problem 8–25. Also construct a 90% confidence interval for the ratio of the two population variances.

8–43.   Test the validity of the equal-variance assumption for the data presented in problem 8–26. Also construct a 98% confidence interval for the ratio of the two population variances.

8–44.   The following data are independent random samples of sales of the Nissan Pulsar model made in a joint venture of Nissan and Alfa Romeo. The data represent sales at dealerships before and after the announcement that the Pulsar model will no longer be made in Italy. Sales numbers are monthly.

> Before: 329, 234, 423, 328, 400, 399, 326, 452, 541, 680, 456, 220
> After: 212, 630, 276, 112, 872, 788, 345, 544, 110, 129, 776

Do you believe that the variance of the number of cars sold per month before the announcement is equal to the variance of the number of cars sold per month after the announcement?

8–45.   A large department store wants to test whether or not the variance of waiting time in two checkout counters is approximately equal. Two independent random samples of 25 waiting times in each of the counters gives: $s_1 = 2.5$ minutes and $s_2 = 3.1$ minutes. Carry out the test of equality of variances using $\alpha = 0.02$.

8–46.   An important measure of the risk associated with a stock is the standard deviation, or variance, of the stock's price movements. A financial analyst wants to test the one-tailed hypothesis that stock A has a greater risk (larger variance of price) than stock B. A random

Answers

8–40.
‾‾‾‾‾
$F = 1.158$
No evidence

8–42.
‾‾‾‾‾
$F = 2.16$
Not significant

8–44.
‾‾‾‾‾
$F = 5.298$
Significant

8–46.
‾‾‾‾‾
$F = 1.879$
Not significant

sample of 25 daily prices of stock A gives $s_A^2 = 6.52$, and a random sample of 22 daily prices of stock B gives a sample variance of $s_B^2 = 3.47$. Carry out the test at $\alpha = 0.01$.

8–47.   Discuss the assumptions made in the solution of the problems in this section.

8–7 Using the Computer

As we progress to more and more complicated statistical analysis, the computer becomes increasingly useful in solving problems. Many of the equations in this chapter can be very tedious to work out by hand. With a computer, however, the calculation of complicated expressions takes a fraction of a second. Let us see how the methods of this section are implementable on a computer. Again, we will use the package MINITAB, with which you now have some familiarity.

A potential buyer of a photocopying machine wants to test which of two models, one made by Savin and one made by Xerox, gives better average copy clarity. An optical device is available for measuring the clarity of copies produced from different originals. The device measures the resolution and the contrast of each copy and translates these characteristics into a single score per copy, measured on a scale of 0 to 100. Two random samples of originals are copied: one sample of 30 different copies done on a random sample of Savin copiers, and another sample of 30 originals copied on randomly chosen Xerox copiers. The results are:

EXAMPLE (k)

```
SAVIN: 95,98,83,97,72,89,86,91,98,98,76,91,85,87,86,92,87,89,86,
       93,95,99,86,96,98,90,98,86,85,79

XEROX: 86,87,89,79,91,92,89,90,84,83,82,99,98,78,98,81,87,82,83,
       88,85,95,80,93,99,98,81,80,90,92
```

Figure 8–13 shows the MINITAB command and the computer output for the analysis of these data. In this case, we requested a two-tailed test of whether or not the two means are equal. Note that the reported statistic is labeled T. This is so because as long as the population standard deviations are not known, the distribution is a t distribution. However, as we noted, when the number of degrees of freedom is large, the t distribution is well approximated by the Z distribution, and this is the case here. Our computed test statistic value is equal to 1.00, and the reported p-value is 0.32. This can be verified

SOLUTION

FIGURE 8–13   MINITAB Commands and Output Example (k)

```
MTB > TWOSAMPLE ALTERNATIVE=0 FOR C1 C2

TWOSAMPLE T FOR C1 VS C2
          N       MEAN      STDEV    SE MEAN
C1   30      89.70      6.92       1.3
C2   30      87.97      6.50       1.2

95 PCT CI FOR MU C1 - MU C2: (-1.7, 5.2)

TTEST MU C1 = MU C2 (VS NE): T= 1.00   P=0.32
```

from the standard normal table (as an approximation). You may also remember that between $+1$ and -1 lies approximately 68% of the area under the normal curve; hence, the area in both tails, the p-value in a two-tailed test, is about 0.32.

EXAMPLE (I)

An economist wants to test whether or not unleaded gasoline prices during a certain period of time were approximately equal, on average, on the East Coast and the West Coast. Two random samples, 15 gas stations in the East and 14 in the West, are collected and the prices per gallon recorded. Data are as follows.

EAST: 95,102,104,99,94,98,105,108,94,106,101,97,99,100,96

WEST: 101,104,99,105,98,107,108,109,98,99,110,97,106,109

SOLUTION

The program and the results of the two-tailed test are shown in Figure 8–14. We use the subcommand POOLED for pooled sample variances. The null hypothesis may be rejected at $\alpha = 0.05$ (consider the p-value!), and we may conclude that, on the average, gasoline was more expensive in the West during the period in question.

FIGURE 8–14 MINITAB Commands and Output for Example (I)

```
MTB > TWOSAMPLE ALTERNATIVE=0 C1 C2;
SUBC> POOLED.


TWOSAMPLE T FOR C1 VS C2
        N       MEAN      STDEV     SE MEAN
C1     15       99.87      4.42       1.1
C2     14      103.57      4.75       1.3


95 PCT CI FOR MU C1 - MU C2: (-7.2, -0.2)


TTEST MU C1 = MU C2 (VS NE) : T= -2.18   P=0.039  DF=   27


POOLED STDEV =          4.58
```

Note that for small samples, and if the POOLED subcommand is not given, MINITAB defaults to the approximate degrees of freedom.

MINITAB can also be used to find probabilities and values for the F distribution. The distribution and the degrees of freedom are specified in a subcommand that follows CDF or INVCDF. This is demonstrated in Figure 8–15. Compare the results with values in the F table.

8–8 Summary and Review of Terms

In this chapter, we extended the ideas of hypothesis tests and confidence intervals to the case of two populations. We discussed the comparisons of two population means, two population proportions, and two population variances. We developed a hypothesis test and confidence interval for the difference between two population means when the population variances were believed to be equal, and in the general case

FIGURE 8–15 Using MINITAB to Find Probabilities or Values of the *F* Distribution

```
MTB > CDF 3.29;
SUBC> F df numerator=7, df denominator= 9.
      3.2900      0.9499


MTB > CDF 1.35;
SUBC> F 120 120.
      1.3500      0.9492


MTB > INVCDF 0.95;
SUBC> F 40 4.
      0.9500      5.7170
```

when they are not assumed equal. We introduced an important family of probability distributions: the **F distributions**. We saw that each *F* distribution has two kinds of degrees of freedom: one associated with the numerator and one associated with the denominator of the expression for *F*. We saw how the *F* distribution is used in testing hypotheses about two population variances. In the next chapter, we will make use of the *F* distribution in tests of the equality of *several* population means: the analysis of variance.

ADDITIONAL PROBLEMS

8–48. Zim Container Service ships containers across both the Atlantic and the Pacific oceans. In 1974, the company had to decide whether to include Kingston, Jamaica, as a port of call instead of Savannah, Georgia, where the company's ships had been calling for some time. Zim's general manager of operations decided to use statistics to determine which of the two ports of call—Savannah or Kingston—would have a greater demand for shipped containers, or whether the average number of containers demanded by the two ports might be approximately equal (in which case the decision would be based on the cost of service). The manager had data on the last 17 calls at Savannah. The data, in number of containers unloaded per call, were: 9, 6, 7, 7, 8, 7, 9, 4, 7, 6, 6, 5, 7, 5, 9, 8, 6. Then, as a test run, company ships unloaded containers at Kingston during 9 arrivals at that port. The data (number of containers unloaded at each trip) were: 10, 5, 8, 8, 9, 10, 4, 9, 11. Use these data to conduct the test, and advise Zim's general manager of operations as to which port should be the regular port of call, or whether the ports will have approximately equal demand for containers.[18] Assume normal populations with equal variances.

8–49. In problem 8–48, construct a 99% confidence interval for the difference between the average number of containers per voyage demanded at Savannah and the average number of containers per voyage demanded at Kingston. Interpret your results.

8–50. The U.S. Census Bureau's *Current Industrial Report on Confectionery* (1986) indicates that the average per capita consumption of candy in the United States was about 19 pounds per person per year for 1984–86 and about 17 pounds per person per year for 1981–83. Suppose that an industry analyst wants to test the claim that average candy consumption in the United States has increased by an average of over 2 pounds per person per year. The analyst is able to obtain a random sample of 30 data items for 1981–83, and finds a sample mean of 16.54 pounds per person per year and a sample standard deviation of 5.3

Answers

8–48.

$t_{(24)} = 1.88$
No evidence

8–50.

$z = 2.29$
Significant

[18] Data provided courtesy of Zim Navigation Company, Ltd.

Answers

pounds. A similar random sample of consumer data consisting of 30 items for 1984–86 gives a sample mean of 21.2 pounds per person per year and a sample standard deviation of 3.5 pounds. Using these data, do you believe that Americans increased their candy consumption by over 2 pounds per person per year from one period to the other?

8–51. For problem 8–50, give a 95% confidence interval for the increase in average candy consumption between the two time periods in question.

8–52.

$z = 0.66$

Not significant

8–52. A study was undertaken by Montgomery Securities to assess average labor and materials costs incurred by Chrysler and General Motors in building a typical four-door, intermediate-sized car. The reported average cost for Chrysler was $9,500, and for GM it was $9,780. Suppose that these data are based on random samples of 25 cars for each company, and suppose that both standard deviations are equal to $1,500. Test the hypothesis that the average GM car of this type is more expensive to build than the average Chrysler car of the same type. Use $\alpha = 0.01$. Assume equal population variances.

8–53. For problem 8–52, give a 99% confidence interval for the difference between the average cost incurred by GM in building the car and the average cost incurred by Chrysler in building the same type of car. Interpret the results.

8–54.

$z = 1.32$

Not significant

8–54. Suppose that the data in problem 8–52 are based on two random samples of 100 data points each. Discuss the advantages of using the method explained in section 8–3 instead of the method presented in section 8–4 in solving the problem. Discuss the various assumptions made when you use each of the two methods. Redo the problem using the results given in problem 8–52.

8–55. Two new movies are screen-tested at two different samples of theaters. *Star Trek VI* is viewed at 80 theaters and is considered a success in terms of box office sales in 60 of these theaters. *Rocky VII* is viewed at a random sample of 100 theaters and is considered a success in 65 of them. Based on these data, do you believe that one of these movies will be a greater success than the other in the coming season? Explain.

8–56.

$[-0.033, 0.233]$

8–56. For problem 8–55, give a 95% confidence interval for the difference in proportion of theaters nationwide where one movie will be preferred over the other. Is the point zero contained in the interval? Discuss.

8–57. Two 12-meter boats, the K boat and the L boat, are tested as possible contenders in the America's Cup races. The following data represent the time, in minutes, to complete a particular tack in independent random trials of the two boats.

K boat: 12.0, 13.1, 11.8, 12.6, 14.0, 11.8, 12.7, 13.5, 12.4, 12.2, 11.6, 12.9
L boat: 11.8, 12.1, 12.0, 11.6, 11.8, 12.0, 11.9, 12.6, 11.4, 12.0, 12.2, 11.7

Test the null hypothesis that the two boats perform equally well. Is one boat faster, on the average, than the other? Assume equal population variances.

8–58.

$t_{(11)} = 2.803$

Significant

8–58. In problem 8–57, assume that the data points are paired as listed and each pair represents performance of the two boats at a single trial. Conduct the test using this assumption. What is the advantage of testing using the paired data versus independent samples?

8–59. As part of an advertising campaign for Nine Lives cat food, the results of a poll were released at a press conference. The results indicated that 70% of the people polled recognized Morris the Cat—the Nine Lives advertising symbol—while only 41% were familiar with the 1988 presidential candidate Michael Dukakis. Assume that the reported results are based on independent random samples of 100 people, each drawn from two different populations. Is there evidence to conclude that, at the time of the poll, more people were familiar with the cat? Discuss the limitations of this analysis.

8–60.

$z = 0.58$

Not significant

8–60. The IIT Technical Institute claims "94% of our graduates get jobs." Assume that the result is based on a random sample of 100 graduates of the program. Suppose that an independent random sample of 125 graduates of a competing technical institute reveals that 92% of these graduates got jobs. Is there evidence to conclude that one institute is more successful than the other in placing its graduates?

8–61. The power of supercomputers derives from the idea of parallel processing. Engineers at Cray Research are interested in determining whether one of two parallel processing designs produces faster average computing time, or whether the two designs are equally fast. The following are the results, in seconds, of independent random computation times using the two designs.

Design 1	Design 2
2.1, 2.2, 1.9, 2.0, 1.8, 2.4,	2.6, 2.5, 2.0, 2.1, 2.6, 3.0,
2.0, 1.7, 2.3, 2.8, 1.9, 3.0,	2.3, 2.0, 2.4, 2.8, 3.1, 2.7,
2.5, 1.8, 2.2	2.6

Assume that the two populations of computing time are normally distributed and that the two population variances are equal. Is there evidence that one parallel processing design allows for faster average computation than the other?

8–62. Test the validity of the equal-variance assumption in problem 8–61. If you reject the null hypothesis of equal population variance, redo the test of problem 8–61 using another method.

8–62.

$F = 1.14$
Not significant

8–63. The senior vice president for marketing at Westin Hotels believes that the company's recent advertising of the Westin Plaza in New York has increased the average occupancy rate at that hotel by a least 5%. To test the hypothesis, a random sample of daily occupancy rates (in percentages) before the advertising is collected. A similar random sample of daily occupancy rates is collected after the advertising took place. The data are as follows.

Before Advertising (%)	After Advertising (%)
86, 92, 83, 88, 79, 81, 90	88, 94, 97, 99, 89, 93, 92
76, 80, 91, 85, 89, 77, 91	98, 89, 90, 97, 91, 87, 80
83	88, 96

Assume normally distributed populations of occupancy rates with equal population variances. Test the vice president's hypothesis.

8–64. For problem 8–63, test the validity of the equal-variance assumption.

8–64.

$F = 1.13$
Not significant

8–65. Refer to problem 8–48. Test the null hypothesis that the variance of the number of containers demanded at Savannah is less than or equal to the variance of the number of containers demanded at Kingston, versus the alternative hypothesis that the variance of the number of containers demanded at Savannah is greater than that of Kingston.

8–66. Refer to problem 8–57. Do you believe that the variance of performance times for the K boat is about the same as the variance of performance times for the L boat? Explain. What are the implications of your result on the analysis of problem 8–57? If needed, redo the analysis in problem 8–57.

8–66.

$F = 5.688$
Significant
New $t_{14} = 2.719$
Significant

8–67. A company is interested in offering its employees one of two employee benefit packages. A random sample of the company's employees is collected, and each person in the sample is asked to rate each of the two packages on an overall preference scale of 0 to 100. The order of presentation of each of the two plans is randomly selected for each person in the sample. The paired data are:

Program A: 45 67 63 59 77 69 45 39 52 58 70 46 60 65 59 80
Program B: 56 70 60 45 85 79 50 46 50 60 82 40 65 55 81 68

Do you believe that the employees of this company prefer, on the average, one package over the other? Explain.

8–68. A company that makes electronic devices for use in hospitals needs to decide on one of two possible suppliers for a certain component to be used in the devices. The company

8–68.

$z = -3.086$
Significant

gathers a random sample of 200 items made by supplier A and finds that 12 items are defective. An independent random sample of 250 items made by supplier B reveals that 38 are defective. Is one supplier more reliable than the other? Explain.

8–69. Refer to problem 8–68. Give a 95% confidence interval for the difference in the proportions of defective items made by suppliers A and B.

8–70.

[3.85, 10.18]

8–70. Refer to problem 8–63. Give a 90% confidence interval for the difference in average occupancy rates at the Westin Plaza hotel before and after the advertising.

8–71. Two machines are tested for the variance of the time they work before failure. A random sample of 25 trials of machine A gives a sample variance of 561 (hours squared), and an independent random sample of 18 trials of machine B gives a sample variance of 386 (hours squared). Assuming that the population of work times before failure for each machine is normally distributed, test for equality of population variances.

8–72. Explain the relationship between the F distribution and the chi-square distribution.

8–73. Refer to problem 8–61. Give a 99% confidence interval for the difference in mean time to complete a computation between each of the two designs.

8–74.

$z = 1.54$
Not significant

8–74. An article on the global labor market reports that 39.5% of the work force in the United States is under age 34, while for Russia the figure is 42.9%.[19] Assuming that these percentages are based on a random sample of 1,000 workers in each country, test the significance of the observed difference.

8–75. Interpret the following computer output.

```
TWOSAMPLE T FOR C1 VS C2
       N      MEAN     STDEV    SE MEAN
C1    16     23.94     1.91      0.48
C2    17     24.82     2.88      0.70


95 PCT C1 FOR MU C1 - MU C2: (-2.62, 0.85)


TTEST MU C1 = MU C2 (VS GT): T= -1.05   P=0.85   DF=  27
```

8–76. Interpret the following computer output.

```
TWOSAMPLE T FOR C1 VS C2
       N      MEAN     STDEV    SE MEAN
C1    16     34.63     2.13      0.53
C2    17     24.82     2.88      0.70


95 PCT C1 FOR MU C1 - MU C2: (8.00, 11.61)


TTEST MU C1 = MU C2 (VS NE): T= 11.07   P=0.0000   DF=  31


POOLED STDEV =          2.54
```

[19] W. B. Johnston, "Global Work Force 2000: The New World Labor Market," *Harvard Business Review* (March–April 1991), p. 120.

PROGRAM TRADING

P *rogram trading* is the name given to stock market buy-and-sell schemes carried out on a computer. About a dozen major members of the New York Stock Exchange, and other companies, engage in this modern way of trading stocks. Usually, the computer programs are designed to follow a hedging strategy known as portfolio insurance or to follow strategies of stock index arbitrage. The computer keeps track of the quoted prices of single securities as well as traded portfolios. Whenever the computer finds that price differences exist, say, between the total quoted prices of a group of stocks and the price of a portfolio containing these stocks, the computer immediately issues an order to buy the cheaper form of the securities and to sell the equivalent, more expensive form of these securities. This is called *arbitrage*. The computer thus aids in determining the existence of price differences and in capitalizing on these differences.

Since the computer can act very quickly and handle large amounts of data, the result is trades of large quantities of stock in very short periods of time whenever a minute price difference is detected. It has recently been asserted that these sudden, large trades result in unnaturally high *volatility* of stock market prices. This volatility is believed to be the source of many recent problems with the operation of the market. On January 15, 1988, the New York Stock Exchange began an experiment lasting six days to determine whether or not program trading is indeed the culprit responsible for high stock price volatility. The Exchange asked its members that engage in program trading to refrain from doing so over the six working days from January 15, 1988, through January 22, 1988.[20]

The following table lists the daily changes in the Dow Jones Industrial Average for the period of January 5, 1988, through January 25, 1988.[21]

Date	Daily Change in Dow Jones Industrial Average	Date	Daily Change in Dow Jones Industrial Average
January 5, 1988	+ 76.42	January 15, 1988	− 8.62
January 6, 1988	+ 16.25	January 18, 1988	+ 39.96
January 7, 1988	+ 6.30	January 19, 1988	+ 7.79
January 8, 1988	+ 14.09	January 20, 1988	− 27.52
January 11, 1988	−140.58	January 21, 1988	− 57.20
January 12, 1988	+ 33.82	January 22, 1988	+ 0.17
January 13, 1988	− 16.58	January 25, 1988	+ 24.20
January 14, 1988	− 3.82		

Separate the data into two groups. Make some necessary assumptions and state them. Analyze the data and, based on your findings, make a recommendation to the New York Stock Exchange.

---

[20] See "Stock Exchange Sets Test to Curb Program Trading," *New York Times* (January 15, 1988).

[21] These data are obtained from various issues of *The Wall Street Journal* and are reproduced by permission of Dow Jones and Company.

9 ANALYSIS OF VARIANCE

INTRODUCTION

BEE IT KNOWNE UNTO ALL MEN BY THESE PRESENTS
IUNE.17.1579.
BY THE GRACE OF GOD AND IN THE NAME OF HERR
MAIESTY QUEEN ELIZABETH OF ENGLAND AND HERR
SUCCESSORS FOREVER. I TAKE POSSESSION OF THIS
KINGDOME WHOSE KING AND PEOPLE FREELY RESIGNE
THEIR RIGHT AND TITLE IN THE WHOLE LAND UNTO HERR
MAIESTIES KEEPING. NOW NAMED BY ME AN TO BEE
KNOWNE UNTO ALL MEN AS NOVA ALBION.
G

FRANCIS DRAKE

In the summer of 1936, a young man named Beryle Shinn chanced upon a brass plate bearing the inscription above while hiking in a hilly area over-looking Point San Quentin and the San Francisco Bay. Mr. Shinn put the plate in the trunk of his car, where it remained for a few years. Later, by chance, the plate came to the attention of Professor Herbert E. Bolton at the Department of History at the University of California, Berkeley.

In a logbook kept during his circumnavigation of the earth, Sir Francis Drake wrote of entering a sheltered area in 1579 on what is now the northern California coast to refit his ship. He also mentioned leaving a brass plate attached to a post to record the event. Thus, upon being presented the Shinn plate, Professor Bolton declared: "One of the world's long-lost historical treasures apparently has been found!"

Although questions about the authenticity of the plate were immediately raised by many scholars—mainly because of the curious forms of many of the letters, and the writing style, which is different from known Elizabethan styles—the plate was nonetheless pronounced genuine and put on permanent display at the Bankroft Library of the University of California.

Contentions that the plate was the work of a modern forger continued to be expressed, and these led the Bankroft Library to order tests of the metallurgic structure of the brass. Finally, in 1976, several tiny holes were drilled in the plate, and a sample of brass particles was sent to the Research Laboratory of Archaeology at Oxford University for analysis. There the sample of brass particles from the plate was statistically compared with two random samples of brass: a sample of brasses made in the 20th century and a sample of English and Continental brasses created between 1540 and 1720. Analysis of the average zinc content of the sample from the discovered plate and that of the two other samples led to the conclusion that the average zinc content of the plate was equal to the average zinc content of modern brasses and very different from the average zinc content of brasses made in the 16th to 18th centuries.[1]

Continued on next page

---

[1] Several tests of the plate of brass were conducted. See "The Plate of Brass Reexamined," a report by the Bankroft Library (1979).

The results of the analysis led Dr. R. Hedges of Oxford University to conclude: "I would regard it as quite unreasonable to continue to believe in the authenticity of the plate." Thus, what was thought to be an ancient artifact was shown to be an ingenious modern forgery. The scientific studies left unanswered the questions of who made the plate, and why.

The statistical method of comparing the means of several populations, such as the mean zinc content of the three brasses relevant to the study of the plate, is the **analysis of variance.** The method is often referred to by its acronym, ANOVA. Analysis of variance is the first of several advanced statistical techniques to be discussed in this book. Along with regression analysis, described in the next two chapters, ANOVA is the most commonly quoted advanced research method in the professional business and economic literature. What is analysis of variance? The name of the technique may seem misleading.

> **ANOVA** is a statistical method for determining the existence of differences among several population means.

While the aim of ANOVA is to detect differences among several population *means,* the technique requires the analysis of different forms of *variance* associated with the random samples under study—hence the name *analysis of variance.*

The original ideas of analysis of variance were developed by the English statistician Sir Ronald A. Fisher during the first part of this century. (Recall our mention of Fisher in Chapter 8 as the discoverer of the F distribution.) Much of the early work in this area dealt with agricultural experiments where crops were given different "treatments," such as being grown using different kinds of fertilizers. The researchers wanted to determine whether all treatments under study were equally effective or whether some treatments were better than others. "Better" referred to those treatments that would produce crops of greater average weight. This question is answerable by the analysis of variance. Since the original work involved different *treatments,* the term remained, and we use it interchangeably with *populations* even when no actual treatment is administered. Thus, for example, if we compare the mean income in four different communities, we may refer to the four populations as four different *treatments.*

In the next section, we will develop the simplest form of analysis of variance, the one-factor, fixed-effects, completely randomized design model. We may ignore this long name for now. ∎

9–2   The Hypothesis Test of Analysis of Variance

> The hypothesis test of analysis of variance:
>
> $H_0: \mu_1 = \mu_2 = \mu_3 = \cdots = \mu_r$
>
> H_1: Not all μ_i ($i = 1, \ldots, r$) are equal   (9–1)

There are r populations, or treatments, under study. We draw an independent random sample from each of the r populations. The size of the sample from population i ($i = 1, \ldots, r$) is n_i, and the total sample size is:

$$n = n_1 + n_2 + \cdots + n_r$$

From the r samples we compute several different quantities, and these lead to a computed value of a test statistic that follows a known F distribution when the null hypothesis is true. From the value of the statistic and the critical point for a given level of significance, we are able to make a determination of whether or not we believe that the r population means are equal.

Usually, the number of compared means, r, is greater than 2. Why greater than 2? If r is equal to 2, then the test in equation 9–1 is just a test for equality of two population means; although we could use ANOVA to conduct such a test, we have seen relatively simple tests of such hypotheses: the two-sample t tests discussed in Chapter 8. In this chapter, we are interested in investigating whether or not *several* population means may be considered equal. This is a test of a *joint hypothesis* about the equality of several population parameters. But why can we not use the two-sample t tests repeatedly? Suppose we are comparing $r = 5$ treatments. Why can we not conduct all possible pairwise comparisons of means using the two-sample t test? There are 10 such possible comparisons (10 choices of five items taken two at a time, found using a combinatorial formula presented in Chapter 2). It should be possible to make all 10 comparisons. However, if we use, say, $\alpha = 0.05$ for each test, then this means that the probability of committing a type I error in any particular test (deciding that the two population means are not equal when indeed they are equal) is 0.05. If each of the 10 tests has a 0.05 probability of a type I error, what is the probability of a type I error if we state "not all the means are equal" (i.e., rejecting H_0 in equation 9–1)? The answer to this question is not known![2]

If we need to compare more than two population means and we want to remain in control of the probability of committing a type I error, we need to conduct a *joint test*. Analysis of variance provides such a joint test of the hypotheses in equation 9–1. The reason for ANOVA's widespread applicability is that there are many situations where we need to compare more than two populations simultaneously. Even in cases where we need to compare only two treatments, say, test the relative effectiveness of two different prescription drugs, our actual test may require the use of a third treatment: a control treatment, or a placebo drug.

We now present the assumptions that must be satisfied so that we can use the analysis of variance procedure in testing our hypotheses of equation 9–1.

The required assumptions of ANOVA:

1. We assume *independent random sampling* from each of the r populations.
2. We assume that the r populations under study are *normally distributed*, with means μ_i that may or may not be equal, but with *equal variances, σ^2*.

Suppose, for example, that we are comparing three populations and want to determine whether or not the three population means μ_1, μ_2, and μ_3 are equal. We draw separate random samples from each of the three populations under study, and we assume that the three populations are distributed as shown in Figure 9–1.

These model assumptions are necessary for the test statistic used in analysis of variance to possess an F distribution when the null hypothesis is true. If the popula-

---

[2] The problem is further complicated because we cannot assume independence of the 10 tests and, therefore, we cannot use a probability computation for independent events. The sample statistics used in the 10 tests are not independent since two such possible statistics are $(\bar{X}_1 - \bar{X}_2)$ and $(\bar{X}_2 - \bar{X}_3)$. Both statistics contain a common term, $\bar{X}_2$, and thus are not independent of each other.

FIGURE 9–1   Three Normally Distributed Populations with Different Means but with Equal Variance

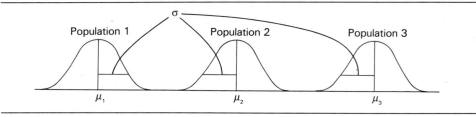

tions are not exactly normally distributed, but have distributions that are close to a normal distribution, the method still yields good results. If, however, the distributions are highly skewed or otherwise different from normality, or if the population variances are not approximately equal, then ANOVA should not be used, and instead we must use a nonparametric technique called the Kruskal-Wallis test. This alternative technique is described in Chapter 14.

The Test Statistic

As mentioned earlier, when the null hypothesis is true, the test statistic of analysis of variance follows an F distribution. As you recall from Chapter 8, the F distribution has two kinds of degrees of freedom: degrees of freedom for the numerator and degrees of freedom for the demoninator.

In the analysis of variance, the numerator degrees of freedom are $r - 1$, and the denominator degrees of freedom are $n - r$. In this section, we will not present the calculations leading to the computed value of the test statistic. Instead, we will assume that the value of the statistic is given. The computations are a topic in themselves and will be presented in the next section. Analysis of variance is an involved technique, and it is difficult and time-consuming to carry out the required computations by hand. Consequently, computers are indispensable in most situations involving analysis of variance, and we will make extensive use of the computer in this chapter. For now, let us assume that a computer is available to us, and that it provides us with the value of the test statistic.

$$\text{ANOVA test statistic} = F_{(r-1,\,n-r)} \qquad\qquad (9–2)$$

Figure 9–2 shows the F distribution with 3 and 50 degrees of freedom, which would

FIGURE 9–2   The Distribution of the ANOVA Test Statistic for $r = 4$ Populations and a Total Sample Size $n = 54$

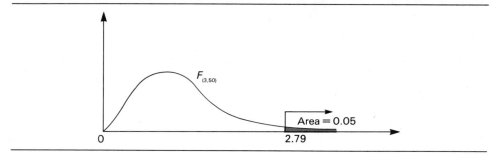

be appropriate for a test of the equality of four population means using a total sample size of 54. Also shown is the critical point for $\alpha = 0.05$, found in Appendix C, Table 5. The critical point is 2.79. For reasons explained in the next section, the test is carried out as a right-hand-tailed test.

We now have the basic elements of a statistical hypothesis test within the context of ANOVA: the null and alternative hypotheses, the required assumptions, and a distribution of the test statistic when the null hypothesis is true. Let us look at an example.

Major roasters and distributors of coffee in the United States have long felt the great uncertainty in the price of coffee beans. Over the course of one year, for example, coffee futures prices went from a low of $1.40 per pound up to $2.50 and then down to $2.03. The main reason for such wild fluctuations in price, which strongly affect the performance of coffee distributors, is the constant danger of drought in Brazil. Since Brazil produces 30% of the world's coffee, the market for coffee beans is very sensitive to the annual rumors of impending drought.[3]

Recently a domestic coffee distributor decided to avert the problem altogether by eliminating Brazilian coffee from all blends the company distributes. Before taking such action, the distributor wanted to minimize the chances of suffering losses in sales volume. Therefore, the distributor hired a marketing research firm to conduct a statistical test of consumers' taste preferences. The research firm made arrangements with several large restaurants to serve randomly chosen groups of their customers different kinds of after-dinner coffee. Three kinds of coffee were served: a group of 21 randomly chosen customers were served pure Brazilian coffee; another group of 20 randomly chosen customers were served pure Colombian coffee; and a third group of 22 randomly chosen customers were served pure African-grown coffee.

This is the *completely randomized design* part of the name of the ANOVA technique we mentioned at the end of the last section. In completely randomized design, the experimental units (in this case, the people involved in the experiment) are randomly assigned to the three treatments, the treatment being the kind of coffee they are served. Later in this chapter, we will encounter other designs useful in many situations. To prevent a response bias, the people in this experiment were not told the kind of coffee they were being served. The coffee was listed as a "house blend."

Suppose that data for the three groups were consumers' ratings of the coffee on a scale of 0 to 100 and that certain computations were carried out with these data (computations will be discussed in the next section), leading to the following value of the ANOVA test statistic: $F = 2.02$. Is there evidence to conclude that any of the three kinds of coffee leads to an average consumer rating different from the other two kinds?

EXAMPLE (a)

SOLUTION

The null and alternative hypotheses here are, by equation 9–1,

$$H_0: \mu_1 = \mu_2 = \mu_3$$
$$H_1: \text{Not all three } \mu_i \text{ are equal}$$

Let us examine the meaning of the null and alternative hypotheses in this example. The null hypothesis states that average consumer responses to each of the three kinds of cof-

---

[3] See "Coffee Nerves that May Not Last Long," *Business Week* (September 8, 1986).

FIGURE 9–3 The Possible Relationships among the Relative Magnitudes of the Three Population Means μ_1, μ_2, and μ_3

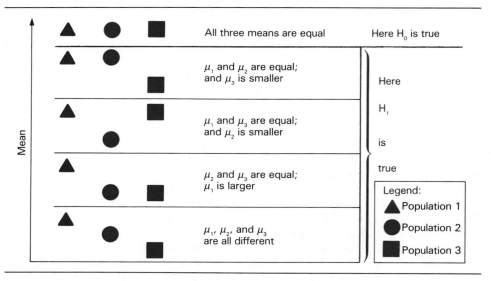

fee are equal. The alternative hypothesis says that not all three population means are equal. What are the possibilities covered under the alternative hypothesis? The possible relationships among the relative magnitudes of any three real numbers μ_1, μ_2, and μ_3 are shown in Figure 9–3.

As you can see from Figure 9–3, the alternative hypothesis is composed of several different possibilities—it includes all the cases where *not all* three means are equal. Thus, if we reject the null hypothesis, all we know is that there is statistical evidence to conclude that not all three population means are equal. However, we do not know in what way the means are different. Therefore, once we reject the null hypothesis, we need to conduct further analysis to determine which population means are different from one another. The further analysis following ANOVA will be discussed in a later section.

We have a null hypothesis and an alternative hypothesis. We also assume that the conditions required for ANOVA are met; that is, we assume that the three populations of consumer responses are (approximately) normally distributed with equal population variance. Now we need to conduct the test.

Since there are three populations, or treatments, under study, the degrees of freedom for the numerator are $r - 1 = 3 - 1 = 2$. Since the total sample size is: $n = n_1 + n_2 + n_3 = 21 + 20 + 22 = 63$, we find that the degrees of freedom for the denominator are $n - r = 63 - 3 = 60$. Thus, when the null hypothesis is true, our test statistic has an F distribution with 2 and 60 degrees of freedom: $F_{(2,60)}$. From Appendix C, Table 5, we find that the right-hand-tail critical point at $\alpha = 0.05$ for an F distribution with 2 and 60 degrees of freedom is $C = 3.15$. Since the computed value of the test statistic is equal to 2.02, we may conclude that at the 0.05 level of significance there is insufficient evidence to conclude that the three means are different. The null hypothesis that all three population means are equal must be accepted. Since the critical point for $\alpha = 0.10$ is 2.39, we find that the p-value is greater than 0.10.

Based on our data, there is no evidence that consumers tend to prefer the Brazilian coffee to the other two brands. The distributor may substitute one of the other brands for the price-unstable Brazilian coffee. Note that we usually prefer to make conclusions

FIGURE 9–4   Carrying Out the Test of Example (a)

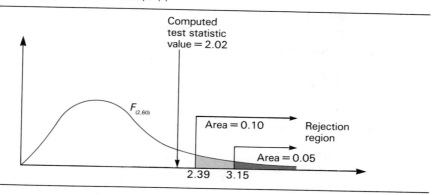

based on the *rejection* of a null hypothesis because acceptance is often considered a weak conclusion. The results of our test are shown in Figure 9–4.

In this section, we have seen the basic elements of the hypothesis test underlying analysis of variance: the null and alternative hypotheses, the required assumptions, the test statistic, and the decision rule. We have not, however, seen how the test statistic is computed from the data or the reasoning behind its computation. The theory and the computations of ANOVA are explained in the following sections.

PROBLEMS

9–1.   Four populations are compared by analysis of variance. What are the possible relations among the four population means covered under the null and alternative hypotheses?

9–2.   What are the assumptions of ANOVA?

9–3.   Three methods of training managers are to be tested for relative effectiveness. The management training institution proposes to test the effectiveness of the three methods by comparing two methods at a time, using a paired *t* test. Explain why this is a poor procedure.

9–4.   In an analysis of variance comparing the output of five plants, data sets of 21 observations per plant are analyzed. The computed *F* statistic value is 3.6. Do you believe that there are differences in average output among the five plants? What is the approximate *p*-value? Explain.

9–5.   A real estate development firm wants to test whether there are differences in the average price of a lot of a given size in the center of each of four cities: Philadelphia, New York, Washington, and Baltimore. Random samples of 52 lots in Philadelphia, 38 lots in New York, 43 lots in Washington, and 47 lots in Baltimore lead to a computed test statistic value of 12.53. Do you believe that average lot prices among the four cities are equal? How confident are you of your conclusion? Explain.

Answer

9–4.

Yes; *p*-value close to 0.01.

9–3   The Theory and the Computations of ANOVA

Recall that the purpose of analysis of variance is to detect differences among several population means based on evidence provided by random samples from these populations. How can this be done? We want to compare *r* population means. We use *r* random samples, one from each population. Each random sample has its own mean. The mean of the sample from population *i* will be denoted by $\bar{x}_i$. We may also compute the mean of all data points in the study, regardless of which population they come from. The mean of all the data points (when all data points are considered a single set) is called the *grand mean* and is denoted by $\overline{\overline{x}}$. These means are given by the following equations.

The mean of sample i ($i = 1, \ldots, r$):

$$\overline{x}_i = \frac{\sum\limits_{j=1}^{n_i} x_{ij}}{n_i} \qquad (9\text{--}3)$$

The **grand mean,** the mean of all the data points:

$$\overline{\overline{x}} = \frac{\sum\limits_{i=1}^{r} \sum\limits_{j=1}^{n_i} x_{ij}}{n} \qquad (9\text{--}4)$$

where x_{ij} is the particular data point in position j within the sample from population i. The subscript i denotes the population, or treatment, and runs from 1 to r. The subscript j denotes the data point within the sample from population i; thus, j runs from 1 to n_i.

In Example (a), $r = 3$, $n_1 = 21$, $n_2 = 20$, $n_3 = 22$, and $n = n_1 + n_2 + n_3 = 63$. The third data point (person) in the group of 21 people who consumed Brazilian coffee is denoted by x_{13} (that is, $i = 1$ denotes treatment 1 and $j = 3$ denotes the third point in that sample).

We will now define the main principle behind the analysis of variance.

> If the r population means are different (that is, at least two of the population means are *not* equal), then it is likely that the variation of the data points about their respective sample means, $\overline{x}_i$, will be *small* when compared with the variation of the r sample means about the grand mean, $\overline{\overline{x}}$.

We will demonstrate the ANOVA principle using three hypothetical populations, which we will call the triangles, the squares, and the circles. Table 9–1 gives the values of the sample points from the three populations. For demonstration purposes, we use very small samples. In real situations, the sample sizes should be much larger. The data given in Table 9–1 are shown in Figure 9–5. The figure also shows

TABLE 9–1 Data and the Various Sample Means for Triangles, Squares, and Circles

Treatment (i)	Sample Point (j)	Value (x_{ij})
$i = 1$ Triangle	1	4
Triangle	2	5
Triangle	3	7
Triangle	4	8
Mean of triangles		6
$i = 2$ Square	1	10
Square	2	11
Square	3	12
Square	4	13
Mean of squares		11.5
$i = 3$ Circle	1	1
Circle	2	2
Circle	3	3
Mean of circles		2
Grand mean of all data points		6.909

FIGURE 9–5 The Deviations of the Triangles, Squares, and Circles from Their Sample Means and the Deviations of the Sample Means from the Grand Mean

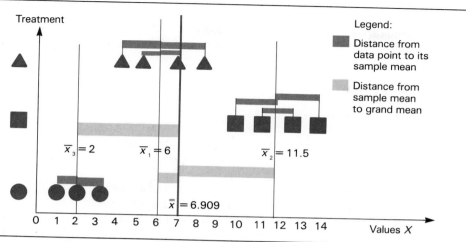

the deviations of the data points from their sample means and the deviations of the sample means from the grand mean.

Look carefully at Figure 9–5. Note that the *average* distance (in absolute value) of data points from their respective group means (that is, the average distance, in absolute value, of a triangle from the mean of the triangles, $\bar{x}_1$; and similarly for the squares and the circles) is *relatively small* compared with the average distance (in absolute value) of the three sample means from the grand mean. If you are not convinced of this, note that there are only three distances of sample means to the grand mean (in the computation, each distance is weighted by the actual number of points in the group), and that only one of them, the smallest distance—that of $\bar{x}_1$ to $\bar{\bar{x}}$—is of the relative magnitude of the distances between the data points and their respective sample means. The two other distances are much greater; hence, the average distance of the sample means from the grand mean is greater than the average distance of all data points to their respective sample means.

The *average* deviation from a mean is zero. We talk about the average absolute deviation—actually, we will use the average *squared* deviation—to prevent the deviations from canceling out. This should remind you of the definition of the sample variance in Chapter 1. Now let us define some terms that will make our discussion simpler.

> We define an **error deviation** as the difference between a data point and its sample mean. Errors are denoted by *e*, and we have:
>
> $$e_{ij} = x_{ij} - \bar{x}_i \qquad (9\text{–}5)$$

Thus, all the distances from the data points to their sample means in Figure 9–5 are errors (some are positive, and some are negative). The reason these distances are called errors is that they are unexplained by the fact that the corresponding data points belong to population *i*. The errors are assumed to be due to natural variation, or pure randomness, within the sample from treatment *i*.

On the other hand,

> We define a **treatment deviation** as the deviation of a sample mean from the grand mean. Treatment deviations, t_i, are given by:
>
> $$t_i = \overline{x}_i - \overline{\overline{x}} \qquad\qquad (9\text{--}6)$$

The ANOVA principle thus says:

When the population means are not equal, the "average" error is relatively small compared with the "average" treatment deviation.

Again, if we actually averaged all the deviations, we would get zero. Therefore, when we apply the principle computationally, we will square the error and treatment deviations before averaging them. This way, we will maintain the relative (squared) magnitudes of these quantities. The averaging process is further complicated because we have to average based on degrees of freedom (recall that degrees of freedom were used in the definition of a sample variance). For now, let the term *average* be used in a simplified, intuitive sense.

Since we noted that the average error in our triangle-square-circle example looks small relative to the average treatment deviation, let us see what the populations that brought about our three samples look like. Figure 9–6 shows the three populations, assumed normally distributed with equal variance. (This can be seen from the equal width of the three normal curves. Note also that the three samples seem to have equal dispersion about their sample means.) The figure also shows that the three population means are not equal.

Figure 9–7, in contrast, shows three samples of triangles, squares, and circles in which the average error deviation is of about the same magnitude (*not* smaller than) as the average treatment deviation. As can be seen from the superimposed nor-

FIGURE 9–6 The Samples of Triangles, Squares, and Circles and Their Respective Populations (the Three Populations Are Normal with Equal Variance but with Different Means)

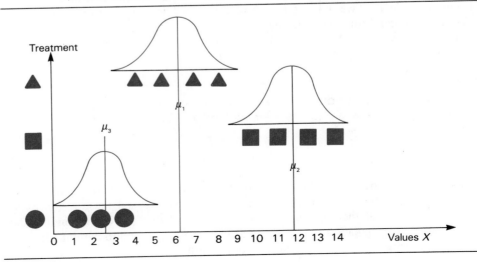

FIGURE 9–7 Samples of Triangles, Squares, and Circles Where the Average Error Deviation Is Not Smaller than the Average Treatment Deviation

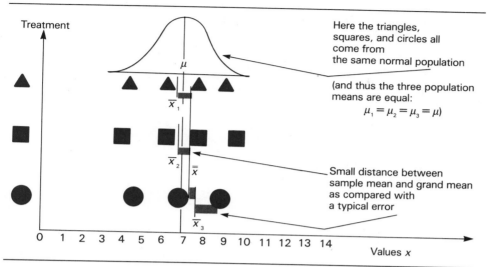

mal populations from which the samples have arisen in this case, the three popula-tion means, μ_1, μ_2, and μ_3, are all equal. Compare the two figures to convince yourself of the ANOVA principle.

The Sum of Squares Principle

We have seen how, when the population means are different, the error deviations in the data are small when compared with the treatment deviations. We made general statements about the average error being small when compared with the average treatment deviation. The error deviations measure how close the data *within* each group are to their respective group means. The treatment deviations measure the dis-tances *between* the various groups. It therefore seems intuitively plausible (as seen in Figures 9–5 to 9–7) that when these two kinds of deviations are of about equal magnitude, the population means are about equal. Why? Because when the average error is about equal to the average treatment deviation, then the treatment deviation may itself be viewed as just another error. That is, the treatment deviation in this case is due to pure chance rather than to any real difference among the population means. In other words, when the average t is of the same magnitude as the average e, then both are estimates of the internal variation within the data and carry no in-formation about a difference between any two groups—about a difference in popula-tion means.

We will now make everything quantifiable, using the *sum of squares principle*. We start by returning to Figure 9–5, looking at a particular data point, and analyz-ing distances associated with the data point. We choose the fourth data point from the sample of squares (population 2). This data point is $x_{24} = 13$ (verify this from Table 9–1). We now magnify a section of Figure 9–5, the section surrounding this particular data point. This is shown in Figure 9–8.

We define the **total deviation** of a data point x_{ij} (denoted by Tot_{ij}) as the deviation of the data point from the grand mean:

$$\text{Tot}_{ij} = x_{ij} - \overline{\overline{x}} \qquad (9\text{–}7)$$

FIGURE 9-8   The Total Deviation as the Sum of the Treatment Deviation and the Error Deviation for a Particular Data Point

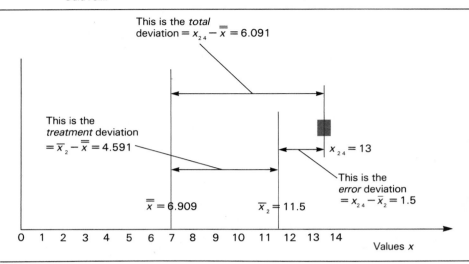

Figure 9-8 shows that the total deviation is equal to the treatment deviation plus the error deviation. This is true for *any* point in our data set (even when some of the numbers are negative).

> For any data point, x_{ij},
>
> $$\text{Tot} = t + e \qquad\qquad (9\text{-}8)$$

In words:

$$\text{Total deviation} = \text{Treatment deviation} + \text{Error deviation}$$

In the case of our chosen data point, x_{24}, we have:

$$t_2 + e_{24} = 4.591 + 1.5 = 6.091 = \text{Tot}_{24}$$

Equation 9-8 works for every data point in our data set. Here is how it is algebraically derived:

$$t_i + e_{ij} = (\bar{x}_i - \bar{\bar{x}}) + (x_{ij} - \bar{x}_i) = x_{ij} - \bar{\bar{x}} = \text{Tot}_{ij} \qquad\qquad (9\text{-}9)$$

As seen in equation 9-9, the term $\bar{x}_i$ cancels out when the two terms in parentheses are added. This shows that for every data point, the total deviation is equal to the treatment part of the deviation plus the error part. This is also seen in Figure 9-8. The *total* deviation of a data point from the grand mean is thus partitioned into a deviation due to *treatment* and a deviation due to *error*. The deviation due to treatment differences is the *between-treatments* deviation, while the deviation due to error is the *within-treatment* deviation.

We have only considered one point, x_{24}. In order to determine whether or not the error deviations are small when compared with the treatment deviations, we need to aggregate the partition over all data points. This is done, as we noted earlier, by averaging the deviations. We take the partition of the deviations in equation

9–9 and we square each of the three terms (otherwise our averaging process would lead to zero).[4] The squaring of the terms in equation 9–9 gives, on one side:

$$t_i^2 + e_{ij}^2 = (\bar{x}_i - \bar{\bar{x}})^2 + (x_{ij} - \bar{x}_i)^2 \tag{9-10}$$

And on the other side:

$$\text{Tot}_{ij}^2 = (x_{ij} - \bar{\bar{x}})^2 \tag{9-11}$$

Note an interesting thing: The two sides of equation 9–9 are equal, but when all three terms are squared, the two sides (now equations 9–10 and 9–11) are *not* equal. Try this with any of the data points. The surprising thing happens next.

We take the squared deviations of equations 9–10 and 9–11, and we *sum them over all our data points*. Interestingly, the sum of the squared error deviations and the sum of the squared treatment deviations do add up to the sum of the squared total deviations. Mathematically, cross-terms in the equation drop out, allowing this to happen. The result is the sum of squares principle.

We have the following:

$$\sum_{i=1}^{r}\sum_{j=1}^{n_i} \text{Tot}_{ij}^2 = \sum_{i=1}^{r} n_i t_i^2 + \sum_{i=1}^{r}\sum_{j=1}^{n_i} e_{ij}^2$$

This can be written in longer form as:

$$\sum_{i=1}^{r}\sum_{j=1}^{n_i} (x_{ij} - \bar{\bar{x}})^2 = \sum_{i=1}^{r} n_i (\bar{x}_i - \bar{\bar{x}})^2 + \sum_{i=1}^{r}\sum_{j=1}^{n_i} (x_{ij} - \bar{x}_i)^2$$

The Sum of Squares Principle

The total sum of squares (SST) is the sum of the two terms: the sum of squares for treatment (SSTR) and the sum of squares for error (SSE).

$$\text{SST} = \text{SSTR} + \text{SSE} \tag{9-12}$$

The sum of squares principle partitions the total sum of squares within the data, SST, into a part due to treatment effect, SSTR, and a part due to errors, SSE. The squared deviations of the treatment means from the grand mean are *counted for every data point*—hence the term n_i in the first summation on the right side (SSTR) of equation 9–12. The second term on the right-hand side is the sum of the squared errors, i.e., the sum of the squared deviations of the data points from their respective sample means.

See Figure 9–8 for the different deviations associated with a single point. Imagine a similar relation among the three kinds of deviations for every one of the data points, as shown in Figure 9–5. Then imagine all these deviations squared and added together—errors to errors, treatments to treatments, and totals to totals. The result is equation 9–12, the sum of squares principle.

Sums of squares measure variation within the data. SST is the total amount of variation within the data set. SSTR is that part of the variation within the data that is due to differences among the groups, and SSE is that part of the variation within the data that is due to error—the part that cannot be explained by differences among the

---

[4] This can be seen from the data in Table 9–1. Note that the sum of the deviations of the triangles from their mean of 6 is $(4 - 6) + (5 - 6) + (7 - 6) + (8 - 6) = 0$; hence, an average of these deviations, or those of the squares or circles, leads to zero.

FIGURE 9–9   Partition of the Total Sum of Squares into Treatment and Error Parts

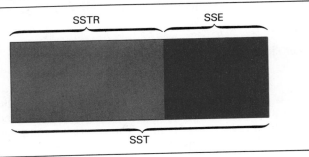

groups. Therefore, SSTR is sometimes called the sum of squares *between* (variation among the groups), and SSE is called the sum of squares *within* (within-group variation). SSTR is also called the *explained variation* (because it is the part of the total variation that can be explained by the fact that the data points belong to several different groups). SSE is, then, called the *unexplained variation*. The partition of the sum of squares in analysis of variance is shown in Figure 9–9.

Breaking down the sum of squares is not enough, however. If we want to determine whether or not the errors are small as compared with the treatment part, we need to find the *average* (squared) error and the *average* (squared) treatment deviation. Averaging, in the context of variances, is achieved by dividing by the appropriate number of degrees of freedom associated with each sum of squares.

The Degrees of Freedom

Recall our definition of degrees of freedom in Chapter 5. The degrees of freedom are the number of data points that are "free to move," that is, the number of elements in the data set, minus the number of restrictions. A restriction on a data set is a quantity already computed from the entire data set under consideration; thus, knowledge of this quantity makes one data point fixed and reduces by one the effective number of data points that are free to move. This is why, as was shown in Chapter 5, knowledge of the sample mean reduces the degrees of freedom of the sample variance to $n - 1$. What are the degrees of freedom in the context of analysis of variance?

Consider the total sum of squares, SST. In computing this sum of squares, we use the entire data set and information about *one* quantity computed from the data: the grand mean (because, by definition, SST is the sum of the squared deviations of all data points from the grand mean). Since we have a total of n data points and one restriction,

The number of degrees of freedom associated with SST is $n - 1$.

The sum of squares for treatment, SSTR, is computed from the deviations of r sample means from the grand mean. The r sample means are considered r independent data points, and the grand mean (which can be considered as having been computed from the r sample means) thus reduces the degrees of freedom by one.

The number of degrees of freedom associated with SSTR is $r - 1$.

The sum of squares for error, SSE, is computed from the deviations of a total of n

data points ($n = n_1 + n_2 + \cdots + n_r$) from r different sample means. Since each of the sample means acts as a restriction on the data set, the degrees of freedom for error are $n - r$. This can be seen another way: There are r groups with n_i data points in group i. Thus, each group, with its own sample mean acting as a restriction, has degrees of freedom equal to $n_i - 1$. The total number of degrees of freedom for error is the sum of the degrees of freedom in the r groups: df $= (n_1 - 1) + (n_2 - 1) + \cdots (n_r - 1) = n - r$.

The number of degrees of freedom associated with SSE is $n - r$.

An important principle in analysis of variance is that the degrees of freedom of the three components are *additive* in the same way that the sums of squares are additive.

$$df(\text{total}) = df(\text{treatment}) + df(\text{error}) \qquad (9\text{--}13)$$

This can easily be verified by noting the following: $n - 1 = (r - 1) + (n - r)$—the r drops out. We are now ready to compute the average squared deviation due to treatment and the average squared deviation due to error.

The Mean Squares

In finding the average squared deviations due to treatment and to error, we divide each sum of squares by its degrees of freedom. We call the two resulting averages **mean square treatment (MSTR)** and **mean square error (MSE),** respectively.

$$\text{MSTR} = \frac{\text{SSTR}}{r - 1} \qquad (9\text{--}14)$$

$$\text{MSE} = \frac{\text{SSE}}{n - r} \qquad (9\text{--}15)$$

The Expected Values of the Statistics MSTR and MSE under the Null Hypothesis

When the null hypothesis of ANOVA is true, all r population means are equal, and in this case there are *no treatment effects*. In such a case, the average squared deviation due to "treatment" is just another realization of an average squared error. In terms of the expected values of the two mean squares, we have:

$$E(\text{MSE}) = \sigma^2 \qquad (9\text{--}16)$$

and

$$E(\text{MSTR}) = \sigma^2 + \frac{\Sigma n_i(\mu_i - \mu)^2}{r - 1} \qquad (9\text{--}17)$$

where μ_i is the mean of population i and μ is the combined mean of all r populations.

Equation 9–16 says that *MSE is an unbiased estimator of σ^2, the assumed common variance of the r populations*. The mean square error in ANOVA is therefore just like the sample variance in the one-population case of earlier chapters.

The mean square treatment, however, comprises two components, as seen from equation 9–17. The first component is σ^2, as in the case of MSE. The second component is a measure of the differences among the r population means, μ_i. If the null hypothesis is true, all r population means are equal—they are all equal to μ. In such a case, the second term in equation 9–17 is equal to *zero*. When this happens, the expected value of MSTR and the expected value of MSE are each equal to σ^2.

> When the null hypothesis of ANOVA is true and all r population means are equal, MSTR and MSE are two independent, unbiased estimators of the common population variance, σ^2.

If, on the other hand, the null hypothesis is not true and differences do exist among the r population means, then *MSTR will tend to be larger than MSE*. This happens because, when not all population means are equal, the second term in equation 9–17 is a positive number.

The F Statistic

The preceding discussion suggests that the ratio of MSTR to MSE is a good indicator of whether or not the r population means are equal. If the r population means are equal, then MSTR/MSE would tend to be close to 1.00. Remember that both MSTR and MSE are sample statistics derived from our data. As such, MSTR and MSE will have some randomness associated with them, and they are not likely to exactly equal their expected values. Thus, when the null hypothesis is true, MSTR/MSE will vary around the value 1.00. When the r population means are not all equal, the ratio MSTR/MSE will tend to be greater than 1.00 because the expected value of MSTR, from equation 9–17, will be larger than the expected value of MSE. How large is "large enough" for us to reject the null hypothesis?

This is where statistical inference comes in. We want to determine whether the difference between our observed value of MSTR/MSE and the number 1.00 is due just to chance variation, or whether MSTR/MSE is *significantly* greater than 1.00— implying that the population means are not all equal. We will make the determination with the aid of the F distribution.

> Under the assumptions of ANOVA, the ratio MSTR/MSE possesses an F distribution with $r - 1$ degrees of freedom for the numerator and $n - r$ degrees of freedom for the denominator when the null hypothesis is true.

In Chapter 8, we saw how the F distribution is used in determining differences between two population variances—noting that if the two variances are equal, then the ratio of the two independent, unbiased estimators of the assumed common variance follows an F distribution. There, too, the appropriate degrees of freedom for the numerator and the denominator of F came from the degrees of freedom of the sample variance in the numerator and the sample variance in the denominator of the ratio. In ANOVA, the numerator is MSTR and has $r - 1$ degrees of freedom; the denominator is MSE and has $n - r$ degrees of freedom. We thus have the following.

The test statistic in analysis of variance:

$$F_{(r-1, n-r)} = \frac{\text{MSTR}}{\text{MSE}} \qquad (9\text{–}18)$$

In this section, we have seen the theoretical rationale for the F statistic we used in section 9–2. We also saw the computations required for arriving at the value of the test statistic. In the next section, we will encounter a convenient tool for keeping track of computations and reporting our results: the ANOVA table.

PROBLEMS

9–6. Define *treatment* and *error*.

9–7. Explain why trying to compute a simple average of all error deviations and of all   Answer
treatment deviations will not lead to any results.

9–8. Explain how the total deviation is partitioned into the treatment deviation and the error deviation.

9–9. Explain the sum of squares principle.

9–10. Where do errors come from, and what do you think are their sources?

9–11. If, in an analysis of variance, you find that MSTR is greater than MSE, why can you not immediately reject the null hypothesis without determining the F ratio and its distribution? Explain.

9–12. What is the main principle behind analysis of variance?

9–13. Explain how information about the variance components in a data set can lead to conclusions about population means.

9–14. Explain the meaning of the terms *within, between, unexplained, explained,* and the context in which these terms arise.

9–15. By the sum of squares principle, SSE and SSTR are additive, and their sum is SST. Does such a relation exist between MSE and MSTR? Explain.

9–16. Does the quantity MSTR/MSE follow an F distribution when the null hypothesis of   9–16.
ANOVA is false? Explain.

9–17. (A mathematically demanding problem) Prove the sum of squares principle, equa-   No.
tion 9–12.

9–4 The ANOVA Table and Examples

Table 9–2 shows the data for our triangles, squares, and circles. In addition, the table shows the deviations from the group means, and their squares. From these quantities, we find the sum of squares and mean squares.

As we see in the last row of the table, the sum of all the deviations of the data points from their group means is zero, as expected. The sum of the *squared* deviations from the sample means (which, from equation 9-12, is SSE) is equal to 17.00.

$$\text{SSE} = \sum_{i=1}^{r} \sum_{j=1}^{n_i} (x_{ij} - \bar{x}_i)^2 = 17.00$$

Now we want to compute the sum of squares for treatment. Recall from Table 9–1 that $\bar{\bar{x}} = 6.909$. Again using the definitions in equation 9–12, we have:

TABLE 9-2 Computations for Triangles, Squares, and Circles

Treatment (i)	j	Value (x_{ij})	($x_{ij} - \bar{x}_i$)	($x_{ij} - \bar{x}_i$)^2
Triangle	1	4	$4 - 6 = -2$	$(-2)^2 = 4$
Triangle	2	5	$5 - 6 = -1$	$(-1)^2 = 1$
Triangle	3	7	$7 - 6 = 1$	$(1)^2 = 1$
Triangle	4	8	$8 - 6 = 2$	$(2)^2 = 4$
Square	1	10	$10 - 11.5 = -1.5$	$(-1.5)^2 = 2.25$
Square	2	11	$11 - 11.5 = -0.5$	$(-0.5)^2 = 0.25$
Square	3	12	$12 - 11.5 = 0.5$	$(0.5)^2 = 0.25$
Square	4	13	$13 - 11.5 = 1.5$	$(1.5)^2 = 2.25$
Circle	1	1	$1 - 2 = -1$	$(-1)^2 = 1$
Circle	2	2	$2 - 2 = 0$	$(0)^2 = 0$
Circle	3	3	$3 - 2 = 1$	$(1)^2 = 1$
			Sum = 0	Sum = 17

$$\text{SSTR} = \sum_{i=1}^{r} n_i(\bar{x}_i - \bar{\bar{x}})^2 = 4(6 - 6.909)^2 + 4(11.5 - 6.909)^2 + 3(2 - 6.909)^2$$

$$= 159.9$$

We now compute the mean squares. From equations 9–14 and 9–15, respectively, we get:

$$\text{MSTR} = \frac{\text{SSTR}}{r - 1} = \frac{159.9}{2} = 79.95$$

$$\text{MSE} = \frac{\text{SSE}}{n - r} = \frac{17}{8} = 2.125$$

Using equation 9–18, we get the computed value of the F statistic:

$$F_{(2,8)} = \frac{\text{MSTR}}{\text{MSE}} = \frac{79.95}{2.125} = 37.62$$

We are finally in a position to conduct the ANOVA hypothesis test to determine whether or not the means of the three populations are equal. From Appendix C, Table 5, we find that the critical point at $\alpha = 0.01$ (for a right-hand-tailed test) for the F distribution with 2 degrees of freedom for the numerator and 8 degrees of freedom for the denominator is 8.65. We can therefore reject the null hypothesis. Since 37.62 is much greater than 8.65, the p-value is much smaller than 0.01. This is shown in Figure 9–10.

FIGURE 9-10 Rejecting the Null Hypothesis in the Triangles, Squares, and Circles Example

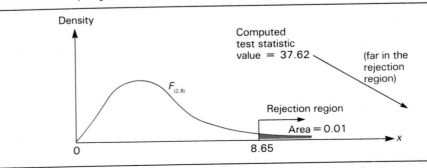

TABLE 9–3   ANOVA Table

Source of Variation	Sum of Squares	Degrees of Freedom	Mean Square	F Ratio
Treatment	SSTR = 159.9	$r - 1 = 2$	$MSTR = \dfrac{SSTR}{r-1}$ $= 79.95$	$F = \dfrac{MSTR}{MSE}$ $= 37.62$
Error	SSE = 17.0	$n - r = 8$	$MSE = \dfrac{SSE}{n-r}$	
Total	SST = 176.9	$n - 1 = 10$	$= 2.125$	

Note that, as usual, we must exercise caution in the interpretation of results based on such small samples. As we noted earlier, in real situations we use large data sets, and the computations are usually done by computer. In the rest of our examples, we will assume that sums of squares and other quantities are produced by a computer.[5] All statistical computer packages contain ANOVA routines, and in section 9–9, we will present examples of input and output.

An essential tool for reporting the results of an analysis of variance is the ANOVA table. An ANOVA table lists the sources of variation: treatment, error, and total. (In the two-factor ANOVA, which we will see in later sections, there will be more sources of variation.) The ANOVA table lists the sums of squares, the degrees of freedom, the mean squares, and the F ratio. The table format simplifies the analysis and the interpretation of the results. The structure of the ANOVA table is based on the fact that both the sums of squares and the degrees of freedom are additive. We will now present an ANOVA table for the triangles, squares, and circles example. Table 9–3 shows the results computed above.

Note that the entries in the second and third columns, sum of squares and degrees of freedom, are both additive. The entries in the fourth column, mean square, are obtained by dividing the appropriate sums of squares by their degrees of freedom. We do not define a mean square total, which is why there is no entry in that particular position in the table. The last entry in the table is the main objective of our analysis: the F ratio, which is computed as the ratio of the two entries in the previous column. There are no other entries in the last column. Example (b), which follows, demonstrates the use of the ANOVA table.

Club Med has over 30 major resorts worldwide, from Tahiti to Switzerland. Many of the beach resorts are in the Caribbean, and at one point the club wanted to test whether or not the resorts on Guadeloupe, Martinique, Haiti, Paradise Island, and St. Lucia were all equally well liked by vacationing club members. The analysis was to be based on a survey questionnaire filled out by a random sample of 40 respondents in each of the resorts. From every returned questionnaire, a general satisfaction score, on a scale of 0 to 100, was computed. Analysis of the survey results yielded the statistics given in Table 9–4.

EXAMPLE (b)

---

[5] If you must carry out ANOVA computations by hand, there are equivalent computational formulas for the sums of squares that may be easier to apply than equation 9–12. These are:

$$SST = \Sigma_i \Sigma_j (x_{ij})^2 - (\Sigma_i \Sigma_j x_{ij})^2/n$$
$$SSTR = \Sigma_i ((\Sigma_j x_{ij})^2/n_i) - (\Sigma_i \Sigma_j x_{ij})^2/n$$

and we obtain SSE by subtraction: SSE = SST − SSTR.

TABLE 9–4   Club Med Survey Results

Resort (i)	Mean Response ($\bar{x}_i$)
1. Guadeloupe	89
2. Martinique	75
3. Haiti	73
4. Paradise Island	91
5. St. Lucia	85

SST = 112,564   SSE = 98,356

The results were computed from the responses using a computer program that calculated the sums of squared deviations from the sample means and from the grand mean. Given the values of SST and SSE, construct an ANOVA table and conduct the hypothesis test. (Note: the reported sample means in Table 9–4 will be used in the next section.)

SOLUTION

Let us first construct an ANOVA table and fill in the information we have: SST = 112,564; SSE = 98,356; $n = 200$; and $r = 5$. This has been done in Table 9–5. We now compute SSTR as the difference between SST and SSE and enter it in the appropriate place in the table. We then divide SSTR and SSE by their respective degrees of freedom to give us MSTR and MSE. Finally, we divide MSTR by MSE to give us the F ratio. All these quantities are entered in the ANOVA table. The result is the complete ANOVA table for the study, Table 9–6.

Table 9–6 contains all the pertinent information for this study. We are now ready to conduct the hypothesis test.

H_0: $\mu_1 = \mu_2 = \mu_3 = \mu_4 = \mu_5$ (average vacationer satisfaction for each of the five resorts is equal)

H_1: Not all μ_i ($i = 1, \ldots , 5$) are equal (on the average, vacationer satisfaction is not equal among the five resorts)

As shown in Table 9–6, the test statistic value is $F_{(4,\ 195)} = 7.04$. As often happens, the exact number of degrees of freedom we need does not appear in Appendix C, Table 5. We use the nearest entry, which is the critical point for F with 4 degrees of freedom for the numerator and 200 degrees of freedom for the denominator. The critical point for $\alpha = 0.01$ is $C = 3.41$. The test is illustrated in Figure 9–11.

TABLE 9–5   Preliminary ANOVA Table for Club Med Example

Source of Variation	Sum of Squares	Degrees of Freedom	Mean Square	F Ratio
Treatment	SSTR =	$r - 1 = $ 4	MSTR =	$F = $
Error	SSE = 98,356	$n - r = 195$	MSE =	
Total	SST = 112,564	$n - 1 = 199$		

TABLE 9–6   ANOVA Table for Club Med Example

Source of Variation	Sum of Squares	Degrees of Freedom	Mean Square	F Ratio
Treatment	SSTR = 14,208	$r - 1 = $ 4	MSTR = 3,552	$F = 7.04$
Error	SSE = 98,356	$n - r = 195$	MSE = 504.4	
Total	SST = 112,564	$n - 1 = 199$		

FIGURE 9–11 Club Med Test

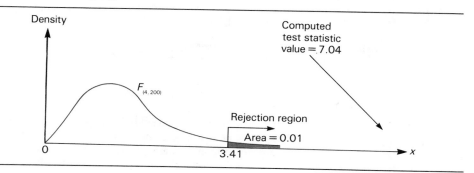

Since the computed test statistic value falls in the rejection region for $\alpha = 0.01$, we reject the null hypothesis and note that the p-value is smaller than 0.01. We may conclude that, based on the survey results and our assumptions, it is likely that the five resorts studied are not equal in terms of average vacationer satisfaction. Which resorts are more satisfying than others? This question will be answered when we return to this example in the next section.

EXAMPLE (c)

An article in the *Journal of Marketing Research* reports the results of a study of job involvement of salespeople in the four major career stages: exploration, establishment, maintenance, and disengagement.[6] As part of the study, the authors report the results of an analysis of variance aimed at determining whether or not salespeople in each of the four career stages are, on the average, equally involved with their jobs. Involvement is measured on a special scale developed by psychologists. The analysis is based on questionnaires returned by a total of 543 respondents, and the reported F value is 8.52. The authors note the result is "significant at $p < .01$." Assuming that MSE = 34.4, construct an ANOVA table for this example. Also verify the authors' claim about the significance of their results.

SOLUTION

In this problem, another exercise in the construction of ANOVA tables, we are doing the opposite of what is usually done: we are going from the final result of an F ratio to the earlier stages of an analysis of variance. First, multiplying the F ratio by MSE gives us MSTR. Then, from the sample size $n = 543$ and from $r = 4$, we get the number of degrees of freedom for treatment, error, and total. Using our information, we construct the ANOVA table (Table 9–7).

From Appendix C, Table 5, we find that the critical point for a right-hand-tailed test at $\alpha = 0.01$ for an F distribution with 3 and 400 degrees of freedom (the entry for

TABLE 9–7 ANOVA Table for Job Involvement

Source of Variation	Sum of Squares	Degrees of Freedom	Mean Square	F Ratio
Treatment	SSTR = 879.3	$r - 1 =$ 3	MSTR = 293.1	$F = 8.52$
Error	SSE = 18,541.6	$n - r =$ 539	MSE = 34.4	
Total	SST = 19,420.9	$n - 1 =$ 542		

[6] W. L. Cron and J. W. Slocum, "The Influence of Career Stages on Salespeople's Performance," *Journal of Marketing Research* (May 1986).

degrees of freedom closest to the needed 3 and 539) is 3.83. Thus, we may conclude that differences do exist among the four career stages with respect to average job involvement. The authors' statement about the p-value is also true: the p-value is much smaller than 0.01.

PROBLEMS

Answer

9–18.

$F_{(2,27)} = 20.71$; reject H_0; p-value < 0.01.

9–18. The Gulfstream Aerospace Company produced three different prototypes as candidates for mass production as the company's newest large-cabin business jet, the Gulfstream IV. Each of the three prototypes has slightly different features, which may bring about differences in performance. Therefore, as part of the decision-making process as to which model to produce, company engineers are interested in determining whether or not the three proposed models have about the same average flight range. Each of the models is assigned a random choice of 10 flight routes and departure times, and the flight range on a full standard fuel tank is measured (the planes carry additional fuel on the test flights, to allow them to land safely at certain destination points). Range data for the three prototypes, in nautical miles (measured to the nearest 10 miles), are as follows.[7]

Prototype A	Prototype B	Prototype C
4,420	4,230	4,110
4,540	4,220	4,090
4,380	4,100	4,070
4,550	4,300	4,160
4,210	4,420	4,230
4,330	4,110	4,120
4,400	4,230	4,000
4,340	4,280	4,200
4,390	4,090	4,150
4,510	4,320	4,220

Do all three prototypes have the same average range? Construct an ANOVA table, and carry out the test. Explain your results.

9–19. In the theory of finance, a market for any asset or commodity is said to be *efficient* if items of identical quality and other attributes (such as risk, in the case of stocks) are sold at the same price. A Geneva-based oil industry analyst wants to test the hypothesis that the spot market for crude oil is efficient. The analyst chooses the Rotterdam oil market, and he selects Arabian Light as the type of oil to be studied. (Differences in location may cause price differences because of transportation costs, and differences in the type of oil—hence, in the quality of oil—also affect the price. Therefore, both the type and the location must be fixed.) The analyst also notes that during the month of February 1987, the "official" price of a barrel of crude oil did not change. A random sample of eight observations from each of four sources of the spot price of a barrel of oil during February is collected. Data, in U.S. dollars per barrel, are as follows.

U.K.	Mexico	U.A.E.	Oman
$17.80	$18.01	$18.10	$18.05
18.00	17.75	17.92	18.01
17.98	18.00	18.01	17.94
18.20	17.77	17.88	18.23
18.00	18.01	18.30	18.20
17.99	18.01	18.22	18.00
18.10	18.12	18.56	17.84
17.90	18.20	18.10	18.11

---

[7] General information about the capabilities of the Gulfstream IV is provided courtesy of the Gulfstream Aerospace Company.

Based on these data, what should the analyst conclude about whether or not the market for crude oil is efficient? Are conclusions valid only for the Rotterdam market? Are conclusions valid for all types of crude oil? What assumptions are necessary for the analysis? Do you believe that all the assumptions are met in this case? What are the limitations, if any, of this study? Discuss.

9–20. The manager of a store wants to decide what kind of hand-knit sweaters to sell. The manager is considering three kinds of sweaters: Irish, Peruvian, and Shetland. The decision will depend on the results of an analysis of which kind of sweater, if any, lasts the longest before wearing out. The manager has some data collected from various customers who in the past bought different sweaters and reported how many years their sweaters lasted before wearing out. There are 20 observations on Irish sweaters, 18 on Peruvian sweaters, and 21 on Shetland sweaters. The data are assumed independent random samples from the three populations of sweaters. The manager hires a statistician, who carries out an ANOVA and finds SSE = 1,240 and SSTR = 740. Construct a complete ANOVA table, and determine whether there is evidence to conclude that the three kinds of sweaters do not have equal average durability.

9–21. An article in the *Journal of Marketing* describes a study of organizational buyer behavior.[8] As part of the analysis, the authors of the study wanted to test whether or not differences exist in the average amount of time buyers need for making a group-purchase decision about one of three different kinds of copying machines. The article reports that the degrees of freedom for error were 82, the mean square treatment was 136.3, and the sum of squares total was 1,701.83. Construct the complete ANOVA table for this study, and determine whether or not there is evidence of differences in the average time to reach a group-purchase decision about copying machines.

9–22. The Fidelity Overseas mutual fund consists of about equal proportions of Japanese and European stocks. The percentage of the fund invested in any individual country varies according to prevailing rates of return on stocks in different countries. At the end of October 1986, the fund manager was considering the possibility of shifting the proportions invested in French, Dutch, and Italian stocks. This change would be made if it could be statistically substantiated that differences in average annualized rates of return during the period ending in October existed among stocks from the three countries. Random samples of 50 French stocks, 32 Dutch stocks, and 28 Italian stocks were collected, and the annualized rate of return for each stock over the period under study was computed. Then an analysis of variance was carried out, which produced the following results: SSE = 22,399.8 and SST = 32,156.1. Based on these results, should the manager shift the proportions of the fund invested in the three countries? How confident are you of your answer? Construct a complete ANOVA table for this problem.

9–23. A study is undertaken to determine whether differences exist in average consumer quality ratings of the following brands of color television sets: Magnavox, General Electric, Panasonic, Zenith, Sears, Philco, Sylvania, and RCA. For each brand, 100 randomly chosen consumer responses are available, and from these the following quantities are computed: SSTR = 45,210; SST = 92,340. Construct an ANOVA table for this study, and test the null hypothesis that all eight brands have equal average consumer quality ratings versus the alternative hypothesis that they do not.

9–5 Further Analysis

You have rejected the ANOVA null hypothesis. What next? This is an important question often overlooked in elementary introductions to analysis of variance. After all, what is the meaning of the statement "not all r population means are equal" if we cannot tell *in what way* the population means are not equal? We need to know

Answers

9–20.
$F_{(2, 56)} = 16.71$; reject H_0; p-value < 0.01.

9–22.
$F_{(2, 107)} = 23.3$; reject H_0; p-value < 0.01.

[8] R. E. Krapfel, "An Advocacy Behavior Model of Organizational Buyers' Vendor Choice," *Journal of Marketing* (Fall 1985).

which of our population means are large, which of them are small, and the magnitudes of the differences among them. These issues are addressed in this section.

ANOVA can be viewed as a machine or a box: in go the data, and out comes a conclusion—"all r population means are equal" or "not all r population means are equal." If the ANOVA null hypothesis, H_0: $\mu_1 = \mu_2 = \cdots = \mu_r$, is accepted and we therefore state that there is no strong evidence to conclude that differences exist among the r population means, there is nothing more to say or do (unless, of course, you believe that differences do exist and you are able to gather more information to prove so). If the ANOVA null hypothesis is rejected, then we have evidence that the r population means are not all equal. This calls for *further analysis*—other hypothesis tests and/or the construction of confidence intervals to determine where the differences exist, their directions, and their magnitudes. The schematic diagram of the "ANOVA box" is shown in Figure 9–12.

Several methods have been developed for further analysis following the rejection of the null hypothesis in ANOVA. All the methods make use of the following two properties.

The sample means, $\overline{X}_i$, are unbiased estimators of the corresponding population means, μ_i.

The mean square error, MSE, is an unbiased estimator of the common population variance, σ^2.

Since MSE can be read directly from the ANOVA table, we have another advantage of using an ANOVA table. This extends the usefulness of the table beyond the primary stages of analysis. The first and simplest post-ANOVA analysis is the estimation of separate population means, μ_i. It can be shown that, under the assumptions of analysis of variance, each sample mean, $\overline{X}_i$, has a normal distribution with mean μ_i and standard deviation $\sigma/\sqrt{n}$, where σ is the common standard deviation of the r populations. Since σ is not known, we estimate it by $\sqrt{\text{MSE}}$. We get the following relation.

$$\frac{\overline{X}_i - \mu_i}{\sqrt{\text{MSE}}/\sqrt{n_i}} \text{ has a } t \text{ distribution with } n - r \text{ degrees of freedom} \qquad (9\text{–}19)$$

This property leads us to the possibility of constructing confidence intervals for individual population means.

FIGURE 9–12 The ANOVA Diagram

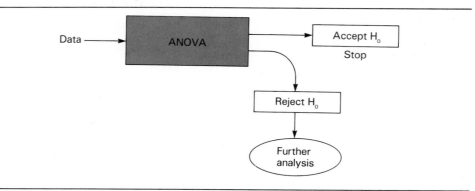

A $(1 - \alpha)$ 100% confidence interval for μ_i, the mean of population i:

$$\bar{x}_i \pm t_{\alpha/2}\frac{\sqrt{MSE}}{\sqrt{n_i}} \qquad (9\text{--}20)$$

where $t_{\alpha/2}$ is the value of the t distribution with $n - r$ degrees of freedom that cuts off a right-hand-tail area equal to $\alpha/2$

Confidence intervals given by equation 9–20 are included in the standard output of ANOVA in many packages, such as MINITAB. This will be seen in section 9–9.

We now demonstrate the use of equation 9–20 with the continuation of Example (b), the Club Med example. From Table 9–4, we get the sample means, $\bar{x}_i$:

$$\begin{aligned}
\text{Guadeloupe:} \quad & \bar{x}_1 = 89 \\
\text{Martinique:} \quad & \bar{x}_2 = 75 \\
\text{Haiti:} \quad & \bar{x}_3 = 73 \\
\text{Paradise Is.:} \quad & \bar{x}_4 = 91 \\
\text{St. Lucia:} \quad & \bar{x}_5 = 85
\end{aligned}$$

From Table 9–6, the ANOVA table for this example, we get: MSE = 504.4 and degrees of freedom for error = $n - r = 195$. We also know that the sample size in each group is $n_i = 40$ for all $i = 1, \ldots, 5$. Since a t distribution with 195 degrees of freedom is, for all practical purposes, a standard normal distribution, we use $z = 1.96$ in constructing 95% confidence intervals for the population mean responses of vacationers on the five islands. We will construct a 95% confidence interval for the mean response on Guadeloupe and leave the construction of the other four confidence intervals as an exercise. For Guadeloupe, we have the following 95% confidence interval for the population mean (μ_1):

$$\bar{x}_1 \pm t_{\alpha/2}\frac{\sqrt{MSE}}{\sqrt{n_1}} = 89 \pm 1.96\frac{\sqrt{504.4}}{\sqrt{40}} = [82.04, 95.96]$$

The real usefulness of ANOVA, however, does not lie in the construction of individual confidence intervals for population means (these are of limited use because the confidence coefficient does not apply to a *series* of estimates). The power of ANOVA lies in providing us with the ability to make *joint* conclusions about population parameters.

As mentioned earlier, several procedures have been developed for further analysis. The method we will discuss here is the *Tukey method* of pairwise comparisons of the population means. The method is also called the HSD (honestly significant differences) test. This method allows us to compare every possible pair of means using a *single level of significance*, say $\alpha = 0.05$ (or a single confidence coefficient, say, $1 - \alpha = 0.95$). The single level of significance applies to the *entire set* of pairwise comparisons.

The Tukey Pairwise Comparisons Test

We will use the *studentized range distribution.*

The **studentized range distribution,** q, is a probability distribution with degrees of freedom r and $n - r$.

Note that the degrees of freedom of q are similar, but not identical, to the degrees of freedom of the F distribution in ANOVA. The F distribution has $r - 1$ and $n - r$ degrees of freedom. The q distribution has degrees of freedom r and $n - r$. Critical points for q with different numbers of degrees of freedom for $\alpha = 0.05$ and for $\alpha = 0.01$ are given in Appendix C, Table 6. Check, for example, that for $\alpha = 0.05$, $r = 3$, and $n - r = 20$, we have the critical point $q_\alpha = 3.58$. The table gives right-hand critical points, which is what we need since our test will be a right-hand-tailed test. We now define the Tukey criterion, T.

The Tukey criterion

$$T = q_\alpha \frac{\sqrt{MSE}}{\sqrt{n_i}} \qquad (9–21)$$

Equation 9–21 gives us a critical point, at a given level α, with which we will compare the computed values of test statistics defined later. Now let us define the hypothesis tests. As mentioned, the usefulness of the Tukey test is that it allows us to *jointly* perform all possible pairwise comparisons of the population means using a single, "family" level of significance. What are all the possible pairwise comparisons associated with an ANOVA?

Suppose that we had $r = 3$. We compared the means of three populations using ANOVA and concluded that the means were not all equal. Now we would like to be able to compare every *pair* of means to determine where the differences among population means exist. How many pairwise comparisons are there? With three populations, there are

$$\binom{3}{2} = \frac{3!}{2! \, 1!} = 3 \text{ comparisons}$$

These comparisons are:

$$1 \text{ with } 2$$
$$2 \text{ with } 3, \text{ and}$$
$$1 \text{ with } 3$$

As a general rule, the number of possible pairwise comparisons of r means is:

$$\binom{r}{2} = \frac{r!}{2!(r - 2)!} \qquad (9–22)$$

You do not really need equation 9–22 for cases where it is relatively easy to list all the possible pairs. In the case of Example (b), there are, by equation 9–22, $5!/2!3! = (5)(4)(3)(2)/(2)(3)(2) = 10$ possible pairwise comparisons. Let us list all the comparisons:

$$\text{Guadeloupe (1)–Martinique (2)}$$
$$\text{Guadeloupe (1)–Haiti (3)}$$
$$\text{Guadeloupe (1)–Paradise Island (4)}$$
$$\text{Guadeloupe (1)–St. Lucia (5)}$$
$$\text{Martinique (2)–Haiti (3)}$$
$$\text{Martinique (2)–Paradise Island (4)}$$

Martinique (2)–St. Lucia (5)

Haiti (3)–Paradise Island (4)

Haiti (3)–St. Lucia (5)

Paradise Island (4)–St. Lucia (5)

These pairings are apparent if you look at Table 9–4 and see that we need to compare the first island, Guadeloupe, with all four islands below it. Then we need to compare the second island, Martinique, with all three islands below it (we already have the comparison of Martinique with Guadeloupe). We do the same with Haiti, and finally with Paradise Island, which has only St. Lucia listed below it; therefore, this is the last comparison. (In the preceding list, we wrote the number of each population in parentheses after the population name.)

The parameter μ_1 denotes the population mean of all vacationer responses for Guadeloupe. The parameters μ_2 to μ_5 have similar meanings. To compare the population mean vacationer responses for every pair of island resorts, we use the following *set of hypothesis tests*.

$$\text{I.} \quad H_0: \mu_1 = \mu_2$$
$$H_1: \mu_1 \neq \mu_2$$

$$\text{II.} \quad H_0: \mu_1 = \mu_3$$
$$H_1: \mu_1 \neq \mu_3$$

$$\text{III.} \quad H_0: \mu_1 = \mu_4$$
$$H_1: \mu_1 \neq \mu_4$$

$$\text{IV.} \quad H_0: \mu_1 = \mu_5$$
$$H_1: \mu_1 \neq \mu_5$$

$$\text{V.} \quad H_0: \mu_2 = \mu_3$$
$$H_1: \mu_2 \neq \mu_3$$

$$\text{VI.} \quad H_0: \mu_2 = \mu_4$$
$$H_1: \mu_2 \neq \mu_4$$

$$\text{VII.} \quad H_0: \mu_2 = \mu_5$$
$$H_1: \mu_2 \neq \mu_5$$

$$\text{VIII.} \quad H_0: \mu_3 = \mu_4$$
$$H_1: \mu_3 \neq \mu_4$$

$$\text{IX.} \quad H_0: \mu_3 = \mu_5$$
$$H_1: \mu_3 \neq \mu_5$$

$$\text{X.} \quad H_0: \mu_4 = \mu_5$$
$$H_1: \mu_4 \neq \mu_5$$

The Tukey method allows us to simultaneously carry out all 10 hypothesis tests at a single given level of significance, say, $\alpha = 0.05$. Thus, if we use the Tukey procedure for reaching conclusions as to which population means are equal and which are not, we know that the probability of reaching at least one erroneous conclusion, stating that two means are not equal when indeed they are equal, is at most 0.05.

The test statistics:

The test statistic for each test is the *absolute difference of the appropriate sample means.*

Thus, the test statistic for the first test (I) is:

$$|\bar{x}_1 - \bar{x}_2| = |89 - 83| = 6$$

Conducting the Tests

We conduct the tests as follows. We compute each of the test statistics and compare them with the value of T that corresponds to the desired level of significance, α. *We reject a particular null hypothesis if the absolute difference between the corresponding pair of sample means exceeds the value of T.*

Using $\alpha = 0.05$, we now conduct the Tukey test for Example (b). All absolute differences of sample means corresponding to the pairwise tests I through X are computed and compared with the value of T. For $\alpha = 0.05$, $r = 5$, and $n - r = 195$ (we use ∞, the last row in the table), we get, from Appendix C, Table 6: $q = 3.86$. We also know that MSE $= 504.4$ and $n_i = 40$ for all i. (Later we will see what to do when not all r samples are of equal size.) Therefore, from equation 9–21:

$$T = q_\alpha \sqrt{\frac{\text{MSE}}{n_i}} = 3.86 \sqrt{\frac{504.4}{40}} = 13.7$$

We now compute all 10 pairwise absolute differences of sample means and compare them with $T = 13.7$ to determine which differences are statistically significant at $\alpha = 0.05$ (these are marked with an asterisk).

$$|\bar{x}_1 - \bar{x}_2| = |89 - 75| = 14 > 13.7*$$
$$|\bar{x}_1 - \bar{x}_3| = |89 - 73| = 16 > 13.7*$$
$$|\bar{x}_1 - \bar{x}_4| = |89 - 91| = 2 < 13.7$$
$$|\bar{x}_1 - \bar{x}_5| = |89 - 85| = 4 < 13.7$$
$$|\bar{x}_2 - \bar{x}_3| = |75 - 73| = 2 < 13.7$$
$$|\bar{x}_2 - \bar{x}_4| = |75 - 91| = 16 > 13.7*$$
$$|\bar{x}_2 - \bar{x}_5| = |75 - 85| = 10 < 13.7$$
$$|\bar{x}_3 - \bar{x}_4| = |73 - 91| = 18 > 13.7*$$
$$|\bar{x}_3 - \bar{x}_5| = |73 - 85| = 12 < 13.7$$
$$|\bar{x}_4 - \bar{x}_5| = |91 - 85| = 6 < 13.7$$

From these comparisons we determine that our data provide statistical evidence to conclude that μ_1 is different from μ_2; μ_1 is different from μ_3; μ_2 is different from μ_4; and μ_3 is different from μ_4. *There are no other statistically significant differences at* $\alpha = 0.05$.

For the purpose of interpretation, it will help to draw a diagram of the significant differences that we found. This has been done in Figure 9–13. Looking at the figure, you may be puzzled by the fact that we believe, for example, that μ_1 is different from μ_2, yet we believe that μ_1 is no different from μ_5 and μ_5 is no different from μ_2. You may say: If A is equal to B, and B is equal to C, then mathematically we must have A equal to C (the transitivity of equality). But remember that we are doing statistics, not discussing mathematical equality. In statistics, accepting the null hypothesis that two parameters are equal does not mean that they are necessarily

FIGURE 9–13   Differences among the Population Means in Example (b) Suggested by the Tukey Procedure

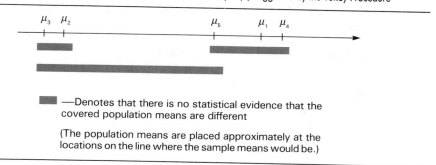

—Denotes that there is no statistical evidence that the covered population means are different

(The population means are placed approximately at the locations on the line where the sample means would be.)

equal. The acceptance just means that we have no statistical evidence to conclude that they are different. Thus, in our present example, we conclude that there is statistical evidence to support the claim that, on the average, vacationers give higher ratings to Guadeloupe (1) than they give to Martinique (2) or Haiti (3); as well as the claim that Paradise Island (4) is, on the average, rated higher than Martinique or Haiti. There is no statistical evidence for any other claim of differences in average ratings among the five island resorts. Note also that we do not have to hypothesize any of the assertions of tests I through X *before* doing the analysis. The Tukey method allows us to make all the above conclusions at a single level of significance, $\alpha = 0.05$.

The Case of Unequal Sample Sizes, and Alternative Procedures

What can we do if the sample sizes are not equal in all groups? We use the *smallest sample size* of all the n_i in computing the criterion T of equation 9–21. The Tukey procedure is the best follow-up to ANOVA when the sample sizes are all equal. The case of equal sample sizes is called the *balanced design*. For very unbalanced designs (i.e., when sample sizes are very different), there are other methods of further analysis to be used following ANOVA. Two of the better-known methods are the Bonferroni method and the Scheffé method. We will not discuss these methods.

PROBLEMS

9–24.   Give 95% confidence intervals for the remaining four population mean responses to the Club Med resorts (the one for Guadeloupe having been given in the text).

9–25.   Use the data of Table 9–1 and the Tukey procedure to determine where differences exist among the triangle, circle, and square population means. Use $\alpha = 0.01$.

9–26.   For problem 9–18, find which, if any, of the three prototype planes has an average range different from the others. Use $\alpha = 0.05$.

9–27.   For problem 9–19, use the Tukey method to determine which oil types, if any, have an average price different from the others. Use $\alpha = 0.05$.

9–28.   For problem 9–20, suppose that the appropriate sample means are 6.4, 2.5, and 4.9 (in years and in order of type listed in problem 9–20). Find where differences, if any, exist among the three population means. Use $\alpha = 0.05$.

9–29.   For problem 9–23, suppose the sample means, in the order listed in that problem, are: 77, 78, 82, 94, 88, 89, 90, 87. Use the Tukey procedure to determine where differences in average population ratings may exist. Use $\alpha = 0.01$.

Answers

9–24.

Martinique [68.04, 81.96]
Haiti [66.04, 79.96]
Paradise Island [84.04, 97.96]
St. Lucia [78.04, 91.96]

9–26.

A has higher range than B and C. B and C show no difference.

Answers

9–28.

$\mu_{Irish} > \mu_{Peruvian}$
No other significant differences.

9–30.

Only investments 1 and 2 have a significant difference.

9–30. An analysis of variance is carried out to determine differences among average annualized returns on four types of investments. The analysis leads to the rejection of the null hypothesis that no differences exist, using $\alpha = 0.05$. The mean square error is 49.5; the sample sizes are all $n_i = 31$. The sample means are: 18, 11, 15, 14. Find the significant differences that exist among the four types of investment.

9–6 Models, Factors, and Designs

A **statistical model** is a set of equations and assumptions that capture the essential characteristics of a real-world situation.

Tne model we have been discussing so far in this chapter is the one-factor ANOVA model. In this model, the populations are assumed to be represented by the following equation.

The one-factor ANOVA model:

$$x_{ij} = \mu_i + \epsilon_{ij} = \mu + \tau_i + \epsilon_{ij} \qquad (9\text{–}23)$$

where ϵ_{ij} is the error associated with the jth member of the ith population. The errors are assumed to be normally distributed with mean zero and variance σ^2.

The ANOVA model assumes that the r populations are normally distributed with means μ_i, which may be different, and with equal variance, σ^2. The right-hand side of equation 9–23 breaks the mean of population i into a common component, μ, and a unique component due to the particular population (or treatment) i. This component is written as τ_i. When we sample, the sample means $\bar{X}_i$ are unbiased estimators of the respective population means, μ_i. The grand mean, $\bar{X}$, is an unbiased estimator of the common component of the means, μ. The treatment deviations, t_i, are estimators of the differences among population means, τ_i. The data errors, e_{ij}, are estimates of the population errors, ϵ_{ij}.

Much more will be said about statistical models in the next chapter, dealing with regression analysis. The one-factor ANOVA null hypothesis, H_0: $\mu_1 = \mu_2 = \cdots = \mu_r$, may be written in an equivalent form, using equation 9–23, as H_0: $\tau_i = 0$ for all i. (This is so because if $\mu_i = \mu$ for all i, then the "extra" components, τ_i, are all zero.) This form of the hypothesis will be extended in the two-factor ANOVA model, also called the two-way ANOVA model, discussed in the following section.

We may want to check that the assumptions of the ANOVA model are indeed met. To check that the errors are approximately normally distributed, we may draw a histogram of the observed errors, e_{ij}, which are called *residuals*. If serious deviations from the normal-distribution assumption exist, the histogram will not resemble a normal curve. Plotting the residuals for each of the r samples under study will reveal whether or not the population variances are indeed (at least approximately) equal. If the *spread* of the data sets around their group means is not approximately equal for all r groups, then the population variances may not be equal. When model assumptions are violated, a nonparametric alternative to ANOVA must be used. An alternative method of analysis is the Kruskal-Wallis test, discussed in Chapter 14. Residual analysis will be discussed in detail in the next chapter.

One-Factor versus Multifactor Models

In each of the examples and problems you have seen so far, we were interested in determining whether or not differences existed among several populations, or treatments. These treatments may be considered as *levels* of a single *factor*.

A **factor** is a set of populations or treatments of a single kind.

Examples of factors are vacationer ratings of a *set of resorts*, the range of different *types of airplanes*, and the durability of different *kinds of sweaters*.

Sometimes, however, we may be interested in studying more than one factor. For example, an accounting researcher may be interested in testing whether there are differences in average error percentage rate among the Big Eight accounting firms, *and* among different geographical locations, such as the Eastern Seaboard, the South, the Midwest, and the West. In such an analysis, there are *two factors:* the different firms (factor A, with eight levels) and the geographical location (factor B, with four levels).

Another example is that of an advertising firm interested in studying how the public is influenced by color, shape, and size in an advertisement. The firm could carry out an ANOVA to test whether or not there are differences in average responses to three different colors, as well as to four different shapes of an ad, and to three different ad sizes. This would be a three-factor ANOVA. There are important statistical reasons for jointly studying the effects of several factors in a multifactor ANOVA. These will be explained in the next section, on two-factor ANOVA.

Fixed-Effects versus Random-Effects Models

Recall Example (b), where we wanted to determine whether differences existed among the five particular island resorts, Guadeloupe, Martinique, Haiti, Paradise Island, and St. Lucia. Once we reject or accept the null hypothesis, *the inference is valid only for the five islands studied*. This is a *fixed-effects model*.

A **fixed-effects model** is a model where the levels of the factor under study (the treatments) are *fixed* in advance. Inference is valid only for the levels under study.

Consider another possible context for the analysis. Suppose that Club Med had no particular interest in the 5 resorts listed, but instead wanted to determine whether differences existed among *any* of its more than 30 resorts. In such a case, we may consider all Club Med resorts as a *population of resorts*, and we may draw a random sample of five (or any other number) of the resorts and carry out an ANOVA to determine differences among population means. The ANOVA would be carried out in exactly the same way. However, since the resorts themselves were randomly selected for analysis out of the population of all Club Med resorts, the inference would be valid for *all* Club Med resorts. This is called the *random-effects model*.

The **random-effects model** is an ANOVA model in which the levels of the factor under study are *randomly chosen* out of an entire population of levels (treatments). Inference is valid for the entire population of levels.

The idea should make sense to you if you recall the principle of inference using random sampling, discussed in Chapter 5, and the story of the *Literary Digest*. In order to make inferences that are valid for an entire population, we must randomly sample from the entire population. Here this principle is applied to a population of treatments.

Experimental Design

Analysis of variance often involves the ideas of **experimental design.** If we want to study the effects of different treatments, we are sometimes in a position to design the experiment by which we plan to study these effects. Designing the experiment involves the choice of elements from a population or populations and the assignment of elements to different treatments. The model we have been using involves a *completely randomized design*.

> A **completely randomized design** is a design in which elements are assigned to treatments *completely at random.* Thus, every element chosen for the study has an equal chance of being assigned to any treatment.

There are other types of design. Some designs, called **blocking designs,** are very useful in reducing experimental errors, that is, reducing variation due to factors other than the ones under study. In the *randomized complete block design,* for example, experimental units are assigned to treatments in blocks of similar elements, with randomized treatment order within each block. In the Club Med situation of Example (b), a randomized complete block design could involve sending each vacationer in the sample to all five resorts, the order of the resorts chosen randomly; each vacationer is then asked to rate all the resorts. A design such as this one, with *experimental units* (here, people) given all the treatments, is called a *repeated measures design.* More will be said about blocking designs later.

PROBLEMS

Answer

9–31.   For problem 9–18, suppose that four more prototype planes are built after the study is completed. Could the inference from the ANOVA involving the first three prototypes be extended to the new planes? Explain.

9–32.   What is a blocking design?

9–33.   For problem 9–18, can you think of a blocking design that would reduce experimental errors?

9–34.   How can we determine whether there are violations of the ANOVA model assumptions? What should we do if such violations exist?

9–35.   Explain why the factor levels must be randomly chosen in the random effects model to allow inference about an entire collection of treatments.

9–36.

No; Rotterdam not randomly chosen.

9–36.   For problem 9–19, based on the given data, can you tell whether or not the world oil market is efficient?

9–7   Two-Way Analysis of Variance

In addition to being interested in possible differences in the general appeal of their five Caribbean resorts [Example (b)], suppose that Club Med is also interested in the respective appeal of four vacation attributes: friendship, sports, culture, and excitement.[9] Club Med would like to have answers to the following two questions.

---
[9] Information on the attributes and the resorts was provided through the courtesy of Club Med.

1. Are there differences in average vacationer satisfaction with the five Caribbean resorts?
2. Are there differences in average vacationer satisfaction in terms of the four vacation attributes?

In cases such as this one, where there is interest in *two* factors—resort and vacation attribute—we can answer the two questions *jointly*. In addition, we can answer a *third*, very important question, which may not be apparent to us.

3. Are there any *interactions* between some resorts and some attributes?

The three questions are statistically answerable by conducting a two-factor, or two-way, ANOVA. Why a two-way ANOVA? Why not conduct each of the two ANOVAs separately?

There are several reasons for conducting a two-way ANOVA. One reason is *efficiency*. When we conduct a two-way ANOVA, we may use a smaller total sample size for the analysis than would be required if we were to conduct each of the two tests separately. Basically, we use the same data resources to answer the two main questions. In the case of Club Med, the club may run a friendship program at each of the five resorts for one week; then the next week (with different vacationers) it may run a sports program in each of the five resorts; and so on. All vacationer responses could then be used for evaluating *both* the satisfaction from the resorts and the satisfaction from the attributes, rather than conducting two separate surveys, requiring twice the effort and number of respondents. A more important reason for conducting a two-way ANOVA is that there really are *three* questions to be answered.

Let us call the first factor of interest (here, resorts) factor A and the second factor (here, attributes) factor B. The effects of each factor alone are the factor's *main effects*. The combined effects of the two factors, beyond what we may expect from the consideration of each factor separately, is the *interaction* between the two factors.

Two factors are said to **interact** if the difference between levels (treatments) of one factor depends on the level of the other factor. Factors that do not interact are called *additive*.

An interaction is thus an *extra effect* that appears as a result of a particular combination of a treatment from one factor with a treatment from another factor. An interaction between two factors exists when, for at least one combination of treatments—say Haiti and sports—the effect of the combination is not additive: there is some special "chemistry" between the two treatments. Suppose that Haiti is rated lowest of all resorts and sports is rated lowest of all attributes. We then expect the Haiti-sports combination to be rated, on average, lowest of all combinations. If this does not happen, the two levels are said to interact.

The three questions answerable by two-way ANOVA are:

1. Are there any factor A main effects?
2. Are there any factor B main effects?
3. Are there any interaction effects of factors A and B?

Let n_{ij} be the sample size in the "cell" corresponding to level i of factor A and level k_j of factor B. Assume there is a uniform sample size for each factor A–factor B combination, say, $n_{ij} = 4$. The layout of the data of a two-way ANOVA, using the Club Med example, is shown in Figure 9–14. Figure 9–15 shows the effects of an

FIGURE 9–14 Two-Way ANOVA Data Layout

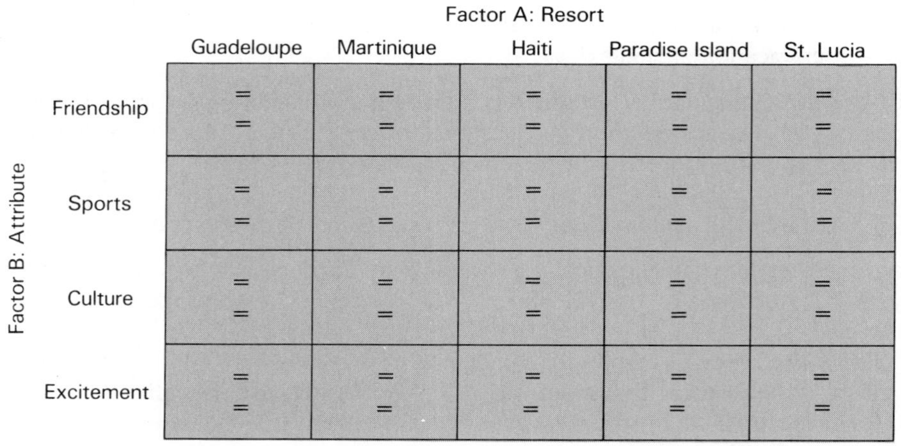

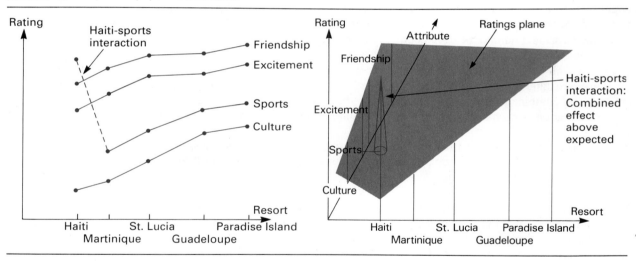

FIGURE 9–15 Graphical Display of Interaction Effects

interaction. We arrange the levels of each factor in increasing order of sample mean responses. The general two-variable trend of increasing average response is the response plane shown in Figure 9–15. An exception to the plane is the Haiti-sports interaction, which leads to a higher-than-expected average response for this combination of levels.

The Two-Way ANOVA Model

There are a levels of factor A ($a = 5$ resorts in the Club Med example) and b levels of factor B ($b = 4$ attributes in the same example). Thus, there are $a \times b$ combinations of levels, or cells, as shown in Figure 9–14. Each one is considered a treatment. We must assume equal sample sizes in all the cells. If we do not have equal sample sizes, we must use an alternative to the method of this chapter and solve the

ANOVA problem using multiple regression analysis (Chapter 11). Since we assume an equal sample size in each cell, we will simplify our notation and call the sample size in each cell n, omitting the subscripts i, j. We will denote the total sample size (formerly called n) by the symbol N. In the two-way ANOVA model, the assumptions of normal populations and equal variance for each two-factor combination treatment are still maintained.

The two-way ANOVA model:

$$x_{ijk} = \mu + \alpha_i + \beta_j + (\alpha\beta)_{ij} + \epsilon_{ijk} \qquad (9\text{--}24)$$

where μ is the overall mean; α_i is the effect of level i ($i = 1, \ldots, a$) of factor A; β_j is the effect of level j ($j = 1, \ldots, b$) of factor B; $(\alpha\beta)_{ij}$ is the interaction effect of levels i and j; and ϵ_{ijk} is the error associated with the kth data point from level i of factor A and level j of factor B. As before, we assume that the error ϵ_{ijk} is normally distributed with mean zero and variance σ^2 for all $i, j,$ and k. [10]

Our data, assumed to be random samples from populations modeled by equation 9–24, give us estimates of the model parameters. These estimates—as well as the different measures of variation, as in the one-way ANOVA case—are used in testing hypotheses. Since, in two-way ANOVA, three questions are to be answered rather than just one, there are three hypothesis tests relevant to any two-way ANOVA. The hypothesis tests that answer questions 1 to 3 are presented next.

The Hypothesis Tests in Two-Way ANOVA

Factor A main-effects test:

$$H_0: \alpha_i = 0 \text{ for all } i = 1, \ldots, a$$
$$H_1: \text{Not all } \alpha_i \text{ are } 0$$

This hypothesis test is designed to determine whether or not there are any factor A main effects. That is, the null hypothesis is true if and only if there are no differences in means due to the different treatments (populations) of factor A.

Factor B main-effects test:

$$H_0: \beta_j = 0 \text{ for all } j = 1, \ldots, b$$
$$H_1: \text{Not all } \beta_j \text{ are } 0$$

This test will detect evidence of any factor B main effects. The null hypothesis is true if and only if there are no differences in means due to the different treatments (populations) of factor B.

Test for (AB) interactions:

$$H_0: (\alpha\beta)_{ij} = 0 \text{ for all } i = 1, \ldots, a \text{ and } j = 1, \ldots, b$$
$$H_1: \text{Not all } (\alpha\beta)_{ij} \text{ are } 0$$

This is a test for the existence of interactions between levels of the two factors. The

---

[10] Since the terms α_i, β_j, and $(\alpha\beta)_{ij}$ are deviations from the overall mean μ, in the fixed-effects model the sums of all these deviations are all zero: $\Sigma\alpha_i = 0$, $\Sigma\beta_j = 0$, and $\Sigma(\alpha\beta)_{ij} = 0$.

null hypothesis is true if and only if there are no two-way interactions between levels of factor A and levels of factor B, that is, if the factor effects are additive.

In carrying out a two-way ANOVA, we should test the third hypothesis first. We do so because it is important to first determine whether or not interactions exist. If interactions do exist, our interpretation of the ANOVA results will be different from the case where no interactions exist (that is, in the case where the effects of the two factors are additive).

Sums of Squares, Degrees of Freedom, and Mean Squares

We define the data, the various means, and the deviations from the means as follows.

x_{ijk} is the kth data point from level i of factor A and level j of factor B.

$\overline{\overline{x}}$ is the grand mean.

$\overline{x}_{ij}$ is the mean of cell ij.

$\overline{x}_i$ is the mean of all data points in level i of factor A.

$\overline{x}_j$ is the mean of all data points in level j of factor B.

Using these definitions, we have:

$$\sum_{1}^{a}\sum_{1}^{b}\sum_{1}^{n}(x_{ijk} - \overline{\overline{x}})^2 = \sum\sum\sum(\overline{x}_{ij} - \overline{\overline{x}})^2 + \sum\sum\sum(x_{ijk} - \overline{x}_{ij})^2 \quad (9\text{--}25)$$

$$\underbrace{\text{SST} = \text{SSTR} + \text{SSE}}$$

(This can be further partitioned)

Equation 9–25 is the usual decomposition of the sum of squares, where each cell (a combination of a level of factor A and a level of factor B) is considered a separate treatment. Deviations of the data points from the cell means are squared and summed. Equation 9–25 is the same as equation 9–12 for the partition of the total sum of squares into sum of squares treatment and sum of squares error in one-way ANOVA. The only difference between the two equations is that here the summations extend over three subscripts: one subscript for levels of each of the two factors and one subscript for the data point number. The interesting thing is that SSTR can be further partitioned into a component due to factor A, a component due to factor B, and a component due to interactions of the two factors. The partition of the total sum of squares into its components is given in equation 9–26.

Do not worry about the mathematics of the summations. Two-way ANOVA is prohibitively tedious for hand computation, and we will always use a computer. The important thing to understand is that the total sum of squares is partitioned into a part due to factor A, a part due to factor B, a part due to interactions of the two factors, and a part due to error. This is shown in Figure 9–16.

What are the degrees of freedom? Since there are a levels of factor A, the degrees of freedom for factor A are $a - 1$. Similarly, there are $b - 1$ degrees of freedom for factor B, and there are $(a - 1)(b - 1)$ degrees of freedom for (AB) interac-

$$\text{SST} = \text{SSTR} + \text{SSE}$$

$$\sum\sum\sum(x - \overline{\overline{x}})^2 = \sum\sum\sum(\overline{x} - \overline{\overline{x}})^2 + \sum\sum\sum(x - \overline{x})^2$$

$$\sum\sum\sum(\overline{x}_i - \overline{\overline{x}})^2 + \sum\sum\sum(\overline{x}_j - \overline{\overline{x}})^2 + \sum\sum\sum(\overline{x}_{ij} - \overline{x}_i - \overline{x}_j + \overline{\overline{x}})^2$$

$$\text{SSA} + \text{SSB} + \text{SS(AB)}$$

Thus,

$$\text{SST} = \text{SSA} + \text{SSB} + \text{SS(AB)} + \text{SSE} \qquad (9\text{--}26)$$

where SSA = sum of squares due to factor A, SSB = sum of squares due to factor B, and SS(AB) = sum of squares due to the interactions of factors A and B

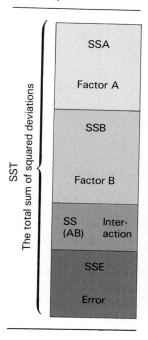

FIGURE 9–16
Partition of the Sum of Squares in Two-Way ANOVA

tions. The degrees of freedom for error are $ab(n - 1)$. The total degrees of freedom are $abn - 1$. But we knew that! $[(a - 1) + (b - 1) + (a - 1)(b - 1) + ab(n - 1) = a + b - 2 + ab - a - b + 1 + abn - ab = abn - 1.]$ Note that since we assume an equal sample size, n, in each cell and since there are ab cells, we have $N = abn$, and the total number of degrees of freedom is $N - 1 = abn - 1$.

Let us now construct an ANOVA table. The table includes the sums of squares, the degrees of freedom, and the mean squares. The mean squares are obtained by dividing each sum of squares by its degrees of freedom. The final products of the table are three F ratios. We define the F ratios as follows.

The F Ratios and the Two-Way ANOVA Table

The F ratio for each one of the hypothesis tests is the ratio of the appropriate mean square to the MSE. That is, for the test of factor A main effects, we use $F = \text{MSA}/\text{MSE}$; for the test of factor B main effects, we use $F = \text{MSB}/\text{MSE}$; and for the test of interactions of the two factors, we use $F = \text{MS(AB)}/\text{MSE}$. We now construct the ANOVA table for two-way analysis, Table 9–8.

The degrees of freedom associated with each F ratio are the degrees of freedom

TABLE 9–8 ANOVA Table for Two-Way Analysis

Source of Variation	Sum of Squares	Degrees of Freedom	Mean Square	F Ratio
Factor A	SSA	$a - 1$	$\text{MSA} = \dfrac{\text{SSA}}{a - 1}$	$F = \dfrac{\text{MSA}}{\text{MSE}}$
Factor B	SSB	$b - 1$	$\text{MSB} = \dfrac{\text{SSB}}{b - 1}$	$F = \dfrac{\text{MSB}}{\text{MSE}}$
Interaction	SS(AB)	$(a - 1)(b - 1)$	$\text{MS(AB)} = \dfrac{\text{SS(AB)}}{(a - 1)(b - 1)}$	$F = \dfrac{\text{MS(AB)}}{\text{MSE}}$
Error	SSE	$ab(n - 1)$	$\text{MSE} = \dfrac{\text{SSE}}{ab(n - 1)}$	
Total	SST	$abn - 1$		

of the respective numerator and denominator (the denominator is the same for all three tests). For the testing of factor A main effects, our test statistic is the first F ratio in the ANOVA table. When the null hypothesis is true (there are no factor A main effects), the ratio $F = \text{MSA}/\text{MSE}$ follows an F distribution with $(a-1)$ degrees of freedom for the numerator and $ab(n-1)$ degrees of freedom for the denominator. We denote this distribution by $F_{[a-1,ab(n-1)]}$. Similarly, for the test of factor B main effects, when the null hypothesis is true, the distribution of the test statistic is $F_{[b-1,ab(n-1)]}$. The test for the existence of (AB) interactions uses the distribution $F_{[(a-1)(b-1),ab(n-1)]}$.

We will demonstrate the use of the ANOVA table in two-way analysis, and the three tests, with a new example.

EXAMPLE (d)

An article in *Financial World* magazine claims that the Japanese have now joined Americans and the English in paying top dollars for paintings at art auctions.[11] Suppose that an art dealer is interested in testing two hypotheses. The first is that paintings sell for the same price, on the average, in London, New York, and Tokyo. The second hypothesis is that works of Picasso, Chagall, and Dali sell for the same average price. The dealer is also aware of a third question. This is the question of a possible interaction between the location (and thus the buyers: Americans, English, Japanese) and the artist. Data on auction prices of 10 works of art by each of the three painters at each of the three cities are collected, and a two-way ANOVA is run on a computer. The results include the following. The sums of squares associated with the location (factor A) is 1,824. The sum of squares associated with the artist (factor B) is 2,230. The sum of squares for interactions is 804. The sum of squares for error is 8,262. Construct the ANOVA table, carry out the hypothesis tests, and state your conclusions.

SOLUTION

We enter the sums of squares into the table. Since there are three levels in each of the two factors, and the sample size in each cell is 10, the degrees of freedom are: $a-1=2$, $b-1=2$, $(a-1)(b-1)=4$, and $ab(n-1)=81$. Also, $abn-1=89$, which checks as the sum of all other degrees of freedom. These values are entered in the table as well. The mean squares are computed, and so are the appropriate F ratios. Check to see how each result in the ANOVA table, Table 9–9, is obtained.

Let us now conduct the three hypothesis tests relevant to this problem. We will state the hypothesis tests in words. The factor A test is:

H_0: There is no difference in the average price of paintings of the kind studied across the three locations

H_1: There are differences in average price across locations

TABLE 9–9 ANOVA Table for Example (d)

Source of Variation	Sum of Squares	Degrees of Freedom	Mean Square	F Ratio
Location	1,824	2	912	8.94
Artist	2,230	2	1,115	10.93
Interaction	804	4	201	1.97
Error	8,262	81	102	
Total	13,120	89		

---

[11] "Japanese Pay Top Prices for Art," *Financial World* (January 20, 1987).

FIGURE 9–17 Example (d): Location Hypothesis Test

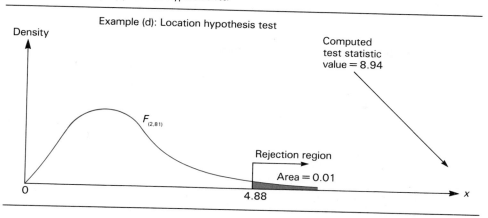

The test statistic is an F random variable with 2 and 81 degrees of freedom (see Table 9–9). The computed value of the test statistic is 8.94. From Appendix C, Table 5, we find that the critical point for $\alpha = 0.01$ is close to 4.88. Thus, the null hypothesis is rejected, and we know that the p-value is much smaller than 0.01. Computer printouts of ANOVA results often list p-values in the ANOVA table, in a column after the F ratios. Often, the computer output will show: $p = 0.0000$. This means that the p-value is smaller than 0.0001. The results of the hypothesis test are shown in Figure 9–17.

Now we perform the hypothesis test for factor B:

H₀: There are no differences in the average price of paintings by the three artists studied

H₁: There are differences in the average price of paintings by the three artists

Here again, the test statistic is an F random variable with 2 and 81 degrees of freedom, and the computed value of the statistic is 10.93. The null hypothesis is rejected, and the p-value is much smaller than 0.01. The test is shown in Figure 9–18.

FIGURE 9–18 Example (d): Artist Hypothesis Test

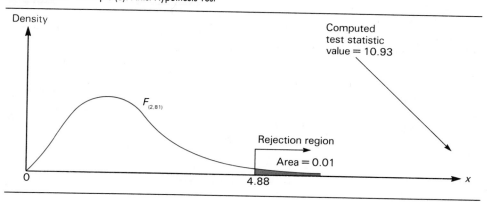

FIGURE 9–19   Example (d): Test for Interaction

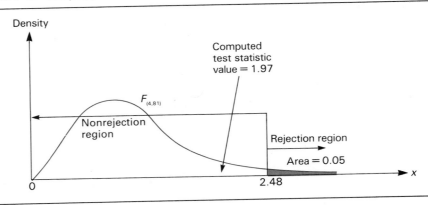

The hypothesis test for interactions is:

H_0: There are no interactions of the locations and the artists under study

H_1: There is at least one interaction of a location and an artist

The test statistic is an F random variable with 4 and 81 degrees of freedom. At a level of significance $\alpha = 0.05$, the critical point (see Appendix C, Table 5) is approximately equal to 2.48, and our computed value of the statistic is 1.97, leading us to accept the null hypothesis of no interaction at levels of significance greater than 0.05. This is shown in Figure 9–19.

As mentioned earlier, we look at the test for interactions first. Since the null hypothesis of no interactions was accepted, we have no statistical evidence of interactions of the two factors. This means, for example, that if a work by Picasso sells at a higher average price than works by the other two artists, then his paintings will fetch—on average—higher prices in all three cities. It also means that if paintings sell for a higher average price in London than in the other two cities, then this holds true—again, on average—for all three artists. Now we may interpret the results of the two main-effects tests.

We may conclude that there is statistical evidence that paintings (by these artists) do not fetch the same average price across the three cities. We may similarly conclude that paintings by the three artists under study do not sell, on average, for the same price. Where do the differences exist? This can be determined by a method for further analysis, such as the Tukey method.

In cases where we *do* find evidence of an interaction effect, our results have a different interpretation. In such cases, we must qualify any statement about differences among levels of one factor (say, factor A) as follows: *There exist differences among levels of factor A, averaged over all levels of factor B.*

We demonstrate this with a brief example. An article in the *Accounting Review* reports the results of a two-way ANOVA on the factors "accounting" and "materiality."[12] The exact nature of the study need not concern us here, as it is very technical. The results of the study include the following.

---

[12] S. Haka, L. Friedman, and V. Jones, "Functional Fixation and Interference Theory," *Accounting Review* (July 1986).

Source	df	Mean Square	F	Probability
Materiality	2	1.3499	4.5	0.0155
Accounting-materiality interaction	4	.8581	2.9	0.0298

From these partial results, we see that the *p*-values ("probability") are each less than 0.05. Therefore, at the 0.05 level of significance for each of the two tests (separately), we find that there is an interaction effect, and we find a main effect for materiality. We may now conclude that, at the 0.05 level of significance, there are differences among the levels of materiality, *averaged over all levels* of accounting.

The Overall Significance Level

Remember our discussion of the Tukey analysis and its importance in allowing us to conduct a family of tests at a single level of significance. In two-way ANOVA, as we have seen, there is a family of *three tests,* each carried out at a given level of significance. Here the question arises: What is the level of significance of the *set* of three tests? A bound on the probability of making at least one type I error in the three tests is given by *Kimball's inequality*. If the hypothesis test for factor A main effects is carried out at α_1, the hypothesis test for factor B main effects is carried out at α_2, and the hypothesis test for interactions is carried out at α_3, then the level of significance, α, of the three tests together is bounded from above as follows.

Kimball's inequality:

$$\alpha \leq 1 - (1 - \alpha_1)(1 - \alpha_2)(1 - \alpha_3) \qquad (9\text{--}27)$$

In Example (d), we conducted the first two tests—the tests for main effects—at the 0.01 level of significance. We conducted the test for interactions at the 0.05 level. Using equation 9–27, we find that the level of significance of the family of three tests is *at most*: $1 - (1 - 0.01)(1 - 0.01)(1 - 0.05) \doteq 0.0689$.

The Tukey Method for Two-Way Analysis

Equation 9–21, the Tukey statistic for pairwise comparisons, is easily extended to two-way ANOVA. We are interested in comparing the levels of a factor once the ANOVA has led us to believe that differences do exist for that factor. The only difference in the Tukey formula is the number of degrees of freedom. In making pairwise comparisons of the levels of factor A, the test statistics are the pairwise differences between the sample means for all levels of factor A, regardless of factor B. For example, the pairwise comparisons of all the mean prices at the three locations in Example (d) will be done as follows. We compute the absolute differences of all the pairs of sample means:

$$\left| \bar{x}_{\text{London}} - \bar{x}_{\text{NY}} \right|$$
$$\left| \bar{x}_{\text{Tokyo}} - \bar{x}_{\text{London}} \right|$$
$$\left| \bar{x}_{\text{NY}} - \bar{x}_{\text{Tokyo}} \right|$$

Now we compare these differences with the Tukey criterion:

Tukey criterion for factor A:

$$T = q_\alpha \sqrt{\frac{MSE}{bn}} \qquad (9\text{--}28)$$

where the degrees of freedom of the q distribution are now a and $ab(n - 1)$. Note also that MSE is divided by bn.

In Example (d), both a and b are 3. The sample size in each cell is $n = 10$. At $\alpha = 0.05$, the Tukey criterion is equal to $(3.4)(\sqrt{102}/\sqrt{30}) = 6.27$. Suppose that the sample mean in New York is 19.6 (hundred thousand dollars), in Tokyo it is 21.4, and in London is 15.1. Comparing all absolute differences of the sample means leads us to the conclusion that the average prices in London and Tokyo are significantly different; but the average prices in Tokyo and New York are not different, and neither are the average prices in New York and London. The overall significance level of these joint conclusions is $\alpha = 0.05$.

Extension of ANOVA to Three Factors

It is possible to carry out a three-way ANOVA. In such cases, we assume that in addition to a levels of factor A and b levels of factor B, there are c levels of factor C. There are three possible pairwise interactions of factors and one possible triple interaction of factors. These are denoted (AB), (BC), (AC), and (ABC). Table 9–10 is the ANOVA table for three-way analysis.

It is beyond the scope of this book to give examples of three-way ANOVA. However, the extension of two-way analysis to this method is straightforward, and if you should need to carry out such an analysis, Table 9–10 will provide you with all the information you need. Three-factor interactions, (ABC), imply that at least some of the two-factor interactions, (AB), (BC), (AC), are dependent on the level of the third factor.

TABLE 9–10   Three-Way ANOVA Table

Source of Variation	Sum of Squares	Degrees of Freedom	Mean Square	F Ratio
Factor A	SSA	$a - 1$	$MSA = \dfrac{SSA}{a - 1}$	$F = \dfrac{MSA}{MSE}$
Factor B	SSB	$b - 1$	$MSB = \dfrac{SSB}{b - 1}$	$F = \dfrac{MSB}{MSE}$
Factor C	SSC	$c - 1$	$MSC = \dfrac{SSC}{c - 1}$	$F = \dfrac{MSC}{MSE}$
(AB)	SS(AB)	$(a - 1)(b - 1)$	$MS(AB) = \dfrac{SS(AB)}{(a - 1)(b - 1)}$	$F = \dfrac{MS(AB)}{MSE}$
(BC)	SS(BC)	$(b - 1)(c - 1)$	$MS(BC) = \dfrac{SS(BC)}{(b - 1)(c - 1)}$	$F = \dfrac{MS(BC)}{MSE}$
(AC)	SS(AC)	$(a - 1)(c - 1)$	$MS(AC) = \dfrac{SS(AC)}{(a - 1)(c - 1)}$	$F = \dfrac{MS(AC)}{MSE}$
(ABC)	SS(ABC)	$(a - 1)(b - 1)(c - 1)$	$MS(ABC)$	$F = \dfrac{MS(ABC)}{MSE}$
Error	SSE	$abc(n - 1)$	MSE	
Total	SST	$abcn - 1$		

FIGURE 9–20 Data Layout in a Two-Way ANOVA with $n = 1$

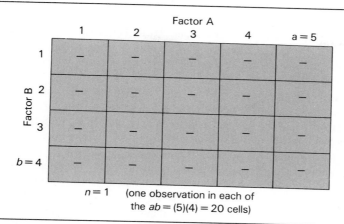

$n = 1$ (one observation in each of
the $ab = (5)(4) = 20$ cells)

Two-Way ANOVA with One Observation per Cell

The case of one data point in every cell presents a problem in two-way ANOVA. Can you guess why? (*Hint:* degrees of freedom for error.) Look at Figure 9–20, which shows the layout of the data in a two-way ANOVA with five levels of factor A and four levels of factor B. Note that the sample size in each of the 20 cells is $n = 1$.

As you may have guessed, there are no degrees of freedom for error! With one observation per cell, $n = 1$; the degrees of freedom for error are $ab(n - 1) = ab(1 - 1) = 0$. This can be seen from Table 9–11. What can we do? If we *believe* that there are no interactions (this assumption cannot be statistically tested when $n = 1$), then our sum of squares SS(AB) is due to error and contains no other information. In such a case, we can use SS(AB) and its associated degrees of freedom, $(a - 1)(b - 1)$, in place of SSE and its degrees of freedom. We can thus conduct the tests for the main effects by dividing MSA by MS(AB) when testing for factor A main effects. The resulting F statistic has $a - 1$ and $(a - 1)(b - 1)$ degrees of freedom. Similarly, when testing for factor B main effects, we divide MSB by MS(AB) and obtain an F statistic with $b - 1$ and $(a - 1)(b - 1)$ degrees of freedom.

Remember that this analysis assumes that there are no interactions between the two factors. Remember also that in statistics it is always desirable to have as much data as possible. Therefore, the two-way ANOVA with one observation per cell is, in itself, of limited use. The idea of two factors and one observation per cell is useful, however, as it brings us closer to the idea of blocking, presented in the next section.

TABLE 9–11 ANOVA Table for Two-Way Analysis with One Observation per Cell Assuming No Interactions

Source of Variation	Sum of Squares	Degrees of Freedom	Mean Square	F Ratio
Factor A	SSA	$(a - 1)$	$MSA = \dfrac{SSA}{a - 1}$	$F = \dfrac{MSA}{MS(AB)}$
Factor B	SSB	$(b - 1)$	$MSB = \dfrac{SSB}{b - 1}$	$F = \dfrac{MSB}{MS(AB)}$
"Error"	SS(AB)	$(a - 1)(b - 1)$	$MS(AB) = \dfrac{SS(AB)}{(a - 1)(b - 1)}$	
Total	SST	$ab - 1$		

PROBLEMS

Answer

9–37. Discuss the context in which Example (d) can be analyzed using a random-effects model.

9–38. What are the reasons for conducting a two-way analysis rather than two separate one-way ANOVAs? Explain.

9–39. What are the limitations of two-way ANOVA? What problems may be encountered?

9–40. (This is a hard problem.) Suppose that a limited data set is available. Explain why it is not desirable to increase the number of factors under study (say, four-way ANOVA, five-way ANOVA, and so on)? Give two reasons for this—one of the reasons a statistical one.

9–41. An article about process tracing and brand extension reports the results of a two-way ANOVA with the two factors "brand extension typicality" and "brand breadth." The article reports an F statistic for interaction of the two factors: $F_{(4,139)} = 4.27$.[13] Is there evidence that the two factors interact with each other, as believed by the authors of the article?

9–42.
———
Location $F = 50.6$, significant.

Job $F = 50.18$, significant.

Interaction $F = 2.14$, not significant.

9–42. The following table reports salaries, in thousands of dollars per year, for executives in three job types and three locations. Conduct a two-way ANOVA on these data.

	Job		
Location	Type I	Type II	Type III
East	54, 61, 59, 56, 70, 62, 63, 57, 68	48, 50, 49, 60, 54, 52, 49, 55, 53	71, 76, 65, 70, 68, 62, 73, 60, 79
Central	52, 50, 58, 59, 62, 57, 58, 64, 61	44, 49, 54, 53, 51, 60, 55, 47, 50	61, 64, 69, 58, 57, 63, 65, 63, 50
West	63, 67, 68, 72, 68, 75, 62, 65, 70	65, 58, 62, 70, 57, 61, 68, 65, 73	82, 75, 79, 77, 80, 69, 84, 83, 76

9–43. The Neilsen Company, which issues television popularity rating reports, is interested in testing for differences in average viewer satisfaction with morning news, evening news, and late news. The company is also interested in determining whether or not differences exist in average viewer satisfaction with the three main networks, CBS, ABC, and NBC. Nine groups of 50 randomly chosen viewers are assigned to each combination cell, CBS-morning, CBS-evening, . . . , NBC-late. The viewers' satisfaction ratings are recorded. The results are analyzed via two-factor ANOVA, one factor being network and the other factor being news time. Complete the following ANOVA table for this study, and give a full interpretation of the results.

Source of Variation	Sum of Squares	Degrees of Freedom	Mean Square	F Ratio
Network	145			
News time	160			
Interaction	240			
Error	6,200			
Total				

9–44. An article reports the results of an analysis of salespersons' performance level as a function of two factors: task difficulty and effort. Included in the article is the following ANOVA table.

---

[13] D.M. Boush and B. Loken, "A Process Tracing Study of Brand Extension Evaluation," *Journal of Marketing Research* (February 1991), p. 21.

Variable	df	F Value	p
Task difficulty	1	0.39	0.5357
Effort	1	53.27	<0.0001
Interaction	1	1.95	0.1649

a. How many levels of task difficulty were studied?

b. How many levels of effort were studied?

c. Are there any significant task difficulty main effects?

d. Are there any significant effort main effects?

e. Are there any significant interactions of the two factors? Explain.

9–45. An article reports the results of a two-way ANOVA on the effects of the two factors—exercise price of an option and the time of expiration of an option—on implied interest rates (the measured variable). Included in the article is the following ANOVA table.

Source of Variance	Degrees of Freedom	Sum of Squares	Mean Square	F
Exercise prices	2	2.866	1.433	.420
Time of expiration	1	16.518	16.518	4.845
Interaction	2	1.315	.658	.193
Explained	5	20.699	4.140	1.214
Residuals (error)	144	490.964	3.409	

a. What is meant by *Explained* in the table, and what is the origin of the information listed under that source?

b. How many levels of exercise price were used?

c. How many levels of time of expiration were used?

d. How large was the total sample size?

e. Assuming an equal number of data points in each cell, how large was the sample in each cell?

f. Are there any exercise price main effects?

g. Are there any time of expiration main effects?

h. Are there any interactions of the two factors?

i. Interpret the findings of this study.

j. Give approximate p-values for the tests.

k. In this particular study, what other, equivalent distribution may be used for testing for time of expiration main effects? (*Hint:* df) Why?

9–8   Blocking Designs

In this section, we discuss alternatives to the completely randomized design. We seek special designs for data analysis that will help us reduce the effects of extraneous factors (factors not under study) on the measured variable. That is, we seek to reduce the errors. These designs allow for *restricted randomization* by grouping the experimental units (people, items in our data) into homogeneous groups called **blocks** and then randomizing the treatments within each block.

The first, and most important, blocking design we will discuss is the *randomized complete block design*.

Randomized Complete Block Design

Recall the first part of the Club Med example, Example (b), where we were interested only in determining possible differences in average ratings among the five resorts (no attributes factor). Suppose that Club Med can get information about its

Answer

9–44.

a. 2
b. 2
c. No
d. Yes
e. No

vacationers' age, sex, marital status, socioeconomic level, etc., and then randomly assign vacationers to the different resorts. The club could form groups of five vacationers each such that the vacationers within each group are similar to each other in age, sex, marital status, etc. Each group of five vacationers is a *block*. Once the blocks are formed, one member from each block is *randomly assigned* to one of the five resorts (Guadeloupe, Martinique, Haiti, Paradise Island, or St. Lucia). Thus, the vacationers sent to each resort will comprise a mixture of ages, of males and females, of married and single people, of different socioeconomic levels, etc. The vacationers within each block, however, will be more or less homogeneous.

The vacationers' ratings of the resorts are then analyzed using an ANOVA that utilizes the blocking structure. Since the members of each block are similar to each other (and different from members of other blocks), we expect them to react to similar conditions in similar ways. This brings about a *reduction in the experimental errors*. Why? If we cannot block, it is possible, for example, that the sample of people we get for Haiti will happen to be wealthier (or predominantly married, predominantly male, or whatever) and will tend to react less favorably to a resort in a developing country than a more balanced sample would react. In such a case, we will have greater experimental error. If, on the other hand, we can *block* and send one member of each homogeneous group of people to each of the resorts and then compare the responses of the block as a whole, we would be more likely to find real differences among the resorts rather than differences among the people. Thus, the errors (differences among people and not among the resorts) are reduced by the blocking design. When all members of every block are randomly assigned to all treatments, such as in this example, our design is called the **randomized complete block design.**

Figure 9–21 shows the formation of blocks in the case of Club Med. We assume that the club is able—for the purpose of a specific study—to randomly assign vacationers to resorts.

The analysis of the results in a randomized complete block design, with a single factor, is very similar to the analysis of two-factor ANOVA with one observation per cell (see Table 9–11). Here, one "factor" is the blocks, and the other is the factor of

FIGURE 9–21   Blocking in the Club Med Example

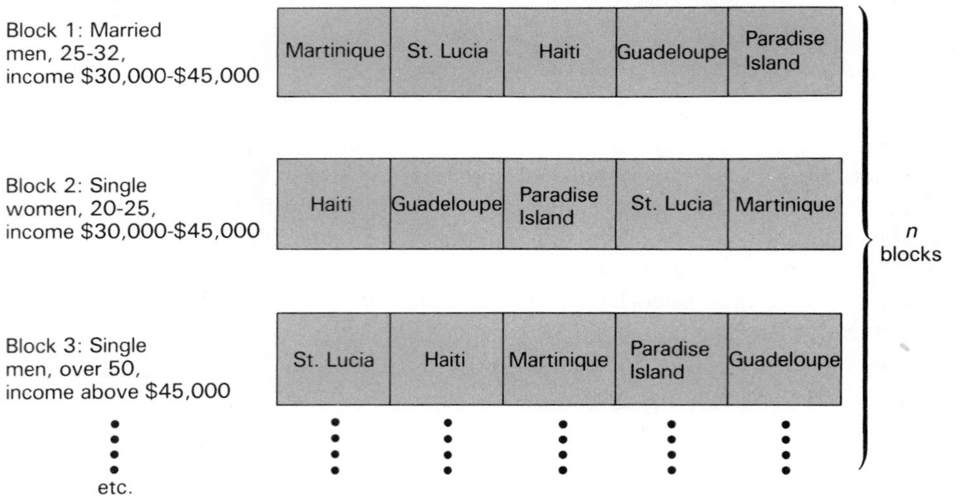

TABLE 9–12 ANOVA Table for Randomized Complete Block Design

Source of Variation	Sum of Squares	Degrees of Freedom	Mean Square	F Ratio
Blocks	SSBL	$n - 1$	MSBL	
Treatments	SSTR	$r - 1$	MSTR	$F = \dfrac{MSTR}{MSE}$
Error	SSE	$(n - 1)(r - 1)$	MSE	
Total		$nr - 1$		

interest (in our example, resorts). The ANOVA table for a randomized complete block design is illustrated in Table 9–12. Compare this table with Table 9–11. There are n blocks of r elements each. We assume that there are no interactions between blocks and treatments; thus, the degrees of freedom for error are $(n - 1)(r - 1)$. The F ratio reported in the table is for use in testing for treatment effects. It is possible to test for block effects with a similar F ratio, although, usually, such a test is of no interest.

As an example, suppose that Club Med did indeed use a blocking design with $n = 10$ blocks. Suppose the results are: SSTR = 3,200, SSBL = 2,800, and SSE = 1,250. Let us conduct the following test.

H$_0$: The average ratings of the five resorts are equal
H$_1$: The average ratings of the five resorts are not all equal

We enter the information into the ANOVA table and compute the remaining entries we need and the F statistic value, which has an F distribution with $(r - 1)$ and $(n - 1)(r - 1)$ degrees of freedom when H$_0$ is true. We have as a result Table 9–13.

We see that the value of the F statistic with 4 and 36 degrees of freedom is 23.04. This value exceeds, by far, the critical point of the F distribution with 4 and 36 degrees of freedom at $\alpha = 0.01$, which is 3.89. The p-value is, therefore, much smaller than 0.01. We thus reject the null hypothesis and conclude that there is evidence that not all resorts are rated equally, on the average. By blocking the respondents into homogeneous groups, Club Med was able to reduce the experimental errors.

You can probably find many examples where blocking can be useful. For example, recall the situation of problem 9–18. Three prototype airplanes were tested on different flight routes to determine whether differences existed in the average range of the planes. A design that would clearly reduce the experimental errors would be a blocking design where all planes are flown over the same routes, at the same time, under the same weather conditions, etc. That is, fly all three planes using each of the sample route conditions. A block in this case is a route condition, and the three "treatments" are the three planes. A numerical example of this problem is given in section 9–9.

TABLE 9–13 Club Med Blocking Design ANOVA Table

Source of Variation	Sum of Squares	Degrees of Freedom	Mean Square	F Ratio
Blocks	2,800	9	311.11	
Resorts	3,200	4	800.00	23.04
Error	1,250	36	34.72	
Total	7,250			

A special case of the randomized complete block design is the **repeated measures design.** In this design, each experimental unit (person or item) is assigned to *all* treatments in a randomly selected order. Suppose that a taste test is to be conducted, where four different flavors are to be rated by consumers. In a repeated measures design, each person in the random sample of consumers is assigned to taste all four flavors, in a randomly determined order, independent from all other consumers. A block in this design is one consumer. We demonstrate the repeated measures design with the following example.

EXAMPLE (e)

Weintraub Entertainment is a new movie company backed by financial support from the Coca-Cola Company. For one of the company's first movies, the director wanted to find the best actress for the leading role. "Best" naturally means the actress who would get the highest average viewer rating. The director was considering three candidates for the role and had each candidate act in a particular test scene. A random group of 40 viewers was selected, and each member of the group watched the same scene enacted by each of the three actresses. The order of actresses was randomly and independently chosen for each viewer. Ratings were on a scale of 0 to 100. The results were analyzed using a block design ANOVA, where each viewer constituted a block of treatments. The results of the analysis are given in Table 9–14. Figure 9–22 shows the layout of the data in this example. Analyze the results. Are all three actresses equally rated, on the average?

SOLUTION

The test statistic has an F distribution with 2 and 78 degrees of freedom when the following null hypothesis is true.

H_0: There are no differences among average population ratings of the three actresses

Check the appropriate critical point for $\alpha = 0.01$ in Appendix C, Table 5 to see that this null hypothesis is rejected in favor of the alternative that differences do exist and that not all three actresses are equally highly rated, on the average. Since the null hy-

TABLE 9–14 The ANOVA Table for Example (e)

Source of Variation	Sum of Squares	Degrees of Freedom	Mean Square	F Ratio
Blocks	2,750	39	70.51	
Treatments	2,640	2	1,320.00	12.93
Error	7,960	78	102.05	
Total	13,350	119		

FIGURE 9–22 Data Layout for Example (e)

	Randomized Viewing Order:		
First sampled person	Actress B	Actress C	Actress A
Second sampled person	Actress C	Actress B	Actress A
Third sampled person	Actress A	Actress C	Actress B
Fourth sampled person	Actress B	Actress A	Actress C
etc.			

pothesis is rejected, there is place for further analysis to determine which actress rates best. Such analysis can be done using the Tukey method or another method of further analysis.

In cases where a repeated measures design is used on *rankings* of several treatments—here, if we had asked each viewer to rank the three actresses as 1, 2, or 3, rather than rate them on a 0 to 100 scale—there is another method of analysis. This method is the *Friedman test,* discussed in Chapter 14.

We will now discuss another type of blocking design. This design is not a randomized complete design. It is *incomplete* in the sense that a block is not assigned to all the treatments. The design is called the *Latin square design.*

Latin Square Design

A Latin square design is a blocking design that uses *two* blocking variables. This is a very compact design that allows us to obtain information using very small data sets. The design reduces much of the extraneous variation by using the two blocking variables. This allows us to use few observations: only one element per treatment per cell. The number of levels of each of the two blocking variables and the number of treatments must all be equal.

> In a **Latin square design,** there are *r* treatments and *r* levels of each of the two blocking variables.

We use a data set of $r \times r = r^2$ elements for the study. Hence the word *square* in the name of this design. As for *Latin,* this is due to our use of Latin letters to denote the treatments (A, B, C, etc.). We demonstrate the use of the Latin square design with the following example.

Fred Meyer, Inc., has five stores in an area of Oregon. The company's advertising manager is planning to advertise fresh produce by using one of five possible in-store advertisements. To determine which of the five ads, if any, is better than the rest and, therefore, the one that should be used in the campaign, the manager proposes an analysis of variance study. The manager knows that sales of produce in a store vary over the five working days of the week. Sales volume on Mondays is generally different from sales volume on Tuesdays, and so on. The manager also knows that sales at the five stores vary from one another. The manager is not interested, however, in determining the differences in average sales volume from store to store or from one weekday to another. She is only interested in finding differences, if they exist, among average sales volumes resulting from the five different advertisements.

Since running the five ads in a test run is expensive, the manager proposes to use the differences among stores and the differences among weekdays to reduce the errors in a study of potential differences among the five proposed advertisements. The manager also wants to minimize the number of times an ad must be tested. The design that blocks using two variables, store and weekday, and tests for differences among the same number of treatments (ads) as the levels of the two blocking variables, is the 5 × 5 Latin square design. We denote the five ads by the Latin letters A, B, C, D and E, and we let the rows of the square stand for the days of the week and the columns of the square stand for the stores (1 through 5). The Latin square is shown in Figure 9–23.

EXAMPLE (f)

FIGURE 9–23   Latin Square for Example (f)

			Store		
Weekdays	**1**	**2**	**3**	**4**	**5**
Monday	B	C	A	D	E
Tuesday	A	D	C	E	B
Wednesday	C	E	B	A	D
Thursday	D	B	E	C	A
Friday	E	A	D	B	C

The figure shows that advertisement B is run on Monday in store 1, on Tuesday in store 5, on Wednesday in store 3, on Thursday in store 2, and on Friday in store 4. Similarly, advertisement C is run on Monday in store 2, on Tuesday in store 3, etc. The important thing to note is that each advertisement is run during every day of the test week at a different store. Each row and column of the design square contains all treatments, and no treatment appears in any row or in any column more than once.

The order of assigning the treatments to the cells of the Latin square is *random*. When preparing a Latin square design, a layout is chosen at random out of a collection of Latin squares with the appropriate number of rows (and columns). There are tables of Latin squares, and one can be randomly chosen using a random number generator. There are 161,280 Latin square designs with five rows and five columns. In the case of 3×3 squares, there are only 12 possible designs. Three of these are shown in Figure 9–24. As you may have noticed, the Latin square design has a limitation. The number of levels of the variable of interest, that is, the number of treatments, must equal the number of levels of the two blocking variables.

The degrees of freedom for each of the two blocking variables and the degrees of freedom associated with the treatments are all equal to $r - 1$. The degrees of freedom for error are $(r - 1)(r - 2)$, and the total degrees of freedom are $r^2 - 1$. These, along with the appropriate sums of squares for the analysis, are shown in Table 9–15.

Since Latin squares are usually small, it is possible to carry out the required computation by hand; therefore, we will give the formulas necessary for obtaining the sums of squares in the ANOVA table, Table 9–15. To avoid complicated notation, however, we will give the formulas in words.

FIGURE 9–24   Selected 3×3 Latin Squares

	A C B			B C A			C A B	
	B A C			A B C			B C A	
	C B A			C A B			A B C	

TABLE 9–15   ANOVA Table for Latin Square Design

Source of Variation	Sum of Squares	Degrees of Freedom	Mean Square	F Ratio
Row Blocks	SSRB	$r - 1$	MSRB	
Column Blocks	SSCB	$r - 1$	MSCB	
Treatments	SSTR	$r - 1$	MSTR	$F = \dfrac{MSTR}{MSE}$
Error	SSE	$(r - 1)(r - 2)$	MSE	
Total	SST	$r^2 - 1$		

The sums of squares for a Latin square design:

$$SST = (\text{Sum of all squared data points}) - (\text{Sum of all data})^2/r^2$$
$$SSRB = (\text{Sum of squared row sums})/r - (\text{Sum of all data})^2/r^2$$
$$SSCB = (\text{Sum of squared column sums})/r - (\text{Sum of all data})^2/r^2$$
$$SSTR = (\text{Sum of squared treatment sums})/r - (\text{Sum of all data})^2/r^2$$
$$SSE = SST - SSRB - SSCB - SSTR \tag{9-29}$$

Table 9–16 shows the data for this example, as well as the sums referred to in the equations. Equations 9–29 are then applied to the data of the problem.

$$SST = (5^2 + 4^2 + 6^2 + 4^2 + 3^2 + 7^2 + 3^2 + \cdots + 6^2 + 5^2) - (114)^2/25 = 58.16$$
$$SSRB = (22^2 + 21^2 + 23^2 + 24^2 + 24^2)/5 - 114^2/25 = 1.36$$
$$SSCB = (22^2 + 22^2 + 22^2 + 25^2 + 23^2)/5 - 114^2/25 = 1.36$$
$$SSTR = (35^2 + 24^2 + 23^2 + 17^2 + 15^2)/5 - 114^2/25 = 48.96$$
$$SSE = SST - SSRB - SSCB - SSTR = 58.16 - 1.36 - 1.36 - 48.96 = 6.48$$

The resulting sums of squares, degrees of freedom, mean squares, and the F ratio required for testing the equality of all treatment means are shown in Table 9–17. All data are in hundreds of units sold per day.

The reported F ratio is the F statistic with 4 and 12 degrees of freedom used for testing the hypotheses:

H_0: The average sales volumes resulting from the five advertisements are equal

H_1: Not all five average sales volumes are equal

TABLE 9–16 The Data for Example (f)

| | Store | | | | | |
Weekday	1	2	3	4	5	Row Total
Monday	B = 5	C = 4	A = 6	D = 4	E = 3	22
Tuesday	A = 7	D = 3	C = 5	E = 2	B = 4	21
Wednesday	C = 4	E = 3	B = 4	A = 8	D = 4	23
Thursday	D = 3	B = 5	E = 4	C = 5	A = 7	24
Friday	E = 3	A = 7	D = 3	B = 6	C = 5	24
Column Total	22	22	22	25	23	114 (Total of all data points)

Treatment totals: $\Sigma A = 35$, $\Sigma B = 24$, $\Sigma C = 23$, $\Sigma D = 17$, $\Sigma E = 15$

TABLE 9–17 ANOVA Table for Example (f)

Source of Variation	Sum of Squares	Degrees of Freedom	Mean Square	F Ratio
Row Blocks	1.36	4	0.34	
Column Blocks	1.36	4	0.34	
Treatments	48.96	4	12.24	F = 22.67
Error	6.48	12	0.54	
Total	58.16	24		

Checking critical points of the F distribution with 4 and 12 degrees of freedom and comparing these critical points with the test statistic value 22.67, we reject the null hypothesis of equal average sales volumes. The p-value is very small. We conclude that there is statistical evidence that not all five advertisements are equally effective. Further analysis should reveal which advertisement is best.

The important thing to remember about blocking designs is that these designs reduce errors in ANOVA and make our tests more efficient. Using a Latin square allows us to reach conclusions based on smaller data sets than would otherwise be required.

PROBLEMS

Answers

9–50.
___
Yes

9–54.
___
$F = 25.84$; reject H_0. Very confident of differences.

9–46. Explain the advantages of blocking designs.

9–47. Explain the advantages and the disadvantages of Latin square designs.

9–48. Suggest a blocking design for the situation in problem 9–19. Explain.

9–49. Suggest a blocking design for the situation in problem 9–21. Explain.

9–50. Is it feasible to design a study utilizing blocks for the situation in problem 9–20? Explain.

9–51. Suggest a blocking design for the situation in problem 9–23.

9–52. How would you design a block ANOVA for the two-way analysis of the situation described in problem 9–42? Which ANOVA method is appropriate for the analysis?

9–53. What important assumption about the relation between blocks and treatments is necessary for carrying out a block design ANOVA?

9–54. Public concern has recently focused on the fact that although Americans often try to lose weight, statistics show that the general population has gained weight, on the average, during the last 10 years. A researcher hired by a weight-loss organization is interested in determining whether three kinds of artificial sweetener currently on the market are approximately equally effective in reducing weight. As part of a study, a random sample of 300 people is chosen. Each person is given one of the three sweeteners to use for a week, and the number of pounds lost is recorded. To reduce experimental errors, the people in the sample are divided into 100 groups of three persons each. The three people in every group all weigh about the same at the beginning of the test week and are of the same sex and approximately the same age. The results are: SSBL = 2,312, SSTR = 3,233, and SSE = 12,386. Are all three sweeteners equally effective in reducing weight? How confident are you of your conclusion? Discuss the merits of blocking in this case as compared with the completely randomized design.

9–55. IBM Corporation has been retraining many of its employees to assume marketing positions. As part of this effort, the company wanted to test four possible methods of training marketing personnel to determine if at least one of the methods was better than the others. Four groups of 70 employees each were assigned to the four training methods. The employees were pretested for marketing ability and grouped into groups of four, each group constituting a block with approximately equal prior ability. Then the four employees in each group were randomly assigned to the four training methods and retested after completion of the three-week training session. The differences between their initial scores and final scores were computed. The results were analyzed using a block design ANOVA. The results of the analysis include: SSTR = 9,875, SSBL = 1,445, and SST = 22,364. Are all four training methods equally effective? Explain.

9–56. In developing its facsimile telephone, FaxPhone model 10, Canon, Inc., wanted to test three possible electronic components for the device to determine whether or not the average transmission speed of a page was approximately equal for the three components. Three different kinds of page were tested: text only, picture only, and mixed text-picture. Also, three kinds of transmitting devices were used. The three components were labeled A, B, and C. The page types were arranged as the rows of the Latin square and the transmitting devices as its columns. A randomly chosen 3×3 Latin square was used. The Latin square and the resulting values, in seconds per page, for the test run are given in the following table. Are there any significant differences in average transmission time for the three tested components? Explain.

Answers

9–56.

$F_{(2, 2)} = 17.7$; accept H_0 at $\alpha = 0.05$.

	Device		
	1	**2**	**3**
Text	B = 17	A = 19	C = 22
Picture	A = 18	C = 24	B = 16
Text-Picture	C = 23	B = 15	A = 19

9–57. A biotech firm is trying to develop a cure for a certain kind of genetic disease. Three possible biological components are to be tested. Since the components are very expensive to manufacture, and since side effects are unknown, it is very important to minimize the testing at this stage. Therefore, a Latin square design is proposed. The three biological agents to be tested are denoted A, B, and C. These are administered to three patients under three test conditions. The randomly chosen 3×3 Latin square and the test results are as follows.

	Patient		
Test Condition	**1**	**2**	**3**
1	A = 8	B = 1	C = 4
2	B = 5	C = 3	A = 7
3	C = 6	A = 9	B = 2

Based on the numerical test results, is there evidence to conclude that patients react differently to the three biological components? Explain.

9–58. A large company is considering buying one of four kinds of word processing machines for use in its offices. The machines, by well-known manufacturers, are labeled for the purpose of a test study as A, B, C, and D. The company would like to purchase machines that would, on the average, lead to the highest average combined score for typing speed and accuracy. Four typists are assigned to the study. One typist is to test machine A on Monday, machine B on Tuesday, and so on. Each typist is to test one machine on one day only. The order of assigning machines and days to typists is determined by a randomly chosen 4×4 Latin square. The chosen square and the test results follow. Based on these results, are there differences in the average adjusted typing score among the four machines? Can you use the results to test for differences among the four typists? Can you use the results for testing whether differences exist in average typing score on different days of the week? Explain.

9–58.

For machines:
$F_{(3, 6)} = 14.54$; reject H_0; p-value < 0.01. No differences among typists or among days.

	Typist			
Day	**1**	**2**	**3**	**4**
Monday	A = 78	C = 70	B = 68	D = 71
Tuesday	D = 68	B = 65	A = 89	C = 50
Wednesday	C = 38	A = 95	D = 70	B = 69
Thursday	B = 67	D = 72	C = 41	A = 90

9–59. What constitutes a block in a repeated measures design?

9–9 Using the Computer

Throughout this chapter, we have emphasized the important role that computers play in the implementation of analysis of variance. All advanced statistical software packages have ANOVA capabilities. The output of such programs includes the ANOVA table, and some packages provide more information. The MINITAB package is capable of carrying out one- and two-way ANOVA and gives individual confidence intervals for treatment means. Recent releases of MINITAB (8 or later) also provide Tukey pairwise comparisons. We demonstrate this in Example (g).

EXAMPLE (g)

The following data set lists the sales resulting from the use of three different sales methods. We want to test the null hypothesis that all three sales methods lead to the same average sales volume, versus the alternative that they do not. The following data are entered into C1, and the levels (populations), coded as 1, 2, and 3, are entered in order into C2.

METHOD A	METHOD B	METHOD C
21	27	18
20	28	17
22	22	19
25	29	24
24	32	20
19	37	17
26	33	19
18	34	22
24	28	20
25	29	21
25	29	24
27	32	18
29	35	18
19	37	22
20	28	21
23	27	21
18	32	17
27	31	21
22	26	20
23	35	19
24	29	18
20	34	23

SOLUTION

Following are the MINITAB command and subcommand necessary for the analysis.

```
ONEWAY C1, C2;
TUKEY 0.05.
```

The MINITAB output for this problem is shown in Figure 9–25. The output includes an ANOVA table for this problem, a table of the sample means and standard deviations, a picture of individual 95% confidence intervals for the three population means, and the Tukey comparisons. We note that the MINITAB command AOVONEWAY (data in columns C1, C2, etc.) will also carry out an ANOVA, but cannot be followed by the Tukey subcommand.

FIGURE 9–25 MINITAB Output for Example (g)

```
MTB > ONEWAY C1 C2;
SUBC> TUKEY 0.05.

ANALYSIS OF VARIANCE ON C1
SOURCE    DF       SS       MS        F        P
C2         2  1348.45   674.23    69.42    0.000
ERROR     63   611.91     9.71
TOTAL     65  1960.36
                              INDIVIDUAL 95 PCT CI'S FOR MEAN
                              BASED ON POOLED STDEV
  LEVEL    N     MEAN    STDEV   ----+---------+---------+---------+--
      1   22   22.773    3.131                (--*--)
      2   22   30.636    3.824                              (--*--)
      3   22   19.955    2.171    (--*--)
                              ----+---------+---------+---------+--
POOLED STDEV =     3.117         20.0      24.0      28.0      32.0

Tukey's pairwise comparisons

     Family error rate = 0.0500
Individual error rate = 0.0193

Critical value = 3.39

Intervals for (column level mean) - (row level mean)

                    1          2

       2     -10.116
              -5.611

       3       0.566      8.429
               5.071     12.934
```

9–10 Summary and Review of Terms

In this chapter, we discussed a method of making statistical comparisons of more than two population means. The method is **analysis of variance,** often referred to as **ANOVA.** We defined **treatments** as the populations under study. A set of treatments is a **factor.** We defined **one-factor ANOVA,** also called one-way ANOVA, as the test for equality of means of treatments belonging to one factor. We defined a **two-factor ANOVA,** also called two-way ANOVA, as a set of three hypothesis tests: (1) a test for main effects for one of the two factors, (2) a test for main effects for the second factor, and (3) a test for the **interaction** of the two factors. We defined the **fixed-effects** model and the **random effects** model. We discussed one method of further analysis to follow an ANOVA once the ANOVA leads to rejection of the null hypothesis of equal treatment means. The method is the **Tukey HSD procedure.** We also mentioned two other alternative methods of further analysis. We discussed **experimental design** in the ANOVA context. Among these designs, we mentioned **blocking** as a method of reducing experimental errors in ANOVA by grouping similar items. We also discussed **Latin square designs,** which use two blocking variables.

ADDITIONAL PROBLEMS

9–60.   An enterprising art historian recently started a new business: the production of walking-tour audiotapes for use by those visiting major cities. She originally produced tapes for eight cities: Paris, Rome, London, Florence, Jerusalem, Washington, New York, and New

Answers

$F_{(7, 152)} = 14.67$; reject H_0; p-value very small.

Haven. A test was carried out to determine whether or not all eight tapes (featuring different aspects of different cities) were equally appealing to potential users. A random sample of 160 prospective tourists was selected, 20 per city. Each person evaluated the tape he or she was given on a scale of 0 to 100. The results were analyzed using one-way ANOVA and included: SSTR = 7,102, SSE = 10,511. Are all eight tapes equally appealing, on the average? What can you say about the p-value?

9–61. NAMELAB® is a San Francisco–based company that uses linguistic analysis and computers to invent catchy names for new products. The company is credited with the invention of Acura, Compaq, Sentra, and other names of successful products. Naturally, statistical analysis plays an important role in choosing the final name for a product. In choosing a name for a compact disc player, NAMELAB is considering four names and uses analysis of variance for determining whether or not all four names are equally liked, on the average, by the public. The results include: $n_1 = 32$, $n_2 = 30$, $n_3 = 28$, $n_4 = 41$, SSTR = 4,537, and MSE = 412. Are all four names approximately equally liked, on the average? What is the approximate p-value?

Reject H_0 for all three at $\alpha = 0.05$.

9–62. An article about gender differences in marketing reports the results of an analysis of variance aimed at assessing whether there was a taste cue positioning effect, a gender effect, and an interaction. The reported results were as follows.[14]

Taste cue positioning: $F_{(1,48)} = 4.79$

Gender: $F_{(1,48)} = 6.93$

Taste cue positioning by gender interaction: $F_{(1,48)} = 8.41$

Interpret the results fully and describe them in a memo to the research director.

9–63. As software for microcomputers becomes more and more sophisticated, the element of time becomes more crucial. Consequently, manufacturers of software packages need to work on reducing the time required for running application programs. Speed of execution also depends on the computer used. A two-way ANOVA is suggested for testing whether or not differences exist among three software packages, and among four microcomputers made by NEC, Toshiba, Kaypro, and Apple, with respect to the average time for performing a certain analysis. The results include: SS(software) = 77,645, SS(computer) = 54,521, SS(interaction) = 88,699, and SSE = 434,557. The analysis used a sample of 60 runs of each software package/computer combination. Complete an ANOVA table for this analysis, carry out the tests, and state your conclusions.

	F	p-value
Process	14.25	< 0.01
Film	117.31	< 0.01
Interaction	10.63	< 0.01

9–64. Recently, the competition between Kodak and Fuji has been intensifying. Kodak has reportedly been analyzing films made by Fuji to determine the secrets of Fuji's bright colors. As part of an analysis, a random sample of five pieces of film by Kodak were developed by a process we will denote as process A, another random sample of five Kodak films were developed by process B, and a third sample by process C. The same was done with three sets of five pieces of film by Fuji. Also, as a third comparison for control, three sets of five pieces of film by Agfa were developed. All the developed films were photochemically tested for color brightness. The results were analyzed by two-way ANOVA aimed at determining whether color brightness differences existed among the three developing processes and among the three kinds of film. Kodak was also interested in finding out whether or not interactions existed—that is, whether one type of film, say, Agfa, resulted in lower-than-expected color brightness when developed by a particular process. The results are given in the following table (the higher the score, the brighter the colors). Use a computer to carry out the two-way ANOVA. State your conclusions.

Film	Process A	Process B	Process C
Kodak	32, 34, 31, 30, 37	26, 29, 27, 30, 31	28, 28, 27, 30, 32
Fuji	43, 41, 44, 50, 47	32, 38, 38, 40, 36	32, 32, 36, 35, 34
Agfa	23, 24, 25, 21, 26	27, 30, 25, 25, 27	25, 27, 26, 22, 25

[14] J. Meyers-Levy and B. Sternthal, "Gender Differences in the Use of Message Cues and Judgments," *Journal of Marketing Research* (February 1991), p. 91.

9–65. The following table summarizes results of ANOVAs of three separate "dependent variables." For each variable, a four-factor ANOVA is carried out.[15] The table reports p-values. Interpret all the results in the table.

Effect Source	Dependent Variable		
	RDIFF	BIAS	BE
METH: factor scoring approach	.008	.009	.457
UNIQ: factor uniqueness	.474	.510	.012
SE: assumed obliqueness relative to true obliqueness	.106	.086	.086
P: number of observed variables	.106	.091	.102
METH × UNIQ	.002	.006	.078
METH × SE	.010	.302	.110
METH × P	.150	.112	.125
UNIQ × SE	.206	.087	.210
UNIQ × P	.001	.176	.008
SE × P	.210	.011	.002

9–66. Among the young affluent professionals in America, there is a growing new demand for exotic pets. The most popular pets are the Shiba Inu dog breed, Rottweilers, Persian cats, and Maine coons. Prices for these pets vary and depend on supply and demand. A breeder of exotic pets wants to know whether these four pets fetch the same average prices, whether prices for these exotic pets are higher in some geographic areas than in others, and whether there are any interactions—one or more of the four pets being more favored in one location than in others. Prices for 10 of each of these pets at four randomly chosen locations around the country are recorded and analyzed. The results are: SS(pet) = 22,245, SS(location) = 34,551, SS(interaction) = 31,778, and SSE = 554,398. Are there any pet main effects? Are there any location main effects? Are there any pet-location interactions? Explain your findings.

	F
Pet	1.93
Location	2.99
Interaction	0.92

No pet effects or interactions. There are location effects at $\alpha = 0.05$.

9–67. Analysis of variance has long been used in providing evidence of the effectiveness of pharmaceutical drugs. Such evidence is required before the FDA will allow a drug to be marketed. In a recent test of the effectiveness of a new sleeping pill, three groups of 25 patients each were given the following treatments. One group was given the drug, the second group was given a placebo, and the third group was given no treatment at all. The number of minutes it took each person to fall asleep was recorded. The results are as follows.

Drug group: 12, 17, 34, 11, 5, 42, 18, 27, 2, 37, 50, 32, 12, 27, 21, 10, 4, 33, 63, 22, 41, 19, 28, 29, 8

Placebo group: 44, 32, 28, 30, 22, 12, 3, 12, 42, 13, 27, 54, 56, 32, 37, 28, 22, 22, 24, 9, 20, 4, 13, 42, 67

No-treatment group: 32, 33, 21, 12, 15, 14, 55, 67, 72, 1, 44, 60, 36, 38, 49, 66, 89, 63, 23, 6, 9, 56, 28, 39, 59

Use a computer (or hand calculations) to determine whether or not the drug is effective. What about the placebo? Give differences in average effectiveness, if any exist.

9–68. A more efficient experiment than the one described in problem 9–67 was carried out to determine whether or not a sleeping pill was effective. Each person in a random sample of 30 people was given the three treatments: drug, placebo, nothing. The order in which these treatments were administered was randomly chosen for each person in the sample.

b. $F_{(2, 58)} = 11.47$; reject H_0.

a. Explain why this experiment is more efficient than the one described for the same investigation in problem 9–67. What is the name of the experimental design used here? Are there any limitations to the present method of analysis?

b. The results of the analysis include: SSTR = 44,572, SSBL = 38,890, and SSE = 112,672. Carry out the analysis, and state your conclusions. Use $\alpha = 0.05$.

---

[15] Reproduced by permission from J. Lastovicka and K. Thamodaran, "Common Factor Score Estimates," *Journal of Marketing Research* (February 1991), p. 109.

9–69. Three new enhanced-definition television models are compared.[16] The distances (in miles) over which a clear signal is received in random trials for each of the models are given below.

General Instrument: 111, 121, 134, 119, 125, 120, 122, 138, 115, 123, 130, 124, 132, 127, 130
Philips: 120, 121, 122, 123, 120, 132, 119, 116, 125, 123, 116, 118, 120, 131, 115
Zenith: 109, 100, 110, 102, 118, 117, 105, 104, 100, 108, 128, 117, 101, 102, 110

Carry out a complete analysis of variance, and report your results in the form of a memorandum. State your hypotheses and your conclusions. Do you believe there are differences among the three models? If so, where do they lie?

9–70.

$F_{(2, 98)} = 0.150$; accept H_0.

9–70. A professor of food chemistry at the University of Wisconsin has recently developed a new system for keeping frozen foods crisp and fresh: coating them with watertight, edible film.[17] The Pillsbury Company wants to test whether the new product is tasty. The company collects a random sample of consumers who are given the following three treatments, in a randomly chosen order for each consumer: regular frozen pizza, frozen pizza packaged in a plastic bag, and the new edible-coating frozen pizza (all reheated, of course). Fifty people take part in the study, and the results include: SSTR = 128,899, SSBL = 538,217, SSE = 42,223,987. (These are ANOVA results for taste scores on a 0–1000 scale.) Based on these results, are all three frozen pizzas perceived as equally tasty or not?

9–71. The manager of a fitness center wants to test whether three of her top athletes are of the same average performance level. The center has three identical exercise machines located at different places in the exercise hall. There are also three daily exercise times: morning, noontime, and evening. The manager assigns each of the athletes to a machine and to an exercise time according to the randomly chosen Latin square that follows. The manager measures the athletes' performance—the number of pullups they can do in a specified time period. The athletes are labeled A, B, and C. Given the data in the Latin square, do all three athletes have the same average performance level?

Time	Machine		
	1	2	3
Morning	B = 24	A = 31	C = 30
Noon	C = 22	B = 29	A = 33
Evening	A = 30	C = 26	B = 32

9–72.

$t^2_{(df)} = F_{(1, df)}$

9–72. Give the statistical reason for the fact that a one-way ANOVA with only two treatments is equivalent to a two-sample t test discussed in Chapter 8.

9–73. An article reports the results of a study aimed at determining whether differences existed between the average rates of return for low-grade versus high-grade bonds. The data were monthly returns for an index of low-grade bonds and for an index of high-grade bonds from January 1977 through December 1989. The reported value of the F statistic was 12.6.[18] Interpret the results.

---

[16] A. Kupfer, "The U.S. Wins One in High-Tech TV," *Fortune* (April 8, 1991), p. 63.

[17] "Edible Packages Keep Frozen Foods Dry," *Business Week* (March 16, 1987).

[18] B. Cornell and K. Green, "The Investment Performance of Low-Grade Bond Funds," *Journal of Finance* (March 1991), p. 37.

9–74. Following is a computer output of an analysis of variance based on randomly chosen rents in four cities. Do you believe that the average rent is equal in the four cities studied? Explain.

```
MTB > AOVONEWAY C1, C2, C3, C4

ANALYSIS OF VARIANCE
SOURCE    DF       SS        MS        F
FACTOR     3     37402     12467     1.76
ERROR     44    311303      7075
TOTAL     47    348706
```

Answers

9–74.

No evidence of any differences.

9–75. Write several paragraphs explaining the meaning of the following excerpt.[19]

Toy awareness level. A two-way ANOVA was conducted with two levels of language and two levels of income as independent factors and toy awareness level as the dependent measure. As hypothesized, English-speaking children were significantly more aware of the toys than were French-speaking children ($F = 400.47$, $p < .0001$). The latter were able to recognize an average of only 8.73 toys correctly, not significantly more than the one in three chance level (i.e., 6.67 toys). In comparison, English-speaking children were able to identify an average of 15.44 toys. A significant income effect is found ($F = 7.08$, $p < .01$). Upper-middle income children recognized more toys (mean = 11.94) than low-income children (mean = 9.94). Contrary to the hypothesis, no significant language by income interaction is found ($F < 1$). The likely reason is a ceiling effect, as all English-speaking children had very high scores. (Of the few mistakes made by English-speaking children, most consisted of boys misidentifying a few girls' toys and vice versa).

9–76. Interpret the following computer output.

9–76.

One-way ANOVA; strongly reject H_0.

```
ANALYSIS OF VARIANCE ON SALES
SOURCE    DF      SS        MS         F         P
STORE      2   1017.33    508.67    156.78     0.000
ERROR     15     48.67      3.24
TOTAL     17   1066.00

                            INDIVIDUAL 95 PCT CI'S FOR MEAN
                            BASED ON POOLED STDEV
LEVEL    N     MEAN    STDEV  -+---------+---------+---------+----
    1    6   53.667    1.862              (-*--)
    2    6   67.000    1.673                              (--*-)
    3    6   49.333    1.862     (-*--)
                               -+---------+---------+---------+----
POOLED STDEV = 1.801         48.0      54.0      60.0      66.0
```

9–77. Interpret the following partial computer output.

```
ANALYSIS OF VARIANCE   SALES

SOURCE         DF       SS
STORE           2     23.11
SIZE            1      1.39
INTERACTION     2      0.44
ERROR          12     14.67
TOTAL          17     39.61
```

---

[19] Reproduced by permission from M. Goldberg, "Assessing the Effectiveness of TV Advertising Directed at Children," *Journal of Marketing Research* (November 1990), p. 450.

NEW COKE, OLD COKE, AND PEPSI

*I*n April 1985, the Coca-Cola Company announced that it would discontinue making its main brand of soft drink, a product the company had been making for 99 years. Instead, the company planned to market a drink based on a new formula. Thus, new Coke was born. Within three months, however, it became apparent that the switch to new Coke was one of the biggest marketing mistakes ever made. The Coca-Cola Company had no choice but to reintroduce the original formula of Coke, under the new name Coca-Cola Classic. In the process, the company's image was tarnished, and its distributors now had to deal with two Cokes.

In 1987, two years after the birth of new Coke and the new-old Coke Classic, a New York marketing research firm conducted a study to determine consumer preferences for the three brands: new Coke, Coke Classic, and Pepsi. The purpose of the study was to determine how well the two Cokes were selling vis-à-vis their competitor. Although Pepsi was known to sell more in supermarkets, Coke was believed to have a wide lead over Pepsi in vending machine sales. As part of the analysis, the researchers wanted to find out whether the three brands sold about equally well, on average, in public buildings that had both a Coke machine (selling both Cokes) and a Pepsi machine. A random sample of nine public buildings in Manhattan fitting the requirements was selected. The data (in number of cans sold over a given period of time) are as follows.

Building	1	2	3	4	5	6	7	8	9
New Coke	3	1	23	11	8	31	28	3	4
Coke Classic	8	9	27	27	29	44	16	8	7
Pepsi	9	6	18	20	10	26	21	0	9

Analyze the data. Discuss any assumptions you are making. Discuss your method of solution. Present the findings, and state your conclusions. What are the advantages of the method used? What are the limitations of the analysis, and how can the study be improved? How useful are the results? Explain.

10

SIMPLE LINEAR REGRESSION AND CORRELATION

INTRODUCTION

I n 1855, a 33-year-old Englishman settled down to a life of leisure in London after several years of travel throughout Europe and Africa. The boredom brought about by a comfortable life induced him to write, and his first book was, naturally, *The Art of Travel*. As his intellectual curiosity grew, he shifted his interests to science and many years later published a paper on heredity, *Natural Inheritance* (1889). He reported his discovery that sizes of seeds of sweet pea plants appeared to "revert," or "regress," to the mean size in successive generations. He also reported results of a study of the relationship between heights of fathers and the heights of their sons. A straight line was fit to the data pairs: height of father versus height of son. Here, too, he found a "regression to mediocrity": the heights of the sons represented a movement away from their fathers, toward the average height. The man was Sir Francis Galton, a cousin of Charles Darwin. We credit him with the idea of statistical regression.

While most applications of regression analysis may have little to do with the "regression to the mean" discovered by Galton, the term **regression** remains. It now refers to the statistical technique of modeling the relationship between variables. In this chapter on **simple linear regression,** we model the relationship between two variables: a **dependent variable,** denoted by Y, and an **independent variable,** denoted by X. The model we use is a *straight-line relationship* between X and Y. When we model the relationship between the dependent variable Y and a set of several independent variables, or when the assumed relationship between Y and X is curved and requires the use of more terms in the model, we use a technique called *multiple regression*. This technique will be discussed in the next chapter.

Figure 10–1 is a general example of simple linear regression: fitting a straight line to describe the relationship between two variables, X and Y. The points on the graph are randomly chosen observations of the two variables, X and Y, and the straight line describes the general *movement* in the data—an increase in Y corresponding to an increase in X. An inverse straight-line relationship is also possible, consisting of a general decrease in Y as X increases (in such cases, the slope of the line is negative).

Regression analysis is one of the most important and widely used statistical techniques and has many applications in business and economics. A firm may be interested in estimating the relationship between advertising and sales (one of the most important topics of research in the field of marketing). Over a short range of values—when advertising is not yet overdone, giving diminishing returns—the relationship between advertising and sales may be well approximated by a straight line. The X variable in Figure 10–1 could denote advertising expenditure, and the Y variable could stand for the resulting sales for the same period. The data points in this case would be pairs of observations of the form: $x_1 = \$75{,}570$, $y_1 = 134{,}679$ units; $x_2 = \$83{,}090$, $y_2 = 151{,}664$ units; etc. That is, the first month the firm spent $\$75{,}570$ on advertising, and sales for the month were 134,679 units; the second month the company spent $\$83{,}090$ on advertising, with resulting sales of 151,664 units for that month, and so on for the entire set of available data.

Continued on next page

FIGURE 10–1 Simple Linear Regression

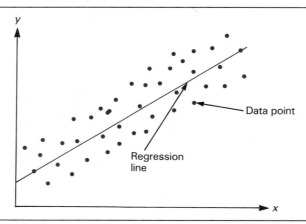

The data pairs, values of X paired with corresponding values of Y, are the points shown in a sketch of the data (such as Figure 10–1). A sketch of data on two variables is called a **scatter plot**. In addition to the scatter plot, Figure 10–1 shows the straight line believed to best show how the general trend of increasing sales corresponds, in this example, to increasing advertising expenditures. This chapter will teach you how to find the best line to fit a data set and how to use the line once you have found it.

Although, in reality, our sample may consist of all available information on the two variables under study, we always assume that our data set constitutes a random sample of observations from a population of possible pairs of values of X and Y. Incidentally, in our hypothetical advertising-sales example, we assume that there is no carryover effect of advertising from month to month; every month's sales depend only on that month's level of advertising. Other common examples of the use of simple linear regression in business and economics are the modeling of the relationship between job performance (the dependent variable Y) and extent of training (the independent variable X); the relationship between returns on a stock (Y) and the riskiness of the stock (X); and the relationship between company profits (Y) and the state of the economy (X).

FIGURE 10–2
A Statistical Model

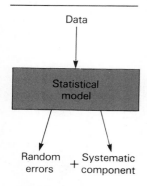

Model extracts everything systematic in the data, leaving purely random errors

Model Building

Like the analysis of variance, both simple linear regression and multiple regression are *statistical models*. Recall that a statistical model is a set of mathematical formulas and assumptions that describe a real-world situation. We would like our model to explain as much as possible about the process underlying our data. However, due to the uncertainty inherent in all real-world situations, our model will probably not explain everything, and we will always have some remaining errors. The errors are due to unknown outside factors that affect the process generating our data.

A good statistical model is *parsimonious,* which means that it uses as few mathematical terms as possible to describe the real situation. The model captures the systematic behavior of the data, leaving out the factors that are nonsystematic and cannot be foreseen or predicted—the errors. The idea of a good statistical model is illustrated in Figure 10–2. The errors, denoted by ϵ, constitute the random component in the model. In a sense, the statistical model breaks down the data into a nonrandom, systematic component, which can be described by a formula, and a purely random component.

How do we deal with the errors? This is where probability theory comes in. Since our model, we hope, captures everything systematic in the data, the remaining random errors are probably due to a large number of minor factors that we cannot trace. We assume that the random errors ϵ are *normally distributed*. If we have a properly constructed model, the resulting observed errors will have an average of zero (although few, if any, will actually equal zero), and they should also be *independent* of each other. We note that the assumption of a normal distribution of the errors is not absolutely necessary in the regression model. The assumption is made so that we can carry out statistical hypothesis tests using the F and t distributions. The only necessary assumption is that the errors ϵ have mean zero and a constant variance σ^2 and that they be uncorrelated with each other. In the next section, we describe the simple linear regression model. We now present a general model-building methodology.

First, we propose a particular model to describe a given situation. For example, we may propose a simple linear regression model for describing the relationship between two variables. Then we estimate the model parameters from the random sample of data we have. The next step is to consider the observed errors resulting from the fit of the model to the data. These observed errors, called **residuals**, represent the information in the data not explained by the model. For example, in the ANOVA model discussed in Chapter 9, the within-group variation (leading to SSE and MSE) is due to the residuals. If the residuals are found to contain some nonrandom, *systematic* component, we reevaluate our proposed model and, if possible, adjust it to incorporate the systematic component found in the residuals; or we may have to discard the model and try another. When we believe that model residuals contain nothing more than pure randomness, we use the model for its intended purpose: *prediction* of a variable, *control* of a variable, or the *explanation* of the relationships among variables.

In the advertising-sales example, once the regression model has been estimated and found to be appropriate, the firm may be able to use the model for predicting sales for a given level of advertising within the range of values studied. Using the model, the firm may also be able to control its sales by setting the level of advertising expenditure. The model may also help explain the effect of advertising on sales within the range of values studied. Figure 10-3 shows the usual steps of building a statistical model. ■

FIGURE 10-3 Steps in Building a Statistical Model

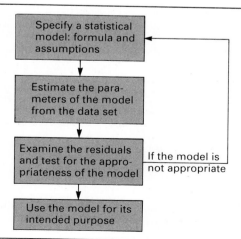

10–2   The Simple Linear Regression Model

Recall from algebra that the equation of a straight line is $Y = A + BX$, where A is the Y-intercept and B is the slope of the line. In simple linear regression, we model the relationship between two variables, X and Y, as a straight line. Therefore, our model must contain two parameters: an intercept parameter and a slope parameter. The usual notation for the **population intercept** is β_0, and the notation for the **population slope** is β_1. If we include the error term, ϵ, the population regression model is given in equation 10–1.

The population simple linear regression model:

$$Y = \beta_0 + \beta_1 X + \epsilon \qquad (10\text{–}1)$$

where Y is the dependent variable, the variable we wish to explain or predict; X is the independent variable, also called the *predictor* variable; and ϵ is the error term, the only random component in the model and, thus, the only source of randomness in Y.

The model parameters are as follows.

β_0 is the Y-intercept of the straight line given by $Y = \beta_0 + \beta_1 X$ (the line does not contain the error term).

β_1 is the slope of the line $Y = \beta_0 + \beta_1 X$.

The simple linear regression model of equation 10–1 is composed of two components: a nonrandom component, which is the line itself, and a purely random component—the error term, ϵ. This is shown in Figure 10–4. The nonrandom part of the model, the straight line, is the equation for the *mean of Y, given X*. We denote the conditional mean of Y, given X, by $E(Y|X)$. Thus, if the model is correct, the *average* value of Y for a given value of X falls right *on* the regression line. The equation for the mean of Y, given X, is given as equation 10–2.

The conditional mean of Y:

$$E(Y \mid X) = \beta_0 + \beta_1 X \qquad (10\text{–}2)$$

Comparing equations 10–1 and 10–2, we see that our model says that each value of Y comprises the average Y for the given value of X (this is the straight line),

FIGURE 10–4   The Simple Linear Regression Model

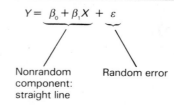

$$Y = \underbrace{\beta_0 + \beta_1 X}_{} + \underbrace{\varepsilon}_{}$$

Nonrandom component: straight line   Random error

FIGURE 10–5 The Population Regression Line

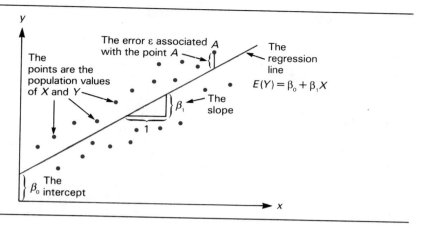

plus a random error. We will sometimes use the simplified notation $E(Y)$ for the line, remembering that this is the *conditional* mean of Y, for a given value of X. As X increases, the average population value of Y also increases, assuming a positive slope of the line (or decreases, if the slope is negative). The *actual* population value of Y is equal to the average Y conditional on X, plus a random error, ϵ. We thus have, for a given value of X:

$$Y = \text{Average } Y \text{ for given } X + \text{Error}$$

Figure 10–5 shows the population regression model.

We now state the assumptions of the simple linear regression model.

Model assumptions:

1. The relationship between X and Y is a straight-line relationship.
2. The values of the independent variable X are assumed fixed (not random); the only randomness in the values of Y comes from the error term, ϵ.
3. The errors, ϵ, are normally distributed with mean 0 and a constant variance σ^2. The errors are uncorrelated (not related) with each other in successive observations.[1] In symbols:

$$\epsilon \sim N(0, \sigma^2) \tag{10–3}$$

Figure 10–6 shows the distributional assumptions of the errors of the simple linear regression model. The population regression errors are normally distributed about the population regression line, with mean zero and equal variance. (The errors are equally spread about the regression line; the error variance does not increase or decrease as X increases.)

FIGURE 10–6
The Distributional Assumptions of the Linear Regression Model

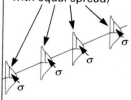

Normal distribution of the regression errors has mean zero and constant variance (the distributions are centered on the line with equal spread)

---

[1] The idea of statistical *correlation* will be discussed in detail in section 10–5. In the case of the regression errors, we assume that successive errors $\epsilon_1, \epsilon_2, \epsilon_3, \ldots$ are uncorrelated: they are not related with each other; there is no trend, no joint movement in successive errors. Incidentally, the assumption of zero correlation together with the assumption of a normal distribution of the errors implies the assumption that the errors are independent of each other. Independence implies noncorrelation, but noncorrelation does not imply independence, except in the case of a normal distribution (this is a technical point).

FIGURE 10–7 Some Possible Relationships between X and Y

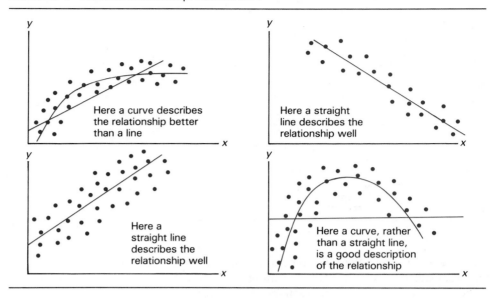

The simple linear regression model applies only if the true relationship between the two variables X and Y is a straight-line relationship. If the relationship is curved (*curvilinear*), then we need to use the more involved methods of the next chapter. In Figure 10–7, we show various relationships between two variables. Some are straight-line relationships that can be modeled by simple linear regression, and others are not.

So far, we have described the population model, that is, the assumed true relationship between the two variables X and Y. Our interest is focused on this unknown population relationship, and we want to *estimate* it using sample information. We obtain a random sample of observations on the two variables, and we estimate the regression model parameters, β_0 and β_1, from this sample. This is done by the *method of least squares*, which is discussed in the next section.

PROBLEMS

10–1. What is a statistical model?

10–2. What are the steps of statistical model building?

10–3. What are the assumptions of the simple linear regression model?

10–4. Define the parameters of the simple linear regression model.

10–5. What is the conditional mean of Y, given X?

10–6. What are the uses of a regression model?

10–7. What is the purpose and meaning of the error term in regression?

10–8. Give examples of business situations where you believe a straight-line relationship exists between two variables. What would be the uses of a regression model in each of these situations?

10–3 Estimation: The Method of Least Squares

We want to find good estimates of the regression parameters, β_0 and β_1. Remember the properties of good estimators, discussed in Chapter 5. Unbiasedness and efficiency are among these properties. A method that will give us good estimates of the regression coefficients is the **method of least squares.** The method of least squares gives us the *best linear unbiased estimators* (BLUE) of the regression parameters, β_0 and β_1. These estimators are both unbiased and have the lowest variance of all possible unbiased estimators of the regression parameters. These properties of the least-squares estimators are specified by a well-known theorem, the *Gauss-Markov theorem*. We denote the least-squares estimators by b_0 and b_1.

The least-squares estimators:

$$b_0 \xrightarrow{\text{estimates}} \beta_0$$
$$b_1 \xrightarrow{\text{estimates}} \beta_1$$

The estimated regression equation:

$$Y = b_0 + b_1 X + e \qquad (10\text{--}4)$$

where b_0 estimates β_0, b_1 estimates β_1, and e stands for the observed errors—the residuals from fitting the line ($b_0 + b_1 X$) to the data set of n points

---

In terms of the data, equation 10–4 can be written with the subscript i to signify each particular data point:

$$y_i = b_0 + b_1 x_i + e_i \qquad (10\text{--}5)$$

where $i = 1, 2, \ldots, n$. Then, e_1 is the first residual, the distance from the first data point to the fitted regression line; e_2 is the distance from the second data point to the line; and so on to e_n, the nth error. The errors, e_i, are viewed as estimates of the true population errors, ϵ_i. The equation of the regression line itself is as follows.

The regression line:

$$\hat{Y} = b_0 + b_1 X \qquad (10\text{--}6)$$

where $\hat{Y}$ (pronounced "Y hat") is the Y value *lying on the fitted regression line* for a given X

Thus, $\hat{y}_1$ is the fitted value corresponding to x_1, that is, the value of y_1 without the error e_1, and so on for all $i = 1, 2, \ldots, n$. The fitted value $\hat{Y}$ is also called the *predicted value of Y* because, if we do not know the actual value of Y, it is the value we would predict for a given value of X using the estimated regression line.

Having defined the estimated regression equation, the errors, and the fitted values of Y, we will now demonstrate the principle of least squares, which gives us the BLUE regression parameter estimates. Consider the data set shown in Figure 10–8(a). In parts (b), (c), and (d) of the figure, we show different lines passing through the data set and the resulting errors, e_i.

As can be seen from Figure 10–8, the regression line proposed in part (b) results in very large errors. The errors corresponding to the line of part (c) are smaller than the ones of part (b), but the errors resulting from using the line proposed in part (d) are by far the smallest. The line in part (d) seems to move with the data and

FIGURE 10–8 A Data Set of *X* and *Y* Pairs, and Different Proposed Straight Lines to Describe the Data

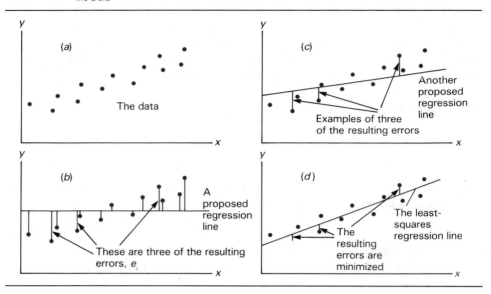

minimize the resulting errors. This should convince you that the line that best describes the trend in the data is the line that lies "inside" the set of points; since some of the points lie above the fitted line and some below the line, some errors will be positive and others will be negative. If we want to minimize all the errors (both positive and negative ones), we should minimize the *sum of the squared errors* (SSE, as in ANOVA). Thus, we want to find the *least-squares* line—the line that minimizes SSE. We note that least squares is not the only method of fitting lines to data. There are other methods, such as minimizing the sum of the absolute errors. The method of least squares, however, is the most commonly used method when estimating a regression relationship. Figure 10–9 shows how the errors lead to the calculation of SSE.

FIGURE 10–9 The Regression Errors Leading to SSE

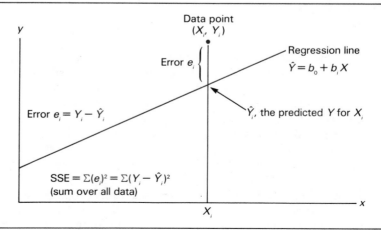

FIGURE 10–10 The Particular Values b_0 and b_1 that Minimize SSE

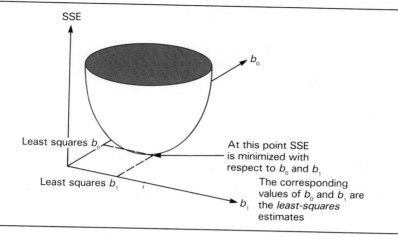

We define the sum of squares for error in regression as:

$$\text{SSE} = \sum_{i=1}^{n} (e_i)^2 = \sum_{i=1}^{n} (y_i - \hat{y}_i)^2 \qquad (10\text{–}7)$$

Figure 10–10 shows different values of SSE corresponding to values of b_0 and b_1. The least-squares line is the particular line specified by values of b_0 and b_1 that minimize SSE, as shown in the figure.

Calculus is used in finding the expressions for b_0 and b_1 that minimize SSE. These expressions are called the *normal equations* and are given as equations 10–8.[2] This system of two equations with two unknowns is solved to give us the values of b_0 and b_1 that minimize SSE. The results are the least-squares estimators, b_0 and b_1, of the simple linear regression parameters, β_0 and β_1.

The **normal equations:**

$$\sum_{i=1}^{n} y_i = nb_0 + b_1 \sum_{i=1}^{n} x_i$$

$$\sum_{i=1}^{n} x_i y_i = b_0 \sum_{i=1}^{n} x_i + b_1 \sum_{i=1}^{n} x_i^2 \qquad (10\text{–}8)$$

Before we present the solutions to the normal equations, we define the sums of squares, SS_X and SS_Y, and the sum of the cross products, SS_{XY}. These will be very useful in defining the least-squares estimates of the regression parameters, as well as in other regression formulas we will see later. The definitions are given in equations 10–9.

---

[2] We leave it as an exercise to the reader with background in calculus to derive the normal equations by taking the partial derivatives of SSE with respect to b_0 and b_1 and setting them to zero.

Definitions of sums of squares and cross products useful in regression analysis:

$$SS_x = \sum (x - \bar{x})^2 = \sum x^2 - \frac{(\sum x)^2}{n}$$

$$SS_Y = \sum (y - \bar{y})^2 = \sum y^2 - \frac{(\sum y)^2}{n} \qquad (10\text{-}9)$$

$$SS_{XY} = \sum (x - \bar{x})(y - \bar{y}) = \sum xy - \frac{(\sum x)(\sum y)}{n}$$

The first definition in each case is the conceptual one using squared distances from the mean; the second part is a computational definition. Summations are over all data.

We now give the solutions of the normal equations, the least-squares estimators b_0 and b_1.

Least-squares regression estimators:
Slope:

$$b_1 = \frac{SS_{XY}}{SS_x} \qquad (10\text{-}10)$$

Intercept:

$$b_0 = \bar{y} - b_1\bar{x}$$

The formula for the estimate of the intercept makes use of the fact that the *least-squares line always passes through the point* $(\bar{x}, \bar{y})$, the intersection of the mean of X and the mean of Y.

It is important to remember that the obtained estimates b_0 and b_1 of the regression relationship are just realizations of *estimators* of the true regression parameters β_0 and β_1. As always, our estimators have standard errors (and variances, which, by the Gauss-Markov theorem, are as small as possible). The estimates can be used, along with the assumption of normality, in the construction of confidence intervals for, and the conducting of hypothesis tests about, the true regression parameters β_0 and β_1. This will be done in the next section.

We demonstrate the process of estimating the parameters of a simple linear regression model in Example (a).

EXAMPLE (a)

The American Express Company has long believed that its cardholders tend to travel more extensively than others—both on business and for pleasure. As part of a comprehensive research effort undertaken by a New York marketing research firm on behalf of American Express, a study was conducted to determine the relationship between travel and charges on the American Express card. The research firm selected a random sample of 25 cardholders from the American Express computer file and recorded their total charges over a specified period of time. For the selected cardholders, information was also obtained, through a mailed questionnaire, on the total number of miles traveled by

TABLE 10–1 American Express Study Data

Miles	Dollars
1,211	1,802
1,345	2,405
1,422	2,005
1,687	2,511
1,849	2,332
2,026	2,305
2,133	3,016
2,253	3,385
2,400	3,090
2,468	3,694
2,699	3,371
2,806	3,998
3,082	3,555
3,209	4,692
3,466	4,244
3,643	5,298
3,852	4,801
4,033	5,147
4,267	5,738
4,498	6,420
4,533	6,059
4,804	6,426
5,090	6,321
5,233	7,026
5,439	6,964

each cardholder during the same period of time. The data for this study are given in Table 10–1. Figure 10–11 is a scatter plot of the data.

As can be seen from the figure, it seems likely that a straight line will describe the trend of increase in dollar amount charged with increase in number of miles traveled. The least-squares line that fits these data is shown in Figure 10–12.

We will now show how the least squares regression line in Figure 10–12 is obtained. Table 10–2 shows the necessary computations. From equations 10–9, using sums at the

SOLUTION

FIGURE 10–11 The Data for the American Express Study

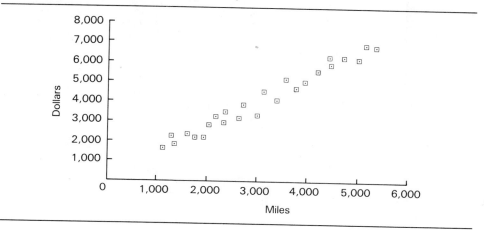

FIGURE 10–12   Least-Squares Line for the American Express Study

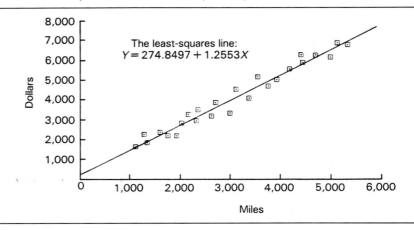

bottom of Table 10–2, we get:

$$SS_X = \sum x^2 - \frac{(\sum x)^2}{n} = 293{,}426{,}946 - \frac{79{,}448^2}{25} = 40{,}947{,}557.84$$

and

$$SS_{XY} = \sum xy - \frac{(\sum x)(\sum y)}{n} = 390{,}185{,}014 - \frac{(79{,}448)\ 106{,}605}{25} = 51{,}402{,}852.4$$

Using equations 10–10 for the least-squares estimates of the slope and intercept parame-

TABLE 10–2   The Computations Required for the American Express Study

Miles (X)	Dollars (Y)	X²	Y²	XY
1,211	1,802	1,466,521	3,247,204	2,182,222
1,345	2,405	1,809,025	5,784,025	3,234,725
1,422	2,005	2,022,084	4,020,025	2,851,110
1,687	2,511	2,845,969	6,305,121	4,236,057
1,849	2,332	3,418,801	5,438,224	4,311,868
2,026	2,305	4,104,676	5,313,025	4,669,930
2,133	3,016	4,549,689	9,096,256	6,433,128
2,253	3,385	5,076,009	11,458,225	7,626,405
2,400	3,090	5,760,000	9,548,100	7,416,000
2,468	3,694	6,091,024	13,645,636	9,116,792
2,699	3,371	7,284,601	11,363,641	9,098,329
2,806	3,998	7,873,636	15,984,004	11,218,388
3,082	3,555	9,498,724	12,638,025	10,956,510
3,209	4,692	10,297,681	22,014,864	15,056,628
3,466	4,244	12,013,156	18,011,536	14,709,704
3,643	5,298	13,271,449	28,068,804	19,300,614
3,852	4,801	14,837,904	23,049,601	18,493,452
4,033	5,147	16,265,089	26,491,609	20,757,851
4,267	5,738	18,207,289	32,924,644	24,484,046
4,498	6,420	20,232,004	41,216,400	28,877,160
4,533	6,059	20,548,089	36,711,481	27,465,447
4,804	6,426	23,078,416	41,293,476	30,870,504
5,090	6,321	25,908,100	39,955,041	32,173,890
5,233	7,026	27,384,289	49,364,676	36,767,058
5,439	6,964	29,582,721	48,497,296	37,877,196
79,448	106,605	293,426,946	521,440,939	390,185,014

ters, we get:

$$b_1 = \frac{SS_{XY}}{SS_X} = \frac{51,402,852.40}{40,947,557.84} = 1.255333776$$

and

$$b_0 = \bar{y} - b_1\bar{x} = \frac{106,605}{25} - (1.255333776)\frac{79,448}{25} = 274.8496866$$

It is important to carry out as many significant digits as you can in these computations. Here we carried out the computations by hand, for demonstration purposes. Usually, all computations are done by computer or by calculator. There are many hand calculators with a built-in routine for simple linear regression. From now on, we will present only the computed results, the least-squares estimates. The estimated least-squares relationship for Example (a) is, reporting estimates to the second significant decimal:

$$Y = 274.85 + 1.26X + e \tag{10-11}$$

The equation of the line itself, that is, the predicted value of Y for a given X, is:

$$\hat{Y} = 274.85 + 1.26X \tag{10-12}$$

In the next section, we will learn how to compute standard errors of the regression estimators using the sums of squares and cross products (equations 10–9). We will also see how these sums of squares are related to sums of squares used in ANOVA.

PROBLEMS

10–9. Explain the advantages of the least squares procedure for fitting lines to data. Explain how the procedure works.

10–10. (A conceptually advanced problem) Can you think of a possible limitation of the least-squares procedure?

10–11. A banking analyst is interested in developing a prediction regression of the prime lending rate using the federal funds rate for the same week as the independent variable. A random sample of 15 weekly observations on both variables is obtained. Data are as follows.

Federal Funds Rate	Prime Lending Rate
6.23	7.75
6.87	8.50
5.54	6.85
5.90	6.78
6.45	8.00
6.55	7.80
5.75	7.05
6.00	7.35
6.20	7.30
6.70	8.00
7.00	8.69
7.23	8.86
5.30	6.25
6.35	7.90
7.15	8.96

Estimate the slope and intercept parameters of the simple linear regression model of the prime rate based on the federal funds rate.

Answers

10–12.

$SS_x = 4.819$
$SS_y = 9.142$
$SS_{xy} = 6.436$

10–14.

$b_0 = 3.057$
$b_1 = 0.187$

10–16.

Cost = 260.728 +
153.596 days + e

10–12. For the data in problem 10–11, what are the values of SS_X, SS_Y, and SS_{XY}?

10–13. A financial analyst at Goldman Sachs ran a regression analysis of monthly returns on a certain investment (Y) versus returns for the same month on the Standard & Poor's Index (X). The regression results included $SS_X = 765.98$ and $SS_{XY} = 934.49$. Give the least-squares estimate of the regression slope parameter.

10–14. Recently, research efforts have focused on the problem of predicting a manufacturer's market share using information on the quality of its product. Suppose that the following data are available on market share, in percentage (Y), and product quality, on a scale of 0 to 100, determined by an objective evaluation procedure (X).

$$X: 27\ 39\ 73\ 66\ 33\ 43\ 47\ 55\ 60\ 68\ 70\ 75\ 82$$
$$Y:\ 2\ \ 3\ 10\ \ 9\ \ 4\ \ 6\ \ 5\ \ 8\ \ 7\ \ 9\ 10\ 13\ 12$$

Estimate the simple linear regression relationship between market share and product quality rating.

10–15. A pharmaceutical manufacturer wants to determine the concentration of a key component of cough medicine that may be used without the drug causing adverse side effects. As part of the analysis, a random sample of 45 patients is administered doses of varying concentration (X), and the severity of side effects (Y) is measured. The results include: $\bar{x} = 88.9$, $\bar{y} = 165.3$, $SS_X = 2,133.9$, $SS_{XY} = 4,502.53$, $SS_Y = 12,500$. Find the least-squares estimates of the regression parameters.

10–16. An analyst for Blue Cross/Blue Shield wants to estimate the linear relationship between an examining physician's estimate of the number of days of hospitalization a patient would require and the total medical costs actually incurred. Results of the analysis are to be used for predicting medical costs based on a physician's preliminary report. The following data constitute a random sample of 11 accounts.

Estimated Number of Days	Total Cost (in dollars)
5	$2,845
6	3,030
2	2,568
7	3,288
1	2,327
4	2,966
8	3,760
3	2,580
2	2,772
5	3,199
9	3,520

Estimate the parameters of the simple linear regression model. Give the equation of the estimated regression line.

10–17. The following table gives the *Financial Times* actuarial indices for April 4, 1991.[3] Estimate the parameters of a linear regression relationship of the U.S. dollar index to the pound sterling index (the independent variable).

National and Regional Markets

	U.S. Dollar Index	Pound Sterling Index
Australia	137.70	114.40
Austria	202.40	168.15
Belgium	141.81	117.82
Canada	138.37	114.96
Denmark	248.09	206.12

[3] Reproduced by permission from *Financial Times* (April 6–7, 1991), p. 19.

National and Regional Markets (concluded)

	U.S. Dollar Index	Pound Sterling Index
Finland	121.82	101.21
France	142.38	118.29
Germany	111.57	92.69
Hong Kong	156.45	129.98
Ireland	170.91	141.99
Italy	82.29	68.36
Japan	143.37	119.12
Malaysia	240.26	199.61
Mexico	824.35	684.88
Netherland	141.62	117.66
New Zealand	46.52	38.65
Norway	201.73	167.60
Singapore	198.62	165.01
South Africa	199.08	165.40
Spain	162.42	134.94
Sweden	195.32	162.27
Switzerland	97.67	81.14
United Kingdom	181.49	150.78
USA	154.09	128.02
Europe	144.73	120.24
Nordic	188.37	156.50
Pacific Basin	143.17	118.95
Euro–Pacific	144.16	119.77
North America	153.04	127.15
Europe Ex. UK	122.55	101.81
Pacific Ex. Japan	139.90	116.23
World Ex. US	144.91	120.40
World Ex. UK	143.54	119.25
World Ex. So. Af.	146.59	121.79
World Ex. Japan	150.19	124.78
The World Index	146.91	122.05

10–18. (A problem requiring knowledge of calculus) Derive the normal equations (10–8) by taking the partial derivatives of SSE with respect to b_0 and b_1 and setting them to zero. (*Hint:* set $\text{SSE} = \Sigma e^2 = \Sigma(y - \hat{y})^2 = \Sigma(y - b_0 - b_1 x)^2$, and take the derivatives of the last expression on the right.)

10–4 Error Variance and the Standard Errors of Regression Estimators

Recall that σ^2 is the variance of the population regression errors, ϵ, and that this variance is assumed to be constant for all values of X in the range under study. The error variance is an important parameter in the context of regression analysis because it is a measure of the spread of the population elements about the regression line. Generally, the smaller the error variance, the more closely the population elements follow the regression line. The error variance is the variance of the dependent variable Y as "seen" by an eye looking in the direction of the regression line (the error variance is not the variance of Y). These properties are demonstrated in Figure 10–13.

The figure shows two regression lines. The top regression line in the figure has a larger error variance than the bottom regression line. The error variance for each regression is the variation in the data points as seen by the eye located at the base of the line, looking *in the direction of the regression line*. The variance of Y, on the other hand, is the variation in the Y values regardless of the regression line. That is, the variance of Y for each of the two data sets in the figure is the variation in the data as seen by an eye looking in a direction parallel to the X-axis. Note also that

FIGURE 10–13 Two Examples of Regression Lines Showing the Error Variance

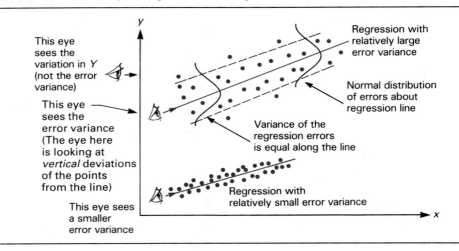

the spread of the data is constant along the regression lines. This is in accordance with our assumption of equal error variance for all X.

Since σ^2 is usually unknown, we need to estimate it from our data. An unbiased estimator of σ^2, denoted by S^2, is the *mean square error* (MSE) of the regression. As you will soon see, sums of squares and mean squares in the context of regression analysis are very similar to those of ANOVA, presented in the preceding chapter. The degrees of freedom for error in the context of simple linear regression are $n - 2$ because we have n data points, from which two parameters, β_0 and β_1, are estimated (thus, two restrictions are imposed on the n points, leaving df $= n - 2$). The sum of squares for error (SSE) in regression analysis is defined as the sum of squared deviations of the data values Y from the fitted values $\hat{Y}$. The sum of squares for error may also be defined in terms of a computational formula using SS_X, SS_Y, and SS_{XY} as defined in equations 10–9. We state these relationships in equations 10–13.

$$\text{df (error)} = n - 2$$

$$\text{SSE} = \sum (Y - \hat{Y})^2$$

$$= SS_Y - \frac{(SS_{XY})^2}{SS_X} \qquad (10\text{–}13)$$

$$= SS_Y - b_1 SS_{XY}$$

An unbiased estimator of σ^2, denoted by S^2, is:

$$\text{MSE} = \frac{\text{SSE}}{n - 2}$$

In Example (a), the sum of squares for error is:

$$\text{SSE} = SS_Y - b_1 SS_{XY} = 66{,}855{,}898 - (1.255333776)(51{,}402{,}852.4)$$

$$= 2{,}328{,}161.2$$

and

$$MSE = \frac{SSE}{n-2} = \frac{2{,}328{,}161.2}{23} = 101{,}224.4$$

An estimate of the standard deviation of the regression errors, σ, is s, which is the square root of MSE. (The estimator S is not unbiased because the square root of an unbiased estimator, such as S^2, is not itself unbiased. The bias, however, is small, and the point is a technical one.) The estimate $s = \sqrt{MSE}$ of the standard deviation of the regression errors is sometimes referred to as *standard error of estimate*. In Example (a), we have:

$$s = \sqrt{MSE} = \sqrt{101{,}224.4} = 318.1578225$$

The computation of SSE and MSE for Example (a) is demonstrated in Figure 10–14.

The standard deviation of the regression errors, σ, and its estimate, s, play an important role in the process of estimation of the values of the regression parameters, β_0 and β_1. This is so because σ is part of the expressions for the standard errors of both parameter estimators. The standard errors are defined next; they give us an idea of the accuracy of the least-squares estimates, b_0 and b_1. *The standard error of b_1 is especially important because it is used in a test for the existence of a linear relationship between X and Y.* This will be seen in section 10–6.

The estimated standard error of b_0 is:

$$s(b_0) = \frac{s\sqrt{\Sigma x^2}}{\sqrt{n\,SS_X}} \tag{10–14}$$

where $s = \sqrt{MSE}$.

The standard error of b_1 is very important, for the reason just mentioned. The true standard error of b_1 is $\sigma/\sqrt{SS_X}$, but since σ is not known, we use the estimated standard deviation of the errors, s.

FIGURE 10–14 Computing SSE and MSE in the American Express Study

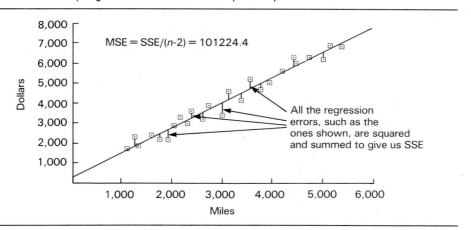

The estimated standard error of b_1 is:

$$s(b_1) = \frac{s}{\sqrt{SS_x}} \qquad (10\text{-}15)$$

Formulas such as equation 10–15 are nice to know, but you should not worry too much about having to use them. Regression analysis is usually done by computer, and the computer output will include the values of the standard errors of the regression estimates. We will now show how the regression parameter estimates and their standard errors can be used in the construction of confidence intervals for the true regression parameters, β_0 and β_1. In section 10–6, as mentioned, we will use the estimated standard error of b_1 for conducting the very important hypothesis test about the existence of a linear relationship between X and Y.

Confidence Intervals for the Regression Parameters

Confidence intervals for the true regression parameters, β_0 and β_1, are easy to compute.

A $(1 - \alpha)100\%$ confidence interval for β_0:

$$b_0 \pm t_{(\alpha/2, n-2)} s(b_0) \qquad (10\text{-}16)$$

where $s(b_0)$ is as given in equation 10–14

A $(1 - \alpha)100\%$ confidence interval for β_1:

$$b_1 \pm t_{(\alpha/2, n-2)} s(b_1) \qquad (10\text{-}17)$$

where $s(b_1)$ is as given in equation 10–15

Let us construct 95% confidence intervals for β_0 and β_1 in the American Express example. Using equations 10–14 to 10–17, we get:

$$s(b_0) = \frac{s\sqrt{\Sigma x^2}}{\sqrt{n SS_x}} = 318.16 \frac{\sqrt{293,426,946}}{\sqrt{(25)(40,947,557.84)}} = 170.338$$

where the various quantities were computed earlier, including Σx^2, which is found at the bottom of Table 10–2.

A 95% confidence interval for β_0 is:

$$b_0 \pm t_{(\alpha/2, n-2)} s(b_0) = 274.85 \pm 2.069(170.338) = [-77.58, 627.28]$$

where the value 2.069 is obtained from Appendix C, Table 3 for $1 - \alpha = 0.95$ and 23 degrees of freedom. We may be 95% confident that the true regression intercept is anywhere from -77.58 to 627.28.

$$s(b_1) = \frac{s}{\sqrt{SS_x}} = \frac{318.16}{\sqrt{40,947,557.84}} = 0.04972 \qquad (10\text{-}18)$$

FIGURE 10–15 Interpretation of the Slope Estimation for Example (a)

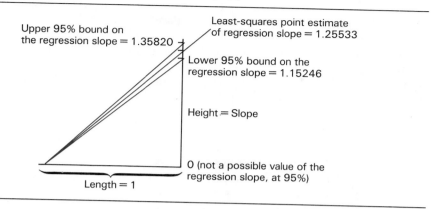

A 95% confidence interval for β_1 is:

$$b_1 \pm t_{(\alpha/2, n-2)} s(b_1) = 1.25533 \pm 2.069(0.04972)$$
$$= [1.15246, 1.35820] \qquad (10-19)$$

From the confidence interval given in equation 10–19, we may be 95% confident that the *true* slope of the (*population*) regression line is anywhere from 1.15246 to 1.3582. This range of values is far from zero, and so we may be quite confident that the true regression slope is not zero. This conclusion is very important, as we will see in following sections. Figure 10–15 demonstrates the meaning of the confidence interval given in equation 10–19.

In the next chapter, we will discuss *joint* confidence intervals for both regression parameters, β_0 and β_1, an advanced topic of secondary importance. (Since the two estimates are related, a joint interval will give us more accuracy and a more meaningful, single confidence coefficient, $1 - \alpha$. This topic is somewhat similar to the Tukey analysis of Chapter 9.) Again, we want to deemphasize the importance of inference about β_0 even though information about the standard error of the estimator of this parameter is reported in computer regression output. It is the inference about β_1 that is of interest to us. Inference about β_1 has implications about the existence of a linear relationship between X and Y; inference about β_0 has no such implications. In addition, there may be a temptation to use the results of the inference about β_0 to "force" this parameter to equal zero or another number. Such temptation should be resisted for reasons that will be explained in a later section; therefore, we deemphasize inference about β_0.

PROBLEMS

10–19. Give a 99% confidence interval for the slope parameter in Example (a). Is zero a credible value for the true regression slope?

10–20. Give an unbiased estimate for the error variance in the situation of problem 10–11. In this problem and others, you may either use a computer or do the computations by hand.

10–21. Find the standard errors of the regression parameter estimates for problem 10–11.

10–22. Give 95% confidence intervals for the regression slope and the regression intercept parameters for the situation of problem 10–11.

Answers

10–20.

MSE = 0.034

10–22.

b_0: [−2.009, 0.315]
b_1: [1.171, 1.533]

10-23. For the situation of problem 10–14, find the standard errors of the estimates of the regression parameters; give an estimate of the variance of the regression errors. Also give a 95% confidence interval for the true regression slope. Is zero a plausible value for the true regression slope at the 95% level of confidence?

10-24.
___

MSE = 28,236.056
$s(b_0) = 108.727$
$s(b_1) = 20.350$
β_1: [107.57, 199.63]
Zero not plausible

10-24. Repeat problem 10–23 for the situation in problem 10–16. Comment on your results.

10-25. In addition to its role in the formulas of the standard errors of the regression estimates, what is the significance of s^2?

10-5   Correlation

We now digress from regression analysis to discuss an important related concept: statistical *correlation*. Recall that one of the assumptions of the regression model is that the independent variable, X, is fixed rather than random and that the only randomness in the values of Y comes from the error term, ϵ. Let us now relax this assumption and *assume that both X and Y are random variables*. In this new context, the study of the relationship between two variables is called *correlation analysis*.

In correlation analysis, we adopt a symmetric approach: we make no distinction between an independent variable and a dependent one. The correlation between two variables is a measure of the linear relationship between them. The correlation gives an indication of how well the two variables move together in a straight-line fashion. The correlation between X and Y is the same as the correlation between Y and X. We now define correlation more formally.

> The **correlation** between two random variables, X and Y, is a measure of the *degree of linear association* between the two variables.

Two variables are highly correlated if they move well together. Correlation is indicated by the **correlation coefficient.**

> The population correlation coefficient is denoted by ρ. The coefficient ρ can take on any value from -1, through 0, to 1.

The possible values of ρ and their interpretations are given below.

1. When ρ is equal to zero, there is no correlation. That is, there is no linear relationship between the two random variables.
2. When $\rho = 1$, there is a perfect, positive, linear relationship between the two variables. That is, whenever one of the variables, X or Y, increases, the other variable also increases; and whenever one of the variables decreases, the other one must also decrease.
3. When $\rho = -1$, there is a perfect negative linear relationship between X and Y. When X or Y increases, the other variable decreases; and when one decreases, the other one must increase.
4. When the value of ρ is between 0 and 1 in absolute value, it reflects the relative strength of the linear relationship between the two variables. For example, a correlation of 0.90 implies a relatively strong positive relationship between the two variables. A correlation of -0.70 implies a weaker, negative (as indicated by the negative sign), linear relationship. A correlation $\rho = 0.30$ implies a relatively weak linear relationship between X and Y.

A few sets of data on two variables, and their corresponding population correlation coefficients, are shown in Figure 10–16.

How do we arrive at the concept of correlation? Consider the pair of random variables, X and Y. In correlation analysis, *we will assume that both X and Y are normally distributed random variables with means μ_X and μ_Y, and standard deviations σ_X and σ_Y, respectively*. We define the *covariance* of X and Y as follows.

FIGURE 10–16
Several Possible Correlations between Two Variables

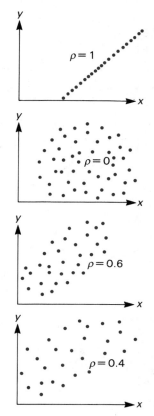

The **covariance** of two variables X and Y:

$$\text{Cov}(X,Y) = E[(X - \mu_X)(Y - \mu_Y)] \qquad (10\text{–}20)$$

where μ_X is the (population) mean of X and μ_Y is the (population) mean of Y

The covariance of X and Y is thus the expected value of the product of the deviation of X from its mean and the deviation of Y from its mean. The covariance is positive when the two random variables move together in the same direction, it is negative when the two random variables move in opposite directions, and it is zero when the two variables are not linearly related. Other than this, the covariance does not convey much. Its magnitude cannot be interpreted as an indication of the *degree* of linear association between the two variables, because this magnitude depends on the magnitudes of the standard deviations of X and Y. But if we divide the covariance by these standard deviations, we get a measure that is constrained to the range of values -1 to 1 and conveys information about the relative strength of the linear relationship between the two variables. This measure is the population correlation coefficient, ρ.

The **population correlation coefficient:**

$$\rho = \frac{\text{Cov}(X,Y)}{\sigma_X \sigma_Y} \qquad (10\text{–}21)$$

Figure 10–16 gives an idea as to what data from populations with different values of ρ may look like.

Like all population parameters, the value of ρ is not known to us, and we need to estimate it from our random sample of (X,Y) observation pairs. It turns out that a sample estimate of $\text{Cov}(X,Y)$ is $SS_{XY}/(n - 1)$; an estimate of σ_X is $\sqrt{SS_X/(n - 1)}$; and an estimate of σ_Y is $\sqrt{SS_Y/(n - 1)}$. Substituting these estimates for their population counterparts in equation 10–21, and noting that the term $n - 1$ cancels out, we get the *sample correlation coefficient*, denoted by r. This estimate of ρ, also referred to as the *Pearson product-moment correlation coefficient*, is given in equation 10–22.

The **sample correlation coefficient:**

$$r = \frac{SS_{XY}}{\sqrt{SS_X \, SS_Y}} \qquad (10\text{–}22)$$

FIGURE 10–16
(concluded)

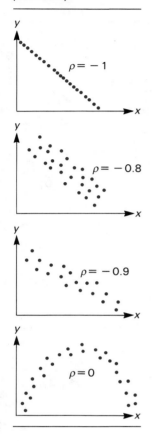

In regression analysis, the square of the sample correlation coefficient, r^2, has a special meaning and importance. This will be seen in section 10–7.

We often use the sample correlation coefficient for descriptive purposes as a point estimator of the population correlation coefficient, ρ. When r is large and positive (closer to $+1$), we say that the two variables are highly correlated in a positive way; when r is large and negative (toward -1), we say that the two variables are highly correlated in an inverse direction, and so on. That is, we view r as if it were the parameter ρ, which r estimates. It is possible, however, to use r as an estimator in testing hypotheses about the true correlation coefficient, ρ. When testing such hypotheses, the assumption of normal distributions of the two variables is required.

The most common test is a test of whether or not two random variables, X and Y, are correlated. The hypothesis test is:

$$H_0: \rho = 0$$
$$H_1: \rho \neq 0$$
(10–23)

The test statistic for this particular test is:

$$t_{(n-2)} = \frac{r}{\sqrt{\dfrac{1 - r^2}{n - 2}}}$$
(10–24)

This test statistic may also be used for carrying out a one-tailed test for the existence of a positive only, or a negative only, correlation between X and Y. These would be one-tailed tests instead of the two-tailed test of equation 10–23, and the only difference is that the critical points for t would be the appropriate one-tailed values for a given α. The test statistic, however, is good *only* for tests where the null hypothesis assumes a zero correlation. When the true correlation between the two variables is anything but zero, the t distribution in equation 10–24 does not apply; in such cases the distribution is more complicated.[4] The test in equation 10–23 is the most common hypothesis test about the population correlation coefficient because it is a test for the existence of a linear relationship between two variables. We demonstrate this test with the following example.

EXAMPLE (b)

An article in the *Journal of Marketing Research* reports the results of a study to determine whether there is a linear relationship between the time spent in negotiating a sale and the resulting profits.[5] A random sample of 27 market transactions was collected, and the time taken to conclude the sale as well as the resulting profit were recorded for each

---

[4] In cases where we want to test $H_0: \rho = a$ versus $H_1: \rho \neq a$, where a is some number other than zero, we may do so by using the Fisher transformation: $z' = (1/2)\log[(1 + r)/(1 - r)]$, where z' is approximately normally distributed with mean $\mu' = (1/2)\log[(1 + \rho)/(1 - \rho)]$ and standard deviation $\sigma' = 1/\sqrt{n - 3}$. (Here *log* is taken to mean *natural logarithm*.) Such tests are less common, and a more complete description may be found in advanced texts. As an exercise, the interested reader may try this test on some data. (You need to transform z' to an approximate standard normal: $z = (z' - \mu')/\sigma'$; use the null-hypothesized value of ρ in the formula for μ'.)

[5] L. McAlister, M. Bazerman, and P. Fader, "Power and Goal Setting in Channel Negotiations," *Journal of Marketing Research* (August 1986).

transaction. The sample correlation coefficient was computed: $r = 0.424$. Is there a linear relationship between the length of negotiations and transaction profits?

We want to conduct the hypothesis test: H_0: $\rho = 0$ versus H_1: $\rho \neq 0$. Using the test statistic in equation 10–24, we get:

SOLUTION

$$t_{(25)} = \frac{r}{\sqrt{(1 - r^2)/(n - 2)}} = \frac{0.424}{\sqrt{(1 - 0.424^2)/25}} = 2.34$$

From Appendix C, Table 3, we find that the critical points for a t distribution with 25 degrees of freedom and $\alpha = 0.05$ are ± 2.060. Therefore, we reject the null hypothesis of no correlation in favor of the alternative that the two variables are linearly related. Since the critical points for $\alpha = 0.01$ are ± 2.787, and $2.787 > 2.34$, we would have to accept the null hypothesis of no correlation between the two variables if we wanted to use the 0.01 level of significance. If we wanted to test (before looking at our data) only for the existence of a positive correlation between the two variables, our test would have been H_0: $\rho \leq 0$ versus H_1: $\rho > 0$, and we would have used only the right-hand tail of the t distribution. At $\alpha = 0.05$, the critical point of t with 25 degrees of freedom is 1.708, and at $\alpha = 0.01$ it is 2.485. The null hypothesis would, again, be rejected at the 0.05 level but accepted at the 0.01 level of significance.

In regression analysis, the test for the existence of a linear relationship between X and Y is a test of whether or not the regression slope, β_1, is equal to zero. The regression slope parameter is related to the correlation coefficient (as an exercise, compare the equations of the estimates r and b_1); when two random variables are uncorrelated, the population regression slope is zero.

We end this section with a word of caution. First, the existence of a correlation between two variables does not necessarily mean that one of the variables *causes* the other one. The determination of **causality** is a difficult question that cannot be directly answered in the context of correlation analysis or regression analysis. Also, the statistical determination that two variables are correlated may not always mean that they are correlated in any direct, meaningful way. For example, if we study any two population-related variables and find that both variables increase "together," this may merely be a reflection of the general increase in population rather than any direct correlation between the two variables. We should look for outside variables that may affect both variables under study.

PROBLEMS

10–26. What is the main difference between correlation analysis and regression analysis?

10–27. Compute the sample correlation coefficient for the data of problem 10–11.

10–28. Compute the sample correlation coefficient for the data of problem 10–14.

10–29. Using the data in problem 10–16, conduct the hypothesis test for the existence of a correlation between the two variables. Use $\alpha = 0.01$.

10–30. Is it possible that a sample correlation of 0.51 between two variables will not indicate that the two variables are really correlated, while a sample correlation of 0.04 between another pair of variables will be statistically significant? Explain.

10–31. The following data, from the September 1986 issue of *International Financial Statistics,* are indexed prices of gold and copper over the last 10 years. Assuming these

Answers

10–28.

$r = 0.960$

10–30.

Yes.

Answer

indexed values constitute a random sample from the population of possible values, test for the existence of a correlation between the indexed prices of the two metals.

> Gold: 76 62 70 59 52 53 53 56 57 56
> Copper: 80 68 73 63 65 68 65 63 65 66

Also, state one limitation of the data set.

10–32.   Follow daily stock price quotations in *The Wall Street Journal* for a pair of stocks of your choice, and compute the sample correlation coefficient. Also, test for the existence of a nonzero correlation in the "population" of prices of the two stocks. For your sample, use as many daily prices as you can.

10–33.   Again using *The Wall Street Journal* as a source of data, determine whether there is a correlation between morning and afternoon price quotations in London for an ounce of gold (for the same day). Any ideas?

10–34.

$t_{(63)} = 3.16$; significant

10–34.   A study was conducted to determine whether a correlation exists between consumers' perceptions of a television commercial (measured on a special scale) and their interest in purchasing the product (measured on a scale). The results are $n = 65$, $r = 0.37$. Is there statistical evidence of a correlation between the two variables?

10–35.   (Optional, advanced problem) Using the Fisher transformation (described in footnote 4), carry out a two-tailed test of the hypothesis that the population correlation coefficient for the situation of problem 10–34 is $\rho = 0.22$. Use $\alpha = 0.05$.

10–6   Hypothesis Tests about the Regression Relationship

When there is no linear relationship between X and Y, the population regression slope, β_1, is equal to zero. Why? The population regression slope is equal to zero in either one of two situations:

1. When Y is *constant* for all values of X. For example, $Y = 457.33$ for all X. This is shown in Figure 10–17(*a*). If Y is constant for all values of X, the slope of Y with respect to X, parameter β_1 is identically zero; there is no linear relationship between the two variables.

2. When the two variables are *uncorrelated*. When the correlation between X and Y is zero, as X increases Y may increase, or it may decrease, or it may remain constant. There is no *systematic* increase or decrease in the values of Y as X increases. This case is shown in Figure 10–17(*b*). As can be seen in the figure, data from this process are not "moving" in any pattern; thus, there is no direction for the line to follow. Since there is no direction, the slope of the line is, again, zero.

Also, remember that the relationship may be curved, with no linear correlation, as was seen in the last part of Figure 10–16. In such cases, the slope may also be zero.

In all cases other than these, there is at least *some* linear relationship between the two variables X and Y; the slope of the line in all such cases would be either positive or negative, but not zero. Therefore, *the most important statistical test in simple linear regression is the test of whether or not the slope parameter, β_1, is equal to zero.* If we conclude in any particular case that the true regression slope is equal to zero, this means that there is no linear relationship between the two variables: either

FIGURE 10–17   The Two Possibilities Where the Population Regression Slope Is Zero

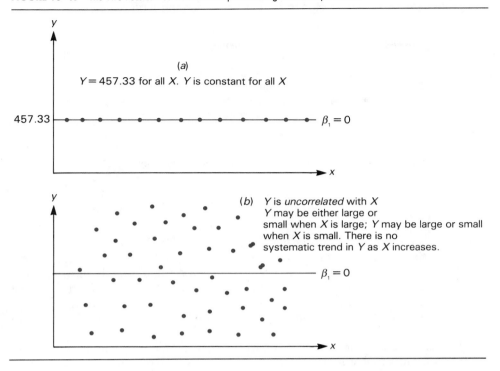

the dependent variable is constant, or—more commonly—the two variables are not linearly related. We thus have the following test for determining the existence of a linear relationship between two variables, X and Y.

A hypothesis test for the existence of a linear relationship between X and Y:

$$H_0: \beta_1 = 0$$
$$H_1: \beta_1 \neq 0$$

(10–25)

This test is, of course, a two-tailed test. Either the true regression slope is equal to zero, or it is not. If it is equal to zero, there is no linear relationship between the two variables; if the slope is not equal to zero, then it is either positive or negative (the two tails of rejection), in which case there is a linear relationship between the two variables. The test statistic for determining the acceptance or rejection of the null hypothesis is given in equation 10–26. Given the assumption of normality of the regression errors, the test statistic possesses the t distribution with $n - 2$ degrees of freedom.

> Test statistic for the existence of a linear relationship between X and Y:
>
> $$t_{(n-2)} = \frac{b_1}{s(b_1)} \qquad (10\text{--}26)$$
>
> where b_1 is the least-squares estimate of the regression slope and $s(b_1)$ is the standard error of b_1. When the null hypothesis is true, the statistic has a t distribution with $n - 2$ degrees of freedom.

This test statistic is a special version of a general test statistic:

$$t_{(n-2)} = \frac{b_1 - \beta_{10}}{s(b_1)} \qquad (10\text{--}27)$$

where β_{10} is the value of β_1 under the null hypothesis. This statistic follows the format: (Estimate − Hypothesized parameter value)/(Standard error of estimator). Since, in the test of equation 10–25, the hypothesized value of β_1 is zero, we have the simplified version of the test statistic, equation 10–26. One advantage of the simple form of our test statistic is that it allows us to conduct the test very quickly. Computer output for regression analysis usually contains a table similar to Table 10–3.

The estimate associated with X (or whatever name the user may have given to the independent variable in the computer program) is b_1. The standard error associated with X is $s(b_1)$. To conduct the test, all you need to do is divide b_1 by $s(b_1)$. In the example of Table 10–3, $4.88/0.1 = 48.8$. The answer is reported in the table as the t ratio. The t ratio can now be compared with critical points of the t distribution with $n - 2$ degrees of freedom. Suppose that the sample size used was 100. Then the critical points for $\alpha = 0.05$ are ± 1.96, and since $48.8 > 1.96$, we conclude that there is evidence of a linear relationship between X and Y in this hypothetical example. (Actually, the p-value is very small. Some computer programs will also report the p-value in an extra column on the right.) What about the first row in the table? The test suggested here is a test of whether or not the intercept β_0 (this is the "constant") is equal to zero. The test statistic is the same as equation 10–26, but with subscripts 0 instead of 1. As we mentioned earlier, this test, although suggested by the output of computer routines, is usually not a meaningful test and should generally be avoided.

We now conduct the hypothesis test for the existence of a linear relationship between miles traveled and amount charged on the American Express card in Example (a). Our hypotheses are: H_0: $\beta_1 = 0$ and H_1: $\beta_1 \neq 0$. Recall that for the American Express study, $b_1 = 1.25533$ and $s(b_1) = 0.04972$ (from equations 10–11 and

TABLE 10–3 An Example of a Part of the Computer Output for Regression

Variable	Estimate	Standard Error	t Ratio
Constant	5.22	0.5	10.44
X	4.88	0.1	48.80

FIGURE 10-18 Test for a Linear Relationship for Example (a)

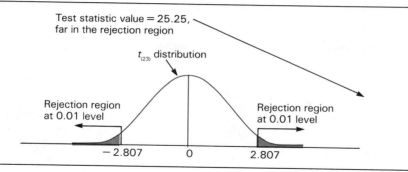

10–18). We now compute the test statistic, using equation 10–26:

$$t = \frac{b_1}{s(b_1)} = \frac{1.25533}{0.04972} = 25.25$$

From the magnitude of the computed value of the statistic, we know that there is statistical evidence of a linear relationship between the variables, because 25.25 is certainly greater than any critical point of a t distribution with 23 degrees of freedom. We show the test in Figure 10–18. The critical points of t with 23 degrees of freedom and $\alpha = 0.01$ are obtained from Appendix C, Table 3. We conclude that there is evidence of a linear relationship between the two variables "miles traveled" and "dollars charged" in Example (a).

Other Tests[6]

Although the test of whether or not the slope parameter is equal to zero is a very important test, because it is a test for the existence of a linear relationship between the two variables, there are other possible tests in the context of regression. These tests serve secondary purposes. In financial analysis, for example, it is often important to determine from past performance data of a particular stock whether or not the stock generally moves with the market as a whole. If the stock does move with the stock market as a whole, the slope parameter of the regression of the stock's returns (Y) versus returns on the market as a whole (X) would be equal to 1.00. That is, $\beta_1 = 1$. We demonstrate this test with Example (c).

The *Market Sensitivity Report*, issued by Merrill Lynch, Inc., lists estimated beta coefficients of common stocks as well as their standard errors. *Beta* is the term used in the finance literature for the estimate b_1 of the regression of returns on a stock versus returns on the stock market as a whole. Returns on the stock market as a whole are taken by Merrill Lynch as returns on the Standard & Poor's 500 Index. The November 1979 issue of the report lists the following findings for common stock of Time, Inc.:

EXAMPLE (c)

---

[6] This subsection may be skipped without loss of continuity.

beta = 1.24, standard error of beta = 0.21, $n = 60$. Is there statistical evidence to re-ject the claim that the Time stock moves, in general, with the market as a whole?

SOLUTION

We want to carry out the special-purpose test: $H_0: \beta_1 = 1$ versus $H_1: \beta_1 \neq 1$. We use the general test of statistic of equation 10–27:

$$t_{(n-2)} = \frac{b_1 - \beta_{10}}{s(b_1)} = \frac{1.24 - 1}{0.21} = 1.14$$

Since $n - 2 = 58$, we use the standard normal distribution. The test statistic value is in the acceptance region for any usual level α, and we conclude that there is no statistical evidence against the claim that Time moves with the market as a whole.

PROBLEMS

Answers

10–36.
———
$t_{(10)} = 1.554$;
accept H_0

10–38.
———
$t_{(13)} = 16.1$;
reject H_0

10–40.
———
$t_{(9)} = 7.548$;
reject H_0

10–42.
———
$t_{(21)} = 4.474$;
reject H_0

10–36. A regression analysis of fuel efficiency (X) versus sales (Y) of different types of corporate aircraft includes the following results: $b_1 = 2.435$, $s(b_1) = 1.567$, $n = 12$. Do you believe there is a linear relationship between sales of corporate aircraft and the aircraft's fuel efficiency?

10–37. An article in the *Journal of Finance* reports the results of a regression analysis of returns on preferred stocks (Y) versus the premium in the preferred-for common stock swap (X).[7] The resulting prediction equation is:

$$\text{Return} = 0.033 + 0.101 \text{ Premium}$$
$$(2.67)$$

where the number in parentheses is the standard error of the slope estimate. The sample size used is $n = 13$. Is there evidence of a linear relationship between returns and premiums?

10–38. In the situation of problem 10–11, test for the existence of a linear relationship between the two variables.

10–39. In the situation of problem 10–14, test for the existence of a linear relationship between the two variables.

10–40. In the situation of problem 10–16, test for the existence of a linear relationship between the two variables.

10–41. For Example (c), test for the existence of a linear relationship between returns on the stock and returns on the market as a whole.

10–42. An advertising research firm conducts a study to determine the relationship between the length of a commercial and the resulting product recall scores of people viewing the commercial. Results of the analysis include $b_1 = 3.467$, $s(b_1) = 0.775$, and $n = 23$. Is there evidence of a linear relationship between commercial length and viewer recall score?

10–43. An article in the *Financial Analysts Journal* discusses results of a regression analysis of average price per share (P) on the independent variable X/k, where X/k is the contemporaneous earnings per share divided by firm-specific discount rate.[8] The regression was run using a random sample of 213 firms listed in the *Value Line Investment Survey*. The reported results are:

$$P = 16.67 + 0.68X/k$$
$$(12.03)$$

---

[7] M. Pinegar and R. Lease, "The Impact of Preferred-for Common Exchange Offers on Firm Value," *Journal of Finance* (September 1986).

[8] L. Johnson, "Dividends and Share Value Revisited," *Financial Analysts Journal* (September–October 1985).

where the number in parentheses is the standard error. Is there a linear relationship between the two variables?

10-44. A management recruiter wants to estimate a linear regression relationship between an executive's experience and the salary the executive may expect to earn after placement with an employer. From data on 28 executives, which are assumed a random sample from the population of executives that the recruiter places, the following regression results are obtained: $b_1 = 5.49$, $s(b_1) = 1.21$. Is there a linear relationship between the experience and the salary of executives placed by the recruiter?

Answer

10-44.

$t_{(26)} = 4.537$;
reject H_0

10-7 How Good Is the Regression?

Once we have determined that a linear relationship exists between the two variables, the question is: How strong is the relationship? If the relationship is a strong one, prediction of the dependent variable can be relatively accurate, and other conclusions drawn from the analysis may be given a high degree of confidence.

We have already seen one measure of the regression fit: the mean square error. The MSE is an estimate of the variance of the true regression errors and is a measure of the variation of the data about the regression line. The MSE, however, depends on the nature of the data, and what may be a large error variation in one situation may not be considered large in another. What we need, therefore, is a *relative* measure of the degree of variation of the data about the regression line. Such a measure allows us to compare the fits of different models.

The relative measure we are looking for is a measure that compares the variation of Y about the regression line with the variation of Y without a regression line. This should remind you of analysis of variance, and we will soon see the relation of ANOVA to regression analysis. It turns out that the relative measure of regression fit we are looking for is the square of the estimated correlation coefficient, r. It is called the *coefficient of determination*.

> The **coefficient of determination, r^2**, is a descriptive measure of the strength of the regression relationship, a measure of how well the regression line fits the data.

The coefficient of determination, r^2, is an estimator of the corresponding population parameter, ρ^2, which is the square of the population coefficient of correlation between two variables X and Y. Usually, however, we use r^2 as a descriptive statistic: a relative measure of how well the regression line fits the data. Ordinarily, we do not use r^2 for reference about ρ^2.

We will now see how the coefficient of determination is obtained directly from a decomposition of the variation in Y into a component due to error and a component due to the regression. Figure 10-19 shows the least-squares line that was fitted to a data set. One of the data points, (x,y), is highlighted. For this data point, the figure shows three kinds of deviations: the deviation of y from its mean $(y - \bar{y})$, the deviation of y from its predicted value using the regression $(y - \hat{y})$, and the deviation of the regression-predicted value of y from the mean of y, which is $(\hat{y} - \bar{y})$. Note that the least-squares line passes through the point $(\bar{x}, \bar{y})$.

We will now follow exactly the same mathematical derivation we used in Chapter 9 when we derived the ANOVA relationships. There we looked at the deviation of a data point from its respective group mean—the error; here the error is the deviation of a data point from its regression-predicted value. In ANOVA, we also looked at the total deviation, the deviation of a data point from the grand mean; here we have the deviation of the data point from the mean of Y. Finally, in ANOVA we also

FIGURE 10–19 The Three Deviations Associated with a Data Point

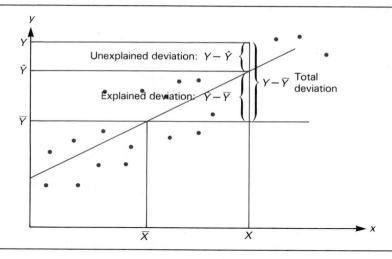

considered the treatment deviation, the deviation of the group mean from the grand mean; here we have the *regression deviation:* the deviation of the predicted value from the mean of Y.

The error is also called the *unexplained deviation* because it is a deviation that cannot be explained by the regression relationship; the regression deviation is also called the *explained deviation* because it is that part of the deviation of a data point from the mean that can be explained by the regression relationship between X and Y. We *explain* why the Y value of a particular data point is above the mean of Y by the fact that its X component happens to be above the mean of X and by the fact that X and Y are linearly (and positively) related. As can be seen from Figure 10–19, and by simple arithmetic, we have:

$$(y - \bar{y}) = (y - \hat{y}) + (\hat{y} - \bar{y})$$

$$\begin{array}{ccccc} \text{Total} & = & \text{Unexplained} & + & \text{Explained} \\ \text{deviation} & & \text{deviation (Error)} & & \text{deviation (Regression)} \end{array} \qquad (10\text{–}28)$$

As in the analysis of variance, we square all three deviations for each one of our data points, and sum over all n points. Here, again, cross terms drop out, and we are left with the following important relationship for the sums of squares:[9]

$$\sum_{i=1}^{n} (y_i - \bar{y})^2 = \sum_{i=1}^{n} (y_i - \hat{y}_i)^2 + \sum_{i=1}^{n} (\hat{y}_i - \bar{y})^2$$

$$\begin{array}{ccccc} \text{SST} & = & \text{SSE} & + & \text{SSR} \qquad (10\text{–}29) \\[4pt] \text{(Total sum} & = & \text{(Sum of} & + & \text{(Sum of} \\ \text{of squares)} & & \text{squares for error)} & & \text{squares for regression)} \end{array}$$

---

[9] The proof of the relation is left as an exercise for the mathematically interested reader.

The term SSR is also called the *explained variation:* it is the part of the variation in Y that is explained by the relationship of Y with the explanatory variable X. Similarly, SSE is the *unexplained variation,* due to error; the sum of the two is the *total variation* in Y.

We define the coefficient of determination as the sum of squares due to the regression divided by the total sum of squares. Also, since by equation 10–29 SSE and SSR add up to SST, the coefficient of determination is equal to 1 minus SSE/SST. We have:

$$r^2 = \frac{\text{SSR}}{\text{SST}} = 1 - \frac{\text{SSE}}{\text{SST}} \qquad (10\text{–}30)$$

The coefficient of determination can be interpreted as *the proportion of the variation in Y that is explained by the regression relationship of Y with X.*

Recall that the correlation coefficient r can be between -1 and 1. Its square, r^2, can therefore be anywhere from 0 to 1. This is in accordance with the interpretation of r^2 as the *percentage of the variation in Y explained by the regression.* The coefficient is a measure of how closely the regression line fits the data; it is a measure of how much the variation in the values of Y is reduced once we regress Y on the variable X. When $r^2 = 1$, we know that 100% of the variation in Y is explained by X. This means that the data all lie right on the regression line, and there are no resulting errors (because, from equation 10–30, SSE must be equal to zero). Since r^2 cannot be negative, we do not know whether the line slopes upward or downward (the direction can be found from b_1 or r), but we know that the line gives a *perfect fit* to the data. Such cases do not occur in business or economics. In fact, when there are no errors, no natural variation, there is no need for statistics.

At the other extreme is the case where the regression line explains nothing. Here the errors account for everything, and SSR is zero. In this case, we see from equation 10–30 that $r^2 = 0$. In such cases, there is no linear relationship between X and Y, and the true regression slope is probably zero (we say "probably" because r^2 is only an estimator, given to chance variation; it could possibly be estimating a nonzero ρ^2). Between the two cases, $r^2 = 0$ and $r^2 = 1$, are values of r^2 that give an indication of the *relative fit* of the regression model to the data. *The higher r^2, the better the fit and the higher our confidence in the regression.* Be wary, however, of situations where the reported r^2 is exceptionally high, such as 0.99 or 0.999. In such cases, something may be wrong. We will see an example of this in the next chapter. Incidentally, in the context of multiple regression, discussed in the next chapter, we will use the notation R^2 for the coefficient of determination to indicate that the relationship is based on several explanatory X variables.

How high should the coefficient of determination be before we can conclude that a regression model fits the data well enough to use the regression with confidence? There is no clear-cut answer to this question. The answer depends on the intended use of the regression model. If we intend to use the regression for *prediction,* the higher the r^2, the more accurate will be our predictions.

An r^2 value of 0.9 or above is very good, a value above 0.8 is good, and a value of 0.6 or above may be satisfactory in some applications, although we must be aware of the fact that, in such cases, errors in prediction may be relatively high. When the r^2 value is 0.5 or below, the regression explains only 50% or less of the variation in the data; therefore, predictions may be poor. If we are interested only in understanding the relationship between the variables, lower values of r^2 may be acceptable, as long as we realize that the model does not explain much.

Figure 10–20 shows several regressions and their corresponding r^2 values. If you think of the total sum of squared deviations as being in a box, then the r^2 is the proportion of the box that is filled with the explained sum of squares, the remaining part being the squared errors. This is shown for each regression in the figure.

It is easy to compute r^2 if we express SSR, SSE, and SST in terms of the computational sums of squares and cross products (equations 10–9):

$$\text{SST} = \text{SS}_Y \qquad \text{SSR} = b_1 \text{SS}_{XY} \qquad \text{SSE} = \text{SS}_Y - b_1 \text{SS}_{XY} \qquad (10\text{–}31)$$

We will now use equation 10–31 in computing the coefficient of determination for Example (a). For this example, we have:

$$\text{SST} = \text{SS}_Y = 66,855,898$$
$$\text{SSR} = b_1 \text{SS}_{XY} = (1.255333776)(51,402,852.4) = 64,527,736.8$$

and

$$\text{SSE} = \text{SST} - \text{SSR} = 2,328,161.2$$

(These were computed when we found the MSE for this example.) We now compute

FIGURE 10–20 The Value of the Coefficient of Determination in Different Regressions

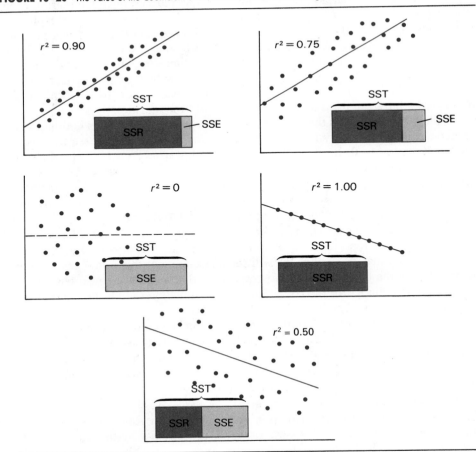

r^2 as:

$$r^2 = \frac{SSR}{SST} = \frac{64,527,736.8}{66,855,898} = 0.96518$$

The r^2 in this example is very high. The interpretation is that over 96.5% of the variation in charges on the American Express card can be explained by the relationship between charges on the card and extent of travel (miles). Again we note that while the computational formulas are easy to use, r^2 is always reported in a prominent place in regression computer output. We will see this in section 10–11.

In the next section, we will see how the sums of squares, along with the corresponding degrees of freedom, lead to mean squares—and to an analysis of variance in the context of regression. In closing this section, we note that in Chapter 11, we will introduce an adjusted coefficient of determination that accounts for degrees of freedom.

PROBLEMS

10–45. In the regression analysis of problem 10–37, the reported coefficient of determination is $r^2 = 0.39$. Does this surprise you? Explain.

10–46. Results of a study reported in the Financial Analysts Journal include a simple linear regression analysis of firms' pension funding (Y) versus profitability (X). The regression coefficient of determination is reported to be $r^2 = 0.02$. (The sample size used is 515.)

a. Would you use the regression model to predict a firm's pension funding?

b. Does the model explain much of the variation in firms' pension funding on the basis of profitability?

c. Do you believe these regression results are worth reporting? Explain.

10–47. What percentage of the variation in Y is explained by the regression in problem 10–11?

10–48. What is the r^2 in the regression of problem 10–14? Interpret its meaning.

10–49. What is the r^2 in the regression of problem 10–16?

10–50. Mita, the manufacturer of copiers, has been spending increasing amounts of money on radio and television advertising in recent years. An analyst employed by Mita wanted to estimate a simple linear regression of the company's annual copier sales versus advertising dollars. The regression results included SSE = 12,745 and SSR = 87,691. What is the coefficient of determination for this regression? Interpret its meaning. Do you believe this regression model would prove a useful tool for predicting sales based on advertising expenditure? Explain.

10–51. An article in the *Journal of Finance* reports the results of simple linear regressions of New York Stock Exchange share price versus after-hours price movements for various firms. Following are the regression r^2 values for various firms:[10] American Express 0.068, DuPont 0.091, Kodak 0.049, IBM 0.188. Comment on the explanatory powers of the linear regression models for these firms.

10–52. Find the r^2 for the regression in problem 10–15.

10–53. (A mathematically demanding problem) Starting with equation 10–28, derive equation 10–29.

10–54. Using equation 10–31 for SSR, show that SSR = $(SS_{XY})^2/SS_X$.

Answers

10–46.

a. No.

b. No.

c. Probably not.

10–48.

$r^2 = 0.922$

10–50.

$r^2 = 0.873$

Model would be useful.

10–52.

$r^2 = 0.76$

[10] D. Neumark, P. A. Tinsley, and S. Tosini, "After-Hours Stock Prices and Post-Crash Hangovers," *Journal of Finance* (March 1991), p. 165.

10–8 Analysis of Variance Table and an F Test of the Regression Model

We know from our discussion of the t test for the existence of a linear relationship that the degrees of freedom for *error* in simple linear regression are $n - 2$. For the *regression,* we have 1 degree of freedom because there is one independent X variable in the regression. The *total* degrees of freedom are $n - 1$ because here we only consider the mean of Y, to which one degree of freedom is lost. These are similar to the degrees of freedom for ANOVA in the last chapter. Mean squares are obtained, as usual, by dividing the sums of squares by their corresponding degrees of freedom. This gives us the mean square regression, MSR, and mean square error (which we encountered earlier), MSE. Further dividing MSR by MSE gives us an F ratio with degrees of freedom 1 and $n - 2$. All these can be put in an ANOVA table for regression. This has been done in Table 10–4.

In regression, there are three sources of variation (see Figure 10–19). These are: *regression*—the explained variation; *error*—the unexplained variation; and their sum, the *total* variation. We know how to obtain the sums of squares and the degrees of freedom, and from them the mean squares. Dividing the mean square regression by the mean square error should give us another measure of the accuracy of our regression because MSR is the average squared explained deviation and MSE is the average squared error (where averaging is done using the appropriate degrees of freedom). The ratio of the two has an F distribution with 1 and $n - 2$ degrees of freedom *when there is no regression relationship between X and Y.* This suggests an F test for the existence of a linear relationship between X and Y. *In simple linear regression, this test is equivalent to the t test*. In multiple regression, as we will see in the next chapter, the F test serves a general role, and separate t tests are used to evaluate the significance of different variables. In simple linear regression, we may conduct either an F test or a t test; the results of the two tests will be the same. The hypothesis test is as given in equation 10–25; the test is carried on the right-hand tail of the F distribution with 1 and $n - 2$ degrees of freedom. We illustrate the analysis with data from Example (a). The ANOVA results are given in Table 10–5.

To carry out the test for the existence of a linear relationship between miles traveled and dollars charged on the card, we compare the computed F ratio of 637.47 with a critical point of the F distribution with 1 degree of freedom for the numerator

TABLE 10–4 ANOVA Table for Regression

Source of Variation	Sum of Squares	Degrees of Freedom	Mean Square	F Ratio
Regression	SSR	1	$\text{MSR} = \dfrac{\text{SSR}}{1}$	$F_{(1,n-2)} = \dfrac{\text{MSR}}{\text{MSE}}$
Error	SSE	$n - 2$	$\text{MSE} = \dfrac{\text{SSE}}{n - 2}$	
Total	SST	$n - 1$		

TABLE 10–5 ANOVA Table for American Express Example

Source of Variation	Sum of Squares	Degrees of Freedom	Mean Square	F Ratio	p
Regression	64,527,736.8	1	64,527,736.8	637.47	0.000
Error	2,328,161.2	23	101,224.4		
Total	66,855,898.0	24			

and 23 degrees of freedom for the denominator. Using $\alpha = 0.01$, the critical point from Appendix C, Table 5 is found to be 7.88. Clearly, the computed value is far in the rejection region, and the p-value is very small. We conclude, again, that there is evidence of a linear relationship between the two variables.

Recall from Chapter 8 that an F distribution with 1 degree of freedom for the numerator and k degrees of freedom for the denominator is the *square* of a t distribution with k degrees of freedom. In Example (a), our computed F statistic value is 637.47, which is the square of our obtained t statistic, 25.25 (to within rounding error). The same relationship holds for the critical points: for $\alpha = 0.01$, we have a critical point for $F_{(1,23)}$ equal to 7.88, and the (right-hand) critical point of a two-tailed test at $\alpha = 0.01$ for t with 23 degrees of freedom is $2.807 = \sqrt{7.88}$.

PROBLEMS

10-55. Conduct the F test for the existence of a linear relationship between the two variables in problem 10-11.

10-56. Carry out an F test for a linear relationship in problem 10-14. Compare your results with those of the t test.

10-57. Repeat problem 10-56 for the data of problem 10-16.

10-58. Conduct an F test for the existence of a linear relationship in the case of problem 10-15.

10-59. For problem 10-50, assume the sample size used was $n = 104$, and conduct an F test for the existence of a linear relationship between the two variables.

10-60. In a simple linear regression analysis, it is found that $b_1 = 2.556$ and $s(b_1) = 4.122$. The sample size is $n = 22$. Conduct an F test for the existence of a linear relationship between the two variables.

10-61. (A mathematically demanding problem) Using the definition of the t statistic in terms of sums of squares, prove (in the context of simple linear regression) that $t^2 = F$.

Answers

10-56.
$F_{(1, 11)} = 129.525$, $t_{(11)} = 11.381$; $t^2 = F$

10-58.
$F_{(1, 43)} = 136.19$; reject H_0

10-60.
$F_{(1, 20)} = 0.385$; accept H_0

10-9 Residual Analysis and Checking for Model Inadequacies

Recall our discussion of statistical models in section 10-1. We said that a good statistical model accounts for the systematic movement in the process, leaving out a series of uncorrelated, purely random errors, ϵ, which are assumed to be normally distributed with mean zero and a constant variance, σ^2. In Figure 10-3, we saw a general methodology for statistical model building, consisting of model identification, estimation, tests of validity, and, finally, use of the model. We are now at the third stage of the analysis of a simple linear regression model: examining the residuals and testing the validity of the model.

Analysis of the residuals could reveal whether or not the assumption of normally distributed errors holds. In addition, the analysis could reveal whether the variance of the errors is indeed constant, that is, whether the spread of the data around the regression line is uniform. The analysis could also indicate whether or not there are any missing variables that should have been included in our model (leading to a multiple regression equation). The analysis may reveal whether the order of data collection (for example, time of observation) has any effect on the data and whether the order should have been incorporated as a variable in the model. Finally, analysis of the residuals may determine whether or not the assumption that the errors are uncorrelated is satisfied. A test of this assumption, the Durbin-Watson test, entails more than a mere examination of the model residuals, and discussion of this test is postponed until the next chapter. We now describe some graphical methods for the examination of the model residuals that may lead to discovery of model inadequacies.

A Check for the Equality of Variance of the Errors

A graph of the regression errors, the residuals, versus the independent variable X, or versus the predicted values $\hat{Y}$, will reveal whether or not the variance of the errors is constant. The variance of the residuals is indicated by the width of the scatter plot of the residuals as X increases. If the width of the scatter plot of the residuals either increases or decreases as X increases, then the assumption of constant variance is not met. This problem is called **heteroscedasticity.** When heteroscedasticity exists, we cannot use the ordinary least-squares method for estimating the regression and should use a more complex method called *generalized least squares*. Figure 10–21 shows how a plot of the residuals versus X or $\hat{Y}$ looks in the case of heteroscedasticity. Figure 10–22 shows a residual plot in a good regression, with no heteroscedasticity.

FIGURE 10–21 A Residual Plot Indicating Heteroscedasticity

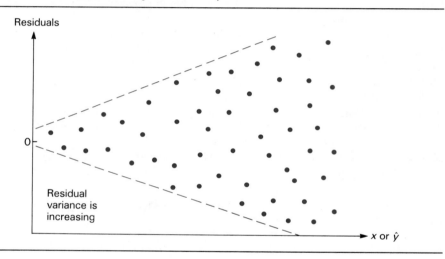

FIGURE 10–22 A Residual Plot Indicating No Heteroscedasticity

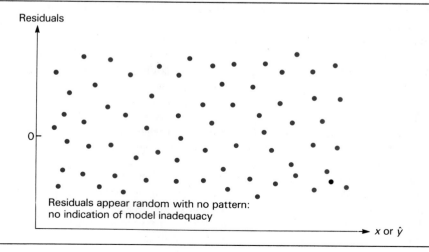

Testing for Missing Variables

Figure 10–22 also shows how the residuals should look when plotted against time (or the order in which data are collected). There should be no trend in the residuals when plotted versus time. A linear trend in the residuals as plotted versus time is shown in Figure 10–23.

If the residuals exhibit a pattern when plotted versus time, then time should be incorporated as an explanatory variable in the model in addition to X. The same is true for any other variable against which we may plot the residuals: if there is any trend in the plot, the variable should be included in our model along with X. Incorporating additional variables leads to a multiple regression model.

Detecting a Curvilinear Relationship between Y and X

If the relationship between X and Y is curved, "forcing" a straight line to fit the data will result in a poor fit. This is shown in Figure 10–24. In this case, the residuals are at first large and negative, then decrease, become positive, and then again become negative. The residuals are not random and independent; they show curvature. This pattern appears in a plot of the residuals versus X, shown in Figure 10–25.

The situation can be corrected by adding the variable X^2 to the model. This also entails the techniques of multiple regression analysis. We note that, in cases where we have repeated Y observations at some levels of X, there is a statistical test for model lack of fit such as that shown in Figure 10–24. The test entails decomposing the sum of squares for error into a component due to lack of fit and a component due to pure error. This gives rise to an F test for lack of fit. This test is described in advanced texts. We point out, however, that examination of the residuals is an excellent tool for detecting such model deficiencies, and this simple technique does not require the special data format needed for the formal test.

FIGURE 10–23 A Residual Plot Indicating a Trend with Time

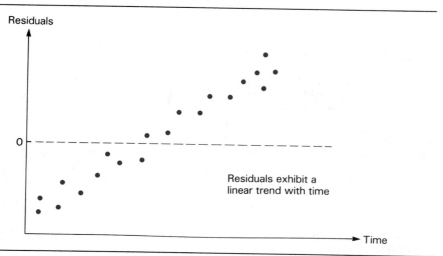

FIGURE 10–24 The Results of Forcing a Straight Line to Fit a Curved Data Set

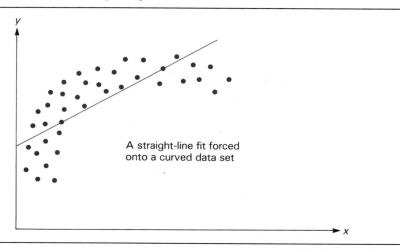

FIGURE 10–25 The Resulting Pattern of the Residuals When a Straight Line Is Forced to Fit a Curved Data Set

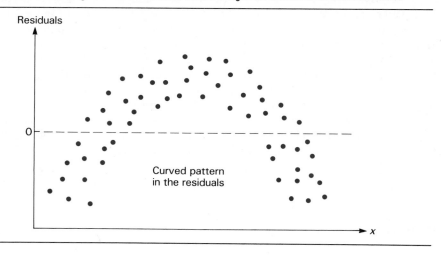

Detecting Deviations from the Normal Distribution Assumption

FIGURE 10–26
Approximately Normally
Distributed Residuals as Plotted
on Probability Scale

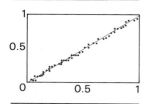

When trying to detect deviations from the normal distribution assumption by use of residual plots, we need to plot the regression residuals on a special "probability paper" scale. Such paper is available in stationery stores. However, if we run the regression on a computer, we may include a command that will produce a residual plot on the required scale. When plotted on a probability-paper scale, *the residuals should form a straight diagonal line*. Serious deviations from the line indicate that the residuals are not approximately normally distributed. An example of approximately normally distributed residuals is shown in Figure 10–26.

It may also be useful to plot *standardized* residuals, that is, the residuals divided by their (sample) standard deviation. (The mean of the residuals should be zero, so we need not subtract it when forming the standardized residuals.) The computer will standardize the residuals upon request. A histogram of the residuals should look similar to a normal curve. In section 10–11, we will see residual plots for the American Express example.

10–62. For each of the following plots of regression residuals versus X, state if there is any indication of model inadequacy, and if so, which inadequacy.

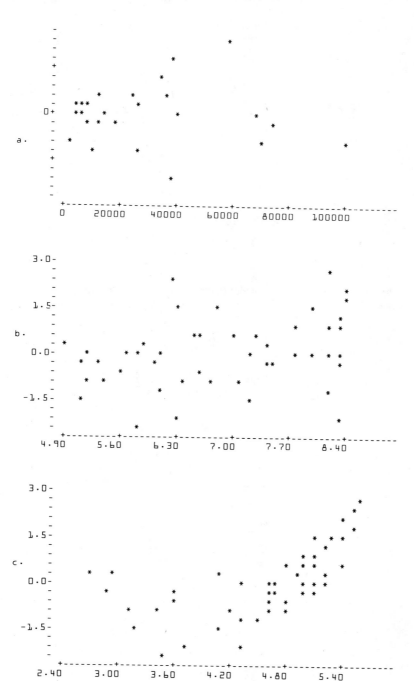

10–63.   In the following plots of the residuals versus time of observation, state if there is evidence of model inadequacy. How would you correct any inadequacy?

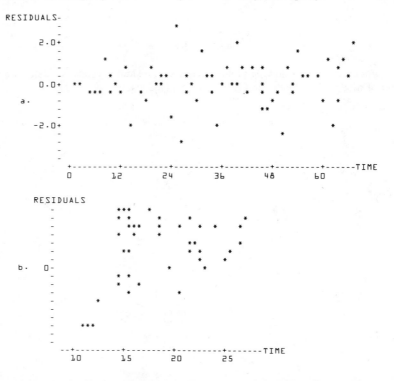

10–64.   Is there any indication of model inadequacy in the following plots of residuals on a normal probability scale?

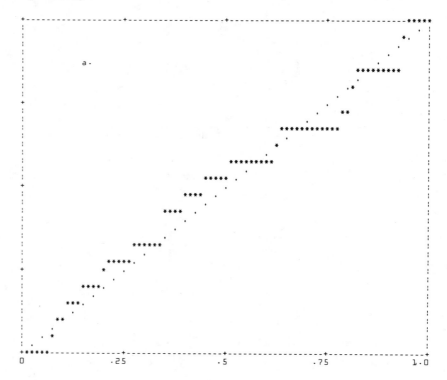

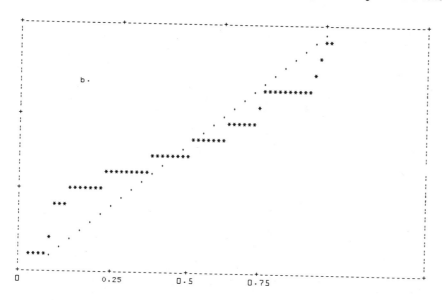

10–65. Produce residual plots for the regression of problem 10–11. Is there any apparent model inadequacy?

10–66. Repeat problem 10–65 for the regression of problem 10–14.

10–67. Repeat problem 10–65 for the regression of problem 10–16.

10–10 Use of the Regression Model for Prediction

As mentioned in the introduction of this chapter, there are several possible uses of a regression model. One is to understand the relationship between the two variables. As with correlation analysis, understanding a relationship between two variables in regression does not imply that one variable causes the other. Causality is a much more complicated issue and cannot be determined by a simple regression analysis.

A more common use of a regression analysis is *prediction:* providing estimates of values of the dependent variable by using the prediction equation: $\hat{Y} = b_0 + b_1 X$. It is important that prediction be done in the region of the data used in the estimation process. *You should be aware that using a regression for extrapolating outside the estimation range is risky, as the estimated relationship may not be appropriate outside this range.* This is demonstrated in Figure 10–27.

Point Predictions

It is very easy to produce point predictions using the estimated regression equation. All we need to do is substitute the value of X for which we want to predict Y into the prediction equation. In Example (a), suppose that American Express wants to predict charges on the card for a member who traveled 4,000 miles during a period equal to the one studied (note that $x = 4,000$ is in the range of X values used in the estimation). We use the prediction equation, equation 10–12, but with higher accuracy for b_1:

$$\hat{y} = 274.85 + 1.2553x = 274.85 + 1.2553(4,000) = 5,296.05 \text{ (dollars)}$$

The process of prediction in this example is demonstrated in Figure 10–28.

FIGURE 10–27 The Danger of Extrapolation

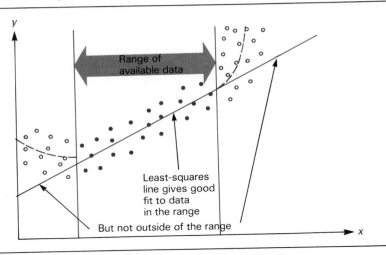

FIGURE 10–28 Prediction in American Express Study

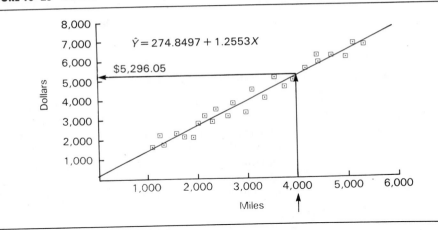

Prediction Intervals

Point predictions are not perfect and are subject to error. The error is due to the uncertainty in estimation as well as the natural variation of points about the regression line. A $(1 - \alpha)100\%$ prediction interval for Y is given in equation 10–32.

A $(1 - \alpha)100\%$ prediction interval for Y:

$$\hat{y} \pm t_{\alpha/2}s\sqrt{1 + \frac{1}{n} + \frac{(x - \overline{x})^2}{SS_x}} \qquad (10\text{–}32)$$

As can be seen from the formula, the width of the interval depends on the distance

FIGURE 10–29 Prediction Band and Its Width

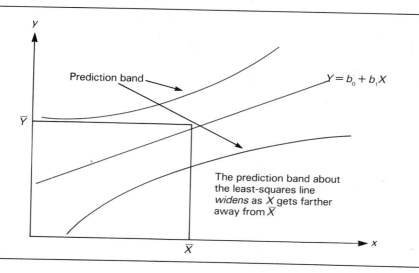

of our value x (for which we wish to predict Y) from the mean, $\bar{x}$. This is shown in Figure 10–29.

We will now use equation 10–32 to compute a 95% prediction interval for the amount charged on the American Express card by a member who traveled 4,000 miles. We know that in this example, $\bar{x} = \Sigma\, x/n = 79{,}448/25 = 3{,}177.92$. We also know that $SS_x = 40{,}947{,}557.84$ and $s = 318.16$. From Appendix C, Table 3 we get the critical point for t with 23 degrees of freedom: 2.069. Applying equation 10–32, we get:

$$5{,}296.05 \pm (2.069)(318.16)\sqrt{1 + 1/25 + (4{,}000 - 3{,}177.92)^2/40{,}947{,}557.84}$$
$$= 5{,}296.05 \pm 676.62 = [4{,}619.43,\ 5{,}972.67]$$

Based on the validity of the study, we are 95% confident that a cardholder who traveled 4,000 miles during a period of the given length will have charges on his or her card totaling anywhere from $4,619.43 to $5,972.67. What about the *average* total charge of all cardholders who traveled 4,000 miles? This is $E(Y \mid x = 4{,}000)$. The point estimate of $E(Y \mid x = 4{,}000)$ is also equal to $\hat{Y}$, but the confidence interval for this quantity is different.

A Confidence Interval for the Average Y, Given a Particular Value of X

We may compute a confidence interval for $E(Y \mid X)$, the expected value of Y for a given X. Here the variation is smaller because we are dealing with the average Y for a given X, rather than a particular Y. Thus, the confidence interval is narrower than a prediction interval of the same confidence level. The confidence interval for $E(Y \mid X)$ is given in equation 10–33.

A $(1 - \alpha)100\%$ confidence interval for $E(Y \mid X)$:

$$\hat{y} \pm t_{\alpha/2}\, s\sqrt{\frac{1}{n} + \frac{(x - \bar{x})^2}{SS_x}} \qquad (10\text{–}33)$$

The confidence band for $E(Y|X)$ around the regression line looks like Figure 10–29 except that the band is narrower. The standard error of the estimator of the conditional mean, $E(Y|X)$, is smaller than the standard error of the predicted Y. Therefore, the 1 is missing from the square root quantity in equation 10–33 as compared with equation 10–32.

For the American Express example, let us now compute a 95% confidence interval for $E(Y|x = 4,000)$. Applying equation 10–33, we have:

$$5,296.05 \pm (2.069)(318.16)\sqrt{1/25 + (4,000 - 3,177.92)^2/40,947,557.84} =$$
$$5,296.05 \pm 156.48 = [5,139.57, 5,452.53]$$

Being a confidence interval for a conditional mean, the interval is much narrower than the prediction interval, which has the same confidence level for covering *any given* observation at the level of X.

PROBLEMS

Answers

10–68.
———
[5,854.4, 7,248.3]

10–70.
———
[5,605.75, 7,496.95]

10–72.
———
[7.793, 8.089]

10–74.
———
[631.513, 1,425.903]

10–68. For the American Express example, give a 95% prediction interval for the amount charged by a member who traveled 5,000 miles. Compare the result with the one for $x = 4,000$ miles.

10–69. Give a 95% confidence interval for $E(Y|x = 5,000)$ in the American Express example. Compare with your answer to problem 10–68.

10–70. For problem 10–68, give a 99% prediction interval.

10–71. For problem 10–11, give a point prediction and a 99% prediction interval for the prime lending rate when the federal funds rate is 6.5%.

10–72. For problem 10–71, give a 99% confidence interval for the average prime lending rate when the federal funds rate is 6.5%.

10–73. For problem 10–16, give a 95% confidence interval for the average cost incurred by patients who stay in the hospital for five days.

10–74. For problem 10–16, give a 95% prediction interval for the cost incurred by a patient who will stay in the hospital for five days.

10–11   Using the Computer

All commonly used statistical packages have regression capabilities. In fact, most advanced calculators can do simple linear regression. In this section, we present a complete computer solution to Example (a) using the MINITAB package.

We enter the data in two columns: miles in column C1 and dollars in column C2. We then name the variables accordingly.

The regression command in MINITAB is very simple:

```
REGRESS (name of dependent variable, or column) ON 1 PREDICTOR (
name of independent variable, or column)
```

If we add a number of another column, such as C3, the computer will put the standardized residuals in that column. If we add the name of another column, such as C4, the computer will put the fitted values (the predicted values of Y for all data points) in that column.

There are also possible subcommands, separated from the main command and from each other by semicolons. The last subcommand must end with a period. One subcommand we use here is RESIDUALS, followed by a column number—here, C5. This will allow us to plot the residuals versus X and versus the fitted values ($\hat{Y}$).

Another subcommand we use is PREDICT, followed by the value of X for which we want a prediction of Y. (We predict Y for $x = \$4,000$.) The prediction gives us a 95% confidence interval for $E(Y \mid X)$ and a 95% prediction interval, along with the point prediction. The command PLOT (variable name or column number) versus (variable name or column number) produces the required plot.

The MINITAB commands and the output are given in Figure 10–30. Note that in the residual plots, there is no evidence of any model inadequacy. Look at all the results: parameter estimates, r^2 (the "adjusted r^2" will be explained in the next chapter), ANOVA table, and the predicted value with its intervals. Compare the results with what we obtained throughout the chapter.

We end this section with a cautionary note. Computer programs allow you to run a regression with no intercept, no "constant." This is a dangerous thing to do. Even if the situation tends to imply that Y should be zero when X is zero (no profit for zero investment, for example), it still is not a good practice to follow. This is so because our data set may not extend to the range of values containing zero, and the relationship may be different in that region (not a continuation of the straight line). If we do force the regression to go through zero, our least-squares estimates may be poor. This is demonstrated in Figure 10–31.

10–12   Summary and Review of Terms

In this chapter, we introduced simple linear regression, a technique for estimating the straight-line relationship between two variables. We defined the **dependent variable** as the variable we wish to predict by, or understand the relation with, the **independent variable** (also called the **explanatory,** or **predictor** variable). We described the **least squares** estimation procedure as the procedure that produces the **best linear unbiased estimators (BLUE)** of the regression coefficients, the **slope** and **intercept** parameters. We learned how to conduct two statistical tests for the existence of a linear relationship between the two variables: the t test and the F test. We noted that in the case of simple linear regression, the two tests are equivalent. We saw how to evaluate the fit of the regression model by considering the **coefficient of determination,** r^2. We learned how to check the validity of the assumptions of the simple linear regression model by examining the **residuals.** Finally, we saw how the regression model can be used for *prediction*. In addition, we discussed a linear **correlation** model. We saw that the correlation model is appropriate when the two variables are viewed in a symmetric role: both being normally distributed random variables, rather than one of them (X) being considered nonrandom, as in regression analysis.

ADDITIONAL PROBLEMS

10–75.   The computer output for a simple linear regression of sales of one product versus sales of another product includes the following: $n = 128$, SSE = 3,343, SSR = 45,678. Compute the remaining sum of squares, the mean squares, the F ratio, and the coefficient of determination. Write an ANOVA table for this regression. What can you say about the relationship between sales of the two products?

10–76.   A real estate agent is looking for a single independent variable to explain the variation in property values in a certain metropolitan area as much as possible. The analyst runs two separate simple linear regression models: model 1—property value (Y) versus distance from the center of town (X); model 2—property values (Y) versus area affluence (X). The first regression analysis gives: SSE = 546, SSR = 1,756. The second regression includes the

Answers

10–76.

Model 1: $r^2 = 0.763$
Model 2: $r^2 = 0.502$
Model 1 is better.

FIGURE 10–30   MINITAB Analysis of the American Express Example

```
MTB > REGRESS 'DOLLARS' ON 1 PREDICTOR 'MILES' TRES IN C3 FITS IN C4;
SUBC>     PREDICT 4000:
SUBC>     RESIDUALS IN C5.

The regression equation is
dollars = 275 + 1.26 miles

Predictor        Coef        Stdev      t-ratio         p
Constant        274.8        170.3         1.61     0.120
miles         1.25533      0.04972        25.25     0.000

s = 318.2        R-sq = 96.5%     R-sq(adj) = 96.4%

Analysis of Variance

SOURCE          DF          SS          MS          F          p
Regression       1    65427736    65427736     634.60     0.000
Error           23     2328161      101224
Total           24    66855896

      Fig   Stdev.Fit         95% C.I.          95% P.I.
   5296.2        75.6   ( 5139.7, 5452.7)   ( 4619.5, 5972.8)

    MTB > name c3 'stres', c4 'fits', c5 'resids'
    MTB > plot 'resids' vs 'fits'


    resids -
           -
           -                                                 *
      350+      *                  *        *
           -                   *
           -                         *
           -         *                 *
        0+     *                  *              *
           -       *                              *    *
           -
           -              *        *           *
     -350+                                 *        *
           -                 *
           -
           -
     -700+
           ----+---------+---------+---------+---------+---------+--fits
             2000      3000      4000      5000      6000      7000
    MTB > plot 'resids' vs 'miles'


    resids -
           -
           -      *                        *        *          *
      350+                       *
           -                  *
           -            *           *                        *
           -                                     *    *   *
        0+     *                                    *
           -        *
           -
           -                 *                   *
     -350+           *            *        *    *              *
           -
           -          *
           -                           *
     -700+
           --------+---------+---------+---------+---------+--------miles
               1600      2400      3200      4000      4800
    MTB > histogram of 'stres'

    Histogram of stress    N = 25
```

FIGURE 10–30 *(concluded)*

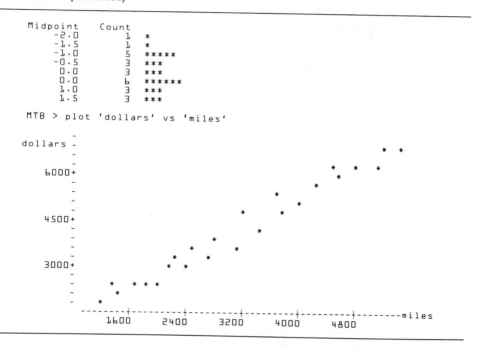

```
Midpoint    Count
    -2.0        1    *
    -1.5        1    *
    -1.0        5    *****
    -0.5        3    ***
     0.0        3    ***
     0.0        6    ******
     1.0        3    ***
     1.5        3    ***

MTB > plot 'dollars' vs 'miles'
```

FIGURE 10–31 The Danger in Forcing the Regression to Go through the Origin

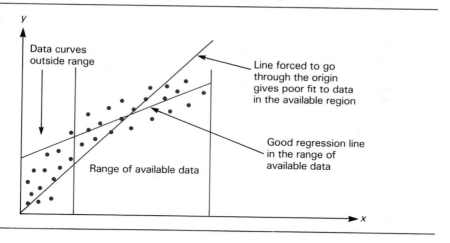

results: SSR = 1,178, SST = 2,345. Which single variable explains more of the variation in property values?

10–77. Recently, interest has centered on the relationship between foreign economic growth and the decline in U.S. exports.[11] A regression of these two variables using a sample of 23 months gave the following results: SSE = 5,432.87, SST = 87,695.98. Conduct the F test for the existence of a linear relationship between the two variables.

---

[11] *Economic Trends, Business Week* (February 4, 1991), p. 20.

Answers

10–78.   An economist conducts a regression analysis of a country's foreign exchange rate versus the country's current money supply. The results of the simple linear regression of 60 monthly observations (five years of data) are: $\Sigma x = 0.0046$, $\Sigma y = 0.5108$, $\Sigma xy = -0.0082$, $\Sigma x^2 = 0.0102$, $\Sigma y^2 = 0.076$. Carry out the required regression calculations. Would you use this regression for predicting the exchange rate? Would you use these results for understanding the effect of the money supply on local exchange rates? Explain.

10–79.   The amount of money a manufacturer is willing to pay for shipping its goods is believed to be inversely related to the length of time the goods are in transit. A shipping company analyst carries out a simple linear regression analysis of the time in transit (X) versus shipping costs (Y) and obtains: $b_1 = -3.453$, $s(b_1) = 0.987$. Conduct the t test for the existence of a linear relationship between shipping costs and length of transit time. From this information, can you also give the F statistic value? (The sample size is $n = 16$ transatlantic crossings.)

10–80.   A retail outlet selling yarn and fabric in California is interested in the relationship between sales of the two product lines. A data set of 16 weekly observations on sales of the two product lines is collected, and the sample correlation coefficient is computed: $r = 0.16$. Conduct a statistical test of whether or not sales of the two product lines are correlated.

10–81.   A computer software manufacturer wants to study the relationship between the number of microcomputers in use in different areas and the number of software packages the company sells in the areas. A simple linear regression analysis of 21 geographical regions reveals the following: $b_0 = 12.43$, $b_1 = 1.076$, $s(b_0) = 13.65$, $s(b_1) = 0.083$, SSE $=$ 1,076.11, $SS_X = 72.641$, $\bar{x} = 12,453$ computers. Using this information, construct 95% confidence intervals for the regression parameters β_0 and β_1, a 95% confidence interval for the *average* number of software packages sold in an area where 10,000 computers are in use, and a 95% prediction interval for the number of packages sold in that area.

10–82.   The management of an international hotel chain is in the process of evaluating the possible sites for a new unit on a beach resort. As part of the analysis, the management is interested in evaluating the relationship between the distance of a hotel from the beach (X) and the hotel's average occupancy rate for the season (Y). A sample of 14 existing hotels in the area is chosen, and each hotel reports its average occupancy rate. The management records the hotel's distance (in miles) from the beach. The following table presents the obtained data. Carry out a complete regression analysis of this data. If building the new hotel is feasible only if the average occupancy rate will be at least 75% during a season, what is the farthest distance from the beach for a possible site of the new hotel?

Distance (miles): 0.1 0.1 0.2 0.3 0.4 0.4 0.5 0.6 0.7 0.7 0.8 0.8 0.9 0.9
Occupancy(%): 92 95 96 90 89 86 90 83 85 80 78 76 72 75

10–83.   A car rental agency is interested in studying the relationship between the mileage of their subcompact cars (X) and the monthly maintenance cost for the cars (Y). Following are data on 15 randomly chosen cars. Carry out a simple linear regression analysis of the relationship between the two variables. What is the expected monthly maintenance cost for a car with 13,000 miles?

Miles (in thousands): 6 7 8 9 10 11 12 13 14 15 16 17 18 19 20
Cost (dollars): 13 16 15 20 19 21 26 24 30 32 30 35 34 40 39

10–84.   (This is a difficult problem.) A financial analyst carried out a regression analysis of the relationship between returns on a stock and a certain characteristic of the stockholders. A sample of 6,154 stockholders was obtained, and the regression results revealed: $r^2 = 0.008$, F ratio $= 12.56$. Explain.

---

[12]"Variety Entertainment Composite," *Variety* (March 25, 1991), p. 1.

10–85. The following data, reprinted by permission from *Variety*, report weekly values (Oct. 5, 1990, to March 22, 1991) of the Entertainment Stock Index versus values of Standard & Poor's 500 Index.[12] Run a complete regression analysis on these data, and report your results in the form of a memorandum to the director of a mutual fund specializing in entertainment stocks.

Answer

Entertainment Stocks	S&P 500	Entertainment Stocks	S&P 500
179.4	367.5	160.6	331.8
180.8	373.6	157.8	326.8
190.1	375.0	156.4	327.8
185.1	370.5	153.6	322.2
181.5	365.7	146.9	315.1
182.6	369.0	145.4	317.1
176.5	359.4	140.1	313.7
171.5	343.1	132.7	311.9
161.2	336.1	134.5	304.7
159.5	332.2	135.2	312.5
150.8	315.2	132.3	300.0
156.1	321.0	144.5	311.5
158.5	328.7		

10–86. The following data, reprinted by permission from *The Economist*, report annual industrial production and gross national product figures for 13 industrial countries.[13] Run a regression analysis of these data aimed at constructing a prediction equation of GNP on industrial production for industrialized nations.

10–86.

GNP = 1.78 + 0.391 production

	Industrial Production	GNP
Australia	−1.5	+0.6
Belgium	+5.0	+4.0
Canada	−6.6	−1.0
France	+0.7	+1.8
Germany	+5.2	+4.5
Holland	+3.9	+3.4
Italy	−5.3	+1.8
Japan	+7.3	+4.7
Spain	−0.7	+3.7
Sweden	−3.4	−0.5
Switzerland	+3.6	+1.7
UK	−3.8	−1.3
USA	−2.6	+0.4

[13] "Economic and Financial Indicators," *The Economist* (March 30, 1991), p. 93.

THE JANUARY INDICATOR

*I*t has been suggested that January is a good indicator of the behavior of the stock market during the entire year. The following data set consists of the changes in stocks in the Standard & Poor's 500 Index during January and the corresponding changes in the same index for the entire year. Data are for the years 1950 to 1987. (Data are obtained from the Hirsch Organization, Inc.)

	January Change	Yearly Change
1950	1.7%	21.8%
1951	6.1%	16.5%
1952	1.6%	11.8%
1953	− 0.7%	− 6.6%
1954	5.1%	45.0%
1955	1.8%	26.4%
1956	− 3.6%	2.6%
1957	− 4.2%	−14.3%
1958	4.3%	38.1%
1959	0.4%	8.5%
1960	− 7.1%	− 3.0%
1961	6.3%	23.1%
1962	− 3.8%	−11.8%
1963	4.9%	18.9%
1964	2.7%	13.0%
1965	3.3%	9.1%
1966	0.5%	−13.1%
1967	7.8%	20.1%
1968	− 4.4%	7.7%
1969	− 0.8%	−11.4%
1970	− 7.6%	0.1%
1971	4.0%	10.8%
1972	1.8%	15.6%
1973	− 1.7%	−17.4%
1974	− 1.0%	−29.7%
1975	12.3%	31.5%
1976	11.8%	19.1%
1977	− 5.1%	−11.5%
1978	− 6.2%	1.1%
1979	4.0%	12.3%
1980	5.8%	25.8%
1981	− 4.6%	− 9.7%
1982	− 1.8%	14.8%
1983	3.3%	17.3%
1984	− 0.9%	1.4%
1985	7.4%	26.0%
1986	0.5%	14.9%
1987	13.2%	2.0%

Conduct an analysis of the reported data, and answer the following questions.

1. Do you believe that January can serve as a predictor of the stock market's performance? Explain.

2. How confident are you of your answer to question 1?

3. In January 1988, the Standard & Poor's 500 Index increased by 4%. Predict the performance of the index for the entire year. Also give a 95% prediction interval.

4. What percentage of the variation in the yearly performance of the Standard & Poor's 500 Index can be explained by the performance of this index in January? Explain the relevance of this percentage (note that January and the year use the same baseline in computing the index).

MULTIPLE REGRESSION

INTRODUCTION

I n regression analysis, it often happens that the variable of interest depends on more than just one other variable. There may be several independent variables that contain information about the variable we are trying to predict or understand. In such cases, it may be worthwhile to formulate a model that allows us to consider the relation of our variable of interest with a set of independent variables. In the American Express example of Chapter 10, the company may be able to more accurately predict the amount charged on the American Express card from knowledge of cardholders' incomes, in addition to miles traveled. When several independent variables are included in a regression equation, our model is called a **multiple regression** model.

How many independent variables should we include in our regression equation? It seems logical that if our equation incorporates information about as many variables as possible, we will have maximum prediction power of the variable of interest. There are, however, some serious limitations to this assertion.

In the summer of 1983, a student of economics had an idea about predicting the nation's economic future. The student decided to collect data on as many economic variables as possible and to formulate a multiple regression equation linking these variables with the gross national product (GNP). The student thought that if the number of variables used was large enough, he would be able to predict the GNP with great accuracy. The student collected 12 years' worth of quarterly data, 48 observations total, and information on 47 economic variables: national income, prime lending rate, unemployment rate, etc., corresponding to the 48 quarters for which GNP values were known. He formulated the regression relation: $Y = \beta_0 + \beta_1 X_1 + \beta_2 X_2 + \beta_3 X_3 + \cdots + \beta_{47} X_{47} + \epsilon$.

In the next section, we will see that this equation is a generalization to k variables (in this case, $k = 47$) of the population regression equation with one variable, introduced in Chapter 10. The student went on to carry out an estimation of the model parameters β_0 to β_{47} using a computer and to compute the multiple coefficient of determination, denoted R^2. (The coefficient R^2 is an extension to multiple regression of the coefficient of determination, r^2, in simple linear regression. This coefficient is a measure of how well the regression equation fits the data.) To his great delight, the student noted that the value of R^2 for his regression was 0.9999. The regression equation apparently had a perfect fit with the data! The student was sure, therefore, that he would be able to predict the GNP from knowledge of the 47 variables with great accuracy. As it turned out, not only were model predictions very poor—the forecasts produced from the model were worse than pure guesses of the GNP[1]—but the model was deemed erroneous, misleading, and in violation of statistical methodology. Why?

---

[1] There are statistical methods for evaluating how good a prediction is, once the actual values become known. These methods consist of looking at the difference between forecast and actuality. Methods of evaluating forecast accuracy will be discussed in the next chapter.

Continued on next page

Recall that in Chapter 10, we said that a good statistical model fits the data well but is also parsimonious, that is, has as few parameters as possible. At the time, you may have wondered why a model should be parsimonious; you may have reasoned that the more parameters in your model, the better the model. Examine Figure 11–1, which demonstrates an important mathematical fact. Given any two points, it is possible to find a one-dimensional surface, a straight line, that will pass through the two points and fit the two points perfectly. Once a third point is obtained, it may not lie on the straight line connecting the original two points. Thus, the line—though providing a perfect fit for two points—may be a poor *predictor* of future observations. With three points, however, we can always find a two-dimensional surface, a plane, that will pass through the three points and thus provide a perfect fit. When a fourth point is added, the point may not lie on the original plane. With four points, we can find a three-dimensional surface (a surface of more than two dimensions is called a *hyperplane*) that will provide a perfect fit. Add a fifth point, and a three-dimensional surface is not enough, but a four-dimensional surface will provide a perfect fit. Thus, given n points, we can find an $(n - 1)$-dimensional surface that will provide a perfect fit for the data. When we do this, however, we are not doing statistics. We are overfitting our data. This procedure leaves no degrees of freedom for error.

Remember that in simple linear regression, there are $n - 2$ degrees of freedom for error. This is so because there are two parameters to be estimated from the data—an intercept and a slope. In a multiple regression model with k variables, there are $k + 1$ parameters to be estimated from the data set—one slope parameter for each of the k variables, and an intercept. Hence, the degrees of freedom for error in a multiple regression model with k independent variables are $n - (k + 1)$. Our student, fitting a regression model with $k = 47$ variables to a data set of $n = 48$ points, is left with $n - (k + 1) = 48 - (47 + 1) = 0$ degrees of freedom for error! This means that there is no allowance for error whatsoever. The model tracks the data, adding a dimension to the regression surface for each data point. The model does not allow for any chance variation. Since real-world data always have some chance variation, future observations do not follow such an overfitted model. Recall that a statistical model should capture as much as possible of the *systematic* move-

FIGURE 11–1   The Dimensionality of Surfaces Fitting Two, Three, and Four Points

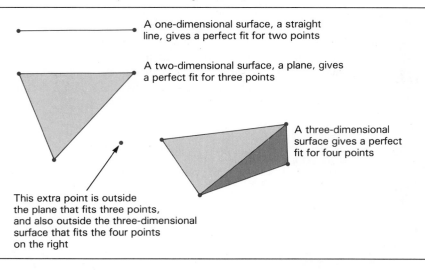

A one-dimensional surface, a straight line, gives a perfect fit for two points

A two-dimensional surface, a plane, gives a perfect fit for three points

A three-dimensional surface gives a perfect fit for four points

This extra point is outside the plane that fits three points, and also outside the three-dimensional surface that fits the four points on the right

FIGURE 11-2 Overfitting a Data Set with a 15-Degree Polynomial

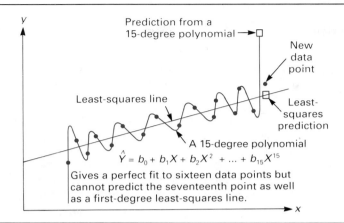

Prediction from a
15-degree polynomial →□

New data point

Least-squares line

Least-squares prediction

A 15-degree polynomial
$\hat{Y} = b_0 + b_1X + b_2X^2 + \ldots + b_{15}X^{15}$
Gives a perfect fit to sixteen data points but cannot predict the seventeenth point as well as a first-degree least-squares line.

ment within the data set, leaving out pure errors—variation due to chance. An overfitted model forces the regression surface to go through every point. This is why the R^2 coefficient is high: the error part of the regression is forced to zero. (The R^2 in the student's model was actually 1.00; the computer-reported value 0.9999 is due to rounding in the computations.)

The idea of overfitting can be seen another way. Multiple regression includes a technique called *polynomial regression*. In polynomial regression, we regress a dependent variable Y on powers of the independent variables. Each power of a variable, say, X_1^2, is considered an independent variable in its own right. For example, a fourth-degree polynomial regression in X is modeled as: $Y = \beta_0 + \beta_1 X + \beta_2 X^2 + \beta_3 X^3 + \beta_4 X^4 + \epsilon$. This is treated as a four-variable regression equation. Overfitting in this context is shown in Figure 11-2.

As shown in the figure, a 15-degree polynomial provides a perfect fit to a set of 16 data points (here again, df for error $= 16 - (15 + 1) = 0$). The prediction of a new data point using this model is worse than the prediction provided by a one-degree model—a least-squares line. The line captures the systematic trend in the data, leaving the rest of the movements within the data to error. In this case, the straight line is a good statistical model, while the 15-degree polynomial—analogous to the model proposed by the student—is not. In the next section, we will formally develop the multiple regression model with k independent variables. ∎

11-2 The *k*-Variable Multiple Regression Model

The population regression model of a dependent variable, Y, on a set of k independent variables, $X_1, X_2, \ldots, X_k$, is given by:

$$Y = \beta_0 + \beta_1 X_1 + \beta_2 X_2 + \cdots + \beta_k X_k + \epsilon \qquad (11-1)$$

where β_0 is the Y-intercept of the regression surface and each $\beta_i, i = 1, \ldots, k$, is the slope of the regression surface—sometimes called the **response surface**—with respect to variable X_i

As with the simple linear regression model, we have some assumptions.

Model assumptions:

1. For each observation, the error term, ϵ, is normally distributed with mean zero and standard deviation σ and is independent of the error terms associated with all other observations. That is:

$$\epsilon_j \sim N(0, \sigma^2) \text{ for all } j = 1, 2, \ldots, n, \qquad (11\text{--}2)$$

independent of other errors.[2]

2. In the context of regression analysis, the variables X_i are considered *fixed quantities*, although in the context of correlational analysis, they are random variables. In any case, X_i *are independent of the error term*, ϵ. When we assume that X_i are fixed quantities, we are assuming that we have realizations of k variables X_i and that the only randomness in Y comes from the error term, ϵ.

For a case with $k = 2$ variables, the response surface is a plane in three dimensions (the dimensions are Y, X_1, and X_2). The plane is the surface of average response $E(Y)$ for any combination of the two variables X_1 and X_2. The response surface is given by the equation for $E(Y)$, which is the expected value of equation 11–1 with two independent variables. The expected value of Y gives the value 0 to the error term, ϵ. The equations for Y and $E(Y)$ in the case of regression with two independent variables are as follows.

$$Y = \beta_0 + \beta_1 X_1 + \beta_2 X_2 + \epsilon \qquad (11\text{--}3)$$
$$E(Y) = \beta_0 + \beta_1 X_1 + \beta_2 X_2 \qquad (11\text{--}4)$$

These are equations analogous to the case of simple linear regression. Here, instead of a regression line, we have a regression plane. Some values of Y (that is, combinations of the X_i variables times their coefficients, β_i, and the errors, ϵ) are shown in Figure 11–3. The figure also shows the response surface, the plane corresponding to equation 11–4.

We estimate the regression parameters of equation 11–3 by the method of least squares. This is an extension of the procedure used in simple linear regression. In the case of two independent variables where the population model is equation 11–3, we need to estimate an equation of a plane that will minimize the sum of the squared errors, $(Y - \hat{Y})^2$, over the entire data set of n points. The method is extendable to any k independent variables. In the case of $k = 2$, there are three normal equations, and their solutions are the least-squares estimators b_0, b_1, and b_2. These are estimators of the Y-intercept, the slope of the plane with respect to X_1, and the slope of the plane with respect to X_2. The normal equations for $k = 2$ are as follows.

FIGURE 11–3
A Two-Dimensional Response Surface $E(Y) = \beta_0 + \beta_1 X_1 + \beta_1 X_2$ and Some Points

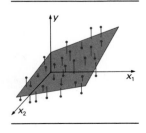

---

[2] The multiple regression model is valid under less restrictive assumptions than these. The assumption of normality of the errors allows us to perform t tests and F tests of model validity. Also, all we need is that the errors are *uncorrelated* with each other. However, normal distribution + noncorrelation = independence.

The normal equations for the case of two independent variables:

$$\sum y = nb_0 + b_1 \sum x_1 + b_2 \sum x_2$$

$$\sum x_1 y = b_0 \sum x_1 + b_1 \sum x_1^2 + b_2 \sum x_1 x_2$$

$$\sum x_2 y = b_0 \sum x_2 + b_1 \sum x_1 x_2 + b_2 \sum x_2^2 \qquad (11\text{--}5)$$

When the various sums, $\sum y$, $\sum x_1$, and the other sums and products, are entered into these equations, it is possible to solve the three equations for the three unknowns b_0, b_1, and b_2. These computations are always done by computer, and, therefore, you need not worry about them. We will, however, demonstrate the solution of equations 11–5 with a simple example.

Alka-Seltzer recently embarked on an in-store promotional campaign, with displays of its antacid featured prominently in supermarkets. The company also ran its usual radio and television commercials. Over a period of 10 weeks, the company kept track of its expenditure on radio and television advertising, variable X_1, as well as its spending on in-store displays, variable X_2. The resulting sales for each week in the area studied were recorded as the dependent variable, Y. The company analyst conducting the study hypothesized a linear regression model of the form

$$Y = \beta_0 + \beta_1 X_1 + \beta_2 X_2 + \epsilon$$

linking sales volume with the two independent variables, advertising and in-store promotions. The analyst wanted to use the available data, considered a random sample of 10 weekly observations, to estimate the parameters of the regression relationship.

EXAMPLE (a)

Table 11–1 gives the data for this study in terms of Y, X_1, and X_2, all in thousands of dollars. The table also gives additional columns of products and squares of data values needed for the solution of the normal equations. These columns are $X_1 X_2$,

SOLUTION

TABLE 11–1 The Various Quantities Needed for the Solution of the Normal Equations for Example (a) (Numbers Are in Thousands of Dollars)

Y	X_1	X_2	$X_1 X_2$	X_1^2	X_2^2	$X_1 Y$	$X_2 Y$
72	12	5	60	144	25	864	360
76	11	8	88	121	64	836	608
78	15	6	90	225	36	1,170	468
70	10	5	50	100	25	700	350
68	11	3	33	121	9	748	204
80	16	9	144	256	81	1,280	720
82	14	12	168	196	144	1,148	984
65	8	4	32	64	16	520	260
62	8	3	24	64	9	496	186
90	18	10	180	324	100	1,620	900
743	123	65	869	1,615	509	9,382	5,040

X_1^2, X_2^2, X_1Y, and X_2Y. The sums of these columns are then substituted into equations 11–5, which are solved for the estimates b_0, b_1, and b_2 of the regression parameters.

From Table 11–1, the sums needed for the solution of the normal equations are: $\Sigma y = 743$, $\Sigma x_1 = 123$, $\Sigma x_2 = 65$, $\Sigma x_1 y = 9,382$, $\Sigma x_2 y = 5,040$, $\Sigma x_1 x_2 = 869$, $\Sigma x_1^2 = 1,615$, $\Sigma x_2^2 = 509$. When these sums are substituted into equations 11–5, we get the resulting normal equations:

$$743 = 10b_0 + 123b_1 + 65b_2$$
$$9,382 = 123b_0 + 1,615b_1 + 869b_2$$
$$5,040 = 65b_0 + 869b_1 + 509b_2$$

Solution of this system of equations by substitution, or by any other method of solution, gives:

$$b_0 = 47.164942, \quad b_1 = 1.5990404, \quad b_2 = 1.1487479$$

These are the *least-squares estimates* of the true regression parameters β_0, β_1, and β_2. Recall that the normal equations (equations 11–5) are originally obtained by calculus methods. (They are the results of differentiating the sum of squared errors with respect to the regression coefficients and setting the results to zero.)

The meaning of the estimates b_0, b_1, and b_2 as the Y-intercept, the slope with respect to X_1, and the slope with respect to X_2, respectively, of the estimated regression surface is illustrated in Figure 11–4.

The general multiple regression model, equation 11–1, has one Y-intercept parameter and k slope parameters. Each slope parameter β_i, $i = 1, \ldots, k$, represents the amount of increase (or decrease, in case it is negative) in $E(Y)$ for an increase of one unit in variable X_i when all other variables are kept constant. The regression coefficients β_i are therefore sometimes referred to as *net regression coefficients* because they represent the net change in $E(Y)$ for a change of one unit in the variable they represent, all else remaining constant.[3] The X_i variables should be independent of each other, as we want each coefficient β_i to reflect change in $E(Y)$ for a unit change in X_i, *with all other independent variables left constant*. This is of-

FIGURE 11–4 The Least-Squares Regression Surface for Example (a)

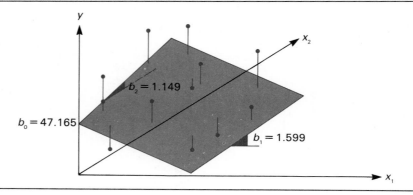

[3] For the reader with knowledge of calculus, we note that the coefficient β_i is the partial derivative of $E(Y)$ with respect to X_i: $\beta_i = \partial E(Y)/\partial X_i$.

ten difficult to achieve in multiple regression analysis since the explanatory variables are often interrelated in some way.

The Estimated Regression Relationship

The **estimated regression relationship:**

$$\hat{Y} = b_0 + b_1 X_1 + b_2 X_2 + \cdots + b_k X_k \qquad (11\text{--}6)$$

where $\hat{Y}$ is the predicted value of Y, the value lying *on* the estimated regression surface. The terms b_i, $i = 0, \ldots, k$, are the least-squares estimates of the population regression parameters β_i.

The least-squares estimators giving us the b_i are BLUE (best linear unbiased estimators).

It is also possible to write the estimated regression relationship in a way showing how each value of Y is expressed as a linear combination of the values of X_i plus an error term. This is given in equation 11–7.

$$y_j = b_0 + b_1 x_{1j} + b_2 x_{2j} + \cdots + b_k x_{kj} + e_j \qquad (11\text{--}7)$$

where $j = 1, \ldots, n$.

In Example (a), the estimated regression relationship of sales volume (Y) on advertising (X_1) and in-store promotions (X_2) is given by:

$$\hat{Y} = 47.164942 + 1.5990404X_1 + 1.1487479X_2$$

PROBLEMS

11–1.   What are the assumptions underlying the multiple regression model? What is the purpose of the assumption of normality of the errors?

11–2.   In a regression analysis of job performance (Y) versus the explanatory variables age (X_1) and experience (X_2), the estimated coefficient b_2 is equal to 1.34. Explain the meaning of this estimate in terms of the impact of experience on performance.

11–3.   In terms of model assumptions, what is the difference between a multiple regression model with k independent variables and a correlational analysis involving these variables?

11–4.   What is a response surface? For a regression model with seven independent variables, what is the dimensionality of the response surface?

11–5.   Again, for a multiple regression model with $k = 7$ independent variables, how many normal equations are there leading to the values of the estimates of the regression parameters?

11–6.   What are the BLUE estimators of the regression parameters?

11–7.   For a multiple regression model with two independent variables, results of the analysis include: $\Sigma y = 852$, $\Sigma x_1 = 155$, $\Sigma x_2 = 88$, $\Sigma x_1 y = 11,423$, $\Sigma x_2 y = 8,320$, $\Sigma x_1 x_2 = 1,055$, $\Sigma x_1^2 = 2,125$, $\Sigma x_2^2 = 768$, $n = 100$. Solve the normal equations for this regression model, and give the estimates of the parameters.

Answer

11-8.
———
$Y = -9.8 + 0.173X_1$
$\qquad + 31.09X_2$

11–8. A realtor is interested in assessing the impact of size (in square feet) and distance from the center of town (in miles) on the value of homes (in thousands of dollars) in a certain area. Nine randomly chosen houses are selected; data are as follows.

Y (value):	345,	238,	452,	422,	328,	375,	660,	466,	290
X_1 (size):	1,650,	1,870,	2,230,	1,740,	1,900,	2,000,	3,200,	1,860,	1,230
X_2 (distance):	3.5,	0.5,	1.5,	4.5,	1.8,	0.1,	3.4,	3.0,	1.0

Compute the estimated regression coefficients and explain their meaning.

11–9. The estimated regression coefficients in Example (a) are $b_0 = 47.165$, $b_1 = 1.599$, and $b_2 = 1.149$ (rounded to three decimal places). Explain the meaning of each of the three numbers in terms of the situation presented in the example.

11–3 The *F* Test of a Multiple Regression Model

The first statistical test we need to conduct in our evaluation of a multiple regression model is a test that will answer the basic question: Is there a regression relationship between the dependent variable Y and *any* of the explanatory, independent variables X_i suggested by the regression equation under consideration? If the proposed regression relationship is as given in equation 11–1, a statistical test that can answer this important question is as follows.

> A statistical hypothesis test for the existence of a linear relationship between Y and any X_i:
>
> $$H_0: \quad \beta_1 = \beta_2 = \beta_3 = \cdots = \beta_k = 0$$
> $$H_1: \quad \text{Not all the } \beta_i \,(i = 1, \ldots, k) \text{ are zero}$$
>
> (11–8)

If the null hypothesis is true, there is no linear relationship between Y and any of the independent variables in the proposed regression equation. In such a case, there is nothing more to do. There is no regression. If, on the other hand, we reject the null hypothesis, there is statistical evidence to conclude that there is a regression relationship between Y and at least one of the independent variables proposed in the regression model.

In order to carry out the important test in equation 11–8, we will perform an analysis of variance. The ANOVA is the same as the one given in Chapter 10 for simple linear regression, except that here we have k independent variables instead of just one. Therefore, the F test of the analysis of variance is not equivalent to the t test for the significance of the slope parameter, as was the case in Chapter 10. Since in multiple regression there are k slope parameters, we have k different t tests to follow the ANOVA.

Figure 11–5 is an extension of Figure 10–19 to the case of $k = 2$ independent variables—to a regression plane instead of a regression line. The figure shows a particular data point, y, the predicted point, $\hat{y}$, which lies on the estimated regression surface, and the mean of the dependent variable, $\bar{y}$. The figure shows the three deviations associated with the data point: the error deviation $y - \hat{y}$, the regression deviation $\hat{y} - \bar{y}$, and the total deviation $y - \bar{y}$. As seen from the figure, the three deviations satisfy the relation: Total deviation = Regression deviation + Error deviation. As in the case of simple linear regression, when we square the deviations and sum them over all n data points, we get the following relation for the sums of

FIGURE 11–5 The Decomposition of the Total Deviation in Multiple Regression Analysis

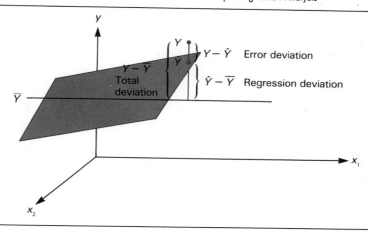

squares. The sums of squares are denoted by SST for the total sum of squares, SSR for the regression sum of squares, and SSE for the error sum of squares.

$$SST = SSR + SSE \qquad (11-9)$$

This is the same as equation 10–29. The difference is in the degrees of freedom. In simple linear regression, the degrees of freedom for error were $n - 2$ because two parameters, an intercept and a slope, were estimated from a data set of n points. In multiple regression, we estimate k slope parameters and an intercept from a data set of n points. Therefore, the degrees of freedom for error are $n - (k + 1)$. The degrees of freedom for the regression are k, and the total degrees of freedom are $n - 1$. Again, the degrees of freedom are additive. Table 11–2 is the ANOVA table for a multiple regression model with k independent variables.

For Example (a), we present the ANOVA table computed using the MINITAB computer package. The results are shown in Table 11–3. Since the p-value is small, we reject the null hypothesis that both slope parameters β_1 and β_2 are zero (equation

TABLE 11–2 ANOVA Table for Multiple Regression

Source of Variation	Sum of Squares	Degrees of Freedom	Mean Square	F Ratio
Regression	SSR	k	$MSR = \dfrac{SSR}{k}$	$F = \dfrac{MSR}{MSE}$
Error	SSE	$n - (k + 1)$	$MSE = \dfrac{SSE}{n - (k + 1)}$	
Total	SST	$n - 1$		

TABLE 11–3 MINITAB-Produced ANOVA Table for the Regression Data of Example (a)

```
Analysis of Variance

   SOURCE      DF        SS         MS        F         P
Regression      2     630.54     315.27     86.34     0.000
Error           7      25.56       3.65
Total           9     656.10
```

FIGURE 11–6   The Regression F Test for Example (a)

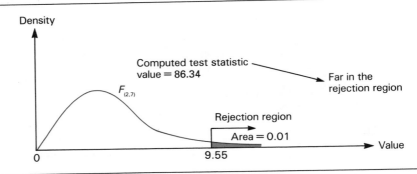

11–8), in favor of the alternative that the slope parameters are not both zero. We conclude that there is evidence of a linear regression relationship between sales and at least one of the two variables, advertising or in-store promotions (or both). The F test is shown in Figure 11–6.

Note that since there are two independent variables in Example (a), we do not yet know whether there is a regression relationship between sales and both advertising and in-store promotions, or whether the relationship exists between sales and one of the two variables only, and if so, which one. All we know is that our data present statistical evidence to conclude that a relationship exists between sales and at least one of the two independent variables. This is, of course, true for all cases where there are two or more independent variables. The F test only tells us that there is evidence of a relationship between the dependent variable and at least one of the independent variables in the full regression equation under consideration. Once we conclude that a relationship exists, we need to conduct separate tests to determine which of the slope parameters β_i, where $i = 1, \ldots, k$, are different from zero. There are, therefore, k further tests.

Compare the use of ANOVA tables in multiple regression with the analysis of variance discussed in Chapter 9. Once we rejected the null hypothesis that all r population means are equal, we required further analysis (the Tukey procedure or an alternative technique) to determine where the differences existed. In multiple regression, the further tests necessary for determining which variables are important are t tests. These tests tell us which variables help explain the variation in the values of the dependent variable and which variables have no explanatory power and should be eliminated from the regression model. Before we get to the separate tests of multiple regression parameters, we want to be able to evaluate how good the regression relationship is as a whole.

PROBLEMS

Answer

11–10.   Explain what is tested by the hypothesis test in equation 11–8. What conclusion should be reached if the null hypothesis is accepted? What conclusion should be reached if the null hypothesis is rejected?

11–11.   In a multiple regression model with 12 independent variables, what are the degrees of freedom for error? Explain.

11–12.

_____

F = 3.54; significant

11–12.   An article about banks' profitability lists four independent variables that may affect profitability.[4] A regression analysis with four independent variables is carried out. The data

4 "Regional, but Less Power," *The Economist* (March 30, 1991), p. 74.

are a random sample of 120 observations. The results of the analysis include: SSE = 4,560, SSR = 562. Is there a regression relationship between the dependent variable and any of the four proposed explanatory variables? Explain.

11–13.   Avis is interested in estimating weekly costs of maintenance of its rental cars of a certain size based on the variables: number of miles driven during the week, number of renters during the week, the car's total mileage, and the car's age. A regression analysis is carried out, and the results include: $n = 45$ cars (each car selected randomly, during a randomly selected week of operation), SSR = 7,768, and SST = 15,673. Construct a complete ANOVA table for this problem, and test for the existence of a linear regression relationship between weekly maintenance costs and any of the four independent variables considered.

11–14.   The Nissan Motor Company wanted to find leverage factors for marketing the Datsun 280Z model in the United States. The company hired a marketing research firm in New York City to carry out an analysis of the factors that make people favor the model in question. As part of the analysis, the marketing research firm selected a random sample of 17 people and asked them to fill out a questionnaire about the importance of three automobile characteristics: prestige, comfort, and economy. Each respondent reported the importance he or she gave to each of the three attributes on a 0 to 100 scale. Each respondent then spent some time becoming acquainted with the car's features and drove it on a test run. Finally, each of the respondents gave an overall appeal score for the model on a 0 to 100 scale. The appeal score was considered the dependent variable, and the three attribute scores were considered independent variables. A multiple regression analysis was carried out, and the results included the following ANOVA table. Complete the table. Based on the results, is there a regression relationship between appeal score and at least one of the attribute variables? Explain.

Answer

11–14.

$F = 48.16$; significant

```
Analysis of Variance

  SOURCE      DF       SS        MS
Regression            7474.0
Error
Total                 8146.5
```

11–4   How Good Is the Regression?

The mean square error, MSE, is an unbiased estimator of the variance of the population errors, ϵ, which we denote by σ^2. The mean square error is defined in equation 11–10.

The mean square error:

$$MSE = \frac{SSE}{n - (k + 1)} = \frac{\sum_{i=1}^{n} (y_i - \hat{y}_i)^2}{n - (k + 1)} \qquad (11\text{–}10)$$

The errors resulting from the fit of a regression surface to our set of n data points are shown in Figure 11–7. The smaller the errors, the better the fit of the regression model. Since the mean square error is the average squared error, where averaging is done by dividing by the degrees of freedom, MSE is a measure of how well the regression fits the data. The square root of MSE is an estimator of the standard deviation of the population regression errors, σ. (Note that a square root of an unbiased estimator is not unbiased; therefore, $\sqrt{MSE}$ is not an unbiased estimator of σ, but it is still a good estimator.) The square root of MSE is usually denoted by s and is referred to as the *standard error of estimate*.

FIGURE 11-7   The Errors in a Multiple Regression Model (Shown for $k = 2$)

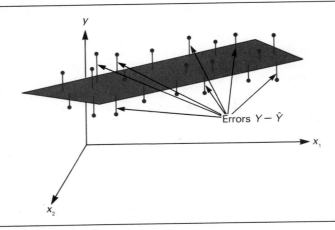

Standard error of estimate:

$$s = \sqrt{MSE} \qquad (11\text{--}11)$$

This statistic is usually reported in computer output of multiple regression analysis. The mean square error and its square root are measures of the size of the errors in regression and do not give an indication about the *explained* component of the regression fit (see Figure 11–5, showing the breakdown of the total deviation of any data point to the error and regression components). A measure of regression fit that does incorporate the explained as well as the unexplained components is the *multiple coefficient of determination*, denoted by R^2. This measure is an extension to multiple regression of the coefficient of determination in simple linear regression, denoted by r^2.

The **multiple coefficient of determination, R^2,** measures the proportion of the variation in the dependent variable that is explained by the combination of the independent variables in the multiple regression model.

$$R^2 = 1 - \frac{SSE}{SST} \qquad (11\text{--}12)$$

Note that R^2 is also equal to SSR/SST because SST $=$ SSR $+$ SSE. We prefer the definition in equation 11–12 for consistency with another measure of how well the regression model fits our data, the *adjusted* multiple coefficient of determination, which will be introduced shortly.

The measures SSE, SSR, and SST are reported in the ANOVA table for multiple regression. Because of the importance of R^2, however, it is reported separately in computer output of multiple regression analysis. The square root of the multiple coefficient of determination, $R = \sqrt{R^2}$, is the **multiple correlation coefficient.** In the context of multiple regression analysis (rather than correlation analysis), the multiple coefficient of determination, R^2, is the important measure, not R. The coefficient of determination measures the percentage of variation in Y explained by the X variables; thus, it is an important measure of how well the regression model fits the data. In correlation analysis, where the X_i variables as well as Y are assumed to be random variables, the multiple correlation coefficient R measures the strength of the linear relationship between Y and the k variables X_i.

Figure 11–8 shows the breakdown of the total sum of squares (the sum of squared deviations of all n data points from the mean of Y; see Figure 11–5) into the sum of squares due to the regression (the explained variation) and the sum of squares due to error (the unexplained variation). The interpretation of R^2 is the same as that of r^2 in simple linear regression. The difference is that here the regression errors are measured as deviations from a regression surface that has higher dimensionality than a regression line. The multiple coefficient of determination, R^2, is a very useful measure of performance of a multiple regression model. It does, however, have some limitations.

Recall the story at the beginning of this chapter about the student who wanted to predict the nation's economic future with a multiple regression model that had many variables. It turns out that, for any given data set of n points, as the number of variables in the regression model increases, so does R^2. You have already seen how this happens: The greater the number of variables in the regression equation, the more the regression surface "chases" the data until it overfits them. Since the fit of the regression model increases as we increase the number of variables, R^2 cannot decrease and approaches 1.00, or 100% explained variation in Y. This can be very deceptive, as the model—while appearing to fit the data very well—would produce poor predictions.

Therefore, a new measure of fit of a multiple regression model must be introduced: the *adjusted* (or corrected) *multiple coefficient of determination*. The adjusted multiple coefficient of determination, denoted $\bar{R}^2$, is the multiple coefficient of determination corrected for degrees of freedom. It accounts, therefore, not only for SSE and SST, but also for their appropriate degrees of freedom. This measure does not always increase as new variables are entered into our regression equation. When $\bar{R}^2$ does increase as a new variable is entered into the regression equation, *it may be worthwhile to include the variable in the equation.* The adjusted measure is defined as follows.

FIGURE 11–8 The Decomposition of the Sum of Squares in Multiple Regression, and the Definition of R^2

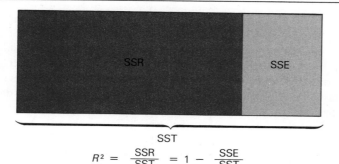

> ### The **adjusted multiple coefficient of determination:**
>
> $$\bar{R}^2 = 1 - \frac{\text{SSE}/(n - (k + 1))}{\text{SST}/(n - 1)} \qquad (11\text{–}13)$$

The adjusted R^2 is the R^2 (defined in equation 11–12) where both SSE and SST are divided by their respective degrees of freedom. Since $\text{SSE}/(n - (k + 1))$ is the MSE, we can say that, in a sense, $\bar{R}^2$ is a mixture of the two measures of the performance of a regression model: MSE and R^2. The denominator on the right-hand side of equation 11–13 would be *mean square total,* were we to define such a measure.

Computer output for multiple regression analysis usually includes the adjusted R^2. If it is not reported, we can get $\bar{R}^2$ from R^2 by a simple formula:

$$\bar{R}^2 = 1 - (1 - R^2)\left(\frac{n - 1}{n - (k + 1)}\right) \qquad (11\text{–}14)$$

It is instructional to prove this relation between R^2 and $\bar{R}^2$, and the proof is left as an exercise. *Note:* Unless the number of variables is relatively large compared to the number of data points (as in the economic student's problem), R^2 and $\bar{R}^2$ are close to each other in value. Thus, in many situations, it suffices to consider the uncorrected measure, R^2. We evaluate the fit of a multiple regression model based on this measure. When considering whether to include an independent variable in a regression model that already contains other independent variables, the increase in R^2 when the new variable is added must be weighed against the loss of one degree of freedom for error resulting from the addition of the variable (a new parameter would be added to the equation). With a relatively small data set and several independent variables in the model, it may not be worthwhile to add a new variable if R^2 increases, say, from 0.85 to 0.86. As mentioned earlier, in such cases, the adjusted measure $\bar{R}^2$ may be a good indicator of whether or not to include the new variable. We may decide to include the variable if $\bar{R}^2$ increases when the variable is added.

Of several possible multiple regression models with different independent variables, the model that minimizes MSE will also maximize $\bar{R}^2$. This should not surprise you, since MSE is related to the adjusted measure, $\bar{R}^2$. The use of the two criteria, MSE and $\bar{R}^2$, in selecting variables to be included in a regression model will be discussed in a later section.

We now present another part of the MINITAB output of the analysis of Example (a), reporting the standard error of estimate, s, as well as R^2 and the adjusted measure, $\bar{R}^2$, for this regression analysis:

```
s = 1.911              R-sq = 96.1%              R-sq(adj) = 95.0%
```

Note that $R^2 = 0.961$, which means that 96.1% of the variation in sales volume is explained by the combination of the two independent variables, advertising and in-store promotions. Note also that the adjusted R^2 is 0.95, which is very close to the unadjusted measure. We conclude that the regression model fits the data very well since a high percentage of the variation in Y is explained by X_1 and/or X_2 (we do not yet know which of the two variables, if not both, is important). The standard error of estimate, s, is an estimate of σ, the standard deviation of the population regression errors. Note that R^2 is also a *statistic*, like s or MSE. It is a sample estimate of

FIGURE 11-9 Measures of Performance of a Regression Model and the ANOVA Table

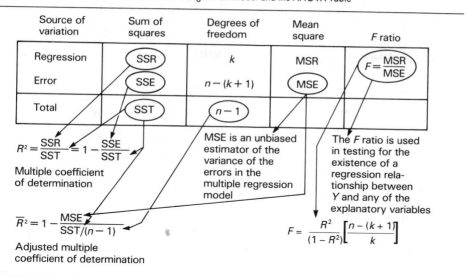

Source of variation	Sum of squares	Degrees of freedom	Mean square	F ratio
Regression	SSR	k	MSR	$F = \dfrac{\text{MSR}}{\text{MSE}}$
Error	SSE	$n - (k + 1)$	MSE	
Total	SST	$n - 1$		

$$R^2 = \frac{\text{SSR}}{\text{SST}} = 1 - \frac{\text{SSE}}{\text{SST}}$$

Multiple coefficient of determination

MSE is an unbiased estimator of the variance of the errors in the multiple regression model

The F ratio is used in testing for the existence of a regression relationship between Y and any of the explanatory variables

$$\overline{R}^2 = 1 - \frac{\text{MSE}}{\text{SST}/(n - 1)}$$

Adjusted multiple coefficient of determination

$$F = \frac{R^2}{(1 - R^2)}\left[\frac{n - (k + 1)}{k}\right]$$

the population multiple coefficient of determination, ρ^2, a measure of the proportion of the explained variation in Y in the entire population of Y and X_i values.

All three measures of the performance of a regression model, MSE (and its square root, s), the coefficient of determination R^2, and the adjusted measure $\overline{R}^2$, are obtainable from quantities reported in the ANOVA table. This is shown in Figure 11-9, which demonstrates the relations among the different measures.

PROBLEMS

11-15. Under what conditions is it important to consider the adjusted multiple coefficient of determination?

Answer

11-16. Explain why the multiple coefficient of determination never decreases as variables are added to the multiple regression model.

11-17. Would it be useful to consider an adjusted coefficient of determination in a simple linear regression situation? Explain.

11-18. Prove equation 11-14.

11-19. Can you judge how well a regression model fits the data by considering the mean square error only? Explain.

11-20. A multiple regression analysis is carried out with three independent variables and a data set of 44 points. The results include: SSE = 6,980 and SSR = 11,778. Construct an ANOVA table, and find MSE, s, R^2, $\overline{R}^2$, and the F ratio. Analyze the results. Is this a good regression model? Why or why not?

11-20.

$R^2 = 0.6279$

$F = 22.5$

11-21. A portion of the MINITAB regression output for the Nissan Motor Company study of problem 11-14 follows. Interpret the findings, and show how these results are obtainable from the ANOVA table results presented in problem 11-14. How good is the regression relationship between the overall appeal score for the automobile and the attribute-importance scores? Also, obtain the adjusted R^2 from the multiple coefficient of determination.

s = 7.192   R-sq = 91.7%   R-sq(adj) = 89.8%

11-22. An article in the *Journal of Marketing Research* reports the results of a regression analysis of brand attitude on the independent variables: "ad reactions" and "brand reactions."[5] The reported results are $n = 103$, $R^2 = 0.67$, $F = 2.53$. Find the adjusted R^2. Also, conduct the F test for the existence of a linear relationship between the dependent variable and at least one of the independent variables. How good is the relationship?

11-23. In the Nissan Motor Company situation in problem 11-21, suppose that a new variable is considered for inclusion in the equation and a new regression relationship is analyzed with the new variable included. Suppose that the resulting multiple coefficient of determination is $R^2 = 91.8\%$. Find the adjusted multiple coefficient of determination. Should the new variable be included in the final regression equation? Give your reasons for including or excluding the variable.

11-24. In the situation of problem 11-22, suppose that a new regression is run with the variable "brand reactions" removed from the equation. The resulting new coefficient of determination is $R^2 = 0.61$. Should the new equation, with the variable omitted, be used for prediction of the dependent variable?

11-25. An article about food production and the economics of developing African countries reports the results of the following regression analysis:[6]

$$\hat{P} = -0.75 + 0.709W + 0.015C + 0.412PM$$

where P is change in industrial prices, W is change in industrial wages, C is change in capacity utilization, and PM is change in price of imported raw materials. The adjusted multiple coefficient of determination is reported as $\bar{R}^2 = 0.873$. The data are yearly figures corresponding to the 12 years 1970-1981.

a. Interpret the meaning of the regression equation and each of the estimated coefficients.

b. What percentage of the variation in industrial prices is explained by the combination of the three independent variables used? (*Caution:* You need to compute something.)

c. What are the limitations of this analysis?

11-26. A study of Dutch tourism behavior included a regression analysis using a sample of 713 respondents. The dependent variable, number of miles traveled on vacation, was regressed on the independent variables, family size and family income, and the multiple coefficient of determination was $R^2 = 0.72$. Find the adjusted multiple coefficient of determination, $\bar{R}^2$. Is this a good regression model? Explain.

11-27. In a regression analysis with six independent variables and a data set of 250 points, it is found that SSE = 5,445 and SST = 22,679. Construct an ANOVA table, conduct the F test, find R^2 and $\bar{R}^2$, and find MSE.

11-5 Tests of the Significance of Individual Regression Parameters

Until now, we have discussed the multiple regression model in general. We saw how to test for the existence of a regression relationship between Y and at least one of a set of independent X_i variables using an F test. We also saw how to evaluate the fit of the general regression model using the multiple coefficient of determination and the adjusted multiple coefficient of determination. We have not yet seen, however, how to evaluate the significance of individual regression parameters, β_i. A test for the significance of an individual parameter is important because it tells us whether or not the variable in question, X_h, has explanatory power with respect to the dependent variable. Such a test tells us whether or not the variable in question should be included in the regression equation.

---

[5] K. Keller, "Cue Compatibility and Framing in Advertising," *Journal of Marketing Research* (February 1991), p. 51.

[6] A. Medani, "Food and Stabilization in Developing Africa," *World Development* (June 1985).

In the last section, we saw that some indication about the benefit from inclusion of a particular variable in the regression equation is given by comparing the adjusted coefficient of determination of a regression that includes the variable of interest with the value of this measure when the variable is not included. In this section, we will perform individual t tests for the significance of each slope parameter, β_i. As we will see, however, we must use caution in interpreting the results of the individual t tests.

In Chapter 10 we saw that the hypothesis test

$$H_0: \beta_1 = 0$$
$$H_1: \beta_1 \neq 0$$

can be carried out using either a t statistic, $t = b_1/s(b_1)$, or an F statistic. Both tests were shown to be equivalent because F with one degree of freedom for the numerator is a squared t random variable with the same number of degrees of freedom as the denominator of F. In simple linear regression, there is only one slope, β_1, and if that slope is zero, there is no linear regression relationship. In multiple regression, where $k > 1$, the two tests are not equivalent. The F test tells us whether or not a relationship exists between Y and at least one of the X_i, and the k ensuing t tests tell us which of the X_i variables are important and should be included in the regression equation. From the similarity of this situation with the situation of analysis of variance discussed in Chapter 9, you probably have guessed at least one of the potential problems: The individual t tests are each carried out at a single level of significance, α, and we cannot determine the level of significance of the family of all k tests of the regression slopes jointly. The problem is further complicated by the fact that the tests are not independent of each other because the regression estimates come from the same data set.

Recall that hypothesis tests and confidence intervals are related. We may test hypotheses about regression slope parameters (in particular, the hypothesis that a slope parameter is equal to zero), or we may construct confidence intervals for the values of the slope parameters. If a 95% confidence interval for a slope parameter, β_h, contains the point zero, then the hypothesis test $H_0: \beta_h = 0$ carried out using $\alpha = 0.05$ would lead to acceptance of the null hypothesis and thus to the conclusion that there is no evidence that the variable X_h has a linear relationship with Y.

We will demonstrate the interdependence of the separate tests of significance of the slope parameters with the use of confidence intervals for these parameters. When $k = 2$, there are two regression slope parameters: β_1 and β_2. (As in simple linear regression, usually there is no interest in testing hypotheses about the intercept parameter.) The sample estimators of the two regression parameters are b_1 and b_2. These estimators (and their standard errors) are correlated with each other (and assumed to be normally distributed). Therefore, the joint confidence region for the pair of parameters (β_1, β_2) is an *ellipse*. If we consider the estimators b_1 and b_2 separately from each other, the joint confidence region would be a rectangle, with each side a separate confidence interval for a single parameter. This is demonstrated in Figure 11–10. A point inside the rectangle formed by the two separate confidence intervals for the parameters, such as point A in the figure, seems like a plausible value for the pair of regression slopes (β_1, β_2) but is not *jointly* plausible for the parameters. Only points inside the ellipse in the figure are jointly plausible for the pair of parameters.

Another problem that may arise in making inferences about individual regression slope coefficients is due to **multicollinearity**—the problem of correlations among the independent variables themselves. In multiple regression, we hope to

FIGURE 11–10   Joint Confidence Region and Individual Confidence Intervals for the Slope Parameters β_1 and β_2

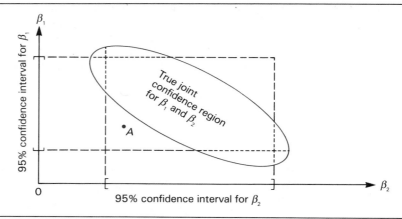

have a strong correlation between each independent variable and the dependent variable, Y. Such correlations give the independent X_i variables predictive power with respect to Y. However, we do not want the independent variables to be correlated with each other. When the independent variables are correlated with each other, we have multicollinearity. When this happens, the independent variables rob each other of explanatory power. Many problems may then arise. One problem is that the standard errors of the individual slope estimators become unusually high, making the slope coefficients seem statistically not significant (not different from zero). For example, if we run a regression of job performance (Y) versus the variables age (X_1) and experience (X_2), we may encounter multicollinearity. Since, in general, as age increases so does experience, the two independent variables are not independent of each other; the two variables rob each other of explanatory power with respect to Y. If we run this regression, it is likely that—even though experience affects job performance—the individual test for significance of the slope parameter β_2 would lead to acceptance of the null hypothesis that this slope parameter is equal to zero. Much will be said later about the problem of multicollinearity. It is important to remember that in the presence of multicollinearity, the significance of any regression parameter depends on the other variables included in the regression equation. Multicollinearity may also cause the signs of some estimated regression parameters to be opposite of what we expect.

Another problem that may affect the individual tests of significance of model parameters occurs when one of the model assumptions is violated. Recall from section 11–2 that one of the assumptions of the regression model is that the error terms, ϵ_j, are uncorrelated with each other. When this condition does not hold, as may happen when our data are time series observations (observations ordered by time: yearly data, monthly data, etc.), we encounter the problem of autocorrelation of the errors. This causes the standard errors of the slope estimators to be unusually small, making some parameters seem more significant than they really are. This problem, too, should be considered, and we will discuss it in detail later.

Forewarned of problems that may arise, let us now consider the tests of the individual regression parameters. In a regression model of Y versus k independent variables $X_1, X_2, \ldots, X_k$, there are k tests of significance of the slope parameters $\beta_1, \beta_2, \ldots, \beta_k$:

Hypothesis tests about individual regression slope parameters:

$$
\begin{array}{ll}
(1) & H_0: \beta_1 = 0 \\
& H_1: \beta_1 \neq 0 \\[6pt]
(2) & H_0: \beta_2 = 0 \\
& H_1: \beta_2 \neq 0 \\
& \quad \vdots \qquad \vdots \\
(k) & H_0: \beta_k = 0 \\
& H_1: \beta_k \neq 0
\end{array}
\tag{11-15}
$$

These tests are carried out by comparing each test statistic with a critical point of the distribution of the test statistic. The distribution of each test statistic, when the appropriate null hypothesis is true, is the t distribution with $n - (k + 1)$ degrees of freedom. The distribution depends on our assumption that the regression errors are normally distributed. The test statistic for each hypothesis test, (i), in equation 11–15 (where $i = 1, 2, \ldots, k$) is the slope estimate b_i divided by the estimated standard error of the estimator, $s(b_i)$. The estimates and the estimated standard errors are reported in the computer output. Each $s(b_i)$ is an estimate of the population standard error of the estimator, $\sigma(b_i)$, which is unknown to us.[7] The test statistics for the hypothesis tests $(1)-(k)$ in equation 11–15 are as follows.

Test statistics for tests about individual regression slope parameters:

$$
\text{For test } i\,(i = 1, \ldots, k): \quad t_{(n-(k+1))} = \frac{b_i - 0}{s(b_i)}
\tag{11-16}
$$

We write each test statistic as the estimate minus zero (the null-hypothesized value of β_i) to stress the fact that we may test the null hypothesis that β_i is equal to any number, not necessarily zero. Testing for equality to zero is most important because it tells us whether there is evidence that variable X_i has a linear relationship with Y. It tells us whether there is statistical evidence that variable X_i has explanatory power with respect to the dependent variable.

Let us look at a quick example. Suppose that a multiple regression analysis is carried out relating the dependent variable Y to five independent variables: X_1, X_2, X_3, X_4, and X_5. In addition, suppose that the F test resulted in rejection of the null hypothesis that none of the predictor variables has any explanatory power with respect to Y; suppose also that the R^2 of the regression is respectably high. As a result, we believe that the regression equation gives a good fit to the data and potentially may be used for prediction purposes. Our task now is to test the importance of each of the X_i variables separately. Suppose that the sample size used in this regression analysis is $n = 150$. The results of the regression estimation procedure are given in Table 11–4.

---

[7] Each $s(b_i)$ is the product of $s = \sqrt{\text{MSE}}$ and a term denoted by c_i, which is a diagonal element in a matrix obtained in the regression computations. You need not worry about matrices. However, the matrix approach to multiple regression is discussed in a section at the end of this chapter for the benefit of students familiar with matrix theory.

TABLE 11−4 Regression Results for Individual Parameters

Variable	Coefficient Estimate	Standard Error
Constant	53.12	5.43
X_1	2.03	0.22
X_2	5.60	1.30
X_3	10.35	6.88
X_4	3.45	2.70
X_5	−4.25	0.38

From the information in Table 11−4, which variables are important, and which are not? Note that the first variable listed is "Constant." This is the Y-intercept. As we noted earlier, testing whether the intercept is zero is less important than testing whether the coefficient parameter of any of the k variables is zero. Still, we may do so by dividing the reported coefficient estimate, 53.12, by its estimated standard error, 5.43. The result is the value of the test statistic that has a t distribution with $n - (k + 1) = 150 - 6 = 144$ degrees of freedom when the null hypothesis that the intercept is zero is true. For all practical purposes, this t random variable is a standard normal variable, Z. The test statistic value is $z = 53.12/5.43 = 9.78$. This value is greater than 1.96, and we may reject the null hypothesis that β_0 is equal to zero at the $\alpha = 0.05$ level of significance. Actually, the p-value is very small. The regression hyperplane, therefore, most probably does not pass through the origin.

Let us now turn to the tests of significance of the slope parameters of the variables in the regression equation. We start with the test for the significance of variable X_1 as a predictor variable. The hypothesis test is: $H_0: \beta_1 = 0$ versus $H_1: \beta_1 \neq 0$. We now compute our test statistic (again, we will use Z for $t_{(144)}$):

$$z = \frac{b_1 - 0}{s(b_1)} = \frac{2.03}{0.22} = 9.227$$

The value of the test statistic, 9.227, lies far in the right-hand rejection region of Z for any conventional level of significance; the p-value is very small. We therefore conclude that there is statistical evidence that the slope of Y with respect to X_1, the population parameter β_1, is not zero. X_1 is shown to have some explanatory power with respect to the dependent variable.

If it is not zero, what is the value of β_1? The parameter, as in the case of all population parameters, is not known to us. An unbiased estimate of the parameter's value is $b_1 = 2.03$. We can also compute a confidence interval for β_1. A 95% confidence interval for β_1 is: $b_1 \pm 1.96 s(b_1) = 2.03 \pm 1.96(0.22) = [1.599, 2.461]$. Based on our data and the validity of our assumptions, we can be 95% confident that the true slope of Y with respect to X_1 is anywhere from 1.599 to 2.461. Figure 11−11 shows the hypothesis test for the significance of variable X_1.

For the other variables, X_2 through X_5, we show the hypothesis tests without figures. The tests are carried out in the same way, with the same distribution. We also do not show the computation of confidence intervals for the slope parameters. These are done exactly as shown for β_1. Note that when the hypothesis test for the significance of a slope parameter leads to acceptance of the null hypothesis that the slope parameter is zero, the point zero will be included in a confidence interval with the same confidence level as the level of significance of the test.

The hypothesis test for β_2 is: $H_0: \beta_2 = 0$ versus $H_1: \beta_2 \neq 0$. The test statistic value is $z = 5.60/1.30 = 4.308$. This value, too, is in the right-hand rejection re-

FIGURE 11–11   Testing Whether or Not $\beta_1 = 0$

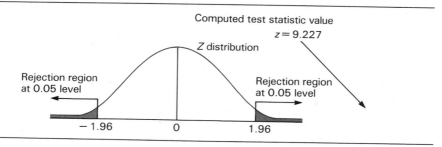

gion for usual levels of significance; the p-value is small. We conclude that X_2 is also an important variable in the regression equation.

The hypothesis test for β_3 is: H_0: $\beta_3 = 0$ versus H_1: $\beta_3 \neq 0$. Here the test statistic value is $z = 10.35/6.88 = 1.504$. This value lies in the acceptance region for levels of α larger than 0.10. The p-value is over 0.133, as you can verify from a normal table. We conclude that variable X_3 is probably not important. Remember our cautionary comments that preceded this discussion—there is a possibility that X_3 is actually an important variable. The variable may *appear* to have a slope that is not different from zero because its standard error, $s(b_3) = 6.88$, may be unduly inflated; the variable may be correlated with another explanatory variable (the problem of multicollinearity). A way out of this problem is to drop another variable, one that we suspect to be correlated with X_3, and see if X_3 becomes significant in the new regression model. We will come back to this problem in the section on multicollinearity and in the section on selection of variables to be included in a regression model.

The hypothesis test about β_4 is: H_0: $\beta_4 = 0$ versus H_1: $\beta_4 \neq 0$. The value of the test statistic for this test is $z = 3.45/2.70 = 1.278$. Again, we accept the null hypothesis that the slope parameter of X_4 is zero and that the variable has no explanatory power. Note, however, the caution in our discussion of the test of β_3. It is possible, for example, that X_3 and X_4 are collinear and that this is the reason for their respective tests resulting in nonsignificance. It would be wise to drop one of these two variables and check whether the other variable then becomes significant. If it does, the reason for our test result is multicollinearity and not the absence of explanatory power of the variable in question. Another point worth mentioning is the idea of joint inference, discussed earlier. Although the separate tests of β_3 and β_4 both may lead to the acceptance of the hypothesis that the parameters are zero, it may be that the two parameters are not jointly equal to zero. This would be the situation if, in Figure 11–10, the rectangle contained the point zero while the ellipse— the true joint confidence region for both parameters—did not contain that point. It is important to note that the t tests are *conditional*. The significance or nonsignificance of a variable in the equation is conditional on the fact that the regression equation contains the other variables.

Finally, the test for the parameter β_5 is: H_0: $\beta_5 = 0$ versus H_1: $\beta_5 \neq 0$. The computed value of the test statistic is $z = -4.25/0.38 = -11.184$. This value falls far in the left-hand rejection region, and we conclude that variable X_5 has explanatory power with respect to the dependent variable and therefore should be included in the regression equation. The slope parameter is negative, which means that, everything else staying constant, the dependent variable Y decreases on the average as X_5 increases. We note that these tests can be carried out very quickly by just considering the p-values.

TABLE 11–5 MINITAB Output for Example (a)

```
MTB > regress 'sales' on 2 predictors, 'advert', 'prom'

The regression equation is
sales = 47.2 + 1.60 advert + 1.15 prom

Predictor       Coef        Stdev       t-ratio       p
Constant       47.165       2.470        19.09       0.000
advert          1.5990      0.2810        5.69       0.000
prom            1.1487      0.3052        3.76       0.007
```

We now return to Example (a) and give the rest of the MINITAB output of the analysis of the relationship between sales and the independent variables, advertising and in-store promotions. Table 11–5 gives the values of the estimates, the standard errors of the estimators, the value of every test statistic, denoted "t-ratio," and the p-values. The output also includes the estimated regression equation. We see that both independent variables are significant.

EXAMPLE (b)

In recent years, many American firms have intensified their efforts to market their products in the Pacific Rim. Among the major economic powers in that area are Japan, Hong Kong, and Singapore. A consortium of U.S. firms that produce raw materials used in Singapore is interested in predicting the level of exports from the United States to Singapore, as well as understanding the relationship between U.S. exports to Singapore and certain variables affecting the economy of that country. Understanding this relationship would allow the consortium members to time their marketing efforts to coincide with favorable conditions in the Singapore economy. Understanding the relationship would also allow the exporters to determine whether or not there is room for expansion of exports to Singapore. The economist hired to do the analysis obtained from the Monetary Authority of Singapore (MAS) monthly data on five economic variables for the period January 1979 to August 1984. The variables were: U.S. exports to Singapore in billions of Singapore dollars (the dependent variable, Exports), money supply figures in billions of Singapore dollars (variable M1), minimum Singapore bank lending rate in percentages (variable Lend), an index of local prices where the base year is 1974 (variable Price), and the exchange rate of Singapore dollars per U.S. dollar (variable Exchange). The monthly data and the MINITAB program that reads them into the computer and names the variables are given in Table 11–6.

SOLUTION

The economist used the MINITAB package to perform a multiple regression analysis with exports as the dependent variable and the four economic variables M1, Lend, Price, and Exchange as the predictor variables. The MINITAB command for this regression and the resulting output are given in Table 11–7.

Let us analyze the regression results. We start with the ANOVA table and the F test for the existence of a linear relationship between the independent variables and exports from the United States to Singapore. We have: $F_{(4,62)} = 73.08$ with a p-value of "0.000". We conclude that there is strong evidence of a linear regression relationship here. This is further confirmed by noting that the coefficient of determination is high: $R^2 = 0.825$. Thus, the combination of the four economic variables explains 82.5% of the variation in exports to Singapore. The adjusted coefficient of determination, $\bar{R}^2$, is a little smaller: 0.814. Now the question is which of the four variables are important as predictors of export volume to Singapore and which are not. Looking at the reported p-values, we see that the Singapore money supply, M1, is an important variable; the level of prices in Singapore is also an important variable. The re-

TABLE 11–6 Example (b) Data as Read into MINITAB

```
MTB > NAME C1 'M1', C2 'LEND', C3 'PRICE', C4 'EXCHANGE', C5 'EXPORTS'
MTB > READ 'REGRESS.DAT' INTO 'M1', 'LEND', 'PRICE', 'EXCHANGE', 'EXPORTS'
      67 ROWS READ
MTB > PRINT 'EXPORTS', 'M1', 'LEND', 'PRICE', 'EXCHANGE'
```

ROW	EXPORTS	M1	LEND	PRICE	EXCHANGE
1	2.6	5.1	7.8	114	2.16
2	2.6	4.9	8.0	116	2.17
3	2.7	5.1	8.1	117	2.18
4	3.0	5.1	8.1	122	2.20
5	2.9	5.1	8.1	124	2.21
6	3.1	5.2	8.1	128	2.17
7	3.2	5.1	8.3	132	2.14
8	3.7	5.2	8.8	133	2.16
9	3.6	5.3	8.9	133	2.15
10	3.4	5.4	9.1	134	2.16
11	3.7	5.7	9.2	135	2.18
12	3.6	5.7	9.5	136	2.17
13	4.1	5.9	10.3	140	2.15
14	3.5	5.8	10.6	147	2.16
15	4.2	5.7	11.3	150	2.21
16	4.3	5.8	12.1	151	2.24
17	4.2	6.0	12.0	151	2.16
18	4.1	6.0	11.4	151	2.12
19	4.6	6.0	11.1	153	2.11
20	4.4	6.0	11.0	154	2.13
21	4.5	6.1	11.3	154	2.11
22	4.6	6.0	12.6	154	2.09
23	4.6	6.1	13.6	155	2.09
24	4.2	6.7	13.6	155	2.10
25	5.5	6.2	14.3	156	2.08
26	3.7	6.3	14.3	156	2.09
27	4.9	7.0	13.7	159	2.10
28	5.2	7.0	12.7	161	2.11
29	4.9	6.6	12.6	161	2.15
30	4.6	6.4	13.4	161	2.14
31	5.4	6.3	14.3	162	2.16
32	5.0	6.5	13.9	160	2.17
33	4.8	6.6	14.5	159	2.15
34	5.1	6.8	15.0	159	2.10
35	4.4	7.2	13.2	158	2.06
36	5.0	7.6	11.8	155	2.05
37	5.1	7.2	11.2	155	2.06
38	4.8	7.1	10.1	154	2.11
39	5.4	7.0	10.0	154	2.12
40	5.0	7.5	10.2	154	2.13
41	5.2	7.4	11.0	153	2.04
42	4.7	7.4	11.0	152	2.14
43	5.1	7.3	10.7	152	2.15
44	4.9	7.6	10.2	152	2.16
45	4.9	7.8	10.0	151	2.17
46	5.3	7.8	9.8	152	2.20
47	4.8	8.2	9.3	152	2.21
48	4.9	8.2	9.3	152	2.15
49	5.1	8.3	9.5	152	2.08
50	4.3	8.3	9.2	150	2.08
51	4.9	8.0	9.1	147	2.09
52	5.3	8.2	9.0	147	2.10
53	4.8	8.2	9.0	146	2.09
54	5.3	8.0	8.9	145	2.12
55	5.0	8.1	9.0	145	2.13
56	5.1	8.1	9.0	146	2.14
57	4.8	8.1	9.0	147	2.14
58	4.8	8.1	8.9	147	2.13
59	5.2	8.6	8.9	147	2.13
60	4.9	8.8	9.0	146	2.13
61	5.5	8.4	9.1	147	2.13
62	4.3	8.2	9.0	146	2.13
63	5.2	8.3	9.2	146	2.09
64	4.7	8.3	9.6	146	2.09
65	5.4	8.4	10.0	146	2.10
66	5.2	8.3	10.0	147	2.11
67	5.6	8.2	10.1	146	2.15

TABLE 11–7 Exports to Singapore Regression Analysis Results

```
MTB > REGRESS 'EXPORTS' ON 4 PREDICTORS, 'M1', 'LEND', 'PRICE', 'EXCHANGE'

The regression equation is
EXPORTS = - 4.02 + 0.368 M1 + 0.0047 LEND + 0.0365 PRICE + 0.27 EXCHANGE

Predictor      Coef        Stdev       t-ratio       P
Constant      -4.015       2.766        -1.45      0.152
M1             0.36846     0.06385       5.77      0.000
LEND           0.00470     0.04922       0.10      0.924
PRICE          0.036511    0.009326      3.91      0.000
EXCHANGE       0.268       1.175         0.23      0.820

s = 0.3358      R-sq = 82.5%      R-sq(adj) = 81.4%

Analysis of Variance

SOURCE       DF      SS          MS         F          P
Regression    4    32.9463     8.2366     73.06      0.000
Error        62     6.9898     0.1127
Total        66    39.9361
```

TABLE 11–8 Exports to Singapore without the Variable M1 in the Equation

```
MTB > REGRESS 'EXPORTS' ON 3 PREDICTORS, 'LEND', 'PRICE', 'EXCHANGE'

The regression equation is
EXPORTS = - 0.29 - 0.211 LEND + 0.0781 PRICE - 2.10 EXCHANGE

Predictor      Coef        Stdev       t-ratio       P
Constant      -0.289       3.308        -0.09      0.931
LEND          -0.21140     0.03929      -5.38      0.000
PRICE          0.078148    0.007268     10.75      0.000
EXCHANGE      -2.095       1.355        -1.55      0.127

s = 0.4130      R-sq = 73.1%      R-sq(adj) = 71.8%
Analysis of Variance

SOURCE       DF      SS          MS         F          P
Regression    3    29.1919     9.7306     57.06      0.000
Error        63    10.7442     0.1705
Total        66    39.9361
```

maining two variables, minimum lending rate and exchange rate, have very large p-values. It is surprising that the lending rate and the exchange rate of Singapore dollars to U.S. dollars seem to have no effect on the volume of Singapore's imports from the United States. Remember, however, that we may have a problem of multicollinearity. This is especially true when dealing with economic variables, which tend to be correlated with each other.[8]

When M1 is dropped from the equation and the new regression analysis considers the independent variables Lend, Price, and Exchange, we see that the lending rate, which was not significant in the full regression equation, now becomes significant! This is seen in Table 11–8. Note that R^2 has dropped greatly with the removal of M1. The fact that the lending rate is significant in the new equation is an indication of *multicollinearity*; the variables M1 and Lend are correlated with each other. Therefore, Lend is not significant when M1 is in the equation, but in the absence of M1, Lend does have explanatory power.

Note that the exchange rate is still not significant. Since R^2 and the adjusted R^2 both decrease significantly when the money supply, M1, is dropped, let us put that variable back into

---

[8] The analysis of economic variables presents special problems. Economists have developed methods that account for the intricate interrelations among economic variables. These methods, based on multiple regression and time series analysis, are usually referred to as *econometric methods*.

TABLE 11–9 Exports to Singapore versus the Variables M1 and Price

```
MTB > REGRESS 'EXPORTS' ON 2 PREDICTORS, 'M1', 'PRICE'

The regression equation is
EXPORTS = - 3.42 + 0.361 M1 + 0.0370 PRICE

Predictor     Coef        Stdev       t-ratio      p
Constant     -3.4230      0.5409       -6.33      0.000
M1            0.36142     0.03925       9.21      0.000
PRICE         0.037033    0.004094      9.05      0.000

s = 0.3306      R-sq = 82.5%      R-sq(adj) = 81.9%

Analysis of Variance

SOURCE       DF       SS         MS        F         p
Regression    2     32.940     16.470    150.67    0.000
Error        64      6.996      0.109
Total        66     39.936
```

the equation and run U.S. exports to Singapore versus the independent variables M1 and Price only. The results are shown in Table 11–9. In this regression equation, both independent variables are significant. Note that R^2 in this regression is the same as R^2 with all four variables in the equation (see Table 11–7); both are 0.825. However, the adjusted coefficient of determination, $\bar{R}^2$, is different. The adjusted R^2 actually *increases* as we drop the variables Lend and Exchange. In the full model with the four variables (Table 11–7), $\bar{R}^2 = 0.814$, while in the reduced model, with variables M1 and Price only (Table 11–9), $\bar{R}^2 = 0.819$. This demonstrates the usefulness of the adjusted R^2. When unimportant variables are added into the equation (unimportant in the presence of other variables), $\bar{R}^2$ decreases even if R^2 increases (here R^2 is reported to first-decimal accuracy, so we do not see an increase). The best model, in terms of explanatory power gauged against the loss of degrees of freedom, is the reduced model in Table 11–9, which relates exports to Singapore with only the money supply and price level. This is also seen by the fact that the other two variables are not significant once M1 and Price are in the equation. Later, when we discuss stepwise regression—a method of letting the computer choose the best variables to be included in the model—we will see that this automatic procedure also chooses the variables M1 and Price as the best combination for predicting U.S. exports to Singapore.

PROBLEMS

11–28. A regression analysis is carried out, and a confidence interval for β_1 is computed to be [1.25, 1.55]; a confidence interval for β_2 is [2.01, 2.12]. Both confidence intervals are of 95%. Explain the possibility that the point (1.26, 2.02) may not lie inside a joint confidence region for (β_1, β_2) at a confidence level of 95%.

Answer

11–29. A regression analysis of total bank deposits versus the independent variable area affluence is carried out. The estimated slope coefficient is 1.27, and its standard error is 0.11. A second independent variable, average value of a single-family home in the area, is added to the model. The estimated slope coefficient of area affluence in the new regression equation is 1.02, and its standard deviation is 0.87. Explain what happened and why.

11–30. Give three reasons why caution must be exercised in interpreting the significance of single regression slope parameters.

11–30.

11–31. Give 95% confidence intervals for the slope parameters β_2 through β_5 using the information in Table 11–4. Which confidence intervals contain the point zero? Explain the interpretation of such outcomes.

Type I error; multi-collinearity; autocorrelation.

Answers

11–32.

Insignificant or collinear.

11–34.

Prestige, n.s.; comfort,
economy are significant.

11–32. Suppose that in a regression equation, two slope parameters are significant and two are not. One of the two insignificant variables is dropped, and the other one remains insignificant in the new equation. Give two possible reasons for this finding, and suggest a way of determining the correct reason.

11–33. A computer program for regression analysis produces a joint confidence region for the two slope parameters considered in the regression equation, β_1 and β_2. The elliptical region of confidence level 95% does not contain the point (0,0). Not knowing the value of the F statistic, or R^2, do you believe there is a linear regression relationship between Y and at least one of the two explanatory variables? Explain.

11–34. In the Nissan Motor Company situation of problems 11–14 and 11–21, part of the information produced by the MINITAB program relevant to tests of separate regression parameters is as follows. Give a complete interpretation of these results.

```
MTB > REGRESS 'RATING' ON 3 PREDICTORS, 'PRESTIGE', 'COMFORT', 'ECONOMY'

The regression equation is
RATING = 24.1 - 0.166 PRESTIGE + 0.324 COMFORT + 0.514 ECONOMY
```

Predictor	Coef	Stdev
Constant	24.14	18.22
PRESTIGE	-0.1658	0.1215
COMFORT	0.3236	0.1228
ECONOMY	0.5139	0.1143

11–35. Refer to Example (b), where exports to Singapore were regressed on several economic variables. Interpret the results of the following analysis, and compare them with the results reported in the text. How does the present model fit with the rest of the analysis? Explain.

```
MTB > REGRESS 'EXPORTS' ON 3 PREDICTORS, 'M1', 'LEND', 'PRICE'

The regression equation is
EXPORTS = - 3.40 + 0.363 M1 + 0.0021 LEND + 0.0367 PRICE
```

Predictor	Coef	Stdev	t-ratio	P
Constant	-3.4047	0.6821	-4.99	0.000
M1	0.36339	0.05940	6.12	0.000
LEND	0.00211	0.04753	0.04	0.965
PRICE	0.036666	0.009231	3.97	0.000

s = 0.3332   R-sq = 82.5%   R-sq(adj) = 81.6%

11–36.

M_1 and Price highest $\overline{R}^2$

11–36. After the model of problem 11–35, the next model was run:

```
MTB > REGRESS 'EXPORTS' ON 2 PREDICTORS, 'M1', 'LEND'

The regression equation is
EXPORTS = - 1.09 + 0.552 M1 + 0.171 LEND
```

Predictor	Coef	Stdev	t-ratio	P
Constant	-1.0859	0.3914	-2.77	0.007
M1	0.55222	0.03950	13.98	0.000
LEND	0.17100	0.02357	7.25	0.000

s = 0.3697   R-sq = 78.1%   R-sq(adj) = 77.4%

Analysis of Variance

SOURCE	DF	SS	MS	F	P
Regression	2	31.189	15.594	114.09	0.000
Error	64	8.748	0.137		
Total	66	39.936			

a. What happened when Price was dropped from the regression equation? Why?

b. Compare this model with all previous models of exports versus the economic variables, and draw conclusions.

c. Which model is best overall? Why?

d. Conduct the F test for this particular model.

e. Compare the reported value of s in this model with the reported s value in the model of problem 11–35. Why is s higher in this model?

f. For the model in problem 11–35, what is the mean square error?

Answer

MSE = 0.111

11–37. A regression analysis of monthly sales versus four independent variables is carried out. One of the variables is known not to have any effect on sales, yet its slope parameter in the regression is significant. In your opinion, what may have caused this to happen?

11–38. An article in the *Journal of Finance* reports the results of a regression analysis of stock returns for firms that are targeted for takeover versus two financial ratios: the Q ratio of the target firm and the Q ratio of the bidder. The results are given in the table below.[9] Give a complete interpretation of the regression results.

	Target Returns
Intercept	0.3270 (0.00)
Target Q is large	−0.1323 (0.00)
Bidder Q is large	−0.0163 (0.70)
F value	5.47 (0.00)
R^2	0.03
N	384

p-values in parentheses.

11–6   Testing the Validity of the Regression Model

In Chapter 10, we stressed the importance of the three stages of statistical model building: model specification, estimation of parameters, and testing the validity of the model assumptions. We will now discuss the third and very important stage of checking the validity of the model assumptions in multiple regression analysis.

Residual Plots

As with simple linear regression, the analysis of regression residuals is an important tool for determining whether the assumptions of the multiple regression model are met. Residual plots are easy to use, and they convey much information quickly. The saying "A picture is worth a thousand words" is a good description of the technique of examining plots of regression residuals. As with simple linear regression, we may plot the residuals against the predicted values of the dependent variable, against each independent variable, against time (or the order of selection of the data points), and on a probability scale, to check the normality assumption. Since we have already discussed the use of residual plots in Chapter 10, we will demonstrate only some of the residual plots using Example (b). Figure 11–12 is a plot of the residuals pro-

---

[9] From H. Servaes, "Tobin's Q and the Gains from Takeovers," *Journal of Finance* 46, no.1 (March 1991), p. 416.

FIGURE 11–12 Residuals against M1 [Example (b)]

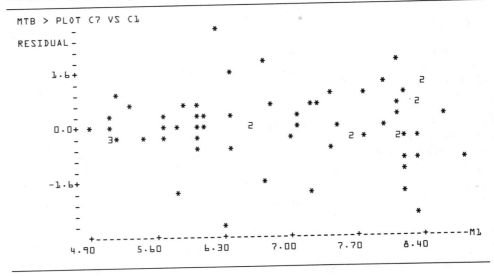

duced from the model with the two independent variables, M1 and Price (Table 11–9), against the variable M1. It appears that the residuals are randomly distributed with no pattern and with equal variance as M1 increases.

Figure 11–13 is a plot of the regression residuals against the variable Price. Here the picture is quite different. As we examine this figure carefully, we see that the spread of the residuals increases as Price increases. Thus, the variance of the residuals is not constant. We have the situation called *heteroscedasticity*—a violation of the assumption of equal error variance. In such cases, the ordinary least squares (OLS) estimation method is not efficient, and an alternative method called

FIGURE 11–13 Residuals against Price [Example (b)]

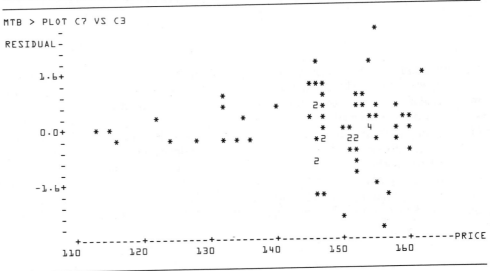

FIGURE 11–14 Residuals against Time [Example (b)]

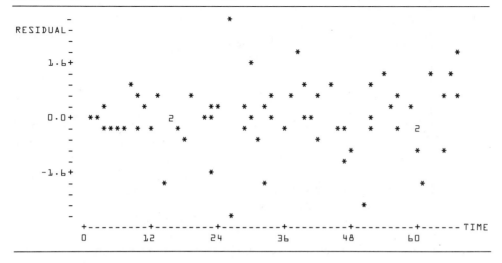

weighted least squares (WLS) should be used instead. The WLS procedure is discussed in advanced texts on regression analysis.

Figure 11–14 is a plot of the regression residuals against the variable Time, that is, the order of the observations. (The observations are a time sequence of monthly data.) This variable was not included in the model, and the plot could reveal whether time should have been included as a variable in our regression model. The plot of the residuals against time reveals no pattern in the residuals as time increases. The residuals seem to be more or less randomly distributed about their mean of zero.

Figure 11–15 is a plot of the regression residuals against the predicted export values, $\hat{Y}$. We leave it as an exercise to the reader to interpret the information in this plot.

FIGURE 11–15 A Plot of the Residuals against the Predicted Y Values [Example (b)]

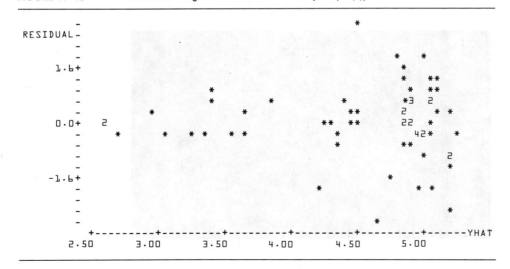

Standardized Residuals

Remember that under the assumptions of the regression model, the population errors, ϵ_j, are normally distributed with mean zero and standard deviation σ. As a result, the errors divided by their standard deviation should follow the standard normal distribution:

$$\frac{\epsilon_j}{\sigma} \sim N(0, 1) \quad \text{for all } j$$

Therefore, dividing the observed regression errors, e_j, by their estimated standard deviation, s, will give us standardized residuals. Examination of a histogram of these residuals may give us an idea as to whether or not the normal assumption is valid.[10]

The MINITAB program produces, on request, the standardized residuals, which may be plotted as a histogram. We give this plot for the data of Example (b), shown in Figure 11–16. These standardized residuals are computed by the more accurate method referred to in the footnote, which accounts for differences in the variance of different error terms. Looking at the plot in Figure 11–16, it seems that the normality assumption is reasonable. There are three observations with standard residuals over 2 in absolute value. Since there are $n = 76$ observations, we expect an average of $76(0.05) = 3.8$ residuals to be above 2 in absolute value purely by chance. Thus, three residuals are within the range we expect under the model assumptions.

Outliers and Influential Observations

An **outlier** is an extreme observation. It is a point that lies away from the rest of the data set. Because of this, outliers may exert greater influence on the least-squares estimates of the regression parameters than do other observations. To see why, consider the data in Figure 11–17. The graph shows the estimated least-squares regression line without the outlier and the line obtained when the outlier is considered.

As can be seen from Figure 11–17, the outlier has a strong effect on the estimation of model parameters. (We used a line showing Y versus variable X_1. The same is

FIGURE 11–16 A Histogram of the Standardized Residuals [Example (b)]

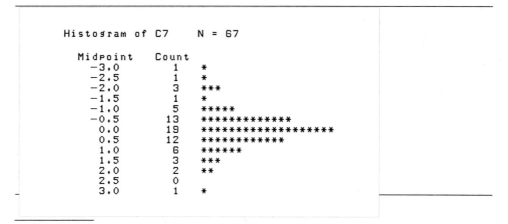

```
Histogram of C7    N = 67

Midpoint   Count
  -3,0       1    *
  -2,5       1    *
  -2,0       3    ***
  -1,5       1    *
  -1,0       5    *****
  -0,5      13    *************
   0,0      19    *******************
   0,5      12    ************
   1,0       6    ******
   1,5       3    ***
   2,0       2    **
   2,5       0
   3,0       1    *
```

---

[10] Actually, the residuals are not independent and do not have equal variance; therefore, we really should divide the residuals, e_j, by something a little more complicated than s. However, the simpler procedure outlined here and implemented in some computer packages is usually sufficiently accurate.

FIGURE 11–17 A Least-Squares Regression Line Estimated with and without the Outlier

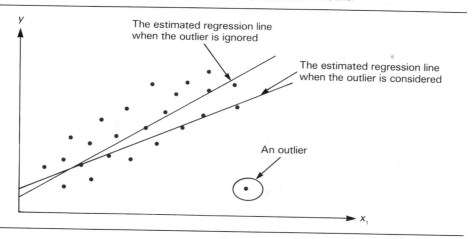

true for a regression plane or hyperplane: the outlier "tilts" the regression surface away from the other points.) The reason for this effect is the nature of least squares: the procedure minimizes the squared deviations of the data points from the regression surface. A point with an unusually large deviation "attracts" the surface toward itself so as to make its squared deviation smaller.

We must, therefore, give special attention to outliers. If an outlier can be traced to an error in recording the data or to another type of error, it should, of course, be removed. On the other hand, if an outlier is not due to error, it may have been caused by special circumstances, and the information it provides may be important. For example, an outlier may be an indication of a missing variable in the regression equation. The data shown in Figure 11–17 may be maximum speed for an automobile as a function of engine displacement. The outlier may be an automobile with four cylinders, while all others are six-cylinder cars. Thus, the fact that the point lies away from the rest may be explained. Because of the possible information content in outliers, they should be carefully scrutinized before one decides to discard them. There are some alternative regression methods that do not use a squared-distance approach and are therefore more robust—less sensitive to the influence of outliers.

Sometimes an outlier is actually a point that is distant from the rest because the value of one of its independent variables is larger than the rest of the data. For example, suppose we measure chemical yield (Y) as a function of temperature (X_1). There may be other variables, but we will consider only these two. Suppose that most of our data are obtained at low temperatures within a certain range, but one observation is taken at a high temperature. This outlying point, far in the X_1 direction, exerts strong influence on the estimation of the model parameters. This is shown in Figure 11–18. Without the point at high temperature, the regression line may have slope zero, and no relationship may be detected, as can be seen from the figure. We must also be careful in such cases to guard against estimating a straight-line relation where a curvilinear one may be more appropriate. This could become evident if we had more data points in the region between the far point and the rest of the data. This is shown in Figure 11–19.

Figure 11–19 serves as a good reminder that regression analysis should not be used for extrapolation. We do not know what happens in the region in which we have no data. This region may be between two regions where we have data, or it may lie

FIGURE 11–18   The Influence of an Observation Far in the X_1 Direction

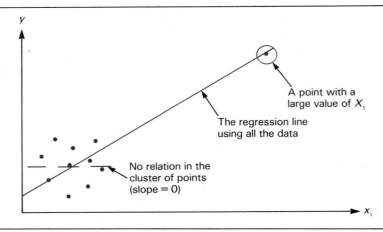

FIGURE 11–19   A Possible Relation in the Region between the Available Cluster of Data and the Far Point

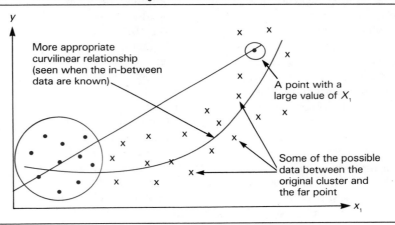

beyond the last observation in a given direction. The relationship may be quite different from what we estimate from the data. This is also a reason why it is not a good idea to force the regression surface to go through the origin (that is, carry out a regression with no constant term: $\beta_0 = 0$), as is done in some applications. The reasoning in such cases follows the idea expressed in the statement "In this particular case, when there is zero input, there must be zero output," which may very well be true. Forcing the regression to go through the origin, however, may make the estimation procedure biased. This is because in the region where the data points are located—assuming they are not near the origin—the best straight line to describe the data may not have an intercept of zero. This happens when the relationship is not a straight-line relationship. We mentioned this problem in Chapter 10.

A data point far from the other points in some X_i direction is called an *influential observation* if it strongly affects the regression fit. There are statistical techniques of testing whether or not the regression fit is strongly affected by a given observation. Computer routines such as MINITAB automatically search for outliers and influential observations. These are reported in the regression output so that the user is alerted to the possible effects of these observations. Table 11–10 shows part of

TABLE 11–10   Part of the MINITAB Output for Example (b)

```
Unusual Observations
Obs.      M1      EXPORTS      Fit    Stdev.Fit    Residual     St.Resid
  1      5.10     2.6000     2.6420    0.1288      -0.0420      -0.14  X
  2      4.90     2.6000     2.6438    0.1234      -0.0438      -0.14  X
 25      6.20     5.5000     4.5949    0.0676       0.9051       2.80R
 26      6.30     3.7000     4.6311    0.0651      -0.9311      -2.87R
 50      8.30     4.3000     5.1317    0.0648      -0.8317      -2.57R
 67      8.20     5.6000     4.9474    0.0668       0.6526       2.02R

R denotes an obs. with a large st. resid.
X denotes an obs. whose X value gives it large influence.
```

the MINITAB output for the analysis of Example (b). The table reports "unusual observations": large residuals and influential observations that affect the estimation of the regression relationship.

Lack of Fit and Other Problems

Model lack of fit occurs if, for example, we try to fit a straight line to curved data. There is a statistical method of determining the existence of lack of fit. The method consists of breaking down the sum of squares for error to a sum of squares due to pure error and a sum of squares due to lack of fit. The method requires that we have observations at equal values of the independent variables or near-neighbor points. This method is described in advanced texts on regression.

A statistical method for determining whether the errors in a regression model are correlated through time (thus violating the regression model assumptions) is the Durbin-Watson test. This test is discussed in a later section of this chapter. Once we determine that our regression model is valid and that there are no serious violations of assumptions, we can use the model for its intended purpose.

PROBLEMS

Analyze the following plot showing the residuals against $\hat{Y}$.

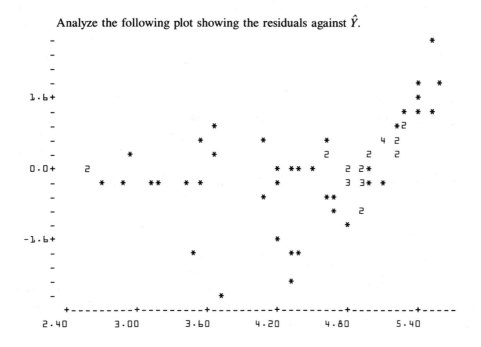

Answers

Nonnormality.

11–40. What is indicated by the following plot of the standardized residuals from a multiple regression analysis?

```
MTB > histogram of c3

Histogram of C3    N = 20

Midpoint    Count
   -1.5       2     **
   -1.0       5     *****
   -0.5       2     **
    0.0       3     ***
    0.5       2     **
    1.0       3     ***
    1.5       2     **
    2.0       1     *
```

11–41. Explain what an outlier is.

11–42.
─────
Computer, plot.

11–42. How can you detect outliers? Discuss two ways of doing so.

11–43. Why should outliers not be discarded and the regression run without them?

11–44. Discuss the possible effects of an outlier on the regression analysis.

11–44.
─────
Bias.

11–45. What is an influential observation? Give a few examples.

11–46. What are the limitations of forcing the regression surface to go through the origin?

11–47. Analyze the residual plot of Figure 11–15.

11–46.
─────
Bias.

11–7 Using the Multiple Regression Model for Prediction

The use of the multiple regression model for prediction follows the same lines as in the case of simple linear regression, discussed in Chapter 10. We obtain a regression model prediction of a value of the dependent variable, Y, based on given values of the independent variables, by substituting the values of the independent variables into the prediction equation. That is, we substitute the values of the X_i variables into the equation for $\hat{Y}$. We demonstrate this in Example (a).

The predicted value of Y is given by substituting the given values of advertising (X_1) and in-store promotions (X_2) for which we want to predict sales (Y) into equation 11–6 using the parameter estimates obtained in section 11–2. Let us predict sales when advertising is at a level of $10,000 and in-store promotions are at a level of $5,000.

$$\hat{Y} = 47.165 + 1.599X_1 + 1.149X_2$$
$$= 47.165 + (1.599)(10) + (1.149)(5) = 68.9 \text{ (thousand dollars)}$$

This prediction is not bad, since the value of Y actually occurring for these values of X_1 and X_2 is known from Table 11–1 to be $Y = 70$ (thousand dollars). Our point estimate of the expected value of Y, $E(Y)$, given these values of X_1 and X_2 is also 68.9 (thousand dollars). Note that our predictions lie *on* the estimated regression surface. The estimated regression surface for Example (a) is the plane shown in Figure 11–20.

We may also compute prediction intervals as well as confidence intervals for $E(Y)$, given values of the independent variables. As you recall, while the predicted value and the estimate of the mean value of Y are equal, the prediction interval is wider than a confidence interval for $E(Y)$ using the same confidence level. There is more uncertainty about the predicted value than there is about the average value of Y given the values X_i. The equation for a $(1 - \alpha)100\%$ prediction interval is an extension of equation 10–32 for simple linear regression. The only difference is that the

FIGURE 11–20   The Estimated Regression Plane for Example (a)

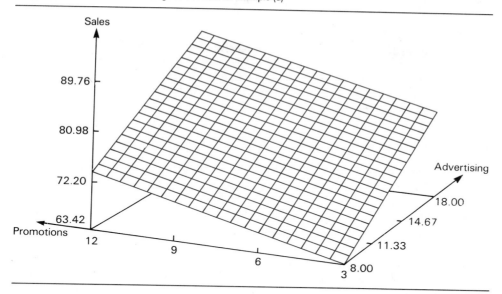

degrees of freedom of the t distribution are $n - (k + 1)$ rather than just $n - 2$, as is the case for $k = 1$. The standard error, when there are several explanatory variables, is a complicated expression, and we will not give it here; we will denote it by $s(\hat{Y})$. The prediction interval is given in equation 11–17.

A $(1 - \alpha)100\%$ prediction interval for a value of Y given values of X_i:

$$\hat{y} \pm t_{[\alpha/2, \, n-(k+1)]}\sqrt{s^2(\hat{Y}) + \text{MSE}} \qquad (11\text{–}17)$$

While the expression in the square root is complex, it is computed by most computer packages for regression. The prediction intervals for any values of the independent variables and a given level of confidence are produced as output.

Similarly, the equation for a $(1 - \alpha)100\%$ confidence interval for the conditional mean of Y is an extension of equation 10–33 for the simple linear regression. It is given as equation 11–18. Again, the degrees of freedom are $n - (k + 1)$. The formula for the standard error is complex and will not be given here. We will call the standard error $s[\hat{E}(Y)]$. The confidence interval for the conditional mean of Y is computable and may be reported, upon request, in the output of most computer packages that include regression analysis.

A $(1 - \alpha)100\%$ confidence interval for the conditional mean of Y:

$$\hat{y} \pm t_{[\alpha/2, \, n-(k+1)]}s(\hat{Y}) \qquad (11\text{–}18)$$

We demonstrate the use of equations 11–17 and 11–18 by computer analysis with Example (b). We use the MINITAB program to produce predictions of the level of U.S. exports to Singapore for given levels of local prices and money supply. We will also obtain a 95% prediction interval for each prediction and a 95% confidence interval for the mean level of exports for the given values of Price and M1. The MINITAB subcommand PREDICT is used for obtaining the output.

We want to predict exports to Singapore at three levels of M1 and Price. These levels are: 6 billion Singapore dollars and 160 (index value), 5 billion Singapore dollars and 150, and 4 billion Singapore dollars and 130. The MINITAB subcommands asking for the predictions and the prediction and confidence intervals (both 95%) are:

```
MTB > regress 'exports' on 2 'M1', 'PRICE';
SUBC>    predict 6 160;
SUBC>    predict 5 150;
SUBC>    predict 4 130.
```

The computer-produced predictions, standard errors, confidence intervals for the conditional means, and prediction intervals are given for the three selected points in Table 11–11.

The predictions are not very reliable because of the heteroscedasticity we discovered in the last section, but they are useful as a demonstration of the procedure. Remember that it is never a good idea to try to predict values outside the region of the data used in the estimation of the regression parameters because the regression relationship may be different outside that range. In this example, all predictions use values of the independent variables within the range of the estimation data.

When using regression models, it is important to know that a regression relationship between the dependent variable and some independent variables does not imply causality. Thus, if we find a linear relationship between Y and X, it does not necessarily mean that X causes Y. Causality is very difficult to determine and to prove. There is also the issue of spurious correlations between variables—correlations that are not real. Montgomery and Peck give an example of a regression analysis of the number of mentally disturbed people in the United Kingdom versus the number of radio receiver licenses issued in that country.[11] The regression relationship is close to a perfect straight line, with $r^2 = 0.9842$. Can the conclusion be drawn that there is a relationship between the number of radio receiver licenses and the incidence of mental illness? Probably not. Both variables—the number of licenses and the incidence of mental illness—are related to a third variable: population size. The increase in both of these variables reflects the growth of the population in general, and there is probably no *direct* connection between the two variables. We must be very careful in our interpretation of regression results.

TABLE 11–11 Predictions, Confidence Intervals, and Prediction Intervals for Example (b)

Fit	Stdev.Fit	95% C. I.	95% P. I.
4.6708	0.0853	(4.5003, 4.8412)	(3.9885, 5.3530)
3.9390	0.0901	(3.7590, 4.1190)	(3.2543, 4.6237)
2.8370	0.1116	(2.6140, 3.0599)	(2.1397, 3.5342)

[11] D. Montgomery and E. Peck, *Introduction to Linear Regression Analysis* (New York: Wiley, 1982).

11–48.   Explain why it is not a good idea to use the regression equation for predicting values outside the range of the estimation data set.

11–49.   Use equation 11–6 to predict sales in Example (a) when the level of advertising is $8,000 and in-store promotions are at a level of $12,000.

11–50.   Using the regression relationship you estimated in problem 11–8, predict the value of a home of 1,800 square feet located 2.0 miles from the center of the town.

11–51.   Using the regression equation from problem 11–25, predict the change in industrial prices (as a percentage) when the change in industrial wages is 4%, the change in capacity utilization is −1%, and the change in the price of imported raw materials is −5%.

11–52.   Using the information in Table 11–11, what is the estimated standard error of $\hat{Y}$? What is the estimated standard error of $\hat{E}(Y)$?

11–53.   Use a computer to produce a prediction interval and a confidence interval for the conditional mean of Y for the prediction in problem 11–49. Use the data in Table 11–1.

11–54.   What is the difference between a predicted value of the dependent variable and the conditional mean of the dependent variable?

11–55.   Why is the prediction interval of 95% wider than the 95% confidence interval for the conditional mean using the same values of the independent variables?

Answers
11–50.
$365,916
11–52.
0.341, 0.085

11–8   Qualitative Independent Variables

The variables we have encountered so far in this chapter have all been *quantitative* variables: variables that can take on values on a scale. Sales volume, advertising expenditure, exports, the money supply, and people's ratings of an automobile are all examples of quantitative variables. In this section, we will discuss the use of *qualitative* variables as explanatory variables in a regression model. Qualitative variables are variables that describe a quality rather than a quantity. This should remind you of analysis of variance in Chapter 9. There we had qualitative variables such as the kind of resort in the Club Med example, type of airplane, type of coffee, etc.

In some cases, it is very useful to include information on one or more qualitative variables in our multiple regression model. For example, a hotel chain may be interested in predicting the number of occupied rooms as a function of the economy of the area in which the hotel is located, as well as advertising level and some other quantitative variables. The hotel may also want to know whether or not the peak season is in progress—a qualitative variable that may have a lot to do with the level of occupancy at the hotel. A property appraiser may be interested in predicting the value of different residential units on the basis of several quantitative variables, such as age of the unit and area in square feet, as well as the qualitative variable of whether the unit is owned or rented.

Each of these qualitative variables has only two *levels:* peak season versus non-peak season, rental unit versus nonrental unit. An easy way to quantify such a qualitative variable is by way of a single **indicator variable,** also called a **dummy variable.** An indicator variable is a variable that indicates whether or not some condition holds. It has the value 1 when the condition holds and the value 0 when the condition does not hold. If you are familiar with computer science, you probably know the indicator variable by another name: *binary variable.* The variable is called *binary* because it takes on only two possible values, 0 and 1.

When included in the model of hotel occupancy, the indicator variable will equal 0 if it is not peak season and 1 if it is (or vice versa; it makes no difference). Similarly, in the property value analysis, the dummy variable will have the value 0 when the unit is rented and 1 when the unit is owned, or vice versa. We define the general form of an indicator variable in equation (11–19).

An indicator variable of qualitative level A:

$$X_h = \begin{cases} 1 \text{ if level A is obtained} \\ 0 \text{ if level A is not obtained} \end{cases} \quad (11-19)$$

The use of indicator variables in regression analysis is very simple. No special computational routines are required. All we do is code the indicator variable as 1 whenever the quality of interest is obtained for a particular data point and as 0 when it is not obtained. The rest of the variables in the regression equation are left the same. We demonstrate the use of an indicator variable in modeling a qualitative variable with two levels in the following example.

EXAMPLE (c)

A motion picture industry analyst wants to estimate the gross earnings generated by a movie. The estimate will be based on different variables involved in the film's production. The independent variables considered are X_1 = production cost of the movie and X_2 = total cost of all promotional activities. A third variable that the analyst wants to consider is the qualitative variable of whether or not the movie is based on a book published before the release of the movie. This third, qualitative variable is handled by the use of an indicator variable: $X_3 = 0$ if the movie is not based on a book, and $X_3 = 1$ if it is. The analyst obtains information on a random sample of 20 Hollywood movies made within the last five years (the inference is to be made only about the population of movies in this particular category). The data are given in Table 11–12. The variable Y is

TABLE 11–12 The Data for Example (c)

Movie	Gross Earnings, Million $ (Y)	Production Cost, Million $ (X_1)	Promotion Cost, Million $ (X_2)	Book (X_3)
1	28	4.2	1	0
2	35	6.0	3	1
3	50	5.5	6	1
4	20	3.3	1	0
5	75	12.5	11	1
6	60	9.6	8	1
7	15	2.5	0.5	0
8	45	10.8	5	0
9	50	8.4	3	1
10	34	6.6	2	0
11	48	10.7	1	1
12	82	11.0	15	1
13	24	3.5	4	0
14	50	6.9	10	0
15	58	7.8	9	1
16	63	10.1	10	0
17	30	5.0	1	1
18	37	7.5	5	0
19	45	6.4	8	1
20	72	10.0	12	1

gross earnings, in millions of dollars. The two quantitative independent variables are also in millions of dollars.

The data are entered into the regression program of the MINITAB package. The resulting output is presented in Table 11–13. The coefficient of determination of this regression is very high; the F statistic value is very significant, and we have a good regression relationship. From the individual t ratios and their p-values, we find that all three independent variables are important in the equation.

From the intercept of 7.84, we could (erroneously, of course) deduce that a movie costing nothing to produce or promote, and that is not based on a book, would still gross \$7.84 million! The point 0 ($X_1 = 0$, $X_2 = 0$, $X_3 = 0$) is outside the estimation region, and the regression relationship may not hold for that region. In our case, it evidently does not. The intercept is merely a reference point used to move the regression surface upward to where it should be in the estimation region.

The estimated slope for the cost variable, 2.85, means that—within the estimation region—an increase of \$1 million in a movie's production cost (the other variables held constant) increases the movie's gross earnings by an average of \$2.85 million. Similarly, the estimated slope coefficient for the promotion variable means that, in the estimation region of the variables, an increase of \$1 million in promotional activities (with the other variables constant) increases the movie's gross earnings by an average of \$2.28 million.

How do we interpret the estimated coefficient of variable X_3? The estimated coefficient of 7.17 means that having the movie based on a published book ($X_3 = 1$) increases the movie's gross earnings by an average of \$7.17 million. Again, the inference is valid only for the region of the data used in the estimation. When $X_3 = 0$, that is, when the movie is not based on a book, the last term in the estimated equation for $\hat{Y}$ in Table 11–13 drops out—there is no added \$7.17 million.

What do we learn from this example about the function of the indicator variable? Note that the predicted value of Y, given the values of the quantitative independent variables, shifts upward (or downward, depending on the sign of the estimated coefficient) by an amount equal to the coefficient of the indicator variable whenever the variable is equal to 1. In this particular case, the surface of the regression—the plane formed by the variables Y, X_1, and X_2—is split into two surfaces: one corresponding to movies based on books and the other corresponding to movies not based on books. The appro-

TABLE 11–13 MINITAB Regression Output for Example (c)

```
MTB > REGRESS 'EARN' ON 3 PREDICTORS 'COST', 'PROM', 'BOOK'

The regression equation is
EARN = 7.84 + 2.85 COST + 2.28 PROM + 7.17 BOOK

Predictor      Coef        Stdev       t-ratio      p
Constant       7.836       2.333       3.36         0.004
COST           2.8477      0.3923      7.26         0.000
PROM           2.2782      0.2534      8.99         0.000
BOOK           7.166       1.818       3.94         0.001

s = 3.690      R-sq = 96.7%      R-sq(adj) = 96.0%

Analysis of Variance

  SOURCE      DF        SS         MS        F         p
Regression     3      6325.2     2108.4    154.89    0.000
Error         16       217.8       13.6
Total         19      6543.0
```

FIGURE 11–21   The Two Regression Planes of Example (c)

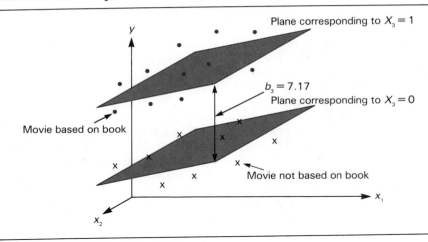

priate surface depends on whether $X_3 = 0$ or $X_3 = 1$; the two estimated surfaces are separated by a distance equal to $b_3 = 7.17$. This is demonstrated in Figure 11–21. The regression surface in this example is a plane, so we can draw its image (for a higher-dimensional surface, the same idea holds).

We will now look at the simpler case, with one independent quantitative variable and one indicator variable. Here we assume an estimated regression relationship of the form: $\hat{Y} = b_0 + b_1 X_1 + b_2 X_2$, where X_1 is a quantitative variable and X_2 is an indicator variable. The regression relationship is a straight line, and the indicator variable splits the line into two parallel straight lines, one for each level (0 or 1) of the qualitative variable. The points belonging to one level [a level could be Book, as in Example (c)] are shown as triangles, and the points belonging to the other level are shown as squares. The distance between the two parallel lines (measured as the difference between the two intercepts) is equal to the estimated coefficient of the dummy variable, X_2. The situation is demonstrated in Figure 11–22.

FIGURE 11–22   A Regression with One Quantitative Variable and One Dummy Variable

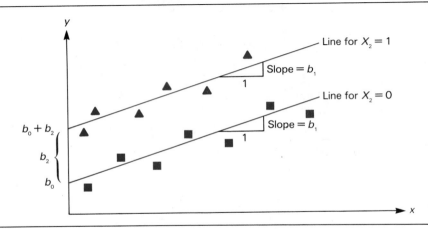

We have been dealing with qualitative variables that have only two levels. Therefore, it has sufficed to use an indicator variable with two possible values, 0 or 1. What about situations where we have a qualitative variable with more than two levels? Should we use an "indicator" variable with more than two values? The answer to this is no. Were we to do this and give our variable values such as 0, 1, 2, 3, . . . to indicate qualitative levels, we would be using a *quantitative* variable that has several discrete values but no values in between. Also, the assignment of the qualities to the values would be arbitrary. Since there may be no justification for using the values 1, 2, 3, etc., we would be imposing a very special measuring scale on the regression problem—a scale that may not be appropriate. Instead, we will use *several* indicator variables.

We account for a qualitative variable with r levels by the use of $r - 1$ indicator $(0 - 1)$ variables.

We will now demonstrate the use of this rule by changing Example (c) somewhat. Suppose that the analyst is not interested in whether or not a movie is based on a book, but rather in using an explanatory variable that represents the category to which each movie belongs: adventure, drama, or romance. Since this qualitative variable has $r = 3$ levels, the rule tells us that we need to model this variable by using $r - 1 = 2$ indicator variables. Each of the two indicator variables will have one of two possible values, as before: 0 or 1. The setup of the two dummy variables indicating the level of the qualitative variable, movie category, is shown in the following table. For simplicity, let us also assume that the only quantitative variable in the equation is production cost (we leave out the promotion variable). This will allow us to have lines rather than planes. We let $X_1 = $ production cost, as before. We now define the two dummy variables, X_2 and X_3.

Category	X_2	X_3
Adventure	0	0
Drama	0	1
Romance	1	0

The definition of the values of X_2 and X_3 for representing the different categories is arbitrary: we could just as well have assigned the values $(X_2 = 0, X_3 = 0)$ to drama or to romance rather than to adventure. The important thing to remember is that the number of dummy variables is one less than the number of categories they represent. Otherwise our model will be overspecified, and problems will occur. In this example, the variable X_2 is the indicator variable for romance; when a movie is in the romance category, the variable has the value 1. Similarly, X_3 is the indicator for drama and has the value 1 in cases where a movie is in the drama category. There are only three categories under consideration, so when both X_2 and X_3 are zero, the movie is neither a drama nor a romance; therefore, it must be an adventure movie.

If we use the model

$$Y = \beta_0 + \beta_1 X_1 + \beta_2 X_2 + \beta_3 X_3 + \epsilon \qquad (11-20)$$

with X_2 and X_3 as defined, we will be estimating three regression lines, one line per category. The line for adventure movies would be $\hat{Y} = b_0 + b_1 X_1$ because here both X_2 and X_3 are zero. The drama line would be $\hat{Y} = b_0 + b_3 + b_1 X_1$ because here $X_3 = 1$ and $X_2 = 0$. In the case of romance movies, our line would be $\hat{Y} = b_0 + b_2 + b_1 X_1$ because in this case $X_2 = 1$ and $X_3 = 0$. Since the estimated coefficients, b_i, may be negative as well as positive, the different parallel lines may position themselves above or below each other, as determined by the data. Of course, the b_i may be estimates of zero. If we should accept the null hypothesis H_0: $\beta_3 = 0$, using the usual t test, it would mean that there is no evidence that the adventure and the drama lines are different. That is, it would mean that, on the average, adventure movies and drama movies have the same gross earnings as determined by the production costs. If we determine that β_2 is not different from zero, the adventure and romance lines will be the same and the drama line may be different. In case the adventure line is different from drama and romance, these two being the same, we would determine statistically that both β_2 and β_3 are different from zero, but not different from each other.

If we have three regression lines, why bother with indicator variables at all? Why not just run three separate regressions, each for a different movie category? One answer to this question has already been given: The use of indicator variables and their estimated regression coefficients with their standard errors allows us to test *statistically* whether the qualitative variable of interest has any effect on the dependent variable. We are able to test whether we have one distinct line, two lines, three lines, or as many lines as there are levels of the qualitative variable. Another reason is that even if we know that there are, say, three distinct lines, estimating them together via a regression analysis with dummy variables allows us to pool the degrees of freedom for the three regressions, leading to better estimation and a more efficient analysis.

Figure 11–23 shows the three regression lines of our new version of Example (c); each line shows the regression relationship between a movie's production cost and the resulting movie's gross earnings in its category. In case there are two independent quantitative variables, say, if we add promotions as a second quantitative variable, we would have three regression *planes* like the two planes shown in Figure 11–21. In Figure 11–23, we show adventure movies as triangles, romance movies as squares, and drama movies as circles. Assuming that adventure movies have the highest average gross earnings, followed by romance and drama, the estimated coefficients b_2 and b_3 would have to be negative, as can be seen from the figure.

Can we run a regression on a qualitative variable (by use of dummy variables)

FIGURE 11–23   The Three Possible Regression Lines, Depending on Movie Category [Modified Example (c)]

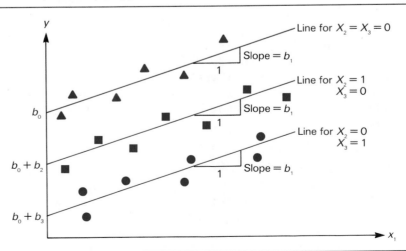

only? Yes. You have already seen this model, essentially. Running a regression on a qualitative variable only means modeling some quantitative response by levels of a qualitative factor: it is the *analysis of variance*, discussed in Chapter 9. Doing the analysis by regression means using a different computational procedure than was done in Chapter 9, but it is still the analysis of variance. Two qualitative variables make the analysis a two-way ANOVA, and interaction terms are cross products of the appropriate dummy variables, such as $X_2 X_3$. We will say more about cross products a little later. For now, we note that the regression approach to ANOVA allows us more freedom. Remember that a two-way ANOVA, using the method in Chapter 9, required a *balanced* design (equal sample size in each cell). If we use the regression approach, we are no longer restricted to the balanced design and may use any sample size.

Let us go back to regressions using quantitative independent variables with some qualitative variables. In some situations, we are not interested in using a regression equation for prediction or for any of the other common uses of regression analysis. Instead, we are intrinsically interested in a qualitative variable used in the regression. Let us be more specific. Recall our original Example (c). Suppose we are not interested in predicting a movie's gross earnings based on the production cost, promotions, and whether or not the movie is based on a book. Suppose instead that we are interested in answering the question: Is there a difference in average gross earnings between movies based on books and movies not based on books?

To answer this question, we use the estimated regression relationship. We use the estimate b_3 and its standard error in testing the null hypothesis H_0: $\beta_3 = 0$ versus the alternative H_1: $\beta_3 \neq 0$. The question is really an ANOVA question. We want to know whether a difference exists in the population means of the two groups movies based on books and movies not based on books. However, we have some quantitative variables that affect the variable we are measuring (gross earnings). We therefore incorporate information on these variables (production cost and promotions) in a regression model aimed at answering our ANOVA question. When we do this, that is, when we attempt to answer the question of whether differences in population means exist, using a regression equation to account for other sources of variation in our data (the quantitative independent variables), we are conducting an **analysis of covariance**. The independent variables used in the analysis of covariance are called **concomitant variables,** and their purpose in the analysis is not to explain or predict the independent variable, but rather to reduce the errors in the test of significance of the indicator variable or variables.

One of the interesting applications of analysis of covariance is in providing statistical evidence in cases of sex or race discrimination. We demonstrate this particular use in the following example.

A large service company was sued by its female employees in a class action suit alleging sex discrimination in salary levels. The claim was that, on the average, a man and a woman of the same education and experience received different salaries: the man's salary was believed higher than the woman's salary. The attorney representing the women employees hired a statistician to provide statistical evidence supporting the women's side of the case. The statistician was allowed access to the company's payroll files and obtained a random sample of 100 employees, 40 of whom were women. In addition to salary, the files contained information on education and experience. The statistician then ran a regression analysis of salary, Y, versus the three variables: education level, X_1 (on a scale based on the total number of years in school, with an additional

EXAMPLE (d)

TABLE 11–14 Regression Results for Example (d)

Variable	Coefficient Estimate	Standard Error
Constant	8,547	32.6
Education	949	45.1
Experience	1,258	78.5
Sex	−3,256	212.4

value added to the score for each college degree earned, by type); years of experience, X_2 (on a scale that combined the number of years of experience directly related to the job assignment with the number of years of similar job experience); and sex, X_3 (0 if the employee was a man and 1 if the employee was a woman). The computer output for the regression included the results: F ratio = 1,237.56 and $R^2 = 0.67$, as well as the coefficient estimates and standard errors given in Table 11–14. Based on this information, does the attorney for the women employees have a case against the company?

SOLUTION

Let us analyze the regression results. Remember that we are using a regression with a dummy variable to perform an analysis of covariance. There is certainly a regression relationship between salary and at least some of the variables, as evidenced by the very large F value, which is beyond any critical point we can find in a table. The p-value is very small. The coefficient of determination is not extremely high, but then we are using very few variables to explain variation in salary levels. This being the case, 67% explained variation, based on these variables only, is quite respectable. Now we consider the information in Table 11–14.

Dividing the four coefficient estimates by their standard errors, we find that all three variables are important, and the intercept is different from zero. However, we are particularly interested in the hypothesis test:

$$H_0: \beta_3 = 0$$
$$H_1: \beta_3 \neq 0$$

Our test statistic is $t_{(96)} = b_3/s(b_3) = -3,256/212.4 = -15.33$. Since t with 96 degrees of freedom [df $= n - (k + 1) = 100 - 4 = 96$] is virtually a standard normal random variable, we conduct this as a Z test. The computed test statistic value of -15.33 lies very far in the left-hand rejection region. This means that there are two regressions: one for men and one for women. Since we coded X_3 as 0 for a man and 1 for a woman, the women's estimated regression plane lies $3,256 below the regression plane for men. Since the parameter of the sex variable is significantly different from zero (with an extremely small p-value) and is negative, there is statistical evidence of sex discrimination in this case. The situation here is as seen in Figure 11–21 for the previous example: we have two regression planes, one below the other. The only difference is that in this example, we were not interested in using the regression for prediction, but rather for an ANOVA-type statistical test.

Interactions between Qualitative and Quantitative Variables

Do the different regression lines or higher-dimensional surfaces have to be parallel? The answer is no. Sometimes, there are *interactions* between a qualitative variable and one or more quantitative variables. The idea of an interaction in regression analysis is the same as the idea of interaction between factors in a two-way ANOVA model (as well as higher-order ANOVAs). In regression analysis with qualitative variables, the interaction between a qualitative variable and a quantitative variable makes the regression lines or planes at different levels of the dummy variables have *different slopes*. Let us look at the simple case where we have one independent quantitative variable, X_1, and one qualitative variable with two levels, modeled by the dummy variable X_2. When an interaction exists between the qualitative and the quantitative variables, the slope of the regression line for $X_2 = 0$ is different from the slope of the regression line for $X_2 = 1$. This is shown in Figure 11–24.

We model the interactions between variables by the cross product of the variables. The interaction of X_1 with X_2 in this case is modeled by adding the term $X_1 X_2$ to the regression equation. We are thus interested in the model:

$$Y = \beta_0 + \beta_1 X_1 + \beta_2 X_2 + \beta_3 X_1 X_2 + \epsilon \qquad (11\text{--}21)$$

We can use the results of the estimation procedure to test for the existence of an interaction. We do so by testing the significance of the parameter β_3.

When the regression parameters β_1, β_2, and β_3 are all nonzero, we have two distinct lines with different intercepts and different slopes. When β_2 is zero, we have two lines with the same intercept and different slopes (this is unlikely to happen, except when both intercepts are zero). When β_3 is zero, we have two parallel lines, as in the case of equation 11–20. If β_1 is zero, of course, we have no regression—just an ANOVA model; we then assume that β_3 is also zero. Assuming the full model of equation 11–21, representing two distinct lines with different slopes and different intercepts, the intercept and the slope of each line will be as shown in Figure 11–24. By substituting $X_2 = 0$ or $X_2 = 1$ into equation 11–21, verify the definition of each slope and each intercept.

Again, there are advantages to estimating a single model for the different levels of the indicator variable. These are the pooling of degrees of freedom (we assume that the spread of the data about the two or more lines is equal) and an understanding of the joint process generating the data. More important, we may use the model to statistically *test* for the equality of intercepts and slopes. Note that when several indicator variables are used in modeling one or more qualitative variables, there are several possible interaction terms in the model. We will learn more about interactions in general in the next section.

FIGURE 11–24 The Effects of an Interaction between a Qualitative Variable and a Quantitative Variable

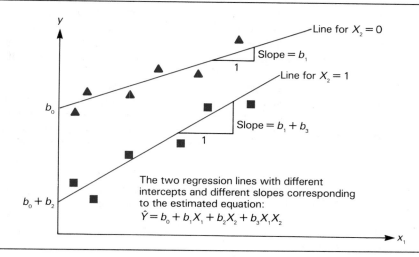

PROBLEMS

Answers

11–56.

Interaction model.
Both variables significant.
Very small R^2.

11–56. An article about stock returns of financial institutions reports the results of a multiple regression analysis of the dependent variable R_P (weekly holding period return on an equally weighted portfolio of savings and loan institutions' stocks) on the independent variable, R_I (weekly holding period return on the GNMA index for the same week) and on a dummy variable, D (0 during January–December 1979, a period during which returns were believed to be different from other periods, and 1 for all other time periods).[12] The estimated regression relationship is:

$$\hat{R}_P = 0.004 + 1.41R_I - 0.874R_I D$$
$$\quad\quad (0.02)\quad (0.287)\quad (0.281)$$

The authors also report $R^2 = 0.142$. The sample size is large (data are weekly, from 1976 to 1982). Give a complete analysis of the results. What kind of model is this? Which parameters are significant? What else can you say about the analysis?

11–57. Echlin, Inc., makes parts for automobiles. The company is engaged in strong competition with Japanese, Taiwanese, and Korean manufacturers of the same auto parts. Recently, the company hired a statistician to study the relationship between monthly sales and the independent variable, number of cars on the road. Data on the explanatory variable are published in national statistical reports. Because of the keen competition with firms in the Orient, an indicator variable was also used. This variable was given the value 1 during months when restrictions on imports from the Orient were in effect, and 0 when such restrictions were not in effect. Denoting sales by Y, total number of cars on the road by X_1, and the import restriction dummy variable by X_2, the following regression equation was estimated:

$$\hat{Y} = -567.3 + 0.006X_1 + 26{,}540X_2$$

The standard error of the intercept estimate was 38.5, that of the coefficient of X_1 was 0.0002, and the standard error of the coefficient of X_2 was 1,534.67. The multiple coefficient of determination was $R^2 = 0.783$. The sample size used was $n = 60$ months (five years of data). Analyze the results presented. What kind of regression model was used? Comment on the significance of the model parameters and the value of R^2. How many distinct regression lines are there? What likely happens during times of restricted trade with the Orient?

11–58.

Should use two dummy
variables.

11–58. A chemical company has three plants. Due to a shortage of labor and the intense heat involved in production, only one plant is operated at a time, and operations are shifted every few days to another plant. The company wants to estimate the relationship between daily production (Y) and the independent variable, labor force present (X_1). Since it is known that differences may exist among the different plants, it is proposed that a qualitative variable, X_2, also be used. This variable is defined as: $X_2 = 1$ if plant A is used, 2 if plant B is used, and 3 if plant C is used during the day. Comment on the proposed regression model.

11–59. If we have a regression model with no quantitative variables and only two qualitative variables, represented by some indicator variables and cross products, what kind of analysis is carried out?

11–60.

Analysis of covariance.
Length of stay; concomi-
tant.

11–60. Recall our Club Med example of Chapter 9. Suppose that vacationers at the Club Med resorts do not all stay an equal length of time at the resort—different people stay different numbers of days. The club's research director knows that people's ratings of the resorts tend to differ depending on the number of days spent at the resort. Design a new method for studying whether or not there are differences among the average population ratings of the five Caribbean resorts. What is the name of your method of analysis, and how is the analysis carried out? Explain.

11–61. A financial institution specializing in venture capital is interested in predicting the success of business operations the institution helps to finance. Success is defined by the insti-

---

[12] J. Brickley and C. James, "Access to Deposit Insurance, Insolvency Rules, and the Stock Returns of Financial Institutions," *Journal of Financial Economics* (July 1986).

tution as return on its investment, as a percentage, after three years of operation. The explanatory variables used are Investment (in thousands of dollars), Early investment (in thousands of dollars), and two dummy variables denoting the category of business. The values of these variables are (0,0) for high-tech industry, (0,1) for bioengineering companies, and (1,0) for aerospace firms. Following is part of the computer output for this analysis, generated by MINITAB. Interpret the output, and give a complete analysis of the results of this study based on the provided information.

```
The regression equation is
RETURN = 6.16 + 0.617 INVEST + 0.151 EARLY + 11.1 DUM1 + 4.15 DUM2
Predictor       Coef        Stdev
Constant        6.162       1.642
INVEST          0.6168      0.1581
EARLY           0.1509      0.1465
DUM1           11.051       1.355
DUM2            4.150       1.315

s = 2.148            R-sq = 91.6%     R-sq(adj) = 89.4%

Analysis of Variance

   SOURCE       DF          SS
Regression       4        755.99
Error           15         69.21
Total           19        825.20
```

11–9 Polynomial Regression

Often, the relationship between the dependent variable, Y, and one or more of the independent X variables is not a straight-line relationship but, rather, has some curvature to it. Several such situations are shown in Figure 11–25 (we show the curved

FIGURE 11–25 Situations Where the Relationship between X and Y Is Curved

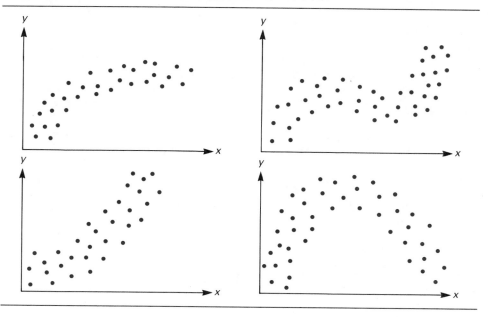

relationship between Y and a *single* explanatory variable, X). In each of the situations shown, a straight line provides a poor fit to the data. Instead, polynomials of order higher than 1, that is, functions of higher powers of X, such as X^2 and X^3, provide much better fit to our data. Such polynomials in the X variable or in several X_i variables are still considered *linear* regression models. Only models where the *parameters*, β_i, are not all of the first power are called nonlinear models. The multiple linear regression model thus covers situations of fitting data to polynomial functions. The general form of a polynomial regression model in one variable, X, is given in equation 11–22.

One-variable polynomial regression model:

$$Y = \beta_0 + \beta_1 X + \beta_2 X^2 + \beta_3 X^3 + \cdots + \beta_m X^m + \epsilon \qquad (11\text{--}22)$$

where m is the *degree* of the polynomial—the highest power of X appearing in the equation. The degree of the polynomial is the *order* of the model.

Figure 11–26 shows how second- and third-degree polynomial models provide good fits for the data sets in Figure 11–25. A straight line is also shown in each case, for comparison. Compare the fit provided in each case by a polynomial with the poor fit provided by a straight line. Also compare the use of low-order polynomials in these examples with the polynomial fit shown in Figure 11–2 in the introduction of this chapter. There the polynomial of a high order was matching the variation in the data and thus modeling the random variation rather than the general trend, unlike the examples shown in Figure 11–26. Some authors, for example, Weisberg, recommend using polynomials of order no greater than 2 (the third-order example in

FIGURE 11–26   The Fits Provided for the Data Sets in Figure 11–25 by Polynomial Models

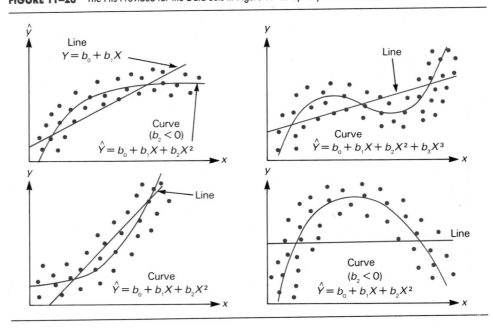

Figure 11–26 would be an exception) because of the overfitting problem.[13] At any rate, models should never be of order 6 or higher (unless the powers of X have been transformed in a special way). Seber shows that when a polynomial of degree 6 or greater is fit to a data set, a matrix involved in regression computations becomes *ill conditioned,* which means that very small errors in the data cause relatively large errors in the estimated model parameters.[14] In short, we must be very careful with polynomial regression models and try to obtain the most parsimonious polynomial model that will fit our data. In the next section, we will discuss *transformations* of data that often can change curved data sets into a straight-line form. If we can find such a transformation for a data set, it is always better to use a first-order model on the transformed data set than to use a higher-order polynomial model on the original data. It should be intuitively clear that problems may arise in polynomial regression. The variables X and X^2, for example, are clearly not independent of each other. This may cause the problem of multicollinearity in cases where the data are confined to a narrow range of values.

Having seen what to beware of in using polynomial regression, let us see how these models are used. Since powers of X can be obtained directly from the value of the variable X, it is relatively easy to run polynomial models. We enter the data into the computer and add a command that uses X to form a new variable. In a second-order model, using the MINITAB package, we add a command to multiply the data column corresponding to X by itself, thus forming the variable X^2. Then we run a multiple regression model with two "independent" variables: X and X^2. We demonstrate this with a new example.

It is well known that sales response to advertising usually follows a curve reflecting the diminishing returns to advertising expenditure. As a firm increases its advertising expenditure, sales increase, but the rate of increase drops continually after a certain point. If we consider company sales profits as a function of advertising expenditure, we find that the response function can be very well approximated by a second-order (quadratic) model of the form:

$$Y = \beta_0 + \beta_1 X + \beta_2 X^2 + \epsilon$$

[see D. Tull et al. (1986)].[15] A quadratic response function such as this one is shown in Figure 11–27.

It is very important for a firm to identify its own point X_m shown in the figure. At this point, a maximum benefit is achieved from advertising in terms of the resulting sales profits. Figure 11–27 shows a general form of the sales response to advertising. In order to find its own maximum point, X_m, a firm needs to estimate its response-to-advertising function from its own operation data, obtained by using different levels of advertising at different time periods and observing the resulting sales profits. For a particular firm, the data on monthly sales (Y) and monthly advertising expenditure (X), both in hundred thousand dollars, are given in Table 11–15. The table shows the data as entered into the MINITAB program. The table also shows the values of X^2 used in the regression analysis.

---

[13] Sanford Weisberg, *Applied Linear Regression,* 2nd ed. (New York: Wiley, 1985).

[14] G. A. F. Seber, *Linear Regression Analysis* (New York: Wiley, 1977).

[15] D. Tull et al., "Leveraged Decision Making in Advertising," *Journal of Marketing Research* (February 1986).

FIGURE 11–27 A Quadratic Response Function of Sales Profits to Advertising Expenditure

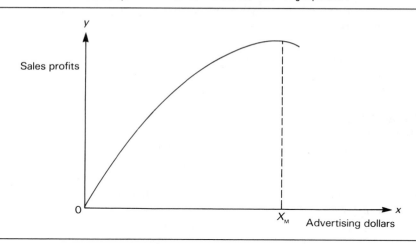

TABLE 11–15 Data for Example (e)

ROW	SALES	ADVERT	ADVSQR
1	5.0	1.0	1.00
2	6.0	1.8	3.24
3	6.5	1.6	2.56
4	7.0	1.7	2.89
5	7.5	2.0	4.00
6	8.0	2.0	4.00
7	10.0	2.3	5.29
8	10.8	2.8	7.84
9	12.0	3.5	12.25
10	13.0	3.3	10.89
11	15.5	4.8	23.04
12	15.0	5.0	25.00
13	16.0	7.0	49.00
14	17.0	8.1	65.61
15	18.0	8.0	64.00
16	18.0	10.0	100.00
17	18.5	8.0	64.00
18	21.0	12.7	161.29
19	20.0	12.0	144.00
20	22.0	15.0	225.00
21	23.0	14.4	207.36

SOLUTION

Figure 11–28 shows the computer-generated plot of the data, sales versus advertising. Above the plot, the figure also shows the MINITAB command that multiplies column C2 (the advertising expenditure column) by itself to form X^2. The next command names the variables, Sales and Advert, and the newly formed variable Advsqr. From the plot, we see that the increases in sales diminish as advertising expenditure increases, and a saturation point will be reached at some level. From the plot, it seems that a quadratic regression model may fit the data well.

Table 11–16 gives the regression command and the output of the regression analysis of sales versus advertising expenditure and squared advertising expenditure, a quadratic regression model. From the results, we see that a second-order regression model, a quadratic model in the advertising variable, fits the data very well. The coefficient of determination is $R^2 = 0.959$, the F ratio is significant, and both Advert and Advsqr are very significant. The negative sign of the squared variable, Advsqr, is logical because a

FIGURE 11–28 MINITAB Commands for Forming an X^2 Variable and a Plot of the Data for Example (e)

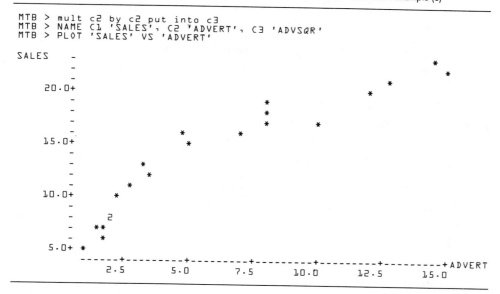

```
MTB > mult c2 by c2 put into c3
MTB > NAME C1 'SALES', C2 'ADVERT', C3 'ADVSQR'
MTB > PLOT 'SALES' VS 'ADVERT'
```

TABLE 11–16 The Regression Results for Example (e)

```
MTB > regress 'SALES' on 2 predictors, 'ADVERT', 'ADVSQR'

The regression equation is
SALES = 3.52 + 2.51 ADVERT - 0.0875 ADVSQR

Predictor      Coef        Stdev       t-ratio      p
Constant       3.5150      0.7385       4.76       0.000
ADVERT         2.5148      0.2580       9.75       0.000
ADVSQR        -0.08745     0.01658     -5.28       0.000

s = 1.228      R-sq = 95.9%      R-sq(adj) = 95.4%

Analysis of Variance

   SOURCE      DF         SS          MS          F          p
Regression      2       630.26      315.13      208.99      0.000
Error          18        27.14        1.51
Total          20       657.40
```

quadratic function with a maximum point has a negative leading coefficient (the coefficient of X^2). We may write the estimated quadratic regression model of Y in terms of X and X^2 as follows.

$$Y = 3.52 + 2.51X - 0.0875X^2 + e \qquad (11-23)$$

The equation of the estimated regression curve itself is given by dropping the error term, e, giving an equation for the predicted values, $\hat{Y}$, that lie on the quadratic curve:

$$\hat{Y} = 3.52 + 2.51X - 0.0875X^2 \qquad (11-24)$$

In our particular example, the equation of the curve (equation 11–24) is of importance, as it can be differentiated with respect to X, with the derivative then set to zero and the result solved for the maximizing value X_m shown in Figure 11–27. (If you have not studied calculus, you may ignore the preceding statement.) The result here is $x_m = 14.34$ (hundred thousand dollars). This value maximizes sales profits with respect to advertising (within estimation error of the regression). Thus, the firm should set its advertising level at $1.434 million. The fact that polynomials can always be differentiated gives these models an advantage over alternative models. Remember, however, to keep the order of the model low.

Other Variables and Cross-Product Terms

The polynomial regression model in one variable, X, given in equation 11–22, can easily be extended to include more than one independent explanatory variable. The new model, which includes several variables at different powers, is a mixture of the usual multiple regression model in k variables (equation 11–1) and the polynomial regression model (equation 11–22). When several variables are in a regression equation, we may also consider *interactions* among variables. We have already encountered interactions in the previous section, where we discussed interactions between an indicator variable and a quantitative variable. We saw that an interaction term is just the cross product of the two variables involved. In this section, we discuss the general concept of interactions between variables, quantitative or not.

The interaction term, $X_i X_j$, is a *second-order* term (the product of two variables is classified the same way as an X^2 term). Similarly, $X_i X_j^2$, for example, is a third-order term. Thus, models that incorporate interaction terms find their natural place within the class of polynomial models. Equation 11–25 is a second-order regression model in two variables, X_1 and X_2. This model includes both first and second powers of both variables and an interaction term.

$$Y = \beta_0 + \beta_1 X_1 + \beta_2 X_2 + \beta_3 X_1^2 + \beta_4 X_2^2 + \beta_5 X_1 X_2 + \epsilon \qquad (11\text{–}25)$$

A regression surface of a model like that of equation 11–25 is shown in Figure 11–29. There are, of course, many possible surfaces depending on the values of the coefficients of all terms in the equation. Equation 11–25 may be generalized to more

FIGURE 11–29 An Example of the Regression Surface of a Second-Order Model in Two Variables

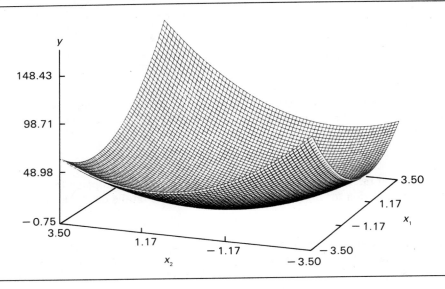

TABLE 11–17 An Example of Regression Output for a Second-Order Model in Two Variables

Variable	Estimate	Standard Error	*t* Ratio
X_1	2.34	0.92	2.54
X_2	3.11	1.05	2.96
X_1^2	4.22	1.00	4.22
X_2^2	3.57	2.12	1.68
$X_1 X_2$	2.77	2.30	1.20

than two explanatory variables, to higher powers of each variable, and to more interaction terms.

When considering polynomial regression models in several variables, it is very important not to get carried away by the number of possible terms one can include in the model. The number of variables, as well as the powers of these variables and the number of interaction terms, should be kept to a minimum.

How do we choose the terms to include in a model? This question will be answered in section 11–13, where we discuss methods of variable selection. You already know several criteria for the inclusion of variables, powers of variables, and interaction terms in a model. One thing to consider is the adjusted coefficient of determination. If this measure decreases when a term is included in the model, then the term should be dropped. Also, the significance of any particular term in a model depends on which other variables, powers, or interaction terms are in the model. We must consider the significance of each term by its *t* statistic, and we must consider what happens to the significance of regression terms once other terms are added to the model or removed from it. For example, let us consider the regression output in Table 11–17.

From the results in the table, it is clear that only X_1, X_2, and X_1^2 are significant. The apparent nonsignificance of X_2^2 and $X_1 X_2$ may be due to multicollinearity. At any rate, a regression without these last two variables should be carried out. We must also look at the R^2 and the adjusted R^2 of the different regressions, and find the most parsimonious model with statistically significant parameters that explain as much as possible of the variation in the values of the dependent variable. Incidentally, the surface in Figure 11–29 was generated by computer using all the coefficient estimates given in Table 11–17 (regardless of their significance) and an intercept of zero.

PROBLEMS

11–62. An article in the *American Economic Review* about contract duration in the coal industry reports the results of a regression relationship of the duration of contractual commitments (DURATION) on the annual quantity of coal contracted for (QUANTITY).[16] The regression model includes a dummy variable (MINE-MOUTH) that has the value 1 for a mine-mouth plant and 0 otherwise. The regression also includes other dummy variables (MIDWEST, WEST) that indicate whether the supply region location is in the Midwest or in the West; when both variables have a value of zero, the location of the supply region is in the

Answer

11–62.

Good regression. Second-order model.

[16] P. Joskow, "Contract Duration and Relationship-Specific Investments," *American Economic Review* 77, no. 1 (March 1987).

Answers

East. Finally, a variable QUANTITY^2 (the square of the QUANTITY variable) is also included. The reported regression results are:

$$\text{DURATION} = 3.933 + 0.409\text{QUANTITY} - 0.002\text{QUANTITY}^2$$
$$(0.811) \quad (0.004) \qquad\qquad (0.00003)$$
$$+ 15.958\text{MINE-MOUTH} + 2.783\text{MIDWEST}$$
$$(1.911) \qquad\qquad\qquad (1.093)$$
$$+ 5.986\text{WEST} + \text{ERROR}$$
$$(1.234)$$

The number of observations used is 169, and the adjusted R^2 is reported to be 0.71. Give a complete interpretation of all regression results.

11–63. Use the data in Table 11–6 to run a polynomial regression model of exports to Singapore versus M1 and M1 squared, as well as Price and Price squared, and an interaction term. Also try to add a squared exchange rate variable into the model. Find the best, most parsimonious regression model for the data.

11–64.
——
Stepwise—chooses Prod, Prom, Book.

11–64. Use the data of Example (c), presented in Table 11–12, to try to fit a polynomial regression model of movie gross earnings on production cost and production cost squared. Also try promotion and promotion squared. What is the best, most parsimonious model?

11–65. Give at least two reasons why a polynomial regression model in one or more independent variables should be kept as parsimonious as possible.

11–66.
——
X_1^2 and cross-product not significant. Rerun regression.

11–66. A regression model of sales (Y) versus advertising (X_1), advertising squared (X_1^2), competitors' advertising (X_2), competitors' advertising squared (X_2^2), and the interaction of X_1 and X_2 is run. The results are as follows.

Variable	Parameter Estimate	Standard Error
X_1	5.324	2.478
X_2	3.229	1.006
X_1^2	4.544	3.080
X_2^2	1.347	0.188
$X_1 X_2$	2.692	1.517

$R^2 = 0.657$ Adjusted $R^2 = 0.611$ $n = 197$

Interpret the regression results. Which regression equation should be tried next? Explain.

11–67. What regression model would you try for the following data? Give your reasons why.

```
20.0+
    -
    -                                              *
    -                                                      *
    -                           *           *
15.0+
    -
    -                     *
    -
    -               *
10.0+         *
    -
    -
    -     *
    -     *
 5.0+  *
   ------+---------+---------+---------+---------+---------+
       2.5       5.0       7.5      10.0      12.5      15.0
```

11–68. The regression model $Y = \beta_0 + \beta_1 X + \beta_2 X^2 + \beta_3 X^3 + \beta_4 X^4 + \epsilon$ was fit to the following data set. Can you suggest a better model? If so, which?

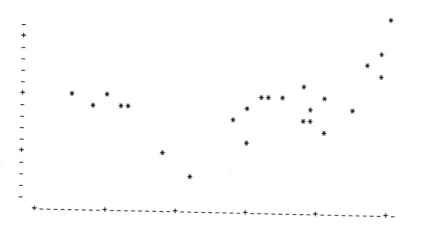

11–68.

Try quadratic and cubic.

11–10   Nonlinear Models and Transformations

Sometimes the relationship between Y and one or more of the independent X_i variables is nonlinear. Remember that powers of the X_i variables in the regression model still keep the model linear, but that powers of the coefficients, β_i, make the model nonlinear. We may have prior knowledge about the process generating the data that indicates that a nonlinear model is appropriate; or we may observe that the data follow one of the general nonlinear curves shown in the figures in this section.

In many cases, a nonlinear model may be changed to a linear model by use of an appropriate **transformation**. Models that can be transformed into linear models are called **intrinsically linear** models. These models are the subject of this section. The "hard-core" nonlinear models, those that cannot be transformed into linear models, are difficult to analyze and therefore are outside the scope of this book.

The first model we will encounter is the *multiplicative model,* given by equation 11–26.

The multiplicative model:

$$Y = \beta_0 X_1^{\beta_1} X_2^{\beta_2} X_3^{\beta_3} \epsilon \qquad (11\text{–}26)$$

This is a multiplicative model in three variables: X_1, X_2, and X_3. The generalization to k variables is clear. The β_i are unknown parameters, and ϵ is a multiplicative random error.

The multiplicative model of equation 11–26 can be transformed into a linear regression model by the use of a **logarithmic transformation**. A logarithmic transformation is the most common transformation of data in statistical analysis. We will use natural logarithms, logs to base e; although any log transformation would do (we may use logs to any base, as long as we are consistent throughout the equation). Taking natural logs (sometimes denoted by ln) of both sides of equation 11–26 gives us the following linear model:

$$\log Y = \log \beta_0 + \beta_1 \log X_1 + \beta_2 \log X_2 + \beta_3 \log X_3 + \log \epsilon \qquad (11\text{–}27)$$

FIGURE 11–30   A Family of Power Curves of the Form $Y = \beta_0 X^{\beta_1}$

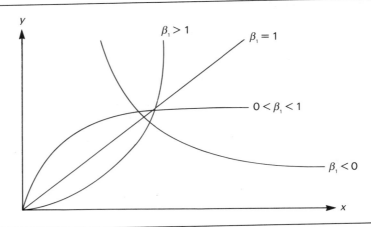

Equation 11–27 is now in the form of equation 11–1: it is a linear regression equation of log Y in terms of log X_1, log X_2, and log X_3 as independent variables. The error term in the linearized model is log ϵ. In order to conform with the assumptions of the multiple regression model and to allow us to perform tests of significance of model parameters, we must assume that the linearized errors, log ϵ, are normally distributed with mean 0 and equal variance σ^2 for successive observations and that these errors are independent of each other.

When we consider only one independent variable, the model of equation 11–26 is a power curve in X, of the form:

$$Y = \beta_0 X^{\beta_1} \epsilon \tag{11–28}$$

Depending on the values of the parameters, β_0 and β_1, equation 11–28 gives rise to a wide-range family of power curves. Several members of this family of curves, showing the relationship between X and Y, leaving out the errors, ϵ, are shown in Figure 11–30. When more than one independent variable is used, as in equation 11–26, the graph of the relationship between the X_i variables and Y is a multidimensional extension of Figure 11–30.

As you can see from the figure, many possible data relationships may be well modeled by a power curve in one variable or its extension to several independent variables. The resemblance of the curves in Figure 11–30 to at least two curves shown in Figure 11–26 is also evident. As you look at Figure 11–30, we repeat our suggestion from the last section that, when possible, a transformed model with few parameters is better than a polynomial model with more parameters.

When dealing with a multiplicative, or power, model, we take logs of both sides of the equation and run a linear regression model on the logs of the variables. Again, it is important to understand that the errors must be multiplicative. This makes sense in situations where the magnitude of an error is proportional to the magnitude of the response variable. We assume that the logs of the errors are normally distributed and satisfy all the assumptions of the linear regression model. Models where the error term is additive rather than multiplicative, such as $Y = \beta_0 X_1^{\beta_1} X_2^{\beta_2} X_3^{\beta_3} + \epsilon$ are *not* intrinsically linear because there is no expression for logs of *sums*.

When using a model such as equation 11–26 or equation 11–28, we enter the data into the computer, form new variables by having the computer take logs of the Y and X_i variables, and run a regression on the transformed variables. In addition to making sure that the model assumptions seem to hold, we must also remember that computer-generated predictions and confidence intervals will be in terms of the transformed variables unless the computer algorithm is designed to convert information back to the original variables. The conversion back to the original variables is done by taking antilogs.

In many situations, it is possible to determine the need for a log transformation by inspecting a scatter plot of the data. We demonstrate the analysis using the data of Example (e). We will assume that a model of the form of equation 11–28 fits the relationship between sales profits (Y) and advertising dollars (X). We assume a power curve with multiplicative errors. Thus, we assume that the relationship between X and Y is given by:

$$Y = \beta_0 X^{\beta_1} \epsilon$$

Taking logs of both sides of the equation, we get the linearized model:

$$\log Y = \log \beta_0 + \beta_1 \log X + \log \epsilon \qquad (11\text{–}29)$$

Our choice of a power curve and a transformation using logarithms is prompted by the fact that our data in this example exhibit curvature that may resemble a member of the family of curves in Figure 11–30, and by the fact that a quadratic regression model, which is similar to a power curve, was found to fit the data well. (Data for this example are shown in Figure 11–28.)

We use the MINITAB program for this analysis. Data are given in column C1 (sales) and C2 (advertising expenditure). The first thing we ask the computer to do is take logs to base e (natural logarithms) of both variables X and Y. The MINITAB command LOGE takes natural logs of the data in the prescribed column and places these logs in a given column. In this case, we put the logs of the Y values and the logs of the X values into columns C3 and C4, respectively. Then we ask the computer to carry out a regression analysis of the logarithms of the two variables. Results of the analysis are given in Table 11–18. The table also shows the MINITAB commands needed for carrying out the analysis. Comparing the results in Table 11–18 with those of the quadratic regression, given in Table 11–16, we find that, in terms of R^2 and the adjusted R^2, the quadratic regression is slightly better than the log Y versus log X regression.

TABLE 11–18 MINITAB Analysis Using a Logarithmic Transformation, Example (e)

```
MTB > LOGE C1, INTO C3
MTB > LOGE C2, INTO C4
MTB > NAME C3 'LOGSALE', C4 'LOGADV'
MTB > REGRESS 'LOGSALE' ON 1 PREDICTOR 'LOGADV'

The regression equation is
LOGSALE = 1.70 + 0.553 LOGADV

Predictor       Coef         Stdev      t-ratio       P
Constant       1.70082      0.05123      33.20      0.000
LOGADV         0.55314      0.03011      18.37      0.000

s = 0.1125      R-sq = 94.7%      R-sq(adj) = 94.4%
Analysis of Variance

  SOURCE      DF       SS          MS          F          P
Regression     1     4.2722      4.2722      336.39     0.000
Error         19     0.2405      0.0127
Total         20     4.5126
```

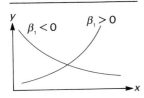

FIGURE 11–31
Exponential Curves

Do we have to take logs of both X and Y, or can we take the log of one of the variables only? That depends on the kind of nonlinear model we wish to linearize. It turns out that there is indeed a nonlinear model that may be linearized by taking the log of one of the variables. Equation 11–30 is a nonlinear regression model of Y versus the independent variable X that may be linearized by taking logs of both sides of the equation. To use the resulting linear model, given in equation 11–31, we run a regression of log Y versus X (not log X). The nonlinear relationship of equation 11–30, an exponential model, is shown in Figure 11–31.

The exponential model:

$$Y = \beta_0 e^{\beta_1 X} \epsilon \qquad (11\text{–}30)$$

The linearized model of the exponential relationship, obtained by taking logs of both sides of equation 11–30, is given by:

$$\log Y = \log \beta_0 + \beta_1 X + \log \epsilon \qquad (11\text{–}31)$$

As can be seen from the plots in Figure 11–31, when the relationship between Y and X is of the exponential form, the relationship is mildly curved upward or downward. Thus, taking log of Y only and running a regression of log Y versus X may be useful when our data display curvature similar to what is seen in Figure 11–31.

The exponential model of equation 11–30 is extendable to several independent X_i variables. The model is given in equation 11–32.

An exponential model in two independent variables:

$$Y = e^{\beta_0 + \beta_1 X_1 + \beta_2 X_2} \epsilon \qquad (11\text{–}32)$$

The letter e in equation 11–32, as in equation 11–30, denotes the natural number $e = 2.7182 \ldots$, the base of the natural logarithm. Taking the natural logs of both sides of equation 11–32 gives us the following linear regression model:

$$\log Y = \beta_0 + \beta_1 X_1 + \beta_2 X_2 + \log \epsilon \qquad (11\text{–}33)$$

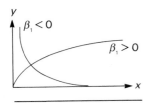

FIGURE 11–32
Curves Corresponding to a
Logarithmic Model

This relationship is extendable to any number of independent variables. The transformation of log Y, leaving the X_i variables in their natural form, allows us to perform linear regression analysis. The data of Example (e), shown in Figure 11–28, do not display a curvature of the type shown in Figure 11–31. The next model we discuss, however, may be more promising.

Figure 11–32 shows curves corresponding to the logarithmic model given in equation 11–34.

The logarithmic model:

$$Y = \beta_0 + \beta_1 \log X + \epsilon \qquad (11\text{–}34)$$

This nonlinear model can be linearized by substituting the variable $X' = \log X$ into the equation. This gives us the linear model in X':

$$Y = \beta_0 + \beta_1 X' + \epsilon \qquad (11\text{–}35)$$

From Figure 11–32, it seems that the logarithmic model with $\beta_1 > 0$ may fit the data of Example (e). We will therefore try to fit this model. The required transformation to obtain the linearized model in equation 11–35 is to take the log of X

TABLE 11–19 Results of a Regression Analysis Fitting a Logarithmic Model to the Data of Example (e)

```
The regression equation is
SALES = 3.67 + 6.78 LOGADV

Predictor      Coef        Stdev      t-ratio      p
Constant     3.6683      0.4016        9.13      0.000
LOGADV       6.7840      0.2360       28.74      0.000

s = 0.8819      R-sq = 97.8%      R-sq(adj) = 97.6%

Analysis of Variance

   SOURCE     DF        SS         MS         F         p
Regression     1     642.62     642.62     823.87     0.000
Error         19      14.78       0.78
Total         20     657.40
```

only, leaving Y as is. We will tell the computer program to run Y versus log X. By doing so, we assume that our data follow the logarithmic model of equation 11–34. The results of the regression analysis of sales profits versus the natural logarithm of advertising expenditure are given in Table 11–19.

As seen from the regression results, the model of equation 11–35 is probably the best model to describe the data of Example (e). The coefficient of determination is $R^2 = 0.978$, which is higher than those of both the quadratic model and the power curve model we tried earlier. Figure 11–33 is a plot of the sales variable versus the log of advertising (the regression model of equation 11–35). As can be seen from the figure, we have a straight-line relationship between log advertising and sales. Compare this figure with Figure 11–34, which is the relationship of log sales versus log advertising, the model of equation 11–31 we tried earlier. In the latter graph, there is some extra curvature, and a straight line does not quite fit the transformed variable. We conclude that the model given by equation 11–34 fits the sales profits versus advertising expenditure relationship best. The estimated regression relationship is as given in Table 11–19: $\widehat{\text{Sales}} = 3.67 + 6.78$ Logadv.

FIGURE 11–33 A Plot of Sales versus the Natural Log of Advertising Expenditure [Example (e)]

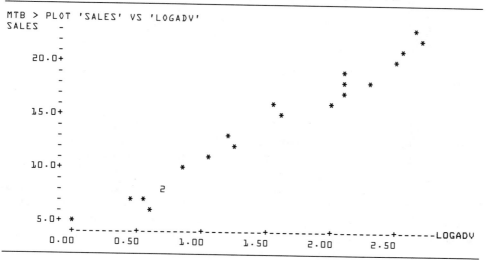

FIGURE 11–34   A Plot of Log Sales versus Log Advertising Expenditure [Example (e)]

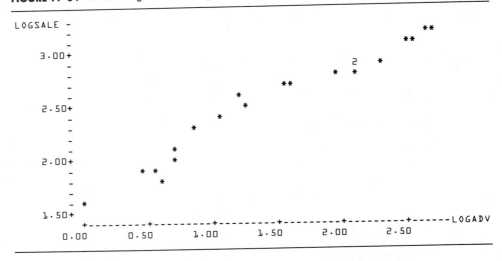

FIGURE 11–35   Residual Plot for the Estimated Model, $\widehat{Sales}$ = 3.67 + 6.78 Logadv [Example (e)]

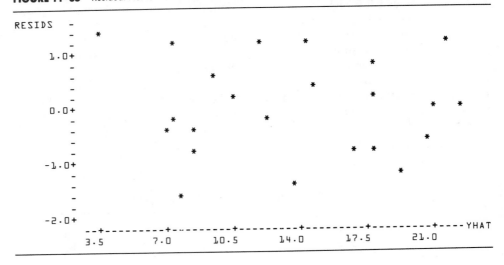

Remember that when we transform our data, the least-squares method minimizes the sum of the squared errors for the *transformed* variables. It is, therefore, very important for us to check for any violations of model assumptions that may occur as a result of the transformations. We must be especially careful with the assumptions about the regression errors and their distribution. This is why residual plots are very important when transformations of variables are used. In our present model for the data of Example (e), a plot of the residuals versus the predicted sales values, $\hat{Y}$, is given in Figure 11–35. The plot of the residuals does not indicate any violation of assumptions, and we therefore conclude that the model is adequate. We note also that confidence intervals for transformed models do not always correspond to correct intervals for the original model.

Another nonlinear model that may be linearized by an appropriate transformation is the *reciprocal model*. A reciprocal model in several variables is given in equation 11–36.

The **reciprocal model**:

$$Y = \frac{1}{\beta_0 + \beta_1 X_1 + \beta_2 X_2 + \beta_3 X_3 + \epsilon} \qquad (11\text{--}36)$$

This model becomes a linear model upon taking the reciprocals of both sides of the equation. In practical terms, we run a regression of $1/Y$ versus the X_i variables unchanged. A particular reciprocal model with one independent variable has a complicated form, which will not be explicitly stated here. This model calls for linearization by taking the reciprocals of both X and Y. Two curves corresponding to this particular reciprocal model are shown in Figure 11–36. When our data display the acute curvature of one of the curves in the figure, running a regression of $1/Y$ versus $1/X$ may be fruitful.

Next we will discuss transformations of the dependent variable, Y, only. These are transformations designed to stabilize the variance of the regression errors.

Variance-Stabilizing Transformations

Remember that one of the assumptions of the regression model is that the regression errors, ϵ, have equal variance. If the variance of the errors increases or decreases as one or more of the independent variables change, we have the problem of heteroscedasticity. When heteroscedasticity is present, our regression coefficient estimates are not efficient. This violation of the regression assumptions may sometimes be corrected by the use of a transformation. We will consider three major transformations of the dependent variable, Y, to correct for heteroscedasticity.

Transformations of Y that may help correct the problem of heteroscedasticity:

1. The square root transformation: $Y' = \sqrt{Y}$

    This is the least "severe" transformation. It is useful when the variance of the regression errors is approximately proportional to the mean of Y, conditional on the values of the independent variables X_i.

2. The logarithmic transformation: $Y' = \log Y$ (to any base)

    This is a transformation of a stronger nature and is useful when the variance of the errors is approximately proportional to the square of the conditional mean of Y.

3. The reciprocal transformation: $Y' = 1/Y$

   This is the most severe of the three transformations and is required when the violation of equal variance is serious. This transformation is useful when the variance of the errors is approximately proportional to the conditional mean of Y to the fourth power.

There are transformations other than these, although the preceding transformations are the most commonly used. In a given situation, we want to find the transformation that makes the errors have approximately equal variance as evidenced by the residual plots. An alternative to using transformations to stabilize the variance is use of the weighted least-squares procedure mentioned in our earlier discussion of the heteroscedasticity problem. We note that a test for heteroscedasticity exists. The test is the Goldfeld-Quandt test, discussed in econometrics books.

It is important to note that transformations may also correct problems of non-normality of the errors. A variance-stabilizing transformation may thus make the distribution of the new errors closer to a normal distribution. In using transformations—whether to stabilize the variance, to make the errors approximate a normal distribution, or to make a nonlinear model linear—it is important to remember that all results should be converted back to the original variables. As a final example of a nonlinear model that can be linearized by using a transformation, we present the *logistic regression model*.

Regression with Dependent Indicator Variable

In section 11–8, we discussed models with indicator variables as independent X_i variables. In this subsection, we discuss regression analysis where the *dependent* variable, Y, is an indicator variable and may obtain only the value 0 or the value 1. This is the case when the response to a set of independent variables is in the binary form: success or failure. An example of such a situation is the following.

A bank is interested in predicting whether or not a given loan applicant would be a good risk, i.e., pay back his or her loan. The bank may have data on past loan applicants, such as applicant's income, years of employment with the same employer, and value of home. All these independent variables may be used in a regression analysis where the dependent variable is binary: $Y = 0$ if the applicant did not repay the loan, and $Y = 1$ if he or she did pay back the loan. When only one explanatory variable, X, is used, the model is the *logistic function*, given in equation 11–37.

The **logistic function**:

$$E(Y|X) = \frac{e^{(\beta_0 + \beta_1 X)}}{1 + e^{(\beta_0 + \beta_1 X)}} \qquad (11\text{–}37)$$

The expected value of Y given X, that is, $E(Y|X)$, has a special meaning: It is the *probability* that Y will equal 1 (the probability of success), given the value of X.

Thus, we write $E(Y|X) = p$. The transformation given below linearizes equation 10–37.

FIGURE 11–37
The Logistic Function

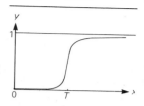

Transformation to linearize the logistic function:

$$p' = \log\left(\frac{p}{1 - p}\right) \qquad (11\text{–}38)$$

We leave it to the reader to show that the resulting regression equation is linear. In practical terms, the transformed model is difficult to employ because resulting errors are intrinsically heteroscedastic. A better approach is to use the more involved methods of nonlinear regression analysis. We present the example to show that, in many cases, the dependent variable may be an indicator variable as well. Much research is being done today on the logistic regression model, which reflects the model's growing importance. Fitting data to the curve of the logistic function is called *logit analysis*. A graph of the logistic function of equation 11–37 is shown in Figure 11–37. Note the typical elongated S shape of the graph. This function is useful as a "threshold model," where the probability that the dependent variable, Y, will be equal to 1 (a success in the experiment) increases as X increases. This increase becomes very dramatic as X reaches a certain threshold value (the point T in the figure).

PROBLEMS

11–69. What are the two main reasons for using transformations?

11–70. Explain why a transformed model may be better than a polynomial model. Under what conditions is this true?

11–71. Refer to the residual plot in Figure 11–13. What transformation would you recommend be tried to correct the situation?

11–72. For the Singapore data of Example (b), presented in Table 11–6, use several different data transformations of the variables Exports, M1, and Price, and find a better model to describe the data. Comment on the properties of your new model.

11–73. Which transformation would you try for modeling the following data set?

Answers

11–70.

Parsimony.

11–72.

Log exports; log M1; log price.

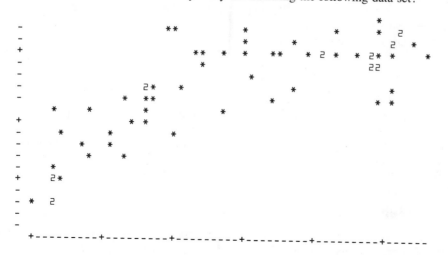

11–74.

Logarithmic model.

11–74. Which transformation would you recommend for the following data set?

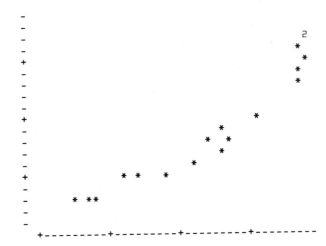

11–75. An analysis of the effect of advertising on consumer price sensitivity is carried out. The log of the quantity purchased ($\ln q$), the dependent variable, is run against the log of an advertising-related variable called RP (the log is variable $\ln RP$). There is an additive error term, ϵ, in the transformed regression. What assumptions about the model relating q and RP are implied by the transformation?

11–76. The following regression model is run.

11–76.

Exponential model.

$$\log Y = 3.79 + 1.66\, X_1 + 2.91\, X_2 + \log e$$

Give the equation of the original, nonlinear model linking the explanatory variables with Y.

11–77. Consider the following nonlinear model.

$$Y = e^{\beta_1 X_1} + e^{\beta_2 X_2} + \epsilon$$

Is this model intrinsically linear? Explain.

11–78.

Take log of both sides.

11–78. The following model is used in economics to describe production.

$$Q = \beta_0 C^{\beta_1} K^{\beta_2} L^{\beta_3} \epsilon$$

where the dependent variable, Q, is the quantity produced; C is the capacity of a production unit; K is the capital invested in the project; and L is labor input, in days. Transform the model to linear regression form.

11–79. Consider the nonlinear model:

$$Y = \frac{1}{\beta_0 + \beta_1 X_1 + \beta_2 X_2 + \epsilon}$$

What transformation linearizes this model?

11–80.

Square root.

11–80. If the residuals from fitting a linear regression model display mild heteroscedasticity, what data transformation may correct the problem?

11–81. The model in problem 11–78 is transformed to a linear regression model and analyzed using a computer. Do the estimated regression coefficients minimize the sum of the squared deviations of the data from the original curve? Explain.

11–11   Multicollinearity

The idea of multicollinearity permeates every aspect of multiple regression, and we have encountered this idea in earlier sections of this chapter. The reason multicollinearity (or simply *collinearity*) has such a pervasive effect on multiple regression is that whenever we study the relationship between Y and several X_i variables, we are bound to encounter some relationships among the X_i variables themselves. Ideally, the X_i variables in a regression equation are uncorrelated with each other; each variable contains a unique piece of information about Y—information that is not contained in any of the other X_i. When the ideal occurs in practice, we have no multicollinearity. On the other extreme, we encounter the case of perfect collinearity. Suppose that we run a regression of Y on two explanatory variables, X_1 and X_2. Perfect collinearity occurs when one X variable can be expressed precisely in terms of the other X variable for all elements in our data set.

Variables X_1 and X_2 are perfectly collinear if:

$$X_1 = a + bX_2 \qquad (11\text{--}39)$$

for some real numbers a and b.

In the case of equation 11–39, the two variables are on a straight line and one of them perfectly determines the other. Here there is no new information about Y to be gained by adding X_2 to a regression equation that already contains X_1 (or vice versa).

In practice, most situations fall between the two extremes. Often, there is some degree of collinearity between several of the independent variables in a regression equation. A measure of the collinearity between two X_i variables is the *correlation* between the two. Recall that in regression analysis we assume that the X_i are constants and not random variables. Here we relax this assumption and measure the correlation between the independent variables (this assumes they are random variables in their own right). When two independent X_i variables are found to be highly correlated with each other, we may expect the adverse effects of multicollinearity on the regression estimation procedure.

In the case of perfect collinearity, the regression algorithm breaks down completely. Even if we were able to get regression coefficient estimates in such a case, their variance would be infinite. When the degree of collinearity is less severe, we may expect the variance of the regression estimators (and the standard errors) to be large. There are other problems that may occur, and we will discuss them shortly. Multicollinearity is a problem of degree. When the correlations among the independent regression variables are minor, the effects of multicollinearity may not be serious. In cases of strong correlations, the problem may affect the regression more adversely, and we may need to take some corrective action. Note that in a multiple regression analysis with several independent variables, *several* of the X_i may be correlated. A set of independent variables that are correlated with each other is called a *multicollinearity set*.

Let us imagine a variable and its information content as a direction in space. Two uncorrelated variables can be viewed as *orthogonal* directions in space: directions that are at 90° to each other. Perfectly correlated variables represent directions that have an angle of 0° or 180° between them, depending on whether the correlation is +1 or −1. Variables that are partly correlated are directions that form an angle greater than 0° but less than 90° (or between 90° and 180° if the correlation is negative). The closer the angle between the directions is to 0° or 180°, the greater the collinearity. This is illustrated in Figure 11–38.

Causes of Multicollinearity

There are several different causes of multicollinearity. A data collection method may produce multicollinearity if, without intention, we tend to gather data with re-

FIGURE 11–38   Collinearity Viewed as the Relationship between Two Directions in Space

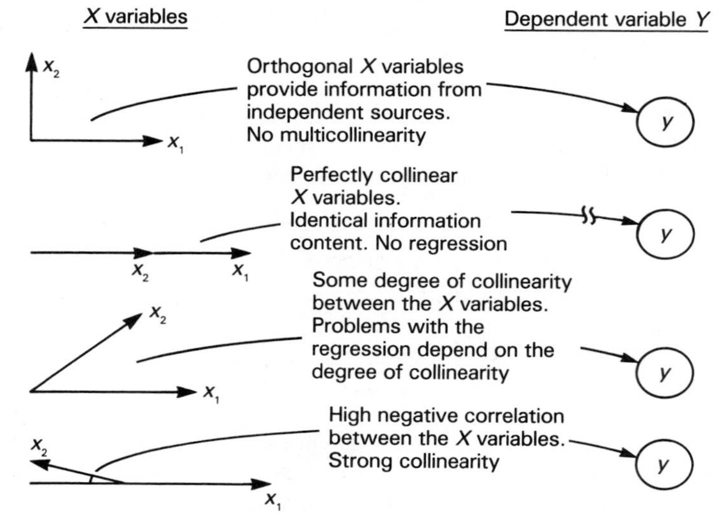

lated values on several variables. For example, we may be interested in running a regression of size of home (Y) versus family income (X_1) and family size (X_2). If, unwittingly, we always sample families with high income and large size (rather than also obtaining sample families with low income and large size or high income and small size), then we have multicollinearity. In such cases, improving the sampling method would solve the problem. In other cases, the variables may by nature be related with each other, and sampling adjustments may not work. In such cases, one of the correlated variables should probably be excluded from the model to avoid the collinearity problem.

In industrial processes, sometimes there are physical constraints on the data. For example, if we run a regression of chemical yield (Y) versus the concentration of two elements $(X_1$ and $X_2)$, and the total amount of material in the process is constant, then as one chemical increases in concentration, we must reduce the concentration of the other. In this case, X_1 and X_2 are (negatively) correlated, and multicollinearity is present.

Yet another source of collinearity is the inclusion of higher powers of the X_i. Including X^2 in a model that contains the variable X may cause collinearity if our data are restricted to a narrow range of values. This was seen in one of the problems in an earlier section.

Whatever the source of the multicollinearity, it is important to be aware of its existence so that we may guard against its adverse effects on the estimation procedure and the ensuing use of the regression equation in prediction, control, or understanding the underlying process. We now present several methods of detecting multicollinearity and a description of its major symptoms.

Detecting the Existence of Multicollinearity

Many statistical computer packages have built-in warnings about severe cases of multicollinearity. When multicollinearity is extreme (that is, when we have near-perfect correlation between some of the explanatory variables), the program may automatically drop collinear variables so that computations may be possible. In such cases, the MINITAB program, for example, will print the following message.

```
[variable name] is highly correlated with other X variables.
[variable name] has been omitted from the equation.
```

In less serious cases, the program prints the first line of the warning above but does not drop the variable.

In cases where multicollinearity is not serious enough to cause computational problems, it may still disturb the statistical estimation procedure and make our estimators have large variances. In such cases, the computer may not print a message telling us about multicollinearity, but we will still want to know about it. There are two methods available in most statistical packages to help us determine the extent of multicollinearity present in our regression.

The first method is the computation of a **correlation matrix** of the independent regression variables. The correlation matrix is an array of all estimated pairwise correlations between the independent variables, X_i. The format of the correlation matrix is shown in Figure 11–39. The correlation matrix allows us to identify those explanatory variables that are highly correlated with each other and thus cause the problem of multicollinearity when they are included together in the regression equation. For example, in the correlation matrix shown in Figure 11–39, we see that the correlation between variable X_1 and variable X_2 is very high (0.92). This means that the two variables represent very much the same direction in space, as was shown in Figure 11–38. Being highly correlated with each other, the two variables contain much of the same information about Y and therefore cause multicollinearity when both are in the regression equation. A similar statement can be made about X_3 and X_6, which have a 0.89 correlation. Remember that multicollinearity is a matter of extent or degree. It is hard to give a rule of thumb as to how high a correlation may be before multicollinearity has adverse effects on the regression analysis. Correlations as high as the ones just mentioned are certainly large enough to cause multicollinearity problems.

We will demonstrate the use of the correlation matrix with the data of Example (b). The MINITAB package features the command CORRELATION, which is followed by the names of specified variables (or columns). This command produces the desired matrix. (The MINITAB output does not include the diagonal of 1s, as do some other packages.) Table 11–20 is the MINITAB-produced correlation matrix showing all pairwise correlations between the independent variables of the Singapore exports example. The table also shows the MINITAB command that produces the output.

FIGURE 11–39 A Correlation Matrix

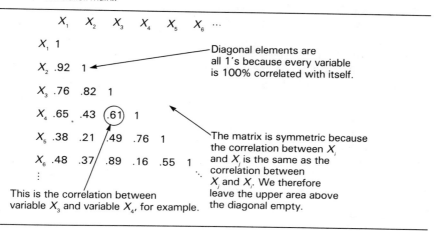

TABLE 11-20 MINITAB-Produced Correlation Matrix for Example (b)

```
MTB > name c1 'm1', c2 'lend', c3 'price', c4 'exch', c5 'export'
MTB > correlation 'm1', 'lend', 'price', 'exch'

              m1       lend      price
lend       -0.112
price       0.447     0.745
exch       -0.410    -0.279    -0.420
```

The highest pairwise correlation exists between Lend and Price. This correlation of 0.745 is the source of the multicollinearity detected in problem 11–36. Recall that the model we chose as best in our solution of Example (b) did not include the lending rate. In our solution of Example (b), we discussed other collinear variables as well. The multicollinearity may have been caused by the smaller pairwise correlations in Table 11–20, or it may have been caused by more complex correlations in the data than just the pairwise correlations. This brings us to the second statistical method of detecting multicollinearity: *variance inflation factors*.

The degree of multicollinearity introduced to the regression by variable X_h, once variables $X_1, \ldots, X_k$ are in the regression equation, is a function of the *multiple correlation* between X_h and the other variables $X_1, \ldots, X_k$. Thus, suppose we run a multiple regression—not of Y, but of X_h on all the other X variables. From this multiple regression, we get an R^2 value. This R^2 is a measure of the multicollinearity "exerted" by the variable X_h. Recall that a major problem caused by multicollinearity is the inflation of the variance of the regression coefficient estimators. To measure this ill effect of multicollinearity, we use the *variance inflation factor* (VIF) associated with variable X_h.

The **variance inflation factor** associated with X_h:

$$\text{VIF } (X_h) = \frac{1}{1 - R_h^2} \qquad (11\text{--}40)$$

where R_h^2 is the R^2 value obtained for the regression of X_h, as dependent variable, on the other X variables in the original equation aimed at predicting Y

It can be shown that the VIF of variable X_h is equal to the ratio of the variance of the coefficient estimator, b_h, in the original regression (with Y as dependent variable) and the variance of the estimator, b_h, in a regression where X_h is *orthogonal* to the other X variables.[17] The VIF is the inflation factor of the variance of the estimator as compared with what that variance would have been if X_h were not collinear with any of the other X variables in the regression. A graph of the relationship between R_h^2 and the VIF is shown in Figure 11–40.

As can be seen from the figure, when the R^2 of X_h versus the other X variables increases from 0.9 to 1, the VIF rises very dramatically. In fact, for $R_h^2 = 1.00$, the VIF is infinite. The graph, however, should not deceive you. Even for values of R_h^2 less than 0.9, the VIF is still large. A VIF of 6, for example, means that the variance of the regression coefficient estimator, b_h, is six times what it should be (when no collinearity exists). Most computer packages will report, on request, the VIFs for all the independent variables in a regression model.

---

[17] J. Johnston, *Econometric Methods* (New York: McGraw-Hill, 1984).

FIGURE 11–40 The Relationship between R_h^2 and VIF

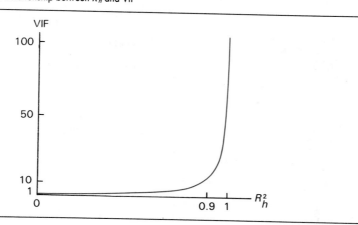

Table 11–21 is the MINITAB output for the full regression model of Example (b), which includes all the variables we considered. Using the regression subcommand VIF, we produce an extra column in the coefficient estimates output that reports the variance inflation factors for all the independent variables. The table also shows the regression command and the VIF subcommand. As we may have expected, multicollinearity is present, as evidenced by the variance inflation factors. Two of these factors are as high as 5 and 6.

What symptoms and effects of multicollinearity would we find without looking at a variable correlation matrix or the VIFs? There are several noticeable effects of multicollinearity. The major ones are presented in the following list.

The effects of multicollinearity:

1. The variances (and standard errors) of regression coefficient estimators are inflated.
2. The magnitudes of the regression coefficient estimates may be different from what we expect them to be.
3. The signs of the regression coefficient estimates may be opposite of what we expect them to be.
4. Adding or removing variables produces large changes in the coefficient estimates or their signs.
5. Removing a data point causes large changes in the coefficient estimates or their signs.
6. In some cases, the *F* ratio is significant, but the *t* ratios are not.

When any or all of these effects are present, multicollinearity is likely to be present. How bad is the problem? What are the adverse consequences of multicollinearity? The problem is not always as bad as it may seem. Actually, if we wish to use the regression model for prediction purposes, multicollinearity may not be a serious problem.

From the effects of multicollinearity just listed (some of them were mentioned in earlier sections), we know that the regression coefficient estimates are not reliable when multicollinearity is present. The most serious effect is the variance inflation,

TABLE 11–21 MINITAB Analysis of the Full Model in Example (b), Including VIFs

```
MTB > regress 'export' on 4 predictors 'm1', 'lend', 'price', 'exch';
SUBC > VIF.

The regression equation is
export = - 4.02 + 0.368 m1 + 0.0047 lend + 0.0365 price + 0.27 exch

Predictor      Coef         Stdev        t-ratio        p        VIF
Constant      -4.015        2.766        -1.45       0.152
m1             0.36846      0.06385       5.77       0.000       3.2
lend           0.00470      0.04922       0.10       0.924       5.4
price          0.036511     0.009326      3.91       0.000       6.3
exch           0.268        1.175         0.23       0.820       1.4

s = 0.3358      R-sq = 82.5%      R-sq(adj) = 81.4%
```

which makes some variables seem not significant. Then there is the problem of the magnitudes of the estimates, which may not be accurate, and the problem of the signs of the estimates. We see that in the presence of multicollinearity, it may not be possible for us to assess the impact of a particular variable on the dependent variable Y because we do not have a reliable estimate of the variable's coefficient. If we are interested in prediction only and do not care about understanding the net effect of each independent variable on Y, the regression model may be adequate even in the presence of multicollinearity. Even though individual regression parameters may be poorly estimated when collinearity exists, the *combination* of all regression coefficients in the regression may, in some cases, be estimated with sufficient accuracy so that satisfactory predictions are possible. In such cases, however, we must be very careful to predict values of Y only within the range of the X variables where the multicollinearity is the same as in the region of estimation. If we try to predict in regions of the X variables where the multicollinearity is not present or is different from that present in the estimation region, large errors will result. We will now explore some of the solutions commonly used to remedy the problem of multicollinearity.

Solutions to the Multicollinearity Problem

1. One of the best solutions to the problem of multicollinearity is to *drop collinear variables from the regression equation.* Suppose that we have a regression of Y on X_1, X_2, X_3, and X_4 and we find that X_1 is highly correlated with X_4. In this case, much of the information about Y in X_1 is also contained in X_4. If we drop one of the two variables from the regression model, we would solve the multicollinearity problem and lose little information about Y. By comparing the R^2 and the adjusted R^2 of different regressions with and without one of the variables, we can decide which of the two independent variables we should drop from the regression. We want to maintain a high R^2 and therefore should drop a variable if the R^2 is not reduced much when the variable is removed from the equation. When the adjusted R^2 *increases* when a variable is deleted, we certainly want to drop the variable. For example, suppose that the R^2 of the regression with all four independent variables is 0.94, the R^2 when X_1 is removed is 0.87, and the R^2 of the regression of X_1, X_2, and X_3 on Y (X_4 removed) is 0.92. In this case, we clearly want to drop X_4 and not X_1. The variable selection methods to be discussed in section 11–13 will help us determine which variables to include in a regression model.

We note a limitation of this remedy to multicollinearity. In some areas, such as economics, theoretical considerations may require that certain variables must be in the equation. In such cases, the bias resulting from deletion of a collinear variable must be weighed against the increase in the variance of the coefficient estimators when the variable is included in the model. The method of weighing the consequences and choosing the best model is presented in advanced books.

2. When the multicollinearity is caused by sampling schemes that, by their nature, tend to favor elements with similar values of some of the independent variables, a change in the sampling plan to include elements outside the multicollinearity range may reduce the extent of this problem.

3. Another method that sometimes helps in reducing the extent of the multicollinearity, or even eliminating it, is changing the form of some of the variables. This can be done in several ways. The best way is to form new combinations of the X variables that are uncorrelated with each other and then run the regression on the new combinations instead of the original variables. (See section 16–5.) This way the information content in the original variables is maintained, but the multicollinearity is removed. There are other ways of changing the form of the variables, such as centering the data: a technique of subtracting the means from the variables and running a regression on the resulting new variables.

4. The problem of multicollinearity may be remedied by using an alternative to the least-squares procedure called *ridge regression*. The coefficient estimators produced by ridge regression are biased, but in some cases, it may be worthwhile to tolerate some bias in the regression estimators in exchange for a reduction in the high variance of the estimators that results from multicollinearity.

In summary, the problem of multicollinearity is an important one. We need to be aware of the problem when it exists and to try to solve it when we can. Removing collinear variables from the equation, when possible, is the simplest method of solving the multicollinearity problem.

PROBLEMS

11–82. For the data of Example (c) presented in Table 11–12, find the sample correlations between every pair of variables (the correlation matrix), and determine whether or not you believe that multicollinearity exists in the regression.

11–83. For the data of Example (c), find the variance inflation factors, and comment on their relative magnitudes.

11–84. Find the correlation between X_1 and X_2 for the data of Example (a) presented in Table 11–1. Is multicollinearity a problem here? Also find the variance inflation factors, and comment on their magnitudes.

11–85. Give an intuitive explanation of the problem of multicollinearity.

11–86. How does multicollinearity manifest itself in a regression situation?

11–87. Explain what is meant by perfect collinearity. What happens when perfect collinearity is present?

11–88. Is it true that the regression equation can never be used adequately for prediction purposes if multicollinearity exists? Explain.

11–89. In a regression of Y on the two explanatory variables X_1 and X_2, the F ratio was found not to be significant. Neither t ratios were found to be significant, and the R^2 was found to be 0.12. Do you believe that multicollinearity is a problem here? Explain.

11–90. In a regression of Y on X_1, X_2, and X_3, the F ratio is very significant, and the R^2 is 0.88, but none of the t ratios are significant. Then X_1 is dropped from the equation, and a new

Answers

11–82.

Prod–earn. .87
Prod–prom. .64
Earn–prom. .88
Others lower.

11–84.

0.74

11–88.

No.

Answers

11–90.

X_2, X_3
Probably collinear.

11–92.

Drop variables; see what
happens to sign.

regression is run of Y on X_2 and X_3 only. The R^2 remains approximately the same, and the F is still very significant, but the two t ratios are still not significant. What do you think is happening here?

11–91. A regression is run of Y versus X_1, X_2, X_3, and X_4. The R^2 is high, and the F is significant, but only the t ratio corresponding to X_1 is significant. What do you propose to do next? Why?

11–92. In a regression analysis with several X variables, the sign of the coefficient estimate of one of the variables is opposite of what you believe it should be. How would you test to determine whether multicollinearity is the cause of this?

11–12 Residual Autocorrelation and the Durbin-Watson Test

Remember that one of the assumptions of the regression model is that the errors, ϵ, are independent from observation to observation. This means that successive errors are not correlated with each other at any lag; that is, the error at position i is not correlated with the error at position $i - 1$, $i - 2$, $i - 3$, etc. The idea of correlation of the values of a variable (in this case we consider the errors as a variable) with values of the *same variable* lagged one, two, three, or more time periods back is called *autocorrelation*.

> An **autocorrelation** is a correlation of the values of a variable with values of the same variable lagged one or more time periods back.

The idea of autocorrelation is one of the most important ideas discussed in the next chapter. Here we demonstrate autocorrelation in the case of regression errors. Suppose that we have 10 observed regression errors: $e_{10} = 1$, $e_9 = 0$, $e_8 = -1$, $e_7 = 2$, $e_6 = 3$, $e_5 = -2$, $e_4 = 1$, $e_3 = 1.5$, $e_2 = 1$, and $e_1 = -2.5$. We arrange the errors in descending order of occurrence, i. Then we form the lag 1 errors, the regression errors lagged one period back in time. The first error is now $e_{10-1} = e_9 = 0$, the second error is now $e_{9-1} = e_8 = -1$, and so on. We demonstrate the formation of the variable e_{i-1} from the variable e_i (that is, the formation of the lag 1 errors from the original errors), as well as the variables e_{i-2}, e_{i-3}, etc., in Table 11–22.

TABLE 11–22 The Formation of the Lagged Errors

i	e_i	e_{i-1}	e_{i-2}	e_{i-3}	e_{i-4}	$\cdots$
10	1	0	-1	2	3	
9	0	-1	2	3	-2	
8	-1	2	3	-2	1	
7	2	3	-2	1	1.5	
6	3	-2	1	1.5	1	
5	-2	1	1.5	1	-2.5	
4	1	1.5	1	-2.5	—	
3	1.5	1	-2.5	—	—	
2	1	-2.5	—	—	—	
1	-2.5	—	—	—	—	

We now define the autocorrelations. The error autocorrelation of lag 1 is the correlation between the *population* errors ϵ_i and ϵ_{i-1}. We denote this correlation by ρ_1. This autocorrelation is estimated by the *sample* error autocorrelation of lag 1, denoted r_1, which is the computed correlation between the variables e_i and e_{i-1}. Similarly ρ_2 is the lag 2 error autocorrelation. This autocorrelation is estimated by r_2, computed from the data for e_i and e_{i-2} in the table. Note that lagging the data makes us lose data points; one data point is lost for each lag. When computing the estimated error autocorrelations, r_j, we use as many points as we have for e_{i-j} and shorten e_i appropriately. We will not do any of these computations in this chapter.

The assumption that the regression errors are uncorrelated means that they are uncorrelated at *any* lag. That is, we assume $\rho_1 = \rho_2 = \rho_3 = \rho_4 = \cdots = 0$. A statistical test was developed in 1951 by Durbin and Watson for the purpose of detecting when the assumption is violated. The test, called the *Durbin-Watson test*, checks for evidence of the existence of a *first-order autocorrelation*.

The Durbin-Watson test:

$$H_0: \rho_1 = 0$$
$$H_1: \rho_1 \neq 0 \qquad\qquad (11\text{--}41)$$

In testing for the existence of a first-order error autocorrelation, we use the Durbin-Watson test statistic. Critical points for this test statistic are given in Appendix C, Table 7. Part of the table is reproduced here as Table 11–23; the formula of the Durbin-Watson test statistic is equation 11–42.

The Durbin-Watson test statistic:

$$d = \frac{\sum_{i=2}^{n}(e_i - e_{i-1})^2}{\sum_{i=1}^{n} e_i^2} \qquad\qquad (11\text{--}42)$$

TABLE 11–23 Critical Points of the Durbin-Watson Statistic d at $\alpha = 0.05$
(n = Sample Size, k = Number of Independent Variables in the Regression) (Partial Table)

n	$k = 1$ d_L	d_U	$k = 2$ d_L	d_U	$k = 3$ d_L	d_U	$k = 4$ d_L	d_U	$k = 5$ d_L	d_U
15	1.08	1.36	0.95	1.54	0.82	1.75	0.69	1.97	0.56	2.21
16	1.10	1.37	0.98	1.54	0.86	1.73	0.74	1.93	0.62	2.15
17	1.13	1.38	1.02	1.54	0.90	1.71	0.78	1.90	0.67	2.10
18	1.16	1.39	1.05	1.53	0.93	1.69	0.82	1.87	0.71	2.06
⋮	⋮	⋮	⋮	⋮	⋮	⋮	⋮	⋮	⋮	⋮
65	1.57	1.63	1.54	1.66	1.50	1.70	1.47	1.73	1.44	1.77
70	1.58	1.64	1.55	1.67	1.52	1.70	1.49	1.74	1.46	1.77
75	1.60	1.65	1.57	1.68	1.54	1.71	1.51	1.74	1.49	1.77
80	1.61	1.66	1.59	1.69	1.56	1.72	1.53	1.74	1.51	1.77
85	1.62	1.67	1.60	1.70	1.57	1.72	1.55	1.75	1.52	1.77
90	1.63	1.68	1.61	1.70	1.59	1.73	1.57	1.75	1.54	1.78
95	1.64	1.69	1.62	1.71	1.60	1.73	1.58	1.75	1.56	1.78
100	1.65	1.69	1.63	1.72	1.61	1.74	1.59	1.76	1.57	1.78

Note that the test statistic, d, is not the sample autocorrelation, r_1.[18] The statistic d has a known, tabulated distribution. Also note that the summation in the numerator extends from 2 to n rather than from 1 to n as in the denominator. An inspection of the first two columns in Table 11–22, corresponding to e_i and e_{i-1}, and our comment on the "lost" data points (here, one point) reveal the reason for this.

Using a given level α from the table (0.05 or 0.01), we may conduct either a test for $\rho_1 < 0$ or a test for $\rho_1 > 0$. The test has *two* critical points for testing for a positive autocorrelation (the one-tailed half of H_1 in equation 11–41). When the test statistic, d, falls to the left of the lower critical point, d_L, we conclude that there is evidence of a positive error autocorrelation of order 1. When d falls between d_L and the upper critical point, d_U, the test is inconclusive. When d falls above d_U, we conclude that there is no evidence of a positive first-order autocorrelation (conclusions are at the appropriate level, α). Similarly, when testing for negative autocorrelation, if d is greater than $4 - d_L$, we conclude that there is evidence of negative first-order error autocorrelation. When d is between $4 - d_U$ and $4 - d_L$, the test is inconclusive; and when d is below $4 - d_U$, there is no evidence of negative first-order autocorrelation of the errors. When we test the two-tailed hypothesis in equation 11–41, the actual level of significance, α, is *double* what is shown in the table. In cases where we have no prior suspicion of one type of autocorrelation (positive or negative), we carry out the two-tailed test and double the α. The critical points for the two-tailed test are shown in Figure 11–41.

For example, suppose we run a regression using $n = 18$ data points and $k = 3$ independent variables, and the computed value of the Durbin-Watson statistic is $d = 3.1$. Suppose that we want to conduct the two-tailed test. From Table 11–23 (or Appendix C, Table 7), we find that at $\alpha = 0.10$ (twice the level of the table) we have: $d_L = 0.93$ and $d_U = 1.69$. We compute $4 - d_L = 3.07$ and $4 - d_U = 2.31$. Since the computed value $d = 3.1$ is greater than $4 - d_L$, we conclude that there is evidence of a negative first-order autocorrelation in the errors. As another example, suppose $n = 80$, $k = 2$, and $d = 1.6$. In this case, the statistic value falls between d_L and d_U, and the test is inconclusive.

The Durbin-Watson statistic helps us test for first-order autocorrelation in the errors. In most cases, when autocorrelation exists, there is a first-order autocorrela-

FIGURE 11–41   Critical Regions of the Durbin-Watson Test

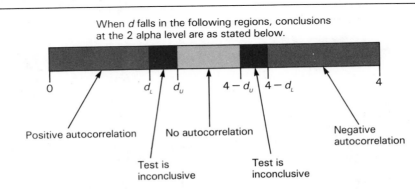

---

[18] Actually, d is approximately equal to $2(1 - r_1)$.

tion. There are cases, however, when second- or higher-order autocorrelation exists without there being a first-order autocorrelation. In such cases, the test does not help us. Fortunately, such cases are not common.

The nice thing about the Durbin-Watson statistic is that it is computed by most statistical computer packages. In MINITAB, the regression subcommand DW produces the value of the Durbin-Watson statistic. We demonstrate the computer output for the Durbin-Watson test with the data of Example (b). The regression command and the DW subcommand are shown, as well as the computed value of the statistic in this example.

```
MTB > regress 'export' on 4 predictors 'm1', 'lend', 'price', 'exch';
SUBC>   DW.

Durbin-Watson statistic = 2.58
```

Recall that for this example, $n = 67$ and $k = 4$ (in this version of the equation). At $\alpha = 0.10$, for a two-tailed test, we have $d_U = 1.73$, $d_L = 1.47$, $4 - d_L = 2.53$, $4 - d_U = 2.27$. We conclude that there is evidence that our regression errors are negatively correlated at lag 1. This, of course, sheds doubt on the regression results; an alternative to least-squares estimation should be used. One alternative procedure that is useful in cases where the ordinary least-squares routine produces autocorrelated errors is a procedure called *generalized least squares* (GLS). This method is described in advanced books. In the next chapter, we will learn much about autocorrelations of variables as well as errors.

PROBLEMS

11-93. What is the purpose of the Durbin-Watson test?

11-94. Discuss the meaning of autocorrelation. What is a third-order autocorrelation?

11-95. What is a first-order autocorrelation? If a fifth-order autocorrelation exists, is it necessarily true that a first-order autocorrelation exists as well? Explain.

11-96. State three limitations of the Durbin-Watson test.

11-97. Find the value of the Durbin-Watson statistic for the data of Example (e), and conduct the Durbin-Watson test. State your conclusion.

11-98. Find the value of the Durbin-Watson statistic for the model of Example (c), and conduct the Durbin-Watson test. Is the assumption of no first-order error autocorrelation satisfied? Explain.

11-99. Do problem 11-98 for the data of Example (a).

11-100. State the conditions under which a one-sided Durbin-Watson test is appropriate (that is, a test for positive autocorrelation only, or a test for a negative autocorrelation only).

11-101. The following table, reprinted by permission from the *Journal of Finance*, reports the results of several regressions of percentage change in the Tokyo and London stock markets on several variables relating to the time following the October 1987 stock market crash.[19] Interpret the results of all the implied Durbin-Watson tests.

Answers

11-96.

Only first order; may be inconclusive; type I error.

11-98.

$DW = 2.13$; accept.

[19] D. Neumark, P. Tinsley, and S. Tosini, "After-Hours Stock Prices and Post-Crash Hangovers," *Journal of Finance* (March 1991), p. 167.

Trading Days Following October 20, 1987

Regressors	Intercept	Days 1–30	Days 30+	Days 1–10	Days 11–20	Days 20+	N	R²	DW
Tokyo Index									
(1)	.000	1.058	.868	—	—	—	104	.93	1.17
	(.001)	(0.045)	(.032)						
(2)	.000	—	—	1.065	1.033	.882	104	.92	1.13
	(.001)			(.057)	(.135)	(.031)			
London Index									
(3)	.000	1.001	.805	—	—	—	129	.89	2.45
	(.001)	(.044)	(.035)						
(4)	.000	—	—	.994	1.038	.821	129	.89	2.40
	(.001)			(.056)	(.103)	(.034)			

11–13   Partial *F* Tests and Variable Selection Methods

Our method of deciding which variables to include in a given multiple regression model has been through trial and error. We started by asserting that several variables may have an effect on our variable of interest, *Y*, and we tried to run a multiple linear regression model of *Y* versus these variables. The "independent" variables have included dummy variables, powers of a variable, transformed variables, and a combination of all the above. Then we scrutinized the regression model and tested the significance of any individual variable (while being cautious about multicollinearity). We also tested the predictive power of the regression equation as a whole. If we found that an independent variable seemed insignificant due to a low *t* ratio, we dropped the variable and reran the regression without it, observing what happened to the remaining independent variables. By a process of adding and deleting variables, powers, or transformations, we hoped to end up with the best model: the most parsimonious model with the highest relative predictive power.

In this section, we present a statistical test, based on the *F* distribution and, in simple cases, the *t* distribution, for evaluating the relative significance of parts of a regression model. The test is sometimes called a *partial F test* because it is an *F* test (or a *t* test, in simple cases) of a *part* of our regression model.

Suppose that a regression model of *Y* versus *k* independent variables is postulated, and the analysis is carried out (the *k* variables may include dummy variables, powers, etc.). Suppose that the equation of the regression model is as given in equation (11–1):

$$Y = \beta_0 + \beta_1 X_1 + \beta_2 X_2 + \beta_3 X_3 + \cdots + \beta_k X_k + \epsilon$$

We will call this model the *full model*. It is the full model in the sense that it includes the maximal set of independent variables, X_i, that we consider as predictors of *Y*. Now suppose that we want to test the relative significance of a subset of *r* out of the *k* independent variables in the full model. (By relative significance we mean the significance of the *r* variables *given* that the remaining *k − r* variables are in the model.) We will do this by comparing the *reduced model*, consisting of *Y* and the *k − r* independent variables that remain once the *r* variables have been removed, with the full model, equation 11–1. The statistical comparison of the reduced model with the full model is done by the **partial F test.**

We will present the partial *F* test using a more specific example. Suppose that we are considering the following two models.

Full model:

$$Y = \beta_0 + \beta_1 X_1 + \beta_2 X_2 + \beta_3 X_3 + \beta_4 X_4 + \epsilon \qquad (11\text{--}43)$$

Reduced model:

$$Y = \beta_0 + \beta_1 X_1 + \beta_2 X_2 + \epsilon \qquad (11\text{--}44)$$

By comparing the two models, we are asking the question: Given that variables X_1 and X_2 are already in the regression model, would we be gaining anything by adding X_3 and X_4 into the model? Will the reduced model be improved in terms of its predictive power by the addition of the two variables X_3 and X_4?

The statistical way of posing and answering this question is, of course, by way of a test of a hypothesis. The null hypothesis that the two variables X_3 and X_4 have no additional value once X_1 and X_2 are in the regression model is the hypothesis that both β_3 and β_4 are zero (*given* that X_1 and X_2 are in the model). The alternative hypothesis is that the two slope coefficients are not both zero. The hypothesis test is stated in equation 11–45.

Partial F test:

H_0: $\beta_3 = \beta_4 = 0$ (given that X_1 and X_2 are in the model)
H_1: β_3 and β_4 are not both zero

$\qquad (11\text{--}45)$

The test statistic for this hypothesis test is the partial F statistic.

The partial F statistic:

$$F_{(r,n-(k+1))} = \frac{(SSE_R - SSE_F)/r}{MSE_F} \qquad (11\text{--}46)$$

where SSE_R is the sum of squares for error of the reduced model; SSE_F is the sum of squares for error of the full model; MSE_F is the mean square error of the full model: $MSE_F = SSE_F/(n - (k + 1))$; k is the number of independent variables in the full model ($k = 4$ in the present example); and r is the number of variables dropped from the full model in creating the reduced model (in the present example, $r = 2$)

The difference $SSE_R - SSE_F$ is called the *extra sum of squares* associated with the reduced model. Since this additional sum of squares for error is due to r variables, it has r degrees of freedom. [Like the sums of squares, degrees of freedom are additive. Thus, the extra sum of squares for error has degrees of freedom: $(n - (k + 1)) - (n - (k - r + 1)) = r$.]

Suppose that the sum of squares for error of the full model, equation 11–43, is 37,653 and that the sum of squares for error of the reduced model, equation 11–44, is 42,900. Suppose also that the regression analysis is based on a data set of $n = 45$ points. Is there a statistical justification for including X_3 and X_4 in a model already including X_1 and X_2?

To answer this question, we conduct the hypothesis test, equation 11–45. To do so, we compute the F statistic of equation 11–46:

$$F_{(2,40)} = \frac{(\text{SSE}_R - \text{SSE}_F)/2}{\text{SSE}_F/40} = \frac{(42,900 - 37,653)/2}{37,653/40} = 2.79$$

This value of the statistic falls in the acceptance region for $\alpha = 0.05$, and so we accept the null hypothesis and conclude that the decrease in the sum of squares for error when we go from the reduced model to the full model, adding X_3 and X_4 to the model that already has X_1 and X_2, is not statistically significant. It is not worthwhile to add the two variables.

In this example, we conducted a partial F test for the conditional significance of a set of $r = 2$ independent variables. This test can be carried out for the significance of any number of independent variables, powers of variables, or transformed variables, considered *jointly* as a set of variables to be added to a model. Frequently, however, we are interested in considering the relative merit of a single variable at a time. We may be interested in sequentially testing the conditional significance of a single independent variable, once other variables are already in the model (when no other variables are in the model, the F test is just a test of the significance of a single-variable regression). The F statistic for this test is still given by equation 11–46, but since the degrees of freedom are 1 and $n - (k + 1)$, this statistic is equal to the square of a t statistic with $n - (k + 1)$ degrees of freedom. Thus, the partial F test for the significance of a *single* variable may be carried out as a t test.

It may have occurred to you that a computer may be programmed to sequentially test the significance of each variable as it is added to a potential regression model, starting with one variable and building up until a whole set of variables has been tested and the best subset of variables chosen for the final regression model. We may also start with a full model, consisting of the entire set of potential variables, and delete variables from the model, one by one, whenever these variables are found not to be significant. Indeed, computers have been programmed to carry out both kinds of sequential single-variable tests and even a combination of the two methods. We will now discuss these three methods of variable selection called, respectively, *forward selection, backward elimination*, and their combination, *stepwise regression*. We will also discuss a fourth method called *all possible regressions*.

Variable Selection Methods

1. **All possible regressions:** This method consists of running all possible regressions when k independent variables are considered and choosing the best model. If we assume that every one of the models we consider has an intercept term, then there are 2^k possible models. This is so because each of the k variables may be either included in the model or not included, which means that there are two possibilities for each variable—2^k possibilities for a model consisting of k potential variables. When four potential variables are considered, such as in Example (b), there are $2^4 = 16$ possible models: four models with a single variable, six models with a pair of variables, four models with three variables, one model with all four vari-

ables, and one model with no variables (an intercept term only). As you can see, the number of possible regression models increases very quickly as the number of variables considered increases.

The different models are evaluated according to some criterion of model performance. There are several possible criteria: We may choose to select the model with the highest adjusted R^2 or the model with the lowest MSE (an equivalent condition). We may also choose to find the model with the highest R^2 for a given number of variables and then assess the increase in R^2 as we go to the best model with one more variable, to see if the increase in R^2 is worth the addition of a parameter to the model. There are other criteria, such as Mallows's C_p statistic described in advanced books. The SAS computer package has a routine called RSQUARE that runs all possible regressions and identifies the model with the highest R^2 for each number of variables included in the model. The all-possible-regressions procedure is thorough but tedious to carry out. The next three methods we describe are all stepwise procedures for building the best model. While the procedure called stepwise regression is indeed stepwise, the other two methods, forward selection and backward elimination, are also stepwise methods. These procedures are usually listed in computer manuals as variations of the stepwise method.

2. **Forward selection:** Forward selection starts with a model with no variables. The method then considers all k models with one independent variable and chooses the model with the highest significant F statistic, assuming that at least one such model has an F statistic with a p-value smaller than some predetermined value (this may be set by the user; otherwise a default value is used). Then the procedure looks at the variables remaining outside the model, considers all partial F statistics (that is, keeping the added variables in the model, the statistic is equation 11–46), and adds the variable with the highest F value to the equation, again assuming at least one variable is found to meet the required level of significance. The procedure is then continued until no variable left outside the model has a partial F statistic that satisfies the level of significance required to enter the model.

3. **Backward elimination:** This procedure works in a manner opposite to forward selection. We start with a model containing all k variables. Then the partial F statistic, equation 11–46, is computed for each variable, treated as if it were the last variable to enter the regression (that is, we evaluate each variable in terms of its contribution to a model that already contains all other variables). When the significance level of a variable's partial F statistic is found not to meet a preset standard (that is, when the p-value is above the preset p-value), the variable is removed from the equation. All statistics are then computed for the new, reduced model, and the remaining variables are screened to see if they meet the significance standard. When a variable is found to have a higher p-value than required, the variable is dropped from the equation. The process continues until all variables left in the equation are significant in terms of their partial F statistic.

4. **Stepwise regression:** This is probably the most commonly used, wholly computerized method of variable selection. The procedure is an interesting mixture of the backward-elimination and the forward-selection methods. In forward selection, once a variable enters the equation, it remains there. This method does not allow for a reevaluation of a variable's significance

once it is in the model. Recall that multicollinearity may cause a variable to become redundant in a model once other variables with much of the same information are included. This is a weakness of the forward-selection technique. Similarly, in the backward-elimination method, once a variable is out of the model, it stays out. Since it is possible that a variable that was not significant due to multicollinearity and was dropped may have predictive power once other variables are removed from the model, there are limitations to backward elimination as well.

Stepwise regression is a combination of forward selection and backward elimination that reevaluates the significance of every variable at every stage. This minimizes the chance of leaving out important variables or keeping unimportant ones. The procedure works as follows. The algorithm starts, as with the forward-selection method, by finding the most significant single-variable regression model. Then the variables left out of the model are checked via a partial F test, and the most significant variable, assuming it meets the entry significance requirement, is added to the model. At this point, the procedure diverges from the forward-selection scheme, and the logic of backward elimination is applied. The original variable in the model is reevaluated to see if it meets preset significance standards for staying in the model once the new variable has been added. If not, the variable is dropped. Then variables still outside the model are screened for entry requirement, and the most significant one, if found, is added. All variables in the model are then checked again for staying-significance once the new variable has been added. The procedure continues until there are no variables outside that should be added to the model and no variables inside the model that should be out.

The minimum significance requirements to enter the model and to stay in the model are often called P_{IN} and P_{OUT}, respectively. These are significance levels of the partial F statistic. For example, suppose that P_{IN} is 0.05 and P_{OUT} is also 0.05. This means that a variable will enter the equation if the p-value associated with its partial F statistic is less than 0.05, and it will stay in the model as long as the p-value of its partial F statistic is less than 0.05 after the addition of other variables. The two significance levels, P_{IN} and P_{OUT}, do not have to be equal, but we must be careful when setting them (or leave their values as programmed) because if P_{IN} is less strict than P_{OUT} (that is $P_{IN} > P_{OUT}$, then we may end up with a circular routine where a variable enters the model, then leaves it, then reenters, etc., in an infinite loop. We demonstrate the stepwise regression procedure as a flowchart in Figure 11–42. Note that since we test the significance of one variable at a time, our partial F test may be carried out as a t test. This is done in some computer packages.

It is important to note that computerized variable selection algorithms may not find the best model. When a model is found, it may not be a *unique* best model: there may be several possibilities. The best model based on one evaluation criterion may not be best using other criteria. Also, since there is order dependence in the selection process, we may not always arrive at the same "best" model. We must remember that computers only do what we tell them to do, and so, if we have not considered some good variables to include in the model, including cross products of variables, powers, and transformations, our model may not be as good as it could be. We must alway use judgment in model selection and not rely blindly on the computer to find the best model. The computer should be used as an *aid*.

FIGURE 11–42   The Stepwise Regression Algorithm

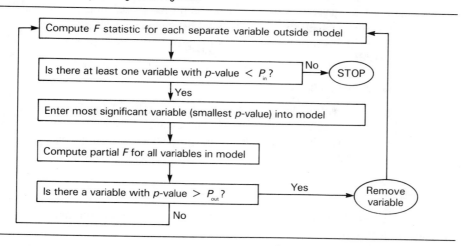

TABLE 11–24   Stepwise Regression Using MINITAB for Example (b)

```
MTB > STEPWISE REGRESSION OF 'EXPORTS', PREDICTORS 'M1', 'LEND', 'PRICE', 'EXCHANGE'

   STEPWISE REGRESSION OF EXPORTS   ON   4 PREDICTORS, WITH N =   67

        STEP         1        2
     CONSTANT     0.9348   -3.4230

     M1            0.520    0.361
     T-RATIO       9.89     9.21

     PRICE                  0.0370
     T-RATIO                9.05

     S            0.495    0.331

     R-SQ         60.08    82.48
```

Table 11–24 shows ouput from a MINITAB stepwise regression for the Singapore exports example, Example (b). Note that the procedure chose the same "best" model (out of the 16 possible regression models) as we did in our analysis. The table also shows the needed commands for the stepwise regression analysis. Note that MINITAB uses t tests rather than the equivalent F tests.

PROBLEMS

11–102.   Use equation 11–46 and the information in Tables 11–7 and 11–9 to conduct a partial F test for the significance of the lending rate and the exchange rate in the model of Example (b).

11–103.   Use a stepwise regression program to find the best set of variables for Example (a).

11–104.   Do problem 11–103 using the data of Example (c).

11–105.   Discuss the relative merits and limitations of the four variable selection methods described in this section.

Answers

11–102.

$F = 0.0275$ N.S.

11–104.

Stepwise chooses all variables.

Answer

11–108.

No.

11–106. In the stepwise regression method, why do we need to test the significance of a variable that is already determined to be included in the model, assuming $P_{IN} = P_{OUT}$?

11–107. Discuss the commonly used criteria for determining the "best" model.

11–108. Is there always a single "best" model in a given situation? Explain.

11–14   Using the Computer

In this chapter, we have made extensive use of the MINITAB package, and by now you should be very familiar with its use in regression analysis. We will review the main commands for regression analysis using this package. Then we will give examples of the use of three other packages: SPSS, SAS, and SYSTAT.

MINITAB

The main regression command in MINITAB is the REGRESS command, which has the following format.

```
REGRESS [name or column of dependent variable] on [number of
independent variables] predictors [names of independent variables,
separated by commas]
```

For example:

```
REGRESS C1 on 3 predictors C2, C3, C4
```

or

```
REGRESS 'Exports' on 2 predictors 'Price', 'M1'
```

Within the REGRESS command, if we mention the name of another column, the standardized residuals will be put into that column. If we then mention another column name, the fitted values $(\hat{Y})$ will be placed in that column. For example:

```
REGRESS C1 on 4 predictors C2, C3, C4, C5 put standardized
residuals into C6
```

and

```
REGRESS C1 on 2 predictors C2, C3 put standardized residuals
into C4, fitted values into C5
```

Other options of the regression program are offered as *subcommands*. Subcommands are separated from the regression command and from each other by a semicolon (;), and the last subcommand is followed by a period (.). Some of the subcommands we have used in this chapter are RESIDUALS, PREDICT, VIF, and DW. Other useful subcommands are described in the MINITAB manual. An example of the use of subcommands is:

```
REGRESS C1 on 2 predictors C2, C3;
  VIF;
  DW.
```

The MINITAB command for carrying out a stepwise regression is of the form:

```
STEPWISE regression of C1, predictors in C2, C3, C4, C5
```

Subcommands that allow us to set the value of the F statistic to enter or leave the equation are FENTER = [number, as critical point] and FREMOVE = [number, as critical point of F]. The default is $F = 4.00$.

SAS

The SAS computer package has several different routines that carry out multiple regression analysis. The simplest one is the REG procedure. This procedure performs general-purpose regression and provides many useful statistics as output. A more comprehensive procedure is the GLM (general linear model) procedure. This procedure is designed to handle complex models, including analysis of variance and analysis of covariance. The procedure automatically generates dummy variables for modeling qualitative variables and is well suited for handling polynomial terms. The RSQUARE procedure is an all-possible-regressions method. The STEPWISE procedure allows the performance of forward selection, backward elimination, and the stepwise regression procedure. The SAS package has other regression routines as well. We will demonstrate the use of the REG procedure using the movie example, Example (c). We use the data in Table 11–12. The program is as follows.

```
DATA MOVIE;
        INPUT EARN 1-3 COST 5-8 PROM 10-12 BOOK 14;
PROC REG DATA=MOVIE;
        MODEL EARN=COST PROM BOOK;
```

In SAS, every command ends with a semicolon (;). Data have been entered separately into the columns indicated (earnings in columns 1–3, etc.). The results of the analysis are given in Table 11–25.

TABLE 11–25 SAS Output for the Analysis of Example (c)

ANALYSIS OF VARIANCE

SOURCE	DF	SUM OF SQUARES	MEAN SQUARE	F VALUE	PROB>F
MODEL	3	6325.151	2108.384	154.887	0.0001
ERROR	16	217.7987	13.61242		
C TOTAL	19	6542.95			

ROOT MSE	3.689501	R-SQUARE	0.9667
DEP MEAN	46.05	ADJ R-SQ	0.9605
C.V.	8.011946		

PARAMETER ESTIMATES

VARIABLE	DF	PARAMETER ESTIMATE	STANDARD ERROR	T FOR H0: PARAMETER=0	PROB > |T|
INTERCEP	1	7.83619	2.33338	3.358	0.0040
COST	1	2.847692	0.3923395	7.258	0.0001
PROM	1	2.278237	0.2534369	8.989	0.0001
BOOK	1	7.166093	1.817964	3.942	0.0012

TABLE 11-26 SPSS Output for Example (b)

```
**** MULTIPLE REGRESSION ****

Listwise Deletion of Missing Data
Equation Number 1   Dependent Variable..   EXPORTS   EXPORTS TO SINGAPORE (THOU)
Beginning Block Number 1.   Method: Stepwise

Variable(s) Entered on Step Number   1..   M1        MONEY SUPPLY (BILLION S$)

Multiple R            .77514          Analysis of Variance
R Square              .60084                              DF      Sum of Squares    Mean Square
Adjusted R Square     .59470          Regression           1         23.99528        23.99528
Standard Error        .49522          Residual            65         15.94084          .24524

                                      F =   97.84259      Signif F =  .0000

------------------ Variables in the Equation ------------------         ----------- Variables not in the Equation -----------

Variable          B        SE B       Beta       T      Sig T           Variable    Beta In    Partial   Min Toler     T      Sig T

M1             .520133    .052584    .775140    9.892   .0000           LEND        .427090    .671750    .987465    7.255    .0000
(Constant)     .934784    .368301               2.538   .0136           PRICE       .529083    .749090    .800141    9.046    .0000
                                                                        EXCHANGE   -.138520   -.200002    .832123   -1.633    .1074

                        ** * * * * * * * * * * * * * * * * * * * * * * *

Variable(s) Entered on Step Number   2..   PRICE     PRICE LEVEL (1975 = 100)

Multiple R            .90820          Analysis of Variance
R Square              .82482                              DF      Sum of Squares    Mean Square
Adjusted R Square     .81935          Regression           2         32.94026        16.47013
Standard Error        .33062          Residual            64          6.99586          .10931

                                      F =  150.67317      Signif F =  .0000

------------------ Variables in the Equation ------------------         ----------- Variables not in the Equation -----------

Variable          B         SE B       Beta       T      Sig T          Variable    Beta In    Partial   Min Toler     T      Sig T

M1             .361417    .039246    .538610    9.209   .0000           LEND        .005276    .005600    .159866    .044    .9647
PRICE          .037033    .004094    .529083    9.046   .0000           EXCHANGE    .012875    .026858    .732976    .213    .8318
(Constant)   -3.422957    .540853              -6.329   .0000

                        ** * *   MULTIPLE   REGRESSION   * * * *

Equation Number 1   Dependent Variable..   EXPORTS   EXPORTS TO SINGAPORE (THOU)

End Block Number   1   PIN =   .050 Limits reached.
```

546

TABLE 11–27   SYSTAT Commands and Output for Example (e)

```
>MGLH
>MODEL SALES = CONSTANT + ADVERT  + ADVERT2
>ESTIMATE


DEP VAR:    SALES        N:       21    MULTIPLE R: 0.979  SQUARED MULTIPLE R: 0.959
ADJUSTED SQUARED MULTIPLE R: 0.954        STANDARD ERROR OF ESTIMATE:        1.228

VARIABLE      COEFFICIENT    STD ERROR      STD COEF   TOLERANCE       T      P(2 TAIL)

CONSTANT        3.515         0.738         0.000         .         4.760     0.000
  ADVERT        2.515         0.258         1.996       0.055       9.749     0.000
 ADVERT2       -0.087         0.017        -1.080       0.055      -5.275     0.000


                            ANALYSIS OF VARIANCE

  SOURCE       SUM-OF-SQUARES      DF      MEAN-SQUARE      F-RATIO        P

REGRESSION        630.258          2        315.129       208.987      0.000
  RESIDUAL         27.142         18          1.508
```

SPSS

In SPSS, the regression methods are all contained in the REGRESSION procedure, which includes a wide variety of options. We demonstrate the use of this package with an example of stepwise regression. We use Example (b) again, and our results parallel the ones obtained using MINITAB in the last section. The output produced by SPSS is more extensive, however, and is given for comparison in Table 11–26. The SPSS commands for carrying out the stepwise regression are:

```
REGRESSION VARIABLES=M1 TO EXPORTS/
        DEPENDENT=EXPORTS/STEPWISE
```

(Data are entered separately).

SYSTAT

In SYSTAT, we first call the module that carries out regression; this is done by the command MGLH. Then we specify the regression as MODEL (variable name) = CONSTANT + (variable names, separated by + signs). Finally, we write the command ESTIMATE. These commands, and the resulting output, are demonstrated for Example (e) in Table 11–27.

11–15   The Matrix Approach to Multiple Regression Analysis[20]

Computers carry out regression calculations by working with arrays of numbers. An array of numbers is called a *matrix* (the plural is *matrices*). The use of matrices vastly simplifies the operations of the computer because rules of matrix algebra make it possible to program the computer to perform operations on matrices that are similar to operations on individual numbers. The use of matrices and their underlying theory also allows the statistician to define properties of regression statistics in clear and concise terms.

---

[20] This section is optional and requires familiarity with linear algebra.

If you are familiar with matrix algebra, the following brief description of the matrix approach to regression analysis will enhance your understanding of regression theory. You will also see definitions of various statistics, such as standard errors of estimators, that are not easily defined without the use of matrices and therefore were not given earlier. If you have not yet studied matrix algebra but will do so sometime in the future, you may always go back to this section and gain a deeper understanding of regression analysis.

Suppose we have a data set of n observations on the dependent variable, Y, and k independent variables, $X_1, X_2, X_3, \ldots, X_k$. We may write the multiple regression equation, equation 11–1, in a format that includes *all* our data points. We do so in terms of arrays of numbers as follows:

$$
\begin{bmatrix} y_1 \\ y_2 \\ y_3 \\ \vdots \\ y_n \end{bmatrix} =
\begin{bmatrix}
1 & x_{11} & x_{12} & x_{13} & \cdots & x_{1k} \\
1 & x_{21} & x_{22} & x_{23} & \cdots & x_{2k} \\
1 & x_{31} & x_{32} & x_{33} & \cdots & x_{3k} \\
\vdots & \vdots & \vdots & \vdots & \cdots & \vdots \\
1 & x_{n1} & x_{n2} & x_{n3} & \cdots & x_{nk}
\end{bmatrix}
\cdot
\begin{bmatrix} \beta_0 \\ \beta_1 \\ \beta_2 \\ \vdots \\ \beta_k \end{bmatrix} +
\begin{bmatrix} \epsilon_1 \\ \epsilon_2 \\ \epsilon_3 \\ \vdots \\ \epsilon_n \end{bmatrix}
\tag{11–47}
$$

Compare equation 11–47 with equation 11–1 and note that here, for each data point, the value of Y is written as the sum of the products of the unknown β parameters and the point's X_i values, plus the error term associated with the data point. The operations are matrix operations.

As an example of the application of equation 11–47, we write the data of Example (a), presented in Table 11–1, in this format. These data are shown in equation 11–48.

$$
\begin{bmatrix} 72 \\ 76 \\ 78 \\ 70 \\ 68 \\ 80 \\ 82 \\ 65 \\ 62 \\ 90 \end{bmatrix} =
\begin{bmatrix}
1 & 12 & 5 \\
1 & 11 & 8 \\
1 & 15 & 6 \\
1 & 10 & 5 \\
1 & 11 & 3 \\
1 & 16 & 9 \\
1 & 14 & 12 \\
1 & 8 & 4 \\
1 & 8 & 3 \\
1 & 18 & 10
\end{bmatrix}
\cdot
\begin{bmatrix} \beta_0 \\ \beta_1 \\ \beta_2 \end{bmatrix} +
\begin{bmatrix} \epsilon_1 \\ \epsilon_2 \\ \epsilon_3 \\ \epsilon_4 \\ \epsilon_5 \\ \epsilon_6 \\ \epsilon_7 \\ \epsilon_8 \\ \epsilon_9 \\ \epsilon_{10} \end{bmatrix}
\tag{11–48}
$$

As an exercise, multiply the matrices as shown, and add the error vector. You will get a set of n equations, one for each data point. Note that the X matrix contains a column of 1s. This is necessary for picking up the intercept term, β_0, which has no X value multiplying it.

We now name the matrices in equation 11–47. We use boldface letters to denote matrices and vectors. The $n \times 1$ matrix (n-dimensional vector) of Y values is called **Y**; the $n \times (k + 1)$ matrix of X values is called **X**; the $(k + 1)$-dimensional vector of β coefficients is called **β**; and the n-dimensional vector of errors is called **ε**. We now may write the regression equation, equation 11–47, in terms of matrices as follows:

$$\mathbf{Y} = \mathbf{X}\boldsymbol{\beta} + \boldsymbol{\epsilon} \tag{11–49}$$

The estimated regression model, with the b estimates replacing the unknown βs, and the observed errors e replacing the unobserved ϵs, can be written in matrix notation as:

$$\mathbf{Y} = \mathbf{Xb} + \mathbf{e} \tag{11-50}$$

As you can see, matrix notation greatly simplifies our regression formulas. Using the definitions of matrix multiplication and addition, the relations between possibly large arrays of numbers can be written with very few symbols. Adding the concept of a transposed matrix, $\mathbf{A}' = $ transpose of matrix $\mathbf{A}$, we can present more results.

The *normal equations* (for a regression with any number of variables and data points) are written in matrix format as follows:

$$\mathbf{X}'\mathbf{Xb} = \mathbf{X}'\mathbf{Y} \tag{11-51}$$

Adding the concept of an inverse of a matrix, $\mathbf{A}^{-1} = $ inverse of matrix $\mathbf{A}$, we can solve the normal equations by premultiplying each side of equation 11–51 by the matrix $(\mathbf{X}'\mathbf{X})^{-1}$:

$$(\mathbf{X}'\mathbf{X})^{-1}(\mathbf{X}'\mathbf{X})\mathbf{b} = (\mathbf{X}'\mathbf{X})^{-1}\mathbf{X}'\mathbf{Y}$$
$$\mathbf{Ib} = (\mathbf{X}'\mathbf{X})^{-1}\mathbf{X}'\mathbf{Y}$$

where $\mathbf{I}$ is the *identity matrix,* resulting from the multiplication of a matrix by its inverse. Since $\mathbf{Ib} = \mathbf{b}$, we arrive at the solution of the normal equations in terms of the least-squares estimate vector $\mathbf{b}$:

$$\mathbf{b} = (\mathbf{X}'\mathbf{X})^{-1}\mathbf{X}'\mathbf{Y} \tag{11-52}$$

Thus, for any number of variables and data points, we obtain the vector of parameter estimates, the transpose of which is $(b_0, b_1, b_2, \ldots, b_k)$, as the result of the matrix operation in equation 11–52. We now present more results.

The predicted values of Y, denoted $\hat{Y}$, corresponding to the observed data (these are called the *fitted values* of Y) are given by:

$$\hat{\mathbf{Y}} = \mathbf{Xb} \tag{11-53}$$

Since $\mathbf{b} = (\mathbf{X}'\mathbf{X})^{-1}\mathbf{X}'\mathbf{Y}$, we can write the fitted values in terms of a transformation of the observed values:

$$\hat{\mathbf{Y}} = \mathbf{X}(\mathbf{X}'\mathbf{X})^{-1}\mathbf{X}'\mathbf{Y} \tag{11-54}$$

The matrix $\mathbf{H} = \mathbf{X}(\mathbf{X}'\mathbf{X})^{-1}\mathbf{X}'$ is called the *hat matrix*. Using it, we may write:

$$\hat{\mathbf{Y}} = \mathbf{HY}$$

The hat matrix, as well as other matrices, such as $\mathbf{X}$ and $(\mathbf{X}'\mathbf{X})^{-1}$, can be obtained from many regression computer programs.

The variance-covariance matrix of the coefficient estimates vector $\mathbf{b}$ is given by:

$$\mathbf{V}(\mathbf{b}) = \sigma^2 (\mathbf{X}'\mathbf{X})^{-1} \tag{11-55}$$

Since σ^2 is unknown and estimated by MSE, we have an estimated variance-covariance matrix of $\mathbf{b}$ given by:

$$\mathbf{s}^2(\mathbf{b}) = \text{MSE}(\mathbf{X}'\mathbf{X})^{-1} \tag{11-56}$$

If we define the matrix $\mathbf{C}$ as $\mathbf{C} = (\mathbf{X}'\mathbf{X})^{-1}$, the estimated standard error of each b_i is given using the diagonal of $\mathbf{C}$, C_{ii}, as:

$$s(b_i) = \sqrt{MSE\ C_{ii}} \qquad (11-57)$$

Another formula that has not been given until now is the definition of the elliptical joint confidence region for p regression parameters (shown in Figure 11–10). The region is defined by the equation:

$$\frac{(\boldsymbol{\beta} - \boldsymbol{b})'\mathbf{X}'\mathbf{X}(\boldsymbol{\beta} - \boldsymbol{b})}{p\ MSE} \leq F_{(\alpha;p,n-p)} \qquad (11-58)$$

A computer may generate values using Equation 11–58 that will give us a joint confidence region for several regression parameters.

What about Multicollinearity?

Earlier we said that in cases of severe multicollinearity, regression calculations cannot be carried out. Stated in terms of matrices, there is a very simple explanation for this.

When perfect multicollinearity exists, the columns of the $\mathbf{X}$ matrix are *linearly dependent*. Perfect multicollinearity means that at least two of the X_i variables are dependent on each other. From equation 11–47, you can see that this means that the columns of the $\mathbf{X}$ matrix are dependent. This dependency carries through to the matrix $\mathbf{X}'\mathbf{X}$, and this matrix, therefore, *cannot be inverted* (its determinant is zero). Thus, we cannot compute $(\mathbf{X}'\mathbf{X})^{-1}$ and cannot obtain the vector of parameter estimates, $\mathbf{b}$. In cases where multicollinearity exists but is not perfect, the matrix is invertible but has much instability in it (the matrix is *ill conditioned*). It is the matrix $(\mathbf{X}'\mathbf{X})^{-1}$ that causes the variance inflation in cases of multicollinearity.

The purpose of this section is just to give you an idea about regression results that are obtained via the matrix approach. Other results are given in advanced books.

11–16   Summary and Review of Terms

In this chapter, we extended the simple linear regression method of Chapter 10 to include several independent variables. We saw how the F test and the t test are adapted to the extension: The F test is aimed at determining the existence of a linear relationship between Y and any of the explanatory variables, and the separate t tests are each aimed at checking the significance of a single variable. We saw how the geometry of least-squares estimation is extended to planes and to higher-dimensional surfaces as more independent variables are included in a model. We extended the coefficient of determination to multiple regression situations, as well as the correlation coefficient. We discussed the problem of **multicollinearity** and its effects on estimation and prediction. We extended our discussion of the use of residual plots and mentioned the problem of **outliers** and the problem of **autocorrelation** of the errors and its detection. We discussed **qualitative variables** and their modeling using **indicator (dummy) variables**. We also talked about higher-order models: **polynomials** and **cross-product terms**. We emphasized the need for parsimony. We showed the relationship between regression and ANOVA, and between regression and **analysis of covariance**. We also talked about **nonlinear** models and about **transformations**. Finally, we discussed methods for selecting variables to find the "best" multiple regression model: **forward selection**, **backward elimination**, **stepwise regression**, and **all possible regressions**.

11–109. The following data, on the market value of firms, their total sales volume, profits, and total assets, all in millions of dollars for the year 1986, are obtained from *Business Week*'s list of the top 1,000 U.S. companies.[21] Assume the data constitute a random sample. Use a computer package of your choice to carry out a stepwise regression analysis of a firm's market value versus the other variables as independent variables. Also, try to add powers of variables, cross-product terms, and transformations. Find the best prediction model; make sure your model is parsimonious.

Answer

Value	Sales	Profits	Assets
90,055	51,250	4,789	57,814
61,610	71,557	5,360	69,165
48,895	35,210	2,492	34,591
27,533	27,148	1,538	26,334
25,728	34,087	314	38,883
24,952	102,814	2,945	73,668
22,336	4,129	675	5,105
21,622	8,414	861	7,966
21,206	62,715	3,285	37,933
20,647	18,281	747	23,706
20,307	25,409	1,478	17,642
19,977	44,866	1,405	39,412
19,757	24,351	715	35,209
19,608	44,281	1,351	68,029
19,438	11,444	1,588	26,218
17,929	8,669	934	8,373
1,993	4,321	261	2,410
2,804	10,372	594	10,382
17,515	11,550	373	12,925
16,930	14,652	1,110	99,476
16,436	11,909	450	4,506
15,850	16,580	757	13,650
15,779	11,113	741	12,242
15,774	4,836	590	4,129
15,680	7,245	523	6,287

11–110. Refer to the regression model in problem 11–62. Another model that was tried by the author of the article yielded the following results.

11–110.

$$\log(\text{DURATION}) = -0.7902 + 0.5057 \log(\text{QUANTITY})$$
$$(0.1089) + (0.0425)$$
$$+ 16.4317\text{MINE-MOUTH}$$
$$(2.0045)$$
$$+ 3.8795 \text{ MIDWEST} + 5.2033 \text{ WEST} + \log(e)$$
$$(0.9821) \qquad (1.1641)$$
$$n = 277$$
$$R^2 = 0.51$$

All variables significant. Three dummies. Untransformed model is multiplicative.

Discuss the type of model used. What is the form of the *untransformed* model? Interpret the regression results. Which model parameters are significant?

[21] "The Top 1000 U.S. Companies Ranked by Stock Market Valuation," *Business Week* (April 17, 1987) pp. 113–63.

Answer

11-111. An article in the *Journal of Management* reports the following results of a regression analysis aimed at predicting performance.[22] The sample size used in section A was $n = 86$, and the sample size used in section B was $n = 74$. Interpret all the findings in the table.

Variable Entered	Step	R^2	ΔR^2	T
Section A				
Feedback condition	1	0.39	0.39	12.01**
Power distance				1.96*
Collectivism				2.17**
Trust in supervisor	2	0.52	0.13	3.45**
Importance of praise				2.11**
Importance of criticism				1.95*
Feedback × power distance	3	0.54	0.02	−1.99*
Feedback × collectivism				−2.01*
Section B				
Importance of praise	1	0.41	0.41	3.42**
Importance of criticism				2.35**
Trust in supervisor				6.71**
Feedback condition	2	0.52	0.11	3.14**
Power distance				0.84
Collectivism				1.07
Feedback × power distance	3	0.54	0.02	−1.99*
Feedback × collectivism				−2.01*

*$p < 0.05$. **$p < 0.01$

11-112.

Both variables are not significant.

11-112. A regression analysis of share price was conducted on standardized dividends per share and standardized retained earnings. The results are given in the following equation. The author also reports that the R^2 is 0.56. What can you say about this regression?

$$P = 22.59 + 5.26D + 5.38R$$
$$(20.87) \quad (21.37)$$

11-113. A front-page article in *The Wall Street Journal* expounds upon a problem that has become serious in recent years: near collisions of airplanes and airline safety.[23] Data on the total number of flights and the total number of near collisions for the years 1980 through 1986 are given in the article and are reproduced here (by permission of Dow Jones & Company):

Year	Flights (in Millions)	Near Collisions
1980	4.95	568
1981	4.65	395
1982	4.55	311
1983	4.90	475
1984	5.56	589
1985	5.75	758
1986	6.25	839

Find the best regression model to fit the relationship between the total number of flights and the total number of near collisions in the sky. What are the implications of your model?

[22] C. Earley, "Trust, Perceived Importance of Praise and Criticism, and Work Performance," *Journal of Management* 12, no. 4 (1986).

[23] "As Air Traffic Rises, So Does Difficulty of Tracking It All," *The Wall Street Journal* (June 4, 1987).

11–114. The following data are on the asking price and other variables for condominiums in Brookline, Massachusetts, in early 1990.[24] Try to construct a prediction equation for the asking price based on any or all of the other reported variables.

Price ($)	Number of Rooms	Number of Bedrooms	Number of Baths	Age	Assessed Value ($)	Area (square feet)
145,000	4	1	1	69	116,500	790
144,900	4	2	1	70	127,200	915
145,900	3	1	1	78	127,600	721
146,500	4	1	1	75	121,700	800
146,900	4	2	1	40	94,800	718
147,900	4	1	1	12	169,700	915
148,000	3	1	1	20	151,800	870
148,900	3	1	1	20	147,800	875
149,000	4	2	1	70	140,500	1078
149,000	4	2	1	60	120,400	705
149,900	4	2	1	65	160,800	834
149,900	3	1	1	20	135,900	725
149,900	4	2	1	65	125,400	900
152,900	5	2	1	37	134,500	792
153,000	3	1	1	100	132,100	820
154,000	3	1	1	18	140,800	782
158,000	5	2	1	89	158,000	955
158,000	4	2	1	69	127,600	920
159,000	4	2	1	60	152,800	1050
159,000	5	2	2	49	157,000	1092
179,900	5	2	2	90	165,800	1180
179,900	6	3	1	89	158,300	1328
179,500	5	2	1	60	148,100	1175
179,000	6	3	1	87	158,500	1253
175,000	4	2	1	80	156,900	650

Answer

11–114.

Stepwise chooses only number of rooms and assessed value.
$b_0 = 910$
$b_1 = 78.5$
$b_2 = 0.234$
$R^2 = 0.591$

11–115. The following table reports the results of a multiple regression of the logarithm of annual earnings in Australia in 1984–85 versus three independent variables and a product of two of them.[25] The sample size was $n = 44$. Discuss the results.

Variable	Coefficient	p-Value	Adj R^2
Injury rate	0.00063	0.8467	
Fatality rate	10.6851	0.3373	
WC benefit	0.000016	0.0031	
Fatality rate * WC benefit	−0.00018	0.4194	0.73

---

[24] I am indebted to Lisa Glucksman of Prudential Edna Kranz Real Estate for the data on condominiums in Brookline in 1990.

[25] Reproduced from T. J. Kniesner and J. D. Leeth, "Compensating Wage Differentials for Fatal Injury Risk in Australia, Japan, and the United States," *Journal of Risk and Uncertainty*, 1991, pp. 75–90.

DIAMOND STATE TELEPHONE COMPANY

*T*he Diamond State Telephone Company is interested in assessing the relationship between the total number of telephone lines that would be demanded by 1,317 new businesses in Delaware and various costs associated with telephone lines. Results of the study would help the company determine the level of monthly service charges per line, the level of installation charges, and the discount for rotary phone service that would maximize revenue.

A random sample of 62 new businesses is selected from the population of 1,317 businesses that submitted requests for telephone service. Each company in the sample is sent a questionnaire listing various possible cost schedules for the installation of new lines and monthly charges, as well as the rotary service discount. For each proposed cost schedule, the respondent is asked to specify how many telephone lines would be requested.

The idea is to use regression analysis to determine the price-elasticity of the demand for telephone lines. When the monthly charges and installation charges are low, businesses will presumably demand a greater number of telephone lines. As the costs involved increase, a business may decide to use fewer telephone lines. Since some new businesses may own the older rotary telephones, the demand for the number of lines may increase as the discount per line for rotary service increases.

The following data are the *total* number of lines that would be demanded by the entire sample of 62 businesses at each corresponding combination of costs.

Number of Lines	Line Installation Charge	Monthly Charge per Line	Rotary Discount
201	$12.50	$10.32	$4.55
199	12.50	10.32	3.05
195	12.50	10.32	1.50
196	18.60	10.32	4.55
187	18.60	15.65	4.55
190	12.50	15.65	3.05
181	18.60	15.65	1.50
167	18.60	20.92	4.55
165	18.60	20.92	3.05
166	25.12	15.65	3.05
150	25.12	20.92	4.55
147	25.12	20.92	1.50
140	37.10	20.92	1.50
121	37.10	27.18	4.55
120	37.10	27.18	3.05
125	25.12	27.18	1.50
145	18.60	27.18	4.55
114	18.60	34.00	4.55
113	18.60	34.00	1.50
108	25.12	34.00	1.50
105	37.10	34.00	3.05

You have been assigned to carry out an analysis of the data. Discuss your suggested methodology. Discuss all the required assumptions. Carry out an analysis, and state your conclusions. Remember that interest centers on the population of 1,317 new businesses. Can the results of the study be applied to other populations? Predict the total demand for lines by the 1,317 new businesses if line installation and monthly charges are set at the highest level used in the study and the rotary discount is set at the lowest level. Predict total population demand for lines using other cost schedules within the range of the estimation data.

12

TIME SERIES, FORECASTING, AND INDEX NUMBERS

INTRODUCTION

The desire to forecast the future is as old as the human race—older if you allow that animals also form anticipations of what the future may bring. A predator may try to predict where the prey will run, and there are other such examples. In ancient times, people relied on prophets, soothsayers, and crystal balls. Today we have computers and with them an impressive, ever-expanding array of quantitative capabilities. Are these powerful quantitative tools useful in predicting the future?

It is important to understand that many economic and business-related variables (as well as others) cannot be forecast well. The future values of these variables cannot be predicted from their past history. This is especially true of the prices of assets traded in efficient markets, such as stocks. The *efficient markets hypothesis* states that the future price of a stock cannot be predicted from its past. This hypothesis is widely held to be true. Stock market analysts who do not believe this hypothesis are known as *chartists,* people who chart stock price movements in an effort to extrapolate them into the future. The rationale behind the efficient markets hypothesis is that the demand for a given stock at any point in time reflects people's expectations of the future value of the stock. If the future value of the stock is expected to increase, people exert buying pressure, and the price increases immediately in fulfillment of this expectation. Mathematically, the theory states that movements of a stock are a *random walk:* the stock moves up or down like a drunk who takes each step randomly and moves with no apparent pattern.

A **time series** is a set of measurements of a variable that are ordered through time.

A time series variable is often denoted by Z_t to distinguish it from the X and Y variables used in regression analysis and other areas. The particular value of the variable at time t is denoted by z_t. We denote the *error* occurring at time t by a_t. The error a_t in a time series model serves the same purpose as the regression error, ϵ. The random error at time t, a_t, is assumed to have mean zero and constant variance σ^2, and successive errors are assumed to be uncorrelated with each other.

Using our new time series notation, a random walk is modeled by equation 12–1.

A random walk:

$$Z_t - Z_{t-1} = a_t \qquad (12\text{–}1)$$

or equivalently:

$$Z_t = Z_{t-1} + a_t$$

Equation 12–1 says that the difference between the value of variable Z at time t and its value at time $t - 1$ is a random error. The time series Z_t is a random walk if each

Continued on next page

FIGURE 12–1   A Random Walk

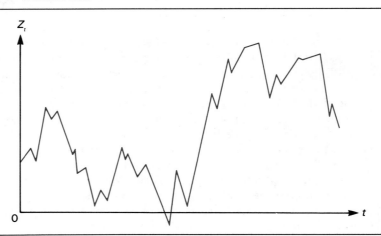

step, as we go from time $t - 1$ to t, is just a random error, a_t. An example of a random walk is shown in Figure 12–1. As can be seen from the figure, there is no persistent pattern or trend in the movement of the variable Z_t through time. The difference between the stock price today and the stock price tomorrow is a purely random "error." Since the error a_t cannot be forecast, because it is purely random, we cannot forecast Z_t. Our best forecast within this framework assumes that a_t will equal its mean of zero, and, therefore, that the price tomorrow will be equal to the price today. This is called the *naive* approach to forecasting.

Many variables, however, such as sales and other business variables, *can* be forecast, and the use of statistics plays an important role in forecasting these variables. While there are many different methods of forecasting—subjective, naive, and others—this is a book on statistics, and we will therefore concentrate our discussion on the *statistical methods of forecasting*.

On January 15, 1884, a physicist, Professor J. H. Poynting of Trinity College, Cambridge, delivered a paper at a meeting of the Royal Statistical Society in London. The paper was entitled "A Comparison of the Fluctuations in the Price of Wheat and in the Cotton and Silk Imports into Great Britain." The paper contained an analysis of these variables and of sunspots. On page 43 of the paper, Poynting described his statistical method. He wrote as follows.

> Suppose that while a full band is playing, we could draw a curve to represent the pressure of the air at a given moment along a line drawn in the direction in which the sound is travelling. Such a curve would appear to fluctuate irregularly. But we know that it is really made up by the superposition of the perfectly regular waves of pressure corresponding to the separate notes sent out by all the various instruments, and a well-trained ear stationed in the line which can pick out the notes practically analyses this irregular pressure curve, that is, breaks it up into its simple harmonics. What is true of this pressure curve is true of all curves however irregularly they fluctuate, and the ear performs for the pressure curve what the mathematician seeks to perform for any other curve by Fourier's theorem.[1]

One of the aims of time series analysis is to forecast future values of time series variables. Incidentally, in this book we make a distinction between the terms *fore-*

---

[1] J. H. Poynting, "A Comparison of the Fluctuations in the Price of Wheat and in the Cotton and Silk Imports into Great Britain," *Statistical Journal* XLVII (March 1884), pp. 34–48.

FIGURE 12-2   A Time Series as a Superposition of Two Regular Wave Functions and a Random Error Component (Not Shown)

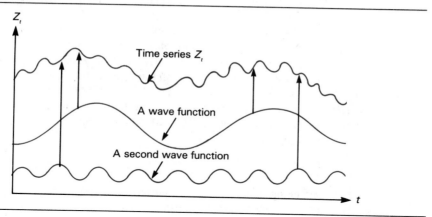

casting and *prediction*. We use the word *prediction* in the context of regression analysis; the word *forecasting* is reserved for time series analysis, where *forecasting is an extrapolation of the series values beyond the region of the estimation data.* Remember the warning we gave about extrapolation in Chapter 10; we will return to that problem later in this chapter.

Now let us return to Professor Poynting. His statements suggest that a time series may look very irregular, but we should be able to break it down into its harmonics. These are regular wavelike functions (sines and cosines) of different frequencies, and they are superimposed on one another. Poynting suggests that we break down a time series into its different wave components. Then we can forecast the time series by forecasting where each wave component is moving. In his paper, Poynting does just that with the different time series: English cotton imports, Italian silk imports, Bengal silk imports, Brutia silk imports, English bank rate, sunspots, and other time series occurring between 1780 and 1880. The decomposition of a time series into wave components is demonstrated in Figure 12-2.

Much of time series analysis makes use of the idea of breaking down a time series into functions like the two shown in Figure 12-2, plus a random error term. The regular (wavelike) functions in the figure have a cycle, and they can be forecast. This reduces the forecasting errors to the magnitude of the nonforecastable residual error once the regularity has been accounted for. Another regularity in a time series may be an increasing or decreasing *trend,* that is, a general movement of increase or decrease. The trend, too, may be accounted for, thus helping us get better forecasts. Remember the idea of a statistical model presented in Chapter 10. Here we see an application of that important idea in the context of time series modeling. A good time series model is one that accounts for as much as possible of the *regular movement* in the time series, leaving out only a random error, which cannot be forecast. By comparison, the random walk series, given in equation 12–1, has *no regular components,* only random errors as the series moves through time. Since there is no regularity, the series cannot be forecast. ∎

12–2   Trend Analysis

Sometimes a time series displays a steady tendency of increase or decrease through time. Such a tendency is called a **trend.** When we plot the observations against time, we may notice that a straight line can describe the increase or decrease in the series as time goes on. This should remind us of simple linear regression, and, indeed, in such cases we will use the method of least squares to estimate the parameters of a straight-line model.

At this point, we make an important remark. *When dealing with time series data, the errors of the regression model may not be independent of each other: time series observations tend to be sequentially correlated.* Therefore, we cannot give much credence to regression results. Our estimation and hypothesis tests may not be accurate. We must be aware of such possible problems and realize that fitting lines to time series data is less an accurate statistical method than a simple, *descriptive* method that may work in some cases. We will now demonstrate the procedure of trend analysis with an example.

EXAMPLE (a)

An economist is researching banking activity and wants to find a model that would help her forecast total net loans by commercial banks. From the *Statistical Abstract of the United States* (Washington, D.C.: U.S. Bureau of the Census, 1987), the economist gets the data presented in Table 12–1. A plot of the data is shown in Figure 12–3.

SOLUTION

As can be seen from the figure, the observations may be described by a straight line. A simple linear regression equation is fit to the data by least squares. A straight-line model to account for a trend is of the form:

$$Z_t = \beta_0 + \beta_1 t + a_t \qquad (12\text{–}2)$$

TABLE 12–1 Annual Total Net Loans by Commercial Banks

Year	Loans ($ billions)
1978	833
1979	936
1980	1,006
1981	1,120
1982	1,212
1983	1,301
1984	1,490
1985	1,608

FIGURE 12–3 Annual Total Net Loans by Commercial Banks

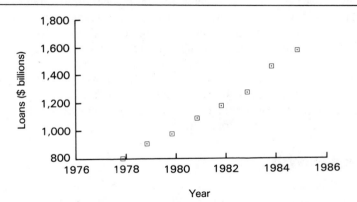

where t is time and a_t is the error term. The coefficients β_0 and β_1 are the regression intercept and slope, respectively.

To carry out the trend analysis, we first *recode* the data to simplify the analysis. Instead of using the years, 1978, 1979, and so on, we renumber the observations so that their mean will be zero. This simplifies computations done by hand, and it makes sense because there is nothing quantitatively meaningful about the numerical value of the year. In order to have a mean of zero and keep the relative scaling correct, we renumber the eight years consecutively as $-7, -5, -3, -1, 1, 3, 5, 7$. (If we had an odd number of years, the middle one would be 0 and the others $1, 2, 3, \ldots$, and $-1, -2, -3, \ldots$, symmetrically on both sides of zero.) We do not show the simple linear regression computations; we have done quite a few in Chapter 10. We show the line, its equation, and the r^2 value in Figure 12–4.

We note that *in the context of time series, the coefficient of determination, r^2, is not a reliable measure*. Also, in this example, we have only eight observations, and the inference drawn from few observations is of limited use. Having pointed out the limitations of our analysis, we note that the line seems to fit our data very well. We may want to use our estimated trend line in forecasting. To forecast total loans in 1986, we note that in

FIGURE 12–4   A Least-Squares Line for the Data of Example (a)

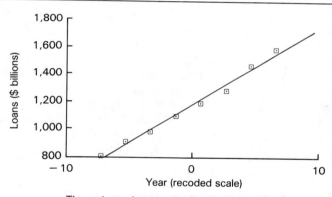

The estimated regression line (in time series notation) is given as:
$$\hat{Z} = 1{,}188 + 54.5119t. \quad \text{We have } r^2 = 0.98.$$

FIGURE 12–5   Least-Squares Line and 1986 Forecast of Total Net Loans by Commercial Banks

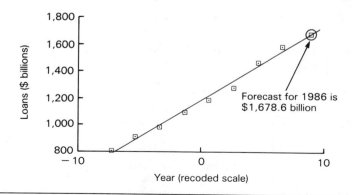

Forecast for 1986 is $1,678.6 billion

the recoded scale, 1986 is 9. We substitute $t = 9$ into the estimated regression equation and get:

$$\hat{z} = 1{,}188 + 54.5119t = 1{,}188 + 54.5119(9) = 1{,}678.6 \text{ (billion dollars)}$$

Remember that forecasting is an extrapolation outside the region of the estimation data. This, in addition to the fact that the regression assumptions are not met in trend analysis, causes our forecast to have an unknown accuracy. We will, therefore, not construct any prediction interval. Figure 12–5 shows our trend line and the forecast total loans for 1986.

Trend analysis includes cases where the trend is not necessarily a straight line. It is possible to model *curved* trends as well, and here we may use either polynomials or transformations, as we have seen in Chapter 11. In fact, a careful examination of the data in Figure 12–3 and of the fitted line in Figure 12–4 reveals that the data are actually curved upward somewhat. We will, therefore, fit an exponential model: $Z = \beta_0 e^{\beta_1 t} a_t$, where β_0 and β_1 are constants and e is the number 2.71828. . . , the base of the natural logarithm. We assume a multiplicative error a_t. We run a regression of the natural log of Z on the variable t. The transformed regression, in terms of the original exponential equation, is shown in Figure 12–6. The coefficient of determination of this model is very close to 1.00. The figure also shows the forecast for 1986, obtained from the equation by substituting $t = 9$, as we did when we tried fitting the straight line.

A polynomial regression with t and t^2 leads to a fit very similar to the one shown in Figure 12–6, and the forecast is very close to the one obtained by the exponential equation. We do not elaborate the details of the analysis here because much was explained about regression models in Chapters 10 and 11. Remember that trend analysis does not enjoy the theoretical strengths that regression analysis does in non-time series contexts; therefore, your forecasts are of questionable accuracy. In the case of Example (a), we conclude that an exponential or quadratic fit is proba-

FIGURE 12–6   Fitting an Exponential Model to the Data of Example (a)

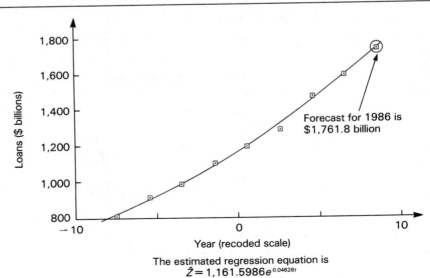

Forecast for 1986 is $1,761.8 billion

Year (recoded scale)

The estimated regression equation is
$\hat{Z} = 1{,}161.5986e^{0.04628t}$

bly better than a straight line, but there is no way to objectively evaluate our forecast. The main advantage of trend analysis is that when the model is appropriate and the data exhibit a clear trend, we may carry out a simple analysis.

PROBLEMS

12–1. What are the advantages and disadvantages of trend analysis? When would you use this method of forecasting?

12–2. As part of the analysis in Example (a), the economist wants to construct a forecasting model for total assets held by banks. From the 1987 *Statistical Abstract of the United States*, the economist gets the following data.

Year:	1978	1979	1980	1981	1982	1983	1984	1985
Assets ($ billions):	276	294	334	352	386	441	386	440

Estimate a trend line for these data, and predict total bank assets for 1986. Compare your forecast with the actual value for 1986, which you may find in the current *Statistical Abstract*.

12–3. The following data are a local newspaper's readership figures, in thousands.

Year:	1976	1977	1978	1979	1980	1981	1982	1983	1984	1985	1986	1987
Readers:	53	65	74	85	92	105	120	128	144	158	179	195

Carry out a trend analysis of these data, and forecast the total number of readers for 1988 and for 1989.

12–4. The following data are annual corporate revenues for a midwestern manufacturing firm, in thousands of dollars. Carry out a trend analysis, and forecast revenues for the next year of operation.

Year:	1977	1978	1979	1980	1981	1982	1983	1984	1985	1986	1987
Revenue:	126	122	125	119	121	120	117	119	115	116	113

12–5. Would trend analysis, by itself, be a useful forecasting tool for monthly sales of swimming suits? Explain.

12–6. A firm's profits are known to vary with a business cycle of several years. Would trend analysis, by itself, be a good forecasting tool of the firm's profits? Why?

Answers

12–2.

$A = -45940 + 23.37Y$
$R^2 = 0.86$
$\hat{A}(1986) = 470.83$

12–4.

$R^2 = 0.85$
$\hat{R}(1988) = 111.54$

12–6.

No.

12–3 Seasonality and Cyclical Behavior

Monthly time series observations very often display *seasonal variation*. The seasonal variation follows a complete cycle throughout a whole year, with the same general pattern repeating itself year after year. The obvious examples of such variation are sales of seasonal items—for example, suntan oil. We expect that sales of suntan oil will be very high during the summer months. We expect sales to taper off during the onset of fall and decline drastically in winter—with another peak during the winter holiday season, when many people travel to sunny places on vacation—and then increase again as spring progresses into summer. The pattern repeats itself the following year.

Seasonal variation, which is very obvious in a case such as suntan oil, actually exists in many time series, even those that may not appear at first to have a seasonal characteristic. Electricity consumption, gasoline consumption, credit card spending, corporate profits, and sales of most discretionary items display distinct seasonal variation. Seasonality is not confined to monthly observations. Monthly time series observations display a 12-month period: a one-year cycle. If our observations of a seasonal variable are quarterly, these observations will have a four-quarter period. Weekly observations of a seasonal time series will display a 52-week period. The term *seasonality*, or *seasonal variation*, frequently refers to a 12-month cycle.

The second wave function in Figure 12–2 describes the seasonality in the time series, and the first wave function—with a longer period—reflects *cyclical variation*. In addition to a linear or curvilinear trend and seasonality, a time series may exhibit cyclical variation (where the period is not one year). In the context of business and economics, cyclical behavior is often referred to as the *business cycle*. The business cycle is marked by troughs and peaks of business activity in a cycle that lasts several years. The cycle is often of irregular, unpredictable pattern, and the period may be anything from 2 to 15 years and may change within the same time series. We repeat the distinction between the terms *seasonal variation* and *cyclical variation*:

> When a cyclical pattern in our data has a period of one year, we usually call the pattern **seasonal variation.** When a cyclical pattern has a period other than a year, we refer to it as **cyclical variation.**

We now give an example of a time series with a linear trend and with seasonal variation and no cyclical variation. Figure 12–7 shows sales data for suntan oil. Note that the data display both a trend (increasing sales as one compares succeeding years), and a seasonal variation.

Figure 12–8 shows a time series of annual corporate gross earnings for a given company. Since the data are annual, there is no seasonal variation. As seen in the figure, the data exhibit both a trend and a cyclical pattern. The business cycle here has a period of approximately four years (the period does change during the time span under study). Figure 12–9 shows monthly total numbers of airline passengers

FIGURE 12–7 Monthly Sales of Suntan Oil

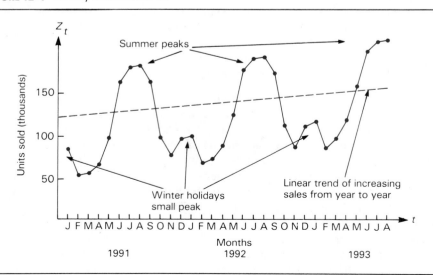

FIGURE 12–8   Annual Corporate Gross Earnings

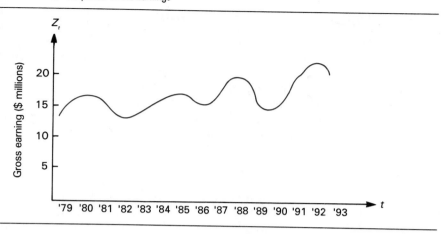

FIGURE 12–9   Monthly Total Numbers of Airline Passengers Traveling between Two Cities

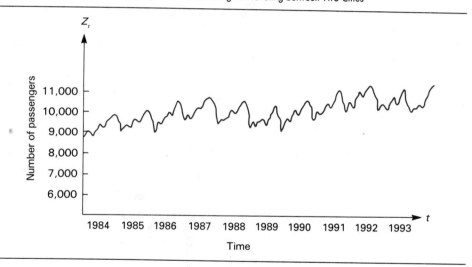

traveling between two cities. See what components you can visually detect in the plot of the time series.

How do we incorporate seasonal behavior in a time series model? There are several different approaches to the problem. Having studied regression analysis, and having used it (somewhat informally) in trend analysis, let us now extend regression analysis to account for seasonal behavior. If you think about it for a while and recall the methods described in Chapter 11, you probably realize that one of the tools of multiple regression—the dummy variable—is applicable here. We can formulate a regression model for the trend, whether linear or curvilinear, and add 11 dummy variables to the model to account for seasonality if our data are monthly. (Why eleven? Reread the appropriate section of Chapter 11 if you don't know.) If data are quarterly, we use three dummy variables to denote the particular quarter. You have probably spotted a limitation to this analysis, in addition to the fact that the assumptions of the regression model are not met in the context of time series. The new limitation is lack of parsimony. If you have two years' worth of monthly data and you use the dummy variable technique along with linear trend, then you have a regression analysis of 24 observations using a model with 12 variables. If, on the other hand, your data are quarterly and you have many years of data, then the problem of the proliferation of variables does not arise. Since the regression assumptions are not met anyway, we will not worry about this problem.

Using the dummy variable regression approach to seasonal time series assumes that the effect of the seasonal component of the series is *additive*. The seasonality is added to the trend and random error, as well as to the cycle (nonseasonal periodicity)—if one exists. We are thus assuming a model of the following form.

An additive model:

$$Z_t = T_t + S_t + C_t + I_t \qquad (12\text{–}3)$$

where T is the trend component of the series, S is the seasonal component, C is the cyclical component, and I is the irregular component

---

(The irregular component is the error, a_t; we use I_t because it is the usual notation in decomposition models.) Equation 12–3 states the philosophy inherent in the use of dummy variable regression to account for seasonality: the time series is viewed as comprising four components that are added to each other to give the observed values of the series.

The particular regression model, assuming our data are quarterly, is given by the following equation.

A regression model with dummy variables for seasonality:

$$Z_t = \beta_0 + \beta_1 t + \beta_2 Q_1 + \beta_3 Q_2 + \beta_4 Q_3 + a_t \qquad (12\text{–}4)$$

where $Q_1 = 1$ if the observation is in the first quarter of the year and 0 otherwise; $Q_2 = 1$ if the observation is in the second quarter of the year and 0 otherwise; $Q_3 = 1$ if the observation is in the third quarter of the year and 0 otherwise; and all three Q_i are 0 if the observation is in the fourth quarter of the year

---

Since the procedure is a straightforward application of the dummy variable regression technique of Chapter 11, we will not give an example.

A second way of modeling seasonality assumes a *multiplicative* model for the components of the time series. This is more commonly used than the additive model, equation 12–3, and is found to appropriately describe time series in a wide range of applications. The overall model is of the following form.

A multiplicative model:

$$Z_t = (T_t)(S_t)(C_t)(I_t) \qquad (12\text{–}5)$$

Here the observed time series values are viewed as the *product* of the four components, when all of them exist. If there is no cyclicity, for example, then $C_t = 1$.

When equation 12–5 is the assumed overall model for the time series, we deal with the seasonality using a method called *ratio to moving average*. Once we account for the seasonality, we may also model the cyclical variation and the trend. We describe the procedure in the next section.

PROBLEMS

12–7. Explain the difference between the terms *seasonal variation* and *cyclical variation*.

12–8. What particular problem would you encounter in fitting a dummy variable regression to 70 weekly observations of a seasonal time series?

12–9. In your opinion, what could be the reasons why the seasonal component is not constant? Give examples where you believe the seasonality may change.

12–10. Cyclical variation may also refer to cycles less than a year. Give examples of time series where you believe there may be a week-long cycle.

Answer

12–8.

Few d.f. for error

12–4 The Ratio-to-Moving-Average Method

A **moving average** of a time series is an *average* of a fixed number of observations (say, five observations) that *moves* as we progress down the series.[2]

A moving average based on five observations is demonstrated in Table 12–2. Figure 12–10 shows how the moving average in Table 12–2 is obtained and how this aver-

TABLE 12–2 Demonstration of a Five-Observation Moving Average

Time, t:	1	2	3	4	5	6	7	8	9	10	11	12	13	14
Series values, Z_t:	15	12	11	18	21	16	14	17	20	18	21	16	14	19
Corresponding series of five-observation moving average:			15.4	15.6	16	17.2	17.6	17	18	18.4	17.8	17.6		

FIGURE 12–10 Computing the Five-Observation Moving Averages for the Data in Table 12–2

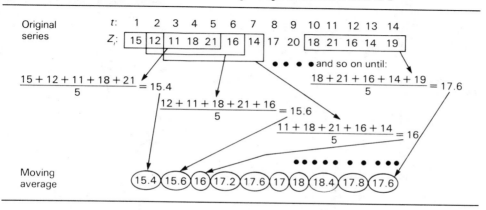

---

[2] The term *moving average* has another meaning within the Box-Jenkins methodology.

age *moves* as the series progresses. Note that the first moving average is obtained from the first five observations, so we must wait until $t = 5$ to produce the first moving average. Therefore, there are fewer observations in the moving-average series than there are in the original series, Z_t. *A moving average smooths the data of its variations.* The original data of Table 12–2 along with the smoothed moving-average series are displayed in Figure 12–11.

The idea may have already occurred to you that if we have a seasonal time series and we compute a moving-average series for the data, then we will smooth out the seasonality. This is indeed the case. Assume a multiplicative time series model of the form given in equation 12–5:

$$Z = TSCI$$

(here we drop the subscript t). If we smooth out the series by using a 12-month moving average when data are monthly, or four-quarter moving average when data are quarterly, then the resulting smoothed series will contain trend and cycle but not seasonality or the irregular component; the last two will have been smoothed out by the moving average. If we then divide each observation by the corresponding value of the moving-average series (MA), we will have isolated the seasonal and irregular components. Notationally,

$$\frac{Z_t}{\text{MA}} = \frac{TSCI}{TC} = SI \tag{12–6}$$

This is the **ratio to moving average.** If we average each seasonal value with all values of Z_t/MA for the same season (that is, for quarterly data, we average all values corresponding to the first quarter, all values of the second quarter, and so on), then we cancel out *most* of the irregular component I_t and isolate the seasonal component of the series. There are two more steps to be followed in the general procedure just described: (1) we compute the seasonal components as percentages by multiplying Z_t/MA by 100; and (2) we *center* the dates of the moving averages by averaging them. In the case of quarterly data, we average every two consecutive moving averages and center them midway between quarters. Centering is required because the number of terms in the moving average is even (4 quarters or 12 months).

FIGURE 12–11 Original Series and Smoothed Moving-Average Series

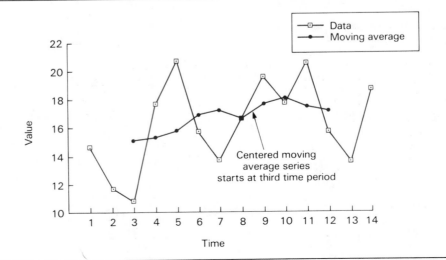

Summary of the ratio-to-moving-average procedure for quarterly data (a similar procedure is carried out when data are monthly):

1. Compute a four-quarter moving-average series.
2. Center the moving averages by averaging every consecutive pair and placing the average between quarters.
3. For each data point, divide the original series value by the corresponding moving average. Then multiply by 100.
4. For each quarter, average all data points corresponding to the quarter. The averaging can be done in one of several ways: find the simple average; find a modified average, which is the average after dropping the highest and lowest points; or find the median. Once we average the ratio-to-moving-average figures for each quarter, we will have four *quarterly indexes*. Finally, we adjust the indexes so that their mean will be 100. This is done by multiplying each by 400 and dividing by their sum.

We demonstrate the procedure with Example (b).

The distribution manager of the Northern Natural Gas Company needs to analyze the time series of quarterly sales of natural gas in a midwestern region served by the company. Quarterly data for 1983 through 1986 are given in Table 12–3. The table also shows the four-quarter moving averages, the centered moving averages, and the ratio to moving average (multiplied by 100 to give percentages). Figure 12–12 shows both the original series and the centered four-quarter moving-average series. Note how the seasonal variation is smoothed out.

    The ratio-to-moving-average column in Table 12–3 gives us the contribution of the seasonal component and the irregular component within the multiplicative model, as seen from equation 12–6. We now come to step 4 of the procedure: averaging each seasonal term so as to average out the irregular effects and isolate the purely seasonal component as much as possible. We will use the simple average in obtaining the four sea-

EXAMPLE (b)

TABLE 12–3 Data and Four-Quarter Moving Averages for Example (b)

Quarter	Sales (Btu in billions)	4-quarter moving average	Centered moving average	Ratio to moving average (percent)
1983 W	170			
S	148			
S	141	152.25	151.125	(141/151.125)100 → 93.3
F	150	150	148.625	100.9
1984 W	161	147.25	146.125	110.2
S	137	145	146	93.8
S	132	147	146.5	90.1
F	158	146	147	107.5
1985 W	157	148	147.5	106.4
S	145	147	144	100.7
S	128	141	141.375	90.5
F	134	141.75	141	95.0
1986 W	160	140.25	140.5	113.9
S	139	140.75	142	97.9
S	130	143.25	(139/142)100	
F	144			

FIGURE 12–12 Northern Natural Gas Sales: Original Series and Moving Average

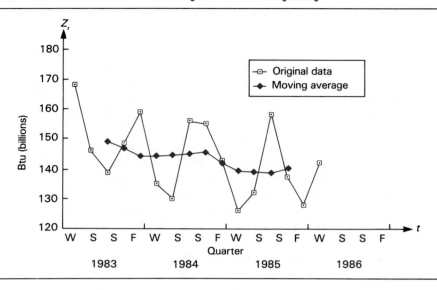

TABLE 12–4 Obtaining the Seasonal Indexes for Example (b)

	Quarter			
	Winter	**Spring**	**Summer**	**Fall**
1983			93.3	100.9
1984	110.2	93.8	90.1	107.5
1985	106.4	100.7	90.5	95.0
1986	113.9	97.9		
Sum	330.5	292.4	273.9	303.4
Average	110.17	97.47	91.3	101.13

Sum of averages = 400.07
Seasonal index = (Average)(400)/(400.07):

	110.15	97.45	91.28	101.11

sonal indexes. This is done in Table 12–4, with the ratio-to-moving-average figures from Table 12–3.

Due to rounding, the indexes do not add to exactly 400, but their sum is very close to 400. The seasonal indexes quantify the seasonal effects in the time series of natural gas sales. We will see shortly how these indexes and other quantities are used in forecasting future values of the time series.

The ratio-to-moving-average procedure, which gives us the seasonal indexes, may also be used for **deseasonalizing** the data. Deseasonalizing a time series is a procedure that is often used to display the general movement of a series without regard to the seasonal effects. Many government economic statistics are reported in the form of deseasonalized time series. To deseasonalize the data, we divide every data point by its appropriate seasonal index. If we assume a multiplicative time series model (equation 12–5), then dividing by the seasonal index gives us a series containing the other components only:

$$\frac{Z}{S} = \frac{TSCI}{S} = CTI \qquad (12\text{--}7)$$

Table 12–5 shows how the series of Example (b) is deseasonalized. The deseasonalized natural gas time series, along with the original time series, is shown in Figure 12–13. Note that we have to multiply our results Z/S by 100 to cancel out the fact that our seasonal indexes were originally multiplied by 100 by convention.

The deseasonalized series in Figure 12–13 does have some variation in it. Comparing this series with the moving-average series in Figure 12–12, containing only

TABLE 12–5 Deseasonalizing the Series for Example (b)

Quarter	Sales (Z) (Btu, in billions)	Seasonal Indexes (S)	Deseasonalized Series (Z/S)(100)
1983 W	170	110.15	154.34
S	148	97.45	151.87
S	141	91.28	154.47
F	150	101.11	148.35
1984 W	161	110.15	146.16
S	137	97.45	140.58
S	132	91.28	144.61
F	158	101.11	156.27
1985 W	157	110.15	142.53
S	145	97.45	148.79
S	128	91.28	140.23
F	134	101.11	132.53
1986 W	160	110.15	145.26
S	139	97.45	142.64
S	130	91.28	142.42
F	144	101.11	142.42

FIGURE 12–13 Original and Deseasonalized Series for the Northern Natural Gas Example

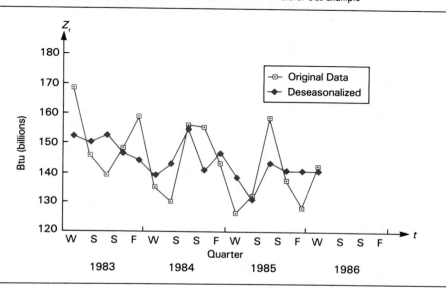

the trend and cyclical components TC, we conclude that the relatively high residual variation in the deseasonalized series is due to the irregular component, I (because the deseasonalized series is TCI and the moving average series is TC). The large irregular component is likely due to variation in the weather throughout the period under study.

The Cyclical Component of the Series

Since the moving-average series is TC, we could isolate the cyclical component of the series by dividing the moving-average series by the trend, T. We must, therefore, first estimate the trend. By visually inspecting the moving-average series in Figure 12–12, we notice a slightly decreasing linear trend and what looks like two cycles. We should therefore try to fit a straight line to the data. The line, fitted by simple linear regression using the original data, is shown in Figure 12–14. The figure also shows the moving-average series. The estimated trend line is:

$$\hat{Z} = 155.275 - 1.1059t \qquad (12\text{–}8)$$

From Figure 12–14, it seems that the cyclical component is relatively small in comparison with the other components of this particular series.

If we want to isolate the cyclical component, we divide the moving-average series (the product TC) by the corresponding trend value for the period. Multiplying the answer by 100 gives us a kind of cyclical index for each data point. There are problems, however, in dealing with the cycle. Unlike the seasonal component, which is fairly regular (with a one-year cycle), the cyclical component of the time series may not have a dependable cycle at all. Both the amplitude and the cycle (peak-to-peak distance) of the cyclical component may be erratic, and it may be very difficult, if not impossible, to predict. This makes it difficult to forecast future series observations.

FIGURE 12–14   The Trend Line and Moving Average for the Northern Natural Gas Example

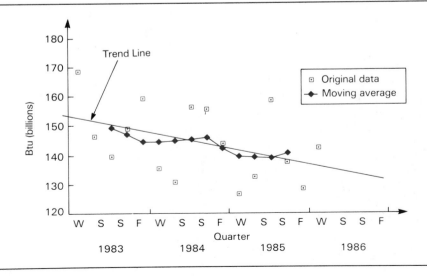

Forecasting a Multiplicative Series

Forecasting a series of the form $Z = TSCI$ entails trying to forecast the three "regular" components C, T, and S. We try to forecast each component separately and then multiply them to get a series forecast:

The forecast of a multiplicative series:

$$\hat{Z} = TSC \qquad\qquad (12\text{--}9)$$

As we noted, it is very difficult to obtain reliable forecasts of the cyclical component. The trend is forecast simply by substituting the appropriate value of t in the least-squares line, as was done in section 12–2. Then we multiply the value by the seasonal index (expressed as a decimal—divided by 100) to give us TS. Finally, we follow the cyclical component and *try* to guess what it may be at the point we need to forecast; then we multiply by this component to get TSC. In our example, since the cyclical component seems small, we may avoid the nebulous task of guessing the future value of the cyclical component. We will therefore forecast using only S and T.

Let us forecast natural gas sales for winter 1987. Equation 12–8 for the trend was estimated with each quarter sequentially numbered from 1 to 16 (we did not renumber so that the mean would be zero, as suggested in Section 12–2). Therefore, winter 1987 is $t = 17$. Substituting this value into equation 12–8, we get:

$$\hat{z} = 155.275 - 1.1059(17) = 136.475 \text{ (billion Btu)}$$

The next stage is to multiply this result by the seasonal index (divided by 100). Since the point is a winter quarter, we use the winter index. From the bottom of Table 12–4 (or the second column of Table 12–5), we get the seasonal index for winter: 110.15. Ignoring the (virtually unforecastable) cyclical component by letting it equal 1, we find, using the forecast equation, equation 12–9:

$$\hat{z} = TSC = (1)(136.475)(1.1015) = 150.327 \text{ (billion Btu)}$$

This is our forecast of sales for winter 1987.

PROBLEMS

12–11. The following data represent average factory worker weekly pay, in dollars, for the months June 1984 to May 1987. Data are from *The Wall Street Journal* (June 11, 1987) and are reprinted by permission of Dow Jones & Company.

375, 370, 374, 378, 376, 380, 384, 380, 378, 380, 382, 383, 382, 381, 385, 387, 390, 392, 403, 398, 393, 389, 394, 392, 393, 391, 392, 396, 395, 400, 409, 404, 404, 405, 399, 402.

Decompose this time series into trend and seasonal components, as well as a cyclical component (if it exists) and the irregular component. Describe each component. Develop the seasonal (monthly) indexes. Use the ratio-to-moving-average method. Also, deseasonalize the series. Forecast average weekly pay for factory workers for June 1987.

12–12. The following data, also from *The Wall Street Journal* (May 28, 1987), are monthly figures of U.S. steel production, in millions of tons, from July 1984 through April 1987.

Answer

12–12.

Prediction for May = 6.525(104.47/100) = 6.817.

7.4, 6.8, 6.4, 6.6, 6.5, 6.0, 7.0, 6.7, 8.2, 7.8, 7.7, 7.3, 7.0, 7.1, 6.9, 7.3, 7.0,
6.7, 7.6, 7.2, 7.9, 7.7, 7.6, 6.7, 6.3, 5.7, 5.6, 6.1, 5.8, 5.9, 6.2, 6.0, 7.3, 7.4.

Decompose the series into its components using the methods of this section, and forecast steel production for May 1987.

12–13.   A company importing Italian cameos needs to forecast the exchange rate of Italian lire to U.S. dollars. Quarterly data from the first quarter of 1987 through the first quarter of 1991 are obtained from *International Financial Statistics* and are as follows (in Italian lire per U.S. dollar):[3]

1,654, 1,695, 1,697, 1,659, 1,708, 1,772, 1,807, 1,757, 1,794, 1,761, 1,747, 1,670,
1,625, 1,624, 1,630, 1,608, 1,594, 1,607, 1,630, 1,629, 1,612, 1,608, 1,604.

Try to forecast the exchange rate for the second quarter of 1991.

12–14.   The following are monthly electrical comsumption data, in megawatts, for a town in Arizona from January 1989 through December 1992:

21, 23, 20, 24, 33, 41, 45, 50, 42, 28, 25, 26, 25, 27, 24, 30, 48, 53, 58, 62, 55, 32, 30, 32,
29, 32, 28, 35, 37, 50, 58, 66, 60, 45, 39, 40, 40, 43, 39, 45, 61, 68, 70, 72, 65, 54, 40, 39.

Decompose the series to its components, and forecast consumption for January 1993.

12–15.   The following are quarterly data of spot prices for a barrel of oil (in U.S. dollars) on the Gulf Coast of the United States, from 1981 through 1985: 42, 40, 39, 41, 40, 38, 35, 37, 39, 35, 34, 37, 36, 32, 30, 33, 32, 28, 27, 31. Decompose the series and forecast the price of a barrel of oil for the first quarter of 1986.

12–5   Exponential Smoothing Methods

One method that is often useful in forecasting time series is *exponential smoothing*. There are exponential smoothing methods of varying complexity, but we will discuss only the simplest model, called *simple exponential smoothing*. Simple exponential smoothing is a useful method for forecasting time series that have no pronounced trend or seasonality. The concept is an extension of the idea of a moving average, introduced in the last section. Look at Figures 12–11 and 12–12, and notice how the moving average *smooths* the original series of its sharp variations. The idea of exponential smoothing is to smooth the original series the way the moving average does and to use the smoothed series in forecasting future values of the variable of interest. In exponential smoothing, however, we want to allow the more recent values of the series to have greater influence on the forecasts of future values than the more distant observations.

> **Exponential smoothing** is a forecasting method where the forecast is based on a *weighted average* of current and past series values. The largest weight is given to the present observation, less weight to the immediately preceding observation, even less weight to the observation before that, and so on. *The weights decline geometrically as we go back in time.*

---

[3] From *International Financial Statistics* (March 1991), p. 136

We define a **weighting factor**, w, as a selected number between zero and one:

$$0 < w < 1 \qquad (12-10)$$

Once we select w—for example, $w = 0.4$—we define the forecast equation. The forecast equation is:

$$\hat{Z}_{t+1} = w(Z_t) + w(1 - w)(Z_{t-1}) + w(1 - w)^2(Z_{t-2})$$
$$+ w(1 - w)^3(Z_{t-3}) + \cdots \qquad (12-11)$$

where $\hat{Z}_{t+1}$ is the *forecast* value of the variable Z at time $t + 1$ from knowledge of the *actual* series values Z_t, Z_{t-1}, Z_{t-2}, and so on back in time to the first known value of the time series, Z_1.

The series of weights used in producing the forecast $\hat{Z}_{t+1}$ is: w, $w(1 - w)$, $w(1 - w)^2$, ... These weights decline toward zero in an *exponential* fashion; thus, as we go back in the series, each value has a smaller weight in terms of its effect on the forecast. If $w = 0.4$, then the rest of the weights are: $w(1 - w) = 0.24$, $w(1 - w)^2 = 0.144$, $w(1 - w)^3 = 0.0864$, $w(1 - w)^4 = 0.0518$, $w(1 - w)^5 = 0.0311$, $w(1 - w)^6 = 0.0187$, and so on. The exponential decline of the weights toward zero is evident. This is shown in Figure 12–15.

Before we go on to show how the exponential smoothing model is used, we will rewrite the model in a recursive form that uses both previous observations and previous forecasts. Let us look at the forecast of the series value at time $t + 1$, denoted $\hat{Z}_{t+1}$. It can be shown that the exponential smoothing model of equation 12–11 is equivalent to the following model.

The exponential smoothing model:

$$\hat{Z}_{t+1} = w(Z_t) + (1 - w)(\hat{Z}_t) \qquad (12-12)$$

where Z_t is the actual, known series value at time t and $\hat{Z}_t$ is the forecast value for time t

---

FIGURE 12–15 Exponentially Declining Weights

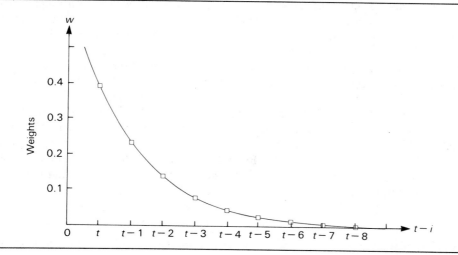

The recursive equation, equation 12–12, can be restated in words as:

Next forecast $= w$(Present actual value) $+ (1 - w)$(Present forecast)

The forecast value for time period $t + 1$ is thus seen as a weighted average of the actual value of the series at time t and the forecast value of the series at time t (the forecast having been made at time $t - 1$). There is yet a third way of writing the formula for the simple exponential smoothing model.

An equivalent form of the exponential smoothing model:

$$\hat{Z}_{t+1} = Z_t + (1 - w)(\hat{Z}_t - Z_t) \qquad (12-13)$$

The proofs of the equivalence of equations 12–11, 12–12, and 12–13 are left as exercises at the end of this section. The importance of equation 12–13 is that it describes the forecast of the value of the variable at time $t + 1$ as the actual value of the variable at the previous time period, t, plus a fraction of the previous *forecast error*. The forecast error is the difference between the forecast, $\hat{Z}_t$, and the actual series value, Z_t. We will formally define the forecast error soon.

The recursive equation (equation 12–12) allows us to compute the forecast value of the series for each time period in a sequential manner. This is done by substituting values for t ($t = 1, 2, 3, 4, \ldots$) and using equation 12–12 for each t to produce the forecast at the next period, $t + 1$. Then the forecast and actual values at the last known time period, $\hat{Z}_t$ and Z_t, are used in producing a forecast of the series into the future. The recursive computation is done by applying equation 12–12 as follows.

$$
\begin{aligned}
\hat{Z}_2 &= w(Z_1) + (1 - w)(\hat{Z}_1) \\
\hat{Z}_3 &= w(Z_2) + (1 - w)(\hat{Z}_2) \\
\hat{Z}_4 &= w(Z_3) + (1 - w)(\hat{Z}_3) \\
\hat{Z}_5 &= w(Z_4) + (1 - w)(\hat{Z}_4) \\
&\;\;\vdots
\end{aligned}
\qquad (12-14)
$$

The problem is how to determine the first forecast, $\hat{Z}_1$. Customarily, we use: $\hat{Z}_1 = Z_1$. Since the effect of the first forecast in a series of values diminishes as the series progresses toward the future, the choice of the first forecast is of little importance (it is an *initial value* of the series of forecasts, and its influence diminishes exponentially).

The choice of w, which is up to the person carrying out the analysis, is of much importance, however. *The larger the value of w, the faster the forecast series responds to change in the original series.* Conversely, the smaller the value of w, the less sensitive is the forecast to changes in the variable Z_t. If we want our forecasts not to respond quickly to changes in the variable, we set w to be a relatively small number. Conversely, if we want the forecast to quickly follow abrupt changes in the variable Z_t, we set w to be relatively large (closer to 1.00 than to 0). We demonstrate this, as well as the computation of the exponentially smoothed series and the forecasts, in Example (c).

EXAMPLE (c)   An investment analyst is interested in forecasting the Dow Jones Transportation Average. The analyst collects 15 daily observations in April and May, 1987, and recursively computes the exponentially smoothed series of forecasts using $w = 0.4$ and the exponentially smoothed forecast series for $w = 0.8$. The original data and both exponentially smoothed series are given in Table 12–6.

The original series and the two exponentially smoothed forecast series, corresponding to $w = 0.4$ and $w = 0.8$, are shown in Figure 12–16. The figure also shows the forecasts of the unknown value of the series at the 16th day produced by the two exponential smoothing procedures ($w = 0.4$ and $w = 0.8$). As was noted earlier, the smoothing coefficient, w, is set at the discretion of the person carrying out the analysis. Since w has a strong effect on the magnitude of the forecast values, the forecast accuracy depends on guessing a "correct" value for the smoothing coefficient. We have presented a simple exponential smoothing method. When the data exhibit a trend or a seasonal variation, or both, more complicated exponential smoothing methods apply.

SOLUTION

TABLE 12–6 Exponential Smoothing Forecasts Using $w = 0.4$ and $w = 0.8$ for Dow Jones Transportation Average

Day	Z_t Original Series	$\hat{Z}_t$ Forecast Using $w = 0.4$	$\hat{Z}_t$ Forecast Using $w = 0.8$
1	925	925	925
2	940	0.4(925) + 0.6(925) = 925	925
3	924	0.4(940) + 0.6(925) = 931	937
4	925	928.2	926.6
5	912	926.9	925.3
6	908	920.9	914.7
7	910	915.7	909.3
8	912	913.4	909.9
9	915	912.8	911.6
10	924	913.7	914.3
11	943	917.8	922.1
12	962	927.9	938.8
13	960	941.5	957.4
14	958	948.9	959.5
15	955	952.5	958.3
16 (Forecasts)		953.5	955.7

FIGURE 12–16 The Dow Jones Transportation Average: Original Series and Two Exponentially Smoothed Series

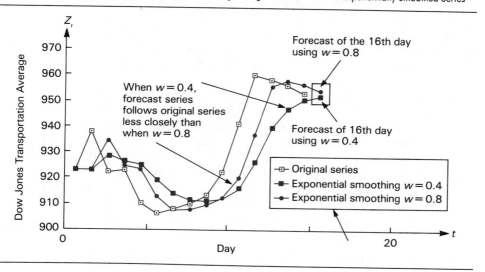

PROBLEMS

Answer

12–16.

Forecast for 1988 is 2.91

12–16.   The following are annual earnings per share data (in dollars) for the years 1971 to 1987 for the CSX Corporation (data are from Value Line, Inc., 1987):

0.54, 1.15, 1.13, 1.69, 1.53, 1.79, 1.34, 1.20, 2.02, 2.38, 2.97, 1.82, 2.07, 3.15, 2.92, 2.73, 3.00

Construct an exponential smoothing model for these data using $w = 0.6$ and forecast earnings per share for 1988. Experiment with other values of w. See if you can improve forecasts of the data points that you have.

12–17.   The following are weekly sales data, in thousands of units, for microcomputer disks: 57, 58, 60, 54, 56, 53, 55, 59, 62, 57, 50, 48, 52, 55, 58, 61. Use $w = 0.3$ and also $w = 0.8$ to produce an exponential smoothing model for these data. Which value of w produces better forecasts? Explain.

12–18.   Construct an exponential smoothing forecasting model, using $w = 0.7$, for new orders reported by manufacturers. Monthly data (in billions of dollars) to April 1987 are:

195, 193, 190, 185, 180, 190, 185, 186, 184, 185, 198, 199, 200, 201,
199, 187, 186, 191, 195, 200, 200, 190, 186, 196, 198, 200, 200

12–19.   The following data are average annual prices, in U.S. dollars, for a barrel of imported crude oil from 1973 to 1990:[4] 6.4, 12.3, 12.7, 13.3, 14.3, 14.4, 21.7, 34.0, 36.5, 33.2, 28.9, 28.5, 26.7, 13.5, 17.7, 14.1, 17.8, 21.2. Construct an exponential smoothing model for these data, and use it to forecast the price of imported oil in 1991.

12–20.   Use *The Wall Street Journal* or another source to gather information on the daily price of gold. Collect a series of prices, and construct an exponential smoothing model. Choose the weighting factor, w, that seems to fit the data best. Forecast the next day's price of gold, and compare the forecast with the actual price once it is known.

12–21.   Prove that equation 12–11 is equivalent to equation 12-12.

12–22.   Prove the equivalence of equations 12–12 and 12–13.

12–6   The Box-Jenkins Methodology

The **Box-Jenkins forecasting methodology**—unlike many other forecasting routines—uses the framework of *statistical model building* developed in Chapter 10. In Figure 10–3, we saw that first we hypothesize an appropriate statistical model, then we estimate the model parameters and test the model's adequacy, and finally, if all is well, we use the model. What separates Box-Jenkins from other forecasting schemes is that it includes these four distinct steps in building the model.

Steps in the construction of a Box-Jenkins forecasting model:

1. *Identify one or more models that describe the time series well.* The identification stage is always the first step in any Box-Jenkins analysis. The identification is done statistically by implicitly testing hypotheses about the correlation structure of the time series.

2. *Estimate the model parameters.* The estimation stage is similar to estimation of the parameters of a multiple regression model, except that we often have to use a nonlinear estimation technique.

---

[4] From U.S. Department of Energy, *Monthly Energy Review* (March 1991), p. 99.

However, this should not concern the analyst, who usually has little control over or interest in the computer algorithm.

3. *Conduct model diagnostic checking.* At this stage, we ascertain that the model is a good one and should produce accurate forecasts with relatively small forecast errors. We also select the best model from among the models identified in step 1, if more than one model was identified as tentatively appropriate.

4. *Use the model.* Now we use the model for forecasting or any other intended use. If the model seems not to perform well, we may go back to earlier stages and find a better model.

The Box-Jenkins methodology is described in advanced books on forecasting.

12–7 A General Discussion of Forecasting

So far in this chapter, we have discussed the method of decomposition of a time series into its components: trend, seasonal component, cyclical component, and irregular component. We saw how the decomposition may aid us in forecasting future values of the time series. The second model we discussed was simple exponential smoothing, and we saw how this method can be used in forecasting a series that does not exhibit trend or seasonality. In cases where the data exhibit a trend, two-parameter exponential smoothing is useful. When the data also exhibit seasonal variation, three-parameter exponential smoothing may be useful. An extension of exponential smoothing to allow the smoothing coefficient, w, to change at any time period is the method of *adaptive filtering*.

The **naive** forecasting method is a method where the forecast value of the variable in the next period is equal to the present value of the variable, that is, $\hat{Z}_{t+1} = Z_t$. The naive forecast is often used as a benchmark for evaluating the success of more complicated forecasting methods. In the case of a random walk, for example, it is hard to beat the naive method because the *step* taken from time t to time $t + 1$ is a purely random error, which cannot be forecast. The best forecast of this error is zero; hence, the best forecast of the value of the variable at time $t + 1$ is the value of the variable at time t, which is Z_t.

So far, we have implicitly assumed that the only information we have about a variable of interest is its past history. Therefore, we have concentrated our efforts on forecasting future values of the variable in question using the available time series of observations of the variable. If, on the other hand, we possess information on *other* variables we believe to be correlated with our variable of interest, we may use the correlations in a regression model of the variable of interest on these other variables. The one example of this that we have seen is regression on time as the independent variable: *trend analysis.* Within the context of regression analysis, we can run a regression of our variable of interest on several variables, including *lagged* values of some or all of the variables we plan to use in the multiple regression model. This is called *lagged-variable regression.* The technique is more complicated than multiple regression analysis, and special methods are required in carrying out the analysis.

In the context of economics, we sometimes specify a particular relationship believed to exist among several variables. Setting up the economic relationship in terms of formulas allows for estimation, testing, and prediction of some variables. Such models are called *econometric models.*

There are also *judgmental* methods of forecasting, where the opinions and information of experts or decision makers are used in formulating forecasts of future values of some variable. Most common among the judgmental methods—and one that has apparently been used with some success—is the *delphi method*. In this method, a group of experts is gathered, and each expert gives his or her judgmental forecast of the variable or variables of interest. The answers are collected and returned to the group for reconsideration until—ideally—a group consensus is reached. In a sense, the delphi method is a combination of forecasts. Recent studies have shown that combinations of forecasts—judgmental, statistical, or other forecasts—are often more accurate than forecasts obtained using a single method.

There are also *Bayesian forecasting methods,* where prior probability distributions of variables of interest are incorporated with the time series data to obtain forecasts. The prior probabilities are often judgmental in nature, and, therefore, Bayesian methods may be viewed as a combination of time series analysis and judgmental, subjective forecasting.

Spectral analysis is a mathematically complex method of analyzing time series data and producing forecasts. This method was mentioned (indirectly) in the introduction to this chapter with reference to the work of Poynting (1884). Spectral analysis entails decomposing a time series into its wave frequency components.

The Forecast Function

In the previous sections, we loosely defined a forecast of variable Z at time $t + 1$ as $\hat{Z}_{t+1}$. This is a **one-step-ahead forecast** of Z at time $t + 1$, where the **forecast origin** is time t. That is, we know the series values up to time t and—"standing" at the last known value, at time t—we *look ahead* one period to time $t + 1$ and forecast the value of our variable at that time period.

We would now like to expand our definition to include forecasts that go further into the future, that is, forecasts of *lead time i*, where $i = 1,2,3, \ldots$. We will now modify our definition and, instead of using $\hat{Z}_{t+1}$, we will use the general notation:

$\hat{Z}_t(i)$ = Forecast of Z, i periods into the future, where the forecast origin is time period t.   (12–15)

For example, $\hat{Z}_{12}(3)$ is a forecast of the variable Z three time periods into the future, using information about any or all of 12 known values of the time series Z_1, Z_2, Z_3, $\ldots$, Z_{12} (think of the forecaster as standing at the 12th known data point and looking three periods into the future). We are assuming that our time series observations are taken at discrete intervals—every day, every week, every month, etc.—rather than being on a continuous scale (instantaneous measurement through time).

Recall from regression analysis that a prediction has a prediction interval associated with it, reflecting the uncertainty about the predicted value. This is true in forecasting as well: with every forecast we can associate a *forecast interval* of a given confidence level. As we look further and further into the future, our forecast interval gets wider to reflect the increasing uncertainty. Incidentally, we may forecast values of the series that are known to us, so that we can compare forecast with actuality and evaluate how well the forecasting model predicts the future. For example, if 12 data points are known, we may choose to use forecast origin 11 and predict the 12th (known) data point and then compare the forecast $\hat{Z}_{11}(1)$ with the known value Z_{12}. The quantity $Z_{12} - \hat{Z}_{11}(1) = e_{12}$ is the one-step-ahead **forecast error** at time $t = 12$.

FIGURE 12–17   The *i*-Step-Ahead Forecast and Forecast Interval

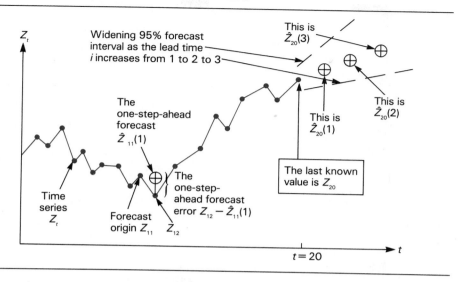

The *i*-step-ahead forecast is the forecast of the value of the variable Z, i periods in the future. This forecast is $\hat{Z}_t(i)$, and $i = 1,2, \ldots$ is the lead time. The idea of an *i*-step-ahead forecast and a forecast interval is demonstrated in Figure 12–17.

A future value of a time series is a random variable. If this random variable has a mean, then this mean—conditional on the values of all known previous values of the random variable—will constitute a good forecast of the future value. Constructing our forecast function in this way leads to *minimum mean-square-error* forecasts. The one-step-ahead forecast having this property is given as follows:

A one-step-ahead forecast as the conditional mean of Z:
$$\hat{Z}_t(1) = E(Z_{t+1} \mid Z_1, Z_2, Z_3, \ldots, Z_t) \qquad (12\text{–}16)$$

That is, the best forecast (in the sense that it minimizes the mean square error) of the value of the series at time $t + 1$, looking one step ahead from time period t, is the *expected value* (the mean) of the random variable Z_{t+1}, *conditional on* the history of the process until time t. The actual construction of minimum mean-square-error forecasts will be seen in the context of Box-Jenkins models in the following sections. We now define mean square error (MSE) and other quantities used in the evaluation of forecasting models.

Criteria for Forecast Evaluation

Several different criteria have been proposed for evaluating the accuracy of forecasting methods. Among the most useful ones are the *mean square error* (MSE), the *mean absolute error* (MAE), and the *mean absolute percentage error* (MAPE). The three measures of forecast accuracy are defined as follows.

Mean square error:

$$MSE = \frac{\Sigma [Z_t - \hat{Z}_{t-1}(1)]^2}{n} \qquad (12\text{--}17)$$

Mean absolute error:

$$MAE = \frac{\Sigma \, | \, Z_t - \hat{Z}_{t-1}(1) \, |}{n} \qquad (12\text{--}18)$$

Mean absolute percentage error:

$$MAPE = \frac{(100)\Sigma \, | \, [Z_t - \hat{Z}_{t-1}(1)]/Z_t \, |}{n} \qquad (12\text{--}19)$$

where n is the number of available pairs of forecast and actual value.

The first measure, MSE, is very frequently used, and so is its square root, $\sqrt{MSE}$, denoted RMSE for root-mean-square error. Both of these measures tend to be strongly affected by outliers: infrequent large forecast errors. The second measure, MAE, has the property of being less sensitive to few large errors, as it is computed from absolute deviations rather than squared deviations. The third measure, MAPE, has the useful property of measuring the forecast errors in proportion to the magnitude of the variable being forecast. Therefore, MAPE is a meaningful measure for comparing forecasts of time series of varying magnitudes.

We now demonstrate the computation of MSE and MAE using the one-step-ahead forecasts of Example (c). Table 12–7 shows the actual values and the one-step-ahead forecasts computed in Table 12–6, as well as absolute forecast errors and squared forecast errors leading to MSE and MAE. (All calculations are rounded up to first-decimal accuracy.)

From the sums shown, we obtain MSE and MAE for both exponential smoothing models, the model using $w = 0.4$ and the model using $w = 0.8$. For the model

TABLE 12–7 The Computations Leading to MSE and MAE for Example (c)

	Forecast		Absolute Error		Squared Error	
Actual	**w = 0.4**	**w = 0.8**	**w = 0.4**	**w = 0.8**	**w = 0.4**	**w = 0.8**
925	925	925	—	—		
940	925	925	15	15	225	225
924	931	937	7	13	49	169
925	928.2	926.6	10.2	1.6	104	2.6
912	926.9	925.3	14.9	13.3	222	176.9
908	920.9	914.7	12.9	6.7	166.4	44.9
910	915.7	909.3	5.7	0.7	32.5	0.5
912	913.4	909.9	1.4	2.1	2	4.4
915	912.8	911.6	2.2	3.4	4.8	11.6
924	913.7	914.3	10.3	9.7	106.1	94.1
943	917.8	922.1	25.2	20.9	635	436.8
962	927.9	938.8	34.1	23.2	1,162.8	538.2
960	941.5	957.4	18.5	2.6	342.3	6.8
958	948.9	959.5	9.1	1.5	82.8	2.3
955	952.5	958.3	2.5	3.3	6.3	10.9
			169.0	117.0	3,141.0	1,728.2

with $w = 0.4$, we find:

$$\text{MSE} = \frac{\Sigma[Z_t - \hat{Z}_{t-1}(1)]^2}{n} = \frac{3,141}{14} = 224.36$$

$$\text{MAE} = \frac{\Sigma\,|\,Z_t - \hat{Z}_{t-1}(1)\,|}{n} = \frac{169}{14} = 12.07$$

For the model with $w = 0.8$, we find:

$$\text{MSE} = \frac{\Sigma\,[Z_t - \hat{Z}_{t-1}(1)]^2}{n} = \frac{1,728.2}{14} = 123.44$$

$$\text{MAE} = \frac{\Sigma\,|\,Z_t - \hat{Z}_{t-1}(1)\,|}{n} = \frac{117}{14} = 8.36$$

We see that—using either of these measures of performance of a forecasting model—the exponential smoothing model with $w = 0.8$ leads to better forecasts than the model with $w = 0.4$ for the particular time series analyzed.

There may be an optimum value of w, leading to *smallest* forecast errors. How can we find the best model in any given situation? There is no clear answer to this question. Trial and error is probably a good way to search for a forecasting model. The usual philosophy in forecasting is along the lines of the adage "The proof of the pudding is in the eating": if a forecasting model leads to good forecasts, then it is a good model.

PROBLEMS

12–23. Name a few statistical forecasting methods and discuss their uses.

12–24. What particular problem do you believe will be encountered in a regression model using time series data? Explain.

12–25. Name a nonstatistical forecasting method.

12–26. What problem do you believe may be encountered in using a Bayesian forecasting model?

12–27. Compute two-steps-ahead and three-steps-ahead forecasts of bank assets in 1987 and 1988 using the trend analysis model you developed in problem 12–2.

12–28. Forecast revenues for 1989 and 1990 using the trend analysis model of problem 12–4.

12–29. Discuss the relative merits of MSE, MAE, RMSE, and MAPE.

12–30. Compute the MAE for both models in problem 12–17. Which model is better?

12–31. Compute the MSE and the MAE for the model in problem 12–19 using several values of w, and choose the best model from among the ones you try.

12–32. In what sense is the conditional mean of Z the best forecast?

Answers

12–24.

Error autocorrelation

12–26.

Prior information

12–28.

$111,540; $110,420

12–30.

3.657; 3.664

12–32.

Minimum MSE

12–8 The Combination of Forecasts

It has been found that *combining* forecasts from two or more different forecasting models can improve the forecast, reducing forecast errors. In a particular situation, for example, suppose we have developed an exponential smoothing model for sales volume of a product, but we also have additional "expert" opinion—management forecasts of sales. It may be beneficial to combine the information from both sources. By doing so, we can improve upon a forecast based solely on the exponential smoothing model (which may model only part of the total information) and also improve upon the purely judgmental forecast given by management (which, too, may not know everything). The combination of forecasts is a good way of pooling information from several sources and using the combination to produce better forecasts.

The combination of forecasts is done in the following way. To each of the forecasting models we plan to use, we assign a weight. In the case of two models, F_1 and F_2, we assign each of them a weight: w_1 and w_2. The weights should be determined in such a way that they are inversely related to the variances of the forecast errors of the two models. Often, the weights are chosen so that their sum is 1.00. When this is done, and our separate models are unbiased, the combined forecast will also be unbiased. The difficulty is, of course, the determination of the weights because the forecast error variances are, in general, not known. We generate forecast errors by withholding some of the data and forecasting the withheld values using a model. Regression analysis can then be used to determine the best weights. Bayesian methods (discussed in Chapter 15) are also a possibility for assigning the weights. Sources of information we believe to be reliable will be given greater weight than ones we find to be less reliable from a subjective-probability point of view. And then, of course, there is trial and error, trying to determine the best forecast combination using the withheld data.

Much has been written about the combination of forecasts, and the reader is referred to C. Granger and R. Ramanathan, "Improved Methods of Combining Forecasts," *Journal of Forecasting*, vol. 3 (1984), pp. 197–204; and D. W. Bunn, "Forecasting with More than One Model," *Journal of Forecasting*, vol. 8 (1989), pp. 161–66.

12–9   Introduction to Index Numbers

It was dubbed the "Crash of '87." Measured as a percentage, the decline was worse than the one that occurred during the same month in 1929 and ushered in the Great Depression. Within a few hours on Monday, October 19, 1987, the Dow Jones Industrial Average plunged 508.32 points, a drop of 22.6%—the greatest percentage drop ever recorded in one day.

What is the Dow Jones Industrial Average, and why is it useful? The Dow Jones average is an example of an index. It is one of several quantitative measures of price movements of stocks through time. Another commonly used index is the New York Stock Exchange (NYSE) Index, and there are others. The Dow Jones captures in one number (the 508.32 points just mentioned, for example) the movements of 30 industrial stocks considered by some to be representative of the entire market. Other indexes are based on a wider proportion of the market than just 30 big firms.

Indexes are useful in many other areas of business and economics. Another commonly quoted index is the consumer price index (CPI), which measures price fluctuations. The CPI is a single number representing the general level of prices that affect consumers. There is a similar measure of the level of prices affecting wholesalers called the wholesale price index. Some business magazines, such as *Business Week*, have their own indexes. When you finish reading these sections, you will be able to construct your own index that will capture the general movement in prices or quantities of any specific commodities, services, or entities that affect you.

We will define index numbers, such as the stock market indexes and the CPI, and show how indexes are constructed and used. Indexes are *descriptive measures;* hence, they diverge from our main emphasis in this book. Index numbers may be used, however, in conjunction with the time series methods discussed in this chapter, and this is why these sections are here. Often, instead of working with a time series of raw numbers, we need to work with a series of numbers that are adjusted to relate to a given point in time. When this is the case, we conduct a time series analysis of the adjusted data in the form of an index.

12–10 Simple Index Numbers

An **index number** is a number that measures the relative change in a set of measurements over time.

When the measurements are of a *single variable,* for example, the price of a certain commodity, the index is called a *simple index number.* A simple index number is the ratio of two values of the variable, expressed as a percentage. First, a *base period* is chosen. The value of the index at any time period is equal to the ratio of the current value of the variable divided by the base period value, times 100.

We will demonstrate this with an example. The following data are average annual cost figures for residential natural gas for the years 1973 to 1986 (in dollars per thousand cubic feet).[5]

121, 121, 133, 146, 162, 164, 172, 187, 197, 224, 255, 247, 238, 222

If we want to describe the relative change in price of residential natural gas, we construct a simple index of these prices. Suppose that we are interested in comparing prices of residential natural gas of any time period to the price in 1973 (the first year in our series). In this case, 1973 is our base year, and the index for that year is defined as 100. The index for any year is defined by equation 12–20.

$$\text{Index number for period } i = 100 \, \frac{\text{Value in period } i}{\text{Value in base period}} \qquad (12\text{--}20)$$

Thus, the index number for 1975 (using the third data point in the series) is computed as:

$$\text{Index number for 1975} = 100 \frac{\text{Price in 1975}}{\text{Price in 1973}}$$

$$= 100 \frac{133}{121} = 109.9$$

This means that the price of residential natural gas increased by 9.9% from 1973 to 1975. Incidentally, the index for 1974 is also 100 since the price did not change from 1973 to 1974. Let us now compute the index for 1976.

$$\text{Index number for 1976} = 100 \frac{146}{121} = 120.66$$

Thus, compared with the price in 1973, the price in 1976 was 20.66% higher. It is very important to understand that changes in the index from year to year *may not be interpreted as percentages* except when one of the two years is the base year. The

---

[5] Data are from the *Monthly Energy Review* (June 1987).

TABLE 12–8   Price Index for Residential Natural Gas, Base Year 1973

Year	Price	Index
1973	121	100
1974	121	100
1975	133	109.9
1976	146	120.7
1977	162	133.9
1978	164	135.5
1979	172	142.1
1980	187	154.5
1981	197	162.8
1982	224	185.1
1983	255	210.7
1984	247	204.1
1985	238	196.7
1986	222	183.5

fact that the index for 1976 is 120.66 and for 1975 is 109.9 does not imply that the price in 1976 was $20.66 - 9.9 = 10.76\%$ higher than in 1975. Comparisons in terms of percentages may only be made with the base year. We can only say that the price in 1975 was 9.9% higher than in 1973, and the price in 1976 was 20.66% higher than in 1973. Table 12–8 shows the year, the price, and the price index for residential natural gas from 1973 to 1986, inclusive.

From the table, we see, for example, that the price in 1983 was over 210% of what it was in 1973 and that by 1986 the price declined to only 183.5% of what it was in 1973. Figure 12–18 shows both the raw price and the index with base year 1973. (The units of the two plots are different, and no comparison between them is suggested.)

If we compute the price indexes for two different items, using the same base year, it is possible to compare how these prices have changed through time. Since the indexes convey information on changes in price relative to a specified point in time, these indexes are free of the units of measurement. Thus, we can compare, for example, the changes in price of cars and price of loaves of bread. Each index will convey information on the percentage change in price of the particular commodity

FIGURE 12–18   Price and Index (Base Year 1973) of Residential Natural Gas

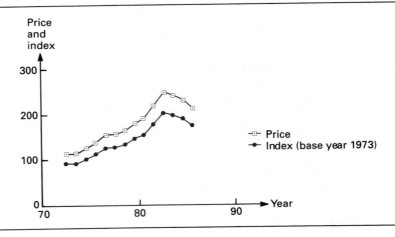

with respect to the price in the base year. The fact that cars cost thousands of dollars and loaves of bread are in the single-dollar range will not affect the comparison. The comparison will focus on percentage of increase or decrease relative to some point in time.

Table 12–9 gives the average price of residential electricity, in cents per kilo-watt hour, for the years 1973 through 1986.[6] Equation 12–20 was used in computing a simple index of the price of residential electricity, with 1973 as the base year. The resulting index is also shown in the table. Comparing the residential electricity price index with the price index for residential natural gas, we see that the changes in the price of natural gas are much more pronounced than the changes in the price of electricity during the years under study. The two price indexes are shown in Figure 12–19.

As time goes on, the relevance of any base period in the past decreases in terms of comparison with values in the present. Therefore, it is sometimes useful to change the base period and move it closer to the present. Many indexed economic variables, for example, use the base year 1967. As we move into more recent years,

TABLE 12–9 Price of Electricity and a Price Index (Base Year 1973)

Year	Price	Index
1973	2.4	100
1974	2.6	108.3
1975	2.7	112.5
1976	2.7	112.5
1977	2.8	116.7
1978	2.8	116.7
1979	2.7	112.5
1980	2.7	112.5
1981	2.9	120.8
1982	3.0	125
1983	3.0	125
1984	3.0	125
1985	3.0	125
1986	3.0	125

FIGURE 12–19 Natural Gas and Electricity Price Indexes (Base Year 1973)

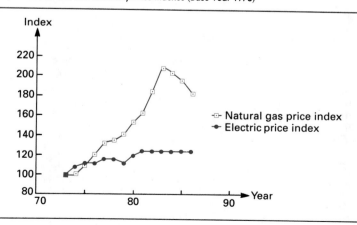

---

[6] Data are from the *Monthly Energy Review* (June 1987).

the base year for these variables is changed to 1980 or later. There is a simple way of changing the base period of an index. All we need to do is change the index number of the new base period so that it will equal 100 and change all other numbers using the *same operation*. Thus, we divide all numbers in the index by the index value of the proposed new base period and multiply them by 100. This is shown in equation 12–21.

Changing the base period of an index:

$$\text{New index value} = \frac{\text{Old index value}}{\text{Index value of new base}} 100 \qquad (12\text{–}21)$$

Suppose that we want to change the base period of the residential natural gas index (Table 12–8) from 1973 to 1980. We want the index for 1980 to equal 100, so we will divide all index values in the table by the current value for 1980, which is 154.5, and multiply these values by 100. For 1981, the new index value is $(162.8/154.5)100 = 105.4$. The new index, using 1980 as base, is shown in Table 12–10.

Figure 12–20 shows the two indexes of the price of residential natural gas using the two different base years. Note that the changes in the index numbers that use 1973 as the base year are more pronounced. This is so because 1980, when used as the base year, is close to the middle of the series, and percentage changes with respect to that year are smaller.

We mentioned that index numbers are useful as a means of comparing changes in prices over time. Such an index is called a *price index*. It is also possible to compare changes in quantity. An index number measuring changes in quantities—for example, the average *amount* of electricity used per year—is called a *quantity index*. Here, too, a base period is chosen, and the index numbers are percentage figures with respect to the base period. The computation is exactly the same, except that the raw numbers are quantities instead of prices.

Another important use of index numbers is as *deflators*. This allows us to compare prices or quantities through time in a meaningful way. Using information on the relative price of natural gas at different years, as measured by the price index for this

TABLE 12–10 Residential Natural Gas Price Index

Year	Index Using 1973 Base	Index Using 1980 Base
1973	100	64.7
1974	100	64.7
1975	109.9	71.1
1976	120.7	78.1
1977	133.9	86.7
1978	135.5	87.7
1979	142.1	92.0
1980	154.5	100
1981	162.8	105.4
1982	185.1	119.8
1983	210.7	136.4
1984	204.1	132.1
1985	196.7	127.3
1986	183.5	118.7

Note: All entries in the righthand column are obtained from the entries in the middle column by multiplication by 100/154.5.

FIGURE 12–20 Comparison of the Two Price Indexes for Residential Natural Gas

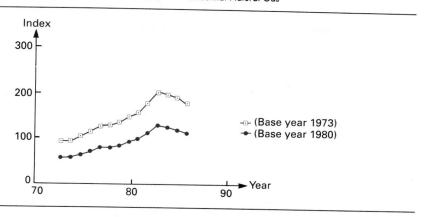

commodity, we can better assess the effect of changes in consumption by consumers. The most important use of index numbers as deflators, however, is in the case of *composite index numbers,* discussed in the next section. In particular, the consumer price index is an overall measure of relative changes in the prices of many goods and thus reflects changes in the value of the dollar. We all know that a dollar today is not worth the same as a dollar 20 years ago. Using the consumer price index, or another composite index, allows us to compare prices through time in "constant" dollars. We will see how this is done in the next section.

PROBLEMS

12–33. Use equation 12–20 and the price data in Table 12–9 to verify the index numbers in that table.

12–34. What is a simple price index?

12–35. What is a simple quantity index?

12–36. What are the uses of index numbers?

12–37. What is the function of the base period?

12–38. The index number for the price of lumber in 1986 is 126.9, and in 1987 it is 134.9. The base year is 1980. Is it true (based on this information) that the price of lumber increased by 8% from 1986 to 1987? Explain.

12–39. The following data, from the *Survey of Current Business* (July 1986), are personal income figures for the United States (in billions of dollars) for the years 1975 to 1984. Construct a simple index of U.S. personal income, using 1979 as the base year.

Year:	1975	1976	1977	1978	1979	1980	1981	1982	1983	1984
Income:	1,265	1,391	1,540	1,733	1,951	2,165	2,429	2,585	2,744	3,012

12–40. Using the index you developed in problem 12–39, change the base year to 1982, and compute the new index.

12–41. The following data are prices of aluminum (in cents per pound) for the years 1975 through 1985. Data are from the *Statistical Abstract of the United States* (Washington, D.C.: U.S. Bureau of the Census, 1987). Construct a price index using 1982 as the base year.

Year:	1975	1976	1977	1978	1979	1980	1981	1982	1983	1984	1985
Price:	39.8	44.5	51.6	54.0	61.0	71.6	76.0	76.0	77.8	81.0	81.0

Answer

12–38.
___
No.

Answer

12–42. The following data are the quantity of steel (in tons) required by a manufacturing plant per week. Construct a simple quantity index for the steel required by the plant using week 5 as the base period.

Week:	1	2	3	4	5	6	7	8	9	10	11	12	13	14	15
Quantity:	54	61	65	71	64	65	74	79	88	87	82	69	90	91	95

12–43. The following data, from the 1986 edition of *International Financial Statistics,* are the price (in dollars per wholesale unit) of Brazilian coffee for the years 1981 to 1986. Construct a simple wholesale price index for Brazilian coffee using 1982 as the base year.

Year:	1981	1982	1983	1984	1985	1986
Price:	25.8	21.2	33.1	52.4	21.3	13.3

12–44.

−37.55%

12–44. Using only the index you developed in problem 12–43 (and not the raw data), perform a computation that will give you the percentage of change in the price of Brazilian coffee from 1985 to 1986.

12–45. Plot the index numbers you computed in problem 12–43, and use the plot to describe the changes in the wholesale price of Brazilian coffee from 1981 to 1986.

12–46. Using the index you developed in problem 12–43, change the base year to 1985, and find the new index. Explain the meaning of numbers smaller than 100 and the meaning of numbers greater than 100.

12–11   Composite Index Numbers

A **composite index number** is an index that measures the relative changes in the values of several variables, taken as a combination.

The combination of variables in a composite index may be a simple aggregation (sums of the prices or the quantities of several items), or the combination may be a *weighted* aggregation. Stock market indexes such as the Dow Jones and the Standard & Poor's 500 are composite indexes of the changes in a group of many stocks. The consumer price index is a weighted composite index of the price of a combination of many consumer items, designed to reflect relative changes in the general level of prices affecting consumers. We will demonstrate the construction of an unweighted (simple) composite price index with Example (d).

EXAMPLE (d)

An investment firm is interested in the stocks of firms in a particular industry group. The firm wants to construct an index of the prices of the four major stocks in the group. Table 12–11 gives prices (in dollars) of the four stocks over a 12-week period.

SOLUTION

In computing a simple aggregate index (an unweighted composite) of the prices of the four stocks, we compute an index of the total price of the four stocks at any given time. Let us choose week 6 as the base period. To compute the index, we just take the numbers in the Total column, divide each of them by the total price in the sixth week (140), and multiply by 100. This gives us the index shown in Table 12–12.

We see, for example, that the aggregate price of the four stocks during week 12 is 11.4% higher than during week 6 (the base week). This kind of composite index is indeed "simple" because it is an index applied to the total price (or quantity) of several items. Commonly quoted stock market indexes are computed similarly to the index in this example. However, stock market indexes use more than just four stocks.

TABLE 12–11 Prices of Four Stocks over a 12-Week Period

Week	Stock				Total
	I	II	III	IV	
1	29	15	32	54	130
2	30.5	16	31	56.5	134
3	31	15	30.5	56.5	133
4	33	15.5	30	57.5	136
5	32	15	29	58	134
6	31	16	32	61	140
7	30	17	32.5	61.5	141
8	29	17	31.5	61.5	139
9	32.5	17.5	32	62	144
10	33	18	32	65	148
11	34	20	34	66	154
12	34	21	33	68	156

TABLE 12–12 Computing a Simple Aggregate Index for Example (d)

Week	Total	Index
1	130	92.9
2	134	95.7
3	133	95.0
4	136	97.1
5	134	95.7
6	140	100.0
7	141	100.7
8	139	99.3
9	144	102.9
10	148	105.7
11	154	110.0
12	156	111.4

Unweighted composite index numbers have their limitation. Often, we need to index prices or quantities of items that differ in importance. In the context of a price index, the quantities of different items consumed may determine the items' relative importance, and this should be considered in the construction of the index. We mentioned a very important index: the consumer price index. The CPI is designed to reflect the level of prices that affect consumers. Since some items are bought often and others not, the index should account for these frequencies of use—or relative quantities required—in aggregating the prices. The CPI is thus an index based on a *weighted* sum of prices of consumer items, the weights being the relative quantities consumed.

A **weighted composite index** is an index based on a weighted combination. This combination can be prices weighted by quantities (for a price index) or quantities weighted by prices (for a quantity index).

We will concentrate on price indexes, which are the more commonly used indexes. For weighting the prices by quantities, there are several approaches that can be used. Two commonly used types of weighted price indexes are the *Laspeyres index* and the *Paasche index*. We will now describe these two kinds of indexes.

The Laspeyres Index

The **Laspeyres index** uses as weights the quantities that apply for the base year (or base time period other than a year).

For the base year, we compute the sum:

$$\sum_{\text{all items}} (\text{Quantity of item}) \times (\text{Price of item})$$

For each year i, we compute the sum:

$$\sum_{\text{all items}} (\text{Quantity of item for base year}) \times (\text{Price of item during year } i)$$

The Laspeyres index is just the ratio of the sum for year i to the sum for the base year, multiplied by 100.

Let q_0 denote all quantities of the items of interest demanded during the base year (year 0). Similarly, let p_0 stand for the prices of all the items of interest during the base year. Let us also define p_i as the prices of the items during year i. The Laspeyres index is given in equation 12–22.

$$\text{Laspeyres index} = \frac{\sum p_i q_0}{\sum p_0 q_0} \, 100 \qquad\qquad (12\text{–}22)$$

Where each summation extends over all items included

Suppose you are interested in computing an index of prices affecting a certain group of consumers and you choose 1980 as the base year. For a Laspeyres index, find the quantities of the different items used, on average, by consumers in 1980. Then multiply each quantity by the price of the appropriate item in the current year, and sum over all items. Next divide the answer by the sum of all quantities in the base year, 1980, each quantity multiplied by the price of the item in 1980. Finally, multiply the result by 100. We demonstrate the computation of a Laspeyres price index with Example (e).

EXAMPLE (e)

A restaurant requires the following raw food supplies: beef, pork, eggs, milk, bread, potatoes, lettuce, tomatoes, and oranges. Prices of these foods, in cents per unit, for the years 1983, 1984, and 1985 are given in Table 12–13. The table also shows the amounts required by the restaurant, in units per week, during the three years. The restaurant manager is interested in developing a Laspeyres-type price index for the raw food items required by the restaurant. The base year is chosen as 1983. Construct the index.

SOLUTION

In a Laspeyres index, only the base year quantities come into play. We compute the price index using equation 12–22. The denominator is obtained as:

$$\sum p_0 q_0 = (238)(50) + (140)(26) + (85)(15) + (105)(85) + (51)(30) + (180)(10) \\ + (46)(5) + (42)(7) + (36)(12) = 30,026$$

TABLE 12–13 Prices and Quantities of Food Items for Example (e)

Item	1983		1984		1985	
	Price	**Quantity**	**Price**	**Quantity**	**Price**	**Quantity**
Beef (lb)	238	50	240	52	233	54
Pork (lb)	140	26	162	24	162	20
Eggs (doz)	85	15	102	12	80	10
Milk (gal)	105	85	112	91	113	92
Bread (lb)	51	30	54	28	55	28
Potatoes (10 lb)	180	10	191	12	160	11
Lettuce (lb)	46	5	50	6	53	4
Tomatoes (lb)	42	7	53	7	52	8
Oranges (lb)	36	12	50	10	53	15

The numerator for 1984 is:

$$\sum p_1 q_0 = (240)(50) + (162)(26) + (102)(15) + (112)(85) + (54)(30)$$
$$+ (191)(10) + (50)(5) + (53)(7) + (50)(12) = 32{,}013$$

The numerator for 1985 is:

$$\sum p_2 q_0 = (233)(50) + (162)(26) + (80)(15) + (113)(85) + (55)(30)$$
$$+ (160)(10) + (53)(5) + (52)(7) + (53)(12) = 31{,}182$$

We now compute the value of the food price index for each of the three years in the sequence. Using equation 12–22, we find:

Year	Index
1983	(30,026/30,026)(100) = 100
1984	(32,013/30,026)(100) = 106.62
1985	(31,182/30,026)(100) = 103.85

We see that the prices, *weighted by the quantities used in the base year,* increased by 6.62% from 1983 to 1984 and decreased somewhat from 1984 to 1985.

The Paasche Index

A Laspeyres-type index is useful when the quantities used do not differ widely from year to year (time period to time period). When large differences occur, the index may not be quite as meaningful. In such cases, we may choose to use another type of index, called a **Paasche index.** In a Paasche index, the quantities used as weights are the current-year quantities. A Paasche index is computed according to equation 12–23.

$$\text{Paasche index} = \frac{\sum p_i q_i}{\sum p_0 q_i} 100 \qquad (12\text{–}23)$$

Although the quantities in Table 12–13 do not vary widely and the Laspeyres index is adequate, we will use these data to demonstrate the computation of a

Paasche-type price index for the food supplies required by the restaurant in Example (e).

For the base year (1983), we have, as usual, index value = 100. For 1984, we compute the numerator and denominator, respectively, as:

$$\sum p_1 q_1 = (240)(52) + (162)(24) + (102)(12) + (112)(91)$$
$$+ (54)(28) + (191)(12) + (50)(6) + (53)(7) + (50)(10) = 32,759$$

$$\sum p_0 q_1 = (238)(52) + (140)(24) + (85)(12) + (105)(91)$$
$$+ (51)(28) + (180)(12) + (46)(6) + (42)(7) + (36)(10) = 30,829$$

Using equation 12–23, we get the value of the index for 1984 as:

$$(32,759/30,829)(100) = 106.26.$$

Similarly, for 1985, we get:

$$\sum p_2 q_2 = (233)(54) + (162)(20) + (80)(10) + (113)(92)$$
$$+ (55)(28) + (160)(11) + (53)(4) + (52)(8) + (53)(15) = 31,741$$

$$\sum p_0 q_2 = (238)(54) + (140)(20) + (85)(10) + (105)(92)$$
$$+ (51)(28) + (180)(11) + (46)(4) + (42)(8) + (36)(15) = 30,630$$

The value of our Paasche price index for 1985 is therefore:

$$(31,741/30,630)(100) = 103.63$$

Note that the values of the Paasche index are very close to the corresponding values of the Laspeyres index in this example. This is so because the quantity weights are not very different from year to year. In such cases, the Laspeyres index should be used.

The Paasche index has several limitations. First, its computation requires knowledge of the quantities needed (or consumed) at every time period. This may be an unrealistic requirement. Often, in the case of economic index numbers, a survey is carried out during the base period in which average consumption rates are estimated. This is costly and involved and cannot be done every year. A second limitation is that it is not very meaningful to use Paasche index figures for two years, neither of which is the base year. If the two index values are different, we may not be able to determine whether the differences we observe are differences in price, differences in quantity, or differences in both price and quantity. For these reasons, the Laspeyres index is usually preferred. If quantities do change with time, it may be preferable to still use the Laspeyres index, but to change the base year from time to time.

The Consumer Price Index

The CPI is probably the best-known Laspeyres-type price index. It is published by the U.S. Bureau of Labor Statistics and is based on the prices of several hundred items. The base year is 1967. For obtaining the base year quantities used as weights, the Bureau of Labor Statistics interviewed thousands of families to determine their consumption patterns. Since the CPI reflects the general price level in the country, it is used, among other purposes, in converting nominal amounts of money to what are called *real* amounts of money: amounts that can be compared through time without requiring us to consider changes in the value of money due to inflation. This use of the CPI is what we referred to earlier as using an index as a *deflator*. By simply dividing X dollars in year i by the CPI value for year i and multiplying by 100, we convert our *X nominal* (year *i*) dollars to *constant* (base year) dollars. This allows us to compare amounts of money across time periods. Let us look at an example.

Table 12–14 gives the CPI values for the years 1950 to 1990. The base year is 1967. This is commonly denoted by [1967 = 100]. The data in Table 12–14 are from the U.S. Bureau of Labor Statistics publication *Monthly Labor Review* (March 1991).

We see, for example, that the general level of prices in the United States in 1985 was over three times what it was in 1967 (the base year). Thus, a dollar in 1985 could buy, on average, only what $1/3.222 = \$0.31$, or 31 cents, could buy in 1967. By dividing any amount of money in a given year by the CPI value for that year and multiplying by 100, we convert the amount to constant (1967) dollars. The term *constant* means dollars of a constant point in time—the base year.

EXAMPLE (f)

TABLE 12–14   The Consumer Price Index [1967 = 100]

Year	CPI
1950	72.1
1951	77.8
1952	79.5
1953	80.1
1954	80.5
1955	80.2
1956	81.4
1957	84.3
1958	86.6
1959	87.3
1960	88.7
1961	89.6
1962	90.6
1963	91.7
1964	92.9
1965	94.5
1966	97.2
1967	100.0
1968	104.2
1969	109.8
1970	116.3
1971	121.3
1972	125.3
1973	133.1
1974	147.7
1975	161.2
1976	170.5
1977	181.5
1978	195.4
1979	217.4
1980	246.8
1981	272.4
1982	289.1
1983	298.4
1984	311.1
1985	322.2
1986	328.4
1987	340.4
1988	354.3
1989	371.3
1990	391.4

FIGURE 12–21   The Consumer Price Index, 1950–1990 (Base Year = 1967)

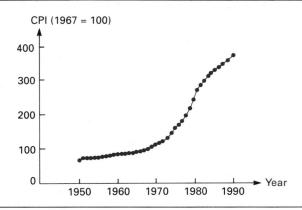

Let us illustrate the use of the CPI as a price deflator. Suppose that during the years 1980 to 1985, an analyst was making the following annual salaries.

1980	$29,500	1983	$35,000
1981	$31,000	1984	$36,700
1982	$33,600	1985	$38,000

Looking at the raw numbers, we may get the impression that this analyst has done rather well. His or her salary has increased from $29,500 to $38,000 in just five years. Actually the analyst's salary has not even kept up with inflation! That is, in *real* terms, or in terms of *actual buying power*, this analyst's 1985 salary is smaller than what it was in 1980. To see why this is true, we use the CPI.

SOLUTION   If we divide the 1980 salary of $29,500 by the CPI value for that year and multiply by 100, we will get the equivalent salary in 1967 dollars: $(29,500/246.8)(100) = \$11,953$. We now take the 1985 salary of $38,000 and divide it by the CPI value for 1985 and multiply by 100. This gives us:$(38,000/322.2)(100) = \$11,794$—*decrease* of $159 (1967)!

If you perform a similar calculation for the salaries of all the other years, you will find that none of them have kept up with inflation. If we transform all salaries to 1967 dollars (or for that matter, to dollars of any single year), the figures can be compared with each other. Often, time series data such as these are converted to constant dollars of a single time period and then analyzed using methods of time series analysis such as the ones presented earlier in this chapter. To convert to dollars of another year (not the base year), you need to divide the salary by the CPI for the current year and multiply by the CPI value for the constant year in which you are interested. For example, let us convert the 1985 salary to 1980 (rather than 1967) dollars. We do this as follows: $(38,000/322.2)(246.8) = \$29,107$. Thus, in terms of 1980 dollars, the analyst was making only $29,107 in 1985, whereas in 1980 he or she was making $29,500 (1980)! Figure 12–21 shows the CPI for the years 1950 to 1990.

PROBLEMS

12–47.   In 1987, the base year was changed to [1982 = 100]. Change the base for all the figures in Table 12–14.

12–48.   *Business Week*, along with several other business publications, has its own indexes of economic activity. The *BW* production index is based on several national production activities and uses base year 1967[1967 = 100]. For the week of October 6, 1987, the magazine reported the following figures for the *BW* production index: latest week, 154.8; week ago, 152.3; month ago, 154.4; year ago, 154.5. Compare national production in the time periods reported by *Business Week* as reflected by the *BW* index.

12–49.   What is the difference between a simple index and a composite index? What is the difference between a simple composite index and a weighted composite index?

12–50.   Why are weights used in certain price indexes, and on what are the weights based? Name two ways of constructing a weighted composite price index.

12–51.   Select an industry group, and follow the prices of several stocks of firms in the group for a period of a few weks. Construct a simple (aggregate) composite index of the values of these stocks. Use the first time period you have as the base period.

12–52.   For Example (f), find the analyst's salaries for 1981, 1982, 1983, and 1984 in 1980 dollars. Find the equivalent salaries for all six years in terms of 1970 dollars. Find the equivalent salaries in terms of 1985 dollars, and use the results in comparing wage increases from year to year.

12–53.   The following data are prices per unit (wholesale) of U.S. wheat, Thai rice, and groundnut meal for the years 1981 to 1985. Data are from the 1986 *International Financial Statistics*. Construct a simple (aggregate) composite price index for the three commodities using 1981 as the base year. Use your index to describe changes in the prices of the three commodities over the five-year period.

	1981	**1982**	**1983**	**1984**	**1985**
Rice (¢/unit)	316	252	323	326	266
Wheat (¢/unit)	332	275	345	345	285
Groundnut meal (¢/unit)	124	108	87	87	84

12–12 Summary and Review of Terms

In this chapter, we discussed forecasting methods. We saw how simple **Cycle ×
Trend × Seasonality × Irregular components models** are created and used. We then talked about **exponential smoothing models.** We also discussed **index numbers**, both **simple** and **composite**.

Answers

12–50.

Weights account for quantities.

12–52.

Real income declined from 1980 to 1981 and from 1984 to 1985.

ADDITIONAL PROBLEMS

12–54.   The following data, obtained from *The Wall Street Journal*, are indexed values of the U.S. dollar as compared with the Japanese yen (index numbers are discussed in the next chapter; here just assume that they are simple numbers representing values).

Date	Index Value	Date	Index Value
September 25, 1987	100	October 4, 1987	100.5
September 26, 1987	100.5	October 5, 1987	100
September 27, 1987	101	October 6, 1987	101
September 28, 1987	102	October 7, 1987	100
September 29, 1987	102.5	October 8, 1987	99
September 30, 1987	102	October 9, 1987	98
October 1, 1987	102.5	October 10, 1987	98.5
October 2, 1987	101	October 11, 1987	99
October 3, 1987	100.5	October 12, 1987	98

Forecast the indexed value of the dollar against the yen for October 13, 1987.

Answer

12–55. The following chart appeared on the front page of *The New York Times* on January 16, 1988 (reproduced by permission of the New York Times Company). Using what you have learned about time series in this chapter, comment on this chart and its caption.

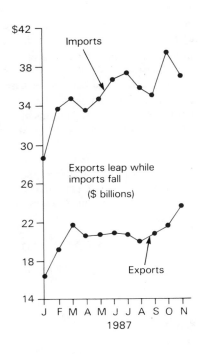

12–56.

Forecast error = 1.4.
Good forecast.

12–56. In the context of problem 12–54, the actual indexed value of the dollar against the yen on October 13, 1987, was 99. Evaluate your forecast accuracy.

12–57. Discuss and compare all the forecasting methods presented in this chapter. What are the relative strengths and weaknesses of each method? Under what conditions would you use any of the methods?

12–58. Discuss the main principle of the exponential smoothing method of forecasting. What effect does the smoothing constant, w, have on the forecasts?

12–59. The following data show the average number of days a single family housing unit has been on the market until sold, recorded for the month in which the unit was sold, in the Boston area (data are from the Greater Boston Real Estate Board).

Month	Average Number of Days	Month	Average Number of Days
January 1986	56	January 1987	69
February 1986	53	February 1987	66
March 1986	57	March 1987	63
April 1986	47	April 1987	60
May 1986	48	May 1987	62
June 1986	46	June 1987	64
July 1986	50	July 1987	66
August 1986	58	August 1987	69
September 1986	55	September 1987	70
October 1986	57	October 1987	71
November 1986	63	November 1987	74
December 1986	72	December 1987	90

a. Is this time series seasonal? Explain.

b. Decompose the series into components, and forecast the average number of days a single family unit was on the market for January 1988.

c. Try another forecasting model. Test both models' performance using available data points. Which model is better?

12–60. The following data are the annual gross earnings, in millions of dollars, for a firm in its first seven years of operation: 1.2, 1.6, 2.2, 2.9, 3.1, 4.3, 6.0. What is the best forecasting model for these data? Now forecast the company's gross earnings for its eighth year of operation. What are the limitations of your forecasting scheme? Discuss.

12–61. The following data are biweekly values of the Dow Jones Industrial Average for the period ending the second week in November 1991.[7] Try to forecast the last two observations in the set using all previous ones.

2800	2925	2950	3000	2875	2975	2500	2600	2450	2500
2350	2500	2450	2460	2480	2470	2600	2625	2500	2650
2950	2900	2950	2940	2880	2900	2890	2975	2900	2925
2890	3050	2990	3000	2900	2990	2970	2980	2970	3050
3060	3050	2970	2980	2950	3075	2975	3070	3050	2925

[7] From *The Wall Street Journal*, November 11, 1991, p. C1.

FORECASTING THE DEMAND FOR SHIPS

S hipbuilding is a risky business. The industry is labor- and capital-intensive, and the required investments are very high. Thus, the profitability of a shipyard depends strongly on management's ability to obtain relatively accurate forecasts of the demand for ships up to several years in the future. This need was accentuated during the 1970s when many shipyards worldwide suffered serious losses due to the sudden drop in demand for supertankers following the oil glut that resulted from the 1973 embargo.

A medium-sized shipyard in Taipei, Taiwan, embarked on a research study aimed at forecasting future demand for ships of a given size (8 to 21 thousand tons displacement). The following data are annual demand figures for ships received by the shipyard from 1924 to 1988.

2, 4, 3, 1, 2, 4, 0, 1, 2, 0, 2, 3, 5, 6, 10, 12, 12, 15, 18, 15, 16, 20, 15, 14, 17, 18, 18, 19, 14, 10, 12, 11, 15, 12, 10, 10, 9, 12, 8, 9, 7, 5, 7, 10, 11, 12, 13, 16, 19, 17, 4, 7, 8, 10, 14, 10, 12, 13, 15, 13, 14, 15, 14, 16, 17

Try several different forecasting methods for these data. Test your models' validity, and produce forecasts. Using your best model, can you forecast the demand for ships with some accuracy? Explain and discuss.

13

QUALITY CONTROL AND IMPROVEMENT

INTRODUCTION

Not long after the Norman Conquest of England, the Royal Mint was established in London. The Mint has been in constant operation from its founding to this very day, producing gold and silver coins for the Crown (and in later periods, coins from cheaper metals). Some time during the reign of Henry II (1154–1189), a mysterious ceremony called the "Trial of the Pyx" was initiated.

The word *pyx* is Old English for "box," and the ceremony was an actual trial by jury of the contents of a box. The ancient trial had religious overtones, and the jurors were all members of the Worshipful Company of Goldsmiths. The box was thrice locked and held under guard in a special room, the Chapel of the Pyx, in Westminster Abbey. It was ceremoniously opened at the trial, which was held once every three or four years.

What did the Pyx box contain, and what was the trial? Every day, a single coin of gold (or silver, depending on what was being minted) was randomly selected by the minters and sent to Westminster Abbey to be put in the Pyx. In three or four years, the Pyx contained a large number of coins. For a given type of coin, say a gold sovereign, the box also contained a royal standard, which was the exact desired weight of a sovereign. At the trial, the contents of the box were carefully inspected, counted, and later some coins were assayed. The total weight of all gold sovereigns was recorded. Then the weight of the royal standard was multiplied by the number of sovereigns in the box and compared with the actual total weight of the sovereigns. A given tolerance was allowed in the total weight, and the trial was declared a success if the total weight was within the tolerance levels established above and below the computed standard.

The trial was designed so that the King or Queen could maintain control of the use of the gold and silver ingots furnished to the Mint for coinage. If, for example, coins were too heavy, then the monarch's gold was being wasted. A shrewd merchant could then melt down such coins and sell them back to the Mint at a profit. This actually happened often enough that such coins were given the name "come again guineas" as they would return to the Mint in melted-down form, much to the minters' embarrassment. On the other hand, if coins contained too little gold, then the currency was being debased and would lose its value. In addition, somebody at the Mint would then be illegally profiting from the leftover gold.

When the trial was successful, a large banquet would be held in celebration. We may surmise that when the trial was not successful . . . the Tower of London was not too far away. The Trial of the Pyx is practiced (with modifications) to this day. Interestingly, the famous scientist and mathematician Isaac Newton was at one time (1699 to 1727) Master of the Mint. In fact, one of the trials during Newton's tenure was not successful, but he survived.[1]

The Trial of the Pyx is a classic example, and probably the earliest on record, of a two-tailed statistical test for the population mean. The Crown wants to test the null

---

[1] Adapted from S. Stigler, "Eight Centuries of Sampling Inspection: The Trial of the Pyx," *Journal of the American Statistical Association* (September 1977), pp. 493–500.

Continued on next page

hypothesis that, on the average, the weight of the coin is as specified. The Crown wants to test this hypothesis against the two-tailed alternative that the average coin is either too heavy or too light—both having negative consequences for the Crown. The test statistic used is the sum of the weights of n coins, and the critical points are obtained as: n times the standard weight, plus and minus the allowed tolerance.[2] The Trial of the Pyx is also a wonderful example of *quality control*. We have a production process, the minting of coins, and we want to ensure that high quality is maintained throughout the operation. We sample from the production process, and we take corrective action whenever we believe that the process is *out of control*—producing items that, on average, lie outside our specified target limits. ∎

13–2   W. Edwards Deming Instructs

We now jump 800 years, to the middle of our present century and to the birth of modern quality-control theory. In 1950 Japan was trying to revive from the devastation of World War II. Japanese industry was all but destroyed, and its leaders knew that industry must be rebuilt well if their nation was to survive. But how? By an ironic twist of fate, Japanese industrialists decided to hire an American statistician as their consultant. The man they chose was W. Edwards Deming, at the time a virtually unknown government statistician. No one in America paid much attention to Deming's theories on how statistics could be used to improve industrial quality. The Japanese wanted to listen. They brought Deming to Japan in 1950, and in July of that year he met with the top management of Japan's leading companies. He then gave the first of many series of lectures to Japanese management. The title of the course was "Elementary Principles of the Statistical Control of Quality," and it was attended by 230 Japanese managers of industrial firms, engineers, and scientists.

The Japanese listened closely to Deming's message. In fact, they listened so well that in a few short decades, Japan became one of the most successful industrial nations on earth. Whereas "Made in Japan" once meant low quality, the phrase has now come to denote the highest quality. In 1960, Emperor Hirohito awarded Dr. Deming the Medal of the Sacred Treasure. The citation with the medal stated that the Japanese people attribute the rebirth of Japanese industry to W. Edwards Deming. In addition, the Deming Award was instituted in Japan to recognize outstanding developments and innovations in the field of quality improvement. On the walls of the main lobby of Toyota's headquarters in Tokyo hang three portraits. One portrait is of the company's founder, another is of the current chairman, and the largest portrait is of Ed Deming.

Ironically, Dr. Deming's ideas did get recognized back in the United States—alas, when he was 80 years old. For years, American manufacturing firms have been feeling the pressure to improve quality, but not much was actually being done while the Japanese were conquering the world markets. In June 1980, Dr. Deming appeared in a network television documentary entitled "If Japan Can, Why Can't We?" Starting the next morning, Dr. Deming's mail quadrupled, and the phone was constantly ringing. Offers came from Ford, General Motors, Xerox, and many others.

Now in his 90s, Dr. Ed Deming is one of the most sought-after consultants to American industry. His appointment book is filled years in advance, and companies are willing to pay very high fees for an hour of his time. He travels around the country lecturing on quality and how to achieve it. The first American company to adopt

---

[2] According to Professor Stigler, the tolerance was computed in a manner incongruent with statistical theory, but he feels we may forgive this error as the trial seems to have served its purpose well through the centuries.

the Deming philosophy and to institute a program of quality improvement at all levels of production was the Nashua Corporation. The company kindly agreed to provide us with actual data of a production process and its quality improvement. This is presented as Case 13 at the end of this chapter. How did Deming do it? How did he apply statistical quality control schemes so powerful that they could catapult a nation to the forefront of the industrialized world and are now helping American firms improve as well? This chapter should give you an idea.

13–3   Statistics and Quality

In all fairness, Dr. Deming did not invent the idea of using statistics to control and improve quality; that honor goes to a colleague of his. What Deming did was to expand the theory and demonstrate how it could be used very successfully in industry. Since then, Deming's theories have gone beyond statistics and quality control, and they now encompass the entire firm. His tenets to management are the well-known "14 Points" he advocates, which deal with the desired corporate approach to costs, prices, profits, labor, and other factors. Now Deming even likes to expound about antitrust laws and capitalism, and to have fun with his audience. At a lecture attended by the author around Deming's 90th birthday, Dr. Deming opened by writing on a transparency: "Deming's Second Theorem: 'Nobody gives a hoot about profits.'" He then stopped and addressed the audience, "Ask me what is Deming's First Theorem." He looked expectantly at his listeners and answered, "I haven't thought of it yet!" The philosophical approach to quality and the whole firm, and how it relates to profits and costs, is described in the ever-growing literature on this subject. It is sometimes referred to as *total quality management* (TQM). Here we want to concentrate on Deming's, and others', *statistical* ideas.

Control Charts

The first modern ideas on how statistics could be used in quality control came in the mid-1920s from a colleague of Deming's, Walter Shewhart of Bell Laboratories. Shewhart invented the **control chart** for industrial processes. A control chart is a graphical display of measurements (usually aggregated in the form of means or other statistics) of an industrial process through time. By carefully scrutinizing the chart, a quality-control engineer can identify any potential problems with the production process. The idea is that when a process is in control, the variable being measured— the mean of every four observations, for example—should remain stable through time. The mean should stay somewhere around the middle line (the grand mean for the process) and not wander off "too much." By now you understand what "too much" means in statistics: more than several standard deviations of the process. The required number of standard deviations is chosen so that there will be a small probability of exceeding them when the process is in control. Addition and subtraction of the required number of standard deviations (generally 3) gives us the **upper control limit** (UCL) and the **lower control limit** (LCL) of the control chart. The UCL and LCL are similar to the "tolerance" limits in the story of the Pyx. When the bounds are breached, the process is deemed **out of control** and must be corrected. A control chart is illustrated in Figure 13–1. We assume throughout that the variable being charted is at least approximately normally distributed.

In addition to looking for the process exceeding the bounds, quality-control workers also look for patterns and trends in the charted variable. For example, if the mean of four observations at a time keeps increasing or decreasing, or it stays too

FIGURE 13–1 A Control Chart

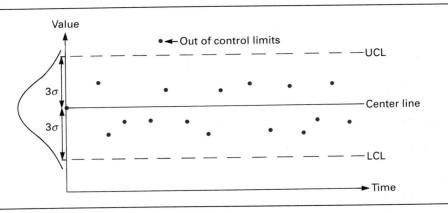

long above or below the center line (even if the UCL and LCL are not breached), the process may be out of control.

> A **control chart** is a time plot of a statistic, such as a sample mean, range, standard deviation, or proportion, with a center line and *upper and lower control limits.* The limits give the desired range of values of the statistic. When the statistic is outside the bounds, or when its time plot reveals certain patterns, the process may be *out of control.*

Central to the idea of a control chart—and, in general, to the use of statistics in quality control—is the concept of **variance.** If we were to summarize the entire field of statistical quality control (also called *statistical process control,* or SPC) in one word, that word would have to be *variance.* Shewhart, Deming, and others wanted to bring the statistical concept of variance down to the shop floor. If foremen and production line workers could understand the existence of variance in the production process, then this awareness itself could be used to help minimize the variance. Furthermore, the variance in the production process could be partitioned into two kinds: the natural, random variation of the process, and variation due to *assignable causes.* Examples of assignable causes are fatigue of workers and breakdown of components. Variation due to assignable causes is especially undesirable because it is due to something being wrong with the production process, and may result in low quality of the produced items. Looking at the chart helps us detect an assignable cause, by asking what has happened at a particular point in time on the chart where the process looks unusual.

> A process is considered in **statistical control** when it has no assignable causes, only natural variation.

Figure 13–2 shows how a process could be in control or out of control. Recall the assumption of a normal distribution—this is what is meant by the normal curves shown on the graphs. These curves stand for the hypothetical populations from which our data are assumed to have been randomly drawn.

Actually, *any* kind of variance is undesirable in a production process. Even the natural variance of a process due to purely random causes rather than to assignable causes can be detrimental. The control chart, however, will detect only assignable

FIGURE 13–2 A Production Process In, and Out of, Statistical Control

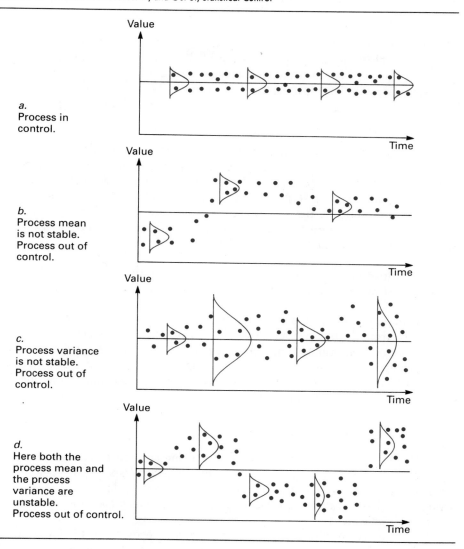

a.
Process in
control.

b.
Process mean
is not stable.
Process out of
control.

c.
Process variance
is not stable.
Process out of
control.

d.
Here both the
process mean and
the process
variance are
unstable.
Process out of control.

causes. As the following story shows, one could do very well by removing all variance.

An American car manufacturer was having problems with transmissions made at one of its domestic plants, and warranty costs were enormous. The identical type of transmission made in Japan was not causing any problems at all. Engineers carefully examined 12 transmissions made at the company's American plant. They found that variations existed among the 12 transmissions, but there were no assignable causes and a control chart revealed nothing unusual. All transmissions were well within specifications. Then they looked at 12 transmissions made at the Japanese plant. The engineer who made the measurements reported that the measuring equipment was broken: in testing one transmission after the other, the needle did not move at all. A closer investigation revealed that the measuring equipment was perfectly fine: the transmissions simply had *no variation*. They did not just satisfy specifications; for all practical purposes, the 12 transmissions were identical![3]

Such perfection may be difficult to achieve, but the use of control charts can go a long way toward improving quality. Control charts are the main topic in this chapter, and we will discuss them in later sections. We devote the remainder of this section to brief descriptions of other quality-control tools.

Pareto Diagrams

In instituting a quality-control and improvement program, one important question to answer is: What are the exact causes of lowered quality in the production process? A ceramics manufacturer may be plagued by several problems: scratches, chips, cracks, surface roughness, uneven surfaces, and so on. It would be very desirable to find out which of these problems are serious and which are not. A good and simple tool for such analysis is the **Pareto diagram**. Although the diagram is named after an Italian economist, its use in quality control is due to J. M. Juran.

> A **Pareto diagram** is a bar chart of the various problems in production and their percentages, which must add to 100%.

A Pareto diagram for the ceramics example above is given in Figure 13–3. As can be seen from the figure, scratches and chips are serious problems, accounting for most of the nonconforming items produced. Cracks occur less frequently, and the other problems are relatively rare. A Pareto diagram thus helps management to identify the most significant problems and concentrate on their solution, rather than wasting time and resources on unimportant causes.

Acceptance Sampling

Finished products are grouped in lots before being shipped to customers. The lots are numbered, and random samples from these lots are inspected for quality. Such checks are made before lots are shipped out, and also when lots arrive at their destination. The random samples are measured to find out which and how many items do not meet specifications.

A lot is rejected whenever the sample mean exceeds or falls below some prespecified limit. For attribute data, the lot is rejected when the number of defective or nonconforming items in the sample exceeds a prespecified limit. Acceptance sampling does not, by itself, improve quality; it simply removes bad lots. To improve quality, it is necessary to control the production process itself, removing any assignable causes and striving to reduce the variation in the process.

Analysis of Variance and Experimental Design

As statistics in general is an important collection of tools to improve quality, so in particular is experimental design. Industrial experiments are performed to find production methods that can bring about high quality. Experiments are designed to

---

[3] From L. Dobyns, "Ed Deming Wants Big Changes and He Wants Them Fast," *Smithsonian* (August 1990), p. 80.

FIGURE 13–3   Pareto Diagram for Ceramics Example

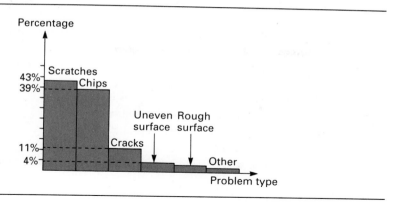

identify the factors that affect the variable of interest, for example, the diameter of a rod. We may find that method B produces rods with diameters that conform to specifications more often than those produced by method A or C. Analysis of variance (as well as regression and other techniques) is used in making such a determination. These tools are more "active" in the quest for improved quality than the control charts, which are merely diagnostic and look at a process already in place. However, both types of tools should be used in a comprehensive quality improvement plan.

Taguchi Methods

The Japanese engineer Genichi Taguchi developed new notions about quality engineering. Taguchi's ideas transcend the customary wisdom of tolerance limits, where we implicitly assume that any value for a parameter within the specified range is as good as any other value. Taguchi aims at the ideal *optimal* value for a parameter in question. For example, if we look at a complete manufactured product, such as a car, the car's quality may not be good even if all of its components are within desired levels when considered alone. The idea is that the quality of a large system deteriorates as we add up the small variations in quality for all of its separate components.

To try to solve this problem, Taguchi developed the idea of a total loss to society due to the lowered quality of any given item. That loss to society is to be minimized. That is, we want to *minimize* the variations in product quality, not simply keep them within limits. This is done by introducing a *loss function* associated with the parameter in question (e.g., rod diameter) and by trying to create production systems that minimize this loss both for components and for finished products.

In the following sections we describe Shewhart's control charts in detail, since they are the main tool currently used for maintaining and improving quality. Information on the other methods we mentioned in this section can be found in the ever-increasing literature on quality improvement. (For example, see the appropriate references in Appendix A at the end of this book.) Our discussion of control charts will roughly follow the order of their frequency of use in industry today. The charts we will discuss are the $\bar{x}$ chart, the R chart, the s chart, the p chart, the c chart, and the x chart.

PROBLEMS

13–1. Discuss what is meant by *quality control* and *quality improvement*.

13–2. What is the main statistical idea behind current methods of quality control?

13–3. Describe the two forms of variation in production systems and how they affect quality.

13–4. What is a quality control chart, and how is it used?

13–5. What are the components of a quality control chart?

13–6. What are the limitations of quality control charts?

13–7. What is acceptance sampling?

13–8. Describe how one would use experimental design in an effort to improve industrial quality.

13–9. What is the main contribution of Genichi Taguchi to the theory of quality improvement?

13–10. Out of 1,000 automobile engines tested for quality, 62 had cracked blocks, 17 had leaky radiators, 106 had oil leaks, 29 had faulty cylinders, and 10 had ignition problems. Draw a Pareto diagram for these data, and identify the key problems in this particular production process.

13–11. In an effort to improve quality, AT&T has been trying to control pollution problems.[4] Problem causes and their relative seriousness, as a percentage of the total, are as follows: chlorofluorocarbons, 61%; air toxins, 30%; manufacturing wastes, 8%; other, 1%. Draw a Pareto diagram of these causes.

13–12. The graph below is reprinted by permission from the article "Turning Software from a Black Art into a Science" (*Business Week*, Quality Issue 1991, pp. 80–81). Discuss the quality implications of the data displayed in this figure.

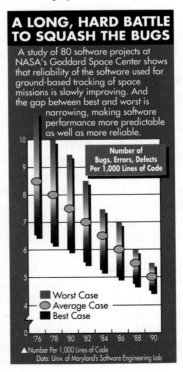

A LONG, HARD BATTLE TO SQUASH THE BUGS

A study of 80 software projects at NASA's Goddard Space Center shows that reliability of the software used for ground-based tracking of space missions is slowly improving. And the gap between best and worst is narrowing, making software performance more predictable as well as more reliable.

Number of Bugs, Errors, Defects Per 1,000 Lines of Code

■ Worst Case
◯ Average Case
■ Best Case

'76 '78 '80 '82 '84 '86 '88 '90

▲ Number Per 1,000 Lines of Code
Data: Univ. of Maryland's Software Engineering Lab

---

[4] "AT&T's Clean Goals," *Business Week* Quality Issue, 1991, p. 49.

13–4   The x̄ Chart

We want to compute the center line and the upper and lower control limits for a process believed to be in control. Then future observations can be checked against these bounds to make sure the process remains in control. To do this, we first conduct an *initial run*. We determine trial control limits to test for control of past data and then we remove out-of-control observations and recompute the control limits. We then apply these improved control limits to future data. This is the philosophy behind all control charts discussed in this chapter. Although we present the x̄ chart first, in an actual quality-control program we would first want to test that the process variation is under control. This is done using the R (range) or the s (standard deviation) chart. Unless the process variability is under statistical control, there is no stable distribution of values with a fixed mean.

An **x̄ chart** can help us to detect shifts in the process mean. One reason for a control chart for the process mean (rather than for a single observation) has to do with the central limit theorem. We want to be able to use the known properties of the normal curve in designing the control limits. By the central limit theorem, the distribution of the sample mean tends toward a normal distribution as the sample size increases. Thus, when we aggregate data from a process, the aggregated statistic, sample mean, becomes closer to a normal random variable than the original, unaggregated quantity. Typically, a set number of observations will be aggregated and averaged. For example, a set of four measurements of rod diameter will be made every hour of production. The four rods will be chosen randomly from all rods made during that hour. If the distribution of rod diameters is roughly mound-shaped, then the sample means of the groups of four diameters will have a distribution closer to normal.

The mean of the random variable $\overline{X}$ is the population mean μ, and the standard deviation of $\overline{X}$ is $\sigma/\sqrt{4}$, where σ is the population standard deviation. We know all this from the theory in Chapter 5. We also know from the theory that the probability that a normal random variable will exceed three of its standard deviations on either side of the mean is 0.0026 (check this using the normal table). Thus, the interval:

$$\mu \pm 3\sigma/\sqrt{n} \qquad (13\text{--}1)$$

should contain about 99.74% of the sample means. This is, in fact, the logic of the control chart for the process mean. The idea is the same as that of a hypothesis test (conducted in a form similar to a confidence interval). We try to select the bounds so that they will be as close as possible to equation 13–1. We then chart the bounds, an estimate of μ in the center (the center line), and the upper and lower bounds (UCL and LCL) as close as possible to the bounds of the interval specified by equation (13–1). Out of 1,000 x̄s, fewer than 3 are expected to be out of bounds. Therefore, with a limited number of x̄s on the control chart, observing even one of them out of bounds is cause to reject the null hypothesis that the process is in control, in favor of the alternative that it is out of control. (One could also compute a *p*-value here, although it is more complicated since we have *several* x̄s on the chart, and in general this is not done.)

We note that the assumption of random sampling is important here as well. If somehow the process is such that successively produced items have values that are correlated—thus violating the independence assumption of random sampling—the interpretation of the chart may be misleading. Various new techniques have been devised to solve this problem.

To construct the control chart for the sample mean, we need estimates of the parameters in equation 13–1. The grand mean of the process, that is, the mean of all the sample means (the mean of all the observations of the process), is our estimate of μ. This is our center line. To estimate σ, we use s, the standard deviation of all the process observations. However, this estimate is only good for large samples, $n > 10$. For smaller sample sizes we use an alternative procedure. When sample sizes are small, we use the *range* of the values in each sample used to compute an $\bar{x}$. Then we average these ranges, giving us a mean range, $\bar{R}$. When the mean range, $\bar{R}$, is multiplied by a constant, which we call A_2, the result is a good estimate for 3σ. Values of A_2 for all sample sizes up to 25 are found in Appendix C, Table 13, at the end of the book. The table also contains the values for all other constants required for the quality-control charts discussed in this chapter.

The following box shows how we compute the center line and the upper and lower control limits when constructing a control chart for the process mean.

Elements of a control chart for the process mean:

Center line: $$\bar{\bar{x}} = \frac{\sum_{i=1}^{k} \bar{x}_i}{k}$$

UCL: $\bar{\bar{x}} + A_2 \bar{R}$ LCL: $\bar{\bar{x}} - A_2 \bar{R}$

where: k = Number of samples, each of size n
$\bar{x}_i$ = Sample mean for the ith sample $\bar{R} = \frac{\sum_{i=1}^{k} R_i}{k}$
R_i = Range of the ith sample

If the sample size in each group is over 10, then:

$$UCL = \bar{\bar{x}} + 3\frac{\bar{s}/c_4}{\sqrt{n}} \qquad LCL = \bar{\bar{x}} - 3\frac{\bar{s}/c_4}{\sqrt{n}}$$

where $\bar{s}$ is the average of the standard deviations of all groups, and c_4 is a constant found in Appendix C, Table 13

In addition to a sample mean being outside the bounds given by the UCL and LCL, other occurrences on the chart may lead us to conclude that there is evidence that the process is out of control. Several such sets of rules have been developed, and the idea behind them is that they represent occurrences that have a very low probability when the process is indeed in control. The set of rules we use is given in Table 13–1.[5]

TABLE 13–1   Tests for Assignable Causes

Test 1: One point beyond 3σ (3s)
Test 2: Nine points in a row on one side of the center line
Test 3: Six points in a row steadily increasing or decreasing
Test 4: Fourteen points in a row alternating up and down
Test 5: Two out of three points in a row beyond 2σ (2s)
Test 6: Four out of five points in a row beyond 1σ (1s)
Test 7: Fifteen points in a row within 1σ (1s) of the center line
Test 8: Eight points in a row on both sides of the center line, all beyond 1σ (1s)

---

[5] This particular set of rules was provided courtesy of Dr. Lloyd S. Nelson of the Nashua Corporation, one of the pioneers in the area of quality control. See L. S. Nelson "The Shewhart Control Chart—Tests for Special Causes," *Journal of Quality Technology* 16 (1984), pp. 237–239. The MINITAB package tests for special causes using Nelson's criteria.

A pharmaceutical manufacturer needs to control the concentration of the active ingredient in a formula used to restore hair to bald people. The concentration should be around 10%, and a control chart is desired to check the sample means of 30 observations, aggregated in groups of three. The data and the MINITAB program, as well as the control chart it produced, are given in Figure 13–4. As can be seen from the control chart, there is no evidence here that the process is out of control.

EXAMPLE (a)

The grand mean is $\bar{\bar{x}} = 10.253$. The ranges of the groups of three observations each are: 0.15, 0.53, 0.69, 0.45, 0.55, 0.71, 0.90, 0.68, 0.11, and 0.24. Thus, $\bar{R} = 0.501$. From Table 13 we find for $n = 3$, $A_2 = 1.023$. Thus, UCL = 10.253 + 1.023(0.501) = 10.766, and LCL = 10.253 − 1.023(0.501) = 9.74. The MINITAB program estimates using the sample standard deviation instead of $\bar{R}$ (the use of $\bar{R}$ is a special option), hence the slight differences.

FIGURE 13–4   MINITAB-Produced Output for Example (a)

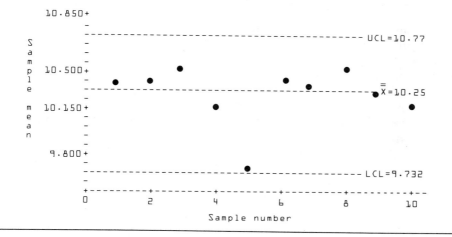

```
MTB > SET C1
DATA> 10.22 10.25 10.37 10.46 10.06 10.59 10.82 10.52 10.13 9.88
DATA> 10.31 10.33 9.92 9.94 9.39 10.15 10.85 10.14 10.69 10.32
DATA> 9.79 10.12 10.80 10.26 10.31 10.23 10.20 10.07 10.15 10.31
DATA> END
MTB > XBARCHART C1 3
```

PROBLEMS

13–13.   What is the logic behind the control chart for the sample mean, and how is the chart constructed?

13–14.   Legal Seafoods in Boston prides itself on having instituted an advanced quality-control system that includes the control of both the food quality and the service quality. The following are successive service times at one of the chain's restaurants on a Saturday night in

May (time is stated in minutes from customer entry to appearance of waitperson):

5, 6, 5, 5.5, 7, 4, 12, 4.5, 2, 5, 5.5, 6, 6, 13, 2, 5, 4, 4.5, 6.5, 4, 1,
2, 3, 5.5, 4, 4, 8, 12, 3, 4.5, 6.5, 6, 7, 10, 6, 6.5, 5, 3, 6.5, 7

13–14.

$\bar{x} = 5.575$
LCL = 1.651
UCL = 9.499
Process in control

13–16.

$\bar{\bar{x}} = 124.2$
LCL = 115.9
UCL = 132.4
Sixth group mean is
beyond UCL.

Aggregate the data into groups of four, and construct a control chart for the process mean. Is the waiting time at the restaurant under control?

13–15.   What assumptions are necessary for constructing an $\bar{x}$ chart?

13–16.   The manufacturer of jet engines needs to control the maximum power delivered by engines. The following are readings related to power for successive engines produced:

121, 122, 121, 125, 123, 121, 129, 123, 122, 122, 120, 121, 119, 118, 121,
125, 139, 150, 121, 122, 120, 123, 127, 123, 128, 129, 122, 120, 128, 120

Aggregate the data in groups of three, and create a control chart for the process mean. Use the chart to test the assumption that the production process is under control.

13–17.   The following data are tensile strengths, in pounds, for a sample of string for industrial use made at a plant. Construct a control chart for the mean, using groups of five observations each. Test for statistical control of the process mean.

5, 6, 4, 6, 5, 7, 7, 7, 6, 5, 3, 5, 5, 5, 6, 5, 5, 6, 7, 7, 7, 7, 6, 7, 5,
5, 5, 6, 7, 7, 7, 7, 7, 5, 5, 6, 4, 6, 6, 6, 7, 6, 6, 6, 6, 6, 7, 5, 7, 6

13–5   The *R* Chart and the *s* Chart

In addition to the process mean, we want to control the process variance as well. When the variation in the production process is high, it means that produced items will have a wider range of values, and this jeopardizes the product's quality. Recall also that in general we want as small a variance as possible. As noted earlier, it is advisable to check the process variance first and then check its mean. Two charts are commonly used to achieve this aim. The more common of the two is a control chart for the process range, called **the *R* chart**. The other is a control chart for the process standard deviation, **the *s* chart**. A third chart is a chart for the actual variance, called the s^2 chart, but we will not discuss it since it is the least commonly used of the three.

The R Chart

Like the $\bar{x}$ chart, the *R* chart also contains a center line and upper and lower control limits. The lower limit is bounded by zero, and sometimes turns out to be zero. Similar to what was done in the previous section for the process mean, we want to specify the upper and lower control limits in the form:

$$\bar{R} \pm 3\sigma_{\bar{R}} \qquad (13\text{–}2)$$

Although the distribution of the sample range is not normal, it is still common in practice to use symmetric bounds such as the ones given above. These bounds still assure us that the probability of breaching them (we are mostly interested in the eventuality of exceeding the upper control limit) is small.

FIGURE 13-5   MINITAB-Produced *R* Chart for Example (a)

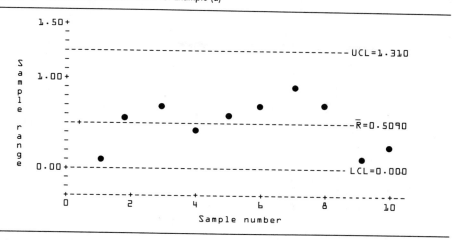

Quality-control experts have calculated that appropriate bounds for small samples (as used in practice) in accordance with the bounds of equation 13–2 are given using constants D_3 and D_4 multiplied by $\overline{R}$. The first gives us the LCL; the second gives us the UCL. The constants D_3 and D_4 are given in Appendix C, Table 13. The center line, UCL, and LCL for the control chart for the process range are given in the following box.

The elements of an *R* chart:

Center Line:	$\overline{R}$
LCL:	$D_3\overline{R}$
UCL:	$D_4\overline{R}$
Where	$\overline{R}$ = Sum of group ranges / Number of groups

---

Returning to Example (a), we find that $\overline{R} = 0.501$, and from Table 13, $D_3 = 0$ and $D_4 = 2.574$. Thus, the center line is 0.501, the lower control limit is 0, and the upper control limit is $(0.501)(2.574) = 1.29$. Figure 13–5 gives the MINITAB-produced control chart for the process range for this example.

There is a small difference in the UCL because of the way MINITAB computes it. The test for control in the case of the process range is just to look for at least one observation outside the bounds. Based on the *R* chart for Example (a), we conclude that the process range seems to be in control.

The s Chart

The *R* chart is in common use because it is easier (by *hand*) to compute ranges rather than to compute standard deviations. Today (as compared with the 1920s, when these charts were invented), computers are usually used to create control charts, and an *s* chart should be at least as good as an *R* chart. We note, however, that the standard deviation suffers from the same nonnormality (skewness) as does

FIGURE 13–6   An s Chart for the Process of Example (a)

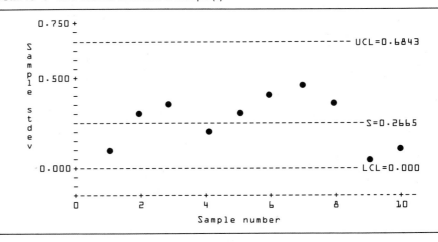

the range. Again, symmetric bounds as suggested by equation 13–2, with s replacing R, are still used. The control chart for the process standard deviation is similar to that for the range. Here we use constants B_3 and B_4, also found in Appendix C, Table 13. The bounds and the center line are given in the following box.

Elements of the s chart:

Center line: $\bar{s}$

LCL: $B_3\bar{s}$

UCL: $B_4\bar{s}$

where $\bar{s}$ is the sum of group standard deviations divided by the number of groups.

The s chart for Example (a) is given in Figure 13–6.

Again, we note that the process standard deviation seems to be in control. Since s charts are done by computer, we will not carry out the computations of the standard deviations of all the groups.

PROBLEMS

Answers

13–22. $\bar{R}$ = 8.059;

LCL = 0; UCL = 20.74.
Sixth range is outside UCL.

13–24. $\bar{s}$ = 2.41; LCL = 0;

UCL = 5.461. Process
std. dev. seems in control

13–18.   Why do we need a control chart for the process range?

13–19.   Compare and contrast the control charts for the process range and the process standard deviation.

13–20.   What are the limitations of symmetric LCL and UCL? Under what conditions are symmetric bounds impossible in practice?

13–21.   Create an R chart for the process in problem 13–14.

13–22.   Create an R chart for the process in problem 13–16.

13–23.   Create an R chart for the process in problem 13–17.

13–24.   Create an s chart for the process in problem 13–14.

13–25.   Create an s chart for the data in problem 13–16.

13–26.   Is the standard deviation of the process in problem 13–17 under control?

13-6   The p Chart

The most common example of a quality-control problem used throughout the book has been that of controlling the proportion of defective items in a production process. This, indeed, is the topic of this section. Here we approach the problem using a control chart.

The number of defective items in a random sample chosen from a population has a binomial distribution: the number of successes, x, out of a number of trials, n, with a constant probability of success, p, in each trial. The parameter p is the proportion of defective items in the population. If the sample size, n, is fixed in repeated samplings, then the sample proportion, $\hat{P}$, also has a binomial distribution. Recall that the binomial distribution is symmetric when $p = 0.5$, and it is skewed for other values of p. By the central limit theorem, as n increases, the distribution of $\hat{P}$ approaches a normal distribution. Thus, a normal approximation to the binomial should work well with large sample sizes; a relatively small sample size would suffice if $p = 0.5$ because of the symmetry of the binomial in this case.

The central limit theorem is the rationale for the control chart for p, called the **p chart**. Using the normal approximation, we want bounds of the form:

$$\hat{p} \pm 3\sigma_{\hat{p}} \tag{13-3}$$

The idea is, again, that the probability of a sample proportion falling outside the bounds is small when the process is under control. When the process is not under control, the proportion of defective or nonconforming items will tend to exceed the upper bound of the control chart. The lower bound is sometimes zero, which happens when $\hat{p}$ is sufficiently small. Being at the lower bound of zero defectives is, of course, a very good occurrence.

Recall that the sample proportion, $\hat{p}$, is given by the number of defectives, x, divided by the sample size, n. We estimate the population proportion, p, by the total number of defectives in all the samples of size n we have obtained, divided by the entire sample size (all the items in all our samples). This is denoted by $\overline{p}$, and serves as the center line of the chart. Also recall that the standard deviation of this statistic is given by:

$$\sqrt{\frac{\overline{p}(1 - \overline{p})}{n}}$$

Thus, the control chart for the proportion of defective items is given in the following box. The process is believed to be out of control when at least one sample proportion falls outside the bounds.

The elements of a control chart for the process proportion:

Center line: $\overline{p}$

LCL: $\overline{p} - 3\sqrt{\dfrac{\overline{p}(1 - \overline{p})}{n}}$

UCL: $\overline{p} + 3\sqrt{\dfrac{\overline{p}(1 - \overline{p})}{n}}$

where n is the number of items in each sample; and $\overline{p}$ is the proportion of defectives in the combined, overall sample.

FIGURE 13–7 MINITAB-Produced p Chart for Example (b)

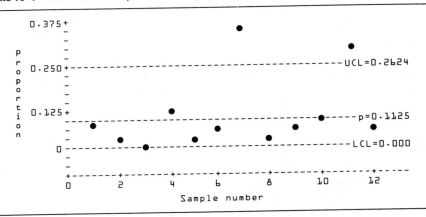

EXAMPLE (b)

A tire manufacturer randomly samples 40 tires at the end of each shift to test for tires that are defective. The number of defectives in 12 shifts are as follows: 4, 2, 0, 5, 2, 3, 14, 2, 3, 4, 12, 3. Construct a control chart for this process. Is the production process under control?

SOLUTION

We use MINITAB. We enter the *number* of defective items for all shifts into column c1 and then state the constant sample size (40 for each shift). The results are shown in Figure 13–7. Our estimate of p, the center line, is the sum of all the defective tires divided by 40 × 12. It is $\bar{p} = 0.1125$. Our estimated standard error of $\bar{p}$ is $\sqrt{\bar{p}(1-\bar{p})/n} = 0.05$; thus, LCL = 0.1125 − 3(0.05) = −0.0375, which means that the LCL should be *zero*. Similarly, UCL = 0.1125 + 3(0.05) = 0.2625.

As we can see from the figure, two sample proportions are outside the UCL. These correspond to the samples with 14 and 12 defective tires, respectively. There is ample evidence that the production process is out of control.

PROBLEMS

Answers

13–28.

$\bar{p} = 0.03333$
LCL = 0
UCL = 0.1317
Twelfth sample is beyond UCL.

13–30.

Nondetection of defectives.

13–27. The manufacturer of steel rods looks at random samples of 20 items from each production shift and notes the number of nonconforming rods in these samples. The results of 10 shifts are: 8, 7, 8, 9, 6, 7, 8, 6, 6, 8. Is there evidence that the process is out of control? Explain.

13–28. A battery manufacturer looks at samples of 30 batteries at the end of every day of production and notes the number of defective batteries. Results (numbers of defectives in samples of 10) are: 1, 1, 0, 0, 1, 2, 0, 1, 0, 0, 2, 5, 0, 1. Is the production process under control?

13–29. BASF Inc. makes 3.5-inch two-sided double-density disks for use in microcomputers. A quality-control engineer at the plant tests batches of 50 disks at a time and plots the proportions of defective disks on a control chart. The first 10 batches used to create the chart had the following numbers of defective disks: 8, 7, 6, 7, 8, 4, 3, 5, 5, 8. Construct the chart and interpret the results.

13–30. If the proportion of defective items in a production process is very small, and few items are tested in each batch, what problems do you foresee? Explain.

13-7 The *c* Chart

It often happens in production activities that we want to control the *number of defects or imperfections per item*. When fabric is woven, for example, it is of interest to keep a record of the number of blemishes per yard and take corrective action when this number is out of control.

Recall from Chapter 3 that the random variable representing the count of the number of errors occurring in a fixed period of time or space is often modeled using the *Poisson distribution*. This is the model we use here. For the Poisson distribution, we know that the mean and the variance are both equal to the same parameter. Here we call that parameter c, and our chart for the number of defects per item (or yard, etc.) is **the *c* chart**. In this chart we plot a random variable, the number of defects per item. We estimate c by $\bar{c}$, which is the average number of defects per item, the total number averaged over all the items we have. The standard deviation of the random variable is thus the square root of c. Now, the Poisson distribution can be approximated by the normal distribution for large sample sizes, and this again suggests the form:

$$\bar{c} \pm 3\sqrt{\bar{c}} \qquad\qquad (13\text{-}4)$$

Equation 13-4 leads to the control bounds and center line given in the box that follows.

Elements of the *c* chart:

Center line:	$\bar{c}$
LCL:	$\bar{c} - 3\sqrt{\bar{c}}$
UCL:	$\bar{c} + 3\sqrt{\bar{c}}$

where $\bar{c}$ is the average number of defects or imperfections per item (or area, volume, etc.).

The following data are the numbers of nonconformities in bolts for use in cars made by the Ford Motor Company:[6] 9, 15, 11, 8, 17, 11, 5, 11, 13, 7, 10, 12, 4, 3, 7, 2, 3, 3, 6, 2, 7, 9, 1, 5, 8. Is there evidence that the process is out of control?

EXAMPLE (c)

We need to find the mean number of nonconformities per item. This is the sum of the numbers divided by 25, or 7.56. The standard deviation of the statistic is the square root of this number, or 2.75, and the control limits are obtained as shown in the box. Figure 13-8 gives the MINITAB solution.

SOLUTION

From the figure we see that one observation is outside the upper control limit, indicating that the production process may be out of control. We also note a general downward trend, which should be investigated (maybe the process is improving).

---

[6] From T. P. Ryan, *Statistical Methods for Quality Improvement* (New York: Wiley, 1989), p. 198.

FIGURE 13–8   MINITAB-Produced Control Chart for Example (c)

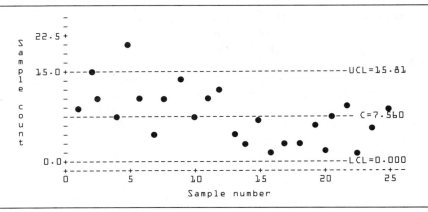

PROBLEMS

Answers

13–32.
_____

$\bar{c}$ = 20.69
LCL = 7.042
UCL = 34.33
Twelfth observation
is beyond UCL.

13–34.

Poisson distribution

13–31.   The following are the numbers of imperfections per yard of yarn: 5, 3, 4, 8, 2, 3, 1, 2, 5, 9, 2, 2, 2, 3, 4, 2, 1. Is there evidence that the process is out of control?

13–32.   The following are the numbers of blemishes in the coat of paint of new automobiles: 12, 25, 13, 20, 5, 22, 8, 17, 31, 40, 9, 62, 14, 16, 9, 28. Is there evidence that the painting process is out of control?

13–33.   The following are the numbers of imperfections in rolls of wallpaper: 5, 6, 3, 4, 5, 2, 7, 4, 5, 3, 5, 5, 3, 2, 0, 5, 5, 6, 7, 6, 9, 3, 3, 4, 2, 6. Construct a _c_ chart for the process, and determine whether there is evidence that the process is out of control.

13–34.   What are the assumptions underlying the use of the _c_ chart?

13–8   The _x_ Chart

Sometimes we are interested in controlling the process mean, but our observations come so slowly from the production process that we cannot aggregate them into groups. In such a case, and in other situations as well, we may consider an **x chart**. An _x_ chart is a chart for the raw values of the variable in question.

As you may guess, the chart is effective if the variable in question has a distribution that is close to normal. We want to have the bounds as: mean of the process ± 3 standard deviations of the process. The mean is estimated by $\bar{x}$, and the standard deviation is estimated by s/c_4.

The tests for special causes in Table 13–1 can be used in conjunction with an _x_ chart as well. Case 13 at the end of this chapter will give you an opportunity to study an actual _x_ chart using all of these tests.

13–9   Using the Computer

MINITAB is an excellent package for quality-control work. The commands are simply: XBARCHART (followed by the column number where data are found and then the number of elements in each group); RCHART (again followed by column number and group number); PCHART (column number where numbers of defects are given and then sample size for all groups); CCHART (followed by a column number). There are numerous subcommands, allowing many different options. There are also many other control charts that the package can produce. These are listed in the MINITAB manual. SYSTAT and other packages also produce control charts.

13–10 Summary and Review of Terms

Quality control and improvement is a fast-growing, important area of application of statistics in both production and services. We discussed **Pareto diagrams**, which are relatively simple graphical ways of looking at problems in production. We discussed quality control in general and how it relates to statistical theory and hypothesis testing. Then we described **control charts**, graphical methods of determining when there is evidence that a process is out of statistical control. The control chart has a **center line**, an **upper control limit**, and a **lower control limit**. The process is believed to be out of control when one of the limits is breached at least once. The control charts we discussed were the $\bar{x}$ **chart**, for the mean; the **R chart**, for the range; the **s chart**, for the standard deviation; the **p chart**, for the proportion; the **c chart**, for the number of defects per item; and, finally, the **x chart**, a chart of individual observations for controlling the process mean.

ADDITIONAL PROBLEMS

13–35. Discuss and compare the various control charts discussed in this chapter.

13–36. The numbers of blemishes in rolls of tape coming out of a production process are as follows: 17, 12, 13, 18, 12, 13, 14, 11, 18, 29, 13, 13, 15, 16. Is there evidence that the production process is out of control?

13–37. The number of defective items out of random samples of 100 windshield wipers selected at the end of each production shift at a factory are as follows: 4, 4, 5, 4, 4, 6, 6, 3, 3, 3, 3, 2, 2, 4, 5, 3, 4, 6, 4, 12, 2, 2, 2, 0, 1, 1, 1, 2, 3, 1. Is there evidence that the production process is out of control?

13–38. Weights of pieces of tile (in ounces) are as follows: 2.5, 2.66, 2.8, 2.3, 2.5, 2.33, 2.41, 2.88, 2.54, 2.11, 2.26, 2.3, 2.41, 2.44, 2.17, 2.52, 2.55, 2.38, 2.89, 2.9, 2.11, 2.12, 2.13, 2.16. Create an R chart for these data, using subgroups of size 4. Is the process variation under control?

13–39. Use the data in problem 13–38 to create an $\bar{x}$ chart to test whether the process mean is under control.

13–40. Create an s chart for the data in problem 13–38.

Answers

13–36.

$\bar{c} = 15.29$
LCL = 3.557
UCL = 27.01
Tenth observation is beyond UCL.

13–38.

$\bar{R} = 0.406$
LCL = 0
UCL = 0.9265
Process in control.

13–40.

$\bar{s} = 0.1817$
LCL = 0
UCL = 0.4117
Process in control.

QUALITY CONTROL AND IMPROVEMENT
AT THE NASHUA CORPORATION*

*I*n 1979, the Nashua Corporation, with an increasing awareness of the importance of always maintaining and improving quality, invited Dr. W. Edwards Deming for a visit and a consultation. Dr. Deming, then almost 80 years old, has been the most sought-after quality guru in America.

Following many suggestions by Deming, Nashua hired Dr. Lloyd S. Nelson the following year as director of statistical methods. The idea was to teach everyone at the company about quality and how it can be maintained and improved using statistics.

Dr. Nelson instituted various courses and workshops lasting 4 to 10 weeks for all the employees. Workers on the shop floor are now familiar with statistical process control (SPC) charts and their use in maintaining and improving quality. Nashua uses individual (x) charts as well as $\bar{x}$, R, and p charts. These are among the most commonly used SPC charts today. Here we will consider the x chart. This chart is used when values come slowly, as in the following example, and it is not practical to take the time to form the subgroups necessary for an $\bar{x}$ or R chart.

Among the many products Nashua makes is thermally responsive paper, which is used in printers and recording instruments. The paper is coated with a chemical mixture that is sensitive to heat, thus producing marks in a printer or instrument when heat is applied by a print head or stylus. The variable of interest is the amount of material coated on the paper (the "weight coat"). Large rolls, some as long as 35,000 feet, are coated, and samples are taken from the ends of the rolls. A template 12 × 18 inches is used in cutting through four layers of the paper—first from an area that was coated and second from an uncoated area. A gravimetric comparison of the coated and uncoated samples gives four measurements of the weight coat. The average of these is the individual x value for that roll.

Assume that 12 rolls are coated per shift and that each roll is tested as described above. For two shifts, the 24 values of weight coat, in pounds per 3,000 square feet, were:

> 3.46, 3.56, 3.58, 3.49, 3.45, 3.51, 3.54, 3.48, 3.54, 3.49, 3.55, 3.60,
> 3.62, 3.60, 3.53, 3.60, 3.51, 3.54, 3.60, 3.61, 3.49, 3.60, 3.60, 3.49

Exhibit 1 shows the individual control chart for this process, using all 24 values to calculate the limits. Is the production process in statistical control? Explain. Discuss any possible actions or solutions.

---

*I am indebted to Dr. Lloyd S. Nelson of the Nashua Corporation for providing me with this interesting and instructive case.

EXHIBIT 1   Standardized *x* Chart

X-bar equals 3.54333

s (est sigma) = 5.12725e-2

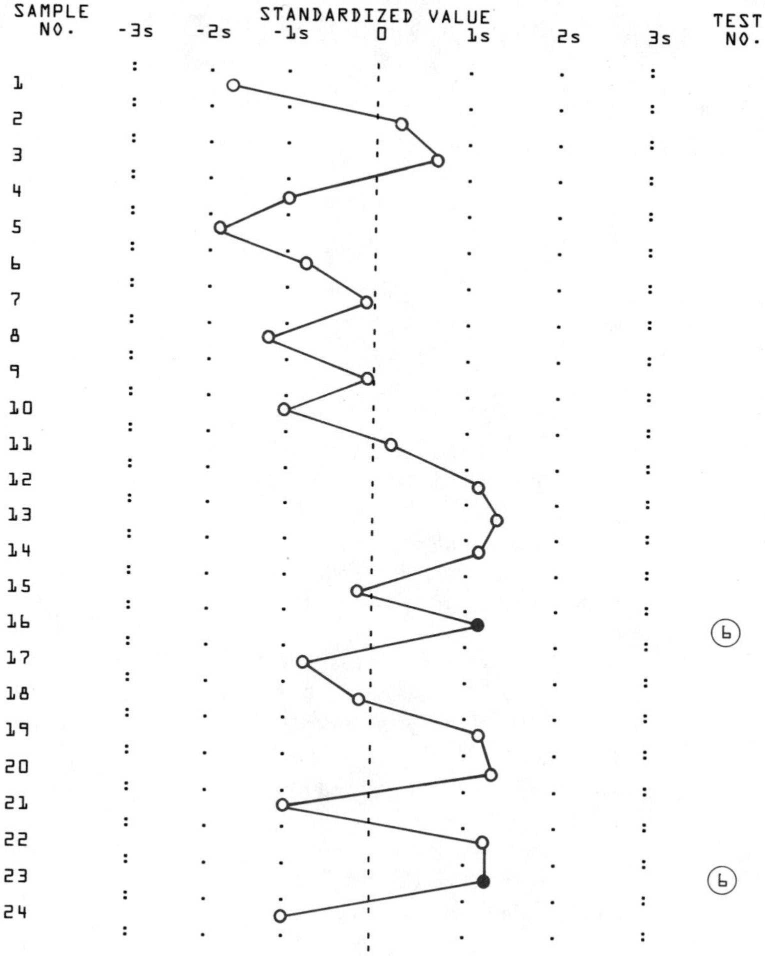

SAMPLE NO.	WEIGHT COAT
1.	3.46
2.	3.56
3.	3.58
4.	3.49
5.	3.45
6.	3.51
7.	3.54
8.	3.48
9.	3.54
10.	3.49
11.	3.55
12.	3.60
13.	3.62
14.	3.60
15.	3.53
16.	3.60
17.	3.51
18.	3.54
19.	3.60
20.	3.61
21.	3.49
22.	3.60
23.	3.60
24.	3.49

14

NONPARAMETRIC METHODS AND CHI-SQUARE TESTS

INTRODUCTION

I n 1710, Dr. John Arbuthnott, Physician in Ordinary to Her Majesty, published an article in the *Philosophical Transactions of the Royal Society of London*. The article was aimed at proving the existence of God and was titled "An Argument for Divine Providence, taken from the constant Regularity observ'd in the Births of both Sexes." While Dr. Arbuthnott may not have proved the existence of God, the scientific method presented in his paper is believed to constitute the oldest known statistical test, the *sign test*. The sign test is a *nonparametric test*.

So far, the statistical procedures we have discussed have dealt with particular population parameters and made use of specific assumptions about the probability distributions of sample estimators, or assumptions about the nature of the population. In particular, we have usually assumed a *normal distribution*. The statistical procedures described in this chapter do not require stringent assumptions. Many of the tests do not deal with particular *parameters* of the population and, thus, are nonparametric. Some tests do not require assumptions about the distributions of the populations of interest. Therefore, nonparametric methods are often called *distribution-free methods*.

The chi-square methods we will discuss do make an assumption of a probability distribution: a limiting normal distribution of sampling outcomes. This assumption leads to a chi-square test statistic. These methods, however, are more general, and our analysis often does not deal with population parameters. In this sense, the chi-square analysis of enumerative data is a nonparametric one.

Typically, nonparametric methods require less stringent assumptions than do their parametric counterparts; on the other hand, they also use less information from the data. This makes the nonparametric tests somewhat less *powerful* than the corresponding parametric tests for the same situations, *when the assumptions of the parametric tests are met*. When the assumptions of the parametric tests are *not* met, the nonparametric tests are the ones we should use. Remember, for example, that in the analysis of variance, we assume that the populations of interest are normally distributed with equal variance. If these assumptions are met, then the *F* test of ANOVA is a powerful method for determining whether several population means are equal. If these assumptions are seriously violated, we must use an alternative method. Here, nonparametric statistics offers a good solution. There is a nonparametric ANOVA procedure called the Kruskal-Wallis test. This test requires no assumptions about the populations involved and uses less of the information in the data: the procedure uses only the *ranks* of the observations.

Many other hypothesis-testing situations have nonparametric alternatives to be used when the usual assumptions we make are not met. In other situations, nonparametric methods offer *unique* solutions to problems at hand. Because a nonparametric test usually requires fewer assumptions and uses less information in the data, it is often said that *a parametric procedure is an exact solution to an approximate problem*, whereas *a nonparametric procedure is an approximate solution to an exact problem*.

In short, we define a **nonparametric method** as one that satisfies at least one of the following criteria.

Continued on next page

1. The method deals with *enumerative data* (data that are frequency counts).
2. The method *does not deal with specific population parameters* such as μ or σ.
3. The method *does not require assumptions about specific population distributions* (in particular, the assumption of normality).

Since nonparametric methods require fewer assumptions than do parametric ones, the methods are useful when the scale of measurement is weaker than required for parametric methods. As we will refer to different measurement scales, you may want to review section 1–7 at this point. ■

14–2   The Sign Test

In Chapter 8, we discussed statistical methods of comparing the means of two populations. There we used the *t* test, which required the assumption that the populations were normally distributed with equal variance. In many situations, one or both of these assumptions are not satisfied. In some situations, it may not even be possible to make exact measurements except for determining the relative magnitudes of the observations. In such cases, the **sign test** is a good alternative. The sign test is also useful in testing for a trend in a series of ordinal values and in testing for a correlation, as we will see soon.

As a test for comparing two populations, the sign test is stated in terms of the probability that values of one population are greater than values of a second population that are paired with the first in some way. For example, we may be interested in testing whether or not consumer responses to one advertisement are about the same as responses to a second advertisement. We would take a random sample of consumers, show them both ads, and ask them to rank the ads on some scale. For each person in our sample, we would then have two responses: one response for each advertisement. The null hypothesis is that the probability that a consumer's response to one ad will be greater than his or her response to the other ad is equal to 0.50. The alternative hypothesis is that the probability is not 0.50. Note that these null and alternative hypotheses are more general than those of the analogous parametric test—the paired *t* test—which is stated in terms of the means of the two populations. When the two populations under study are symmetric, the test is equivalent to a test of the equality of two means, like the parametric *t* test. As stated, however, the sign test is more general and requires fewer assumptions.

We define *p* as the probability that *X* will be greater than *Y*, where *X* is the value from population 1 and *Y* is the value from population 2. Thus:

$$p = P(X > Y) \qquad (14-1)$$

The test could be a two-tailed test, or a one-tailed test in either direction. Under the null hypothesis, it is as likely that *X* will exceed *Y* as it is likely that *Y* will exceed *X*: the probability of either occurrence is 0.50. We leave out the possibility of a tie, that is, the possibility that $X = Y$. When we gather our random sample of observations, we denote every pair *X*, *Y* where *X* is greater than *Y* by a plus sign (+), and we denote every pair where *Y* is greater than *X* by a minus sign (−) (hence the name *sign test*). In terms of signs, the null hypothesis is that the probability of a + sign [that is, $P(X > Y)$] is equal to the probability of a − sign [that is, $P(X < Y)$], and both are equal to 0.50. These are the possible hypothesis tests:

Possible hypotheses for the sign test:

Two-tailed test

$$H_0: p = 0.50$$
$$H_1: p \neq 0.50 \tag{14-2}$$

Right-hand-tailed test

$$H_0: p \leq 0.50$$
$$H_1: p > 0.50 \tag{14-3}$$

Left-hand-tailed test

$$H_0: p \geq 0.50$$
$$H_1: p < 0.50 \tag{14-4}$$

The test assumes that the pairs of (X, Y) values are independent and that the measurement scale within each pair is at least *ordinal*. After discarding any ties, we are left with the number of $+$ signs and the number of $-$ signs. These are used in defining the test statistic.

The test statistic:

$$T = \text{Number of } + \text{ signs} \tag{14-5}$$

We define n as the number of paired data points, once tied values have been discarded. The test is a *binomial* test with parameter $p = 0.50$: that is, when the null hypothesis $p = 0.50$ is true, the distribution of the number of $+$ signs is the binomial distribution with parameter $p = 0.50$ and n trials. We look at values in the binomial table, Appendix C, Table 1, and determine the appropriate cutoff value(s) that corresponds as closely as possible to the desired level of significance, α. Then we compare T with the cutoff point(s).

The decision rule:

For a two-tailed test (equation 14-2), we find a critical point corresponding as closely as possible to $\alpha/2$ and call it C_1, and we define C_2 as $n - C_1$. We reject the null hypothesis at a level of (approximately) α if T is either less than or equal to C_1 or is greater than or equal to C_2.

For a right-hand-tailed test (equation 14-3), we reject H_0 if T is greater than or equal to $n - C$, where C is that value of the binomial distribution with parameters n and $p = 0.5$ such that the sum of the probabilities of all values less than or equal to C is as close as possible to our chosen level of significance, α.

For a left-hand-tailed test (equation 14-4), we reject H_0 at an approximate level of significance α if T is less than or equal to C, where C is defined as above.

Note that instead of $n - C$, we could use C if we define the test statistic T in equation 14–5 as the number of $-$ signs instead of the number of $+$ signs.

When the sample size is large enough to use the normal approximation to the binomial distribution, we may do so. In such cases, the test becomes the Z test for proportions, discussed in Chapter 7. Our test statistic (in a simplified form) is as follows.

A large-sample test statistic for the sign test:

$$z = \frac{2T - n}{\sqrt{n}}$$

(14–6)

The decision rule is to compare z with critical point(s) of the standard normal distribution for the appropriate level of α (and according to whether or not the test is one- or two-tailed). For example, in a left-hand-tailed test at $\alpha = 0.05$, we reject the null hypothesis if and only if z is less than -1.645.

We now demonstrate the use of the sign test with Example (a).

EXAMPLE (a)

According to a recent survey of 220 chief executive officers of *Fortune 1000* companies (Heidrick and Struggles, 1987), 18.3% of the CEOs in these firms hold MBA degrees. A management consultant wants to test whether there are differences in attitude toward CEOs who hold MBA degrees. In order to control for extraneous factors affecting attitudes toward different CEOs, the consultant designed a study that recorded the attitudes toward the same group of 19 CEOs before and after these people completed an MBA program. The consultant had no prior intention of proving one kind of attitudinal change; she believed it was possible that the attitude toward a CEO could change for the better, change for the worse, or not change at all following the completion of an MBA program. Therefore, the consultant decided to use the following two-tailed test.

H₀: There is no change in attitude toward a CEO following his/her being awarded an MBA degree

versus

H₁: There is a change in attitude toward a CEO following the award of an MBA degree

The consultant defined variable X_i as the attitude toward CEO i before receipt of the MBA degree, as rated by his or her professional associates on a scale of 1 to 5 (5 being highest). Similarly, she defined Y_i as the attitude toward CEO i following receipt of the MBA degree, as rated by his or her professional associates on the same scale.

SOLUTION

In this framework, the null and alternative hypotheses may be stated in terms of the probability that the attitude score *after* (Y) is greater than the attitude *before* (X). The null hypothesis is that the probability that the attitude after receipt of the degree is higher than the attitude before is 0.50 (i.e., the attitude is as likely to improve as it is to become worse, where *worse* means a lower numerical score). The alternative hypothesis is that the probability is not 0.50 (i.e., the attitude is likely to change in one or the other direction). The null and alternative hypotheses can now be stated in the form of equation 14–2:

H₀: $p = 0.50$

versus

$$H_1: p \neq 0.50$$

The consultant looked at her data of general attitude scores toward the 19 randomly chosen CEOs both before and after these CEOs received their MBAs. Data are given in Table 14–1. The first thing to note is that there are two ties: for CEOs number 2 and 5. We thus remove these two from our data set and reduce the sample size to $n = 17$. We now (arbitrarily) define a + sign to be any data point where the *after* attitude score is greater than the *before* score. In terms of + and − symbols, the data in Table 14–1 are as follows:

$$+ + + + + - + - + + + + + - + + +$$

According to our definition of the test statistic, equation 14–5, we have:

$$T = \text{Number of } +s = 14$$

We now carry out the statistical hypothesis test. From Appendix C, Table 1, the binomial table, we find for $p = 0.5$ and $n = 17$ that the point $C_1 = 4$ corresponds to a "tail" probability of 0.0245. That is, $F(4) = 0.0245$. This is as close as we can get to an $\alpha/2 = 0.025$ level, which would be needed for a two-tailed test at the level of significance $\alpha = 0.05$. Using our rule for defining the rejection region in a two-tailed test, we find the second critical point: $C_2 = n - C_1 = 17 - 4 = 13$. Our rejection region is thus defined as all points of the statistic that are greater than or equal to 13, or less than or equal to 4. The significance level of this test is $2(0.0245) = 0.049$, which is as close as we can get to $\alpha = 0.05$ with a discrete distribution such as the binomial. [Incidentally, we put *tail* in quotation marks because the probability is the sum of the masses at the points 0, 1, 2, 3, and 4. Recall that for a discrete random variable, $F(4) = p(0) + p(1) + p(2) + p(3) + p(4)$.] The definition of the right-hand rejection region as points to the right of and including $n - C_1$ relies on the fact that a binomial distribution with $p = 0.50$ (and only this particular binomial distribution) is *symmetric*. The distribution and the decision rule for this particular test are illustrated in Figure 14–1.

Since our computed test statistic value is $T = 14$, which is in the right-hand rejection region, we reject the null hypothesis. Since, from Appendix C, Table 1, $F(3) = 0.0064$ and $14 = 17 - 3$, you should be able to see that the p-value is $2(0.0064) = 0.0128$, which is a little over 0.01. Since the rejection happened in the right-hand rejection region, the consultant may conclude that there is evidence that attitudes toward CEOs who recently received their MBA degrees have become more positive (as defined by the attitude test).

Now suppose that the consultant had originally intended to test for a *particular* attitudinal change: an *improvement* in attitude. In this case, the test would be a right-hand-tailed test. Looking at Table 1, we find that there is no value C for which $F(C) = 0.05$. The closest value is $C = 5$, for which $F(5) = 0.0717$. We could also use $C = 4$, where $F(4) = 0.0245$. In either case, the critical point for a right-hand-tailed test is $n - C$. This gives us 13, if we wish to underestimate $\alpha = 0.05$, and 12 if we wish to overestimate it. In either case, the null hypothesis is rejected and—in the one-tailed test—the p-value is half what it was for a two-tailed test. Here the p-value is 0.0064.

TABLE 14–1   Data for Example (a)

CEO:	1	2	3	4	5	6	7	8	9	10	11	12	13	14	15	16	17	18	19
Attitude Before:	3	5	2	2	4	2	1	5	4	5	3	2	2	2	1	3	4	4	2
Attitude After:	4	5	3	4	4	3	2	4	5	4	4	5	5	3	2	2	5	5	5

FIGURE 14-1   Carrying Out the Test for Example (a)

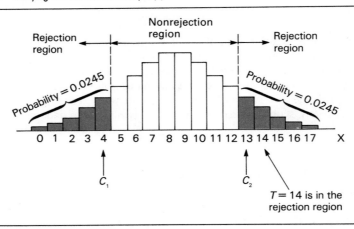

Let us now look at the normal approximation to the binomial. Since here $np = 17(0.5) = 8.5$ and $n(1 - p) = 8.5$, both of which are over 5, we may use the normal approximation to the binomial and carry out the test as a Z test. We use the test statistic of equation 14-6:

$$z = \frac{2T - n}{\sqrt{n}} = \frac{2(14) - 17}{\sqrt{17}} = 2.667$$

This value of the test statistic falls in the right-hand rejection region for a two-tailed Z test at $\alpha = 0.05$ and at $\alpha = 0.01$. In fact, the p-value is found from the standard normal table to be 0.0076 for a two-tailed test. For a right-hand-tailed test, the p-value would be half of 0.0076, or 0.0038 (both numbers are approximate).

The sign test can be viewed as a test of the hypothesis that the *median* difference between two populations is zero. As such, the test may be adapted for testing whether the median of a single population is equal to any prespecified number. The null and alternative hypotheses here are:

H_0: Population median $= a$

H_1: Population median $\neq a$

where a is some number. One-tailed tests of this hypothesis are also possible, and the extension is straightforward.

To conduct the test, we pair our data observations with the null-hypothesized value of the median and perform the sign test. If the null hypothesis is true, then we expect that about half the signs will be +s and half −s because, by the definition of the median, half the population values are above it and half are below it.

Suppose that we wish to test the null hypothesis that median income in a certain region is $24,000 per family per year. The following random sample of family incomes is available (in thousands of dollars): 22, 30, 28, 22, 34, 19, 42, 18, 16, 26, 30, 25, 29, 20, 17, 33, 32, 24, 40, 21. In terms of + signs, − signs, and ties (t), the data are as follows when paired with the hypothesized median of 24: − + + − + − + − − + + + + − − − + + t + −. (The choice of how to define a + versus a − is, again, arbitrary). Discarding the single tie, we see that the number of + signs is 10, and the sample size is $n = 19$.

If we use the normal approximation to the binomial distribution, we find from equation 14–6 that the value of the test statistic is as follows:

$$z = \frac{2T - n}{\sqrt{n}} = \frac{20 - 19}{4.36} = 0.23$$

This value is, of course, well inside the acceptance region for any commonly used level of significance, α. The p-value is 0.82. We could have used the binomial distribution. Note that obtaining 10 or more successes with 19 trials where $p = 0.5$ (that is, assuming H_0 is true) is very probable.

We now discuss two variations of the sign test.

The McNemar Test

The McNemar test is designed for determining the existence of differences in pairs of *qualitative* variables (X, Y). Suppose that X may equal either 0 or 1 and that the same is true for Y. We define a $+$ as the event that $X = 0$ and $Y = 1$; similarly, we define a $-$ as the event that $X = 1$ and $Y = 0$. Applying the sign test to these possibilities allows us to test whether or not the probability that $X = 0$ and $Y = 1$ is the same as the probability that $X = 1$ and $Y = 0$.

This test is useful in testing whether changes occur as a result of an experiment. In this context, X may be a consumer's response (yes or no) before he or she is exposed to an advertisement, and Y is the response (yes or no) after exposure to the ad. There are four possibilities: $X = 0$, $Y = 0$; $X = 0$, $Y = 1$; $X = 1$, $Y = 0$; and $X = 1$, $Y = 1$. The cases $(X = 0, Y = 0)$ and $(X = 1, Y = 1)$ are considered ties; as in the simple sign test, ties are discarded from the analysis. The two other possibilities—$X = 0$, $Y = 1$ and $X = 1$, $Y = 0$—contain information about possible change in the population from yes to no or vice versa. We denote the first case by a $+$ and the second one by a $-$. The sample size is $n =$ (total number of $+$s and $-$s). We conduct the usual sign test for determining whether or not we can reject the null hypothesis that no change from yes to no or vice versa is evident in the population.

When the sample size (without the ties) is large, we may use the chi-square distribution, and we use a different test statistic. For such cases, we define a *contingency table*—a table of all possibilities. Table 14–2 is the contingency table for this situation. We see that a and d are the numbers of ties $(X = 0, Y = 0$ and $X = 1, Y = 1$, respectively), b is the number of $+$ signs $(X = 0, Y = 1)$, and c is the number of $-$ signs $(X = 1, Y = 0)$. The test statistic is simply $b =$ number of $+$ signs. When the sample size $n = b + c$ is large, we use the following test statistic.

TABLE 14–2 Contingency Table for the McNemar Test

	$Y = 0$	$Y = 1$
$X = 0$	a	b
$X = 1$	c	d

Large-sample test statistic for the McNemar test:

$$T = \frac{(b - c)^2}{(b + c)}$$

(14–7)

When the null hypothesis of no change is true, the test statistic T in equation 14–7 approximately follows a chi-square distribution with 1 degree of freedom when the sample size is large (the sample size must be large enough for the normal approximation to the binomial distribution to hold).

We will demonstrate the use of the McNemar test with Example (b). Since the small-sample case is identical to the sign test with a binomial decision rule, we will demonstrate the McNemar test with a large sample and show how a chi-square analysis of a simple two-cell × two-cell contingency table is carried out.

EXAMPLE (b)

As part of the ever-raging market war between Pepsi and Coke, taste tests are conducted from time to time, aimed at showing that the public prefers one brand over the other. A market research analyst was interested in finding out whether people tend to change their taste preference from Pepsi to Coke Classic or vice versa following a taste test. A random sample of 120 people was selected prior to a taste test. The people were interviewed and asked about their soft drink preferences. It was found that 70 people preferred Coke Classic while 50 preferred Pepsi. Following the taste test, 15 Pepsi drinkers stated that they now preferred the taste of Coke Classic and 22 Coke Classic drinkers said that they now preferred Pepsi. Is there evidence that the taste tests tend to make people change their preferences toward one of the two soft drinks?

SOLUTION

Our null and alternative hypotheses are:

$$H_0: P(X = 0, Y = 1) = P(X = 1, Y = 0)$$
$$H_1: P(X = 0, Y = 1) \neq P(X = 1, Y = 0)$$

(14–8)

where 0 denotes preference for Coke Classic and 1 denotes preference for Pepsi; X is the pretest preference, and Y denotes preference after the test. The null hypothesis is that the probability that a Coke Classic drinker will change to Pepsi following a taste test is the same as the probability that a Pepsi drinker will change to Coke Classic.

To test the hypotheses in equation 14–8, we carry out the McNemar test. First we construct the contingency table for this experiment. This is Table 14–3. The relevant in-

TABLE 14–3 Contingency Table for Example (b)

		After the test		Total before:
		$Y = 0$ (Coke Classic)	$Y = 1$ (Pepsi)	
Before the test	$X = 0$ (Coke Classic)	$a = 48$	$b = 22$	70
	$X = 1$ (Pepsi)	$c = 15$	$d = 35$	50
	Total after:	63	57	

FIGURE 14–2 Carrying Out the Test for Example (b)

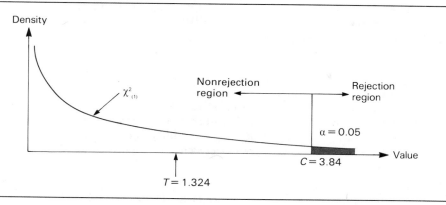

formation in the table is contained in the diagonal cells: $b = 22$ and $c = 15$. We use this information in computing our test statistic (equation 14–7):

$$T = \frac{(b - c)^2}{(b + c)} = \frac{(22 - 15)^2}{(22 + 15)} = \frac{49}{37} = 1.324$$

We now conduct the test by comparing the computed value of the statistic with a critical point of the chi-square distribution with 1 degree of freedom. If we choose $\alpha = 0.05$, we find from Appendix C, Table 4 that the critical point is $C = 3.84$. We must, therefore, accept the null hypothesis that people are no more likely to switch from Pepsi to Coke Classic than they are to switch from Coke Classic to Pepsi following a taste test. As usual, acceptance of the null hypothesis is not a strong conclusion. Note that the test is a two-tailed test, but that it is carried out on the *right tail* of the chi-square distribution. The test is demonstrated in Figure 14–2. (Note that the chi-square distribution with 1 degree of freedom does not have the characteristic shape of chi-square distributions.) We will return to contingency tables in a later section and explore their use in other contexts.

We now present another variation of the sign test. This one is designed for determining the existence of a trend in a series of numbers.

The Cox and Stuart Test

The Cox and Stuart test is a test for the existence of a trend. The test consists of dividing a sequence of data points into two groups. If the number of data points, n, is even, the division into two groups is straightforward. If n is odd, we discard the middle observation. The data points can now be paired. Let $k = n/2$, where n is the sample size, or the sample size less one point if there was originally an odd number of points. We pair the data points, X_i, as (X_1, X_{1+k}), (X_2, X_{2+k}), etc. That is, if we have 10 data points, we pair the first with the sixth, the second with the seventh, and so on until the last pair, which is point 5 paired with point 10. We now perform the sign test on the pairs of points thus formed. Again, we have three possible tests: a two-tailed test (equation 14–2), a right-hand-tailed test (equation 14–3), and a left-hand-tailed test (equation 14–4). In accordance with our definition of the sign test, and with X denoting the first number and Y the second number in any pair, equation 14–2 is a two-tailed test for *any trend*, up or down; equation 14–3 is a test for a *neg-*

ative trend; and equation 14–4 is a test for a *positive trend.* We may redefine our + and − signs, however, so that the test for either a positive or a negative trend may be carried out as either a right-hand-tailed test or a left-hand-tailed test. We demonstrate the Cox and Stuart test with Example (c).

EXAMPLE (c)

An article in *Business Week* discusses industrial growth in Canada in recent years.[1] The article claims that exports of Canadian manufactured goods have been increasing and that this represents a general trend of increasing exports for Canada. The reported export data for the years 1979 through 1986 are (in billions of U.S. dollars): 67, 72, 65, 75, 82, 83, 81, 83. Do these data present evidence of a positive trend in exports of Canadian manufactured goods?

SOLUTION

First we pair the observations. Since there are eight observations, we pair the first with the fifth, the second with the sixth, and so on:

$$
\begin{array}{cc}
67 & 82 \\
72 & 83 \\
65 & 81 \\
75 & 83 \\
\end{array}
$$

We want to test for an increasing trend, as claimed in the article. Therefore, we will define every pair where the second data point is greater than the first as a + (this corresponds to an increase in the series values as time goes on—a positive trend). Our null and alternative hypotheses are:

$$H_0: P(+) \leq 0.5$$

$$H_1: P(+) > 0.5$$

The pairs (67, 82), (72, 83), (65, 81), (75, 83) all correspond to +s; therefore, the value of our test statistic is $T = 4$ where $n = 4$. Looking at the binomial table (Appendix C, Table 1), we find that the probability of obtaining four successes in four trials is 0.0625. This is the smallest probability in the table for $n = 4$. Because of the very discrete nature of the distribution, we are not able to get a finer probability division. We may conclude that the p-value is 0.0625 and reject the null hypothesis, realizing that it is not possible with $n = 4$ to get p-values smaller than 0.0625. We may also seek more data.

We now present one more possible application of the sign test. This test is aimed at determining whether a correlation exists between two variables.

Extension of the Cox and Stuart Test as a Test for Correlation

When our data are paired observations on two variables, we may arrange them in increasing order of one of the variables and then apply the Cox and Stuart test for a trend. If a trend—either up or down—exists in the *second* variable, then a correlation exists between the two variables. This is demonstrated with Example (d).

---

[1] "Industry's Surprising Revival North of the Border," *Business Week* (July 27, 1987).

An accountant wants to test whether a correlation exists between a firm's price/earnings ratio and its percentage return on equity. The following data for firms in various industries are available:[2]

EXAMPLE (d)

Percentage return on equity:	15.9	13.6	15.4	7.0	13.1	15.8	14.9	15.1	9.0	15.2	18.6	13.9
P/E ratio:	8	6	8	13	8	6	8	6	12	11	9	7

SOLUTION

First we arrange the data pairs according to increasing values of the first variable, percentage return:

(7,13), (9,12), (13.1,8), (13.6,6), (13.9,7), (14.9,8), (15.1,6), (15.2,11), (15.4,8), (15.8,6), (15.9,8), (18.6,9)

We now split the second variable, as we did with the Cox and Stuart test, and form pairs—the first observation with the seventh, the second with the eighth, and so on:

$$(13,6), (12,11), (8,8), (6,6), (7,8), (8,9)$$

We have two ties, two + signs, and two − signs. The probability of getting two or more successes in four trials of a binomial random variable with $p = 0.5$ is 0.6875 (using Appendix C, Table 1); hence, we conclude that there is no evidence of a correlation between the two variables. Clearly, a test with so few data points is not very powerful. More data may be necessary for a more conclusive test. The nice thing about nonparametric procedures, however, is that they may be applied even with small data sets. The limitation is that we may not always be able to reach conclusive results.

PROBLEMS

14–1. An investment analyst wants to test whether differences exist between the returns on two mutual funds. Paired data of annualized rates of return for the two mutual funds during 15 randomly chosen months are as follows.

Month	Fund A return (%)	Fund B return (%)
1	12	14
2	11	15
3	14	16
4	10	9
5	12	10
6	8	9
7	16	18
8	13	12
9	12	17
10	10	13
11	6	10
12	9	12
13	16	15
14	13	19
15	10	14

Conduct the sign test for determining whether or not returns on the two mutual funds are equal.

---

[2] Data are from R. Anthony and J. Reece, *Accounting: Text and Cases* (Homewood, Ill.: Richard D. Irwin, Inc., 1983)

Answers

14-2.

$\sum + = 10$

p-value = 0.006

14-2. A randomly chosen group of 12 consumers was asked to rate two products on a scale of 1 to 5 (5 being the highest). For each consumer, the first rating in the pair is of product 1, and the second is of product 2. The data are: (2,5), (3,2), (1,4), (2,4), (3,4), (4,4), (4,5), (1,5), (4,5), (2,3), (2,3), (3,4). The aim of the study was to prove that product 2 is favored over product 1. Do these data present evidence to justify this claim?

14-3. The following data are performance scores of managers before and after completing a management training program (the second score is *after*).

(32,45), (49,88), (61,95), (78,74), (21,30), (79,86), (62,70) (20,46), (48,24), (54,55), (93,88), (61,77), (97,99), (32,39), (55,65), (81,84) (12,30), (42,50), (93,67), (45,67), (88,70), (42,60), (47,64), (20,65), (33,81)

Is there evidence that the program is effective? Which distribution are you using? Why?

14-4.

$\sum + = 19$

p-value = 0.0015

14-4. In 1987, Japanese automakers decided to make a bid for the luxury auto market in the United States. Honda, and later the Nissan Auto Company, decided that the American luxury car market had been dominated too long by German firms. As a result, Honda and Nissan designed prestige cars they hoped would penetrate the American market. The first Japanese personal luxury car to be introduced in the United States was Honda's Acura Legend. In searching for marketing strategies for the new car, Honda decided to test the driver satisfaction of this car against that of a comparable BMW model. Twenty-eight randomly chosen drivers from within the target market for the Acura Legend (American professional people in their mid-thirties with incomes of at least $40,000—according to company sources) were asked to test-drive both the Acura and the comparable BMW model. The order—which car was driven first—was randomly chosen for each driver. Each driver then gave a comprehensive satisfaction score for each of the two cars driven. Scores were on a scale of 1 to 10 (ten being the best). The data follow. The first score for each driver is the BMW score, and the second is the Acura score. Honda wanted to prove that drivers in the target market preferred the Acura Legend. Can you help them?

(6,9), (7,10), (8,8), (9,10), (5,7), (6,5), (9,9), (8,9), (9,10), (6,9), (4,6), (8,7), (6,10), (7,8), (8,9), (9,10), (10,9), (9,9), (3,5), (7,9), (6,10), (10,10), (9,10), (8,7), (8,9), (7,10), (8,8), (9,10)

14-5. The Breakstone Company makes whipped butter and whipped margarine. A company marketing analyst wanted to test whether people prefer the taste of one of these products over the other. A random sample of consumers was selected, and each one was asked to taste both the butter and the margarine and then state a preference. The data are as follows. Is there evidence that one of the two products is preferred over the other? (M denotes margarine and B is for butter.) M B B B M B B M B B B B M M B M M M B B M B M B B B B (no pref.) M B B B (no pref.) M M M B M B B B B B M B

14-6.

T = 1.52;
cannot reject.

14-6. Much has been said and debated recently about insider trading and the value of information. An attorney representing a client accused of insider trading argued that even information considered private is probabilistic in nature and does not *necessarily* lead to abnormal market returns. To prove this point, the attorney simulated a trading experiment. Portfolios of a random sample of 100 independent investors were analyzed for their average returns in the past year. The portfolios were then classified as having provided above-market returns (classification A) or below-market returns (classification B). Then the investors were monitored as they were given authentic inside information about various companies. The investors made buy-and-sell decisions at their own discretion based on the new information. At the end of the experiment, which lasted several months, the investors' portfolios were again classified as A or B, based on their performance during the experimental period. Originally, 42 portfolios were classified A and 58 classified B. After the experiment, 17 A portfolios were now classified B, and 25 B portfolios improved and were now classified A. What should the attorney argue, and how?

14-7. The Nielsen Company produces ratings of television programs, which national advertisers use in determining where to advertise and how much to pay for the commercials. To produce accurate ratings, Nielsen is constantly conducting statistical surveys aimed at assessing the popularity of television programs. A major national network recently decided to substitute a ball game for the evening news and to give only late-night and morning news during the days a game was telecast. Following the implementation of the new programming, Nielsen wanted to assess the program's effectiveness in terms of viewer popularity. A random sample of 1,000 viewers was selected. It was found that before the new programming, 324 viewers tuned in to the network's evening program on a regular basis. After the change to the sports program, 129 viewers changed to another network, while 75 of the 676 viewers who used to watch other networks' programs turned to the ball games. Do these findings provide evidence of a significant change in the network's popularity?

14–8. Western tourists have been reaching the island of Bali in noticeable numbers only since 1975. The Bali Hyatt hotel in Sanur reported the following numbers of tourists from the United States and Europe during the high season in the years 1975 through 1987: 839, 736, 1,005, 1,020, 1,049, 1,202, 1,345, 1,509, 1,400, 1,556, 1,769, 1,033, 1,448. Is there evidence of a trend of increasing numbers of Western tourists staying at the Bali Hyatt?

14–9. A marketing research firm was hired to conduct a wine tracking study for Paul Masson. A random sample of 600 wine drinkers was selected from different geographical areas. It was found that 126 of these people consumed Paul Masson wines at least occasionally. At the end of the marketing campaign, which lasted eight months, the original sample of 600 people was tracked. It was found that of the original Paul Masson consumers, 15 switched over to other wines. The results also showed that of the non–Paul Masson consumers, 58 switched to drinking Paul Masson wines at least occasionally. Do you believe that the marketing campaign was effective? Explain.

14–10. Mahi Mahi, the favorite fish of the Hawaiians, is now sold to many restaurants on the U.S. mainland, thanks to a local Hawaiian marketer who realized the potential appeal of the fish outside the Islands. After 20 months of operation, the fish exporter wanted to find out whether or not an increasing trend in sales was evident. Use the following data to test for the existence of such a trend (numbers are in tons of fish sold per month): 76, 68, 79, 80, 65, 88, 92, 91, 85, 87, 99, 78, 101, 90, 105, 95, 89, 97, 106, 101.

14–11. The following data are the average monthly stock price of Time, Inc., from December 1985 through June 1987 (Source: *Business Week,* August 3, 1987). Is there evidence of any trend (up or down) in the price of this stock? 57, 61, 72, 77, 80, 84, 80, 81, 73, 71, 72, 69, 72, 85, 83, 84, 88, 94, 96.

14–12. One of the suburbs of a large city is near a waste dump. A researcher wants to test whether or not there is a positive correlation between the distance of a residential unit from the waste dump and the unit's price. The following data are available. All units are single-family homes of approximately the same size.

| Price (in $1,000s): | 67 | 128 | 234 | 88 | 95 | 120 | 187 | 166 | 213 | 200 | 150 | 108 | 125 |
| Distance (miles): | 0.5 | 1 | 6 | 0.4 | 1 | 1.5 | 4 | 5 | 7 | 6.5 | 3 | 2 | 2.5 |

Do you believe that a positive correlation exists between the two variables?

14–13. Under what circumstances would you use a variation of the sign test for correlation rather than the usual Pearson product-moment statistic and a *t* test?

14–14. Under what circumstances would you use the sign test as a test that the population median is a specified value, as opposed to using the *t* test for a population mean? What are the advantages of either test vis-à-vis the other? Explain.

14–15. The median amount of accounts payable to a retailer is believed to be $78.50. A test is designed to assess whether this assumption is still true after several changes in company operations have taken place. A random sample of 30 accounts is collected. The data follow (in dollars).

34.12, 58.90, 73.25, 33.70, 69.00, 70.53, 12.68, 100.00, 82.55, 23.12, 57.55, 124.20, 89.60, 79.00, 150.13, 30.35, 42.45, 50.00, 90.25, 65.20, 22.28, 165.00, 120.00, 97.25, 78.45, 24.57, 12.11, 5.30, 234.00, 76.65

Answers

14–8.

$\sum + = 5$

p-value = 0.1095

14–10.

$T = 9$

p-value = 0.01

14–12.

$T = 6$

p-value = 0.016

Answers

$T = 5$
p-value $= 0.032$

14–16.   The Skate Source, Inc., specializes in arranging ice skating shows as special events. The company proprietors wanted to find out whether there is an increasing trend in demand for their services. The number of shows per quarter for the company's first 12 quarters of operation are as follows: 4, 6, 5, 5, 7, 6, 8, 9, 11, 10, 8, 9. Is there evidence of an increasing trend?

14–17.   A publishing magnate took over a large Eastern newspaper and made changes in the paper's format and news coverage. One of the paper's major advertisers wanted to test whether the changes brought more readers, or instead caused the paper to lose readership. A survey of 2,000 readers, randomly selected from the area served by the newspaper, revealed that originally 1,200 were regular readers of the newspaper and 800 were not. After the changes were instituted, 355 readers switched to other newspapers, while 122 people who originally were not regular readers switched to the newspaper. Conduct the test, and state your conclusions.

14–18.
$T = 4$
p-value $= 0.1875$

14–18.   The following data are total amounts of loans made by a bank and the corresponding interest rate. Test for a negative correlation between total amount of loans and the interest rate. (Loans are in millions of dollars, and interest rates are stated as percentages.) (1.4, 18), (2.3, 12), (1.8, 16), (1.1, 20), (2.5, 11), (2.8, 10), (1.9, 17), (2.2, 13), (1.0, 11), (1.7, 14), (1.8, 15).

14–3   The Runs Test—A Test for Randomness

In his well-known book *Introduction to Probability Theory and Its Applications* (New York: John Wiley & Sons, Inc., 1973), William Feller tells of noticing how people occupy bar stools. Let S denote an occupied seat and E an empty seat. Suppose that, entering a bar, you find the following sequence:

S E S E S E S E S E S E S E S E S E   (Case 1)

Do you believe that this sequence was formed at random? Is it likely that the 10 seated persons took their seats by a random choice, or did they purposely make sure they sat at a distance of one seat away from their neighbors? Just looking at the perfect regularity of this sequence makes us doubt its randomness.

Let us now look at another way the people at the bar might have been occupying the 10 out of 20 seats:

S S S S S S S S S S E E E E E E E E E E   (Case 2)

Is it likely that this sequence was formed at random? In this case, rather than perfect separation between people, there is a perfect clustering together. This, too, is a form of regularity not likely to have arisen by chance.

Let us now look at yet a third case:

S E E S S E E E S E S S E S E E S S S E   (Case 3)

This last sequence seems more random. It is much more likely that this sequence was formed by chance than the sequences in cases 1 and 2. There does not seem to be any consistent regularity in the series in case 3.

What we feel intuitively about order versus randomness in these cases can indeed be *quantified*. There is a statistical test that can help us determine whether or not we believe that a sequence of symbols, items, or numbers resulted from a random process. The statistical test for randomness depends on the concept of a *run*.

> A **run** is a sequence of like elements that are preceded and followed by different elements or no element at all.

FIGURE 14–3　Examples of Runs

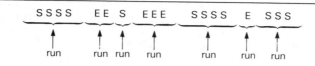

Using the symbols S and E, Figure 14–3 demonstrates the definition of a run by showing all runs in a particular sequence of symbols. There are seven runs in the sequence of elements in Figure 14–3.

Applying the definition of runs to cases 1, 2, and 3, we see that in case 1 there are 20 runs in a sequence of 20 elements! This is clearly the largest possible number of runs. The sequence in case 2 has only two runs. In the first case, there are too many runs, and in the second case, there are too few runs for randomness to be a probable generator of the process. In case 3, there are 12 runs—neither too few nor too many. This sequence could very well have been generated by a random process. To quantify how many runs are acceptable before we begin to doubt the randomness of the process, we use a probability distribution. This distribution leads to a *statistical test for randomness*.

Let us call the number of elements of one kind (S) n_1 and the number of elements of the second kind (E) n_2. The total sample size is $n = n_1 + n_2$. In all three cases, both n_1 and n_2 are equal to 10. For a given pair (n_1, n_2) and a given number of runs, Appendix C, Table 8 gives the probability that the number of runs will be *less than or equal to* the given number (i.e., left-hand "tail" probabilities).

Based on our example, look at the row in Table 8 corresponding to $(n_1, n_2) = (10, 10)$. We find that the probability that four or fewer runs will occur is 0.001; the probability that five or fewer will occur is 0.004; the probability that six or fewer runs will occur is 0.019; and so on.

The logic of the test for randomness is as follows. We know the probabilities of obtaining any number of runs, and if we obtain an extreme number of runs—too many or too few—we will decide that the elements in our sequence were not generated in a random fashion.

A two-tailed hypothesis test for randomness:

H_0: Observations are generated randomly
H_1: Observations are not randomly generated　　　(14–9)

The test statistic:

$$R = \text{Number of runs} \qquad (14\text{–}10)$$

The decision rule is to reject H_0 at level α if $R \le C_1$ or $R \ge C_2$, where C_1 and C_2 are critical values obtained from Appendix C, Table 8 with total tail probability $P(R \le C_1) + P(R \ge C_2) = \alpha$.

Let us conduct the hypothesis test for randomness (equation 14–9) for the sequences in cases 1, 2, and 3. Note that the tail probability for six or fewer runs is

0.019, and the probability for 16 or more runs is $P(R \geq 16) = 1 - F(15) = 1 - 0.981 = 0.019$. Thus, if we choose $\alpha = 2(0.019) = 0.038$, which is as close to 0.05 as we can get with this discrete distribution, our decision rule would be to reject H_0 for $R \geq 16$ or $R \leq 6$.

In case 1, we have $R = 20$. We reject the null hypothesis. In fact, the p-value obtained by looking in the table is less than 0.001. The same is true in case 2, where $R = 2$. In case 3, we have $R = 12$. We find the p-value as follows: $2[P(R \geq 12)] = 2[1 - F(11)] = 2(1 - 0.586) = 2(0.414) = 0.828$. The null hypothesis must be accepted.

Large-Sample Properties

As you may have guessed, as the sample sizes n_1 and n_2 increase, the distribution of the number of runs approaches a normal distribution.

The mean of the normal distribution of the number of runs:

$$E(R) = \frac{2n_1 n_2}{n_1 + n_2} + 1 \qquad (14\text{--}11)$$

The standard deviation:

$$\sigma_R = \sqrt{\frac{2n_1 n_2 (2n_1 n_2 - n_1 - n_2)}{(n_1 + n_2)^2 (n_1 + n_2 - 1)}} \qquad (14\text{--}12)$$

Therefore, when the sample size is large, we may use a *standard normal test statistic* given by:

$$z = \frac{R - E(R)}{\sigma_R} \qquad (14\text{--}13)$$

We demonstrate the large-sample test for randomness with Example (e).

EXAMPLE (e)

One of the most important uses of the test for randomness is its application in residual analysis. Recall that a regression model, or a time series model, is adequate if the errors are random (no regular pattern). A time series model was fitted to sales data of multiple-vitamin pills. After the model was fitted to the data, the following residual series was obtained from the computer. Is there any statistical evidence to conclude that the time series errors are not random and, hence, that the model should be corrected?

−23, 30, 12, −10, −5, −17, −22, 57, 43, −23, 31, 42, 50, 61, −28, −52, 10, 34, 28, 55, 60, 32, 88, −75, −22, −56, −89, −34, −20, −2, −5, 29, 12, 45, 77, 78, 91, 25, 60, −25, 45, 42, 30, −59, −60, −40, −75, −25, −34, −66, −90, 10, −20

(The sequence of residuals continues, and their sum is zero.) Using this part of the sequence, we reason that since the mean residual is zero, we may look at the sign of the residuals and write them as + or − signs. Then we may count the number of runs of positive and negative residuals and perform the runs test for randomness.

We have the following signs.

$$- + + - - - - + + - + + + + - - + + + + + + + - - - - - - - - - + + + + +$$
$$+ + + - + + + - - - - - - - - + -$$

Letting n_1 be the number of positive residuals and n_2 the number of negative ones, we have: $n_1 = 27$, $n_2 = 26$. We count the number of runs and find that $R = 15$.

We now compute the value of the Z statistic from equation 14–13. We have, for the mean and standard deviation given in equations 14–11 and 14–12, respectively:

$$E(R) = \frac{2(27)(26)}{27 + 26} + 1 = 27.49$$

and

$$\sigma_R = \sqrt{\frac{2(27)(26)[2(27)(26) - 27 - 26]}{(27 + 26)^2(27 + 26 - 1)}} = 3.6$$

The computed value of the Z test statistic is:

$$z = \frac{R - E(R)}{\sigma_R} = \frac{15 - 27.49}{3.6} = -3.47$$

From the Z table we know that the p-value is 0.0006 (this is a two-tailed test). We reject the null hypothesis that the residuals are random and conclude that the time series model needs to be corrected.

The Wald-Wolfowitz Test

An extension of the runs test for determining whether or not two populations have the same distribution is the **Wald-Wolfowitz test.**

> The null and alternative hypotheses for Wald-Wolfowitz test:
>
> H_0: The two populations have the same distribution
> H_1: The two populations have different distributions $\qquad$ (14–14)

This is one nonparametric analogue to the t test for equality of two population means. Since the test is nonparametric, it is stated in terms of the distributions of the two populations rather than their means; however, the test is aimed at determining the difference between the two means. The test is two-tailed, but it is carried out on one tail of the distribution of the number of runs.

The only assumptions required for this test are that the two samples are independently and randomly chosen from the two populations of interest, and that values are on a continuous scale. The test statistic is, as before, $R =$ Number of runs.

We arrange the values of the two samples in increasing order in one sequence, regardless of the population from which each is taken. We denote each value by the symbol representing its population, and this gives us a sequence of symbols of two types. We then count the number of runs in the sequence. This gives us the value of R.

Logically, if the two populations have the same distribution, we may expect a higher degree of overlapping of the symbols of the two populations (i.e., a large

FIGURE 14–4   Overlap versus Clustering of Two Samples

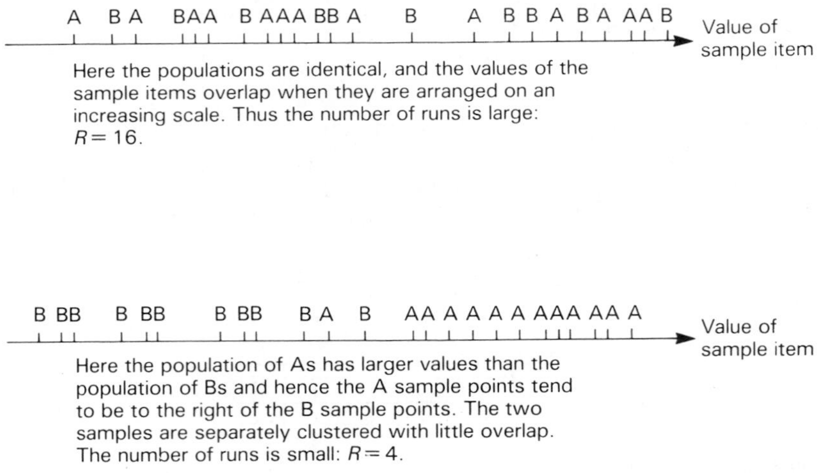

A   B A   BAA   B AAA BB A   B   A   B B A B A AA B   Value of
                                                                    sample item

Here the populations are identical, and the values of the
sample items overlap when they are arranged on an
increasing scale. Thus the number of runs is large:
$R = 16$.

B BB   B BB   B BB   B A   B   AA A A A A AAA AA A   Value of
                                                              sample item

Here the population of As has larger values than the
population of Bs and hence the A sample points tend
to be to the right of the B sample points. The two
samples are separately clustered with little overlap.
The number of runs is small: $R = 4$.

number of runs). If, on the other hand, the two populations are different, we may
expect a clustering of the sample items from each of the groups. If, for example, the
values in population 1 tend to be larger than the values in population 2, then we may
expect the items from sample 1 to be clustered to the right of the items of sample 2.
This produces a small number of runs. We would like to reject the null hypothesis
when the number of runs is too small. We illustrate the idea of overlapping versus
clustering in Figure 14–4.

We demonstrate the Wald-Wolfowitz test with Example (f).

EXAMPLE (f)

The manager of a record store wants to test whether her two salespeople are equally effective.
That is, she wants to test whether the number of sales made by each salesperson is about the
same or whether one is better than the other. The manager gets the following random samples of daily sales made by each salesperson.

Salesperson A: 35, 44, 39, 50, 48, 29, 60, 75, 49, 66
Salesperson B: 17, 23, 13, 24, 33, 21, 18, 16, 32

SOLUTION

We have $n_1 = 10$ and $n_2 = 9$. We arrange the items from the two samples in increasing
order and denote them by A or B based on which population they came from. We get:

B B B B B B B A B B A A A A A A A A A

The total number of runs is $R = 4$.

From Appendix C, Table 8, we find that the probability of four or fewer runs for
sample sizes of 9 and 10 is 0.002. As the p-value is 0.002, we reject the null hypothesis
that the two salespeople are equally effective. Since salesperson A had the larger values,
we conclude that he or she tends to sell more than salesperson B.

We have assumed here that the sales of the two salespersons cannot be paired as
taking place on the same days. Otherwise, a paired test would be more efficient, as
it would reduce day-to-day variations.

The Wald-Wolfowitz test is a *weak test*. There are other nonparametric tests, as we will see, that are more powerful than this test in determining differences between two populations. The advantage of the present test is that it is easy to carry out. There is no need to compute any quantity from the data values—all we need to do is order the data on an increasing scale and count the number of runs of elements from the two samples.

PROBLEMS

14–19. Some items produced by a machine are defective. If the machine follows some pattern where defective items are not randomly produced throughout the process, the machine needs to be adjusted. A quality control engineer wants to determine whether the sequence of defective (D) versus good (G) items is random. The data are:

G G G G G D D D G G G G G G G D D D G G G G G G G G G G G D D D D G G G
G G G G G G G D D D G G G G G G G G G D D D D

Conduct the test for randomness, and state your conclusions.

14–20. A computer is used for generating random numbers. It is necessary to test whether the numbers produced are indeed random. A common method of doing this is to look at runs of odd versus even digits. Conduct the test using the following sequence of numbers produced by the computer.

    2765898376445449986752138797563745876453426789876334821911093473640898763

14–21. In a regression analysis, 12 out of 30 residuals are above 1.00 in value, and the rest are not. With A denoting a residual greater than 1 and B a residual below 1, the residuals are as follows:

            BBBBBBBBBBAAAAAAAAAAAABBBBBBBBBBAA

Do you believe that the regression errors are random? Explain.

14–22. A messenger service employs eight men and nine women. Every day, the assignments of errands are supposed to be done at random. On a certain day, all the best jobs, in order of desirability, were given to the eight men. Is there evidence of sex discrimination? Discuss this also in the context of a continuing, daily operation. What would happen if you tested the randomness hypothesis every day?

14–23. Bids for a government contract are supposed to be opened in a random order. For a given contract, there were 42 bids, 30 of them from domestic firms and 12 from foreign firms. The order in which the sealed bids were opened was as follows (D denotes a domestic firm and F a foreign one):

D D D D D D D D F D D D D D D D F F D D D D D D D D D D F D D F D D D D D D
F F F F F F F

Could the foreign firms claim that they have been discriminated against? Explain.

14–24. Two advertisements are to be compared for their appeal. A random sample of eight people was selected, and their responses to ad 1 were recorded. Another random sample, of nine people, was shown ad 2, and their responses were also recorded. The response data are as follows (10 is highest appeal).

                    Ad 1: 7, 8, 6, 7, 8, 9, 9, 10
                    Ad 2: 3, 4, 3, 5, 5, 4, 2, 5, 4

Is there a quick statistical proof that one ad is better than the other?

Answers

14–20.
———
46 runs;
p-value = 0.032

14–22.
———
2 runs;
small *p*-value.

14–24.
———
2 runs;
small *p*-value.

14–25.   The following data are salaries of seven randomly chosen owners of furniture-making firms and eight randomly chosen owners of paper-product firms [Source: *Business Week* (July 27, 1987)]. The data are in thousands of dollars per year.

> Furniture: 175, 170, 166, 168, 204, 96, 147
> Paper Products: 89, 120, 136, 160, 111, 101, 98, 80

Use the Wald-Wolfowitz test, and find whether there is evidence that average owner salaries in the two business lines are not equal.

14–4   The Mann-Whitney *U* Test

In this section, we present the first of several statistical procedures that are based on *ranks*. In these procedures, we rank the observations from smallest to largest and then use the ranks instead of the actual sample values in our computations. Sometimes, our data are themselves ranks. Methods based on ranks are useful when the data are at least on an *ordinal* scale of measurement. Surprisingly, when we substitute ranks for actual observations, the loss of information does not weaken the tests very much. In fact, when the assumptions of the corresponding parametric tests are met, the nonparametric tests based on ranks are often about 95% as efficient as the parametric tests. When the assumptions needed for the parametric tests (usually, a normal distribution) are *not* met, the tests based on ranks are excellent, powerful alternatives.

We demonstrate the ranking procedure with a simple set of numbers: 17, 32, 99, 12, 14, 44, 50. We rank the observations from smallest to largest. This gives us: 3, 4, 7, 1, 2, 5, 6. (Because the smallest observation is 12, the next one up is 14, and so on. The largest observation—the seventh—is 99.) This simple ranking procedure is the basis of the test presented in this section, as well as of the tests presented in the next few sections. Tests based on ranks are probably the most widely used nonparametric procedures.

In this section, we present the **Mann-Whitney *U* test,** also called the *Wilcoxon rank sum test,* or just the *rank sum test*. This test is different from the test we discuss in the next section, called the Wilcoxon *signed-rank* test. Try not to get confused by these names. The Mann-Whitney test is an adaptation of a procedure due to Wilcoxon, who also developed the signed-rank test. The most commonly used name for the rank sum test, however, is the Mann-Whitney *U* test.

The Mann-Whitney *U* test is a test of equality of two population distributions. The test is most useful, however, in testing for equality of two population means. As such, the test is an alternative to the two-sample *t* test and is used when the assumption of normal population distributions is not met. The test is only slightly weaker than the *t* test and is more powerful than the Wald-Wolfowitz runs test described in the previous section.

The null and alternative hypotheses for the Mann-Whitney *U* test:

> H_0: The distributions of the two populations are identical
>
> H_1: The two population distributions are not identical   (14–15)

Often, the hypothesis test in equation 14–15 is written in terms of equality versus nonequality of two population means or equality versus nonequality of two population medians. As such, we may also have one-tailed versions of the test. We may test whether one population mean is greater than the other. We may state these hypotheses in terms of population medians.

The only assumptions required by the test are that the samples are random samples from the two populations of interest and that they are also drawn independently of each other. If we want to state the hypotheses in terms of population means or medians, however, we need to add an assumption, namely, that if a difference exists between the two populations, the difference is in *location* (mean, median).

The Computational Procedure

We combine the two random samples and rank all our observations from smallest to largest. To any ties we assign the *average* rank of the tied observations. Then we sum all the ranks of the observations from one of the populations and denote that population as population 1. The sum of the sample ranks is R_1.

The Mann-Whitney U statistic:

$$U = n_1 n_2 + \frac{n_1(n_1 + 1)}{2} - R_1 \qquad (14\text{--}16)$$

where n_1 is the sample size from population 1 and n_2 is the sample size from population 2

The U statistic is a measure of the difference between the ranks of the two samples. Large values of the statistic, or small ones, provide evidence of a difference between the two populations. If we assume that differences between the two populations are only in location, then large or small values of the statistic provide evidence of a difference in the location (mean, median) of the two populations.

The distribution of the U statistic for small samples is given in Appendix C, Table 9. The table assumes that n_1 is the smaller sample size. For large samples, we may, again, use a normal approximation. The convergence to the normal distribution is relatively fast, and when both n_1 and n_2 are above 10 or so, the normal approximation is good.

The mean of the distribution of U:

$$E(U) = \frac{n_1 n_2}{2} \qquad (14\text{--}17)$$

The standard deviation of U:

$$\sigma_U = \sqrt{\frac{n_1 n_2 (n_1 + n_2 + 1)}{12}} \qquad (14\text{--}18)$$

The large-sample test statistic:

$$z = \frac{U - E(U)}{\sigma_U} \qquad (14\text{--}19)$$

For large samples, the test is straightforward. In a two-tailed test, we reject the null hypothesis if z is greater than or less than the values that correspond to our chosen level of α (for example, ± 1.96 for $\alpha = 0.05$). Similarly, in a one-tailed test, we reject H_0 if z is greater than (or less than) the appropriate critical point. Note that U is large when R_1 is small and vice versa. Thus, if we want to prove the alternative hypothesis that the location parameter of population 1 is greater than the location parameter of population 2, we reject on the *left* tail of the normal distribution.

With small samples, we have a problem because the U table lists only left-hand-side probabilities of the statistic (the table gives $F(U)$ values). Here we will use the following procedure. For a two-tailed test, we define R_1 as the larger of the two sums of ranks. This will make U small so it can be tested against a left-hand critical point with tail probability $\alpha/2$. For a one-tailed test, if we want to prove that the location parameter of population 1 is greater than that of population 2, we look at the sum of the ranks of sample 1 and accept H_0 if this sum is smaller than that for sample 2. Otherwise, we compute the statistic and test on the left side of the distribution. We choose the left-hand critical point corresponding to α. Relabel populations 1 and 2 if you want to prove the other one-tailed possibility.

We demonstrate the Mann-Whitney test with two examples.

EXAMPLE (g)

Federal aviation officials tested two proposed versions of the Copter-plane, a twin-engine plane with tilting propellers that make takeoffs and landings easy and save time during short flights. The two models, made by Bell Helicopter Textron, Inc., were tested on the New York–Washington route. The officials wanted to know whether the two models were equally fast or whether one was faster than the other. Each of the models was flown six times, at randomly chosen departure times. The data, in minutes of total flight time for models A and B, are as follows.

Model A: 35, 38, 40, 42, 41, 36
Model B: 29, 27, 30, 33, 39, 37

SOLUTION

First we order the data so that they can be ranked. This has been done in Figure 14–5. We note that the sum of the ranks of the sample points from the population of model A should be higher since the ranks for this model are higher. We will thus define R_1 as the sum of the ranks from this sample because we need a small value of U (which happens when R_1 is large) for comparison with table values. We find the value of R_1 as: $R_1 = 5 + 6 + 8 + 10 + 11 + 12 = 52$. This is the sum of the circled ranks in Figure 14–5, the ranks belonging to the sample for model A.

We now compute the test statistic, U. From equation 14–16, we find:

$$U = n_1 n_2 + \frac{n_1(n_1 + 1)}{2} - R_1 = (6)(6) + \frac{(6)(7)}{2} - 52 = 5$$

Looking at Appendix C, Table 9, we find that the probability that U will attain a value of 5 or less is 0.0206. Since this is a two-tailed test, we want to reject the null hypothe-

FIGURE 14–5 Ordering and Ranking the Data for Example (g)

Model A:					35	36		38		40	41	42
Model B:		27	29	30	33			37		39			
Rank:		1	2	3	4	⑤	⑥	7	⑧	9	⑩	⑪	⑫

sis if the value of the statistic is less than or equal to the (left-hand) critical point corresponding to $\alpha/2$; if we choose $\alpha = 0.05$, then $\alpha/2 = 0.025$. Since 0.0206 is less than 0.025, we reject the null hypothesis at the 0.05 level. The p-value for this test is $2(0.0206) = 0.0412$. (Why?)

Suppose that we had chosen to conduct this as a one-tailed test. If we had originally wanted to test whether model B is slower than model A, then we would have to accept the null hypothesis that model B is *not* slower because the sum of the ranks of model B is smaller than the sum of ranks of model A, and, hence, U would be large and not in the (left-side) rejection region. If, on the other hand, we wanted to test whether model A is slower, the test statistic would have been the same as the one we used, except that we could have rejected with a value of U as high as 7 (from Table 9, the tail probability for $U = 7$ is 0.0465, which is less than $\alpha = 0.05$). Remember that in a one-tailed test, we use the (left-hand) critical point corresponding to α and not $\alpha/2$. In any case, we reject the null hypothesis and state that there is evidence to conclude that model B is generally faster.

When the sample sizes are large and we use the normal approximation, conducting the test is much easier since we do not have to redefine U so that it is always on the left-hand side of the distribution. We just compute the standardized Z statistic, using equations 14–17 through 14–19, and consult the standard normal table. This is demonstrated in Example (h).

A multinational corporation is about to open a subsidiary in Greece. Since the operation will involve a large number of executives who will have to move to that country, the company plans to offer an extensive program of teaching the language to the executives who will operate in Greece. For its previous operation starts in France and Italy, the company used cassettes and books provided by Educational Services Teaching Cassettes, Inc. Recently one of the company directors suggested that the book-and-cassette program offered by Metacom, Inc., sold under the name The Learning Curve, might provide a better introduction to the language. The company therefore decided to test the null hypothesis that the two programs were equally effective versus the one-tailed alternative that students who go through The Learning Curve program achieve better proficiency scores in a comprehensive examination following the course. Two groups of 15 executives were randomly selected, and each group studied the language under a different program. The final scores for the two groups, Educational Services (ES) and Learning Curve (LC), are as follows. Is there evidence that The Learning Curve method is more effective?

EXAMPLE (h)

ES: 65, 57, 74, 43, 39, 88, 62, 69, 70, 72, 59, 60, 80, 83, 50
LC: 85, 87, 92, 98, 90, 88, 75, 72, 60, 93, 88, 89, 96, 73, 62

We order the scores and rank them. When ties occur, we assign to each tied observation the average rank of the ties.

SOLUTION

ES: 39 43 50 57 59 60 62 65 69 70 72   74   80 83   88
LC: 60 62   72 73   75   85 87 88 89 90 92 93 96 98
                                                          88

The tied observations are: 60 (two—one from each group), 62 (two—one from each group), 72 (two—one from each group), and 88 (three—one from ES and two from LC). If we disregarded ties, the two observations of 60 would have received ranks 6 and

7. Since either one of them could have been rank 6 or rank 7, they each get the *average* rank of 6.5 (and the next rank up is 8). The next two observations are also tied (both are 62). They would have received ranks 8 and 9, so each gets the average rank of 8.5, and we continue with rank 10, which goes to the observation 65. The two 72 observations each get the average rank of 13.5 [(13 + 14)/2]. There are three 88 observations; they occupy ranks 22, 23, and 24. Therefore, each of them gets the average rank of 23.

We now list the ranks of all the observations in each of the two groups:

| ES: | 1 | 2 | 3 | 4 | 5 | 6.5 | 8.5 | 10 | 11 | 12 | 13.5 | 16 | 18 | 19 | 23 |
| LC: | 6.5 | 8.5 | 13.5 | 15 | 17 | 20 | 21 | 23 | 23 | 25 | 26 | 27 | 28 | 29 | 30 |

Note that two of the 23 ranks belong to LC and one belongs to ES. We may now compute the test statistic, U. To be consistent with the small-sample procedure, let us define LC as population 1. We have:

$$R_1 = 6.5 + 8.5 + 13.5 + 15 + 17 + 20 + 21 + 23 + 23 + 25 + 26 + 27 + 28 + 29 + 30 = 312.5$$

Thus, the value of the statistic is:

$$U = (15)(15) + \frac{(15)(16)}{2} - 312.5 = 32.5$$

We now compute the value of the standardized Z statistic, equation 14–19. From equation 14–17,

$$E(U) = \frac{(15)(15)}{2} = 112.5$$

and from equation 14–18,

$$\sigma_U = \sqrt{\frac{(15)(15)(31)}{12}} = 24.1$$

We get:

$$z = \frac{U - E(U)}{\sigma_U} = \frac{32.5 - 112.5}{24.1} = -3.32$$

We want to reject the null hypothesis if we believe that LC gives *higher* scores. Our test statistic is defined to give a negative value in such a case. Since the computed value of the statistic is in the rejection region for any common α value, we reject the null hypothesis and conclude that there is evidence that the LC program is more effective. Our p-value is 0.0005.

In Example (h) we used the Mann-Whitney test instead of the parametric t test because some people have a facility with language and tend to score high on language tests, whereas others do not and tend to score low. This can create a bimodal distribution (one with two modes) rather than a normal curve, which is required for the t test.

In Example (g), we had small samples. When small samples are used, the parametric tests are sensitive to deviations from the normal assumption required for the t distribution. In such cases, it is usually better to use a nonparametric method such as the Mann-Whitney test, unless there is a good indication that the populations in question are approximately normally distributed.

14–26. Gotex® is considering two possible bathing suit designs for the new season. One is called Nautical Design, and the other is Geometric Prints. Since the fashion industry is very competitive, Gotex needs to test before marketing the bathing suits. Ten randomly chosen top models are selected for modeling the Nautical Design, and 10 other randomly chosen top models are selected to model the Geometric Prints bathing suits. The results of the judges' ratings of the 20 bathing suits follows.

ND: 86, 90, 77, 81, 86, 95, 99, 92, 93, 85
GP: 67, 72, 60, 59, 78, 69, 70, 85, 65, 62

Is there evidence to conclude that one design is better than the other? If so, which one is it, and why?

14–27. Following reports by scientists that a large hole in the atmospheric ozone revolves around Antarctica, two U.S. jets of the U-2 type were sent to collect samples of air for comparison with samples collected elsewhere to see if the ozone layer is indeed depleted. If so, controls on the manufacture of ozone-depleting fluorocarbons would have to be imposed to prevent further dangerous depletion of ozone around the world. Using the following data, test the null hypothesis that the ozone concentration over Antarctica is approximately equal to the concentration found in other areas against the alternative hypothesis that the concentration over Antarctica is lower than that found elsewhere.

Antarctica (%): 6, 10, 12, 23, 11, 31, 25, 11, 8, 7, 34, 14, 16, 18, 40, 31, 22, 5
Other places (%): 17, 32, 41, 29, 16, 30, 19, 51, 65, 22, 40, 47, 29, 30, 16, 70

14–28. Explain when you would use the Mann-Whitney test, when you would use the two-sample *t* test, and when you would use the Wald-Wolfowitz test. Discuss your reasons for choosing each test in the appropriate situation.

14–29. Superconductors, materials that carry electricity without losing energy, are believed to be the key to technology in the 21st century. Currently, two types of ceramics are considered for potential use—one designed at an IBM laboratory in the United States and one designed at the University of Tokyo, Japan. The efficiency of electrical conductivity is measured using a special formula; the higher the measurement, the more efficient the conductor. Using the following data, determine whether there is statistical evidence to conclude that one of the two superconductors is more efficient than the other.

IBM conductor: 143, 121, 120, 101, 107, 142, 118, 130, 128, 107, 108, 126
Tokyo conductor: 102, 119, 121, 113, 126, 116, 117, 129, 104, 109, 110

14–30. Shearson Lehman Brothers, Inc., now encourages its investors to consider real estate limited partnerships. The company offers two limited partnerships—one in a condominium project in Chicago and one in Dallas. Annualized rates of return for the two investments during separate eight-month periods are as follows. Is one type of investment better than the other? Explain.

Chicago (%): 12, 13, 10, 14, 15, 9, 11, 10
Dallas (%): 10, 9, 8, 7, 9, 11, 6, 13

14–31. According to a recent *Business Week* article, the average Taiwanese is as likely to use a bank as to use a black-marketeer for changing money. Since rates vary from place to place, it may be of interest to determine whether black-market foreign exchange commissions are approximately equal to those of banks. A random sample of 16 bank commissions and a random sample of 17 black-market commissions are collected. Data, in percentage charged per transaction, are as follows. Conduct a two-tailed test of equality of commission rates.

Black market: 1, 1.5, 1.3, 1.2, 2, 2.1, 1.8, 1.4, 1.5, 2.3, 1.7, 1.2, 1.4, 1.1, 1.9, 2.3, 2.6
Banks: 1.8, 1.7, 1.9, 1.5, 1.7, 1.3, 2.4, 2.8, 1.9, 2.1, 2.2, 2.6, 1.9, 2.5, 2.0, 2.1

Answers

14–26.

$U = 3.5$
p-value < 0.0002

14–30.

$U = 12$
p-value $= 0.038$

14–5   The Wilcoxon Signed-Rank Test

The **Wilcoxon signed-rank** test is useful in comparing two populations for which we have paired observations. As such, the test is a good alternative to the paired-observations t test in cases where the differences between paired observations are not believed to be normally distributed. We have already seen a nonparametric test for such a situation—the sign test. Unlike the sign test, the Wilcoxon test accounts for the magnitude of differences between paired values, not only their signs. The test does so by considering the *ranks* of these differences. The test is therefore more efficient than the sign test when the differences may be quantified rather than just given a positive or negative sign. The sign test, on the other hand, is easier to carry out.

The Wilcoxon procedure may also be adapted for testing whether the location parameter of a single population (its median or its mean) is equal to any given value. There are one-tailed and two-tailed versions of each test. We start with the paired-observations test for the equality of two population distributions (or the equality of the location parameters of the two populations).

The Paired-Observations Two-Sample Test

The null hypothesis is that the median difference between the two populations is zero. The alternative hypothesis is that it is not zero.

> The hypothesis test:
>
> H_0: The median difference between populations 1 and 2 is zero
> H_1: The median difference between populations 1 and 2 is not
>   zero   (14–20)

We assume that the distribution of differences between the two populations is symmetric, that the differences are mutually independent, and that the measurement scale is at least interval. By the assumption of symmetry, hypotheses may be stated in terms of means. The alternative hypothesis may also be a directed one: that the mean (or median) of one population is greater than the mean (or median) of the other population.

First, we list the pairs of observations we have on the two variables (the two populations). The data are assumed to be a random sample of paired observations. For each pair, we compute the difference:

$$D = x_1 - x_2 \qquad (14-21)$$

Then we rank the absolute values of the differences, D.

In the next step, we form sums of the ranks of the positive and of the negative differences.

> The Wilcoxon T statistic is defined as the smaller of the two sums of ranks—the sum of the negative or the positive ones.
>
> $$T = \min\left(\sum(+), \sum(-)\right) \qquad (14-22)$$
>
> where $\sum(+)$ is the sum of the ranks of the positive differences and $\sum(-)$ is the sum of the ranks of the negative differences

The decision rule: Critical points of the distribution of the test statistic T (when the null hypothesis is true) are given in Appendix C, Table 10. We carry out the test on the left tail, that is, we reject the null hypothesis if the computed value of the statistic is *less than* a critical point from the table, for a given level of significance.

For a one-tailed test, suppose that the alternative hypothesis is that the mean (median) of population 1 is greater than that of population 2, that is:

$$H_0: \mu_1 \le \mu_2$$
$$H_1: \mu_1 > \mu_2 \qquad (14\text{-}23)$$

Here we use the sum of the ranks of the negative differences. If the alternative hypothesis is reversed (populations 1 and 2 switched), then we use the sum of the ranks of the positive differences as the statistic. In either case, the test is carried out on the left "tail" of the distribution. Appendix C, Table 10 gives critical points for both one-tailed and two-tailed tests.

Large-Sample Version of the Test

As in other situations, as the sample size increases, the distribution of the Wilcoxon statistic, T, approaches the normal probability distribution. In the Wilcoxon test, n is defined as the number of *pairs* of observations from populations 1 and 2. As the number of pairs, n, gets large (as a rule of thumb, $n > 25$ or so), T may be approximated by a normal random variable as follows.

The mean of T:

$$E(T) = \frac{n(n + 1)}{4} \qquad (14\text{-}24)$$

The standard deviation of T:

$$\sigma_T = \sqrt{\frac{n(n + 1)(2n + 1)}{24}} \qquad (14\text{-}25)$$

The standardized z statistic:

$$z = \frac{T - E(T)}{\sigma_T} \qquad (14\text{-}26)$$

We now demonstrate the Wilcoxon signed-rank test with Example (i).

The Sunglass Hut of America, Inc., operates kiosks occupying previously unused space in the well-traveled aisles of shopping malls. Sunglass Hut owner, Sanford Ziff, hopes to expand within a few years to every major shopping mall in America. He is using the present $4.5 million business as a test of the marketability of different types of sunglasses. Two types of sunglasses are sold: violet and pink. Ziff wants to know whether there is a difference in the quantities sold of each type. The numbers of sunglasses sold of each kind are paired by store; these data for each of 16 stores during the first month of operation are given in Table 14–4. The table also shows how the differences and their absolute values are computed and ranked, and how the signed ranks are summed, leading to the computed value of T.

EXAMPLE (i)

TABLE 14-4 Data and Computations for Example (i)

Store	Number Violet Sold (X_1)	Number Pink Sold (X_2)	Difference ($D = X_1 - X_2$)	Rank of Absolute Difference $\lvert D \rvert$	Rank of Positive D	Rank of Negative D
1	56	40	16	9	9	
2	48	70	−22	12		12
3	100	60	40	15	15	
4	85	70	15	8	8	
5	22	8	14	7	7	
6	44	40	4	2	2	
7	35	45	−10	6		6
8	28	7	21	11	11	
9	52	60	−8	5		5
10	77	70	7	3.5	3.5	
11	89	90	−1	1		1
12	10	10	0			
13	65	85	20	10	10	
14	90	61	29	13	13	
15	70	40	30	14	14	
16	33	26	7	3.5	3.5	
					$\Sigma(+) = 96$	$\Sigma(-) = 24$

SOLUTION

Note that a difference of zero is discarded, and the sample size is reduced by one. The effective sample size for this experiment is now $n = 15$. Note also that ties are handled as before: We assign the average rank to tied differences. Since the smaller sum is the one associated with the negative ranks, we define T as that sum. We therefore have the following value of the Wilcoxon test statistic.

$$T = \sum(-) = 24$$

We now conduct the test of the hypotheses in equation 14–20. We compare the computed value of the statistic, $T = 24$, with critical points of T from Table 10. For a two-tailed test, we find that for $\alpha = 0.05$ ($P = 0.05$ in the table) and $n = 15$, the critical point is 25. Since the test is carried out on the "left tail"—that is, we reject the null hypothesis if the computed value of T is *less than or equal* to the table value—we reject the null hypothesis that the distribution of sales of the violet sunglasses is identical to the distribution of sales of the pink sunglasses. Furthermore, since the sum of the ranks of the negative differences is smaller, and since we defined violet as 1 and pink as 2, we further believe that the violet glasses sell better than the pink ones. If we allow the assumption that if differences occur, they are differences in the mean of the distributions, we may conclude that there is statistical evidence that the *average* sales of violet sunglasses in the *population* of stores will be higher than those of the pink sunglasses.

A Test for the Mean or Median of a Single Population

As stated earlier, the Wilcoxon signed-rank test may be adapted for testing whether or not the mean (or median) of a *single* population is equal to any given number. There are three possible tests. The first is a left-hand-tailed test where the alternative hypothesis is that the mean (or median—both are equal if we assume a *symmetric* population distribution) is smaller than some value specified in the null hypothesis. The second is a right-hand-tailed test where the alternative hypothesis is that the mean (or median) is greater than some value. The third is a two-tailed test where the alternative hypothesis is that the mean (or median) is not equal to the value specified in the null hypothesis.

The computational procedure is as follows. Using our n data points, $x_1, x_2, \ldots,$ x_n, we form pairs: $(x_1, m), (x_2, m), \ldots, (x_n, m)$ where m is the value of the mean (or median) specified in the null hypothesis. Then we perform the usual Wilcoxon signed-rank test on these pairs.

In a right-hand-tailed test, if the negative ranks have a larger sum than the positive ranks, we accept the null hypothesis. If the negative ranks have a smaller sum than the positive ones, we conduct the test (on the "left tail" of the distribution, as usual) and use the critical points in the table corresponding to the one-tailed test. We use the same procedure in the left-hand-tailed test. For a two-tailed test, we use the two-tailed critical points. In any case, we always reject the null hypothesis if the computed value of T is less than or equal to the appropriate critical point from Appendix C, Table 10.

We will now demonstrate the single-sample Wilcoxon test for a mean using the large-sample normal approximation.

EXAMPLE (j)

The average hourly number of messages transmitted by a private communications satellite is believed to be 149. The satellite's owners have recently been worried about the possibility that demand for this service may be declining. They therefore want to test the null hypothesis that the average number of messages is 149 (or more) versus the alternative hypothesis that the average hourly number of relayed messages is less than 149. A random sample of 25 operation hours are selected. The data (numbers of messages relayed per hour) are:

151, 144, 123, 178, 105, 112, 140, 167, 177, 185, 129, 160, 110, 170, 198, 165, 109, 118, 155, 102, 164, 180, 139, 166, 182

Is there evidence of declining use of the satellite?

SOLUTION

We form 25 pairs, each pair consisting of a data point and the null-hypothesized mean of 149. Then we subtract the second number from the first number in each pair (that is, we subtract 149 from every data point). This gives us the differences, D.

2, −5, −26, 29, −44, −37, −9, 18, 28, 36, −20, 11, −39, 21, 49, 16, −40, −31, 6, −47, 15, 31, −10, 17, 33

The next step is to rank the absolute value of the differences from smallest to largest. We have the following ranks, in the order of the data

1, 2, 13, 15, 23, 20, 4, 10, 14, 19, 11, 6, 21, 12, 25, 8, 22, 16.5, 3, 24, 7, 16.5, 5, 9, 18

Note that the differences 31 and −31 are tied and, since they would occupy positions 16 and 17, each is assigned the average of these two ranks, 16.5.

The next step is to compute the sum of the ranks of the positive differences and the sum of the ranks of the negative differences. The ranks associated with the positive differences are: 1, 15, 10, 14, 19, 6, 12, 25, 8, 3, 7, 16.5, 9, and 18. (Check this.) The sum of these ranks is $\Sigma(+) = 163.5$. When using the normal approximation, we may use either sum of ranks. Since this is a left-hand-tailed test, we want to reject the null hypothesis that the mean is 149 only if there is evidence that the mean is less than 149, that is, when the sum of the positive ranks is too small. We will therefore carry out the test on the left tail of the normal distribution.

Using equations 14–24 to 14–26, we compute the value of the test statistic, Z, as:

$$z = \frac{T - E(T)}{\sigma_T} = \frac{T - [n(n+1)/4]}{\sqrt{n(n+1)(2n+1)/24}} = \frac{163.5 - [(25)(26)/4]}{\sqrt{(25)(26)(51)/24}} = 0.027$$

This value of the statistic lies inside the acceptance region, far from the critical point for any conventional level of significance. (If we had decided to carry out the test at $\alpha = 0.05$, our critical point would have been $C = -1.645$.) We accept the null hypothesis and conclude that there is no evidence that use of the satellite is declining.

In closing this section, we note that the Wilcoxon signed-rank test assumes that the distribution of the population is symmetric in the case of the single-sample test, and that the distribution of differences between the two populations in the paired, two-sample case is symmetric. This assumption allows us to make inferences about population means or medians. Another assumption inherent in our analysis is that the random variables in question are continuous. The measurement scale of the data is at least ordinal.

PROBLEMS

Answers

14–34.
———
$T = 23$;
accept H_0.

14–32. Explain the purpose of the Wilcoxon signed-rank test. When is this test useful? Why?

14–33. For problem 14–30, suppose that the returns for the Chicago and Dallas investments are paired by month: the first observation for each investment is for the first month (say, January), the second is for the next month, and so on. Conduct the analysis again, using the Wilcoxon signed-rank test. Is there a difference in your conclusion? Explain.

14–34. An article in the *Canadian Business Review* discusses differences in management style between North American and European corporations.[3] The following are paired management achievement scores for a European subsidiary and a North American subsidiary of the same firm for a random sample of 10 firms. Test the hypothesis of no difference in management style.

(25, 41), (28, 18), (37, 35), (10, 56), (14, 15), (51, 72), (30, 43), (28, 66), (33, 31), (20, 29)

14–35. The average life of a 100 watt light bulb is stated on the package to be 750 hours. The quality-control director at the plant making the light bulbs needs to check whether the statement is correct. The director is only concerned about a possible reduction in quality and will stop the production process only if statistical evidence exists to conclude that the average life of a light bulb is less than 750 hours. A random sample of 20 bulbs is collected and left on until they burn out. The lifetime of each bulb is recorded. The data are (in hours of continuous use): 738, 752, 710, 701, 689, 779, 650, 541, 902, 700, 488, 555, 870, 609, 745, 712, 881, 599, 659, 793. Should the process be stopped and corrected? Explain why or why not.

14–36.
———
Sign test.

14–36. A retailer of records and compact discs wants to test whether people can differentiate—by the quality of sound only—between the two products. A random sample of consumers who agreed to participate in the test and who have no particular experience with high-quality audio equipment is selected. The same musical performance is played for each person, once on a disc and once on a record. The listeners do not know which is playing, and the order has been determined randomly. Each person is asked to state which of the two performances he or she prefers. What statistical test is most appropriate here? Why?

14–37. From experience, a manager knows that the commissions earned by her salespeople are very well approximated by a normal distribution. The manager wants to test whether the average commission is $439 per month. A random sample of 100 observations is available. What statistical test is best in this situation? Why?

---

[3] R. Gray and T. Thone, "Differences between North American and European Corporate Cultures," *Canadian Business Review* (Autumn 1990), p. 26.

14–38. Returns on stock of small firms have been shown to be symmetrically distributed, but the distributions are believed to be "long-tailed"—not well approximated by the normal distribution. If it is desired to test whether or not the average return on a stock of a small firm is equal to 12% per year, what test would you recommend? Why?

14–39. Sky Pies® is a recently opened shop at O'Hare International Airport in Chicago that sells frozen, packaged-to-go pizzas. "You can bring sourdough bread from San Francisco, then why not pizza from Chicago?" says founder Bill Gramas. Bill calculated that his business will turn a profit if he can sell at least 120 pizzas per day. Sales data, in number sold per day for the first 15 days, are as follows (assume these data are a random sample of daily sales): 145, 190, 206, 167, 120, 178, 110, 102, 119, 201, 100, 118, 127, 148, 155. Test the null hypothesis that average sales are less than or equal to 120 per day versus the alternative that the average is over 120. What is the main, serious limitation of this analysis?

14–40. Air New Zealand offers two package tours from the United States to New Zealand. One, which includes airfare and five nights' hotel accommodation in Auckland, is advertised at $799. The other includes only two nights' accommodation and is advertised at $710. For a random sample of 12 days, the airline records the number of bookings for each package. The paired observations are as follows. Do you believe that one package is more popular than the other? Explain.

14–40.
———
$T = 27$; do not reject H_0

$799 package: 56, 79, 85, 77, 32, 48, 88, 95, 57, 70, 52, 90
$710 package: 60, 85, 70, 82, 41, 60, 89, 80, 77, 86, 66, 75

14–41. A stock market analyst wants to test whether there are higher-than-usual returns on stocks following a two-for-one split. A random sample of 10 stocks that recently split is available. For each stock, the analyst records the percentage return during the month preceding the split and the percentage return for the month following the split. The data are:

Before split (%): 0.5, −0.2, 0.9, 1.1, −0.7, 1.5, 2.0, 1.3, 1.6, 2.1
After split (%):   1.1, 0.3, 1.2, 1.9, −0.2, 1.4, 1.8, 1.8, 2.4, 2.2

Is there evidence that a stock split causes excess returns for the month following the split? Redo the problem using the sign test. Compare the results of the sign test with those of the Wilcoxon test.

14–42. Much has been said about airline deregulation and the effects it has had on the airline industry and its performance. Following a deluge of complaints from passengers, the public relations officer of one of the major airlines asked the company's operations manager to look into the problem. The operations manager obtained average takeoff delay figures for a random sample of the company's routes over time periods of equal length before and after the deregulation. The data, in minutes of average delay per route, are as follows.

14–42.
———
p-value < 0.001

Before: 3, 2, 4, 5, 1, 0, 1, 5, 6, 3, 10, 4, 11, 7
After: 6, 8, 2, 9, 8, 2, 6, 12, 5, 9, 8, 12, 11, 10

Is there evidence in these data that the airline's delays have increased after deregulation?

14–43. The average score on a vocational training test has been known to be 64. Recently, several changes have been instituted in the program; the effect of these changes on performance on the test is unknown. It is therefore desirable to test the null hypothesis that the average score for all people who will complete the program will be 64 versus the alternative that it will not be 64. The following random sample of scores is available.

87, 91, 65, 31, 8, 53, 99, 44, 42, 60, 77, 73, 42, 50, 79, 90, 54, 39, 77, 60, 33, 41, 42, 85, 71, 50, 63, 58, 89, 5, 66, 99, 57, 12, 47, 72, 80, 84

Conduct the test.

14–6 The Kruskal-Wallis Test—
A Nonparametric Alternative to One-Way ANOVA

Remember that the ANOVA procedure discussed in Chapter 9 requires the assumption that the populations being compared are all normally distributed with equal variance. When there is reason to believe that the populations under study are *not* normally distributed, we cannot use the ANOVA procedure. There is, however, a nonparametric test designed to detect differences among populations that does not require any assumptions about the shape of the population distributions. This test is the **Kruskal-Wallis test**. The test is the nonparametric alternative to the (completely randomized design) one-way analysis of variance. In the next section, we will see a nonparametric alternative to the randomized block design analysis of variance, the *Friedman test*. Both of these tests use ranks.

The Kruskal-Wallis test is an analysis of variance that uses the ranks of the observations rather than the data themselves. This assumes, of course, that the observations are on an interval scale. If our data are in the form of ranks, we use them as they are. The Kruskal-Wallis test is identical to the Mann-Whitney test when only two populations are involved. We thus use the Kruskal-Wallis test for comparing k populations, where k is greater than 2. The null hypothesis is that the k populations under study have the same distribution, and the alternative hypothesis is that at least two of the population distributions are different from each other.

The Kruskal-Wallis hypothesis test:

> H_0: All k populations have the same distribution
>
> H_1: Not all k populations have the same distribution   (14–27)

Although the hypothesis test is stated in terms of the distributions of the populations of interest, the test is most sensitive to differences in the *locations* of the populations. Therefore, the test is actually used to test the ANOVA hypothesis of equality of k population means. The only assumptions required for the Kruskal-Wallis test are that the k samples are random and are independently drawn from the respective populations. The random variables under study are continuous, and the measurement scale used is at least ordinal.

We rank all data points in the entire set from smallest to largest, without regard to which sample they come from. Then we sum all the ranks from each separate sample. Let n_1 be the sample size from population 1, n_2 the sample size from population 2, and so on up to n_k, which is the sample size from population k. Define n as the total sample size: $n = n_1 + n_2 + \cdots n_k$. We define R_1 as the sum of the ranks from sample 1, R_2 as the sum of the ranks from sample 2, and so on to R_k, the sum of the ranks from sample k. We now define the Kruskal-Wallis test statistic, H.

The Kruskal-Wallis test statistic

$$ H = \frac{12}{n(n+1)} \left(\sum_{j=1}^{k} \frac{R_j^2}{n_j} \right) - 3(n+1) \qquad (14–28) $$

For very small samples ($n_j < 5$), there are tables for the exact distribution of H under the null hypothesis; these are found in books devoted to nonparametric statistics. Usually, however, we have samples that are greater than 5 for each group (remember the serious limitations of inference based on very small samples). For larger samples, as long as each n_j is at least 5, the distribution of the test statistic H under the null hypothesis is well approximated by the chi-square distribution with $k - 1$ degrees of freedom.

We reject the null hypothesis on the right-hand tail of the chi-square distribution. That is, we reject the null hypothesis if the computed value of H is too large, exceeding a critical point of $\chi^2_{(k-1)}$ for a given level of significance, α. We demonstrate the Kruskal-Wallis test with an example.

EXAMPLE (k)

A company is planning to buy a word processing software package to be used by its office staff. Three available packages, made by different companies, are considered: Multimate™, WordPerfect™, and Microsoft Word™. Demonstration packages of the three alternatives are available, and the company selects a random sample of 18 staff members, 6 members assigned to each package. Every person in the sample learns how to use the particular package to which he or she is assigned. The time it takes every member to learn how to use the word processing package is recorded. The question is: Does it take approximately the same amount of time to learn how to use each package proficiently?

None of the office staff has used any of these packages before, and, because of similarity in use, each person is assigned to learn only one package. The staff, however, have varying degrees of experience. In particular, some are very experienced typists, and others are beginners. Therefore, it is believed that the three populations of time it takes to learn how to use a package are not normally distributed. If a conclusion is reached that one package takes longer to learn than the others, then learning time will be a consideration in the purchase decision. Otherwise, the decision will be based only on package capabilities and price. Table 14–5 gives the data, in minutes, for every person in the three samples. It also shows the ranks and the sum of the ranks for each group.

SOLUTION

Using the obtained sums of ranks for the three groups, we compute the Kruskal-Wallis statistic, H. From equation 14–28 we get:

$$H = \frac{12}{n(n + 1)}\left(\sum \frac{R_j^2}{n_j}\right) - 3(n + 1) = \frac{12}{(18)(19)}\left(\frac{90^2}{6} + \frac{56^2}{6} + \frac{25^2}{6}\right) - 3(19)$$

$$= 12.3625$$

We now perform the test of the hypothesis that the populations of the learning times of the three software packages are identical. We compare the computed value of H with

TABLE 14–5 The Data (in Minutes) and the Ranks for Example (k)

Multimate		WordPerfect		Microsoft Word	
Time	Rank	Time	Rank	Time	Rank
45	14	30	8	22	4
38	10	40	11	19	3
56	16	28	7	15	1
60	17	44	13	31	9
47	15	25	5	27	6
65	18	42	12	17	2
	$R_1 = 90$		$R_2 = 56$		$R_3 = 25$

FIGURE 14–6   Carrying Out the Test for Example (k)

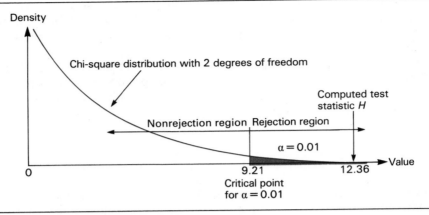

critical points of the chi-square distribution with $k - 1 = 3 - 1 = 2$ degrees of freedom. Using Appendix C, Table 4, we find that $H = 12.36$ exceeds the critical point for $\alpha = 0.01$, which is given as 9.21. We therefore reject the null hypothesis and conclude that there is evidence that the time it takes to learn how to use the word processing packages is not the same for all three; at least one package takes longer to learn. Our p-value is smaller than 0.01. The test is demonstrated in Figure 14–6.

We note that even though our example had a balanced design (equal sample sizes in all groups), the Kruskal-Wallis test can also be performed if sample sizes are different. We also note that we had no ties in this example. If ties do exist, we assign them the average rank, as we have done in previous tests based on ranks. It is possible to correct for the effect of ties by using a correction formula, which may be found in advanced books.

Further Analysis

As in the case of the usual ANOVA, once we reject the null hypothesis of no difference among populations, the question arises: Where are the differences? That is, which populations are different from which? Here we use a procedure that is similar to the Tukey method of further analysis following ANOVA. For every pair of populations we wish to compare (populations i and j, for example), we compute the average rank of the sample.

$$\bar{R}_i = \frac{R_i}{n_i} \quad \text{and} \quad \bar{R}_j = \frac{R_j}{n_j} \qquad (14\text{–}29)$$

where R_i and R_j are the sums of the ranks from samples i and j, respectively, computed as part of the original Kruskal-Wallis test. We now define the test statistic D as the absolute difference between $\bar{R}_i$ and $\bar{R}_j$.

> The test statistic for determining whether there is evidence to reject the null hypothesis that populations i and j are identical:
>
> $$D = |\bar{R}_i - \bar{R}_j| \qquad (14\text{–}30)$$

We carry out the test by comparing the test statistic D with a quantity that we compute from the critical point of the chi-square distribution at the same level, α, at which we carried out the Kruskal-Wallis test. The quantity is computed as follows.

The critical point for the paired comparisons:

$$C_{KW} = \sqrt{(\chi^2_{\alpha, k-1})\left[\frac{n(n+1)}{12}\right]\left(\frac{1}{n_i} + \frac{1}{n_j}\right)} \qquad (14\text{--}31)$$

where $\chi^2_{\alpha, k-1}$ is the critical point of the chi-square distribution used in the original, overall test

By comparing the value of the statistic D with C_{KW} for every pair of populations, we can perform all pairwise comparisons *jointly* at the level of significance, α, at which we performed the overall test. We reject the null hypothesis if and only if $D > C_{KW}$. We demonstrate the procedure by performing all three pairwise comparisons of the populations in Example (k).

Since we have a balanced design, $n_i = n_j = 6$ for all three samples, the critical point, C_{KW}, will be the same for all pairwise comparisons. Using equation 14–31, and 9.21 as the value of chi-square for the overall test at $\alpha = 0.01$, we get:

$$C_{KW} = \sqrt{(9.21)\left[\frac{(18)(19)}{12}\right]\left(\frac{1}{6} + \frac{1}{6}\right)} = 9.35$$

Comparing populations 1 and 2: From the bottom of Table 14–5, we find that $R_1 = 90$ and $R_2 = 56$. Since the sample sizes are each 6, we find that the average rank for sample 1 is $90/6 = 15$, and the average rank for sample 2 is $56/6 = 9.33$. Hence, the test statistic for comparing these two populations is the absolute value of the difference between 15 and 9.33, which is 5.67. This value is less than C_{KW}, and we must conclude that there is no evidence, at $\alpha = 0.01$, of a difference between populations 1 and 2.

Comparing populations 1 and 3: Here the absolute value of the difference between the average ranks is $|(90/6) - (25/6)| = 10.83$. Since 10.83 is greater than $C_{KW} = 9.35$, we conclude that there is evidence, at $\alpha = 0.01$, that population 1 is different from population 3.

Comparing populations 2 and 3: Here we have $D = |(56/6) - (25/6)| = 5.17$, which is less than 9.35. Therefore we conclude that there is no evidence, at $\alpha = 0.01$, that populations 2 and 3 are different.

Our interpretation of the data is that at $\alpha = 0.01$, there are significant differences only between the time it takes to learn Multimate and the time it takes to learn Microsoft Word. Since the values for Multimate are larger, we conclude that the study provides evidence that Multimate takes longer to learn.

PROBLEMS

14–44. Electronic data interchange (EDI) is an electronic pipeline linking suppliers with their customers. The system cuts the delivery time of goods by as much as 50% compared with other means of communication. The system allows specially formatted documents, such as purchase orders, to be sent from one company's computer to that of another. Currently, the system is used mainly by three industries: grocery, transportation, and pharmaceutical. EDI's management plans great expansion in the next few years and wants to know whether

Answer

14–44.

$H = 12.5$
p-value $= 0.002$

the three industry groups make about equal use of the system, or whether one group uses it more frequently than another group. A random sample of 10 grocery retailers using the system is gathered, as well as a random sample of 8 transportation users and 7 pharmaceutical users. For each company, the number of times EDI was used in the last month is recorded. The data are as follows. Is the frequency of use of EDI's services about the same for all three industry groups?

Groceries:	12, 14, 30, 5, 9, 18, 52, 19, 65, 25
Transportation:	48, 72, 99, 30, 62, 79, 120, 88
Pharmaceuticals:	40, 48, 67, 112, 31, 141, 69

14–45. An analyst in the publishing industry wants to find out whether the cost of a newspaper advertisement of a given size is about the same in four large newspaper groups. Random samples of seven newspapers from each group are selected, and the cost of an ad is recorded. The data follow (in dollars). Do you believe that there are differences in the price of an ad across the four groups?

Group A:	57, 65, 50, 45, 70, 62, 48
Group B:	72, 81, 64, 55, 90, 38, 75
Group C:	35, 42, 58, 59, 46, 60, 61
Group D:	73, 85, 92, 68, 82, 94, 66

14–46.

H = 29.61
p-value < 0.001

14–46. On July 28, 1987, lawyers representing the Beatles filed a $15 million suit in New York against Nike, Inc., over Nike's Air Max shoe commercial set to the Beatles' 1968 hit song "Revolution." As part of all such lawsuits, the plaintiff must prove a financial damage—in this case, that Nike improperly gained from the unlicensed use of the Beatles' song. In proving their case, lawyers for the Beatles had to show that "Revolution," or any Beatles' song, is not just a tune played with the commercial and that, in fact, the use of the song made the Nike commercial more appealing than it would have been if it had featured another song or melody. A statistician was hired to aid in proving this point. The statistician designed a study in which the Air Max commercial was recast using two other randomly chosen songs that were in the public domain and did not require permission, and that were not sung by the Beatles. Then three groups of 12 people each were randomly selected. Each group was shown one of the commercials, and every person's appeal score for the commercial was recorded. Using the following appeal scores, determine whether there is statistical evidence that not all three songs would be equally effective in the commercial. If you do reject the null hypothesis of equal appeal, go the required extra step to prove that the Beatles' "Revolution" does indeed have extra appeal over other songs, and that Nike should pay the Beatles for using it.

"Revolution":	95, 98, 96, 99, 91, 90, 97, 100, 96, 92, 88, 93
Random alternative A:	65, 67, 66, 69, 60, 58, 70, 64, 64, 68, 61, 62
Random alternative B:	59, 57, 55, 63, 59, 44, 49, 48, 46, 60, 47, 45

14–47. A researcher at an accounting firm wants to find out whether the current ratio for three industries is about the same. Random samples of eight firms in Industry A, six firms in Industry B, and six firms in Industry C are available. The current ratios are:

Industry A:	1.38, 1.55, 1.90, 2.00, 1.22, 2.11, 1.98, 1.61
Industry B:	2.33, 2.50, 2.79, 3.01, 1.99, 2.45
Industry C:	1.06, 1.37, 1.09, 1.65, 1.44, 1.11

Conduct the test at $\alpha = 0.05$, and state your conclusion.

14–48.

H = 13.01
p-value = 0.001

14–48. Recently, Japan's asset-rich life insurance companies have been venturing overseas and becoming a force in world financial markets. The insurance companies invest in real estate in New York, Canada, and the U.S. Sun Belt. A real estate investment broker hired by one Japanese insurance company wanted to find out whether or not the return on investment in comparable real estate in each of these three areas is approximately the same. Random sample data for investments in the three areas follow (figures represent annualized percentage return).

New York: 15, 18, 17, 19, 18, 10, 12, 16
Canada: 10, 9, 8, 11, 7, 13
Sun Belt: 21, 20, 22, 14, 23, 16, 24

Conduct the test. Are returns approximately equal in the three areas?

14–49. The following data are small random samples of rents (in dollars) in five American cities. The New York data are for Manhattan only.

New York (Manhattan): 900, 1,200, 850, 1,320, 1,400, 1,150, 975,
Chicago: 625, 640, 775, 1,000, 690, 550, 840, 750
Detroit: 415, 400, 420, 560, 780, 620, 800, 390
Tampa: 410, 310, 320, 280, 500, 385, 440
Orlando: 340, 425, 275, 210, 575, 360

Conduct the Kruskal-Wallis test to determine whether evidence exists that there are differences in the rents in these cities. If differences exist, where are they?

14–50. What assumptions have you used when solving problems 14–44 through 14–49? What assumptions did you *not* make about the populations in question? Explain.

14–7 The Friedman Test for a Randomized Block Design

Recall the randomized block design, which was discussed in Chapter 9. In this design, each *block* of units is assigned all k treatments, and our aim is to determine possible differences among treatments or treatment means (in the context of ANOVA). A *block* may be one person who is given all k treatments (asked to try k different products, to rate k different items, etc.). The Kruskal-Wallis test discussed in the previous section is a nonparametric version of the one-way ANOVA with completely randomized design. Similarly, the **Friedman test,** the subject of this section, is a nonparametric version of the randomized block design ANOVA. Sometimes this design is referred to as a two-way ANOVA with one item per cell because it is possible to view the blocks as one factor and the treatment levels as the other. In the randomized block design, however, we are interested in the treatments as a factor and not in the blocks themselves. Like the methods we discussed in preceding sections, the Friedman test is based on ranks. The test may be viewed as an extension of the Wilcoxon signed-rank test or an extension of the sign test to more than two treatments per block. Recall that in each of these tests, there are two treatments assigned to each element in the sample—the observations are paired. In the Friedman test, the observations are more than paired: each block, or person, is assigned to all $k > 2$ treatments.

Since the Friedman test is based on the use of ranks, it is especially useful for testing treatment effects when the observations are in the form of ranks. In fact, in such situations, we cannot use the randomized block design ANOVA because the assumption of a normal distribution cannot hold for very discrete data such as ranks. The Friedman test is a unique test for a situation where data are in the form of ranks within each block. Our example will demonstrate the use of the test in this particular situation. When our data are on an interval scale and not in the form of ranks, but we believe that the assumption of normality may not hold, we use the Friedman test instead of the parametric ANOVA and transform our data to ranks.

> The null and alternative hypotheses of the Friedman test:
>
> H_0: The distributions of the k treatment populations are identical
>
> H_1: Not all k distributions are identical   (14–32)

The data for the Friedman test are arranged in a table in which the rows are blocks (or units, if each unit is a block). There are n blocks. The columns are the treatments, and there are k of them. Let us assume that each block is one person who is assigned to all treatments. The data in this case are arranged as in Table 14–6.

If the data are not already in the form of ranks within each block, we rank the observations within each block from 1 to k. That is, the smallest observation in the block is given rank 1, the second smallest gets rank 2, and the largest gets rank k. Then we sum all the ranks for every treatment. The sum of all the ranks for treatment 1 is R_1, the sum of the ranks for treatment 2 is R_2, and so on to R_k, the sum of all the ranks given to treatment k.

If the distributions of the k populations are indeed identical, as stated in the null hypothesis, then we expect that the sum of the ranks for each treatment would not differ much from the sum of the ranks of any other treatment. The differences among the sums of the ranks are measured by the Friedman test statistic, denoted by X^2. When this statistic is too large, we reject the null hypothesis and conclude that at least two treatments do not have the same distribution.

> The Friedman test statistic:
>
> $$X^2 = \frac{12}{nk(k+1)} \sum_{j=1}^{k} R_j^2 - 3n(k+1) \qquad (14\text{–}33)$$

When the null hypothesis is true, the distribution of X^2 approaches the chi-square distribution with $k - 1$ degrees of freedom as n increases. For small values of k and n, tables of the exact distribution of X^2 under the null hypothesis may be found in

TABLE 14–6 The Data Layout for the Friedman Test

	Treatment 1	Treatment 2	Treatment 3	. . .	Treatment k
Person 1					
Person 2					
Person 3					
⋮	⋮	⋮	⋮	. . .	⋮
Person n					
Sum of ranks:	R_1	R_2	R_3	. . .	R_k

nonparametric statistics books. Here we will use the chi-square distribution as our decision rule. We note that for small n, the chi-square approximation is *conservative*; that is, we may not be able to reject the null hypothesis as easily as we would if we use the exact distribution table. Our decision rule is to reject H_0 at a given level, α, if X^2 exceeds the critical point of the chi-square distribution with $k - 1$ degrees of freedom and right-tail area α. We now demonstrate the use of the Friedman test with an example.

EXAMPLE (I)

There is a segment of the population, mostly retired people, who frequently go on low-budget cruises. Many travel agents specialize in this market and maintain mailing lists of people who take frequent cruises. One such travel agent in Fort Lauderdale wanted to find out whether "frequent cruisers" prefer some of the cruise lines in the low-budget range over others. If so, the agent would concentrate on selling tickets on the preferred line(s) rather than on a wider variety of lines. From a mailing list of people who have taken at least one cruise on each of the three cruise lines Carnival, Costa, and Sitmar, the agent selected a random sample of 15 people and asked them to rank their overall experiences with the three lines. The ranks were 1 (best), 2 (second best), and 3 (worst). The results are given in Table 14–7. Are the three cruise lines equally preferred by people in the target population?

SOLUTION

Using the sums of the ranks of the three treatments (the three cruise lines), we compute the Friedman test statistic. From equation 14–33, we get:

$$X^2 = \frac{12}{nk(k+1)}(R_1^2 + R_2^2 + R_3^2) - 3n(k+1)$$

$$= \frac{12}{(15)(3)(4)}(31^2 + 21^2 + 38^2) - 3(15)(4) = 9.73$$

We now compare the computed value of the statistic with values of the right tail of the chi-square distribution with $k - 1 = 2$ degrees of freedom. The critical point for $\alpha = 0.01$ is found from Appendix C, Table 4 to be 9.21. Since 9.73 is greater than 9.21, we conclude that there is evidence that not all three low-budget cruise lines are equally preferred by the frequent cruiser population.

TABLE 14–7 Sample Results of Example (I)

Respondent	Carnival	Costa	Sitmar
1	1	2	3
2	2	1	3
3	1	3	2
4	2	1	3
5	3	1	2
6	3	1	2
7	1	2	3
8	3	1	2
9	2	1	3
10	1	2	3
11	2	1	3
12	3	1	2
13	1	2	3
14	3	1	2
15	3	1	2
	$R_1 = 31$	$R_2 = 21$	$R_3 = 38$

PROBLEMS

14–51. A random sample of 12 consumers are asked to rank their preferences of four new fragrances that a perfume manufacturer wants to introduce to the market in the coming fall. The data are as follows (best liked denoted by 1 and least liked denoted by 4). Do you believe that all four fragrances are equally liked? Explain.

Respondent	Fragrance 1	Fragrance 2	Fragrance 3	Fragrance 4
1	1	2	4	3
2	2	1	3	4
3	1	3	4	2
4	1	2	3	4
5	1	3	4	2
6	1	4	3	2
7	1	3	4	2
8	2	1	4	3
9	1	3	4	2
10	1	3	2	4
11	1	4	3	2
12	1	3	4	2

14–52.

$X^2 = 12.6$
p-value = 0.002

14–52. While considering three managers for a possible promotion, the company president decided to solicit information from employees about the managers' relative effectiveness. Each person in a random sample of 10 employees who had worked with all three managers was asked to rank the managers, where best is denoted by 1, second best by 2, and worst by 3. The data follow. Based on the survey, are all three managers perceived as equally effective? Explain.

Respondent	Manager 1	Manager 2	Manager 3
1	3	2	1
2	3	2	1
3	3	1	2
4	3	2	1
5	2	3	1
6	3	1	2
7	3	2	1
8	3	2	1
9	3	1	2
10	3	1	2

14–53. In testing to find a cure for a nervous problem, it is not possible to directly quantify the condition of a patient after he or she has been treated with a drug, except to compare the patient's condition with those of other patients with the same illness severity who were treated with other drugs. A pharmaceutical firm conducting clinical trials therefore selects a random sample of 27 patients. The sample is then separated into blocks of three patients each, with the three patients in each block having about the same pretreatment condition. Each person in a block is then randomly assigned to be treated by one of the three drugs under consideration. After the treatment, a physician evaluates each person's condition and ranks the patient in comparison with the others in the same block (with 1 indicating the most improvement and 3 indicating the least improvement). Using the following data, do you believe that all three drugs are equally effective?

Block	Drug A	Drug B	Drug C
1	2	3	1
2	2	3	1
3	2	3	1
4	2	3	1
5	1	3	2
6	2	3	1
7	2	1	3
8	2	3	1
9	1	2	3

14–54. Four different processes for baking cakes commercially are considered. The cakes produced by each process are evaluated in terms of their overall quality. Since the cakes sometimes may not rise, the distribution of quality ratings is different from a normal distribution. When conducting a test of the quality of the four processes, cakes are blocked into groups of four according to the type of ingredients used. The ratings of the cakes baked by the four processes are as follows. (Ratings are on a scale of 0 to 100.) Are the four processes equally good? Explain.

Answer

14–54.

$X^2 = 16.35$
p-value $= 0.001$

Block	Process 1	Process 2	Process 3	Process 4
1	87	65	73	20
2	98	60	39	45
3	85	70	50	60
4	90	80	85	50
5	78	40	60	45
6	95	35	70	25
7	70	60	55	40
8	99	70	45	60

14–8   The Spearman Rank Correlation Coefficient

Recall our discussion of correlation in Chapter 10. There we stressed the assumption that the distributions of the two variables in question, X and Y, are normal. In cases where this assumption is not realistic, or in cases where our data are themselves in the form of ranks or are otherwise on an ordinal scale, we have alternative measures of the degree of association between the two variables. The most commonly used nonparametric measure of the correlation between two variables is the *Spearman rank correlation coefficient*, denoted by r_s.

Our data are pairs of n observations on two variables X and Y—pairs of the form (x_i, y_i), where $i = 1, \ldots, n$. To compute the Spearman correlation coefficient, we first rank all the observations of one variable within themselves from smallest to largest. Then, we independently rank the values of the second variable from smallest to largest. *The Spearman rank correlation coefficient is the usual (Pearson) correlation coefficient applied to the ranks.* When no ties exist, that is when there are no two values of X or two values of Y with the same rank, there is an easier computational formula for the Spearman correlation coefficient. The formula is given below.

The **Spearman rank correlation coefficient** (assuming no ties):

$$r_s = 1 - \frac{6 \sum_{i=1}^{n} d_i^2}{n(n^2 - 1)} \qquad (14\text{–}34)$$

where d_i, $i = 1, \ldots, n$, are the differences in the ranks of x_i and y_i:
$d_i = R(x_i) - R(y_i)$

If we do have ties within the X values or the Y values, but the number of ties is small compared with n, equation 14–34 is still useful.

The Spearman correlation coefficient satisfies the usual requirements of correlation measures. It is equal to 1 when the variables X and Y are perfectly positively related, that is, when Y increases whenever X does and vice versa. It is equal to -1 in the opposite situation, where X increases whenever Y decreases. It is equal to 0 when there is no relation between X and Y. Values between these extremes give a relative indication of the degree of association between X and Y.

As with the parametric Pearson correlation coefficient, there are two possible uses for the Spearman statistic. It may be used as a descriptive statistic giving us an indication of the association between X and Y. We may also use it for *statistical inference*. In the context of inference, we assume that there is a certain correlation in the ranks of the values of the bivariate population of X and Y. This population rank correlation is denoted by ρ_s. We want to test whether $\rho_s = 0$, that is, whether or not there is an association between the two variables X and Y.

Hypothesis test for association between two variables:

$$H_0: \rho_s = 0$$
$$H_1: \rho_s \neq 0 \qquad\qquad (14\text{–}35)$$

This is a two-tailed test for the existence of a relation between X and Y. One-tailed versions of the test are also possible. If we want to test for a positive association between the variables, then the alternative hypothesis is that the parameter ρ_s is strictly greater than zero. If we want to test for a negative association only, then the alternative hypothesis is that ρ_s is strictly less than zero. The test statistic is simply r_s, as defined in equation 14–34.

When the sample size is less than or equal to 30, we use Appendix C, Table 11. The table gives critical points for various levels of significance, α. For a two-tailed test, we double the α level given in the table and reject the null hypothesis if r_s is either greater than or equal to the table value, C, or less than or equal to $-C$. In a right-hand-tailed test, we reject only if r_s is greater than or equal to C; and in a left-hand-tailed test, we reject only if r_s is less than or equal to $-C$. In either one-tailed case, we use the α given in one of the columns in the table (we do not double it).

For larger sample sizes, we use the normal approximation to the distribution of r_s under the null hypothesis. The Z statistic for such a case is as follows.

A large-sample test statistic for association:

$$z = r_s \sqrt{n - 1} \qquad\qquad (14\text{–}36)$$

We demonstrate the computation of Spearman's statistic, and a test of whether the population rank correlation is zero, with Example (m).

EXAMPLE (m)

The S&P100 Index is an index of 100 stock options traded on the Chicago Board of Options Exchange. The MMI is an index of 20 stocks with options traded on the American Stock Exchange. Since options are volatile, the assumption of a normal distribution may not be appropriate, and the Spearman rank correlation coefficient may provide us with information about the association between the two indexes.[4] Using the reported data on the two indexes, given in Table 14–8, compute the r_s statistic, and test the null hypothesis that the MMI and the S&P100 are not related against the alternative that they are positively correlated.

---

[4] *Volatility* means that there are jumps to very small and very large values. This gives the distribution long tails and makes it different from the normal distribution. For *stock returns*, however, the normal assumption is a good one, as was mentioned in previous chapters.

TABLE 14–8 Data on the MMI and S&P100 Indexes [Example (m)]

Date	MMI	S&P100
6/26/84	220	151
7/6/84	218	150
7/11/84	216	148
7/16/84	217	149
7/21/84	215	147
7/26/84	213	146
8/1/84	219	152
8/5/84	236	165
8/10/84	237	162
8/15/84	235	161

TABLE 14–9 The Ranks and Rank Differences for Example (m)

Rank(MMI)	Rank(S&P100)	Difference
7	6	1
5	5	0
3	3	0
4	4	0
2	2	0
1	1	0
6	7	−1
9	10	−1
10	9	1
8	8	0

SOLUTION

We rank the MMI values and the S&P100 values and compute the 10 differences: $d_i = \text{Rank }(\text{MMI}_i) - \text{Rank}(\text{S\&P100}_i)$. This is shown in Table 14–9. The order of the values in the table corresponds to their order in Table 14–8.

We now use equation 14–34 and compute r_s.

$$r_s = 1 - \frac{6(d_1^2 + d_2^2 + \cdots + d_{10}^2)}{10(10^2 - 1)} = 1 - \frac{24}{990} = 0.9758$$

The sample correlation is very high.

We now use the r_s statistic in testing the hypotheses:

$$H_0: \rho_s \leq 0$$
$$H_1: \rho_s > 0 \qquad\qquad (14-37)$$

We want to test for the existence of a positive rank correlation between MMI and S&P100 in the *population* of values of the two indexes. We want to test whether the high sample rank correlation we found is statistically significant. Since this is a right-hand-tailed test, we reject the null hypothesis if r_s is greater than or equal to a point C found in Table 11 at a level of α given in the table. We find from the table that for $\alpha = 0.005$ and $n = 10$, the critical point is 0.794. Since $r_s = 0.9758 > 0.794$, we reject the null hypothesis and conclude that the MMI and the S&P100 are positively correlated. The p-value is less than 0.005.

In closing this section, we note that Spearman's rank correlation coefficient is sometimes referred to as *Spearman's rho* (the Greek letter ρ). There is another commonly used nonparametric measure of correlation. This one was developed by

Kendall and is called Kendall's tau (the Greek letter τ). Since Kendall's measure is not as simple to compute as the Spearman coefficient of rank correlation, we leave it to texts on nonparametric statistics.

PROBLEMS

Answers

14–55. The director of a management training program wants to test whether there is a positive association between an applicant's score on a test prior to his or her being admitted to the program and the same person's success in the program. The director ranks 15 participants according to their performance on the pretest and separately ranks them according to their performance in the program:

Participant:	1	2	3	4	5	6	7	8	9	10	11	12	13	14	15
Pretest rank:	8	9	4	2	3	10	1	5	6	15	13	14	12	7	11
Performance rank:	7	5	9	6	1	8	2	10	15	14	4	3	11	12	13

Using these data, carry out the test for a positive rank correlation between pretest scores and success in the program.

14–56.

$r_s = 0.791$
Significant.

14–56. The following data are a random sample of consumers' income and expenditure on certain luxury items. Compute the Spearman rank correlation coefficient, and test for the existence of a population correlation.

Income ($1000's/year):	23,	17,	34,	56,	49,	31,	28,	80,	65,	40,	26
Luxury Item Spending ($/Month):	10,	50,	120,	225,	90,	60,	55,	340,	170,	25,	80

14–57. The following table is a listing from the Fortune 500 and gives profits as percent of sales and assets for 10 firms.[5] Is there a rank correlation between the two variables?

	Profits as Percent of:	
	Sales	**Assets**
International Business Machines, Armonk, N.Y.	8.7	6.9
Mobil, Fairfax, Va.	3.3	4.6
General Electric, Fairfield, Conn.	7.4	2.8
Philip Morris, New York	8.0	7.6
Texaco, White Plains, N.Y.	3.5	5.6
E. I. du Pont de Nemours, Wilmington, Del.	5.8	6.1
Chevron, San Francisco	5.5	6.1
Chrysler, Highland Park, Mich.	0.2	0.1
Amoco, Chicago	6.8	5.9
Boeing, Seattle	5.0	9.5

14–58.

$r_s = -0.755$
No positive correlation.

14–58. Recently the European Economic Community (EEC) decided to lower its subsidies to makers of pasta. In deciding by what amount to reduce total subsidies, experiments were carried out for determining the possible reduction in exports, mainly to the United States, that would result from the subsidy reduction. Over a small range of values, economists wanted to test whether there is a positive correlation between level of subsidy and level of exports. A computer simulation of the economic variables involved in the pasta exports market was carried out. The results are as follows. Assuming that the simulation is an accurate description of reality and that the values obtained may be viewed as a random sample of the populations of possible outcomes, state whether you believe that a positive rank correlation exists between subsidy level and exports level over the short range of values studied.

---

[5] "The Fortune 500 Largest U.S. Industrial Corporations," *Fortune* (April 22, 1991), p. 286.

Subsidy (millions of dollars/year):	5.1	5.3	5.2	4.9	4.8	4.7	4.5	5.0	4.6	4.4	5.4
Exports (millions of dollars/year):	22	30	35	29	27	36	40	39	42	45	21

14–59.   An advertising research analyst wanted to test whether there is any relationship between a magazine advertisement's color intensity and the ad's appeal. Ten ads of varying degrees of color intensity, but identical in other ways, were shown to randomly selected groups of respondents. The respondents rated each ad for its general appeal. The respondents were segmented in such a way that each group viewed a different ad, and every group's responses were aggregated. The results were ranked as follows.

Color intensity:	8	7	2	1	3	4	10	6	5	9
Appeal score:	1	3	4	2	5	8	7	6	9	10

Is there a rank correlation between color intensity and appeal?

14–9   A Chi-Square Test for Goodness of Fit

In this section and the next two, we describe tests that make use of the chi-square distribution. The data used in these tests are *enumerative:* the data are counts, or frequencies. Our actual observations may be on a nominal (or higher) scale of measurement. Because many real-world situations in business and other areas allow for the collection of count data (for example, the number of people in a sample who fall into different categories of age, sex, income, and job classification), chi-square analysis is very common and very useful. The tests are easy to carry out and are versatile: we can employ them in a wide variety of situations. The tests presented in this and the next two sections are among the most useful statistical techniques of analyzing data. Quite often, in fact, a computer program designed merely to count the number of items falling in some categories automatically prints out a chi-square value. The user then has to consider the question: What statistical test is implied by the chi-square statistic in this particular situation? Among their other purposes, these sections should help you answer this question.

There is a common principle in all the chi-square tests we will discuss. The principle is summarized in the following steps:

Steps in a chi-square analysis:

1. We hypothesize about a population by stating the null and alternative hypotheses.
2. We compute frequencies of occurrence of certain events that we expect under the null hypothesis. These give us the *expected* counts of data points in different cells.
3. We note the *observed* counts of data points falling in the different cells.
4. We consider the difference between the observed and the expected. This difference leads us to a computed value of the chi-square statistic. The formula of the statistic is given as equation 14–38.
5. We compare the value of the statistic with critical points of the chi-square distribution and make a decision.

The analysis in this section and the next two involves tables of data counts. The chi-square statistic has the same form in the applications in all three sections. The statistic is equal to the *squared difference between the observed count and the expected count in each cell, divided by the expected count, summed over all cells.* If our data table has k cells, let the observed count in cell i be O_i and the expected count (expected under H_0) be E_i. The definition is for all cells $i = 1, 2, \ldots, k$.

The chi-square statistic:

$$X^2 = \sum_{i=1}^{k} \frac{(O_i - E_i)^2}{E_i} \qquad (14\text{--}38)$$

As the total sample size increases, for a given number of cells, k, the distribution of the statistic X^2 in equation 14–38 approaches the chi-square distribution. The degrees of freedom of the chi-square distribution are determined separately in each situation.

The reason for the chi-square limiting distribution is the central limit theorem. Remember the binomial experiment, where the number of *successes* (items falling in a particular category) is a random variable. The probability of a success is a fixed number, p. Recall from the beginning of Chapter 4 that as the number of trials, n, increases, the distribution of the number of binomial successes approaches a normal distribution. In the situations in this and the next two sections, the number of items falling in any of *several* categories is a random variable, and as the number of trials increases, the observed number in any cell, O_i, approaches a normal random variable. Remember also that the sum of several squared standard normal random variables has a chi-square distribution. The terms summed in equation 14–38 are standardized random variables that are squared. Each one of these variables approaches a normal random variable. Their sum, therefore, approaches a chi-square distribution as the sample size, n, gets large.

> A **goodness-of-fit test** is a statistical test of how well our data support an assumption about the distribution of a population or random variable of interest. The test determines how well an assumed distribution fits the data.

For example, we often make an assumption of a normal population. It may be of interest to test how well a normal distribution fits a given data set. Shortly we will see how to carry out a test of the normal distribution assumption.

We start our discussion of goodness-of-fit tests with a simpler test, and a very useful one—a test of goodness of fit in the case of a **multinomial distribution**. The multinomial distribution is a generalization of the binomial distribution to more than two possibilities (success vs. failure). In the multinomial situation, we have $k > 2$ possible categories for the data. A data point can fall into only one of the k categories, and the probability that the point will fall in category i (where $i = 1, 2, \ldots, k$) is constant and equal to p_i. The sum of all k probabilities p_i is 1.

Given five categories, for example, such as five age groups, a respondent can fall into only one of the (nonoverlapping) groups. If the probabilities that the respondent will fall into any of the k groups are given by the five parameters p_1, p_2, p_3, p_4, and p_5, then the multinomial distribution with these parameters and n, the number of people in a random sample, specifies the probability of any combination of cell counts. For example, if $n = 100$ people, the multinomial distribution gives us the probability that 10 people will fall in category 1, 15 in category 2, 12 in category 3, 50 in category 4, and the remaining 13 in category 5. The distribution gives us the probabilities of *all possible counts* of 100 people (or items) distributed into five cells.

When we have a situation such as this, we may use the multinomial distribution to test how well our data fit the assumption of k fixed probabilities $p_1, \ldots, p_k$ of falling into k cells. However, working with the multinomial distribution is difficult, and the chi-square distribution is a very good alternative when sample size considerations allow its use.

A Goodness-of-Fit Test for the Multinomial Distribution

The null and the alternative hypotheses for the multinomial distribution:

H_0: The probabilities of occurrence of events $E_1, \ldots E_k$ are given by the specified probabilities $p_1, p_2, \ldots, p_k$

H_1: The probabilities of the k events are not the p_i stated in the null hypothesis   (14–39)

The test statistic is as given in equation 14–38. For large enough n (a rule for how large is "enough" will be given shortly), the distribution of the statistic may be approximated by a chi-square distribution with $k - 1$ degrees of freedom. We demonstrate the test with Example (n).

Raymond Weil is about to come out with a new watch and wants to find out whether people have special preferences for the color of the watchband, or whether all four colors under consideration are equally preferred. A random sample of 80 prospective watch buyers is selected. Each person is shown the watch with four different band colors and asked to state his or her preference. The results—the *observed counts*—are given in Table 14–10.

EXAMPLE (n)

The null and alternative hypotheses, equation 14–39, take the following specific form:

SOLUTION

H_0: The four band colors are equally preferred; that is, the probabilities of choosing any of the four colors are equal: $p_1 = p_2 = p_3 = p_4 = 0.25$

H_1: Not all four colors are equally preferred (the probabilities of choosing the four colors are not all equal)

To compute the value of our test statistic (equation 14–38), we need to find the *expected* counts in all four cells (in this example, each cell corresponds to a color).

TABLE 14–10   Watchband Color Preferences

Tan	Brown	Maroon	Black	Total
12	40	8	20	80

Recall that for a binomial random variable, the mean—the *expected value*—is equal to the number of trials, n, times the probability of success in a single trial, p. Here, in the multinomial experiment, we have k cells, each with probability p_i, where $i = 1, 2, \ldots, k$. For each cell, we have a binomial experiment with probability p_i and number of trials n. The expected number in each cell is therefore equal to n times p_i.

The expected count in cell i:

$$E_i = np_i \qquad\qquad (14\text{--}40)$$

In this example, the number of trials is the number of people in the random sample: $n = 80$. Under the null hypothesis, the expected number of people who will choose color i is equal to $E_i = np_i$. Furthermore, since all the probabilities in this case are equal to 0.25, we have the following:

$$E_1 = E_2 = E_3 = E_4 = (80)(0.25) = 20$$

When the null hypothesis is true, and the probability that any person will choose any one of the four colors is equal to 0.25, we may not observe 20 people in every cell. In fact, observing *exactly* 20 people in each of the four cells is an event with a small probability. However, the number of people we observe in each cell should not be too far from the expected number, 20. Just how far is "too far" is determined by the chi-square distribution. We use the expected counts and the observed counts in computing the value of the chi-square test statistic. From equation 14–38, we get the following:

$$X^2 = \sum_{i=1}^{k} \frac{(O_i - E_i)^2}{E_i} = \frac{(12 - 20)^2}{20} + \frac{(40 - 20)^2}{20} + \frac{(8 - 20)^2}{20} + \frac{(20 - 20)^2}{20}$$

$$= \frac{64}{20} + \frac{400}{20} + \frac{144}{20} + 0 = 3.2 + 20 + 7.2 + 0 = 30.4$$

We now conduct the test by comparing the computed value of our statistic, $X^2 = 30.4$, with critical points of the chi-square distribution with $k - 1 = 4 - 1 = 3$ degrees of freedom. From Appendix C, Table 4, we find that the critical point for a chi-square random variable with 3 degrees of freedom and right-hand-tail area $\alpha = 0.01$ is 11.3. (*Note that all the chi-square tests in this chapter are carried out only on the right-hand tail of the distribution.*) Since the computed value is much greater than the critical point at $\alpha = 0.01$, we conclude that there is evidence to reject the null hypothesis that all four colors are equally likely to be chosen. Some colors are probably preferable to others. Our p-value is very small.

The test for multinomial probabilities does not always entail equal probabilities, as was the case in our example. The probabilities may very well be different. All we need to do is specify the probabilities in the null hypothesis and then use the hypothesized probabilities in computing the expected cell counts (using equation 14–40). Then we use the expected counts along with the observed counts in computing the value of the chi-square statistic.

Under what conditions can we assume that, under the null hypothesis, the distribution of the test statistic in equation 14–38 is well-approximated by a chi-square distribution? This important question has no exact answer. As the sample size, n, increases, the approximation gets better and better. On the other hand, there is also a dependence on the cell, k. If the expected number of counts in some cells is too small, the approximation may not be valid. We will give a good rule of thumb that specifies the minimum expected count in each cell needed for the chi-square approximation to be valid. The rule is conservative in the sense that other rules have been given that allow smaller expected counts under certain conditions. If we follow the rule given here, we will usually be safe using the chi-square distribution.

> The chi-square distribution may be used as long as the expected count in every cell is at least 5.0.

Suppose that while conducting an analysis, we find that for one or more cells, the expected number of items is less than 5. We may still continue our analysis if we can *combine cells* so that the expected number has a total of at least 5. For example, suppose that our null hypothesis is that the distribution of ages in a certain population is as follows: 20% are between the ages of 0 to 15, 10% are in the age group of 16 to 25, 10% are in the age group of 26 to 35, 20% are in the age group of 36 to 45, 30% are in the age group of 45 to 60, and 10% are 61 or over. If we number the age group cells consecutively from 1 to 6, then the null hypothesis is: H_0: $p_1 = 0.20$, $p_2 = 0.10$, $p_3 = 0.10$, $p_4 = 0.20$, $p_5 = 0.30$, $p_6 = 0.10$.

Now suppose that we gather a random sample of $n = 40$ people from this population and use this group to test for goodness of fit of the multinomial assumption in the null hypothesis. What are our expected cell counts? In the 0–15 cell, the expected number of people is $np_1 = (40)(0.20) = 8$, which is fine. But for the next age group, 16–25, we find that the expected number is $np_2 = (40)(0.10) = 4$, which is less than 5. If we want to continue the analysis, we may combine age groups that have small expected counts with other age groups. We may combine the 16–25 age group with the 26–35 age group, which also has a low expected count. Or we may combine the 16–25 group with the 0–15 group, and the 26–35 group with the 36–45 group—whichever makes more sense in terms of the interpretation of the analysis. We also need to combine the 61-and-over group with the 45–60 age group. Once we make sure that all expected counts are at least 5, we may use the chi-square distribution. Instead of combining groups, we may choose to increase the sample size.

We will now discuss the determination of the number of degrees of freedom. Figure 14–7 shows the table of counts for Example (n). Note that there are four cells, corresponding to the four colors in the analysis, *and* there is a fifth outside cell, which we have so far ignored. This is the cell containing the *total count* of the four cells—the total sample size, $n = 80$. The total count acts similarly to the way $\bar{x}$ does when we use it in computing the sample standard deviation. *The total count reduces the number of degrees of freedom by 1.* Why? Because knowing the total allows us not to know directly *any one* of the cell counts. If we knew, for example, the counts in the cells corresponding to tan, black, and maroon but did not know the

FIGURE 14–7   Demonstration of a Loss of 1 Degree of Freedom

There are four cells *inside* the table. The *total* (outside the table) makes any one cell redundant (here we cross out one cell), reducing the number of degrees of freedom by 1.

| 1 | 2 | 3 | 4 | Total |

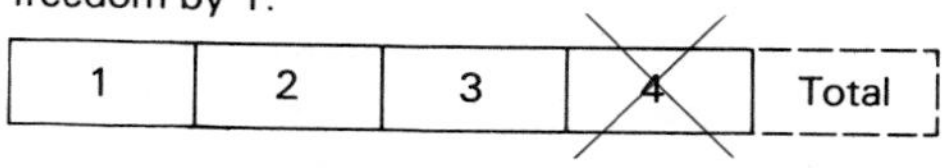

count in the brown cell, we could still figure out the count for this cell by subtracting the sum of the three cell counts we do know from the total of 80. Thus, when we know the total, one degree of freedom is lost from the category cells. Out of four cells in this example, *any three* are free to move. Out of k cells, since we know their total, only $k - 1$ are free to move: df $= k - 1$.

As a general rule, we know that the number of degrees of freedom is equal to the number of items (here items are cells inside the table) less the number of restrictions. The total count acts as a restriction on the cell counts and so one cell is lost. Any time you have such a table, cross out any one column (as shown in Figure 14–7) and count the remaining number of cells. This will give you the number of degrees of freedom. Later, when we show tables with several rows and several columns, this principle will still hold. We will cross out any one row (due to our knowledge of the column totals) and any one column (due to our knowledge of row totals) and the remaining number of cells inside the table will give us the number of degrees of freedom of the chi-square statistic.

We now note another fact that will be important in our next example.

> If we have to use the data for estimating the parameters of the probability distribution stated in the null hypothesis, then for every parameter we estimate from the data, we lose an additional degree of freedom.

The chi-square goodness-of-fit test may be applied to testing any hypothesis about the distribution of a population or a random variable. As mentioned earlier, the test may be applied in particular to testing how well an assumption of a normal distribution is supported by a given data set. The standard normal distribution table, Appendix C, Table 2, gives us the probability that a standard normal random variable will be between any two given values. Through the transformation $X = \mu + \sigma Z$, we may then find boundaries in terms of the original variable, X, for any given probabilities of occurrence. These boundaries can be used in forming cells with known probabilities and, hence, known expected counts for a given sample size. This analysis, however, assumes that we know μ and σ, the mean and the standard deviation of the population or variable in question.

When μ and σ are *not* known, and the null and alternative hypotheses are stated as:

H_0: The population (or random variable) has a normal distribution

H_1: The population (or random variable) is not normally distributed   (14–41)

there is no mention in the statement of the hypotheses of what the mean or standard may be, and we need to estimate them directly from our data. When this happens, we lose a degree of freedom for each parameter estimated from the data (unless we use another data set for the estimation). We estimate μ by $\overline{X}$ and σ by S, as usual. The degrees of freedom of the chi-square statistic are df $= k - 2 - 1 = k - 3$ (instead of $k - 1$, as before). We will now demonstrate the test for a normal distribution with Example (o).

EXAMPLE (o)   An analyst working for a department store chain wants to test the assumption that the amount of money spent by a customer in any store is approximately normally distributed. It is important to test this assumption because the analyst plans to conduct an analysis of variance to determine whether average sales per customer are equal at several stores in the same chain (as we recall, the normal-distribution assumption is required for

ANOVA). A random sample of 100 shoppers at one of the department stores reveals that the average spending is $\bar{x} = \$125$ and the standard deviation is $s = \$40$. These are sample estimates of the *population* mean and standard deviation. (The breakdown of the data into cells is included in the solution.)

We begin by defining boundaries with known probabilities for the standard normal random variable, Z. We know that the probability that the value of Z will be between -1 and $+1$ is about 0.68. We also know that the probability that Z will be between -2 and $+2$ is about 0.95, and we know other such probabilities. We may use Appendix C, Table 2 to find more exact probabilities. Let us use the table and define several nonoverlapping intervals for Z with known probabilities. We will form intervals of about the same probability. Figure 14–8 shows one possible partition of the standard normal distribution to intervals and their probabilities, obtained from Table 2. You may use any partition you desire.

The partition was obtained as follows. We know that the area under the curve between 0 and 1 is 0.3413 (from Table 2). Looking for an area of about half that size, 0.1700, we find that the appropriate point is $z = 0.44$. A similar relationship exists on the negative side of the numbers line. Thus, using just the values 0.44 and 1 and their negatives, we get a complete partition of the Z scale into the six intervals: $-\infty$ to -1, with associated probability of 0.1587; -1 to -0.44, with probability 0.1713; -0.44 to 0, with probability 0.1700; 0 to 0.44, with probability 0.1700; 0.44 to 1, with probability 0.1713; and, finally, 1 to ∞, with probability 0.1587. Breakdowns into other intervals may also be used.

Now we transform the Z scale values into interval boundaries for the original problem. Taking $\bar{x}$ and s as if they were the mean and the standard deviation of the *population*, we use the transformation $X = \mu + \sigma Z$, with $\bar{x} = 125$ and $s = 40$ substituted for the unknown parameters. The Z value boundaries we just obtained are substituted into the transformation, giving us the following cell boundaries:

$$x_1 = 125 + (-1)(40) = 85$$
$$x_2 = 125 + (-0.44)(40) = 107.4$$
$$x_3 = 125 + (0)(40) = 125$$
$$x_4 = 125 + (0.44)(40) = 142.6$$
$$x_5 = 125 + (1)(40) = 165$$

The cells and their expected counts are given in Table 14–11. Cell boundaries are broken at the nearest cent. Recall that the expected count in each cell is equal to the cell probability times the sample size: $E_i = np_i$. In this example, the p_i are obtained from

FIGURE 14–8 Intervals and Their Standard Normal Probabilities

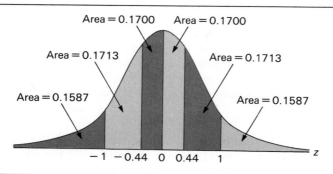

TABLE 14–11   Cells and Their Expected Counts

0–$84.99	$85.00–$107.39	$107.4–$124.99	$125–$142.59	$142.6–$164.99	$165 and above	
15.87	17.13	17.00	17.00	17.13	15.87	Total = 100

TABLE 14–12   Observed Cell Counts

0–$84.99	$85.00–$107.39	$107.4–$124.99	$125–$142.59	$142.6–$164.99	$165 and above	
14	20	16	19	16	15	Total = 100

TABLE 14–13   Computing the Value of the Chi-Square Statistic for Example (o)

Cell	i	O_i	E_i	$(O_i - E_i)$	$(O_i - E_i)^2$	$(O_i - E_i)^2/E_i$
0–$84.99	1	14	15.87	−1.87	3.50	0.22
$85.00–$107.39	2	20	17.13	2.87	8.24	0.48
$107.40–$124.99	3	16	17.00	−1.00	1.00	0.06
$125.00–$142.59	4	19	17.00	2.00	4.00	0.24
$142.60–$164.99	5	16	17.13	−1.13	1.28	0.07
$165.00 and above	6	15	15.87	−0.87	0.76	0.05
						1.12

the normal table and are, in order, 0.1587, 0.1713, 0.1700, 0.1700, 0.1713, and 0.1587. Multiplying these probabilities by $n = 100$ gives us the expected counts. (Note that the theoretical boundaries of $-\infty$ and $+\infty$ have no practical meaning; therefore, the lowest bound is replaced by 0 and the highest bound by *and above*.) Note that all expected cell counts are above 5, and, therefore, the chi-square distribution is an adequate approximation to the distribution of the test statistic X^2 in equation 14–38 under the null hypothesis.

Table 14–12 gives the observed counts of the sales amounts falling in each of the cells. The table was obtained by the analyst by looking at each data point in the sample and classifying the amount into one of the chosen categories.

To facilitate the computation of the chi-square statistic, we arrange the observed and expected cell counts in a single table and show the computations necessary for obtaining the value of the test statistic. This has been done in Table 14–13. The sum of all the entries in the last column in the table is the value of the chi-square statistic. The appropriate distribution has $k - 3 = 6 - 3 = 3$ degrees of freedom. We now consult the chi-square table, Appendix C, Table 4, and we find that the computed statistic value $X^2 = 1.12$ falls in the acceptance region for any level of α in the table. There is therefore no statistical evidence that the population is not normally distributed.

The chi-square goodness-of-fit test may be applied to testing the fit of any hypothesized distribution. In general, we use an appropriate probability table for obtaining probabilities of intervals of values. The intervals define our data cells. Using the sample size, we then find the expected count in each cell. We compare the expected counts with the observed counts and compute the value of the chi-square test statistic.

The chi-square statistic is useful in other areas as well. In the next section, we will describe the use of the chi-square statistic in the analysis of *contingency tables*—an analysis of whether two principles of classification are contingent on one another or independent of each other. The following section extends the contingency table analysis to a test of homogeneity of several populations.

14–60. An article in the *Columbia Journal of World Business* reports on foreign ownership of U.S. assets.[6] A table in the article suggests that the national breakdown (in percentages) of European firms owning U.S. investments is as follows: United Kingdom, 40.2%; Germany, 9.1%; Netherlands, 19.5%; and other nations, 31.2%. A random sample of 212 European firms that bought American assets in 1992 revealed the following breakdown (in number of firms): 91 firms from the United Kingdom, 22 from the Netherlands, 10 from Germany, and 89 from other countries. Do you believe that the percentages of all European firms who invested in the United States in 1992 are the same as reported in the journal? Explain.

14–61. A company is considering five possible names for its new product. Before choosing a name, the firm decides to test whether all five names are equally appealing. A random sample of 100 people is chosen, and each person is asked to state his or her choice of the best name among the five possibilities. The numbers of people who chose each one of the names are as follows.

Name:	A	B	C	D	E
Number of choices:	4	12	34	40	10

Conduct the test.

14–62. A study reports an analysis of 35 key product categories. At the time of the study, 72.9% of the products sold were of a national brand, 23% were private-label, and 4.1% were generic. Suppose that you want to test whether these percentages are still valid for the market today. You collect a random sample of 1,000 products in the 35 product categories studied, and you find the following: 610 products are of a national brand, 290 are private-label, and 100 are generic. Conduct the test, and state your conclusions.

14–63. An industry analyst wants to test the null hypothesis that the market share figures for firms in the industry are as follows.

Firm:	A	B	C	D	E	Other
Share:	1%	9%	14%	26%	0.5%	49.5%

The analysis is to be based on a classification of 100 randomly chosen products.

a. Can you use the chi-square statistic to conduct this test?

b. If you cannot use the chi-square statistic, can you make changes that will allow you to use it?

c. Suppose that the 100 products in the sample are classified as follows: firm A, 0; firm B, 0; firm C, 26; firm D, 15; firm E, 2; other, 57. Conduct the analysis (if you can), and state your conclusion.

14–64. Returns on an investment have been known to be normally distributed with mean 11% (annualized rate) and standard deviation 2%. A brokerage firm wants to test the null hy-

Answers

14–60.

$X^2 = 21.79$
Significant.

14–62.

$X^2 = 119.97$
Very significant.

14–64.

$X^2 = 0.586$
Not significant.

[6] B. Majumdar, "Foreign Ownership of America: A Matter of Concern," *Columbia Journal of World Business* (Fall 1990), p. 17.

pothesis that this statement is true and collects the following returns data (assumed a random sample): 8%, 9%, 9.5%, 9.5%, 8.6%, 13%, 14.5%, 12%, 12.4%, 19%, 9%, 10%, 10%, 11.7%, 15%, 10.1%, 12.7%, 17%, 8%, 9.9%, 11%, 12.5%, 12.8%, 10.6%, 8.8%, 9.4%, 10%, 12.3%, 12.9%, 7%. Conduct the analysis and state your conclusion.

14–65. Using the data provided in problem 14–64, test the null hypothesis that returns on the investment are normally distributed, but with *unknown* mean and standard deviation. That is, test only for the validity of the normal-distribution assumption. How is this test different from the one in problem 14–64?

14–10 Contingency Table Analysis— A Chi-Square Test for Independence

Recall the important concept of *independence* of events, which we discussed in Chapter 2. Two events, A and B, are independent if the probability of their joint occurrence is equal to the product of their marginal (i.e., separate) probabilities. This was given as equation 2–13.

$$\text{A and B are independent if } P(A \cap B) = P(A)P(B)$$

In this chapter, we will develop a statistical test that will help us determine whether or not two classification criteria, such as sex and job performance, are independent of each other. The technique will make use of **contingency tables:** tables with cells corresponding to cross-classifications of attributes or events. In marketing research studies, such tables are referred to as *cross-tabs*. The basis for our analysis will be the property of independent events just stated.

The contingency tables may have several rows and several columns. The rows correspond to levels of one classification category, and the columns correspond to another. We will denote the number of rows by r, and the number of columns by c. The total sample size is n, as before. The count of the elements in cell (i, j), that is, the cell in row i and column j (where $i = 1, 2, \ldots, r$ and $j = 1, 2, \ldots, c$) is denoted by O_{ij}. The total count for row i is R_i, and the total count for column j is C_j. The general form of a contingency table is shown in Figure 14–9. The table is demonstrated for $r = 5$ and $c = 6$. Note that n is also the sum of all r row totals and the sum of all c column totals.

Let us now state the null and alternative hypotheses.

Hypothesis test for independence:

H_0: The two classification variables are independent of each other

H_1: The two classification variables are not independent   (14–42)

FIGURE 14–9   The Layout of a Contingency Table

Second Classification Category	First Classification Category						Total
	1	2	3	4	5	6	
1	O_{11}	O_{12}	O_{13}	O_{14}	O_{15}	O_{16}	R_1
2	O_{21}	O_{22}	O_{23}	O_{24}	O_{25}	O_{26}	R_2
3	O_{31}	O_{32}	O_{33}	O_{34}	O_{35}	O_{36}	R_3
4	O_{41}	O_{42}	O_{43}	O_{44}	O_{45}	O_{46}	R_4
5	O_{51}	O_{52}	O_{53}	O_{54}	O_{55}	O_{56}	R_5
Total	C_1	C_2	C_3	C_4	C_5	C_6	n

The principle of our analysis is the same as that used in the previous section. The chi-square test statistic for this set of hypotheses is the one we used before, given in equation 14–38. The only difference is that the summation extends over all cells in the table: the c columns and the r rows (in the previous application, goodness-of-fit tests, we only had one row). We will rewrite the statistic to make it clearer:

Chi-square test statistic for independence:

$$X^2 = \sum_{i=1}^{r}\sum_{j=1}^{c} \frac{(O_{ij} - E_{ij})^2}{E_{ij}} \qquad (14\text{–}43)$$

The double summation in equation 14–43 means summation over all rows and all columns.

The degrees of freedom of the chi-square statistic are:

$$df = (r - 1)(c - 1)$$

Now all we need to do is find the expected cell counts, E_{ij}. Here is where we use the assumption that the two classification variables are independent. Remember that the philosophy of hypothesis testing is to assume that H_0 is true and to use this assumption in determining the distribution of the test statistic. Then we try to show that the result is unlikely under H_0 and thus reject the null hypothesis.

Assuming that the two classification variables are independent, let us derive the expected counts in all cells. Look at a particular cell in row i and column j. Recall from equation 14–40 that the expected number of items in a cell is equal to the sample size times the probability of the occurrence of the event signified by the particular cell. In the context of an $r \times c$ contingency table, the probability associated with cell (i, j) is the probability of occurrence of event i *and* event j. Thus, the expected count in cell (i, j) is: $E_{ij} = nP(i \cap j)$. If we assume independence of the two classification variables, then event i and event j are independent events, and, by the law of independence of events, $P(i \cap j) = P(i)P(j)$.

From the row totals, we can estimate the probability of event i as R_i/n. Similarly, we estimate the probability of event j by C_j/n. Substituting these estimates of the marginal probabilities, we get the following expression for the expected count in cell (i, j): $E_{ij} = n(R_i/n)(C_j/n) = R_iC_j/n$.

The expected count in cell (i, j):

$$E_{ij} = \frac{R_i C_j}{n} \qquad (14\text{–}44)$$

Equation 14–44 allows us to compute the expected cell counts. These, along with the observed cell counts, are used in computing the value of the chi-square statistic, which leads us to a decision about the null hypothesis of independence.

We will now illustrate the analysis with two examples. The first example is an illustration of an analysis of the simplest contingency table: a 2×2 table. In such tables, the two rows correspond to the occurrence versus nonoccurrence of one event, and the two columns correspond to the occurrence or nonoccurrence of another event.

EXAMPLE (p)

An article in *Business Week* reports profits and losses of firms by industry.[7] A random sample of 100 firms is selected, and for each firm in the sample, we record whether the company made money or lost money, and whether or not the firm is a service company. The data are summarized in the 2×2 contingency table, Table 14–14. Using the information in the table, determine whether or not you believe that the two events "the company made a profit this year" and "the company is in the service industry" are independent.

SOLUTION

Table 14–14 is the table of observed counts. We now use its marginal totals, R_1, R_2, C_1, and C_2, as well as the sample size, n, in creating a table of expected counts. Using equation 14–44,

$$E_{11} = R_1 C_1/n = (60)(48)/100 = 28.8$$
$$E_{12} = R_1 C_2/n = (60)(52)/100 = 31.2$$
$$E_{21} = R_2 C_1/n = (40)(48)/100 = 19.2$$
$$E_{22} = R_2 C_2/n = (40)(52)/100 = 20.8$$

We now arrange these values in a table of expected counts, Table 14–15. Using the values shown in the table, we now compute the chi-square test statistic of equation 14–43:

$$X^2 = \frac{(42 - 28.8)^2}{28.8} + \frac{(18 - 31.2)^2}{31.2} + \frac{(6 - 19.2)^2}{19.2} + \frac{(34 - 20.8)^2}{20.8} = 29.09$$

To conduct the test, we compare the computed value of the statistic with critical points of the chi-square distribution with $(r - 1)(c - 1) = (2 - 1)(2 - 1) = 1$ degree of freedom. From Appendix C, Table 4, we find that the critical point for $\alpha = 0.01$ is 6.63, and, since our computed value of the X^2 statistic is much greater than the critical point, we reject the null hypothesis and conclude that the two qualities, profit/loss and industry type, are probably not independent.

TABLE 14–14   Contingency Table of Profit/Loss versus Industry Type

	Industry Type		
	Service	Nonservice	Total
Profit	42	18	60
Loss	6	34	40
Total	48	52	100

TABLE 14–15   Expected Counts (with the Observed Counts Shown in Parentheses) for Example (p)

	Service	Nonservice
Profit	28.8 (42)	31.2 (18)
Loss	19.2 (6)	20.8 (34)

[7] *Business Week* (August 17, 1987).

In the analysis of 2×2 contingency tables, our chi-square statistic has *1 degree of freedom*. In such cases, it is often recommended that the value of the statistic be "corrected" so that its discrete distribution will be better approximated by the *continuous* chi-square distribution. The correction is called the **Yates correction** and entails subtracting the number $1/2$ from the absolute value of the difference between the observed and the expected counts before squaring them, as required by equation 14–43. The Yates-corrected form of the statistic is as follows.

$$\text{Yates-corrected } X^2 = \sum_{\text{all cells}}\sum \frac{(|O_{ij} - E_{ij}| - 0.5)^2}{E_{ij}} \qquad (14\text{–}45)$$

For our example, the corrected value of the chi-square statistic is found as:

Yates-corrected X^2

$$= \frac{(13.2 - 0.5)^2}{28.8} + \frac{(13.2 - 0.5)^2}{31.2} + \frac{(13.2 - 0.5)^2}{19.2} + \frac{(13.2 - 0.5)^2}{20.8}$$
$$= 26.92$$

As we see, the correction yields a smaller computed value. This value still leads to a strong rejection of the null hypothesis of independence. In many cases, the correction will not significantly change the results of the analysis. We will not emphasize the correction in the applications in this book.

As the number of cells in the contingency table becomes large, the use of a computer in the analysis becomes indispensable. As mentioned earlier, many computer programs automatically give a computed value of the chi-square statistic with any cross-tabulation of data. In section 14–12, we give a description of the use of the MINITAB package in chi-square analysis (as well as in many nonparametric tests). The following example is analyzed using the MINITAB program for chi-square analysis.

EXAMPLE (q)

To better identify its target market, Alfa Romeo conducted a market research study. A random sample of 669 respondents was chosen, each of whom was asked to select one of four qualities that he or she believed described him or her best as a driver. The four possible self-descriptive qualities were *defensive, aggressive, enjoying,* and *prestigious.* Each respondent was then asked to choose one of three Alfa Romeo models as his or her choice of the most suitable car. The three models were Alfasud, Giulia, and Spider. The purpose of the study was to determine whether a relationship existed between a driver's self-image and his or her choice of an Alfa Romeo model. The response data are given in Table 14–16.

SOLUTION

For each cell, we need to multiply the row total by the column total and divide by the sample size, $n = 669$, to get the expected cell count. Then we use the expected counts and the observed counts in computing the value of the chi-square statistic given by equa-

TABLE 14–16   The Observed Counts: Alfa Romeo Study

Alfa Romeo Model	Self-Image				Total
	Defensive	Aggressive	Enjoying	Prestigious	
Alfasud	22	21	34	56	133
Giulia	39	45	42	68	194
Spider	77	89	96	80	342
Total	138	155	172	204	669

FIGURE 14–10   MINITAB Output for Example (q)

```
MTB > CHISQUARE ANALYSIS ON C1, C2, C3, C4

Expected counts are printed below observed counts


             C1       C2       C3       C4     Total
    1        22       21       34       56       133
           27.4     30.8     34.2     40.6

    2        39       45       42       68       194
           40.0     44.9     49.9     59.2

    3        77       89       96       80       342
           70.5     79.2     87.9    104.3

 Total      138      155      172      204       669

 ChiSq =   1.08 +   3.13 +   0.00 +   5.88 +
           0.03 +   0.00 +   1.24 +   1.32 +
           0.59 +   1.20 +   0.74 +   5.66 = 20.87
 df = 6
```

tion 14–43. These operations are performed by the MINITAB program. The computer output is shown in Figure 14–10.

Follow the computations indicated in the figure, and make sure that you understand how each number is obtained. The degrees of freedom are $(r - 1)(c - 1) = (3 - 1)(4 - 1) = 6$. The computed value of the statistic is $X^2 = 20.87$. Comparing this value with critical points of the chi-square distribution with 6 degrees of freedom, we reject the null hypothesis with a p-value less than 0.01. We conclude that there is evidence of a dependence between a driver's self-image and his or her preference for one of the Alfa Romeo models.

Degrees of Freedom

Why are the degrees of freedom for the test statistic based on a contingency table with r rows and c columns equal to $(r - 1)(c - 1)$? Recall from our earlier discussion that the degrees of freedom are obtained by subtracting the number of restrictions from the number of cells under consideration. In the goodness-of-fit tests, we

FIGURE 14–11 Degrees of Freedom = Number of Cells Left in the Table after One Row and One Column Have Been Crossed Out

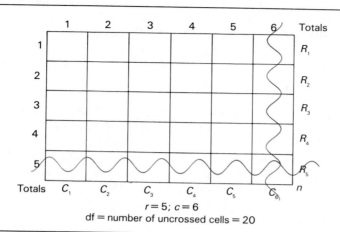

$$r = 5; c = 6$$
df = number of uncrossed cells = 20

had k cells and one restriction—the total count. In the context of a two-dimensional contingency table, we have *one row restriction for each row* (the row total, R_i) *and one column restriction for each column* (the column total, C_j). This leaves us with $(r - 1)(c - 1)$ cells that are "free to move."

This idea is demonstrated in Figure 14–11. The example in the figure parallels the setup in Figure 14–9, demonstrating a situation with $r = 5$ rows and $c = 6$ columns. Since many people prefer a visual explanation (and aid to memory) rather than an algebraic one, you may find the idea shown in Figure 14–11 useful in determining the number of degrees of freedom in the analysis of any contingency table. The idea is to cross out any one row and any one column in the table, then count the remaining cells. The number of cells left intact is the number of degrees of freedom of the statistic.

Measuring the Degree of Dependence

In tests of dependence between two classification variables, as well as in tests for goodness of fit, it is often possible to reject the null hypothesis as long as our sample is large enough. That is, as the sample size increases, the probability of rejecting the null hypothesis increases, even if the *degree of dependence* between the two variables is very small. For this reason, the chi-square statistic is often used not merely in testing for a dependence between the two variables, but also as a measure of the degree of dependence. The computed value of the statistic is not enough, however, because its meaning depends on the number of degrees of freedom. For example, a computed value $X^2 = 20$ is not significant (at $\alpha = 0.10$) when the degrees of freedom are 16, but such a value is highly significant when the associated degrees of freedom are 2.

Several measures of dependence, all making use of the value of the X^2 statistic and some adjustment for degrees of freedom, have been suggested. Two of the better known measures are Cramer's contingency coefficient and Pearson's contingency coefficient. These are described in advanced texts.

Further Analysis

As in the case of analysis of variance, once we reject the overall null hypothesis, we may be interested in answering questions about *subsets* of our variable levels. In Example (q), interest may center on whether the dependence that was found between the chosen Alfa Romeo model and the driver's self-image level exists if we consider *only* the two self-image levels *defensive* versus *aggressive,* leaving out the other two levels. It is possible to partition the chi-square variable into components corresponding to parts of the original contingency table.

Stringent rules apply, however, for carrying out such analysis. First, the parts of the table targeted for special scrutiny must be identified *before* we have looked at the results of the overall test. Second, we may partition along rows *or* columns, but not both; and in the subset tables chosen for analysis, no two cells may be in a different column and a different row more than once. The degrees of freedom associated with each subset table are determined as usual. The overall significance level of the set of tests is given by $\alpha = [(1 - \alpha_1)(1 - \alpha_2)]$ when two tests are carried out—one at level α_1 and the other at level α_2.[8]

Higher-Order Contingency Tables

The contingency tables we have discussed are two-dimensional tables, which compare two classification variables. It is possible to extend the idea to more than two variables. Although drawing a three-dimensional table on paper is difficult, the analysis itself is not complicated. In the case of three variables, we are testing for the mutual independence of the three variables from one another. The test statistic is an extension of the formula for X^2 given in equation 14–43, with summation extending over all cells in the three-dimensional table. Figuring the number of degrees of freedom is more complicated. Such tests are discussed in advanced texts.

PROBLEMS

Answer

14–66.

$X^2 = 12.193$
Significant.

14–66. An article in *Business Week* reports that smaller firms seem to be hiring more than large ones as the economy picks up its pace.[9] The table below gives numbers of employees hired and those laid off, out of a random sample of 1,032, broken down by firm size. Is there evidence that hiring practices are dependent on firm size?

	Small Firm	Medium-Sized Firm	Large Firm	Total
Number hired	210	290	325	825
Number laid off	32	95	80	207
Total	242	385	405	1,032

14–67. An analyst in the soft drink industry wants to conduct a statistical test to determine whether there is a relationship between a person's preference for one of the four brands: Coke, Pepsi, 7Up, and Dr. Pepper; and whether the person drinks regular or diet drinks. A random sample of 330 people is selected, and their responses are as follows.

---

[8] Some significant dependencies between rows and columns may be washed out in the larger analysis.

[9] "Small Business Expects to Be Hiring Before the Big Guys," *Business Week* (April 22, 1991), p. 20.

Soft Drink Preference				
	Coke	**Pepsi**	**7Up**	**Dr Pepper**	**Total**
Diet	55	32	47	21	155
Regular	60	43	35	37	175
Total	115	75	82	58	330

Conduct the test, and state your conclusion.

14–68. *Fortune* reports on the competition among car rental companies.[10] The table below gives the number of cars, out of a random sample of 100 rental cars, belonging to each of the listed firms in 1979 and in 1990. Is there evidence of a change in the market shares of the car rental firms?

	Hertz	**Avis**	**National**	**Budget**	**Other**	**Total**
1979	39	26	18	14	3	100
1990	29	25	16	19	11	100

14–69. Northwest Airlines and Eastern Airlines compete with each other on many flight routes in the eastern part of the country. In early July 1987, both airlines began offering off-peak flights at reduced fares. The fares on both airlines, for the same flight routes, were virtually identical. The marketing manager at Northwest's headquarters in Minneapolis wanted to find out whether passengers' preferences for one of the two airlines were independent of whether the flight was peak or off-peak. If, on the other hand, a dependence were found, then the decision would be to concentrate on the type of flight (peak or off-peak) that tended to favor Northwest. A random sample of 100 passengers who had flown on one of the two airlines in the region of interest was obtained from travel industry computer files. For each flier, the airline and the type of flight were recorded. The data are as follows. Conduct the test, and state your conclusion. What is your recommendation to the marketing manager?

	Northwest	**Eastern**
Peak	25	32
Off-peak	30	13

14–70. A study was conducted to determine whether a relationship existed between certain shareholder characteristics and the level of risk associated with the shareholders' investment portfolios. As part of the analysis, portfolio risk (measured by the portfolio beta) was divided into three categories: low risk, medium risk, and high risk; and the portfolios were cross-tabulated according to the three risk levels and seven family-income levels. The results of the analysis, conducted using a random sample of 180 investors, are shown in the following contingency table. Test for the existence of a relationship between income and investment risk taking. [Be careful here! (Why?)]

Income Level ($)	**Portfolio Risk Level**			
	Low	**Medium**	**High**	**Total**
0 to 19,999	5	4	1	10
20,000 to 24,999	6	3	0	9
25,000 to 29,999	22	30	11	63
30,000 to 34,999	11	20	20	51
35,000 to 39,999	8	10	4	22
40,000 to 44,999	2	0	10	12
45,000 and above	1	1	11	13
Total	55	68	57	180

---

[10] "Rental Firms Race for Market Share," *Fortune* (April 22, 1991), p. 17.

14–71. When new paperback novels are promoted at bookstores, a display is often arranged with copies of the same book with differently colored covers. A publishing house wanted to find out whether there is a dependence between the place where the book is sold and the color of its cover. For one of its latest novels, the publisher sent displays and a supply of copies of the novel to large bookstores in five major cities. The resulting sales of the novel for each city-color combination are as follows. Numbers are in thousands of copies sold over a three-month period.

	Color				
City	**Red**	**Blue**	**Green**	**Yellow**	**Total**
New York	21	27	40	15	103
Washington	14	18	28	8	68
Boston	11	13	21	7	52
Chicago	3	33	30	9	75
Los Angeles	30	11	34	10	85
Total	79	102	153	49	383

a. Assume that the data are random samples for each particular color-city combination and that the inference may apply to all novels. Conduct the overall test for independence of color and location.

b. Before the analysis, the publisher stated a special interest in the issue of whether there is any dependence between the red versus blue preference and the two cities Chicago versus Los Angeles. Conduct the test. Explain.

14–11 A Chi-Square Test for Equality among Proportions

Contingency tables and the chi-square statistic are also useful in another kind of analysis. Sometimes we are interested in whether the proportion of some characteristic is equal in several populations. An insurance company, for example, may be interested in finding out whether the proportion of people who submit claims for automobile accidents is about the same for the three age groups: 25 and under, over 25 and under 50, and 50 and over. In a sense, the question of whether the proportions are equal is a question of whether the three age populations are *homogeneous* with respect to accident claims. Therefore, tests of equality of proportions across several populations are also called tests of *homogeneity*.

The analysis is carried out in exactly the same way as in the previous application. We arrange the data in cells corresponding to population-characteristic combinations, and for each cell, we compute the expected count based on its row and column totals. The chi-square statistic is computed exactly as before. Two things are different in this analysis. First, we identify our populations of interest *before* the analysis and sample directly from these populations. Contrast this with the previous application, where we sampled from *one* population and then cross-classified according to two criteria. Second, because we identify populations and sample from them directly, the sizes of the samples from the different populations of interest are *fixed*. This is called *a chi-square analysis with fixed marginal totals*. This fact, however, does not affect the analysis.

We will demonstrate the analysis with the insurance company example just mentioned. The null and alternative hypotheses are:

H_0: The proportion of claims is the same for all three age groups (i.e., the age groups are homogeneous with respect to claim proportions)

H_1: The proportion of claims is not the
same across age groups (the age groups
are not homogeneous) $\qquad$ (14–46)

Suppose that random samples, selected from company records for the three age categories, are classified according to *claim* versus *no claim* and counted. The data are presented in Table 14–17.

To carry out the test, we first calculate the expected counts in all the cells. The expected cell counts are obtained, as before, by using equation 14–44. The expected count in each cell is equal to the row total times the column total, divided by the total sample size (the pooled sample size from all populations). The reason for the formula in this new context is that if the proportion of items in the class of interest (here, the proportion of people who submit a claim) is equal across all populations, as stated in the null hypothesis, then *pooling* this proportion across populations gives us the expected proportion in the cells for the class. Thus, the expected proportion in the claim class is estimated by the total in the claim class divided by the grand total, or $R_1/n = 135/300 = 0.45$. If we multiply this pooled proportion by the total number in the sample from the population of interest (say, the sample of people 25 and under), this should give us the *expected* count in the cell *claim—25 and under*. We get: $E_{11} = C_1(R_1/n) = (C_1 R_1)/n$. This is exactly as prescribed by equation 14–44 in the test for independence. Here we get: $E_{11} = (100)(0.45) = 45$. This is the expected count under the null hypothesis. We compute the expected counts for all other cells in the table in a similar manner. Table 14–18 is the table of expected counts in this example.

Note that since we have used equal sample sizes (100 from each age population), the expected count is equal in all cells corresponding to the same class. The proportions are expected to be equal under the null hypothesis. Since these proportions are multiplied by the same sample size, the counts are also equal.

We are now ready to compute the value of the chi-square test statistic. From equation 14–43, we get:

$$X^2 = \sum_{\text{all cells}} \frac{(O-E)^2}{E} = \frac{(40-45)^2}{45} + \frac{(35-45)^2}{45} + \frac{(60-45)^2}{45}$$
$$+ \frac{(60-55)^2}{55} + \frac{(65-55)^2}{55} + \frac{(40-55)^2}{55} = 14.14$$

TABLE 14–17 Data for the Insurance Company Example

	Age Group			
	25 and under	Over 25 and under 50	50 and over	Total
Claim	40	35	60	135
No Claim	60	65	40	165
Total	100	100	100	300

There are fixed sample sizes for all three populations.

TABLE 14–18 The Expected Counts for the Insurance Company Example

	25 and under	Over 25 and under 50	50 and over	Total
Claim	45	45	45	135
No Claim	55	55	55	165
Total	100	100	100	300

The degrees of freedom are obtained as usual. We have three rows and two columns, so the degrees of freedom are $(3 - 1)(2 - 1) = 2$. Alternatively, cross out any one row and any one column in Table 14–17 or 14–18 (ignoring the *Total* row and column). This leaves you with two cells, giving df $= 2$.

Comparing the computed value of the statistic with critical points of the chi-square distribution with 2 degrees of freedom, we find that the null hypothesis may be rejected and that the p-value is less than 0.01. (Check this, using Appendix C, Table 4.) We conclude that the proportions of people who submit claims to the insurance company are not the same across the age groups studied.

In general, when we compare c populations (or r populations, if they are arranged as the rows of the table rather than the columns), the hypotheses in equation 14–46 may be written as:

$$H_0: p_1 = p_2 = \cdots = p_c$$
$$H_1: \text{Not all } p_i, \, i = 1, \ldots, c, \text{ are equal} \qquad (14\text{--}47)$$

where p_i $(i = 1, \ldots, c)$ is the proportion in population i of the characteristic of interest. The test of equation 14–47 is a generalization to c populations of the test of equality of two population proportions discussed in Chapter 8. In fact, when $c = 2$, the test is identical to the simple test for equality of two population proportions. In our present context, the two-population test for proportion may be carried out using a 2×2 contingency table. The results of such a test would be identical to the results of a test using the method of Chapter 8 (a Z test).

The test presented in this section may also be applied to *several* proportions within each population. That is, instead of just testing for the proportion of *claim* versus *no claim,* we could be testing a more general hypothesis about the proportions of *several* different types of claims: no claim, claim under \$1,000, claim of \$1,000 to \$5,000, and claim over \$5,000. Here the null hypothesis would be that the proportion of each type of claim is equal across all populations. (This does not mean that the proportions of all types of claims are equal within a population.) The alternative hypothesis would be that not all proportions are equal across all populations under study. The analysis is done using an $r \times c$ contingency table (instead of the $2 \times c$ table we used in the preceding example). The test statistic is the same, and the degrees of freedom are as before: $(r - 1)(c - 1)$. We will now discuss another extension of the test presented in this section.

The Median Test

The hypotheses for the median test:

$$H_0: \text{The } c \text{ populations have the same median}$$
$$H_1: \text{Not all } c \text{ populations have the same median} \qquad (14\text{--}48)$$

Using the c random samples from the populations of interest, we determine the grand median, that is, the median of all our data points regardless of which population they are from. Then we divide each sample into two sets. One set contains all points that are greater than the grand median, and the second set contains all points in the sample that are less than or equal to the grand median. We construct a $2 \times c$ contingency table in which the cells in the top row contain the counts of all points above the median for all c samples. The second row contains cells with the counts of the data points in each sample that are less than or equal to the grand median. Then we conduct the usual chi-square analysis of the contingency table. If we reject H_0, then we may conclude that there is evidence that not all c population medians are equal. Further analysis by a breakdown of the original table to smaller parts is also possible. Remember, however, that the level of significance of all further tests is questionable and subject to restrictions if it is to retain its meaning. We now demonstrate the median test with Example (r).

An economist wants to test the null hypothesis that the median family income across three rural areas is approximately equal. Random samples of family incomes in the three regions (in thousands of dollars per year) are given in Table 14–19.

EXAMPLE (r)

For simplicity, we chose an equal sample size of 10 in each population. This is not necessary; the sample sizes may be different. There is a total of 30 observations, and the median is therefore the average of the 15th and the 16th observations. Since the 15th observation (counting from smallest to largest) is 31, and the 16th is 32, the grand median is 31.5. Table 14–20 shows the counts of the sample points in each sample that are above the grand median and those that are less than or equal to the grand median. The table also shows the expected cell counts (in parentheses). Note that all expected counts are 5—the minimum required for the chi-square test. We now compute the value of the chi-square statistic.

SOLUTION

$$X^2 = \frac{1}{5}[(4 - 5)^2 + (5 - 5)^2 + (6 - 5)^2 + (6 - 5)^2 + (5 - 5)^2 + (4 - 5)^2]$$

$$= \frac{4}{5} = 0.8$$

TABLE 14–19 Family Incomes ($1,000s per Year)

Region A	Region B	Region C
22	31	28
29	37	42
36	26	21
40	25	47
35	20	18
50	43	23
38	27	51
25	41	16
62	57	30
16	32	48

TABLE 14–20 Observed and Expected Counts for Example (r)

	Region A	Region B	Region C	Total
Above grand median	4	5	6	15
	(5)	(5)	(5)	
Less than or equal to grand median	6	5	4	15
	(5)	(5)	(5)	
Total	10	10	10	30

Comparing this value with critical points of the chi-square distribution with 2 degrees of freedom, we conclude that there is no evidence to reject the null hypothesis. The p-value is greater than 0.20.

Note that the median test is a weak test. Other tests could have resulted in the rejection of the null hypothesis (try them). We presented the test as an illustration of the wide variety of possible uses of the chi-square statistic. Other uses may be found in advanced books. We note that if the test had led to rejection, then other tests would probably have done so, too. Sometimes this test is easier to carry out and may lead to a quick answer (when we reject the null hypothesis).

PROBLEMS

Answers

14–72.

$X^2 = 109.56$
Very significant.

14–74.

$X^2 = 16.15$
Significant.

14–76.

$X^2 = 24.36$
Significant.

14–72. An advertiser runs a commercial on national television and wants to determine whether the proportion of people exposed to the commercial is equal throughout the country. A random sample of 100 people is selected at each of five locations, and the number of people in each location who have seen the commercial at least once during the week is recorded. The numbers are as follows: location A, 32 people; location B, 59 people; location C, 78 people; location D, 40 people; and location E, 10 people. Do you believe that the proportion of people exposed to the commercial is equal across the five locations?

14–73. An accountant wants to test the hypothesis that the proportion of incorrect transactions at four client accounts is about the same. A random sample of 80 transactions of one client reveals that 21 are incorrect; for the second client, the sample proportion is 25 out of 100; for the third client, the proportion is 30 out of 90 sampled; and for the fourth, 40 are incorrect out of a sample of 110. Conduct the test at $\alpha = 0.05$.

14–74. An article in the *Financial Times* raises the question of whether experienced fund managers are performing about the same as less experienced ones in the new bull market.[11] A sample of 128 fund managers with at least eight years of experience revealed that 54 of them beat the market, 43 of them did about as well as the market, and 31 did worse than the market. In a sample of 95 less experienced fund managers, 65 were found to beat the market, 21 did about the same as the market, and 9 did poorer than the market. Test the null hypothesis that experienced fund managers do as well as inexperienced ones versus the alternative that differences in performance exist between the two groups.

14–75. A quality-control engineer wants to test the null hypothesis that the proportion of defective components in three large shipments is approximately equal. A random sample of 100 components is selected from each shipment. The first sample reveals 25 defective items, the second has 15, and the third has 8. Conduct the test at $\alpha = 0.05$.

14–76. As markets become more and more international, many firms invest in research aimed at determining the maximum possible extent of sales in foreign markets. An American manufacturer of coffee makers wants to find out whether the company's market share and the market shares of two main competitors are about the same in three European countries to which all three companies export their products. The results of a market survey are summarized in the following table. The data are random samples of 150 consumers in each country. Conduct the test of equality of population proportions across the three countries.

---

[11] "Old Hands Get Set for a Comeback," *Financial Times* (August 8, 1987).

| | **Country** | | | |
	France	England	Spain	**Total**
Company	55	38	24	117
First competitor	28	30	21	79
Second competitor	20	18	31	69
Other	47	64	74	185
Total	150	150	150	450

14–77. New production methods stressing teamwork have recently been instituted at car manufacturing plants in Detroit. Three teamwork production methods are to be compared to see if they are equally effective. Since large deviations often occur in the numbers produced daily, it is desired to test for equality of medians (rather than means). Samples of daily production volume for the three methods are as follows. Assume that these are random samples from the populations of daily production volume. Use the median test to help determine whether the three methods are equally effective.

Method A: 5, 7, 19, 8, 10, 16, 14, 9, 22, 4, 7, 8, 15, 18, 7
Method B: 8, 12, 15, 28, 5, 14, 19, 16, 23, 19, 25, 17, 20
Method C: 14, 28, 13, 10, 8, 29, 30, 26, 17, 13, 10, 31, 27, 20

14–12 Using the Computer

While many nonparametric tests are easy to carry out by hand, other tests, such as the chi-square tests, are more tedious, and a computer is very useful in carrying out the computations. Companies involved with research often use their own in-house computer programs for chi-square analysis (cross-tabs). The computer programs produce high-quality reports with values of the chi-square statistic and its associated p-value for every possible comparison of data attributes.

All commonly used computer packages have nonparametric capabilities. In this section, we will present examples of the use of MINITAB in nonparametric analysis. The MINITAB commands are very simple. Usually, all that is needed is to enter the data and specify the name of the nonparametric test required. We start with the runs test.

Figure 14–12 shows the results of a runs test carried out on a data set where the aim is to find whether runs of numbers above and below 30 indicate that the series of numbers is a random one. As seen in the output, the p-value is 0.0128. We may conclude (at levels of α greater than 0.0128) that the sequence probably does not represent a random process.

We now demonstrate the use of the Mann-Whitney test. Two sales techniques are tested, and the null hypothesis is that both techniques are equally effective. The alternative hypothesis is that the first method is more effective than the second (a right-hand-tailed test). The MINITAB command is:

```
MANN-WHITNEY (ALTERNATIVE=1) C1, C2
```

The data are in C1 and C2. The specification ALTERNATIVE=1 tells the program that the test is a right-hand-tailed test for the location parameter (mean, median) of the population from which the C1 data came, minus that of the population from which the data in C2 came. ALTERNATIVE=−1 would indicate a left-hand-tailed test, and the default (that is, no ALTERNATIVE statement) indicates a two-tailed test.

A list of the data, 10 points from each method (the data are *not* paired), as well as the output, are given in Figure 14–13. The words ETA1 and ETA2 are the

FIGURE 14–12 A MINITAB-Computed Runs Test

```
C1
    21   13   14   53   44   37   49   11    3    6   16   36   55
    44   33   21   18   19   17   61   18   22   21   23   24   38
    34   35   31   28   26   44   16   33   32   27   21   12   34
    21   22   14   16   33   38   45   66   71   29   28   37   45

MTB > RUNS ABOVE AND BELOW 30,  C1

    C1

    K =    30. 0000


THE OBSERVED NO. OF RUNS =   18
THE EXPECTED NO. OF RUNS =   26.8462
24 OBSERVATIONS ABOVE K    28 BELOW
          THE TEST IS SIGNIFICANT AT   0.0128
```

FIGURE 14–13 MINITAB-Computed Mann-Whitney Test

```
MTB > PRINT C1, C2
  ROW   C1    C2
    1   35    26
    2   38    29
    3   44    18
    4   59    30
    5   27    28
    6   36    22
    7   37    21
    8   40    29
    9   38    19
   10   28    31
MTB > MANN-WHITNEY (ALTERNATIVE=1) C1, C2
Mann-Whitney Confidence Interval and Test

C1          N =  10     MEDIAN =       37.500
C2          N =  10     MEDIAN =       27.000
POINT ESTIMATE FOR ETA1-ETA2 IS      10.9992
95.5  PCT C.I. FOR ETA1-ETA2 IS (     7.0,      18.0)
W =    145.5
TEST OF ETA1 = ETA2 VS. ETA1 G.T. ETA2 IS SIGNIFICANT AT   0.0012
```

MINITAB terms for the population parameters (mean or median) of populations 1 and 2, respectively. Note that a confidence interval for the difference between the parameters of the two populations is also provided. Throughout this chapter we have discussed only tests and not confidence intervals. We have done so because the most common applications of nonparametric methods are in the area of hypothesis testing. The computation of confidence intervals is also possible (recall the relationship between hypothesis tests and confidence intervals). The construction of confidence intervals, however, is often more difficult than in the parametric case and we have not emphasized them here.

FIGURE 14–14 MINITAB-Computed Wilcoxon Signed-Rank Test

```
ROW      C1      C2

  1     143     165
  2     124     170
  3     179     231
  4     166     154
  5     133     200
  6     167     169
  7     134     149
  8     104     111
  9     190     202
 10     121      98
 11     144     152

MTB > SUBTRACT C1 FROM C2, PUT IN C3
MTB > WTEST C3

TEST OF MEDIAN = 0.000000000 VERSUS MEDIAN N.E.  0.000000000

                 N FOR     WILCOXON            ESTIMATED
           N     TEST     STATISTIC  P-VALUE     MEDIAN
C3        11      11        53.5      0.075      14.75
```

We see that the test leads to rejection of the null hypothesis and the p-value is very small (0.0012). We conclude that there is statistical evidence that method 1 is more effective than method 2.

We now demonstrate the MINITAB solution to a problem using the Wilcoxon signed-rank test. Paired data are available constituting a random sample of ratings of two managers by 10 randomly chosen employees. Figure 14–14 shows the listing of the data entered into columns C1 and C2 and the output of the analysis. We need to ask the computer to subtract one column from the other; we are testing the null hypothesis that the median difference is zero versus the two-tailed alternative that it is not zero. As in the case of the Mann-Whitney test, an ALTERNATIVE= statement tells the computer to conduct a one-tailed test. For a two-tailed test, we leave out this command. The main command to perform the Wilcoxon signed-rank test is: WTEST data in C3. (We put the difference between the columns C1 and C2 into C3 prior to this command.) The results of the test indicate that the p-value is 0.075, so we accept the null hypothesis that the median difference is zero (assuming we want to reject at levels of α less than or equal to 0.05).

For the Kruskal-Wallis test, data are entered into two columns, C1 and C2. In C1 we put the data elements; in C2 we put indicators: 1, 2, 3, and so on, denoting the population to which any given data point belongs. In the example shown in Figure 14–15, there are three samples to be analyzed, as evidenced by the indicators 1, 2, and 3 in column C2. The data have presumably been entered into the two columns prior to the analysis. The data represent random samples of mpg ratings for three types of high-performance V-8 engines. The null hypothesis is that the three engines have about the same mpg rating, and the alternative is that they do not.

The computed value of the Kruskal-Wallis statistic is $H = 14.52$ (14.72 when adjusted for ties). We compare this value with critical points of the chi-square distribution with $k - 1 = 3 - 1 = 2$ degrees of freedom. We conclude that there is evidence that the three engines do not have equal mpg ratings. The p-value is 0.001.

Computing rank correlation is simple in MINITAB. First, we replace values by their ranks. This is done by the commands:

```
RANK C1, put into C3
RANK C2, put into C4
```

FIGURE 14–15   MINITAB-Computed Kruskal-Wallis Test

```
MTB > PRINT C1, C2
  ROW    C1    C2

    1    12     1
    2    14     1
    3    15     1
    4    12     1
    5    15     1
    6    17     1
    7    15     1
    8    17     1
    9    16     1
   10    18     2
   11    16     2
   12    17     2
   13    19     2
   14    18     2
   15    21     2
   16    20     2
   17    11     3
   18    12     3
   19    10     3
   20    12     3
   21    14     3

MTB > KRUSKAL WALLIS FOR DATA IN C1 SUBSCRIPTS IN C2

  LEVEL      NOBS      MEDIAN   AVE. RANK    Z VALUE
      1         9       15.00        9.9      -0.71
      2         7       18.00       17.5       3.39
      3         5       12.00        3.9      -2.93
OVERALL        21                   11.0

H = 14.52            df = 2           P = 0.001
H = 14.72            df = 2           P = 0.001 (ADJ. FOR TIES)
```

(The RANK command may also be used in conjunction with other nonparametric methods requiring analysis of ranks rather than raw data.) Afterwards, we simply write the command:

```
CORRELATION between C3 and C4
```

Recall that the Spearman coefficient is the correlation between the ranks of the observations. The result of the analysis is therefore the Spearman statistic, r_s.

An analysis of the rank correlation between two variables is shown in Figure 14–16. The result is $r_s = -0.236$. With $n = 10$ observations, we find from Appendix C, Table 11 that the critical point for r_s at $\alpha = 0.05$ is ± 0.564. Since $-0.236 > -0.564$, we accept the null hypothesis. The data do not present evidence of a nonzero rank correlation.

The use of MINITAB in chi-square analysis was demonstrated in section 14–10 (the output was shown in Figure 14–10). There we used the MINITAB command CHISQUARE analysis on C1, C2, . . . , Ck. The ith entry in column C_j was the *count* in cell (i, j). The same analysis could be done using the command TABLE and the subcommand CHISQUARE.

FIGURE 14-16   MINITAB-Computed Rank Correlation

```
MTB > PRINT C1, C2
 ROW    C1    C2
   1    86    54
   2    89    59
   3    97    66
   4    54    20
   5    66    70
   6    49    57
   7    40    81
   8    69    90
   9    22    60
  10    39    95
MTB > RANK C1, PUT IN C3
MTB > RANK C2, PUT IN C4
MTB > CORRELATION BETWEEN C3 AND C4
Correlation of C3 and C4 = -0.236

MTB > STOP
```

FIGURE 14-17   MINITAB-Produced Contingency Table Analysis

```
MTB > CONTINGENCY TABLE ANALYSIS ON C1, C2

Expected counts are printed below observed counts

Rows C1  Columns C2
              1        2        3      Total

    3         4        0        0        4
            1.6      1.2      1.1

    4        10        2        9       21
            8.6      6.4      6.0

    5         6       13        5       24
            9.8      7.3      6.9

Total        20       15       14       49

ChiSq =   3.43 +   1.22 +   1.14 +
          0.24 +   3.05 +   1.50 +
          1.47 +   4.35 +   0.50 = 16.91
df = 4
3 cells with expected counts less than 5.0
```

The MINITAB package automatically checks for the validity of the chi-square distribution assumption. The package will warn us every time it finds a cell with expected count less than 5.0; the output will list all such occurrences. The program uses a less stringent rule for the validity of the chi-square approximation—a rule due to Cochran that states that the approximation may be valid as long as none of the expected cell counts are less than 1.0 and no more than 20% of the expected counts are less than 5.0. This is demonstrated in Figure 14–17. The program will also list all cells with expected counts less than 1.0, and, if it finds such cells, will state that the chi-square approximation is probably not valid.

14–13   Summary and Review of Terms

This chapter was devoted to **nonparametric tests** (summarized in Table 14–21). Interpreted loosely, the term refers to statistical tests in situations where stringent assumptions about the populations of interest may not be warranted. Most notably, the very common assumption of a normal distribution—required for the parametric t and F tests—is not necessary for the application of nonparametric methods. The methods often use less of the information in the data and thus tend to be less powerful than parametric methods, when the assumptions of the parametric methods are met. The nonparametric methods include methods for handling categorical data, and here the analysis entails use of a limiting chi-square distribution for our test statistic. **Chi-square analysis** is often discussed separately from nonparametric methods, although the analysis is indeed "nonparametric," as it usually involves no specific reference to population *parameters* such as μ and σ. The other nonparametric methods (ones that require no assumptions about the distribution of the population) are often called *distribution-free* methods.

Besides chi-square analyses of **goodness of fit, independence,** and tests for **equality of proportions,** the methods we discussed included many methods based on **ranks.** These included a **rank correlation coefficient** due to Spearman; a test analogous to the parametric paired-sample t test—the **Wilcoxon signed-rank test;** a ranks-based ANOVA—the **Kruskal-Wallis test;** and a method for investigating two independent samples analogous to the parametric two-sample t test, called the **Mann-Whitney test.** We also discussed a test for randomness—the **runs test;** a paired-difference test called the **sign test,** which uses less information than the Wilcoxon signed-rank test; and several other methods.

TABLE 14–21   Summary of Nonparametric Tests

Situation	Nonparametric Test(s)	Corresponding Parametric Test
Single-sample test for location	Sign test Wilcoxon test (more powerful)	Single-sample t test
Goodness of fit	Chi-square test	
Randomness	Runs test	
Paired test for changes	McNemar test	
Paired differences test	Sign test Wilcoxon test (more powerful)	Paired-data t test
Test for difference of two independent samples	Wald-Wolfowitz (weaker) Mann-Whitney (more powerful) Median test (weaker)	Two-sample t test
Test for difference of more than two independent samples	Kruskal-Wallis test Median test (weaker)	ANOVA
Test for difference of more than two samples, blocked	Friedman test	Randomized block-design ANOVA
Test for trend in single series	Cox and Stuart test	Time series tests
Correlation	Cox and Stuart test Spearman's statistic and test Chi-square test for independence	Pearson's product-moment
Equality of several population proportions	Chi-square test	

14–78. At the conclusion of the first episode of "Infiltrator," a message flashed onto the screen asking viewers to call one of two "800" phone numbers if they liked the program and to call the other number if they did not. The program's sponsor wanted to know if the program was likely to be equally popular in several regions of the country. Since at different regions different "800" numbers were used, counting the yes and no votes for the separate regions was relatively easy. Assume that the following results were presented to the sponsor, producer, and network executives the next day. What would be your recommendation as a hired statistician?

	Region				
	Northeast	**Midwest**	**Southwest**	**South**	**West**
Yes	13,278	7,091	2,310	3,106	15,442
No	871	308	119	565	101

14–79. In July 1987, six consecutive incidents occurred involving Delta Airlines. The incidents consisted of near misses and similar safety violations. Such events, though relatively rare, do occur from time to time in the airline industry. The problem was that all six *consecutive* events involved the same airline. Delta, which until the occurrence of the incidents enjoyed one of the finest reputations for safety in the air, suddenly found itself under investigation by the FAA. The big question facing the airline, the FAA, and the country as a whole (the case received much attention in the media) was: Is it possible that Delta was involved in all six consecutive incidents purely by chance? Since, as mentioned, such incidents do occur from time to time, and are recorded, it is possible to go back to FAA records and identify the six incidents that occurred preceding the reported Delta incidents. Suppose that all six previous incidents did not involve Delta Airlines.

a. What test would you suggest for this problem?

b. Conduct the test. What is your conclusion?

c. What is the effect of the assumption that all six previous incidents did not involve Delta on the results of your test? Discuss.

14–80. *Forbes* reports on the increasing success of Hollywood movies in Europe.[12] In Germany, 12 out of 70 theaters selected at random showed American-made movies; in France the number was 10 out of 65; and in Italy, 15 out of 100 movie theaters showed Hollywood movies. Test for equality of the proportion of theaters showing American-made movies in these three countries.

14–81. Jordan Furniture Store advertises on the radio. Before hiring the announcer for its ad, the store tested four different announcers. A random sample of 10 people was asked to rank the voice quality of the four announcers from best (1) to worst (4). The data are as follows.

Announcer			
A	**B**	**C**	**D**
1	3	2	4
3	4	2	1
4	2	1	3
3	1	2	4
1	2	4	3
3	1	2	4
3	2	4	1
2	3	4	1
3	4	1	2
4	2	3	1

a. What is the appropriate test in this situation?

b. Conduct the test. Are the voices of all four announcers equally well liked?

Answers

14–78.

$X^2 = 1626$
Extremely significant.

14–80.

$X^2 = 0.15$
n.s.

---

[12] J. Marcom, "Dream Factory to the World," *Forbes* (April 29, 1991), p. 98.

14–82.

$X^2 = 58.3$
Significant.

14–82. A recent article in *The Wall Street Journal* discusses the perceived demand in Europe for the new Eurotunnel under the English Channel, linking England and France.[13] As part of the analysis leading to the decision to build the tunnel, a test was proposed for determining which nation, if any, would benefit most from the tunnel. A random sample of 437 English tourists revealed that 321 of these tourists would use the tunnel for crossing the channel, while the rest would prefer to fly or use a ferry. A random sample of 248 Dutch tourists traveling to England revealed that 111 of them would use the tunnel, while the rest would use other means of transportation to England. A random sample of 502 French tourists traveling to England revealed that 289 of them would prefer to use the tunnel over other means of transportation to England. The three random samples were independent of each other. Do you believe that an equal proportion of tourists from the three countries studied would use the Eurotunnel once it is completed? Explain.

14–83. In the study described in problem 14–82, it was hypothesized that the average French tourist spends eight days in England. A random sample of nine French tourists indicated that they each spent more than eight days in England. Based on these data, conduct a quick test of the hypothesis, and state your conclusion. What assumptions are you making in carrying out this test?

14–84.

Wilcoxon signed-rank

14–84. For problem 14–83, suppose that you recorded the actual number of days spent in England by each of the nine French tourists. What other test could you then use for the null hypothesis that the average stay is eight days? Discuss the relative advantages and disadvantages of the two statistical tests.

14–85. A random sample of 12 consumers ranked four brands of hair conditioner, labeled A, B, C, and D. The results follow.

A	B	C	D
2	1	3	4
1	4	3	2
2	1	4	3
1	3	4	2
1	2	4	3
1	3	2	4
1	3	4	2
2	1	4	3
3	1	4	2
1	3	2	4
2	3	1	4
1	2	4	3

Are there differences in the appeal of the four brands? Explain.

14–86. Discuss the different measures of correlation, their use, the required assumptions, and their limitations.

14–87. In April 1988, representatives of the OPEC nations met for the first time with representatives of non-OPEC oil-producing nations in an effort to raise the price of oil. An oil industry analyst in the United States wanted to find out whether or not this meeting brought about changes in people's attitudes toward OPEC. A random sample of 120 people revealed that before the meeting, 85 of the people in the sample were resentful of OPEC, while the remaining 35 people had no opinion. After the April meeting, two people who originally expressed resentment toward the organization said that they now had no opinion. In addition, 29 people who originally stated that they had no opinion stated after the April meeting that they now felt resentment toward the organization. Analyze these data, and state your conclusion.

---

[13] "Strong U.K. Demand Seen for Eurotunnel," *The Wall Street Journal* (November 13, 1987).

14–88. The following data are annual corporate revenues for the years 1976 to 1988 (data are in millions of dollars): 4.5, 4.1, 5.0, 4.4, 4.3, 3.9, 5.6, 5.8, 4.9, 6.0, 5.4, 4.8, 5.5. Is there evidence of a trend in the series of annual revenues? Explain.

14–89. The following data are daily price quotations of two stocks.

Stock A:	12.50,	12.75,	12.50,	13.00,	13.25,	13.00,	13.50,	14.25,	14.00
Stock B:	35.25,	36.00,	37.25,	37.25,	36.50,	36.50,	36.00,	36.00,	36.25

Is there a correlation between the two stocks? Explain.

14–90. The Hyatt Gold Passport® is a card designed to allow frequent guests at Hyatt hotels to enjoy privileges similar to the ones enjoyed by frequent air travelers. When the program was initiated, a random sample of 15 Hyatt Gold Passport members was asked to rate the program on a scale of 0 to 100 and also to rate (on the same scale) an airline frequent-flier card that all of them had. The results are as follows.

Hyatt card:	98,	99,	87,	56,	79,	89,	86,	90,	95,	99,	76,	88,	90,	95
Airline card:	84,	62,	90,	77,	80,	98,	65,	97,	58,	74,	80,	90,	85,	70

Is the Hyatt Gold Passport better liked than the airline frequent-flier card by holders of both cards? Explain.

14–91. Two telecommunication systems are to be compared. A random sample of 14 users of one system independently rate the system on a scale of 0 to 100. An independent random sample of 12 users of the other system rate their system on the same scale. The data are as follows. System A: 65, 67, 83, 39, 45, 20, 95, 64, 99, 98, 76, 78, 82, 90. System B: 45, 57, 76, 54, 60, 72, 34, 50, 63, 39, 44, 70. Based on these data, are the two telecommunication systems equally liked? Explain.

14–92. Refer to problem 14–91. Suppose that a third telecommunication system is to be compared with the two systems of problem 14–91. Ratings by a random sample of 13 users of the third system, on the same scale of 0 to 100, are as follows: 56, 58, 64, 59, 48, 49, 60, 75, 33, 72, 48, 51, 37. Are all three systems equally liked? Explain.

14–93. Explain why you used the statistical methods you chose in problems 14–91 and 14–92. Compare your methods with the corresponding parametric methods, and discuss the relative advantages and disadvantages of the different methods.

14–94. What is the distinction between *distribution-free* methods and *nonparametric* methods?

14–95. The following data are salaries, in thousands of dollars per year, of a random sample of employees in a certain industry.

28.5,	29,	29.7,	31,	28,	32.5,	32.6,	33,	31.8,	37.4,	24.6,
38.1,	28.8,	30.1,	32.5,	34.4,	26.7,	28.1,	39.2,	40.3,	33.5,	33.8,
38.2,	23.0,	22.9,	29.9,	31.2,	33.0,	31.7,	37,	35,	32.1,	37,
29.9,	22,	23.8,	27,	35,	37.5,	40.1,	22.1,	26.3,	30.0,	40.1

Do you believe that salaries in this industry are normally distributed? Explain.

14–96. In a chi-square analysis, the expected count in one of the cells is 2.1. Can you conduct the analysis? If not, what can be done?

Answers

14–88.

p-value $= 0.031$
increase trend

14–90.

p-value $= 0.209$

14–92.

$H = 7.43$
p-value $= 0.024$

14–96.

combine cells

CASE 14

THE NINE NATIONS OF NORTH AMERICA

I in a fascinating article in the *Journal of Marketing* (April 1986), "The Nine Nations of North America and the Value Basis of Geographic Segmentation," Professor Lynn Kahle explores the possible marketing implications of Joel Garreau's idea of the nine nations.

Garreau traveled extensively throughout North America, studying people, customs, traditions, and ways of life. This research led Garreau to the conclusion that state boundaries or the census bureau's division of the United States into regions are not very indicative of the cultural and social boundaries that really exist on the continent. Instead, Garreau suggested in his best-selling book *The Nine Nations of North America* (New York: Avon, 1981) that the real boundaries divide the entire North American continent into nine separate, homogeneous regions, which he called "nations." Each nation, according to Garreau, is inhabited by people who share the same traditions, values, hopes, and world outlook and are different from the people of the other nations. The nine nations cross national boundaries of the United States, Canada, and the Caribbean. Garreau named his nations very descriptively, as follows: New England, Quebec, The Foundry, Dixie, The Islands, Empty Quarter, Breadbasket, MexAmerica, and Ectopia. Exhibit 1 shows the boundaries of these nations.

Geographic segmentation is a very important concept in marketing. Thus, Garreau's novel idea promised potential gains in marketing. Professor Kahle suggested

EXHIBIT 1

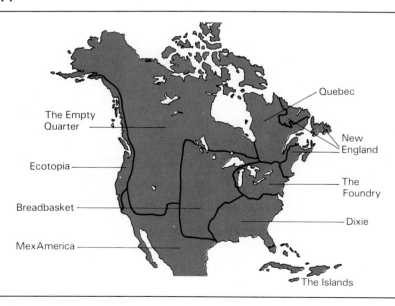

EXHIBIT 2 Distribution of Values across Census Regions of the United States

Values	New England	Middle Atlantic	South Atlantic	East South Central	East North Central	West North Central	West South Central	Mountain	Pacific	N
Self-respect	22.6%	18.6%	23.1%	23.4%	20.2%	16.7%	23.8%	29.2%	19.8%	471
Security	21.2	18.0	18.3	26.9	22.1	20.6	23.8	18.1	18.5	461
Warm relationships with others	13.9	16.8	15.7	11.4	16.0	21.6	14.9	15.3	17.6	362
Sense of accomplishment	13.9	13.0	10.7	9.6	11.4	14.7	6.8	8.3	12.1	254
Self-fulfillment	8.0	10.0	10.1	7.8	9.3	8.3	5.5	6.9	15.0	214
Being well respected	8.8	7.7	9.8	12.0	10.0	7.4	14.0	4.2	3.5	196
Sense of belonging	7.3	8.8	9.2	7.8	7.4	6.9	6.4	13.9	7.0	177
Fun—enjoyment—excitement	4.4	7.1	3.3	1.2	3.5	3.9	4.7	4.2	6.4	100
Total	100.0	100.0	100.0	100.0	100.0	100.0	100.0	100.0	100.0	2,235
N	137	339	338	167	430	204	235	72	313	

EXHIBIT 3 Distribution of Values across the Nine Nations

Values	New England	The Foundry	Dixie	The Islands	Bread-basket	Mex-America	Empty Quarter	Eco-topia	N
Self-respect	22.5%	20.5%	22.5%	25.0%	17.9%	22.7%	35.3%	18.0%	471
Security	21.7	19.6	23.3	15.6	20.2	17.3	17.6	19.6	461
Warm relationships with others	14.2	16.7	13.8	9.4	20.5	18.0	5.9	18.5	362
Sense of accomplishment	14.2	11.7	10.0	9.4	12.4	11.3	8.8	12.2	254
Self-fulfillment	9.2	9.9	8.4	3.1	7.5	16.0	5.9	12.7	214
Being well respected	8.3	8.7	11.0	15.6	10.1	2.7	2.9	4.2	196
Sense of belonging	5.0	8.4	7.5	12.5	7.8	6.7	17.6	7.9	177
Fun—enjoyment—excitement	5.0	4.5	3.5	9.4	3.6	5.3	5.9	6.9	100
Total	100.0	100.0	100.0	100.0	100.0	100.0	100.0	100.0	2,235
N	120	750	653	32	307	150	34	189	

a statistical test of whether or not Garreau's division of the country (without the nation of Quebec, which lies entirely outside the United States) could be found valid with respect to marketing-related values. Such a division could then replace currently used geographic segmentation methods.

Two currently used segmentation schemes studied by Kahle were the quadrants and the census bureau regions. Kahle used a random sample of 2,235 people across the country and collected responses pertaining to eight self-assessed personal attributes: self-respect, security, warm relationships with others, sense of accomplishment, self-fulfillment, being well respected, sense of belonging, and fun-enjoyment-excitement. Kahle showed that these self-assessment attributes were directly related to marketing variables. The attributes determine, for example, the magazines a person is likely to read and the television programs he or she is likely to watch.

Kahle's results, using the nine nations division (without Quebec), the quadrants division, and the census division of the country, are presented in Exhibits 2 through 4. These tables are reprinted by permission from Kahle (1986). (Values reported in the exhibits are percentages.)

Carefully analyze the results presented in the exhibits. Is the nine nations segmentation a useful alternative to the quadrants or the census bureau divisions of the country? Explain.

EXHIBIT 4 Distribution of Values across Quadrants of the United States

Values	East	Midwest	South	West	N
Self-respect	19.7%	19.1%	23.4%	21.6%	471
Security	18.9	21.6	22.0	18.4	461
Warm relationships with others	16.0	17.8	14.5	17.1	362
Sense of accomplishment	13.2	12.5	9.2	11.4	254
Self-fulfillment	9.5	9.0	8.1	13.5	214
Being well respected	8.0	9.1	11.6	3.6	196
Sense of belonging	8.4	7.3	8.0	8.3	177
Fun—enjoyment—excitement	6.3	3.3	3.4	6.2	100
Total	100.0	100.0	100.0	100.0	2,235
N	476	634	740	385	

15

BAYESIAN STATISTICS AND DECISION ANALYSIS

INTRODUCTION

O nly two hours after the polls closed in the Spanish general election on October 28, 1982, the statistician José M. Bernardo made a stunning prediction about the outcome of the election. Bernardo accurately forecast that the Spanish Socialist party would win a landslide victory and be returned to power for the first time since the Spanish Civil War in the late 1930s. Furthermore, Bernardo predicted (to within a fraction of 1%) the number of votes that each political party would receive. He also estimated the number of seats (to within a single seat) that each party would hold in the new parliament. Bernardo made these amazing predictions hours before any other attempt was made to forecast the outcome of the election.

How did Bernardo do it? Instead of using the usual statistical approach to inference, an approach based solely on random sampling and usually referred to as the *classical* approach, Bernardo chose to follow a different statistical philosophy. He chose to use the **Bayesian** approach.[1]

The Bayesian approach allows the statistician to use *prior information* about a particular problem in addition to sampling. This approach is called *Bayesian* because the mathematical link between the probabilities associated with data results and the probabilities associated with the prior information is Bayes' theorem, which was introduced in Chapter 2. The theorem allows us to combine the prior information with the results of our sampling, giving us *posterior* (postsampling) information. A schematic comparison of the classical and the Bayesian approaches is shown in Figure 15–1.

In the case of the Spanish election, Bernardo used the results of the 1979 general election as his prior information. He used the 1979 results in identifying polling stations that seemed to be representative of the political behavior of Spanish voters as a whole and sampled from these stations. The undecided votes were distributed using information about proportions obtained in the 1979 election. The use of prior information led to more precise statistical conclusions than would have been obtained by pure random sampling. It is the *mixing* (using Bayes' theorem) of the prior information with sampling information from the 1982 election that gave Bernardo his fantastically accurate conclusions.

The Bayesian philosophy does not necessarily lead to conclusions that are more accurate than those obtained by using the classical approach. If the prior information we have is accurate, then using it in conjunction with sample information leads to more accurate results than would be obtained without prior information. If, on the other hand, the prior information is inaccurate, then using it in conjunction with our sampling results leads to a less accurate outcome than would be obtained by using classical statistical inference. It is the very use of prior knowledge in a statistical analysis that often brings the entire Bayesian methodology under attack.

---

[1] A description of Professor Bernardo's study may be found in his article: J. M. Bernardo, "Monitoring the 1982 Spanish Socialist Victory: A Bayesian Analysis," *Journal of the American Statistical Association*, 79 (September 1984), pp. 510–515.

Continued on next page

FIGURE 15–1   A Comparison of the Bayesian and the Classical Approaches

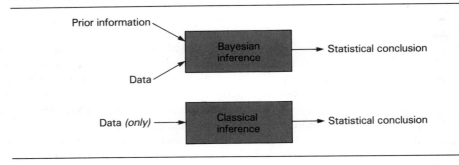

When prior information is a direct result of previous statistical surveys, or when prior information reflects no knowledge about the problem at hand (in which case the prior probabilities are called *noninformative*), the Bayesian analysis is purely *objective,* and few people would argue with its validity. Often, however, the prior information reflects the personal ideas of the individual doing the analysis—or possibly those of an expert who has knowledge of the particular problem at hand. In such cases, where the prior information is of a *subjective* nature, one may criticize the results of the analysis.

One way to classify statisticians is according to whether they are Bayesian or non-Bayesian (i.e., classical). The Bayesian group used to be a minority, but in recent years its numbers have grown. Even though differences between the two groups exist, it can be shown that when noninformative prior probabilities are used, the Bayesian results parallel the classical statistical results. This fact lends credibility to the Bayesian approach. If we are careful with the use of any prior information, we may avoid criticism and produce good results via the Bayesian methodology. Bernardo, for example, used no subjective elements in his analysis of the Spanish election: his prior knowledge—his prior probabilities—all came from the known results of the 1979 election. There is, of course, the question: Why would one believe that any results obtained in 1979 should have any relevance to the 1982 election? We may assume that Bernardo's answer to this question was subjective. If indeed it were, he certainly made a good bet.

In the next two sections, we give some basic elements of *Bayesian statistics.* These sections extend the idea of Bayes' theorem, first to discrete random variables and then to continuous ones. Section 15–4 discusses some aspects of subjective probabilities and how they can be elicited from a person who has knowledge of the situation at hand.

There is another important area, not entirely in the realm of statistics, that makes use of Bayes' theorem as well as subjective probabilities. This is the area of **decision analysis.** Decision analysis is a methodology developed in the 1960s that quantifies the elements of a decision-making process in an effort to determine the optimal decision. ∎

15–2   Bayes' Theorem and Discrete Probability Models

In section 2–8, we introduced Bayes' theorem. The theorem was presented in terms of *events.* The theorem was shown to transform *prior probabilities* of the occurrence of certain events into *posterior probabilities* of occurrence of the same events. Recall Example (k) of Chapter 2. In that example, we started with a prior probability that a randomly chosen person is sick with a certain disease, given by $P(I) = 0.001$. Through the information that the person tested positive for the disease, and the reliability of the test, known to be $P(Z \mid I) = 0.92$ and $P(Z \mid \bar{I}) = 0.04$, we obtained through Bayes' theorem (equation 2–27) the posterior probability that the person was sick:

$$P(I \mid Z) = \frac{P(Z \mid I)P(I)}{P(Z \mid I)P(I) + P(Z \mid \bar{I})P(\bar{I})} = 0.0225$$

The fact that the person had a positive reaction to the test may be considered our *data*. The conditional probabilities $P(Z \mid I)$ and $P(Z \mid \bar{I})$ help incorporate the data information in the computation. We will now extend these probabilities to include more than just an event and its complement, as was done in this example, or one of three events, as was the case in Example (1) of Chapter 2. Our extension will cover a whole *set* of values and their prior probabilities. The *conditional* probabilities, when extended over the entire set of values of a random variable, are called the *likelihood function*.

> The **likelihood function** is the set of conditional probabilities $P(x \mid \theta)$ for given data x, considered a function of an unknown population parameter, θ.

Using the likelihood function and the prior probabilities $P(\theta)$ of the values of the parameter in question, we define Bayes' theorem in the following form:

Bayes' theorem for a discrete random variable:

$$P(\theta \mid x) = \frac{P(x \mid \theta)\, P(\theta)}{\Sigma_i\, P(x \mid \theta_i)P(\theta_i)} \qquad (15\text{–}1)$$

where θ is an unknown population parameter to be estimated from the data. The summation in the denominator is over all possible values of the parameter of interest, θ_i, and x stands for our particular data set.

> In Bayesian statistics, we assume that population parameters such as the mean, the variance, or the population proportion are *random variables* rather than fixed (but unknown) quantities, as in the classical approach.

We assume that the parameter of interest is a random variable; thus, we may specify our prior information about the parameter as a **prior probability distribution** of the parameter. Then we obtain our data, and from them we get the likelihood function, that is, a measure of how likely we are to obtain our particular data, *given* different values of the parameter specified in the parameter's prior probability distribution. This information is transformed via Bayes' theorem, equation 15–1, to a **posterior probability distribution** of the value of the parameter in question. The posterior distribution includes the prior information as well as the data results. The posterior distribution can then be used in statistical inference. Such inference may include computing confidence intervals. Bayesian confidence intervals are often called **credible sets** of given posterior probability.

The following example illustrates the use of Bayes' theorem when the population parameter of interest is the population proportion, p.

EXAMPLE (a)

A market research analyst is interested in estimating the proportion of people in a certain area who use a product made by her client. That is, the analyst is interested in estimating her client's *market share*. The analyst denotes the parameter in question—the true (population) market share of her client—by S. From previous studies of a similar nature, and from other sources of information about the industry, the analyst constructs the following table of prior probabilities of the possible values of the market share, S. This is the analyst's prior probability distribution of S. It contains different values of the parameter in question and the analyst's degree of belief that the parameter is equal to any of the values, given as a probability. The prior probability distribution is presented in Table 15–1.

As seen from the prior probabilities table, the analyst does not believe that her client's market share could be above 0.6 (60% of the market). For example, she may know that a competitor controls 40% of the market, so values above 60% are impossible as her client's share. Similarly, she may know for certain that her client's market share is at least 10%. The assumption that S may equal one of six discrete values is a restrictive approximation. In the next section, we will explore a continuous space of values.

The analyst now gathers a random sample of 20 people and finds out that 4 out of the 20 in the sample do use her client's product. The analyst wishes to use Bayes' theorem to combine her prior distribution of market share with the data results to obtain a posterior distribution of market share. Recall that in the classical approach, all that can be used is the sample estimate of the market share, which is $\hat{p} = x/n = 4/20 = 0.2$ and may be used in the construction of a confidence interval or a hypothesis test.

TABLE 15–1 Prior Probabilities of Market Share, S

S	$P(S)$
0.1	0.05
0.2	0.15
0.3	0.20
0.4	0.30
0.5	0.20
0.6	0.10
	1.00

TABLE 15–2 Prior Distribution, Likelihood, and Posterior Distribution of Market Share [Example (a)]

S	$P(S)$	$P(x\mid S)$	$P(S)P(x\mid S)$	$P(S\mid x)$
0.1	0.05	0.0898	0.00449	0.06007
0.2	0.15	0.2182	0.03273	0.43786
0.3	0.20	0.1304	0.02608	0.34890
0.4	0.30	0.0350	0.01050	0.14047
0.5	0.20	0.0046	0.00092	0.01230
0.6	0.10	0.0003	0.00003	0.00040
	1.00		0.07475	1.00000

Using Bayes' theorem for discrete random variables (equation 15–1), the analyst updates her prior information to incorporate the data results. This is done in a tabular format and is shown in Table 15–2. As required by equation 15–1, the conditional probabilities $P(x \mid S)$ are evaluated. These conditional probabilities are our likelihood function. To evaluate these probabilities, we ask the following questions:

1. How likely are we to obtain the data results we have, that is, 4 successes out of 20 trials, if the probability of success in a single trial (the true *population proportion*) is equal to 0.1?
2. How likely are we to obtain the results we have if the population proportion is 0.2?
3. How likely are we to obtain these results when the population proportion is 0.3?
4. How likely are we to obtain these results when the population proportion is 0.4?
5. How likely are we to obtain these results when the population proportion is 0.5?
6. How likely are we to obtain these results when the population proportion is 0.6?

The answers to these six questions are obtained from a table of the binomial distribution (Appendix C, Table 1) and written in the appropriate places in the third column of Table 15–2. The fourth column is the product, for each value of S, of the prior probability of S and its likelihood. The sum of the entries in the fourth column is equal to the denominator in equation 15–1. When each entry in column 4 is divided by the sum of that column, we get the posterior probabilities, which are written in column 5. This procedure corresponds to an application of equation 15–1 for each one of the possible values of the population proportion, S.

By comparing the values in column 2 of Table 15–2 with the values in column 5, we see how the prior probabilities of different possible market share values changed by the incorporation, via Bayes' theorem, of the information in the data (i.e., the fact that 4 people in a sample of 20 were found to be product users). The influence of the prior beliefs about the actual market share is evident in the posterior distribution. This is illustrated in Figure 15–2, which shows the prior probability distribution of S, and Figure 15–3, which shows the posterior probability distribution of S.

As the two figures show, starting with a prior distribution that is spread in a somewhat symmetric fashion over the six possible values of S, we end up, after the incorporation of data results, with a posterior distribution that is concentrated over the three values 0.2, 0.3, and 0.4, with the remaining values having small probabilities. The total posterior probability of the three values 0.2, 0.3, and 0.4 is equal to 0.92723 (from summing Table 15–2 entries). The three adjacent values are thus a set of *highest posterior probability* and can be taken as a *credible set* of values for S with posterior probability close to the standard 95% confidence level. Recall that with discrete random variables, it is hard to get values corresponding to exact, prespecified levels such as 95%, and we are fortunate in this case to be close to 95%. We may state as our conclusion that we are about 93% confident that the market share is anywhere between 0.2 and 0.4. Our result is a Bayesian conclusion, which may be stated in terms of a *probability*; it includes both the data results and our prior information. (As a comparison, compute an approximate classical confidence interval based on the sampling result.)

SOLUTION

FIGURE 15–2
The Prior Distribution of Market Share [Example (a)]

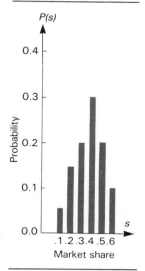

FIGURE 15–3
The Posterior Distribution of Market Share [Example (a)]

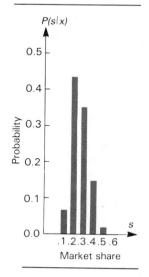

One of the great advantages of the Bayesian approach is the possibility of carrying out the analysis in a *sequential* fashion. Information obtained from one sampling study can be used as the prior information set when new information becomes available. The second survey results are considered the data set, and the two sources are combined by use of Bayes' theorem. The resulting posterior distribution may then be used as the prior distribution when new data become available, and so on.

TABLE 15–3   Prior Distribution, Likelihood, and Posterior Distribution of Market Share for Second Sampling

S	P(S)	P(x|S)	P(S)P(x|S)	P(S|x)
0.1	0.06007	0.1423	0.0085480	0.049074
0.2	0.43786	0.2463	0.1078449	0.619138
0.3	0.34890	0.1465	0.0511138	0.293444
0.4	0.14047	0.0468	0.0065740	0.037741
0.5	0.01230	0.0085	0.0001046	0.000601
0.6	0.00040	0.0008	0.0000003	0.000002
	1.00000		0.1741856	1.000000

We now illustrate the sequential property by continuing Example (a). Suppose that the analyst is able to obtain a *second* sample after her analysis of the first sample is completed. She obtains a sample of 16 people and finds that there are 3 users of the product of interest in this sample. The analyst now wants to combine this new sampling information with what she already knows about the market share. To do this, the analyst considers her last posterior distribution, from column 5 of Table 15–2, as her new *prior* distribution when the new data come in. Note that the last posterior distribution contains *all* of the analyst's information about market share before the incorporation of the new data, because it includes both her prior information and the results of the first sampling. Table 15–3 shows how this information is transformed into a new posterior probability distribution by incorporating the new sample results. The likelihood function is again obtained by consulting Appendix C, Table 1. We look for the binomial probabilities of obtaining 3 successes of 16 trials, using the given values of $S(0.1, 0.2, \ldots, 0.6)$, each in turn taken as the binomial parameter, p.

The new posterior distribution of S is shown in Figure 15–4. Note that the highest posterior probability after the second sampling is given to the value $S = 0.2$, the posterior probability being 0.6191. With every additional sampling, the posterior distribution will get more peaked at values indicated by the data. The posterior distribution keeps moving toward data-derived results, and the effects of the prior distribution become less and less important. This fact becomes clear as we compare the distributions shown in Figures 15–2, 15–3, and 15–4. This property of Bayesian analysis is reassuring. It allows the data to speak for themselves, thus moving away from prior beliefs if these beliefs are away from reality. In the presence of limited data, Bayesian analysis allows us to compensate for the small data set by allowing us to use previous information—obtained either by prior sampling or by other means.

Incidentally, what would have happened if our analyst had decided to combine the results of the two surveys before considering them in conjunction with her prior information? That is, what would have happened if the analyst had decided to consider the two samples as one, where the total number of trials is $20 + 16 = 36$ and the total number of successes is $4 + 3 = 7$ users? Surprisingly, the posterior probability distribution for the combined sample incorporated with the prior distribution would have been exactly the same as the posterior distribution presented in Table 15–3. This fact demonstrates how well the Bayesian approach handles successive pieces of information. It does not matter when or how information is incorporated in the model—the posterior distribution will contain *all* information available at any given time.

In the next section, we discuss Bayesian statistics in the context of continuous probability distributions. In particular, we develop the normal probability model for

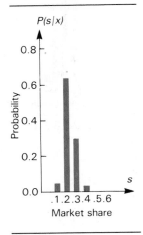

FIGURE 15–4
The Second Posterior Distribution of Market Share

Bayesian analysis. As will be seen in the next section, the normal distribution is particularly amenable to Bayesian analysis. If our prior distribution is normal and the likelihood function is normal, then the posterior distribution is also normal. We will develop two simple formulas: one for the posterior mean and one for the posterior variance (and standard deviation) in terms of the prior distribution parameters and the likelihood function.

PROBLEMS

15–1. In 1987, the Wells Fargo Bank of San Francisco launched a special credit card. The card was designed to reward people who pay their bills on time by allowing them to pay a lower-than-usual interest rate. Some research went into designing the new program. The director of the bank's regular credit card systems was consulted, and she gave her prior probability distribution of the proportion of cardholders who would qualify for the new program. Then a random sample of 20 cardholders was selected and traced over several months. It was found that 6 of them paid all their credit card bills on time. Using this information and the information in the following table—the director's prior distribution of the proportion of all cardholders who pay their bills on time—construct the posterior probability distribution for this parameter. Also give a credible set of highest posterior probability close to 95% for the parameter in question. Plot both the prior and the posterior distributions of the parameter.

Answers

Proportion	Probability
0.1	0.2
0.2	0.3
0.3	0.1
0.4	0.1
0.5	0.1
0.6	0.1
0.7	0.1

15–2. In the situation of problem 15–1, suppose that a second random sample of cardholders was selected, and it was found that 7 out of the 17 people in the sample paid their bills on time. Construct the new posterior distribution containing information from the prior distribution and both samplings. Again, give a credible set of highest posterior probability close to 95%, and plot the posterior distribution.

15–2.

90.6% credible set: [0.2, 0.4]

15–3. For Example (a), suppose that a third sample is obtained. Three out of 10 people in the sample are product users. Update the probabilities of market share after the third sampling, and produce the new posterior distribution.

15–4. The company that markets the Yugoslav car Yugo in the United States needed to estimate the proportion of the market that the car would capture once it was introduced. Based on experience with Korean, French, and other foreign cars marketed in the country, one of the company's executives gave his prior probability distribution of the proportion of the foreign-car market that would go to Yugo. The prior probability distribution of this proportion (M = market share) is as follows.

15–4.

$P(M|X)$
0.538
0.407
0.039
0.016

M	$P(M)$
0.05	0.3
0.15	0.5
0.20	0.1
0.25	0.1

A random sample of 18 potential buyers of new foreign cars revealed that one of them would buy a Yugo. Compute the posterior probability distribution of M.

15–5. Recent years have seen a sharp decline in the Alaska king crab fishery. One problem identified as a potential cause of the decline has been the prevalence of a deadly parasite

Answers

believed to infect a large proportion of the adult king crab population. A fisheries manage-ment agency monitoring crab catches needed to estimate the proportion of the adult crab pop-ulation infected by the parasite. The agency's biologists constructed the following prior prob-ability distribution for the proportion of infected adult crabs (denoted by R).

R	P(R)
0.25	0.1
0.30	0.2
0.35	0.2
0.40	0.3
0.45	0.1
0.50	0.1

A random sample of 10 adult king crabs was collected, and it was found that 3 of them were infected with the parasite. Construct the posterior probability distribution of the proportion of infected adult crabs, and plot it.

15–6.

97% credible
set: [0.25, 0.45]

15–6.   Continuing problem 15–5, a second random sample of 12 adult crabs was collected, and it revealed that 4 individual crabs had been infected. Revise your probability distribution, and plot it. Give a credible set of highest posterior probability close to 95%.

15–7.   For problem 15–5, suppose the biologists believed the proportion of infected crabs in the population was equally likely to be anywhere from 10% to 90%. Using the discrete points 0.1, 0.2, etc., construct a uniform prior distribution for the proportion of infected crabs, and compute the posterior distribution after the results of the sampling in problem 15–5.

15–8.

$P(S|X)$
.0423
.1584
.3644
.2872
.1124
.0352

15–8.   An airline is interested in the proportion of flights that are full during a given sea-son. The airline uses data from past experience and constructs the following prior distribution of the proportion of flights that are full to capacity.

S	P(S)
0.70	0.1
0.75	0.2
0.80	0.3
0.85	0.2
0.90	0.1
0.95	0.1
	1.0

A sample of 20 flights shows that 17 of these flights are full. Update the probability distribu-tion to obtain a posterior distribution for the proportion of full flights.

15–9.   In the situation of problem 15–8, another sample of 20 flights reveals that 18 of them are full. Obtain the second posterior distribution of the proportion of full flights. Graph the prior distribution of problem 15–8, as well as the first posterior and the second posterior distributions. How did the distribution of the proportion in question change as more informa-tion became available?

15–10.

94.45% credible
set: [0.10, 0.25]

15–10.   A quality-control engineer has the following prior probability distribution for the proportion of defective items in a production process.

x	P(x)
0.05	0.1
0.10	0.2
0.15	0.4
0.20	0.2
0.25	0.1
	1.0

The engineer collects a random sample of 15 items and finds that 2 are defective. Compute the posterior distribution for the proportion of defective items, and give a credible set for the population proportion of defective items with posterior probability close to 95%.

15–3   Bayes' Theorem and Continuous Probability Distributions

We will now extend the results of the preceding section to the case of continuous probability models. Recall that a continuous random variable has a probability density function, denoted by $f(x)$. The function $f(x)$ is nonnegative, and the total area under the curve of $f(x)$ must equal 1.00. Recall that the probability of an event is defined as the area under the curve of $f(x)$ over the interval or intervals corresponding to the event.

> We define $f(\theta)$ as the **prior probability density** of the parameter θ. We define $f(x \mid \theta)$ as the **conditional density** of the data x, *given* the value of θ. This is the likelihood function.

The **joint density** of θ and x is obtained as the product:

$$f(\theta, x) = f(x \mid \theta) f(\theta) \qquad (15\text{–}2)$$

Using these functions, we may now write Bayes' theorem for continuous probability distributions. The theorem gives us the **posterior density** of the parameter θ, *given* the data x.

Bayes' theorem for continuous distributions:[2]

$$f(\theta \mid x) = \frac{f(x \mid \theta) f(\theta)}{\text{Total area under } f(\theta, x)} \qquad (15\text{–}3)$$

Equation 15–3 is the analog for continuous random variables of equation 15–1. We may use the equation for updating a prior probability density function of a parameter θ once data, x, are available. In general, computing the posterior density is a complicated operation. However, in the case of a normal prior distribution and a normal data-generating process (or large samples, leading to central-limit conditions), the posterior distribution is also a normal distribution. The parameters of the posterior distribution are easy to calculate, as will be shown next.

The Normal Probability Model

Suppose that you want to estimate the population mean, μ, of a normal population that has a *known* standard deviation, σ. Also suppose that you have some prior beliefs about the population in question. Namely, you view the population mean as a random variable with a normal (prior) distribution with mean M' and standard deviation σ'.

If you draw a random sample of size n from the normal population in question and obtain a sample mean M, then the posterior distribution for the population mean, μ, is a *normal distribution with mean M'' and standard deviation σ''* obtained, respectively, from equations 15–4 and 15–5.

---

[2] For the reader with knowledge of calculus, we note that Bayes' theorem is written as: $f(\theta \mid x) = f(x \mid \theta) f(\theta) / [\int_{-\infty}^{\infty} f(x \mid \theta) f(\theta) d\theta]$.

> The posterior mean and variance of the normal distribution of the population mean, μ:
>
> $$M'' = \frac{(1/\sigma'^2)M' + (n/\sigma^2)M}{(1/\sigma'^2) + (n/\sigma^2)} \qquad (15\text{--}4)$$
>
> $$\sigma''^2 = \frac{1}{(1/\sigma'^2) + (n/\sigma^2)} \qquad (15\text{--}5)$$

The two equations are very useful in many applications. We are fortunate that the normal distribution family is *closed*, that is, when the prior distribution of a parameter is normal and the population (or process) is normal, the posterior distribution of the parameter in question is also normal. Be sure that you understand the distinction among the various quantities involved in the computations—especially the distinction between σ^2 and σ'^2. The quantity σ^2 is the variance of the population, and σ'^2 is the prior variance of the population mean, μ. We demonstrate the methodology with Example (b).

EXAMPLE (b)

A stockbroker is interested in the return on investment for a particular stock. Since Bayesian analysis is especially suited for the incorporation of opinion or prior knowledge with data, the stockbroker wishes to use a Bayesian model. The stockbroker quantifies his beliefs about the *average return* on the stock by a normal probability distribution with mean 15 (percent return per year) and a standard deviation of 8. Since it is relatively large, as compared with the mean, the stockbroker's prior standard deviation of μ reflects a state of relatively little prior knowledge about the stock in question. However, the prior distribution allows the broker to incorporate in the analysis some of his limited knowledge about the stock. The broker collects a sample of 10 monthly observations on the stock and computes the annualized average percentage return. He gets a mean $M = 11.54$ (percent) and a standard deviation $s = 6.8$. Assuming that the population standard deviation is equal to 6.8 and that returns are normally distributed, what is the posterior distribution of average stock returns?

SOLUTION

We know that the posterior distribution is normal, with mean and variance given by equations 15–4 and 15–5, respectively. We have:

$$M'' = \frac{(1/64)15 + (10/46.24)11.54}{(1/64) + (10/46.24)} = 11.77$$

$$\sigma'' = \sqrt{\frac{1}{(1/64) + (10/46.24)}} = 2.077$$

Note how simple it is to update probabilities when one starts with a normal prior distribution, and a normal population. Incidentally, the assumption of a normal population is very appropriate in our case, as the theory of finance demonstrates that stock returns are well approximated by the normal curve. If the population standard deviation is unknown, the sample standard deviation provides a reasonable estimate.

Figure 15–5 shows the stockbroker's prior distribution, the normal likelihood function (normalized to have a unit area), and the posterior density of the average return on the stock of interest. Note that the prior distribution is relatively flat—this is due to the relatively large standard deviation. The standard deviation is a measure of uncertainty, and here it reflects the fact that the broker does not know much about the stock. Prior

FIGURE 15–5 The Prior Distribution, the Likelihood Function, and the Posterior Distribution of Average Return, μ [Example (b)]

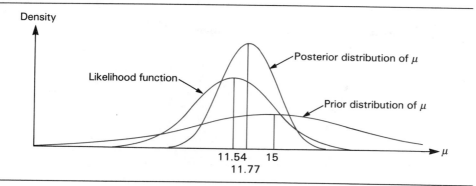

distributions such as the one used here are called **diffuse priors.** They convey *little* a priori knowledge about the process in question. A relatively flat prior normal distribution conveys *some* information but lets the data tell us more.

Credible Sets

Unlike the discrete case, it is possible in the continuous case to construct credible sets for parameters with an exact, prespecified probability level. These are easy to construct. In Example (b), the stockbroker may construct a 95% highest-posterior-density (HPD) credible set for the average return on the stock directly from the posterior density. The posterior distribution is normal, with mean 11.77 and standard deviation 2.077. Therefore, the 95% HPD credible set for μ is simply:

$$M'' \pm 1.96 \, \sigma'' = 11.77 + 1.96(2.077)$$

$$= [7.699, \ 15.841]$$

Thus, the stockbroker may conclude there is a 0.95 probability that the average return on the stock is anywhere from 7.699 to 15.841% per year.

Recall that in the classical approach, we would have to rely only on the data and not be able to use prior knowledge. As a conclusion, we would have to say: "Ninety-five percent of the intervals constructed in this manner will contain the parameter of interest." In the Bayesian approach, we are free to make *probability* statements as conclusions. Incidentally, the idea of attaching a probability to a result extends to the Bayesian way of testing hypotheses. A Bayesian statistician can give a posterior probability to the null hypothesis. Contrast this with the classical p-value, as defined in Chapter 7.

Suppose the stockbroker believed differently. Suppose that he believed that returns on the stock had a mean of 15 and a standard deviation of 4. In this case, the broker admits less uncertainty in his knowledge about average stock returns. The sampling results are the same, so the likelihood is unchanged. However, the posterior distribution does change as it now incorporates the data (through the likelihood) with a prior distribution that is not diffuse, as in the last case, but more peaked over its mean of 15. In our present case, the broker has a stronger belief that the average return is around 15% per year, as indicated by a normal distribution more peaked

FIGURE 15-6   The Prior Distribution, the Likelihood Function, and the Posterior Distribution of Average Return Using a More Peaked Prior Distribution

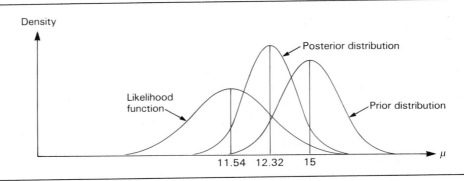

around its mean. Using equations 15–4 and 15–5, we obtain the posterior mean and standard deviation:

$$M'' = \frac{(1/16)15 + (10/46.24)11.54}{(1/16) + (10/46.24)} = 12.32$$

$$\sigma'' = \sqrt{\frac{1}{(1/16) + (10/46.24)}} = 1.89$$

As can be seen, the fact that the broker felt more confident about the average return being around 15% (as manifested by the smaller standard deviation of his prior probability distribution) caused the posterior mean to be closer to 15% than it was when the same data were used with a more diffuse prior (the new mean is 12.32, compared with 11.77, obtained earlier). The prior distribution, the likelihood function, and the posterior distribution of the mean return on the stock are shown in Figure 15–6. Compare this figure with Figure 15–5, which corresponds to the earlier case with a more diffuse prior.

PROBLEMS

Answer

15–11.   The partner-manager of a franchise of Au Bon Pain, Inc., the French bakery-restaurant chain, believes that the *average* daily revenue of her business may be viewed as a random variable (she adheres to the Bayesian philosophy) with mean $8,500 and standard deviation $1,000. Her prior probability distribution of average daily revenue is normal. A random sample of 35 days reveals a mean daily revenue of $9,210 and a standard deviation of $365. Construct the posterior distribution of average daily revenue. Assume a normal distribution of daily revenues.

15–12.

95% HPD
region is:
[9,301.39, 10,491.77]

15–12.   Video Dog™ is an ingenious invention. It allows you to enjoy the pleasures of owning a pet without having to feed it, take it for walks, or worry about fleas and ticks. Before marketing the idea, the manufacturer wanted to estimate average monthly sales that would result in an area with a given population. From experience with similar products (probably the Pet Rock), the manufacturer assessed a normal prior probability distribution for average monthly sales in the area, with mean 15,000 and standard deviation 4,000. A random sample of 12 monthly sales in an area of about the same population and in the same geographical region gave a mean of 9,867 and a standard deviation of 1,055. Give a 95% highest-posterior-density credible set for the average monthly sales the manufacturer may expect in a region of the given size. Assume sales are normally distributed.

15–13.   Mr. Claude Vrinat, owner of Taillevent—one of Europe's most highly acclaimed restaurants—is reported to regularly sample the tastes of his patrons.[3] From experience, Vrinat believes that the average rating (on a scale of 0 to 100) that his clients give his *foie gras de canard* may be viewed as normally distributed with mean 94 and standard deviation 2. A random sample of 10 diners gives an average rating of 96 and standard deviation of 1. What should be Vrinat's posterior distribution of average rating of *foie gras de canard*, assuming ratings are normally distributed?

15–14.   In the context of problem 15–13, a second random sample of 15 diners is asked to rate the *foie gras*, giving a mean rating of 95 and standard deviation of 1. Incorporate the new information to give a posterior distribution that accounts for both samplings and the prior distribution. Give a 95% HPD credible set for mean rating.

15–15.   The operator of a film developing business believes that the average time it takes to develop a roll of film of a particular type is uncertain and may be described by a normal distribution with mean 22 minutes and standard deviation 2 minutes. Using this information as the prior distribution, and the fact that a random sample of 14 rolls had an average development time of 24 minutes per roll and a standard deviation of 3 minutes, construct the posterior distribution of average development time. Assume normality.

15–16.   Continuing problem 15–15, a second random sample of 20 rolls of film gave a mean development time of 25 minutes and a standard deviation of 2 minutes. Construct the second posterior distribution, and use it in constructing a 99% HPD credible set for average development time.

15–17.   In an effort to predict Alaska's oil-related state revenues, a delphi session is regularly held where experts in the field give their expectations of the average future price of crude oil over the next year (see Chapter 12 for a brief description of a delphi session). The views of five prominent experts who participated in the last delphi session may be stated as normal prior distributions with means and standard deviations given in the following table. To protect their identities (the delphi sessions are closed to the public), we will denote them by the letters A through E. Data are in dollars per barrel.

Expert	Mean	Standard Deviation
A	23	4
B	19	7
C	25	1
D	20	9
E	27	3

Compare the views of the five experts using this information. What can you say about the different experts' degrees of belief in their own respective knowledge? One of the experts is the governor of Alaska, who, due to the nature of his post, devotes little time to following oil prices. All other experts have varying degrees of experience with price analysis; one of them is the ARCO expert who assesses oil prices on a daily basis. Looking *only* at the reported prior standard deviations, who is likely to be the governor, and who is likely to be the ARCO expert? Now suppose that at the end of the year it was found that the average daily price of crude oil was $18 per barrel. Who should be most surprised (and embarrassed), and why?

15–4   The Evaluation of Subjective Probabilities

Since Bayesian analysis makes extensive use of people's subjective beliefs in the form of prior probabilities, it is only natural that the field should include methods for the elicitation of personal probabilities. We begin by presenting some simple ideas on how to identify a normal prior probability distribution and give a rough estimate of its mean and standard deviation. Then we present the de Finetti game, which is a

Answers

15–14.
———
[94.996, 95.776]

15–16.
———
[23.67, 25.65]

[3] Patricia Wells, "Three-Star Galaxy," in *Beloved Cities: Europe*, ed. A. Rosenthal and A. Gelb (New York: Viking Penguin, 1985), pp. 240–255.

useful tool for calibrating one's personal probability of occurrence of an event. We also give an interactive computer program that can be used for this purpose.

Assessing a Normal Prior Distribution

As you well know by now, the normal probability model is useful in a wide variety of applications. Furthermore, since we know probabilities associated with the normal distribution, results can easily be obtained if we do make the assumption of normality. How can we estimate a decision maker's subjective normal probability distribution? For example, how did the stockbroker of Example (b) decide that his prior distribution of average returns was normal with mean 15 and standard deviation 8?

The normal distribution appears naturally and as an approximation in many situations due to the central limit theorem. Therefore, in many instances, it makes sense to assume a normal distribution. In other cases, it frequently happens that we have a distribution that is not normal but still is *symmetric* with a *single mode*. In such cases, it may still make sense to assume a normal distribution as an approximation because this distribution is easily estimated as a subjective distribution, and the resulting inaccuracies will not be great. In cases where the distribution is *skewed*, however, the normal approximation will not be adequate.

Once we determine that the normal distribution is appropriate for describing our personal beliefs about the situation at hand, we need to estimate the mean and the standard deviation of the distribution. For a symmetric distribution with one mode, the mean is equal to the median and to the mode. Therefore, we may ask the decision maker whose subjective probability we are trying to assess what he or she believes to be the center of the distribution. We may also ask for the most likely value. We may ask for the average, or we may ask for the point that splits the distribution into two equal parts. All of these questions would lead us to the central value, which we take to be the mean of the subjective distribution. It is useful to ask the person whose probabilities we are trying to elicit *several* of these questions, so that we have a few checks on the answer. Any discrepancies in the answers may lead to possible violations of our assumption of the symmetry of the distribution or its unimodality (having only one mode), which would obviate the normal approximation. Presumably, questions such as these lead the stockbroker of Example (b) to determine that the mean of his prior distribution for average returns is 15%.

How do we estimate the standard deviation of a subjective distribution? Recall the simple rules of thumb for the normal probability model:

Approximately 68% of the distribution lies within *one* standard deviation of the mean.

Approximately 95% of the distribution lies within *two* standard deviations of the mean.

These rules lead us to the following questions for the decision maker whose probabilities we are trying to assess: "Give me two values of the distribution in question such that you are 95% sure that the variable in question is between the two values," or equivalently, "give me two values such that 95% of the distribution lies between them." We may also ask for two values such that 68% of the distribution is between these values.

For 95% sureness, assuming symmetry, we know that the two values we obtain as answers are *each* two standard deviations away from the mean. In the case of the stockbroker, he must have felt there was a 0.95 chance that the average return on the stock was anywhere from -1% to 31%. The two points, -1 and 31, are 2×8 units on either side of the mean, 15. Hence, the standard deviation is 8. The stockbroker could also have said that he was 68% sure that the average return was anywhere from 7% to 23% (each of these two values is one standard deviation away from the mean, 15). Using 95% bounds is more useful than 68% limits because people are more likely to think in terms of 95% sureness. Be sure you understand the difference between this method of obtaining bounds on values of a population (or random variable) and the construction of confidence intervals (or credible sets) for population *parameters*.

The de Finetti Game

One of the most active statisticians in the area of subjective probability was the late Italian statistician Bruno de Finetti. De Finetti embarked on a thorough investigation of the way people perceive probability and obtained some profound results in this area as early as 1937. In later years he developed a game that he played with his students at the University of Rome. In this game, each student stated his or her estimated probability that a given soccer team would win in a game to be played on the coming weekend. Each student was then asked a series of questions designed to gauge the probability that the team in question would win, against a certain *lottery* with known probabilities. This game led to a more precise assessment of the probability of the event in question. Most people playing this game find that the probabilities they state initially for an event are changed by the end of the game. This gives the player a better feel for what his or her true beliefs are with regard to the event in question. The game proceeds as follows.

As an example, let us take the event that a particular presidential candidate will win the election; you must state what you think are the candidate's chances. Suppose you say that the chances are 0.40. We then present you with the following choices. (1) "A bag contains 50 red balls and 50 black balls. If you choose to do so, you may reach inside the bag and pick a ball at random. If the ball turns out to be red, then we will give you one million dollars! (2) On the other hand, you may choose not to draw a ball out of the bag. Instead we will wait until after the presidential election in November, and if your candidate wins you will get one million dollars. You must state now if you choose to draw a ball or await the outcome of the election (you cannot do both)."

Suppose your answer is that you will wait until the election and collect your million dollars if the candidate wins. We would then present you with the following choice. "The bag now contains 60 red balls and 40 black ones. If you draw a red ball, you will win one million dollars as before. You must choose whether to draw a ball now or wait until the election results are known." Suppose that you think about this and decide to draw a ball out of the bag. The next question will be: "There are now 55 red balls in the bag and 45 black ones. Will you draw now or wait until November?" Suppose you now say that you will wait until the election; the next question will then be: "There are 57 red balls and 43 black ones. Will you draw or wait?" Suppose that you say that you will draw. If you draw when there are 57 red balls in the bag and wait when there are 55 red balls, then the last question is: "What will you do if there are 56 red balls in the bag?" Suppose you say that you are indifferent at this point. This means that you actually believe that the probability that the candidate will win the election is 0.56. Here the weighing of the probability of a win against an objective lottery with an exact, known probability of success revealed that you really feel that the probability of success of the candidate in question is 0.56, which is a change from your originally stated probability of 0.40. As mentioned earlier, most people do change their stated probabilities during the course of the game. The game allows you to gauge your probability against a precisely measured analog: the hypothetical lottery.

Figure 15–7 shows sample output of a run of an interactive program written in the BASIC language for playing the de Finetti game of eliciting personal probabilities. A listing of the program itself is given in section 15–10. It should be noted that our version of the game is not the most sophisticated or accurate one possible. Our program does not check for *consistency* by checking probabilities of the complement of the event in question. Additional checks would complicate our game somewhat. The interested reader is referred to Bruno de Finetti's book *Probability, Induction, and Statistics* (New York: John Wiley & Sons, Inc, 1972).

FIGURE 15–7 Sample Computer Output of the de Finetti Game

```
HELLO!
LET US ASSESS THE PROBABILITY OF AN EVENT OF INTEREST TO YOU.
IMAGINE THAT I HAVE AN URN CONTAINING 100 BALLS. THERE ARE AS MANY
RED BALLS AS INDICATED BELOW, AND THE REST OF THEM ARE BLACK. NOW,
IF YOU DRAW A RED BALL FROM THE URN, I WILL GIVE YOU ONE MILLION
DOLLARS!!! ON THE OTHER HAND, IF YOU WAIT FOR THE EVENT OF INTEREST
TO OCCUR, THEN I WILL GIVE YOU ONE MILLION DOLLARS IF IT DOES
INDEED OCCUR. HOWEVER, YOU MUST MAKE THE DECISION NOW AS TO WHETHER
TO DRAW A BALL, OR TO WAIT TO SEE IF THE EVENT WILL OCCUR AND
COLLECT THE MONEY IF IT DOES. YOU CANNOT DO BOTH. DEPENDING ON THE
COMPOSITION OF THE URN AT EACH STAGE, TYPE A 'D' FOR DRAW, OR A 'W'
FOR WAIT OR AN 'I' IF YOU ARE INDIFFERENT AT THAT PARTICULAR POINT
THERE ARE      50
RED BALLS IN THE URN
WAIT, DRAW, OR INDIFFERENT? W
THERE ARE      75
RED BALLS IN THE URN
WAIT, DRAW, OR INDIFFERENT? W
THERE ARE      87
RED BALLS IN THE URN
WAIT, DRAW, OR INDIFFERENT? D
THERE ARE      81
RED BALLS IN THE URN
WAIT, DRAW, OR INDIFFERENT? D
THERE ARE      78
RED BALLS IN THE URN
WAIT, DRAW, OR INDIFFERENT? D
THERE ARE      76
RED BALLS IN THE URN
WAIT, DRAW, OR INDIFFERENT? W
THERE ARE      77
RED BALLS IN THE URN
WAIT, DRAW, OR INDIFFERENT? W
THERE ARE      77
RED BALLS IN THE URN
THE PROBABILITY OF YOUR EVENT IS
   77       PERCENT
PLAY ANOTHER ONE?
```

15–18.   Choose an event of interest to you, and play the de Finetti game to quantify your degree of belief in the occurrence of the event.

15–19.   In answering your questions as you try to elicit a personal probability distribution, an executive tells you that she believes that profits are approximately normally distributed and that she is 95% sure that profits will be anywhere from $1.5 million to $3.5 million. What are the mean and the standard deviation of the distribution of profits?

15–5   Decision Analysis: An Overview

Some years ago, the state of Massachusetts had to solve a serious problem: There was an alarming number of road fatalities due to icy roads in the winter. The state department of transportation wanted to solve the problem by salting the roads to reduce ice buildup. The introduction of large amounts of salt into the environment, however, would eventually cause an increase in the sodium content of drinking water, thus increasing the risk of heart problems in the general population.

This is the kind of problem that can be solved by *decision analysis*. There is a decision to be made: to salt or not to salt. With each of the two possible *actions*, we may associate a final *outcome*, and each outcome has a *probability* of occurrence. An additional number of deaths from heart disease would result if roads are salted. The number of deaths is uncertain, but its probability may be assessed. On the other hand, a number of highway deaths could be prevented if salt were used. Here again, the number is uncertain and governed by some probability law. In decision analysis we seek the *best* decision in a given situation. Although it is unpleasant to think of deaths, the best (optimal) decision here is the decision that would minimize the expected total number of deaths. *Expected* means averaged using the different probabilities as weights.

The area of decision analysis is independent of most of the material in this book. To be able to perform decision analysis, you need to have a rudimentary understanding of probability and of expected values. Some problems make use of additional information, obtained either by sampling or by other means. In such cases, we may have an idea about the *reliability* of our information—which may be stated as a probability—and the information is incorporated in the analysis by use of Bayes' theorem.

When a company is interested in introducing a new product, decision analysis offers an excellent *aid* in coming to a final decision. When one company considers a merger with another, decision analysis may be used as a way of evaluating all possible outcomes of the move and deciding whether or not to go ahead based on the best expected outcome. Decision analysis can help you decide which investment or combination of investments to choose. It could help you choose a job or career. It could help you decide whether or not to pursue an MBA degree.

We emphasize the use of decision analysis as an *aid* in corporate decision making. Since it is often difficult to *quantify* the aspects of human decision making, it is important to understand that decision analysis should not be the only criterion for making a decision. A stockbroker's hunch, for example, may be a much better indication of the best investment decision than a formal mathematical analysis, which may very well miss some important variables.

Decision analysis, as described in this book, has several elements.

The elements of a decision analysis:

1. Actions
2. Chance occurrences
3. Probabilities
4. Final outcomes
5. Additional information
6. Decision

Actions

By an action, we mean anything that the decision maker can do. An action is some-thing you, the decision maker, can control. You may choose to take an action, or you may choose not to take it. Often, there are several choices for action: you may buy one of several different products, travel one of several possible routes, etc. Many decision problems are *sequential* in nature: you choose one action from among several possibilities; later, you are again in a position to take an action. You may keep taking actions until a final outcome is reached; you keep playing the game until the game is over. Finally, you have reached some final outcome—you have gained a certain amount or lost an amount, achieved a goal or failed.

Chance Occurrences

Even if the decision problem is essentially nonsequential in nature (you take an ac-tion, something happens, and that's it), we may gain a better understanding of the problem if we view the problem as sequential. We assume that the decision maker takes an action, and afterwards "chance takes an action." The action of *chance* is the chance occurrence. When you decide to buy ABC stock, you have taken an ac-tion. When the stock falls three points the next day, chance has taken an action.

Probabilities

All actions of chance are governed by probabilities, or at least we view them that way because we cannot predict chance occurrences. The probabilities are obtained by some method. Often, the probabilities of chance occurrences are the decision maker's (or consulted expert's) subjective probabilities. Thus, the chief executive officer of a firm bidding for another firm will assign certain probabilities to the vari-ous outcomes that may result from the attempted merger.

In other cases, the probabilities of chance occurrences are more objective in na-ture. If we use sampling results as an aid in the analysis (see the section on addi-tional information, which follows), then statistical theory gives us measures of the reliability of results and, hence, probabilities of relevant chance occurrences.

Final Outcomes

We assume that the decision problem is of finite duration. After you, the decision maker, have taken an action or a sequence of actions, and after chance has taken ac-tion or a sequence of actions, there is a final outcome. An outcome may be viewed as a *payoff* or *reward*, or it may be viewed as a *loss*. We will look at outcomes as rewards (positive or negative). A payoff is an amount of money (or other measure of benefit, called a *utility*) that you receive at the end of the game—at the end of the decision problem.

Additional Information

Each time chance takes over, a random occurrence takes place. We may have some prior information that allows us to assess the probability of any chance occurrence. Often, however, we may be able to purchase additional information. We may consult an expert, for a price, or we may sample from the population of interest (assuming there is such a population), for a price. The costs of obtaining additional information are subtracted from our final payoff. Therefore, buying new information is, in itself, an action that we may choose to take or not to take. Deciding whether or not to obtain such information is part of the entire decision process. We must weigh the benefit of the additional information against its cost.

Decision

The action, or sequential set of actions, we decide to take is called our *decision*. The decision obtained through a useful analysis is that set of actions that maximizes our expected final-outcome payoff. The decision will often give us a set of *alternative actions* in addition to the optimal set of actions. In a decision to introduce a new product, suppose that the result of the decision analysis indicates that we should proceed with the introduction of the product without any market testing—that is, without any sampling. Suppose, however, that a higher official in the company requires us to test the product even though we may not want to do so. A comprehensive solution to the decision problem would provide us not only with the optimal action (market the product), but also with information on how to proceed in the best possible way when we are forced to take some suboptimal actions along the way. The complete solution to the decision problem would thus include information on how to treat the results of the market test. If the results are unfavorable, the optimal action at this point may be not to go ahead with introducing the product. The solution to the decision problem—the *decision*—gives us all information on how to proceed at any given stage or circumstance.

As you see, we have stressed a sequential approach to decision making. At the very least, a decision analysis consists of two stages: the decision maker takes an

FIGURE 15–8 An Example of a Decision Tree for New-Product Introduction

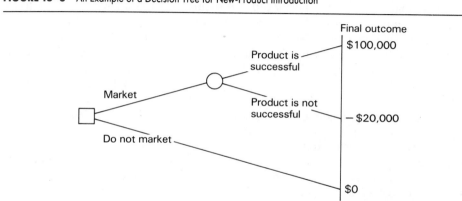

action out of several possible ones, and then chance takes an action. This sequential approach to decision making is very well modeled and visualized by what is called a **decision tree.**

A decision tree is a set of nodes and branches. At a *decision node*, the decision maker takes an action; the action is the choice of a branch to be followed. The branch leads to a *chance node*, where chance determines the outcome; that is, chance chooses the branch to be followed. Then either the final outcome is reached (the branch ends) or the decision maker gets to take another action, and so on. We mark a decision node by a square and a chance node by a circle. These are connected by the branches of the decision tree. An example of a decision tree is shown in Figure 15–8. The decision tree shown in the figure is a simple one: it consists of only four branches, one decision node, and one chance node. In addition, there is no product-testing option. As we go on, we will see more complicated decision trees, and we will explore related topics.

PROBLEMS

15–20. What are the uses of decision analysis?

15–21. What are the limitations of decision analysis?

15–22. List the elements of a decision problem, and explain how they interrelate.

15–23. What is the role of probabilities in a decision problem, and how do these probabilities arise?

15–24. What is a decision tree?

15–6   Decision Trees

As mentioned in the last section, a decision tree is a useful aid in carrying out a decision analysis because it allows us to visualize the decision problem. If nothing else, the tree gives us a good perspective on our decision problem: it lets us see when we, as decision makers, are in control of our actions and when we are not. To handle the instances when we are not in control, we use probabilities. These probabilities—assuming they are assessed in some accurate, logical, and consistent way—are our educated guesses as to what will happen when we are not in control.

The aforementioned use of decision trees in clarifying our perspective on a decision problem may not seem terribly important, say, compared with a quantitatively rigorous solution to a problem involving exact numbers. However, this use of decision trees is actually more important than it seems. After you have seen how to use a decision tree in computing the expected payoff at each chance node and the choice of the optimal action at each decision node, and after you have tried several decision problems, you will find that the trees have an added advantage. You will find that just drawing the decision tree helps you better understand the decision problem you need to solve. Then, even if the probabilities and payoffs are not accurately assessed, making you doubt the optimality of the solution you have obtained, you will have gained a better understanding of your decision problem. This in itself should help you find a good solution to the problem.

In a sense, a decision tree is a good psychological tool. People are often confused about decisions. They are not always perfectly aware of what they can do and what they cannot do, and they often lack an understanding of uncertainty and how it affects the outcomes of their decisions. This is especially true of large-scale decision problems, where there are several possible actions at several different points, each followed by chance outcomes that lead to a distant final outcome. In such cases, drawing a decision tree is an indispensable way of gaining familiarity with all aspects of the decision problem. The tree shows us which actions affect which, and how the actions interrelate with chance outcomes. The tree shows us how combinations of actions and chance outcomes lead to possible final outcomes and payoffs.

Having said all this, let us see how decision problems are transformed into visual decision trees and how these trees are analyzed. Let us see how decision trees can lead us to optimal solutions to decision problems. We will start with the simple new-product introduction example shown in the decision tree in Figure 15-8. Going step-by-step, we will show how that simple tree was constructed. The same technique is used in constructing more complicated trees, with many branches and nodes.

The Payoff Table

The first step in the solution of any decision problem is to prepare the *payoff table* (also called the *payoff matrix*). The payoff table is a table of the possible payoffs we would receive if we took certain actions, and certain chance occurrences followed. Generally, what takes place will be called *state of nature* and what we do will be called the *decision*. This leads us to a table that is very similar to Table 7-2. There we dealt with hypothesis testing, and the state of nature was whether or not the null hypothesis was true; our decision was either to accept or reject the null hypothesis. In that context, we could have associated the result "accept H_0 when H_0 is true" with some *payoff* (because a correct decision was made); the outcome "accept H_0 when H_0 is false" could have been associated with another (negative) payoff, and similarly for the other two possible outcomes. In the context of decision analysis, we might view the hypothesis testing as a sequential process. We make a decision (to accept or to reject H_0), and then "chance" takes over and either makes H_0 true or makes it false.

Let us now write the payoff table for the new-product introduction problem. Here we assume that if we do not introduce the product, there is nothing gained and nothing lost. This assumes we have not invested anything in developing the product, and it assumes no opportunity loss. If we do not introduce the new product, our payoff is zero.

If our action is to introduce the product, two things may happen: the product may be successful, or it may not. If the product is successful, our payoff will be $100,000, and if it is not successful, we will lose $20,000, so our payoff will be −$20,000. The payoff table for this simple problem is Table 15-4. In real-world situations, we may assess more possible outcomes: finely divided *degrees* of success. For example, the product may be extremely successful—with payoff $150,000; very successful—payoff $120,000; successful—payoff $100,000; somewhat successful—payoff $80,000; barely successful—payoff $40,000; breakeven—payoff $0; unsuccessful—payoff −$20,000; or disastrous—payoff −$50,000. Table 15-4 can be easily extended to cover these expanded states of nature. Instead of two columns,

TABLE 15-4 Payoff Table: New-Product Introduction

	Product Is:	
Action	**Successful**	**Not Successful**
Market the product	+$100,000	−$20,000
Do not market the product	0	0

we would have eight, and we would still have two rows corresponding to the two possible actions.

The values in Table 15–4 give rise to the decision tree that was shown in Figure 15–8. We take an action: If we do not market the product, the payoff is zero, as shown by the arc from the decision node to the final outcome of zero. If we choose to market the product, chance will either take us to success and a payoff of $100,000, or it will lead us to failure and a loss of $20,000. We now need to deal with chance. We do so by assigning probabilities to the two possible states of nature, that is, to the two possible actions of chance. Here, some elicitation of personal probabilities is done. Suppose that our marketing manager plays the de Finetti game and concludes that the probability of success of the new product is 0.75. The probability of failure then must be $1 - 0.75 = 0.25$. Let us write these probabilities on the appropriate branches of our decision tree. The tree, with payoffs and probabilities, is shown in Figure 15–9.

We now have all the elements of the decision tree, and we are ready to solve the decision problem.

> The solution of decision tree problems is achieved by working backward from the final outcomes.

The method we use is called **averaging out and folding back.** Working backward from the final outcomes, we *average out all chance occurrences.* This means that we find the *expected value* at each chance node. At each chance node (each circle in the tree), we write the expected monetary value of all branches leading out of the node; we *fold back* the tree. At each decision node (each square in the tree), we *choose the action that maximizes our (expected) payoff.* That is, we look at all branches emanating from the decision node, and we choose the branch leading to the highest monetary value. Other branches may be *clipped;* they are not optimal. The problem is solved once we reach the beginning: the first decision node.

Let us solve the decision problem of the new-product introduction. We start at the final outcomes. There are three such outcomes, as seen in Figure 15–9. The outcome with payoff zero emanates directly from the decision node; we leave it for now. The other two payoffs, $100,000 and −$20,000, both emanate from a chance node. We therefore average them out—using their respective probabilities—and fold

FIGURE 15–9   Decision Tree for New-Product Introduction

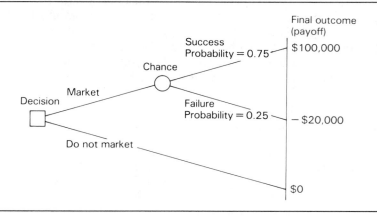

back to the chance node. To do this, we find the expected monetary value at the chance node (the circle in Figure 15–9). Recall the definition of the expected value of a random variable, given as equation 3–4.

The expected value of X, denoted $E(X)$:

$$E(X) = \sum_{\text{all } x} xP(x)$$

The outcome as you leave the chance node is a random variable with two possible values: 100,000 and −20,000. The probability of the outcome 100,000 is 0.75, and the probability of the outcome −20,000 is 0.25. To find the expected value at the chance node, we apply equation 3–4:

$$E(\text{outcome at chance node}) = (100,000)(0.75) + (-20,000)(0.25)$$
$$= 70,000$$

Thus, the expected value associated with the chance node is +$70,000; we will write this value next to the circle in our decision tree. We can now look at the decision node (the square), since we have folded back and reached the first node in the tree. We know the (expected) monetary values associated with the two branches emanating from this node. Recall that at decision nodes, we do not average. Rather, we choose the best branch to be followed and clip the other branches, as they are not optimal. Thus, at the decision node, we compare the two values +$70,000 and $0. Since 70,000 is greater than 0, the expected monetary outcome of the decision to market the new product is greater than the monetary outcome of the decision not to market the new product. We follow the rule of choosing the decision that maximizes the expected payoff, so we choose to market the product. (We clip the branch corresponding to "not market" and put a little arrow by the branch corresponding to "market.") In section 15–8, where we discuss *utility*, we will see an alternative to the "maximum expected monetary value" rule, that takes into account our attitudes toward risk rather than simply aiming for highest *average* payoff, as we have done here. The solution of the decision tree is shown in Figure 15–10.

We follow the arrow and make the decision to market the new product. Then chance takes over, and the product either becomes successful (an event which,

FIGURE 15–10   Solution of the New-Product Introduction Decision Tree

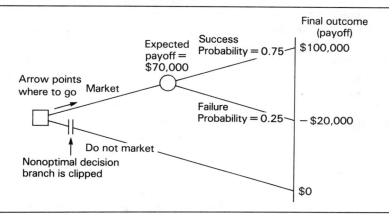

TABLE 15–5 Possible Outcomes and Their Probabilities

Outcome	Payoff	Probability
Extremely successful	$150,000	0.1
Very successful	120,000	0.2
Successful	100,000	0.3
Somewhat successful	80,000	0.1
Barely successful	40,000	0.1
Breakeven	0	0.1
Unsuccessful	−20,000	0.05
Disastrous	−50,000	0.05

FIGURE 15–11 Extended–Possibilities Decision Tree for New-Product Introduction

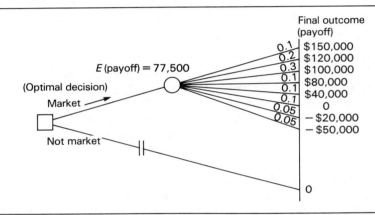

a priori, we believe to have a 0.75 probability of occurring), or does not become successful. On the average—that is, if we make decisions such as this one very many times—we should expect to make $70,000.

Let us now consider the extended market possibilities mentioned earlier. Suppose that the outcomes and their probabilities in the case of extended possibilities are as given in Table 15–5. In this new, extended example, the payoff is more realistic: it has many possible states. Our payoff is a random variable. The expected value of this random variable is computed, as usual, by multiplying the values by their probabilities and adding (equation 3–4). This can easily be done by adding a column for Payoff × Probability to Table 15–5 and adding all entries in the column. This gives us: $E(\text{payoff}) = \$77,500$ (verify this). The decision tree for this example—with many branches emanating from the chance node—is shown in Figure 15–11. The optimal decision in this case is, again, to market the product.

We have seen how to analyze a decision problem by using a decision tree. Let us now look at an example. In Example (c), chance takes over after *either* action we take, and the problem involves more than one action. We will take an action, then a chance occurrence will take place. Then we will again decide on an action, after which chance will again take over, leading us to a final outcome.

EXAMPLE (c)   In 1987, Digital Equipment Corporation arranged to get the Cunard Lines ship *Queen Elizabeth 2* (QE2) for use as a floating hotel for the company's annual convention. The meeting took place in September and lasted nine days. In agreeing to lease the QE2, Cunard had to make a decision. If the cruise ship were leased to Digital, Cunard would get a flat fee and an additional percentage of profits from the gala convention, which could attract as many as 50,000 people. Cunard analysts therefore estimated that if the ship were leased, there would be a 0.50 probability that the company would make $700,000 for the nine days; a 0.30 probability that profits from the venture would be about $800,000; a 0.15 probability that profits would be about $900,000; and a 0.05 probability that profits would be as high as $1 million. If the ship were not leased to Digital, the vessel would be used for its usual Atlantic crossing voyage, also lasting nine days. If this happened, there would be a 0.90 probability that profits would be $750,000 and a 0.10 probability that profits would be about $780,000. The tighter distribution of profits on the voyage was due to the fact that Cunard analysts knew much about the company's usual business of Atlantic crossings but knew relatively little about the proposed venture.

Cunard had one additional option. If the ship were leased to Digital, and it became clear within the first few days of the convention that Cunard's profits from the venture were going to be in the range of only $700,000, the steamship company could choose to promote the convention on its own by offering participants discounts on QE2 cruises. The company's analysts believed that if this action were chosen, there would be a 0.60 probability that profits would increase to about $740,000 and a 0.40 probability that the promotion would fail, lowering profits to $680,000 due to the cost of the promotional campaign and the discounts offered. What should Cunard have done?

SOLUTION

Let us analyze all the components of this decision problem. There are two possible actions, one of which must be chosen: to lease or not to lease. We can start constructing our tree by drawing the square denoting this decision node and showing the two appropriate branches leading out of it.

Once we make our choice, chance takes over. If we choose to lease, chance will lead us to one of four possible outcomes. We show these possibilities by attaching a circle node at the end of the Lease action branch, with four branches emanating from it. If we choose not to lease, chance again takes over, leading us to two possible outcomes. This is shown by a chance node attached at the end of the Not lease action branch, with two branches leading out of it and into the possible final outcome payoffs of $750,000 and $780,000.

We now go back to the chance occurrences following the Lease decision. At the end of the branch corresponding to an outcome of $700,000, we attach another decision node corresponding to the promotion option. This decision node has two branches leaving it: one goes to the final outcome of $700,000, corresponding to nonpromotion of the convention; and the other, the one corresponding to promotion, leads to a chance node, which in turn leads to two possible final outcomes: a profit of $740,000 and a profit of $680,000. All other chance outcomes following the Lease decision lead directly to final outcomes. These outcomes are profits of $800,000, $900,000, and $1 million. At each chance branch, we note its probability. The chance outcomes of the Lease action have probabilities 0.5, 0.3, 0.15, and 0.05 (in order of increasing monetary outcome). The probabilities of the outcomes following the Not lease action are 0.9 and 0.1, respectively. Finally, the probabilities corresponding to the chance outcomes following the Promote action are 0.4 and 0.6, again in order of increasing profit.

Our decision tree for the problem is shown in Figure 15–12. Having read the preceding description of the details of the tree, you will surely agree that "a picture is worth a thousand words."

We now solve the decision tree. Our method of solution, as you recall, is averaging out and folding back. We start at the end; that is, we look at the final-outcome payoffs and work backward from these values. At every chance node, we average the payoffs using their respective probabilities. This gives us the expected monetary value associated with the chance node. At every decision node, we choose the action with the

FIGURE 15–12   The Decision Tree for the Cunard Lease Example

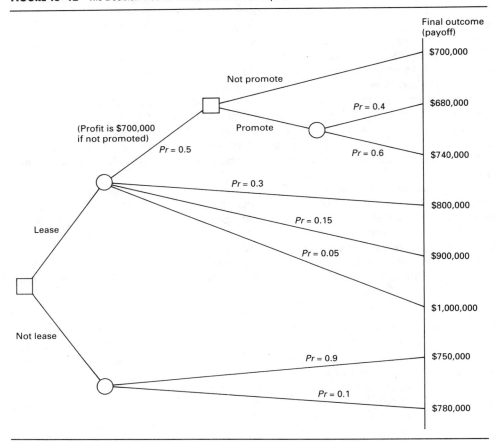

highest expected payoff and clip the branches corresponding to all other, nonoptimal actions. Once we reach the first decision node in the tree, we are done and will have obtained a complete solution to the decision problem.

Let us start with the closest chance node to the final outcomes—the one corresponding to the possible outcomes of the Promote action. The expected payoff at this chance node is obtained as:

$$E(\text{payoff}) = (680,000)(0.4) + (740,000)(0.6) = \$716,000$$

We now move back to the Promote/Not promote decision node. Here we must choose the action that maximizes the expected payoff. This is done by comparing the two payoffs: the payoff of $700,000 associated with the Not promote action and the expected payoff of $716,000 associated with the Promote action. Since the *expected* value of $716,000 is greater, we choose to promote. We show this with an arrow, and we clip the nonoptimal action not to promote. The expected value of $716,000 now becomes associated with the decision node, and we write it next to the node.

We now fold back to the chance node following the Lease action. There are four branches leading out of that node. One of them leads to the Promote decision node, which, as we just decided, is associated with an (expected) outcome of $716,000. The probability of reaching the decision node is 0.5. The next branch leads to an outcome of $800,000 and has a probability of 0.3; and the next two outcomes are $900,000 and

$1 million, with probabilities 0.15 and 0.05, respectively. We now average out the payoffs at this chance node as follows.

$$E(\text{payoff}) = (716,000)(0.5) + (800,000)(0.3) + (900,000)(0.15) + (1,000,000)(0.05)$$
$$= \$783,000$$

This expected monetary value is now written next to the chance node.

Let us now look at the last chance node, the one corresponding to outcomes associated with the Not lease action. Here, we have two possible outcomes: a payoff of $750,000, with probability 0.9; and a payoff of $780,000, with probability 0.1. We now find the expected monetary value of the chance node:

$$E(\text{payoff}) = (750,000)(0.9) + (780,000)(0.1) = \$753,000$$

We are now finally at the first decision node of the entire tree. Here we must choose the action that maximizes the expected payoff. The choice is done by comparing the expected payoff associated with the Lease action, $783,000, and the expected payoff associated with not leasing, $753,000. Since the higher expected payoff is that associated with leasing, the decision is to lease. This is shown by an arrow on the tree and by clipping the Not lease action as nonoptimal. The stages of the solution are shown in Figure 15–13.

FIGURE 15–13 Solution of the Cunard Leasing Problem

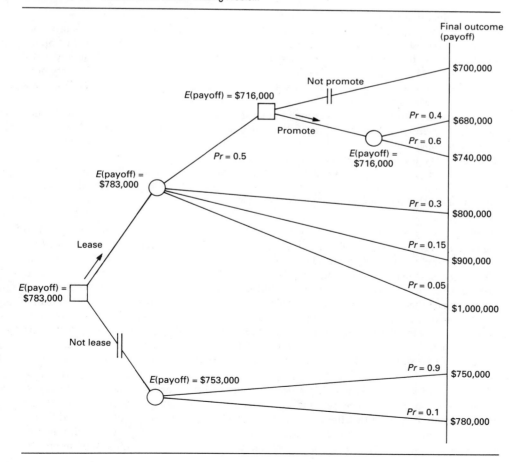

We now have a final solution to the decision problem: We choose to *lease* our ship to Digital Equipment Corporation. Then, if we should find out that our profit from the lease is going to be in the range of only $700,000, our action would be to *promote* the convention. Note that in this decision problem, the decision consists of a pair of actions. The decision tells us what to do in any eventuality.

If the tree had more than just two decision nodes, the final solution to the problem would have consisted of a set of optimal actions at all decision nodes. The solution would have told us what to do at any decision node to maximize our expected payoff, *given* that we arrive at that decision node. Note, again, that our solution is optimal only in an *expected monetary value* sense. If Cunard is very conservative and does not want to take *any* risk of getting a profit lower than the minimum of $750,000 it is assured of receiving from an Atlantic crossing, then, clearly, the decision to lease would not be optimal because it does admit such a risk. If the steamship company has some risk aversion but would accept some risk of lower profits, then the analysis should be done using *utilities* rather than pure monetary values. The use of utility in a way that accounts for people's attitudes toward risk is discussed in section 15–8.

PROBLEMS

Answer

15–25. Spuds MacKenzie, Dean of Partyology, the Original Party Animal—the stocky, bow-legged, white English bull terrier featured in Bud Light beer commercials—is probably one of the greatest advertising discoveries of all time. Few people know, however, that Spuds began appearing for Anheuser-Busch, the makers of Bud Light, in 1983 but played only a minor role in Bud Light advertising. Spuds's career really started four years (almost thirty dog-years!) later, at the Super Bowl in January 1987, when Anheuser-Busch paid CBS *$20,000 a second* to put Spuds on the air.

What went into that fateful decision? Let us say that Anheuser-Busch's marketing director felt that there would be a 0.35 probability that a series of three 60-second commercials during the Super Bowl could boost sales volume of Bud Light beer by $8 million during the following three months. The director also believed that there was a 0.65 probability that the resulting excess sales would be about $4 million. Considering also the cost of airing the company's commercials, carry out the decision analysis of whether or not to advertise on television featuring the then-unknown Spuds MacKenzie. Construct a complete decision tree, and solve it.

15–26.

New plane;
E = $270 million.

15–26. Boeing has drawn up plans for a new fuel-saving jet, the 7J7, that is designed to compete with the European-built Airbus 320. Boeing is currently conducting research to assess the feasibility of building the 7J7. Company experts believe there is a 0.20 chance that sales of the new plane would bring in gross revenues of $400 million over a period of two years; a 0.30 chance that sales of the plane during this period would bring $300 million; and a 0.50 chance that sales would bring in only $200 million. Were Boeing not to manufacture the plane and instead use its resources to make other planes that are currently being used by airlines all over the world, there is a 0.75 chance that sales of these other planes during the period in question will bring in gross revenues of $250 million, and a 0.25 chance that sales will bring in $300 million. Draw a decision tree for this problem, and solve it. What should Boeing do?

15–27. Atari Corporation is facing a decision about whether or not to acquire all the outstanding stock of Federated Stores, Inc., a stereo and electronic equipment retailer. Atari's financial analysts believe that there is a 0.40 probability that ownership of Federated Stores would bring Atari profits of $55 million over the next three years, a 0.45 probability of $70 million in profits over the period in question, and a 0.15 probability of $80 million in profits.

Atari is considering two alternative plans. One plan is to start its own chain of retail outlets. Analysts believe that this plan has a 0.10 probability of failing, producing a loss of $10 million over the next three years; it has a 0.30 probability of bringing in profits of $30 million; a 0.40 probability of producing profits of $75 million over the same period; and a 0.20 probability of bringing in $100 million in profits. The second plan is to divert the efforts to manufacturing a new computer. This plan is believed to have a 0.5 probability of bringing in profits of $150 million over the next three years, a 0.3 probability of bringing in only $50 million, and a 0.2 probability of causing a loss of $20 million over the period in question. Construct and solve the decision tree. Advise Atari about what to do and why.

15–28. Predicting the styles that will prevail in a coming year is one of the most important and difficult problems in the fashion industry. A fashion designer must work on designs for the coming fall long before he or she can find out for certain what styles are going to be "in." A well-known designer believes that there is a 0.20 chance that short dresses and skirts will be popular in the coming fall; a 0.35 chance that popular styles will be of medium length; and a 0.45 chance that long dresses and skirts will dominate fall fashions. The designer must now choose the styles on which to concentrate. If she chooses one style and another turns out to be more popular, profits will be lower than if the new style were guessed correctly. The following table shows what the designer believes she would make, in hundreds of thousands of dollars, for any given combination of her choice of style and the one that prevails in the new season.

	Prevailing Style		
Designer's Choice	**Short**	**Medium**	**Long**
Short	8	3	1
Medium	1	9	2
Long	4	3	10

Construct a decision tree, and determine what style the designer should choose to maximize her expected profits.

15–29. For problem 15–28, suppose that if the designer starts working on long designs, she can change them to medium designs after the prevailing style for the season becomes known—although she must then pay a price for this change because of delays in delivery to manufacturers. In particular, if the designer chooses long and the prevailing style is medium, and she then chooses to change to medium, there is a 0.30 chance that her profits will be $200,000 and a 0.70 chance that her profits will be $600,000. No other change from one style to another is possible. Incorporate this information in your decision tree of problem 15–28, and solve the new tree. Give a complete solution in the form of a pair of decisions under given circumstances that maximize the designer's expected profits.

15–30. Commodity futures provide an opportunity for buyers and suppliers of commodities such as wheat to arrange in advance sales of a commodity, with delivery and payment taking place at a prespecified time in the future. The price is decided at the time the order is placed, and the buyer is asked to deposit an amount less than the value of the order, but enough to protect the seller from loss in case the buyer should decide not to meet his or her obligation.

An investor is considering investing $15,000 in wheat futures and believes that there is a 0.10 probability that he will lose $5,000 by the expiration of the contract, a 0.20 probability that he will make $2,000, a 0.25 probability that he will make $3,000, a 0.15 probability he will make $4,000, a 0.15 probability he will make $5,000, a 0.10 probability he will make $6,000, and a 0.05 probability that he will make $7,000. If the investor should find out that he is going to lose $5,000, he can pull out of his contract, losing $3,500 for certain and an additional $3,000 with probability 0.20 (the latter amount deposited with a brokerage firm as a guarantee). Draw the decision tree for this problem, and solve it. What should the investor do?

15–31. For problem 15–30, suppose that the investor is considering another investment as an alternative to wheat. He is considering investing his $15,000 in a limited partnership for the same duration of time as the futures contract. This alternative has a 0.50 chance of earning $5,000 and a 0.50 chance of earning nothing. Add this information to your decision tree of problem 15–30, and solve it.

15–7   Handling Additional Information Using Bayes' Theorem

In any kind of decision problem, it is very natural to ask: Can I gain additional information about the situation? Any additional information will help in making a decision under uncertainty. The more we know, the better able we are to make decisions that are likely to maximize our payoffs. If our information is perfect, that is, if we can find out exactly what chance will do, then there really is no randomness, and the situation is perfectly determined. In such cases, there is no need for decision analysis because we can determine the exact action that will maximize the *actual* (rather than the *expected*) payoff. Here we are concerned with making decisions under uncertainty, and we assume that when additional information is available, such information is probabilistic in nature. Our information has a certain degree of *reliability*. The reliability is stated as a set of conditional probabilities.

If we are considering the introduction of a new product into the market, it would be wise to try and gain information about the prospects for success of the new product by sampling potential consumers and soliciting their views about the product. (Isn't this what statistics is all about?) Results obtained from random sampling are always probabilistic in nature; the probabilities originate in the sampling distributions of our statistics. The reliability of survey results may be stated as a set of *conditional probabilities* in the following way. *Given* that the market is ripe for our product and that it is in fact going to be successful, there is a certain probability that the sampling results will tell us so. Conversely, given that the market will not accept the new product, there is a certain probability that the random sample of people we select will be representative enough of the population in question to tell us so.

To show the use of the conditional probabilities, let S denote the event that the product will be a success and $F = \overline{S}$ (the complement of S) be the event that the product will fail. Let IS be the event that the sample indicates that the product will be a success, and IF the event that the sample indicates that the product will fail. The reliability of the sampling results may be stated by the conditional probabilities: $P(\text{IS} \mid \text{S})$, $P(\text{IS} \mid \text{F})$, $P(\text{IF} \mid \text{S})$, and $P(\text{IF} \mid \text{F})$. (Each pair of conditional probabilities with the same condition has a sum of 1.00. Thus, $P(\text{IS} \mid \text{S}) + P(\text{IF} \mid \text{S}) = 1$, and $P(\text{IS} \mid \text{F}) + P(\text{IF} \mid \text{F}) = 1$. So we only need to be given two of the four conditional probabilities.)

Once we have sampled, we know the sample outcome: either the event IS (the sample telling us that the product will be successful) or the event IF (the sample telling us that our product will not be a success). What we need is the probability that the product will be successful *given* that the sample told us so or the probability that the product will fail, if that is what the sample told us. In symbols, what we need is $P(\text{S} \mid \text{IS})$ and $P(\text{F} \mid \text{IS})$ (its complement), or the pair of probabilities $P(\text{S} \mid \text{IF})$ and $P(\text{F} \mid \text{IF})$. We have $P(\text{IS} \mid \text{S})$, and we need $P(\text{S} \mid \text{IS})$. The conditions in the two probabilities are *reversed*. Remember that Bayes' theorem reverses the conditionality of events. This is why decision analysis is usually associated with Bayesian theory. In order to transform information about the reliability of additional information in a decision problem to *usable* information about the likelihood of states of nature, we need to use Bayes' theorem.

Restating the theorem in this context, suppose that the sample told us that the product will be a success. The (posterior) probability that the product will indeed be a success is given by:

$$P(S \mid IS) = \frac{P(IS \mid S)P(S)}{P(IS \mid S)P(S) + P(IS \mid F)P(F)} \qquad (15-6)$$

The probabilities $P(S)$ and $P(F)$ are our *prior* probabilities of the two possible outcomes: successful product versus unsuccessful product. Knowing these prior probabilities and knowing the reliability of survey results, here in the form of $P(IS \mid S)$ and $P(IS \mid F)$, allows us to compute the posterior, *updated* probability that the product will be successful given that the sample told us that it will be successful.

How is all this used in a decision tree? We extend our decision problem to include two possible actions: to test or not to test, that is, to obtain additional information or not to obtain such information. The decision of whether or not to test must be made *before* we make any other decision. In the case of a new-product introduction decision problem, our decision tree must be augmented to include the possibility of testing or not testing before deciding on whether or not to market our new product. We will assume that the test costs $5,000. Our new decision tree is shown in Figure 15–14.

FIGURE 15–14 New–Product Decision Tree with Testing

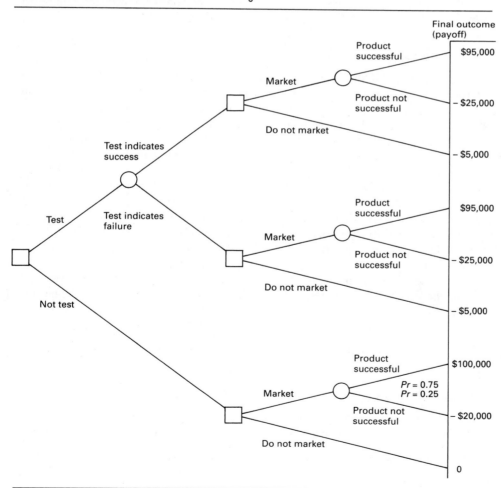

As shown in Figure 15–14, we first decide whether or not to test. If we test, we get a test result. The result is a *chance outcome*—the test indicates success, or the test indicates failure (event IS or event IF). If the test indicates success, we may choose to market, or we may choose not to market. The same happens if the test indicates failure: we may *still* choose to market, or we may choose not to market. If the test is worthwhile, it is not logical to market once the test tells us the product will fail. But the point of the decision analysis is that *we do not know* whether the test is worthwhile; this is one of the things on which we need to decide. Therefore, we allow for the possibility of marketing even if the test tells us not to market, as well as allowing for all other possible combinations of decisions.

Determining the Payoffs

Recall that if the product is successful, we make $100,000, and if it is not successful, we lose $20,000. The test is assumed to cost $5,000. Thus, *we must subtract $5,000* from all final-outcome payoffs that are reached via testing. If we test, we spend $5,000. If we then market and the product is successful, we make $100,000, but we must deduct the $5,000 we had to pay for the test, leaving us a net profit of $95,000. Similarly, we must add the $5,000 cost of the market test to the possible loss of $20,000. This brings the payoff that corresponds to product failure to −$25,000.

Determining the Probabilities

We have now reached the crucial step of determining the probabilities associated with the different branches of our decision tree. As shown in Figure 15–14, we only know two probabilities: the probability of a successful product without any testing and the probability of an unsuccessful product without any testing. (These are our old probabilities from the decision tree of Figure 15–9.) These probabilities are $P(S) = 0.75$ and $P(F) = 0.25$. The two probabilities are also our *prior* probabilities—the probabilities before any sampling or testing is undertaken. As such, we will use them in conjunction with Bayes' theorem for determining the posterior probabilities of success and of failure, and the probabilities of the two possible test results: $P(\text{IS})$ and $P(\text{IF})$. The latter are the total probabilities of IS and IF, respectively, and are obtained from the *denominator* in equation 15–6 and its analog using the event IF. These are sometimes called *predictive probabilities* because they *predict* the test results.

For the decision tree in Figure 15–14, we have *two* probabilities, and we need to fill in the other six. First, let us look at the particular branches and define our probabilities. The probabilities of the two upper branches of the chance node immediately preceding the payoffs correspond to the two sequences:

Test → Test indicates success → Market → Product is successful

and

Test → Test indicates success → Market → Product is not successful

These are the two sequences of events leading to the payoffs $95,000 and −$25,000, respectively. The probabilities we seek for the two final branches are:

$P(\text{Product is successful} \mid \text{Test has indicated success})$

and

$P(\text{Product is not successful} \mid \text{Test has indicated success})$

These are the required probabilities because we have reached the branches Success and No success via the route: Test → Test indicates success. In symbols, the two probabilities we seek are: $P(S \mid IS)$ and $P(F \mid IS)$. The first probability will be obtained from Bayes' theorem, equation 15−6, and the second will be obtained as $P(F \mid IS) = 1 - P(S \mid IS)$. What we need for Bayes' theorem—in addition to the prior probabilities—are the conditional probabilities that contain the information about the reliability of the market test. Let us suppose that these probabilities are:

$$P(IS \mid S) = 0.9; \ P(IF \mid S) = 0.1; \ P(IF \mid F) = 0.85; \ P(IS \mid F) = 0.15$$

Thus, when the product is indeed going to be successful, the test has a 0.90 chance of telling us so. Ten percent of the time, however, when the product is going to be successful, the test erroneously indicates failure. When the product is *not* going to be successful, the test so indicates with probability 0.85 and fails to do so with probability 0.15. This information is assumed to be known to us at the time we consider whether or not to test.

Applying Bayes' theorem, equation 15−6, we get:

$$P(S \mid IS) = \frac{P(IS \mid S)P(S)}{P(IS \mid S)P(S) + P(IS \mid F)P(F)} = \frac{(0.9)(0.75)}{(0.9)(0.75) + (0.15)(0.25)}$$
$$= \frac{0.675}{0.7125} = 0.9474$$

The denominator in the equation, 0.7125, is an important number. Recall from section 2−8 that this is the *total probability* of the conditioning event; it is the probability of IS. We therefore have:

$$P(S \mid IS) = 0.9474 \quad \text{and} \quad P(IS) = 0.7125$$

These two probabilities give rise to two more probabilities (namely, those of their complements): $P(F \mid IS) = 1 - 0.9474 = 0.0526$ and $P(IF) = 1 - P(IS) = 1 - 0.7125 = 0.2875$.

Using Bayes' theorem and its denominator, we have found that the probability that the test will indicate success is 0.7125, and the probability that it will indicate failure is 0.2875. Once the test indicates success, there is a probability of 0.9474 that the product will indeed be successful and a probability of 0.0526 that it will not be successful. This gives us four more probabilities to attach to branches of the decision tree. Now all we need are the last two probabilities: $P(S \mid IF)$ and $P(F \mid IF)$. These are obtained via an analog of equation 15−6 for when the test indicates failure. It is given as equation 15−7.

$$P(S \mid IF) = \frac{P(IF \mid S)P(S)}{P(IF \mid S)P(S) + P(IF \mid F)P(F)} \tag{15−7}$$

The denominator of equation 15−7 is, by the law of total probability, simply the probability of the event IF, and we have just solved for it: $P(IF) = 0.2875$. The numerator is equal to $(0.1)(0.75) = 0.075$. We thus get $P(S \mid IF) = 0.075/0.2875 = 0.2609$. The last probability we need is $P(F \mid IF) = 1 - P(S \mid IF) = 1 - 0.2609 = 0.7391$.

We will now enter all these probabilities into our decision tree. The complete tree with all probabilities and payoffs is shown in Figure 15−15. (To save space in the figure, events are denoted by their symbols: S, F, IS, etc.)

We are finally in a position to solve the decision problem by averaging out and folding back our tree. Let us start by averaging out the three chance nodes closest to

FIGURE 15–15   New–Product Decision Tree with Probabilities

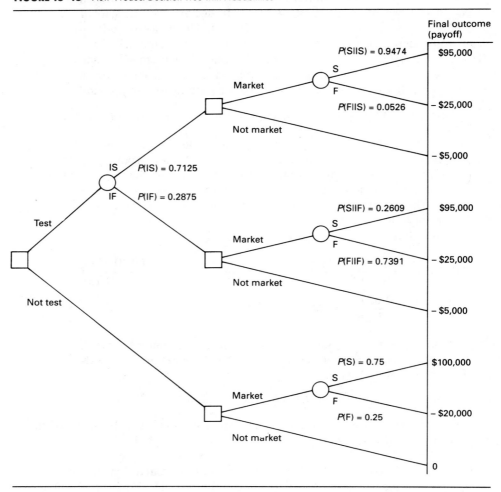

the final outcomes:

$$E(\text{payoff}) = (0.9474)(95,000) + (0.0526)(-25,000)$$
$$= \$88,688 \quad \text{(Top chance node)}$$
$$E(\text{payoff}) = (0.2609)(95,000) + (0.7391)(-25,000)$$
$$= \$6,308 \quad \text{(Middle chance node)}$$
$$E(\text{payoff}) = (0.75)(100,000) + (0.25)(-20,000)$$
$$= \$70,000 \quad \text{(Bottom chance node)}$$

We can now fold back and look for the optimal actions at each of the three preceding decision nodes. Again, starting from top to bottom, we first compare $88,688 with −$5,000 and conclude that—once the test indicates success—we should market the product. Then, comparing $6,308 with −$5,000, we conclude that even if the test says that the product will fail, we are still better off if we go ahead and market the product (remember, all our conclusions are based on the expected monetary value and have no allowance for risk aversion). The third comparison again tells us to market the product, because $70,000 is greater than zero.

FIGURE 15–16   New–Product Introduction: Expected Values and Optimal Decision

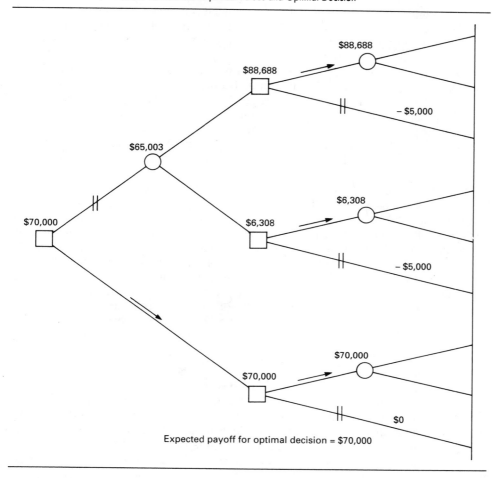

Expected payoff for optimal decision = $70,000

We are now at the chance node corresponding to the outcome of the test. At this point, we need to average out $88,688 and $6,308, with probabilities 0.7125 and 0.2875, respectively. This gives us:

$$E(\text{payoff}) = (0.7125)(88,688) + (0.2875)(6,308) = \$65,003.75$$

Finally, we are at the very first decision node, and here we need to compare $65,003.75 with $70,000. Since $70,000 is greater, our optimal decision is *not* to test and to go right ahead and market the new product. If we *must*, for some reason, test the product, then we should go ahead and market it regardless of the outcome of the test if we want to maximize our expected monetary payoff. Note that our solution is, of course, strongly dependent on the numbers we have used. If these numbers were different—for example, if the prior probability of success were not as high as it is—the optimal solution could very well have been to test first and then follow the result of the test. Our solution to this problem is shown in Figure 15–16.

We now demonstrate the entire procedure of decision analysis with additional information by Example (d). To simplify the calculations, which were explained earlier on a conceptual level using equations, we will use tables.

EXAMPLE (d)

Insurance companies need to invest large amounts of money in opportunities that provide high yields and are long-term in nature. One type of investment that has recently attracted some insurance companies is real estate.

The Aetna life and casualty company is considering an investment in real estate in central Florida. The investment is for a period of ten years, and company analysts believe that the investment will lead to returns that depend on future levels of economic activity in the area. In particular, the analysts believe that the invested amount would bring the profits listed in Table 15–6, depending on the listed levels of economic activity and their given (prior) probabilities. The alternative to this investment plan—one that the company has used in the past—is a particular investment that has a 0.5 probability of yielding a profit of $4 million and a 0.5 probability of yielding $7 million over the period in question.

The company may also seek some expert advice on economic conditions in central Florida. For an amount that would be equivalent to $1 million 10 years from now (when invested at a risk-free rate), the company could hire an economic consulting firm to study the future economic prospects in central Florida. From past dealings with the consulting firm, Aetna analysts believe that the reliability of the consulting firm's conclusions is as listed in Table 15–7. The table lists as columns the three conclusions the consultants may reach about the future of the area's economy. The rows of the table correspond to the true level of the economy 10 years in the future, and the table entries are conditional probabilities. For example, if the future level of the economy is going to be high, then the consultants' statement will be "high" with probability 0.85. What should Aetna do?

SOLUTION

First, we construct the decision tree, including all the known information. The decision tree is shown in Figure 15–17. Now we need to use the prior probabilities in Table 15–6 and the conditional probabilities in Table 15–7 in computing both the posterior probabilities of the different payoffs from the investment *given* the three possible consultants' conclusions, and the predictive probabilities of the three consultants' conclusions. This is done in Tables 15–8, 15–9, and 15–10. Note that the probabilities of the outcomes of the alternative investment do not change with the consultants' conclusions (the consultants' conclusions pertain only to the central Florida investment prospects, not to the alternative investment).

TABLE 15–6 Information for Example (d)

Profit from Investment	Level of Economic Activity	Probability
$3 million	Low	0.20
$6 million	Medium	0.50
$12 million	High	0.30

TABLE 15–7 The Reliability of the Consulting Firm

	Consultants' Conclusion		
True Future State of Economy	**High**	**Medium**	**Low**
Low	0.05	0.05	0.90
Medium	0.15	0.80	0.05
High	0.85	0.10	0.05

FIGURE 15–17 Decision Tree for Example (d)

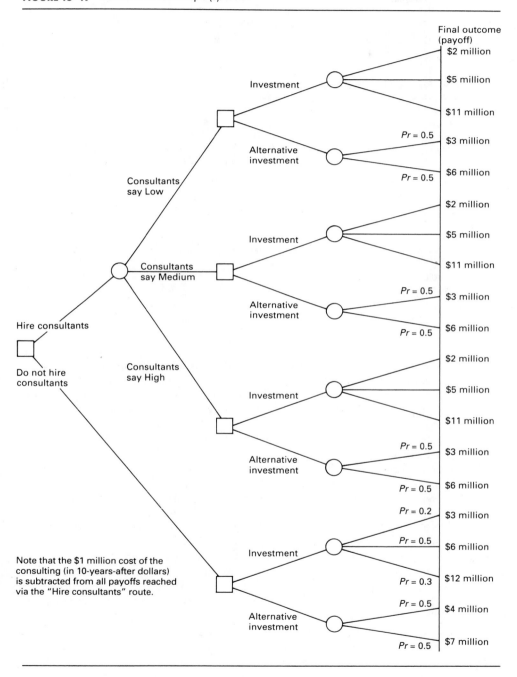

Final outcome (payoff)

- $2 million
- $5 million
- $11 million
- $3 million ($Pr = 0.5$)
- $6 million ($Pr = 0.5$)
- $2 million
- $5 million
- $11 million
- $3 million ($Pr = 0.5$)
- $6 million ($Pr = 0.5$)
- $2 million
- $5 million
- $11 million
- $3 million ($Pr = 0.5$)
- $6 million ($Pr = 0.5$)
- $3 million ($Pr = 0.2$)
- $6 million ($Pr = 0.5$)
- $12 million ($Pr = 0.3$)
- $4 million ($Pr = 0.5$)
- $7 million ($Pr = 0.5$)

Investment / Alternative investment

Consultants say Low / Consultants say Medium / Consultants say High

Hire consultants / Do not hire consultants

Note that the $1 million cost of the consulting (in 10-years-after dollars) is subtracted from all payoffs reached via the "Hire consultants" route.

TABLE 15–8 Events and Their Probabilities: Consultants Say "Low"

Event	Prior	Conditional	Joint	Posterior
Low	0.20	0.90	0.180	0.818
Medium	0.50	0.05	0.025	0.114
High	0.30	0.05	0.015	0.068
		P(Consultants say "Low") =	0.220	1.000

TABLE 15–9 Events and Their Probabilities: Consultants Say "Medium"

Event	Prior	Conditional	Joint	Posterior
Low	0.20	0.05	0.01	0.023
Medium	0.50	0.80	0.40	0.909
High	0.30	0.10	0.03	0.068
		P(Consultants say "Medium") =	0.44	1.000

TABLE 15–10 Events and Their Probabilities: Consultants Say "High"

Event	Prior	Conditional	Joint	Posterior
Low	0.20	0.05	0.010	0.029
Medium	0.50	0.15	0.075	0.221
High	0.30	0.85	0.255	0.750
		P(Consultants say "High") =	0.340	1.000

These tables represent a way of using Bayes' theorem in an efficient manner. Each of the tables gives us the three posterior probabilities and the predictive probability for a particular consultants' statement. The structure of the tables is the same as that of Table 15–2, for example. Let us define our events in shortened form. H indicates that the level of economic activity will be high; L and M are defined similarly. We let H be the event that the consultants will predict a high level of economic activity. We similarly define L and M. Using this notation, the following is a breakdown of Table 15–8.

The prior probabilities are just the probabilities of events H, L, and M, as given in Table 15–6. Next we consider the event that the consultants predict a low economy: event L. The next column in Table 15–8 consists of the conditional probabilities: $P(L \mid L)$, $P(L \mid M)$, and $P(L \mid H)$. These probabilities come from the last column of Table 15–7. The joint probabilities column in Table 15–8 consists of the products of the entries in the first two probabilities columns. The *sum* of the entries in this column is the denominator in Bayes' theorem: it is the total (or predictive) probability of the event L. Finally, dividing each entry in the joint probabilities column by the sum of that column [i.e., by $P(L)$], gives us the posterior probabilities: $P(L \mid L)$, $P(M \mid L)$, and $P(H \mid L)$. Tables 15–9 and 15–10 are interpreted in the same way, for events M and H, respectively.

Now that we have all the required probabilities, we can enter them in the tree. We can then average out at the chance nodes and fold back the tree. At each decision node, we choose the action that maximizes the expected payoff. The tree, with all its probabilities, final-outcome payoffs, expected payoffs at the chance nodes, and indicators of the optimal action at each decision node, is shown in Figure 15–18. The figure is a complete solution to this problem.

FIGURE 15–18 Solution to Aetna Decision Problem

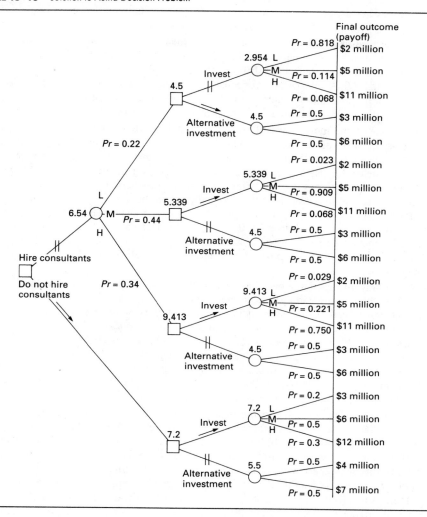

The final solution is not to hire the consultants and to invest in the central Florida project. If we have to consult, then we should choose the alternative investment if the consultants predict a low level of economic activity for the region, and invest in the central Florida project if they predict either a medium or a high level of economic activity. The expected value of the investment project is $7.2 million.

PROBLEMS

15–32. Explain why Bayes' theorem is necessary for handling additional information in a decision problem.

15–33. Explain the meaning of the term *predictive probability*.

Answers

15–34.

Hire;
E = $7.46 million.

15–36.

Test, then do as test
tells you;
E = $37,160.

15–38.

Test, then do as test says;
E = $752,000.

15–40.

Discount broker;
E = $225.

15–34. For Example (d), suppose that hiring the economic consultants costs only $100,000 (in 10-years-after dollars). Redo the analysis. What is the optimal decision? Explain.

15–35. For problem 15–25, suppose that before deciding whether or not to advertise on television, Anheuser-Busch has a choice of testing the commercial. Suppose that the test costs $200,000 and has the following reliability. If we call sales of $8 million the high state and $4 million in sales the low state, then if the true state is high, the test has a 0.96 chance of detecting this and a 0.04 chance of erroneously indicating "low." If the true state is low, then the test has a 0.93 chance of determining this and a 0.07 chance of erroneously concluding "high." Use this information, and redo the problem. What is the optimal decision?

15–36. One of the most powerful people in Hollywood is not an actor, director, or producer. It is Richard Soames, an insurance director for the London-based Film Finances Ltd. Soames is a leading provider of movie completion bond guarantees. The guarantees are like insurance policies that pay the extra costs when films go over budget or are not completed on time. Suppose that Soames is considering insuring the production of a movie and feels there is a 0.65 chance that his company will make $80,000 on the deal (i.e., the production will be on time and not exceed budget). He believes there is a 0.35 chance that the movie will exceed budget and his company will lose $120,000, which would have to be paid to complete production. Soames could pay a movie industry expert $5,000 for an evaluation of the project's success. He believes that the expert's conclusions are true 90% of the time. What should Soames do?

15–37. Many airlines flying overseas have recently considered changing the kinds of goods they sell at their in-flight duty-free services. Swissair, for example, is considering selling Swiss watches instead of the usual liquor and cigarettes. A Swiss Air executive believes that there is a 0.60 chance that passengers would prefer these goods to the usual items and that revenues from in-flight sales would increase by $40,000 over a period of several months. She believes there is a 0.40 chance that revenues would decrease by $20,000, which would happen should people not buy the watches and instead desire the usual items. Testing the new idea on actual flights would cost $6,000, and the results would have a 0.85 probability of correctly detecting the state of nature. What should Swissair do?

15–38. For problem 15–28, suppose that the designer can obtain some expert advice for a cost of $30,000. If the fashion is going to be short, there is a 0.90 probability that the expert will predict short, a 0.05 probability that the expert will predict medium, and a 0.05 probability that the expert will predict long. If the fashion is going to be medium, there is a 0.10 probability that the expert will predict short, a 0.75 probability that the expert will predict medium, and a 0.15 probability that the expert will predict long. If the fashion is going to be long, there is a 0.10 probability that the expert will predict short, a 0.10 probability that the expert will predict medium, and a 0.80 probability that the expert will predict long. Construct the decision tree for this problem. What is the optimal decision for the designer?

15–39. A cable television company is considering extending its services to a rural community. The company's managing director believes that there is a 0.50 chance that profits from the service will be high and amount to $760,000 in the first year, and a 0.50 chance that profits will be low and amount to $400,000 for the year. An alternative operation promises a sure profit of $500,000 for the period in question. The company may test the potential of the rural market for a cost of $25,000. The test has a 90% reliability of correctly detecting the state of nature. Construct the decision tree, and determine the optimal decision.

15–40. An investor is considering two brokerage firms. One is a discount broker offering no investment advice, but charging only $50 for the amount the investor intends to invest. The other is a full-service broker who charges $200 for the amount of the intended investment. If the investor chooses the discount broker, there is a 0.45 chance of a $500 profit (before charges) over the period of the investment, a 0.35 chance of making only $200, and 0.20 chance of losing $100. If the investor chooses the full-service broker, then there is a 0.60 chance that the investment will earn $500, a 0.35 chance that it will earn $200, and a 0.05 chance that it will lose $100. What is the best investment advice in this case?

15–8 Utility

Often we have to make decisions where the rewards are not easily quantifiable. The reputation of a company, for example, is not easily measured in terms of dollars and cents. Such rewards as job satisfaction, pride, and a sense of well-being also fall into this category. Although you may feel that a stroll on the beach is "priceless," it is sometimes possible to order such things on a scale of values by gauging them against the amount of money you would require for giving them up. When such scaling is possible, the value system used is called a **utility.**

If a decision affecting a firm involves rewards or losses that are either nonmonetary or—more commonly—represent a mixture of dollars and other benefits such as reputation, long-term market share, and customer satisfaction, we need to convert all the benefits to a single scale. The scale, often measured in dollars or other units, is a *utility scale*. Once utilities are assessed, the analysis proceeds as before, with the utility units acting as dollars and cents. If the utility function was correctly evaluated, results of the decision analysis may be meaningful.

The concept of utility is derived not only from seemingly nonquantifiable rewards. Utility is a part of the very way we deal with money. For most people, the value of a thousand dollars is not constant. For example, suppose you were offered a thousand dollars to wash someone's dirty dishes. Would you do it? Probably yes. Now suppose that you were given a million dollars and then asked if you would do the dishes for a thousand dollars. Most people would refuse because the value of an additional thousand dollars seems insignificant once you have a million dollars (or more), as compared with the value of a thousand dollars if you do not have a million.

The value you attach to money—the *utility* of money—is not a straight-line function, but a curve. Such a curve is shown in Figure 15–19. Looking at the figure, we see that the utility (the value) of one additional dollar, as measured on the vertical axis, *decreases* as our wealth (measured on the horizontal axis) increases. The type of function shown in Figure 15–19 is well suited for modeling a situation where

FIGURE 15–19 A Utility-of-Money Curve

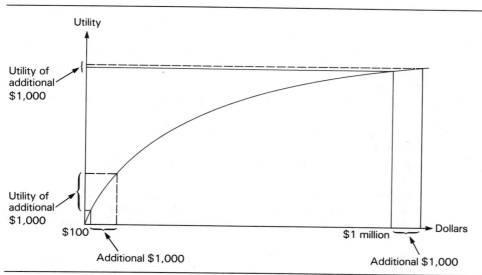

FIGURE 15-20   Utility of a Risk Avoider

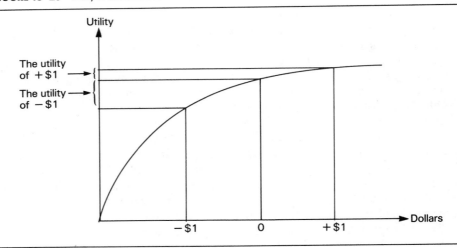

an additional amount of money, $x, has different worth to us depending on our wealth, that is, where the utility of each additional dollar decreases as we acquire more money. This utility function is the utility curve of a *risk-averse* individual. Indeed, utility can be used to model people's attitudes toward risk. Let us see why and how.

Suppose that you are offered the following choice. You can get $5,000 for certain, or you could get a lottery ticket where you have a 0.5 chance of winning $20,000 and a 0.5 chance of losing $2,000. Which would you choose? The expected payoff from the lottery is $E(\text{payoff}) = (0.5)(20,000) + (0.5)(-2,000) = \$9,000$. This is almost *twice* the amount you could get with probability 1.0, the $5,000. Expected monetary payoff would tell us to choose the lottery. However, few people would really do so; most would choose the $5,000, a sure amount. This shows us that a possible loss of $2,000 is not worth the possible gain of $20,000, even if the expected payoff is large. Such behavior is typical of a risk-averse individual. For such a person, the reward of a possible gain of one dollar is not worth the "pain" of a possible loss of the same amount.

Risk aversion is modeled by a utility function (the value-of-money function) such as the one shown in Figure 15-19. Again, let us look at such a function. Figure 15-20 shows how, for a risk-averse individual, the utility of one dollar earned (one dollar to the *right* of zero) is less than the value of a dollar lost (one dollar to the *left* of zero).

Not everyone is risk-averse, especially if we consider companies rather than individuals. The utility functions in Figures 15-19 and 15-20 are *concave* functions: they are functions with a decreasing slope, and these are characteristic of a risk-averse person. For a *risk-seeking* person, the utility is a *convex* function: a function with an increasing slope. Such a function is shown in Figure 15-21. Look at the curve in the figure, and convince yourself that an added dollar is worth *more* to the risk taker than the pain of a lost dollar (use the same technique used in Figure 15-20).

For a *risk-neutral* person, a dollar is a dollar no matter what. Such an individual gives the same value to one dollar whether he or she has $10 million or nothing. For such a person, the pain of the loss of a dollar is the same as the reward of gaining

FIGURE 15-21
Utility of a Risk Taker

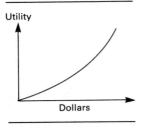

FIGURE 15-22
Utility of a Risk-Neutral Person

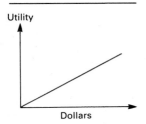

one dollar. The utility function for a risk-neutral person is a straight line. Such a utility function is shown in Figure 15–22. Again, convince yourself that the utility of
+$1 is equal (in absolute value) to the utility of −$1 for such a person. Figure
15–23 shows a mixed utility function. The individual is a risk avoider when his or
her wealth is small, and a risk taker when his or her wealth is great. We now present
a method that may be used for assessing an individual's utility function.

A Method of Assessing Utility

One way of assessing the utility curve of an individual is to do the following.

1. Identify the maximum payoff in a decision problem, and assign it the utility
   1: $U(\text{Max value}) = 1$.
2. Identify the minimum payoff in a decision problem, and assign it the value
   0: $U(\text{Min value}) = 0$.
3. Conduct the following game to determine the utility of any intermediate
   value in the decision problem (in this chosen scale of numbers). Ask the
   person whose utility you are trying to assess to determine the probability p
   such that he or she expresses *indifference* between the two choices: receive
   the payoff R with certainty or have probability p of receiving the maximum
   value and probability $1 - p$ of receiving the minimum value. The determined p is the utility of the value R. This is done for all values R for which
   we want to assess the utility.

The assessment of a utility is demonstrated in Figure 15–24. The utility curve passes
through all the points R_i, p_i $(i = 1, 2 \ldots)$ for which the utility was assessed. Let
us look at an example.

FIGURE 15–23
A Mixed Utility

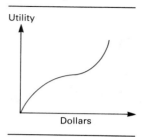

FIGURE 15–24
The Assessment of a Utility
Function

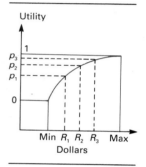

Suppose that an investor is considering decisions that lead to the following possible payoffs: $1,500, $4,300, $22,000, $31,000, and $56,000 (the investments have different
levels of risk). We now try to assess the investor's utility function.

EXAMPLE (e)

Starting with step 1, we identify the minimum payoff as $1,500. This value is assigned
the utility of 0. The maximum payoff is $56,000, and we assign the utility 1 to that
figure. We now ask the investor a series of questions that should lead us to the determination of the utilities of the intermediate payoff values. Let us suppose the investor
states that he is indifferent between receiving $4,300 for certain and receiving $56,000
with probability 0.2 and $1,500 with probability 0.8. This means that the utility of the
payoff $4,300 is 0.2. We now continue to the next payoff, of $22,000. Suppose that the
investor is indifferent between receiving $22,000 with certainty and $56,000 with probability 0.7 and $1,500 with probability 0.3. The investor's utility of $22,000 is therefore 0.7. Finally, the investor indicates indifference between a certain payoff of $31,000
and receiving $56,000 with probability 0.8 and $1,500 with probability 0.2. The utility
of $31,000 is thus equal to 0.8. We now plot the corresponding pairs (payoff, utility)
and run a rough curve through them.

The curve—the utility function of the investor—is shown in Figure 15–25. Whatever the decision problem facing the investor, the *utilities* rather than the actual payoffs
are the values to be used in the analysis. The analysis is based on maximizing the investor's *expected utility* rather than the expected monetary outcome.

SOLUTION

FIGURE 15–25
Investor's Utility

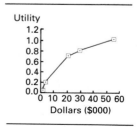

Note that utility is not unique. Many possible scales of values may be used to represent a person's attitude toward risk, as long as the general shape of the curve, for a given individual, remains the same—convex, concave, or linear—and with the same relative curvature. In practice, the assessment of utilities may not always be a feasible procedure, as it requires the decision maker to play the hypothetical game of assessing the indifference probabilities.

PROBLEMS

Answer

15–44.

Risk-averse.

15–41. What is a utility function?

15–42. What are the advantages of using a utility function?

15–43. What are the characteristics of the utility function of a risk-averse individual? Of a risk taker?

15–44. What can you say about the risk attitude of the investor in Example (e)?

15–45. Choose a few hypothetical monetary payoffs, and determine your own utility function. From the resulting curve, draw a conclusion about your attitude toward risk.

15–9   The Value of Information

In decision-making problems, the question often arises as to the *value* of information: How much should we be willing to pay for additional information about the situation at hand? The first step in answering this question is to find out how much we should be willing to pay for perfect information, that is, how much we should pay for a crystal ball that would tell us *exactly* what will happen: what the exact state of nature will be. If we can determine the value of perfect information, this will give us an *upper bound* on the value of any (imperfect) information. If we are willing to pay D dollars to know exactly what will happen, then we should be willing to pay an amount no greater than D for information that is less reliable. Since sample information is imperfect (in fact, it is probabilistic in nature, as we well know from our discussion of sampling), the value of sample information is less than the value of perfect information. It will only equal the value of perfect information if the entire population is sampled.

Let us see how the upper bound on the value of information is obtained. Since we do not know what the perfect information is, we can only compute the *expected value of perfect information* in a given decision-making situation. The expected value is a *mean* computed using the prior probabilities of the various states of nature. It assumes, however, that at any given point when we actually take an action, we know its exact outcome. Before we (hypothetically) buy the perfect information, we do not know what the state of nature will be, and therefore we must average payoffs using our prior probabilities.

The expected value of perfect information (EVPI):

EVPI = The expected monetary value of the decision situation when perfect information is available *minus* the expected value of the decision situation when no additional information is available

This definition of the expected value of perfect information is logical: it says that the (expected) maximum amount we should be willing to pay for perfect information is equal to the difference between our expected payoff from the decision situation when we have the information and our expected payoff from the decision situation without the information. The expected value of information is equal to what we stand to gain from this information. We will demonstrate the computation of the expected value of perfect information with an example.

An article in the *Journal of Marketing Research* gives an example of decision making in the airline industry.[4] The situation involves a price war that ensues when one airline determines the fare it will set for a particular route. Profits depend on the fare that will be set by a competing airline for the same route. Competitive situations such as this one are modeled using game theory. In this example, however, we will look at the competitor's action as a chance occurrence and consider the problem within the realm of decision analysis.

EXAMPLE (f)

Table 15–11 shows the payoffs (in millions of dollars) to the airline over a given period of time, for a given fare set by the airline and by its competitor. We assume that there is a certain probability that the competitor will choose the low ($200) price and a certain probability that the competitor will choose the high price. Suppose that the probability of the low price is 0.6 and that the probability of the high price is 0.4.

The decision tree for this situation is given in Figure 15–26. Solving the tree, we find that if we set our price at $200, the expected payoff is equal to: $E(\text{payoff}) =$

SOLUTION

TABLE 15–11   Airline Payoffs (in Millions of Dollars)

Airline's Fare (Action)	Competitor's Fare (State of Nature)	
	$200	**$300**
$200	8	9
$300	4	10

FIGURE 15–26   Decision Tree for Example (f)

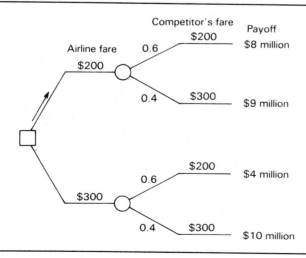

---

[4] K. Moorthy, "Using Game Theory to Model Competition," *Journal of Marketing Research* (August 1985).

(0.6)(8) + (0.4)(9) = \$8.4 million. If we set our price at \$300, then our expected pay-off is: $E(\text{payoff}) = (0.6)(4) + (0.4)(10) = \$6.4$ million. The optimal action is, there-fore, to set our price at \$200. This is shown with an arrow in Figure 15–26.

Now we may ask the question of whether or not it may be worthwhile to obtain more information. Obtaining new information in this case may entail hiring a consultant who is knowledgeable about the operating philosophy of the competing airline. We may seek other ways of obtaining information; we may, for example, make an analysis of the competitor's past pricing behavior. The important question is: What do we stand to gain from the new information? Suppose that we know exactly what our competitor plans to do. If we know that the competitor plans to set the price at \$200, then our optimal action is to set ours at \$200 as well; this is seen by comparing the two amounts in the first payoff column of Table 15–11, the column corresponding to the competitor's setting the price at \$200. We see that our maximum payoff is then \$8 million, obtained by choosing \$200 as our own price as well. If the competitor chooses to set its price at \$300, then our optimal action is to set our price at \$300 as well and obtain a payoff of \$9 million.

We know that without any additional information, the optimal decision is to set the price at \$200, obtaining an *expected* payoff of \$8.4 million (the expected value of the decision situation without any information). What is the expected payoff with *perfect* information? We do not know what the perfect information may be, but we assume that the prior probabilities we have are a true reflection of the long-run proportion of the time our competitor sets either price. Therefore, 60% of the time our competitor sets the low price, and 40% of the time the competitor sets the high price. If we had perfect information, we would know—at the time—how high to set the price. If we knew that the competitor planned to set the price at \$200, we would do the same because this would give us the maximum payoff, \$8 million. Conversely, when our perfect informa-tion tells us that the competitor is setting the price at \$300, we would again follow suit and gain a maximum payoff, \$10 million. Analyzing the situation *now*, we do not know what the competitor will do (we do not have the perfect information), but we do know the probabilities. We therefore average the maximum payoff in each case, that is, the payoff that would be obtained under perfect information, using our probabilities. This gives us the *expected payoff* under perfect information. We get: E(payoff under perfect information) = (Maximum payoff if the competitor chooses \$200) × (Probability that the competitor will choose \$200) + (Maximum payoff if the competitor chooses \$300) × (Probability that the competitor will choose \$300) = (8)(0.6) + (10)(0.4) = \$8.8 million. If we could get perfect information, we could *expect* (on the average) to make a profit of \$8.8 million. Without perfect information, we expect to make \$8.4 million (the optimal decision without any additional information).

We now use the definition of the expected value of perfect information:

$$\text{EVPI} = E(\text{payoff under perfect information}) - E(\text{payoff without information})$$

Applying the rule in this case, we get: EVPI = 8.8 − 8.4 = \$0.4 million, or simply \$400,000. Therefore, \$400,000 is the *maximum* amount of money we should be willing to pay for additional information about our competitor's price intentions. This is the amount of money we should be willing to pay to know for certain what our competitor plans to do. We should pay *less* than this amount for all information that is not as reli-able.

What about sampling, when sampling is possible? (In the airlines example, it probably is not possible to sample.) The expected value of sample information is equal to the expected value of perfect information, minus the expected cost of sam-pling errors. The expected cost of sampling errors is obtained from the probabilities of errors—known from sampling theory—and the resulting loss of payoff due to making less-than-optimal decisions. The *expected net gain* from sampling is equal to

FIGURE 15–27 The Expected Net Gain from Sampling (in Dollars) as a Function of the Sample Size

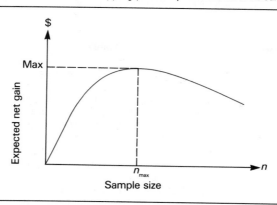

the expected value of sampling information, minus the cost of sampling. As the sample size increases, the expected net gain from sampling first increases, as our new information is valuable and improves our decision-making ability. Then the expected net gain decreases because we are paying for the information at a constant rate, while the information content in each additional data point becomes less and less important as we get more and more data. (A sample of 1,100 does not contain much more information than a sample of 1,000. However, the same 100 data points may be *very* valuable if they are all we have.)

At some particular sample size, n, we maximize our expected net gain from sampling. Determining the optimal sample size to be used in a decision situation is a difficult problem, and we will not say more about it here. We will, however, show the relationship between sample size and the expected net gain from sampling in Figure 15–27. The interested reader is referred to advanced works on the subject.[5]

PROBLEMS

15–46. Explain the value of additional information within the context of decision making.

15–47. Explain how we compute the expected value of perfect information, and why it is computed that way.

15–48. Compute the expected value of perfect information for the situation in problem 15–28.

15–49. For the situation in problem 15–28, suppose the designer is offered expert opinion about the new fall styles for a price of $300,000. Should she buy the advice? Explain why or why not.

15–50. What is the expected value of perfect information in the situation of problem 15–25? Explain.

Answers

15–48.
___
$290,000

15–50.
___
EVPI = 0

15–10 Using the Computer

Most statistical computer packages do not have extensive Bayesian statistics or decision analysis capabilities. There are, however, some computer programs for microcomputers that do decision analysis. One such program is *Arborist*.™[6] It is also possi-

---

[5] See C. Barenghi, A. Aczel, and R. Best, "Determining the Optimal Sample Size for Decision Making," *Journal of Statistical Computation and Simulation* (Spring 1986), pp. 135–45. Figure 15–27 is reprinted, by permission, from that article.

[6] Arborist™ is a trademark of Texas Instruments Incorporated.

FIGURE 15–28   Computer Program for the de Finetti Game

```
1 CLS
2 PRINT "HELLO!!"
3 PRINT"*********************************************************"
4 PRINT "LET US ASSESS THE PROBABILITY OF AN EVENT OF INTEREST TO"
5 PRINT " YOU, IMAGINE THAT I HAVE AN URN CONTAINING 100 BALLS."
6 PRINT " THERE ARE AS MANY RED BALLS AS INDICATED BELOW, AND THE"
7 PRINT "REST OF THEM ARE BLACK, NOW, IF YOU DRAW A RED BALL FROM"
8 PRINT "THE URN, I WILL GIVE YOU ONE MILLION DOLLARS!!!"
9 PRINT "ON THE OTHER HAND, IF YOU WAIT FOR THE EVENT OF INTEREST"
10 PRINT "TO OCCUR, THEN I WILL GIVE YOU ONE MILLION DOLLARS IF IT"
11 PRINT "DOES INDEED OCCUR, HOWEVER, YOU MUST MAKE THE DECISION"
12 PRINT "NOW AS TO WHETHER TO DRAW A BALL, OR TO WAIT TO SEE IF"
13 PRINT "THE EVENT WILL OCCUR, AND COLLECT THE MONEY IF IT DOES."
14 PRINT "YOU CANNOT DO BOTH. DEPENDING ON THE COMPOSITION OF THE"
15 PRINT "URN, AT EACH STAGE, TYPE A 'D' FOR DRAW, OR A 'W' FOR"
16 PRINT "WAIT! OR AN 'I' IF YOU ARE INDIFFERENT AT THAT"
17 PRINT "PARTICULAR POINT"
18 PRINT "$$$$$$$$$$$$$$$$$$$$$$$$$$$$$$$$$$$$$$$$$$$$$$$$$$$$$$$$$$$"
20 LET A = 100
30 LET B = 0
40 LET D = A + B
50 LET C = INT(D/2)
55 PRINT "THERE ARE"   , C
56 PRINT "RED BALLS IN THE URN"
60 IF C = B THEN 370
70 IF C = A THEN 370
125 INPUT "WAIT, DRAW, OR INDIFFERENT"; ANSWER$
130 CLS
140 IF ANSWER$ = "I" THEN 370
150 IF ANSWER$ = "D" THEN 300
159 IF ANSWER$ = "W" AND C = 99 THEN GOSUB 500
160 IF ANSWER$ = "W" THEN 350
170 PRINT "SORRY, YOU USED THE WRONG ANSWER SYMBOL TRY AGAIN"
180 GOTO 55
300 LET A = C
310 GOTO 40
350 LET B = C
360 GOTO 40
370 CLS
375 PRINT "THE PROBABILITY OF YOUR EVENT IS"
380 PRINT C, "PERCENT"
381 INPUT "PLAY ANOTHER ONE?"   , D$
382 IF D$ = "Y" THEN GOSUB 600
383 IF D$ = "YES" THEN GOSUB 600
384 CLS
385 PRINT "GOODBYE AND THANK YOU FOR PLAYING THE PROBABILITY -"
386 PRINT "GAME. I HOPE THAT YOU NOW HAVE A BETTER FEELING"
387 PRINT "FOR YOUR TRUE SUBJECTIVE PROBABILITY OF THE"
388 PRINT "EVENT."
389 PRINT "ZZZZZZZZZZZZZZZZZZZZZZZZZZZZZZZZZZZZZZZZZZZZZZZZ"
390 END
500 C = 100
501 RETURN
600 CLS
601 GOTO 20
```

ble to write your own computer program for solving a decision tree; such programs are not difficult to write in any of the commonly used programming languages. Figure 15–28 is a listing of a program in BASIC that allows you to play the de Finetti game for assessing personal probabilities.

15–11   Summary and Review of Terms

In this chapter, we presented two related topics: **Bayesian statistics** and **decision analysis.** We saw that the Bayesian statistical methods are extensions of Bayes' theorem to discrete and continuous random variables. We saw how the Bayesian approach allows the statistician to use, along with the data, **prior information** about the situation at hand. The prior information is stated in terms of a **prior probability distribution** of population parameters. We saw that the Bayesian approach is less restrictive in that it allows us to consider an unknown parameter as a random variable. In this context, as more sampling information about a parameter becomes available to us, we can update our prior probability distribution of the parameter, thus creating a **posterior probability distribution.** The posterior distribution may then serve as a prior distribution when more data become available. We saw that the sequential nature of the analysis is also an asset. We discussed the possible dangers in using the Bayesian approach and the fact that we must be careful in our choice of prior distributions.

We saw how decision analysis may be used to find the decision that maximizes our **expected payoff** from an uncertain situation. We discussed personal, or **subjective probabilities** and saw how these can be assessed and used in a Bayesian statistics problem or in a decision problem. We saw that a **decision tree** is a good method of solving problems of decision making under uncertainty. We learned how to use the method of **averaging out and folding back,** a method that leads to the determination of the **optimal decision**—the decision that maximizes the expected monetary payoff. We saw how to assess the usefulness of obtaining additional information within the context of the decision problem, using a decision tree and Bayes' theorem. Finally, we saw how to incorporate people's attitudes toward risk in our analysis and how these attitudes lead to a **utility function,** which may be used instead of the pure monetary values of the problem. We saw that this leads to solutions to decision problems that maximize the **expected utility** rather than the expected monetary payoff. We also discussed the **expected value of perfect information** and saw how this value serves as an upper bound for the amount of money we are willing to pay for additional information about a decision-making situation.

ADDITIONAL PROBLEMS

15–51.   A quality-control engineer believes that the proportion of defective items in a production process is a random variable with a probability distribution that is approximated by the following probability mass function.

x	P(x)
0.1	0.1
0.2	0.3
0.3	0.2
0.4	0.2
0.5	0.1
0.6	0.1

Answers

The engineer collects a random sample of items and finds that 5 out the 16 items in the sample are defective. Find the engineer's posterior probability distribution of the proportion of defective items.

15–52.

92.11%:

[0.2, 0.4]

15–52.   Continuing problem 15–51, determine a credible set for the proportion of defective items with probability close to 0.95. Interpret the meaning of the credible set.

15–53.   For problem 15–51, suppose that the engineer collects a second sample of 20 items and finds that 5 items are defective. Update the probability distribution of the population proportion you computed in problem 15–51 to incorporate the new information.

15–54.   What are the main differences between the Bayesian approach to statistics and the classical approach? Discuss these differences.

15–55.   What is the added advantage of the normal probability distribution in the context of Bayesian statistics?

15–56.

$M'' = 99.81$

$\sigma'' = 0.9806$

15–56.   The average life of a battery is believed to be normally distributed with an unknown mean, μ. The mean is viewed as a random variable with expected value of 45 hours and standard deviation of 5 hours. The population standard deviation is believed to be 10 hours. A random sample of 100 batteries gives a sample mean of 102 hours. Find the posterior probability distribution of the population mean, μ.

15–57.   For problem 15–56, give a highest-posterior-density credible set of probability 0.95 for the population mean.

15–58.

[98.89, 101.96]

15–58.   For problem 15–56, a second sample of 60 batteries gives a sample mean of 101.5 hours. Update the distribution of the population mean, and give a new HPD credible set of probability 0.95 for μ.

15–59.   What is a payoff table? What is a decision tree? Can a payoff table be used in decision making without a decision tree?

15–60.   What is a subjective probability, and what are its limitations?

15–61.   Discuss the advantages and the limitations of the de Finetti game. What is the main principle behind the game?

15–62.   Why is Bayesian statistics controversial? Try to argue for, and then against, the Bayesian methodology.

15–63.   Suppose that I am indifferent in terms of the following two choices: a sure $3,000 payoff, and a payoff of $5,000 with probability 0.2 and $500 with probability 0.8. Am I a risk taker or a risk-averse individual (within the range $500 to $5,000)? Explain.

15–64.

Alternative

$E = \$4,000$

is optimal.

15–64.   An investment is believed to earn $2,000 with probability 0.2, $2,500 with probability 0.3, and $3,000 with probability 0.5. An alternative investment may earn zero with probability 0.1, $3,000 with probability 0.2, $4,000 with probability 0.5, and $7,000 with probability 0.2. Construct a decision tree for this problem, and determine the investment with the highest expected monetary outcome. What are the limitations of the analysis?

15–65.   Assess your own utility in the range of values of problem 15–64, and redo that problem using utilities instead of dollars. Has the optimal decision changed? Explain.

15–66.

Merge;

$E = \$2.45$ million.

15–66.   A company is considering merging with a smaller firm in a related industry. The company's chief executive officer believes that the merger has a 0.55 probability of success. If the merger is successful, the company stands to gain in the next two years $5 million with probability 0.2; $6 million with probability 0.3; $7 million with probability 0.3; and $8 million with probability 0.2. If the attempted merger should fail, the company stands to lose $2 million (due to loss of public goodwill) over the next two years with probability 0.5 and to lose $3 million over this period with probability 0.5. Should the merger be attempted? Explain.

15–67.   For problem 15–66, suppose that the chief executive may hire a consulting firm for a fee of $725,000. The consulting firm will advise the CEO about the possibility of success of the merger. This consulting firm is known to have correctly predicted the outcomes of 89% of all successful mergers and the outcomes of 97% of all unsuccessful ones. What is the optimal decision?

15–68.   What is the expected value of perfect information about the success or failure of the merger in problem 15–66?

15–69.   A company is interested in hiring a new manager. There are two candidates for the position. Candidate A successfully managed two out of three firms that he headed and improved profits by an average of 10%. In his third previous job, the candidate caused a profit loss of 4%. Candidate B successfully managed four out of five firms she previously headed. Ths candidate increased profits by an average of 6% at the firms she successfully managed, and caused a profit loss of 5% at the firm she managed unsuccessfully. Which candidate should be hired, and why?

15–70.   For problem 15–69, add the option of not hiring a new manager, and assume no change in profits. Redo the problem.

15–71.   For a cost of 1% of profits, the firm may allow one of the two candidates in problem 15–69 to manage the company for a trial period to determine whether the candidate will be successful. Such a test has a reliability of 90%. What is the optimal decision?

Answers

15–68.

$1.125 million

15–70.

Hire A.

GETTING BUMPED

*T*he overbooking of airplane seats is not a new phenomenon. However, as airlines become more and more competitive, their profit margins narrow, and they find it increasingly necessary to fill every possible seat. Virtually the only way of achieving a flight that is as full as possible is to overbook the seats on the plane, counting on the fact that some people will fail to show up for the flight. If the number of no-shows is smaller than the number of overbooked seats, the plane will be full and some ticketed passengers will have to get "bumped" —for a suitable compensation. Often, the compensation is in the form of a free round-trip flight ticket between any two domestic airports served by the airline.

The operations managers of airlines have ready access to all information on flight capacities, peak and off-peak demand, and any other relevant information directly from computers. This has enabled some of these managers to make surprisingly accurate calculations of the probabilities of the number of no-shows for any given flight. The operations manager of Western Airlines (before the company was taken over by Delta) used such probability calculations. The manager was able to predict to within a few people the number of passengers expected to show up for some flights. This allowed the airline to determine the extent of overbooking that would maximize the number of filled seats and minimize the number of free tickets offered.

Instead of looking at airline seat overbooking from the airlines' point of view, let us look at it from the point of view of an individual traveler. Let us see how an airline passenger can (in fact, at least one *did*) use decision analysis to beat the airline in this game, maximizing the *passenger's* expected payoff. Let us suppose that you are the passenger and that this is your decision problem.

You are staying at the Hilton Hawaiian Village on Waikiki beach. You have been attending a professional conference at the hotel, paid for by your organization. It is the day before Thanksgiving, and this is your last night at the hotel. The front desk has just informed you that the hotel is full and that if you decide that you want to stay an extra night, you will have to call in the morning and ask if there is a vacancy. The desk attendant tells you that the chances of a vacancy tomorrow morning are about 0.30. You also know that most hotel rooms in Hawaii are full for the Thanksgiving holiday, and you believe that the chances of finding a hotel room tomorrow, assuming the Hilton will not be able to accommodate you, are about 0.50.

If you find a room at the Hilton, then—since your conference is over—you will have to pay for the room. Your room costs $110 per day. The pleasure you will derive from staying an extra day in Hawaii is worth $500 to you. This is your utility for staying a day: the amount someone would have to pay you to forgo your one-day vacation at the Hilton, assuming you can stay there. This amount is inclusive of the cost of your stay.

If you cannot stay at the Hilton, you will have to spend much of the next day searching for a room, thus reducing your pleasure from staying. In addition, since you are likely to find a less comfortable hotel than the Hilton (if you find one at all), these factors reduce your utility from staying an extra day to about $150. A room at another hotel will cost you $50.

What about flying home? You can either fly home tonight, the day before Thanksgiving, or you can fly back tomorrow, Thanksgiving Day. You can also fly home the day after Thanksgiving. Your flight ticket is good for any of the three flights, but you cannot leave any later than the day after tomorrow.

Reading a newspaper, you find that about 250,000 people were bumped from their flights in the last four months. Using this information in conjunction with what you know about the total number of flights and other information, you estimate that the *overall* probability of being bumped from a flight is about 0.4. The newspaper article further tells you that the worst time for the airlines—and the best time for you if you want to get bumped and earn a free ticket—is today: the day before Thanksgiving, when everyone is rushing home.

The worst day to fly, from your point of view, is tomorrow. Then everyone will be home; few people will fly, and you are not very likely to be bumped. You therefore estimate that the chances of being bumped from your flight today, if you try to return home right now and not stay the night, which has already been paid for, is about 0.16 (four times the "usual" probability). You believe that the chances of being bumped tomorrow are only 0.01, and the probability of being bumped if you try to fly the next day is 0.06. If you get bumped that third day, you will stay at the airport until the late-night flight. You believe that you will surely find a place on that flight.

Getting bumped from a flight is worth $1,100 to you. You are planning a long-distance trip, which will cost this much, and if you get bumped and earn a free ticket, you will use it for the trip.

You allow yourself one more possibility: If you decide to go to the airport tonight in the hope of getting bumped, and you see that your plane is not going to be full, you can return to your hotel. In this case, you will only lose the taxi fare to the airport and back—$40—and you will miss a hula show worth $50 in utility for you but costing nothing. You will not allow yourself such an option tomorrow or the next day. Then, if you are bumped, you will collect your free ticket and fly home on the late-night flight; if you are not bumped, you will take the regular flight. What should you do to maximize your expected payoff from this unusual situation?

16 MULTIVARIATE ANALYSIS

INTRODUCTION

Multivariate statistical methods, or simply **multivariate methods,** are statistical methods for the simultaneous analysis of data on several variables. Suppose that a company markets two related products, say, toothbrushes and toothpaste. The company's marketing director may be interested in analyzing consumers' preferences for the two products. The exact type of analysis may vary depending on what the company needs to know. What distinguishes the analysis—whatever form it may take—is that it should consider people's perceptions of both products *jointly*. Why? If the two products are related, it is likely that consumers' perceptions of the two products will be correlated. Incorporating knowledge of such correlations in our analysis makes the analysis more accurate and more meaningful.

Recall that regression analysis and correlation analysis are methods involving several variables. In a sense, they are multivariate methods even though, strictly speaking, in regression analysis we make the assumption that the independent variable or variables are not random but are fixed quantities. In this chapter, we discuss statistical methods that are usually referred to as *multivariate*. These are more advanced than regression analysis or simple correlational analysis. In a multivariate analysis, we usually consider data on several variables as a single element—for example, an ordered set of values such as (x_1, x_2, x_3, x_4) is considered a single element in an analysis that concerns four variables. In the case of the analysis of consumers' preference scores for two products, we will have a consumer's response as the *pair* of scores (x_1, x_2), where x_1 is the consumer's preference for the toothbrush, measured on some scale, and x_2 is his or her preference for the toothpaste, measured on some scale. In the analysis, we consider the pair of scores (x_1, x_2) as one sample point. When k variables are involved in the analysis, we will consider the *k-tuple* of numbers $(x_1, x_2, \ldots, x_k)$ as one element—one data point. Such an ordered set of numbers is called a **vector.** Vectors form the basic elements of our analysis in this chapter.

As you recall, the normal distribution plays a crucial role in most areas of statistical analysis. You should therefore not be surprised that the normal distribution plays an equally important role in multivariate analysis. Interestingly, the normal distribution is easily extendable to several variables. As such, it is the distribution of *vector random variables* of the form: $\mathbf{X} = (X_1, X_2, X_3, \ldots, X_k)$. The distribution is called the **multivariate normal distribution.** When $k = 2$, the *bivariate* case, we have a two-dimensional normal distribution. Instead of a bell-shaped curve, we have a (three dimensional) bell-shaped *mound* as our density function. When k is greater than 2, the probability function is a surface of higher dimensionality than 3, and we cannot graph it. The multivariate normal distribution will be discussed in the next section.

The bivariate normal distribution, which, along with its higher-dimensional extensions, forms the basis for multivariate methods, originates in the work of Francis Galton in the second half of the last century. Galton once wrote to each of his friends asking them to grow peas. Then he asked them to take measurements of the

Continued on next page

peas of two generations and send him the data. Based on these data, Galton discovered the correlation coefficient as a measure of association and used it to describe the relationship between the sizes of peas of two generations. Later work by Karl Pearson and others led to theories of different kinds of correlation that may exist among variables. These theories opened the way to the formulation of various multivariate techniques. The main multivariate methods are:

1. Multivariate tests for population means
2. Multivariate analysis of variance (MANOVA)
3. Discriminant analysis
4. Factor analysis
5. Cluster analysis
6. Multidimensional scaling
7. Conjoint analysis
8. Canonical correlation analysis

We will discuss the first four methods, and briefly describe the latter four. These methods are interesting and useful. The usefulness of multivariate methods derives from the fact that real-world problems are rarely simple: they usually involve more than just a single variable. These multivariate methods allow us to perform different kinds of analyses that account for more than one variable. Some of the methods, such as the multivariate analysis of variance, are extensions of single-variable analyses; others, such as factor analysis, are unique techniques for dealing with several variables and have no single-variable analogs.

Multivariate methods are usually avoided in elementary or intermediate-level statistics courses because these methods are perceived as advanced, complex, or mathematically sophisticated. There is a degree of truth to such assertions. In recent years, however, the fast growth in computer technology has put the use of these "complicated" methods within easy reach of people who require analysis of complex problems in marketing research and other areas of business and economics. Anyone can enter data into a computer and obtain results. This chapter will teach you how to *interpret* these results. The chapter will also show you how to use the advanced computer programs at your disposal to solve problems that could not be solved (or at least not solved well) without the use of multivariate methods.

Our approach will avoid the use of complicated mathematical expressions. Instead we will concentrate on the application of the methods to real problems and on the interpretation of results. We will need, however, a thorough introduction to the multivariate normal distribution. We will also introduce new statistics and their distributions. The next section should give you everything you need to know about the multivariate distributions used in this chapter. We will also present the Hotelling T^2 statistic, which is used in testing hypotheses about multivariate population means. ■

16–2 The Multivariate Normal Distribution

In the introduction, we mentioned that in multivariate analysis our elements are vectors rather than single observations. We did not define a vector, counting on the intuitive interpretation that a vector is an ordered set of numbers. For our purposes, a vector is just that: an ordered set of numbers, with each number representing a value of one of the k variables in our analysis.

A k-dimensional random variable **X**:

$$\mathbf{X} = (X_1, X_2, \ldots, X_k) \qquad (16\text{--}1)$$

where k is some integer

A realization of the random variable **X** is a drawing from the populations of values of the k variables and will be denoted, as usual, by lower-case letters.

A realization of a k-dimensional random variable **X**:

$$\mathbf{x} = (x_1, x_2, \ldots, x_k) \qquad (16\text{--}2)$$

Thus, in our simple example of consumer preferences for two products, we will be interested in the bivariate (two-component) random variable $\mathbf{X} = (X_1, X_2)$, where X_1 denotes a consumer's preference for the toothbrush and X_2 is the same consumer's preference for the toothpaste. A particular realization of the bivariate random variable may be (89, 78). If this is a result of random sampling from a population, it means that the particular sampled individual rates the toothbrush an 89 (on a scale of 0 to 100) and the toothpaste a 78.

For the k-dimensional random variable $\mathbf{X} = (X_1, X_2, X_3, \ldots, X_k)$, we may define a cumulative probability distribution function $F(x_1, x_2, x_3, \ldots, x_k)$. This is a joint probability function for all k random variables X_i, where $i = 1, 2, 3, \ldots, k$.

A joint cumulative probability distribution function of a k-dimensional random variable **X**:

$$F(x_1, x_2, \ldots, x_k) = P(X_1 \leq x_1, X_2 \leq x_2, \ldots, X_k \leq x_k) \qquad (16\text{--}3)$$

Equation 16–3 is a statement of the probability that X_1 is less than or equal to some value x_1, *and* X_2 is less than or equal to some value x_2, *and* . . . , *and* X_k is less than or equal to some value x_k. In our simple example, $F(55, 60)$ is the *joint* probability that a consumer's preference score for the toothbrush is less than or equal to 55 and that his or her preference score for the toothpaste is less than or equal to 60.

The *marginal* probability distribution of any one of the k variables X_i is the probability distribution of that variable alone, regardless of whatever values may be taken by all other component random variables in the vector.

The **marginal distribution** of X_i:

$$F(x_i) = P(X_i \leq x_i) \qquad (16\text{--}4)$$

where x_i is some value

If the k random variables are independent of each other, and only if they are independent of each other, the probability function in equation 16–3 can be factored as the product of the individual marginal probability distribution functions of the k variables. In such cases, we have the following.

For independent random variables:

$$F(x_1, x_2, \ldots, x_k) = F(x_1)F(x_2) \cdots F(x_k) \qquad (16\text{--}5)$$

This should be clear to you from the definition of each $F(x_i)$ as the probability $P(X_i \leq x_i)$ and the rule for independence of events. The expression $F(x_1, x_2, \ldots, x_k)$ is the probability that the random variable X_1 is less than or equal to some value x_1 and the random variable X_2 is less than or equal to x_2, and so on to X_k. Thus, $F(x_1, x_2, \ldots, x_k)$ is an expression of joint probability. As we know, the joint probability of k events is equal to the product of the marginal probabilities of the k events $\{X_i \leq x_i\}$, $i = 1, \ldots, k$, if and only if the events are independent (see Chapter 2).

In general, the joint probability distribution function is not factorable to the product of the marginal probability distributions. There will be some *correlations* among the random variables: they will not be independent. If the random variables are independent, there is less of an advantage to a multivariate analysis. We now define the multivariate normal distribution.

A multivariate normal random variable has the following probability density function.

$$f(x_1, x_2, \ldots, x_k) = \frac{1}{(2\pi)^{k/2}|\boldsymbol{\Sigma}|^{1/2}} e^{-(1/2)(\mathbf{X}-\boldsymbol{\mu})'\boldsymbol{\Sigma}^{-1}(\mathbf{X}-\boldsymbol{\mu})} \qquad (16\text{--}6)$$

where **X** is the vector random variable defined in equation 16–1; the term $\boldsymbol{\mu} = (\mu_1, \mu_2, \ldots, \mu_k)$ is the *vector of means* of the component variables X_i; and $\boldsymbol{\Sigma}$ is the *variance-covariance matrix*, which we will define shortly. The operations $'$ and $^{-1}$ are transposition and inversion of matrices, respectively, and $|\ \ |$ denotes the determinant of a matrix.

If you have had some linear algebra, then you know what equation 16–6 means, in terms of matrix operations. It is not necessary, however, to know any linear algebra to understand multivariate methods. We present equation 16–6 for the mere purpose of showing that the density function of a multivariate normal random variable is very similar to that of a univariate normal random variable. The formula is very much the same, with $\boldsymbol{\Sigma}$ replacing σ and $\boldsymbol{\mu}$ being a vector rather than a single number. The operations are matrix operations rather than operations involving simple numbers, but you need not understand them in order to carry out an analysis. Compare equation 16–6 with equation 4–1 for the single-variable normal density function.

The probabilities relevant to a multivariate normal random variable are obtained, in principle, by integration of the function in equation 16–6. However, since the single-variable normal density is not integrable, you have probably guessed that the multivariate one is not integrable either. We will obtain probabilities by other means.

The simplest multivariate normal distribution is the bivariate one. It is defined as follows. For the bivariate normal random variable $\mathbf{X} = (X_1, X_2)$, we have the mean vector

$$\boldsymbol{\mu} = \begin{bmatrix} \mu_1 \\ \mu_2 \end{bmatrix}$$

and the variance-covariance matrix $\boldsymbol{\Sigma}$ defined below.

The variance-covariance matrix of a bivariate random variable:

$$\boldsymbol{\Sigma} = \begin{bmatrix} \sigma_1^2 & \rho\sigma_1\sigma_2 \\ \rho\sigma_1\sigma_2 & \sigma_2^2 \end{bmatrix} \qquad (16\text{--}7)$$

It is important to understand the meaning of the variance-covariance matrix. This matrix contains much information about the bivariate random variable. The matrix is symmetric and each of the two off-diagonal elements (lower left and upper right) are equal to the *covariance* of X_1 and X_2.

The covariance of the random variables X_1 and X_2:

$$\text{Cov}(X_1, X_2) = \rho\sigma_1\sigma_2 \qquad (16\text{--}8)$$

where ρ is the (population) correlation coefficient of X_1 and X_2; and σ_1 is the standard deviation of X_1 and σ_2 is the standard deviation of X_2

The two diagonal elements of the matrix $\boldsymbol{\Sigma}$ are the squares of each of the two standard deviations and are, therefore, the variance of random variable X_1 and the variance of random variable X_2, respectively.

Using equation 16–7 and the definition of the multivariate normal density, equation 16–6, we get the following expression for the probability density function of the bivariate normal random variable.

$$f(x_1, x_2) = \frac{1}{2\pi\sigma_1\sigma_2\sqrt{1-\rho^2}} e^{\{-1/2(1-\rho^2)\}\{[(x_1-\mu_1)/\sigma_1]^2 - 2\rho[(x_1-\mu_1)/\sigma_1][(x_2-\mu_2)/\sigma_2] + [(x_2-\mu_2)/\sigma_2]^2\}}$$

$$(16\text{--}9)$$

As you see, it is possible to write down the density function of the bivariate normal random variable without the use of matrices or linear algebra. The expression is, of course, much more complicated than when matrix notation is used. Again, you will never have to use this expression. Probabilities of the bivariate normal random variable have been tabulated by numerical integration but, as stated earlier, we will not need these tables and will obtain probabilities in a different manner.

The density function given in equation 16–6 or 16–9 is a bivariate extension of the single-variable normal distribution—the bell-shaped curve. The new function is a mound-shaped function of two variables, X_1 and X_2. An example of a bivariate normal density function $f(x_1, x_2)$ is shown in Figure 16–1. The probability density function is a three-dimensional surface, where the value of the function—its height—is determined by the values of the two variables X_1 and X_2. The width of the mound and its orientation in the X_1-X_2 plane are determined by the elements of the

FIGURE 16–1   The Bivariate Normal Probability Density Function

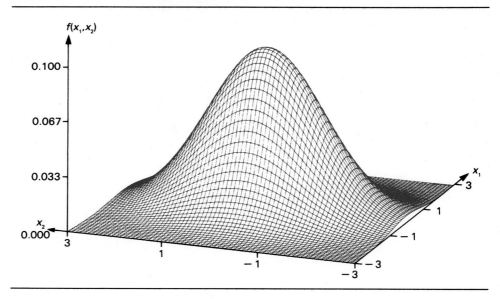

variance-covariance matrix: the two standard deviations of the component random variables in the vector and the correlation between the two random variables. The exponent in the multivariate density function, $(\mathbf{X} - \boldsymbol{\mu})'\boldsymbol{\Sigma}^{-1}(\mathbf{X} - \boldsymbol{\mu})$, specifies the equation of an *ellipsoid* when it is set equal to some positive value, c. In the bivariate case, this gives the equation of an ellipse in the X_1-X_2 plane. Each ellipse has equal

FIGURE 16–2   Ellipses of Fixed Density for a Bivariate Normal Distribution with $\rho = 0$, $\sigma_1 = 1$, and $\sigma_2 = 1$

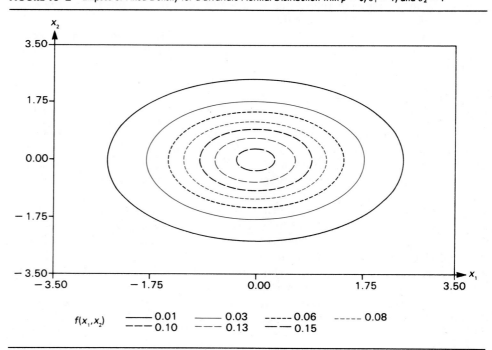

FIGURE 16–3 Ellipses of Fixed Density for a Bivariate Normal Distribution with $\rho = 0.8$, $\sigma_1 = 1$, and $\sigma_2 = 2$

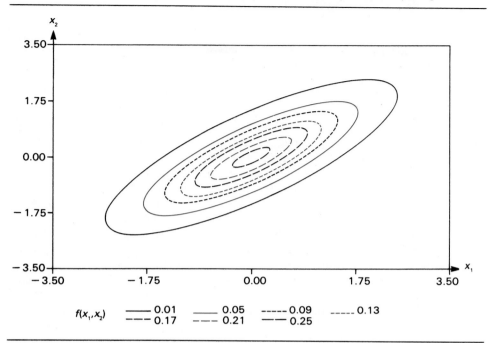

$$f(x_1, x_2) \quad \text{——} \ 0.01 \quad \text{——} \ 0.05 \quad \text{-----} \ 0.09 \quad \text{----} \ 0.13$$
$$\text{---} \ 0.17 \quad \text{– – –} \ 0.21 \quad \text{—— } \ 0.25$$

density at all of its points. For given values of c, we can draw the ellipses, and this forms a kind of topographical map of the bivariate density mound. Every ellipse represents a certain height of the function. Two examples of bivariate normal density functions, drawn as sets of ellipses, are shown in Figures 16–2 and 16–3. The two density functions correspond to bivariate random variables with different variances and correlation coefficients.

The center of all the ellipses of the bivariate density function is the point corresponding to the means of the two component variables: (μ_1, μ_2). In the case of higher-dimensional normal variables, the center of all ellipsoids (they cannot be drawn in higher dimensions) of a k-variate normal distribution is $(\mu_1, \mu_2, \ldots, \mu_k)$.

> The multivariate mean of a population or distribution, given by $(\mu_1, \mu_2, \ldots, \mu_k)$, is called the **centroid** of the population or distribution.

Evaluating Probabilities

In the single-variable case, the probability that a normal random variable is within two bounds on the real line is given by the area under the normal curve between the two bounds. In the bivariate case, the probability that the bivariate vector random variable (X_1, X_2) will be within any region in the X_1-X_2 plane is given by the *volume* of the bivariate normal density mound above the region in question.

Look at the ellipses in Figure 16–2 or 16–3. For a given ellipse, it is possible to find the probability that the bivariate random variable will fall within the region of the ellipse by using the chi-square distribution.

We define the following quantity:

$$(\mathbf{X} - \boldsymbol{\mu})'\boldsymbol{\Sigma}^{-1}(\mathbf{X} - \boldsymbol{\mu}) = \chi^2 \qquad (16\text{--}10)$$

where $\mathbf{X}$ and $\boldsymbol{\mu}$ are k-dimensional vectors and $\boldsymbol{\Sigma}$ is the variance-covariance matrix. The quantity χ^2 has a chi-square distribution with k degrees of freedom.

In the case of $k = 2$, the density function is a mound in three-dimensional space. The volume of the mound above the ellipse is given by the probability corresponding to the value of the χ^2 statistic computed in equation 16–10. For example, the probability that the bivariate random variable will fall in the region of the ellipse given by fixing $\chi^2 = 5.99$ is 0.95. This is seen by checking Appendix C, Table 4, which shows that the point 5.99 is the critical point of the chi-square distribution with 2 degrees of freedom that has an area of 0.95 to its left. The identification of the ellipse assumes that we know both the centroid, $\boldsymbol{\mu} = (\mu_1, \mu_2)$, and the variance-covariance matrix, $\boldsymbol{\Sigma}$. The procedure is illustrated in Figure 16–4. It is this procedure, and others we will discuss later, that allow us to compute probabilities of the multivariate normal distribution without tables computed specifically for the multivariate distribution in question. Equation 16–10 holds also for values of k larger than $k=2$. In such higher-dimensional cases, we deal with ellipsoids rather than ellipses in the plane, and the density function has higher dimensionality than three and cannot be easily visualized. At higher dimensions, we use chi-square distributions with more degrees of freedom. For example, the probability that the five-dimensional normal random variable $\mathbf{X} = (X_1, X_2, X_3, X_4, X_5)$ will fall in the (five-dimensional) region in space defined by the ellipsoid $(\mathbf{X} - \boldsymbol{\mu})'\boldsymbol{\Sigma}^{-1}(\mathbf{X} - \boldsymbol{\mu}) = 15.1$ is 0.99 (verify this from Table 4). All the elements of $\boldsymbol{\mu}$ and $\boldsymbol{\Sigma}$ are assumed known.

For a k-dimensional random variable, we have a general k-dimensional variance-covariance matrix $\boldsymbol{\Sigma}$:

$$\boldsymbol{\Sigma} = \begin{bmatrix} \sigma_1^2 & \rho_{12}\sigma_1\sigma_2 & \cdots & \rho_{1k}\sigma_1\sigma_k \\ \rho_{21}\sigma_2\sigma_1 & \sigma_2^2 & & \rho_{2k}\sigma_2\sigma_k \\ \vdots & \vdots & \ddots & \vdots \\ \rho_{k1}\sigma_k\sigma_1 & \rho_{k2}\sigma_k\sigma_2 & \cdots & \sigma_k^2 \end{bmatrix} \qquad (16\text{--}11)$$

where σ_i is the standard deviation of the component variable X_i, and ρ_{ij} is the coefficient of correlation between X_i and $X_j(i, j = 1, \ldots, k)$

Sample Estimates

In our discussion of statistical inference in the univariate case, we noted that the standard deviation, σ, is rarely—if ever—known to us. We therefore estimated the standard deviation from our sample and used the estimate, s, in its place. The distribution of statistics relevant to inference about the population mean was then shown to be the t distribution instead of the normal distribution. Similarly to the univariate situation, the true variance-covariance matrix $\boldsymbol{\Sigma}$ of a multivariate population is rarely, if ever, known to us. Therefore, when we conduct an inferential analysis in

FIGURE 16–4   The Probability that a Bivariate Normal Random Variable Will Fall in the Region of an Ellipse

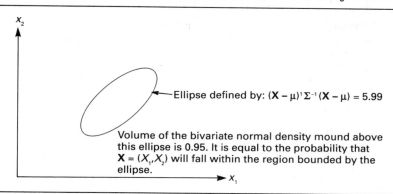

x_2

Ellipse defined by: $(\mathbf{X} - \mathbf{\mu})'\mathbf{\Sigma}^{-1}(\mathbf{X} - \mathbf{\mu}) = 5.99$

Volume of the bivariate normal density mound above this ellipse is 0.95. It is equal to the probability that $\mathbf{X} = (X_1, X_2)$ will fall within the region bounded by the ellipse.

x_1

the multivariate case, we need both a sample estimate of $\mathbf{\Sigma}$ and a related probability distribution analogous to the student t distribution. Fortunately, both of these are available to us. A sample-derived matrix that helps us estimate $\mathbf{\Sigma}$ is the matrix of sums of squares and cross products (SSCP). Shortly, we will define this matrix. It is denoted by $\mathbf{S}$, and it can be shown that $\mathbf{S}/(n - 1)$ is an unbiased estimator matrix for $\mathbf{\Sigma}$.

We now define the sample statistics for a multivariate analysis. The multivariate sample mean is called the *sample centroid* and is the vector of the sample means of the k variables under study.

The sample centroid:

$$\bar{\mathbf{X}} = \begin{bmatrix} \bar{X}_1 \\ \bar{X}_2 \\ \vdots \\ \bar{X}_k \end{bmatrix}$$

(16–12)

The matrix of sums of squares and cross products (SSCP):

$$\mathbf{S} = \begin{bmatrix} \Sigma w_1^2 & \Sigma w_1 w_2 & \cdots & \Sigma w_1 w_k \\ \Sigma w_2 w_1 & \Sigma w_2^2 & \cdots & \Sigma w_2 w_k \\ \vdots & \vdots & \ddots & \vdots \\ \Sigma w_k w_1 & \Sigma w_k w_2 & \cdots & \Sigma w_k^2 \end{bmatrix}$$

(16–13)

where the summation in each element extends over all data items from the relevant population. The w_i ($i = 1, \ldots, k$) are *deviations* of the data points $x_{i,j}$ from their respective sample means $\bar{x}_i$ (the subscript j, denoting the number of the point within the sample of size n, is suppressed in the matrix for simplicity).

The SSCP matrix, $\mathbf{S}$, is calculated by the computer in any analysis, and we need not worry about the exact computation of each of its elements. All you need to know is that the matrix $S/(n - 1)$ is an unbiased estimator of the variance-covariance matrix Σ. The diagonal elements of $S/(n - 1)$ are estimates of the variances of the k populations under study, and the off-diagonal elements of $S/(n - 1)$ are estimates of the covariances of the appropriate pairs of random variables (or populations). Our equations will involve the matrix S, not $S/(n - 1)$. We can now discuss some simple multivariate statistical inference about population means.

The Sampling Distribution of the Sample Centroids

Recall that in the univariate case, when we obtain a random sample of size n from a normal population, the sample mean, $\overline{X}$, is normally distributed with mean μ and variance σ^2/n. Similarly, when we draw a random sample of size n from a multivariate normal distribution (with k components) we have the following:

> The sampling distribution of $\overline{X}$ is multivariate normal with mean vector μ and variance-covariance matrix Σ/n.

In a similar way to our construction of confidence intervals for the population mean in the univariate case, we can construct a confidence region for the population centroid, μ (where μ is a k-dimensional vector).

> If the population variance-covariance matrix Σ is known, then a $(1 - \alpha)100\%$ confidence region for the k-dimensional population centroid, μ, is given by the ellipsoid:
>
> $$(x - \overline{x})'\Sigma^{-1}(x - \overline{x}) = \chi^2_{(1-\alpha)}/n \qquad (16\text{--}14)$$

Let us look at an example. Suppose that we know that the variance-covariance matrix of a bivariate normal population is:

$$\Sigma = \begin{bmatrix} 2 & 1 \\ 1 & 3 \end{bmatrix}$$

Suppose also that we used a random sample of $n = 20$ observations and obtained the sample centroid:

$$\overline{x} = \begin{bmatrix} 10 \\ 12 \end{bmatrix}$$

We want to construct a 95% confidence region for the bivariate population centroid, μ. According to equation 16–14, the region we seek is given by the area outlined by the ellipse in the X_1-X_2 plane satisfying the equation:

$$[x_1 - \overline{x}_1, \, x_2 - \overline{x}_2]\begin{bmatrix} 2 & 1 \\ 1 & 3 \end{bmatrix}^{-1}\begin{bmatrix} x_1 - \overline{x}_1 \\ x_2 - \overline{x}_2 \end{bmatrix} = \frac{\chi^2_{(0.95,\,df=2)}}{20}$$

Inverting the matrix Σ (using methods from linear algebra—or a computer), we find:

$$\Sigma^{-1} = \begin{bmatrix} 3/5 & -1/5 \\ -1/5 & 2/5 \end{bmatrix}$$

We premultiply the matrix Σ^{-1} by the vector $[x_1 - 10, \, x_2 - 12]$ and postmultiply the result by the vector

$$\begin{bmatrix} x_1 - 10 \\ x_2 - 12 \end{bmatrix}$$

FIGURE 16–5
A Confidence Region for the
Population Centroid

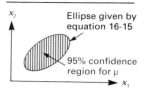

From Table 4, we find that the appropriate chi-square value is 5.99, which we then divide by 20. Putting all this together, we get:

$$0.6x_1^2 - 7.2x_1 + 0.6x_2^2 - 5.6x_2 - 0.4x_1 x_2 + 69.6 = \frac{5.99}{20} \qquad (16{-}15)$$

This is the equation of the ellipse that constitutes a 95% confidence region for the population centroid

$$\mu = \begin{bmatrix} \mu_1 \\ \mu_2 \end{bmatrix}$$

This is shown schematically in Figure 16–5.

Do not worry about such computations; they are done by computer. The whole purpose of this section is just to give you some feel for the multidimensionality of multivariate analysis and the way we handle it by using vectors and matrices. Incidentally, can you interpret the numerical meaning of the variance-covariance matrix in our example:

$$\Sigma = \begin{bmatrix} 2 & 1 \\ 1 & 3 \end{bmatrix}$$

Recall from equation 16–7 that the element in the first row and first column in the matrix is the variance of X_1, and the element in the second row and second column is the variance of X_2. Thus, we have: $\sigma_1^2 = 2$, $\sigma_2^2 = 3$. The off-diagonal elements are both equal to the covariance of X_1 and X_2, so we have $\rho \sigma_1 \sigma_2 = 1$. Since σ_1 must equal $\sqrt{2}$ and σ_2 must equal $\sqrt{3}$, we have $\rho = 1/(1.414)(1.732) = 0.408$. This is the population correlation of X_1 and X_2.

Hypothesis Tests about the Population Centroid μ

To conduct the hypothesis test:

$$H_0: \mu = \mu_0$$
$$H_1: \mu \neq \mu_0$$

we compute the test statistic:

$$Q = n(\mu_0 - \overline{\mathbf{x}})' \Sigma^{-1} (\mu_0 - \overline{\mathbf{x}}) \qquad (16{-}16)$$

Our decision rule is to reject H_0 at the level of significance α if and only if $Q > \chi^2_{(k,\, 1-\alpha)}$. That is, we reject the null hypothesis that the population centroid μ is equal to μ_0 if and only if the test statistic value Q is greater than the $(1 - \alpha)$ point of the chi-square distribution with k degrees of freedom.

The test statistic Q will exceed the critical point for chi-square if and only if the $(1 - \alpha)100\%$ confidence region (ellipsoid) given by equation 16–14 does not contain the point μ_0. The equivalence may be seen by comparing equations 16–16 and 16–14.

As mentioned earlier, Σ is usually not known to us. We therefore need to use its unbiased estimator: the matrix $S/(n - 1)$ where S is the SSCP matrix defined in equation 16–13. When Σ is not known, the distribution of $\overline{X}$ is no longer a multivariate normal distribution, and we therefore cannot use the chi-square device in computing confidence regions or testing hypotheses about the population centroid. Recall that in the univariate case, we used the statistic:

$$t = \frac{\overline{X} - \mu_0}{S/\sqrt{n}}$$

If we square the statistic above, we get: $t^2 = n(\overline{X} - \mu_0)(S^2)^{-1}(\overline{X} - \mu_0)$. This expression was generalized to the multivariate case by H. Hotelling in 1931. The new statistic is called *Hotelling's T^2 statistic*.

Hotelling's T^2 statistic:

$$T^2 = n(n - 1)(\overline{\mathbf{x}} - \mathbf{\mu}_0)'\mathbf{S}^{-1}(\overline{\mathbf{x}} - \mathbf{\mu}_0) \qquad (16\text{–}17)$$

where $\overline{\mathbf{x}}$ is the k-dimensional sample centroid, $\mathbf{\mu}_0$ is the hypothesized k-dimensional population centroid, and $\mathbf{S}^{-1}$ is the inverse of the SSCP matrix, $\mathbf{S}$

Hotelling's T^2 statistic can be transformed to an F statistic with an F distribution with k degrees of freedom for the numerator and $n - k$ degrees of freedom for the denominator when the null hypothesis is true. The transformation is simply a multiplication by $(n - k)/(n - 1)k$. We get the following.

The transformation of Hotelling's T^2 statistic to an F statistic:

$$\frac{n - k}{(n - 1)k} T^2 = F_{(k, n-k)} \qquad (16\text{–}18)$$

Equations 16–17 and 16–18 allow us to conduct hypothesis tests about the population centroid when the variance-covariance matrix Σ is not known. We demonstrate the use of Hotelling's T^2 statistic with Example (a).

EXAMPLE (a)

Unilever is a $25-billion-a-year Anglo-Dutch conglomerate with two chairpersons, two headquarters, and two sets of shareholders: one set in the Netherlands and one in the United Kingdom. Much of the company's business involves sales of food products Unilever makes. Company experts believe that production of margarine in the Dutch division averages 900 tons per day and production of margarine in the English division averages 1,200 tons per day. To test this hypothesis, a random sample of 100 days is chosen. It is found that the average margarine production in Unilever's Dutch division during the 100 days is 1,005 tons per day, and in the English division production is 1,150 tons per day. The following matrix of sums of squares and cross products is computed.

$$S = \begin{bmatrix} 10,000 & 5,000 \\ 5,000 & 40,000 \end{bmatrix}$$

Test the hypotheses:

$$H_0: \boldsymbol{\mu} = \begin{bmatrix} 900 \\ 1,200 \end{bmatrix}$$

$$H_1: \boldsymbol{\mu} \neq \begin{bmatrix} 900 \\ 1,200 \end{bmatrix}$$

First, we invert the matrix S. This can be done by hand, using any method of matrix inversion from linear algebra. The inverse is found to be (check this):

$$S^{-1} = \begin{bmatrix} 16/150,000 & -2/150,000 \\ -2/150,000 & 4/150,000 \end{bmatrix}.$$

SOLUTION

Now, using equation 16–17, we compute the value of Hotelling's statistic, T^2:

$$T^2 = n(n-1)(\overline{\mathbf{x}} - \boldsymbol{\mu}_0)' S^{-1}(\overline{\mathbf{x}} - \boldsymbol{\mu}_0)$$

$$= (100)(99)[1,005 - 900, \ 1,150 - 1,200]\left(\frac{1}{150,000}\right)\begin{bmatrix} 16 & -2 \\ -2 & 4 \end{bmatrix}\begin{bmatrix} 1,005 - 900 \\ 1,150 - 1,200 \end{bmatrix}$$

$$= (9,900)[105, -50]\left(\frac{1}{150,000}\right)\begin{bmatrix} 16 & -2 \\ -2 & 4 \end{bmatrix}\begin{bmatrix} 105 \\ -50 \end{bmatrix} = 13,688.4$$

If you are not familiar with matrix operations, do not worry about these computations. These are usually done by computer, and we will present computer results from now on. These calculations—in a simple multivariate case—were done by hand to give you a feel for what goes into multivariate statistical computations. These calculations were also done for the benefit of the reader who is well versed in matrix algebra and who may find in multivariate statistics an interesting application of the linear algebra he or she spent many hours learning.

Having obtained the value of Hotelling's T^2 statistic, we now transform it to an F statistic. Using equation 16–18, we get:

$$F_{(2,98)} = \frac{100 - 2}{(99)(2)}(13,688.4) = 6,775.07$$

We now compare the computed value of the statistic, $F = 6,775.07$, with critical points of the F distribution with 2 and 98 degrees of freedom. From Appendix C, Table 5, we find that the critical point for $\alpha = 0.01$ is close to 4.8. We can therefore strongly reject the null hypothesis that the means are 900 and 1,200 tons per day, respectively.

Equations 16–17 and 16–18, with a variable vector $\mathbf{X}$ substituted for $\boldsymbol{\mu}_0$, may also be used for defining the boundaries of a $(1 - \alpha)100\%$ confidence region for the population centroid $\boldsymbol{\mu}$. We will not give an example of this.

The Shape and the Orientation of the Bivariate Normal Density

We close this section with a discussion of some interesting geometrical properties of the bivariate normal distribution. As we know, the center of the distribution, its *centroid*, is the point (μ_1, μ_2). This point is the concentric center of all the *isodensity* (equal-density) ellipses we used in drawing the distribution in two dimensions. The major or the minor axis of the ellipses makes an angle, θ, with the positive X_1 axis.

FIGURE 16–6
Three-Dimensional Plots of Several
Bivariate Normal Densities

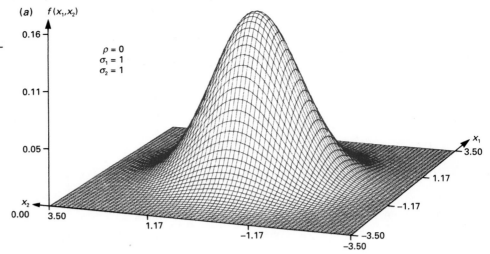

(a) $f(x_1,x_2)$

0.16

0.11

$\rho = 0$
$\sigma_1 = 1$
$\sigma_2 = 1$

0.05

x_2
0.00   3.50   1.17   −1.17   −3.50

1.17

−1.17

x_1
3.50

−3.50

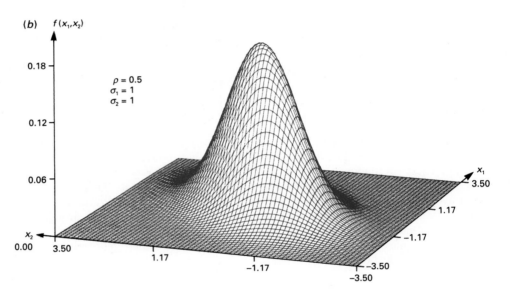

(b) $f(x_1,x_2)$

0.18

$\rho = 0.5$
$\sigma_1 = 1$
$\sigma_2 = 1$

0.12

0.06

x_2
0.00   3.50   1.17   −1.17   −3.50

1.17

−1.17

x_1
3.50

−3.50

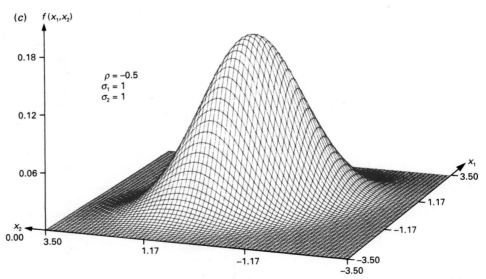

(c) $f(x_1,x_2)$

0.18

0.12

$\rho = -0.5$
$\sigma_1 = 1$
$\sigma_2 = 1$

0.06

x_2
0.00   3.50   1.17   −1.17   −3.50

1.17

−1.17

x_1
3.50

−3.50

FIGURE 16–6 *(concluded)*

(d) $f(x_1, x_2)$

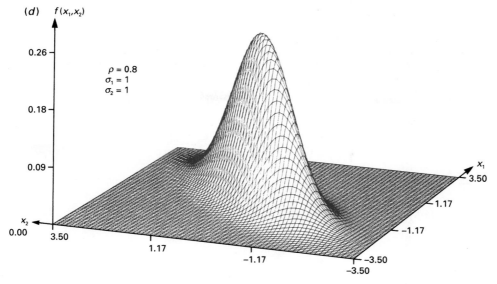

$\rho = 0.8$
$\sigma_1 = 1$
$\sigma_2 = 1$

(e) $f(x_1, x_2)$

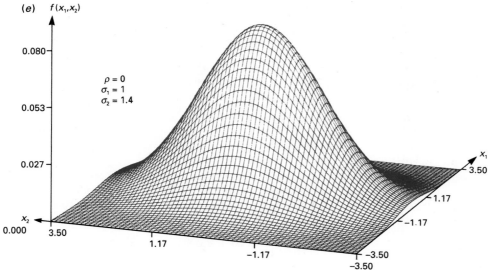

$\rho = 0$
$\sigma_1 = 1$
$\sigma_2 = 1.4$

(f) $f(x_1, x_2)$

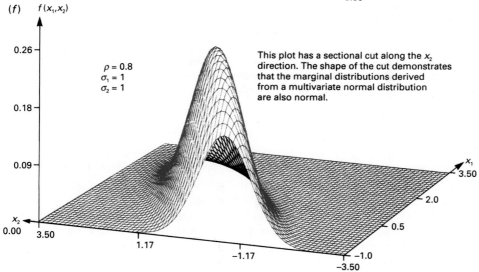

$\rho = 0.8$
$\sigma_1 = 1$
$\sigma_2 = 1$

This plot has a sectional cut along the x_2 direction. The shape of the cut demonstrates that the marginal distributions derived from a multivariate normal distribution are also normal.

The angle is equal to $45°$ when $\sigma_1 = \sigma_2$. When the two standard deviations are not equal, the angle is given as follows.

When $\sigma_1 \neq \sigma_2$:

$$\theta = \frac{1}{2} \text{ Arctangent } \frac{2\rho\sigma_1\sigma_2}{\sigma_1^2 - \sigma_2^2} \qquad (16\text{–}19)$$

Some examples are shown in the graphs in Figure 16–6.

PROBLEMS

Answer

16–1.   Explain the advantages of a multivariate analysis in comparison with a set of univariate analyses.

16–2.   What are the parameters of a multivariate normal probability density function, and what corresponds to probabilities?

16–3.   What are the elements of the variance-covariance matrix of a bivariate normal distribution, and what is the significance of each of the elements?

16–4.   Define a centroid. What is the population centroid? The sample centroid?

16–5.   For a bivariate normal distribution, suppose that the standard deviation of X_1 is 50, the standard deviation of X_2 is 60, and the correlation between X_1 and X_2 is 0.65. Write the variance-covariance matrix of the distribution.

16–6.   What is the SSCP matrix, and what are its uses?

16–7.   Sales of Honda and Subaru cars in a midwestern state are believed to average 800 units per month and 650 units per month, respectively. To test this hypothesis, a random sample of 24 months is selected, and it is found that the sample means are 1,100 for Honda and 750 for Subaru. The SSCP matrix is:

$$\mathbf{S} = \begin{bmatrix} 12{,}000 & 8{,}000 \\ 8{,}000 & 16{,}000 \end{bmatrix}$$

Conduct the test. Assume multivariate normality.

16–8.   Why are tables of probabilities of the multivariate normal distribution not necessary?

16–9.   In an analysis of seven variables in a multivariate process, define the element in the seventh row, first column of the variance-covariance matrix.

16–10.   Again, in a seven-variable analysis, assuming the variables follow a multivariate normal distribution, what is the probability distribution of the following quantity?

$$(\mathbf{X} - \boldsymbol{\mu})'\boldsymbol{\Sigma}^{-1}(\mathbf{X} - \boldsymbol{\mu})$$

16–11.   Define a 99% confidence interval for the population centroid of a bivariate normal population for a given $\overline{\mathbf{x}}$ vector and known matrix $\boldsymbol{\Sigma}$, where the sample size is $n = 50$.

16–12.   What is the multivariate analog of the sample variance s^2?

16–13.   What are the uses of Hotelling's T^2 statistic?

16–14.
_____
$F_{(2, 18)} = 19.999$
Reject H_0.

16–14.   Nightly sales of pizza and beer at a small establishment are known to be normally distributed. Management wants to test the null hypothesis that average nightly sales have means of 120 pizzas and 400 mugs of beer. A random sample of 20 nights is selected, and it is found that the sample means are 110 pizzas and 420 mugs of beer. The matrix of sums of squares and cross products is computed to be:

$$S = \begin{bmatrix} 2,000 & 400 \\ 400 & 8,000 \end{bmatrix}$$

Carry out the test.

16–15. Describe how you would test the hypothesis that the centroid of four related populations is equal to a given (four-dimensional) vector.

16–16. The two ellipses in the exhibit below correspond to 90% and 95% confidence regions for the bivariate population centroid, μ. Interpret the meaning of the four vectors shown in the exhibit: A, B, C, and D.

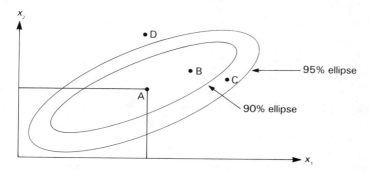

16–17. What is the shape of surfaces and equal probability density of the multivariate normal disribution? Describe their shape in the bivariate case.

16–3 Multivariate Analysis of Variance

Multivariate analysis of variance, often called MANOVA, is one of the most common multivariate techniques. It is an extension of the univariate technique, ANOVA. We use MANOVA when we want to test for differences among several populations (or treatments) with respect to more than one variable. That is, *we use MANOVA to test for differences among the centroids of several populations*. We call the number of populations under study r and the number of variables k.

The null and alternative hypotheses of MANOVA:

$$H_0: \mu_1 = \mu_2 = \mu_3 = \cdots = \mu_r$$
$$H_1: \text{Not all } \mu_i (i = 1, 2, \ldots, r) \text{ are equal}$$

where

$$\mu_i = \begin{bmatrix} \mu_{i1} \\ \mu_{i2} \\ \mu_{i3} \\ \vdots \\ \mu_{ik} \end{bmatrix}$$

is the vector of the means, in population i, of the k variables under study. It is the centroid of population i. We may say that while ANOVA is a test of equality of r population means, MANOVA is a test of the equality of r population *centroids*, or multivariate means.

When $r = 2$, the test is an extension to k variables of the two-sample t test of Chapter 8. As you should guess from the discussion in the last section, the multivariate analog of the t statistic is Hotelling's T^2 statistic, adapted for use with two samples. The T^2 statistic for two-sample analysis has a rather complicated formula, and we will not give it here; its value is reported by the computer. Like the single-sample T^2 statistic, the one for use with two samples may be transformed to an F statistic with an F distribution with k and $n_1 + n_2 - k - 1$ degrees of freedom when the null hypothesis is true (n_1 is the sample size in population 1, and n_2 is the sample size in population 2). The transformation of Hotelling's T^2 to F is given in equation 16–20.

The transformation of T^2 to F in two-sample analysis:

$$\frac{n_1 + n_2 - k - 1}{(n_1 + n_2 - 2)k} T^2 = F_{(k, n_1+n_2-k-1)} \qquad (16\text{–}20)$$

For example, suppose that we want to test whether two different methods of teaching a task are equally effective. We have two groups, assumed to be random samples from two populations. One population represents the "treatment" of being taught using method 1, and the other population represents the "treatment" of being taught using method 2. In each group, we measure two variables: the speed at which trained people perform the required task and the accuracy with which they perform the task. Both of these variables are measured on ordinal scales. The null hypothesis is that the two methods are equally effective, that is, the graduates of each of the two programs perform the task at the same average speed and with the same average accuracy. We perform a multivariate test (here, bivariate) because there certainly is a correlation between the speed and the accuracy at which the task is performed.

Suppose that the scores for speed and accuracy for the method 1 group of 30 students and the method 2 group of 35 students are analyzed by computer, and the result is a computed T^2 statistic given as: $T^2 = 47.05$. We test the null hypothesis H_0: $\boldsymbol{\mu}_1 = \boldsymbol{\mu}_2$ versus the alternative hypothesis H_1: $\boldsymbol{\mu}_1 \neq \boldsymbol{\mu}_2$, where $\boldsymbol{\mu}_i = [\mu_{i1}, \mu_{i2}]$; μ_{i1} is the average speed score in population (method) i, and μ_{i2} is the average accuracy score in population (method) i, where $i = 1, 2$.

To conduct the test, we use equation 16–20 and transform the T^2 statistic to an F value. We get: $F_{(2,62)} = (62/126)(47.05) = 23.15$. We now need to compare this computed value of the statistic with critical points of the F distribution with 2 degrees of freedom for the numerator and 62 degrees of freedom for the denominator. From Appendix C, Table 5, we find that the critical point for $\alpha = 0.01$ is approximately 4.97 (by interpolation). Since the computed value of the statistic, 23.15, is much greater than this critical point, we may conclude that there is statistical evidence that the two methods are not equally effective. One method produces either accuracy scores or speed scores, or both, that are different on the average from those produced by the other method. We note that the computer results will usually include the F statistic that corresponds to the computed T^2. All the user needs to do is to consider the reported F value. Often, the computer results also include the p-value of the F test, and all the user needs to do is to interpret the results.

What about multivariate analysis with more than two populations, or, in other words, the extension of ANOVA to several variables? Before we answer this question, let us state the assumptions we make in any multivariate analysis of variance, regardless of the number of populations to be compared.

MANOVA Assumptions

The assumptions necessary for multivariate analysis of variance are extensions of the ANOVA assumptions of normal distributions of the r populations under study and equal population variances. Thus, in MANOVA we assume the following:

1. The r populations under study have multivariate normal distributions.
2. The r populations have equal variance-covariance matrices, $\mathbf{\Sigma}$.

We will now define several different kinds of SSCP matrices that will lead to the development of test statistics to help us determine whether or not we believe the r populations under study have equal centroids. These matrices are extensions to k variables of the sums of squares, SSTR, SSE, and SST, of single-variable ANOVA discussed in Chapter 9.

Recall how (in section 16–2) we defined the SSCP matrix in equation 16–13. In MANOVA, we deal with r samples, one sample from each population. Each sample is, itself, k-variate. Therefore, for each one of our r samples, we can define the SSCP matrix as in equation 16–13. This gives us the r matrices: $\mathbf{S}_1, \mathbf{S}_2, \ldots, \mathbf{S}_r$. Each of the r matrices has dimension $k \times k$. We now define the matrix $\mathbf{S}_e$, which is also $k \times k$. The matrix $\mathbf{S}_e$ is obtained as the sum of the r matrices $\mathbf{S}_i$, $i = 1, 2, \ldots, r$. We have:

$$\mathbf{S}_e = \mathbf{S}_1 + \mathbf{S}_2 + \cdots + \mathbf{S}_r \tag{16–21}$$

The matrix $\mathbf{S}_e$ is the *error* sum of squares and cross products matrix. It is the *within* SSCP matrix for the r samples. The matrix $\mathbf{S}_e$ resembles the SSE in the univariate case of ANOVA. Similarly, we define the matrix $\mathbf{S}_T$ as the *total* SSCP matrix. This is the matrix of sums of squares and cross products of our *entire*, combined sample, regardless of which population gave rise to the sample items. This matrix is like the SST of ANOVA. Remember that in ANOVA we had SSTR + SSE = SST. In MANOVA, we have a similar relation:

$$\mathbf{S}_T = \mathbf{S}_A + \mathbf{S}_e \tag{16–22}$$

where $\mathbf{S}_A$ is the *among* SSCP matrix. The extension to MANOVA of the ANOVA relation SST = SSTR + SSE has matrices taking the place of numbers. We are now ready to define an important statistic.

Wilks' Lambda

We define *Wilks' lambda* (Λ), also called *Wilks' likelihood ratio criterion*, as follows.

Wilks' lambda:

$$\Lambda = \frac{|\mathbf{S}_e|}{|\mathbf{S}_T|} \tag{16–23}$$

where $|\mathbf{M}|$ stands for the *determinant* of the matrix $\mathbf{M}$

Again, if you have had no linear algebra, do not worry about the meaning of the determinant. For a 2×2 matrix, $\begin{bmatrix} a & b \\ c & d \end{bmatrix}$ where a, b, c, *and* d are numbers, the deter-

TABLE 16–1   Transformation of Wilks' Lambda to F for Selected Values of k and r

r	k	Transformation		F (Degrees of Freedom)
2	Any	$\dfrac{1-\Lambda}{\Lambda}\dfrac{n-k-1}{k}$	$=$	$F_{(k,\,n-k-1)}$
3	Any	$\dfrac{1-\sqrt{\Lambda}}{\sqrt{\Lambda}}\dfrac{n-k-2}{k}$	$=$	$F_{[2k,\,2(n-k-2)]}$
Any	1	$\dfrac{1-\Lambda}{\Lambda}\dfrac{n-r}{r-1}$	$=$	$F_{(r-1,\,n-r)}$
Any	2	$\dfrac{1-\sqrt{\Lambda}}{\sqrt{\Lambda}}\dfrac{n-r-1}{r-1}$	$=$	$F_{[2(r-1),\,2(n-r-1)]}$

minant is equal to $(a)(d) - (b)(c)$. For higher-order matrices, the determinant is slightly more complicated; but again, all the computations are done by computer.

In our context, the determinant may be viewed as a measure of volume. When the r groups are really separated from each other, that is, when the population centroids are not equal, we expect (generalizing from the single-variable ANOVA case) that the volume of the *within* variation will be small compared with the volume of the *total* variation. Remember from ANOVA that *error* is small when compared with *total* in cases where the null hypothesis is false and the population means are not equal. Thus Wilks' lambda is expected to be relatively small when H_0 should be rejected.

The exact distribution of Wilks' lambda is complicated, but there are transformations of Λ to statistics that have at least an approximate F distribution when the null hypothesis is true. The degree of approximation accuracy depends on the values of k and r. The computer output will usually include a transformed F statistic and will state whether it is exact or approximate. Table 16–1 shows the cases where an exact transformation of Λ to F is possible. In other cases, the transformed Λ has an approximate F distribution. In the cases where $r = 2$ (two groups only), it can be shown that Wilks' lambda is equivalent to Hotelling's T^2 in that one of them can be transformed exactly into the other. You need not know which transformation is used: the computer will output an F statistic along with Wilks' lambda. It will also give the p-value.

Look at the third case in Table 16–1. Do you recognize this case? We have $r =$ any value and $k = 1$. The fact that $k = 1$ means that the analysis is univariate. This is the comparison of r population means with respect to a single variable: it is ANOVA. Recall from Chapter 9 that in ANOVA, our F statistic has degrees of freedom $(r - 1)$ and $(n - r)$. This is exactly what we have here.

The first case in Table 16–1, $r = 2$ and any k, is the case we described earlier: a two-population comparison. As noted earlier, Hotelling's T^2 statistic is appropriate in this situation. The statistic $(1 - \Lambda)/\Lambda$ is equal to $T^2/(n - 2)$. The appropriate F statistic from Table 16–1 is identical to the F statistic obtained by transforming Hotelling's T^2 using equation 16–20 with $n = n_1 + n_2$ as the total sample size (prove this).

Other Statistics

There are several other statistics that are often reported by computer programs of MANOVA. Some of these are: *Pillai's trace, Roy's largest root, Hotelling's trace, Rao's statistic,* and *Bartlett's statistic.* Rao's statistic covers the transformations of Λ

shown in Table 16–1. Some of the statistics are transformations of Wilks' lambda; others depend on other information in the matrices involved in the computations. Most of the statistics are transformable in some way to an F statistic, and the value of F will be reported along with them in the computer output. Let us look at an example of the use of MANOVA.

EXAMPLE (b)

One of the most remarkable import product successes in recent years has been the introduction of the Australian mineral drink Koala Springs into the North American market. The drink, mineral water with added natural flavor, comes in two main flavors: lemon-lime and orange-mango. The importer wants to find out whether the drinks sell equally well in three geographical regions, denoted 1, 2, and 3. That is, the importer wants to know whether the centroids of the three populations 1, 2, and 3 are equal. The three centroids are each a bivariate vector of means: $\mu_i = [\mu_{i1}, \mu_{i2}]'$, where μ_{i1} is the mean weekly sales of lemon in region i and μ_{i2} is the mean weekly sales of orange in region i ($i = 1, 2, 3$) (we call the drinks lemon and orange for short). The null and alternative hypotheses are, then:

$$H_0: \begin{bmatrix} \mu_{11} \\ \mu_{12} \end{bmatrix} = \begin{bmatrix} \mu_{21} \\ \mu_{22} \end{bmatrix} = \begin{bmatrix} \mu_{31} \\ \mu_{32} \end{bmatrix}$$

$$H_1: \text{Not all three } \mu_i \text{ vectors are equal}$$

To test the hypotheses, we carry out a MANOVA. The available data, assumed to be random samples from the three bivariate populations under study, are 20 weekly sales (in thousands of cases) of the lemon and orange drinks in the three regions. Our data are presented in Table 16–2.

The data are entered into a computer and analyzed using the SPSS program MANOVA. The results of the analysis are shown as the computer output in Figure 16–7. The output

SOLUTION

TABLE 16–2 Number of Cases Sold (in Thousands) of the Lemon and Orange Koala Springs Drinks in Three Geographic Regions

Region 1		Region 2		Region 3	
Lemon	**Orange**	**Lemon**	**Orange**	**Lemon**	**Orange**
22	34	41	44	61	60
23	35	42	43	62	65
24	32	43	45	62	64
25	30	42	50	60	60
27	33	43	48	64	69
23	30	41	47	65	69
24	32	45	51	66	70
28	34	46	53	61	65
24	29	47	49	56	60
27	31	48	50	55	61
28	33	50	53	62	63
29	35	42	40	68	73
25	36	41	46	63	67
21	30	42	47	66	68
20	35	39	42	65	72
22	33	41	43	66	68
20	34	40	42	57	61
18	28	45	51	55	62
19	29	44	50	59	68
20	30	48	54	60	66

FIGURE 16–7   SPSS Output for the MANOVA of Example (b)

```
                         ANALYSIS OF VARIANCE--DESIGN 1

Multivariate Tests of Significance (S = 2, M = -1/2, N = 27)

Test Name         Value        Approx. F     Hypoth. DF      Error DF      Sig. of F

Pillais          1.10749        35.36508        4.00          114.00         .000
Hotellings      23.06778       317.18195        4.00          110.00         .000
Wilks             .03560       120.39192        4.00          112.00         .000
Roys              .95815

Note: F statistic for WILKS' Lambda is exact.



EFFECT   REGION   (CONT.)

Univariate F-tests with (2, 57) D. F.

Variable    Hypoth. SS    Error SS      Hypoth. MS     Error MS        F        Sig. of F

LEMON      14604.43333    654.50000    7302.21667    11.48246    635.94553      .000
ORANGE     11183.63333    752.30000    5591.81667    13.19825    423.67879      .000

        3952 BYTES OF WORKSPACE NEEDED FOR MANOVA EXECUTION
```

gives the values of several statistics: Pillai's, Hotelling's, Wilks', and Roy's. A note in the output states that the F statistic for Wilks' lambda is exact. The reported value of Wilks' lambda is $\Lambda = 0.03560$. From Table 16–1, we know that either the second or the fourth transformation would be appropriate here. The two are identical in this case (show this). Using the transformation, we get:

$$F_{(4,112)} = \frac{1 - \sqrt{0.0356}}{\sqrt{0.0356}} \frac{60 - 4}{2} = 120.39$$

which is the exact value of the corresponding F statistic reported in the output. Comparing this value with critical points of the F distribution with 4 degrees of freedom for the numerator and 112 degrees of freedom for the denominator, we conclude that H_0 can be strongly rejected. The reported p-value (denoted "Sig. of F" in the output) is very small. It is reported as .000 because the computer is not programmed to report values smaller than 0.001. The transformed statistic follows an exact F distribution (when the null hypothesis is true) because $k = 2$ and $r = 3$, which is one of the situations listed in Table 16–1. Wilks' lambda is the most commonly used statistic, and we concentrated on its use. The other reported statistics may be considered as well. Those that are transformed to F statistics in the output also have their reported p-values. All of these statistics are very significant as well, which is not surprising, as the statistics are related. We will usually consider Wilks' lambda.

Next, the output in Figure 16–7 shows the results of individual ANOVAs performed on each of the two single variables in our bivariate vector: an ANOVA of sales of the lemon drink in the three regions and an ANOVA of sales of the orange drink in the three regions. The results of the separate ANOVAs show that the null hypothesis that sales of the lemon drink have the same average at the three regions may be rejected (Sig. of F = .000); the same can be said about mean sales of the orange drink.

Further Analysis

The individual ANOVAs for each of the two variables are an example of further analysis following the rejection of the null hypothesis in MANOVA. It is possible to base the critical value for F tests of the separate ANOVAs on a statistic of the MANOVA that ensures a single overall level of significance α for the univariate ANOVAs and pairwise or other follow-up tests. We will present the results of another procedure that ensures the meaning of an overall level of significance: the *stepdown procedure*. The stepdown procedure computes a univariate F statistic for one of the variables in the vector after eliminating the effects of the other variables. Then another variable is chosen. Each variable (in our example, there are only two of them) is examined on the unique information it provides about differences among the r populations under study. Output for the stepdown procedure in our example is shown in Figure 16–8.

Looking at the results in the figure we see that there are significant differences among regions with respect to sales of both the lemon and the orange drinks. The only difference between the results of the stepdown procedure and the univariate ANOVAs shown in Figure 16–7 is that using the stepdown procedure, the p-value for the orange ANOVA is shown to be higher than that for lemon, once lemon is removed from the analysis. The new p-value is shown as .005 instead of .000. As it turns out, both variables are still highly significant.

Another method of further analysis to follow MANOVA is the *Dunn-Bonferroni method*. Here, if we carry out k univariate ANOVAs following a MANOVA, then any ANOVA will be considered significant—at an overall level of significance α—if its p-value is smaller than α/k. Letting $\alpha = 0.05$, our univariate ANOVAs will be considered significant at an overall level $\alpha = 0.05$ if each is significant at a level $0.05/2 = 0.025$ (or less). Clearly, both univariate ANOVAs in our example are significant. Another method of further analysis following MANOVA makes use of discriminant functions. *Discriminant analysis* is discussed in the next section.

Two-Way MANOVA

We will now say a few things about two-factor, or two-way, MANOVA. First, let us generalize Wilks' lambda statistic. Recall from univariate ANOVA that in two-factor or higher-order ANOVAs, there are several possible hypotheses to be tested: main effects of factor A, main effects of factor B, and AB interactions (with more possibilities in higher-order designs). Whatever our hypothesis may be, let us call the sum

FIGURE 16–8   SPSS-Produced Stepdown Procedure for Example (b)

Variable	Hypoth. MS	Error MS	StepDown F	Hypoth. DF	Error DF	Sig. of F
LEMON	7302.21667	11.48246	635.94553	2	57	.000
ORANGE	39.38055	6.86975	5.73246	2	56	.005

Roy-Bargman Stepdown F - tests

of squares and cross products matrix corresponding to what we want to test $\mathbf{S}_h$. This is the SSCP matrix for hypothesis h. This matrix will be produced by the computer for any given hypothesis.

Wilks' lambda for hypothesis h:

$$\Lambda_h = \frac{|\mathbf{S}_e|}{|\mathbf{S}_h + \mathbf{S}_e|} \qquad (16\text{--}24)$$

where $|\mathbf{M}|$ is the determinant of matrix $\mathbf{M}$

The matrix $\mathbf{S}_e$ is the SSCP matrix for error. In some multifactor designs, we use the interaction SSCP matrix for $\mathbf{S}_e$, but usually we use the *within* SSCP matrix $\mathbf{S}_e$ in computing this statistic. In single-factor MANOVA, there is only one hypothesis (before we go to further analysis). Thus, in single-factor MANOVA, we see that the *hypothesis* SSCP matrix $\mathbf{S}_h$ is just $\mathbf{S}_A$. Since, in such cases, $\mathbf{S}_T = \mathbf{S}_A + \mathbf{S}_e$, the statistic in equation 16–24 is exactly the same as the one in equation 16–23. The matrices $\mathbf{S}_h$ and $\mathbf{S}_e$ for Example (b) are shown in Figure 16–9.

Note that the matrices in the output do not list the upper right off-diagonal elements. This is because the off-diagonal elements of an SSCP matrix are equal. Write the other off-diagonal element where the missing element should be. Then add the two matrices and find the determinant of the resulting matrix. This is your denominator. The numerator is the determinant of the $\mathbf{S}_e$ matrix. Compute it as well, and find the value of Wilks' lambda. Compare it with the value given in Figure 16–7. (Recall that the determinant of a 2×2 matrix $\begin{bmatrix} a & b \\ c & d \end{bmatrix}$ is just $(a)(d) - (b)(c)$.) Your answer for Λ_h in our example should agree with the value reported in Figure 16–7.

In two-factor MANOVA, there will be an SSCP matrix for factor A, matrix $\mathbf{S}_A$, which will be used along with $\mathbf{S}_e$ in computing Wilks' lambda for the test of factor A main effects using equation 16–24. Similarly, an appropriate SSCP matrix will be used along with $\mathbf{S}_e$ in computing a value of Wilks' lambda for factor B main effects; and similarly for an interaction between the two factors. The SSCP matrices are ad-

---

FIGURE 16–9   The Matrices $\mathbf{S}_h$ and $\mathbf{S}_e$ for Example (b)

EFFECT   REGION
Adjusted Hypothesis Sum-of-Squares and Cross-Products

	LEMON	ORANGE
LEMON	14604.43333	
ORANGE	12740.43333	11183.63333

- -

WITHIN CELLS Sum-of-Squares and Cross-Products

	LEMON	ORANGE
LEMON	654.50000	
ORANGE	490.50000	752.30000

- -

ditive in a similar way to the additivity of the sums of squares SSA, SSB, SS(AB), and SSE in univariate ANOVA.

In two-way MANOVA we have:

$$\mathbf{S}_T = \mathbf{S}_A + \mathbf{S}_B + \mathbf{S}_{AB} + \mathbf{S}_e \qquad (16\text{--}25)$$

The SSCP matrices and their associated degrees of freedom for two-way MANOVA are given in Table 16–3. Here n is the number of sample points in each cell (we use a balanced design), a is the number of levels of factor A, and b is the number of levels of factor B. In a fixed-effects MANOVA, we use $\mathbf{S}_e$ in computing Wilks' lambda in equation 16–24. (We do not substitute $\mathbf{S}_{AB}$ for it.) The degrees of freedom from Table 16–3 are then transformed into *new* degrees of freedom for the F statistic corresponding to Wilks' lambda, via complicated formulas that may be found in advanced books.

We will now look at a simple two-way MANOVA example. Suppose in Example (b) that the importer wants to test for equality of the bivariate sales not only across the three geographic regions, but also at two different kinds of stores: supermarkets and convenience stores. Thus, the importer wants the MANOVA to provide answers to the *three* preliminary questions:

1. Are average sales of the bivariate vector (lemon drink, orange drink) equal across all three geographical regions?
2. Are average sales of the vector of the two drinks equal at supermarkets and at convenience stores?
3. Is there any interaction between the two factors, geographical region and type of store, with respect to sales of the two products?

New data are gathered that reflect weekly sales of the two kinds of drinks at each of the three regions and at each of the two types of stores. Figure 16–10 shows the output of the four SSCP matrices needed for our analysis.

We will now demonstrate the computation of Wilks' lambda, using equation 16–24, for testing the null hypothesis of no interaction between the two factors (recall from the univariate ANOVA of Chapter 9 that this hypothesis is to be tested first). From the data in Figure 16–10, we have:

$$\mathbf{S}_h = \mathbf{S}_{AB} = \begin{bmatrix} 29.43 & 36.80 \\ 36.80 & 54.70 \end{bmatrix} \quad \text{and} \quad \mathbf{S}_e = \begin{bmatrix} 416.0 & 184.9 \\ 184.9 & 352.0 \end{bmatrix}$$

TABLE 16–3 Two-Way MANOVA Table

Source	SSCP Matrix	Degrees of Freedom
Factor A	$\mathbf{S}_A$	$a - 1$
Factor B	$\mathbf{S}_B$	$b - 1$
AB interaction	$\mathbf{S}_{AB}$	$(a - 1)(b - 1)$
Error	$\mathbf{S}_e$	$ab(n - 1)$
Total	$\mathbf{S}_T$	$nab - 1$

FIGURE 16–10   SPSS-Produced SSCP Matrices for Two-Way MANOVA [Extended Example (b)]

Factor A: region (S_A)	EFFECT REGION Adjusted Hypothesis Sum-of-Squares and Cross-Products

```
                              LEMON              ORANGE
         LEMON           14604.43333
         ORANGE          12740.43333         11183.63333
```

Factor B: store (S_B)

```
EFFECT      STORE
Adjusted Hypothesis Sum-of-Squares and Cross-Products
                              LEMON              ORANGE
         LEMON             209.06667
         ORANGE            268.80000          345.60000
```

Region-store interaction (S_{AB})

```
EFFECT      REGION BY STORE
Adjusted Hypothesis Sum-of-Squares and Cross-Products
                              LEMON              ORANGE
         LEMON              29.43333
         ORANGE             36.80000           54.70000
```

Error: within cells (S_e)

```
WITHIN CELLS Sum-of-Squares and Cross-Products
                              LEMON              ORANGE
         LEMON             416.00000
         ORANGE            184.90000          352.00000
```

Hence, their sum (needed for the denominator in equation 16–24) is:

$$\mathbf{S}_h + \mathbf{S}_e = \begin{bmatrix} 445.43 & 221.70 \\ 221.70 & 406.70 \end{bmatrix}$$

The denominator in equation 16–24 is the determinant of the matrix $\mathbf{S}_h + \mathbf{S}_e$. We compute it as:

$$\begin{vmatrix} 445.43 & 221.70 \\ 221.70 & 406.70 \end{vmatrix} = (445.43)(406.70) - (221.70)(221.70) = 132{,}005.49$$

Now we need the numerator of equation 16–24, which is the determinant of the matrix $\mathbf{S}_e$. We get:

$$\begin{vmatrix} 416.0 & 184.9 \\ 184.9 & 352.0 \end{vmatrix} = (416.0)(352.0) - (184.9)(184.9) = 112{,}243.99$$

Finally, dividing the two results, we get the value of Wilks' lambda for this test:

$$\Lambda_h = \frac{|\mathbf{S}_e|}{|\mathbf{S}_h + \mathbf{S}_e|} = \frac{112{,}243.99}{132{,}005.49} = 0.85029$$

This value agrees with the reported value of Wilks' lambda for the test for interaction shown in Figure 16–11. The output also shows the transformation of Wilks' lambda to an F statistic. The reported p-value of the statistic, "Sig. of F," is 0.070. Thus, using the customary $\alpha = 0.05$, we may conclude that there are no significant interactions between the two factors. As you recall from Chapter 9, this simplifies our conclusions in that we need not qualify our statements about each main effect by the phrase " . . . averaged over the levels of the other factor. . . ." Figure 16–11 also shows the results of the MANOVA tests for the main effects of region and store.

Looking at the p-values of the F statistics corresponding to the Wilks' lambdas for the three tests shown in Figure 16–11, we conclude the following: There are no significant interactions between type of store and region as far as sales of the two drinks are involved (at $\alpha = 0.05$). There are significant differences among the three

FIGURE 16–11 SPSS-Produced Two-Way MANOVA Results [Extended Example (b)]

```
                    ANALYSIS OF VARIANCE--DESIGN 1

EFFECT       REGION BY STORE
Multivariate Tests of Significance (S = 2, M = -1/2, N = 25 1/2)

Test Name         Value      Approx. F      Hypoth. DF      Error DF      Sig. of F

Pillais          .15165      2.21522          4.00          108.00          .072
Hotellings       .17379      2.25929          4.00          104.00          .068
Wilks            .85029      2.23840          4.00          106.00          .070
Roys             .13756

Note: F statistic for WILKS' Lambda is exact.



EFFECT       REGION
Multivariate Tests of Significance (S = 2, M = -1/2, N = 25 1/2)

Test Name         Value      Approx. F      Hypoth. DF      Error DF      Sig. of F

Pillais         1.14498     36.15642          4.00          108.00          .000
Hotellings     45.27405    588.56262          4.00          104.00          .000
Wilks            .01809    170.54669          4.00          106.00          .000
Roys             .97830

Note: F statistic for WILKS' Lambda is exact.



EFFECT       STORE
Multivariate Tests of Significance (S = 1, M = 0, N = 25 1/2)

Test Name         Value      Approx. F      Hypoth. DF      Error DF      Sig. of F

Pillais          .51241     27.84923          2.00          53.00           .000
Hotellings      1.05091     27.84923          2.00          53.00           .000
Wilks            .48759     27.84923          2.00          53.00           .000
Roys             .51241

Note: F statistics are exact.
```

regions with respect to average sales of (the vector of) the two drinks. That is, the population centroids (μ_1, μ_2) of sales of the two drinks are not equal at all three regions. We make a similar conclusion about the two types of store. At this point, we cannot determine *where* the differences exist. All we know is that the centroids are probably not equal. This does not mean that every pair of centroids is unequal. It may be that average sales are the same in two regions but differ from the average sales in the third region. Also, we do not know whether average sales of *both* drinks are different in different regions, or whether the differences that exist are with respect to only one of the two drinks (i.e., one of the components of the bivariate vector).

All these questions need to be answered by methods of further analysis. We would need to perform further analysis on each of the two components of the vector (i.e., separate ANOVAs). We would also need to perform pairwise or other comparisons among the levels of each of the factors (in this example, the store factor need not be further analyzed beyond univariate ANOVAs because it only has two levels). The further analysis may be done using the stepdown procedure or any other procedure that maintains an overall level of significance for all separate tests. As mentioned earlier, discriminant analysis, discussed in the next section, will provide us with an additional method of further analysis to follow MANOVA.

The MANOVA procedure may be extended to cover multivariate analysis of covariance, called MANCOVA for short. It may also be extended to cover many different types of factorial designs, such as the ones discussed in Chapter 9 as well as many others. Whatever special design you may need to use in the analysis of your data, you will find a description of the procedure in a manual of the statistical package you plan to use, such as SPSS or SAS. Technical details of the method may be found in advanced texts on multivariate methods. This section should give you everything you need to know to get started on the more complicated multivariate designs described in other sources. Computer packages that perform MANOVA also provide routines for checking the validity of the assumptions required for the MANOVA procedure. As in the case of ANOVA, the MANOVA procedure is not very sensitive to deviations from the assumptions of multivariate normality and equal variance-covariance matrices, as long as the deviations are not extreme.

PROBLEMS

Answers

16-22.

Reject

16-24.

$F = 18.74$
Reject H_0.

16-26.

$F = 28.95$
Reject H_0.

16-18.   Under what conditions are Hotelling's T^2 statistic and Wilks' lambda equivalent?

16-19.   Define the matrices S_e, S_A, and S_T. What does each of them measure?

16-20.   What are the assumptions of MANOVA?

16-21.   Define Wilks' lambda by a formula, and discuss its meaning in terms of different measures of variability.

16-22.   Suppose that you run a multivariate analysis of variance and find that Λ is very close to zero. Without knowing the value of the corresponding F statistic and its degrees of freedom, should you accept or reject the null hypothesis? Explain.

16-23.   Redo problem 16–22, except that now Λ is close to 1.00.

16-24.   A MANOVA is carried out to determine whether differences exist in the average qualification level, measured by the two variables education and experience, of top managers at three industry groups. The total sample size is $n = 90$ (thirty executives are randomly selected from each of the three industry groups). The computed value of Wilks' lambda is $\Lambda = 0.485$. Transform Λ to the appropriate F statistic using the information in Table 16–1, and conduct the test for equality of population centroids. State your conclusions.

16-25.   Explain the difference between a univariate two-factor ANOVA and a one-factor MANOVA with two variables.

16-26.   The makers of desks and chairs for schools want to determine whether the average number of years it takes before replacement of chairs or desks is necessary is approximately equal at four different kinds of schools. Data on 100 pairs of items at each kind of school are available, and the analysis yields Wilks' lambda equal to 0.672. Use the appropriate transformation from Table 16–1, and conduct the F test. What are your conclusions?

16-27.   Discuss the general principle behind the stepdown procedure. What are the uses of the procedure?

16-28.   Name other methods of further analysis to follow MANOVA in addition to the stepdown procedure.

16-29.   Using the SSCP matrices shown in Figure 16–9, compute the value of Wilks' lambda, and compare it with the value reported in the output in Figure 16–7.

16-30.   In a two-factor MANOVA, describe the meaning of each of the following matrices: S_A, S_B, S_{AB}, S_e, and S_T. Give a simple formula that links all of these matrices.

16-31.   Using the information in the output shown in Figure 16–10, compute the values of Wilks' lambda for the factor A (region), and the factor B (store) main effects. Compare with the values reported in Figure 16–11.

16–32. An article in the *Journal of Marketing Research* reports the results of an analysis aimed at determining the effectiveness of the use of humor in advertising. Two ad types were used, humorous and nonhumorous; and five ad-response variables were measured. The total sample size was 80 people, and the resulting F statistic value from the MANOVA was 7.57.[1] Is there evidence of differences between humorous and nonhumorous ads with respect to at least one of the response variables?

16–33. The *Journal of Marketing* reports the results of a MANOVA aimed at comparing purchasers of goods with purchasers of services. The sample size used was 252 people in total, and four consumer behavior attributes were measured. The resulting F statistic was 254.00.[2] Comment on the significance of the results.

Answer

16–32.

Yes

16–4 Discriminant Analysis

A bank is faced with the following problem: Due to economic conditions in the area the bank serves, a large percentage of the bank's mortgage holders are defaulting on their loans. It therefore is very important for the bank to develop some criteria for making a statistical determination about whether or not any particular loan applicant is likely to be able to repay his or her loan. Is such a determination possible?

There is a very useful multivariate technique aimed at answering such a question. The idea is very similar to that of multiple regression analysis. In multiple regression, we try to predict values of a continuous-scale variable—the dependent variable—based on the values of a set of independent variables. The independent variables may be continuous or they may be qualitative (in which case we use dummy variables to model them, as you recall from Chapter 11). In **discriminant analysis,** the situation is similar. We try to develop an equation that will help us predict the value of a dependent variable based on values of a set of independent variables. The difference is that the dependent variable is *qualitative*. In the bank loan example, the qualitative dependent variable is a classification: repay or default. The independent variables that help us make a classification of the loan outcome category may be: family income, family assets, job stability (number of years with present employer), and any other variables we think may have an effect on whether or not the loan will be repaid. There is also an option where the algorithm itself chooses which variables should be included in the prediction equation. This is similar to a stepwise regression procedure.

If we let our dependent, qualitative variable be D and we consider k independent variables, then our prediction equation has the following form.

The form of an estimated prediction equation:

$$D = b_0 + b_1 X_1 + b_2 X_2 + \cdots + b_k X_k \qquad (16\text{–}26)$$

where the b_i, $i = 1, \ldots, k$, are the *discriminant weights*—they are like the estimated regression coefficients in multiple regression; b_0 is a constant

---

[1] A Chattopadhyay and K. Basu, "Humor in Advertising," *Journal of Marketing Research* (November 1990), p. 470.

[2] K. Murray, "A Test of Services Marketing Theory," *Journal of Marketing* (January 1991), p. 17.

Developing a Discriminant Function

In discriminant analysis, we aim at deriving the linear combination of the independent variables that *discriminates best* between the two or more a priori defined
groups (the repay group versus the default group in the bank loan example). This is
done by finding coefficient estimates b_i in equation 16–26 that maximize the among-
groups variation relative to the within-groups variation.

Figure 16–12 shows how we develop a **discriminant function.** We look for a *direction in space*, a combination of variables (here, two variables, X_1 and X_2) that
maximizes the separation between the two groups. As seen in the figure, if we consider only the X_2 component of every point in the two groups, we do not have much
separation between the two groups. Look at the data in Figure 16–12 from the direction specified by having the eye located by the X_2 axis. As you see from your
vantage point, the two groups overlap, and some of the upper points in group 2 look
like they belong in group 1. Now look at the data with the eye located below the X_1
axis. Here you have better separation between the two groups. From this vantage
point, however, the points blend together into one big group, and you will still not
be able to easily classify a point as belonging to a single group based solely on its
location. Now look at the data with the eye above and perpendicular to line L. Here
you have perfect separation of the two groups, and if you were given the coordinate
along line L of a new point, you would probably be able to logically classify that
point as belonging to one group or the other. (Such classification will never be *perfect* with real data because there will always be the chance that a point belonging to
population 1 will somehow happen to have a low X_2 component and/or a large X_1
component that would throw it into the region we classify as belonging to population
2.) In discriminant analysis, we find the combination of variables (i.e., the direction
in space) that maximizes the discrimination between groups. Then we classify new
observations as belonging to one group or the other based on their score on the
weighted combination of variables chosen as the discriminant function.

FIGURE 16–12   Maximizing the Separation between Two Groups

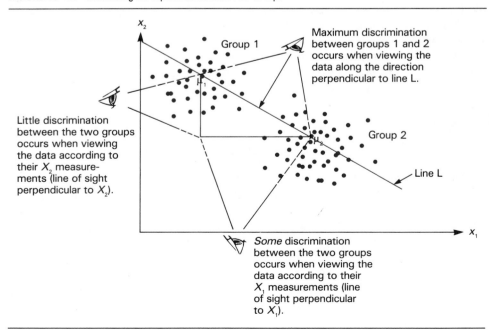

Since in multivariate analysis we assume that the points in each group have a multivariate normal distribution (with possibly different centroids), the marginal distribution of each of the two populations, when viewed along the direction that maximizes the differentiation between groups, is univariate *normal*. This is shown in Figure 16–13.

The point C on the discriminant scale is the *cutting score*. When a data point gets a score smaller than C, we classify that point as belonging to population 1, and when a data point receives a score greater than C, we classify that point as belonging to population 2. This assumes, of course, that we do not know which population the point really belongs to and we use the discriminant function to classify the point based on the values the point has with respect to the independent variables. In our bank loan example, we use the variables family income, assets, job stability, and other variables to estimate a discriminant function that will maximize the differences (i.e., the multivariate distance) between the two groups: the repay group and the default group. Then, when new applicants arrive, we find their score on our discriminant scale and classify the applicants as to whether we believe they are going to repay or default. Errors will, of course, occur. Someone we classify as a defaulter may (if given the loan) actually repay it, and someone we classify in the repay group may not.

Look at Figure 16–13. There is an area under the univariate normal projection of group 1 to the right of C. This is the probability of erroneously classifying an observation in population 1 as belonging to population 2. Similarly, the area under the right-hand normal curve to the left of the cutting score C is the probability of misclassifying a point that belongs to population 2 as being from population 1.

When the population centroids of the two groups are equal (i.e., when a MANOVA should lead us to accept the null hypothesis of equal multivariate means), there would be *no discrimination* between the groups based on the values of the independent variables considered in the analysis. In such a case, the univariate normal distributions of the discriminant scores will be identical (the two curves will overlap). The reason the curves overlap is due to the model assumptions. In discriminant analysis, as in MANOVA, we assume that the populations under study have multivariate normal distributions with equal variance-covariance matrices and possibly different means.

FIGURE 16–13 The Discriminant Function

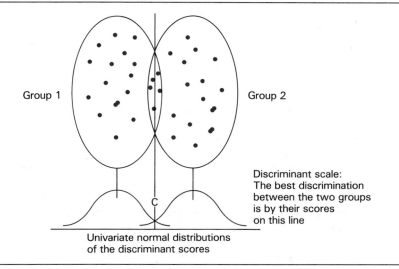

Group 1   Group 2

Discriminant scale:
The best discrimination
between the two groups
is by their scores
on this line

C

Univariate normal distributions
of the discriminant scores

Evaluating the Performance of the Model

We test the accuracy of our discriminant function by evaluating its success rate when the function is applied to cases with *known* group memberships. It is best to withhold some of our data when we carry out the estimation phase of the analysis, and then use the withheld observations in testing the accuracy of the predictions based on our estimated discriminant function. If we try to evaluate the success rate of our discriminant function based only on observations used in the estimation phase, then we run the risk of overestimating the success rate. Still, we will use our estimation data in estimating the success rate because it usually will not be efficient to withhold many observations for use solely in assessing our classification success rate. A *classification summary table* will be produced by the computer. This table will show us how many cases were correctly classified and will also report the *percentage* of correctly classified cases in each group. This will give us the *hit rate* or *hitting probabilities*.

We assume that the cost of making one kind of error (classifying an element as belonging to population 1 when the element actually belongs to population 2) is equal to the cost of making the other kind of error (classifying an element as belonging to population 2 when the element actually belongs to population 1). When the costs are unequal, an adjustment to the procedure may be made.

The procedure may also be adjusted for prior probabilities of group membership. That is, when assigning an element to one of the two groups, we may account not only for its discriminant score, but also for its prior probability of belonging to the particular population, based on the relative size of the population as compared with the other populations under study. In the bank loan example, suppose that defaulting on the loan is a very rare event, with a priori probability 0.001. We may wish to adjust our discriminant criterion to account for this fact, appropriately reducing our rate of classifying people as belonging to the default category. Such adjustments are based on the use of Bayes' theorem. We demonstrate discriminant analysis with the example we used at the beginning of this section—the bank loan example—which we will call Example (c).

EXAMPLE (c)

The bank we have been discussing has data on 32 loan applicants. Data are available on each applicant's total family assets, total family income, total debt outstanding, family size, number of years with present employer for household head, and a qualitative variable that equals 1 if the applicant has repaid the loan and 0 if he or she has not repaid the loan. Data are presented in Table 16–4. The bank is interested in using the data to estimate a discriminant function. The bank intends to use this function in classifying future loan applicants.

SOLUTION

The data, a random sample of 32 cases, are analyzed using the SPSS program DISCRIMINANT. The output of the analysis is given in the following figures. We use a stepwise procedure similar to stepwise multiple regression. At each stage, the computer chooses a variable to enter the discriminant function. The criterion for entering the equation may be specified by the user. Here we choose the Wilks lambda criterion. The variable to enter is the variable that best fits the entry requirements in terms of the associated Wilks' lambda value. Variables may enter and leave the equation at each step in the same way that they are processed in stepwise regression. The reason for this is that multicollinearity may exist. Therefore, we need to allow variables to leave the equation once other variables are in the equation. Figure 16–14 shows the variables that enter and leave the equation at each stage of the discriminant analysis.

TABLE 16–4 The Data of Example (c) (Assets, Income, and Debt, in Thousands of Dollars)

Assets	Income	Debt	Family Size	Number of Years with Present Employer	Repay/Default
98	35	12	4	4	1
65	44	5	3	1	1
22	50	0	2	7	1
78	60	34	5	5	1
50	31	4	2	2	1
21	30	5	3	7	1
42	32	21	4	11	1
20	41	10	2	3	1
33	25	0	3	6	1
57	32	8	2	5	1
8	23	12	2	1	0
0	15	10	4	2	0
12	18	7	3	4	0
7	21	19	4	2	0
15	14	28	2	1	0
30	27	50	4	4	0
29	18	30	3	6	0
9	22	10	4	5	0
12	25	39	5	3	0
23	30	65	3	1	0
34	45	21	2	5	0
21	12	28	3	2	1
10	17	0	2	3	1
57	39	13	5	8	0
60	40	10	3	2	1
78	60	8	3	5	1
45	33	9	4	7	0
9	18	9	3	5	1
12	23	10	4	4	1
55	36	12	2	5	1
67	33	35	2	4	1
42	45	12	3	8	0

FIGURE 16–14 SPSS-Produced Stepwise Discriminant Analysis for Example (c)

```
- - - - - - - - - - - - - - - - - - - - - D I S C R I M I N A N T   A N A L Y S I S

ON GROUPS DEFINED BY REPAY


ANALYSIS NUMBER        1

STEPWISE VARIABLE SELECTION

        SELECTION RULE:  MINIMIZE WILKS' LAMBDA
        MAXIMUM NUMBER OF STEPS. . . . . . . . . .    10
        MINIMUM TOLERANCE LEVEL. . . . . . . . . . 0.00100
        MINIMUM F TO ENTER . . . . . . . . . . . . 1.0000
        MAXIMUM F TO REMOVE. . . . . . . . . . . . 1.0000

CANONICAL DISCRIMINANT FUNCTIONS

        MAXIMUM NUMBER OF FUNCTIONS. . . . . . . .     1
        MINIMUM CUMULATIVE PERCENT OF VARIANCE . . 100.00
        MAXIMUM SIGNIFICANCE OF WILKS' LAMBDA. . . 1.0000

PRIOR PROBABILITY FOR EACH GROUP IS 0.50000
```

FIGURE 16–14 *(continued)*

```
--------------- VARIABLES NOT IN THE ANALYSIS AFTER STEP    0 ---------------

                     MINIMUM
VARIABLE   TOLERANCE   TOLERANCE   F TO ENTER    WILKS' LAMBDA

ASSETS     1.0000000   1.0000000    6.6152          0.81933
INCOME     1.0000000   1.0000000    3.0672          0.90724
DEBT       1.0000000   1.0000000    5.2263          0.85164
FAMSIZE    1.0000000   1.0000000    2.5292          0.92225
JOB        1.0000000   1.0000000    0.24457         0.99191


* * * * * * * * * * * * * * * * * * * * * * * * * * * * * * * * * * * * * * *


AT STEP    1, ASSETS    WAS INCLUDED IN THE ANALYSIS.

                                    DEGREES OF FREEDOM   SIGNIF.   BETWEEN GROUPS
WILKS' LAMBDA         0.81933         1      1      30.0
EQUIVALENT F          6.61516                1      30.0    0.0153

----------------- VARIABLES IN THE ANALYSIS AFTER STEP    1 -----------------

VARIABLE   TOLERANCE   F TO REMOVE   WILKS' LAMBDA

ASSETS     1.0000000      6.6152

---------------- VARIABLES NOT IN THE ANALYSIS AFTER STEP    1 ----------------

                     MINIMUM
VARIABLE   TOLERANCE   TOLERANCE   F TO ENTER    WILKS' LAMBDA

INCOME     0.5784563   0.5784563   0.90821E-02      0.81908
DEBT       0.9706667   0.9706667    6.0662          0.67759
FAMSIZE    0.9492947   0.9492947    3.9269          0.72162
JOB        0.9631433   0.9631433   0.47688E-06      0.81933

F STATISTICS AND SIGNIFICANCES BETWEEN PAIRS OF GROUPS AFTER STEP    1
EACH F STATISTIC HAS    1 AND        30.0 DEGREES OF FREEDOM.

                    GROUP         0

      GROUP
         1                  6.6152
                           0.0153


* * * * * * * * * * * * * * * * * * * * * * * * * * * * * * * * * * * * * * *


AT STEP    2, DEBT     WAS INCLUDED IN THE ANALYSIS.

                                    DEGREES OF FREEDOM   SIGNIF.   BETWEEN GROUPS
WILKS' LAMBDA         0.67759         2      1      30.0
EQUIVALENT F          6.89923                2      29.0    0.0035

----------------- VARIABLES IN THE ANALYSIS AFTER STEP    2 -----------------

VARIABLE   TOLERANCE   F TO REMOVE   WILKS' LAMBDA

ASSETS     0.9706667      7.4487          0.85164
DEBT       0.9706667      6.0662          0.81933
```

FIGURE 16-14 *(concluded)*

```
---------------- VARIABLES NOT IN THE ANALYSIS AFTER STEP    2 ----------------

                         MINIMUM
VARIABLE   TOLERANCE   TOLERANCE   F TO ENTER     WILKS' LAMBDA

INCOME     0.5728383   0.5568120   0.17524E-01       0.67717
FAMSIZE    0.9323959   0.9308959   2.2214            0.62779
JOB        0.9105435   0.9105435   0.27914           0.67091

F STATISTICS AND SIGNIFICANCES BETWEEN PAIRS OF GROUPS AFTER STEP    2
EACH F STATISTIC HAS    2 AND        29.0 DEGREES OF FREEDOM.

                    GROUP          0

    GROUP
      1                   6.8992
                          0.0035


* * * * * * * * * * * * * * * * * * * * * * * * * * * * * * * * * * * * * * * *

AT STEP    3, FAMSIZE  WAS INCLUDED IN THE ANALYSIS.

                                   DEGREES OF FREEDOM    SIGNIF.  BETWEEN GROUPS
WILKS' LAMBDA          0.62779      3     1       30.0
EQUIVALENT F           5.53369            3       28.0    0.0041

----------------- VARIABLES IN THE ANALYSIS AFTER STEP    3 ------------------

VARIABLE   TOLERANCE   F TO REMOVE    WILKS' LAMBDA

ASSETS     0.9308959   8.4282            0.81676
DEBT       0.9533874   4.1849            0.72162
FAMSIZE    0.9323959   2.2214            0.67759

---------------- VARIABLES NOT IN THE ANALYSIS AFTER STEP    3 ----------------

                         MINIMUM
VARIABLE   TOLERANCE   TOLERANCE   F TO ENTER     WILKS' LAMBDA

INCOME     0.5725772   0.5410775   0.24098E-01       0.62723
JOB        0.8333526   0.8333526   0.86952E-02       0.62759


F STATISTICS AND SIGNIFICANCES BETWEEN PAIRS OF GROUPS AFTER STEP    3
EACH F STATISTIC HAS    3 AND        28.0 DEGREES OF FREEDOM.

                    GROUP          0

    GROUP
      1                   5.5337
                          0.0041


F LEVEL OR TOLERANCE OR VIN INSUFFICIENT FOR FURTHER COMPUTATION

                              SUMMARY TABLE

              ACTION       VARS   WILKS'
STEP  ENTERED  REMOVED      IN    LAMBDA    SIG.    LABEL

  1   ASSETS                1     .81933   .0153
  2   DEBT                  2     .67759   .0035
  3   FAMSIZE               3     .62779   .0041
```

We see that the procedure chose total family assets, total debt, and family size as the three most discriminating variables between the repay and the default groups. The summary table in Figure 16–14 shows that all three variables are significant, the largest p-value being 0.0153. The three variables have some discriminating power. Figure 16–15 shows the estimated discriminant function coefficients. The results in the figure give us the following estimated discriminant function:

$$D = -0.995 - 0.0352 \text{ ASSETS} + 0.0429 \text{ DEBT} + 0.483 \text{ FAMILY SIZE} \quad (16\text{–}27)$$

The cutting score is zero. Discriminant scores greater than zero (i.e., positive scores) indicate a predicted membership in the default group (population 0), while negative scores imply predicted membership in the repay group (population 1). This can be seen by looking at the predicted group membership chart, Figure 16–16. The figure shows all cases used in the analysis. Since we have no holdout sample for testing the effectiveness of prediction of group membership, the results are for the estimation sample only. For each case, the table gives the *actual group* to which the data point (person, in our example) belongs. A double asterisk (**) next to the actual group indicates that the point was incorrectly classified. The next column, under the heading "Highest probability: Group," gives the predicted group membership (0 or 1) for every element in our sample.

The next column, "Highest probability: $P(D|G)$," gives the likelihood—the probability of obtaining the discriminant score received, given that the point belongs to the group to which it is predicted to belong. The following column, "Highest probability: $P(G|D)$," is the posterior probability of membership in the predicted group, given the obtained discriminant score. Posterior probabilities are obtained using Bayes' theorem. We did not specify prior probabilities here, and the assumption is that the *sample* proportions reflect the true *population* proportions of the two groups.

The next set of two columns labeled "Second highest," gives the other possibility: group membership in the opposite group and its probability. Since there are only two possible groups, this probability is $1 - P(G|D)$, where G is the predicted group. The last column in the table gives the discriminant score. For example, the first case belongs to group 1; it is predicted by the discriminant function to belong to group 1; its likelihood, $P(D|G)$ is 0.1798; its posterior probability of belonging to group 1 is $P(G|D) = 0.9587$. This point has the second highest probability of belonging to group 0 (there are only two groups, so the other group must, of course, be second). This probability is $0.0413(= 1 - 0.9587)$. Finally, the discriminant score for this point is -1.999. Figure 16–17 gives the summary results of the classification of the data in the estimation set (we have no holdout data set) using the discriminant function.

The classification results table shown in Figure 16–17 gives us a summary of the results in Figure 16–16, as well as the resulting percentages. The table in Figure 16–17 is often called the *hit ratio table*. Let us analyze the results presented in the table. In our data, there were 14 cases belonging to group 0 and 18 cases belonging to group 1. The next column shows us that

FIGURE 16–15 SPSS-Produced Estimates of the Discriminant Function Coefficients for Example (c)

```
UNSTANDARDIZED CANONICAL DISCRIMINANT FUNCTION COEFFICIENTS

                    FUNC    1

    ASSETS       -0.3522450E-01
    DEBT          0.4291033E-01
    FAMSIZE       0.4832695
    (CONSTANT)   -0.9950070
```

FIGURE 16–16 Predicted Group Membership Chart for Example (c)

CASE SEGNUM	MIS VAL	SEL	ACTUAL GROUP	HIGHEST PROBABILITY GROUP	P(D/G)	P(G/D)	2ND HIGHEST GROUP	P(G/D)	DISCRIMINANT SCORES...
1			1		1 0.1798	0.9587	0	0.0413	-1.9990
2			1		1 0.3357	0.9293	0	0.0707	-1.6202
3			1		1 0.8840	0.7939	0	0.2061	-0.8034
4			1	**	0 0.4761	0.5146	1	0.4854	0.1328
5			1		1 0.3368	0.9291	0	0.0709	-1.6181
6			1		1 0.5571	0.5614	0	0.4386	-0.0704
7			1	**	0 0.6272	0.5986	1	0.4014	0.3598
8			1		1 0.7236	0.6452	0	0.3548	-0.3039
9			1		1 0.9600	0.7693	0	0.2307	-0.7076
10			1		1 0.3004	0.9362	0	0.0638	-1.6930
11			0		0 0.5217	0.5415	1	0.4585	0.2047
12			0		0 0.6018	0.8714	1	0.1286	1.3672
13			0		0 0.6080	0.5887	1	0.4113	0.3325
14			0		0 0.5083	0.8932	1	0.1068	1.5068
15			0		0 0.8409	0.6959	1	0.3041	0.6447
16			0		0 0.2374	0.9481	1	0.0519	2.0269
17			0		0 0.9007	0.7195	1	0.2805	0.7206
18			0		0 0.8377	0.8080	1	0.1920	1.0502
19			0		0 0.0677	0.9797	1	0.0203	2.6721
20			0		0 0.1122	0.9712	1	0.0288	2.4338
21			0	**	1 0.7395	0.6524	0	0.3476	-0.3250
22			1	**	0 0.9432	0.7749	1	0.2251	0.9166
23			1		1 0.7819	0.6711	0	0.3289	-0.3807
24			0	**	1 0.5294	0.5459	0	0.4541	-0.0286
25			1		1 0.5673	0.8796	0	0.1204	-1.2296
26			1		1 0.1964	0.9557	0	0.0443	-1.9494
27			0	**	1 0.6916	0.6302	0	0.3698	-0.2608
28			1	**	0 0.7479	0.6562	1	0.3438	0.5240
29			1	**	0 0.9211	0.7822	1	0.2178	0.9445
30			1		1 0.4276	0.9107	0	0.0893	-1.4509
31			1		1 0.8188	0.8136	0	0.1864	-0.8866
32			0	**	1 0.8825	0.7124	0	0.2876	-0.5097

FIGURE 16–17 Summary Table of Classification Results for Example (c)

```
CLASSIFICATION RESULTS -

                          NO. OF    PREDICTED GROUP MEMBERSHIP
       ACTUAL GROUP        CASES        0            1
-------------------------  ------   -------      --------

GROUP      0                 14        10            4
                                     71.4%        28.6%

GROUP      1                 18         5           13
                                     27.8%        72.2%

PERCENT OF `GROUPED` CASES CORRECTLY CLASSIFIED: 71.88%
```

10 of the group 0 cases were correctly classified by the discriminant function and that these 10 observations constitute 71.4% of the group 0 cases. Four cases belonging to category 0 were incorrectly classified as belonging to category 1. Similarly, the table shows that 72.2% of the group 1 cases were correctly classified by the discriminant function, while 27.8% (five cases) were not. The diagonal elements in the table, here 71.4% and 72.2%, are the important figures. They give us the prediction accuracy of the discriminant function. The percentage of the total number of cases that were correctly classified is given at the bottom of the table. Here the table shows "Percent of 'grouped' cases correctly classified: 71.88%." This is the *overall* success rate, or hit ratio, of the discriminant function. This value is obtained by dividing the number of correctly classified cases by the total number of cases and multiplying by 100 to get a percentage: $[(10 + 13)/32]100 = 71.88\%$.

In a sense, the hit ratio, the overall percentage of cases that were correctly classified by the discriminant function, is similar to the R^2 statistic in multiple regression. The hit ratio is a measure of how well the discriminant function discriminates between groups. When this measure is 100%, the discrimination is very good; when it is small, the discrimination is poor. How small is "small"? Let us consider this problem logically. Suppose that our data set contains 100 observations: 50 in each of the two groups. Now, if we arbitrarily assign all 100 observations to one of the groups, we would have a 50% prediction accuracy! We should expect the discriminant function to give us better than 50% correct classification ratio; otherwise we can do as well without it. Similarly, suppose that one group has 75 observations and the other 25. In this case, we would get 75% correct classification if we assigned all our observations to the large group. Here the discriminant function should give us better than 75% correct classification if it is to be useful.

Another criterion for evaluating the success of the discriminant function is the *proportional chance criterion*.

The **proportional chance criterion:**

$$C = p^2 + (1 - p)^2 \qquad\qquad (16\text{--}28)$$

where p is the proportion of observations in one of the two groups (given as a decimal-quantity)

In our example, the discriminant function passes both of these tests. The proportions of people in each of the two groups are: $14/32 = 0.4375$, and $18/32 = 0.5625$. From Figure 16–17, we know that the hit ratio of the discriminant function is 0.7188 (71.88%). This figure is much higher than that we could obtain by arbitrary assignment (56.25%). The proportional chance criterion, equation 16–28, gives us: $C = (0.4375)^2 + (0.5625)^2 = 0.5078$. The hit ratio is clearly larger than this criterion as well. While the hit ratio is better than expected under arbitrary classification, it is not great. We would probably like to have a greater hit ratio if we are to classify loan applicants in a meaningful way. In this case, over 28% may be expected to be incorrectly classified. We must also keep in mind two facts: (1) Our sample size was relatively small, and therefore our inference may be subject to large errors; and (2) our hit ratio is overestimated because it is based on the estimation data. To get a better idea, we would need to use the discriminant function in classifying cases not used in the estimation and see how well the function performs with this data set.

Figure 16–18 shows the locations of the data points in the two groups in relation to their discriminant scores. It is a *map* of the locations of the two groups along the direction of greatest differentiation between the groups (the direction of the discriminant function). Note the overlap of the two groups in the middle of the graph and the separation on the two sides. (Group 0 is denoted by 1s and group 1 by 2s.)

FIGURE 16–18   A Map of the Location of the Two Groups for Example (c)

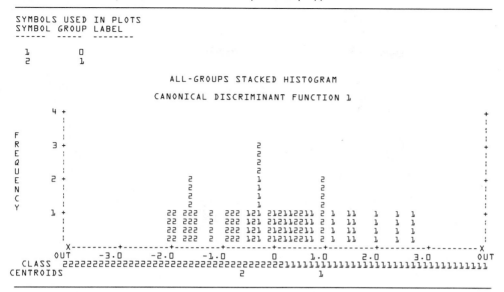

Discriminant Analysis with More than Two Groups

Discriminant analysis is extendable to more than two groups. When we carry out an analysis with more than two groups, however, we have more than one discriminant function. The first discriminant function is the function that discriminates best among the r groups. The second discriminant function is a function that has zero correlation with the first and has second-best discriminating power among the r groups, and so on. With r groups, there are $r - 1$ discriminant functions. Thus, with three groups, for example, there are two discriminant functions.

For Example (c), suppose that the bank distinguishes three categories: people who repay the loan (group 1), people who default (group 0), and people who have some difficulties and are several months late with payments, but do not default (group 2). The bank has data on a random sample of 46 people, each person falling into one of the three categories. Figure 16–19 shows the classification probabilities and the predicted groups for the new analysis. The classification is based on scores on both discriminant functions. The discriminant scores of each person on each of the two discriminant functions are also shown. Again, double asterisks denote a misclassified case. Figure 16–20 gives the estimated coefficients of the two discriminant functions.

Figure 16–21 gives the classification summary. We see that 86.7% of the group 0 cases were correctly classified by the two discriminant functions, 78.6% of group 1 were correctly classified, and 82.4% of group 2 were correctly classified. The overall percentage of correctly classified cases is 82.61%, which is fairly high.

Figure 16–22 is a scatter plot of the data in the three groups. The figure also shows the three group centroids. The following figure, Figure 16–23, is especially useful. This is a *territorial map* of the three groups as determined by the pair of estimated discriminant functions. The map shows the boundaries of the plane formed by looking at the pair of scores: (discriminant function 1 score, discriminant function 2 score). Any *new* point may be classified as belonging to one of the groups depending

FIGURE 16–19 Predicted Group Membership Chart for Three Groups [Extended Example (c)]

CASE SEGNUM	MIS VAL	SEL	ACTUAL GROUP	HIGHEST PROBABILITY GROUP P(D/G) P(G/D)			2ND HIGHEST GROUP P(G/D)		DISCRIMINANT SCORES...	
1			1	1	0.6966	0.9781	2	0.0198	-2.3023	-0.4206
2			1	1	0.3304	0.9854	2	0.0142	-2.8760	-0.1267
3			1	1	0.9252	0.8584	2	0.1060	-1.2282	-0.3592
4			1	1	0.5982	0.9936	2	0.0040	-2.3031	-1.2574
5		**	1	0	0.6971	0.8513	1	0.1098	0.6072	-1.3190
6			1	1	0.8917	0.8293	2	0.1226	-1.1074	-0.3643
7		**	1	0	0.2512	0.5769	1	0.4032	-0.0298	-1.8240
8			1	1	0.7886	0.9855	2	0.0083	-1.9517	-1.1657
9			0	0	0.3132	0.4869	1	0.4675	-0.1210	-1.3934
10			0	0	0.4604	0.9951	2	0.0032	2.1534	-1.7015
11			0	0	0.5333	0.9572	1	0.0348	1.0323	-1.9002
12			0	0	0.8044	0.9762	2	0.0204	1.9347	-0.9280
13			0	0	0.6697	0.8395	1	0.1217	0.5641	-1.3381
14			0	0	0.2209	0.7170	2	0.2815	2.2185	0.6586
15			0	0	0.6520	0.9900	2	0.0075	2.0176	-1.3735
16			0	0	0.0848	0.9458	2	0.0541	3.2112	0.3004
17		**	0	2	0.2951	0.7983	0	0.1995	1.6393	1.4480
18		**	1	0	0.1217	0.6092	1	0.3843	-0.0234	-2.3885
19			0	0	0.6545	0.6144	2	0.3130	0.7054	-0.0932
20			1	1	0.7386	0.9606	2	0.0362	-2.1369	-0.2312
21			1	1	0.0613	0.9498	2	0.0501	-3.2772	0.8831
22			0	0	0.6667	0.6961	1	0.1797	0.3857	-0.7874
23			1	1	0.7659	0.8561	2	0.1320	-1.6001	0.0635
24		**	0	1	0.5040	0.4938	2	0.3454	-0.4694	-0.0770
25		**	2	1	0.9715	0.8941	2	0.0731	-1.2811	-0.5314
26			2	2	0.6241	0.5767	0	0.2936	0.2503	0.2971
27			2	2	0.9608	0.9420	0	0.0353	0.1808	1.5221
28			2	2	0.9594	0.9183	0	0.0589	0.3557	1.3629
29		**	2	0	0.2982	0.5458	2	0.4492	1.6705	0.6994
30		**	2	1	0.9627	0.9160	2	0.0462	-1.2538	-0.8067
31			2	2	0.0400	0.9923	0	0.0076	1.7304	3.1894
32			2	2	0.9426	0.9077	1	0.0620	-0.2467	1.3298
33			2	2	0.7863	0.7575	0	0.2075	0.6256	0.8154
34			2	2	0.3220	0.9927	0	0.0060	0.6198	2.6635
35			2	2	0.9093	0.8322	1	0.1113	-0.2519	0.9826
36			2	2	0.5387	0.5528	0	0.4147	0.8843	0.4770
37			2	2	0.7285	0.9752	1	0.0160	-0.1655	2.0088
38			2	2	0.7446	0.9662	1	0.0248	-0.3220	1.9034
39			0	0	0.6216	0.9039	1	0.0770	0.7409	-1.6165
40			2	2	0.9461	0.8737	1	0.0823	-0.2246	1.1434
41			1	1	0.7824	0.9250	2	0.0690	-1.8845	-0.0819
42			0	0	0.3184	0.9647	1	0.0319	1.0456	-2.3016
43			1	1	0.7266	0.7304	0	0.1409	-0.6875	-0.6183
44			2	2	0.8738	0.9561	1	0.0278	-0.1642	1.7082
45			0	0	0.6271	0.9864	2	0.0121	2.2294	-1.0154
46			2	2	0.2616	0.9813	1	0.0175	-0.8946	2.5641

on where its pair of computed scores make it fall on the map. For example, a point with the scores: 2 on function 1 and −4 on function 2 falls in the territory of group 0 (this group is denoted by 1 in the plot, as indicated). A group territory is marked by its symbol on the inside of its boundaries with other groups. Group centroids are also shown, denoted by asterisks.

```
UNSTANDARDIZED CANONICAL DISCRIMINANT FUNCTION COEFFICIENTS

                    FUNC   1          FUNC   2

    ASSETS        -0.4103059E-01  -0.5688170E-03
    INCOME        -0.4325325E-01   0.6726829E-01
    DEBT           0.3644035E-01   0.4154356E-01
    FAMSIZE        0.7471749       0.1772388
    JOB            0.1787231      -0.4592559E-01
    (CONSTANT)    -0.9083139      -3.743060
```

FIGURE 16–21   Summary Table of Classification Results [Extended Example (c)]

```
CLASSIFICATION RESULTS -
```

ACTUAL GROUP		NO. OF CASES	PREDICTED GROUP MEMBERSHIP		
			0	1	2
GROUP	0	15	13 86.7%	1 6.7%	1 6.7%
GROUP	1	14	3 21.4%	11 78.6%	0 0.0%
GROUP	2	17	1 5.9%	2 11.8%	14 82.4%

```
PERCENT OF 'GROUPED' CASES CORRECTLY CLASSIFIED:  82.61%
```

FIGURE 16–22   Scatter Plot of the Data [Extended Example (c)]

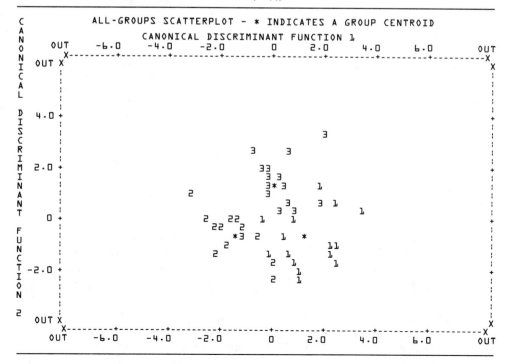

FIGURE 16–23   Territorial Map [Extended Example (c)]

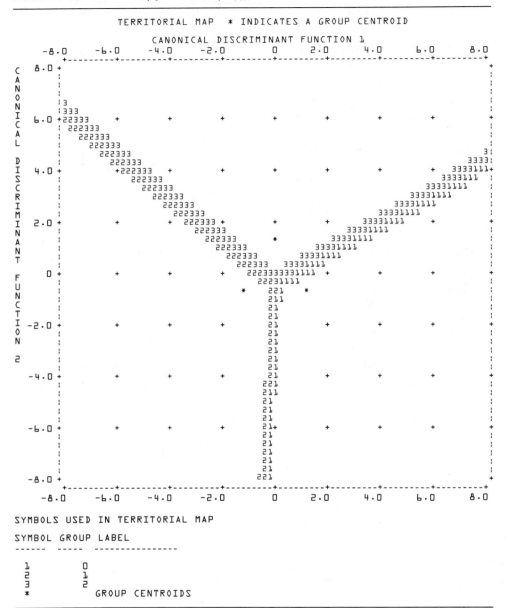

Many more statistics relevant to discriminant analysis may be computed and re-ported by computer packages. These are beyond the scope of our discussion, but ex-planations of these statistics may be found in books on multivariate analysis. This section should give you the basic ideas of discriminant analysis so that you may build on the knowledge acquired here.

There is a strong connection between discriminant analysis and multivariate analysis of variance. For one thing, when the group centroids are equal (the case where the null hypothesis of MANOVA should be accepted), there is no discrimi-nant function (in the population) that will distinguish among groups. On the other hand, when group differences do exist, the discriminant functions may help us identify where such differences lie. In our Koala Springs example, Example (b), both lemon and orange sales variables were chosen by the stepwise discriminant analysis and found to be highly significant using the Wilks' criterion. Both the territorial map and the scatter plot show the separation among the three groups—the three geographical regions. The classification summary table shows that 100% of all cases were correctly classified using the two discriminant functions. This is seen in the results of the discriminant analysis of the data of Example (b), shown in Figure 16–24.

FIGURE 16–24   Result of Discriminant Analysis for Example (b)

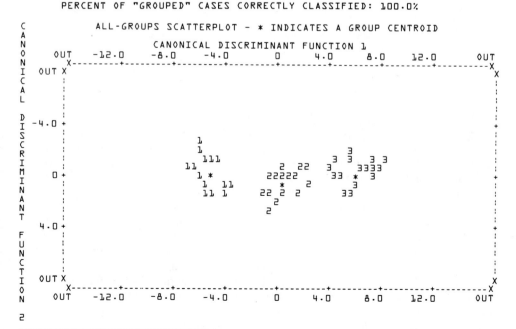

```
                              SUMMARY TABLE


                 ACTION          VARS   WILKS'
       STEP ENTERED REMOVED       IN    LAMBDA      SIG.    LABEL
         1   LEMON                 1    .04289     .0000
         2   ORANGE                2    .03560     .0000

       UNSTANDARDIZED CANONICAL DISCRIMINANT FUNCTION COEFFICIENTS

                      FUNC  1           FUNC  2

       LEMON         0.2453008        -0.3318621
       ORANGE        0.6141705E-01     0.3799908
       (CONSTANT)   -13.48576         -4.153066


       CLASSIFICATION RESULTS -

                                 NO. OF    PREDICATED GROUP MEMBERSHIP
            ACTUAL GROUP         CASES        1          2          3
       -------------------      ------    ---------  --------  --------

       GROUP        1             20          20         0          0
                                            100.0%      0.0%       0.0%

       GROUP        2             20           0         20          0
                                              0.0%    100.0%       0.0%

       GROUP        3             20           0          0         20
                                              0.0%      0.0%     100.0%

       PERCENT OF "GROUPED" CASES CORRECTLY CLASSIFIED: 100.0%
```

FIGURE 16–24 *(concluded)*

```
                    TERRITORIAL MAP  * INDICATES A GROUP CENTROID
                         CANONICAL DISCRIMINANT FUNCTION 1
           -16.0    -12.0     -8.0     -4.0      .0      4.0      8.0     12.0     16.0
          +---------+---------+---------+---------+---------+---------+---------+---------+
  C   16.0+                                    1223                                      +
  A       :                                   11223                                     :
  N       :                                  122233                                     :
  O       :                                  12 223                                     :
  N       :                                  12  23                                     :
  I       :                                 112  23                                     :
  C   12.0+    +         +         +        122+ 233    +         +         +        +    :
  A       :                                 12   223                                    :
  L       :                                 12    23                                    :
          :                                 12    23                                    :
  D       :                                112   233                                    :
  I       :                                122   223                                    :
  S    8.0+    +         +         +       12  +  23    +         +         +        +    :
  C       :                               12     23                                     :
  R       :                              112    233                                     :
  I       :                              122    223                                     :
  M       :                              12     23                                      :
  I       :                              12     23                                      :
  I    4.0+    +         +         +    + 112 +  233  +         +         +        +     :
  N       :                             122    223                                      :
  A       :                             12     23                                       :
  N       :                             12     23                                       :
  T       :                            112    233                                       :
          :                            122    223                                       :
  F     .0+    +         +         + *  + 12 +   23+   *        +         +        +     :
  U       :                             12   *  233                                     :
  N       :                            112    223                                       :
  C       :                            122    23                                        :
  T       :                            12     23                                        :
  I       :                            12     233                                       :
  I   -4.0+    +         +         +    112 +  223    +         +         +        +     :
  O       :                            122    23                                        :
  N       :                            12     23                                         :
          :                            12     233                                        :
  2       :                           112    223                                         :
          :                           122    23                                          :
     -8.0+    +         +         +    12  +   23    +         +         +        +      :
          :                           12     233                                         :
          :                          112    223                                          :
          :                          122    23                                           :
          :                          12     23                                           :
          :                          12     233                                          :
    -12.0+    +         +         +  112  +  +223    +         +         +        +      :
          :                          122    23                                           :
          :                          12     233                                          :
          :                          12     223                                          :
          :                         112    23                                            :
          :                         122    23                                            :
    -16.0+                          12     233                                           :
          +---------+---------+---------+---------+---------+---------+---------+---------+
           -16.0    -12.0     -8.0     -4.0      .0      4.0      8.0     12.0     16.0
```

PROBLEMS

16–34.   What are the purposes of discriminant analysis?

16–35.   Suppose that a discriminant analysis is carried out on a data set consisting of two groups. The larger group constitutes 125 observations and the smaller one 89. It is believed that the relative sizes of the two groups reflect their relative sizes within the population. If the classification summary table indicates that the overall percentage of correct classification is 57%, would you use the results of this analysis? Why or why not?

16–36.

$D = 0.1592$
Classify default.

16–36.   Refer to the results in Figure 16–15 and to equation 16–27. Suppose that a loan applicant has assets of $23,000, debt of $12,000, and a family with three members. How should you classify this person, if you are to use the results of the discriminant analysis? (Remember that debt and assets values are listed without the "000" digits in the program.)

16–37.   For problem 16–36, suppose an applicant has $54,000 in assets, $10,000 of debt, and a family of four. How would you classify this applicant? In this problem and the preceding one, be careful to interpret the *sign* of the score correctly.

16–38.   Why should you use a holdout data set and try to use the discriminant function for classifying its members? How would you go about doing this?

16–39.   A mail-order firm wants to be able to classify people as prospective buyers versus nonbuyers based on some of the people's demographics provided on mailing lists. From prior experience, it is known that only 8% of those who receive a brochure end up buying from the company. Use two criteria to determine the minimum overall prediction success rate you would expect from a discriminant function in this case.

16–40.   In the situation of problem 16–39, how would you account for the prior knowledge that 8% of the population of those who receive a brochure actually buy?

16–41.   Suppose that a multivariate analysis of variance is carried out to determine whether or not there are differences among consumers in four different countries in relation to five consumption characteristics variables. If the MANOVA leads to acceptance of the null hypothesis of no differences, what would you expect to be the results of a discriminant analysis (assuming one was attempted)?

16–42.   For problem 16–41, suppose that the MANOVA led to a rejection of the null hypothesis. How would you then use the results of a discriminant analysis?

16–43.   Use the territorial map shown in Figure 16–23 to predict group membership for a point with a score of −3 on discriminant function 1 and a score of 0 on discriminant function 2. What about a point with a score of 2 on function 1 and 4 on function 2?

16–44.   Use the territorial map in Figure 16–24 to classify a point that received the score −2 on function 1 and 15 on function 2.

16–45.   Use the information in Figure 16–20 and the territorial map in Figure 16–23 to classify a person with assets of $50,000, income of $37,500, debt of $23,000, family size of 2, and 3 years' employment at the current job.

16–46.   What are the advantages of a stepwise routine for selection of variables to be included in the discriminant function(s)?

16–47.   A discriminant function is estimated, and the p-value based on Wilks' lambda is found to be 0.239. Would you use this function? Explain.

16–48.   What is the meaning of $P(G|D)$, and how is it computed when prior information is specified?

16–49.   The results in Figure 16–24 include the statement: "Percent of 'grouped' cases correctly classified: 100.00%." Does this statement imply that when a new observation becomes available, there will be a probability of 1.00 of classifying it correctly? Explain.

16–50.   In trying to classify members of a population into one of six groups, how many discriminant functions are possible? Will all of these functions necessarily be found significant? Explain.

16–51.   A discriminant analysis was carried out to determine whether a firm belongs to one of three classes: build, hold, or pull back. The results, reported in an article in the *Journal of*

Answers

16–44.
———
Group 1

16–50.
———
5, some may be N.S.

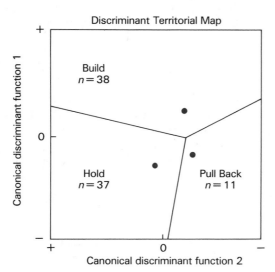

Discriminant Territorial Map

Marketing Research, include the preceding territorial map.[3] How would you classify a firm that received a score of 0 on both discriminant functions?

16–5   Principal Components and Factor Analysis

In this section, we discuss two related methods for decomposing the information content in a set of variables into information about an inherent set of latent components. The first method is called **principal component analysis.** Our aim with this method is to decompose the variation in a multivariate data set into a set of components such that the first component accounts for as much of the variation in the data as possible, the second component accounts for the second largest portion of the variation, and so on. In addition, each component in this method of analysis is *orthogonal* to the others; that is, each component is uncorrelated with the others: as a direction in space, each component is at right angles to the others.

In **factor analysis,** which is the second method for decomposing the information in a set of variables, our approach to the decomposition is different. We are not always interested in the orthogonality of the components (in this context, called *factors*); neither do we care whether the proportion of the variance accounted for by the factors decreases as each factor is extracted. Instead, we look for meaningful factors in terms of the particular application at hand. The factors we seek are the underlying, latent dimensions of the problem. The factors *summarize* the larger set of original variables.

For example, consider the results of a test consisting of answers to many questions administered to a sample of students. If we apply principal components analysis, we will decompose the answers to the questions into scores on a (usually smaller) set of components that account for successively smaller portions of the variation in the student answers and that are independent of each other. If we apply factor analysis, on the other hand, we seek to group the question variables into a smaller set of meaningful factors. One factor, consisting of responses to several questions, may be a measure of raw intelligence; another factor may be a measure of verbal ability and will consist of another set of questions; and so on.

We will start by discussing principal components and then present a detailed description of the techniques of factor analysis. There are two kinds of factor analysis. One is called *R*-factor analysis, and this is the method we will describe. Another is called *Q*-factor analysis. *Q*-factor analysis is a technique where we group the respondents, people or data elements, into sets with certain meanings rather than grouping the variables. *Q*-factor analysis is similar in its aims to cluster analysis, which is briefly discussed in the next section.

Principal Components

Figure 16–25 shows a data set in two dimensions. Each point in the ellipsoid-shaped cluster has two components: *X* and *Y*. If we look at the direction of the data cluster, however, we see that it is not oriented along either of the two axes *X* and *Y*. In fact, the data are oriented in space at a certain angle to the *X* axis. Look at the two principal axes of the ellipse of data, and you will notice that one contains much variation along its direction. The other axis, at 90° to the first, represents less variation of the data along its direction. We choose that direction in space about which the data are

---

[3] M. Burke, "Strategic Choice and Marketing Managers," *Journal of Marketing Research* (November 1984).

FIGURE 16–25 The Principal Components of a Bivariate Data Set

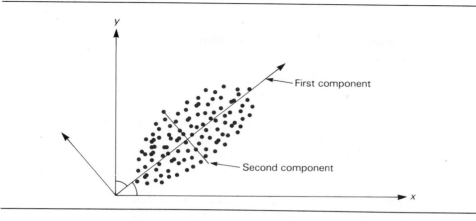

most variable (the principal axis of the ellipse) and call it the *first principal component*. The *second principal component* is at 90° to the first (it is **orthogonal** to the first). These axes are shown in Figure 16–25. Note that all we really have to do is rotate the original *X* and *Y* axes until we find a direction in space where the principal axis of the elliptical cluster of data lies along this direction. Since this is the larger axis, it represents the largest variation in the data, the data vary most along the direction we labeled *first component*. The second component captures the second largest variation in the data.

With three variables, there are three directions in space. We find that rotation of the axes of the three variables *X*, *Y*, and *Z* such that the first component is the direction in which the ellipsoid of data is widest. The second component is the direction with the second largest proportion of variance, and the third component is the direction with the third largest variation. All three components are at 90° to each other. Such rotations, which preserve the orthogonality (90° angle) of the axes, are called *rigid rotations*. With more variables, the procedure is the same (except that we can no longer graph it). The successive reduction in the variation in the data with the extraction of each component is shown schematically in Figure 16–26.

FIGURE 16–26 The Reduction in the Variance in a Data Set with Successive Extraction of Components

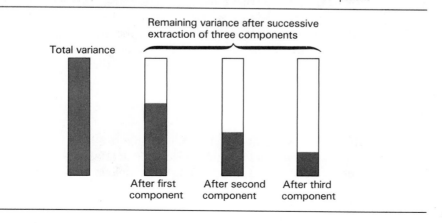

The Extraction of the Components

There is a remarkable mathematical theorem, the fundamental theorem of principal components, that allows us to find the components. The theorem says that if we have any set of k variables $X_1, X_2, \ldots, X_k$, where the variance-covariance matrix of these variables, denoted Σ, *is invertible* (an algebraic condition you need not worry about), we can always transform the original variables to a set of k uncorrelated variables $Y_1, Y_2, \ldots, Y_k$ by an appropriate rotation. Note that we do not require a normal distribution assumption.

Can you think of one very good use of principal component analysis as a preliminary stage for an important statistical technique? Remember the ever-present problem of *multicollinearity* in multiple regression analysis? There the fact that k "independent" variables turned out to be dependent on each other caused many problems. One solution to the problem of multicollinearity is to transform the original k variables, which are correlated with each other, into a new set of k uncorrelated variables. These uncorrelated variables are the principal components of the data set. Then we can run the regression on the new set, the principal components, and avoid the multicollinearity altogether. We still have to consider, however, the contribution of each original variable to the dependent variable in the regression.

Equation 16–29 is the equation of the first principal component, which is a linear combination of the original k variables $X_1, X_2, \ldots, X_k$.

$$Y_1 = a_{11}X_1 + a_{12}X_2 + \cdots + a_{1k}X_k \qquad (16\text{--}29)$$

Similarly, the second principal component is given by:

$$Y_2 = a_{21}X_1 + a_{22}X_2 + \cdots + a_{2k}X_k \qquad (16\text{--}30)$$

and so on. The a_{ij} are constants, like regression coefficients. The linear combinations are formed by the rotation of the axes.

If we use k new independent variables $Y_1, Y_2, \ldots, Y_k$, then we have accounted for all the variance in the observations. In that case, all we have done is to transform the original variables into linear combinations that are uncorrelated with each other (orthogonal) and that account for all the variance in the observations, the first component accounting for the largest portion, the second for less, and so on. When we use k new variables, however, there is no *economy* in the number of new variables. If, on the other hand, we want to reduce the number of original variables to a smaller set where each new variable has some meaning—each new variable represents a hidden *factor*—we need to use factor analysis. Factor analysis (the R-factor kind), also called *common factor analysis,* is one of the most commonly used multivariate methods, and we devote the rest of this section to a description of this important method. In factor analysis, we assume a multivariate normal distribution.

Factor Analysis

In factor analysis, we assume that each of the variables we have is made up of a linear combination of *common factors* (hidden factors that affect the variable and possibly affect other variables) and a *specific* component unique to the variable.

The k original X_i variables written as linear combinations of a smaller set of m common factors and a unique component for each variable:

$$X_1 = b_{11} F_1 + b_{12} F_2 + \cdots + b_{1m} F_m + U_1$$
$$X_2 = b_{21} F_1 + b_{22} F_2 + \cdots + b_{2m} F_m + U_2$$
$$\vdots$$
$$X_k = b_{k1} F_1 + b_{k2} F_2 + \cdots + b_{km} F_m + U_k \qquad (16\text{--}31)$$

The F_j, $j = 1, \ldots, m$, are the common factors. Each U_i, $i = 1, \ldots, k$, is the unique component of variable X_i. The coefficients b_{ij} are called *factor loadings*.

The total variance in the data in factor analysis is composed of the common-factor component, called the *communality* and the *specific* part, due to each variable alone.

The Extraction of Factors

The factors are extracted according to the communality. We determine the number of factors in an analysis based on the percentage of the variation explained by each factor. Sometimes prior considerations lead to the determination of the number of factors. One rule of thumb in determining the number of factors to be extracted considers the total variance explained by the factor. In computer output, the total variance explained by a factor is listed as the *eigenvalue*. (Eigenvalues are roots of determinantal equations and are fundamental to much of multivariate analysis. Since understanding them requires some familiarity with linear algebra, we will not say much about eigenvalues, except that they are used as measures of the variance explained by factors.) The rule just mentioned says that a factor with an eigenvalue less than 1.00 should not be used because it accounts for less than the variation explained by a single variable. This rule is conservative in the sense that we probably want to summarize the variables with a set of factors smaller than indicated by this rule. Another, less conservative, rule says that the factors should account for a relatively large portion of the variation in the variables: 80%, 70%, 65%, or any relatively high percentage of the variance. The consideration in setting the percentage is similar to our evaluation of R^2 in regression. There really is no absolute rule.

We start the factor analysis by computing a correlation matrix of all the variables. This diagonal matrix has 1s on the diagonal because the correlation of each variable with itself is equal to 1.00. The correlation in row i and column j of this matrix is the correlation between variables X_i and X_j. The correlation matrix is then used by the computer in extracting the factors and producing the factor matrix. The factor matrix is a matrix showing the factor loadings—the sample correlations between each factor and each variable. These are the coefficients b_{ij} in equation 16–31. Principal component analysis is often used in the preliminary factor extraction procedure, although other methods are useful as well.

The Rotation of Factors

Once the factors are extracted, the next stage of the analysis begins. In this stage, the factors are *rotated*. The purpose of the rotation is to find the best distribution of the factor loadings in terms of the meaning of the factors. If you think of our hypothetical example of scores of students on an examination, it could be that the initial factors derived (these could be just the principal components) explain proportions of the variation in scores, but not in any meaningful way. The rotation may then lead us to find a factor that accounts for intelligence, a factor that accounts for verbal ability, a third factor that accounts for artistic talent, and so on. The rotation is an integral part of factor analysis and helps us derive factors that are as meaningful as possible. Usually, each of the initially derived factors will tend to be correlated with *many* of the variables. The purpose of the rotation is to identify each factor with only *some* of the variables—different variables with each factor—so that each factor may be interpreted in a meaningful way. Each factor will then be associated with *one* hidden attribute: intelligence, verbal ability, or artistic talent.

There are two classes of rotation methods. One is **orthogonal, or rigid, rotation.** Here the axes maintain their orthogonality; that is, they maintain an angle of 90° between every two of them. This means that the factors, once they are rotated, will

FIGURE 16–27 An Orthogonal Factor Rotation and an Oblique Factor Rotation

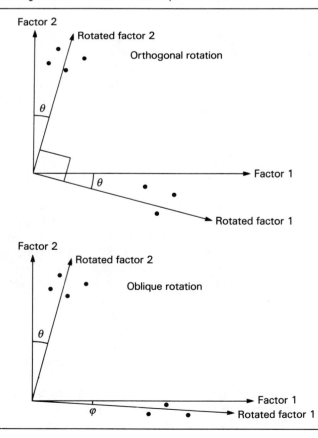

maintain the quality of being uncorrelated with each other. This may be useful if we believe that the inherent, hidden dimensions in our problem are independent of each other (here this would mean that we believe intelligence is independent of verbal ability and that both are independent of artistic talent). The rigid rotation is also more simple to carry out than nonrigid rotation. A nonrigid rotation is called an **oblique rotation.** In an oblique rotation, we allow the factors to have some correlations among them. We break the initial 90° angles between pairs of axes (pairs of factors), and we seek the *best association* between factors and variables that are included in them, regardless of whether the factors are independent of each other (i.e., at 90° to each other).

Figure 16–27 shows the two possible kinds of rotation. The dots on the graph in each part of the figure correspond to variables, and the axes correspond to factors. In the first example, orthogonal rotation, look at the projections of the seven points (seven variables) along the two axes. These are the factor loadings. When we rotate the axes (the factors), maintaining their 90° angle, we find a better fit of the variables with the factors. The top four variables load highly on the shifted vertical axis, while the bottom three variables load highly on the shifted horizontal axis. In the lower figure, we see that an oblique rotation provides a better association of the factors with the variables.

There are several algorithms for orthogonal rotation. The most commonly used algorithm is call VARIMAX. The VARIMAX rotation aims at finding a solution where a variable loads highly on one particular factor and loads as low as possible on other factors. The algorithm maximizes the sum of the variances of the loadings in the factor matrix; hence the name VARIMAX. When we use this method, our final solution will have factors with loadings that are high on some variables and low on others. This simplifies the interpretation of the factors. Two other methods are QUARTIMAX and EQUIMAX. Since they are less commonly used, we will not discuss them. Let us look at an example.

An analysis of the responses of 1,076 randomly sampled people to a survey about job satisfaction was carried out. The questionnaire contained 14 questions related to satisfaction on the job. The responses to the questions were analyzed using factor analysis with VARIMAX rotation of factors. The results, the 4 factors extracted and their loadings with respect to each of the original 14 variables, are shown in Table 16–5.

EXAMPLE (d)

The highest loading variables are chosen for each factor. Thus, the first factor has loadings of 0.87, 0.88, 0.92, and 0.65 on the questions relabeled as 1, 2, 3, and 4, respectively. After looking at the questions, the analysts named this factor *satisfaction with information.* After looking at the highest-loading variables on the next factor, factor 2, the analysts named this factor *satisfaction with variety.* The two remaining factors were named in a similar way. The key to identifying and interpreting the factors is to look for the variables with highest loadings on each factor and to find a common meaning: a summary name for all the variables loading high on that factor. The VARIMAX rotation is especially useful for such interpretations because it will make each factor have some variables with high loadings and the rest of the variables with low loadings. The factor is then identified with the high-loading variables.

The factor loadings are the standardized regression coefficients in a multiple regression equation of each original variable as dependent, and with the factors as independent

SOLUTION

TABLE 16–5   Factor Analysis of Satisfaction Items

	Factor Loadings[a]			
	1	**2**	**3**	**4**
Satisfaction with Information				
1. I am satisfied with the information I receive from my superior about my job performance	0.87	0.19	0.13	0.22
2. I receive enough information from my supervisor about my job performance	0.88	0.14	0.15	0.13
3. I receive enough feedback from my supervisor on how well I'm doing	0.92	0.09	0.11	0.12
4. There is enough opportunity in my job to find out how I am doing	0.65	0.29	0.31	0.15
Satisfaction with Variety				
5. I am satisfied with the variety of activities my job offers	0.13	0.82	0.07	0.17
6. I am satisfied with the freedom I have to do what I want on my job	0.17	0.59	0.45	0.14
7. I am satisfied with the opportunities my job provides me to interact with others	0.18	0.48	0.32	0.22
8. There is enough variety in my job	0.11	0.75	0.02	0.12
9. I have enough freedom to do what I want in my job	0.17	0.62	0.46	0.12
10. My job has enough opportunity for independent thought and action	0.20	0.62	0.47	0.06
Satisfaction with Closure				
11. I am satisfied with the opportunities my job gives me to complete tasks from beginning to end	0.17	0.21	0.76	0.11
12. My job has enough opportunity to complete the work I start	0.12	0.10	0.71	0.12
Satisfaction with Pay				
13. I am satisfied with the pay I receive for my job	0.17	0.14	0.05	0.51
14. I am satisfied with the security my job provides me	0.10	0.11	0.15	0.66

[a]Varimax rotation. R^2 for each of the four factors is 41.0, 13.5, 8.5, and 7.8, respectively.

variables. When the factors are uncorrelated, as is the case when we use an orthogonal rotation, the total proportion of the variance explained for each variable is equal to the sum of the proportions of the variance explained by all the factors. The proportion of the variance of each variable that is explained by the common factors is the communality. For each variable we therefore have:

$$\text{Communality} = \% \text{ variance explained} = \sum_i (b_{ij})^2 \qquad (16\text{--}32)$$

where b_{ij} are the coefficients from the appropriate equation for the variable in question from equation 16–31. In this example, we have for the variable "I am satisfied with the information I receive from my superior about my job performance" (variable 1):

$$\text{Communality} = (0.87)^2 + (0.19)^2 + (0.13)^2 + (0.22)^2 = 0.8583, \text{ or } 85.83\%$$

(See the loadings of this variable on the four factors in Table 16–5.) This means that 85.83% of the variation in values of variable 1 is explained by the four factors. We may similarly compute the communality of all other variables. Variable 1 is assigned to factor 1, as indicated in the table. That factor accounts for $(0.87)^2 = 0.7569$, or 75.69% of the variation in this variable. Variable 5, for example, is assigned to factor 2, and factor 2 accounts for $(0.82)^2 = 0.6724$, or 67.24% of the variation in variable 5.

Finally, we mention a use of factor analysis as a preliminary stage for other forms of analysis. We can assign factor scores to each of the respondents (each member of our data set) and then conduct whatever analysis we are interested in, using the factor scores instead of scores on the original variables. This is meaningful when the factors summarize the information in a way that can be interpreted easily.

PROBLEMS

16–52. What is the main purpose of factor analysis?

16–53. What are the differences between factor analysis and principal components analysis?

Answer

16–54. What are the two kinds of factor analysis, and why is one of them more commonly used than the other?

16–55. What are the two kinds of factor rotation? What is the aim of rotating the factors? What is achieved by each of the two kinds of rotation?

16–56. What is achieved by the VARIMAX rotation, and what are two other rotation methods?

In the following problems, we present tables of results of factor analyses in different contexts reported in the marketing research literature. The reference *JMR* stands for *Journal of Marketing Research,* and *JM* stands for *Journal of Marketing.* Give a brief interpretation of the findings in each problem.

16–57. From P. Schurr and B. Calder, "Psychological Effects of Restaurant Meetings on Industrial Buyers," *JM* (January 1986):

	Rotated Factor Loadings		
	Factor 1 **(Scale 3)**	**Factor 2** **(Scale 2)**	**Factor 3** **(Scale 1)**
1. Argument evaluation			
a. Supplier's argument	0.31	0.38	0.76
b. User's argument	0.15	0.35	0.85
2. Who-must-yield			
a. Who must give in	0.15	0.85	0.29
b. Who has best case	0.18	0.78	0.37
3. Overall supplier evaluation			
a. Overall impression	0.90	0.18	0.26
b. Buy from in future	0.94	0.14	0.12

16–58. For the following result, from J. Gaski and J. Etzel,"The Index of Consumer Sentiment toward Marketing," *JM* (July 1986), interpret the meaning of the *negative* loadings on factor 4.

	Pattern Matrix			
	Factor 1 **Price**	**Factor 2** **Retailing/Selling**	**Factor 3** **Advertising**	**Factor 4** **Product**
Price item 1	0.37964	−0.11218	0.21009	−0.16767
Price item 2	0.34560	−0.11200	0.18910	−0.09073
Price item 3	0.60497	0.07133	−0.04858	0.03024
Price item 6	0.81856	0.03963	−0.01044	0.01738
Price item 7	0.74661	0.03967	0.00884	−0.06703

16–58.

Factor 1 = Price
Factor 2 = Retail/Sell
Factor 3 = Advertising
Factor 4 = Opposite of product rating

(continued)

Answer

Pattern Matrix

	Factor 1 Price	Factor 2 Retailing/Selling	Factor 3 Advertising	Factor 4 Product
Retailing/selling item 1	0.07910	0.74098	−0.02888	0.07095
Retailing/selling item 2	−0.13690	0.58813	0.15950	−0.14141
Retailing/selling item 3	0.01484	0.74749	−0.02151	0.02269
Retailing/selling item 6	−0.05868	0.56753	0.10925	−0.13337
Retailing/selling item 7	0.07788	0.69284	−0.02320	−0.00457
Advertising item 2	−0.03460	−0.03414	0.65854	−0.01691
Advertising item 3	−0.06838	0.01973	0.71499	−0.06951
Advertising item 4	0.01481	−0.00748	0.57196	−0.03100
Advertising item 5	0.20779	0.13434	0.38402	0.12561
Advertising item 7	0.00921	0.11200	0.64330	−0.02534
Product item 2	0.24372	0.16809	−0.05254	−0.33600
Product item 3	−0.00370	0.02951	−0.00013	−0.61145
Product item 5	−0.03193	0.00631	0.04031	−0.78286
Product item 6	0.02346	0.01814	0.09122	−0.73298
Product item 7	0.03854	0.08088	−0.05244	−0.33921

16–59. Give a name to each one of the factors in the following table, reprinted from G. Laurent and J. Kapferer, "Measuring Consumer Involvement Profiles," *JMR* (February 1985). Be sure to consider the signs of the loadings.

	Factor 1	Factor 2	Factor 3	Factor 4
Importance 1	0.59			
Importance 2	0.56			
Importance 3	0.62			
Importance 4	0.74			
Pleasure 1		−0.73		
Pleasure 2		−0.68		
Pleasure 3		−0.82		
Pleasure 4		−0.67		
Pleasure 5		−0.58		
Sign 1			0.78	
Sign 2			0.94	
Sign 3			0.73	
Sign 4			0.77	
Risk importance 1	0.62			
Risk importance 2	0.74			
Risk importance 3	0.74			
Risk probability 1				0.76
Risk probability 2				0.64
Risk probability 3				0.50

Omitted loadings are inferior to 0.25.

16–60.

Pricing policy associated with Factor 2
comm = 0.501

16–60. In the following table, from J. Eliashberg and D. Michie, "Multiple Business Goals," *JMR* (February 1984), identify each of the variables with one factor only. Also find the communality of each variable.

Business Policy	Factor 1 Market Penetration Issues	Factor 2 Project Quality Issues
Pricing policies	0.331	0.626
Record and reporting procedures	0.136	0.242
Advertising copy and expenditures	0.468	0.101
Selection of sources of operating supplies	0.214	0.126
Customer service and complaints	−0.152	0.792
Market forecasting and performance standards	0.459	0.669
Warranty decisions	0.438	0.528
Personnel staffing and training	0.162	0.193
Product delivery scheduling	0.020	0.782

(continued)

Business Policy	Factor 1 Market Penetration Issues	Factor 2 Project Quality Issues
Construction/installation procedures	0.237	0.724
Subcontracting agreements	−0.015	0.112
Number of dealerships	0.899	0.138
Location of dealerships	0.926	0.122
Trade areas	0.885	0.033
Size of building projects	0.206	0.436
Building design capabilities	−0.047	0.076
Sales promotion materials	0.286	0.096
Financial resources	0.029	0.427
Builder reputation	0.076	0.166
Offering competitors' lines	0.213	0.111
Variance explained	3.528	3.479
Percentage of total variance	17.64	17.39
Reliability (coefficient alpha)	.94	.83

16–61. The following table is from G. Frazier and R. Rody, "The Use of Influence Strategies in Interim Relationships in Industrial Product Channels," *JM* (January 1991). Name the factors in the table.

	Factor 1	Factor 2
Developing end-user preferences	−.04	.88
Product quality and technical leadership	.19	.65
Sales promotion programs and promotional aids	−.11	.86
Pricing policy	.78	−.03
Return goods policy	.79	−.04
Product availability (delivery and reliability)	.63	.26
Cooperativeness and technical competence of its personnel	.59	.45

16–62. Try to carry out a factor analysis on random samples of rows of data in the Federal Reserve data set at the end of the book (Appendix D).

16–6 A Brief Description of Other Multivariate Methods

In the last sections, we discussed the most commonly used multivariate techniques. These techniques, however, are not the only ones. There is a wide spectrum of multivariate techniques, and new ones are developed from time to time to meet special needs. In the business world, multivariate techniques are used most often in marketing research, as you may have surmised from the last section. We will now say a few words about other techniques useful in marketing research and in other areas.

Cluster Analysis

Cluster analysis is a technique for grouping people or items into clusters of similar elements. In cluster analysis, we try to identify similar elements by their characteristics. We form groups, or clusters, that are homogeneous and different from other groups. Correlations and functions of distance between elements are used in defining the clusters.

Conjoint Analysis

Conjoint analysis is a technique that attempts to find scales of measurement that relate predictor variables to a response variable using some selected composition rule. In evaluating a product purchase decision, for example, a customer may be seen as making a decision about purchasing a composition of product attributes. Conjoint analysis seeks to determine the rule the customer follows in evaluating this composition.

Canonical Correlation Analysis

In canonical correlation analysis, we try to evaluate the correlation between a *set* of variables that may be considered the independent, or predictor, variables and a *set* of dependent variables. Canonical correlation is thus similar to multiple regression analysis with a set of *several* dependent variables of interest. The canonical correlation is a correlation between two linear compositions of variables (one set designated dependent and the other designated independent). In discriminant analysis, we often measure a canonical correlation. This is the correlation of some variable with the linear composition of the discriminating variables, the discriminant function.

Multidimensional Scaling

Multidimensional scaling is a collection of statistical methods for graphing data sets in a way that allows a visual understanding of relationships among variables.

16–7   Using the Computer

In MINITAB, the command PCA, followed by column numbers C1, C2, and so on, will result in a principal components analysis on data in the specified columns. Similarly, the command DISCRIMINANT will produce a discriminant analysis. In SPSS, the commands for factor analysis, discriminant analysis, and MANOVA are simply FACTOR, DISCRIMINANT, and MANOVA, respectively. In addition to the SPSS User's Guide, there is a book called *SPSS Advanced Statistics User's Guide* by Marija J. Norusis (Chicago: SPSS Inc., 1990). This guide is highly recommended. The background you have acquired in this chapter should allow you to conduct any multivariate analysis using the guidebook.

To show the commands necessary for multivariate analysis, we present Figure 16–28, which illustrates the program commands for running the three analyses just

FIGURE 16–28   Examples of SPSS Program Commands for MANOVA, Discriminant Analysis, and Factor Analysis

```
DATA LIST FILE=QUALA
        /1 LEMON 1-2 ORANGE 4-5 REGION 7 STORE 9
MANOVA LEMON ORANGE BY REGION(1,3) STORE(1,2)
        /PRINT=SIGNIF(HYPOTH MULTIV UNIV)
        /DESIGN
DISCRIMINANT GROUPS=REGION(1,3)
        /VARIABLES=LEMON TO ORANGE
        /METHOD=WILKS
STATISTICS ALL
UNNUMBERED
INPUT PROGRAM
N OF CASES 100
NUMERIC A B C D E F G H I J K
INPUT MATRIX FREE
END INPUT PROGRAM
FACTOR READ=CORRELATION TRIANGLE
        /VARIABLES=A TO K
```

mentioned. The MANOVA and DISCRIMINANT analysis programs shown are the ones that were used in Example (b) and its extension.

16–8   Summary and Review of Terms

There is a large body of statistical techniques called **multivariate methods.** These methods are useful in analyzing data in situations that involve several variables. In this chapter, we discussed some of these methods. We began by describing the **multivariate normal distribution.** Then we presented simple tests for population parameters using **Hotelling's T^2** statistic. Then we discussed **multivariate analysis of variance (MANOVA),** which is an extension of the univariate ANOVA technique to several variables. The main statistical tool we discussed in the context of this method was **Wilks' lambda,** a statistic shown to be transformable to an F statistic with varying degrees of approximation accuracy. We then discussed **discriminant analysis,** a method of classifying members of a population into one of two (or more) groups. The analysis entailed the postulation and estimation of one or more **discriminant functions.** We then discussed **factor analysis,** a statistical technique for reducing the dimensionality of a problem by summarizing a set of variables as a smaller set of inherent, latent common factors. We also discussed a related technique often used as a first stage in factor analysis: **principal components analysis.** We discussed the concept of independence in several dimensions: the concept of **orthogonality** of factors or variables. We discussed rotations used in factor analysis: **orthogonal rotations,** which maintain the independence of the factors, and **oblique rotations,** which do not. Finally, we mentioned a few other multivariate techniques that were not discussed in detail: conjoint analysis, cluster analysis, multidimensional scaling, and canonical correlation analysis.

PROBLEMS

16–63. What are the uses of the multivariate normal distribution? Why is it needed? What allows us to assume that such a distribution fits our population?

16–64. What statistic is equivalent to Wilks' lambda when two populations are compared?

16–65. Suppose that you want to determine whether differences exist among the centroids of several multivariate normal populations, but for some reason you cannot perform a MANOVA. What other multivariate techniques may help you make such a determination? Why?

16–66. How many discriminant functions may be found significant in classifying an observation into one of four groups?

16–67. Is it possible that only one discriminant function will be found significant in discriminating among three groups? Explain.

16–68. What is a hit ratio? Would a hit ratio of 67% be sufficient when one group has 100 observations, another group has 200 observations, and the ratio of these groups is believed to reflect their ratio in the population? Explain.

16–69. Name other statistics, beside Wilks' lambda, that may be used in MANOVA.

16–70. What is achieved by further analysis to follow MANOVA?

16–71. What is achieved by principal components analysis? How can it be used as a preliminary stage in factor analysis? What important stages must follow it, and why?

16–72. In a factor analysis of 17 variables, a solution is found consisting of 17 factors. Comment on the analysis.

16–73. When is an oblique rotation superior to an orthogonal one, and why?

16–74. What is a communality, and what does it indicate?

Answers

16–64.

T^2

16–66.

3

Answer

16-78.

Lambda = 0.169
F = 40.03
Salary
F = 91.47
Benefit
F = 11.80
All significant

16-75. What is the communality of variable 9 listed in Table 16-5?

16-76. Name a statistical method of analysis for which principal components may be a first stage. Explain.

16-77. What are factor loadings, and what do they measure?

16-78. An employment agency wants to determine whether the average salary and benefits offered to employees with a given level of training and experience are equal at three different industries. A random sample of 20 workers with the same level of training and experience is selected from each one of the three industries under study. The data, salary in thousands of dollars per year, and benefits on a scale of 0 to 200, are as follows.

Industry A		Industry B		Industry C	
Salary	Benefits	Salary	Benefits	Salary	Benefits
31.5	160	36.2	187	43.1	148
30.0	177	35.5	190	41.2	156
32.0	155	34.8	172	36.8	161
31.1	145	33.9	188	39.1	157
32.2	168	31.1	165	38.2	146
31.8	171	35.9	173	40.7	135
30.2	140	34.5	167	44.6	188
29.6	162	38.6	195	42.2	170
33.1	178	37.7	168	38.6	155
31.6	180	39.2	179	39.0	178
28.7	150	33.3	188	36.5	160
32.2	141	37.8	176	38.8	172
31.8	160	38.5	180	39.8	175
32.4	110	35.9	196	42.6	180
28.2	150	34.8	160	42.1	178
29.9	147	36.1	179	40.8	182
32.5	166	39.9	190	37.7	164
33.2	182	40.1	195	39.2	160
31.6	151	32.2	180	40.4	174
32.0	172	37.6	166	42.8	158

Conduct a MANOVA, and state your conclusions.

16-79. Discuss the uses of several-factors MANOVA.

16-80. Describe the shape of a bivariate normal distribution with $\rho = -0.9$, $\sigma_1 = 5$, and $\sigma_2 = 10$.

16-81. A television producer wants to predict the success of new television programs. A program is considered successful if it survives its first season. Data on production costs, number of sponsors, and the total amount spent on promoting the program are available. A random sample of programs is selected, and the data are presented in the following table. Production costs are in millions of dollars, and promotions in hundreds of thousands of dollars: S denotes success and F failure.

Success/Failure	Production Cost	Number of Sponsors	Promotions
S	2.5	1	2.1
F	1.1	1	3.7
S	2.0	1	2.8
F	2.5	1	1.8
F	2.5	1	1.0
S	3.7	2	5.5
S	3.6	3	5.0
S	2.7	1	4.1
S	1.9	1	6.9
F	1.3	1	1.5
S	2.6	2	2.0
S	3.5	3	3.8
F	1.9	1	1.0
S	6.8	1	2.1

Success/Failure	Production Cost	Number of Sponsors	Promotions
S	5.0	1	1.9
S	4.6	3	4.1
S	3.0	2	3.9
S	2.5	3	7.0
S	1.8	2	6.6
F	2.0	2	1.1
S	3.5	3	3.8
S	1.8	3	8.1
S	5.6	1	4.2
F	1.5	2	3.0
S	4.4	4	5.0

Conduct a discriminant analysis, and state your conclusions.

16–82.   A factor analysis was conducted with 24 variables. The VARIMAX rotation was used, and the results were 2 factors. Comment on the analysis.

CASE
16

PREDICTING COMPANY FAILURE

*T*he following article is reprinted in its entirety by permission from *Forbes* (April 1, 1991). Discuss the statistical method alluded to in this article. Could you reproduce (or improve upon) Professor Platt's results? Explain.

Is a former $40 stock now trading at $2.50 a bargain?
Or an invitation to get wiped out? Depends.

How cheap?

By Steve Kichen

HARLAN PLATT, an associate professor of finance at Northeastern University, has written *Why Companies Fail*, a study that should be of considerable interest to bargain-hunting investors. Platt's study can be useful in helping determine whether a stock that has fallen sharply in price is a bargain or a prospective piece of wallpaper.

Platt developed a mathematical model that predicts the probability of bankruptcy from certain ratios on a company's balance sheet.

Here's the thesis: Some companies trading very cheaply still have large sales, considerable brand recognition and a chance at recovery, or at least takeover at a premium. Their stocks could double or triple despite losses and weak balance sheets. Other borderline companies will land in bankruptcy court and leave common shareholders with nothing.

Even though it more than tripled from its October low, Unisys, with $10 billion in sales, is not a Wall Street favorite: At a recent 5 1/2, its market capitalization is only $890 million. Will Unysis fail? Almost certainly not within the next 12 months, according to Platt.

For the list below, we found cheap stocks with low price-to-sales ratios. Then we eliminated all but the ones Platt says are highly unlikely to fail within a year. Platt put cheap stocks such as Gaylord Container, Masco Industries, and Kinder-Care Learning Centers in the danger zone.

Among low-priced stocks, Unisys and Navistar, however, make the safety grade. So does Wang Laboratories. Says Platt, "They are still selling over $2 billion worth of computers and their $575 million in bank debt is now down to almost nothing."

Platt, who furnishes his probabilities to Prospect Street Investment Management Co., a Boston fund manager, refuses to disclose his proprietary formula. But among the ratios he considers are total debt to total assets, cash flow to sales, short-term debt to total debt, and fixed assets to total assets.

"Companies with large fixed assets are more likely to have trouble because these assets are less liquid," Platt says. But norms for a company's industry are also important. An unusually high level of such current assets as inventory and receivables may itself be a sign of weakness.

The low-priced stocks on the list may or may not rise sharply in the near future, but they are not likely to disappear into insolvency.

Big Companies with Little Prices

These 10 companies are in poor financial shape, but not so poor, according to calculations by finance professor Harlan Platt, that they are likely to go bankrupt within the next year. Thus, these stocks are plausible bets for rebounds.

Company/Industry	Recent Price	Earnings per Share Latest 12 Months	1991 Estimated	Total Assets ($mil)	Total Debt/Total Assets	Sales ($mil)	Cash Flow/ Sales	Price/ Sales
Highland Superstores/ consumer electronics stores	2¹/₈	$−0.89	NA	$320	57%	$892	−1.6%	0.04
Businessland/computer stores	2¹/₂	−1.65	$−1.02	616	72	1,306	−2.0	0.06
Jamesway/discount stores	3¹/₂	−0.06	0.18	435	61	909	1.6	0.06
Merisel/computer equipment wholesaler	3¹/₈	0.03	0.33	432	73	1,192	0.4	0.06
Unisys/computers	5¹/₂	−3.45	−0.56	10,484	65	10,111	3.1	0.09
National Convenience Stores/convenience stores	5¹/₈	−0.43	0.21	406	65	1,067	2.0	0.11
TW Holdings/restaurants	4⁷/₁₆	−0.61	−0.43	3,531	79	3,682	3.9	0.13
Varity/farm and construction equipment	2³/₄	0.35	0.32	3,177	61	3,472	6.4	0.20
Wang Laboratories Cl B/ minicomputers	3³/₈	4.04	−0.29	1,750	72	2,369	−20.1	0.24
Navistar International/trucks	4¹/₈	−0.24	−0.08	3,795	60	3,810	−0.6	0.27

NA: Not available.

Sources: Harlan Platt, Northeastern University; Institutional Brokers Estimate System (a service of Lynch, Jones & Ryan), via Lotus One Source; *FORBES.*

SAMPLING METHODS

I N T R O D U C T I O N

T hroughout this book, we have always assumed that information is obtained through random sampling. The method we have used until now is called simple random sampling. In simple random sampling, we assume that our sample is randomly chosen from the entire population of interest, and that every set of n elements in the population has an equal chance of being selected as our sample.

We assume that a randomization device is always available to the experimenter. We also assume that the entire population of interest is known, in the sense that it is possible to draw a random sample from the entire population where every element has an equal chance of being included in our sample. Randomly choosing our sample from the entire population in question is our insurance against sampling bias. This was demonstrated in Chapter 5 with the story of the *Literary Digest*.

But do these conditions always hold in real sampling situations? Also, are there any easier ways—more efficient, more economical ways—of drawing random samples? Are there any situations where, instead of randomly drawing every single sample point, we may randomize less frequently and still obtain an adequately random sample for use in statistical inference? Consider the situation where our population is made up of several groups and the elements within each group are similar to each other, but different from the elements in other groups (for example, sampling an economic variable in a city where some people live in rich neighborhoods and thus form one group, while others live in poorer neighborhoods, forming other groups). Is there a way of using the homogeneity within the groups to make our sampling more efficient? The answers to these questions, as well as many other questions related to sampling methodology, are the subject of this chapter.

In the next section, we will thoroughly explore the idea of random sampling and discuss its practical limitations. We will see that biases may occur if samples are chosen without randomization. We will also discuss criteria for the prevention of such selection biases. In the following sections, we will present more efficient and more involved methods of drawing random samples that are appropriate in different situations. ∎

17–2 Nonprobability Sampling and Bias

The advantage of random sampling is that the probabilities that the sample estimator will be within a given number of units from the population parameter it estimates are known. Sampling methods that do not use samples with known probabilities of selection are known as *nonprobability sampling methods*. In such sampling methods, we have no objective way of evaluating how far away from the population parameter our estimate may be. In addition, when we do not select our sample randomly out of the entire population of interest, our sampling results may be biased. That is, the average value of the estimate in repeated sampling is not equal to the parameter of interest. Put simply, our sample may not be a true representative of the population of interest.

EXAMPLE (a)

A marketing research firm wants to estimate the proportion of consumers who might be interested in purchasing the Spanish sherry Jerez if this product were available at liquor stores in this country. How should information for this study be obtained?

SOLUTION

The population relevant to our case is not a clear-cut one. Before embarking on our study, we need to define our population more precisely. Do we mean all consumers in the United States? Do we mean all families of consumers? Do we mean only people of drinking age? Perhaps we should consider our population to be only those people who, at least occasionally, consume similar drinks. These are important questions that we need to answer before we begin the sampling survey. The population must be defined in accordance with the *purpose of the study*. In the case of a proposed new product like Jerez, we are interested in the product's potential market share. We are interested in estimating the proportion of the market for alcoholic beverages that will go to Jerez, once it is introduced. Therefore, we define our population as all people who, at least occasionally, consume alcoholic beverages.

Now we need to know how to obtain a random sample from this population. To obtain a random sample out of the whole population of people who drink alcoholic beverages at least occasionally, we must have a *frame*. That is, we need a list of all such people, from which we can randomly choose as many people as we need for our sample. In reality, of course, no such list is available. Therefore, we must obtain our sample in some other way. Market researchers send field workers to places where consumers may be found, usually shopping malls. There shoppers are randomly selected and pre-screened to ascertain whether they are in the population of interest—in this case, whether they are people who at least occasionally consume alcoholic beverages. Then the selected people are given a taste test of the new product and asked to fill out a questionnaire about their response to the product and their future purchase intent. This method of obtaining a random sample works as long as the interviewers do not choose people in a nonrandom fashion, for example, choosing certain types of people because of their appearance. If this should happen, a bias may be introduced if the variable favoring selection is somehow related to interest in the product.

Another point we must consider is the requirement that people selected at the shopping mall should constitute a representative sample from the entire population in which we are interested. We must consider the possibility that potential buyers of Jerez may not be found in shopping malls, and if their proportion outside the malls is different from what it is in the malls where surveys take place, a bias will be introduced. We must consider the location of shopping malls and ascertain that we are not favoring some segments of the population over others. Preferably, several shopping malls, located in different areas, should be chosen.

We should randomize the selection of people or elements in our sample. However, if our sample is not chosen in a purely random way, it may still suffice for our purposes as long as it *behaves* as a purely random sample and no biases are introduced. In designing the study, we should collect a few random samples at different locations, chosen at different times and handled by different field workers, to minimize the chances of a bias. The results of different samples validate the assumption that we are indeed getting a representative sample.

17–3   Stratified Random Sampling

In some cases, a population may be viewed as comprising different groups where elements in each group are similar to each other in some way. In such cases, we may gain sampling precision (that is, reduce the variance of our estimators) as well as reduce the costs of the survey by treating the different groups separately. If we consider these groups, or *strata,* as separate subpopulations and draw a separate random sample from each stratum and combine the results, our sampling method is called *stratified random sampling.*

> In **stratified random sampling,** we assume that the population of N units may be divided into m groups with N_i units in group $i, i = 1, \ldots, m$. The m strata are nonoverlapping and together they make up the total population: $N_1 + N_2 + \cdots + N_m = N$.

We define the true *weight* of stratum i as $W_i = N_i/N$. That is, the weight of stratum i is equal to the proportion of the size of stratum i in the whole population. Our total sample, of size n, is divided into subsamples from each of the strata. We sample n_i items in stratum i, and $n_1 + n_2 + \cdots n_m = n$. We define the sampling fraction in stratum i as: $f_i = n_i/N_i$.

The true mean of the entire population is μ, and the true mean in stratum i is μ_i. The variance of stratum i is σ_i^2, and the variance of the entire population is σ^2. The sample mean in stratum i is $\bar{X}_i$, and the combined estimator, the sample mean in stratified random sampling, $\bar{X}_{st}$, is defined as follows.

> The **estimator of the population mean in stratified random sampling**:
> $$\bar{X}_{st} = \sum_{i=1}^{m} W_i \bar{X}_i \qquad (17\text{–}1)$$

In simple random sampling with no stratification, the stratified estimator in equation 17–1 is, in general, *not equal* to the simple estimator of the population mean. The reason is that the estimator in equation 17–1 uses the true weights of the strata, W_i. The simple random sampling estimator of the population mean is $\bar{X} = (\sum_{\text{all data}} X)/n = (\sum_{i=1}^{m} n_i \bar{X}_i)/n$. This is equal to $\bar{X}_{st}$ only if we have $n_i/n = N_i/N$ for each stratum, that is, if the proportion of the sample taken from each stratum is equal to the proportion of each stratum in the entire population. Such a stratification is called stratification with *proportional allocation.*

Following are some important properties of the stratified estimator of the population mean.

1. If the estimator of the mean in each stratum, $\bar{X}_i$, is *unbiased,* then the stratified estimator of the mean, $\bar{X}_{st}$, is an unbiased estimator of the population mean, μ.

2. If the samples in the different strata are drawn *independently* of each other, then the variance of the stratified estimator of the population mean, $\bar{X}_{st}$, is given by:

$$V(\bar{X}_{st}) = \sum_{i=1}^{m} W_i^2 V(\bar{X}_i) \qquad (17-2)$$

where $V(\bar{X}_i)$ is the variance of the sample mean in stratum i.

3. If sampling in all strata is *random,* then the variance of the estimator, given in equation 17–2, is further equal to:

$$V(\bar{X}_{st}) = \sum_{i=1}^{m} W_i^2 \left(\frac{\sigma_i^2}{n_i}\right)(1 - f_i) \qquad (17-3)$$

When the sampling fractions, f_i, are small and may be ignored, we get:

$$V(\bar{X}_{st}) = \sum_{i=1}^{m} W_i^2 \frac{\sigma_i^2}{n_i} \qquad (17-4)$$

4. If the sample allocation is proportional ($n_i = n(N_i/N)$ for all i), then:

$$V(\bar{X}_{st}) = \left(\frac{1-f}{n}\right) \sum_{i=1}^{m} W_i \sigma_i^2 \qquad (17-5)$$

which reduces to $(1/n) \sum_{i=1}^{m} W_i \sigma_i^2$ when the sampling fraction is small.

In addition, if the population variances in all the strata are equal, then:

$$V(\bar{X}_{st}) = \frac{\sigma^2}{n} \qquad (17-6)$$

when the sampling fraction is small.

Practical Applications

In practice, the true population variances in the different strata are usually not known. When the variances are not known, we estimate them from our data. An unbiased estimator of σ_i^2, the population variance in stratum i, is given by:

$$S_i^2 = \sum_{\text{data in stratum } i} \frac{(X - \bar{X}_i)^2}{n_i - 1} \qquad (17-7)$$

The estimator in equation 17–7 is the usual unbiased sample estimator of the population variance in each stratum as a separate population. A particular estimate of the variance in stratum i will be denoted by s_i^2. If sampling in each stratum is random, then an unbiased estimator of the variance of the sample estimator of the population mean is:

$$s^2(\bar{X}_{st}) = \sum_{i=1}^{m} \left(\frac{W_i^2 S_i^2}{n_i}\right)(1 - f_i) \qquad (17-8)$$

Any of the preceding formulas apply in the special situations where they can be used with the estimated variances substituted for the population variances.

Confidence Intervals

We now give a confidence interval for the population mean, μ, obtained from stratified random sampling.

A $(1 - \alpha)$ 100% confidence interval for the population mean, μ, using stratified sampling:

$$\overline{X}_{st} \pm z_{\alpha/2} s(\overline{X}_{st}) \qquad (17\text{--}9)$$

where $s(\overline{X}_{st})$ is the square root of the estimate of the variance of $\overline{X}_{st}$ given in equation 17–8.

When the sample sizes in at least some of the strata are small and the population variances are unknown, but the populations are at least approximately normal, we use the t distribution instead of Z. We denote the degrees of freedom of the t distribution by df. The exact value of df is difficult to determine, but it lies somewhere between the smallest $n_i - 1$ (the degrees of freedom associated with the sample from stratum i) and the sum of the degrees of freedom associated with the samples from all strata, $\sum_{i=1}^{m} (n_i - 1)$. An approximation for the effective number of degrees of freedom is given by:

$$\text{Effective df} = \frac{\left[\sum_{i=1}^{m} N_i (N_i - n_i) s_i^2 / n_i \right]^2}{\sum_{i=1}^{m} [N_i (N_i - n_i)/n_i]^2 s_i^4/(n_i - 1)} \qquad (17\text{--}10)$$

We demonstrate the application of the theory of stratified random sampling presented so far by the following example.

Once a year, *Fortune* magazine publishes the Fortune Service 500: a list of the largest service companies in America. The 500 firms belong to six major industry groups. The industry groups and the number of firms in each group are listed in Table 17–1.

The 500 firms are considered a complete population: the population of the top 500 service companies in the United States. An economist who is interested in this popula-

EXAMPLE (b)

TABLE 17–1　The Fortune Service 500

Group	Number of Firms
1.　Diversified service companies	100
2.　Commercial banking companies	100
3.　Financial service companies (including savings and insurance)	150
4.　Retailing companies	50
5.　Transportation companies	50
6.　Utilities	50
	$\overline{500}$

tion wants to estimate the mean net income of all firms in the index. However, obtaining the data for all 500 firms in the index is either difficult, time-consuming, or costly. Therefore, the economist wants to gather a random sample of the firms, compute a quick average of the net income for the firms in the sample, and use it to estimate the mean net income for the entire population of 500 firms.

SOLUTION

The economist believes that firms in the same industry group share common characteristics related to net income. Therefore, the six groups are treated as different strata, and a random sample is drawn from each stratum. The weights of each of the strata are known exactly as computed from the strata sizes in Table 17−1. Using the definition of the population weights, $W_i = N_i/N$, we get the following weights.

$$W_1 = N_1/N = 100/500 = 0.2$$
$$W_2 = N_2/N = 100/500 = 0.2$$
$$W_3 = N_3/N = 150/500 = 0.3$$
$$W_4 = N_4/N = 50/500 = 0.1$$
$$W_5 = N_5/N = 50/500 = 0.1$$
$$W_6 = N_6/N = 50/500 = 0.1$$

The economist decides to select a random sample of 100 of the 500 firms listed in *Fortune*. (Data appeared in the June 9, 1986, issue.) The economist chooses to use a proportional allocation of the total sample to the six strata (another method of allocation will be presented shortly). With proportional allocation, the total sample of 100 must be allocated to the different strata in proportion to the strata weights computed. Thus, for each i, $i = 1, \ldots, 6$, we compute n_i as: $n_i = nW_i$. This gives the following sample sizes.

$$n_1 = 20, \ n_2 = 20, \ n_3 = 30, \ n_4 = 10, \ n_5 = 10, \ n_6 = 10$$

We will assume that the net income values in the different strata are approximately normally distributed and that the estimated strata variances (to be estimated from the data) are the true strata variances, σ_i^2, so that the normal distribution may be used.

The economist draws the random samples and computes the sample means and variances. The results, in millions of dollars (for the means) and in millions of dollars squared (for the variances), are given in Table 17−2, along with the sample sizes in the different strata and the strata weights. From the table, and with the aid of equation 17−1 for the mean and equation 17−5 for the variance of the sample mean (with the estimated sample variances substituted for the population variances in the different strata), we will now compute the stratified sample mean and the estimated variance of the stratified sample mean.

TABLE 17−2 The Sampling Results for Example (b)

Stratum	Mean	Variance	n_i	W_i
1	52.7	97,650	20	0.2
2	112.6	64,300	20	0.2
3	85.6	76,990	30	0.3
4	12.6	18,320	10	0.1
5	8.9	9,037	10	0.1
6	52.3	83,500	10	0.1

$$\bar{x}_{st} = \sum_{i=1}^{6} W_i\bar{x}_i = (0.2)(52.7) + (0.2)(112.6) + (0.3)(85.6) + (0.1)(12.6) + (0.1)(8.9) + (0.1)(52.3)$$

$$= \$66.12 \text{ million}$$

and

$$s(\bar{X}_{st}) = \sqrt{\frac{1-f}{n} \sum_{i=1}^{6} W_i s_i^2}$$

$$= \sqrt{\frac{0.8}{100}[(0.2)(97,650)+(0.2)(64,300)+(0.3)(76,990)+(0.1)(18,320)+(0.1)(9,037)+(0.1)(83,500)]}$$

$$= 23.08$$

(Our sampling fraction is $f = 100/500 = 0.2$.) Our unbiased point estimate of the average net income of all firms in the Fortune Service 500 is \$66.12 million.

Using equation 17–9, we now compute a 95% confidence interval for μ, the mean net income of all firms in the index. We have the following:

$$\bar{x}_{st} \pm z_{\alpha/2}s(\bar{X}_{st}) = 66.12 \pm (1.96)(23.08) = [20.88, 111.36]$$

Thus, the economist may be 95% confident that the average net income for all firms in the Fortune Service 500 is anywhere from 20.88 to 111.36 million dollars. Incidentally, the true population mean net income for all 500 firms in the index is $\mu = \$61.496$ million.

Stratified Sampling for the Population Proportion

The theory of stratified sampling extends in a natural way to sampling for the population proportion, p. Let the sample proportion in stratum i be $\hat{P}_i = X_i/n_i$, where X_i is the number of successes in a sample of size n_i. Then the stratified estimator of the population proportion p is the following.

Stratified estimator of the population proportion, p:

$$\hat{P}_{st} = \sum_{i=1}^{m} W_i\hat{P}_i \tag{17–11}$$

where the weights, W_i, are defined as in the case of sampling for the population mean: $W_i = N_i/N$

The following is an approximate expression for the variance of the estimator of the population proportion $\hat{P}_{st}$, for use with large samples.

The approximate variance of $\hat{P}_{st}$:

$$V(\hat{P}_{st}) = \sum W_i^2 \frac{\hat{P}_i\hat{Q}_i}{n_i} \tag{17–12}$$

where $\hat{Q}_i = 1 - \hat{P}_i$

When finite-population correction factors, f_i, must be considered, the following expression is appropriate for the variance of $\hat{P}_{st}$:

$$V(\hat{P}_{st}) = \frac{1}{N^2} \sum_{i=1}^{m} N_i^2 (N_i - n_i) \frac{\hat{P}_i \hat{Q}_i}{(N_i - 1)n_i} \qquad (17\text{-}13)$$

When proportional allocation is used, an approximate expression is:

$$V(\hat{P}_{st}) = \frac{1 - f}{n} \sum_{i=1}^{m} W_i \hat{P}_i \hat{Q}_i \qquad (17\text{-}14)$$

Let us now return to Example (a), sampling for the proportion of people who might be interested in purchasing the Spanish sherry Jerez. Suppose that the marketing researchers believe that preferences for imported wines differ between consumers in metropolitan areas and those in other areas. The area of interest for the survey covers a few states in the Northeast, where it is known that 65% of the people live in metropolitan areas and 35% live in nonmetropolitan areas. A sample of 130 people randomly chosen at shopping malls in metropolitan areas shows that 28 of them are interested in Jerez, while a random sample of 70 people selected at malls outside the metropolitan areas shows that 18 of them are interested in the sherry.

Let us use these results in constructing a 90% confidence interval for the proportion of people in the entire population who are interested in the product. From equation 17-11, using two strata with weights 0.65 and 0.35, we get:

$$\hat{p}_{st} = \sum_{i=1}^{2} W_i \hat{p}_i = (0.65)\frac{28}{130} + (0.35)\frac{18}{70} = 0.23$$

Our allocation is proportional because $n_1 = 130$, $n_2 = 70$, and $n = 130 + 70 = 200$, so that $n_1/n = 0.65 = W_1$ and $n_2/n = 0.35 = W_2$. In addition, the sample sizes of 130 and 70 represent tiny fractions of the two strata; hence, no finite-population correction factor is required. The equation for the estimated variance of the sample estimator of the proportion is therefore equation 17-14 without the finite-population correction:

$$V(\hat{P}_{st}) = \frac{1}{n} \sum_{i=1}^{2} W_i \hat{p}_i \hat{q}_i = \frac{1}{200}[(0.65)(0.215)(0.785) + (0.35)(0.257)(0.743)]$$

$$= 0.0008825$$

The estimated standard error of $\hat{P}_{st}$ is therefore $\sqrt{V(\hat{P}_{st})} = \sqrt{0.0008825} = 0.0297$. Thus, our 90% confidence interval for the population proportion of people interested in Jerez is:

$$\hat{p}_{st} \pm z_{\alpha/2} s(\hat{P}_{st}) = 0.23 \pm (1.645)(0.0297) = [0.181, 0.279]$$

The stratified point estimate of the percentage of people in the proposed market area for Jerez who may be interested in the product, if it is introduced, is 23%. A 90% confidence interval for the population percentage is 18.1% to 27.9%. In the next subsections, we will explore some optional, advanced aspects of stratified sampling.

What Do We Do When the Population Strata Weights Are Unknown?

When the true strata weights, $W_i = N_i/N$, are unknown—that is, when we do not know what percentage of the whole population belongs to each stratum—we may still use stratified random sampling. In such cases, we use estimates of the true weights, denoted by w_i. The consequence of using estimated weights instead of the true weights is the introduction of a bias into our sampling results. The interesting thing about this kind of bias is that it is not eliminated as the sample size increases. When errors in the strata weights exist, our results are always biased; the greater the errors, the greater the bias. These errors also cause the estimated standard error of the sample mean, $s(\bar{X}_{st})$, to underestimate the true standard error. Consequently, confidence intervals for the population parameter of interest tend to be narrower than they should be.

How Many Strata Should We Use?

The number of strata to be used is an important question to consider when designing any survey that uses stratified sampling. In many cases, there is a natural breakdown of the population into a given number of strata. In other cases, there may be no clear, unique way of separating the population into groups. For example, if age is to be used as a stratifying variable, there are many ways of breaking the variable and forming strata. There are two guidance rules for constructing strata. The rules are presented below.

Rules for Constructing Strata

1. The number of strata should preferably be less than or equal to 6.
2. Choose the strata in such a way that Cum $\sqrt{f(x)}$ is approximately constant for all strata (where Cum $\sqrt{f(x)}$ is the cumulative square root of the frequency of X, the variable of interest).

The first rule is clear. The second rule says that in the absence of other guidelines for breaking down a population into strata, we partition the variable used for stratification into categories so that the cumulative square root of the frequency function of the variable is approximately equal for all strata. We illustrate this rule in the hypothetical case of Table 17–3. As can be seen in this simplified example, the *combined* age groups 20–30, 31–35, and 36–45 all have a sum of $\sqrt{f}$ equal to 5; hence, these groups make good strata with respect to age as a stratifying variable according to rule 2.

Post-Sampling Stratification

At times, we conduct a survey using simple random sampling with no stratification, and, after obtaining our results, we may note that the data may be broken into categories of similar elements. Can we now use the techniques of stratified random sampling and enjoy its benefits in terms of reduced variances of the estimators? Surpris-

TABLE 17–3 Constructing Strata by Age

Age	Frequency (f)	$\sqrt{f}$	Cum $\sqrt{f}$
20–25	1	1	
26–30	16	4	5
31–35	25	5	5
36–40	4	2	
41–45	9	3	5

ingly, the answer is yes. In fact, if the subsamples in each of our strata contain at least 20 elements, and if our estimated weights of the different strata, w_i (computed from the data as n_i/n, or from more accurate information), are close to the true population strata weights, W_i, then our stratified estimator will be almost as good as that of stratified random sampling with proportional allocation. This procedure is called *post-stratification*. We close this section with a discussion of an alternative to proportional allocation of the sample in stratified random sampling, called *optimum allocation*.

Optimum Allocation

With optimum allocation, we select the sample sizes to be allocated to each of the strata so as to minimize one of two criteria. We either minimize the cost of the survey for a given value of the variance of our estimator, or we minimize the variance of our estimator for a given cost of taking the survey.

We assume a cost function of the form:

$$C = C_0 + \sum_{i=1}^{m} C_i n_i \qquad (17-15)$$

where C is the total cost of the survey, C_0 is the fixed cost of setting up the survey, and C_i is the cost per item sampled in stratum i. Clearly, the total cost of the survey is the sum of the fixed cost and the costs of sampling in all the strata (where the cost of sampling in stratum i is equal to the sample size, n_i, times the cost per item sampled, C_i).

Under the assumption of a cost function given in equation 17–15, the optimum allocation that will minimize our total cost for a fixed variance of the estimator, or minimize the variance of the estimator for a fixed total cost, is as follows.

Optimum allocation:

$$\frac{n_i}{n} = \frac{W_i \sigma_i / \sqrt{C_i}}{\sum_{i=1}^{m} W_i \sigma_i / \sqrt{C_i}} \qquad (17-16)$$

Equation 17–16 has an intuitive appeal. It says that for a given stratum, we should take a larger sample if the stratum is *more variable internally* (greater σ_i), if the relative *size of the stratum is larger* (greater W_i), or if *sampling in the stratum is cheaper* (smaller C_i).

If the cost per unit sampled is the same in all the strata (that is, if $C_i = c$ for all i), then the optimum allocation for a fixed total cost is the same as the optimum allocation for fixed sample size, and we have what is called the *Neyman allocation* (after J. Neyman, athough this allocation was actually discovered earlier by A. A. Tschuprow in 1923).

The Neyman allocation:

$$\frac{n_i}{n} = \frac{W_i \sigma_i}{\sum_{i=1}^{m} W_i \sigma_i} \qquad (17-17)$$

Suppose that we want to allocate a total sample of size 1,000 to three strata, where stratum 1 has weight 0.4, standard deviation 1, and cost per sampled item 4 cents; stratum 2 has weight 0.5, standard deviation 2, and cost per item 9 cents; and stratum 3 has weight 0.1, standard deviation 3, and cost per item 16 cents. How should we allocate this sample if optimum allocation is to be used? We have:

$$\sum_{i=1}^{3} \frac{W_i \sigma_i}{\sqrt{C_i}} = \frac{(0.4)(1)}{\sqrt{4}} + \frac{(0.5)(2)}{\sqrt{9}} + \frac{(0.1)(3)}{\sqrt{16}} = 0.608$$

From equation 17–16, we get:

$$\frac{n_1}{n} = \frac{W_1 \sigma_1 / \sqrt{C_1}}{\sum\limits_{i=1}^{3} (W_i \sigma_i / \sqrt{C_i})} = \frac{(0.4)(1)/\sqrt{4}}{0.608} = 0.329$$

$$\frac{n_2}{n} = \frac{W_2 \sigma_2 / \sqrt{C_2}}{\sum\limits_{i=1}^{3} (W_i \sigma_i / \sqrt{C_i})} = \frac{(0.5)(2)/\sqrt{9}}{0.608} = 0.548$$

$$\frac{n_3}{n} = \frac{W_3 \sigma_3 / \sqrt{C_3}}{\sum\limits_{i=1}^{3} (W_i \sigma_i / \sqrt{C_i})} = \frac{(0.1)(3)/\sqrt{16}}{0.608} = 0.123$$

The optimum allocation in this case is 329 items from stratum 1, 548 items from stratum 2, and 123 items from stratum 3 (making a total of 1,000 sample items, as specified).

Let us now compare this allocation with proportional allocation. With a sample of size 1,000 and a proportional allocation, we would allocate our sample only by the strata weights, which are 0.4, 0.5, and 0.1, respectively. Therefore, our allocation will be 400 from stratum 1, 500 from stratum 2, and 100 from stratum 3. The optimum allocation is different, as it incorporates the cost and variance considerations. Here, the difference between the two sets of sample sizes is not large.

Suppose, in this example, that the costs of sampling from the three strata are the same. In this case, we can use the Neyman allocation and get, from equation 17–17:

$$\frac{n_1}{n} = \frac{W_1 \sigma_1}{\sum\limits_{i=1}^{3} W_i \sigma_i} = \frac{(0.4)(1)}{1.7} = 0.235$$

$$\frac{n_2}{n} = \frac{W_2 \sigma_2}{\sum\limits_{i=1}^{3} W_i \sigma_i} = \frac{(0.5)(2)}{1.7} = 0.588$$

$$\frac{n_3}{n} = \frac{W_3 \sigma_3}{\sum\limits_{i=1}^{3} W_i \sigma_i} = \frac{(0.1)(3)}{1.7} = 0.176$$

Thus, the Neyman allocation gives a sample of size 235 to stratum 1, 588 to stratum 2, and 176 to stratum 3. Note that these subsamples add only to 999, due to rounding error. The last sample point may be allocated to any of the strata.

In general, stratified random sampling gives more precise results than those obtained from simple random sampling: the standard errors of our estimators from stratified random sampling are usually smaller than those of simple random sampling. Furthermore, in stratified random sampling, an optimum allocation will produce more precise results than a proportional allocation if some strata are more expensive to sample than others or if the variances within strata are different from each other.

PROBLEMS

Answers

17–1.   A securities analyst wants to estimate the average percentage of institutional holding of all publicly traded stocks in the United States. The analyst believes that stocks traded on the three major exchanges have different characteristics and therefore decides to use stratified random sampling. The three strata are the New York Stock Exchange (NYSE), the American Exchange (AMEX), and the Over the Counter (OTC) exchange. The weights of the three strata, as measured by the number of stocks listed in each exchange divided by the total number of stocks, are: NYSE, 0.44; AMEX, 0.15; OTC, 0.41. A total random sample of 200 stocks is selected, with proportional allocation. It is found that the average percentage of institutional holdings of the subsample selected from the issues of the NYSE is 46% and the standard deviation is 8%. The corresponding results for the AMEX are 9% average institutional holdings and a standard deviation of 4%, and the corresponding results for the OTC stocks are 29% average institutional holdings and a standard deviation of 16%.

a. Give a stratified estimate of the mean percentage of institutional holdings per stock.

b. Give the standard error of the estimate in *a*.

c. Give a 95% confidence interval for the mean percentage of institutional holdings.

d. Explain the advantages of using stratified random sampling in this case. Compare with simple random sampling.

17–2.

Production, 57.1%; marketing, 28.6%; management, 4.8%; other 9.5%.

17–2.   A company has 2,100 employees belonging to the following groups: production, 1,200; marketing, 600; management, 100; other, 200. The company president wants to obtain an estimate of the views of all employees about a certain impending executive decision. The president knows that the management employees' views are most variable, along with employees in the "other" category, while the marketing and production people have rather uniform views within their groups. The production people are the most costly to sample, in terms of the time required to find them at their different jobs, and the management people are easiest to sample.

a. Suppose that a total sample of 100 employees is required. What are the sample sizes in the different strata under proportional allocation?

b. Discuss how you would design an optimum allocation in this case.

17–3.   Last year, consumers increasingly bought fleece (industry jargon for hot-selling jogging suits, which now rival jeans as the uniform for casual attire). A New York designer of jogging suits is interested in the new trend and wants to estimate the amount spent per person on jogging suits during the year. The designer knows that people who belong to health-and-fitness clubs will have different buying behavior than people who do not. Furthermore, the designer finds that, within the proposed study area, 18% of the population are members of health-and-fitness clubs. A random sample of 300 people is selected, and the sample is proportionally allocated to the two strata: members of health clubs and nonmembers of health clubs. It is found that among members, the average amount spent is $152.43 and the standard deviation is $25.77, while among the nonmembers, the average amount spent is $15.33 and the standard deviation is $5.11.

a. What is the stratified estimate of the mean?

b. What is the standard error of the estimator?

c. Give a 90% confidence interval for the population mean, μ.

d. Discuss one possible problem with the data. (*Hint:* Can the data be considered normally distributed? Why?)

17–4.

0.189, 0.154, 0.120,
0.109, 0.109, 0.091,
0.091, 0.086, 0.051

17–4.   A financial analyst is interested in estimating the average amount of a foreign loan by American banks. The analyst believes that the amount of a loan may be different depending on the bank, or, more precisely, on the extent of the bank's involvement in foreign loans. The analyst obtains the following data on the percentage of profits of U.S. banks from loans to Mexico and proposes to use these data in the construction of strata weights. The strata are the different banks: First Chicago: 33%; Manufacturers Hanover: 27%; Bankers Trust: 21%; Chemical Bank: 19%; Wells Fargo Bank: 19%; Citicorp: 16%; Mellon Bank: 16%; Chase Manhattan: 15%; Morgan Guarantee Trust: 9%.

a. Construct the strata weights for proportional allocation.

b. Discuss two possible problems with this study.

17–4 Cluster Sampling

Let us consider the case where we have no frame (i.e., no list of all the elements in the population) and the elements are *clustered* in larger units. Each unit, or cluster, contains several elements of the population. In this case, we may choose to use the method of **cluster sampling.** This may also be the case when the population is large and spread over a geographical area in which smaller subregions are easily sampled and where a simple random sample or a stratified random sample may not be carried out as easily.

Suppose that the population is composed of M clusters and there is a list of all M clusters from which a random sample of m clusters is selected. There are two possibilities. First, we may sample *every element* in every one of the m selected clusters. In this case, our sampling method is called *single-stage cluster sampling.* Second, we may select a random sample of m clusters and then select a random sample of n elements from each of the selected clusters. In this case, our sampling method is called *two-stage cluster sampling.*

Single-Stage Cluster Sampling for the Population Mean

Let $n_1, n_2, \ldots, n_m$ be the number of elements in each of the m sampled clusters. Let $\bar{X}_1, \bar{X}_2, \ldots, \bar{X}_m$ be the means of the sampled clusters. The cluster sampling unbiased estimator of the population mean, μ, is given as follows.

Cluster sampling estimator of μ:

$$\bar{X}_{\text{cl}} = \frac{\sum\limits_{i=1}^{m} n_i \bar{X}_i}{\sum\limits_{i=1}^{m} n_i} \tag{17–18}$$

An estimator of the variance of the estimator of μ in equation 17–18 is:

$$s^2(\bar{X}_{\text{cl}}) = \left(\frac{M - m}{Mm\bar{n}^2}\right) \frac{\sum\limits_{i=1}^{m} n_i^2(\bar{X}_i - \bar{X}_{\text{cl}})^2}{m - 1} \tag{17–19}$$

where $\bar{n} = (\sum_{i=1}^{m} n_i)/m$ is the average number of units in the sampled clusters.

Single-Stage Cluster Sampling for the Population Proportion

The cluster sampling estimator of the population proportion, p:

$$\hat{P}_{\text{cl}} = \frac{\sum\limits_{i=1}^{m} n_i \hat{P}_i}{\sum\limits_{i=1}^{m} n_i} \tag{17–20}$$

where the $\hat{P}_i$ are the proportions of interest within the sampled clusters

The estimated variance of the estimator in equation 17–20 is given by:

$$s^2(\hat{P}_{cl}) = \frac{M-m}{Mm\overline{n}^2} \frac{\sum\limits_{i=1}^{m} n_i^2(\hat{P}_i - \hat{P}_{cl})^2}{m-1} \qquad (17-21)$$

We now demonstrate the use of cluster sampling for the population mean with the following example.

EXAMPLE (c)

The J. B. Hunt Transport Company is especially interested in lowering fuel costs in order to survive in the tough world of deregulated trucking. Recently, the company introduced new measures to reduce fuel costs for all its trucks. Suppose that company trucks are based in 110 centers throughout the country and that the company's management wants to estimate the average amount of fuel saved per truck for the week following the institution of the new measures. For reasons of lower cost and administrative ease, management decides to use single-stage cluster sampling and to select a random sample of 20 trucking centers and measure the weekly fuel saving for each of the trucks in the selected centers (each center is a cluster). The average fuel savings per truck, in gallons, for each of the 20 selected centers are as follows (the number of trucks in each center is given in parentheses): 21 (8), 22 (8), 11 (9), 34 (10), 28 (7), 25 (8), 18 (10), 24 (12), 19 (11), 20 (6), 30 (8), 26 (9), 12 (9), 17 (8), 13 (10), 29 (8), 24 (8), 26 (10), 18 (10), 22 (11). From these data, compute an estimate of the average amount of fuel saved per truck for all of Hunt's trucks over the week in question. Also give a 95% confidence interval for this parameter.

SOLUTION

From equation 17–18, we get:

$$\overline{x}_{cl} = \frac{\sum\limits_{i=1}^{m} n_i \overline{x}_i}{\sum\limits_{i=1}^{m} n_i} = [21(8) + 22(8) + 11(9) + 34(10) + 28(7) + 25(8) + 18(10) + 24(12) +$$
$$19(11) + 20(6) + 30(8) + 26(9) + 12(9) + 17(8) + 13(10) + 29(8) +$$
$$24(8) + 26(10) + 18(10) + 22(11)]/(8 + 8 + 9 + 10 + 7 + 8 + 10 +$$
$$12 + 11 + 6 + 8 + 9 + 9 + 8 + 10 + 8 + 8 + 10 + 10 + 11) = 21.83$$

From equation 17–19, we find that the estimated variance of our sample estimator of the mean is:

$$s^2(\overline{X}_{cl}) = \left(\frac{M-m}{Mm\overline{n}^2}\right) \frac{\sum\limits_{i=1}^{20} n_i^2(\overline{x}_i - \overline{x}_{cl})^2}{m-1}$$

$$= \frac{110 - 20}{(110)(20)(9)^2} [8^2(21-21.83)^2 + 8^2(22-21.83)^2 +$$
$$9^2(11-21.83)^2 + \cdots + 11^2(22-21.83)^2]/19$$

$$= 1.587$$

Using the preceding information, we construct a 95% confidence interval for μ as follows:

$$\overline{x}_{cl} \pm 1.96s(\overline{X}_{cl}) = 21.83 \pm 1.96\sqrt{1.587} = [19.36, 24.30]$$

Thus, based on the sampling results, Hunt's management may be 95% confident that average fuel savings per truck for all of their trucks over the week in question is anywhere from 19.36 to 24.30 gallons.

Two-Stage Cluster Sampling

When clusters are very large or when elements within each cluster tend to be similar, we may gain little information by selecting every element within the selected clusters. In such cases, it may be more economical to select more clusters and to sample only some of the elements within the chosen clusters. The formulas for the estimators and their variances in the case of two-stage cluster sampling are more complicated and may be found in advanced books on sampling methodology.

The Relation with Stratified Sampling

In stratified sampling, we sample elements from every one of our strata, and this assures us of full representation of all segments of the population in the sample. In cluster sampling, we sample only some of the clusters, and although elements within any cluster may tend to be homogeneous, as is the case with strata, not all of the clusters are represented in the sample; this leads to lowered precision of the cluster sampling method. In stratified random sampling, we use the fact that the population may be broken into subgroups. This usually leads to a smaller variance of our estimators. In cluster sampling, however, the method is used mainly because of ease of implementation or reduction in sampling costs, and the estimates do not usually lead to more precise results.

PROBLEMS

17–5. There are 602 aerobics-and-fitness centers in Japan (up from 170 five years ago). Adidas, the European maker of sports shoes and apparel, is very interested in this fast-growing potential market for its products. As part of a marketing survey, Adidas wants to estimate the average income of all members of Japanese fitness centers. (Members of one such club pay $62 to join and another $62 per month. Adidas believes that the average income of all fitness club members in Japan may be higher than that of the general population, for which census data exist.) Since travel and administrative costs for conducting a simple random sample of all members of fitness clubs throughout Japan would be prohibitively high, Adidas decided to conduct a cluster sampling survey. Five clubs were chosen at random out of the entire collection of 602 clubs, and all members of the 5 clubs were interviewed. The following are the average incomes (in U.S. dollars) for the members of each of the 5 clubs (the number of members in each club is given in parentheses): $37,237 (560), $41,338 (435), $28,800 (890), $35,498 (711), $47,446 (230). Give the cluster sampling estimate of the population mean income for all fitness club members in Japan. Also give a 90% confidence interval for the population mean. Are there any limitations to the methodology in this case?

17–6. Israel's kibbutzim are by now well diversified beyond their agrarian roots, producing everything from lollipops to plastic pipe. These 282 widely scattered communes of several hundred members maintain hundreds of factories and other production facilities.[1] An economist wants to estimate the average annual revenues of all kibbutz production facilities. Since each kibbutz has several production units, and since travel and other costs are high, the economist wants to consider a sample of 15 randomly chosen kibbutzim and find the annual revenues of all production units in the selected kibbutzim. From these data, the economist hopes to estimate the average annual revenue per production unit in all 282 kibbutzim. The sample results are as follows.

Answer

17–6.
———
[0.912, 1.945]
Million dollars

---

[1] *Forbes* (January 26, 1987).

Answer

Kibbutz	Number of Production Units	Total Kibbutz Annual Revenues (in Millions of Dollars)
1	4	4.5
2	2	2.8
3	6	8.9
4	2	1.2
5	5	7.0
6	3	2.2
7	2	2.3
8	1	0.8
9	8	12.5
10	4	6.2
11	3	5.5
12	3	6.2
13	2	3.8
14	5	9.0
15	2	1.4

From these data, compute the cluster sampling estimate of the mean annual revenue of all kibbutzim production units, and give a 95% confidence interval for the mean.

17–7.   Under what conditions would you use cluster sampling? Explain the differences among cluster sampling, simple random sampling, and stratified random sampling. Under what conditions would you use two-stage cluster sampling? Explain the difference between single-stage and two-stage cluster sampling? What are the limitations of cluster sampling?

17–8

[0.478, 0.752]

17–8.   Recently a survey was conducted to assess the quality of investment brokers.[2] A random sample of 6 brokerage houses was selected from a total of 27 brokerage houses. Each of the brokers in the selected brokerage houses was evaluated by an independent panel of industry experts as "highly qualified" or was given an evaluation below this rating. The designers of the survey wanted to estimate the proportion of all brokers in the entire industry who would be considered highly qualified. The survey results are in the following table.

Brokerage House	Total Number of Brokers	Number of HQ Brokers
1	120	80
2	150	75
3	200	100
4	100	65
5	88	45
6	260	200

Use the cluster sampling estimator of the population proportion to estimate the proportion of all highly qualified brokers in the investment industry. Also give a 99% confidence interval for the population proportion you estimated.

17–9.   Forty-two cruise ships come to Alaska's Glacier Bay every year. The state tourist board wants to estimate the average cruise passenger's satisfaction from this experience, rated on a scale of 0 to 100. Since the ships' arrivals are evenly spread throughout the season, simple random sampling is costly and time-consuming. Therefore, the agency decides to send its volunteers to board the first five ships of the season, consider them as clusters, and randomly choose 50 passengers in each ship for interviewing.

a. Is the method employed single-stage cluster sampling? Explain.

b. Is the method employed two-stage cluster sampling? Explain.

c. Suppose that each of the ships has exactly 50 passengers. Is the proposed method single-stage cluster sampling?

d. The 42 ships belong to 12 cruise ship companies. Each company has its own characteristics in terms of price, luxury, services, and type of passengers. Suggest an alternative sampling method, and explain its benefits.

---

[2] *Financial World* (January 20, 1987).

17–5 Systematic Sampling

Sometimes a population is arranged in some order: files in a cabinet, crops in a field, goods in a warehouse, etc. In such cases it may be easier to draw our random sample in a *systematic* way rather than generate a simple random sample that would entail looking for particular items within the population. To select a **systematic sample** of n elements from a population of N elements, we divide the N elements in the population into n groups of k elements and then use the following rule.

> We randomly select the first element out of the first k elements in the population, and then we select every kth unit afterwards until we have a sample of n elements.

For example, suppose $k = 20$, and we need a sample of $n = 30$ items. We randomly select the first item from among the integers 1 to 20. If the random number selected is 11, then our systematic sample will contain the elements: 11, $11 + 20 = 31$, $31 + 20 = 51, \ldots$, and so on until we have 30 elements in our sample.

A variant of this rule, which solves the problems that may be encountered when k is not an integer multiple of the sample size, n (their product being N), is to let k be the nearest integer to N/n. We now regard the N elements as being arranged in a circle (with the last element preceding the first element). We randomly select the first element from all N population members and then select every kth item until we have n items in our sample.

The Advantages of Systematic Sampling

In addition to the ease of drawing samples in a systematic way—for example, by simply measuring distances with a ruler in a file cabinet and sampling every fixed number of inches—the method has some statistical advantages as well. First, when $k = N/n$, the sample estimator of the population mean is unbiased. Second, systematic sampling is usually more precise than simple random sampling because it actually stratifies the population into n strata, each stratum containing k elements. Therefore, systematic sampling is approximately as precise as stratified random sampling with one unit per stratum. The difference between the two methods is that the systematic sample is spread more evenly over the entire population than a stratified sample, because in stratified sampling the samples in the strata are drawn separately. This adds precision in some cases. Systematic sampling is also related to cluster sampling in that it amounts to selecting one cluster out of a population of k clusters.

Estimation of the Population Mean in Systematic Sampling

> The systematic sampling estimator of the population mean, μ:
>
> $$\bar{X}_{sy} = \frac{\sum_{i=1}^{n} X_i}{n} \qquad (17\text{–}22)$$

The estimator is, of course, the same as the simple random sampling estimator of the population mean based on a sample of size n. The variance of the estimator in equation 17–22 is difficult to estimate from the results of a single sample. The estimation requires some assumptions about the order of the population. The estimated variances of $\bar{X}_{sy}$ in different situations are given below.

1. When the population values are assumed to be in no particular order with respect to the variable of interest, the estimated variance of the estimator of the mean is the same as in the case of simple random sampling:

$$s^2(\bar{X}_{sy}) = \left(\frac{N - n}{Nn}\right) S^2 \qquad (17\text{–}23)$$

where S^2 is the usual sample variance, and the first term accounts for finite-population correction as well as division by n.

2. When the mean is constant within each stratum of k elements but different from stratum to stratum, the estimated variance of the sample mean is:

$$s^2(\bar{X}_{sy}) = \frac{N - n}{Nn} \frac{\sum\limits_{i=1}^{n} (X_i - X_{i+k})^2}{2(n - 1)} \qquad (17\text{–}24)$$

3. When the population is assumed to be either increasing or decreasing linearly in the variable of interest, and when the sample size is large, the appropriate estimator of the variance of our estimator of the mean is:

$$s^2(\bar{X}_{sy}) = \left(\frac{N - n}{Nn}\right) \frac{\sum\limits_{i=1}^{n} (X_i - 2X_{i+k} + X_{i+2k})^2}{6(n - 2)} \qquad (17\text{–}25)$$

for $1 \leq i \leq n - 2$.

There are formulas that apply in more complicated situations as well.
We demonstrate the use of systematic sampling with the following example.

EXAMPLE (d)

An investor obtains a copy of *The Wall Street Journal* and wants to get a quick estimate of how the New York Stock Market has performed since the previous day. The investor knows that there are about 2,100 stocks listed on the NYSE and wants to look at a quick sample of 100 stocks and determine the average price change for the sample. The investor thus decides on an "every 21st" systematic sampling scheme. The investor uses a ruler and finds that this means that a stock should be selected about every 1.5 inches along the listings columns in the *Journal*. The first stock is randomly selected from among the first 21 stocks listed on the NYSE by using a random-number generator in a calculator. The selected stock is the seventh from the top, which happens to be ANR. For the day in question (January 22, 1987), the price change for ANR is $-1/4$. The next stock to be included in the sample is the one in position $7 + 21 = 28$th from the top. The stock is Aflpb, which on this date had a price change of 0 from the previous day. As mentioned, the selection is not done by counting the stocks, but by the faster method of successively measuring 1.5 inches down the column from each selected stock. The resulting sample of 100 stocks gives a sample mean of $\bar{x}_{sy} = +0.5$ and $s^2 = 0.36$. Give a 95% confidence interval for the average price change of all stocks listed on the NYSE.

SOLUTION

We have absolutely no reason to believe that the order in which the NYSE stocks are listed in *The Wall Street Journal* (i.e., alphabetically) has any relationship to the stocks' price changes. Therefore, the appropriate equation for the estimated variance of $\overline{X}_{sy}$ is equation 17–23. Using this equation, we get:

$$s^2(\overline{X}_{sy}) = \left(\frac{N-n}{Nn}\right)s^2 = \left(\frac{2,100-100}{210,000}\right)0.36 = 0.0034$$

A 95% confidence interval for μ, the average price change on this day for all stocks on the NYSE, is therefore:

$$\overline{x}_{sy} \pm 1.96s(\overline{X}_{sy}) = 0.5 \pm (1.96)(\sqrt{0.0034}) = [0.386, 0.614]$$

The investor may be 95% sure that the average stock on the NYSE gained anywhere from \$0.386 to \$0.614.

When sampling for the population proportion, use the same equations as the ones used for simple random sampling if it may be assumed that no inherent order exists in the population. Otherwise use variance estimators given in advanced texts.

PROBLEMS

17–10. The Bridgestone Corporation maintains strict quality control of its tire production. This entails frequent sampling of tires from large stocks shipped to retailers. Samples of tires are selected and run continuously until they are worn out, and the average number of miles "driven" in the laboratory is noted. Suppose a warehouse contains 11,000 tires arranged in a certain order. The company wants to select a systematic sample of 50 tires to be tested in the laboratory. Use randomization to determine the first item to be sampled, and give the rule for obtaining the rest of the sample in this case.

17–11. A large discount store gives its sales personnel bonuses based on their average sale amount. Since each salesperson makes hundreds of sales each month, the store management decided to base average sale amount for each salesperson on a random sample of the person's sales. Since records of sales are kept in books, it is convenient to use systematic sampling. Suppose a salesperson has made 855 sales over the month, and management wants to choose a sample of 30 sales for estimation of the average amount of all sales. Suggest a way of doing this in such a way that no problems would result due to the fact that 855 is not an integer multiple of 30. Give the first element you choose to select, and explain how the rest of the sample is obtained.

17–12. An accountant always audits the second account and every fourth account thereafter when sampling a client's accounts.

a. Does the accountant use systematic sampling? Explain.

b. Explain the problems that may be encountered when this sampling scheme is used.

17–13. Beer sales in a tavern are cyclical over the week, with large volume during weekend nights, lower volume during the beginning of the week, and somewhat higher volume at midweek. Explain the possible problems that could arise, and the conditions under which they might arise, if systematic sampling were used to estimate beer sales volume per night.

17–14. A population is composed of 100 items arranged in some order. It is known that every stratum of 10 items in the order of arrangement tends to be similar in its values. An "every 10th" systematic sample is selected. The first item, randomly chosen, is the 6th item, and its value is 20. The following items in the sample are, of course, the 16th, the 26th, etc. The values of all items in the systematic sample are as follows: 20, 25, 27, 34, 28, 22, 28, 21, 37, 31. Give a 90% confidence interval for the population mean.

17–15. Explain the relationship between the method employed in problem 17–14 and the method of stratified random sampling. Explain the differences between the two methods.

Answers

17–12

No.
Bias may occur.

17–14.

[24.55, 30.05]

17–6   Other Methods

In addition to the method of two-stage cluster sampling, which was mentioned but not discussed in detail, there are several other advanced sampling methods that are useful in various situations. Two such methods are the *ratio estimator method* and the *regression estimator method*. These methods are useful when, in addition to the variable in which we are interested, we also have information about another variable correlated with it. These two methods make use of the relationship between the two variables to improve our estimation of the mean, or proportion, of the variable of interest. The ratio method is a regression model through the origin. That is, we assume a relationship between x and y of the form $y = Rx$, and knowledge about one of the variables thus improves our estimation of the other variable.

The second model, regression estimator, allows for a more involved relationship between x and y, a relationship of the simple linear regression form: $y = A + Bx$. In Chapter 10, we discussed this model in detail. An application of the theory developed in that chapter in the context of sampling leads to sampling models with increased precision. Ratio and regression estimators are discussed in advanced texts on sampling methodology. Another sampling method worth mentioning is the method of *double sampling*. In this method, a preliminary sample is collected in order to obtain information about an auxiliary variable that is correlated with the variable of interest. This information is then used in a ratio or regression estimation procedure. In addition, a preliminary sample may be drawn in the context of stratified random sampling to establish strata and obtain information about their respective weights. This information is then used in stratified sampling.

17–7   Nonresponse

Nonresponse to sample surveys is one of the most serious problems that occur in practical applications of sampling methodology. The problem is one of loss of information. For example, suppose that a survey questionnaire dealing with some issue is mailed to a randomly chosen sample of 500 people and that only 300 people respond to the survey. The question is: What can you say about the 200 people who did not respond? This is a very important question, and there is no immediate answer to it precisely because the people did not respond; we know nothing about them. Suppose that the questionnaire asks for a yes or no answer to a particular public issue over which people have differing views, and we want to estimate the proportion of people who would respond yes. People may have such strong views about the issue that those who would respond no may refuse to respond altogether. In this case, the 200 nonrespondents to our survey will contain a higher proportion of "no" answers than the 300 responses we have. But, again, we would not know about this. The result will be a bias. How can we compensate for such a possible bias?

We may want to consider the population as made up of two *strata:* the respondents' stratum and the nonrespondents' stratum. In the original survey, we managed to sample only the respondents' stratum, and this caused the bias. What we need to do is to obtain a random sample from the nonrespondents' stratum. This is easier said than done. Still, there are ways we can at least reduce the bias and get some idea about the proportion of "yes" answers in the nonresponse stratum. This entails *callbacks:* returning to the nonrespondents and asking them again. In some mail questionnaires, it is common to send several requests for response, and these reduce the uncertainty. There may, however, be hard-core refusers who just do not want to answer the questionnaire. It is likely that these people have very distinct views about the issue in question, and if you leave them out, there will be a significant bias in your conclusions. In such a situation, it may be useful to gather a small random sample of the hard-core refusers and offer them some monetary reward for their answers. In cases where people may find the question embarrassing or may worry about revealing their personal views, there is the possibility of using a random-response mechanism whereby the respondent randomly answers one of two questions: one is the sensitive question, and the other is an innocuous question of no relevance. The interviewer does not know which question any particular respondent answered but does know the probability of answering the sensitive question. This still allows for computation of the aggregated response to the sensitive question while protecting any given respondent's privacy.

17-8   Summary and Review of Terms

In this chapter, we considered some advanced sampling methods that allow for better precision than simple random sampling, or for lowered costs and easier survey implementation. We concentrated on **stratified random sampling,** the most important and useful of the advanced methods and one that offers statistical advantages of improved precision. We then discussed **cluster sampling** and **systematic sampling,** two methods that are used primarily for their ease of implementation and reduced sampling costs. We mentioned a few other advanced methods, which are described in books devoted to sampling methodology.

ADDITIONAL PROBLEMS

17-16.   Bloomingdale's in New York has the following departments on its mezzanine level: Stendahl, Ralph Lauren, The Beauty Spot, and Lauder Prescriptives. The mezzanine level is managed separately from the other levels, and during the store's post-holiday sale, the level manager wanted to estimate the average sales amount per customer throughout the sale. The following table gives the relative weights of the different departments (known from previous operation of the store), as well as the sample means and variances of the different strata for a total sample of 1,000 customers, proportionally allocated to the four strata. Give a 95% confidence interval for the average sale (in dollars) per customer for the entire level over the period of the post-holiday sale.

Answer

17-16.

[67.207, 68.743]

Stratum	Weight	Sample Mean	Sample Variance
Stendahl	0.25	65.00	123.00
Ralph Lauren	0.35	87.00	211.80
Beauty Spot	0.15	52.00	88.85
Lauder Prescriptives	0.35	38.50	100.40

Note: We assume that shoppers visit the mezzanine level to purchase from only one of its departments. Since the brands and designers are competitors, and since shoppers are known to have a strong brand loyalty in this market, the assumption seems reasonable.

17-17.   A state department of transportation is interested in sampling commuters to determine certain of their characteristics. The department arranges for its field workers to board buses at random, as well as stop private vehicles at intersections and ask the commuters to fill out a short questionnaire. Is this method cluster sampling? Explain.

17-18.   Use systematic sampling to estimate the average performance of all stocks in one of the listed stock exchanges on a given day. Compare your results with those reported in the media for the day in question.

Answers

17–20.
_____

17, 40, 63, 86, 109, 12

17–22.
_____

Stratified r.s.

17–24.
_____

[84.646, 85.754]

17–28.
_____

Poststratification

17–19.   An economist wants to estimate average annual profits for all businesses in a given community and proposes to draw a systematic sample of all businesses listed in the local Yellow Pages. Comment on the proposed methodology. What potential problem do you foresee?

17–20.   In an "every 23d" systematic sampling scheme, the first item was randomly chosen to be the 17th element. Give the numbers of 6 sample items out of a population of 120.

17–21.   A quality-control sampling scheme was carried out by Sony for estimating the percentage of defective radios in a large shipment of 1,000 containers with 100 radios in each container. Twelve containers were chosen at random, and every radio in them was checked. The numbers of defective radios in each of the containers are: 8, 10, 4, 3, 11, 6, 9, 10, 2, 7, 6, 12. Give a 95% confidence interval for the proportion of defective radios in the entire shipment.

17–22.   Suppose that the radios in the 1,000 containers of problem 17–21 were produced in five different factories, each factory known to have different internal production controls. Each container is marked with a number denoting the factory where the radios were made. Suggest an appropriate sampling method in this case, and discuss its advantages.

17–23.   The makers of Taster's Choice® instant coffee want to estimate the proportion of underfilled jars of a given size. The jars are in 14 warehouses around the country, and each warehouse contains crates of cases of jars of coffee. Suggest a sampling method, and discuss it.

17–24.   Cadbury, Inc., is interested in estimating people's responses to a new chocolate. The company believes that people in different age groups differ in their preferences for chocolate. The company believes that in the region of interest, 25% of the population are children, 55% are young adults, and 20% are older people. A proportional allocation of a total random sample of size 1,000 is undertaken, and people's responses on a scale of 0 to 100 are solicited. The results are as follows. For the children, $\bar{x} = 90$ and $s = 5$; for the young adults, $\bar{x} = 82$ and $s = 11$; and for the older people, $\bar{x} = 88$ and $s = 6$. Give a 95% confidence interval for the population average rating for the new chocolate.

17–25.   For problem 17–24, suppose that it costs twice as much money to sample a child compared with the younger and older adults, where costs are the same per sampled person. Use the information in problem 17–24 (the weights and standard deviations) to determine an optimal allocation of the total sample.

17–26.   Refer to the situation in problem 17–24. Suppose that the following relative age frequencies in the population are known.

Age Group	Frequency
under 10	0.10
10 to 15	0.10
16 to 18	0.05
19 to 22	0.05
23 to 25	0.15
26 to 30	0.15
31 to 35	0.10
36 to 40	0.10
41 to 45	0.05
46 to 50	0.05
51 to 55	0.05
56 and over	0.05

Define strata to be used in the survey.

17–27.   Name two sampling methods that are useful when there is information about a variable related to the variable of interest.

17–28.   Suppose that a study was undertaken using a simple random sample from a particular population. When the results of the study became available, it was apparent that the population could be viewed as consisting of several strata. What can be done now?

17–29.   For problem 17–28, suppose that the population is viewed as comprising 18 strata. Is using this number of strata advantageous? Are there any alternative solutions?

17–30.   Discuss and compare the three sampling methods: cluster sampling, stratified sampling, and systematic sampling.

17–31.   The following table reports return on capital for insurance companies.[3] Consider the data a population of U.S. insurance companies, and select a random sample of firms to estimate mean return on capital. Do the sampling two ways: first, as a systematic sample considering the entire list as a uniform, ordered population; and second, use stratified random sampling, the strata being the types of insurance company. Compare your results.

Company	Return on Capital Latest 12 Mos. %	Company	Return on Capital Latest 12 Mos. %	Company	Return on Capital Latest 12 Mos. %
Diversified		**Life & health**		**Property & casualty**	
Marsh & McLennan Cos	25.4	Conseco	13.7	20th Century Inds	25.1
Loews	13.8	First Capital Holding	10.7	Geico	20.4
American Intl Group	14.6	Torchmark	18.4	Argonaut Group	17.1
General Re	17.4	Capital Holding	9.9	Hartford Steam Boiler	19.1
Safeco	11.6	American Family	8.5	Progressive	10.1
Leucadia National	27.0	Kentucky Central Life	6.3	WR Berkley	11.5
CNA Financial	8.6	Provident Life & Acc	13.1	Mercury General	28.3
Aon	12.8	NWNL	8.4	Selective Insurance	13.6
Kemper	1.4	UNUM	13.2	Hanover Insurance	6.3
Cincinnati Financial	10.7	Liberty Corp	10.1	St Paul Cos	16.9
Reliance Group	23.1	Jefferson-Pilot	9.5	Chubb	14.3
Alexander & Alexander	9.9	USLife	6.7	Ohio Casualty	9.3
Zenith National Ins	9.8	American Natl Ins	5.2	First American Finl	4.8
Old Republic Intl	13.4	Monarch Capital	0	Berkshire Hathaway	7.3
Transamerica	7.5	Washington National	1.2	ITT	10.2
Uslico	7.7	Broad	8.0	USF&G	6.6
Aetna Life & Cas	8.0	First Executive	0	Xerox	5.3
American General	8.2	ICH	0	Orion Capital	10.8
Lincoln National	9.2			Fremont General	12.6
Sears, Roebuck	7.2			Foremost Corp of Amer	0
Independent Insurance	7.8			Continental Corp	6.6
Cigna	7.0			Alleghany	9.0
Travelers	0				
American Bankers	8.3				
Unitrin	6.1				

[3] Reproduced by permission from "Annual Report on American Industry," *Forbes* (January 7, 1991), p. 176.

CASE 17

THE BOSTON REDEVELOPMENT AUTHORITY

*T*he Boston Redevelopment Authority is mandated the task of improving and developing urban areas in Boston. One of the Authority's main concerns is with the development of the community of Roxbury. This community has undergone many changes in recent years, and much interest is given to its future development.

Currently, only 2% of the total land in this community is used in industry, and 9% is used commercially. As part of its efforts to develop the community, the Boston Redevelopment Authority is interested in determining the attitudes of the residents of Roxbury toward the development of more business and industry in their region. The authority therefore plans to sample residents of the community to determine their views and use the sample or samples to infer about the views of all residents of the community. Roxbury is divided into 11 planning subdistricts. The population density is believed to be uniform across all 11 subdistricts, and the population of each subdistrict is approximately proportional to the subdistrict's size. There is no known list of all the people in Roxbury. A map of the community is shown in Exhibit 1. Advise the Boston Redevelopment Authority on designing their survey.

EXHIBIT 1   Roxbury Planning Subdistricts

APPENDIX
A

REFERENCES

Books on Data Analysis (Chapter 1):

Chambers, J. M.; W. S. Cleveland; B. Kleiner; and P. A. Tukey. *Graphical Methods for Data Analysis*. Boston: Duxbury Press, 1983. An interesting approach to graphical techniques and EDA using computer-intensive methods. The book requires no mathematical training.

Tukey, J. W. *Exploratory Data Analysis*. Reading, Mass.: Addison-Wesley Publishing, 1977. This is the original EDA book. Some material in our Chapter 1 is based on this text.

Books Primarily about Probability and Random Variables (Chapters 2, 3, 4):

Chung, K. L. *Probability Theory with Stochastic Processes*. New York: Springer-Verlag, 1979. This is a lucidly written book. The approach to the theory of probability is similar to the one used in our text.

Feller, William. *An Introduction to Probability Theory and Its Applications*. Vol. 1, 3rd ed.; vol. 2, 2nd ed. New York: John Wiley & Sons, 1968, 1971. This is a classic textbook in probability theory. Volume 1 should be understandable to a reader of our text. Volume 2, which deals with continuous probability models, is more difficult and requires considerable mathematical ability.

Loève, Michel. *Probability Theory*. 4th ed. New York: Springer-Verlag, 1977. This is a mathematically demanding classic text in probability (an understanding of mathematical analysis is required).

Ross, Sheldon M. *A First Course in Probability*. 3rd ed. New York: Macmillan, 1988. An intuitive introduction to probability that requires a knowledge of calculus.

Ross, Sheldon M. *Introduction to Probability Models*. 4th ed. New York: Academic Press, 1989. A very intuitive introduction to probability theory that is consistent with the development in our text.

Statistical Theory and Sampling (Chapters 5, 6, 7, 8, and 17):

Cochran, William G. *Sampling Techniques*. 3rd ed. New York: John Wiley & Sons, 1977. This is a classic text on sampling methodology. Much of the material in our Chapter 17 draws on the results in this book.

Cox, D. R., and D. V. Hinkley. *Theoretical Statistics*. London: Chapman and Hall, 1974. A thorough discussion of the theory of statistics.

Fisher, Sir Ronald A. *The Design of Experiments*. 7th ed. Edinburgh: Oliver and Boyd, 1960. A classic treatise on statistical inference.

Fisher, Sir Ronald A. *Statistical Methods for Research Workers*. Edinburgh: Oliver and Boyd, 1941.

Hogg, R. V., and A. T. Craig. *Introduction to Mathematical Statistics*. 4th ed. New York: Macmillan, 1978. A good introduction to mathematical statistics that re-quires an understanding of calculus.

Kendall, M. G., and A. Stuart. *The Advanced Theory of Statistics*. Vol. 1, 2nd ed.; vols. 2, 3. London: Charles W. Griffin, 1963, 1961, 1966.

Mood, A. M.; F. A. Graybill; and D. C. Boes. *Introduction to the Theory of Statistics*. 3rd ed. New York: McGraw-Hill, 1974.

Rao, C. R. *Linear Statistical Inference and Its Applications*. 2nd ed. New York: John Wiley & Sons, 1973. This is a classic book on statistical inference that provides in-depth coverage of topics ranging from probability to analysis of variance, regression analysis, and multivariate methods. This book contains theoretical results that are the basis of statistical inference. The book requires advanced mathematical ability.

Books Primarily about Experimental Design, Analysis of Variance, Regression Analysis, and Econometrics (Chapters 9, 10, and 11):

Chatterjee, S., and B. Price. *Regression Analysis by Example*. 2nd ed. New York: John Wiley & Sons, 1991.

Cochran, W. G., and G. M. Cox. *Experimental Designs*. 2nd ed. New York: John Wiley & Sons, 1957.

Draper, N. R., and H. Smith. *Applied Regression Analysis*. 2nd ed. New York: John Wiley & Sons, 1981. A thorough text on regression analysis that requires an understanding of matrix algebra.

Johnston, J. *Econometric Methods.* 3rd ed. New York: McGraw-Hill, 1984. A good, comprehensive introduction to econometric models and regression analysis at a somewhat higher level than that of our text.

Judge, G. R.; C. Hill; W. Griffiths; H. Lutkepohl; and T. Lee. *Introduction to the Theory and Practice of Econometrics.* New York: John Wiley & Sons, 1982.

Montgomery, D. C., and E. A. Peck. *Introduction to Linear Regression Analysis.* 2nd ed. New York: John Wiley & Sons, 1992. A very readable book on regression analysis that is recommended for further reading after our Chapter 11.

Neter, J.; W. Wasserman; and M. H. Kutner. *Applied Linear Regression Models.* 2nd ed. Homewood, Ill.: Richard D. Irwin, 1989. A good introduction to regression analysis.

Neter, J.; W. Wasserman; and M. H. Kutner. *Applied Linear Statistical Models.* 3rd ed. Homewood, Ill.: Richard D. Irwin, 1990. A good introduction to regression and analysis of variance that requires no advanced mathematics.

Scheffé, H. *The Analysis of Variance.* New York: John Wiley & Sons, 1959. This is a classic text on analysis of variance that requires advanced mathematical ability.

Seber, G. A. F. *Linear Regression Analysis.* New York: John Wiley and Sons, 1977. An advanced book on regression analysis. Some of the results in this book are used in our Chapter 11.

Snedecor, George W., and William G. Cochran. *Statistical Methods.* 7th ed. Ames: Iowa State University Press, 1980. This well-known book is an excellent introduction to analysis of variance and experimental design, as well as regression analysis. The book is very readable and requires no advanced mathematics.

Weisberg, S. *Applied Linear Regression.* 2nd ed. New York: John Wiley & Sons, 1985. A good introduction to regression analysis.

Books on Forecasting (Chapter 12):

Abraham, B., and J. Ledolter. *Statistical Methods for Forecasting.* New York: John Wiley & Sons, 1983. This is an excellent book on forecasting methods.

Armstrong, S. *Long-Range Forecasting.* 2nd ed. New York: John Wiley & Sons, 1985.

Granger, C. W. J., and P. Newbold. *Forecasting Economic Time Series.* 2nd ed. New York: Academic Press, 1986. A good introduction to forecasting models.

Books on Quality Control (Chapter 13):

Duncan, A. J. *Quality Control and Industrial Statistics.* 5th ed. Homewood, Ill.: Richard D. Irwin, 1986.

Gitlow, H.; S. Gitlow; A. Oppenheim; and R. Oppenheim. *Tools and Methods for the Improvement of Quality.* Homewood, Ill.: Richard D. Irwin, 1989.

Ott, E. R., and E. G. Schilling. *Process Quality Control.* 2nd ed. New York: McGraw-Hill, 1990.

Ryan, T. P. *Statistical Methods for Quality Improvement.* New York: John Wiley & Sons, 1989. Much of the material in our Chapter 13 is inspired by the approach in this book.

Books on Nonparametric Methods (Chapter 14):

Conover, W. J. *Practical Nonparametric Statistics.* 2nd ed. New York: John Wiley & Sons, 1980. This is an excellent, readable textbook covering a wide range of nonparametric methods. Much of the material in our Chapter 14 is based on results in this book.

Hollander, M., and D. A. Wolfe. *Nonparametric Statistical Methods.* New York: John Wiley & Sons, 1973.

Siegel, S. *Nonparametric Statistics for the Behavioral Sciences.* 2nd ed. New York: McGraw-Hill, 1988.

Books on Subjective Probability, Bayesian Statistics, and Decision Analysis (Chapter 15 and Chapter 2):

Berger, James O. *Statistical Decision Theory and Bayesian Analysis.* 2nd ed. New York: Springer-Verlag, 1985. A comprehensive book on Bayesian methods at an advanced level.

de Finetti, Bruno. *Probability, Induction, and Statistics.* New York: John Wiley & Sons, 1972. This excellent book on subjective probability and the Bayesian philosophy is the source of the de Finetti game in our Chapter 15. The book is readable at about the level of our text.

de Finetti, Bruno. *Theory of Probability.* Vols. 1 and 2. New York: John Wiley & Sons, 1974, 1975. An excellent introduction to subjective probability and the Bayesian approach by one of its pioneers.

DeGroot, M. H. *Optimal Statistical Decisions.* New York: McGraw-Hill, 1970.

Good, I. J. *Good Thinking: The Foundations of Probability and Its Applications.* Minneapolis: University of Minnesota Press, 1983.

Jeffreys, Sir Harold. *Theory of Probability.* 3rd rev. ed. London: Oxford University Press, 1983. First published in 1939, this book truly came before its time. The book explains the Bayesian philosophy of science and its application in probability and statistics. It is readable and thought-provoking and is highly recommended for anyone with an interest in the ideas underlying Bayesian inference.

Books on Multivariate Analysis (Chapter 16):

Anderson, T. W. *An Introduction to Multivariate Statistical Analysis*. 2nd ed. New York: John Wiley & Sons, 1984. First published in 1958, this advanced book contains much of the theory underlying the more commonly used multivariate methods.

Morrison, Donald F. *Multivariate Statistical Methods*. 3rd ed. New York: McGraw-Hill, 1990. This is an applied text explaining some of the more important multivariate techniques and illustrating their use with many examples.

Norusis, M. *Advanced Statistics Guide SPSS*. Chicago, Ill.: SPSS, 1990. This is an excellent introduction to the use of multivariate statistics and other advanced statistical techniques from a computer-user point of view. The book contains detailed examples of how to carry out a multivariate analysis using the SPSS package.

Tatsuoka, M. M. *Multivariate Analysis*. 2nd ed. New York: Macmillan, 1987. This is an excellent book on the theory of multivariate analysis that requires a knowledge of matrix algebra. Much of the material in our Chapter 16 is based on results in this book.

ANSWERS TO MOST ODD-NUMBERED PROBLEMS

APPENDIX

B

NOTE: Many of the answers are obtained using a linear interpolation.

Chapter 1

1–1 LQ = 121, MQ = 128, UQ = 133.5, 10th percentile = 114.8, 15th percentile = 118.1, 65th percentile = 131.1, IQR = 12.5.

1–3 Median = 70, 20th percentile = 45, 30th percentile = 53.8, 60th percentile = 76.8, 90th percentile = 89.4.

1–5 Median = 51, LQ = 30.5, UQ = 194.25, IQR = 163.75, 45th percentile = 42.2.

1–7 Mean = 126.63, median = 128, modes = 128, 134, 136.

1–9 Mean = 66.954, median = 70, mode = 45.

1–11 Mean = 199.875, median = 51, mode = none.

1–15 Range = 27, variance = 57.74, standard deviation = 7.599 (assume a sample).

1–17 Range = 60, variance = 321.38, standard deviation = 17.93.

1–19 Range = 1186, variance = 110,287.75, standard deviation = 332.096

1–21 Mean = 73.78, modal class: 71–80, median class: 71–80, standard deviation = 15. Relative frequencies: 0.09, 0.12, 0.17, 0.28, 0.19, 0.15.

1–23 Mean = 3.54, standard deviation = 0.77. Modal class: 3.1–3.5.

1–55 A: $\bar{x}$ = 965.67, s = 21.08, CV = 0.0218.
B: $\bar{x}$ = 147.08, s = 25.98, CV = 0.177.

1–61 Mean = 504.69, standard deviation = 94.55.

1–65 80th percentile = 20.6, IQR = 12.25.

1–67 Modal class: 35,000–39,999, mean = 38,760.87, standard deviation = 7,003.87.

1–75 In order of table appearance:

Range	s^2	s
79.6	409.25	20.23
8.9	10.63	3.26
19.5	33.87	5.82
10.5	7.08	2.66
6.6	8.76	2.96
35.4	225.30	15.01
35.3	160.78	12.68
23.9	61.78	7.86
48.8	186.32	13.65

1–77 Mean = 19.23, median = 15.6, modes are 10.3, 14.5, and 16.8, range = 81.6, standard deviation = 13.12, Q1 = 12.6, Q3 = 22.9, 10th percentile = 7.4, 90th percentile = 39.3

1–79 s^2 = 0.0299, s = 0.1729.

Chapter 2

2–1 Objective and subjective.

2–5 R ∪ T: exposed to radio or television ad. R ∩ T: exposed to both radio and television ads.

2–7 39/28,000,000.

2–9 2/3.

2–11 0.99.

2–13 0.6, 0.1.

2–15 0.49.

2–17 1/3.

2–19 0.791.

2–21 $\overline{A \cup B \cup C} = \overline{A} \cap \overline{B} \cap \overline{C}$.

2–23 0.75.

2–25 0.000246.

2–27 0.6.

2–29
a. 0.100.
b. 0.206.
c. 0.590; mutually exclusive events.
d. 0.144.
e. 0.451.
f. 0.571.
g. 0.168.
h. 0.454.
i. 0.569.

2–31 0.4.

2–33
a. 3/10.
b. 3/10.
c. 2/3.
d. 1/3.

2–35 0.138 ≠ 0.2202; therefore, the events are not independent.

2–37 Yes; 0.2 × 0.3 = 6%.

2–39 0.814.

2–41 1/(1,600 × 146,000).

2–43 0.522.

2–45 0.267.

2–49 One executive calls both flips. If he gets both right or both wrong, he attends the meeting, otherwise the other one goes.

2–51 450,450.

2–53 259,459,200.

2–55 21.

2–57 1/1,947,792.

2–59 1/12,271,512.

2–61 0.545.

2–63 0.37.

2–65 0.8809.

2–67 0.1602.

2–69 0.85.

2–71 1/3.

2–73 0.0248.

2–75 0.60.

2–77 0.666.

2–79 0.18.

2–81 0.7254.

2–83 51% of the people.

2–85 0.524.

2–87 0.41.

2–89 0.0715.

2–91 0.811.

2–93 0.203.

2–95 0.551.

2–97 Yes; 0.770.

2–99 $1 - 1/2^{n-1}$

Chapter 3

3–1 a. $\Sigma P(x) = 1.00$.
  b. x: 0   1   2
     $F(x)$: 0.3 0.5 0.7
     x: 3   4   5
     $F(x)$: 0.8 0.9 1.00
  c. $P(X > 2) = 1 - F(2)$
     $= 0.3$.

3–3 a. $\Sigma P(x) = 1.00$.
  b. x: 0   10
     $F(x)$: 0.10 0.30
     x: 20   30
     $F(x)$: 0.65 0.85
     x: 40   50
     $F(x)$: 0.95 1.00
  c. $P(X > 20) = 1 - F(20)$
     $= 0.35$.

3–5 | x | $P(x)$ | $F(x)$ |
|---|---|---|
| 2 | 1/36 | 1/36 |
| 3 | 2/36 | 3/36 |
| 4 | 3/36 | 6/36 |
| 5 | 4/36 | 10/36 |
| 6 | 5/36 | 15/36 |
| 7 | 6/36 | 21/36 |
| 8 | 5/36 | 26/36 |
| 9 | 4/36 | 30/36 |
| 10 | 3/36 | 33/36 |
| 11 | 2/36 | 35/36 |
| 12 | 1/36 | 36/36 |

3–7 a. $P(4 \leq X \leq 7) = P(4)$
     $+ P(5) + P(6) + P(7)$
     $= 0.55$.
  b. x: 2   3
     $F(x)$: 0.2 0.4
     x: 4   5
     $F(x)$: 0.7 0.8
     x: 6   7   8
     $F(x)$: 0.9 0.95 1.00
  c. $P(X \leq 6) = F(6) = 0.9$.
  d. $P(3 < X \leq 6) = F(6)$
     $- F(3) = 0.9 - 0.4$
     $= 0.5$.

3–9 b. 0.5
  c. | x | $F(x)$ |
|---|---|
| 9 | 0.05 |
| 10 | 0.20 |
| 11 | 0.50 |
| 12 | 0.70 |
| 13 | 0.85 |
| 14 | 0.95 |
| 15 | 1.00 |

3–11 Mean = 3.19, variance = 2.214, standard deviation = 1.488.

3–13 Mean = 2.8, variance = 2.16, standard deviation = 1.47.

3–15 $E(X) = 2.2$, $P(X > E(X))$
       $= P(3) + P(4) + P(5)$
       $= 0.3$.

3–17 By Chebyshev's theorem, the probability is at least 0.9375.

3–19 Stock Y is riskier because $V(Y) > V(X)$, while $E(X)$ is close to $E(Y)$.

3–21 Raise by amount
       $E(X) = (0)P(\text{No claim}) +$
       $(600)P(\text{Claim}) = 0 +$
       $600(0.005) = \$3$.

3–23 $E(\text{Cost}) = \$465.85$.

3–29 a. Random sampling from a large population.
  b. 0.2373. Use the method of Chapter 1.
  c. s: 0   1
     $P(s)$: 0.0010 0.0146
     s: 2   3
     $P(s)$: 0.0879 0.2637
     s: 4   5
     $P(s)$: 0.3955 0.2373
  d. 0.9990, using Chapter 1.
  e. 0.2637.
  f. 0.1035.
  g. 3.75.
  h. 0.9375.

3–31 Binomial, if sales calls are independent of each other.

3–33 Not binomial, because members of the same family are not independent of each other (genetically and behaviorally).

3–35 $P(\text{at least } 5) = 0.0328$, $P(\text{at most } 2) = 0.6778$.

3–37 0.794.

3–39 0.033.

3–41 $P(0) = 0.905$.
       $P(1) = 0.0905$.
       $P(2) = 0.00452$.
       $P(3) = 0.000151$.

3–43 0.148.

3–45 0.953.

3–47 0.197.

3–53 a. A triangle with base 0–2 and height at right angle on right equal to 1.
  b. Area under $f(x) =$ (base)(height)/2 = 1.00.
  c. Area of triangle from 0 to 1, which is $(1)(1/2)/2 = 0.25$.

3–55 2/7.

3–57 0.4375.

3–61 b. x: 0   1   2
     $F(x)$: 0.05 0.10 0.20
     x: 3   4   5
     $F(x)$: 0.35 0.55 0.70
     x: 6   7   8
     $F(x)$: 0.85 0.95 1.00
  c. 0.65.

d. 0.70.

e. 4.25.

f. Variance = 4.188, standard deviation = 2.046.

g. [0.157, 8.343].

3-63 *a.* Binomial, $n = 52$, $p = 0.1$.

b. 5.2.

3-65 Expected value = \$1,130. Standard deviation = 1,874.46.

3-67 *a.* Cars independent of each other.

b.

x:	0	1
P(x):	0.599	0.315

x:	2	3
P(x):	0.075	0.011

x:	4	5 or more
P(x):	0.011	≤ 0.0001

c. 0.086.

d. 0.5 car.

3-71 *c.* 0.75.

3-73 0.995.

3-77 *a.* 0.222.

b. 23.889.

3-79 *a.* 0.31.

b. 10.980.

c. 1.233.

Chapter 4

4-1 0.6826, 0.95, 0.9802, 0.9951, 0.9974.

4-3 0.1828.

4-5 0.0215.

4-7 0.9901.

4-9 A number very close to zero.

4-11 0.9544.

4-13 Not likely; probability = 0.00003.

4-15 $z = 0.19$.

4-17 $z = 0.583$.

4-19 $z = 1.96$ and -1.96.

4-21 0.0164.

4-23 0.927.

4-25 0.003.

4-27 0.8609, 0.2107, 0.8306.

4-29 0.0931.

4-31 0.121, 0.0037, less than

0.00003—do not believe claim.

4-33 126.6.

4-35 20,321.6.

4-37 13.94 and 50.06.

4-39 103.5.

4-41 \$30,185.

4-43 9.65 and 12.75.

4-45 [303.88, 496.13].

4-47 0.423.

4-49 13,155.8.

4-51 Mean = 5.83, standard deviation = 2.41.

4-53 5,224.92.

4-55 2.138.

4-57 Assume independence of parties arriving for dinner. Using binomial: 0.2375. Using normal approximation: 0.2321.

4-59 0.9922.

4-61 Assume independence of students. 0.0738.

4-63 Very close to 0.

4-65 0.4013, 0.5808, 0.0228.

4-67 0.0228, 0.9772, 0.9088, 0.5394. Limitation: stock prices are very discrete.

4-69 \$6.39.

4-71 [42,275, 57,725].

4-73 10.4125%, 13.7875%

4-75 10.22.

4-77 Mean = 666,523.4, standard deviation = 35,528.6.

4-79 Mean = 650, standard deviation = 273.44.

4-81 37,153 papers.

4-83 Greater than 0.999.

4-85 23.92, so set warranty at 24 months.

4-87 0.242.

4-89 \$741,272.

4-91 Very close to 1.

Chapter 5

5-3 0.4166.

5-5 0.75, \$4,276,250.

5-13 $E(\bar{X}) = \mu = 125$, $\mathrm{SE}(\bar{X}) = \sigma/\sqrt{n} = 8.944$.

5-15 When the distribution of the population is unknown.

5-17 Binomial. Cannot use normal approximation because $np = 1.2$.

5-19 0.075.

5-21 0.999.

5-23 0.2308.

5-25 0.0016.

5-27 0.0502.

5-29 0.0552.

5-31 A generous budget means we can get a large sample; a consistent estimator is good, as its probability of being close to the parameter increases with the sample size.

5-37 df = $n - 2$ because there are two restrictions: intercept and slope.

5-39 Yes, can solve an equation for the missing check.

5-41 $E(\bar{X}) = 1,065, V(\bar{X}) = 2,500$.

5-43 $E(\bar{X}) = 53$, $\mathrm{SE}(\bar{X}) = 0.5$.

5-45 $E(\hat{P}) = 0.2, \mathrm{SE}(\hat{P}) = 0.042$.

5-47 When the population is highly skewed, the central limit theorem does not apply unless the sample size is very large. Solve by taking a very large sample.

5-49 0.9544.

5-51 $P(Z < -12.88)$, which is a very small number. Therefore, do not believe the claim.

5-57 0.1727.

5-59 0.0499.

5-61 0.9503.

5-63 No minimum ($n = 1$ will do for normality).

5-65 This estimator is consistent, and is more efficient than $\bar{X}$ because: $\sigma^2/n^2 < \sigma^2/n$. Since both are unbiased, use the new estimator.

5–67 Relative minimum sample sizes: $n_a < n_b < n_d < n_e < n_c$.

5–69 Conduct a simulation: draw repeated samples using a computer, and determine the distribution empirically.

5–71 $P(Z < -5) = 0.0000003$. Not probable.

5–73 0.923.

Chapter 6

6–5 [86,978.12, 92,368.12] dollars.

6–7 [31.1, 32.9] mpg.

6–9 [9.05, 9.55] percent.

6–11 All values in the 99% confidence interval are above 245, so the manager may be 99% confident that the average number of documents transmitted is over 245.

6–13 95%: [136.99, 156.51], 90%: [138.56, 154.94], 99%: [133.93, 159.57].

6–15 [9.263, 9.337].

6–17 8.393.

6–19 95%: [15,684.37, 17,375.63], 99%: [15,418.6, 17,641.4].

6–21 [27.93, 33.19] thousand miles.

6–23 [72.599, 89.881].

6–25 [29.87, 59.33] dollars.

6–27 [2.34, 2.86] days.

6–29 [93.75, 108.71] sales.

6–31 [15.86, 17.14] dollars.

6–33 [5.44, 7.96] years.

6–35 [55.85, 67.48] containers.

6–37 [9.074, 10.660].

6–39 [0.158, 0.309].

6–41 [0.710, 0.790].

6–43 [0.120, 0.178].

6–45 [0.431, 0.569].

6–47 [0.038, 0.270].

6–49 [0.536, 0.623].

6–51 [0.500, 0.680].

6–53 [625.92, 670.72].

6–55 [0.459, 0.603].

6–57 [0.058, 0.182].

6–61 [4.74, 16.34].

6–63 [869.77, 1,788.94].

6–65 [200.58, 1,412.95].

6–67 [0.093, 0.341].

6–69 271.

6–71 39.

6–73 131.

6–75 865.

6–77 0.209.

6–79 0.0997.

6–81 $15,477.75.

6–83 0.283.

6–85 [8.883, 13.757] million dollars.

6–87 96.

6–89 [619,948.5, 1,305,649.1].

6–91 [0.189, 0.351].

6–93 [5.625, 26.102].

6–95 [2.279, 2.721].

6–97 [−0.000376, 0.00538]. Lower bound is really 0.

6–99 [339,817.73, 372,342.27].

6–101 [4.145, 15.291].

6–103 Normal population distribution.

6–107 50%

Chapter 7

7–1 $z = -2.575$. Reject H_0 almost at $\alpha = 0.01$. Average mpg is different.

7–3 $z = -19.72$. Reject H_0 very strongly (p-value is very small).

7–5 $z = -1.456$. Accept H_0 (p-value = 0.1454)

7–7 $t_{19} = 8.944$. Reject H_0.

7–9 $t_{11} = 2.617-$ Reject H_0.

7–11 $t_{24} = 2.25$. Reject H_0 at $\alpha = .05$, accept at $\alpha = .01$.

7–13 Normal population distribution.

7–15 $t_{27} = 0.248$. Accept H_0.

7–17 $z = -1.037$. Accept H_0.

7–19 $z = 2.653$. Reject H_0 at both levels.

7–23 $t_{18} = -8.97$. Reject H_0; ad is probably false.

7–25 $z = 5.354$. Reject H_0.

7–27 $z = 2.44$. Reject H_0.

7–29 $t_9 = -1.581$. Accept H_0 (claim not rejected).

7–31 Since $\hat{p} = 0.12 > 0.11 = p$, accept H_0 that the unemployment rate has not decreased.

7–33 $z = 6.708$. Reject H_0.

7–35 Since $\bar{x} = 33.8 < 35 = \mu_0$, accept H_0 that the true mean $\mu_0 \leq 35$. The fund's claim would only be unsupportable if $\mu_0 > 35$.

7–37 $z = -2.582$. Reject H_0 at $\alpha = 0.01$ (p-value = 0.0098). The proportion has probably decreased.

7–39 $z = 3.016$. Reject H_0 (p-value = 0.0026).

7–41 p-value is $P(z < -3.05) = 0.0011$. Reject H_0 at levels as low as 0.0011.

7–45 $z = 51.02$. Reject H_0, p-value very close to 0. z is still very large even without the finite population correction.

7–47 $z = -0.898$. Accept H_0 (p-value: 0.185).

7–49 $X^2_{24} = 47.04$. Reject H_0 (p-value < 0.005).

7–51 $X^2_{299} = 306.9$. Accept H_0.

7–53 0.909.

7–55 Power at $\mu_1 = 60$ is 0.984.

7–57 1,241.

7–59 737.

7–61 591.

7–65 $z = 8.0$. Reject H_0 (p-value very close to 0).

7–77 $z = -5.0$. Reject H_0 (p-value very close to 0).

7–79 *a.* 14.
b. Reject (p-value very close to 0).

7–81 Two-tailed test. $z = 2.07$. Reject H_0 (p-value: 0.038).

7–83 $z = 4.25$. Reject H_0 (p-value very close to 0).

7–87 $z = -4.86$. Reject H_0 (p-value very close to 0). Power for $p_1 = 4\%$ is 0.521.

7–89 $X_{24}^2 = 26.92$. Accept H_0 (p-value > 0.10).

7–91 $z = -5.33$. Reject H_0 (p-value very close to 0).

7–93 $z = 1.705$. Reject H_0 (p-value = 0.0441).

7–95 $t_{13} = -3.987-$ Reject H_0 (p-value < 0.005).

7–97 $z = 2.53$. Reject H_0 (p-value = 0.0057).

7–99 $t_{17} = 2.828$. Reject H_0 (p-value is between 0.01 and 0.005).

7–101 $z = -4.896$. Reject H_0 (p-value is very small).

7–103 p-values (in order): 0.4592, 0.968, 0.8026, less than 0.0004, 0.0818. Only form is significant at $\alpha = 0.05$.

7–105 Left-hand test of H_0: $p_0 \geq 0.25$ gives $z = -0.146$, p-value = 0.442. Accept H_0 at any level.

Chapter 8

8–1 $t_{24} = 3.11$. Reject H_0 (p-value < 0.01).

8–3 $t_{11} = 2.034$. Must accept H_0 at $\alpha = 0.05$.

8–5 $t_{14} = 1.469$. Must accept H_0 at $\alpha = 0.05$.

8–7 Power = $P(Z > 1.55)$ = 0.0606.

8–9 $z = -3.13$. Reject H_0.

8–11 $z = 3.3$. Reject H_0.

8–13 $z = 4.24$. Reject H_0.

8–15 *a.* One-tailed: H_0: $\mu_1 - \mu_2 \leq 0$.
b. $z = 1.53$.
c. Accept H_0 at the 0.05 significance level.
d. 0.063.
e. $t_{19} = 0.846$. Accept H_0.

8–17 [2.416%, 2.664%]

8–19 $t_{26} = 1.132$. Accept H_0 (p-value > 0.10).

8–21 $z = 8.24$. Reject H_0 (p-value is very small).

8–23 $t_{13} = 1.164$. Accept H_0 (p-value > 0.10).

8–25 $z = 2.785$. Reject H_0 (p-value: 0.0026).

8–27 $t_{28} = 5.136$. Reject H_0 of equal lending (p-value close to 0).

8–29 $z = 2.835$. Reject H_0 of no effect on on-time rate (p-value: 0.0023).

8–31 $z = -0.228$. Accept H_0 of equal success.

8–33 [0.0419, 0.0781].

8–35 $z = 1.601$. Accept H_0 at $\alpha = 0.05$ (p-value: 0.0547).

8–37 [-0.027, 0.033].

8–39 $z = 5.33$. Reject H_0 (p-value very close to 0).

8–41 $F_{(17, 11)} = 2.16$. Accept H_0 at $\alpha = 0.10$.

8–43 $F_{(27, 20)} = 1.838$. Accept H_0 at $\alpha = 0.10$. [0.652, 4.837].

8–45 $F_{(24, 24)} = 1.538$. Accept H_0 at $\alpha = 0.01$.

8–49 [-3.478, 0.680].

8–51 [2.387, 6.933].

8–53 [-812.9, 1,372.9].

8–55 $z = 1.447$. Accept H_0 of equal success (p-value: 0.148).

8–57 $t_{22} = 2.719$. Reject H_0 at $\alpha = 0.02$ (p-value > 0.01, < 0.02).

8–59 $z = 4.126$. Reject H_0 (that the cat was not better known) (p-value very close to 0).

8–61 $t_{26} = 2.479$. Reject H_0 of equal results (p-value: 0.02).

8–63 $t_{29} = 1.08$. Accept H_0 of no effect.

8–65 Since $s_1^2 < s_2^2$, accept H_0.

8–67 $t_{15} = -0.975$. Accept H_0 of equal ratings.

8–69 [0.0366, 0.1474].

8–71 $F_{(24, 17)} = 1.453$. Accept H_0 at $\alpha = 0.10$.

8–73 [-0.0413, 0.7254].

8–75 t-test for H_0: $\mu_1 \leq \mu_2$ of two independent samples of sizes 16, 17. H_0 is accepted, p-value is 0.85.

Chapter 9

9–1 H_0: All four means are equal. H_1: All four means are different; three are equal and one is different; two are equal and two are different; two are equal and the other two are equal.

9–3 Series of paired tests are dependent on each other. There is no control on the overall probability of a type I error.

9–5 $F_{3,176} = 12.53$. Reject H_0 (p-value < 0.01).

9–7 The sum of all the deviations from a mean is zero.

9–11 Both MSTR and MSE are sample statistics given to natural variation about their means.

9–15 Example: let
SST = 10,500,
SSTR = 10,000,
SSE = 500, $n = 106$, $r = 6$.
$10{,}000 + 500 = 10{,}500$,
but MSTR + MSE = 100 + 100 ≠ 100.

9–19

Source	df	SS	MS	F
Treatment	3	0.1152	0.0384	1.47
Error	28	0.7315	0.0261	
Total	31	0.8467		

Critical point for $F_{3,28}$ at $\alpha = 0.10$ is 2.29, so we must accept H_0. There is no evidence of differences in the average price in the populations.

9–21

Source	df	SS	MS	F
Treatment	2	272.6	136.3	7.82
Error	82	1429.2	17.4	
Total	84	1701.8		

Reject H_0 (p-value < 0.01). The average time to reach a decision is probably not the same for all three copying machines.

9–23 $F_{7,792} = 108.5$. Reject H_0 (p-value is very small).

9–25 $T = 4.738$. The mean for squares is significantly greater than that for the circles and triangles. No significant difference in the means of the circles and triangles.

9–27 $T = 0.22$. No differences are significant, as expected from the solution of problem 9–19.

9–29 $T = 3.85$. The mean for Zenith is significantly greater than all others; Sylvania, Philco, Sears, and RCA are next, not significantly different from one another; then comes Panasonic, different from them; and finally come GE and Magnavox, not significantly different from each other.

9–31 No. The three prototypes were not randomly chosen from a population of proto- types.

9–33 Fly all three planes on the same routes.

9–37 Random-effects model if the locations and the artists are randomly chosen from some populations.

9–41 Reject H_0 of no interaction, p-value < 0.01.

9–43 Network: $F_{2,441} = 5.16$; news time: $F_{2,441} = 5.69$; interac- tions: $F_{4,441} = 4.27$. At $\alpha = 0.01$, there exist network main effects when averaged over levels of news time; there exist news time main effects when averaged over levels of network; there exist interactions between levels of network and news time.

9–45
a. Explained = treatment = factor A + factor B + (AB).
b. $a = 3$.
c. $b = 2$.
d. $N = 150$.
e. $n = 25$.
f. There are no significant exercise price main ef- fects.
g. At $\alpha = 0.05$, there are time of expiration main effects, but not at $\alpha = 0.01$.
h. There are no significant interactions.
i. Some evidence for time of expiration main effects; no evidence for exercise price main effects and interactions.
j. For time of expiration, p-value is between 0.01 and 0.05. For the other two tests, p-value is very high.
k. Could use the t distribu- tion with 144 degrees of freedom (practically a normal distribution) be- cause F with 1 degree of freedom for the numera- tor is the same as a t random variable squared: $t_{144}^2 = F_{1,144}$.

9–47 Advantages: reduced experi- mental error and efficient use of a small sample. Dis- advantages: must have r = number of columns = number of rows, and the test may be weak due to a small sample size.

9–49 Use a repeated measures de- sign: have every person eval- uate all three copying ma- chines.

9–51 Use repeated measures: have every person evaluate all eight television brands.

9–53 We must assume no block- factor interactions.

9–55 $F_{3,207} = 61.7$. Reject H_0 (p-value is very small).

9–57 $F_{2,2} = 9.58$. Must accept H_0.

9–59 Every person is a block.

9–61 $F_{3,137} = 3.67$. p-value is be- tween 0.01 and 0.05. There is some evidence that not all names are equally liked.

9–63 Software: $F_{2,708} = 63.25$; computer: $F_{3,708} = 29.60$; interactions: $F_{6,708} = 24.09$. All are significant.

9–65 Only the factors with p-value ≤ 0.05 are significant.

9–67 $F_{2,72} = 4.547$. p-value (using a computer) $= 0.0138$. At $\alpha = 0.05$, only the drug group and the no-treatment group are significantly differ- ent from each other.

9–69 One-way ANOVA give $F = 22.21$, so reject H_0 of three equal means (p-value < 0.001). Using Tukey cri- terion at $\alpha = 0.01$, reject H_0: $\bar{x}_{GI} = \bar{x}_z$ and reject H_0: $\bar{x}_p = \bar{x}_z$, but accept H_0: $\bar{x}_{GI} = \bar{x}_p$.

9–71 $F_{2,2} = 6.88$. Must accept H_0.

9–73 $F_{(1,310)} \doteq F_{(1,00)}$, so reject H_0 of equal means at $\alpha = 0.05$.

9–77 Two-way ANOVA with 3 lev- els of factor "store," 2 levels of factor "size," using 3 sam- ple points in each cell. F ratios not shown, but only main "store" effect is signifi- cant.

Chapter 10

10–11 $b_1 = 1.35$, $b_0 = -0.835$.

10–13 $b_1 = 0.287$, $b_0 = -0.104$.

10–15 $b_1 = 2.11$, $b_0 = -22.28$.

10–17 $b_0 = 0.00170$, $b_1 = 1.204$.

10–19 [1.116, 1.395].

10–21 $s(b_0) = 0.538$, $s(b_1) = 0.084$.

10–23 [0.106, 0.488].

10–27 0.976.

10–29 $t_9 = 7.53$. Reject H_0 of zero correlation (p-value very close to 0).

10–31 $t_8 = 5.11$. Reject H_0 of zero correlation.

10–35 $z = 1.297$. Accept H_0.

10–37 $t_{11} = 0.0378$. Accept H_0; no evidence of a linear relationship at any α.

10–39 $t_{11} = 11.69$. Reject H_0 of no linear relationship.

10–41 $t_{58} = 5.90$. Reject H_0 of no linear relationship.

10–43 $t_{211} = z = 0.0565$. Accept H_0 of no linear relationship.

10–45 No, since there is no evidence of a linear relationship.

10–47 95.117%.

10–49 $r^2 = 0.8636$.

10–51 No linear relations in evidence for any of the firms.

10–55 $F_{(1,13)} = 256.3$. p-value is very close to 0.

10–57 $F_{(1,9)} = 56.97$; $t_9 = 7.548$; $t^2 = F$ statistic.

10–59 $F_{(1,102)} = 701.8$. p-value is very close to 0.

10–63 *a.* No inadequacy.
b. Pattern of increase with time.

10–65 No inadequacy.

10–67 No inadequacy.

10–69 [6,322.3, 6,780.4].

10–71 7.941; [7.367, 8.515].

10–73 [913.42, 1,144.00].

10–75 $F = 1,721.64$; there is evidence of a relationship. $r^2 = 0.93$.

10–77 $F = 317.98$. Yes.

10–79 $t_{(14)} = -3.498$. Yes. $F_{(1,14)} = t_{(14)}^2 = 12.24$.

10–81 For intercept: [−16.14, 41.00]; for slope: [0.90228,

1.250]; 95% C.I. for average Y when $X = 10,000$ is [6,238.86, 15,306.00].

10–83 $b_0 = 1.195$, $b_1 = 1.929$, $t = 18.512$, $r^2 = 0.96345$, $\hat{Y}$ (for $X = 13$) = \$26.27.

10–85 (Entertainment) = −81.04 + 0.7183 (S&P). $R^2 = 0.942$. F value = 374.6 (p-value very close to 0). Excellent linear relationship.

Chapter 11:

11–5 Eight equations.

11–7 $b_0 = -1.145$, $b_1 = 0.049$, $b_2 = 10.898$.

11–11 $n - 13$.

11–13 $F_{(4,40)} = 9.827$. There is evidence of a relationship.

11–21 Good regression, high R^2.

11–23 $\bar{R}^2 = 0.89$, which is smaller than before—do not include new variable.

11–25 *b.* $R^2 = 0.9076$. *c.* small sample, and time-series data.

11–27 $F_{(6,243)} = 128.19$, $R^2 = 0.7599$, $\bar{R}^2 = 0.754$. MSE = 22.4.

11–31 [3.052, 8.148], [−3.135, 23.835], [−1.842, 8.742], [−4.995, −3.505].

11–33 Yes.

11–35 Lend seems insignificant because of collinearity with M1 or Price.

11–37 Autocorrelation.

11–39 Heteroscedasticity and curvature not accounted for in the model.

11–47 Strong heteroscedasticity.

11–49 \$73,745.

11–51 0.011%.

11–53 P.I. (65.793, 81.692). C.I. (67.203, 80.281).

11–59 Two-way ANOVA.

11–65 Loss of degrees of freedom for error; correlations among the power terms.

11–67 Curvature—use a quadratic model.

11–71 Square root or log.

11–73 Logarithmic transformation.

11–75 A power curve with multiplicative error term.

11–77 Cannot transform to a linear model.

11–79 Take reciprocals of both sides of the equation.

11–81 No.

11–89 No. There is no relationship between Y and any of the variables.

11–91 Delete some variables to check for multicollinearity.

11–101 Using $\alpha = 0.05$ and the $n = 100$ row of the table, regressors (1) and (2) both have DW statistics $< d_L$, indicating positive autocorrelation. For (3) and (4), DW $> 4 - d_L$, indicating negative autocorrelation.

11–103 $E(Y) = 47.16 + 1.599X_1 + 1.149X_2$.

11–109 Stepwise chooses Value^2 and Profit^2.

11–111 All variables except Power distance and Collectivism in section B are significant.

11–113 The model is exponential (or quadratic). This implies increasing danger.

Chapter 12

12–3 Exponential trend model. Forecast for 1988 is 226,399 readers and for 1989, 253,660 readers.

12–5 No (because of seasonality).

12–13 Forecast using trend and seasonal index: 1582.61.

12–15 Forecast using trend and seasonal index: \$29.65.

12–17 Both models are about equally effective.

12–39 64.84, 71.30, 78.93, 88.83, 100, 110.97, 124.50, 132.50, 140.65, 154.38.

12–41 52.37, 58.55, 67.89, 71.05, 80.26, 94.21, 100, 100, 102.37, 106.58, 106.58.

12–43 121.70, 100, 156.13, 247.17, 100.47, 62.74.

12–47 Multiply each number in Table 12–18 by 100/289.1.

12–53 772, 635, 755, 758, 635, 100, 82.25, 97.80, 98.19, 82.25.

12–55 Clear increasing *trend* in the data regardless of small local variations.

12–59 *a.* Seasonal series.
         b. Best model is STI. Forecast is 87.41.

Chapter 13

13–15 Random sampling.

13–17 Passes all eight tests; process in control.

13–27 All points well within the p-chart limits; process in control.

13–29 All points well within the p-chart limits; process in control.

13–31 All points within c-chart limits (one is *on* the UCL); process in control.

13–33 All points within c-chart limits; process in control.

13–37 Yes: the 12 sample point is well above the UCL of the p-chart for these data.

13–39 Last group of four points have mean $<$ LCL for the $\bar{x}$-chart. (The other seven tests pass.)

Chapter 14

14–1 Do not reject H_0 (p-value is approximately 0.118).

14–3 $z = 3$—reject H_0.

14–5 $z = 1.85$—cannot reject H_0 at $\alpha = 0.05$.

14–7 $T = 14.29$, critical point for chi-square(1) at 0.005 = 7.88—reject H_0.

14–9 $T = 25.33$—reject H_0.

14–11 $T = 7$, p-value = 0.0156—reject H_0. There is evidence of an increasing trend.

14–15 $T = 19$, $z = 1.46$—cannot reject H_0.

14–17 $T = 113.8$—reject H_0.

14–19 $z = -4.82$—reject H_0.

14–21 $z = -4.42$—reject randomness hypothesis.

14–23 $z = -3.13$—reject H_0.

14–25 $R = 6$—cannot reject H_0 (p-value = 0.298).

14–27 $z = 3.00$—reject H_0.

14–29 $z = -0.984$—do not reject H_0.

14–31 $z = 2.14$—reject H_0.

14–33 $T = 6$—cannot reject H_0 (p-value = 0.10).

14–35 $T = 56$—reject H_0 at $\alpha = 0.05$.

14–37 Parametric t (z) test.

14–39 $T = 18$—reject H_0 at $\alpha = 0.025$.

14–41 $T = 4.5$—reject at $\alpha = 0.01$.

14–43 $T = 320.5$. Do not reject H_0.

14–45 $H = 13.716$—reject H_0 (p-value < 0.005).

14–47 $H = 13.54$—reject H_0 (p-value < 0.005).

14–49 $H = 26.49$—reject H_0 (p-value < 0.005). Only New York and Orlando are significantly different at $\alpha = 0.05$.

14–51 $X^2 = 20.4$—reject H_0 (p-value < 0.005).

14–53 $X^2 = 6.22$—reject H_0 (p-value < 0.05).

14–55 $r_s = 0.275$—accept H_0 of no positive correlation.

14–57 $r_s = 0.524$—significant.

14–59 $r_s = 0.297$—not significant.

14–61 Chi-square(4) = 50.8—reject H_0 (p-value < 0.005).

14–63 *a.* No. Some expected counts are less than 5.
          b. Combine cells A and B,

and combine cells E and Other.
          c. Chi-square(3) = 26.56—reject H_0 (p-value $<$ 0.005).

14–65 Chi-square has 2 df less: df = k − 3, $\bar{x}$ = 11.21, s = 2.71, chi-square(1) = 2.88—must accept H_0.

14–67 Chi-square(3) = 6.8—accept H_0.

14–69 Using the Yates correction, chi-square(1) = 5.64—reject H_0 (p-value $<$ 0.025). (Chi-square = 6.65 without correction.)

14–71 Chi-square(12) = 33.9—reject H_0 (p-value < 0.005).

14–73 Chi-square(3) = 4.23—accept H_0 (p-value > 0.10).

14–75 Chi-square(2) = 10.86—reject H_0 (p-value < 0.005).

14–77 Chi-square(2) = 4.14—must accept H_0.

14–79 *a.* Runs test.
          b. Two runs—reject H_0 (p-value = 0.004).
          c. Results depend on the assumption of six previous incidents.

14–81 *a.* Friedman test.
          b. $X^2 = 0.36$—accept H_0.

14–83 Use the sign test. Assume independence and a symmetric distribution. p-value = 0.004—reject H_0.

14–85 $X^2 = 13.5$—reject H_0 (p-value < 0.005).

14–87 $T = 23.51$—reject H_0 (p-value < 0.005).

14–91 $U = 40.5$, $z = -2.24$—reject H_0.

14–95 Chi-square(1) = 1.65—accept H_0; $\bar{x}$ = 31.55, s = 5.09.

Chapter 15

15–1 0.02531, 0.46544, 0.27247, 0.17691, 0.05262, 0.00697, 0.00028. 96.7% credible set is from 0.2 to 0.5.

15–3 0.0126, 0.5831, 0.3659, 0.0384, a number close to zero.

15–5 0.1129, 0.2407, 0.2275, 0.2909, 0.0751, 0.0529.

15–7 0.0633, 0.2216, 0.2928, 0.2364, 0.1286, 0.0465, 0.0099.

15–9 0.0071, 0.0638, 0.3001, 0.3962, 0.1929, 0.0399.

15–11 Normal: mean $= 9{,}207.3$, standard deviation $= 61.58$.

15–13 Normal: mean $= 95.95$, standard deviation $= 0.312$.

15–15 Normal: mean $= 23.72$, standard deviation $= 0.7442$.

15–17 Governor $=$ D (largest S.D.), ARCO expert $=$ C (smallest S.D.); most surprised is C.

15–19 Mean $= 2.5$, S.D. $= 0.5$.

15–25 Expected profit $= \$1.8$ million. Decide to advertise.

15–27 Expected profit $= \$86$ million; optimal decision is to make a new computer.

15–29 Optimal decision is *long*— change if you can, when fashion is known. $E(\text{profit}) = \$698{,}000$.

15–31 Optimal decision is wheat futures; expected payoff $= \$3{,}040$.

15–35 Don't test, $E(\text{payoff}) = \$1.8$ million. If you must test, ignore test result and advertise.

15–37 Don't test. Sell watches. If you must test, still sell watches $[E(\text{payoff}) = \$16{,}000]$.

15–39 Optimal decision is to test and follow the result of the test $[E(\text{payoff}) = \$587{,}000]$.

15–49 EVPI $= \$290{,}000$. Buy information if very reliable.

15–51 0.0114, 0.3004, 0.3500, 0.2707, 0.0556, 0.0118.

15–53 0.0026, 0.3844, 0.4589, 0.1480, 0.0060, 0.0001.

15–57 95% HPD region $= [97.888, 101.732]$.

15–63 $1{,}400 < 3{,}000$—a risk taker.

15–67 Merge. Do not consult. If you must consult, do what they say $[E(\text{payoff}) = \$2.45$ million$]$.

15–69 Candidate A should be chosen.

Chapter 16

16–5 $\begin{bmatrix} 2{,}500 & 1{,}950 \\ 1{,}950 & 3{,}600 \end{bmatrix}$

16–7 $T^2 = 4{,}657.5$; $F_{(2,22)} = 2{,}227.5$. Reject H_0.

16–9 $\rho_{7,1}\sigma_7\rho_1$.

16–11 Ellipse given by $(\mathbf{X} - \bar{\mathbf{X}})'\Sigma^{-1}(\mathbf{X} - \bar{\mathbf{X}}) = \chi^2_{0.99}/n = 9.21/50$.

16–17 Ellipsoid; ellipse.

16–23 Accept H_0.

16–33 $n = 252$, $r = 2$ (goods buyers *vs.* services buyers), $k = 4$. $F_{(4,247)} = 254$ has p-value close to 0; strong evidence of unequal centroids.

16–35 No. Can do as well by arbitrarily assigning everyone to the larger group.

16–37 Classify as repay.

16–39 Hit ratio must be better than 92%; use proportional chance criterion.

16–41 No discrimination ability.

16–43 Group 2.

16–45 Group 3.

16–47 Discriminant function not statistically significant; should not be used.

16–51 Hold.

16–55 Orthogonal and oblique.

16–57 Factor 1 is Overall Supplier Evaluation, Factor 2 is Who Must Yield, Factor 3 is Argument Evaluation.

16–61 Factor 1 is Customer Satisfaction, Factor 2 is Development/Promotion.

16–65 Discriminant analysis. If one discriminant function is significant, MANOVA would also lead to rejection of H_0.

16–67 Yes.

16–69 Pillai's trace, Roy's largest root, Hotelling's trace, Rao's statistic, Bartlett's statistic.

16–73 When the latent factors are not mutually independent.

16–75 0.6393.

16–81 Wilks' lambda $= 0.412$. $F_{(3,21)} = 9.987$, p-value very close to 0. Production cost p-value $= 0.009$. No. of sponsors p-value $= 0.066$ (not significant). Promotions p-value $= 0.004$. Discriminant function coefficients: production cost, 0.945; promotions, 0.996. 84% correct prediction.

Chapter 17

17–1 *a.* $\bar{x}_{\text{st}} = 33.48\%$.

    b. S.D. $= 0.823\%$.

    c. [31.87, 35.09].

17–3 *a.* 40.01.

    b. 0.685.

    c. [38.88, 41.14].

    d. Data may have many zero values.

17–5 $\$35{,}604.5$, [32,790, 38,420].

17–9 *a*, *b*, and *c*: no. The clusters need to be randomly chosen. *d.* Consider the cruise ship companies as strata. Randomly draw clusters from the strata.

17–13 If k is a multiple of 7, we would sample the same day during different weeks and lose information about other days.

17–17 Yes.

17–19 Bias due to businesses not listed.

17–21 $0.0733 \pm 0.018 = [0.055, 0.091]$.

17–25 Sample about 109 children, 744 young adults, and 147 older people.

APPENDIX C

STATISTICAL TABLES

TABLE 1 Cumulative Binomial Distribution

$$F(x) = P(X \le x) = \sum_{i=0}^{x} \binom{n}{i} p^i (1-p)^{n-i} \qquad \textit{Example: if } p = 0.10, \ n = 5, \text{ and } x = 2, \text{ then } F(x) = 0.991$$

n	x	.01	.05	.10	.20	.30	.40	.50	.60	.70	.80	.90	.95	.99
5	0	.951	.774	.590	.328	.168	.078	.031	.010	.002	.000	.000	.000	.000
	1	.999	.977	.919	.737	.528	.337	.187	.087	.031	.007	.000	.000	.000
	2	1.000	.999	.991	.942	.837	.683	.500	.317	.163	.058	.009	.001	.000
	3	1.000	1.000	1.000	.993	.969	.913	.813	.663	.472	.263	.081	.023	.001
	4	1.000	1.000	1.000	1.000	.998	.990	.969	.922	.832	.672	.410	.226	.049
6	0	.941	.735	.531	.262	.118	.047	.016	.004	.001	.000	.000	.000	.000
	1	.999	.967	.886	.655	.420	.233	.109	.041	.011	.002	.000	.000	.000
	2	1.000	.998	.984	.901	.744	.544	.344	.179	.070	.017	.001	.000	.000
	3	1.000	1.000	.999	.983	.930	.821	.656	.456	.256	.099	.016	.002	.000
	4	1.000	1.000	1.000	.998	.989	.959	.891	.767	.580	.345	.114	.033	.001
	5	1.000	1.000	1.000	1.000	.999	.996	.984	.953	.882	.738	.469	.265	.059
7	0	.932	.698	.478	.210	.082	.028	.008	.002	.000	.000	.000	.000	.000
	1	.998	.956	.850	.577	.329	.159	.063	.019	.004	.000	.000	.000	.000
	2	1.000	.996	.974	.852	.647	.420	.227	.096	.029	.005	.000	.000	.000
	3	1.000	1.000	.997	.967	.874	.710	.500	.290	.126	.033	.003	.000	.000
	4	1.000	1.000	1.000	.995	.971	.904	.773	.580	.353	.148	.026	.004	.000
	5	1.000	1.000	1.000	1.000	.996	.981	.937	.841	.671	.423	.150	.044	.002
	6	1.000	1.000	1.000	1.000	1.000	.998	.992	.972	.918	.790	.522	.302	.068
8	0	.923	.663	.430	.168	.058	.017	.004	.001	.000	.000	.000	.000	.000
	1	.997	.943	.813	.503	.255	.106	.035	.009	.001	.000	.000	.000	.000
	2	1.000	.994	.962	.797	.552	.315	.145	.050	.011	.001	.000	.000	.000
	3	1.000	1.000	.995	.944	.806	.594	.363	.174	.058	.010	.000	.000	.000
	4	1.000	1.000	1.000	.990	.942	.826	.637	.406	.194	.056	.005	.000	.000
	5	1.000	1.000	1.000	.999	.989	.950	.855	.685	.448	.203	.038	.006	.000
	6	1.000	1.000	1.000	1.000	.999	.991	.965	.894	.745	.497	.187	.057	.003
	7	1.000	1.000	1.000	1.000	1.000	.999	.996	.983	.942	.832	.570	.337	.077
9	0	.914	.630	.387	.134	.040	.010	.002	.000	.000	.000	.000	.000	.000
	1	.997	.929	.775	.436	.196	.071	.020	.004	.000	.000	.000	.000	.000
	2	1.000	.992	.947	.738	.463	.232	.090	.025	.004	.000	.000	.000	.000
	3	1.000	.999	.992	.914	.730	.483	.254	.099	.025	.003	.000	.000	.000
	4	1.000	1.000	.999	.980	.901	.733	.500	.267	.099	.020	.001	.000	.000
	5	1.000	1.000	1.000	.997	.975	.901	.746	.517	.270	.086	.008	.001	.000
	6	1.000	1.000	1.000	1.000	.996	.975	.910	.768	.537	.262	.053	.008	.000
	7	1.000	1.000	1.000	1.000	1.000	.996	.980	.929	.804	.564	.225	.071	.003
	8	1.000	1.000	1.000	1.000	1.000	1.000	.998	.990	.960	.866	.613	.370	.086
10	0	.904	.599	.349	.107	.028	.006	.001	.000	.000	.000	.000	.000	.000
	1	.996	.914	.736	.376	.149	.046	.011	.002	.000	.000	.000	.000	.000
	2	1.000	.988	.930	.678	.383	.167	.055	.012	.002	.000	.000	.000	.000
	3	1.000	.999	.987	.879	.650	.382	.172	.055	.011	.001	.000	.000	.000
	4	1.000	1.000	.998	.967	.850	.633	.377	.166	.047	.006	.000	.000	.000
	5	1.000	1.000	1.000	.994	.953	.834	.623	.367	.150	.033	.002	.000	.000
	6	1.000	1.000	1.000	.999	.989	.945	.828	.618	.350	.121	.013	.001	.000
	7	1.000	1.000	1.000	1.000	.998	.988	.945	.833	.617	.322	.070	.012	.000
	8	1.000	1.000	1.000	1.000	1.000	.998	.989	.954	.851	.624	.264	.086	.004
	9	1.000	1.000	1.000	1.000	1.000	1.000	.999	.994	.972	.893	.651	.401	.096

							p							
n	*x*	.01	.05	.10	.20	.30	.40	.50	.60	.70	.80	.90	.95	.99
15	0	.860	.463	.206	.035	.005	.000	.000	.000	.000	.000	.000	.000	.000
	1	.990	.829	.549	.167	.035	.005	.000	.000	.000	.000	.000	.000	.000
	2	1.000	.964	.816	.398	.127	.027	.004	.000	.000	.000	.000	.000	.000
	3	1.000	.995	.944	.648	.297	.091	.018	.002	.000	.000	.000	.000	.000
	4	1.000	.999	.987	.836	.515	.217	.059	.009	.001	.000	.000	.000	.000
	5	1.000	1.000	.998	.939	.722	.403	.151	.034	.004	.000	.000	.000	.000
	6	1.000	1.000	1.000	.982	.869	.610	.304	.095	.015	.001	.000	.000	.000
	7	1.000	1.000	1.000	.996	.950	.787	.500	.213	.050	.004	.000	.000	.000
	8	1.000	1.000	1.000	.999	.985	.905	.696	.390	.131	.018	.000	.000	.000
	9	1.000	1.000	1.000	1.000	.996	.966	.849	.597	.278	.061	.002	.000	.000
	10	1.000	1.000	1.000	1.000	.999	.991	.941	.783	.485	.164	.013	.001	.000
	11	1.000	1.000	1.000	1.000	1.000	.998	.982	.909	.703	.352	.056	.005	.000
	12	1.000	1.000	1.000	1.000	1.000	1.000	.996	.973	.873	.602	.184	.036	.000
	13	1.000	1.000	1.000	1.000	1.000	1.000	1.000	.995	.965	.833	.451	.171	.010
	14	1.000	1.000	1.000	1.000	1.000	1.000	1.000	1.000	.995	.965	.794	.537	.140
20	0	.818	.358	.122	.012	.001	.000	.000	.000	.000	.000	.000	.000	.000
	1	983	.736	.392	.069	.008	.001	.000	.000	.000	.000	.000	.000	.000
	2	.999	.925	.677	.206	.035	.004	.000	.000	.000	.000	.000	.000	.000
	3	1.000	.984	.867	.411	.107	.016	.001	.000	.000	.000	.000	.000	.000
	4	1.000	.997	.957	.630	.238	.051	.006	.000	.000	.000	.000	.000	.000
	5	1.000	1.000	.989	.804	.416	.126	.021	.002	.000	.000	.000	.000	.000
	6	1.000	1.000	.998	.913	.608	.250	.058	.006	.000	.000	.000	.000	.000
	7	1.000	1.000	1.000	.968	.772	.416	.132	.021	.001	.000	.000	.000	.000
	8	1.000	1.000	1.000	.990	.887	.596	.252	.057	.005	.000	.000	.000	.000
	9	1.000	1.000	1.000	.997	.952	.755	.412	.128	.017	.001	.000	.000	.000
	10	1.000	1.000	1.000	.999	.983	.872	.588	.245	.048	.003	.000	.000	.000
	11	1.000	1.000	1.000	1.000	.995	.943	.748	.404	.113	.010	.000	.000	.000
	12	1.000	1.000	1.000	1.000	.999	.979	.868	.584	.228	.032	.000	.000	.000
	13	1.000	1.000	1.000	1.000	1.000	.994	.942	.750	.392	.087	.002	.000	.000
	14	1.000	1.000	1.000	1.000	1.000	.998	.979	.874	.584	.196	.011	.000	.000
	15	1.000	1.000	1.000	1.000	1.000	1.000	.994	.949	.762	.370	.043	.003	.000
	16	1.000	1.000	1.000	1.000	1.000	1.000	.999	.984	.893	.589	.133	.016	.000
	17	1.000	1.000	1.000	1.000	1.000	1.000	1.000	.996	.965	.794	.323	.075	.001
	18	1.000	1.000	1.000	1.000	1.000	1.000	1.000	.999	.992	.931	.608	.264	.017
	19	1.000	1.000	1.000	1.000	1.000	1.000	1.000	1.000	.999	.988	.878	.642	.182
25	0	.778	.277	.072	.004	.000	.000	.000	.000	.000	.000	.000	.000	.000
	1	.974	.642	.271	.027	.002	.000	.000	.000	.000	.000	.000	.000	.000
	2	.998	.873	.537	.098	.009	.000	.000	.000	.000	.000	.000	.000	.000
	3	1.000	.966	.764	.234	.033	.002	.000	.000	.000	.000	.000	.000	.000
	4	1.000	.993	.902	.421	.090	.009	.000	.000	.000	.000	.000	.000	.000
	5	1.000	.999	.967	.617	.193	.029	.002	.000	.000	.000	.000	.000	.000
	6	1.000	1.000	.991	.780	.341	.074	.007	.000	.000	.000	.000	.000	.000
	7	1.000	1.000	.998	.891	.512	.154	.022	.001	.000	.000	.000	.000	.000
	8	1.000	1.000	1.000	.953	.677	.274	.054	.004	.000	.000	.000	.000	.000
	9	1.000	1.000	1.000	.983	.811	.425	.115	.013	.000	.000	.000	.000	.000
	10	1.000	1.000	1.000	.994	.902	.586	.212	.034	.002	.000	.000	.000	.000
	11	1.000	1.000	1.000	.998	.953	.732	.345	.078	.006	.000	.000	.000	.000
	12	1.000	1.000	1.000	1.000	.983	.846	.500	.154	.017	.000	.000	.000	.000
	13	1.000	1.000	1.000	1.000	.994	.922	.655	.268	.044	.002	.000	.000	.000
	14	1.000	1.000	1.000	1.000	.998	.966	.788	.414	.098	.006	.000	.000	.000
	15	1.000	1.000	1.000	1.000	1.000	.987	.885	.575	.189	.017	.000	.000	.000
	16	1.000	1.000	1.000	1.000	1.000	.996	.946	.726	.323	.047	.000	.000	.000
	17	1.000	1.000	1.000	1.000	1.000	.999	.978	.846	.488	.109	.002	.000	.000
	18	1.000	1.000	1.000	1.000	1.000	1.000	993	.926	.659	.220	.009	.000	.000
	19	1.000	1.000	1.000	1.000	1.000	1.000	.998	.971	.807	.383	.033	.001	.000
	20	1.000	1.000	1.000	1.000	1.000	1.000	1.000	.991	.910	.579	.098	.007	.000
	21	1.000	1.000	1.000	1.000	1.000	1.000	1.000	.998	.967	.766	.236	.034	.000
	22	1.000	1.000	1.000	1.000	1.000	1.000	1.000	1.000	.991	.902	.463	.127	.002
	23	1.000	1.000	1.000	1.000	1.000	1.000	1.000	1.000	.998	.973	.729	.358	.026
	24	1.000	1.000	1.000	1.000	1.000	1.000	1.000	1.000	1.000	.996	.928	.723	.222

TABLE 2 Areas of the Standard Normal Distribution

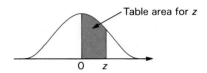

Table area for *z*

The table areas are probabilities that the standard normal random variable is between 0 and z.

Second Decimal Place in *z*

z	0.00	0.01	0.02	0.03	0.04	0.05	0.06	0.07	0.08	0.09
0.0	0.0000	0.0040	0.0080	0.0120	0.0160	0.0199	0.0239	0.0279	0.0319	0.0359
0.1	0.0398	0.0438	0.0478	0.0517	0.0557	0.0596	0.0636	0.0675	0.0714	0.0753
0.2	0.0793	0.0832	0.0871	0.0910	0.0948	0.0987	0.1026	0.1064	0.1103	0.1141
0.3	0.1179	0.1217	0.1255	0.1293	0.1331	0.1368	0.1406	0.1443	0.1480	0.1517
0.4	0.1554	0.1591	0.1628	0.1664	0.1700	0.1736	0.1772	0.1808	0.1844	0.1879
0.5	0.1915	0.1950	0.1985	0.2019	0.2054	0.2088	0.2123	0.2157	0.2190	0.2224
0.6	0.2257	0.2291	0.2324	0.2357	0.2389	0.2422	0.2454	0.2486	0.2517	0.2549
0.7	0.2580	0.2611	0.2642	0.2673	0.2704	0.2734	0.2764	0.2794	0.2823	0.2852
0.8	0.2881	0.2910	0.2939	0.2967	0.2995	0.3023	0.3051	0.3078	0.3106	0.3133
0.9	0.3159	0.3186	0.3212	0.3238	0.3264	0.3289	0.3315	0.3340	0.3365	0.3389
1.0	0.3413	0.3438	0.3461	0.3485	0.3508	0.3531	0.3554	0.3577	0.3599	0.3621
1.1	0.3643	0.3665	0.3686	0.3708	0.3729	0.3749	0.3770	0.3790	0.3810	0.3830
1.2	0.3849	0.3869	0.3888	0.3907	0.3925	0.3944	0.3962	0.3980	0.3997	0.4015
1.3	0.4032	0.4049	0.4066	0.4082	0.4099	0.4115	0.4131	0.4147	0.4162	0.4177
1.4	0.4192	0.4207	0.4222	0.4236	0.4251	0.4265	0.4279	0.4292	0.4306	0.4319
1.5	0.4332	0.4345	0.4357	0.4370	0.4382	0.4394	0.4406	0.4418	0.4429	0.4441
1.6	0.4452	0.4463	0.4474	0.4484	0.4495	0.4505	0.4515	0.4525	0.4535	0.4545
1.7	0.4554	0.4564	0.4573	0.4582	0.4591	0.4599	0.4608	0.4616	0.4625	0.4633
1.8	0.4641	0.4649	0.4656	0.4664	0.4671	0.4678	0.4686	0.4693	0.4699	0.4706
1.9	0.4713	0.4719	0.4726	0.4732	0.4738	0.4744	0.4750	0.4756	0.4761	0.4767
2.0	0.4772	0.4778	0.4783	0.4788	0.4793	0.4798	0.4803	0.4808	0.4812	0.4817
2.1	0.4821	0.4826	0.4830	0.4834	0.4838	0.4842	0.4846	0.4850	0.4854	0.4857
2.2	0.4861	0.4864	0.4868	0.4871	0.4875	0.4878	0.4881	0.4884	0.4887	0.4890
2.3	0.4893	0.4896	0.4898	0.4901	0.4904	0.4906	0.4909	0.4911	0.4913	0.4916
2.4	0.4918	0.4920	0.4922	0.4925	0.4927	0.4929	0.4931	0.4932	0.4934	0.4936
2.5	0.4938	0.4940	0.4941	0.4943	0.4945	0.4946	0.4948	0.4949	0.4951	0.4952
2.6	0.4953	0.4955	0.4956	0.4957	0.4959	0.4960	0.4961	0.4962	0.4963	0.4964
2.7	0.4965	0.4966	0.4967	0.4968	0.4969	0.4970	0.4971	0.4972	0.4973	0.4974
2.8	0.4974	0.4975	0.4976	0.4977	0.4977	0.4978	0.4979	0.4979	0.4980	0.4981
2.9	0.4981	0.4982	0.4982	0.4983	0.4984	0.4984	0.4985	0.4985	0.4986	0.4986
3.0	0.4987	0.4987	0.4987	0.4988	0.4988	0.4989	0.4989	0.4989	0.4990	0.4990
3.1	0.4990	0.4991	0.4991	0.4991	0.4992	0.4992	0.4992	0.4992	0.4993	0.4993
3.2	0.4993	0.4993	0.4994	0.4994	0.4994	0.4994	0.4994	0.4995	0.4995	0.4995
3.3	0.4995	0.4995	0.4995	0.4996	0.4996	0.4996	0.4996	0.4996	0.4996	0.4997
3.4	0.4997	0.4997	0.4997	0.4997	0.4997	0.4997	0.4997	0.4997	0.4997	0.4998
3.5	0.4998									
4.0	0.49997									
4.5	0.499997									
5.0	0.4999997									
6.0	0.499999999									

TABLE 3   Critical Values of the *t* Distribution

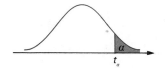

Degrees of Freedom	$t_{.100}$	$t_{.050}$	$t_{.025}$	$t_{.010}$	$t_{.005}$
1	3.078	6.314	12.706	31.821	63.657
2	1.886	2.920	4.303	6.965	9.925
3	1.638	2.353	3.182	4.541	5.841
4	1.533	2.132	2.776	3.747	4.604
5	1.476	2.015	2.571	3.365	4.032
6	1.440	1.943	2.447	3.143	3.707
7	1.415	1.895	2.365	2.998	3.499
8	1.397	1.860	2.306	2.896	3.355
9	1.383	1.833	2.262	2.821	3.250
10	1.372	1.812	2.228	2.764	3.169
11	1.363	1.796	2.201	2.718	3.106
12	1.356	1.782	2.179	2.681	3.055
13	1.350	1.771	2.160	2.650	3.012
14	1.345	1.761	2.145	2.624	2.977
15	1.341	1.753	2.131	2.602	2.947
16	1.337	1.746	2.120	2.583	2.921
17	1.333	1.740	2.110	2.567	2.898
18	1.330	1.734	2.101	2.552	2.878
19	1.328	1.729	2.093	2.539	2.861
20	1.325	1.725	2.086	2.528	2.845
21	1.323	1.721	2.080	2.518	2.831
22	1.321	1.717	2.074	2.508	2.819
23	1.319	1.714	2.069	2.500	2.807
24	1.318	1.711	2.064	2.492	2.797
25	1.316	1.708	2.060	2.485	2.787
26	1.315	1.706	2.056	2.479	2.779
27	1.314	1.703	2.052	2.473	2.771
28	1.313	1.701	2.048	2.467	2.763
29	1.311	1.699	2.045	2.462	2.756
30	1.310	1.697	2.042	2.457	2.750
40	1.303	1.684	2.021	2.423	2.704
60	1.296	1.671	2.000	2.390	2.660
120	1.289	1.658	1.980	2.358	2.617
∞	1.282	1.645	1.960	2.326	2.576

Source: M. Merrington, "Table of Percentage Points of the *t*-Distribution," *Biometrika* 32 (1941) p. 300. Reproduced by permission of the *Biometrika* trustees.

TABLE 4   Critical Values of the Chi-Square Distribution

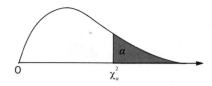

Degrees of Freedom	$\chi^2_{.995}$	$\chi^2_{.990}$	$\chi^2_{.975}$	$\chi^2_{.950}$	$\chi^2_{.900}$
1	0.0000393	0.0001571	0.0009821	0.0039321	0.0157908
2	0.0100251	0.0201007	0.0506356	0.102587	0.210720
3	0.0717212	0.114832	0.215795	0.351846	0.584375
4	0.206990	0.297110	0.484419	0.710721	1.063623
5	0.411740	0.554300	0.831211	1.145476	1.61031
6	0.675727	0.872085	1.237347	1.63539	2.20413
7	0.989265	1.239043	1.68987	2.16735	2.83311
8	1.344419	1.646482	2.17973	2.73264	3.48954
9	1.734926	2.087912	2.70039	3.32511	4.16816
10	2.15585	2.55821	3.24697	3.94030	4.86518
11	2.60321	3.05347	3.81575	4.57481	5.57779
12	3.07382	3.57056	4.40379	5.22603	6.30380
13	3.56503	4.10691	5.00874	5.89186	7.04150
14	4.07468	4.66043	5.62872	6.57063	7.78953
15	4.60094	5.22935	6.26214	7.26094	8.54675
16	5.14224	5.81221	6.90766	7.96164	9.31223
17	5.69724	6.40776	7.56418	8.67176	10.0852
18	6.26481	7.01491	8.23075	9.39046	10.8649
19	6.84398	7.63273	8.90655	10.1170	11.6509
20	7.43386	8.26040	9.59083	10.8508	12.4426
21	8.03366	8.89720	10.28293	11.5913	13.2396
22	8.64272	9.54249	10.9823	12.3380	14.0415
23	9.26042	10.19567	11.6885	13.0905	14.8479
24	9.88623	10.8564	12.4011	13.8484	15.6587
25	10.5197	11.5240	13.1197	14.6114	16.4734
26	11.1603	12.1981	13.8439	15.3791	17.2919
27	11.8076	12.8786	14.5733	16.1513	18.1138
28	12.4613	13.5648	15.3079	16.9279	18.9392
29	13.1211	14.2565	16.0471	17.7083	19.7677
30	13.7867	14.9535	16.7908	18.4926	20.5992
40	20.7065	22.1643	24.4331	26.5093	29.0505
50	27.9907	29.7067	32.3574	34.7642	37.6886
60	35.5346	37.4848	40.4817	43.1879	46.4589
70	43.2752	45.4418	48.7576	51.7393	55.3290
80	51.1720	53.5400	57.1532	60.3915	64.2778
90	59.1963	61.7541	65.6466	69.1260	73.2912
100	67.3276	70.0648	74.2219	77.9295	82.3581

Degrees of Freedom	$\chi^2_{.100}$	$\chi^2_{.050}$	$\chi^2_{.025}$	$\chi^2_{.010}$	$\chi^2_{.005}$
1	2.70554	3.84146	5.02389	6.63490	7.87944
2	4.60517	5.99147	7.37776	9.21034	10.5966
3	6.25139	7.81473	9.34840	11.3449	12.8381
4	7.77944	9.48773	11.1433	13.2767	14.8602
5	9.23635	11.0705	12.8325	15.0863	16.7496
6	10.6446	12.5916	14.4494	16.8119	18.5476
7	12.0170	14.0671	16.0128	18.4753	20.2777
8	13.3616	15.5073	17.5346	20.0902	21.9550
9	14.6837	16.9190	19.0228	21.6660	23.5893
10	15.9871	18.3070	20.4831	23.2093	25.1882
11	17.2750	19.6751	21.9200	24.7250	26.7569
12	18.5494	21.0261	23.3367	26.2170	28.2995
13	19.8119	22.3621	24.7356	27.6883	29.8194
14	21.0642	23.6848	26.1190	29.1413	31.3193
15	22.3072	24.9958	27.4884	30.5779	32.8013
16	23.5418	26.2962	28.8454	31.9999	34.2672
17	24.7690	27.5871	30.1910	33.4087	35.7185
18	25.9894	28.8693	31.5264	34.8053	37.1564
19	27.2036	30.1435	32.8523	36.1908	38.5822
20	28.4120	31.4104	34.1696	37.5662	39.9968
21	29.6151	32.6705	35.4789	38.9321	41.4010
22	30.8133	33.9244	36.7807	40.2894	42.7956
23	32.0069	35.1725	38.0757	41.6384	44.1813
24	33.1963	36.4151	39.3641	42.9798	45.5585
25	34.3816	37.6525	40.6465	44.3141	46.9278
26	35.5631	38.8852	41.9232	45.6417	48.2899
27	36.7412	40.1133	43.1944	46.9630	49.6449
28	37.9159	41.3372	44.4607	48.2782	50.9933
29	39.0875	42.5569	45.7222	49.5879	52.3356
30	40.2560	43.7729	46.9792	50.8922	53.6720
40	51.8050	55.7585	59.3417	63.6907	66.7659
50	63.1671	67.5048	71.4202	76.1539	79.4900
60	74.3970	79.0819	83.2976	88.3794	91.9517
70	85.5271	90.5312	95.0231	100.425	104.215
80	96.5782	101.879	106.629	112.329	116.321
90	107.565	113.145	118.136	124.116	128.299
100	118.498	124.342	129.561	135.807	140.169

Source: C. M. Thompson, "Tables of the Percentage Points of the χ^2-Distribution," *Biometrika* 32 (1941), pp. 188–89. Reproduced by permission of the *Biometrika* Trustees.

Appendix C

TABLE 5 Critical Values of the F Distribution for $\alpha = 0.10$

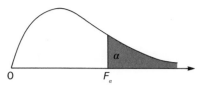

Denominator Degrees of Freedom (k_2)	Numerator Degrees of Freedom (k_1)								
	1	**2**	**3**	**4**	**5**	**6**	**7**	**8**	**9**
1	39.86	49.50	53.59	55.83	57.24	58.20	58.91	59.44	59.86
2	8.53	9.00	9.16	9.24	9.29	9.33	9.35	9.37	9.38
3	5.54	5.46	5.39	5.34	5.31	5.28	5.27	5.25	5.24
4	4.54	4.32	4.19	4.11	4.05	4.01	3.98	3.95	3.94
5	4.06	3.78	3.62	3.52	3.45	3.40	3.37	3.34	3.32
6	3.78	3.46	3.29	3.18	3.11	3.05	3.01	2.98	2.96
7	3.59	3.26	3.07	2.96	2.88	2.83	2.78	2.75	2.72
8	3.46	3.11	2.92	2.81	2.73	2.67	2.62	2.59	2.56
9	3.36	3.01	2.81	2.69	2.61	2.55	2.51	2.47	2.44
10	3.29	2.92	2.73	2.61	2.52	2.46	2.41	2.38	2.35
11	3.23	2.86	2.66	2.54	2.45	2.39	2.34	2.30	2.27
12	3.18	2.81	2.61	2.48	2.39	2.33	2.28	2.24	2.21
13	3.14	2.76	2.56	2.43	2.35	2.28	2.23	2.20	2.16
14	3.10	2.73	2.52	2.39	2.31	2.24	2.19	2.15	2.12
15	3.07	2.70	2.49	2.36	2.27	2.21	2.16	2.12	2.09
16	3.05	2.67	2.46	2.33	2.24	2.18	2.13	2.09	2.06
17	3.03	2.64	2.44	2.31	2.22	2.15	2.10	2.06	2.03
18	3.01	2.62	2.42	2.29	2.20	2.13	2.08	2.04	2.00
19	2.99	2.61	2.40	2.27	2.18	2.11	2.06	2.02	1.98
20	2.97	2.59	2.38	2.25	2.16	2.09	2.04	2.00	1.96
21	2.96	2.57	2.36	2.23	2.14	2.08	2.02	1.98	1.95
22	2.95	2.56	2.35	2.22	2.13	2.06	2.01	1.97	1.93
23	2.94	2.55	2.34	2.21	2.11	2.05	1.99	1.95	1.92
24	2.93	2.54	2.33	2.19	2.10	2.04	1.98	1.94	1.91
25	2.92	2.53	2.32	2.18	2.09	2.02	1.97	1.93	1.89
26	2.91	2.52	2.31	2.17	2.08	2.01	1.96	1.92	1.88
27	2.90	2.51	2.30	2.17	2.07	2.00	1.95	1.91	1.87
28	2.89	2.50	2.29	2.16	2.06	2.00	1.94	1.90	1.87
29	2.89	2.50	2.28	2.15	2.06	1.99	1.93	1.89	1.86
30	2.88	2.49	2.28	2.14	2.05	1.98	1.93	1.88	1.85
40	2.84	2.44	2.23	2.09	2.00	1.93	1.87	1.83	1.79
60	2.79	2.39	2.18	2.04	1.95	1.87	1.82	1.77	1.74
120	2.75	2.35	2.13	1.99	1.90	1.82	1.77	1.72	1.68
∞	2.71	2.30	2.08	1.94	1.85	1.77	1.72	1.67	1.63

Denominator Degrees of Freedom (k_2)	Numerator Degrees of Freedom (k_1)									
	10	12	15	20	24	30	40	60	120	∞
1	60.19	60.71	61.22	61.74	62.00	62.26	62.53	62.79	63.06	63.33
2	9.39	9.41	9.42	9.44	9.45	9.46	9.47	9.47	9.48	9.49
3	5.23	5.22	5.20	5.18	5.18	5.17	5.16	5.15	5.14	5.13
4	3.92	3.90	3.87	3.84	3.83	3.82	3.80	3.79	3.78	3.76
5	3.30	3.27	3.24	3.21	3.19	3.17	3.16	3.14	3.12	3.10
6	2.94	2.90	2.87	2.84	2.82	2.80	2.78	2.76	2.74	2.72
7	2.70	2.67	2.63	2.59	2.58	2.56	2.54	2.51	2.49	2.47
8	2.54	2.50	2.46	2.42	2.40	2.38	2.36	2.34	2.32	2.29
9	2.42	2.38	2.34	2.30	2.28	2.25	2.23	2.21	2.18	2.16
10	2.32	2.28	2.24	2.20	2.18	2.16	2.13	2.11	2.08	2.06
11	2.25	2.21	2.17	2.12	2.10	2.08	2.05	2.03	2.00	1.97
12	2.19	2.15	2.10	2.06	2.04	2.01	1.99	1.96	1.93	1.90
13	2.14	2.10	2.05	2.01	1.98	1.96	1.93	1.90	1.88	1.85
14	2.10	2.05	2.01	1.96	1.94	1.91	1.89	1.86	1.83	1.80
15	2.06	2.02	1.97	1.92	1.90	1.87	1.85	1.82	1.79	1.76
16	2.03	1.99	1.94	1.89	1.87	1.84	1.81	1.78	1.75	1.72
17	2.00	1.96	1.91	1.86	1.84	1.81	1.78	1.75	1.72	1.69
18	1.98	1.93	1.89	1.84	1.81	1.78	1.75	1.72	1.69	1.66
19	1.96	1.91	1.86	1.81	1.79	1.76	1.73	1.70	1.67	1.63
20	1.94	1.89	1.84	1.79	1.77	1.74	1.71	1.68	1.64	1.61
21	1.92	1.87	1.83	1.78	1.75	1.72	1.69	1.66	1.62	1.59
22	1.90	1.86	1.81	1.76	1.73	1.70	1.67	1.64	1.60	1.57
23	1.89	1.84	1.80	1.74	1.72	1.69	1.66	1.62	1.59	1.55
24	1.88	1.83	1.78	1.73	1.70	1.67	1.64	1.61	1.57	1.53
25	1.87	1.82	1.77	1.72	1.69	1.66	1.63	1.59	1.56	1.52
26	1.86	1.81	1.76	1.71	1.68	1.65	1.61	1.58	1.54	1.50
27	1.85	1.80	1.75	1.70	1.67	1.64	1.60	1.57	1.53	1.49
28	1.84	1.79	1.74	1.69	1.66	1.63	1.59	1.56	1.52	1.48
29	1.83	1.78	1.73	1.68	1.65	1.62	1.58	1.55	1.51	1.47
30	1.82	1.77	1.72	1.67	1.64	1.61	1.57	1.54	1.50	1.46
40	1.76	1.71	1.66	1.61	1.57	1.54	1.51	1.47	1.42	1.38
60	1.71	1.66	1.60	1.54	1.51	1.48	1.44	1.40	1.35	1.29
120	1.65	1.60	1.55	1.48	1.45	1.41	1.37	1.32	1.26	1.19
∞	1.60	1.55	1.49	1.42	1.38	1.34	1.30	1.24	1.17	1.00

TABLE 5 *(continued)*   Critical Values of the F Distribution for $\alpha = 0.05$

Denominator Degrees of Freedom (k_2)	Numerator Degrees of Freedom (k_1)								
	1	2	3	4	5	6	7	8	9
1	161.4	199.5	215.7	224.6	230.2	234.0	236.8	238.9	240.5
2	18.51	19.00	19.16	19.25	19.30	19.33	19.35	19.37	19.38
3	10.13	9.55	9.28	9.12	9.01	8.94	8.89	8.85	8.81
4	7.71	6.94	6.59	6.39	6.26	6.16	6.09	6.04	6.00
5	6.61	5.79	5.41	5.19	5.05	4.95	4.88	4.82	4.77
6	5.99	5.14	4.76	4.53	4.39	4.28	4.21	4.15	4.10
7	5.59	4.74	4.35	4.12	3.97	3.87	3.79	3.73	3.68
8	5.32	4.46	4.07	3.84	3.69	3.58	3.50	3.44	3.39
9	5.12	4.26	3.86	3.63	3.48	3.37	3.29	3.23	3.18
10	4.96	4.10	3.71	3.48	3.33	3.22	3.14	3.07	3.02
11	4.84	3.98	3.59	3.36	3.20	3.09	3.01	2.95	2.90
12	4.75	3.89	3.49	3.26	3.11	3.00	2.91	2.85	2.80
13	4.67	3.81	3.41	3.18	3.03	2.92	2.83	2.77	2.71
14	4.60	3.74	3.34	3.11	2.96	2.85	2.76	2.70	2.65
15	4.54	3.68	3.29	3.06	2.90	2.79	2.71	2.64	2.59
16	4.49	3.63	3.24	3.01	2.85	2.74	2.66	2.59	2.54
17	4.45	3.59	3.20	2.96	2.81	2.70	2.61	2.55	2.49
18	4.41	3.55	3.16	2.93	2.77	2.66	2.58	2.51	2.46
19	4.38	3.52	3.13	2.90	2.74	2.63	2.54	2.48	2.42
20	4.35	3.49	3.10	2.87	2.71	2.60	2.51	2.45	2.39
21	4.32	3.47	3.07	2.84	2.68	2.57	2.49	2.42	2.37
22	4.30	3.44	3.05	2.82	2.66	2.55	2.46	2.40	2.34
23	4.28	3.42	3.03	2.80	2.64	2.53	2.44	2.37	2.32
24	4.26	3.40	3.01	2.78	2.62	2.51	2.42	2.36	2.30
25	4.24	3.39	2.99	2.76	2.60	2.49	2.40	2.34	2.28
26	4.23	3.37	2.98	2.74	2.59	2.47	2.39	2.32	2.27
27	4.21	3.35	2.96	2.73	2.57	2.46	2.37	2.31	2.25
28	4.20	3.34	2.95	2.71	2.56	2.45	2.36	2.29	2.24
29	4.18	3.33	2.93	2.70	2.55	2.43	2.35	2.28	2.22
30	4.17	3.32	2.92	2.69	2.53	2.42	2.33	2.27	2.21
40	4.08	3.23	2.84	2.61	2.45	2.34	2.25	2.18	2.12
60	4.00	3.15	2.76	2.53	2.37	2.25	2.17	2.10	2.04
120	3.92	3.07	2.68	2.45	2.29	2.17	2.09	2.02	1.96
∞	3.84	3.00	2.60	2.37	2.21	2.10	2.01	1.94	1.88

Denominator Degrees of Freedom (k_2)	Numerator Degrees of Freedom (k_1)									
	10	12	15	20	24	30	40	60	120	∞
1	241.9	243.9	245.9	248.0	249.1	250.1	251.1	252.2	253.3	254.3
2	19.40	19.41	19.43	19.45	19.45	19.46	19.47	19.48	19.49	19.50
3	8.79	8.74	8.70	8.66	8.64	8.62	8.59	8.57	8.55	8.53
4	5.96	5.91	5.86	5.80	5.77	5.75	5.72	5.69	5.66	5.63
5	4.74	4.68	4.62	4.56	4.53	4.50	4.46	4.43	4.40	4.36
6	4.06	4.00	3.94	3.87	3.84	3.81	3.77	3.74	3.70	3.67
7	3.64	3.57	3.51	3.44	3.41	3.38	3.34	3.30	3.27	3.23
8	3.35	3.28	3.22	3.15	3.12	3.08	3.04	3.01	2.97	2.93
9	3.14	3.07	3.01	2.94	2.90	2.86	2.83	2.79	2.75	2.71
10	2.98	2.91	2.85	2.77	2.74	2.70	2.66	2.62	2.58	2.54
11	2.85	2.79	2.72	2.65	2.61	2.57	2.53	2.49	2.45	2.40
12	2.75	2.69	2.62	2.54	2.51	2.47	2.43	2.38	2.34	2.30
13	2.67	2.60	2.53	2.46	2.42	2.38	2.34	2.30	2.25	2.21
14	2.60	2.53	2.46	2.39	2.35	2.31	2.27	2.22	2.18	2.13
15	2.54	2.48	2.40	2.33	2.29	2.25	2.20	2.16	2.11	2.07
16	2.49	2.42	2.35	2.28	2.24	2.19	2.15	2.11	2.06	2.01
17	2.45	2.38	2.31	2.23	2.19	2.15	2.10	2.06	2.01	1.96
18	2.41	2.34	2.27	2.19	2.15	2.11	2.06	2.02	1.97	1.92
19	2.38	2.31	2.23	2.16	2.11	2.07	2.03	1.98	1.93	1.88
20	2.35	2.28	2.20	2.12	2.08	2.04	1.99	1.95	1.90	1.84
21	2.32	2.25	2.18	2.10	2.05	2.01	1.96	1.92	1.87	1.81
22	2.30	2.23	2.15	2.07	2.03	1.98	1.94	1.89	1.84	1.78
23	2.27	2.20	2.13	2.05	2.01	1.96	1.91	1.86	1.81	1.76
24	2.25	2.18	2.11	2.03	1.98	1.94	1.89	1.84	1.79	1.73
25	2.24	2.16	2.09	2.01	1.96	1.92	1.87	1.82	1.77	1.71
26	2.22	2.15	2.07	1.99	1.95	1.90	1.85	1.80	1.75	1.69
27	2.20	2.13	2.06	1.97	1.93	1.88	1.84	1.79	1.73	1.67
28	2.19	2.12	2.04	1.96	1.91	1.87	1.82	1.77	1.71	1.65
29	2.18	2.10	2.03	1.94	1.90	1.85	1.81	1.75	1.70	1.64
30	2.16	2.09	2.01	1.93	1.89	1.84	1.79	1.74	1.68	1.62
40	2.08	2.00	1.92	1.84	1.79	1.74	1.69	1.64	1.58	1.51
60	1.99	1.92	1.84	1.75	1.70	1.65	1.59	1.53	1.47	1.39
120	1.91	1.83	1.75	1.66	1.61	1.55	1.50	1.43	1.35	1.25
∞	1.83	1.75	1.67	1.57	1.52	1.46	1.39	1.32	1.22	1.00

TABLE 5 *(continued)* Critical Values of the *F* Distribution for $\alpha = 0.025$

Denominator Degrees of Freedom (k_2)	Numerator Degrees of Freedom (k_1)								
	1	2	3	4	5	6	7	8	9
1	647.8	799.5	864.2	899.6	921.8	937.1	948.2	956.7	963.3
2	38.51	39.00	39.17	39.25	39.30	39.33	39.36	39.37	39.39
3	17.44	16.04	15.44	15.10	14.88	14.73	14.62	14.54	14.47
4	12.22	10.65	9.98	9.60	9.36	9.20	9.07	8.98	8.90
5	10.01	8.43	7.76	7.39	7.15	6.98	6.85	6.76	6.68
6	8.81	7.26	6.60	6.23	5.99	5.82	5.70	5.60	5.52
7	8.07	6.54	5.89	5.52	5.29	5.12	4.99	4.90	4.82
8	7.57	6.06	5.42	5.05	4.82	4.65	4.53	4.43	4.36
9	7.21	5.71	5.08	4.72	4.48	4.32	4.20	4.10	4.03
10	6.94	5.46	4.83	4.47	4.24	4.07	3.95	3.85	3.78
11	6.72	5.26	4.63	4.28	4.04	3.88	3.76	3.66	3.59
12	6.55	5.10	4.47	4.12	3.89	3.73	3.61	3.51	3.44
13	6.41	4.97	4.35	4.00	3.77	3.60	3.48	3.39	3.31
14	6.30	4.86	4.24	3.89	3.66	3.50	3.38	3.29	3.21
15	6.20	4.77	4.15	3.80	3.58	3.41	3.29	3.20	3.12
16	6.12	4.69	4.08	3.73	3.50	3.34	3.22	3.12	3.05
17	6.04	4.62	4.01	3.66	3.44	3.28	3.16	3.06	2.98
18	5.98	4.56	3.95	3.61	3.38	3.22	3.10	3.01	2.93
19	5.92	4.51	3.90	3.56	3.33	3.17	3.05	2.96	2.88
20	5.87	4.46	3.86	3.51	3.29	3.13	3.01	2.91	2.84
21	5.83	4.42	3.82	3.48	3.25	3.09	2.97	2.87	2.80
22	5.79	4.38	3.78	3.44	3.22	3.05	2.93	2.84	2.76
23	5.75	4.35	3.75	3.41	3.18	3.02	2.90	2.81	2.73
24	5.72	4.32	3.72	3.38	3.15	2.99	2.87	2.78	2.70
25	5.69	4.29	3.69	3.35	3.13	2.97	2.85	2.75	2.68
26	5.66	4.27	3.67	3.33	3.10	2.94	2.82	2.73	2.65
27	5.63	4.24	3.65	3.31	3.08	2.92	2.80	2.71	2.63
28	5.61	4.22	3.63	3.29	3.06	2.90	2.78	2.69	2.61
29	5.59	4.20	3.61	3.27	3.04	2.88	2.76	2.67	2.59
30	5.57	4.18	3.59	3.25	3.03	2.87	2.75	2.65	2.57
40	5.42	4.05	3.46	3.13	2.90	2.74	2.62	2.53	2.45
60	5.29	3.93	3.34	3.01	2.79	2.63	2.51	2.41	2.33
120	5.15	3.80	3.23	2.89	2.67	2.52	2.39	2.30	2.22
∞	5.02	3.69	3.12	2.79	2.57	2.41	2.29	2.19	2.11

Denominator Degrees of Freedom (k_2)	Numerator Degrees of Freedom (k_1)									
	10	12	15	20	24	30	40	60	120	∞
1	968.6	976.7	984.9	993.1	997.2	1001	1006	1010	1014	1018
2	39.40	39.41	39.43	39.45	39.46	39.46	39.47	39.48	39.49	39.50
3	14.42	14.34	14.25	14.17	14.12	14.08	14.04	13.99	13.95	13.90
4	8.84	8.75	8.66	8.56	8.51	8.46	8.41	8.36	8.31	8.26
5	6.62	6.52	6.43	6.33	6.28	6.23	6.18	6.12	6.07	6.02
6	5.46	5.37	5.27	5.17	5.12	5.07	5.01	4.96	4.90	4.85
7	4.76	4.67	4.57	4.47	4.42	4.36	4.31	4.25	4.20	4.14
8	4.30	4.20	4.10	4.00	3.95	3.89	3.84	3.78	3.73	3.67
9	3.96	3.87	3.77	3.67	3.61	3.56	3.51	3.45	3.39	3.33
10	3.72	3.62	3.52	3.42	3.37	3.31	3.26	3.20	3.14	3.08
11	3.53	3.43	3.33	3.23	3.17	3.12	3.06	3.00	2.94	2.88
12	3.37	3.28	3.18	3.07	3.02	2.96	2.91	2.85	2.79	2.72
13	3.25	3.15	3.05	2.95	2.89	2.84	2.78	2.72	2.66	2.60
14	3.15	3.05	2.95	2.84	2.79	2.73	2.67	2.61	2.55	2.49
15	3.06	2.96	2.86	2.76	2.70	2.64	2.59	2.52	2.46	2.40
16	2.99	2.89	2.79	2.68	2.63	2.57	2.51	2.45	2.38	2.32
17	2.92	2.82	2.72	2.62	2.56	2.50	2.44	2.38	2.32	2.25
18	2.87	2.77	2.67	2.56	2.50	2.44	2.38	2.32	2.26	2.19
19	2.82	2.72	2.62	2.51	2.45	2.39	2.33	2.27	2.20	2.13
20	2.77	2.68	2.57	2.46	2.41	2.35	2.29	2.22	2.16	2.09
21	2.73	2.64	2.53	2.42	2.37	2.31	2.25	2.18	2.11	2.04
22	2.70	2.60	2.50	2.39	2.33	2.27	2.21	2.14	2.08	2.00
23	2.67	2.57	2.47	2.36	2.30	2.24	2.18	2.11	2.04	1.97
24	2.64	2.54	2.44	2.33	2.27	2.21	2.15	2.08	2.01	1.94
25	2.61	2.51	2.41	2.30	2.24	2.18	2.12	2.05	1.98	1.91
26	2.59	2.49	2.39	2.28	2.22	2.16	2.09	2.03	1.95	1.88
27	2.57	2.47	2.36	2.25	2.19	2.13	2.07	2.00	1.93	1.85
28	2.55	2.45	2.34	2.23	2.17	2.11	2.05	1.98	1.91	1.83
29	2.53	2.43	2.32	2.21	2.15	2.09	2.03	1.96	1.89	1.81
30	2.51	2.41	2.31	2.20	2.14	2.07	2.01	1.94	1.87	1.79
40	2.39	2.29	2.18	2.07	2.01	1.94	1.88	1.80	1.72	1.64
60	2.27	2.17	2.06	1.94	1.88	1.82	1.74	1.67	1.58	1.48
120	2.16	2.05	1.94	1.82	1.76	1.69	1.61	1.53	1.43	1.31
∞	2.05	1.94	1.83	1.71	1.64	1.57	1.48	1.39	1.27	1.00

TABLE 5 (concluded)   Critical Values of the F Distribution for $\alpha = 0.01$

Denominator Degrees of Freedom (k_2)	Numerator Degrees of Freedom (k_1)								
	1	2	3	4	5	6	7	8	9
1	4,052	4,999.5	5,403	5,625	5,764	5,859	5,928	5,982	6,022
2	98.50	99.00	99.17	99.25	99.30	99.33	99.36	99.37	99.39
3	34.12	30.82	29.46	28.71	28.24	27.91	27.67	27.49	27.35
4	21.20	18.00	16.69	15.98	15.52	15.21	14.98	14.80	14.66
5	16.26	13.27	12.06	11.39	10.97	10.67	10.46	10.29	10.16
6	13.75	10.92	9.78	9.15	8.75	8.47	8.26	8.10	7.98
7	12.25	9.55	8.45	7.85	7.46	7.19	6.99	6.84	6.72
8	11.26	8.65	7.59	7.01	6.63	6.37	6.18	6.03	5.91
9	10.56	8.02	6.99	6.42	6.06	5.80	5.61	5.47	5.35
10	10.04	7.56	6.55	5.99	5.64	5.39	5.20	5.06	4.94
11	9.65	7.21	6.22	5.67	5.32	5.07	4.89	4.74	4.63
12	9.33	6.93	5.95	5.41	5.06	4.82	4.64	4.50	4.39
13	9.07	6.70	5.74	5.21	4.86	4.62	4.44	4.30	4.19
14	8.86	6.51	5.56	5.04	4.69	4.46	4.28	4.14	4.03
15	8.68	6.36	5.42	4.89	4.56	4.32	4.14	4.00	3.89
16	8.53	6.23	5.29	4.77	4.44	4.20	4.03	3.89	3.78
17	8.40	6.11	5.18	4.67	4.34	4.10	3.93	3.79	3.68
18	8.29	6.01	5.09	4.58	4.25	4.01	3.84	3.71	3.60
19	8.18	5.93	5.01	4.50	4.17	3.94	3.77	3.63	3.52
20	8.10	5.85	4.94	4.43	4.10	3.87	3.70	3.56	3.46
21	8.02	5.78	4.87	4.37	4.04	3.81	3.64	3.51	3.40
22	7.95	5.72	4.82	4.31	3.99	3.76	3.59	3.45	3.35
23	7.88	5.66	4.76	4.26	3.94	3.71	3.54	3.41	3.30
24	7.82	5.61	4.72	4.22	3.90	3.67	3.50	3.36	3.26
25	7.77	5.57	4.68	4.18	3.85	3.63	3.46	3.32	3.22
26	7.72	5.53	4.64	4.14	3.82	3.59	3.42	3.29	3.18
27	7.68	5.49	4.60	4.11	3.78	3.56	3.39	3.26	3.15
28	7.64	5.45	4.57	4.07	3.75	3.53	3.36	3.23	3.12
29	7.60	5.42	4.54	4.04	3.73	3.50	3.33	3.20	3.09
30	7.56	5.39	4.51	4.02	3.70	3.47	3.30	3.17	3.07
40	7.31	5.18	4.31	3.83	3.51	3.29	3.12	2.99	2.89
60	7.08	4.98	4.13	3.65	3.34	3.12	2.95	2.82	2.72
120	6.85	4.79	3.95	3.48	3.17	2.96	2.79	2.66	2.56
∞	6.63	4.61	3.78	3.32	3.02	2.80	2.64	2.51	2.41

Denominator Degrees of Freedom (k_2)	Numerator of Degrees of Freedom (k_1)									
	10	12	15	20	24	30	40	60	120	∞
1	6,056	6,106	6,157	6,209	6,235	6,261	6,287	6,313	6,339	6,366
2	99.40	99.42	99.43	99.45	99.46	99.47	99.47	99.48	99.49	99.50
3	27.23	27.05	26.87	26.69	26.60	26.50	26.41	26.32	26.22	26.13
4	14.55	14.37	14.20	14.02	13.93	13.84	13.75	13.65	13.56	13.46
5	10.05	9.89	9.72	9.55	9.47	9.38	9.29	9.20	9.11	9.02
6	7.87	7.72	7.56	7.40	7.31	7.23	7.14	7.06	6.97	6.88
7	6.62	6.47	6.31	6.16	6.07	5.99	5.91	5.82	5.74	5.65
8	5.81	5.67	5.52	5.36	5.28	5.20	5.12	5.03	4.95	4.86
9	5.26	5.11	4.96	4.81	4.73	4.65	4.57	4.48	4.40	4.31
10	4.85	4.71	4.56	4.41	4.33	4.25	4.17	4.08	4.00	3.91
11	4.54	4.40	4.25	4.10	4.02	3.94	3.86	3.78	3.69	3.60
12	4.30	4.16	4.01	3.86	3.78	3.70	3.62	3.54	3.45	3.36
13	4.10	3.96	3.82	3.66	3.59	3.51	3.43	3.34	3.25	3.17
14	3.94	3.80	3.66	3.51	3.43	3.35	3.27	3.18	3.09	3.00
15	3.80	3.67	3.52	3.37	3.29	3.21	3.13	3.05	2.96	2.87
16	3.69	3.55	3.41	3.26	3.18	3.10	3.02	2.93	2.84	2.75
17	3.59	3.46	3.31	3.16	3.08	3.00	2.92	2.83	2.75	2.65
18	3.51	3.37	3.23	3.08	3.00	2.92	2.84	2.75	2.66	2.57
19	3.43	3.30	3.15	3.00	2.92	2.84	2.76	2.67	2.58	2.49
20	3.37	3.23	3.09	2.94	2.86	2.78	2.69	2.61	2.52	2.42
21	3.31	3.17	3.03	2.88	2.80	2.72	2.64	2.55	2.46	2.36
22	3.26	3.12	2.98	2.83	2.75	2.67	2.58	2.50	2.40	2.31
23	3.21	3.07	2.93	2.78	2.70	2.62	2.54	2.45	2.35	2.26
24	3.17	3.03	2.89	2.74	2.66	2.58	2.49	2.40	2.31	2.21
25	3.13	2.99	2.85	2.70	2.62	2.54	2.45	2.36	2.27	2.17
26	3.09	2.96	2.81	2.66	2.58	2.50	2.42	2.33	2.23	2.13
27	3.06	2.93	2.78	2.63	2.55	2.47	2.38	2.29	2.20	2.10
28	3.03	2.90	2.75	2.60	2.52	2.44	2.35	2.26	2.17	2.06
29	3.00	2.87	2.73	2.57	2.49	2.41	2.33	2.23	2.14	2.03
30	2.98	2.84	2.70	2.55	2.47	2.39	2.30	2.21	2.11	2.01
40	2.80	2.66	2.52	2.37	2.29	2.20	2.11	2.02	1.92	1.80
60	2.63	2.50	2.35	2.20	2.12	2.03	1.94	1.84	1.73	1.60
120	2.47	2.34	2.19	2.03	1.95	1.86	1.76	1.66	1.53	1.38
∞	2.32	2.18	2.04	1.88	1.79	1.70	1.59	1.47	1.32	1.00

Source: M. Merrington and C. M. Thompson, "Tables of Percentage Points of the Inverted Beta (F)-Distribution," *Biometrika* 33 (1943) pp. 73–88. Reproduced by permission of the *Biometrika* Trustees.

TABLE 5A The F Distribution for $\alpha = 0.05$ and $\alpha = 0.01$ (**Bold**) for Many Possible Degrees of Freedom

Denominator Degrees of Freedom (k_2)	Numerator Degrees of Freedom (k_1)																							
	1	2	3	4	5	6	7	8	9	10	11	12	14	16	20	24	30	40	50	75	100	200	500	∞
1	161	200	216	225	230	234	237	239	241	242	243	244	245	246	248	249	250	251	252	253	253	254	254	254
	4,052	**4,999**	**5,403**	**5,625**	**5,764**	**5,859**	**5,928**	**5,981**	**6,022**	**6,056**	**6,082**	**6,106**	**6,142**	**6,169**	**6,208**	**6,234**	**6,261**	**6,286**	**6,302**	**6,323**	**6,334**	**6,352**	**6,361**	**6,366**
2	18.51	19.00	19.16	19.25	19.30	19.33	19.36	19.37	19.38	19.39	19.40	19.41	19.42	19.43	19.44	19.45	19.46	19.47	19.47	19.48	19.49	19.49	19.50	19.50
	98.49	**99.00**	**99.17**	**99.25**	**99.30**	**99.33**	**99.36**	**99.37**	**99.39**	**99.40**	**99.41**	**99.42**	**99.43**	**99.44**	**99.45**	**99.46**	**99.47**	**99.48**	**99.48**	**99.49**	**99.49**	**99.49**	**99.50**	**99.50**
3	10.13	9.55	9.28	9.12	9.01	8.94	8.88	8.84	8.81	8.78	8.76	8.74	8.71	8.69	8.66	8.64	8.62	8.60	8.58	8.57	8.56	8.54	8.54	8.53
	34.12	**30.82**	**29.46**	**28.71**	**28.24**	**27.91**	**27.67**	**27.49**	**27.34**	**27.23**	**27.13**	**27.05**	**26.92**	**26.83**	**26.69**	**26.60**	**26.50**	**26.41**	**26.35**	**26.27**	**26.23**	**26.18**	**26.14**	**26.12**
4	7.71	6.94	6.59	6.39	6.26	6.16	6.09	6.04	6.00	5.96	5.93	5.91	5.87	5.84	5.80	5.77	5.74	5.71	5.70	5.68	5.66	5.65	5.64	5.63
	21.20	**18.00**	**16.69**	**15.98**	**15.52**	**15.21**	**14.98**	**14.80**	**14.66**	**14.54**	**14.45**	**14.37**	**14.24**	**14.15**	**14.02**	**13.93**	**13.83**	**13.74**	**13.69**	**13.61**	**13.57**	**13.52**	**13.48**	**13.46**
5	6.61	5.79	5.41	5.19	5.05	4.95	4.88	4.82	4.78	4.74	4.70	4.68	4.64	4.60	4.56	4.53	4.50	4.46	4.44	4.42	4.40	4.38	4.37	4.36
	16.26	**13.27**	**12.06**	**11.39**	**10.97**	**10.67**	**10.45**	**10.29**	**10.15**	**10.05**	**9.96**	**9.89**	**9.77**	**9.68**	**9.55**	**9.47**	**9.38**	**9.29**	**9.24**	**9.17**	**9.13**	**9.07**	**9.04**	**9.02**
6	5.99	5.14	4.76	4.53	4.39	4.28	4.21	4.15	4.10	4.06	4.03	4.00	3.96	3.92	3.87	3.84	3.81	3.77	3.75	3.72	3.71	3.69	3.68	3.67
	13.74	**10.92**	**9.78**	**9.15**	**8.75**	**8.47**	**8.26**	**8.10**	**7.98**	**7.87**	**7.79**	**7.72**	**7.60**	**7.52**	**7.39**	**7.31**	**7.23**	**7.14**	**7.09**	**7.02**	**6.99**	**6.94**	**6.90**	**6.88**
7	5.59	4.74	4.35	4.12	3.97	3.87	3.79	3.73	3.68	3.63	3.60	3.57	3.52	3.49	3.44	3.41	3.38	3.34	3.32	3.29	3.28	3.25	3.24	3.23
	12.25	**9.55**	**8.45**	**7.85**	**7.46**	**7.19**	**7.00**	**6.84**	**6.71**	**6.62**	**6.54**	**6.47**	**6.35**	**6.27**	**6.15**	**6.07**	**5.98**	**5.90**	**5.85**	**5.78**	**5.75**	**5.70**	**5.67**	**5.65**
8	5.32	4.46	4.07	3.84	3.69	3.58	3.50	3.44	3.39	3.34	3.31	3.28	3.23	3.20	3.15	3.12	3.08	3.05	3.03	3.00	2.98	2.96	2.94	2.93
	11.26	**8.65**	**7.59**	**7.01**	**6.63**	**6.37**	**6.19**	**6.03**	**5.91**	**5.82**	**5.74**	**5.67**	**5.56**	**5.48**	**5.36**	**5.28**	**5.20**	**5.11**	**5.06**	**5.00**	**4.96**	**4.91**	**4.88**	**4.86**
9	5.12	4.26	3.86	3.63	3.48	3.37	3.29	3.23	3.18	3.13	3.10	3.07	3.02	2.98	2.93	2.90	2.86	2.82	2.80	2.77	2.76	2.73	2.72	2.71
	10.56	**8.02**	**6.99**	**6.42**	**6.06**	**5.80**	**5.62**	**5.47**	**5.35**	**5.26**	**5.18**	**5.11**	**5.00**	**4.92**	**4.80**	**4.73**	**4.64**	**4.56**	**4.51**	**4.45**	**4.41**	**4.36**	**4.33**	**4.31**
10	4.96	4.10	3.71	3.48	3.33	3.22	3.14	3.07	3.02	2.97	2.94	2.91	2.86	2.82	2.77	2.74	2.70	2.67	2.64	2.61	2.59	2.56	2.55	2.54
	10.04	**7.56**	**6.55**	**5.99**	**5.64**	**5.39**	**5.21**	**5.06**	**4.95**	**4.85**	**4.78**	**4.71**	**4.60**	**4.52**	**4.41**	**4.33**	**4.25**	**4.17**	**4.12**	**4.05**	**4.01**	**3.96**	**3.93**	**3.91**
11	4.84	3.98	3.59	3.36	3.20	3.09	3.01	2.95	2.90	2.86	2.82	2.79	2.74	2.70	2.65	2.61	2.57	2.53	2.50	2.47	2.45	2.42	2.41	2.40
	9.65	**7.20**	**6.22**	**5.67**	**5.32**	**5.07**	**4.88**	**4.74**	**4.63**	**4.54**	**4.46**	**4.40**	**4.29**	**4.21**	**4.10**	**4.02**	**3.94**	**3.86**	**3.80**	**3.74**	**3.70**	**3.66**	**3.62**	**3.60**
12	4.75	3.88	3.49	3.26	3.11	3.00	2.92	2.85	2.80	2.76	2.72	2.69	2.64	2.60	2.54	2.50	2.46	2.42	2.40	2.36	2.35	2.32	2.31	2.30
	9.33	**6.93**	**5.95**	**5.41**	**5.06**	**4.82**	**4.65**	**4.50**	**4.39**	**4.30**	**4.22**	**4.16**	**4.05**	**3.98**	**3.86**	**3.78**	**3.70**	**3.61**	**3.56**	**3.49**	**3.46**	**3.41**	**3.38**	**3.36**

13	4.67 **9.07**	3.80 **6.70**	3.41 **5.74**	3.18 **5.20**	3.02 **4.86**	2.92 **4.62**	2.84 **4.44**	2.77 **4.30**	2.72 **4.19**	2.67 **4.10**	2.63 **4.02**	2.60 **3.96**	2.55 **3.85**	2.51 **3.78**	2.46 **3.67**	2.42 **3.59**	2.38 **3.51**	2.34 **3.42**	2.32 **3.37**	2.28 **3.30**	2.26 **3.27**	2.24 **3.21**	2.22 **3.18**	2.21 **3.16**
14	4.60 **8.86**	3.74 **6.51**	3.34 **5.56**	3.11 **5.03**	2.96 **4.69**	2.85 **4.46**	2.77 **4.28**	2.70 **4.14**	2.65 **4.03**	2.60 **3.94**	2.56 **3.86**	2.53 **3.80**	2.48 **3.70**	2.44 **3.62**	2.39 **3.51**	2.35 **3.43**	2.31 **3.34**	2.27 **3.26**	2.24 **3.21**	2.21 **3.14**	2.19 **3.11**	2.16 **3.06**	2.14 **3.02**	2.13 **3.00**
15	4.54 **8.68**	3.68 **6.36**	3.29 **5.42**	3.06 **4.89**	2.90 **4.56**	2.79 **4.32**	2.70 **4.14**	2.64 **4.00**	2.59 **3.89**	2.55 **3.80**	2.51 **3.73**	2.48 **3.67**	2.43 **3.56**	2.39 **3.48**	2.33 **3.36**	2.29 **3.29**	2.25 **3.20**	2.21 **3.12**	2.18 **3.07**	2.15 **3.00**	2.12 **2.97**	2.10 **2.92**	2.08 **2.89**	2.07 **2.87**
16	4.49 **8.53**	3.63 **6.23**	3.24 **5.29**	3.01 **4.77**	2.85 **4.44**	2.74 **4.20**	2.66 **4.03**	2.59 **3.89**	2.54 **3.78**	2.49 **3.69**	2.45 **3.61**	2.42 **3.55**	2.37 **3.45**	2.33 **3.37**	2.28 **3.25**	2.24 **3.18**	2.20 **3.10**	2.16 **3.01**	2.13 **2.96**	2.09 **2.89**	2.07 **2.86**	2.04 **2.80**	2.02 **2.77**	2.01 **2.75**
17	4.45 **8.40**	3.59 **6.11**	3.20 **5.18**	2.96 **4.67**	2.81 **4.34**	2.70 **4.10**	2.62 **3.93**	2.55 **3.79**	2.50 **3.68**	2.45 **3.59**	2.41 **3.52**	2.38 **3.45**	2.33 **3.35**	2.29 **3.27**	2.23 **3.16**	2.19 **3.08**	2.15 **3.00**	2.11 **2.92**	2.08 **2.86**	2.04 **2.79**	2.02 **2.76**	1.99 **2.70**	1.97 **2.67**	1.96 **2.65**
18	4.41 **8.28**	3.55 **6.01**	3.16 **5.09**	2.93 **4.58**	2.77 **4.25**	2.66 **4.01**	2.58 **3.85**	2.51 **3.71**	2.46 **3.60**	2.41 **3.51**	2.37 **3.44**	2.34 **3.37**	2.29 **3.27**	2.25 **3.19**	2.19 **3.07**	2.15 **3.00**	2.11 **2.91**	2.07 **2.83**	2.04 **2.78**	2.00 **2.71**	1.98 **2.68**	1.95 **2.62**	1.93 **2.59**	1.92 **2.57**
19	4.38 **8.18**	3.52 **5.93**	3.13 **5.01**	2.90 **4.50**	2.74 **4.17**	2.63 **3.94**	2.55 **3.77**	2.48 **3.63**	2.43 **3.52**	2.38 **3.43**	2.34 **3.36**	2.31 **3.30**	2.26 **3.19**	2.21 **3.12**	2.15 **3.00**	2.11 **2.92**	2.07 **2.84**	2.02 **2.76**	2.00 **2.70**	1.96 **2.63**	1.94 **2.60**	1.91 **2.54**	1.90 **2.51**	1.88 **2.49**
20	4.35 **8.10**	3.49 **5.85**	3.10 **4.94**	2.87 **4.43**	2.71 **4.10**	2.60 **3.87**	2.52 **3.71**	2.45 **3.56**	2.40 **3.45**	2.35 **3.37**	2.31 **3.30**	2.28 **3.23**	2.23 **3.13**	2.18 **3.05**	2.12 **2.94**	2.08 **2.86**	2.04 **2.77**	1.99 **2.69**	1.96 **2.63**	1.92 **2.56**	1.90 **2.53**	1.87 **2.47**	1.85 **2.44**	1.84 **2.42**
21	4.32 **8.02**	3.47 **5.78**	3.07 **4.87**	2.84 **4.37**	2.68 **4.04**	2.57 **3.81**	2.49 **3.65**	2.42 **3.51**	2.37 **3.40**	2.32 **3.31**	2.28 **3.24**	2.25 **3.17**	2.20 **3.07**	2.15 **2.99**	2.09 **2.88**	2.05 **2.80**	2.00 **2.72**	1.96 **2.63**	1.93 **2.58**	1.89 **2.51**	1.87 **2.47**	1.84 **2.42**	1.82 **2.38**	1.81 **2.36**
22	4.30 **7.94**	3.44 **5.72**	3.05 **4.82**	2.82 **4.31**	2.66 **3.99**	2.55 **3.76**	2.47 **3.59**	2.40 **3.45**	2.35 **3.35**	2.30 **3.26**	2.26 **3.18**	2.23 **3.12**	2.18 **3.02**	2.13 **2.94**	2.07 **2.83**	2.03 **2.75**	1.98 **2.67**	1.93 **2.58**	1.91 **2.53**	1.87 **2.46**	1.84 **2.42**	1.81 **2.37**	1.80 **2.33**	1.78 **2.31**
23	4.28 **7.88**	3.42 **5.66**	3.03 **4.76**	2.80 **4.26**	2.64 **3.94**	2.53 **3.71**	2.45 **3.54**	2.38 **3.41**	2.32 **3.30**	2.28 **3.21**	2.24 **3.14**	2.20 **3.07**	2.14 **2.97**	2.10 **2.89**	2.04 **2.78**	2.00 **2.70**	1.96 **2.62**	1.91 **2.53**	1.88 **2.48**	1.84 **2.41**	1.82 **2.37**	1.79 **2.32**	1.77 **2.28**	1.76 **2.26**
24	4.26 **7.82**	3.40 **5.61**	3.01 **4.72**	2.78 **4.22**	2.62 **3.90**	2.51 **3.67**	2.43 **3.50**	2.36 **3.36**	2.30 **3.25**	2.26 **3.17**	2.22 **3.09**	2.18 **3.03**	2.13 **2.93**	2.09 **2.85**	2.02 **2.74**	1.98 **2.66**	1.94 **2.58**	1.89 **2.49**	1.86 **2.44**	1.82 **2.36**	1.80 **2.33**	1.76 **2.27**	1.74 **2.23**	1.73 **2.21**
25	4.24 **7.77**	3.38 **5.57**	2.99 **4.68**	2.76 **4.18**	2.60 **3.86**	2.49 **3.63**	2.41 **3.46**	2.34 **3.32**	2.28 **3.21**	2.24 **3.13**	2.20 **3.05**	2.16 **2.99**	2.11 **2.89**	2.06 **2.81**	2.00 **2.70**	1.96 **2.62**	1.92 **2.54**	1.87 **2.45**	1.84 **2.40**	1.80 **2.32**	1.77 **2.29**	1.74 **2.23**	1.72 **2.19**	1.71 **2.17**
26	4.22 **7.72**	3.37 **5.53**	2.98 **4.64**	2.74 **4.14**	2.59 **3.82**	2.47 **3.59**	2.39 **3.42**	2.32 **3.29**	2.27 **3.17**	2.22 **3.09**	2.18 **3.02**	2.15 **2.96**	2.10 **2.86**	2.05 **2.77**	1.99 **2.66**	1.95 **2.58**	1.90 **2.50**	1.85 **2.41**	1.82 **2.36**	1.78 **2.28**	1.76 **2.25**	1.72 **2.19**	1.70 **2.15**	1.69 **2.13**

TABLE 5A *(concluded)*

Numerator Degrees of Freedom (k_1)

Denominator Degrees of Freedom (k_2)	1	2	3	4	5	6	7	8	9	10	11	12	14	16	20	24	30	40	50	75	100	200	500	∞
27	4.21 **7.68**	3.35 **5.49**	2.96 **4.60**	2.73 **4.11**	2.57 **3.79**	2.46 **3.56**	2.37 **3.39**	2.30 **3.26**	2.25 **3.14**	2.20 **3.06**	2.16 **2.98**	2.13 **2.93**	2.08 **2.83**	2.03 **2.74**	1.97 **2.63**	1.93 **2.55**	1.88 **2.47**	1.84 **2.38**	1.80 **2.33**	1.76 **2.25**	1.74 **2.21**	1.71 **2.16**	1.68 **2.12**	1.67 **2.10**
28	4.20 **7.64**	3.34 **5.45**	2.95 **4.57**	2.71 **4.07**	2.56 **3.76**	2.44 **3.53**	2.36 **3.36**	2.29 **3.23**	2.24 **3.11**	2.19 **3.03**	2.15 **2.95**	2.12 **2.90**	2.06 **2.80**	2.02 **2.71**	1.96 **2.60**	1.91 **2.52**	1.87 **2.44**	1.81 **2.35**	1.78 **2.30**	1.75 **2.22**	1.72 **2.18**	1.69 **2.13**	1.67 **2.09**	1.65 **2.06**
29	4.18 **7.60**	3.33 **5.42**	2.93 **4.54**	2.70 **4.04**	2.54 **3.73**	2.43 **3.50**	2.35 **3.33**	2.28 **3.20**	2.22 **3.08**	2.18 **3.00**	2.14 **2.92**	2.10 **2.87**	2.05 **2.77**	2.00 **2.68**	1.94 **2.57**	1.90 **2.49**	1.85 **2.41**	1.80 **2.32**	1.77 **2.27**	1.73 **2.19**	1.71 **2.15**	1.68 **2.10**	1.65 **2.06**	1.64 **2.03**
30	4.17 **7.56**	3.32 **5.39**	2.92 **4.51**	2.69 **4.02**	2.53 **3.70**	2.42 **3.47**	2.34 **3.30**	2.27 **3.17**	2.21 **3.06**	2.16 **2.98**	2.12 **2.90**	2.09 **2.84**	2.04 **2.74**	1.99 **2.66**	1.93 **2.55**	1.89 **2.47**	1.84 **2.38**	1.79 **2.29**	1.76 **2.24**	1.72 **2.16**	1.69 **2.13**	1.66 **2.07**	1.64 **2.03**	1.62 **2.01**
32	4.15 **7.50**	3.30 **5.34**	2.90 **4.46**	2.67 **3.97**	2.51 **3.66**	2.40 **3.42**	2.32 **3.25**	2.25 **3.12**	2.19 **3.01**	2.14 **2.94**	2.10 **2.86**	2.07 **2.80**	2.02 **2.70**	1.97 **2.62**	1.91 **2.51**	1.86 **2.42**	1.82 **2.34**	1.76 **2.25**	1.74 **2.20**	1.69 **2.12**	1.67 **2.08**	1.64 **2.02**	1.61 **1.98**	1.59 **1.96**
34	4.13 **7.44**	3.28 **5.29**	2.88 **4.42**	2.65 **3.93**	2.49 **3.61**	2.38 **3.38**	2.30 **3.21**	2.23 **3.08**	2.17 **2.97**	2.12 **2.89**	2.08 **2.82**	2.05 **2.76**	2.00 **2.66**	1.95 **2.58**	1.89 **2.47**	1.84 **2.38**	1.80 **2.30**	1.74 **2.21**	1.71 **2.15**	1.67 **2.08**	1.64 **2.04**	1.61 **1.98**	1.59 **1.94**	1.57 **1.91**
36	4.11 **7.39**	3.26 **5.25**	2.86 **4.38**	2.63 **3.89**	2.48 **3.58**	2.36 **3.35**	2.28 **3.18**	2.21 **3.04**	2.15 **2.94**	2.10 **2.86**	2.06 **2.78**	2.03 **2.72**	1.98 **2.62**	1.93 **2.54**	1.87 **2.43**	1.82 **2.35**	1.78 **2.26**	1.72 **2.17**	1.69 **2.12**	1.65 **2.04**	1.62 **2.00**	1.59 **1.94**	1.56 **1.90**	1.55 **1.87**
38	4.10 **7.35**	3.25 **5.21**	2.85 **4.34**	2.62 **3.86**	2.46 **3.54**	2.35 **3.32**	2.26 **3.15**	2.19 **3.02**	2.14 **2.91**	2.09 **2.82**	2.05 **2.75**	2.02 **2.69**	1.96 **2.59**	1.92 **2.51**	1.85 **2.40**	1.80 **2.32**	1.76 **2.22**	1.71 **2.14**	1.67 **2.08**	1.63 **2.00**	1.60 **1.97**	1.57 **1.90**	1.54 **1.86**	1.53 **1.84**
40	4.08 **7.31**	3.23 **5.18**	2.84 **4.31**	2.61 **3.83**	2.45 **3.51**	2.34 **3.29**	2.25 **3.12**	2.18 **2.99**	2.12 **2.88**	2.07 **2.80**	2.04 **2.73**	2.00 **2.66**	1.95 **2.56**	1.90 **2.49**	1.84 **2.37**	1.79 **2.29**	1.74 **2.20**	1.69 **2.11**	1.66 **2.05**	1.61 **1.97**	1.59 **1.94**	1.55 **1.88**	1.53 **1.84**	1.51 **1.81**
42	4.07 **7.27**	3.22 **5.15**	2.83 **4.29**	2.59 **3.80**	2.44 **3.49**	2.32 **3.26**	2.24 **3.10**	2.17 **2.96**	2.11 **2.86**	2.06 **2.77**	2.02 **2.70**	1.99 **2.64**	1.94 **2.54**	1.89 **2.46**	1.82 **2.35**	1.78 **2.26**	1.73 **2.17**	1.68 **2.08**	1.64 **2.02**	1.60 **1.94**	1.57 **1.91**	1.54 **1.85**	1.51 **1.80**	1.49 **1.78**
44	4.06 **7.24**	3.21 **5.12**	2.82 **4.26**	2.58 **3.78**	2.43 **3.46**	2.31 **3.24**	2.23 **3.07**	2.16 **2.94**	2.10 **2.84**	2.05 **2.75**	2.01 **2.68**	1.98 **2.62**	1.92 **2.52**	1.88 **2.44**	1.81 **2.32**	1.76 **2.24**	1.72 **2.15**	1.66 **2.06**	1.63 **2.00**	1.58 **1.92**	1.56 **1.88**	1.52 **1.82**	1.50 **1.78**	1.48 **1.75**
46	4.05 **7.21**	3.20 **5.10**	2.81 **4.24**	2.57 **3.76**	2.42 **3.44**	2.30 **3.22**	2.22 **3.05**	2.14 **2.92**	2.09 **2.82**	2.04 **2.73**	2.00 **2.66**	1.97 **2.60**	1.91 **2.50**	1.87 **2.42**	1.80 **2.30**	1.75 **2.22**	1.71 **2.13**	1.65 **2.04**	1.62 **1.98**	1.57 **1.90**	1.54 **1.86**	1.51 **1.80**	1.48 **1.76**	1.46 **1.72**
48	4.04 **7.19**	3.19 **5.08**	2.80 **4.22**	2.56 **3.74**	2.41 **3.42**	2.30 **3.20**	2.21 **3.04**	2.14 **2.90**	2.08 **2.80**	2.03 **2.71**	1.99 **2.64**	1.96 **2.58**	1.90 **2.48**	1.86 **2.40**	1.79 **2.28**	1.74 **2.20**	1.70 **2.11**	1.64 **2.02**	1.61 **1.96**	1.56 **1.88**	1.53 **1.84**	1.50 **1.78**	1.47 **1.73**	1.45 **1.70**

df																								
50	4.03 **7.17**	3.18 **5.06**	2.79 **4.20**	2.56 **3.72**	2.40 **3.41**	2.29 **3.18**	2.20 **3.02**	2.13 **2.88**	2.07 **2.78**	2.02 **2.70**	1.98 **2.62**	1.95 **2.56**	1.90 **2.46**	1.85 **2.39**	1.78 **2.26**	1.74 **2.18**	1.69 **2.10**	1.63 **2.00**	1.60 **1.94**	1.55 **1.86**	1.52 **1.82**	1.48 **1.76**	1.46 **1.71**	1.44 **1.68**
55	4.02 **7.12**	3.17 **5.01**	2.78 **4.16**	2.54 **3.68**	2.38 **3.37**	2.27 **3.15**	2.18 **2.98**	2.11 **2.85**	2.05 **2.75**	2.00 **2.66**	1.97 **2.59**	1.93 **2.53**	1.88 **2.43**	1.83 **2.35**	1.76 **2.23**	1.72 **2.15**	1.67 **2.06**	1.61 **1.96**	1.58 **1.90**	1.52 **1.82**	1.50 **1.78**	1.46 **1.71**	1.43 **1.66**	1.41 **1.64**
60	4.00 **7.08**	3.15 **4.98**	2.76 **4.13**	2.52 **3.65**	2.37 **3.34**	2.25 **3.12**	2.17 **2.95**	2.10 **2.82**	2.04 **2.72**	1.99 **2.63**	1.95 **2.56**	1.92 **2.50**	1.86 **2.40**	1.81 **2.32**	1.75 **2.20**	1.70 **2.12**	1.65 **2.03**	1.59 **1.93**	1.56 **1.87**	1.50 **1.79**	1.48 **1.74**	1.44 **1.68**	1.41 **1.63**	1.39 **1.60**
65	3.99 **7.04**	3.14 **4.95**	2.75 **4.10**	2.51 **3.62**	2.36 **3.31**	2.24 **3.09**	2.15 **2.93**	2.08 **2.79**	2.02 **2.70**	1.98 **2.61**	1.94 **2.54**	1.90 **2.47**	1.85 **2.37**	1.80 **2.30**	1.73 **2.18**	1.68 **2.09**	1.63 **2.00**	1.57 **1.90**	1.54 **1.84**	1.49 **1.76**	1.46 **1.71**	1.42 **1.64**	1.39 **1.60**	1.37 **1.56**
70	3.98 **7.01**	3.13 **4.92**	2.74 **4.08**	2.50 **3.60**	2.35 **3.29**	2.23 **3.07**	2.14 **2.91**	2.07 **2.77**	2.01 **2.67**	1.97 **2.59**	1.93 **2.51**	1.89 **2.45**	1.84 **2.35**	1.79 **2.28**	1.72 **2.15**	1.67 **2.07**	1.62 **1.98**	1.56 **1.88**	1.53 **1.82**	1.47 **1.74**	1.45 **1.69**	1.40 **1.62**	1.37 **1.56**	1.35 **1.53**
80	3.96 **6.96**	3.11 **4.88**	2.72 **4.04**	2.48 **3.56**	2.33 **3.25**	2.21 **3.04**	2.12 **2.87**	2.05 **2.74**	1.99 **2.64**	1.95 **2.55**	1.91 **2.48**	1.88 **2.41**	1.82 **2.32**	1.77 **2.24**	1.70 **2.11**	1.65 **2.03**	1.60 **1.94**	1.54 **1.84**	1.51 **1.78**	1.45 **1.70**	1.42 **1.65**	1.38 **1.57**	1.35 **1.52**	1.32 **1.49**
100	3.94 **6.90**	3.09 **4.82**	2.70 **3.98**	2.46 **3.51**	2.30 **3.20**	2.19 **2.99**	2.10 **2.82**	2.03 **2.69**	1.97 **2.59**	1.92 **2.51**	1.88 **2.43**	1.85 **2.36**	1.79 **2.26**	1.75 **2.19**	1.68 **2.06**	1.63 **1.98**	1.57 **1.89**	1.51 **1.79**	1.48 **1.73**	1.42 **1.64**	1.39 **1.59**	1.34 **1.51**	1.30 **1.46**	1.28 **1.43**
125	3.92 **6.84**	3.07 **4.78**	2.68 **3.94**	2.44 **3.47**	2.29 **3.17**	2.17 **2.95**	2.08 **2.79**	2.01 **2.65**	1.95 **2.56**	1.90 **2.47**	1.86 **2.40**	1.83 **2.33**	1.77 **2.23**	1.72 **2.15**	1.65 **2.03**	1.60 **1.94**	1.55 **1.85**	1.49 **1.75**	1.45 **1.68**	1.39 **1.59**	1.36 **1.54**	1.31 **1.46**	1.27 **1.40**	1.25 **1.37**
150	3.91 **6.81**	3.06 **4.75**	2.67 **3.91**	2.43 **3.44**	2.27 **3.14**	2.16 **2.92**	2.07 **2.76**	2.00 **2.62**	1.94 **2.53**	1.89 **2.44**	1.85 **2.37**	1.82 **2.30**	1.76 **2.20**	1.71 **2.12**	1.64 **2.00**	1.59 **1.91**	1.54 **1.83**	1.47 **1.72**	1.44 **1.66**	1.37 **1.56**	1.34 **1.51**	1.29 **1.43**	1.25 **1.37**	1.22 **1.33**
200	3.89 **6.76**	3.04 **4.71**	2.65 **3.88**	2.41 **3.41**	2.26 **3.11**	2.14 **2.90**	2.05 **2.73**	1.98 **2.60**	1.92 **2.50**	1.87 **2.41**	1.83 **2.34**	1.80 **2.28**	1.74 **2.17**	1.69 **2.09**	1.62 **1.97**	1.57 **1.88**	1.52 **1.79**	1.45 **1.69**	1.42 **1.62**	1.35 **1.53**	1.32 **1.48**	1.26 **1.39**	1.22 **1.33**	1.19 **1.28**
400	3.86 **6.70**	3.02 **4.66**	2.62 **3.83**	2.39 **3.36**	2.23 **3.06**	2.12 **2.85**	2.03 **2.69**	1.96 **2.55**	1.90 **2.46**	1.85 **2.37**	1.81 **2.29**	1.78 **2.23**	1.72 **2.12**	1.67 **2.04**	1.60 **1.92**	1.54 **1.84**	1.49 **1.74**	1.42 **1.64**	1.38 **1.57**	1.32 **1.47**	1.28 **1.42**	1.22 **1.32**	1.16 **1.24**	1.13 **1.19**
1,000	3.85 **6.66**	3.00 **4.62**	2.61 **3.80**	2.38 **3.34**	2.22 **3.04**	2.10 **2.82**	2.02 **2.66**	1.95 **2.53**	1.89 **2.43**	1.84 **2.34**	1.80 **2.26**	1.76 **2.20**	1.70 **2.09**	1.65 **2.01**	1.58 **1.89**	1.53 **1.81**	1.47 **1.71**	1.41 **1.61**	1.36 **1.54**	1.30 **1.44**	1.26 **1.38**	1.19 **1.28**	1.13 **1.19**	1.08 **1.11**
∞	3.84 **6.63**	2.99 **4.60**	2.60 **3.78**	2.37 **3.32**	2.21 **3.02**	2.09 **2.80**	2.01 **2.64**	1.94 **2.51**	1.88 **2.41**	1.83 **2.32**	1.79 **2.24**	1.75 **2.18**	1.69 **2.07**	1.64 **1.99**	1.57 **1.87**	1.52 **1.79**	1.46 **1.69**	1.40 **1.59**	1.35 **1.52**	1.28 **1.41**	1.24 **1.36**	1.17 **1.25**	1.11 **1.15**	1.00 **1.00**

Reprinted by permission from *Statistical Methods*, 7th ed. by George W. Snedecor and William G. Cochran, © 1980 by the Iowa State University Press, Ames, Iowa 50010

TABLE 6 Critical Values of the Studentized Range Distribution for $\alpha = 0.05$

r

$n-r$	2	3	4	5	6	7	8	9	10	11	12	13	14	15	16	17	18	19	20
1	18.0	27.0	32.8	37.1	40.4	43.1	45.4	47.4	49.1	50.6	52.0	53.2	54.3	55.4	56.3	57.2	58.0	58.8	59.6
2	6.08	8.33	9.80	10.9	11.7	12.4	13.0	13.5	14.0	14.4	14.7	15.1	15.4	15.7	15.9	16.1	16.4	16.6	16.8
3	4.50	5.91	6.82	7.50	8.04	8.48	8.85	9.18	9.46	9.72	9.95	10.2	10.3	10.5	10.7	10.8	11.0	11.1	11.2
4	3.93	5.04	5.76	6.29	6.71	7.05	7.35	7.60	7.83	8.03	8.21	8.37	8.52	8.66	8.79	8.91	9.03	9.13	9.23
5	3.64	4.60	5.22	5.67	6.03	6.33	6.58	6.80	6.99	7.17	7.32	7.47	7.60	7.72	7.83	7.93	8.03	8.12	8.21
6	3.46	4.34	4.90	5.30	5.63	5.90	6.12	6.32	6.49	6.65	6.79	6.92	7.03	7.14	7.24	7.34	7.43	7.51	7.59
7	3.34	4.16	4.68	5.06	5.36	5.61	5.82	6.00	6.16	6.30	6.43	6.55	6.66	6.76	6.85	6.94	7.02	7.10	7.17
8	3.26	4.04	4.53	4.89	5.17	5.40	5.60	5.77	5.92	6.05	6.18	6.29	6.39	6.48	6.57	6.65	6.73	6.80	6.87
9	3.20	3.95	4.41	4.76	5.02	5.24	5.43	5.59	5.74	5.87	5.98	6.09	6.19	6.28	6.36	6.44	6.51	6.58	6.64
10	3.15	3.88	4.33	4.65	4.91	5.12	5.30	5.46	5.60	5.72	5.83	5.93	6.03	6.11	6.19	6.27	6.34	6.40	6.47
11	3.11	3.82	4.26	4.57	4.82	5.03	5.20	5.35	5.49	5.61	5.71	5.81	5.90	5.98	6.06	6.13	6.20	6.27	6.33
12	3.08	3.77	4.20	4.51	4.75	4.95	5.12	5.27	5.39	5.51	5.61	5.71	5.80	5.88	5.95	6.02	6.09	6.15	6.21
13	3.06	3.73	4.15	4.45	4.69	4.88	5.05	5.19	5.32	5.43	5.53	5.63	5.71	5.79	5.86	5.93	5.99	6.05	6.11
14	3.03	3.70	4.11	4.41	4.64	4.83	4.99	5.13	5.25	5.36	5.46	5.55	5.64	5.71	5.79	5.85	5.91	5.97	6.03
15	3.01	3.67	4.08	4.37	4.59	4.78	4.94	5.08	5.20	5.31	5.40	5.49	5.57	5.65	5.72	5.78	5.85	5.90	5.96
16	3.00	3.65	4.05	4.33	4.56	4.74	4.90	5.03	5.15	5.26	5.35	5.44	5.52	5.59	5.66	5.73	5.79	5.84	5.90
17	2.98	3.63	4.02	4.30	4.52	4.70	4.86	4.99	5.11	5.21	5.31	5.39	5.47	5.54	5.61	5.67	5.73	5.79	5.84
18	2.97	3.61	4.00	4.28	4.49	4.67	4.82	4.96	5.07	5.17	5.27	5.35	5.43	5.50	5.57	5.63	5.69	5.74	5.79
19	2.96	3.59	3.98	4.25	4.47	4.65	4.79	4.92	5.04	5.14	5.23	5.31	5.39	5.46	5.53	5.59	5.65	5.70	5.75
20	2.95	3.58	3.96	4.23	4.45	4.62	4.77	4.90	5.01	5.11	5.20	5.28	5.36	5.43	5.49	5.55	5.61	5.66	5.71
24	2.92	3.53	3.90	4.17	4.37	4.54	4.68	4.81	4.92	5.01	5.10	5.18	5.25	5.32	5.38	5.44	5.49	5.55	5.59
30	2.89	3.49	3.85	4.10	4.30	4.46	4.60	4.72	4.82	4.92	5.00	5.08	5.15	5.21	5.27	5.33	5.38	5.43	5.47
40	2.86	3.44	3.79	4.04	4.23	4.39	4.52	4.63	4.73	4.82	4.90	4.98	5.04	5.11	5.16	5.22	5.27	5.31	5.36
60	2.83	3.40	3.74	3.98	4.16	4.31	4.44	4.55	4.65	4.73	4.81	4.88	4.94	5.00	5.06	5.11	5.15	5.20	5.24
120	2.80	3.36	3.68	3.92	4.10	4.24	4.36	4.47	4.56	4.64	4.71	4.78	4.84	4.90	4.95	5.00	5.04	5.09	5.13
∞	2.77	3.31	3.63	3.86	4.03	4.17	4.29	4.39	4.47	4.55	4.62	4.68	4.74	4.80	4.85	4.89	4.93	4.97	5.01

TABLE 6 *(concluded)*   Critical Values of the Studentized Range Distribution for $\alpha = 0.01$

$n-r$	2	3	4	5	6	7	8	9	10	11	12	13	14	15	16	17	18	19	20
1	90.0	135	164	186	202	216	227	237	246	253	260	266	272	277	282	286	290	294	298
2	14.0	19.0	22.3	24.7	26.6	28.2	29.5	30.7	31.7	32.6	33.4	34.1	34.8	35.4	36.0	36.5	37.0	37.5	37.9
3	8.26	10.6	12.2	13.3	14.2	15.0	15.6	16.2	16.7	17.1	17.5	17.9	18.2	18.5	18.8	19.1	19.3	19.5	19.8
4	6.51	8.12	9.17	9.96	10.6	11.1	11.5	11.9	12.3	12.6	12.8	13.1	13.3	13.5	13.7	13.9	14.1	14.2	14.4
5	5.70	6.97	7.80	8.42	8.91	9.32	9.67	9.97	10.2	10.5	10.7	10.9	11.1	11.2	11.4	11.6	11.7	11.8	11.9
6	5.24	6.33	7.03	7.56	7.97	8.32	8.61	8.87	9.10	9.30	9.49	9.65	9.81	9.95	10.1	10.2	10.3	10.4	10.5
7	4.95	5.92	6.54	7.01	7.37	7.68	7.94	8.17	8.37	8.55	8.71	8.86	9.00	9.12	9.24	9.35	9.46	9.55	9.65
8	4.74	5.63	6.20	6.63	6.96	7.24	7.47	7.68	7.87	8.03	8.18	8.31	8.44	8.55	8.66	8.76	8.85	8.94	9.03
9	4.60	5.43	5.96	6.35	6.66	6.91	7.13	7.32	7.49	7.65	7.78	7.91	8.03	8.13	8.23	8.32	8.41	8.49	8.57
10	4.48	5.27	5.77	6.14	6.43	6.67	6.87	7.05	7.21	7.36	7.48	7.60	7.71	7.81	7.91	7.99	8.07	8.15	8.22
11	4.39	5.14	5.62	5.97	6.25	6.48	6.67	6.84	6.99	7.13	7.25	7.36	7.46	7.56	7.65	7.73	7.81	7.88	7.95
12	4.32	5.04	5.50	5.84	6.10	6.32	6.51	6.67	6.81	6.94	7.06	7.17	7.26	7.36	7.44	7.52	7.59	7.66	7.73
13	4.26	4.96	5.40	5.73	5.98	6.19	6.37	6.53	6.67	6.79	6.90	7.01	7.10	7.19	7.27	7.34	7.42	7.48	7.55
14	4.21	4.89	5.32	5.63	5.88	6.08	6.26	6.41	6.54	6.66	6.77	6.87	6.96	7.05	7.12	7.20	7.27	7.33	7.39
15	4.17	4.83	5.25	5.56	5.80	5.99	6.16	6.31	6.44	6.55	6.66	6.76	6.84	6.93	7.00	7.07	7.14	7.20	7.26
16	4.13	4.78	5.19	5.49	5.72	5.92	6.08	6.22	6.35	6.46	6.56	6.66	6.74	6.82	6.90	6.97	7.03	7.09	7.15
17	4.10	4.74	5.14	5.43	5.66	5.85	6.01	6.15	6.27	6.38	6.48	6.57	6.66	6.73	6.80	6.87	6.94	7.00	7.05
18	4.07	4.70	5.09	5.38	5.60	5.79	5.94	6.08	6.20	6.31	6.41	6.50	6.58	6.65	6.72	6.79	6.85	6.91	6.96
19	4.05	4.67	5.05	5.33	5.55	5.73	5.89	6.02	6.14	6.25	6.34	6.43	6.51	6.58	6.65	6.72	6.78	6.84	6.89
20	4.02	4.64	5.02	5.29	5.51	5.69	5.84	5.97	6.09	6.19	6.29	6.37	6.45	6.52	6.59	6.65	6.71	6.76	6.82
24	3.96	4.54	4.91	5.17	5.37	5.54	5.69	5.81	5.92	6.02	6.11	6.19	6.26	6.33	6.39	6.45	6.51	6.56	6.61
30	3.89	4.45	4.80	5.05	5.24	5.40	5.54	5.65	5.76	5.85	5.93	6.01	6.08	6.14	6.20	6.26	6.31	6.36	6.41
40	3.82	4.37	4.70	4.93	5.11	5.27	5.39	5.50	5.60	5.69	5.77	5.84	5.90	5.96	6.02	6.07	6.12	6.17	6.21
60	3.76	4.28	4.60	4.82	4.99	5.13	5.25	5.36	5.45	5.53	5.60	5.67	5.73	5.79	5.84	5.89	5.93	5.98	6.02
120	3.70	4.20	4.50	4.71	4.87	5.01	5.12	5.21	5.30	5.38	5.44	5.51	5.56	5.61	5.66	5.71	5.75	5.79	5.83
∞	3.64	4.12	4.40	4.60	4.76	4.88	4.99	5.08	5.16	5.23	5.29	5.35	5.40	5.45	5.49	5.54	5.57	5.61	5.65

r

Reprinted by permission of the *Biometrika* Trustees from E. S. Pearson and H. O Hartley, eds., *Biometrika Tables for Statisticians*, vol. I, 3rd ed., (Cambridge University Press, 1966).

TABLE 7   Critical Values of the Durbin-Watson Test Statistic for $\alpha = 0.05$

n	k = 1		k = 2		k = 3		k = 4		k = 5	
	d_L	d_U	d_L	d_U	d_L	d_U	d_L	d_U	d_L	d_U
15	1.08	1.36	0.95	1.54	0.82	1.75	0.69	1.97	0.56	2.21
16	1.10	1.37	0.98	1.54	0.86	1.73	0.74	1.93	0.62	2.15
17	1.13	1.38	1.02	1.54	0.90	1.71	0.78	1.90	0.67	2.10
18	1.16	1.39	1.05	1.53	0.93	1.69	0.82	1.87	0.71	2.06
19	1.18	1.40	1.08	1.53	0.97	1.68	0.86	1.85	0.75	2.02
20	1.20	1.41	1.10	1.54	1.00	1.68	0.90	1.83	0.79	1.99
21	1.22	1.42	1.13	1.54	1.03	1.67	0.93	1.81	0.83	1.96
22	1.24	1.43	1.15	1.54	1.05	1.66	0.96	1.80	0.86	1.94
23	1.26	1.44	1.17	1.54	1.08	1.66	0.99	1.79	0.90	1.92
24	1.27	1.45	1.19	1.55	1.10	1.66	1.01	1.78	0.93	1.90
25	1.29	1.45	1.21	1.55	1.12	1.66	1.04	1.77	0.95	1.89
26	1.30	1.46	1.22	1.55	1.14	1.65	1.06	1.76	0.98	1.88
27	1.32	1.47	1.24	1.56	1.16	1.65	1.08	1.76	1.01	1.86
28	1.33	1.48	1.26	1.56	1.18	1.65	1.10	1.75	1.03	1.85
29	1.34	1.48	1.27	1.56	1.20	1.65	1.12	1.74	1.05	1.84
30	1.35	1.49	1.28	1.57	1.21	1.65	1.14	1.74	1.07	1.83
31	1.36	1.50	1.30	1.57	1.23	1.65	1.16	1.74	1.09	1.83
32	1.37	1.50	1.31	1.57	1.24	1.65	1.18	1.73	1.11	1.82
33	1.38	1.51	1.32	1.58	1.26	1.65	1.19	1.73	1.13	1.81
34	1.39	1.51	1.33	1.58	1.27	1.65	1.21	1.73	1.15	1.81
35	1.40	1.52	1.34	1.58	1.28	1.65	1.22	1.73	1.16	1.80
36	1.41	1.52	1.35	1.59	1.29	1.65	1.24	1.73	1.18	1.80
37	1.42	1.53	1.36	1.59	1.31	1.66	1.25	1.72	1.19	1.80
38	1.43	1.54	1.37	1.59	1.32	1.66	1.26	1.72	1.21	1.79
39	1.43	1.54	1.38	1.60	1.33	1.66	1.27	1.72	1.22	1.79
40	1.44	1.54	1.39	1.60	1.34	1.66	1.29	1.72	1.23	1.79
45	1.48	1.57	1.43	1.62	1.38	1.67	1.34	1.72	1.29	1.78
50	1.50	1.59	1.46	1.63	1.42	1.67	1.38	1.72	1.34	1.77
55	1.53	1.60	1.49	1.64	1.45	1.68	1.41	1.72	1.38	1.77
60	1.55	1.62	1.51	1.65	1.48	1.69	1.44	1.73	1.41	1.77
65	1.57	1.63	1.54	1.66	1.50	1.70	1.47	1.73	1.44	1.77
70	1.58	1.64	1.55	1.67	1.52	1.70	1.49	1.74	1.46	1.77
75	1.60	1.65	1.57	1.68	1.54	1.71	1.51	1.74	1.49	1.77
80	1.61	1.66	1.59	1.69	1.56	1.72	1.53	1.74	1.51	1.77
85	1.62	1.67	1.60	1.70	1.57	1.72	1.55	1.75	1.52	1.77
90	1.63	1.68	1.61	1.70	1.59	1.73	1.57	1.75	1.54	1.78
95	1.64	1.69	1.62	1.71	1.60	1.73	1.58	1.75	1.56	1.78
100	1.65	1.69	1.63	1.72	1.61	1.74	1.59	1.76	1.57	1.78

TABLE 7 *(concluded)* Critical Values of the Durbin-Watson Test Statistic for $\alpha = 0.01$

	k = 1		k = 2		k = 3		k = 4		k = 5	
n	d_L	d_U	d_L	d_U	d_L	d_U	d_L	d_U	d_L	d_U
15	0.81	1.07	0.70	1.25	0.59	1.46	0.49	1.70	0.39	1.96
16	0.84	1.09	0.74	1.25	0.63	1.44	0.53	1.66	0.44	1.90
17	0.87	1.10	0.77	1.25	0.67	1.43	0.57	1.63	0.48	1.85
18	0.90	1.12	0.80	1.26	0.71	1.42	0.61	1.60	0.52	1.80
19	0.93	1.13	0.83	1.26	0.74	1.41	0.65	1.58	0.56	1.77
20	0.95	1.15	0.86	1.27	0.77	1.41	0.68	1.57	0.60	1.74
21	0.97	1.16	0.89	1.27	0.80	1.41	0.72	1.55	0.63	1.71
22	1.00	1.17	0.91	1.28	0.83	1.40	0.75	1.54	0.66	1.69
23	1.02	1.19	0.94	1.29	0.86	1.40	0.77	1.53	0.70	1.67
24	1.05	1.20	0.96	1.30	0.88	1.41	0.80	1.53	0.72	1.66
25	1.05	1.21	0.98	1.30	0.90	1.41	0.83	1.52	0.75	1.65
26	1.07	1.22	1.00	1.31	0.93	1.41	0.85	1.52	0.78	1.64
27	1.09	1.23	1.02	1.32	0.95	1.41	0.88	1.51	0.81	1.63
28	1.10	1.24	1.04	1.32	0.97	1.41	0.90	1.51	0.83	1.62
29	1.12	1.25	1.05	1.33	0.99	1.42	0.92	1.51	0.85	1.61
30	1.13	1.26	1.07	1.34	1.01	1.42	0.94	1.51	0.88	1.61
31	1.15	1.27	1.08	1.34	1.02	1.42	0.96	1.51	0.90	1.60
32	1.16	1.28	1.10	1.35	1.04	1.43	0.98	1.51	0.92	1.60
33	1.17	1.29	1.11	1.36	1.05	1.43	1.00	1.51	0.94	1.59
34	1.18	1.30	1.13	1.36	1.07	1.43	1.01	1.51	0.95	1.59
35	1.19	1.31	1.14	1.37	1.08	1.44	1.03	1.51	0.97	1.59
36	1.21	1.32	1.15	1.38	1.10	1.44	1.04	1.51	0.99	1.59
37	1.22	1.32	1.16	1.38	1.11	1.45	1.06	1.51	1.00	1.59
38	1.23	1.33	1.18	1.39	1.12	1.45	1.07	1.52	1.02	1.58
39	1.24	1.34	1.19	1.39	1.14	1.45	1.09	1.52	1.03	1.58
40	1.25	1.34	1.20	1.40	1.15	1.46	1.10	1.52	1.05	1.58
45	1.29	1.38	1.24	1.42	1.20	1.48	1.16	1.53	1.11	1.58
50	1.32	1.40	1.28	1.45	1.24	1.49	1.20	1.54	1.16	1.59
55	1.36	1.43	1.32	1.47	1.28	1.51	1.25	1.55	1.21	1.59
60	1.38	1.45	1.35	1.48	1.32	1.52	1.28	1.56	1.25	1.60
65	1.41	1.47	1.38	1.50	1.35	1.53	1.31	1.57	1.28	1.61
70	1.43	1.49	1.40	1.52	1.37	1.55	1.34	1.58	1.31	1.61
75	1.45	1.50	1.42	1.53	1.39	1.56	1.37	1.59	1.34	1.62
80	1.47	1.52	1.44	1.54	1.42	1.57	1.39	1.60	1.36	1.62
85	1.48	1.53	1.46	1.55	1.43	1.58	1.41	1.60	1.39	1.63
90	1.50	1.54	1.47	1.56	1.45	1.59	1.43	1.61	1.41	1.64
95	1.51	1.55	1.49	1.57	1.47	1.60	1.45	1.62	1.42	1.64
100	1.52	1.56	1.50	1.58	1.48	1.60	1.46	1.63	1.44	1.65

Reproduced by permission from J. Durbin and G. S. Watson, "Testing for Serial Correlation in Least Squares Regression, II," *Biometrika* 38 (1951), pp. 159–78.

TABLE 8　Cumulative Distribution Function: $F(r)$ for the Total Number of Runs R in Samples of Sizes n_1 and n_2

	Number of Runs, r								
(n_1, n_2)	2	3	4	5	6	7	8	9	10
(2,3)	0.200	0.500	0.900	1.000					
(2,4)	0.133	0.400	0.800	1.000					
(2,5)	0.095	0.333	0.714	1.000					
(2,6)	0.071	0.286	0.643	1.000					
(2,7)	0.056	0.250	0.583	1.000					
(2,8)	0.044	0.222	0.533	1.000					
(2,9)	0.036	0.200	0.491	1.000					
(2,10)	0.030	0.182	0.455	1.000					
(3,3)	0.100	0.300	0.700	0.900	1.000				
(3,4)	0.057	0.200	0.543	0.800	0.971	1.000			
(3,5)	0.036	0.143	0.429	0.714	0.929	1.000			
(3,6)	0.024	0.107	0.345	0.643	0.881	1.000			
(3,7)	0.017	0.083	0.283	0.583	0.833	1.000			
(3,8)	0.012	0.067	0.236	0.533	0.788	1.000			
(3,9)	0.009	0.055	0.200	0.491	0.745	1.000			
(3,10)	0.007	0.045	0.171	0.455	0.706	1.000			
(4,4)	0.029	0.114	0.371	0.629	0.886	0.971	1.000		
(4,5)	0.016	0.071	0.262	0.500	0.786	0.929	0.992	1.000	
(4,6)	0.010	0.048	0.190	0.405	0.690	0.881	0.976	1.000	
(4,7)	0.006	0.033	0.142	0.333	0.606	0.833	0.954	1.000	
(4,8)	0.004	0.024	0.109	0.279	0.533	0.788	0.929	1.000	
(4,9)	0.003	0.018	0.085	0.236	0.471	0.745	0.902	1.000	
(4,10)	0.002	0.014	0.068	0.203	0.419	0.706	0.874	1.000	
(5,5)	0.008	0.040	0.167	0.357	0.643	0.833	0.960	0.992	1.000
(5,6)	0.004	0.024	0.110	0.262	0.522	0.738	0.911	0.976	0.998
(5,7)	0.003	0.015	0.076	0.197	0.424	0.652	0.854	0.955	0.992
(5,8)	0.002	0.010	0.054	0.152	0.347	0.576	0.793	0.929	0.984
(5,9)	0.001	0.007	0.039	0.119	0.287	0.510	0.734	0.902	0.972
(5,10)	0.001	0.005	0.029	0.095	0.239	0.455	0.678	0.874	0.958
(6,6)	0.002	0.013	0.067	0.175	0.392	0.608	0.825	0.933	0.987
(6,7)	0.001	0.008	0.043	0.121	0.296	0.500	0.733	0.879	0.966
(6,8)	0.001	0.005	0.028	0.086	0.226	0.413	0.646	0.821	0.937
(6,9)	0.000	0.003	0.019	0.063	0.175	0.343	0.566	0.762	0.902
(6,10)	0.000	0.002	0.013	0.047	0.137	0.288	0.497	0.706	0.864
(7,7)	0.001	0.004	0.025	0.078	0.209	0.383	0.617	0.791	0.922
(7,8)	0.000	0.002	0.015	0.051	0.149	0.296	0.514	0.704	0.867
(7,9)	0.000	0.001	0.010	0.035	0.108	0.231	0.427	0.622	0.806
(7,10)	0.000	0.001	0.006	0.024	0.080	0.182	0.355	0.549	0.743
(8,8)	0.000	0.001	0.009	0.032	0.100	0.214	0.405	0.595	0.786
(8,9)	0.000	0.001	0.005	0.020	0.069	0.157	0.319	0.500	0.702
(8,10)	0.000	0.000	0.003	0.013	0.048	0.117	0.251	0.419	0.621
(9,9)	0.000	0.000	0.003	0.012	0.044	0.109	0.238	0.399	0.601
(9,10)	0.000	0.000	0.002	0.008	0.029	0.077	0.179	0.319	0.510
(10,10)	0.000	0.000	0.001	0.004	0.019	0.051	0.128	0.242	0.414

					Number of Runs, r						
(n_1, n_2)	11	12	13	14	15	16	17	18	19	20
(2,3)										
(2,4)										
(2,5)										
(2,6)										
(2,7)										
(2,8)										
(2,9)										
(2,10)										
(3,3)										
(3,4)										
(3,5)										
(3,6)										
(3,7)										
(3,8)										
(3,9)										
(3,10)										
(4,4)										
(4,5)										
(4,6)										
(4,7)										
(4,8)										
(4,9)										
(4,10)										
(5,5)										
(5,6)	1.000									
(5,7)	1.000									
(5,8)	1.000									
(5,9)	1.000									
(5,10)	1.000									
(6,6)	0.998	1.000								
(6,7)	0.992	0.999	1.000							
(6,8)	0.984	0.998	1.000							
(6,9)	0.972	0.994	1.000							
(6,10)	0.958	0.990	1.000							
(7,7)	0.975	0.996	0.999	1.000						
(7,8)	0.949	0.988	0.998	1.000	1.000					
(7,9)	0.916	0.975	0.994	0.999	1.000					
(7,10)	0.879	0.957	0.990	0.998	1.000					
(8,8)	0.900	0.968	0.991	0.999	1.000	1.000				
(8,9)	0.843	0.939	0.980	0.996	0.999	1.000	1.000			
(8,10)	0.782	0.903	0.964	0.990	0.998	1.000	1.000			
(9,9)	0.762	0.891	0.956	0.988	0.997	1.000	1.000	1.000		
(9,10)	0.681	0.834	0.923	0.974	0.992	0.999	1.000	1.000	1.000	
(10,10)	0.586	0.758	0.872	0.949	0.981	0.996	0.999	1.000	1.000	1.000

Reproduced from F. Swed and C. Eisenhart, "Tables for Testing Randomness of Grouping in a Sequence of Alternatives," *Annals of Mathematical Statistics* 14 (1943) by permission of the authors and of the Editor, *Annals of Mathematical Statistics*.

TABLE 9   Cumulative Distribution Function of the Mann-Whitney U Statistic: $F(u)$ for $n_1 \leq n_2$ and $3 \leq n_2 \leq 10$

$n_2 = 3$

		n_1	
u	1	2	3
0	0.25	0.10	0.05
1	0.50	0.20	0.10
2		0.40	0.20
3		0.60	0.35
4			0.50

$n_2 = 4$

			n_1	
u	1	2	3	4
0	0.2000	0.0667	0.0286	0.0143
1	0.4000	0.1333	0.0571	0.0286
2	0.6000	0.2667	0.1143	0.0571
3		0.4000	0.2000	0.1000
4		0.6000	0.3143	0.1714
5			0.4286	0.2429
6			0.5714	0.3429
7				0.4429
8				0.5571

$n_2 = 5$

			n_1		
u	1	2	3	4	5
0	0.1667	0.0476	0.0179	0.0079	0.0040
1	0.3333	0.0952	0.0357	0.0159	0.0079
2	0.5000	0.1905	0.0714	0.0317	0.0159
3		0.2857	0.1250	0.0556	0.0278
4		0.4286	0.1964	0.0952	0.0476
5		0.5714	0.2857	0.1429	0.0754
6			0.3929	0.2063	0.1111
7			0.5000	0.2778	0.1548
8				0.3651	0.2103
9				0.4524	0.2738
10				0.5476	0.3452
11					0.4206
12					0.5000

$n_2 = 6$

n_1

u	1	2	3	4	5	6
0	0.1429	0.0357	0.0119	0.0048	0.0022	0.0011
1	0.2857	0.0714	0.0238	0.0095	0.0043	0.0022
2	0.4286	0.1429	0.0476	0.0190	0.0087	0.0043
3	0.5714	0.2143	0.0833	0.0333	0.0152	0.0076
4		0.3214	0.1310	0.0571	0.0260	0.0130
5		0.4286	0.1905	0.0857	0.0411	0.0206
6		0.5714	0.2738	0.1286	0.0628	0.0325
7			0.3571	0.1762	0.0887	0.0465
8			0.4524	0.2381	0.1234	0.0660
9			0.5476	0.3048	0.1645	0.0898
10				0.3810	0.2143	0.1201
11				0.4571	0.2684	0.1548
12				0.5429	0.3312	0.1970
13					0.3961	0.2424
14					0.4654	0.2944
15					0.5346	0.3496
16						0.4091
17						0.4686
18						0.5314

$n_2 = 7$

n_1

u	1	2	3	4	5	6	7
0	0.1250	0.0278	0.0083	0.0030	0.0013	0.0006	0.0003
1	0.2500	0.0556	0.0167	0.0061	0.0025	0.0012	0.0006
2	0.3750	0.1111	0.0333	0.0121	0.0051	0.0023	0.0012
3	0.5000	0.1667	0.0583	0.0212	0.0088	0.0041	0.0020
4		0.2500	0.0917	0.0364	0.0152	0.0070	0.0035
5		0.3333	0.1333	0.0545	0.0240	0.0111	0.0055
6		0.4444	0.1917	0.0818	0.0366	0.0175	0.0087
7		0.5556	0.2583	0.1152	0.0530	0.0256	0.0131
8			0.3333	0.1576	0.0745	0.0367	0.0189
9			0.4167	0.2061	0.1010	0.0507	0.0265
10			0.5000	0.2636	0.1338	0.0688	0.0364
11				0.3242	0.1717	0.0903	0.0487
12				0.3939	0.2159	0.1171	0.0641
13				0.4636	0.2652	0.1474	0.0825
14				0.5364	0.3194	0.1830	0.1043
15					0.3775	0.2226	0.1297
16					0.4381	0.2669	0.1588
17					0.5000	0.3141	0.1914
18						0.3654	0.2279
19						0.4178	0.2675
20						0.4726	0.3100
21						0.5274	0.3552
22							0.4024
23							0.4508
24							0.5000

TABLE 9 *(continued)*

| | | | | | $n_2 = 8$ | | | |
| | | | | | n_1 | | | |
u	1	2	3	4	5	6	7	8
0	0.1111	0.0222	0.0061	0.0020	0.0008	0.0003	0.0002	0.0001
1	0.2222	0.0444	0.0121	0.0040	0.0016	0.0007	0.0003	0.0002
2	0.3333	0.0889	0.0242	0.0081	0.0031	0.0013	0.0006	0.0003
3	0.4444	0.1333	0.0424	0.0141	0.0054	0.0023	0.0011	0.0005
4	0.5556	0.2000	0.0667	0.0242	0.0093	0.0040	0.0019	0.0009
5		0.2667	0.0970	0.0364	0.0148	0.0063	0.0030	0.0015
6		0.3556	0.1394	0.0545	0.0225	0.0100	0.0047	0.0023
7		0.4444	0.1879	0.0768	0.0326	0.0147	0.0070	0.0035
8		0.5556	0.2485	0.1071	0.0466	0.0213	0.0103	0.0052
9			0.3152	0.1414	0.0637	0.0296	0.0145	0.0074
10			0.3879	0.1838	0.0855	0.0406	0.0200	0.0103
11			0.4606	0.2303	0.1111	0.0539	0.0270	0.0141
12			0.5394	0.2848	0.1422	0.0709	0.0361	0.0190
13				0.3414	0.1772	0.0906	0.0469	0.0249
14				0.4040	0.2176	0.1142	0.0603	0.0325
15				0.4667	0.2618	0.1412	0.0760	0.0415
16				0.5333	0.3108	0.1725	0.0946	0.0524
17					0.3621	0.2068	0.1159	0.0652
18					0.4165	0.2454	0.1405	0.0803
19					0.4716	0.2864	0.1678	0.0974
20					0.5284	0.3310	0.1984	0.1172
21						0.3773	0.2317	0.1393
22						0.4259	0.2679	0.1641
23						0.4749	0.3063	0.1911
24						0.5251	0.3472	0.2209
25							0.3894	0.2527
26							0.4333	0.2869
27							0.4775	0.3227
28							0.5225	0.3605
29								0.3992
30								0.4392
31								0.4796
32								0.5204

					$n_2 = 9$				
					n_1				
u	1	2	3	4	5	6	7	8	9
0	0.1000	0.0182	0.0045	0.0014	0.0005	0.0002	0.0001	0.0000	0.0000
1	0.2000	0.0364	0.0091	0.0028	0.0010	0.0004	0.0002	0.0001	0.0000
2	0.3000	0.0727	0.0182	0.0056	0.0020	0.0008	0.0003	0.0002	0.0001
3	0.4000	0.1091	0.0318	0.0098	0.0035	0.0014	0.0006	0.0003	0.0001
4	0.5000	0.1636	0.0500	0.0168	0.0060	0.0024	0.0010	0.0005	0.0002
5		0.2182	0.0727	0.0252	0.0095	0.0038	0.0017	0.0008	0.0004
6		0.2909	0.1045	0.0378	0.0145	0.0060	0.0026	0.0012	0.0006
7		0.3636	0.1409	0.0531	0.0210	0.0088	0.0039	0.0019	0.0009
8		0.4545	0.1864	0.0741	0.0300	0.0128	0.0058	0.0028	0.0014
9		0.5455	0.2409	0.0993	0.0415	0.0180	0.0082	0.0039	0.0020
10			0.3000	0.1301	0.0559	0.0248	0.0115	0.0056	0.0028
11			0.3636	0.1650	0.0734	0.0332	0.0156	0.0076	0.0039
12			0.4318	0.2070	0.0949	0.0440	0.0209	0.0103	0.0053
13			0.5000	0.2517	0.1199	0.0567	0.0274	0.0137	0.0071
14				0.3021	0.1489	0.0723	0.0356	0.0180	0.0094
15				0.3552	0.1818	0.0905	0.0454	0.0232	0.0122
16				0.4126	0.2188	0.1119	0.0571	0.0296	0.0157
17				0.4699	0.2592	0.1361	0.0708	0.0372	0.0200
18				0.5301	0.3032	0.1638	0.0869	0.0464	0.0252
19					0.3497	0.1924	0.1052	0.0570	0.0313
20					0.3986	0.2280	0.1261	0.0694	0.0385
21					0.4491	0.2643	0.1496	0.0836	0.0470
22					0.5000	0.3035	0.1755	0.0998	0.0567
23						0.3445	0.2039	0.1179	0.0680
24						0.3878	0.2349	0.1383	0.0807
25						0.4320	0.2680	0.1606	0.0951
26						0.4773	0.3032	0.1852	0.1112
27						0.5227	0.3403	0.2117	0.1290
28							0.3788	0.2404	0.1487
29							0.4185	0.2707	0.1701
30							0.4591	0.3029	0.1933
31							0.5000	0.3365	0.2181
32								0.3715	0.2447
33								0.4074	0.2729
34								0.4442	0.3024
35								0.4813	0.3332
36								0.5187	0.3652
37									0.3981
38									0.4317
39									0.4657
40									0.5000

TABLE 9 *(concluded)*

| | | | | | $n_2 = 10$ | | | | | |
| | | | | | n_1 | | | | | |
u	1	2	3	4	5	6	7	8	9	10
0	0.0909	0.0152	0.0035	0.0010	0.0003	0.0001	0.0001	0.0000	0.0000	0.0000
1	0.1818	0.0303	0.0070	0.0020	0.0007	0.0002	0.0001	0.0000	0.0000	0.0000
2	0.2727	0.0606	0.0140	0.0040	0.0013	0.0005	0.0002	0.0001	0.0000	0.0000
3	0.3636	0.0909	0.0245	0.0070	0.0023	0.0009	0.0004	0.0002	0.0001	0.0000
4	0.4545	0.1364	0.0385	0.0120	0.0040	0.0015	0.0006	0.0003	0.0001	0.0001
5	0.5455	0.1818	0.0559	0.0180	0.0063	0.0024	0.0010	0.0004	0.0002	0.0001
6		0.2424	0.0804	0.0270	0.0097	0.0037	0.0015	0.0007	0.0003	0.0002
7		0.3030	0.1084	0.0380	0.0140	0.0055	0.0023	0.0010	0.0005	0.0002
8		0.3788	0.1434	0.0529	0.0200	0.0080	0.0034	0.0015	0.0007	0.0004
9		0.4545	0.1853	0.0709	0.0276	0.0112	0.0048	0.0022	0.0011	0.0005
10		0.5455	0.2343	0.0939	0.0376	0.0156	0.0068	0.0031	0.0015	0.0008
11			0.2867	0.1199	0.0496	0.0210	0.0093	0.0043	0.0021	0.0010
12			0.3462	0.1518	0.0646	0.0280	0.0125	0.0058	0.0028	0.0014
13			0.4056	0.1868	0.0823	0.0363	0.0165	0.0078	0.0038	0.0019
14			0.4685	0.2268	0.1032	0.0467	0.0215	0.0103	0.0051	0.0026
15			0.5315	0.2697	0.1272	0.0589	0.0277	0.0133	0.0066	0.0034
16				0.3177	0.1548	0.0736	0.0351	0.0171	0.0086	0.0045
17				0.3666	0.1855	0.0903	0.0439	0.0217	0.0110	0.0057
18				0.4196	0.2198	0.1099	0.0544	0.0273	0.0140	0.0073
19				0.4725	0.2567	0.1317	0.0665	0.0338	0.0175	0.0093
20				0.5275	0.2970	0.1566	0.0806	0.0416	0.0217	0.0116
21					0.3393	0.1838	0.0966	0.0506	0.0267	0.0144
22					0.3839	0.2139	0.1148	0.0610	0.0326	0.0177
23					0.4296	0.2461	0.1349	0.0729	0.0394	0.0216
24					0.4765	0.2811	0.1574	0.0864	0.0474	0.0262
25					0.5235	0.3177	0.1819	0.1015	0.0564	0.0315
26						0.3564	0.2087	0.1185	0.0667	0.0376
27						0.3962	0.2374	0.1371	0.0782	0.0446
28						0.4374	0.2681	0.1577	0.0912	0.0526
29						0.4789	0.3004	0.1800	0.1055	0.0615
30						0.5211	0.3345	0.2041	0.1214	0.0716
31							0.3698	0.2299	0.1388	0.0827
32							0.4063	0.2574	0.1577	0.0952
33							0.4434	0.2863	0.1781	0.1088
34							0.4811	0.3167	0.2001	0.1237
35							0.5189	0.3482	0.2235	0.1399
36								0.3809	0.2483	0.1575
37								0.4143	0.2745	0.1763
38								0.4484	0.3019	0.1965
39								0.4827	0.3304	0.2179
40								0.5173	0.3598	0.2406
41									0.3901	0.2644
42									0.4211	0.2894
43									0.4524	0.3153
44									0.4841	0.3421
45									0.5159	0.3697
46										0.3980
47										0.4267
48										0.4559
49										0.4853
50										0.5147

TABLE 10 Critical Values of the Wilcoxon *T* Statistic

One-Tailed	Two-Tailed	*n* = 5	*n* = 6	*n* = 7	*n* = 8	*n* = 9	*n* = 10
$P = 0.05$	$P = 0.10$	1	2	4	6	8	11
$P = 0.025$	$P = 0.05$		1	2	4	6	8
$P = 0.01$	$P = 0.02$			0	2	3	5
$P = 0.005$	$P = 0.01$				0	2	3

One-Tailed	Two-Tailed	*n* = 11	*n* = 12	*n* = 13	*n* = 14	*n* = 15	*n* = 16
$p = 0.05$	$P = 0.10$	14	17	21	26	30	36
$P = 0.025$	$P = 0.05$	11	14	17	21	25	30
$P = 0.01$	$P = 0.02$	7	10	13	16	20	24
$P = 0.005$	$P = 0.01$	5	7	10	13	16	19

One-Tailed	Two-Tailed	*n* = 17	*n* = 18	*n* = 19	*n* = 20	*n* = 21	*n* = 22
$P = 0.05$	$P = 0.10$	41	47	54	60	68	75
$P = 0.025$	$P = 0.05$	35	40	46	52	59	66
$P = 0.01$	$P = 0.02$	28	33	38	43	49	56
$P = 0.005$	$P = 0.01$	23	28	32	37	43	49

One-Tailed	Two-Tailed	*n* = 23	*n* = 24	*n* = 25	*n* = 26	*n* = 27	*n* = 28
$P = 0.05$	$P = 0.10$	83	92	101	110	120	130
$P = 0.025$	$P = 0.05$	73	81	90	98	107	117
$P = 0.01$	$P = 0.02$	62	69	77	85	93	102
$P = 0.005$	$P = 0.01$	55	68	68	76	84	92

One-Tailed	Two-Tailed	*n* = 29	*n* = 30	*n* = 31	*n* = 32	*n* = 33	*n* = 34
$P = 0.05$	$P = 0.10$	141	152	163	175	188	201
$P = 0.025$	$P = 0.05$	127	137	148	159	171	183
$P = 0.01$	$P = 0.02$	111	120	130	141	151	162
$P = 0.005$	$P = 0.01$	100	109	118	128	138	149

One-Tailed	Two-Tailed	*n* = 35	*n* = 36	*n* = 37	*n* = 38	*n* = 39
$P = 0.05$	$P = 0.10$	214	228	242	256	271
$P = 0.025$	$P = 0.05$	195	208	222	235	250
$P = 0.01$	$P = 0.02$	174	186	198	211	224
$P = 0.005$	$P = 0.01$	160	171	183	195	208

One-Tailed	Two-Tailed	*n* = 40	*n* = 41	*n* = 42	*n* = 43	*n* = 44	*n* = 45
$P = 0.05$	$P = 0.10$	287	303	319	336	353	371
$P = 0.025$	$P = 0.05$	264	279	295	311	327	344
$P = 0.01$	$P = 0.02$	238	252	267	281	297	313
$P = 0.005$	$P = 0.01$	221	234	248	262	277	292

One-Tailed	Two-Tailed	*n* = 46	*n* = 47	*n* = 48	*n* = 49	*n* = 50
$P = 0.05$	$P = 0.10$	389	408	427	446	466
$P = 0.025$	$P = 0.05$	361	379	397	415	434
$P = 0.01$	$P = 0.02$	329	345	362	380	398
$P = 0.005$	$P = 0.01$	307	323	339	356	373

Reproduced from F. Wilcoxon and R. A. Wilcox, *Some Rapid Approximate Statistical Procedures* (1964), p. 28, with the permission of the American Cyanamid Company.

TABLE 11   Critical Values of Spearman's Rank Correlation Coefficient

n	$\alpha = 0.05$	$\alpha = 0.025$	$\alpha = 0.01$	$\alpha = 0.005$
5	0.900	—	—	—
6	0.829	0.886	0.943	—
7	0.714	0.786	0.893	—
8	0.643	0.738	0.833	0.881
9	0.600	0.683	0.783	0.833
10	0.564	0.648	0.745	0.794
11	0.523	0.623	0.736	0.818
12	0.497	0.591	0.703	0.780
13	0.475	0.566	0.673	0.745
14	0.457	0.545	0.646	0.716
15	0.441	0.525	0.623	0.689
16	0.425	0.507	0.601	0.666
17	0.412	0.490	0.582	0.645
18	0.399	0.476	0.564	0.625
19	0.388	0.462	0.549	0.608
20	0.377	0.450	0.534	0.591
21	0.368	0.438	0.521	0.576
22	0.359	0.428	0.508	0.562
23	0.351	0.418	0.496	0.549
24	0.343	0.409	0.485	0.537
25	0.336	0.400	0.475	0.526
26	0.329	0.392	0.465	0.515
27	0.323	0.385	0.456	0.505
28	0.317	0.377	0.448	0.496
29	0.311	0.370	0.440	0.487
30	0.305	0.364	0.432	0.478

Reproduced by permission from E. G. Olds, "Distribution of Sums of Squares of Rank Differences for Small Samples," *Annals of Mathematical Statistics* 9 (1938).

TABLE 12 Poisson Probability Distribution

This table gives values of

$$P(x) = \frac{\mu^x e^{-\mu}}{x!}$$

					μ					
x	.005	.01	.02	.03	.04	.05	.06	.07	.08	.09
0	.9950	.9900	.9802	.9704	.9608	.9512	.9418	.9324	.9231	.9139
1	.0050	.0099	.0192	.0291	.0384	.0476	.0565	.0653	.0738	.0823
2	.0000	.0000	.0002	.0004	.0008	.0012	.0017	.0023	.0030	.0037
3	.0000	.0000	.0000	.0000	.0000	.0000	.0000	..0001	.0001	.0001

					μ					
x	0.1	0.2	0.3	0.4	0.5	0.6	0.7	0.8	0.9	1.0
0	.9048	.8187	.7408	.6703	.6065	.5488	.4966	.4493	.4066	.3679
1	.0905	.1637	.2222	.2681	.3033	.3293	.3476	.3595	.3659	.3679
2	.0045	.0164	.0333	.0536	.0758	.0988	.1217	.1438	.1647	.1839
3	.0002	.0011	.0033	.0072	.0126	.0198	.0284	.0383	.0494	.0613
4	.0000	.0001	.0002	.0007	.0016	.0030	.0050	.0077	.0111	.0153
5	.0000	.0000	.0000	.0001	.0002	.0004	.0007	.0012	.0020	.0031
6	.0000	.0000	.0000	.0000	.0000	.0000	.0001	.0002	.0003	.0005
7	.0000	.0000	.0000	.0000	.0000	.0000	.0000	0000	.0000	.0001

					μ					
x	1.1	1.2	1.3	1.4	1.5	1.6	1.7	1.8	1.9	2.0
0	.3329	.3012	.2725	.2466	.2231	.2019	.1827	.1653	.1496	.1353
1	.3662	.3614	.3543	.3452	.3347	.3230	.3106	.2975	.2842	.2707
2	.2014	.2169	.2303	.2417	.2510	.2584	.2640	.2678	.2700	.2707
3	.0738	.0867	.0998	.1128	.1255	.1378	.1496	.1607	.1710	.1804
4	.0203	.0260	.0324	.0395	.0471	.0551	.0636	.0723	.0812	.0902
5	.0045	.0062	.0084	.0111	.0141	.0176	.0216	.0260	.0309	.0361
6	.0008	.0012	.0018	.0026	.0035	.0047	.0061	.0078	.0098	.0120
7	.0001	.0002	.0003	.0005	.0008	.0011	.0015	.0020	.0027	.0034
8	.0000	.0000	.0001	.0001	.0001	.0002	.0003	.0005	.0006	.0009
9	.0000	.0000	.0000	.0000	.0000	.0000	.0001	.0001	.0001	.0002

					μ					
x	2.1	2.2	2.3	2.4	2.5	2.6	2.7	2.8	2.9	3.0
0	.1225	.1108	.1003	.0907	.0821	.0743	.0672	.0608	.0550	.0498
1	.2572	.2438	.2306	.2177	.2052	.1931	.1815	.1703	.1596	.1494
2	.2700	.2681	.2652	.2613	.2565	.2510	.2450	.2384	.2314	.2240
3	.1890	.1966	.2033	.2090	.2138	.2176	.2205	.2225	.2237	.2240
4	.0992	.1082	.1169	.1254	.1336	.1414	.1488	.1557	.1622	.1680

TABLE 12   *(continued)*

					μ					
x	**2.1**	**2.2**	**2.3**	**2.4**	**2.5**	**2.6**	**2.7**	**2.8**	**2.9**	**3.0**
5	.0417	.0476	.0538	.0602	.0668	.0735	.0804	.0872	.0940	.1008
6	.0146	.0174	.0206	.0241	.0278	.0319	.0362	.0407	.0455	.0504
7	.0044	.0055	.0068	.0083	.0099	.0118	.0139	.0163	.0188	.0216
8	.0011	.0015	.0019	.0025	.0031	.0038	.0047	.0057	.0068	.0081
9	.0003	.0004	.0005	.0007	.0009	.0011	.0014	.0018	.0022	.0027
10	.0001	.0001	.0001	.0002	.0002	.0003	.0004	.0005	.0006	.0008
11	.0000	.0000	.0000	.0000	.0000	.0001	.0001	.0001	.0002	.0002
12	.0000	.0000	.0000	.0000	.0000	.0000	.0000	.0000	.0000	.0001

					μ					
x	**3.1**	**3.2**	**3.3**	**3.4**	**3.5**	**3.6**	**3.7**	**3.8**	**3.9**	**4.0**
0	.0450	.0408	.0369	.0334	.0302	.0273	.0247	.0224	.0202	.0183
1	.1397	.1304	.1217	.1135	.1057	.0984	.0915	.0850	.0789	.0733
2	.2165	.2087	.2008	.1929	.1850	.1771	.1692	.1615	.1539	.1465
3	.2237	.2226	.2209	.2186	.2158	.2125	.2087	.2046	.2001	.1954
4	.1734	.1781	.1823	.1858	.1888	.1912	.1931	.1944	.1951	.1954
5	.1075	.1140	.1203	.1264	.1322	.1377	.1429	.1477	.1522	.1563
6	.0555	.0608	.0662	.0716	.0771	.0826	.0881	.0936	.0989	.1042
7	.0246	.0278	.0312	.0348	.0385	.0425	.0466	.0508	.0551	.0595
8	.0095	.0111	.0129	.0148	.0169	.0191	.0215	.0241	.0269	.0298
9	.0033	.0040	.0047	.0056	.0066	.0076	.0089	.0102	.0116	.0132
10	.0010	.0013	.0016	.0019	.0023	.0028	.0033	.0039	.0045	.0053
11	.0003	.0004	.0005	.0006	.0007	.0009	.0011	.0013	.0016	.0019
12	.0001	.0001	.0001	.0002	.0002	.0003	.0003	.0004	.0005	.0006
13	.0000	.0000	.0000	.0000	.0001	.0001	.0001	.0001	.0002	.0002
14	.0000	.0000	.0000	.0000	.0000	.0000	.0000	.0000	.0000	.0001

					μ					
x	**4.1**	**4.2**	**4.3**	**4.4**	**4.5**	**4.6**	**4.7**	**4.8**	**4.9**	**5.0**
0	.0166	.0150	.0136	.0123	.0111	.0101	.0091	.0082	.0074	.0067
1	.0679	.0630	.0583	.0540	.0500	.0462	.0427	.0395	.0365	.0337
2	.1393	.1323	.1254	.1188	.1125	.1063	.1005	.0948	.0894	.0842
3	.1904	.1852	.1798	.1743	.1687	.1631	.1574	.1517	.1460	.1404
4	.1951	.1944	.1933	.1917	.1898	.1875	.1849	.1820	.1789	.1755
5	.1600	.1633	.1662	.1687	.1708	.1725	.1738	.1747	.1753	.1755
6	.1093	.1143	.1191	.1237	.1281	.1323	.1362	.1398	.1432	.1462
7	0640	.0686	.0732	.0778	.0824	.0869	.0914	.0959	.1002	.1044
8	.0328	.0360	.0393	.0428	.0463	.0500	.0537	.0575	.0614	.0653
9	.0150	.0168	.0188	.0209	.0232	.0255	.0280	.0307	.0334	.0363

					μ					
x	**4.1**	**4.2**	**4.3**	**4.4**	**4.5**	**4.6**	**4.7**	**4.8**	**4.9**	**5.0**
10	.0061	.0071	.0081	.0092	.0104	.0118	.0132	.0147	.0164	.0181
11	.0023	.0027	.0032	.0037	.0043	.0049	.0056	.0064	.0073	.0082
12	.0008	.0009	.0011	.0014	.0016	.0019	.0022	.0026	.0030	.0034
13	.0002	.0003	.0004	.0005	.0006	.0007	.0008	.0009	.0011	.0013
14	.0001	.0001	.0001	.0001	.0002	.0002	.0003	.0003	.0004	.0005
15	.0000	.0000	.0000	.0000	.0001	.0001	.0001	.0001	.0001	.0002

					μ					
x	**5.1**	**5.2**	**5.3**	**5.4**	**5.5**	**5.6**	**5.7**	**5.8**	**5.9**	**6.0**
0	.0061	.0055	.0050	.0045	.0041	.0037	.0033	.0030	.0027	.0025
1	.0311	.0287	.0265	.0244	.0225	.0207	.0191	.0176	.0162	.0149
2	.0793	.0746	.0701	.0659	.0618	.0580	.0544	.0509	.0477	.0446
3	.1348	.1293	.1239	.1185	.1133	.1082	.1033	.0985	.0938	.0892
4	.1719	.1681	.1641	.1600	.1558	.1515	.1472	.1428	.1383	.1339
5	.1753	.1748	.1740	.1728	.1714	.1697	.1678	.1656	.1632	.1606
6	.1490	.1515	.1537	.1555	.1571	.1584	.1594	.1601	.1605	.1606
7	.1086	.1125	.1163	.1200	.1234	.1267	.1298	.1326	.1353	.1377
8	.0692	.0731	.0771	.0810	.0849	.0887	.0925	.0962	.0998	.1033
9	.0392	.0423	.0454	.0486	.0519	.0552	.0586	.0620	.0654	.0688
10	.0200	.0220	.0241	.0262	.0285	.0309	.0334	.0359	.0386	.0413
11	.0093	.0104	.0116	.0129	.0143	.0157	.0173	.0190	.0207	.0225
12	.0039	.0045	.0051	.0058	.0065	.0073	.0082	.0092	.0102	.0113
13	.0015	.0018	.0021	.0024	.0028	.0032	.0036	.0041	.0046	.0052
14	.0006	.0007	.0008	.0009	.0011	.0013	.0015	.0017	.0019	.0022
15	.0002	.0002	.0003	.0003	.0004	.0005	.0006	.0007	.0008	.0009
16	.0001	.0001	.0001	.0001	.0001	.0002	.0002	.0002	.0003	.0003
17	.0000	.0000	.0000	.0000	.0000	.0001	.0001	0001	.0001	.0001

					μ					
x	**6.1**	**6.2**	**6.3**	**6.4**	**6.5**	**6.6**	**6.7**	**6.8**	**6.9**	**7.0**
0	.0022	.0020	.0019	.0017	.0015	.0014	.0012	.0011	.0010	.0009
1	.0137	.0126	.0116	.0106	.0098	.0090	.0082	.0076	.0070	.0064
2	.0417	.0390	.0364	.0340	.0318	.0296	.0276	.0258	.0240	.0223
3	.0848	.0806	.0765	.0726	.0688	.0652	.0617	.0584	.0552	.0521
4	.1294	.1249	.1205	.1162	.1118	.1076	.1034	.0992	.0952	.0912
5	.1579	.1549	.1519	.1487	.1454	.1420	.1385	.1349	.1314	.1277
6	.1605	.1601	.1595	.1586	.1575	.1562	.1546	.1529	.1511	.1490
7	.1399	.1418	.1435	.1450	.1462	.1472	.1480	.1486	.1489	.1490
8	.1066	.1099	.1130	.1160	.1188	.1215	.1240	.1263	.1284	.1304
9	.0723	.0757	.0791	.0825	.0858	.0891	.0923	.0954	.0985	.1014

TABLE 12 *(concluded)*

					μ					
x	6.1	6.2	6.3	6.4	6.5	6.6	6.7	6.8	6.9	7.0
10	.0441	.0469	.0498	.0528	.0558	.0588	.0618	.0649	.0679	.0710
11	.0245	.0265	.0285	.0307	.0330	.0353	.0377	.0401	.0426	.0452
12	.0124	.0137	.0150	.0164	.0179	.0194	.0210	.0227	.0245	.0264
13	.0058	.0065	.0073	.0081	.0089	.0098	.0108	.0119	.0130	.0142
14	.0025	.0029	.0033	.0037	.0041	.0046	.0052	.0058	.0064	.0071
15	.0010	.0012	.0014	.0016	.0018	.0020	.0023	.0026	.0029	.0033
16	.0004	.0005	.0005	.0006	.0007	.0008	.0010	.0011	.0013	.0014
17	.0001	.0002	.0002	.0002	.0003	.0003	.0004	.0004	.0005	.0006
18	.0000	.0001	.0001	.0001	.0001	.0001	.0001	.0002	.0002	.0002
19	.0000	.0000	.0000	.0000	.0000	.0000	.0000	.0001	.0001	.0001

					μ					
x	7.1	7.2	7.3	7.4	7.5	7.6	7.7	7.8	7.9	8.0
0	.0008	.0007	.0007	.0006	.0006	.0005	.0005	.0004	.0004	.0003
1	.0059	.0054	.0049	.0045	.0041	.0038	.0035	.0032	.0029	.0027
2	.0208	.0194	.0180	.0167	.0156	.0145	.0134	.0125	.0116	.0107
3	.0492	.0464	.0438	.0413	.0389	.0366	.0345	.0324	.0305	.0286
4	.0874	.0836	.0799	.0764	.0729	.0696	.0663	.0632	.0602	.0573
5	.1241	.1204	.1167	.1130	.1094	.1057	.1021	.0986	.0951	.0916
6	.1468	.1445	.1420	.1394	.1367	.1339	.1311	.1282	.1252	.1221
7	.1489	.1486	.1481	.1474	.1465	.1454	.1442	.1428	.1413	.1396
8	.1321	.1337	.1351	.1363	.1373	.1382	.1388	.1392	.1395	.1396
9	.1042	.1070	.1096	.1121	.1144	.1167	.1187	.1207	.1224	.1241
10	.0740	.0770	.0800	.0829	.0858	.0887	.0914	.0941	.0967	.0993
11	.0478	.0504	.0531	.0558	.0585	.0613	.0640	.0667	.0695	.0722
12	.0283	.0303	.0323	.0344	.0366	.0388	.0411	.0434	.0457	.0481
13	.0154	.0168	.0181	.0196	.0211	.0227	.0243	.0260	.0278	.0296
14	.0078	.0086	.0095	.0104	.0113	.0123	.0134	.0145	.0157	.0169
15	.0037	.0041	.0046	.0051	.0057	.0062	.0069	.0075	.0083	.0090
16	.0016	.0019	.0021	.0024	.0026	.0030	.0033	.0037	.0041	.0045
17	.0007	.0008	.0009	.0010	.0012	.0013	.0015	0017	.0019	.0021
18	.0003	.0003	.0004	.0004	.0005	.0006	.0006	.0007	.0008	.0009
19	.0001	.0001	.0001	.0002	.0002	.0002	.0003	.0003	.0003	.0004
20	.0000	.0000	.0001	.0001	.0001	.0001	.0001	.0001	.0001	.0002
21	.0000	.0000	.0000	.0000	.0000	.0000	.0000	.0000	.0001	.0001

TABLE 13 Control Chart Constants

n	For Estimating Sigma		For X̄ Chart		For X̄ Chart (Standard Given)	For R Chart		For R Chart (Standard Given)			For s Chart (Standard Given)			
	c_4	d_2	A_2	A_3	A	D_3	D_4	D_1	D_2	B_3	B_4	B_5	B_6	
2	0.7979	1.128	1.880	2.659	2.121	0	3.267	0	3.686	0	3.267	0	2.606	
3	0.8862	1.693	1.023	1.954	1.732	0	2.575	0	4.358	0	2.568	0	2.276	
4	0.9213	2.059	0.729	1.628	1.500	0	2.282	0	4.698	0	2.266	0	2.088	
5	0.9400	2.326	0.577	1.427	1.342	0	2.115	0	4.918	0	2.089	0	1.964	
6	0.9515	2.534	0.483	1.287	1.225	0	2.004	0	5.078	0.030	1.970	0.029	1.874	
7	0.9594	2.704	0.419	1.182	1.134	0.076	1.924	0.205	5.203	0.118	1.882	0.113	1.806	
8	0.9650	2.847	0.373	1.099	1.061	0.136	1.864	0.387	5.307	0.185	1.815	0.179	1.751	
9	0.9693	2.970	0.337	1.032	1.000	0.184	1.816	0.546	5.394	0.239	1.761	0.232	1.707	
10	0.9727	3.078	0.308	0.975	0.949	0.223	1.777	0.687	5.469	0.284	1.716	0.276	1.669	
15	0.9823	3.472	0.223	0.789	0.775	0.348	1.652	1.207	5.737	0.428	1.572	0.421	1.544	
20	0.9869	3.735	0.180	0.680	0.671	0.414	1.586	1.548	5.922	0.510	1.490	0.504	1.470	
25	0.9896	3.931	0.153	0.606	0.600	0.459	1.541	1.804	6.058	0.565	1.435	0.559	1.420	

Reprinted by permission from T. P. Ryan, *Statistical Methods for Quality Improvement* (New York: John Wiley and Sons, 1989).

TABLE 14   Random Numbers

1559	9068	9290	8303	8508	8954	1051	6677	6415	0342
5550	6245	7313	0117	7652	5069	6354	7668	1096	5780
4735	6214	8037	1385	1882	0828	2957	0530	9210	0177
5333	1313	3063	1134	8676	6241	9960	5304	1582	6198
8495	2956	1121	8484	2920	7934	0670	5263	0968	0069
1947	3353	1197	7363	9003	9313	3434	4261	0066	2714
4785	6325	1868	5020	9100	0823	7379	7391	1250	5501
9972	9163	5833	0100	5758	3696	6496	6297	5653	7782
0472	4629	2007	4464	3312	8728	1193	2497	4219	5339
4727	6994	1175	5622	2341	8562	5192	1471	7206	2027
3658	3226	5981	9025	1080	1437	6721	7331	0792	5383
6906	9758	0244	0259	4609	1269	5957	7556	1975	7898
3793	6916	0132	8873	8987	4975	4814	2098	6683	0901
3376	5966	1614	4025	0721	1537	6695	6090	8083	5450
6126	0224	7169	3596	1593	5097	7286	2686	1796	1150
0466	7566	1320	8777	8470	5448	9575	4669	1402	3905
9908	9832	8185	8835	0384	3699	1272	1181	8627	1968
7594	3636	1224	6808	1184	3404	6752	4391	2016	6167
5715	9301	5847	3524	0077	6674	8061	5438	6508	9673
7932	4739	4567	6797	4540	8488	3639	9777	1621	7244
6311	2025	5250	6099	6718	7539	9681	3204	9637	1091
0476	1624	3470	1600	0675	3261	7749	4195	2660	2150
5317	3903	6098	9438	3482	5505	5167	9993	8191	8488
7474	8876	1918	9828	2061	6664	0391	9170	2776	4025
7460	6800	1987	2758	0737	6880	1500	5763	2061	9373
1002	1494	9972	3877	6104	4006	0477	0669	8557	0513
5449	6891	9047	6297	1075	7762	8091	7153	8881	3367
9453	0809	7151	9982	0411	1120	6129	5090	2053	7570
0471	2725	7588	6573	0546	0110	6132	1224	3124	6563
5469	2668	1996	2249	3857	6637	8010	1701	3141	6147
2782	9603	1877	4159	9809	2570	4544	0544	2660	6737
3129	7217	5020	3788	0853	9465	2186	3945	1696	2286
7092	9885	3714	8557	7804	9524	6228	7774	6674	2775
9566	0501	8352	1062	0634	2401	0379	1697	7153	6208
5863	7000	1714	9276	7218	6922	1032	4838	1954	1680
5881	9151	2321	3147	6755	2510	5759	6947	7102	0097
6416	9939	9569	0439	1705	4680	9881	7071	9596	8758
9568	3012	6316	9065	0710	2158	1639	9149	4848	8634
0452	9538	5730	1893	1186	9245	6558	9562	8534	9321
8762	5920	8989	4777	2169	7073	7082	9495	1594	8600
0194	0270	7601	0342	3897	4133	7650	9228	5558	3597
3306	5478	2797	1605	4996	0023	9780	9429	3937	7573
7198	3079	2171	6972	0928	6599	9328	0597	5948	5753
8350	4846	1309	0612	4584	4988	4642	4430	9481	9048
7449	4279	4224	1018	2496	2091	9750	6086	1955	9860
6126	5399	0852	5491	6557	4946	9918	1541	7894	1843
1851	7940	9908	3860	1536	8011	4314	7269	7047	0382
7698	4218	2726	5130	3132	1722	8592	9662	4795	7718
0810	0118	4979	0458	1059	5739	7919	4557	0245	4861
6647	7149	1409	6809	3313	0082	9024	7477	7320	5822
3867	7111	5549	9439	3427	9793	3071	6651	4267	8099
1172	7278	7527	2492	6211	9457	5120	4903	1023	5745
6701	1668	5067	0413	7961	7825	9261	8572	0634	1140
8244	0620	8736	2649	1429	6253	4181	8120	6500	8127
8009	4031	7884	2215	2382	1931	1252	8088	2490	9122
1947	8315	9755	7187	4074	4743	6669	6060	2319	0635
9562	4821	8050	0106	2782	4665	9436	4973	4879	8900
0729	9026	9631	8096	8906	5713	3212	8854	3435	4206
6904	2569	3251	0079	8838	8738	8503	6333	0952	1641

Reproduced by permission from T. P. Ryan, *Statistical Methods for Quality Improvement* (New York: John Wiley & Sons, 1989).

THE FEDERAL RESERVE DATA SET

The following are monthly observations on six economic variables from September 1981 through November 1991. These data are obtained from the *Federal Reserve Bulletin,* vols. 68 to 74 (Washington, D.C.: Board of Governors of the Federal Reserve System). The variables are defined as follows.

FFR = Monthly average of the federal funds rate (%).

FT = Foreign trade: U.S. exports of domestic and foreign merchandise, excluding grant-aid shipments. Data are in millions of dollars, seasonally adjusted.

IP = Seasonally adjusted U.S. industrial production index (1967 = 100 from September 1981 to August 1984, 1977 = 100 from September 1984 to February 1988, and 1987 = 100 from March 1989 onward).

HS = Number of new-unit private residential housing permits authorized, in thousands of units.

ER = Index of weighted-average exchange value of the U.S. dollar against currencies of 10 industrial nations (1973 = 100).

NSE = New York Stock Exchange common stock price index (1965 = 50).

	Month	FFR	FT	IP	HS	ER	NSE
1981	September	15.87	19,655	151.6	850	107.78	68.37
	October	15.08	19,044	149.2	722	106.34	69.40
	November	13.31	19,153	146.3	743	104.53	71.49
	December	12.37	18,885	143.4	797	105.21	71.81
1982	January	13.22	18,737	140.7	803	106.96	67.91
	February	14.78	18,704	142.9	792	110.36	66.16
	March	14.68	18,602	141.7	851	112.45	63.86
	April	14.94	17,843	140.2	871	114.07	66.97
	May	14.45	18,218	139.2	944	111.03	67.07
	June	14.15	18,822	138.7	929	116.97	63.10
	July	12.59	18,026	138.8	1,062	118.91	62.82
	August	10.12	17,463	138.4	888	119.63	62.91
	September	10.31	17,320	137.3	1,029	120.93	70.21
	October	9.71	16,671	135.7	1,154	123.16	76.10
	November	9.20	15,852	134.9	1,227	124.27	79.75
	December	8.95	16,347	135.2	1,326	119.22	80.30
1983	January	8.68	17,393	137.4	1,447	117.73	83.25
	February	8.51	16,326	138.1	1,479	119.70	84.74
	March	8.77	16,752	140.0	1,467	120.71	87.50
	April	8.80	16,074	142.6	1,536	121.82	90.61
	May	8.63	15,566	144.4	1,635	122.05	94.61
	June	8.98	17,008	146.4	1,761	125.16	96.43
	July	9.37	16,486	149.7	1,752	126.62	96.74
	August	9.56	16,582	151.8	1,671	129.77	93.96
	September	9.45	17,257	153.8	1,540	129.74	96.70
	October	9.04	17,033	155.0	1,650	127.50	96.78
	November	9.34	17,063	155.3	1,649	130.26	95.36
	December	9.47	17,298	156.2	1,602	132.84	94.92
1984	January	9.56	18,326	158.5	1,799	135.07	96.16
	February	9.59	17,212	160.0	1,902	131.71	90.60
	March	9.91	17,727	160.8	1,756	128.07	90.66
	April	10.29	17,521	162.1	1,802	130.01	90.67
	May	10.32	17,950	162.8	1,774	133.49	90.07
	June	11.06	17,633	164.4	1,819	134.31	88.28
	July	11.23	19,442	165.9	1,590	139.30	87.08

	Month	FFR	FT	IP	HS	ER	NSE
	August	11.64	18,036	166.0	1,508	140.21	94.49
	September	11.30	18,210	123.3	1,481	145.70	95.68
	October	9.99	18,411	122.7	1,436	147.56	95.09
	November	9.43	18,395	123.4	1,616	144.92	95.85
	December	8.38	19,142	123.3	1,599	149.24	94.85
1985	January	8.35	19,401	123.6	1,635	152.85	99.11
	February	8.50	17,853	123.7	1,624	158.43	104.73
	March	8.58	18,446	124.0	1,741	158.14	103.42
	April	8.27	17,779	124.1	1,704	149.56	104.66
	May	7.97	17,414	124.1	1,778	149.92	107.00
	June	7.53	17,438	124.3	1,717	147.71	109.52
	July	7.88	17,411	124.1	1,709	140.94	111.64
	August	7.90	17,423	125.2	1,782	137.55	109.09
	September	7.92	17,034	125.1	1,846	139.14	106.62
	October	7.99	17,618	124.4	1,703	130.71	107.57
	November	8.05	17,721	125.4	1,668	128.08	113.93
	December	8.27	16,994	126.4	1,839	125.80	119.33
1986	January	8.14	17,006	126.2	1,861	123.65	120.16
	February	7.86	17,735	125.3	1,808	118.77	126.43
	March	7.48	18,913	123.6	1,834	116.05	133.97
	April	6.99	17,965	124.7	1,885	115.67	137.25
	May	6.85	17,431	124.2	1,788	113.27	137.37
	June	6.92	19,070	124.2	1,792	113.77	140.82
	July	6.56	17,707	124.9	1,759	110.38	138.32
	August	6.17	17,604	125.1	1,673	107.50	140.91
	September	5.89	17,518	125.2	1,603	107.15	137.06
	October	5.85	19,330	125.3	1,565	106.58	136.74
	November	6.04	18,595	126.0	1,613	107.90	140.84
	December	6.91	18,431	126.7	1,910	106.54	142.12
1987	January	6.43	16,421	126.5	1,652	101.13	151.17
	February	6.10	18,660	127.2	1,676	89.46	161.23
	March	6.13	21,776	127.3	1,719	98.99	166.43
	April	6.37	20,496	127.4	1,598	97.09	163.88
	May	6.85	20,784	128.4	1,493	96.05	163.00
	June	6.73	21,126	129.1	1,517	97.78	169.58
	July	6.58	21,008	130.6	1,487	99.36	174.28
	August	6.73	20,222	131.0	1,502	99.43	184.18
	September	7.22	20,986	130.9	1,502	97.23	178.39
	October	7.29	21,752	131.7	1,463	96.65	157.13
	November	6.69	23,799	133.2	1,469	91.49	137.21
	December	6.77	24,801	133.9	1,361	88.70	134.88
1988	January	6.83	22,330	134.4	1,257	89.29	140.55
	February	6.58	23,559	134.4	1,422	91.08	145.13
	March	6.58	29,106	134.7	1,476	89.73	149.88
	April	6.87	26,335	135.4	1,449	88.95	148.46
	May	7.09	27,478	136.1	1,436	89.74	144.99
	June	7.51	26,283	136.5	1,485	92.58	152.72
	July	7.75	26,516	138.0	1,425	96.53	152.12
	August	8.01	27,493	138.5	1,466	98.29	149.25
	September	8.19	27,989	138.6	1,432	97.91	151.47
	October	8.30	27,816	139.4	1,526	95.10	156.36
	November	8.35	27,538	139.9	1,508	91.91	152.67
	December	8.76	28,864	140.4	1,518	91.88	155.35
1989	January	9.12	28,980	140.8	1,486	95.12	160.35
	February	9.36	28,839	140.5	1,403	95.77	165.08
	March	9.85	30,065	107.7	1,230	96.99	164.56
	April	9.84	30,759	108.6	1,334	97.24	169.38
	May	9.81	30,455	108.3	1,347	100.81	175.30
	June	9.53	31,286	108.4	1,323	103.09	180.76
	July	9.24	29,662	107.8	1,281	99.12	185.15
	August	8.99	30,249	108.2	1,334	100.44	192.93
	September	9.02	30,367	108.2	1,310	101.87	193.02
	October	8.84	31,474	107.7	1,362	98.92	192.49
	November	8.55	30,618	108.1	1,364	97.99	188.50
	December	8.45	31,262	108.6	1,416	94.88	192.67

	Month	FFR	FT	IP	HS	ER	NSE
1990	January	8.23	31,372	107.5	1,739	93.00	187.96
	February	8.24	31,576	108.5	1,297	92.25	182.55
	March	8.28	33,266	108.9	1,232	94.11	186.26
	April	8.26	32,058	108.8	1,108	93.51	185.61
	May	8.18	32,774	109.4	1,065	92.04	191.35
	June	8.29	34,221	110.1	1,123	92.43	196.68
	July	8.15	32,125	110.4	1,086	89.68	196.61
	August	8.13	32,515	110.5	1,055	86.55	181.45
	September	8.20	32,231	110.6	989	86.10	173.22
	October	8.11	34,631	109.9	925	83.43	168.05
	November	7.81	33,586	108.3	916	82.12	172.21
	December	7.31	33,570	107.2	854	83.35	179.57
1991	January	6.91	34,144	106.6	802	83.51	177.95
	February	6.25	33,599	105.7	876	82.12	197.75
	March	6.12	34,031	105.0	892	88.12	203.56
	April	5.91	35,632	105.5	913	91.41	207.71
	May	5.78	35,271	106.4	966	92.29	207.07
	June	5.90	34,975	107.3	999	95.18	207.32
	July	5.82	35,227	108.1	1,005	95.19	208.29
	August	5.66	34,380	108.0	953	93.47	213.33
	September	5.45	35,348	108.4	982	91.18	212.55
	October	5.21	37,114	108.2	1,028	90.69	213.10
	November	4.81	37,462	108.0	993	87.98	213.25

INDEX

Critical Values of the Chi-Square Distribution

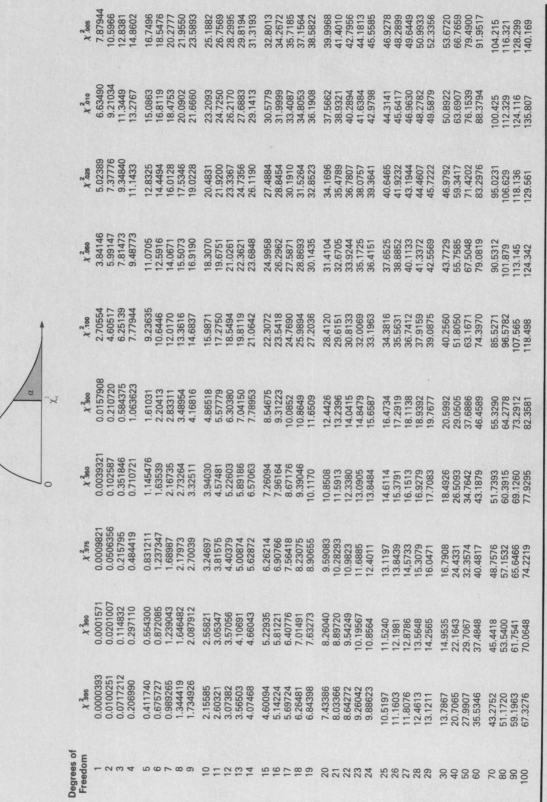

Degrees of Freedom	$\chi^2_{.995}$	$\chi^2_{.990}$	$\chi^2_{.975}$	$\chi^2_{.950}$	$\chi^2_{.900}$	$\chi^2_{.100}$	$\chi^2_{.050}$	$\chi^2_{.025}$	$\chi^2_{.010}$	$\chi^2_{.005}$
1	0.0000393	0.0001571	0.0009821	0.0039321	0.0157908	2.70554	3.84146	5.02389	6.63490	7.87944
2	0.0100251	0.0201007	0.0506356	0.102587	0.210720	4.60517	5.99147	7.37776	9.21034	10.5966
3	0.0717212	0.114832	0.215795	0.351846	0.584375	6.25139	7.81473	9.34840	11.3449	12.8381
4	0.206990	0.297110	0.484419	0.710721	1.063623	7.77944	9.48773	11.1433	13.2767	14.8602
5	0.411740	0.554300	0.831211	1.145476	1.61031	9.23635	11.0705	12.8325	15.0863	16.7496
6	0.675727	0.872085	1.237347	1.63539	2.20413	10.6446	12.5916	14.4494	16.8119	18.5476
7	0.989265	1.239043	1.68987	2.16735	2.83311	12.0170	14.0671	16.0128	18.4753	20.2777
8	1.344419	1.646482	2.17973	2.73264	3.48954	13.3616	15.5073	17.5346	20.0902	21.9550
9	1.734926	2.087912	2.70039	3.32511	4.16816	14.6837	16.9190	19.0228	21.6660	23.5893
10	2.15585	2.55821	3.24697	3.94030	4.86518	15.9871	18.3070	20.4831	23.2093	25.1882
11	2.60321	3.05347	3.81575	4.57481	5.57779	17.2750	19.6751	21.9200	24.7250	26.7569
12	3.07382	3.57056	4.40379	5.22603	6.30380	18.5494	21.0261	23.3367	26.2170	28.2995
13	3.56503	4.10691	5.00874	5.89186	7.04150	19.8119	22.3621	24.7356	27.6883	29.8194
14	4.07468	4.66043	5.62872	6.57063	7.78953	21.0642	23.6848	26.1190	29.1413	31.3193
15	4.60094	5.22935	6.26214	7.26094	8.54675	22.3072	24.9958	27.4884	30.5779	32.8013
16	5.14224	5.81221	6.90766	7.96164	9.31223	23.5418	26.2962	28.8454	31.9999	34.2672
17	5.69724	6.40776	7.56418	8.67176	10.0852	24.7690	27.5871	30.1910	33.4087	35.7185
18	6.26481	7.01491	8.23075	9.39046	10.8649	25.9894	28.8693	31.5264	34.8053	37.1564
19	6.84398	7.63273	8.90655	10.1170	11.6509	27.2036	30.1435	32.8523	36.1908	38.5822
20	7.43386	8.26040	9.59083	10.8508	12.4426	28.4120	31.4104	34.1696	37.5662	39.9968
21	8.03366	8.89720	10.28293	11.5913	13.2396	29.6151	32.6705	35.4789	38.9321	41.4010
22	8.64272	9.54249	10.9823	12.3380	14.0415	30.8133	33.9244	36.7807	40.2894	42.7956
23	9.26042	10.19567	11.6885	13.0905	14.8479	32.0069	35.1725	38.0757	41.6384	44.1813
24	9.88623	10.8564	12.4011	13.8484	15.6587	33.1963	36.4151	39.3641	42.9798	45.5585
25	10.5197	11.5240	13.1197	14.6114	16.4734	34.3816	37.6525	40.6465	44.3141	46.9278
26	11.1603	12.1981	13.8439	15.3791	17.2919	35.5631	38.8852	41.9232	45.6417	48.2899
27	11.8076	12.8786	14.5733	16.1513	18.1138	36.7412	40.1133	43.1944	46.9630	49.6449
28	12.4613	13.5648	15.3079	16.9279	18.9392	37.9159	41.3372	44.4607	48.2782	50.9933
29	13.1211	14.2565	16.0471	17.7083	19.7677	39.0875	42.5569	45.7222	49.5879	52.3356
30	13.7867	14.9535	16.7908	18.4926	20.5992	40.2560	43.7729	46.9792	50.8922	53.6720
40	20.7065	22.1643	24.4331	26.5093	29.0505	51.8050	55.7585	59.3417	63.6907	66.7659
50	27.9907	29.7067	32.3574	34.7642	37.6886	63.1671	67.5048	71.4202	76.1539	79.4900
60	35.5346	37.4848	40.4817	43.1879	46.4589	74.3970	79.0819	83.2976	88.3794	91.9517
70	43.2752	45.4418	48.7576	51.7393	55.3290	85.5271	90.5312	95.0231	100.425	104.215
80	51.1720	53.5400	57.1532	60.3915	64.2778	96.5782	101.879	106.629	112.329	116.321
90	59.1963	61.7541	65.6466	69.1260	73.2912	107.565	113.145	118.136	124.116	128.299
100	67.3276	70.0648	74.2219	77.9295	82.3581	118.498	124.342	129.561	135.807	140.169

Source: C. M. Thompson, "Tables of the Percentage Points of the χ^2-Distribution," *Biometrika* 32 (1941), pp. 188–89. Reproduced by permission of the *Biometrika* Trustees.